IS CHRISTIAN APOLOGETICS BIBLICAL?

IS CHRISTIAN APOLOGETICS VIABLE IN A
POST-CHRISTIAN CULTURE?

HOW DOES CHRISTIAN APOLOGETICS
RELATE TO EVANGELISM, WORSHIP
AND PASTORAL CARE?

These are but a few of the questions

that the *New Dictionary of Christian*

Apologetics undertakes to answer.

Crafted by leading Christian philoso-

phers and theologians and filled with

hundreds of essays and articles, the

dictionary both informs and guides

readers to better understand and articu-

late the Christian faith in today's world.

This book is an indispensable resource

for teachers, stu

of Christian a

NEW DICTIONARY OF
CHRISTIAN APOLOGETICS

NEW DICTIONARY OF
CHRISTIAN APOLOGETICS

Editors:

Campbell Campbell-Jack
Minister, Possilpark Church of Scotland, Glasgow

Gavin J. McGrath
Associate Minister, St Luke's Church, Wimbledon Park, London;
formerly Associate Professor of Theology,
Trinity Episcopal School for Ministry, USA

Consulting editor:

C. Stephen Evans
University Professor of Philosophy and Humanities,
Baylor University, USA

Organizing editor:

Steve Carter
Reference Books Editor, Inter-Varsity Press, Leicester

Inter-Varsity Press
Leicester, England

InterVarsity Press
Downers Grove, Illinois, USA

INTER-VARSITY PRESS
38 De Montfort Street, Leicester LE1 7GP, England
Website: www.ivpbooks.com
Email: ivp@ivp-editorial.co.uk

INTERVARSITY PRESS
PO Box 1400, Downers Grove, Illinois 60515, USA
Website: www.ivpress.com
Email: mail@ivpress.com

First published 2006

British Library Cataloguing in Publication Data
A catalogue record for this book is available from the British Library.

UK ISBN-10: 1-84474-093-5
UK ISBN-13: 978-1-84474-093-2

Library of Congress Cataloging-in-Publication Data has been requested

US ISBN-10: 0-8308-2451-0
US ISBN-13: 978-0-8308-2451-9

Set in Sabon
Typeset in Great Britain by CRB Associates, Reepham, Norfolk
Printed in Great Britain by CPI Bath

Inter-Varsity Press is closely linked with the Universities and Colleges Christian Fellowship, a student movement connecting Christian Unions in universities and colleges throughout Great Britain, and a member movement of the International Fellowship of Evangelical Students. Website: www.uccf.org.uk

InterVarsity Press is the book-publishing division of InterVarsity Christian Fellowship/USA®, a student movement active on campus at hundreds of universities, colleges and schools of nursing in the United States of America, and a member movement of the International Fellowship of Evangelical Students. For information about local and regional activities, write to Public Relations Dept., InterVarsity Christian Fellowship USA, 6400 Schroeder Road, PO Box 7895, Madison, WI 53707-7895, or visit the IVCF website at <www.ivcf.org>.

Contents

Preface

In every generation Christian people face the challenges, questions, prejudices and concerns of those who find the Christian faith incredible, confusing, problematic and, on the other hand, intriguing. At times Christians respond in what we might call defensive situations: answering specific criticisms and challenges. At other times Christians respond in more positive situations: participating in the public discourse by commending the gospel of the Lord Jesus Christ and its accompanying world-view. In both cases, Christian people seek not only to explain their beliefs but also to commend their beliefs. This is what Christian apologetics is all about; it is, as 1 Peter 3:15, the *locus classicus* of biblical texts concerning apologetics, instructs, 'always being prepared to make a defence [Gk *apologia*] to anyone who asks you for the reason for the hope that is in you' (ESV).

This *apologia*, from which we get the word 'apologetics', arises out of particular convictions. First, as 1 Peter 3:15 also states, Christ Jesus is Lord and he is holy. In other words, Christian apologetics, while Trinitarian, is Christ-focused and Christ-centred. Christian apologetics assumes and articulates a distinctive – namely, a conviction that Jesus Christ is Lord, the Son of the one, true, holy God, and to him God the Holy Spirit witnesses. Secondly, and as an important consequence, Christian apologetics is essentially hopeful (again as 1 Peter 3:15 instructs). In the truest sense, Christian apologetics is hopeful because it is gospel-focused and gospel-centred. Because God offers humanity good news (gospel) in the death and resurrection of his Son, Christian apologetics is determined by this good news and the hope of which it speaks (both present and future). Thirdly, Christian apologetics, according to 1 Peter 3:16, has a special character: 'gentleness and respect'. Sadly, Christian people do not consistently demonstrate this character in Christian apologetics. Too often Christian apologetics degenerates into a desire to win debates and counter arguments with supposed clever reasoning. Today's Christian people would do well to see again the biblical pattern of apologetics, expressly the gospel point (or, better, heart) of Christian apologetics.

This Dictionary aims to provide resources for Christian apologetics in our contemporary contexts. The various articles aim not so much to provide a single 'answer' as to introduce theological, historical, philosophical and pastoral insights which, in turn, all contribute to create an *apologia*. While the Dictionary is arranged topically for the sake of convenience, it is hoped that readers will see the whole – the interrelatedness of all the various topics. This is because Christian apologetics is not so much a set of answers or responses as a way of seeing (as well as being and living) consistent with a biblical world-view – seeing all of reality and existence through biblical revelation, the chief focus of which is the gospel of the Lord Jesus Christ. Only in this primary sense are there then Christian answers and responses.

Producing this volume would have been impossible without the contributions of those who wrote the articles; the editors are indebted to each author. Special acknowledgment must go to C. Stephen Evans for his assistance in suggesting various topics and contributors as well as for his own articles. Supremely, the editors commend Steve Carter, the organizing editor of this volume at Inter-Varsity Press, for his skill, insights and wisdom. He patiently endured lengthy delays on the part of the editors and extended gracious encouragement to them to see this project through to its published conclusion.

This volume will serve its desired purpose if it helps today's Christian people to offer our troubled, fragile and confused world a truly Christian *apologia*.

C. CAMPBELL-JACK
GAVIN J. MCGRATH

How to use this Dictionary

This introduction provides some guidance on how to use the Dictionary to the best advantage.

Arrangement
The Dictionary is arranged in two parts. Part One consists of six major introductory articles, arranged thematically, on key methodological issues in Christian apologetics. A list of subjects is provided on the Contents page. Part Two consists of numerous shorter articles, arranged alphabetically, on the various forms and aspects of apologetics.

Cross-references
It has been editorial policy in the Dictionary to group smaller topics together and treat them in a single larger article. For example, 'suffering' is dealt with in the article on EVIL, and 'evolution' in the article on ORIGINS, THEORIES OF.
    Cross-referencing is therefore an important feature of the Dictionary.

1. Numerous one-line entries refer the reader to the title of the article in which the topic is treated, *e.g.* ANNIHILATIONISM, see HELL.
2. An asterisk before a word or phrase indicates that further relevant information will be found in the article under that title. It is equivalent to the abbreviation *q.v.* Please note that the form of the asterisked word will not always be precisely the same as that of the article to which the asterisk refers. So '*reasoning' refers to the article on REASON, and '*science' to SCIENCE AND FAITH and SCIENCE AND THE BIBLE.
3. A reference in brackets in the body of an article, such as '(see *Christianity, Protestant)', is self-explanatory.

Abbreviations
A list of abbreviations used in the Dictionary will be found on p. xi.

Authorship of articles
The author's name is given at the end of each article. A complete list of contributors, in alphabetical order of surname, will be found on pp. xiii–xx. To the best of the editors' knowledge, this information was correct at the time of publication.

Bibliographies
Guidance for further study has been provided in most articles, sometimes in the body of the article, but mainly in the bibliography at the end. The works listed in the bibliography may include studies that take a different position from that of the author of the article. The listed websites were live, to the best of the authors' knowledge, when they submitted their articles, but some will become unavailable after a time.

Abbreviations

1. Biblical books

Books of the Old Testament
Gen., Exod., Lev., Num., Deut., Josh., Judg., Ruth, 1,2 Sam., 1,2 Kgs, 1,2 Chr., Ezra, Neh., Esth., Job, Ps. (Pss.), Prov., Eccl., Song, Isa., Jer., Lam., Ezek., Dan., Hos., Joel, Amos, Obad., Jon., Mic., Nah., Hab., Zeph., Hag., Zech., Mal.

Books of the New Testament
Matt., Mark, Luke, John, Acts, Rom., 1,2 Cor., Gal., Eph., Phil., Col., 1,2 Thess., 1,2 Tim., Titus, Philm., Heb., Jas, 1,2 Pet., 1,2,3 John, Jude, Rev.

2. General abbreviations

ad loc	at the place	LXX	Septuagint (Gk Version of OT)
b.	born	MS(S)	manuscripts
c.	about, approximately	MT	Masoretic Text
cf.	compare	n	note
ch(s).	chapter(s)	n.d.	no date
d.	died	no.	number
ed(s).	editor(s)	n.s.	new series
edn	edition	NT	New Testament
e.g.	for example	*op. cit.*	in the work cited above
ET	English translation	OT	Old Testament
et al.	and others	p(pp).	page(s)
etc.	and so on	par.	and parallel
f. ff.	and the following	repr.	reprinted
Gk	Greek	*sic.*	thus
Heb.	Hebrew	tr.	translated, translation
ibid.	the same work	v., vv.	verse, verses
idem	the same author	*viz.*	namely
i.e.	that is to say	vol(s).	volume(s)
lit.	literally	vss	versions
loc. cit.	in the place already quoted		

List of contributors

To the best of the editors' knowledge, this information was correct at the time of publication.

A Y Aghamkar, BA, MTh, BD, PhD, Professor and Head of Missiology Department, SAIACS, Bangalore, India

T D Alexander, BA, PhD, Director of Christian Training, Union Theological College, Belfast

M Alsford, BA, PhD, PGCE, Senior Lecturer, University of Greenwich, London

S E Alsford, BA(Hons), PGCE, PhD, Senior Lecturer, University of Greenwich, London

W P Alston, BMus, PhD, Professor Emeritus of Philosophy, Syracuse University, USA

R S Anderson, BD, PhD, Senior Professor of Theology and Ministry, Fuller Theological Seminary, Pasadena, USA

F D Aquino, BA, MA, MDiv, PhD, Assistant Professor of Theology, Abilene Christian University, USA

C B G Ash, MA, BA, Director of Cornhill Training Course, London

P Bassett, PhD, Professor Emeritus of the History of Christianity, Nazarene Theological Seminary, Kansas City, USA

O J Batchelor, BSc, MSc, CQSW, Regional Drug Interventions Manager, Gateshead

R Beaton, BA, MDiv, PhD, Associate Professor of New Testament, Fuller Theological Seminary, Pasadena, USA

D W Bebbington, MA, PhD, FRHistS, Professor of History, University of Stirling

W D Beck, PhD, MA, BA, Dean of Graduate Studies, Professor of Philosophy, Liberty University, Lynchburg, USA

J K Beilby, MATS, PhD, Associate Professor of Systematic and Philosophical Theology, Bethel University, St Paul, USA

B E Benson, PhD, PhL(Masters), BA, Associate Professor of Philosophy, Wheaton College, USA

H R Bercovici, PhD, MDiv, BA, Scholar-in-Residence, Trinity Institute, Greenwich, USA

M A Bergmann, BBS, BA, MA, PhD, Associate Professor of Philosophy, Purdue University, West Lafayette, USA

R J Berry, MA, DSc, FIBiol, FRSE, Professor of Genetics, University College London

E P Beukes, BSc, MA, PhD, Professor of Economics, The King's University College, Edmonton, Canada

A Billington, BA, MA, Lecturer in Hermeneutics, London School of Theology

J J Bimson, BA, PhD, Tutor in Old Testament, Trinity College, Bristol

Kirsten R Birkett, BSc(Hons), PhD, Lecturer, Oak Hill Theological College, London

H A G Blocher, BD, Diplôme d'Etudes Supérieures de Théologie, DD, Professor of Systematic Theology, Faculté Libre de Théologie Evangélique, Vaux-sur-Seine, France, and Gunther H. Knoedler Professor of Theology, Wheaton College, USA

Peter G Bolt, ThL, BD, MCDipA(Theol), MTh, MA(Hons), PhD, Head of New Testament, Moore Theological College, Sydney, Australia

G Bonner, MA, Former Distinguished Professor, Catholic University of America, Washington, D.C., USA, Visiting Professor, Villanova University, USA, and sometime Reader in Theology, Durham University

Ruth A C Bradby, BA, MMus, MTh, PhD Research Student, Chester College

Wade F Bradshaw, BS, MA, DVM, Worker, L'Abri Fellowship, England

G L Bray, BA, MLitt, DLitt, Anglican Professor of Divinity, Beeson Divinity School, Samford University, Birmingham, USA

R S Briggs, MA, PhD, Tutor in Old Testament and Hermeneutics, St John's College, Durham University

D M Bruce, BSc, DipTh, PhD, Director, Science, Religion and Technology Project, Church of Scotland, Edinburgh

J Budziszewski, PhD, Professor of Government and Philosophy, University of Texas, Austin, USA

R K Bufford, PhD, MA, BA, Professor of Psychology, George Fox University, Newberg, USA

W H A Bunting, BA, MA, PhD, Lecturer in Philosophy, University of Ulster

T J Burke, Jr, BA, MA, MDiv, PhD, Professor of Philosophy and Religion, Hillsdale College, USA

D G Burnett, BSc, PhD, DipTheol, MA, Lecturer/Tutor, All Nations Christian College, Ware

J L Burns, PhD, Senior Research Professor in Theology, Dallas Theological Seminary, USA; co-founder and co-president, Asian Christian Academy, India

R W Caldwell III, PhD, Assistant Professor of American Church History, Southwestern Baptist Theological Seminary, Fort Worth, USA

C M Cameron, BA, BD, PhD, Minister, Darvel Parish Church, Ayrshire

C Campbell-Jack, BD, MTh, PhD, Minister, Possilpark Church of Scotland, Glasgow

R C J Carling, BSc, MSc, PhD, freelance editor, Canterbury

J P Chaplin, BA, MPhil, PhD, Associate Professor of Political Theory, Institute for Christian Studies, Toronto, Canada

D M Ciocchi, BA, MA, MA, PhD, Associate Professor of Philosophy, Biola University, La Mirada, USA

Kelly James Clark, PhD, MA, MA, BA, Department of Philosophy, Calvin College, Grand Rapids, USA

R S Clark, BA, MDiv, DPhil, Associate Professor of Historical and Systematic Theology, Westminster Seminary, California, USA

D Closson, BS, MS, MA, Director of Administration, Probe Ministries, Richardson, USA

D L Clough, MA, MSt, PhD, Tutor in Ethics and Systematic Theology, Cranmer Hall, Durham

G Cole, BA, BD, MTh, ThD, Professor of Biblical and Systematic Theology, Trinity Evangelical Divinity School, Deerfield, USA

W L Craig, PhD, DTheol, Research Professor of Philosophy, Talbot School of Theology, La Mirada, USA

E David Cook, BA, MA, PhD, MA, DHLH, A Holmes Professor of Faith and Learning, Wheaton College, USA, and Fellow, Green College, Oxford

W Corduan, BS, MA, PhD, Professor of Philosophy and Religion, Taylor University, Upland, USA

S B Cowan, PhD, MA, MDiv, BA, Associate Director, Apologetics Resource Center, Birmingham, USA

Nicola Hoggard Creegan, BA(Hons), MATS, MPhil, PhD, Lecturer in Theology, Bible College of New Zealand, Auckland, New Zealand

O D Crisp, BD, MTh, PhD, Lecturer in Christian Studies, University of Bristol

D Daniels, BA, MDiv, PhD, Professor of Church History, McCormick Theological Seminary, Chicago, USA

G Daniels, BA, BD, General Director, Christians in Sport, Bicester

W A Dembski, PhD, Carl F. H. Henry Professor of Theology and Science and Director of Center for Science and Theology, Southern Baptist Theological Seminary, Louisville, USA

C C DiCello, BS, MDiv, DTS, Adjunct Professor, Columbia Evangelical Seminary, Longview, USA, and High School Public School Teacher, Pottsville, USA

J W Drane, MA, PhD, Adjunct Professor, School of Theology, Fuller Theological Seminary, Pasadena, USA

S J Duffin, BA, MA, Senior Tutor, School of History, Philosophy and Politics, Massey University, Palmerston North, New Zealand

Colin Duriez, BA(Hons), PGCE, writer, editor and lecturer, Keswick

William Edgar, Dr Théol, MDiv, BA(Hons), Professor of Apologetics, Co-ordinator of the Apologetics Department and Chairman of the Faculty, Westminster Theological Seminary, Philadelphia, USA

J H Elias, BSc, BD, Minister, Tabernacle Welsh Congregational Church, Ynsysbwl

M W Elliott, BA, BD, PhD, Teaching Fellow in Church History, University of St Andrews

E E Ericson, Jr, BA, MA, PhD, Professor of English, Emeritus, Calvin College, Grand Rapids, USA

C Stephen Evans, BA, MPhil, PhD, University Professor of Philosophy and Humanities, Baylor University, Waco, USA

G J Fackre, BD, PhD, Abbot Professor of Christian Theology, Emeritus, Andover Newton Theological School, Newton Centre, USA

L P Fairfield, BA, MA, PhD, Professor of Church History, Trinity Episcopal School for Ministry, Ambridge, USA

E Ferguson, BA, MA, STB, PhD, Distinguished Scholar in Residence, Abilene Christian University, USA

David B Fletcher, BA, MA, PhD, Associate Professor of Philosophy, Wheaton College, USA

T P Flint, BA, PhD, Professor, Department of Philosophy, University of Notre Dame, USA

B A Follis, BA(Hons), PhD, Rector, All Saints Church, Belfast

J A Fortna, MDiv, Adjunct Professor of Church History, Denver Seminary, USA

J M Frame, DD, MPhil, BD, AB, Professor of Systematic Theology and Philosophy, Reformed Theological Seminary, Orlando, USA

R T France, MA, BD, PhD, formerly Principal, Wycliffe Hall, Oxford

R S Fyall, MA, BD, PhD, Director of Rutherford House, Edinburgh

Robert A J Gagnon, BA, MTS, PhD, Associate Professor of New Testament, Pittsburgh Theological Seminary, USA

S S Gassanov, BA, MPhil, LLB, Law Student, Gowlings, Lafleur, Hendeison LLP, Canada

C M Gay, BS, MCS, PhD, Associate Professor of Interdisciplinary Studies, Regent College, Vancouver, Canada

R D Geivett, PhD, MA, Professor of Philosophy, Biola University, La Mirada, USA

D W J Gill, BA, DPhil, FSA, Senior Lecturer in Ancient History, and Associate Dean, University of Wales, Swansea

J W Gladwin, MA, DipTh, Bishop of Chelmsford

Martin F Goldsmith, MA, Lecturer, All Nations Christian College, Ware

T G Grass, BA, PhD, Associate Lecturer, Spurgeon's College, London, and freelance writer

J B Green, BS, MTh, PhD, Vice President of Academic Affairs and Professor of New Testament Interpretation, Asbury Theological Seminary, Wilmore, USA

The late S E Grenz, BA, MDiv, DTheol, formerly Pioneer McDonald Professor of Theology, Carey Theological College, Vancouver, Canada, and Professor of Theological Studies, Mars Hill Graduate School, Seattle, USA

R E Groenhout, BA, PhD, Professor of Philosophy, Calvin College, Grand Rapids, USA

D R Groothuis, BS, MA, PhD, Professor of Philosophy, Denver Seminary, USA

G R Habermas, PhD, MA, BRE, Research Distinguished Professor of Apologetics and Philosophy, Liberty University, Lynchburg, USA

Christopher A Hall, BA, MA, ThM, PhD, Professor of Biblical and Theological Studies, Eastern University, St Davids, USA

G Harp, BA, MA, PhD, Professor of History, Grove City College, USA

D G Hart, PhD, MA, MTS, MAR, BA, Director of Fellowship Programs and Scholar-in-Residence, Intercollegiate Studies Institute, Wilmington, USA

H Hart, PhD, Director for Honors Programs & Faculty Development Intercollegiate Studies Institute, Wilmington, USA

R S Harvey, BA, MA, PGCE, Tutor in Hebrew Bible and Jewish Studies, All Nations Christian College, Ware

L Hegedűs, PhD, Dr.h.c., Professor Emeritus, Karoly Gaspar Reformed University, Budapest, Hungary, and M. Bishop, Consultative Synod, Hungarian Reformed Churches, Hungary

P Helm, MA, Emeritus Professor of the History and Philosophy of Religion, University of London

J C Helt, BA, MDiv, PhD, Interim Pastor, Westminster Presbyterian Church, Madison, USA

E D Herbert, PhD, BA, BSc, Vice-Principal, International Christian College, Glasgow

A I C Heron, MA, BD, Dr Theol, Professor of Reformed Theology, University of Erlangen, Nuremberg, Germany

P S Heslam, MA, BA, DPhil, FRSA, Carts Fellow and Director of Transforming Business, Faculty of Divinity, Cambridge University, and Associate Tutor, Ridley Hall, Cambridge, and Research Associate, the London Institute for Contemporary Christianity

I Hexham, BA, MA, PhD, Full Professor, Department of Religious Studies, University of Calgary, Canada

Peter Hicks, MA, BD, PhD, formerly Lecturer in Philosophy, London School of Theology

D H K Hilborn, BA, MA, PhD, Head of Theology, Evangelical Alliance, and Associate Research Fellow, London School of Theology

D J Hill, MA, PhD, Temporary Lecturer in Philosophy, University of Liverpool

P N Hillyer, BD, PhD, freelance theological author and editor, and formerly Lecturer in Theology, Bishop's College, Calcutta, India

J P Hochschild, BA, MA, PhD, Assistant Professor, Department of Philosophy, Mount St Mary's University, Emmitsburg, USA

D J Hoitenga, Jr, AB, PhD, Professor of Philosophy Emeritus, Grand Valley State University, Allendale, USA

D Hollinger, PhD, Vice Provost and Professor of Christian Ethics, Messiah College, Grantham, USA

A F Holmes, BA, MA, PhD, Emeritus Professor of Philosophy, Wheaton College, USA

Graham R Houston, BSc(Hons), BD(Hons), MTh, PhD, Minister of Cairngryffe with Symington, Church of Scotland Presbytery of Lanark

R F Hurding, MA, MB BChir, DRCOG, Retired Medical Practitioner; Counsellor and Visiting Lecturer in Pastoral Studies, Trinity College, Bristol

Gordon L Isaac, BA, MDiv, MTh, PhD, Professor of Church History, Gordon-Conwell Theological Seminary, South Hamilton, USA

Trig Johnson, BA, MA, MSt, DPhil, Adjunct Assistant Professor, University of North Caroline, Asheville, USA

P S Johnston, BA, BD, MTh, PhD, Director of Studies, Wycliffe Hall, Oxford

A J Jones, BSc, MEd, PhD, CBiol, MIBiol, Senior Tutor, West Yorkshire School of Christian Studies, Leeds

V M Kärkkäinen, Dr Theol, Professor of Systematic Theology, Fuller Theological Seminary, Pasadena, USA

W K Kay, BA, MA, MEd, PhD (Educ), PhD (Theol), Director of the Centre for Pentecostal and Charismatic Studies, University of Wales, Bangor

R Kearsley, BD, PhD, Lecturer, South Wales Baptist College, and Department of Religious and Theological Studies, Cardiff University

Sylvia C Keesmaat, BA, MA, DPhil, Adjunct Professor of Biblical Studies, Institute for Christian Studies, Toronto, Canada

T D Kennedy, AB, PhD, Professor of Philosophy, Valparaiso University, USA

R B Keyes, BA, MDiv, Director of L'Abri Fellowship, Southborough, USA

D P Kingdon, MA, BD, Joint Managing Editor, Grace Publications Trust

R C Koons, MA, PhD, BA, Professor of Philosophy, University of Texas, Austin, USA

D T Koyzis, BA, MPhil, PhD, Professor of Political Science, Redeemer University College, Ancaster, Canada

S G Lebhar, BA, MDiv, PhD Student in Old Testament, University of Cambridge

B J Lee, PhD, MAR, Associate Editor, Ad Fontes, Alexandria, USA

G R LeMarquand, BA, STM, MA, ThD, Associate Professor of Biblical Studies and Mission, Trinity Episcopal School for Ministry, Ambridge, USA

Julian D Linnell, BA, PGCE, MA, MSc, MDiv, PhD, Associate Pastor, Galilee Church, Virginia Beach, USA

R Lints, MA, PhD, AM, Professor of Theology and Apologetics, Gordon-Conwell Theological Seminary, South Hamilton, USA

B A Little, BRE, MA, MRE, DMin, PhD, Associate Professor of Philosophy of Religion, Southeastern Baptist Theological Seminary, Wake Forest, USA

J McDermond, BA, MDiv, MLitt, DMin, Associate Professor of Christian Ministry and Spirituality, Messiah College, Grantham, USA

F Macdonald, MS, BD, formerly General Secretary, United Bible Societies, Reading

John C McDowell, BA (Hons), PhD, Meldrum Lecturer in Systematic Theology, New College, University of Edinburgh

Jock McGregor, BSc, MDiv, L'Abri Fellowship, Rochester, USA

J L McPake, BA, BD, PhD, Parish Minister, Mossneuk Parish Church, East Kilbride, and formerly Convener of the Panel on Doctrine of the Church of Scotland

I Howard Marshall, PhD, DD, Honorary Research Professor of New Testament, University of Aberdeen

P A Marshall, BSc, MSc, MA, MPhil, PhD, Senior Fellow, Freedom House's Center for Religious Freedom, Washington, USA

E N Martin, BA, MA, PhD, Associate Professor of Philosophy and Theology, Liberty University, Lynchburg, USA

K G Molyneux, MA, PhD, Lecturer/Tutor and Academic Dean, All Nations Christian College

J W Montgomery, AB, BLS, MA, BD, STM, PhD, MPhil, LLM, LLD, Docteur d'Université, Barrister-at-Law, DUJ, Professor Emeritus of Law and Humanities, University of Luton, and Distinguished Professor of Apologetics and Law, Trinity College and Theological Seminary, USA

E Moore, PhD, MAR, BA, Assistant Professor of Hebrew and Biblical Studies, Trinity Episcopal School of Ministry, Ambridge, USA

J P Moreland, BS(Hons), ThM(Hons), MA(Highest Hons), PhD, Distinguished Professor of Philosophy, Talbot School of Theology, Biola University, La Mirada, USA

P K Moser, PhD, MA, BA, Professor and Chairperson of Philosophy, Loyola University of Chicago, USA

C A Mosser, BA, MA, ThM, PhD, Assistant Professor of Biblical Studies, Eastern University, St David's, USA

C G Moucarry, MA, PhD, Lecturer in Islamic and Middle Eastern Studies, All Nations Christian College

F Namdaran, MB, ChB, MTh, retired doctor

H A Netland, BA, MA, PhD, Associate Professor of Philosophy of Religion and Intercultural Studies, Trinity Evangelical Divinity School, Deerfield, USA

S J Nichols, MA, MAR, PhD, Professor, Lancaster Bible College and Graduate School, USA

Thomas A Noble, MA, BD, PhD, Professor of Theology, Nazarene Theological Seminary, Kansas City, USA

S F Noll, BA, MA, MDiv, PhD, Vice Chancellor, Uganda Christian University, Mukono, Uganda

K Scott Oliphint, MAR, ThM, PhD, Associate Professor of Apologetics, Westminster Theological Seminary, Philadelphia, USA

M A Ovey, BA, MA, Mth, BCL, PhD, Kingham Hill Lecturer in Doctrine, Apologetics & Philosophy, Oak Hill College, London

J I Packer, MA, DPhil, DD, Board of Governors Professor of Theology, Regent College, Vancouver, Canada

Christopher Partridge, PhD, BD, DipRS, Professor of Contemporary Religion and Co-director of Centre for Religion, Film and Contemporary Culture, University of Chester

Thomas C Pfizenmaier, PhD, MDiv, MA, BA, Senior Minister, Bonhomme Presbyterian Church, Chesterfield, USA

The late David R L Porter, ALA, BA, writer and editor, Greatham

G T Prance, MA, DPhil, FRS, VMH, Scientific Director, The Eden Project, St Austell

D Ratzsch, PhD, Professor of Philosophy, Calvin College, Grand Rapids, USA

M C Rea, PhD, MA, BA, Associate Professor of Philosophy, University of Notre Dame, USA

B W Reynolds, BA, MA, PhD, Professor of History and Chairman of the Department, Asbury College, Wilmore, USA

J M Reynolds, PhD, MA, BA, Director, Torrey Honors Institute, Biola University, La Mirada, USA

W G Rietkerk, drs, Chairman, Board of Trustees, L'Abri Fellowship, and Member of City Council, Utrecht, the Netherlands

A Julian Rivers, MA, LLM, MIur, PhD, Senior Lecturer in Law, University of Bristol

A M Robbins, BA, MRE, MA, PhD, Director of Training and Lecturer in Theology and Contemporary Culture, London School of Theology, Northwood

E Rowlands, BD(Hons), BA/BA(Hons), Theology Course Leader and Lecturer in Hebrew and Old Testament, International Christian College, Glasgow

D Scott Russell, BA, MDiv, Episcopal Campus Minister, Virginia Polytechnic Institute and State University, Blacksburg, USA

R A Russell, BA, MA, MA, PGCE, MEd, DipHE Theology, formerly Vicar of Widcombe, Bath, and Director of the Christian Studies Unit, Radstock

D M Scholer, BA, MA, ThD, Professor of New Testament and Associate Dean, Center for Advanced Theological Studies, School of Theology, Fuller Theological Seminary, USA

P A Schouls, BA, MA, PhD, Adjunct Professor, Graduate Liberal Studies, Simon Fraser University, Vancouver, Canada

Q J Schultze, PhD, Arthur H DeKruyter Chair in Faith and Communication, Calvin College, Grand Rapids, USA

G G Scorgie, BTh, MA, MCS, PhD, Professor of Theology, Bethel Seminary, San Diego, USA

B J M Scott, MA, formerly with Interserve India and Ministry among Asians in Britain

Charles Henry Sherlock, BA, MA, ThL, BD, ThD, Director of Ministry Studies, Melbourne College of Divinity, Australia

C Sinkinson, BA, MA, PhD, Minister of Alderholt Evangelical Congregational Church

David Smith, DLitt, Lecturer in Urban Mission and World Christianity, International Christian College, Glasgow

J Sode-Woodhead, PhD, Director, Heritage International, Edinburgh

J G Stackhouse, Jr, BA, MA, PhD, Sangwoo Youtong Chee Professor of Theology and Culture, Regent College, Vancouver, Canada

J A Studebaker, Jr, PhD, MDiv, BS, Adjunct Professor, Cornerstone University, Spring Arbor University and Taylor University, USA

Richard L Sturch, MA, DPhil, formerly Rector of Islip, Oxfordshire

C C Taliaferro, PhD, MA, MTS, BA, Professor of Philosophy, St Olaf College, Northfield, USA

S Theron, PhD, MA, BA, formerly Head of Philosophy Department (Senior Lecturer), National University of Lesotho

D E H Thistlethwaite, BA Hons, MA, Administrator, the John Ray Initiative, Cheltenham

M D Thompson, BA, BTh, MTh, DPhil, Senior Lecturer in Theology and Director of Studies, Moore College, Sydney, Australia

T R Thompson, BA, MDiv, PhD, Professor of Religion, Calvin College, Grand Rapids, USA

D J Tidball, BA, BD, PhD, Principal, London School of Theology, Northwood

M J Tracey, PhD, Associate Professor of Philosophy, Benedictine University, Lisle, USA

C R Trueman, MA, PhD, Professor of Historical Theology and Church History, Westminster Theological Seminary, USA

The late N T van der Merwe, Doctorandus Philosophiae, MA, BA(Hons), formerly Professor of Philosophy, PU for CHE Potchefstroom, South Africa

K J Vanhoozer, BA, MDiv, PhD, Research Professor of Systematic Theology, Trinity Evangelical Divinity School, Deerfield, USA

G E Veith, BA, MA, PhD, Professor of English, Concordia University, Cedarburg, USA

A G Vos, AB, MA, PhD, Professor of Philosophy, Western Kentucky University, Bowling Green, USA

Julian W Ward, BSc, BD, MSc, MPhil, formerly Dean of Students, Regents Theological College, Nantwich

T J Ward, BA, MA, PhD, Church Minister, Hinckley

C W Weber, BA, MA, PhD, Professor of History, Wheaton College, USA

P J Weigel, BA, MPhil, PhD, Assistant Professor of Philosophy and Religion, Washington College, Chestertown, USA

J S Weir, BA, Head of International Ministry, Christians in Sport, Bicester

G J Wenham, MA, PhD, formerly Professor of Old Testament, University of Gloucestershire, Cheltenham

P D A Weston, MA, MPhil, PhD, Lecturer in Mission Studies, Ridley Hall, Cambridge

R A Whitacre, AB, MTS, PhD, DD, Professor of Biblical Studies, Trinity Episcopal School for Ministry, Ambridge, USA

R S White, BA, MA, PhD, FRS, Professor of Geophysics, University of Cambridge

D A Wilkinson, BSc, PhD, MA, PhD, FRAS, Wesley Research Lecturer in Theology and Science, University of Durham

S N Williams, MA, PhD, Professor of Systematic Theology, Union Theological College, Belfast

T Williams, BA, MA, PhD, Associate Professor of Philosophy and Religious Studies, University of South Florida, Tampa, USA

A I Wilson, BA, BD, PhD, Principal-Designate, Dumisani Theological Institute, King William's Town, South Africa, and Extraordinary Associate Professor of New Testament, North-West University, Potchefstroom, South Africa

R D Winter, MB, BS, MRC Psych, Professor of Practical Theology and Director of Counselling, Covenant Theological Seminary, St Louis, USA

A M Wolters, BA, MA, PhD, Professor of Religion and Theology and Classical Languages, Redeemer University College, Ancaster, Canada

W J Wood, MA, PhD, Professor of Philosophy, Wheaton College, USA

E M Yamauchi, BA, MA, PhD, Professor of History, Miami University, Oxford, USA

J W Yates III, BA, MDiv, MA, PhD Student and Decani Scholar, Clare College, University of Cambridge

J C Zellman, BA, MA, PhD, Instructor, Penn State University, Pennsylvania, USA

PART ONE

PART ONE

Christian Apologetics for a New Century: Where We Have Come from, Where We are Going

Delineating apologetics

Apologetics is the art of persuasion, the discipline which considers ways to commend and defend the living God to those without faith. As such it can be practised by every believer. It is also a branch of *theology concerned to meet the questions and objections raised by Christian beliefs with credible and cogent answers. Apologetics seeks to build arguments based on criteria which are true and compelling at the same time. The practice of apologetics involves more than articulating solid reasons for one's Christian hope. Following texts such as 1 Pet. 3:15, it begins with a spiritual disposition, sustaining the worship of Christ in one's heart and exercising gentleness and respect for the questioner, in hopes of vindicating God's honour. In addition, there is a community dimension meant to complement the verbal argument. The Greek word *apologia*, from which we derive the English word apologetics, is often translated 'give an answer', but its meaning is more forceful than this. In classical Greek it is a legal term, meaning to get oneself off a charge, and that is carried through in many biblical instances. Though apologetics is primarily intended to defend the faith when facing outsiders, it can also be used for the correction and edification of believers.

While we are responsible to develop the best arguments we can, it is the *Holy Spirit who will function as the ultimate persuader, and who will elicit a response. This is because apologetics is fundamentally the recommendation of God himself. It is a critical component of evangelism, of announcing the good news of the gospel to a fallen, often hostile world. In the ultimate sense, God is the primary apologist. Graciously, he addresses his people with arguments meant to bring them to repentance and faith, owing to his redemptive mercy: ' "Come now, let us reason together," says the LORD. "Though your sins are like scarlet, they shall be as white as snow" ' (Isa. 1:18).

Three defining episodes

One could identify three eras in the history of apologetics, corresponding to three epochs in the history of the church. The first is during the earliest years of the church, when Christianity was spreading throughout the Roman Empire and beyond. The second is the long stretch of time when the church was more settled and established, the period known as Christendom. The third is the mode of society known as modernity, the period to which we still belong, where the church is losing ground in the West, but yet gaining ground throughout the southern hemisphere. These are hardly airtight categories, but they do represent distinct backgrounds for the major types of apologetic systems.

The early church

The theologians in the first generation after the close of the apostolic age are known as the Church Fathers, and they functioned primarily as apologists. It was a time when the church's international role was growing, despite many odds. Understandably, apologetics in this period aimed to prove the legitimacy of Christian faith and had to respond to two major threats, one from outside the church and one from within: persecution and heresy. In addition, the early church had to define itself in relation to *Judaism, showing both continuity with the faith of the OT (understood as fulfilled in Christ) and discontinuity with the hardened Judaism which had rejected Christ as Messiah.

Responding to persecution

Persecution came in waves throughout the period from Nero (64) to Diocletian (284–305). To begin with, Christians had been considered a group within Judaism and as such had benefited from the long established Roman tolerance of the Jews. It soon became clear, however, that they were a distinct body, often opposed by the Jews, and eventually by the Romans. The Romans had social reasons for their persecution of the church as they considered Christians to be a threat to the status quo because they refused to participate in such public activities as making vows, burning incense to the emperor or consulting the gods. Because the state was absolute, the primary allegiance of Christians to their Lord was interpreted as disloyalty to the system. Furthermore, various church practices were open to misunderstanding and brought charges of cannibalism (the Lord's Supper), incest (the holy kiss) and atheism ('no other gods before me'). It is also true to say that some early Christians welcomed persecution and rejoiced in the opportunity to suffer like their Lord.

The first significant apologist of the period was *Justin Martyr (d. 165), who set the tone for many who would follow. His *Dialogue with Trypho* was an attempt to persuade a Jew of the truth of the gospel, and so it used proofs of Christ's messiahship from prophecy and arguments for the fulfilment of the Old Testament in the New. Justin's *First Apology* was a plea to the Emperor Antonius Pius to listen to the voice of reason, rather than rumour, as he investigated charges against Christians. Much of Justin's argument centred on the person of Christ, whom he believed to be the true *logos*, a term he used in an idiomatic way. *Tertullian (c. 155–220) was far more critical of Greek philosophy, contending that after *Jesus Christ, 'we have no need of speculation'. His finest work is the *Apology*, a passionate polemic in which he asks the Romans to use their own juridical principles against the irrational persecution of Christians.

The challenge of heresy

The second threat in the life of the early church was heresy, and the two issues are not unrelated. Persecution is a form of testing, and a church under external pressure is tempted to seek relief in all kinds of extreme forms. One of the most persistent heterodox views was *Gnosticism, a complex system of mythologies which centred on the idea that matter is *evil, and salvation comes through spiritual awakening and being reunited with the divine fullness. Marcionism was another heresy, which was very popular, and it taught that Jewish elements had corrupted the pure message of God's love and that the Pauline gospel was the only true one. Montanism stressed the imminence of Christ's return and the need to listen to contemporary prophets whether or not they

harmonized with Scripture. Perhaps the most threatening heresy was Arianism, which held that Christ was not fully divine, because God was incapable of communicating his substance to a human being.

A number of apologists argued against such heresies. One of the most prolific was *Irenaeus (c. 130 – c. 200). His *Against Heresies* is a lengthy polemic against 'The Gnosis falsely so called'. Against Gnosticism's spiritual elitism, Irenaeus taught the eternal validity of the 'rule of truth', the summary of apostolic teaching based on Scripture. Significantly, his writings helped establish the *authority of appointed bishops as the only certified teachers of apostolic doctrine. Unlike the gnostic masters, they taught one message, and did so publicly. It was not apologists as individuals only who responded to heresy. Church councils were called upon to settle various doctrinal disputes and to issue clear statements of faith. For example, the Council of Nicea (325) condemned Arianism, asserting that there was 'one Lord Jesus Christ the Son of God, begotten of the Father, only-begotten, that is from the substance of the Father'.

Apologetics in Christendom

The second great episode in church history, and thus in Christian apologetics, was introduced when the Emperor Constantine published the Edict of Milan in 312. This gave Christians freedom of worship and returned all confiscated properties to the church. In the centuries that followed, the church moved from the status of outsider into full legitimacy. As Christendom became established, apologetics developed both in form and content, giving it a far more systematic character. In the early church, being a philosopher and being a Christian were considered mutually exclusive, but beginning with *Augustine (354–430) theology began to draw upon philosophy more and more and Christianity was seen as a more perfect philosophy. Augustine, while strongly influenced by *Plato and neo-*Platonism, had nevertheless a strong biblical base. He justified using the wisdom of philosophy as 'spoiling the Egyptians'. His *City of God* is a masterpiece of polemical writing. It critiques paganism, establishes a linear philosophy of history and defends Christians from the charge of complicity in the sack of Rome.

The Venerable Bede (673–735) encouraged monks to develop a style of Christian scholarship which would benefit from a philosopher's way of thinking and living. Peter *Abelard (1049–1172) wrote a dialogue between a philosopher, a Christian and a Jew, in which the philosopher is a Greek who is acquainted with wisdom, while the Jew is bound to his senses, needing *miracles and earthly signs. By the time of *Thomas Aquinas (1225–74), philosophy became the 'handmaid' of theology. In the *Summa Theologica*, Aquinas affirms that theology supplies further doctrine than philosophy, but only as a different order, because some matters can only be grasped through faith in revealed truth.

It should be noted that early missionaries to Europe, such as Patrick (c. 389–461), who evangelized the Irish, and Augustine, the evangelist of England, used the love of books, the liturgy and also imagery for their apologetic outreach. Patrick's stress on missions inspired many Celtic monks, who then evangelized Europe and arguably 'saved' civilization. Similarly, the vast Russian Orthodox church, beginning with the 'baptism' of Russia in 988 and living through a strong coalition of church and state, practised a sort of apologetics based on the beauty of the liturgy and the strong testimony of saintly believers. The *Autobiography* of Avvakum (d. 1682) stands as a masterpiece of Russian apologetical literature. Despite state oppression, and rivalries with the Greek Orthodox church, strong devotional and apologetic literature was produced in Russia. One need think of *Dostoevsky's portrait of Father Zosima, and of Alyosha, in *The Brothers Karamazov*, or, again, of the piety, the 'Godmanhood', proclaimed by Tolstoy and Soloviev.

The *theistic proofs

In keeping with this new confidence in philosophy, various arguments were developed in the Middle Ages which relied on methods handed down from the ancient Greeks. *Anselm of Canterbury (1033–1109) set forth what we now call the *ontological argument, in his book, the *Proslogion*, whose original title was *Faith Seeking Understanding*. His procedure is first to define God as 'that than which nothing greater can be conceived'. From there he proves that God must exist, since were he only in the mind, he would no longer be the greatest conceivable being. This argument did not go unopposed, and yet it has had remarkable numbers of adherents, down to our own times. Karl *Barth wrote his own *Fides Quaerens*

Intellectum (1931), in which he declared his debt to Anselm.

Another kind of theistic proof was found in several medieval theologians, including Anselm. The most influential version was offered by Thomas Aquinas. Though not found set forth in a systematic fashion in any one place, significant portions of it occur in the *Summa Contra Gentiles*, which, significantly, was intended as a manual for missionaries to the Islamic world. The premise is that because Muslims cannot be expected to believe the Scriptures, an argument from reason must be developed in order to clear the ground for the deeper doctrines. Known today as the *cosmological argument, it states that all natural things are dependent for their existence on something else. In turn, dependent things must depend on a being which is non-dependent and which exists necessarily. For example, though everything here on earth is in motion, there must be an unmoved mover, who is God. This kind of *a posteriori* argument, though attacked by David *Hume and Immanuel *Kant, has also survived down to our own times.

*Scholasticism

The content of medieval apologetics was intertwined with its form, which was most often scholastic. In essence, the term refers to a way of arguing and presenting views which synthesized Greek philosophy, particularly that of Aristotle, with the Church Fathers and the Bible. The idea was that through both faith and reason, certain questions could be settled. The standard format was that questions about such issues as the *Trinity, the problem of the will and the sacraments, were raised, answered wrongly but plausibly, and then answered correctly. Peter Abelard (1079–1142) used this scholastic form in *Sic et non* (Yes and No), which consisted of resolving differences between recognized authorities on such questions as whether *universals are real, or only names.

Despite various attempts to purge theology of scholasticism, it lasted well into the seventeenth century. Francisco de Suarez (1548–1617), author of *Defence of the Faith* and the *Metaphysical Disputations*, was a scholastic with a major influence both on theology and secular philosophy. Scholasticism also had many Protestant adherents, including Petrus Ramus (1515–72), who had considerable influence on the Puritans, and François Turretini (1623–87), whose *Institutio theologiae elenticae*, written according to the scholastic format, became a major textbook for Protestant theologians on both continents. While the strictly scholastic method is no longer used in our own times, its influence is still felt in various types of apologetics today. The fundamental idea of basing arguments on known *first principles and then moving to religious affirmations is very much present in certain contemporary polemics.

Reform and the theology of knowledge
Various movements of reform came to characterize the theology and the apologetics of the late medieval and the Renaissance periods. While not intending to be innovative, the effect of Martin Luther's (1483–1546) insistence on *sola scriptura* and *sola fide* was to set off, among other things, a revolution in the approach to human knowledge that would eventually change the way apologetics was approached. Luther found the teaching of the Church Fathers useful, but only as a secondary guide. Scripture alone was authoritative. He rejected the popular allegorical method of interpretation in favour of the simplicity of the text, which always presented Jesus Christ to the reader. He disputed the value of scholastic theology, challenging *Duns Scotus and Biel, as well as much of the Aristotelian method of knowledge, putting in their place the grace of God, his freely given 'alien righteousness', to which faith is the only appropriate response. Thus, Luther was able to stand against John Eck in the famous disputation at Leipzig (1519), denying the infallibility of church councils and the primacy of Rome. Though excommunicated for his views at the Diet of Worms (1521), he declared before the emperor that unless convinced by Scripture and sound reason he would not recant. In his polemic against *Erasmus on the *Bondage of the Will* (1525), he argued that human reason was incapable, in and of itself, of arriving at the truth.

John *Calvin (1509–64) consolidated and developed Luther's approach, centred on the glory of God in all things, including *epistemology. His *Institutes of the Christian Religion* (1559) opened with a discussion of the knowledge of God. This work is among the most arresting and learned in the annals of theology and relates the knowledge of God to the knowledge of the self. To know God, we must know ourselves, and most especially our own 'ignorance, vanity, poverty, infamy, indeed, our corruption', without which understanding we

can never know God. At the same time, it is the knowledge of God which vouchsafes the true understanding of the self, because 'no drop will be found either of wisdom and light, or of righteousness or power or rectitude, or of genuine truth, which does not flow from him, and of which he is not the cause'. Calvin questioned the ability of the unaided mind to arrive at a true knowledge of God, as depravity has affected the reasoning process, not only our moral behaviour. His view has been called the '*noetic effects of sin'. Though external proofs for the authority of Scripture were good and necessary, ultimately Scripture is self-authenticating. Because of our sin, however, only the inward testimony of the Holy Spirit can bring final assurance that it is the word of God. Neither Calvin nor Luther were philosophical apologists in the traditional sense, but both were in fact responsible for a turning point in *epistemology that had vast implications for Christian apologetics.

Modernity

Modernity is a broad movement of ideas and institutions based on a bias in favour of the new, the *modo*, over against traditional ideals. Its intellectual roots are in the *Enlightenment of the seventeenth and eighteenth centuries, while its institutional roots are in the nineteenth century. Human rationality, faith in progress and the beginning point of human self-consciousness were placed in the centre, challenging the claims of revealed religion. The scientific method, despite origins in considerable part generated from a Christian worldview, became more and more an independent test for *truth, seeming to place God in the gaps rather than as the underlying ground of all phenomena. While anything but a uniform movement, and certainly not irreligious in a monolithic way, there was nevertheless a considerable *secularization during this time. Centralized, bureaucratic government gradually replaced government by divine right, and a market economy began to replace traditional trade conventions.

Into this context, deism arose in England and spread to Germany and France. Following the views of Lord *Herbert of Cherbury, and becoming more radical through Lord Shaftsbury and Matthew *Tindal (author of the telling, *Christianity As Old As Creation*), it held that God was a loving supreme being for all people, the Father of mankind, not the

God of a particular people such as Israel. This view denied the Trinity, the incarnation, miracles and the *atonement, asserting instead the need for tolerance and kindness in human society. In the writings of French deists such as Pierre *Bayle (1647–1746) and Jean-Jacques *Rousseau (1712–78) 'free examination' replaced the inward testimony of the Holy Spirit as the favoured arbiter of truth.

Evidentialism
Not surprisingly, Christian apologetics during this time concentrated on questions provoked by these views: the nature of *doubt, tolerance, religious indifferentism and, increasingly, the problem of theodicy, or of justifying the existence of God in the face of evil. In Great Britain works of popular apologetics spread rapidly in the eighteenth century. A lectureship, named after Robert Boyle, a chief opponent of deism, was set up, bringing many defenders of the faith to the fore. Beginning in the sixteenth century, the *teleological argument, or argument from design, was introduced. It was used by such luminaries as Philippe de Mornay, Hugo *Grotius, Jacques Abbadie and, especially, William *Paley.

Bishop *Joseph Butler (1692–1752) was the most famous of the spokesmen against scepticism. His book, *The Analogy of Religion, Natural and Revealed, to the Constitution and Course of Nature* (1736) was a best-seller. It argued, among other things, that the soul was immortal, based on the theory of inertia. Miracles were believable because nature was full of surprises. While popular, his approach was not decisive. David Hume (1711–76) argued that miracles were in violation of the laws of nature, and that human testimony was so steeped in the uniformity of nature that it could not be trusted to report miracles accurately. William Paley (1743–1805) replied to Hume with a point of view that makes him the father of modern evidentialism. His approach was to amass evidences of all kinds, some based on prophecy, some on the changed lives of those who encountered Christ, some on the impossibility of Easter faith unless the resurrection were true. Paley is best known for his rehabilitation of the watchmaker *analogy. In his *Natural Theology* (1802) he opens with the comparison between the world and a watch. Just as it is unthinkable for the watch not to have been made by a craftsman, so the world, which is far more complex than a watch, cannot be conceived to have come about without a designer.

Evidentialism, modified along the way by various approaches, such as the Common Sense philosophy of Thomas Chalmers (1780–1847), has become one the of the major tools of Christian apologetics. In the twentieth century evidentialism was developed most thoughtfully by authors such as J. N. D. Anderson, in *Christianity: The Witness of History* (1969), and E. J. *Carnell, in *The Case for Biblical Christianity* (1969). Their approach is to match the claims of the Christian religion with historical and empirical data that are open to *verification by rational means. Richard Swinburne uses high level philosophical arguments in defence of the validity of miracles and other evidences as testimonies to the claims of Christ. At the more popular level, we could cite the works of John Warwick Montgomery and the evangelist Josh McDowell, whose series *Evidence that Demands a Verdict* has become widely known in evangelical circles.

Theodicy
In this same atmosphere, the problem of evil became one of the central issues in apologetics. Here, the works of G. W. *Leibniz (1646–1716) are important. He hoped in his *Demonstrationes Catholicae* (1669) to set forth a programme for the religious unity of all of Europe and also for the best way to evangelize the rest of the world. The text discusses proofs for God's existence and various evidences for the veracity of the Bible and of Christian doctrine. In his *Theodicy* (1710) Leibniz argues against Pierre Bayle that faith and *logic are compatible. Even evil can be present in a world in which God is perfect, while the rest of creation enjoys various degrees of imperfection. We live, as he put it, in 'the best of all possible worlds'. We may remember *Voltaire's vigorous and sardonic reply in *Candide*.

The most significant figure in this context is Blaise *Pascal (1623–62). Both a scientist and an apologist, he was an Augustinian, with strong sympathies with Jansenism (an anti-Pelagian reform movement within the *Roman Catholic Church in the seventeenth century). His unfinished *Pensées* is a masterpiece of French literature as well as a powerful apology against the religious indifference of his day, particularly the group known as libertines, the decadent nobility, lulled into spiritual lethargy by constant *entertainment. In addition to the sort of evidentialism he shared with his times, Pascal also argued from the grandeur of God and the misery of mankind. In his famous wager, he tells his decadent, freethinking readers that if Christianity is true then one has gained everything by believing it, but even if it is false, one has lost nothing. Though hardly opposed to reason, he insisted that 'the heart has its reasons which reason cannot know'.

Safeguarding religion
Despite the popularity of evidentialism, in the judgment of many it has not successfully been able to answer David Hume and his successors. A very different kind of answer was given by the Enlightenment's greatest philosopher, Immanuel Kant (1724–1804). He opposed traditional deductive theology, which he deemed dogmatic. He rejected all the classical proofs because they were human constructs that reasoned their way up to God and declared that only moral consciousness was certain. This resulted from his need to answer Hume, whose scepticism awoke him, as he put it, from his dogmatic slumbers. He needed to provide a warrant for *a priori* knowledge and to guarantee a 'transcendental deduction' from timeless laws, without which experience is impossible. *Ethics is not a matter of obedience to divine *law but categorical imperatives based on the good will as the *summum bonum*. Religious faith is not subject to scientific verification because it belongs to pure reason. While Kant meant to be safeguarding religion at the same time as allowing *science to progress unhampered, the effect of his philosophy was to reduce religion to morals and to cut it off from *history.

Friedrich *Schleiermacher (1768–1834) stepped into the breech and became the defining apologist for the entire nineteenth century. Along with Kant, he judged orthodoxy outdated and sterile, but unlike Kant he insisted on connecting faith to history, science and *culture. Yet he refused so to attach religion either to science or *morality that it lost its savour. His answer was to explain religion as the universal feeling (*Gefühl*) of utter dependence. Like a sacred music, religious feeling accompanied all of life, but was reducible to no single part of it. His best known apological work is the manifesto, *Speeches on Religion*, with the telling subtitle, *To the Cultured among Its Despisers* (1799). Schleiermacher intended

by this approach to place Christian faith on a sure footing, one that was not tied down to specific dogmas. While his readers could see that the Christian faith was but one of many, an honest look at the person of Jesus should have convinced them it was the most admirable. Schleiermacher was a pioneer in hermeneutics, the interpretation of Scripture and the analysis of *language's ability to express faith. Thus, though religion is a feeling of dependence, science should have free reign, especially in the exegesis of Scripture and in the development of theology as a discipline. In his *Brief Outline on the Study of Theology* (1830) he elaborated his programme for apologetics. The traditional disciplines, biblical, historical and practical theology, should be prefaced by a new discipline, to be called 'philosophical theology', which in turn is divided into two branches, apologetics and polemics. The task of the former is not so much to evangelize (which is part of practical theology) but to give believers intellectual underpinnings for the continuity of Christian faith from its early days.

In a way Schleiermacher set the tone for much of the discussion throughout both the nineteenth and the twentieth centuries. How can one relate the subjective to the objective realities of religion? Whether in the form of earlier liberalism or in various modified versions, apologists have had to wrestle with ways to honour the proper place for *religious experience while engaging the work of science. Paul *Tillich (1886–1965) developed the 'method of correlation', which tracked the way our basic religious questions are raised in any given culture, and then correlated them with theological answers meant to lead believers back to the ground of being.

Apologetics in question

Shattered by the carnage of the First World War and rendered implausible for its overly human theology, the older liberalism and its *a posteriori* apologetics were deemed bankrupt. Karl Barth (1886–1968) opposed Schleiermacher's arguments and put into question the entire enterprise of apologetics. Though still dependent on the terms set for the discussion by Kant and Schleiermacher, Christian faith for Barth was not a series of propositional truths but a dynamic relationship between Christ and the sinner. He also argued that the Bible and the Word, which are not *per se* identical, are in a dialectical relationship. In this light, he saw in apologetics a regrettable tendency to allow unbelief to define the issues. He was no doubt thinking of Schleiermacher's apologetics, far too human for a sovereign God. Ironically, Barth's works are nothing if not strongly polemical in their form.

In our own day there has been much discussion about whether modernity has exhausted itself. The favourite term employed in asserting the demise of the modern is postmodernism or, more exactly, the postmodern condition. It is meant to signify that 'meta-narratives', i.e. rationally warranted, exhaustive world-views, are no longer believable. In their place, any number of substitutes, from the modest to the more ambitious, have been proposed. Christian apologetics is thus obliged to wrestle with two issues: are we indeed in postmodern times and what is the best way to respond? Apologists such as Thomas Oden in *After Modernity ... What?* (1990), and the team of Brian Walsh and J. R. Middleton, in *Truth Is Stranger than It Used to Be* (1995), believe there has been a significant shift away from modernity and that apologists need to respond to the postmodern condition. Others disagree, accepting with Jürgen Habermas and Anthony Giddens that modernity cannot be supplanted because it is too well-rooted in its institutional forms. Swiss theologian Pierre Gisel believes Christians can work well within a postmodern framework and that even the philosophy of Michel *Foucault can be marshalled into service. Others are far more sceptical. In the wide-ranging works of social commentators David Wells and Ken Meyers, the assumptions of postmodernist claims are challenged and the church is invited to exercise a more critically enlightened faith and life.

Transcendental apologetics

Several, more theologically orthodox, responses to modernity and the Enlightenment's challenge should be noted. The first is a loose-knit school of thought that has become known as presuppositionalism, or the transcendental approach. Claiming an essential continuity with historic Christian views, it began in earnest with a conservative reaction to the French Revolution. Early nineteenth-century Roman Catholic historians such as Joseph de Maistre and Guillaume Groen Van Prinsterer denounced the French Revolution, believing it to have been guided by a fundamentally anti-Christian spiritual principle. Groen's greatest student

Abraham *Kuyper (1837–1920) expanded this idea of an underlying spiritual ground motive and reckoned that cultures could be either regenerate or unregenerate in their basic identity. This was the beginning of modern world-view thinking. Kuyper hoped to find a religious principle behind every cultural expression, whether it be political, artistic, scientific or educational. He developed the idea of sphere sovereignty, the notion that each institution, the church, the state, the school, the family, occupied a sovereign, though overlapping territory.

Kuyper had considerable influence. Among his notable progeny were the members of the so-called Amsterdam philosophers, D. H. Th. *Vollenhoven, H. G. *Stoker and, especially, Herman Dooyeweerd (1894–1977), co-founders of the 'Philosophy of the Cosmonomic Idea'. *Dooyeweerd's monumental *New Critique of Theoretical Thought* (1953) was a 'transcendental critique' of various philosophies and sought to unmask their pretensions to autonomy by laying bare their ground motives. These were inevitably dualistic and dialectical, since unbelief is by nature unstable. Only the biblical ground motive of creation-fall-redemption is stable enough to hold up.

Closely tied to the Amsterdam school, but far more committed to the interface of theology with philosophy, Cornelius *Van Til (1895–1987) became one of the twentieth century's most original, and controversial, apologists. He founded the school of apologetics to be known as presuppositionalism, a term he did not use much but which became a major alternative to both the classical and the evidentialist views. As the name implies, the method insists on acknowledging that an ultimate conceptual framework must govern every argument and every appeal to data. Neither laws of *logic nor evidences are neutral. In *The Defense of the Faith* (1967) Van Til vigorously challenges traditional apologetics for being unable to go to the root of an unbelieving system, and thus ending up conceding too much ground. Instead, apologists must demonstrate that only from a self-attesting, triune God can reality hold together and have any meaning.

A host of apologists were influenced, at least in part, by Van Til's presuppositional approach. The most philosophically capable is the American epistemologist, John Frame, whose work on the theological basis for knowledge continues the Van Til tradition with a precision and creativity exceeding the master. The most notable is Francis A. *Schaeffer (1912–84), the leader of the community called *L'Abri* in the Swiss Alps. With his collaborator, the art historian H. R. *Rookmaaker, he developed a critique of Western culture which formed the background for his lectures and writings on apologetics. Not an academic, his method was to use broad strokes, with illustrations drawn from the sciences, the arts, popular culture and current events. Like Dooyeweerd and Van Til, Schaeffer described unbelief as dualistic and unstable. Yet there was always a latent conservatism in his outlook which led him to hold to a declinist historiography and to a right-leaning approach to various social issues. Schaeffer's most noteworthy follower is Os *Guinness, prolific writer and the director of the Trinity Forum, an 'academy without walls' dedicated to reaching the gate-keepers of society with a concern for truth and moral integrity. Guinness and others have made apologists aware of the social dimension of belief and unbelief. Using concepts drawn from the sociology of knowledge, they argue from plausibility and cultural factors rather than from exclusively logical philosophical constructs.

Authentic faith

Many other exponents of a more orthodox theology, not related to the presuppositionalist school, have arisen in response to modernity. Chief among them in the nineteenth century was the enigmatic Danish thinker Søren *Kierkegaard (1813–55). He reacted strongly to *Hegel's grand, rational system, and pleaded instead for an individual discovery of God's call. There is a certain absurdity in trusting God, he held, not because faith is irrational but because God may ask us to go beyond the conventional path of conformity if we are to be authentic Christians. It is almost impossible to trace with accuracy the considerable influence of Kierkegaard on the following generations, both inside and outside the church. He left his mark on Karl Barth. One of his most creative followers was Jacques Ellul (1912–94), a French Reformed apologist whose work on the rise of technical society, *La technique ou l'enjeu du siècle* (1954), was prescient of a culture based on efficiency rather than meaning. He was also the perceptive critic of the secularization theory that held we were evolving into a religionless state, an impossibility according to

Ellul, since we are religious by nature. The best we can do is substitute 'new demons' like *hedonism or totalitarianism for the older beliefs of Christendom.

Imaginative apologetics

In yet another tradition, mostly in the United Kingdom, an original and creative group of apologists with extraordinary literary faculties emerged. The prolific writer G. K. *Chesterton (1874–1936) is one of the most quoted pundits in the English language. His use of *paradox in argumentation was deployed throughout his writings in an attempt to subvert unbelief, e.g. he called orthodoxy 'the one and only really unpardonable heresy'.

C. S. *Lewis (1898–1963) was perhaps the twentieth century's greatest apologist, though he is hard to put into a standard category. A scholar of medieval literature, he wrote novels, mostly fantasies with a Christian subtext, and also theological works defending miracles, the need for *absolutes in education and God's goodness in the face of evil. His children's stories the *Chronicles of Narnia* have sold in the millions. His direct apologetic writings, while not immune from criticism, are lucid and compelling. In many ways Lewis resembles his mentor George *MacDonald, the Scottish man of letters whose *The Golden Key* and other stories have spoken to many readers. Lewis was also a close associate of J. R. R. *Tolkien and Dorothy *Sayers, both 'apologists' with enormous literary gifts. It is quite possible that we have this circle of literati to thank for the very survival of Christian apologetics in our times.

Into a new century

Here, we must move from the more assured into the realm of conjecture. What appears certain is that the centre of gravity will continue to move from Europe and North America to the rest of the world. This will bring with it challenges new and old. Ten issues (among others) merit attention.

Apologetic theology

The very way in which we do theology will no doubt be modified in the future. Though originally Middle Eastern and North African, mainstream theology has been dominated by the West for many centuries. This has given it certain characteristics. But now non-Western theologies are emerging which have certain original accents. For example, most are far more missiological in nature, and it could be said that because of that they are more apologetical in character. Even in the West, Jürgen Moltmann has suggested that all theology should be apologetic. Much of Hans Urs von Balthasar's theological writing is in the vein of *cultural apologetics. But theology done in the two-thirds world is already openly apologetical, and this should reverberate on theology worldwide.

Back to the Fathers

There is no doubt that in many places around the world, apologetics will pick up on the defining themes of the early church, persecutions and heresies. In our own times, Christians are severely oppressed in many parts of the world. The example of the persecuted church in China is particularly poignant. Recently, a number of leaders in the house church network have drafted a declaration of faith to be presented to the government. It resembles classical statements of faith by covering topics such as God, mankind, sin, redemption, etc., but it also spells out the mutual responsibilities of believers and those in authority and argues that not only must government not persecute the church but it is in the State's own best interests to treat the church with respect. Unfortunately, this document met mostly with hostility. In the West, terrorist attacks on the free world mean that apologetics will need to steer believers into the clear distinctions of church and state, the need for loving one's enemies and the need for public *justice.

Numerous organizations exist to assist Christians who are oppressed for their faith. Not only do they call on the church around the world, and the international community, to rally in support of the oppressed, but they counsel various ways to use Christian apologetics as a defence of the faith. Persecution may be direct and violent, as in countries such as China, but it can be more subtle, stemming from prevailing cultural ideologies even in free countries. Wisdom is needed in those circumstances to know which battles to fight and which to overlook. In North America, one campus Christian ministry has faced opposition from advocates of radical diversity. Wary of the dangers, it published guidelines for its leaders on how to handle those with whom they disagree. It contains statements about being persuasive without being offensive, reminding them of the rules for civil discussions.

Heresies, too, are found in abundance today. As in the early church, responding to heresy is a way of defining the church in its unity. The challenge is, first, to define heresy in order properly to identify it, and then, second, to know how to respond with an appropriate defence of the truth. It is not always simple to know what is an unbiblical variant on Christian faith and what is squarely outside the faith. Yet, it is telling that most heresies today are but the earlier ones in a slightly different guise. For example, Gnosticism, with its spiritual elitism, has many forms today, and the theologians of 'open theism' are moving in the same direction as Pelagianism. Many of the patterns found in Arianism are also repeated in places like Unitarianism and the Jehovah's Witnesses.

*Pluralism and diversity

Surely the theology of religions will become a principal item on the agenda for the new century's apologetics. This has become abundantly clear after the end of the cold war, and the beginning of the intensive threats of international *terrorism. From the beginning, missionaries and theologians have reached out to adherents of the *world religions. The letter to the Romans outlines unbelief in terms of the knowledge of God gone wrong (Rom. 1:18–27), but what of the Hindu who is seeking to escape the slavery of the life-death cycle and practise good karma and the Confucianist trying to honour parents and ancestors? Are these religions entirely off course and groundless? May we find in them parallels to the Christian story and discover redemptive analogies there? Today the question of the status of non-Christians is particularly urgent. What of people who have never heard the gospel? Apologetics will have to provide some careful guidelines here.

In this connection, *New Age thought and the fascination with Eastern religions continues to grow in the West. Part of the attraction stems from resentment of an overly technological society and the need to find solace in less rational experience. From soft medicines, to vegetarian diets, to transactional *psychology in corporate culture, there is no end of quasi-mystical variants. Various cults continue to multiply as well, some of them aggressive, others more syncretistic.

This raises the related matter of how people

can live side by side with others who differ significantly in culture and confession. Because of the increasing plurality of cultures and ethnic groups living in close communication, apologetics will have to be concerned with issues such as public policy and justice for all peoples, without sacrificing truth and Christian conviction. Conflict resolution will become a sister discipline to apologetics. It is widely believed that many of the world's conflicts are related to religious identity. Richard Dawkins asserts that religion causes wars by 'generating certainty'. This is not as evident as it may appear, but apologetics will have to provide some answers. Because of its increasing presence in the world, Islam will become a special subject of apologetic discussion.

Good models are needed for conflict resolution and cohabitation. Related issues include: the danger of the privatization of our faith while we avoid illegitimate ways of transforming culture; the proper relation of the church to the state; how Christians can work towards a just society without attempting to legislate one particular faith; the legitimacy of going to war; and how to answer the increasing violence in society, especially among young people.

Ethnicity and *gender

Furthermore, although the ultimate gospel truths are universal, responsible apologetics will have to apply its discourse to specific communities. This is already beginning to occur, e.g. the American team Craig S. Keener and Glenn Usry have written on a number of occasions addressing African-American consciousness. In *Defending Black Faith* (1997), they address questions such as, Afrocentrism, the Nation of Islam and *slavery in the OT. Similarly, work is coming out on apologetics to modern Jews, to university students and even to the teenaged skateboard culture.

In a similar vein, more attention will need to be paid to *gender issues in apologetics. Both the church and the world have been made more aware of women's rights in the last few decades, but feminists often accuse the Bible of being misogynist because of its apparent patriarchy. Apologists are already addressing this kind of issue, but more will have to be done. Related to this, the question of homosexual identity will become an issue needing clarification. This matter will be critical for apologetics in our new century. Finally, *marriage and the family will have to be affirmed in a way that does no injury to single persons.

*Globalization

Certainly, globalization raises many questions which Christian apologists will be obliged to answer. At its most basic level, globalization means the unprecedented mobility of capital, people and ideas around the world and across cultural barriers. It has both a political and an economic dimension, but it also has a religious dimension, relating to the need to find meaning in the midst of an economically driven world market. According to some sociologists, a powerful few will be able to annul time and space, resulting in the dispossessing of local communities. Churches, particularly in urban settings, will have a special responsibility to defend the gospel in the face of a global hyperculture. More reflection will be needed on the uses and abuses of mass communication, especially the internet, the cell phone, e-mail, and the like.

Intelligent design

In the arena of science, many voices are being raised to speak against a chance or purely evolutionary origin of the universe. For example, Oxford philosopher Richard Swinburne, affirms in *The Existence of God* (1979) that the cumulative effect of a series of inductive arguments (reasoning from a part to the whole) is persuasive of theism. Another sort of argument from design, one which interfaces with science and *natural theology, is enormously popular at the present. Spearheaded by Hugh Ross, Michael Behe and Philip Johnson, it centres on the notion of 'irreducible complexity'. One cannot explain the complex phenomenon of the eye, for example, with a series of consecutive evolutionary steps. Like the mousetrap, no component makes sense without all the others, which is proof that it has a teleology. Despite their tendency toward 'concordism', overharmonizing Scripture and science, this school has made considerable inroads into both the academic and the popular mind.

Philosophical apologetics

In many ways, philosophical apologetics is not only alive and well, but on the rise. Stemming from the neo-Thomist revivals, Roman Catholic apologists continue to work as serious philosophers defending Christian faith, e.g. Joseph Maréchal, Karl *Rahner and Bernard

Lonergan. Many Protestants have adhered to this tradition as well. In the twentieth century the most notable were E. L. Mascall and August LeCerf. On the more popular level, John Gerstner, Arthur Lindsley and R. C. Sproul have kept the theistic proofs alive, albeit in somewhat modified versions, careful to avoid the charge of rationalism. In their *Classical Apologetics* (Preface, p. x), these authors state, 'We affirm reason without *rationalism, personal love without personalism, faith without *fideism.' Again, in North America, the Talbot School of Theology is the seat of a revival of the classical approach. Drawing partly on the work of George Mavrodes and William Alston, Christian philosophers William Lane Craig and J. P. Moreland believe that although the fundamental work of conviction must be that of the Holy Spirit, sound argument can and must play a supplemental role. They rely on updated versions of the cosmological argument and the human ability to judge empirical data and conclude, inductively, that the Christian message is the most likely explanation for the evidence.

Christian philosophers have recently risen to prominence in the academic world. It is quite remarkable to note that because of the influence of Alvin Plantinga, Nicholas Wolterstorff, Paul Helm, William Alston, Eleanor Stump and many others, the American academic philosophical community has been strongly marked by a conservative Christian theology. Almost all their work has a forceful apologetic character. This stands in stark contrast to the previous consensus of positivism, the theory that claims only hard facts and verification by empirical measurement will yield any knowledge worthy of its name. Perhaps the most notable is Alvin Plantinga. In his earlier works, *The Nature of Necessity* and *God, Freedom, and Evil*, he used a variant on the ontological argument. More recently he has argued that belief in God is 'properly basic', without needing outside evidence. In 1978 The Society of Christian Philosophers was formed through the leadership of Plantinga, George Mavrodes, Arthur Holmes and Robert and Marilyn Adams. It has grown to a membership of 1,200, and publishes the influential journal, *Faith and Philosophy*.

World ethics

Apologetics in the new century will interface a good deal more with ethics. Particular areas such as medical- and bio-ethics, ecology, work and rest, will become prominent on the agenda. Finding a proper moral framework with which to decide questions such as the status of the unborn child, stem cell research, euthanasia, genetic engineering and the like is a part of commending the veracity of Christian faith. Certain related particular challenges, especially the AIDS pandemic, are closely related to apologetics, because they raise so many questions about God's goodness, styles of life and the relation of scientific research to cultural issues. What is the proper balance between development and care for the earth? What is meant by rest, and by leisure?

Along these lines, the whole area of guilt, shame and atonement will become a strong feature of apologetics in the emerging century. It is likely that apologetics will increasingly need to find ways to explain atonement for human guilt, both corporate and individual. At the corporate level, in the more developed countries guilt is often hidden or avoided. This masking is produced by the surrounding affluence and refusal to be as generous as we could be. Ironically, all kinds of disorders and abnormalities plague us. Also, the uneasy legacy of misspent military ventures can produce a bad conscience for generations.

In less developed countries guilt often takes the form of shame. This is because in more hierarchical societies protocol requires honour in relationships. When honour is breeched, shame and loss of face result. On the individual level many are experiencing the kind of guilt that comes from keeping secrets and hiding illicit behaviour. This can produce serious psychological consequences. Ultimately, all of this is rooted in our universal guilt before God. Reparations will undoubtedly be required by troubled countries and by oppressed ethnic groups across the world. Further, the church will have to decide when and how to respond with the demand for apologies, as illustrated by the Pope's apology to the Jews for the evils visited upon them in the past.

The shape of meaning

While the gospel message remains unchanged, new circumstances require new ways of shaping that message. A greater use of paradox, of the *arts, of healing communities and of imagination, will be called for. Here, lessons may be learned from the Orthodox Church, which has always had a stronger place for aesthetics than Western theologies.

There are signs that the mood for deconstruction and postmodernism is on the wane. Part of the reason is exhaustion, and part is the changing configuration of the world after the demise of totalitarian ideologies. This means that after living in hibernation for some time, questions of meaning, of beauty and of absolutes will reemerge. In France today, after *Derrida, it is acceptable once again to discuss the meaning of life as a philosophical issue. It is likely that the arts will be a major forum for the revival of truth. In this vein, the work of Jeremy Begbie's forum on theology through the arts, and Mako Fujimura's *International Arts Ministry* are promising and an example of the church returning to its roots. The cultivation of the imagination will become ever more important, with the need to cultivate metaphor, analogy and imagery in order to point to the truth of God's ways and of his person. Hermeneutics will continue to be a central concern, from the defence of biblical authority to questions of criticism and interpretation of texts of all kinds. It will be important to avoid the Scylla of *modern* bare propositional truth without falling into the Charybdis of *postmodern* randomness.

The gospel

Specific issues to be addressed in the new century could well be multiplied. Undoubtedly, there is an apologetical facet to almost everything that matters deeply in human experience. But surely the most central issue of all, one which has always been primary, and which is more crucial than ever, is the call to know God and to worship him. The centre of apologetics should quite naturally be the centre of the Christian message. Though we have fallen from God's presence, Jesus Christ has come into the world to save sinners. Because of Christ's finished work at Calvary, and because of his resurrection from the dead, we now have access to the grace of God through faith in his Son. The first task of apologetics is to persuade men and women that salvation is freely offered to all, and that their only hope in life or in death is in Jesus Christ, God's Son, the Saviour of the world.

Bibliography

L. R. Bush (ed.), *Classical Readings in Christian Apologetics, AD 100–1800* (Grand Rapids, 1983); A. Dulles, *A History of Apologetics* (Philadelphia, 1971); W. Dyrness, *Christian Apologetics in a World Community* (Downers Grove, 1983); W. R. Everdell, *Christian Apologetics in France, 1730–1790: The Roots of Romantic Religion* (Lewiston, 1987); P. J. Griffiths, *An Apology for Apologetics: A Study in the Logic of Interreligious Dialogue* (Maryknoll, 1991); R. M. Grant, *Greek Apologists of the Second Century* (Philadelphia, 1988); D. J. Hoitenga, Jr, *Faith and Reason from Plato to Plantinga: An Introduction to Reformed Epistemology* (Albany, 1991); F. Laplanche, *L'évidence du Dieu Chrétien, Religion, Culture et Societé dans l'Apologétique Protestante de la France Classique 1576–1670* (Strasbourg, 1983); R. Palmer, *Catholics and Unbelievers in Eighteenth Century France* (Princeton, 1939); B. Ramm, *Varieties of Christian Apologetics* (Grand Rapids, 1962); A. P. F. Sell, *Defending and Declaring the Faith: Some Scottish Examples 1860–1920* (Exeter and Colorado Springs, 1987); R. C. Sproul, J. Gerstner and A. Lindsley, *Classical Apologetics: A Rational Defense of the Christian Faith and a Critique of Presuppositional Apologetics* (Grand Rapids, 1984).

W. EDGAR

Approaches to Christian Apologetics

From the earliest days of the church, Christians have been concerned with apologetics, the attempt to defend and support Christian faith by arguments. The apologist for the faith is one who attempts to show the truth and/or reasonableness of Christian faith, either positively or by rebutting objections to faith. Throughout the history of apologetics, there have been various attempts to categorize apologetic arguments. Many have distinguished positive apologetics, which tries to support Christian faith directly, from negative apologetics, which tries to remove barriers to faith by repelling attacks of various kinds. Another helpful categorization, particularly for understanding different approaches to *natural theology, is between apologetic approaches that take as their starting place reflection on the self, as in *Augustine, and approaches that take as their starting place reflection on the cosmos or the natural world, as in *Thomas Aquinas.

Gordon Lewis has classified types of apologetics according to their underlying religious epistemologies, distinguishing, e.g., between the empiricist approach exemplified by J. Oliver Buswell Jr and the *rationalism illustrated in Gordon Clark. In 1953 Bernard *Ramm published a book, *Types of Apologetic Systems*, that distinguished between approaches centring on subjective immediacy (*Pascal, *Kierkegaard), those centring on natural theology (Aquinas, *Butler) and those centring on *revelation (*Augustine, Edward John *Carnell).

Steven B. Cowan's recent *Five Views on Apologetics* (Grand Rapids, 2000) distinguishes the following types of approaches. The classical method involves a 'two-step' apologetic in which arguments for God's existence are followed by historical evidences for *miracles, the *resurrection of Jesus, and the *authority of the Bible. What Cowan calls the evidential method disputes the need for this first step (natural theology or its analogue) and argues directly for both the existence of God and the truth of Christianity from miracles, fulfilled prophecies and other historical evidences. The cumulative case method regards evidences of

many different kinds as providing an 'inference to the best explanation' for Christian faith. The presuppositionalist attempts to show that all systems of thought begin with *first principles or presuppositions and argues that Christianity alone provides presuppositions that can be consistently developed and lived. Finally, the Reformed epistemologist argues that belief in God, and even full-orbed Christian belief, can be rational even if not based on evidence at all.

In looking at these approaches to apologetics, one can view them as 'ideal types', using that term as Max Weber did to represent pure constructs that may not be perfectly exemplified. When we look at actual individuals instead of ideal types, the differences between these types may be significantly reduced. For example, William Craig, who represents the 'classical' approach in the Cowan volume, concedes to his 'evidential' opponents that one might well argue directly from miracles to the truth of Christianity in a 'one-step' apologetic. He also concedes to the Reformed epistemologist that one can rationally believe in God and even have knowledge of God that is not based on arguments or evidence at all, but rather on the work of the Spirit of God within the life of a person. From the other side, the 'Reformed epistemologist' Kelly Clark, while maintaining that faith without arguments or evidence is reasonable, agrees that arguments can be given and that they can be useful. Practically, there may not be nearly so much disagreement about the methodology of apologetics as might at first be thought.

The ideal types that inspired the organization of Cowan's book do, however, make a useful starting point for sorting out questions concerning apologetics. We may begin by noting that three of the approaches form a natural grouping or family. The classical, evidential and cumulative case views all seem to assume that the task of apologetics is to provide evidence for Christianity, either to show that Christianity is true, probably true, or more likely to be true than its rivals. Alternatively, one could think of the goal as providing evidence that shows Christian belief

15

to be reasonable or more reasonable than its rivals. The three views disagree about the kind of evidence needed to do the job, and perhaps in some cases about the strength of the evidence and how the evidence supports Christianity (what one might call the logical form of the evidence). By and large, however, all three think of the task of apologetics as providing evidence. We could call all three of these views 'evidentialist' approaches as there is no good reason to give to the approach that emphasizes historical and empirical evidence sole possession of this label.

The other two approaches, the 'presuppositional' and the 'Reformed epistemology' views, both have some roots in Reformed theology. Although they do not seem to have much in common that is positive, they both seem to agree that knowledge of Christianity, or even reasonable belief, does not have to rest on evidence. We could usefully group these views as well, then, and call them 'non-evidentialist' approaches.

It is more important to focus on the fundamental questions raised by the distinction between evidentialists and non-evidentialists (in my sense) than to focus on the relatively finer distinctions between types of evidentialists. The crucial questions raised by the disagreements between evidentialists and non-evidentialists would seem to be the following: What role does evidence play in Christian belief? Is it essential, helpful, or could it even be harmful?

These questions are best answered in the context of actual apologists. Two outstanding Christian philosophers, Richard Swinburne and Alvin Plantinga, have developed comprehensive accounts that are regarded even by their opponents as models of powerful argument. We shall therefore turn to them as, respectively, exemplars of the evidentialist and non-evidentialist approaches. A careful look at the particulars of their work will help us to see why they give different answers to the questions raised. In conclusion we will suggest some lessons to be drawn from each and tentatively suggest ways in which evidentialist and non-evidentialist strategies may be regarded as complementary.

Richard Swinburne's evidentialist apologetic

Over the last thirty years Richard Swinburne has published a formidable series of works that mount a case for the reasonableness of Christian faith as understood in the ecumenical

Christian creeds. The case begins with an argument that the concept of God is logically coherent, and thus the central claims of Christian faith are not logically inconsistent. It then proceeds to a complex argument for the reasonableness of belief in God. The argument is really a series of converging arguments, thus providing what some would call a 'cumulative case' or 'inference to the best explanation'. Swinburne's arguments are, broadly speaking, inductive in nature, in that they take as their starting point observable facts, and they are probabilistic in character as well.

For Swinburne, a good explanation is one that is simple, that allows us to predict many facts (and different types of facts), that fits well with our background knowledge, and that has no rival that does a better job of satisfying these criteria. In general, Swinburne uses the probability calculus to assess the adequacy of a theory, and determines the probability of a theory by a combination of its prior probability (or the probability it has in itself apart from the evidence to be explained) and its explanatory power, its ability to account for the evidence under consideration. In the case of God's existence, since the theory is basically one that is supposed to explain everything, there is no 'background knowledge' from adjacent fields that is relevant. In such a case, Swinburne believes that the prior probability of God's existence is basically a function of the simplicity of the theory. Since the existence of God, understood as a being with infinite power, knowledge, freedom and goodness, is a very simple theory, then the prior probability is relatively high in comparison with alternatives such as *materialism (which is also a 'theory of everything').

Furthermore, the view that there is a God does have explanatory power. Here Swinburne appeals to the kind of considerations traditionally treated by natural theology, including especially *cosmological arguments, *teleological arguments, and arguments from *religious experience. The existence of God explains such facts as that there is a universe at all, that the universe is one that operates according to orderly laws, and that the universe produces animals and humans with consciousness and with complex, intricately ordered bodies. The view that there is a God also explains the fact that humans have religious experiences and that some have experienced miracles and answers to prayer. Swinburne also argues that *evil provides no evidence against God's existence. All of these things together 'make it significantly more probable than not that there is a God' (*Is There a God?*, p. 139).

Swinburne goes on to employ the same kind of inductive, probabilistic, cumulative case argument to defend more specifically Christian beliefs. In these arguments the evidence from natural theology plays an important role in providing background knowledge; if we have good reason to believe in God then it will be much more reasonable to believe that God might reveal himself and authenticate that revelation by doing miracles. Furthermore, Swinburne argues that we have some reason to expect that the revelation would include an *atonement and involve an incarnation. The evidence that a particular individual was God incarnate would include such things as living a morally perfect life, teaching deep moral truths, showing that he himself believed he was God incarnate, teaching that his life included an atonement for sins, and founding a *community to carry on his work. In addition to these 'marks', Swinburne holds that in the case of a true incarnation, God would provide a 'super-miracle' as an authentication of the incarnation. *Jesus of Nazareth satisfies all of these criteria, but no other religious figure from human history has ever come close to doing so.

Swinburne's apologetic case can be seen to have some of the features of all of the three forms of 'evidentialism' treated in Cowan's volume. It provides a classic two-step evidential argument, but it allows, as part of that broader case, for miracles and special religious experiences to have independent evidential value. And the overall argument is clearly a rigorous form of a cumulative case argument.

Swinburne's apologetic strategy rests on a view of belief as linked to evidence. For Swinburne, to believe a proposition *p* is to believe that *p* is more probable than some alternative, and he understands probability to be a function of evidence. A defence of the reasonableness of Christian belief must then take the form of showing that there is evidence for Christian beliefs. As we shall see, Alvin Plantinga's version of Reformed epistemology questions this basic assumption.

Alvin Plantinga's Reformed epistemology

It is not an overstatement to say that Alvin Plantinga and his fellow Reformed epistemologists have revolutionized discussions in

apologetics and philosophy of religion in the past twenty-five years. Previously, debates hinged around the question of what kind of evidence is required for religious belief and whether enough evidence of that kind is available. Reformed epistemology changed the terms of the debate by arguing that belief in God, and even more specific Christian beliefs, can be 'properly basic' and not founded on evidence at all.

'Warrant' is Plantinga's term for that quality (whatever it is) which, when possessed in sufficient quantity, and added to true belief, makes such belief knowledge. In *Warrant and Proper Function* (New York, 1993) Plantinga developed his account of warrant in some detail and applied it to various types of knowledge. *Warranted Christian Belief* (New York, 2000) draws on this epistemological theory and develops an account of how a person might know Christian doctrines to be true.

The central thrust of Plantinga's argument is that Christian doctrines are not known to be true on the basis of evidence. Many philosophers have held that not all of our beliefs can be based on other beliefs; to avoid an infinite regress some must be basic or foundational in character. It has commonly been assumed, however, that belief in God could not be basic because, according to the epistemology of classical *foundationalism, only beliefs that are highly certain (self-evident, incorrigible or evident to the senses) can properly be basic. Plantinga criticizes classical foundationalism both for being self-stultifying, since the claim that only highly certain beliefs should be properly basic is not itself highly certain and cannot be shown to be probable on the basis of such highly certain beliefs, and for leading to the counter-intuitive result that most of the things we think we know (such as what we ate for breakfast this morning) we do not in fact know (*Warranted Christian Belief*, pp. 94–99).

Plantinga therefore adopts a fallibilist version of foundationalism. Memory beliefs and perceptual beliefs are typical examples of properly basic beliefs and they can have this status, even though they can be mistaken, because they often possess warrant. Roughly, beliefs possess warrant when they are the result of faculties that are functioning properly in a congenial epistemic environment according to a design plan successfully aimed at *truth (*Warranted Christian Belief*, pp. 153–161).

This account of warrant commits Plantinga to a version of 'externalism', an *epistemology that sees knowledge as a matter of being related in a proper way to the external reality we know. One way we acquire such a relation is through evidence, but on this view not all cases of knowledge require evidence that is 'internal' to us in the sense of being accessible to our consciousness.

On the basis of this epistemological framework, Plantinga centres his critical fire on what he terms the 'evidentialist objection' to Christian belief, the claim that Christian belief, even if true, is unreasonable or unjustified because there is not enough evidence for its truth. Evidence here is understood as propositional evidence, the kind of evidence that could serve as a premise in an argument. Basic beliefs, however, do not gain warrant from other beliefs that serve as evidence for them. If Christian beliefs can be properly basic, then the evidentialist objection will fail.

In 'Reason and Belief in God' (in A. Plantinga and N. Wolterstorff [eds.], *Faith and Rationality: Reason and Belief in God* [Notre Dame, 1983]), Plantinga defends the claim that belief in God can be properly basic in this way. There is, he thinks, a natural knowledge of God that does not depend on philosophical argument. God has created us with a sense of divinity that makes it possible for humans to know God's reality. John *Calvin has of course developed this theme in some detail: 'There is within the human mind, and indeed by natural instinct, an awareness of divinity ... God himself has implanted in all men a certain understanding of his divine majesty.' In *Warranted Christian Belief* Plantinga recapitulates this earlier account of how theistic belief can be properly basic and designates it ecumenically as the 'Aquinas/Calvin model'.

In claiming that belief on this model can be properly basic, Plantinga does not deny that there are circumstances and experiences that may be seen as grounding the belief. Beliefs that are properly basic are not, therefore, groundless or arbitrary. Thus, on beholding a sunset or a flower, a person may naturally think that God created this wonderful and beautiful thing. In such a case, however, the belief is still basic. The person does not treat the sunset or flower as evidence and attempt to construct an argument for God's existence, but simply spontaneously forms a belief in God as a result of the experience. This is possible according to the model because God has created humans with a natural tendency or disposition to form a belief in himself in these kinds of circumstances.

In calling this account a 'model' Plantinga means several things (see *Warranted Christian Belief*, pp. 169–170). First, he wants to claim the model is possible, not merely logically possible but epistemically possible, 'consistent with what we know'. Secondly, there are no objections to the model that are cogent; at least no objections that do not presuppose the falsity of Christian belief. This means that any objections will have to take the form of a challenge to the truth of Christianity. A critic cannot argue that he or she does not know whether or not Christianity is true, but does know that Christian belief is irrational or unjustified. The only way a critic could know that such beliefs are unwarranted is to know that they are false. Thirdly, Plantinga affirms, though he says he cannot philosophically show it to be the case, that the model he proposes is actually true or at least close to the truth. Finally, he says that there are a number of similar models of how Christian beliefs could be known to be true, and that if Christianity is true, then one of those models is very likely to be true as well. His model, or a similar one, thus provides a good way for Christians to think about their faith and how it is known.

Plantinga affirms that if the *sensus divinitatis* is a divinely implanted faculty that is designed to produce true beliefs, and if it is functioning properly in a congenial epistemic environment so as to do that successfully, then a belief in God that is the output of this faculty possesses warrant. If these conditions are met and the belief is true and held with the requisite degree of firmness, then the belief in question will even amount to knowledge, and the believer will know that God exists even if he or she does not know any arguments for God's existence and has no propositional evidence for the belief.

Although Plantinga thinks that the *sensus divinitatis* can indeed lead to belief in God that is properly basic, the focus of *Warranted Christian Belief* is not on this faculty, for two reasons. First of all, Plantinga is interested not simply in whether theistic belief is warranted, but whether full-blooded Christian belief – belief in a trinitarian God who has acted in Jesus to redeem the world – is warranted. For such beliefs a natural faculty that leads to belief in God is clearly inadequate. Secondly,

Plantinga recognizes that the *sensus divinitatis* does not always, or even usually, function properly in the actual world, due to human sin. Human beings have rebelled against God and this rebellion has damaged their natural epistemic powers, particularly with respect to the knowledge of God.

To deal with the damage due to sin and also the particularities of Christian belief, Plantinga develops what he terms the 'extended Aquinas/ Calvin model', which purports to give an account of how Christian beliefs could be known to be true by humans whose cognitive faculties have been damaged by sin. The model represents how God could communicate to humans his plan to repair the damage caused by human sin and give them the knowledge they need to receive the benefits of this plan.

Once more, John Calvin's views, particularly Calvin's doctrine of the internal testimony or witness of the *Holy Spirit, play a dominant role in the development of Plantinga's extended model. However, Plantinga again claims that Calvin's account can be seen as an elaboration of views found in Thomas Aquinas, according to whom 'the believer has sufficient motive for believing, for he is moved by the authority of divine teaching confirmed by miracles and, what is more, *by the inward instigation of the divine invitation*' (Plantinga's italics).

Almost all traditional Christians would agree that God's plan of salvation includes the life, atoning death and resurrection of Jesus, the incarnate Son of God. Through the work of Jesus, God has founded the church, the new people of God, and invited people to become part of this new community. On Plantinga's account, this plan of salvation has an epistemological dimension; God would not want to develop a scheme for human salvation and then leave people ignorant of it. This epistemological dimension has three main constituents: Scripture, the presence and work of the Holy Spirit and faith as a reality in the believer (see *Warranted Christian Belief*, pp. 243–252). The Bible is viewed as 'a library of books or writings each of which has a human author, but each of which is also specially inspired by God in such a way that he himself is its principal author'. Within its pages are to be found the 'stunning good news of the way of salvation God has graciously offered'. The 'great things of the Gospel' found therein are things that Christians come to 'grasp, believe, accept, endorse, and rejoice in' by virtue of the work of the Holy Spirit in creating faith in their hearts, a work that over time repairs the damage done by sin.

Plantinga uses the term 'faith' not only for the third element in the model, but also as a useful shorthand designator of the whole process. Thus, one can say that Christian doctrines are known by faith and not by reason, if we think of reason as the natural faculty whereby we come to know some things by way of inference from other things we know. Plantinga is well aware that faith includes more than belief; he claims only that belief is a necessary part of faith.

Plantinga makes the same claims for his extended model as he did for his original model. It is possible (epistemically) that this is how Christian truths are known; there are no cogent objections, philosophical or otherwise, to the model that do not presuppose the falsity of Christianity. If Christianity is true, then the model, or something similar to the model, is very likely true as well, and thus the model provides Christians with a good way of thinking about their faith. If the model is indeed true, then Christians who believe the great things of the gospel are warranted in doing so, and if their degree of confidence is high enough, the warrant is sufficient for knowledge.

How is it possible for faith (using the term to refer to the whole process) to have warrant? The answer is simply that according to the model, the standard conditions for warrant are met: the beliefs in question come into existence 'by a belief-producing process that is functioning properly in an appropriate cognitive environment (the one for which they were designed), according to a design plan successfully aimed at the production of true beliefs'.

Plantinga does recognize one significant difference between the extended model and other cases of warranted belief. The extended model views the beliefs in question as produced not by a natural human faculty, but by a cognitive process 'that involves a special, supernatural activity on the part of the Holy Spirit'. However, Plantinga claims that this makes no difference. The 'deliverances' of this process can enjoy warrant, even 'warrant sufficient for knowledge'. Plantinga's externalism is most evident at this point. What matters is not that the believer has historical evidence for Jesus' miracles or the resurrection, but that the believer has convictions that are produced by a process aimed at truth and objectively likely to arrive at truth.

Strictly speaking, the Reformed epistemologist does not claim that one cannot provide evidence for Christian faith, but only that such evidence is unnecessary for belief to be reasonable and even for such belief to amount to knowledge. Plantinga himself has offered arguments for belief in God, though he has expressed doubts about aspects of Swinburne's case, particularly the claim that theism has an 'intrinsic probability'. However, in the case of fully developed Christian belief, Plantinga seems to go beyond the claim that evidence is not necessary to the claim that a strong evidential case cannot be made: the major difficulty is that what we are asked to believe is so amazing, so improbable, it is hard to imagine any historical evidence that would be sufficient. The Christian gospel concerns the resurrection of a person from the dead, a person who claimed to be God, and such an account is completely unlike the stories about wars, cruelty, and ambition that fill the pages of historical texts. The problem is really not that the historical evidence we have is of inferior quality, but that the beliefs in question are such that it is hard to see how any amount of historical evidence would be sufficient to warrant their acceptance.

Plantinga's thinking here seems somewhat close to *Kierkegaard, who is of course well known for his claim that the incarnation is the 'absolute paradox'. If we put aside what I have argued is the erroneous interpretation of Kierkegaard that sees the *paradox of the incarnation as a logical contradiction, the two views seem very similar. The incarnation is seen by Kierkegaard as the most improbable and strange of events, and the content of faith is such that differences in the quality of the historical evidence make no difference. If the evidence were as complete and solid as possible, the evidence alone would still be insufficient for faith, because of the amazing character of the gospel.

Evidentialism and non-evidentialism as complementary accounts

Though these two apologetic strategies have often been viewed as mutually exclusive rivals, it is possible to see the two as complementary accounts that have different goals. Fundamentally, one may see the non-evidentialist as providing an account of how the Christian knows the gospel to be true, while the evidentialist provides an account that is supposed to persuade the non-Christian or allay the doubts of the Christian. The key to seeing how the two are complementary is to recognize that there is a difference between being justified (or warranted) in holding a belief, and being able to justify a belief to someone else. The two tasks are logically distinct.

Strictly speaking, one might think that only the evidentialist provides an apologetic, by providing arguments for Christian belief. Evidentialism then would be the proper account of apologetics, while non-evidentialism might provide an account of faith that is in some sense internal to the life of faith, an account of how faith arises and functions that presupposes the truth of Christianity. However, to say this would underestimate the apologetic value of the non-evidentialist approach. Christianity has frequently been attacked as irrational because there is not sufficient evidence to warrant belief. An argument that belief that is not based on evidence can be rational can then have great value for the Christian in rebutting such a charge of irrationality, and even for the non-Christian who is considering Christianity but who might be deterred from commitment to Christ by a mistaken conviction that Christian belief must be based on evidence.

The two approaches are complementary in a number of ways. First of all, even the non-evidentialists must recognize that there are many objections to Christian faith and that these objections sometimes seem powerful. An evidential case may be useful in rebutting such alleged defeaters even for a belief that is not based primarily on evidence. Secondly, there are levels of knowledge. One can speak not only of knowing a proposition, but of knowing that one knows a proposition, and an evidential case could be part of the way such second-level knowledge could be acquired. This would be a case of 'faith seeking understanding'. Thirdly, since the non-evidentialist denies not the possibility of evidence but only its necessity, he can admit that one way God's Spirit might operate to produce faith is through evidence. For some people, an evidential case might then be part of the process by which God produces faith through the work of the Spirit.

How does Reformed epistemology differ from what Cowan terms 'presuppositionalism'? The point of similarity is that Reformed epistemology, like presuppositionalism, emphasizes that coming to know the truths of Christian faith is ultimately the work of God, and thus gives an account of that process that in some ways presupposes the truth of Christianity. The difference is that the presuppositionalist typically goes on to claim that a person's belief structure forms a tightly linked system, and that the non-Christian who does not begin with the right presuppositions will inevitably fall into contradictions. This suggests an apologetic strategy that has been fruitfully employed by thinkers such as Francis *Schaeffer, but sometimes it has led presuppositionalists to make exaggerated claims to the effect that non-believers can have no knowledge, and that there is no '*common ground' or points where believers and non-believers can agree. One does not have to make such exaggerated claims in order to see that what has been called the 'pressure of God's reality' does indeed pinch the non-Christian in various ways and lead to inconsistencies that can be pointed out by apologists. If the non-believer could not discover any truth at all, then it is hard to see why he should be driven into inconsistency.

The non-evidentialist's misgivings about evidential arguments can be allayed if the two are seen as complementary. The non-evidentialist stresses that coming to faith is a total transformation of the person and that such a transformation cannot occur merely through the consideration of evidence. The evidentialist may cheerfully concede this, and even agree that evidence is not a substitute for faith, insofar as the latter is understood as involving such a transformation. The improbability of the gospel that the non-evidentialist sees as problematic may be partly a function of the presence or lack of faith. It may well be that faith must be present in order for certain types of evidence to be properly appreciated and assessed, and yet that the evidence can be seen to support Christian when faith is present. If that is so, then we can understand why in the NT there is stress both on evidence (as in John 20:31) and on the evident fact that the evidence often did not lead to faith.

C. S. EVANS

Legitimacy of Apologetics

Legitimacy is a matter of utmost significance for the field of apologetics in the contemporary Western world. Legitimacy refers to the logical admissibility of apologetics as a valid intellectual and practical activity. It considers whether it is possible to have knowledge of God and *truth, and how such knowledge may be understood and imparted. Establishing the legitimacy or plausibility of apologetics is a necessary precursor to engaging the task itself. As a prologue to apologetic practice, a consideration of legitimacy provides a defence of the apologetic task; an apologetic for apologetics. It further clarifies how we may speak of God, and understand religious knowledge in a cultural context where such knowledge is continually challenged and undermined, both from within and without the Christian faith. It is further relevant for appraising the usefulness of various apologetic methods, from *evidentialism to *fideism.

The issue of truth

The matter of truth, and our understanding of it, is central to the legitimacy of the apologetic task. Engaging apologetics means there must be some commitment to the existence of truth, and a degree of confidence that we can apprehend something of it, in order to commend it to others.

Origins and development

The early Christians struggled with the reality of truth against various heresies that emphasized the non-reality of truth. Against *Docetism and Gnosticsm, the apostles Paul and John stressed the reality of their Christian experience, and reinforced the historicity and materiality of a Christ who was both completely God and completely human. For them, and others, apologetics became a matter of active proclamation against threats to the church, as well as the readiness to give account of the hope that they had. At the same time, the witness provided by the alternative *cultural community added merit to their apologetic, earning attention, respect and conversions, as recorded by writers both within and without the NT. For these early believers, apologetic legitimacy was rooted in the immediacy of the events of the life of Christ, as witnessed by his disciples, and in his expected soon return. Truth was revealed, seen, understood and believed in the community of the Spirit. This sense of realism allowed for a sense of *mystery, but mystery did not overwhelm their confidence in knowledge of God.

Philosophical challenges and contextual concerns encouraged the church's early theologians to launch a defence of the faith in response to particular concerns amongst communities of believers. Indeed, much of the content of the epistles is devoted to elaboration of the faith in response to specific questions, and apologetics was legitimized by the external challenges launched against the church and the truth to which it was committed. In the West, this prompted the development of the *creeds, and writings of the Church Fathers. Later, in the medieval period, observation and reason would figure prominently in the apologetics of thinkers like *Thomas Aquinas and *Anselm. Meanwhile, Eastern Christianity developed a more apophatic approach to apologetics that largely nullified the apologetic task. By describing God as ineffable mystery, the Eastern church did not consider the apologetic task to comprise a rational defence of faith; though it should be noted that Eastern theologians still considered conversion to Christianity to be an essential prerequisite for continued growth into God.

The modern period

Subsequent historical periods were marked variously by trends of *rationalism, *romanticism and other forms of idealist and realist thought. Apologetics for some needed to be rationally demonstrated in order for the Christian faith to be true. For others, the focus was more on emotion and experience. In the modern period, Friedrich *Schleiermacher, in his famous *On Religion: Speeches to its Cultured Despisers*, sought to rescue the faith of his friends in a particularly idealist culture by pointing to the truth of Christianity as an answer to the universal 'feeling of ultimate dependence'. John *Locke, on the other hand, while highlighting the supremacy of reason, viewed *revelation as a supplement to reason, though they should not logically conflict, if both are true. Defenders of the faith were to be found on both sides of, and at various points across, an increasing divide, as a wedge between reason and revelation became forced unnecessarily by *Descartes, *Hume and *Kant.

An ensuing divorce for some between faith and reason did not prevent scores of Christians from seeking to hold reason and revelation together, at least through method of argument, though the weight of their approaches usually fell on one side or the other. In more recent times, the faith-and-reason divide has become further complicated as social change and philosophical postmodernisms influence the apologetics field. Christians increasingly find themselves in an intellectual and cultural environment that rejects *first principles of reason and doubts the communicability of truth beyond individual faith commitment and context. This scepticism takes on many forms but the outcome is the same: individuals become the arbiters of their own truths. Even if *reality exists independently of our arbitration, we are no longer confident that our apprehension of reality corresponds with its inherent truth. When a culture is no longer committed to a discovery of what is real and true, have we come to the end of the apologetic task?

The contemporary situation: A crisis of apologetic legitimacy

The condition of contemporary Western society represents a late modernity, or even a hypermodernity (modernity pushed to its extreme limits), and is most often described as postmodernity (simply, that which comes after modernity). Postmodern society is characterized by information *technology, consumerism, rugged individualism, *globalization, *secularism and *pluralism. Changes that have taken place since the Second World War brought about increased social and geographical mobility, instant access to information and goods, and growing personal freedom and independence. At the same time, a globalized economy attests to cultural interdependence, even as some cultural values have come to dominate our ability and preference to master our individual existences. An increasing lack of shared values or norms, save those dictated by the market, leaves apologetics floundering. *Authority is questioned rather than respected in most sectors of society, from politics to family life. To express confidence, let alone *certainty, in religious matters is considered imperialistic and arrogant at best; an infraction of the rights of others at worst. The privatization of religion combined with consumerist and pluralist influences often leads to a spirituality that is relativistic, vague, syncretistic and individualistic. No longer interested in whether something is true, but whether it suits their temperament and lifestyle, many people in contemporary Western culture question the legitimacy of religious apologetics altogether.

At the same time, in Western society, there are many still who prefer a rational approach to life. They trust *science and the advances technology has brought to human existence. For them, truth is more about discovering cause and effect than meaning. They might engage in dialogue with a religious apologist, but would demand scientific evidence and proof beyond a call to faith. Many such people encountered at least the cultural remnants of Christianity by virtue of living in a predominantly Christian society. Their rejection of invitations to faith often expresses rebellion against such cultural exposure, leaving the apologetic challenge in a post-Christian society in some ways more difficult than if Christianity were never known. Although plausibility structures of Western society contrive to undermine the legitimacy of apologetics, there may yet be reason to hope for a renewal of apologetics amongst an emerging generation of Christians. In such a situation the justification of apologetics may be rooted simply in the creative retelling of the gospel story, where basic knowledge cannot be assumed.

If postmodernity may be described as a sociological condition, postmodernism is a broad term applied to various philosophies that have emerged in recent decades. Developing from the limits of analytical philosophy, and resting on a crisis of meaning in *language, it highlights a contemporary disbelief of meta-narratives (stories that explain everything), rejecting the big stories that have structured culture and given it meaning. Failures of Marxism and other ideologies to bring about world revolution contributed significantly to

the disillusionment of many intellectuals. With a rejection of big stories that give our culture meaning, we are left with fragmentation and individualism, perhaps to the point of violence; a potential war of all against all, according to Jean-François *Lyotard. The suggestion that one has access to a story that explains and embraces all others is itself to enact totalizing violence on them and their individual right to difference. If apologetics is about commending a grand meta-narrative, then we should not be surprised to have its legitimacy as an activity questioned in the contemporary environment.

After the divide between faith and reason encouraged by Descartes and Kant, the door to scepticism was firmly and widely opened. Hume was able to suggest that we are nothing more than the sum of our perceptions, an assertion pushed even further by Nietzsche. In response to a search for meaning in discourse, there was a marked turn to the analysis of language in the twentieth century. For many philosophers, particularly the logical positivists, language was considered meaningful only if its postulates could be verified by sensory experience. The *verification principle meant that much of language was relegated to the realm of preference at best, insignificance or irrelevance at worst. Ludwig *Wittgenstein nudged analytical philosophy past its potential stagnation. He suggested that language functions as a game; players understand the rules of the game and use language accordingly. There is a multiplicity of games, none of which functions in isolation from another, but all are enacted in a social context. In its contextual function, language becomes useful to describe certain experiences, but it cannot be relied upon to explain reality. Transcendent, objective points of view must be denied.

Following these ideas, deconstructionists such as *Derrida and *Foucault suggested that words may refer to other words, but not to a reality outside of themselves. Indeed, all language use may be reduced to expressions of *power. Such ideas have a destructive effect on *epistemology; if language is not connected in any sense to reality, what is it possible to know with confidence? Are we able to trust our own apprehension of words and their meaning when they are used to describe and explain God? First principles, upon which the rest of language and epistemology may be built, are destroyed. Many evangelicals, including Nicholas Wolterstorff, have conceded that *foundationalism is in rough shape. If this is so, it has important repercussions for apologetics, particularly evidentialism. The idea of building a rational case on logical principles that rest one on another, forming an impenetrable fortress, collapses.

Combined with the sociological condition of postmodernity, the philosophical climate is nurturing extreme forms of pluralism and *relativism regarding truth. For many Christians, if faith is to be shared at all, it must be done in a way that does not rely on evidentialism and epistemological propositions. Some turn to *pragmatism, as a measure of apologetic validity, hoping to show not that Christianity is true, but that it works. Still others herald the end of the apologetic task, preferring instead to 'live out' the truth of faith in community, rather than use language to provoke or challenge. The contemporary situation leads us to consider how we know what we know, and to discover whether we really have reached an impasse for apologetics in the Western world.

Means of knowledge

The study of knowledge, and how we come to know what we know, is called epistemology. Traditionally, religious epistemology encompasses several elements: our reasoned thoughts about God; God's self-disclosure through revelation; our sensory experience of the world; and our belief or faith, expressed through confession. Such knowledge depended heavily on the authority of God, the Scriptures and the church. All of these types of knowledge are affirmed in Scripture, and provide various starting points for apologetics, though none should stand in complete isolation from the others, as though they were independent entities. Nevertheless, the matter of epistemological starting points is increasingly important for the legitimacy of apologetics. The starting point for apologetics is largely what renders it legitimate for a particular audience, depending on shared values and presuppositions. For the Reformers, faith would always be pre-eminent, though an appreciation of creation and grace would not shut out the role of reason. For others, rationalism, or even experience, would be the starting place for their apologetic systems.

Reason

Reason has been employed in Christian apologetics from the earliest times. Indeed, any attempt to communicate in word or deed necessarily involves an expectation that the mind is capable of understanding what is being communicated. Even postmodern philosophers who seek to undermine the suitability of language as a conduit for truth use language to put forth their arguments. *Augustine of Hippo set out an early approach to theological elaboration of the faith that was largely self-legitimizing as he 'believed in order to understand'. His was no mere fideism, however, as belief demanded to be understood in order to increase faith, and demonstrate its truth. Like many of his predecessors, reason and revelation, experience and faith all had their roles to play.

As Christianity spread and became adopted as the state religion in the West, the development of arguments for Christian truth took on the more scholarly and reflective quality of the Middle Ages, and adopted increasingly rational approaches to faith. The traditional *ontological arguments of Anselm and the teleological approach of Aquinas all depended on postulates of reason to establish their cases. Nevertheless, from Anselm's ontology to Aquinas' *natural theology, apologetic systems continued to rest primarily on foundations of biblical authority and faith, and not rational proof. Even though Anselm's discussion with the fool may prove unsatisfactory as a demonstration of God's existence, it is significant that his theological engagement grew out of an Augustinian 'faith seeking understanding'.

For some, however, reason is the very starting point for apologetics, and retains a pre-eminent role throughout. They may point to scriptural exhortations to 'Come now, let us reason together' (Isa. 1:18) and to 'be prepared to give an answer to everyone who asks you to give the reason for the hope that you have' (1 Pet. 3:15). In terms of *theology, they will consider importance of creation and the endowment of humanity with special gifts and abilities of reason as a result of bearing the image of God. They are likely to downplay the significance of the fall, and focus on the human potential, evident in the life of Christ, and the enlightenment of reason available to all through the *Holy Spirit.

For idealists like Edward *Caird, the very being of God was viewed as eternal and absolute mind, whose reflection or presence in humanity resided in the faculty of reason. His approach to theistic arguments for the existence of God rested on such premises as the role of reason and the existence of rational mind. This depended on the principles of rationalism developed by thinkers of the *Enlightenment period, such as Descartes. Descartes wanted to seek a rational certainty of knowledge that could be demonstrated with precision. Although his approach did not eliminate the possibility of knowledge about God, it set rational thought logically prior to belief, and opened a door to scepticism about unseen authorities. An awkward schism between faith and reason ensued. Despite their personal faith, and commitment to revelation, John Locke and Immanuel Kant, amongst others, also left intellectual legacies that further re-inforced the rational divide. As an empiricist, Locke emphasized the imprint of sensory experience upon the mind as the primary means of gaining knowledge about the world. He also believed that people may have some sense of how things in themselves really are. He did not discount the possibility of revelation, but believed it should not contradict what is reasonably true.

Kant believed that the eternal mind was present in the moral inclinations of humanity. But moral knowledge and knowledge of God could not rest on a strictly rational basis. Eventually, a wedge between universal know-ledge and personal knowledge reinforced the separation of reason and faith for Kant, as he distinguished between how things are in them-selves and how they appear to individual observers. Such a view resonates in the con-temporary situation, where truth is often individualized and foundationalism rejected. The idea that there are first principles of reason upon which other ideas may be built as indis-putable evidence for the existence of divine truth is no longer accepted as legitimate by many. Although evidentialists like Richard Swinburne still believe in the legitimacy of using the *theistic proofs in apologetics, for many, reason no longer helps us to understand things as they are, but only as they appear 'to me'. Indeed, David Hume and Friedrich *Nietzsche would deny that knowledge is much other than a string of perceptions, leading to scepticism of epistemology and crises of meaning. If we cannot have knowledge of things in themselves, especially those which we cannot encounter through sensory experience, then faith is forever divorced from reason, and the plausibility of recommending Christ as anything other than a personal preference is nullified.

Theologically, a divide between faith and reason may be reinforced by a view of the fall that posits the total depravity of the human mind. For many Reformers, Luther included, the image of God – often equated with human ability to reason – was all but obliterated by the fall. Reason cannot be trusted, as it bears the marks of the sinful nature. The *noetic effects of sin prevent reason from being a reliable means of thinking about God, though, as *Calvin suggested, grace to the believer and the non-believer redeems reason to some degree. At least this concession is necessary in order to retain some measure of human responsibility (Rom. 1:1).

For John Wesley, amongst others, reason is part of God's nature and the eternal order of the universe. It is not that humans reason their way to God, but that reason works together with grace, revelation, faith and experience to assist humans to understand themselves and their predicament and to work out their salva-tion in ways that are consistent with the faith they profess. Such a holistic view challenges contemporary rejections of reason in apolo-getics. It reminds us that reason is to be seen less as a faculty of mind and more as a process to be engaged, insofar as we reason about things. It may well serve to undermine systems of apologetics built solely on evidences and propositions. But it affirms that the process of *reasoning is basic to human existence and is an inevitable part of working out what it means to be a follower of Christ.

Revelation

Revelation, as God's self-disclosure, represents for many the legitimate corollary to reason in apologetics. If human reason is flawed because of sin, then in order to save humans from their striving after a god of their imaginations, God must show himself. God speaks through word and image to communicate himself and his truth. His revelation is recorded in Scripture, through his dealings with his covenant people, and supremely in the person and work of *Jesus Christ, who is both the word (logos) and the image (eikōn) of God. Knowledge of revealed truth comes through divine–human encounter, especially through the intimacy of a personal relationship with God in Christ, sealed with the Holy Spirit. Theologically, God's general revelation begins with creation and continues through the special revelation of covenant and redemption, and awaits consummation.

Though now we 'see through a glass darkly', in the eschaton we shall 'see face to face'. God's self-revelation will render the apologetic task redundant when 'every knee shall bow and tongue confess that Jesus Christ is Lord, to the glory of God the Father'.

The task of apologetics cannot, however, be obsolete in the present day, since not all have seen and believed. Either God has chosen to keep himself hidden from some and they are blind to his revelation, or they will yet have opportunity to respond. If the latter, then apologetic engagement becomes a legitimate activity even for those who stress the centrality of revelation; if the former, then the apologist ought to be willing at least to account for God's hiddenness and favouritism. Such discussion recalls the Calvinist–Arminian debate, in which the Calvinist highlights the action of God in salvation and the Arminian focuses on the human response of faith. If all is *predestination, there is no need for apologetics, save as apologists are chosen by God to engage in this activity as part of his eternal plan. It is helpful to recognize, though, that the prevenient grace of the moderate Arminian and the effectual calling of the moderate Calvinist are not a universe apart. Both remind us that knowledge of God through revelation at his initiative is as much about right standing and relationship as about information and understanding.

The question remains, how do reason and revelation work together? Does revelation supplement or supplant reason as a means of knowledge of God? Some believe that revelation works merely to enlighten and enliven what is already known by reason. But this has implications for a Christian understanding of conversion and salvation. If one is required to assent intellectually to faith in order for salvation to be effective, then those who are, for various reasons, unable to respond intellectually are beyond redemption. Surely God's grace extends to the humble and the incapacitated. It would seem, from this perspective, that an emphasis on natural theology is largely untenable, with significance for the legitimacy of apologetics.

Not surprisingly, some who advocate the primacy of revelation with respect to our knowledge of God sometimes downplay the importance of the apologetic task. Supposing that the only possible knowledge of God is entirely by his initiative and self-disclosure, they believe that to offer a defence of one's faith is absurd if it has no effect whatsoever on others, or contributes nothing to the development of one's own knowledge and understanding of God. Such a view has found renewed favour amongst some Christians who, in a rejection of evidentialist apologetics, have committed never to offer words of evangelical challenge or commendation regarding their faith. It may be argued that such an approach is experience-based in the first instance, but there is a clear emphasis on the *mystery of God and a trust that he will, in his way and time, reveal himself to those he has chosen to follow him.

This view has affinities with Karl *Barth's rejection of natural theology. Some believe that Barth's view reflects a Kantian epistemology that separates divine knowledge from knowledge of the world gained through sensory experience. He famously argued with Emil *Brunner, who wanted to allow that there could be some knowledge of God from general revelation. Barth's outright rejection of any sort of natural theology reinforced the idea that there is no knowledge of God apart from the Word in Christ, apprehended simply by a Kierkegaardian 'leap of faith'. He went so far as to suggest that the God apprehended even in part by reason was not the same God as the Father of our Lord Jesus Christ. This line of thought is picked up and expanded by the contemporary self-styled scholars of 'radical orthodoxy', who wish to reject the antique of reason in favour of a restored vision of tradition, with *theology reigning again as the queen of the sciences, rather than serving as their lowly handmaiden.

Such ideas will resonate with those who adhere to the uniqueness of God's special revelation in Christ, as they explain some of the apologetic ambivalence experienced today. But if a biblical doctrine of creation is to be taken seriously, there must be room for discussion over whether the God of creation reveals himself in creation and in reason. Though saving knowledge of God in Christ may not result from traditional theistic proofs, such discussions may go some way in eliminating stumbling blocks or pointing to the possibility that a theistic God is active in the universe. There are further implications for dialogue with other religions in the contemporary world, as we seek to understand what sort of knowledge of God is obtainable by those who worship other than a Christian God. Even for those who reject meta-narratives of human existence, an apologetic for a strong view of revelation will itself be required to legitimate claims to unique knowledge of the divine through revelation. Such legitimization is often found in referring to the believer's knowledge of revelation through experience, which once again lets reason into the picture, though when reason conflicts with experience, for many in the contemporary world, reason becomes dispensable.

Experience

The appeal to experience for legitimate knowledge of God is not at all new. The words of the old gospel chorus, 'You ask me know I know he lives ... he lives within my heart!' reflect a sentiment that is as old as Christianity itself. Though John and Paul confessed the risen Christ through revelation, it was the power of their experience that reinforced their commitment. Indeed, their experience was provided as evidence for their knowledge of God as 'that which we have seen with our eyes, touched with our hands'. This is no mere reasonable conclusion brought about by sensory perception. The power of the revelation they received was brought home in their experience of God that changed their lives and the way they viewed the world.

Context as experience in time and space has always played an important part in what it means to know God. As embodied people, we can do no other than encounter him in the context of our own culture, regardless of how the divine–human encounter may eventually transform our cultural point of view. This idea is reinforced in the fact that early doctrine was developed in response to particular questions and challenges to particular communities of believers at particular times in history. Even the creeds of the church were developed for such reasons. Once again, a biblical doctrine of creation will affirm God's presence in his handiwork, and his sustenance of human *culture by grace.

Are there limits to knowledge of God through experience? Can we 'just know' truth when we encounter it? Is it self-legitimizing? The experience of the Christian journey, without defined points of commitment, is increasingly heralded as a plausible approach to knowledge of God, even for those who consider themselves to be evangelicals. Looking for God in contemporary culture, through film, *television, literature and art, is growing rapidly in popularity as a pastime (or even devotional time) for Christians. Seeing it as more than mere entertainment, many expect a worshipful encounter with God when they participate in cultural activities. Increasingly, some Christians suggest that they experience God most in cinemas or when socializing with friends rather than in church, during formal worship. Is this means of gaining knowledge of God apologetically legitimate?

Friedrich *Schleiermacher, the father of modern liberal Protestantism, would think so. His exhortation to his friends to interpret their feelings of inspiration and need in the culture of Romanticism as legitimate encounter with God rings a familiar tone. Like the Idealists, who exalted reason as reflecting the mind of God, others upheld feeling and emotion as reflecting the presence of God. Some would go so far as to say that such experiences represent our participation in God, who is working out his existence through encounter with humans in the world. But just as rational proofs do not necessarily lead to saving knowledge of God in Christ, neither do experiences of culture alone provide any divine knowledge that is verifiable, outside of individual subjective interpretation. Experience may well affirm or challenge what knowledge we already possess, but it is difficult to understand experience as doing more than pointing us in particular directions; sometimes towards knowledge of God, and sometimes away from it. Experience without interpretation or understanding will not necessarily lead to divine truth, despite some veridical aspects. As we tend to interpret our experiences subjectively, according to previously held commitments, experience serves as a legitimate apologetic insofar as it is offered as a personal commendation. Working together with reason and revelation, however, experience becomes far more useful. Study of contemporary culture becomes a relevant apologetic exercise itself, testing ways in which our experiences demonstrate knowledge of God that is like and unlike the knowledge we have of God through Christ, and recorded in the Scriptures. In reality, the reason why most people persist in faith, is not because their daily experience confirms it, but because of the few times when it did strike like lightning. Faith initiated by God persists, despite experiences in contemporary life that militate against belief.

Faith

Faith represents assent to the Christian confession and commitment to its content. More than that, it constitutes personal belief in what is held to be true about God and his dealings with humanity. It is the context of the confession we hold as Christians, bearing witness to the tradition of the church and acknowledging our assent to the believing tradition. In this sense, faith, though personal, is not independent.

Faith is connected to reason, revelation and experience, insofar as those things come together to enable, empower, confirm or challenge faith. As belief, faith may or may not be based on reason, revelation or experience; belief that is self-legitimizing cannot be apologetic. Even those who adhere to such a perspective would have to admit that they do, in fact, have experiences and think thoughts, and that those experiences or thoughts influence their faith development in some way. However, where faith is primary for a Christian, everything else will be measured against beliefs that are inseparable from the content of the faith professed. Though such beliefs may evolve over time, generally they form a world-view through which all other knowledge is filtered.

In essence this leads us to the presuppositionalist apologetics of Cornelius *Van Til, Francis *Schaeffer, Alvin Plantinga and various Reformed thinkers. Although they vary significantly in their approaches to apologetics, they understand the metaphysical or ontological claim of God's existence to be properly basic. Giving priority to revelation apprehended by faith, most presuppositionalists resist the existentialist 'leap of faith' to differing degrees. For Schaeffer, the 'God who is there' is simply the presupposition upon which a Christian view of the world hinges. For Plantinga, there is sufficient philosophical warrant to consider the existence of God as a basic assumption around which Christian belief may cohere. Recent work on worldview as a concept serves to demonstrate the presuppositionalist nature of much of human knowledge, scientific and otherwise. Many evangelicals are uncomfortable with the necessary pluralism that such conclusions may imply. Still others welcome the postmodern opportunity to push beyond world-view theory and to deconstruct integrated approaches to knowledge of God whilst developing ever new applications.

In response to various challenges to apologetic legitimacy, Alan Sell has helpfully pointed to the confession of the Christian faith as a legitimate starting point for apologetics. Its community aspect, rooted in tradition and revelation, yet apprehended personally by faith and lived in a life of commitment, offers a way forward for apologetic legitimacy and world-view theory in a postmodern context. The basic confession that Jesus is Lord, he argues, has been the centrepiece of the Christian faith from its inception, and remains a unifying concept in theory and practice. The Christian confession is not only the starting point for apologetic method, but represents the very content of faith that Christians hope to commend to others. Such an approach defends the legitimacy of the apologetic task in light of epistemological and linguistic challenges against the nature of what Christians can legitimately know and communicate about God.

In practice, most Christians have a commitment to faith that brings together reason, revelation and experience to form a world-view that at least organizes their knowledge, even if it does not predetermine it. No matter how strong our faith commitments may be, we are not excused from the challenge to form a world-view that is *coherent*, and that responds reasonably to challenges that come either through experience or revelation. The challenge of revelation is necessary if growth and discipleship are to take place; the challenge of experience either proves faith, or encourages an adjustment to the world-view; the challenge of reason means that even though reason may not be reliable for establishing knowledge of God, such knowledge should still be reasonable, and we ought to be able to offer reasons for believing as we do. Some may not require such knowledge themselves, being content fideists. But if Christians hope to become all things to all people in order that some might be saved, they cannot be averse to removing obstacles to belief for others, who may yet come to confess Jesus Christ as Lord.

Bibliography

K. Boa and R. Bowman Jr, *Faith Has Its Reasons* (Colorado Springs, 2001); S. Cowan (ed.), *Five Views on Apologetics* (Grand Rapids, 2000); D. Groothuis, *Truth Decay* (Downers Grove, 2000); D. Naugle, *Worldview* (Cambridge, 2000); J. Orr, *The Christian View of*

God and the World (Edinburgh, 1893); A. P. F. Sell, *Confessing and Commending the Faith: Historic Witness and Apologetic Method* (Cardiff, 2002); J. Stackhouse, *Humble Apologetics* (Oxford, 2002); K. Vanhoozer, *Is There a Meaning in This Text?* (Leicester, 1998).

A. M. ROBBINS

Christian Apologetics: Is it Viable in a Post-Christian Culture?

The word 'apologetics' comes from the Greek root *apologia*, meaning 'to defend, make reply, give an answer', and was originally used of a formal courtroom defence. Within Christianity, apologetics is, in general, the activity of defending one's Christian faith through some kind of rational argument. The question of whether this is still viable in today's *culture is, in some senses, an odd one. If we take *apologia* in its basic sense, of giving a defence for what we believe, then obviously such an activity is relevant at any time. If apologetics was useful in a pre-Christian era, as the apostle Paul demonstrates in a number of sermons, then it is useful now in a post-Christian one. Peter commands Christians to be ready to give a reason for the hope they have (1 Pet. 3:15). Although our culture may have changed, theologically we are still in the same post-Christ, pre-heaven era as the NT writers, and people still need to be convinced to follow Christ. It is still the time when people will turn their ears away from the truth (2 Tim. 4:4), still the time when we are exhorted to 'be prepared in season and out of season; correct, rebuke and encourage – with great patience and careful instruction' (2 Tim. 4:2).

Any time that Christianity is preached amongst the educated – as the early Christian theologians and philosophers who came to be known as 'apologists' demonstrated – there is a place for the reasoned defence and recommendation of the faith. There is always value in attempting to gain a fair hearing for Christianity and dispel popular objections. As long as there are complaints against Christianity – and there always will be – answers to them can be given. Perhaps, however, the question 'Is apologetics viable in a post-Christian era?' could be motivated by a view that apologetics is not viable in any era. There has been a powerful strand of *Protestant theology that has stood against apologetics or *natural theology. Karl *Barth, for instance, influentially argued that to engage in apologetics is to give up the Christian standpoint in favour of non-Christian assumptions. The presuppositions of a Christian, the entire framework of ontology, *epistemology and the role of *reason, are so different from the non-Christian that there is no common ground for discussion.

There has also been traditionally wide disagreement about the *noetic effects of sin, i.e. how much the fall affected humanity's mental capabilities. If humans are simply not capable of accurate *reasoning, then there is no point in trying to reason with them. It is unlikely any theologians would take this extreme view, but the place of reason in conversion has been a matter of great debate. How much can an unregenerate mind understand the gospel, and how much does that mind need illuminating by the *Holy Spirit for that understanding to be possible? There are good reasons for questioning the capacity of sinful, unregenerate humans to reason clearly. Scripture testifies that truths about God are hidden from humanity, and some of these we deliberately suppress in our rejection of God, to the detriment of our own minds (Rom. 1:18–22). There is a veil over human hearts, obscuring God's message, which is taken away only in Christ (2 Cor. 3:14–15). For the unregenerate mind, no matter how clear the explanation nor how intelligent the hearer, the *truth about God and salvation can never be understood without supernatural intervention. This concept lies behind such passages as 1 Cor. 1:18 – 2:16. The message of the cross is 'foolishness' to those without the Holy Spirit, not because it is an inherently foolish or irrational message but because the unregenerate simply do not have access to spiritual truths.

These emphases have led to a long tradition within Christian thought that downplays the role of reason in various ways. Luther, *Pascal and *Lessing had little faith in the unregenerate mind. Kierkegaard advocated the primacy of spiritual experience in convincing the believer, even advocating irrational belief as being better (because more risky) than rational belief. In fact, this became for *Kierkegaard a kind of backwards argument for Christianity: the fact so many people place their faith in such an irrational system is reason to embrace it. The idea that eternal happiness depends on an obscure historical event is so bizarre that it could not have been invented by human beings.

Nonetheless, the biblical data do not allow us to dismiss the role of reason and persuasion, even given the necessity of the Spirit. Throughout the Acts account we see how Paul persuaded his hearers as he travelled around the ancient world, defended the truth of his claims and argued that Jesus was the Christ, reasoning and debating with his opponents. It appears that although the work of the Spirit is essential, it does not engender arational knowledge, but rather removes a 'blockage' in the rational processes. This is similar to the line taken by Christian thinkers such as *Augustine. The process of persuasion is important, even crucial, but alone will not convert the sinner. Only the Holy Spirit can so remove the spiritual blindness of the unregenerate that a human is able to understand the truth of the gospel. Both the need for argument and persuasion and the need for the illuminating work of the Holy Spirit are emphasized in Scripture.

Why else might one ask whether apologetics is still viable in our post-Christian era? It could be that apologetics is assumed to depend on such ideas of rationality and *logic that are now under attack in Western society. What is relevant, then, is not so much that we are post-Christian as postmodern. Postmodernism is the name given to a broad shift in ideas and values that took place in the latter part of the twentieth century. It is defined in contrast to *modernism, the name given to the philosophical mood which dominated Western thought from the *Enlightenment onwards. Modernism upheld various ideals, such as the belief that humankind was progressing and could solve the world's problems. *Science, the objective study of *reality, would enable us to discover truth; education and social organization would equip us to overcome the problems of crime and establish the perfect, equitable state. There were right answers to every question, and we were going to find them. The 'Enlightenment' referred to the way in which the human race was to be enlightened through knowledge and education, and would inevitably improve.

In the twentieth century, however, this optimistic certainty began to crumble. In most disciplines which have some philosophical aspect, the old idea of *certainty and rules for obtaining it have slowly disappeared. Jean-François *Lyotard, a prominent postmodern writer, says that modernity's prime characteristic was its dependence on 'meta-narratives' (i.e. on universal 'narratives' or accounts of reality, of the way things are, e.g. Marxism, Christianity, *Hegel's theory of universal spirit or the concept of progress). These meta-narratives were held to be objectively true and to transcend time and circumstance. Now, however, not only is there a greater awareness of different competing world philosophies, but an ethic has arisen that says no one philosophy can claim to be the truth. Each culture constructs its cultural framework for the world; and since each framework is simply another way of seeing things, it is meaningless to say that one framework is 'more true' than another.

Overall, people are asking where this objective truth is that *modernism told us we could discover. Now, it seems that even if there is such a thing as objective truth (which we doubt), there is no way of knowing what it is. After all, every way of looking at the world is culturally conditioned. The old arguments that were meant to convince us of another person's truth are now seen as mere *power struggles. No one way of looking at the world can be wrong, and neither can it be right but just different. Another person's framework of belief cannot be dismissed, because that requires some objective criterion by which to judge it, and there is no such thing. The best we ever have is our own culturally conditioned framework. This is the mood of postmodernism. This is the atmosphere in which a great deal of academic study of the humanities is undertaken, and the attitude which has filtered down into public life.

How can we defend the truth of Christianity if there is no such thing as truth? How can we argue for the exclusive rightness of one viewpoint, when such exclusivity is dismissed as evil and the practise of argument itself is subject to deconstruction? It is easy to feel that apologetics, if it ever worked, has little chance when our hearers have a postmodern outlook.

Yet this is to be too pessimistic. For one thing, it is hardly the case that postmodernism governs all intellectual discussion. There are many influential philosophers who dismiss much of postmodern thought, and it certainly has very vocal opponents. For many people, it is a fashionable view to espouse in public rather than a serious philosophy of life. For the great majority, it is an academic issue and has nothing to do with real life.

Even if a listener has been seriously influenced by postmodern thought, this in no way makes apologetics impossible. It may be the case that concepts of absolute truth, and the practice of evaluating religious beliefs in terms of truth, is unfashionable. This does not, however, take away the task of persuasion. If truth as a concept must be defended, then that is what we do. There are various ways to persuade listeners that truth exists outside the mind of the thinker. It is not the concern of this article to go into details of such arguments here, but some indication of tactics can be given. We might, for instance, simply appeal to common sense. We might point out the areas in which postmodern people usually do believe in absolute truth, e.g. the truth that child abuse is never acceptable, that people have inherent human rights, that suffering is bad. We might demonstrate the impossibility of living without assumptions of truth, e.g. that relationships matter, that traffic is dangerous. We might even discuss the intangibility of some truths, which are knowably true even if they cannot be proved beyond any *doubt, e.g. that I love my mother and she loves me. Postmodern attitudes do not mean we give up in despair. At most, they mean we change our topic of argument a little.

In any case, if we are Christian we know that the epistemological fatalism of postmodern thought is not true. There is communication, because there is a God who created us with the ability to communicate and understand, and who communicates to us. There is *logic and rationality, because we are created in the image of God to rule the world, which requires understanding. We have reason for hope, and reason to be positive about our capacity both to understand and to be understood. So, even though our opponents might insist that a rational argument cannot operate upon them, or that linear discussion is not relevant, we can still have confidence that our rational argument can affect their minds. Even if popular wisdom tells us that no-one will be convinced by propositional apologetics, that the only thing people will react to is stories, Christians know that propositions can be convincing. We believe in a God who communicates both through propositions and *history.

The postmodern atmosphere in which we operate means that certain approaches to Christianity may be more effective than others. A recognition of the importance of presuppositions, for instance, may be more inviting to postmodern listeners than, say, an appeal to history. At any time, we should take the trouble to understand our listener's thoughts and objections and answer in ways that matter to them. Apologetics may be different in style when a listener holds postmodern assumptions, but apologetics is still a viable activity.

Having established that there is good reason to assert that apologetics, the task of defending the Christian faith by rational argument, always has a place, is there anything different about the role of apologetics in our current time? Does our post-Christian society make any difference at all?

Despite the foregoing defence of the timelessness of apologetics, there is also reason to say that our post-Christian society is different. It does change the very role of apologetics. At least, it makes far more obvious a potential problem that apologetics is always prone to, and which is crucial now. Consider the statement, 'Apologetics attempts to render the Christian faith persuasive.' This would no doubt pass as a fairly standard description of apologetics. However, it gives us a clue that there is often some confusion as to the role of apologetics. For the Christian faith itself is always capable of persuading. It does not need to be rendered persuasive, it already is. It is a radical and compelling message for many people. The gospel itself, the message that *Jesus died to take the penalty for our sins and that in his resurrection we can have new life and relationship with God, is a sensible and coherent one, offering a philosophical resolution to existential problems as well as the enticing prospect of a different way of living. The gospel answers such questions as why there is suffering in the world, whether people matter, whether there is life after death and so on. For many people, just hearing these answers is convincing.

It may be that people are not convinced of the truth of this message, not because the gospel needs to be made more persuasive, but because they do not realize what the gospel says. Sometimes what we need to do is to stop arguing and make sure that our hearers realize what we are arguing about. In these post-Christian days especially, the need to do this becomes even more obvious. As in the early days of evangelism, the Western world may not need a defence of the faith so much as simply an explanation of what it is. Our culture is 'post-Christian' not just in that Christian values and beliefs no longer hold the public place they once did, but also in that levels of biblical literacy have fallen dramatically. Sunday School attendance, once a social norm even for nominally believing families, has fallen off dramatically. Exposure to Bible teaching cannot be assumed any more, with the result that an increasing number of adults simply do not know what the Christian gospel is. The remnants of Christian thought in our culture only confuse the picture, so that Christianity is associated with moralism (usually of the most repressive kind), conservative social views, weak sentimentality and seventies musicals. We are facing a population of people who are not only profoundly ignorant of the Christian gospel but, worse still, think they know it since they live in a 'Christian' culture. This means that Christians may not even be asked to explain the hope that they have, let alone give reasons for it. Their non-Christian audience thinks they already understand it, and despise it as an emotional weakness, or some such thing. The opportunity for apologetics, then, is all the more remote, for who is interested in hearing the defence of something they think they already know and reject?

The primary task in a post-Christian era, then, may be evangelism rather than apologetics. Indeed, one can argue that it is the primary task in any era, it is just that our current times make the issue more obvious. This is not to say that apologetics is non-viable, merely that the gospel needs to be explained before it can be defended. There is no point launching into a lengthy list of the historical evidences for the New Testament if the hearer does not know why the New Testament is important. A spirited defence of Jesus' fulfilment of prophecy is premature if a listener has no real idea who Jesus is.

It is often surprising in these post-Christian times how persuasive the Christian gospel is. Evangelism can, in fact, be its own apologetic. The gospel message in itself, the truth that God died for us in Jesus to reconcile us to him for all eternity, answers many of the questions people have concerning worldly philosophies. For instance, it sometimes seems to be the case that people doubt the possibility of a meta-narrative simply because they have never heard a plausible one. Telling them of Christianity gives them an excellent example of a meta-narrative that has great explanatory power. People may be wondering whether there is truth at all. In examining Chrisitanity, they can study a prime contender for truth. How do I make moral decisions? Is there any hope for community, family, relationships? Where is the spiritual, where is God? The Christian gospel answers all these questions.

It may also be the case that traditional apologetics are not necessary in this post-Christian era, for the simple reason that the gospel is marvellously strong when seen against the hopelessness and despair of its competitors. People who have never heard of the Christian answer, who know nothing of it, can be amazed by its good sense. It truly is good news, overcoming the existential problems that plague us, problems to which many philosophies simply insist there is no answer. Christians can easily forget how terrible a godless world is. It is only when we become blasé about the gospel's astounding solutions to philosophical problems that familiarity breeds contempt. But the solution to ignorance, and the solution to being blasé, is to re-tell the powerful and shocking original story. In a real-life communication, with the give and take that naturally occurs between friends in conversations that may take place over years, evangelism and apologetics may blend into one. It is, after all, part of the same dialogue. Christian faith is explained, answers are given in response to questions and criticisms are made of opposing views.

Christianity does have answers. It is an entirely respectable intellectual framework to hold, and rather better than most. We do not need to struggle to defend Christianity as if it is somehow lost and floundering in the new world. The answers are there. What we need to do is remind the modern world of the answers it has forgotten. Christianity has not been disproved by the modern intellectual estate, despite what the popular media would have us believe.

In this dialogue we will do more than just defend the faith. In a world where Christianity is not attacked so much as ignored, we need to be a little more assertive. We need to do some attacking of our own, to show up non-Christian philosophies for their failures. There is some precedent for this in the literature on apologetics. It is similar to Francis *Schaeffer's 'taking the lid off', i.e. exposing the weaknesses, of secular philosophies as a prelude to explaining the Christian alternative. This moves beyond apologia and is more outward-looking, less on the defensive. An appropriate word for this activity might be 'kategoria', which describes the critical activity which apologia answers. It goes beyond apologetics to critique our society, its philosophies and ideas. It is something the non-Christian world hardly expects of Christianity with its reputation of fluffy and woolly-minded thinking.

Perhaps our times may even encourage us to be more bold in our attacks on non-Christian answers. If Christianity is no longer the mainstream, no longer the power-broker, then it no longer has to maintain a middle-class respectability. It is more free to be presented as the radical and subversive message that it is – subversive of culture, subversive of entrenched ideas, subversive of all the techniques that sinful humans use to avoid God.

There are particular topics which we will probably need to address as part of re-educating the post-Christian public about what the Christian religion is. One crucial topic will be the concept of 'faith' itself. There is very little understanding in contemporary discourse as to what the Bible means when it talks of faith. Religious faith is often treated as an entity which you either have or have not and which you may have in varying amounts. It is something that happens to you or something you leap into, not an act of will. To 'have faith'

means you are a religious person who believes something for which there is no evidence. Since it is something not open to rational discussion, or even personal control, being something that comes upon you in an arational way, then it is foolish to talk of faith being true or false. It is not something that exists within those categories.

Part of the problem is that although the English word 'faith' translates a fairly uniform concept in the Bible, it is used in the English language more generally to mean a whole lot of things. It can be very derogatory when used by atheists or it can be held as the high ideal by all kinds of religions, and in each case it can mean totally different things. There is nothing wrong with using the word faith to refer to an anti-rational apprehension of knowledge, contrary to reason, if that is what people want to do. It may be useful to have a word that describes an epistemic path that is quite separate from the normal mental processes of rational thought. The trouble is, that is not what the Bible talks about. To use the same English word faith, to describe both a mystical concept and the Bible's idea of commitment to God is highly misleading.

In much of modern discussion it is as if faith is an intuitive apprehension of ideas or some mystical source of information. We can have knowledge from reason meaning from using rational mental processes, or we can have faith, meaning some mysterious, irrational other *certainty. Yet both reason and faith can be part of the same process. Reason is generally a series of logical steps, which has to start from somewhere. It can start from things we make up, that just seem self-evidently true, or it can start from things we have been told on *authority. Faith, in the biblical sense, is our decision about where to start, about whether we trust our own heads or some other authority. Faith is also our decision about what to do with the conclusions (regardless of where the premises came from). Do we trust our own mental ability to deduce correctly? Do we trust someone else's conclusions? The question is not 'Do you have faith?' but 'In what do you place your faith?'.

Faith is different from reason, but is not something without reason. It is something more than just the mental conclusion. It is a decision to act, and the act itself. Faith is not contrary to reason, or opposed to the mental act of reason. Quite the opposite, for to have faith without reason is foolish, just as to have reason without faith is foolish. It is demonstrably foolish to believe something for no reason. It is idiotic to step out of an aeroplane having faith that you can fly to the ground. Faith without reasons for faith is nonsense. If one is going to trust or have faith in something – a person, an authority, a bridge – then one ought to make sure that thing is trustworthy. If the bridge looks unstable, it is foolish to trust it. There is no point in having faith it will hold you up, when all the evidence you have points to the contrary. At the same time, it is foolish to see the good sense of some action but still refuse to do it. If you have good reason to trust a person, then trust them. If you need to cross a river and it is entirely reasonable to have faith in the strength of the bridge, then go across. The process of reason will not get you across the river. At some point you have to act on your conclusions.

So what is the relationship between faith and reason? This is something we need to make absolutely clear to a post-Christian world. Faith is an action of trust. Reason is the activity of making logical deductions from given premises. We are all capable of both, within the range of human abilities. God has created us as rational beings with the ability to make correct deductions. Our mental power is evident in the great success of science and *technology and other intellectual pursuits. We also have a wealth of information in the world to act as premises. We are capable of considerable feats of reason.

There is information we have not been given in the created world. So there are some things that cannot be worked out, simply because of lack of information, e.g. God's plans, the mind of God, his personal relationships and so on. God has graciously given us this information in Scripture. To believe what God has told us in Scripture is entirely reasonable. We can sensibly have faith in God, because God has demonstrated himself to be faithful. He keeps his promises and he tells the truth; these are good reasons to trust him. Our faith in God is not something apart from our reason. Having faith in God is simply taking the logical step once we

have seen the good reasons for trusting him. We do have good reason to trust him. Our trust is not mystical, or irrational. It is entirely reasonable.

Faith and reason are different, but by no means contradictory. One should always follow the other. Those who come to a reasonable conclusion and fail to act on it are as foolish as those who act without reason. The difference is not one of opposition, nor is it an essential epistemic difference. In this post-Christian era, as in any era, we need to be aware of the misunderstandings people may have which keep them from becoming Christian. The definition of 'faith' is just one example of a word commonly used in Christian evangelism which is used differently by most non-Christian hearers. We must do all we can to make sure our words communicate accurately what we mean and always be sensitive to our context. This is as true now as it ever was, and no doubt forms part of the 'gentleness and respect' that Peter urges us to have as we give answers (1 Pet. 3:15).

As Christian evangelism goes on in any era, it is crucial that we do not leave out the most important part, explaining what, or whom, our faith is in. We trust Jesus, who is God himself, who demonstrated his love for us by dying in our place. God dealt with the *evil and suffering in this world by paying for it himself. This message is itself the answer to the questions humanity has about our nonsensical, confusing, painful life. This is a radical and life-changing message.

Non-Christians are frequently surprised by how substantial the Christian philosophy is. The secular media provide little idea about what Christianity says and generally assume it is just as weak as any other answer. We practise Christianity in the midst of misunderstanding and misinformation, in which our beliefs are seen as at worst immoral and at best outdated. It is our task, our powerful, convincing task, to demonstrate otherwise.

K. R. BIRKETT

Theology and Apologetics

If theology is 'faith seeking understanding', and apologetics is the rational defence of the faith, does it follow that apologetics enjoys a certain priority over, and independence from, theology? Theology may be queen of the sciences, but when intellectually challenged, should the queen defer to the apologist, her white knight? Or, does the apologist argue not only to but from a position of faith, not only to but from doctrines such as revelation, creation, sin and redemption? To what extent should apologetics be distinctly Christian, not only in its conclusions, but also in its method?

Faith seeking understanding and/or defence?

The question is whether the rationality that commends faith is distinctive and unique to faith or not. Can one defend Christian beliefs on the basis of other beliefs without according ultimate *authority to something other than *revelation? Perhaps the most important insight in recent discussions concerning *epistemology is that knowledge is now seen to be something that is established *within* fiduciary frameworks rather than independently of them. It was not, however, always so.

Apologetics and natural theology

The first aim of the so-called 'classical method' of apologetics was to devise arguments that established *theism as the correct world-view. After the supreme being's existence had been demonstrated, usually on the basis of arguments from nature, attention was then given to adducing historical evidences for the truth of the biblical accounts of God's mighty acts, especially the resurrection of *Jesus Christ. Theology has two initial questions for classical apologetics.

In the first place, the theologian wants to know whether a defence of theism *per se* counts as *Christian* apologetics. For the God of Jesus Christ is not a generic 'supreme being', the same deity as professed by the other monotheistic faiths, but the specifically triune God who is Father, Son and Spirit. Arguments for generic theism are not yet defences of Christian faith.

Secondly, the theologian wants to know whether one can argue to specifically Christian conclusions on the basis of appeals to nature and historical evidences. Better: the theologian wonders whether the evidence will be rightly interpreted apart from the divine interpretation of *history provided through special revelation. Can an appeal to evidences ever move beyond the existence of a generic deity to acknowledge the triune God – Father, Son and Spirit – at work in the history of Jesus Christ?

Apologetics and revealed theology: Which God? Whose reason?

Classical apologists see their task as removing impediments to belief in God. But which God? Can one by searching find out the one true God apart from the testimony of the OT and NT? Arguments for the existence of God, even if successful, may be pyrrhic victories if they fail to lead one to the triune God or if they secure only intellectual assent. Neither proofs nor evidences will get us very far unless we think about God and the world in terms of a biblical framework.

Does reason represent the view of 'everyman', or a God's eye point of view, or the view of modern science? What counts as the epistemic norm, the standard or criterion of knowledge, in apologetics? Must faith stand before the bar of reason, or may certain faith commitments (e.g. presuppositions) be normative too? Should apologists work with a 'quadrilateral', appealing to Scripture, tradition, reason and experience alike, or with a 'bilateral', where arguments are made only on the basis of reason and experience, or with some 'unilateral' approach?

The working hypothesis of the present article is that apologetics should not proceed as if Christian doctrines were irrelevant to the defence, or to the understanding, of faith. Indeed, we might apply to the apologist what *Bultmann said of the exegete: apologetics without presuppositions is impossible. Consider, for example, the following decisions that every apologist needs to make on doctrinal issues such as revelation, the existence of God, human beings as created and fallen and the Holy Spirit.

Can God be adequately known on the basis of general revelation alone? Is demonstrating the existence of 'God', the supreme being, a defence of the Christian God in particular or of *monotheism (or deism) in general? Is the God of the gospel the same as the 'perfect being' of the classical monotheistic tradition? What do human beings know of God and when – under what conditions – do they know it? Is there a *common ground between believers and unbelievers that stems from their common creaturehood? What are the *noetic effects of sin, i.e. the effects of human fallenness on human thought processes? (If Christianity is indeed true, then everything in the world may serve as corroborative evidence. The problem, however, is that unbelievers often resist letting any kind of evidence *count* as such. Sinful biases colour and predispose persons to take the evidence one way rather than another, and the question therefore arises as to the objectivity of human beings.) What is the *Holy Spirit's role in testifying to the truth of Christianity? Some apologists (e.g. William Craig) distinguish between *knowing* God, which is possible only because of the inner work of the Holy Spirit, and *showing* Christianity to be true. The testimony of the Spirit to the truth of Christianity is self-authenticating, but it is not, strictly speaking, an argument. Others (e.g. Alvin Plantinga) contend that it is entirely proper to incorporate the Spirit into one's account of warranted belief.

Theology and apologetics in modernity

The relation between theology and apologetics is, of course, hardly new. In the second century, the 'Apologists', Christian thinkers such as *Justin Martyr, commended Christian faith to their contemporaries by demonstrating its compatibility with the best of Greek philosophy. Justin's aim was to present Jesus Christ as the epitome of knowledge and *truth. Philosophy played a ministerial role as apologetic handmaiden to theology. Human reason was governed by assumptions that were largely Christian. Such has not been the case in modernity, in which secular reason assumed a near magisterial role.

Secular reason

According to modern philosophers as diverse as *Locke, *Kant and *Hegel, reason stands over revelation like a judge. In the age of criticism, religious beliefs are guilty until proven innocent. *Science rather than Scripture dictates the 'plausibility structure' (Berger, *Newbigin *et al.*) that in turn influences what beliefs were felt to be reasonable.

Can one employ secular reason – the critical method that has been applied to fields as diverse as physics and biblical studies – to find out God? Can the apologist make evangelical bricks out of the mud and straw of the scientific method or human experience? Is it possible to defend the intelligibility of the faith while continuing to speak in a distinctively Christian voice? Do modern methods, norms and sources of knowledge represent new tools in the hands of the white knight, or a Trojan horse that ultimately takes faith, not secular thought, captive? Should those who wish to commend the rationality and truth of Christian faith concede to modernity the very standards of rationality? Is the meaning of rationality exhausted by the scientific or critical approach?

The method of correlation

Should Christians seek to engage modernity on terms that modernity sets? A fair amount of the evangelical apologetics produced in the twentieth century bore more than a passing resemblance to the theological method employed by the arch-liberal theologian, Paul *Tillich. Tillich too was concerned to make Christianity intelligible in terms of contemporary *culture.

The concern to make the faith intelligible to contemporary ears – call it the 'apologetic' impulse – stands in some tension with the impulse of faith to seek understanding on its own terms, however. Indeed, Hans Frei has argued that a preoccupation with apologetics led many modern theologians to revise how they interpreted and understood the Bible (*The Eclipse of Biblical Narrative* [New Haven, 1974]). If the literal sense offends thee, pluck it out – or rather, interpret it as meaning something other than what it literally says in order to make it more palatable. These apologetic or 'mediating' theologians met the intellectual standards of modernity, however, only by an often drastic revision of central Christian beliefs. Specifically, the problem with these revisionists' attempts is that they invariably eclipsed the biblical narrative, and hence lost the true identity of Jesus Christ. Apologetic points, i.e. contemporary intelligibility, are gained at the expense of fidelity to the biblical text. Frei contends that it is simply not possible to reach gospel truth via arguments that do not begin with specifically Christian premises and presuppositions.

There is some irony in evangelical apologists using the same tools and strategies as modern liberal theologians. The issue Frei's account raises is whether it is possible to fight modernity on its own terms, with its own weapons. What reasons do theologians have for thinking there may be something wrong with 'modern' apologetics?

First, its assumption that knowing subjects are neutral, objective and unbiased. One cannot simply follow a method and arrive at a proof for God's existence as if the meaning and status of one's own existence were not on the line. And precisely because one's own life is implicated in such a debate, one cannot expect neutrality.

Secondly, its capitulation at the outset to a secular view of *reality and to a sub-evangelical view of God. One of the most successful attempts at correlating Christian faith with modern science is process theology. The basis for this correlation is a rationally established process *metaphysics. Process theism, besides reconciling modern learning and (a revised) Christian faith, has the extra benefit of 'solving' the problem of *evil. For according to process thinkers, God is not 'over' creation but in relation to it; and if God does not coerce but only 'persuades', then we can explain evil by saying it is the result of the world's refusal of God's loving persuasion. The problem, of course, is that on this view God is loving, in an inclusivist sense, but not sovereign. What one gains (God's love) cannot compensate for what one loses (God's lordship). Process theology thus represents a cautionary tale of the cost involved in trying to defend Christian belief by correlating it with what contemporary culture finds intelligible.

Thirdly, its pride in thinking that secular reason is universal. Lesslie Newbigin rightly saw that modernity was in fact not a universal framework but a very particularized *culture*, a local, Western culture. Newbigin argues that Enlightenment thinkers refused to acknowledge that human knowledge always presupposes some fiduciary framework or other, some normative set of beliefs and practices (e.g. a culture). What happens in modernity is that faith in the stories of the Bible was replaced by faith in another set of stories, stories about

science and secular reason. Instead of questioning the new story, however, modern theologians and apologists alike typically accepted the new framework and then laboured mightily to find room for the old, old story. However, one cannot commend a counter-cultural message in terms that leave the most important assumptions of that culture unchallenged.

Theology and apologetics in postmodernity

To the extent that postmodernity represents a crisis of legitimation in the very idea of knowledge, justification and truth, it follows that postmodernity also represents a *prima facie* challenge to the very idea of apologetics.

Thanks to the postmodern critique of the *Enlightenment project, we have come to see that all thinking takes place within certain interpretative frameworks. Our situation – our location in space and time – partially shapes what we see and how we assess the evidence. On this point, postmodern thinkers are hardly radical; Christians have always known that humans do not know like God. Humans lack even the knowledge of angels, for we cannot wholly transcend our situated identity. It is no longer sufficient to ask which beliefs have sufficient evidence; rather, one must ask people to give an account of the way they view the evidence.

Evidentialists have typically focused on 'exegeting' the facts, on the assumption that everyone sees and reasons in more or less the same way. This is 'outside/in' thinking: one supposedly stands outside a faith commitment and reasons one way in. Presuppositionalists, famous for having pressed the hermeneutical point (e.g. with what framework does one interpret the facts?) are 'inside/out' thinkers who acknowledge the inevitability of thinking within some fiduciary framework. Interestingly enough, the final two of the three postmodern developments in theology discussed below share significant family resemblances with more traditional presuppositionalist approaches.

Cultural apologetics

Christian apologists would do well to concede the postmodern point that human beings are not autonomous knowing subjects or disembodied minds. What one comes to believe and to accept as reasonable involves the whole person: mind, emotions, will and *imagination – or in biblical terms, the 'heart'. Postmodernity has brought to the fore the need for an apologetics that addresses the whole person. Logical argumentation may be only one form of apologetics, and a rather truncated one at that.

While Keats may have overstated himself when he penned the line, 'Beauty is truth, truth beauty', modernity has consistently overlooked the ancient wisdom that viewed truth, beauty and goodness as an integral unity. C. S. *Lewis is perhaps an exception to the modern rule. On the one hand, Lewis offered proofs for the existence of God and arguments in favour of *miracles. Yet alongside these more traditional reasoned defences of the Christian faith, Lewis also provided an indirect, more imaginative argument in his fiction, a 'poetic apologetic', as it were. Through his fictional narratives, Lewis enabled readers both to 'see' and to 'taste' the truth, goodness and beauty of reality bathed in Christian colours and light. Lewis's literary works seek to convince readers of the Christian vision as a whole.

This does not mean that rhetoric, much less sophistry, should take the place of *logic. No, it leads rather to an enlarged concept of argument, and of apologetics, that appeals to the imagination and that acknowledges the theological significance of culture and aesthetics as aspects of the Christian world-view. It is possible to render Christian truth artistically as well as argumentatively. These are new waters for apologetics, but a trail is being blazed, by, among others, musician theologians Jeremy Begbie and William Edgar.

Post-liberal apologetics

A number of theologians associated with Yale University have opened up new vistas in apologetics as well as theology that stem from their critique of modern liberal theology. George Lindbeck has criticized the modernist attempt to demonstrate the intelligibility of Christian belief on the basis of universal principles or structures. For Lindbeck, the question is not whether there are norms for rationality (there are), but whether they can be formulated in some neutral, framework-independent manner (they cannot). From a post-liberal perspective, philosophy must never become either the magister or the manager of rational conversation, but must rather be content to serve as a part-time adjunct labourer in the mission fields of apologetics.

William Placher believes that Christians in North America find it difficult to engage culture effectively because they have accepted too many of its basic assumptions. Such was the price to be paid for intellectual respectability. Yet the price is too great if it entails that Christians can no longer speak, or think, in a distinctive (and faithful) manner. Perhaps, says Placher, the time has come for an 'unapologetic' theology, and apologetics, that refuse to let non-Christians set the intellectual agenda.

Post-liberal apologists seek to dialogue with those of other faiths or no faith without the benefit of any overarching theoretical foundation or framework. Common ground there may be, but it is not epistemological. Placher denies that we can converse with others only on the allegedly neutral ground of reason. It is mere pretence to speak and act as if we do not hold Christian convictions. We should instead admit that we stand in a particular tradition – in what A. *MacIntyre calls a 'socially embodied argument' – and remind our interlocutor that he or she does too. Unlike their modern liberal forebears, post-liberals are unapologetic in their commitment to the tradition that locates its identity in the biblical narrative.

All reasons are internal to a particular tradition, be it the tradition of modern science or of Christian orthodoxy. Truth, however, is not context dependent: if something is true, it is true for everyone, regardless of the tradition to which they belong. Placher's 'unapologetic apologetics' seeks to describe the world so as to demonstrate its true pattern as held together in Christ. Apologetics in a post-liberal mode is a hermeneutical exercise that appeals to the data of human history and experience and infers a Christian world-view as the best explanation. In particular, the reasonableness of Christianity is a function of its persuasive and assimilative powers. Its argumentative style is not universal but *ad hoc*. *Ad hoc* apologetics is a matter not of redescribing Christian belief in terms that moderns or postmoderns can readily understand, but rather of redescribing all of life and human experience with categories derived from the biblical narrative.

Apologetics is about helping others to develop the 'discerning vision' that allows Christians to see the world in terms of biblical patterns. One of the best ways of cultivating this vision is to invite others to participate in the life and language of the Christian community. Ultimately, the intelligibility of Christian belief comes from learning the skills that enable one to interpret and perform life in biblical terms:

'An "ad hoc" apologetics would make a case for the reasonableness of Christian belief not by referring to some putatively neutral datum of experience to which the Christian religion conforms but, rather, through the skilful demonstration of how our common and everyday world in its variety really conforms to the biblical world' (W. Werpehowski, 'Ad Hoc Apologetics', *Journal of Religion*, 66 [1986], p. 284). The best defence, one might say, is a good catechesis. Conversely, arguments for the existence of a generic deity are decidedly sub-evangelical.

Radical apologetics

Radical orthodoxy, the upstart theological movement associated with John Milbank, has yet to produce a work of explicit apologetics. Nevertheless, radical orthodoxy is probably the best contemporary example of the adage that the best defence is a good offence. In bravura style, Milbank denounces secular modernity as the misbegotten child of a theological error. Similarly, he sees the opposition between reason and revelation as a peculiarly modern corruption.

Briefly, Milbank argues that all thought which seeks to make do without God is ultimately nihilistic. In *Theology and Social Theory: Beyond Secular Reason* (Oxford and Cambridge, 1990), for example, Milbank accuses the secular theories of *Weber and Marx of being anti-theologies in disguise and refuses to let them 'position' theology. Modern social theory is governed by the assumption that reality is ultimately conflictual and violent. On this view, politics is all about force and counter-force. Only on a Christian world-view can one think about society in terms of interpersonal (e.g. trinitarian) harmony. The aim of radical orthodoxy is to reinterpret all of reality on the basis of Christian rather than secular assumptions. Its proponents believe that if one does not presuppose Christian doctrine from the outset, then it will be virtually impossible to find room for it later on: either creation *ex nihilo* and ontological harmony or *nihilism and ontological violence.

The authors of a collection of essays on topics as diverse as language, friendship and music repeatedly make the point that when one tries to think about some segment of reality independently of God, one is invariably driven to nihilism, to what earlier presuppositional apologists termed 'chance' (J. Milbank,

C. Pickstock and G. Ward [eds.], *Radical Orthodoxy: A New Theology* [London, 1999]). Of special note is Milbank's essay on 'knowledge'. Milbank rejects the very premise that philosophy has its own autonomy and legitimacy apart from faith. Philosophy must not be allowed to set the conditions for knowledge, for when it is does so it dictates the terms on which Christians can come to know God. Philosophers like Kant have done precisely that, and modern theologians (and apologists) have bowed the knee to these standards more often than not. For Milbank, both reason and revelation are part of a larger scheme in which human beings are allowed to participate in the mind of God. What *Augustine termed 'the light of the mind' is neither merely reason or revelation, but both together.

Theology as apologetics?

Ironically, it is partly due to postmodern criticisms of modernity that we have come to appreciate certain apologetic, even epistemological, resources that are intrinsic to theology. It is now time to make these explicit. The gospel of Jesus Christ entails certain claims about the nature of reality. We come to know God, the world and ourselves only in light of the biblical account of creation, fall and redemption. All human thinking takes place within fiduciary frameworks, but only the biblical framework enables us to interpret reality correctly.

The epistemic primacy of Jesus Christ

'The best Christian apologetics is a *Christological* apologetics' is a good rallying cry, to be sure, but what exactly does it mean? Bruce Marshall has recently advanced the cause of post-liberal apologetics by explicitly addressing the related questions of the truth and justification of belief. Like other post-liberal thinkers, Marshall thinks it dangerous to defend Christian beliefs on other than Christian grounds. Accordingly, he attacks the dependence thesis, which states that one can argue for Christian beliefs only on the basis of another set of beliefs (e.g. science, philosophy, history). When other beliefs are allowed to determine the truth of Christian beliefs, the meaning of Christian beliefs often gets revised as well. Tillich's theology was intelligible to the intellectuals of his day, yet its existential scaffolding affected the very meaning of the resurrection, salvation and the uniqueness of

Jesus Christ. It is not enough to confess Christian beliefs to be true, says Marshall; Bultmann and Tillich could do that. One must also make the core Christian beliefs the *primary criteria* of truth.

According to Marshall (*Trinity and Truth* [Cambridge, 2000]), Christian beliefs must be regarded as epistemically primary: 'What we need is a way of giving reasons for beliefs without creating epistemic subordination and dependence.' We do not argue *to* the truth of Christian doctrines, but *from* them. If it is indeed the case that 'in [Christ] all things hold together' (Col. 1:17), then the narratives that identify Jesus should have 'unrestricted epistemic primacy'. A belief is justified, therefore, if it coheres with the gospel of Jesus Christ: 'The narratives which identify Jesus are epistemic trump.'

Marshall is not proposing a mere *fideism. Though he does not seek to justify Christian beliefs on the basis of other beliefs, he does seek to justify them on the basis of their assimilative and explanatory power with regard to everything else. When Christian beliefs are taken as true on their own terms, all other truths in the world fall into their proper place. For example, no beliefs that are inconsistent with the truth of Jesus Christ can themselves be true. Jesus is the truth that Christian apologists ultimately must defend, for it is Jesus who makes God the Father known. The best way to demonstrate the rationality of the gospel is to display its assimilative power, that is, its ability to illumine all other narratives.

Finally, Christians demonstrate the truth of Jesus when they conform to or 'bear' his image. Bearing Christ's image – being a Christ to one's neighbour – is a compelling demonstration of the truth in action. The way Christians live, therefore, can also serve as a kind of 'correspondence' claim to the truth of Jesus Christ.

Word and Spirit: warranted Christian belief

Alvin Plantinga refuses to let non-Christian systems of philosophy claim the high ground with regard to definitions of knowledge and accounts of rationality. What one takes as rational depends on what one believes about reality: 'It is at bottom not merely an epistemological dispute, but an ontological or theological dispute.' For example, evolutionary naturalists who deny the biblical account must then try to explain how and why reason is a reliable belief-forming mechanism. Plantinga, by contrast, defends the rationality of Christian belief by appealing explicitly to Christian doctrine. Specifically, Christian belief is justified – or in Plantinga's terms, has 'warrant' – because God has designed our cognitive faculties to produce such beliefs in the context of the witness of Word and Spirit.

For Plantinga, faith is as legitimate a faculty for producing true beliefs as is perception. This is a more radical apologetics in that it, like presuppositional approaches, recognizes that the first objective of the discussion is to challenge the business-as-usual epistemological assumptions as to what counts as a rational belief. Plantinga argues that these business-as-usual assumptions actually derive from non-Christian assumptions. They are ultimately as 'circular', therefore, as Christian fideism is typically alleged to be.

The central section of Plantinga's *Warranted Christian Belief* is an exposition of the 'A/C model', i.e. the account given by the Christian tradition, paradigmatically represented by *Thomas Aquinas and Calvin, of how minds rationally come to hold Christian beliefs. On Plantinga's account, when the mind is functioning properly, a *sensus divinitatis* yields theistic beliefs. At the same time, he acknowledges that this 'natural' knowledge of God has been corrupted by sin. The A/C model consequently explains the rationality of Christian beliefs in terms of Word and Spirit: the truths of the gospel revealed to our minds (Word) and sealed upon our hearts (Spirit). Faith based on biblical testimony and the internal witness of the Spirit to the truth of the gospel just *is* warranted Christian belief. For part of the design plan of the mind consists in believing what we learn through testimony. Believing the divine testimony – the witness of Scripture and Spirit – is, therefore, entirely proper. Indeed, to deprive oneself of these sources of knowledge is, for Plantinga, irrational and unjustifiable.

The role of doctrine in defending doctrine

Marshall and Plantinga are two examples of what we could term a theological apologetics. Reason here does not stand over the gospel, deciding what to accept and what to reject, but rather assumes the gospel as its ultimate explanatory and interpretative framework with which to make sense of all other knowledge and experience. The biblical narrative provides the fiduciary framework, or explanatory hypothesis, for making sense of everything else. (John Frame's intriguing suggestion that the Reformation principle of *sola scriptura* applies to apologetics too resonates with the position advocated here. Reason here plays a *ministerial* role.)

It is not necessary to apologize for taking Scripture as one's ultimate epistemic norm. As postmoderns and presuppositionalists have reminded us, everyone thinks and reasons on the basis of some interpretative framework or another. On this view, rationality is less a matter of starting points or neutral ground than it is a matter of being willing to put one's faith commitments to any number of critical and, as we shall see below, existential tests. Jesus staked his own claim to be the way, truth, and life of God by his words and by the 'argument', so to speak, of his cross. Similarly, our rational defence of the gospel unfolds within faith's interpretative framework.

Inasmuch as doctrines represent sustained reflection on the focal points of biblical narrative, the following topics may be taken as representing how a scriptural framework might inform apologetics.

1. *Creation: reliable cognitive faculties.* Classical apologists often rely on the laws of logic – universal rational principles – and ground them either in our being created in the image of God or on God's 'design plan' for the human mind. The point is that God has created human beings such that their cognitive faculties will, given optimal conditions, yield true beliefs. The doctrine of creation serves as a powerful warrant for affirming the reliability and universality of human thought processes.

2. *The fall: fallible cognitive faculties.* Cognitive conditions are, alas, far from optimal. Because of sin, all dimensions of human being, including our thinking, are distorted – out of order. Sinners find it easier to rationalize than to be rational, to suppress the truth than to acknowledge it. Yet, to deny the truth of God the Creator is to be deceived about the world and oneself as well. Given the noetic effects of sin, rationality cannot be a matter of disinterested thinking; this kind of objectivity is not possible for rebels, at least not when the discussion touches on the subject of God and humanity. In the light of human fallenness, then, it is preferable to think of rationality in terms of criticizability. To be rational is to be willing to submit one's belief to critical testing.

One must therefore be open to criticism because one must be open to the possibility that one's cognitive and spiritual equipment may not be functioning according to the divine design plan. Rationality here converges with intellectual honesty and humility – with admitting the provisionality of our beliefs, the possibility that we may be (and often are) mistaken.

3. *Redemption: renewed cognitive faculties.* Christians believe that, thanks to the work of Christ and the gift of the *Holy Spirit, all things can be made new. We can come back to our senses through the renewing of our minds (Rom. 12:2). Recent work in virtue epistemology has recast debates about justifying beliefs away from an emphasis on following correct procedures (e.g. the scientific method) in favour of an emphasis on becoming the right sort of person, namely, a person of intellectual virtue. An intellectual virtue is a habit of mind that is conducive to obtaining truth. For example, honesty is truth conducive; close-mindedness is not. Similarly, coherence and consistency are virtues; indeed, it has been said that logic is simply 'ethics applied to the intellect'. A belief is justified, on this view, when it is held by a person of intellectual virtue. As the doctrines of creation and fall lend support to reliabilism and fallibilism in the domain of epistemology, so here too the doctrine of redemption confirms and deepens virtue epistemology's point that rationality has less to do with following scholarly procedures and more to do with becoming a saint.

4. *Ecclesiology: the rationality of church tradition.* Even the doctrine of the church, the anticipation of the new creation in Christ, has something to contribute to how one conceives the task of apologetics. Sadly, the church is as often invoked as evidence against the truth of Christianity as for it. At its best, however, the church is a socially embodied argument that grasps, and embodies, the meaning and truth of the gospel of Jesus Christ. In short, the church is itself a 'tradition of rationality', whose life, language and thought employ the biblical narrative as its fiduciary framework for making sense of reality. The real opposition is not between reason and revelation, but between traditions – two masters! – that reason serves: the Christian and the secular. For MacIntyre, a tradition is rationally justified when, like a research programme in science, it solves more problems (e.g. intellectual, social, spiritual) than its competitors. In this

light, it is significant that the Christian church is flourishing in all parts of the world while, say, communism is not.

Towards a sapiential apologetics

Theology exists to make the faith comprehensible (meaningful), apologetics to demonstrate its plausibility (truth). Maintaining a faithful *and* credible witness to the gospel should be a vital concern of all Christians. It is probably unhelpful, therefore, to draw too sharp a distinction between theology and apologetics, for each seeks to preserve the integrity of Christian faith in its own way. Indeed, theology and apologetics are not so much two separate specializations as they are two moments or stages in the lifelong witness of the Christian disciple. The mission of the church is to demonstrate the gospel's meaning *and* truth.

The wisdom of God

What is ultimately at stake in defending Christian belief, preserving the integrity of Christian witness and demonstrating the meaning and truth of the gospel is not the sheer existence but rather the wisdom of God. The mere existence of God, in an age of religious *pluralism, is almost a moot point. Apologetics would be better served by arguments that focus on God's identity, not his existence, and in particular, by arguments that defended the wisdom of what God was doing in Israel and preeminently in Jesus Christ. As Plantinga points out, the propositional object of Christian faith involves the central teachings of the gospel, of which the cross, the great display of the wisdom and power of God, is at the centre (*Warranted*, p. 248). This wisdom appears as 'foolishness to the Greeks' and to the moderns alike. The main object of apologetics, I submit, is defending the wisdom of God as displayed in the cross of Christ.

Consider the most telling objection not only to God's existence but to the notion that God is all-good and all-powerful: the problem of evil. Those who believe that the reality of evil is incompatible with that of God err primarily not in denying God's existence but rather in misidentifying God. They assume a perfect being of their own devising. The implicit assumption is that, if *I* were a perfect being, there would be no place for evil in my universe. But this assumption refuses to recognize the identity of God as described in Scripture.

Consider, secondly, the most telling objection to Christian faith in particular: the scandal of particularity. Why is Jesus Christ the only way to truth and life? Why this man, this name, this faith only? The cross is the most telling expression of both problems: of evil, of particularity. Yet it is also the place where the solution is to be found: the place where the triune God decisively reveals himself; the place where the divine wisdom is most manifest, at least for those with the eyes and the spectacles of faith (Scripture) to see it.

In order to demonstrate the wisdom of the cross, one must display the logic of biblical narrative, which is to say redemptive history, that alone identifies the one true God as the triune God – Father, Son and Spirit – who creates and redeems a human people for the sake of eternal communion. To commend the cross as the wisdom of God involves claims not only for truth and logic, but also for goodness and beauty. According to Prov. 8:30, God's created order is the result of a craftsmanship which, while more than aesthetic, is surely not less. Surely it is relevant that the answer to the problem of evil that God gives Job is not a proposition that Job needs to believe but rather an appeal to the greatness – the beauty – of the created order. How much more are the cross and resurrection, twin events that reconcile and renew this same created order, a matter of the wisdom of God! The Christ event, together with the broader narrative of which it is the climax, contains *in nuce* the clue to the meaning of everything else. To repeat: the main burden of Christian apologetics is to demonstrate the wisdom – the truth, goodness and beauty – of the cross.

Knights of the Lord's Table

What is needed today is an enlarged vision of what apologetics involves that integrates logical arguments, the narrative imagination and faithful practices all for the sake of bearing witness in word and deed to the wisdom of God embodied in Jesus Christ. The Christian apologist should be as concerned with storied and socially embodied arguments (e.g. with the church as a bearer of the evangelical tradition of rationality) as with propositional proofs. This more costly kind of argument requires not only validity, a quality of argumentation, but virtue, a quality of character.

S. Hauerwas makes this point even more provocatively by saying that if the Holy Spirit does not witness to the Father and Son through the witnesses of Christians, then Christians have no arguments to make. Christianity is unintelligible without witnesses, i.e. without people whose practices exhibit their committed assent to a particular way of structuring the whole.

While truth is not relative to the Christian community, its contemporary demonstration may be. It is not necessary to choose between propositions, plots and practices; an enlarged conception of apologetics should include all three. Arguments alone are not enough; we need a biblically informed imagination and biblically informed shape of community life fully to see, and to taste, the wisdom of God in a consistent and compelling manner.

Every Christian represents a crucial premise, and together these premises comprise the socially embodied argument which is the body of Christ. The believer-disciple is a 'knight of faith' (S. *Kierkegaard), or better, a 'knight of the Lord's Table'. For everything these knights say and do, they say and do in remembrance of him who is the wisdom of God. These knights will be 'critical fideists' who acknowledge their faith commitments but are at the same time willing to put these commitments to critical tests of all kinds: intellectual as well as existential. The ensuing apologies will therefore take many forms: not only argumentative demonstrations but also, and perhaps more compellingly, more costly attestations.

Martyrology and apologetics

The competent apologist is one who witnesses to the intellectual and existential integrity of the gospel, the extraordinary message that the triune God has enabled sinners, through the cross and resurrection of Jesus Christ, to share in the divine life. It is not irrational to accept testimony, especially the compelling testimony of a life well lived. Those who speak the truth in love will find themselves not only proclaiming the passion narrative but in a sense performing it; for all who bear witness to the truth of God's wisdom – a wisdom at odds with the wisdom of this world – must be prepared to endure opposition. Knights of the Lord's Table seek to live well and, if necessary, to die well in a demonstration of the wisdom of the cross.

They are less conquerors than sufferers for the truth.

Theology sees apologetics as a vital aspect of its martyrology, of the study of its ongoing mission to bear witness to the truth, goodness and beauty of the wisdom of God and the cross of Christ. Apologetics should be in the business not merely of justifying certain propositions in a manner that appeals to the intellect only, but of rendering a powerful and compelling witness to the wisdom of the Christian way that appeals to the will, emotions and imagination as well (Vanhoozer, *The Drama of Doctrine*). For what is at stake in defending the faith is not only establishing this or that proposition, but also convincing people of the wisdom of the Christian vision as a whole. This includes, of course, showing the deficiencies of the false wisdom of the world. In sum: we need a broader conception of apologetics that defends not simply the existence of God or the historicity of Jesus' *miracles, but the logic, and dynamics, of the cross, the power and wisdom of God.

A sapiential, martyrological apologetics stands in continuity with classical apologetics too. Justin Martyr's apology, as his name indicates, included his willingness to die for his faith. In the final analysis, the best apologetic is the whole people of God speaking and acting as faithful disciples of Jesus Christ, arguing, living, and dying as wise witnesses to the way, the truth and the life.

Bibliography

B. Marshall, *Trinity and Truth* (Cambridge, 2000); N. Murphy, *Beyond Liberalism and Fundamentalism: How Modern and Postmodern Philosophy Set the Theological Agenda* (Valley Forge, 1996); L. Newbigin, *The Gospel in a Pluralist Society* (London and Grand Rapids, 1989); W. Placher, *Unapologetic Theology* (Westminster, 1989); A. Plantinga, *Warranted Christian Belief* (Oxford, 2000); K. Vanhoozer, *The Drama of Doctrine: A Canonical–Linguistic Approach to Christian Theology* (Louisville, 2005).

K. J. VANHOOZER

Christian Apologetics in the Non-Western World

Christian apologetics in the non-Western world is a complex, multi-layered and exhaustive subject area. It has the potential to help contemporary Christians to deal with issues that they confront in the postmodern era, where often a hybrid of Western marketing techniques and Eastern mythology – a devastating combination of seduction through media and mysticism – is evident. Non-Western apologetics covers vast and complex situations, and is written from numerous perspectives in order to address a variety of issues which confront the non-Western world. This article surveys the context in which apologetic writings emerged in the non-Western world, then compares and contrasts the Western and non-Western contexts and issues that are addressed by non-Western apologists, and finally focuses on key apologetic approaches developed in the South Asian context.

In an era of rapid *globalization, many of the issues that are faced by non-Western apologists are bound to have global relevance. The non-Western world includes countries from South America to Africa, to Asia. The issues, concerns and themes that are addressed in these continents are so diverse and complex that it is not possible to discuss them fully in a short article like this. Although these regions each represent a unique socio-religious context, however, there are several common issues and concerns that are tackled by Christian apologists in each. The way the Christian faith was introduced in these regions also differs drastically. For example, in most of South America, so-called 'Christianization' involved imposing Western or European Christianity, along with its culture, on the local inhabitants. This was primarily done through the colonial powers that were in control of the situation. Granted that several missionary efforts were also at work to bring the native population under the Christian banner, the fact that the process of Christianization seemed to go hand in glove with the colonization of South America cannot be denied. So the issues and concerns that emerged out of such a context did not warrant a strong apologetic response. It was only towards the middle of the twentieth century, with the emergence of 'liberation theology', that a number of issues began to be addressed by Christian (evangelical) apologists.

In Africa (though generalization is risky), the penetration of missionary societies along with the colonial powers meant that the Christian faith generally spread through the coastal areas. The patterns of conversion and the spread of Christianity differ drastically from those in South America. Here again, the missionary endeavours and colonial powers, to a large extent, went hand in hand, with the Dutch, Portuguese, English and French-speaking countries taking the lead. Both in South America and in Africa, missionaries confronted local animistic and tribal religions and introduced the Christian faith with comparative ease. Segments of tribes and regions were converted to the Christian faith through group or mass conversions. Christian apologetics did not have a significant part to play in such contexts, because of the animistic cultures and a lack of literacy among the local people in addition to the complexities of *language and *culture. In most cases, animism did not pose a substantial challenge to the Christian faith, nor did the missionaries or the local Christians feel much need to develop any apologetic literature. Partly because Christianity sailed smoothly along in these countries, bringing most people *en masse* into the Christian fold, the need for apologetic literature was rarely sensed. It was only in the wake of the advance of *Islam in Northern and Western Africa that Christian apologetics emerged, and that only scantily.

Asia, though not a continent, is more complex than normally perceived. It is a complicated region of the world, where the classical religions of *Hinduism, *Buddhism, Confucianism and Islam were born, and where they dominated for centuries. These religions and their adherents posed a strong challenge to the spread of the Christian faith, even though the Western colonial powers were equally present in most Asian countries. In the midst of the prevalent classical religions, Christian faith was often attacked, challenged and criticized; hence the

44

need for apologetics was evident right from the introduction of the Christian faith in these countries. That explains why early missionary writing has a dominant theme of Christian apologetics. If Christian apologetics in its strict sense means 'defending the faith', then, when it came to the Asian context, it truly meant defending the faith. For the non-Western context, which is so religiously and culturally diverse and where the issues are so complex, different types of Christian apologetics were bound to emerge. But they did not necessarily fit into strict apologetic methods or types. Rather, each type took its own shape in line with its contextual realities. It is not possible to fit Christian apologetics in Asia into the Western mould of apologetics, even though it took Western classical, experiential and historical aspects into consideration. At times it tended to be negative and defensive, but in most cases it has been positive, taking the initiative in providing answers to some of the issues and questions raised in its contemporary contexts.

South Asia has been a fertile ground for missionary experiments since Christian missions faced at least three classical religions (Hinduism, Islam and Buddhism) and multiple cultures and languages. It was in South Asia that many initial apologetic approaches were formulated and popularized around the world. This region also produced more contextual theological reflection than any other part of the non-Western world. Therefore, studying some of the key approaches and theological trends that emerged out of South Asia will help us to understand the challenge of Christian apologetics in the non-Western world.

Differences between Western and non-Western apologetics

Differences between Western and non-Western approaches to apologetics become evident when we compare their theological, philosophical and conceptual frameworks. The Western way of thinking is generally influenced by Greek philosophy, which holds a linear understanding of *history or time. It signifies the progression in one direction. It also places emphasis on rationality; reason plays a dominant role, and feelings, emotion and even the role of subjective experience are given a secondary position. Approaches to Christian apologetics in the Western world have followed systematic and logical ways of argument, based on conceptual and theological foundations, whereas the non-Western context

demanded a more experiential and practical approach. Bear in mind that Christian apologetics in the non-Western world has taken a form different from that in the developed Western world because of its complex cultural, religious and social context.

Western apologetics seems to be more systematic and logical in its approach and arguments. It assumes a strong methodological as well as conceptual approach to the subject. This assumption is further evident in the way the methodology and structure are developed by Western apologists. While making the sharp distinction between the Western theological system and Asian Christian theology, Saphir Athyal points out that 'in Western theologies, the concept of *monotheism, the personal character of God, the reality of sin, understanding of the world as God's sphere of action, etc., need not get any thorough treatment at all, while in Asia these might be some of the most alive issues in theology'. Granted that there are different approaches to apologetic writings in the West, the basic rational and conceptual assumption is clearly seen. For example, two of the methods Gordon R. Lewis distinguishes are pure *empiricism, as defended by J. Oliver Buswell Jr, and *rationalism, as defended by Gordon H. Clark. Obviously, faith and reason go hand in hand in Western apologetic methods, but this is not necessarily the case in Eastern or Asian apologetics, since it is experience, rather than rationalism that plays a central role in Eastern thinking.

Non-Western apologetics emerged out of a necessity to defend the faith in a strong religiously and culturally plural context, where Christianity tended to be a minority religion. Religious *pluralism has always been a reality in the non-Western world, where both classical and animistic religions have always posed a fundamental challenge to Christianity. Pluralism rejects any religion's claim to be unique, final or decisive, and argues for the equal validity of all religions. The apologists that emerged out of such a context therefore had to address the concerns of a pluralistic cultural and religious context. This was essential, partly because, in most non-Western countries (except in South America), Christianity has been a minority religion, and Christian assumptions could not be taken for granted while developing apologetics. Therefore, the basic issues, the approaches and the degree of freedom to express one's opinion as a Christian were drastically different in the non-Western context. At times, this led to negative apologetics that tended to be defensive. Christianity, as a minority faith among many dominant faiths in these non-Western countries, was often subjected to close scrutiny, interrogation and criticism. Much apologetic writing thus tended to be reactionary, since its authors had to respond to the criticism levelled by the proponents of other religions.

Another reality that has to be taken into consideration is that much of non-Western apologetics is not primarily in written form, much less written in English. Most non-Western contexts represent a multiplicity of languages, and most apologetic writing is done in local or regional languages. Oral apologetics takes place at a very grassroots level, and is either not available for our study or cannot be analysed because it is not availabile in written form. Thus a large segment of apologetics remains untouched and unexplored.

Apologetics has had to be expressed in the form of contextual *theology rather than as pure apologetics. The noted theologian Robin Boyd, who served in India as a missionary for a number of years, includes apologetics under the heading of revealed theology. He contends that within revealed theology five classifications can be made: biblical theology, dogmatic theology, history of dogma, apologetics, and practical theology. Boyd states: 'Apologetics is that branch of theology in which the Christian faith is defended against those who attack it. It can also refer to the task of formulating the faith in a way which will make it attractive to non-Christians, and so the word "apologetics" can be used to describe the task of proclamation.'

In that sense, very little real apologetics is being produced in the Asian context, since most of it has taken the form of theological reflection in response to issues faced by the apologetics in their pluralistic context. However, contextual theology has not only focused on apologetic concerns; rather, it has responded to the contextual issues that demanded comprehensive theological articulation of the Christian faith in an appropriate manner. Sadly, however, much contextual theology in Asia, and particularly in South Asia, is influenced by the ecumenical thought that tends to accommodate the Christian faith to the local cultural and religious context. In doing so, it appears to have lost a biblical focus and tends to lean towards a more syncretistic and compromising expression of the faith. Here Bruce Nicholls' observations on Indian contextual theology are noteworthy: 'Most attempts to contextualize theology in India have tended to follow the same path of relativizing the Gospel and absolutising one or other of the Hindu conceptual frameworks.' If this is true, most Indian contextual theology does not fit into the category of pure Christian apologetics, since it does not necessarily provide a defence of the Christian faith. Nevertheless, the value of contextual theology is not diminished, since it demonstrates the natural struggle to respond to the objections, questions and issues raised by the context itself.

Added to that, the issue of the colonial dominance of the so-called 'Christian West' has to be taken into consideration, since it has affected both the content of and the approaches to Christian apologetics in the non-Western world. Traditional Christianity in its historic manifestation has been predominantly Western, and has demonstrated an aggressive, superior, colonial and imperialistic attitude. The dilemma of defending the Christian faith without being associated with the 'sins of colonialism' has been a delicate task for most apologists, though some of them seem to have been left with no alternative to defending 'Western Christianity'. Most Christian apologists have had to maintain a delicate balance between being Christians and not being a part of the 'Christian colonial' power. Because many early apologists in non-Western countries were missionaries from Western countries, the tendency to uphold the colonial powers as part of God's plan seems to have been evident to a certain extent in their writings. The tendency to condemn local religions and religious systems in the light of supposedly 'Western Christianity and culture' has evidently cast a shadow over their apologetic writings. This is seen in early nineteenth-century missionary writings where elements of judgment and condemnation seem apparent. Some converts from local religions who undertook apologetic writings were trained under the Western missionaries, thus consciously or unconsciously demonstrating a similar bias in their writings. That, however, changed when the national Christians took over and began to reflect on their religiously plural context and to articulate their response to it. In so doing, non-Western theologians developed different approaches and methods which they considered appropriate for and relevant to their context.

Apologetics in the pluralistic context of South Asia

Christian apologetics in the South Asian context necessarily emerged in response to the reality of non-Christian religions. When Western missionaries were confronted with the problem of religious plurality, the question of their attitude towards other religions was raised. They found it difficult to call other religions simply 'unbelief' or 'superstition'. The relationship between the Christian faith and other religions and cultures therefore became the primary concern for those engaged in Christian mission and theology. As a result, different ways of making the Christian gospel meaningful to people in their own context have been tried. Christian apologetics in the South Asian context is thus largely based on the reflections of missionaries with different attitudes towards other religions. Though these are categorized in theological terms, they also contain certain elements of apologetics.

The exclusive approach

The first approach, normally called '*exclusivism' and associated with Karl *Barth and Hendrik Kraemer, affirms *Jesus Christ as the full and final *revelation of God and the only way of salvation. All other religions and their manifestations are perceived to be deviations from the 'Truth'; therefore, they should be totally rejected. They are under God's judgment and condemned as inadequate. The advocates of this approach believe that people of other religions must come to know God only through faith in Christ. Most early evangelism in South Asia was based on this assumption, and this was reflected in the missionaries' writings in general and their apologetic writings in particular. Apart from biblical support for this approach, most early missionaries took it for granted that, in going from Christendom to paganism, they were going from a higher civilization to a lower, and that they were taking light into darkness. They did not generally make a clear distinction between the gospel and the culture of Christendom. This provoked strong reaction from the native advocates of local religions, to which the Christian apologists had to respond. The exclusivist approach was further developed into a 'Christ *against* culture' attitude that was heavily criticized by native people such as Keshub Chander Sen and Raja Rammohan Roy, who rejected this Christian claim of exclusivism.

The inclusive approach

In the early twentieth century, indigenous theology was being influenced by the spirit of nationalism and nation-building. As a result, a 'Christ *of* culture' attitude was developed by Christian theologians demonstrating a keen interest for a more relevant and contextual theology in the South Asian context. This inclusivist attitude attempted to include all religions under the redemptive influence of Jesus Christ. Karl *Rahner, a primary proponent of this position, asserted that non-Christian religions contain elements of not merely natural knowledge of God, but also supernatural elements arising out of grace, which is given to humans as a gratuitous gift on account of Christ. P. D. Devanandan, a well-known Indian theologian, attempted to refine this thinking by finding a 'meeting point' between Christianity and Hinduism, so that both could work together for the nation, building on their religious and spiritual bases. Then there were those who put their efforts into examining the philosophical framework between Christianity and Hinduism. They worked on the assumption that there is a broader philosophical framework through which we can explain Christ and his work. A. J. Appasamy and P. Chenchiah attempted to use the Hindu philosophical system to interpret Christ and his work in a better way.

Raymond Panikkar took this further and attempted to find a meeting point between Christianity and Hinduism. In his book *The Unknown Christ of Hinduism* Panikkar insisted that this meeting point is Christ himself, and that, following Paul, we may speak not only of the unknown God of the Greeks but also of the hidden Christ of Hinduism. Hidden and unknown indeed! Since Panikkar held that Hinduism has the presence of the 'unknown Christ' within it, he saw Hinduism as a legitimate way of salvation. Hence, for him, salvation is found in all the other faiths, including Christianity, and is not confined to Christianity alone. Although Panikkar's work was in many ways in line with Rahner's theology, there is a significant difference in their understanding of salvation in other religions. For Rahner, 'anonymous Christianity' was anticipated in Hinduism, and salvation was, through God's grace, offered to 'anonymous Christians'; whereas Panikkar affirmed Hinduism itself as a way of salvation. As is evident in their theologies, their focus shifts from the exclusivity of Christ to the universality of God.

In line with this approach, a search for a relevant spirituality can be seen in the work of Abhishiktananda, and of Bede Griffiths, who sought to relate to Hinduism through the *ashram* and ascetic life. This type of theological approach was felt to be essential in response to Christianity's confrontation with other religions along with 'secular' humanism. South Asian Christian theologians proposed the concept of inclusive 'Christocentrism', in which Christ is seen as normative and has revealed himself in other religions also.

Most South Asian Christian theologians have been affected by a 'Copernican revolution', in which Christ and Christianity are no longer seen as being at the centre of the saving and revealing work of God, but as being in 'orbit', along with other religions, around God, who is at the centre in the universe of faith. Ultimately it is God who manifests himself in different civilizations and in different revelations and religions. Even though the various revelations differ, however, such theologians believe that God is at work in every religion. Those who advocate this theory of the presence of Christ in all religions say that this sympathetic approach to other religions puts an end to Christian attempts at conversion and encourages Christians to see the divine expression of faith in this multi-religious society.

In discussing the role of other religions in Asian and specifically Indian Christian theology, K. P. Aleaz proposes a perspective on the theology of religions which he calls 'pluralistic inclusivism'. He points out that this perspective is different from that of exclusivism, inclusivism or pluralism, and will enrich not only Christian theology but also the theology of other religions. He also emphasized that these different religions will contribute to each other in arriving at the content of the faith-experience.

Another expression of this inclusive attitude is seen in the theological reflections of J. N. Farquhar, who articulated a basis for the 'fulfilment theory' from Jesus' words, 'I came not to destroy but to fulfil.' In his interpretation of fulfilment, Farquhar makes a distinction between traditional Christianity and the Christianity that springs from Christ himself. He concluded that Christianity, or rather Christ himself, is the 'crown of Hinduism.' According to him, there is an aspiration in Hinduism which

could be considered a preparation for Christ, since every religion is instrumental in leading men and women to God. Therefore, every important Christian truth is foreshadowed in Hinduism. It should be noted that he did not think that every aspect of Hinduism found its fulfilment in Christ. Rather, he explains this idea in an evolutionary framework in which Hinduism is radically displaced by Christianity.

Following this approach, Hans Staffer, an Austrian Jesuit, and Bede Griffiths, an English Benedictine, applied the inculturation approach by attempting a synthesis of Christian faith and Hindu culture. Staffer, in line with Brahmabandhav Upadhyay's Hindu-Catholic approach, regarded religions as having two dimensions: *samaj dharma* (social customs, ritual purity, diet, etc.) and *sadhana dharma* (the way of salvation). He believed that Christianity is primarily *sadhana dharma*, since it accommodates all social customs and cultures. Therefore, Christianity and Hinduism complement each other and can be synthesized. This being the case, conversion to Christianity is not required, since adherents can conveniently embrace the essence of other religious traditions while remaining in their own community and not renouncing it. This involves, not an uncritical admiration for everything Hindu, but 'purifying' anything that is erroneous or corrupt. Staffer also denied that all the religions have salvific value, asserting that they are only a providential preparation for Christianity. Taking the analogy of the relationship between seed and soil, he affirmed that every sincere religious person is saved by Christ. Christ has secretly sown the 'seeds of his Word' in their hearts, because they have generously responded to God's secret calling.

Writing on the uniqueness of Christ in a multi-religious country like India, where millions are sincerely searching for God, Ken Gnanakan points out that they are misled by the fallacy that this sincere search will ultimately lead them to the true God, no matter by what name or in what form this God is now worshipped. Within this atmosphere, the Christian is asked to be more accommodating, and to that end theories of the 'hidden Christ in Hinduism' or of the 'anonymous Christian' have been encouraged. Bishop Stephen Neill, along the same lines, stated that 'Jesus cannot be understood in any dimension other than his own'. These arguments amount to a defence of the uniqueness of Jesus Christ and his salvation for humankind. In the midst of these debates one can see elements of apologetics emerging.

However, some leading figures within Hinduism, such as Swami Devananda, Ram Swarup and Sita Ram Goel, have raised objections to this movement, leading to vigourous debates with Griffiths. Devananda strongly criticized both Griffiths' use of the term *sanyasin* (a person who renounces all ties to family and belongings and endorses asceticism), which, for Devananda, could be applied only to Hindus, and his use of the *pranava* symbol (Om, the most revered symbol in Hinduism) over the cross, which pained Hindu religious sentiments. He suspected that the Catholic *ashram* movement to synthesize Christianity and Hinduism was really just another attempt to convert Hindus.

This 'fulfilment theory' has also faced much criticism by the noted Hindu apologist Ram Swarup. He held that the Christian approach of 'fulfilment', that is, of Christianity as 'revealed' religion and Hinduism as 'preparatory' to Christianity, results from self-centred and self-righteous thinking that shows no evidence of the spirituality, respect and genuineness which the Christians claimed to have. The proponents of the fulfilment theory insisted that Hinduism is primarily a cultural and social concept and not a religion. Attempts were made to separate the spiritual and socio-cultural elements of Hinduism, and a religious synthesis was sought. But this attempt to separate religion and culture failed in the context of *polytheism and the caste system of Hinduism.

In line with this, David Mosse, in his study of Catholic–Hindu synthesis, observed that the attempt to inculturate the gospel in Hindu society was based on the high-caste or Brahmanical tradition. As a result, the *Dalits*, who were a majority in the church, strongly objected to the approach because it was in favour of the caste system.

These theologians, however, tried their best to inculcate Christianity in the Hindu culture and tradition through the approach of inculturation. But history shows that this approach failed in many areas. As Pieris puts it, 'inculturation is something that happens naturally. It can never be induced artificially.' He also observed that the inculturationists perpetuate the cultural gap by maintaining social divisions in the church.

Then there are those who maintain the uniqueness of Christ among multiple religions.

Taking into consideration general revelation, they agree that God has manifested himself in other religions. In Christianity, however, we have a special revelation of God in Jesus Christ. The knowledge of God in other religions is not sufficient to save a person. While refusing the concept of 'many ways', Ravi Zacharias, an influential Christian apologist of Indian origin, asserts: 'All religions are not the same. All religions do not point to God. All religions *do not say* that all religions are the same. At the heart of *every* religion is an uncompromising commitment to a particular way of defining who God is or is not and, accordingly, of defining life's purpose.' In the midst of pluralistic cultures the gospel can vary in its expression, but its core content cannot be changed or compromised. But 'all-inclusive philosophies can only come at the cost of truth. And no religion denies its core belief'. Zacharias also agrees that although there are some similarities in all religions, including Christianity, at the core they are fundamentally different. For instance, some have seen parallels between Christ and Buddha, or Christ and Krishna. In his apologetic work, however, Zacharias brings out the fundamental differences between these central figures and says that although those differences may be discomforting, they are real. In addition to this, every claim that Christ made about himself challenges the other religions and their gods and asserts that he is the only way to God.

Contemporary Christian apologetic reflections

In the wake of a systematic attack on the Christian community in the recent past, there arose a strong debate over the uniqueness of Christ, salvation from sin and especially conversion. Ken Gnanakan discussed the theological problem in the context of India. Writing about the general revelation of God in other religions, he is of the opinion that 'this revelation does not directly bring salvation', and maintained that it is through Christ alone that salvation is available for all who believe. Along the same line of thought, Sunand Sumithra argues that Christian conversion is an 'unrepeatable decision' before God and is possible only through Christ. Some key national consultations initiated both by Protestants and Catholics addressed various aspects of conversion, the need for it, and the fundamental right to convert. The outcome of these consultations provided a strong base for Christian apologetics. Stanley Samartha, in his attempt to formulate Christology in India today, said, 'It is only as we share in the struggles and conflicts and tragedies of our national life and, in that context, seek to answer what it means to affirm that Christ, crucified and risen, is the Lord of all life that we can hope to make the gospel trustingly relevant to human need in contemporary India.' While his was an attempt to take the middle and more balanced way, there were others who tried to articulate their response in a more contextualized manner.

There is, however, always a danger of syncretism when attempting to contextualize the gospel in a religiously pluralistic setting. Contextualizing biblical truth within the Asian situation involves what Filipino theologian Carlos Abesamis calls 'bracketing off' the Western, Greek, tradition of theology. Sunand Sumithra and Bruce Nicholls emphasize that a boundary needs to be drawn between contextualization and syncretism. They point out the danger, if Indian theologians fail to do so, of making the 'Hindu religious cultural framework primary and the biblical context secondary'. So there is a need to draw a line between true contextualization and false syncretism. They significantly point out that it all 'depends on exercising the prophetic rebuke of the Christian faith, judging what is contrary to revelation, purifying and transforming what reflects God's work as creator and bringing to all men in salvation history'. Ken Gnanakan, while not against contextualization of the message, states that 'Indian biblical theology must be just as strong in order to be able to effectively confront other Indian theologies with the uniqueness of Christian revelation and the inexorable claims of Christ upon the country'. Both these theologians attempt to respond to the objects raised by the Hindu fundamentalists in the wake of systematic attacks on Christians, both physically and intellectually. South Asian theologians evidently have struggled with the issue of making the gospel of Jesus Christ relevant to the context, and, in so doing, some of them have entered the realm of Christian apologetics.

Other attempts to respond to the issue of the uniqueness of Christ in the midst of religious pluralism in Asia have been made by groups of theologians representing certain strands of theology. For example, in 1990 the major concern of the Theological Consultation of the Asian Theological Association (ATA) was 'Salvation in Asian context', in response to the question of salvation in other religions. It affirmed in its 'Confession of Faith' statement that 'salvation is only in the cross of Christ and is efficacious for all time'. At the same time, the Roman Catholic encyclical *Redemtoris Missio* (December 1990) reasserted the exclusiveness of Christ and stressed the universal scope of salvation. It clearly stated that only in Christ are we set free from all alienation and doubt, and from slavery to the power of sin and death.

Towards the end of the twentieth century, a wave of persecution of Christians in South Asia and particularly in India forced the Christians to defend their faith in various ways. It was primarily the exclusivity of Christ and Christianity, along with the Christian insistence on religious conversion, which led to great opposition by Hindu fundamentalists. During the 1980s and 1990s the Rashtriay Swanmsevak Sangh, and all its associate organizations (the Bhartiya Janata Party, Vishwa Hindu Parishad and Bajrang Dal) appeared to have influenced the country by promoting their ideology of Hindutva – excluding the ideologies of *secularism and *communism and the religions of Islam and Christianity in order to make India a Hindu *rashtra* (a Hindu nation). Following this, India experienced many communal riots between Hindus and Muslims and Christians. Not only this, the party's main aim seemed to be to promote Hindutva as a theological and practical alternative by finding fault with Islam's dogmatism and Christianity's exclusive claims and their practice of converting Hindus. In their writings they criticized and attacked Nehruvian secularism and communalism. Ram Swarup and Sita Ram Goel are notable critics of Islam and Christianity who, through their extensive research, provided important resources for Hindus in their opposition to these religions. Both authors saw Islamic and Christian claims to exclusive truth and their campaigns of conversion as the root of the emerging political disturbance in the country.

Some apologetic responses were developed by mission thinkers such as Ebe Sunder Raj, who attempted to respond to the allegations surrounding conversion and called for a national debate on the issues related to it. At the national level, the All India Christian Council, the United National Christian Forum and other similar bodies attempted to promote dialogue between the Hindutva forces and Christian leaders. Sadly, the outcome of these attempts was not published; but the value of their practical apologetic response cannot be undermined, since they attempted to respond to the issues raised by the Hindu fundamentalist forces at the grass-roots level.

Academic and philosophical attacks on the Christian faith were also initiated by the Hindu journalist Arun Shourie and other Hindu members of the intelligentsia. Shourie heavily criticized the missionaries' social activities as another attempt to produce conversions. He also appealed to Christians to ask whether it can be claimed, in the light of contemporary scholarship, that the Bible is free of error and the Pope infallible. For him, whatever the church said about contextualization, inculturation and dialogue was merely a change in its methods of evangelization. In his arguments against Christianity, he made extensive use of material from the writings of Vivekananda and *Gandhi, and tried to convince his Hindu readers that these objections still held and can be used to refute Christian conversion activities.

Responding to Shourie's intellectual attack on Christianity and particularly on Christian mission, Vishal Mangalwadi, a noted Christian activist and writer, strongly objected to Shourie's attacks, seeing him as a 'postmodern Hindu' who neither sought the 'truth' nor regarded finding it as possible. According to Mangalwadi, some Hindus objected to conversion, not because of a commitment to pluralism, but because of a cosy *relativism. More Christian apologetic response needs to emerge at the intellectual level to enable educated thinking people to see the real truth behind these attacks and counter-attacks.

Conclusion

Christian apologetics in the non-Western world is a complex and multifaceted discipline that cannot be understood or interpreted in the light of a Western apologetic framework. Several basic elements of apologetic are evident in non-Western or Asian contextual theology, though at times it tends to be leaning towards syncretism. Several strands of apologetic writing have emerged within the non-Western context, especially in the South Asian region, all of which have contributed to various aspects of a Christian defence of the faith.

Bibliography

Abhishiktananda, *Hindu–Christian Meeting Point* (Delhi, 1997); K. P. Aleaz, 'Religious Pluralism and Christian Witness: A Biblical-Theological Analysis', *Bangalore Theological Forum*, 21.4 and 22.1; 'The Role of Asian Religions in Asian Christian Theology', *Asia Journal of Theology*. 15.2; S. Athyal, 'Toward an Asian Christian Theology', in D. J. Elwood (ed.), *Asian Christian Theologies: Emerging Themes* (Philadelphia, 1980); R. H. S. Boyd, *The Kristadvaita: A Theology for India* (Madras, 1977); P. Chenchiah, *Rethinking Christianity in India* (Madras, 1938); S. B. Cowan (ed.), *Five Views on Apologetics* (Secunderabad, 2000); P. D. Devanandan, *Preparing for Dialogue* (Bangalore, 1961); D. J. Elwood, (ed.), *Asian Christian Theologies: Emerging Themes* (Philadelphia, 1980); K. R. Gnanakan, *Proclaiming Christ in a Pluralistic Context* (Bangalore, 2002); S. R. Goel, *Catholic Ashrams: Sannyasins or Swindlers?* (New Delhi, 1994); J. Hick and B. Hebblethwaite, *Christianity and Other Religions* (London, 1980); H. Kraemer, *The Christian Message in a Non-Christian World* (London, 1938); V. Mangawadi, *Missionary Conspiracy: Letters to a Postmodern Hindu* (Carlisle, 1996); B. Nicholls, 'Towards a Theology of Gospel and Culture', in J. Stott and R. T. Coote (eds.), *Gospel and Culture* (Pasadena, 1979); R. Panikkar, *The Unknown Christ of Hinduism* (London, 1964); E. Sunder Raj, *The Confusion Called Conversion* (Chennai, 1998); M. M. Thomas, *The Acknowledged Christ of the Indian Renaissance* (Madras, 1976); R. Zacharias, *Jesus Among Other Gods: The Absolute Claims of the Christian Message* (Nashville, 2000); *The Lotus and the Cross* (Sisters, OR, 2001).

A. AGHAMKAR

PART TWO

PART TWO

ABELARD, PETER

In Peter Abelard (1079–1142) we have one of the most daring figures of the medieval Renaissance. He was a master of dialectic who dared to apply *Aristotelian *logic to both philosophy and theology. Born in Pallett in Brittany in 1079, he later studied under Roscelin (1050–1120?) and under William of Champeaux (1070–1121), archdeacon of Paris. Abelard established fame as a brilliant lecturer in both Melun and Corbeil and later as the holder of the chair of dialectics at the cathedral school in Paris. Early on in his career Abelard departed from both of his primary teachers to give his own answer to the unsolved question of *universals that exercised the best minds of his time. Intrigue and his own willingness to antagonize those around him characterized Abelard's restless career.

Among the writings of Abelard is a work entitled *Sic et Non* ('Yes and No'), in which contrasting and sometimes contradictory statements are placed side by side without resolution. This practice did not start with Abelard. There is no good reason to believe that Abelard wrote this work as a modern rationalist might, in order to bring Christian belief into disrepute. Rather, his concern was, 'to provoke young readers by conflicting questions to the maximum of inquiry into the truth'. His desire was to see the varied voices of the tradition brought into the service of understanding the faith of the church.

Recent scholars have insisted that reason is the point of departure for all of Abelard's theology. It is true that Abelard was inclined to emphasize reason and dialectic over a mysticism of faith. However, Abelard also denied that reason alone can establish the truth of any doctrine. Thus, it may be that a greater recognition of the moral character of Abelard's thought is necessary if he is to be fully understood. Nevertheless, he insisted that one must endeavour to understand rationally the doctrines of the Christian faith because it is the duty of the theologian not only to teach the faith, but also to defend it against its enemies. Abelard is here not thinking of unbelievers so much as heretics who err through an excessive reliance on reason.

Bibliography

M. T. Clanchy, *Abelard: A Medieval Life* (Oxford, 1997); S. Kreis, 'Peter Abelard', *The History Guide* (Spring 2003); P. L. Williams, *The Moral Philosophy of Peter Abelard* (Lanham, 1980).

G. L. Isaac

ABORTION

An apologetic response to abortion requires both a critique of pro-abortion positions and a positive presentation of Christian perspectives. This will involve reflection on a woman's view of ownership of her own body, freedom, the status of the foetus, when life begins and the value of that life, conflicts of rights and how to deal with hard cases.

Critique

The claim that a woman's body belongs to herself alone defies the reality of relationships in society, the nature of sexual intercourse and the presence and being of foetal life. None of us is totally free to do whatever we wish with our own bodies, and there are laws restricting what we may and may not do. Seat belts, crash helmets, alcohol and sexual expression are all controlled by *law and limited by our human relationships.

The foetus is not only a part of a woman, it has its own unique history, genetic make-up, life and being. That there is dependence is a fact of human nature rather than a mark of insignificance. If the significance of life is denied from the moment of fertilization, then some other moment or defining qualities need to be offered as a criterion for when life is to be protected. Any argument allowing abortion by denying the worth of the foetus has to show why life after birth is more important than life in the womb, when the dependency is very similar.

The pro-choice position strictly interpreted allows a woman to choose either to have or not have an abortion. It is the woman's choosing itself which matters. But often the pro-choice stress seems to be pro-abortion. It stresses the right of the woman to do whatever she wants with her own body. That implies that society has a responsibility to supply or permit a woman to have whatever she wants. This is not just a demand on the medical and financial resources of society, but implies that a woman's rights are more important than the rights of the foetus, the father, doctors and nurses, the wider family and society. Law often permits abortion under certain circumstances. That shows that there are limits to rights and part of that will be dealing with conflicting rights' claims. One focus is to ask if a woman should be allowed to abort a child simply on the grounds that it is female. Once grounds for abortion are at stake, there is clearly no absolute right to abort on demand.

The hard cases of threat to the life of the mother from continuing the pregnancy, rape, incest and severe handicap are often used to justify abortion and challenge the Christian views of compassion and the sanctity of life. While Christians do show a variety of responses to these cases, they are consistent in stressing that an abortion is always an human tragedy. Both the taking of life, whatever its state, and the conditions which have led to that 'killing' are *evil. The debate is whether or not it is a necessary evil, unavoidable, and a less than perfect act which requires regret, sorrow and repentance.

There is no necessary contradiction between holding that human life is sacred and the recognition that in extreme circumstances the taking of life may be a necessary evil. A totally consistent view of sanctity of life would be anti-abortion, euthanasia, war and capital punishment. For those who hold to abortion in extremes as a necessary evil, there is a clear debate with the pro-abortionist over when and under what circumstances abortion may be justified.

Positive presentation

All Christians hold that human life is a gift of God and to be treated with respect from the earliest stage. For some that will guide their choice of contraception, avoiding abortifacients like the coil and 'morning after' pill as well as their attitude towards abortion.

Christians need to show that they can and do offer a genuine alternative for any woman who is considering an abortion. That will take the form of counselling and practical and financial support for the length of the pregnancy and far beyond. That a woman who has had an abortion may suffer from post-abortive trauma and *depression is both a warning and concern in counselling and caring for women dealing with a possible abortion.

Christians must show the wonder of human life and development from the earliest stages and stress the fact that from the moment of fertilization, the complete genetic content of a unique human life is present. From that moment, the result will be a human being exactly as we are, if other things are equal. We know that sadly miscarriages and abortion do happen, but that does not change the nature and status of humanity. The value of humanity rests on being made in the image of God, and Christians will try to reflect God's perspectives on human life and origins looking at Ps. 139, the prophets and the meeting of the pregnant Mary and the pregnant Elizabeth in Luke 1.

Christians should challenge the idea that our bodies are our own and that we are free to do whatever we want with them. Both God and society set limits to individual freedom to protect the individual from harm and to protect others. The interrelationship between human beings is part of sharing the image of God and the responsibility we have for each other. Compassion for the woman and her unique circumstances does not imply agreement with whatever decision is made. While there is a responsibility to help people think through what abortion is, what it means and its results, individuals must have the freedom to make their own decisions. Our responsibility does not undercut that of the individual.

The basis of talk about 'rights' must be explored and the challenge of how to judge between competing rights, especially those of the father, other family members and doctors who may have strong views opposed to abortion. It is appropriate to ask how the pro-abortionist distinguishes infanticide from abortion and whether some frivolous or even immoral grounds can really justify abortion.

Winning the personal and social debate must be matched with compassionate commitment to offer alternatives to and support for those who decide for or against abortion.

Bibliography

R. F. R. Gardner, *Abortion: The Personal Dilemma* (Exeter, 1972); C. Everett Koop and F. A. Schaeffer, *Whatever Happened to the Human Race?* (Wheaton, 1983).

E. D. COOK

ABSOLUTES

Absolutes are rules of conduct that are assumed to apply universally, regardless of culture or context. Motives and outcomes feature less prominently than obedience to a moral obligation. For Christians, absolutes are considered to be those rules that God intends humans, as his creatures, to obey in every circumstance. Absolutes are often understood to be rooted in God's directives through Scripture. At other times, absolutes may be regarded as those universally accessible tenets of reason which guide human actions and bind them with obligations.

Divine command

Scripture affirms that God gives commands and expects his commands to be obeyed by his people. He holds people responsible for their obedience or disobedience to his revealed directives. This is sometimes referred to as the 'divine command' theory of *ethics. The Ten Commandments are perhaps the most obvious examples of God-given rules which are to be followed by those who seek to honour him. Implicit in divine command theory is the idea that what God wills for his creation is good, and following the Ten Commandments is not simply a matter of blind obedience. Rather, it establishes the priorities for human life and offers the best guidance for a life of wholeness or shalom. Nevertheless, the matter of God's authority to command and require obedience cannot be disregarded. God's authority remains central to divine command theory.

This opens up an ancient dilemma of absolutism highlighted by *Plato's *Euthyphro*: Are actions wrong because they are forbidden, or are they forbidden because they are wrong? Conversely, does God command something because it is good, or is something good because God commands it? Christians may be reluctant to draw too firm a line between the two. If God's commands emanate from his character, then it is fair to say that God both wills the good and defines what is good. As God is the author of all creation, he has placed inherent good in creation, but it is not to be understood as independent of the character of the Creator. So God commands the good because he has made it good; it is good because it *is* good and also because he commands it.

The idea of obedience to the divine command has opened for many an entire arena of ethical speculation about why God's commands ought to be obeyed. Some indicate that if obedience does not lie in the goodness of the command itself, then it must lie in the status of the person in relation to God. Some have posited the 'ought' from 'is' notion, sometimes referred to

as the naturalistic fallacy. They suggest that God *ought* to be obeyed absolutely because he *is* the Father of creation. The moral obligation in this case arises from his position of fatherhood. It has been objected that the fact of fatherhood does not necessarily instil obligation in the child. Rather, the quality of the relationship is what defines the obligation. A tyrannical father who demands absolute obedience to absurd commands does not instil confidence. For the Christian, God's commands are seen to be absolute not only because of the *authority of his power and position, but also because of the quality of the relationship of love he has generally with his creation, and specifically with his church through *Jesus Christ. For it is only through a relationship of grace that obedience to God's commands is made possible through the empowerment of the Holy Spirit.

Categorical imperatives

For some, absolutes are seen less as divine commands than as rules that humans understand, through reason, to be universally good. Immanuel *Kant is the most famous advocate of such a position. He suggested that there are certain imperatives that extend beyond personal preference to a matter of duty. These are not hypothetical imperatives but categorical imperatives, because any reasonable creature can see that they are universally beneficial and thus ought to be obeyed. For Kant, one such imperative was to 'do only that which you would wish to become a universal law'. For example, one should always tell the truth in every circumstance.

The matter is complicated when imperatives are applied to life. Truth-telling may be compromised when certain situational constraints are introduced. If a person arrives at your house begging you to hide them from a pursuing murderer, and the murderer then knocks at the door and asks if you are hiding their intended victim, do you tell the truth? The case of Rahab in the OT provides an example of how failing to tell the truth in a situation worked to the benefit of God's people. She was not rebuked for failing her duty to the absolute rule never to tell a lie.

Graded absolutism

There has been a recognition amongst many Christian ethicists that sometimes divine absolutes appear to conflict when applied to particular situations. For example, a pregnant woman may have a physical complication that means almost certain death for both her and her unborn child. The doctors indicate that if they abort the child, they may be able to save her life. In order for her life to be spared, another must be sacrificed.

While some may say that the answer is obvious, for most of us, it is not. Injunctions against killing and the imperative to preserve life appear to conflict. In such a dreadful situation, the possibility of sparing at least one life will seem for some to outweigh the absolute 'You shall not kill'. Whether absolutes actually do conflict in theory or practice, or whether it seems that way from a limited human perspective, some have suggested that Christians should deal with such situations from a perspective of 'graded absolutism'. Graded absolutism indicates that some absolutes may take higher precedence in situations where two absolutes seem to come into conflict. In this example, they may indicate that the preservation of the life of the mother, as it exists in relationship with many others, outweighs the absolute directive not to kill the unborn child, especially in a situation where both are almost certain to die otherwise.

The difficulty of weighing absolutes against one another in applied ethics has led many to suggest that it is not a helpful approach to ethics for Christians, who must constantly wrestle with the interpretation of Scripture for the development of biblical principles rather than absolute rules that apply in every situation. Nevertheless, it points to the importance of engaging the hermeneutical task with diligence in ethical matters, rather than simply adopting a legalistic and moralistic stance.

Challenges to absolutism

It is not surprising that challenges have come to absolutism from many directions. Not only have issues of biblical interpretation served to erode a sense of moral absolutism, but changing philosophies and cultures also have had a significant impact. Subjectivism, *relativism, the issues of experience and context all challenge the idea of moral or epistemological absolutes.

Joseph Fletcher was one ethicist who developed an ethic based on situationism. Fletcher believed that love is the single absolute for the Christian. He did not think that it could be determined in advance what love might do in a given situation. Therefore, although love was an absolute command, it was tempered and determined by the circumstances of the context in which love had to be applied. Love was subject to the situation, compromising its absolute nature.

In recent times, there has been a resurgence of interest in virtue ethics. This revival was encouraged by the work of Alasdair *MacIntyre and others, who pointed out some of the difficulties of pursuing revealed or reasoned absolutes. In the place of absolutes, MacIntyre posited the development of virtue as an appropriate ethical approach. Against Kant, and with Richard *Rorty, he suggests that absolutes are really context-bound understandings of what the good is. For MacIntyre, it is impossible to reason beyond this, and so he begins with practices and from there derives virtues which are necessary for realizing the goods inherent in them. Such an Aristotelian and Thomist view is historically bound and teleologically oriented. As such, virtues are not derived deontologically from absolutes. However, if the good lay in realizing the fulfilment of the good of practices, rather than merely developing character, then they may have, in some sense, an absolute quality about them. But they do not, as such, address the matter of absolutes in the sense of duty or obedience to rules.

A virtue approach finds popularity in an era where moral absolutes have fallen on hard times and the notion of God's authority to command is in crisis. Helpful though an appreciation of virtues may be, Christians should not be eager to deny absolutes *per se*. Some Christian ethicists are suggesting ways of portraying and preserving God's moral authority that do not mean reverting to a thoughtless *legalism. If God is the author of creation and through Christ has shown the measure and demand of his love, then in the life-giving Spirit he offers the resources for obedience to that greatest command to 'love as I have loved you'. With Paul Ramsey, and echoing Paul *Tillich, we may affirm that love, as the ultimate principle of ethics, is both an unconditional command and the power breaking through all commands.

Bibliography

M. Beaty, C. Fisher and M. Nelson, *Christian Theism and Moral Philosophy* (Macon, 1998); D. Bloesch, *Freedom for Obedience* (Eugene, 2002); J. Rachels, *The Elements of*

Moral Philosophy (London and New York, 2002).

A. M. ROBBINS

ACCOMMODATION THEORY

Introduction

The phrase 'accommodation theory' is used in communication studies to describe the way we adjust our speech depending on our audience. The term has also been used by critics of Christianity to argue that Jesus accommodated his teaching (e.g. on the flood [Matt. 24:37–39] and Jonah [Matt. 12:39–41]) to his Jewish hearers. Apart from the historical disjunctions this introduces, it simply is not the case that Jesus accommodated this way when confronted with error (Matt. 15; 23). (And it is not easy to explain why an 'accommodating' Jewish teacher was crucified.) All of which goes to show that there are limits to accommodation.

Accommodation theory as outlined here, however, has to do with God speaking in a form appropriate to the capacity of human beings. This understanding of accommodation has a long history, permeating Christian thought from the first century onwards. It has been, and remains, a fundamental issue for *theology and apologetics.

Accommodation in Christian thought

Early Christian apologists appealed to accommodation to explain why the Mosaic law was no longer binding on new-covenant believers. Justin argued that God gave Israel rituals to perform because he was accommodating himself to human weakness; the law was a means of leading the people away from idolatry and was intended only for that stage of salvation history. *Augustine used the picture of a physician who prescribes one medicine to some patients through assistants and another medicine by himself to other patients, the analogy being that 'the divine providence remains entirely without change, but comes to the aid of mutable creatures in various ways, and commands or forbids different things at different times according to the different stages of their disease'. Accommodation was also drawn on in disputes over anthropomorphic *language used to describe God. Origen offered the analogy of baby talk, noting that 'when we are talking to very small children we do not

assume as the object of our instruction any strong understanding in them, but say what we have to say accommodating it to the small understanding of those whom we have before us'.

Accommodation was a central feature of *Calvin's theology. Like Origen, he used the analogy of baby talk, noting that 'as nurses commonly do with infants, God is wont ... to "lisp" in speaking to us ... not so much [to] express clearly what God is like as accommodate the knowledge of him to our slight capacity'. Recent scholarship has been careful to note that Calvin's concept of accommodation cannot be reduced to a single understanding (such as for *revelation), but is diverse in character and more subtle than its use in earlier theologians. In Calvin's handling, a distinction can be drawn between God's accommodation to humanity in general and his accommodation to Israel in particular.

Accommodation provides an apologetic tool to tackle apparent inconsistencies in Scripture. When the Bible speaks of God's mouth, ears, eyes and hands, it is as though, according to Calvin, God is using baby talk to accommodate himself. Language about God 'changing his mind' shows that he represents himself not as he is but as he seems to us, particularly given our time- and space-bound perspective. God uses the language of 'change' to accommodate himself to human beings who must exist and act in time and history. It is not a pedagogical choice to do so (as if accommodation were merely a useful teaching device); rather, it is a *necessity*, given the distinction between the timeless Creator and time-bound creatures.

Elsewhere in Calvin's work, the dominant motif is that of God accommodating, not because of his people's 'childishness', but because of their primitiveness and stubbornness. This apologetic element is seen especially when he deals with the alleged barbarity of parts of the OT such as less-than-perfect aspects of legislation and military campaigns, which God tolerated on account of his people's hardness of heart (cf. Matt. 19:8). This was different from the response of Origen and Augustine, who frequently resorted to allegorical interpretations of 'difficult' passages.

Some implications

Apart from whatever insights emerge out of a consideration of accommodation through

Christian history, a number of implications for apologists can be set out briefly.

1. Accommodation reminds us of the graciousness that characterizes God's dealings with humanity and the importance of his self-disclosure in Scripture. In one sense, all knowledge of God is accommodated in that it is tailored to us. In the Bible itself God limits his expression to the grammar and vocabulary of human languages, and yet not in such a way that distortion is thereby introduced – just as to speak childishly is not necessarily to communicate without intelligence or in error.

2. Accommodation provides an appropriate perspective on the nature of humanity and human knowledge. A Christian *epistemology will recognize that men and women are finite, stubborn and sinful, and in need of God's revelation.

3. Accommodation calls us to faithful biblical interpretation and biblical theology. With Calvin and others, accommodation helps us understand that so-called difficulties in biblical texts related to imprecision, hyperbole, reports of natural phenomena, etc. are not threats to a traditional stance on the infallibility of Scripture. Nor does accommodation entail a metaphorical theology where *reality is reduced to mere metaphor. Texts which suggest God has a physical body (say) can be understood appropriately in the light of other texts which declare God is spirit, when we adopt an approach which looks at the wider context of Scripture as a whole, compares texts with texts and engages in careful biblical theology.

Christian theologians since Calvin have continued to explore the significance of divine accommodation for theology and biblical interpretation. It has become especially important in recent debates about the 'openness' of God, such as how much he knows about the future and whether he 'changes his mind' as a result of prayer. In deploying the notion of 'accommodation', however, we should heed the advice of those who have warned against introducing an unnecessary disjunction between the *mode* of God's revelation and the *content* of revelation, as if what really matters is the theological kernel which can be extracted from the formal husk, the latter seen as a mere 'vehicle' for *truth. God's revelation in Scripture is inextricably bound to human language with all the implications that carries for hermeneutics and epistemology.

Bibliography

J. Balserak, ' "The Accommodating Act Par Excellence?": An Inquiry into the Incarnation and Calvin's Understanding of Accommodation', *Scottish Journal of Theology* 55.4 (2002), pp. 408–423; F. L. Battles, 'God Was Accommodating Himself to Human Capacity', *Interpretation* 31.1 (1977), pp. 19–38; S. D. Benin, *The Footprints of God: Divine Accommodation in Jewish and Christian Thought* (Albany, 1993); K. Sparks, 'The Sun Also Rises: Accommodation in Inscripturation and Interpretation', in V. Bacote, L. C. Miguélez and D. L. Okolm (eds.), *Evangelicals and Scripture: Tradition, Authority and Hermeneutics* (Downers Grove, 2004), pp. 112–132; D. F. Wright, 'Calvin's Accommodating God', in W. H. Neuser and B. G. Armstrong (eds.), *Calvinus Sincerioris Religionis Vindex* (Kirksville, 1997), pp. 3–19.

A. BILLINGTON

ACTS, HISTORICITY OF, see HISTORICAL DIFFICULTIES IN THE NEW TESTAMENT
ADAM, HISTORICITY OF, see ORIGINS, THEORIES OF

ADVERTISING

Advertising is the most common form of mass persuasion in market economies. Although advertisers are not always successful at selling particular products or services, they do collectively nurture consumer identities. Advertisements implicitly proclaim that people can achieve greater happiness merely by purchasing products and services and conspicuously impressing others with their resulting acquisitions.

Some scholars compare this conspicuous consumption to *pagan 'magic'. They suggest that advertising transforms consumption into rituals for overcoming unpopularity and low self-esteem. Even the simple act of buying and using laundry detergent can become a means of impressing friends and expressing love to a spouse or children. Consumers are asked implicitly to have 'faith' in the power of advertised brands to improve their lives.

In advanced industrial societies, this consumer

magic generally competes with the gospel of *Jesus Christ. Both messages appeal to human beings' basic need to be appreciated and especially loved.

As secular evangelism, however, advertising has to persuade consumers over and over again, since new products and services are continually being released. Advertisements nearly always look to the future, offering consumers new, improved and presumably more effective ways of achieving happiness. Any resulting consumer benefits are always short-lived, however, as new products are announced in print advertisements and broadcast commercials. Deeper, lasting happiness is always around the corner, never fully achieved.

By contrast, the gospel proclaims a completed act, and Christ's sacrifice for human sin is an historically validated source of hope rather than the latest hype about future happiness. God accepts the repentant heart fully, just as the father unconditionally welcomes home the prodigal son. Perhaps the most compelling defence of the Christian faith in a consumer *culture is that Jesus Christ accepts people as they are, in their broken relationships, with all of their feelings of inadequacy and rejection. Advertising creates only more demands, new burdens, ongoing unhappiness and competition for attention, whereas the gospel reveals that Jesus has already paid for sin and promised eternal life.

In the NT Jesus proclaims freedom from the burdens imposed by the religious establishment, saying, 'Come to me, all you who are weary and burdened, and I will give you rest' (Matt. 11:28). Today people face secular burdens, including trying to achieve happiness with the latest goods and services. In response, Jesus offers real hope to all who are struggling to find happiness under advertising-induced burdens.

Redemption in Christ addresses the underlying condition of the human heart, not merely external images or personae. Scripture even warns against the human tendency to evaluate persons based on external images (1 Sam. 16:7). God looks for a contrite heart, for those who admit their brokenness rather than try to cover it over through consumption.

Created in the image and likeness of God, human beings have an inherent worth that transcends popular fads and fashions. In addition, saved by the blood of Christ, people are precious individuals, not mere consumers.

Eternal life is guaranteed, not wishful thinking or pagan magic.

Probably the most potent defence against never-ending advertising claims is authentic Christian living that testifies to faith in Christ by reaching out to others in love and acceptance. Communities of Christian love can inoculate believers against advertising even in the midst of a consumer culture. St Francis's dictum remains prophetic in image-oriented consumer cultures: Preach the gospel always; if necessary, use words.

Bibliography

R. Clapp (ed.), *The Consuming Passion: Christianity and The Consumer Culture* (Downers Grove, 1998); R. W. Fox and T. J. Lears (eds.), *The Culture of Consumption: Critical Essays in American History, 1880–1980* (New York, 1983); Q. J. Schultze, *Christianity and the Mass Media in America: Toward a Democratic Accommodation* (Lansing, 2003); J. B. Twitchell, *Adcult USA: The Triumph of Advertising in American Culture* (New York, 1996); T. Veblen, *The Theory of the Leisure Class* (New York, 1912); R. Williams, 'Advertising: the Magic System,' in R. Williams, *Problems in Materialism and Culture* (London, 1980), pp. 170–195.

Q. J. SCHULTZE

AFRICAN AMERICAN/CARIBBEAN RELIGION

Christian apologetics by African Americans and Afro-Caribbean theologians has addressed various critiques of the Christian faith, in particular Christianity as a white man's religion and God as a white racist. These theologians were the founders and leaders of the modern black theology movement, a school of thought founded during the late 1960s in the United States. The leading theologian to address these topics was the American scholar, James Hal Cone. Other black theologians include Gayraud Wilmore, J. Deotis Roberts, Delores Williams, Noel Erskine, Dwight Hopkins and Jacqueline Grant. Among the group, Noel Erskine, a Jamaican-born scholar, is the leading Afro-Caribbean theologian.

Within North America and the Caribbean, the religious choice of the vast majority of people of African descent, or diasporic Africans, is Christianity. The other *world religions practised among diasporic Africans are *Islam, Yoruban and *Judaism. Islamic communities include those associated with Sunni and Sufi streams of Islam as well as African American developments such as the Moorish Science Temple and the Nation of Islam. The Yoruban religious communities consist of Santeria and Shango. The black Jewish communities include reformed Jewish congregations and the Church of God (black Hebrews). The other major religious communities are Vodun, a Fon-derived religion, and Rastafarianism, a messianic faith. These alternatives to Christianity within the African diaspora in North America and the Caribbean represent challenges to the tenets of the Christian faith.

The challenge that Christianity is a white man's religion comes especially from African American Muslims. The most stringent proponent of the position was Malcolm X, an African American leader within the Nation of Islam during the mid-twentieth century. Malcolm X contended that Christianity was the white man's religion because of its historical development, legitimation of white supremacy and delegitimation of the humanity and self-determination of diasporic Africans. Christianity, according to Malcolm X, had served as the 'perfect slave religion', a religion that enslaved and pacified African peoples with its white *Jesus and theology of submission. Malcolm stated that even the Bible 'in the white man's hands and his interpretation of it' had served as the 'greatest ideological weapon for enslaving millions of non-white human beings'.

African American theologians responded to this accusation in a variety of ways. First, Gayraud Wilmore and others identified the European moment in the history of Christianity as one among many, highlighting the role of Africa and Africans in the development of early Christianity prior to the rise of European hegemony within Christianity. Related to this historical project, they spotlighted the ancient and medieval African Christian kingdoms of Egypt, Nubia and Ethiopia, the early modern Christian kingdom of Kongo, and the rise and development of the black church in North America and the Caribbean by African Americans and other diasporic African Christians. Secondly, Cone and others concurred with Malcolm X and the other critics about the role of Christian doctrine in legitimizing white supremacy and delegitimizing the struggle for African American self-determination and liberation. They contended that these Christian theologies were distortions of the Christian faith and, along with other white misinterpretations of the gospel, should be opposed. They also argued for the preservation of the 'perceived truths of the biblical texts', and the transformation of 'past understandings of the gospel' into interpretations that were biblically sound and relevant to the struggle for liberation. They challenged the theological complicity of Christianity with white supremacy in the United States.

The apologetic espoused by black theologians contends that the Christian God is against *racism and identifies with, and is in solidarity with, the victims of racism. They asserted that the Christian gospel, as opposed to certain white Christian theologies, did not legitimate racism, because it supported the emancipation of 'black people from white racism, thus providing authentic freedom for both white and black people'.

Cain Hope Felder and others noted how interpretation of the Bible differed when it moved from white to black hands. Black hermeneutics exposes the presence in the biblical record of Africans such as Keturah, the Queen of Sheba, Solomon, Simon of Cyrene, the Ethiopian eunuch and others, as well as the role of Egypt/Africa as a safe haven for the infant Jesus. Afrocentric and feminist biblical scholars explore the emancipatory themes in Scripture. Theologians such as Cone argue for the blackness of Jesus, regarding blackness as the symbol of oppression and identifying Jesus as the 'oppressed one' who stood in solidarity with the oppressed. Kelly Brown Douglass speaks of the black Christ, rejecting the white Jesus for the historical Jesus, Jesus as a revolutionary, and for the Jesus of faith, especially the faith of African Americans. Finally, scholars such as Vincent Harding and Wilmore demonstrate that historically there existed an ecclesial trajectory within the black church that resisted white supremacy and fostered radical Christian activity. Consequently, Christianity is not a white man's religion; if anything, Christianity is a black religion, emancipatory in nature and empowering the oppressed to join God in the liberation struggle. This is because through the cross and resurrection the 'oppressed are set free to struggle politically against the imposed injustice of rulers', according to Cone.

Critics of Christianity from within the

African American/Caribbean community have raised theological questions, including whether God is a white racist. The major articulator of this question is William R. Jones. Jones considered it theologically impossible to defend the goodness of God in the light of the enormity of black suffering in the world. Jones contended that Christianity promoted divine racism, the unequal bestowal of God's love and favour upon different races and ethnicities. He suggested the reality of divine malevolence by doubting 'God's intrinsic goodness relative to blacks' because of the maldistribution of black suffering. He pondered the 'possibility of a demonic God', even questioning 'God's existence and relevance in the struggle for black freedom'. Jones regarded God as a white racist because the doctrine of God either directly or indirectly justifies black suffering.

The majority of black theologians, however, affirm the goodness of God in the face of black suffering, engaging the biblical conception of the Christian God. They refute the theologies of divine racism and divine disfavour with African people. For them, black oppression was not a sign of divine disfavour; rather it is a product of structural sin, of white supremacy and patriarchy. The contradiction became a challenge to the theological enterprise. God opposed *slavery, emancipated the enslaved and participated in the liberation of the oppressed in the exodus. The exodus event is central to theological exploration. According to J. Deotis Roberts, it supplied 'a central category for interpreting' the Hebrew Scriptures, the work of Jesus Christ and the mission of the church in the world. The God revealed in Jesus Christ demonstrated the same solidarity with the poor, outcast, and marginalized as the God of the exodus. Cone articulated this position forcefully.

According to Cone, Jesus expressed solidarity with the oppressed by being born among them, ministering to them, and proclaiming God's reign as 'usurping the powers that enslave human lives'. Jesus as the oppressed one revealed through his life, death and resurrection 'that God is present in all dimensions of human liberation'. In death, Jesus revealed 'the freedom of God, taking upon himself the totality of human oppression', and in the resurrection he disclosed 'that God is not defeated by oppression but transforms it into the possibility of freedom'. Cone argues that 'the resurrection, therefore, is God breaking into history and liberating the oppressed from their present suffering, thereby opening up humanity to a divine realization beyond history'. In Christ 'God becomes oppressed humanity and thus reveals that the achievement of full humanity is consistent with divine being'. The exodus, the crucifixion and the resurrection all became intertwined in Christ as acts of liberation.

Cone summarized the discussion in the following way: 'Whatever else may be said about the philosophical difficulties that the problem of evil poses ... faith arising out of the cross and the resurrection of Jesus renders their questions ['Is God evil?' or 'Is God a white racist?'] absurd from the biblical point of view. The absurdity of the question is derived from the fact that its origins ignores the very foundation of biblical faith itself, that is, God becoming the Suffering Servant in Christ in order that we might be liberated from injustice and pain.'

Moral outrage instead of awe or the quest for truth is the starting point for theological reflection of black theologians. The theological questions revolve around divine solidarity with racial and human equality, racial and human freedom, and racial and human liberation rather than questions about the existence or holiness or impassibility of God. The Christological questions focus on Jesus being the oppressed one and being black rather than on the virgin birth or divine miracles or the co-existence of the humanity and divinity of Christ. And the theological anthropology explores freedom from injustice and oppression more than the free will or moral capacity/incapacity of humanity. African Americans, the poor and the oppressed become the subjects of the theological task.

The apologetics of black theology entails emancipating the Christian doctrine from captivity to white supremacy and oppression, exposing the link between theology and racism along with other forms of oppression, denouncing spurious forms of Christian theology, utilizing doctrine in the eradication of oppression and making liberation cardinal to the gospel. Theological and ethical inquiry is interwined. Apologetics participates in the liberation of the oppression.

Bibliography

J. H. Cone, *God of the Oppressed* (Maryknoll, 1997); C. H. Felder (ed.), *Stony the Road We Trod: African American Biblical*

Interpretation (Minneapolis, 1991); W. R. Jones, *Is God a White Racist?* (New York, 1973); J. D. Roberts, *Liberation and Reconciliation: A Black Theology* (Maryknoll, 1994).

D. D. DANIELS

AGNOSTICISM

The word 'agnosticism' was coined by the Victorian intellectual T. H. Huxley to describe his own professed inability to know whether or not God exists. Agnosticism has been described as 'a profession of ignorance' on the part of people who find both dogmatic faith and secular *materialism unacceptable. With regard to the former, agnostics view orthodox Christianity as making claims to a knowledge of God which far exceed what is reasonable within the confines of a scientific culture. On the other hand, they are inclined to treat outright *atheism as another species of unacceptable dogmatism which threatens to destroy the foundation of *ethics. This ambivalence, combined with an often passionate concern to retain a clear moral foundation for human life, is characteristic of classic agnosticism. It can be seen in Huxley's own rejection of his earlier confidence in the benign process of evolution. In later life he came to recognize that the survivors in the evolutionary struggle depicted by Darwin may often be 'the ethically worst', and he acknowledged that the doctrines of the theologians, despite their apparently antiquated formulation, were 'vastly nearer the truth than the "liberal" popular illusions that babies are all born good'.

The historical context within which agnosticism appeared was marked by an increasing incidence of religious *doubt. The emergence of what came to be called 'modern thought' raised new questions concerning the interpretation of the Bible both indirectly, as the outcome of the development of the hard *sciences, and directly, with the application of historical-critical studies to the understanding of Scripture itself. As early as 1844 Tennyson penned the famous lines of *In Memoriam* which speak of faltering where once men 'firmly trod':

> I stretch lame hands of faith, and grope,
> And gather dust and chaff, and call
> To what I feel is Lord of all,
> And faintly trust the larger hope.

The seeds of agnosticism are clearly evident here. This poem gave eloquent expression to the spiritual and intellectual struggles of a large number of Victorian people who felt the once firm ground beneath their feet moving and saw the picture of the world bequeathed to them by devout parents breaking up before their eyes.

Unfortunately, the crisis of faith was often deepened by the reaction of those who attempted to defend belief in the face of the new questions raised by a younger generation. Christian apologists, understandably alarmed at modern trends, had a tendency to react with a militant defence of the status quo, adopting an apologetic stance which frequently ignored the doubters' real questions and involved merely repeating standard positions with little modification, other than turning up the volume. The results of such an apologetic could be disastrous because when honest, thoughtful men and women were told that they must accept all or nothing, and that capitulation to modern thought on a single point would involve abandoning Christianity altogether, the intellectual travail involved in attempting to relate faith to a changing culture became a life-and-death struggle.

When in 1888 Mrs Humphry Ward published the novel *Robert Elsmere*, with its detailed description of the manner in which the loss of an orthodox faith by the central character created emotional havoc both for himself and for his devout evangelical wife, she struck a chord in many Victorian homes. This book was immensely popular because many readers saw in it a mirror reflecting the chasm that was opening up within their families between agnostic sons and daughters, who felt that honesty and integrity demanded their rejection of inherited certainties, and devout parents, heartbroken at the rejection of a faith that gave life meaning and value. It may be difficult for postmodern Christians to understand the extent and intensity of such a struggle, but in a world that now lives after Christendom the questions raised by the Victorian agnostics and the response of faith to them are by no means irrelevant.

A new apologetic

By the end of the nineteenth century a new generation of evangelical theologians appeared who recognized the vital need for a fresh approach to apologetics. The most distinguished representatives of this movement were the Scottish theologians, James Denney and James Orr. Christian scholars like these retained an unwavering commitment to the orthodox faith, yet were willing to listen and respond to the scientists and philosophers who were increasingly shaping Western culture. Denney insisted that 'the attempt to appreciate the mind of our time is forced upon us' since there were 'latent presuppositions of the modern mind' which prevented its understanding the conceptions of atonement and forgiveness that are at the heart of the gospel. Evangelical theologians of this kind felt far more relaxed about engaging modern thought than the previous generation had been; indeed, they acknowledged that there were positive gains from the new sciences and, adopting a dialogical approach to contemporary agnostics, they set themselves the task of exposing the inadequacies of the modern mind, insisting that there are wider dimensions of reality than can be perceived within a secular framework of knowledge. For James Orr, the supreme challenge facing the church in a world being transformed both by science and by the destructive force of unbridled capitalism was to bring Christianity 'as an applied power on the life and conditions of society'. This broad conception of mission provided a valuable point of contact with agnostics who, as we have seen, retained deep ethical concerns.

Twentieth-century agnostics

Agnosticism, which was always more of a mood than a movement, persisted into the twentieth century, represented, for example, by the English composer, Ralph Vaughan Williams. Describing himself as a 'Christian agnostic', Vaughan Williams hesitated to affirm belief in the historic creeds, yet with the ambivalence we have seen to be characteristic of such people, his beautiful and spiritually sensitive hymn settings contributed much to the renewal of the worship of the English church. In addition, Vaughan Williams freely confessed that he could never escape the attractions of John Bunyan, for whose work he retained a lifelong love. The *Romanza* in the Fifth Symphony was inspired by Bunyan's famous description of the pilgrim's arrival at the foot of the cross and is music of unsurpassed tenderness and beauty.

The spirit of agnosticism as described above can be detected in many people who have not used this term to identify themselves and, indeed, were probably unaware of it. For example, the French writer Albert Camus teetered on the brink of faith, recognizing the attractiveness of belief in transcendent realities and worrying about the ethical consequences of the loss of religion. Yet Camus held back from commitment on the grounds that *theology seemed incapable of dealing satisfactorily with the issue of human suffering. Camus saw all too clearly the terrible consequences for human life, both for individuals and for society, of the absence of God since, as he memorably expressed it, when the sky becomes empty the earth is 'delivered into the hands of power without principles'. In the preface to *The Myth of Sisyphus* he indicated that he was wrestling with profound existential issues 'without the aid of eternal values which, temporarily perhaps, are absent or distorted in contemporary Europe'. Here again is the classic agnostic ambivalence: a deep concern with morality, *and* a professed incapacity to believe that is related to a perceived failure of the Christian apologetic. In this case, as Camus made clear in his novel *The Plague*, the stumbling stone was an inadequate, even offensive, Catholic theodicy in the face of the horrors that occurred across Europe in the twentieth century.

It is worth considering at this point whether the issues raised by agnosticism, either in its overt Victorian forms or in the shape of twentieth-century thought such as that cited above, may not have unexpected significance in relation to the postmodern challenge. The contemporary suspicion of meta-narratives was certainly anticipated in the agnostic suspicion of theological dogmas, while the renewed concern to discover a basis for values in a globalized world has a clear parallel in the Victorian attempt to retain a hold on general ethics. While T. H. Huxley would have been horrified by the lunatic fringe of the *New Age movement, his doubts about traditional Christian dogmas, together with his anxiety concerning the survival of moral values, are not so far removed from the positions taken by those postmodern people who are searching for religious and ethical values. If this observation has validity, then the apologetic task facing Christians today may not be dissimilar from that which confronted evangelical theologians at the beginning of the twentieth century, and we may have important lessons to learn from them.

Agnosticism and Christian apologetics

How then should Christian apologists respond to agnostics today? First, the history of the encounter with classical agnosticism suggests that it is important to engage in missionary conversation in which there is a critical, but not entirely unsympathetic, understanding of the thinking and motivation of the dialogue-partner. Any response that is based on ignorance and driven by fear easily results in the caricaturing, or even the demonizing, of the agnostic and may rather quickly descend into a fruitless shouting match. Such an apologetic, as the Victorians discovered, is likely only to widen the gulf between Christians and sincere doubters. The most effective apologist is likely to be someone who understands the real anguish and travail that often accompany religious doubt and so can approach the other person with a genuine pastoral concern and an ability to utilize the relevant biblical resources in relation to the struggles between faith and doubt.

Secondly, it is vital that the position held by those with whom we speak is properly understood; which is to say that listening is an indispensable pre-requisite to apologetics if we are to discover and understand the true causes of doubt. Such careful listening may often reveal the fact that the doubter's uncertainties are related not to the person of Christ, or even necessarily to the central affirmations of the gospel, but to peripheral aspects of Christianity as an empirical religion – things about which we ourselves may have reason to be concerned. Quite clearly this was the case in the examples mentioned earlier, and one wonders what might have been the outcome for Albert Camus, for example, had he encountered Christians who were able to relate the doctrine of the cross to the agonies of a suffering humankind in a manner that offered a truly biblical theodicy.

Thirdly, it is critically important to be able to demonstrate in both word and deed what faith *does*. A recent literary study of the Bible suggests that the story told in the NT has resulted in millions of people worshipping a crucified God, while other millions who never worship at all carry 'within their cultural DNA a religiously derived suspicion that somehow, someday, "the last will be first, and the first last"' (Jack Miles). In other words, among these millions, including those who can be classified as agnostic, there is a moral sense that is ultimately derived from gospel. In such a context we need an apologetic that goes beyond the expression of *truth in purely conceptual, abstract terms and is based on living evidence of individual and social transformation as the outcome of faith. In this way, very many people whose cultural DNA connects them, however remotely, to Christ may have a chance of coming home and rediscovering who they really are.

Finally, it needs to be said that for the agnostic the point must eventually come at which the ambivalence which almost defines this stance is challenged and the moment of decision is reached. No matter how sensitive and sympathetic our apologetics may be, the dialogue must reach a stage at which the almost congenital 'wavering between two opinions' is challenged by the prophetic word: 'If the LORD is God, follow him.'

Bibliography

A. Camus, *The Myth of Sisyphus* (Harmondsworth, 1975); R. Caporale and A. Grumelli (eds.), *The Culture of Unbelief* (Berkeley, 1971); H. Carrier, 'The New Evangelization Facing Agnostic Culture', in *Evangelizing the Culture of Modernity* (New York, 1993), pp. 133–149; E. Jay, *Faith and Doubt in Victorian Britain* (Basingstoke, 1986); T. Phillips and D. Okholm (eds.), *Christian Apologetics in the Postmodern World* (Downers Grove, 1995).

D. W. SMITH

ALBERTUS MAGNUS

Albertus Magnus (c. 1200–80), also called Albert the Great, was a German theologian and bishop. In 1220 Albert joined the Dominicans, a controversial new religious order dedicated to apologetic preaching and mendicancy. As his theological works attest, Albert shared the Dominican conviction that the falsity of Christian heresies and insufficiency of non-Christian religious faiths can be established rationally. In 1256 Albert successfully cleared the Dominicans and other mendicants of the charges brought against them at the papal court by William of St-Amour.

In 1250, contrary to the letter of the Dominican order's statutes, Albert made a pagan philosophical text, *Aristotle's *Nicomachean*

Ethics, the subject of a lecture course at the Dominican seminary in Cologne. Albert justified his choice in several ways, arguing, for instance, that Aristotle's text shows what unaided human reason can know about happiness and virtue, and that to know this is to know something of great value for Christian apologetics. Such arguments prevailed in 1259 at the General Chapter in Valenciennes, when the Dominican order revised its seminary curriculum to include the study of philosophical authors, in particular Aristotle. With the stated purpose of 'making Aristotle intelligible to Latins', Albert spent twenty years paraphrasing every available work believed in his day to have been written by Aristotle.

Critics claimed that Albert's paraphrases failed to name and to refute those Aristotelian teachings that are false and contrary to Christian faith. Albert replied that his aim was merely to clarify Aristotle's teachings and not to assess them. He also argued that because *theology and philosophy proceed from different *first principles, the fact that a theological conclusion contradicts a philosophical one does not itself establish, as some maintain, that the philosophical conclusion has been falsely derived. Seen from this perspective, faith and reason are not complementary but rather incommensurable modes of human knowing. Albert's controversial position on faith and reason was appropriated by Latin Averroists and challenged his most celebrated student, *Thomas Aquinas.

Bibliography

S. Tugwell, 'Introduction', in S. Tugwell (ed.), *Albert & Thomas: Selected Writings* (New York, 1988), pp. 3–130; D. B. Twetten, 'Albert the Great, Double Truth, and Celestial Causality', *Documenti e studi sulla tradizione filosofica medievale* 12 (2001), pp. 275–358; J. A. Weisheipl, 'Albert's Disclaimers in the Aristotelian Paraphrases', in J. C. Schnaubelt *et al.* (eds.), *Proceedings of the PMR Conference* 5 (Villanova, 1983), pp. 1–27.

M. J. TRACEY

ALLEN, WOODY

Woody Allen (b. 1935) has earned his place among the most important filmmakers of our time largely by capturing his own fears and neuroses on camera for thirty-five years. Typically best when comical, often heavy-handed when serious, Allen's films are, for the most part, not easily forgotten. The self-effacing wit and relentless self-analysis at the core of most of his films make them readily accessible, at least to self-aware neurotics.

If for no other film, Allen deserves mention for *Crimes and Misdemeanors* (1989). Judah Rosenthal, a successful opthamologist, is desperate to rid himself of his mistress who is threatening to expose him in a desperate appeal for attention. Judah, instead of capitulating, hires his brother to kill her. Afterwards, Judah is consumed with guilt and grief. In the course of the film, Allen carefully examines the *conscience and moral consequence of Judah's choice. Both mortality and *morality come centre-stage. While Judah appears to win, in that he 'gets away with murder', he is forced to live with near paralysing guilt, and thus loses. In a remarkable plot twist, Judah seeks religious counsel from his rabbi, a deeply moral man who is going blind. In the midst of the moral wrangling and conscience tending that drives the plot, the question 'Does God truly see all?' provides a haunting subtext to this memorable film. Likewise, *ethics and the issues of revenge and infidelity are presented so powerfully that any group could easily find substance to discuss.

Bibliography

R. R. Curry, *Perspectives on Woody Allen* (New York, 1996); S. B. Girgus, *The Films of Woody Allen* (Cambridge, 1993); F. Hirsch, *Love, Sex, Death, and the Meaning of Life: The Films of Woody Allen* (New York, 2001); M. P. Nichols, *Reconstructing Woody: Art, Love, and Life in the Films of Woody Allen* (Lanham, 1998); R. A. Schwartz, *Woody, from Antz to Zelig: A Reference Guide to Woody Allen's Creative Work, 1964–1998* (Westport, 2000).

D. S. RUSSELL

AMBROSE OF MILAN

One of the four canonical doctors of the Latin church, Ambrose (c. 339–97) was prefect of Milan in 374 when he was elected bishop by the acclamation of the local populace. He was admitted to the three orders of ministry (deacon, priest and bishop) in a single day, a rare procedure which came to be known as *ordination per saltum*. As bishop of Milan, which was then the effective capital of the western half of the Roman Empire, Ambrose played a prominent part in both ecclesiastical and political affairs. His preaching was famous all over the world and attracted even the sceptical *Augustine, who was converted to Christianity in 386 largely under Ambrose's influence. Shortly afterwards, Ambrose rebuked the Emperor Theodosius I after his unjustified massacre of the inhabitants of Thessalonica (390) and forced him to do penance for his action. Such behaviour was unprecedented at that time and made Ambrose a model for the prince bishops of the Middle Ages in their dealings with secular rulers.

As a writer, Ambrose's reputation rests on a substantial body of works which have survived. Most of them are commentaries on the Bible, including treatises on the six days of creation, the Psalms and the Gospel of Luke. His dependence on earlier writers, both Latin and Greek, was considerable, but as time went on he became more independent in his thinking. In particular, he abandoned the literal approach to exegesis which had characterized most of his immediate predecessors, and returned to the more allegorical approach, ultimately inherited from *Origen. He often pushed this to extremes, as e.g. when he compared Bathsheba to the church, David to Christ, and Uriah – the husband from whom David stole Bathsheba – to the devil! Ambrose justified such an extraordinary interpretation by claiming that Holy Scripture could never portray the sins of a great saint like David except as a foundation for moral and spiritual lessons which were meant to edify the church. He was particularly prone to a suggestive type of interpretation, where a single word in one text might touch off a series of reflections on other, unrelated passages where the same word happened to recur.

In theology, Ambrose wrote a spirited defence of orthodoxy against the claims of the Arians, addressing the work to the Emperor Gratian (378–80). The approach he took was heavily dependent on various predecessors in the Greek world, notably *Athanasius and Basil of Caesarea, but there was little of comparable depth in Latin, and the book appeared at a key moment in Roman history. The last Arian emperor, Valens, was killed at Adrianople, but by the Arian Goths, who would become a permanent presence inside the empire and

eventually sack Rome itself (in 410). For this reason, Ambrose's clear assertion that the Son is truly God made a deep impression on his contemporaries and turned him into a leading defender of orthodox Christology in the Latin world.

In social and political affairs, Ambrose presided over a culture which was gradually changing from paganism to Christianity. He was preoccupied with practical moral questions like greed and adultery, and became a great advocate of celibacy as a holy calling for believers. He was also prominent in making Easter a major public festival, and he encouraged the cult of the martyrs and the establishment of close spiritual links between the living and the dead which such a cult implied. Ambrose was happy to borrow ideas from pagan sources, in particular from the neoplatonists, but his knowledge of them was limited and it cannot be said that he was unduly influenced by Greek philosophical ideas. More important to him by far was the OT, which he took very much to heart and used as the basis for much of his teaching and preaching. He regarded those two activities as the chief calling of a bishop and did his best to train up clergy to follow in his footsteps. In all these respects he became a model for the Middle Ages, though his reputation was bound to suffer after the Reformation, when his allegorical approach to biblical interpretation was widely rejected. A particularly serious blow fell when Erasmus demonstrated that a superb commentary on the Pauline epistles, which everyone had attributed to Ambrose, in fact came from an earlier writer, whom Erasmus playfully dubbed the Ambrosiaster, the name by which he continues to be known today.

Ambrose is now appreciated more for his historical role in the conversion of ancient Rome to Christianity, and notably his influence on Augustine, than for his own writings, which are little studied. On the other had, his somewhat eclectic and poetic approach to the Bible has a certain appeal to the postmodern generation, and it is possible that his particular genius will be better appreciated in the future than it has been in the more recent past.

Bibliography

Ambrose's works are available in the original Latin, either in J. P. Migne's classic *Patrologia Latina* (vols. 14–15) or more recently in a series of excellent editions produced by the Corpus Scriptorum Ecclesiasticorum Latinorum (vols. 32 and 73). Translations are not particularly easy to find, though several treatises have been published at different times in the Fathers of the Church series and others can be found in B. Ramsey, *Ambrose* (London, 1997).

D. F. Homes, *The Life and Times of St Ambrose* (Oxford, 1935); N. McLynn, *Ambrose of Milan* (Berkeley, 1994); J. Moorhead, *Ambrose: Church and Society in the Late Roman World* (Harlow, 1999); B. Ramsey, *Ambrose* (London, 1997); D. H. Williams, *Ambrose of Milan and the End of the Nicene-Arian Conflicts* (Oxford, 1995).

G. L. BRAY

ANALOGY, PRINCIPLE OF

The belief that God possesses certain attributes is a familiar feature of Judaic-Christian thought and worship, indeed a feature of all theistic religions. He is, for example, wise, truthful, just and forgiving. Throughout the history of Christian thought, however, such attributions have given rise to intellectual perplexities for believers and unbelievers alike; for how can the *language of finite human beings adequately describe the attributes of a transcendent God? And if divine attributes cannot be known, then a form of radical scepticism seems to threaten orthodox theism.

The principle of analogy is a response to this problem. It is a philosophical device designed to clarify the meanings of predicates which are commonly attributed to God and to do so in a way that overcomes the scepticism concerning their meaningfulness which we have just described. In exploring the principle I will first clarify the sceptical challenge and some of the assumptions about meaning on which it rests. I will then explain and critically examine some of the ways in which the principle has been formulated. Finally, I will offer a brief critique of the philosophical assumptions which underlie the principle, indicating how an alternative approach might overcome some of the difficulties which have been addressed.

The sceptical challenge

The sceptical challenge argues that terms can be used meaningfully to refer to God only when certain semantic and theological background conditions are satisfied. It goes on to argue that theistic terms fail to satisfy the relevant background conditions and concludes that the terms familiarly used to refer to God are meaningless.

Consider some of the terms with which, as I have said, we typically refer to God – wise, truthful, just and forgiving. Let us suppose that we accept what might be called 'the empiricist principle' to the effect that the meanings of such 'essentially human terms' are learned in empirical contexts. In other words, I learn what wisdom is by contrasting the people whom I know who possess it with those I know who do not possess it; I learn what love is by contrasting behaviour which is loving with behaviour which is less loving and so on. Let us accept, also, the logical truth that the property terms in question, when applied to God, either preserve or do not preserve the meanings which they have in everyday human contexts. In the former case the meanings are said to be 'univocal', in the latter they are said to be 'equivocal'. We may now enquire as to whether predicates which apply to human beings apply also, and with the same meaning, to God. To suppose the meaning to be univocal renders an understanding of their meaning unproblematical; divine love is continuous with (though greater than) human love, divine wisdom is continuous with (though greater than) human wisdom and so on. Hence, if we know the meanings of the terms in human contexts, we can know them, by extension, in divine contexts. However, attractive though it first appears, some consider this account to be unacceptable. Theologians have argued that it compromises divine 'otherness' or transcendence, it confuses the finite with the infinite, and it leaves us with a wholly 'anthropomorphic' conception of God. These convictions form the first horn of the dilemma. The alternative assumption, that property terms referring to God are to be understood in an equivocal sense, also generates problems. If we know the meanings of terms only in empirical contexts and so can know nothing of their meaning in transcendent contexts, then since God is a transcendent being the properties cannot intelligibly be attributed to him. And what then can we meaningfully say about God? The terms which we familiarly use of God have been emptied of all intelligible content, and we are left with a conception of God which is so attenuated that we are in danger of lapsing into scepticism concerning the divine nature. This is the second horn of the dilemma. That these alternatives appear exhaustive and that each is unacceptable is the sceptical problem to which the principle of analogy is offered as a solution.

The problem just described has consistently engaged the Christian church over the centuries. Seeds of a theory of analogical prediction are to be found in the writings of the patristic period. *Augustine is influenced by it when, in *De Trinitate*, he illustrates the mysteries of the triune being by drawing attention to analogous mysteries surrounding human psychology, and in the late medieval period a rigorous examination of the issues was undertaken, especially by *Thomas Aquinas and Suarez. In the early modern period sceptical doubts still lingered. For example, Archbishop King argued that our conceptions of God's nature are as different from true knowledge of God as is a map from the land which it represents; Bishop Browne maintained that since our knowledge of God is composed of worldly ideas we have no more notion of divine things 'than a blind man hath of light'. The neo-Kantian framework of phenomenal and noumenal worlds revived similar agnostic worries, and even in the closing decades of the twentieth century the issue engaged theists such as H. L. Mansel as well as sceptics such as A. G. N. *Flew.

Responses to the sceptical argument either accept the basic philosophical framework which I have just described or they challenge it. The latter possibility should be noted because the empiricist principle was rejected in the last century by philosophers such as Chomsky, Fodor, Quine and *Wittgenstein, a point to which I will return in the conclusion.

More commonly, theists have accepted the sceptic's underlying empiricist assumptions and as a consequence have been led to accept some form of the theory of analogy which forms the subject matter of this article. The principle of analogy is an important and influencial response and it is to it, especially to its classical expression in the scholastic period, that we must now turn.

The principle of analogy

When Aquinas looked for a theory of the divine attributes, he drew upon the philosophical traditions of the Greeks, especially upon the ideas of *Aristotle, whose works were at that time becoming available in the universities of Paris, Oxford and Bologna. Here he found both the basic philosophical assumptions and the detailed categories of thought within which the theory of analogical prediction was formulated. Prominent in the former were, first, Aristotle's theory of concepts (especially his distinction between equivocal and univocal terms and his account of the different kinds of equivocation) and, secondly, his account of the different senses of being (in particular his stress that the different senses of being may be unified by their relationship to one fundamental sense). Even more important to the needs of the Schoolmen was Aristotle's account of how we acquire knowledge of attributes. According to this view we have no direct knowledge of Forms such as wisdom, love or justice; rather we come to know these things only indirectly by experiencing the imperfect embodiments of them in particular persons and actions.

The theory of analogy drew on these basic Aristotelian categories so as to explain how, granted our finite understanding, we can have knowledge of the infinite divine character. In so doing Aquinas distinguished, first, between the two forms that analogy may take, *duorum ad tertuim* and *unius ad alterum*, and then distinguished between two subdivisions of the latter, namely the analogy of attribution and the analogy of proportionality. As we shall see, each of these elements played an influential role in the development of the theory of analogy and it is to an exposition and criticism of these theories that we must now turn.

Analogy duorum ad tertium

This form of analogy links two analogates, or bearers of properties, by virtue of their relationship to a third analogate in which the property which is the basis for the resemblance is *paradigmatically displayed. Suppose then, that analogates Ai, Aii and Aiii all exhibit, non-univocallly, a property P. An analogy *duorum ad tertium* obtains between P as exhibited in Ai and Aii if, and only if, the following conditions are satisfied: Ai resembles Aii; Ai and Aii both resemble Aiii; the property P is displayed paradigmatically in Aiii, so that, in scholastic terms, Aiii is the 'prime analogate' or Form of the property in question. Finally, it is by virtue of the presence of P in Aiii that Ai resembles Aii. Consider the property of being healthy. Fresh fruit is a healthy form of food, walking is a healthy form of exercise and Jones is a healthy person. The health that Jones enjoys is the prime analogate; fresh fruit and walking are healthy by analogy in the sense that they enjoy similar relationships to the prime analogate. In our present context, humans and God are analogates which resemble each other by virtue of their relation to another analogate, which is the Form of the property in respect of which God and humans are alike.

Analogy *duorum ad tertium* is rarely invoked as an account of divine attributes. Recall the problem with which the principle of analogy is centrally concerned: the meanings of all human property terms are derived from empirical contexts ('the empirical principle'), and we wonder if they can be meaningfully applied beyond those contexts. The problem is that if the empirical principle is accepted, then the meaning of prime analogates is as inaccessible as the meanings of the terms which describe divine attributes. We may state the problem in the form of a dilemma. If we accept the empirical principle, then we can never know the meaning of prime analogates because, as Forms, by reference to which attributes are ascribed both to God and to humans beings, their meanings necessarily go beyond these contexts. On the other hand, if we reject the empirical principle and assert that meanings can transcend human experience, then the meanings of prime analogates are, in principle, accessible. However, if that is the case then the whole theory of analogy *duorum ad tertium* loses its rationale. If human empirical contexts can, after all, be transcended and we have direct access to the meanings of prime analogates, then there is no reason, in principle, why we should not have direct knowledge of the meaning of terms that refer to divine attributes. Analogy *duorum ad tertium* is redundant.

Analogy unus ad alterum

If the scholastic principle of analogy is to be plausible, therefore, we must turn to the form that it took in *unus ad alterum*. This type of analogy postulates only a non-univocal relationship between two analogates; no third independent analogate is involved. In its turn, however, it subdivides into the analogy of attribution and the analogy of proportionality and it is to these forms that we must now look for a more coherent account of the theory.

The most important feature of the analogy of attribution is that the attribute properly belongs to one of the two analogates, the prime analogate, and only relatively or derivatively to the other analogate. Some technical terms will require elucidation, however, in the process of expounding this conception.

First, consider primacy. It is tempting to think that the primacy in question is ontological and that, since all perfections are most fully realized in the divine nature, the prime analogate is God. In the present context, however, this would be a mistake. We are interested in the extent to which terms whose meaning is learned in human experience can, if at all, be applied to God, and, by implication, whether we can ever know the meaning of such terms when applied to God. Consequently, the primacy in question is semantic and epistemological, not ontological, and it is the meaning of terms in finite, empirical contexts that is primary and their application to God that is derivative. Secondly, when we speak of derivative attributions the relationship is usually thought of as being causal, the derivative attribution being causally effective in relation to the primary analogate. To take the standard example, fresh fruit is healthy because eating it is causally linked to the health of the healthy person. In the theistic context, therefore, a divine attribute is whatever is causally necessary to bring about the attribute which is properly displayed in the prime analogate, namely human beings. Thus when we say that God and humans are both good we are, so far as analogy of attribution is concerned, saying no more than that God has goodness to the degree and in the form that are causally effective in producing human goodness.

This having been made clear, the difficulty with the analogy of attribution is evident. We wish to know in what ways divine attributes resemble human attributes and the answer is this: the analogates apply non-univocally to both God and humans and God's attributes are causally sufficient in relation to human attributes. But this does not enable us to say whether, in what respect or to what degree, divine attributes are like human attributes. Our agnostic and sceptical doubts are not relieved by the analogy of attribution. We must either find a more plausible rendering of primacy or reformulate the theory without any conception of primacy.

This reformulation brings us to the analogy of proportionality. In this, as in the previous case, the principle of analogy involves a common attribute ascribed, non-univocally, to two analogates. In the case of proportionality, however, the relationship is not hierarchical; neither of the analogates is primary. The attribute is found formally in both analogates but the mode of their presence is determined by the nature of the bearer. There is not, then, a literal equivalence between wisdom or love or justice as found in God and the same attributes in humans. Both possess the attributes, but the essential nature of the bearer determines the form of the attribute that each possesses. As A. M. *Farrer explains, 'Divine intelligence is appropriate to divine existence as creaturely to creaturely.' In summary, in the analogy of proportionality an attribute is exemplified in each of two analogates in the form that is appropriate to each analogate and quite independently of any relation to a prime analogate.

This conception of analogy has its origins in Greek mathematics in which it is referred to the proportionality, that is to the common or reciprocal relations (e.g. double, triple etc.), which exist between two proportions. However, it was best known in the context of direct comparisons between terms with similar meanings and resemblances between relations. Thus:

$$\frac{\text{divine wisdom}}{\text{divine nature}} = \frac{\text{human wisdom}}{\text{human nature}}$$

and

$$\frac{\text{divine love}}{\text{divine nature}} = \frac{\text{human love}}{\text{human nature}}$$

and so on for all of the other virtues.

This conception of analogy has much to commend it. On the one hand, it seems to do justice to the sense of divine 'otherness', to the sense that God's attributes differ in kind as well as in degree, from human attributes, and so it is not open to the charge of anthropomorphism to which some accounts seem vulnerable. Yet, on the other hand, it does seem to recognize a continuity between divine attributes and human attributes, thus avoiding the threat of scepticism.

The difficulty with the analogy of proportionality is not so much that what it asserts is false: how, after all, could one fault the contention that God's attributes are appropriate to his divine nature? The problem is more that the theory does not say enough and that what it says does not show how agnostic doubts about the nature of divine attributes can be answered. The theory attempts to throw light on the divine attributes by drawing attention to the fact that the relationship between God's attributes and God's nature is the same as the relationship between human attributes and human nature. Since we know the latter relationship, it is assumed that we can move to the former and that we can move from knowledge of the former to knowledge of the nature of God's attributes. However, we do not come to know human attributes by grasping their relationship with some conception of human nature. Rather, we have direct non-analogical knowledge of human attributes. That being the case, the problem in connection with divine attributes is that on the present theory we do not possess a knowledge of the divine nature which enables us to qualify the relevant attribute, nor do we know what the appropriate qualification would be. In place of a theory there is merely the promise of one.

Consider a specific example. We are told that human love is relative to human nature. But how does that differ from merely saying that there are certain characteristic ways in which human beings show their love? And, correspondingly, it is not clear how the view that divine love is relative to the divine nature differs from merely saying that divine love manifests itself in various characteristic forms. The analogy of proportion seems to take us no closer to a knowledge of the nature of the divine attributes.

Conclusion

If an intermediate position between univocal and equivocal accounts of divine attribute terms cannot be found, then Christian philosophers might be expected to explore radical alternatives which would challenge the framework within which the basic problem arose. One such radical alternative, to which I alluded briefly at the end of the first section, would be to challenge the empirical principle, and it is to this suggestion that I now return. There are both philosophical and theological strands to such an alternative.

First, at a philosophical level we should note the precarious status in contemporary philosophy of the empiricist principle itself. The empiricist principle (the meaning of all property terms derived from experience) is not self-evidently true, so on what grounds is it asserted? It has been challenged from many philosophical quarters in recent decades. Chomsky has argued that one cannot explain the acquisition of basic linguistic structures without postulating innate cognitive capacities, and Fodor has extended this thesis to the acquisition of all concepts. More generally, Quine and Wittgenstein have mounted sustained attacks on the empiricist conceptions of concept formulation. If we follow Quine in replacing the 'two dogmas of empiricism' by a form of holism, constrained by simplicity, consistency and epistemic conservatism, we would have an alternative framework for defending human knowledge of divine attributes. The alternative to *empiricism would be a nativism which held that our knowledge of meanings is a function of our innate cognative structures together with experience which shapes and informs those innate structures.

Secondly, at a theological level, the account of human knowledge of divine attributes would form one part of the general belief that humans were created in the image of God. On such an account, empiricist conceptions of concept formulation would be replaced by what I shall refer to as 'strong theistic nativism'. Nativism is the view that concept formulation is, at least in part, a function of the structure of the cognitive capacities of the knowing subject. Theistic nativism is the view that nativism is true and that human cognitive capacities are the result of God's creative activity. Strong theistic nativism is the view that nativism is true and that God has created human cognitive capacities so that they can recognize and respond to God's own character.

Empiricist incomprehension concerning the divine attributes would be overcome on such a view. Acceptance of the empiricist principle made it seem strange, if not incomprehensible, that our finite cognitive structures could provide us with knowledge of the divine nature. However, on strong theistic nativism this is not in the least strange: humans have knowledge of the divine attributes precisely because God created them in such a fashion that they might know, love and serve him.

Bibliography

W. Alston, 'Functionalism and Theological Language', in *American Philosophical Quarterly* (1985); F. Ferre, *Language, Logic and God* (New York, 1961); G. C. Joyce, 'Analogy', in J. Hastings (ed.), *The Encyclopaedia of Religion and Ethics*, vol. 1 (New York, 1910); E. L. Mascall, *Existence and Analogy* (New York, 1949); Thomas Aquinas, *Summa Theologica* (London, 1964).

H. BUNTING

ANGELS

Angels, along with the Y2K frenzy, enjoyed a flurry of publicity in the 1990s but have since receded again into the shadows of Christian consciousness. This is the latest stage in the dismissal of angels from the realm of contemporary thought that has been going on since the heyday of *Thomas Aquinas (1225–74), the so-called 'angelic doctor', who wrote extensively about angels.

The tradition of angelology

Aquinas was part of a long philosophical tradition going back to the ancient Greeks, according to which elements of reality were represented by *daimones* (not 'demons' as such but intermediate entities). These essences were harmonized with biblical figures by 'Pseudo-*Dionysius', a sixth-century Christian Neoplatonist, and arranged in a 'celestial hierarchy' of nine choirs of angels. Pseudo-Dionysius combined intellectual speculation with a sense of awesome worship in a way still characteristic of the Eastern Orthodox Church's approach to angelology.

For Aquinas, however, angels posed the supreme philosophical case of 'minds without bodies' and, according to his principle of plenitude, formed a necessary link in the chain of being between the immortal God and mortal creatures. Aquinas treated angels as subjects of rational understanding rather than revealed knowledge, and his rationalism led to a reaction in the work of *William of Ockham, whose principle of parsimony reduced natural knowledge to the simplest truth.

Ockham's approach was taken up by John *Calvin in his *Institutes of the Christian Religion*. Calvin confined knowledge of angels to scriptural examples and the identity of angels to their function as messengers. Many evangelicals, following Calvin, tend to pay lip service to the existence of angels but have little place for them in teaching or worship. Indeed, an interest in angels is often seen as a distraction from pure worship of the one God (cf. Heb. 1:14).

The reserve about angels that was characteristic of the Reformation developed into a complete rejection of them during the Enlightenment. Taking the principle of parsimony to its limit, René *Descartes argued that only God and human consciousness could be rationally proved and, therefore, the existence of other intelligences in the universe was purely conjectural and unnecessary to the conduct of everyday life. Descartes' method, extended by John *Locke in his *Essay on Human Understanding*, has formed the fundamental mindset of modern scepticism towards angels.

At the same time that philosophers and theologians were becoming dubious about the existence of angels, artists and poets constructed a sanctuary for them. Renaissance and Baroque art is noted for its *putti*, babies with wings, which seem to be a throwback to pagan figures like Cupid. John Milton (*Paradise Lost*), William Blake (*The Marriage of Heaven and Hell*) and J. W. Goethe (*Faust*) all portray good and evil angels as protagonists in their works. This tendency represents an ongoing romantic sensibility that wishes to 'remythologize' the angels in worship and art, after having 'demythologized' them as real beings.

Twentieth-century approaches

The twentieth century witnessed several attempts to rehabilitate the status of angels and angelology. To begin with, neo-Thomists like Mortimer Adler and Peter Kreeft defended the traditional Roman Catholic dogmas about angels as reaffirmed by the *Catechism of the Catholic Church*.

On the Protestant side, Karl *Barth devotes a large section of his *Church Dogmatics* to 'the Representatives of Heaven'. While criticizing Aquinas' speculation, Barth nevertheless concludes that 'to deny the angels is to deny God himself' (p. 486). Angels serve as a reminder, Barth avers, that salvation comes from above but at the same time is directed to earth. 'The supreme glory and true honour of the Creator', Barth argues, 'are displayed in the fact that in Jesus Christ He has not taken to Himself heaven and the angels but man and the earth' (p. 420).

C. S. *Lewis does not devote much space to angels in his non-fiction apologetic works, but he makes use of them in his fiction. In addition to his famous devil Screwtape, he describes angelic archetypes in his science fiction novels. In *Perelandra*, the hero Ransom is granted a vision of a pair of primordial male and female figures: 'Pure, spiritual, intellectual love shot from their faces like barbed lightning' (pp. 199–200). From this encounter Ransom understands 'why mythology was what it was – gleams of celestial strength and beauty falling on a jungle of filth and imbecility' (p. 201).

From the postmodernist movement have come attempts to reinstate the role of angels. Stuart Schneiderman, a Lacanian psychoanalyst, has attempted to recover the psychological reality of angels. Along similar lines, Walter Wink, biblical scholar and theologian, has tried to rehabilitate the idea of 'principalities and powers'. 'People may never again regard them as quasi-material beings flapping around the sky', he asserts, 'but perhaps they will come to see them as the actual spirituality of actual entities in the real world' (*Unmasking the Powers*, p. 173).

Interest in angels among contemporary evangelical Christians was rekindled by Billy Graham's *Angels*, which has sold over three million copies since it appeared in 1975. Frank Peretti's fictionalized account of principalities and powers in *This Present Darkness* has also been popular and has been supplemented by C. Peter Wagner's claim that mission breakthroughs require prayer engaging the 'territorial spirits' of unreached peoples. Among recent dogmatic textbooks, Wayne Grudem gives a particularly extensive treatment of angelology.

Biblical theology of angels

Whatever the current philosophical trends, we as Christians are called on to think about the angelic figures that are presented in Scripture and to find a coherent explanation of them that takes into account the variety of contexts in the Old and New Testaments where angels appear. What conclusions can be reached from a consideration of the scriptural passages? We can divide these conclusions according to ontological and epistemological questions.

Do angels exist? Angels exist, unequivocally. So do *Satan, demons and principalities and powers.

Are angels distinct personalities or are they impersonal entities? Angels and Satan have personalities as they have names, albeit mostly unknown to us. 'Principalities', however, seem to be hidden forces which maintain a degree of control in the fallen world.

Do angels have bodies, or are they pure intelligences? Scripture is not perfectly clear about this, but it seems reasonable to infer that angels have some kind of spiritual bodies like that of the risen Christ.

Do angels and devils have the same origin and nature? Yes, they are all creatures of God, but their destinies differ. 'Elect angels' (1 Tim. 5:21) are holy for all eternity, whereas Satan and his host are fallen angels, utterly evil and forever damned. 'Principalities and powers' are corrupt angelic beings who retain certain forms of authority in the fallen world but who will be ultimately damned.

Do angels have a life of their own? Angels appear in the Bible primarily as ministering spirits. On occasion, however, Scripture gives glimpses of the angels worshipping God in their own community of praise (Rev. 4 – 5).

Can we know about angels by reason, or by revelation only? Angels appear in Scripture largely in the context of salvation history. By contrast, the creation accounts and wisdom literature are largely silent about them. Thus, Thomas Aquinas' intellectual quest may have been a probing of mysteries too deep for philosophy.

Are angels better understood in terms of myth and metaphor? To the extent that myth and metaphor are necessary ways to explain the invisible world, then angels must be approached with the sensibility of a literary critic rather than that of a scientific investigator.

Are angels of marginal importance to a full Christian faith? Nowhere does Scripture require belief in angels. Angels are never at centre stage in the biblical accounts, but they do appear in major passages dealing with the nature of the triune God, God's rule and his final judgment of the world. The contemporary attack on angels seems to be the spearhead of a larger attack on biblical Christianity, and so we may well take warning not to neglect them.

If it is true that an interest in angels is still on the decline in Western culture, Christian apologists will need to take the basic biblical teaching on them seriously and engage once again the contemporary world-view with courage and insight.

Bibliography

M. Adler, *The Angels and Us* (New York and London, 1982); K. Barth, *Church Dogmatics* III/3 (Edinburgh, 1960); *The Catechism of the Catholic Church* (London and Ligouri, 1994), sections 325–336; W. Grudem, *Systematic Theology: An Introduction to Biblical Doctrine* (Leicester, 1994); P. Kreeft, *Angels and Demons: What Do We Really Know about Them?* (San Francisco, 1995); S. F. Noll, *Angels of Light, Powers of Darkness: Thinking Biblically about Angels, Satan and Principalities* (Downers Grove, 1998); W. Wink, *Unmasking the Powers: The Invisible Forces that Determine Human Existence* (Philadelphia, 1986).

S. F. NOLL

ANIMALS AND ANIMAL RIGHTS

The question of how we treat and use animals often evokes very strong feelings. Some Christians argue that human beings are much more important than animals – citing humanity's God-given dominion over animals (Gen. 1:26) and using such verses as Matt. 10:29–31; 12:11–12 and Luke 12:6–7 to say that even *Jesus himself taught that animals are less important than humans. However, others find it hard to understand why there is such indifference to animal suffering amongst many in the Christian community. Others feel that God has providentially given us animals for food and for other uses, but yet others feel that *vegetarianism should be the norm for the Christian. Some even eschew pet ownership. Making sense of this diversity of ideas concerning animals demands a careful 'theology of the beasts'.

It is surprising that until recently so little has been written about animals from a Christian point of view, despite the ongoing controversy in society about animal exploitation and animal rights. This is particularly surprising when one is reminded of the close link in the nineteenth century between animal welfare and human welfare issues. Evangelical Christians and other reformers, such as *Wilberforce and Shaftesbury, who took seriously the biblical concept of careful stewardship of God's world, played a major part not only in the reform of human welfare issues (such as children's rights and the abolition of slavery) but also in animal welfare. John Colam, who was secretary of the Royal Society for the Prevention of Cruelty to Animals (RSPCA), was also active in the founding of the National Society for the Prevention of Cruelty to Children (NSPCC).

How should we treat animals?

The Bible mentions over 120 species of animals, which is perhaps not surprising since it was a commonplace that the biblical writers had direct interaction with animals through their animal husbandry and the pastoral control of predators. In contrast, certainly in many of the 'developed' nations of the world, we are largely insulated from animals, encountering them only in 'non-natural' contexts, such as in pre-packaged food on supermarket shelves or in the keeping of pets or in zoos. This disconnectedness from the natural world will inevitably colour our viewpoint of how we treat animals.

Despite so many mentions of animals in the Bible, only a very few verses specifically teach about how we should care for animals. Clearly there is a link between godliness and caring for one's animals, e.g. 'a righteous man cares for the needs of his animal' (Prov. 12:10), and there is the curious prohibition against what seems like the particularly barbaric practice of cooking a kid in its mother's milk (Exod. 23:19; 34:26; Deut. 14:21). There are also examples of kindness towards animals (e.g. the erection of shelters for cattle, Gen. 33:17).

However, many of the biblical writers used animals as examples to teach us about how we should conduct ourselves (e.g. Prov. 6:6) or about God's character (e.g. Matt. 6:26; 10:29; 23:37; Luke 12:24) rather than to teach us an ethic of animal care.

Despite so little biblical material specifically about animal care, according to Hume, 'Neighbourliness towards animals was such a deeply rooted tradition among the Jews that it was taken for granted', and consequently there are many references in the OT to God leading his flock like a shepherd (e.g. Ps. 23:1, 6; Isa. 40:11). Linzey talks of the Christ-like innocence of animals and what they can teach us about God's love for us and about the gospel.

Jesus' view of animals

With his deep knowledge of the OT, Jesus would have known of those verses that argue for kindness towards animals (e.g. Exod. 23:19; Deut. 22:6–7; 25:4 [cf. 1 Tim. 5:18]; Prov. 12:10). There are several indications of Jesus' high regard for animals (e.g. Luke 13:15; 14:5) and he referred to labouring oxen as a picture of his compassion (Matt. 11:28–30). Moreover, it must be remembered that as part of the Trinity, Jesus was actively involved in the creation of the natural world (John 1:3; Col. 1:15–17; Heb. 1:2), and his was an intimate knowledge of the natural world (see

Matt. 8:20; Luke 9:58). It is difficult to imagine that Jesus, our moral exemplar, would condone cruelty.

It is also difficult to envisage Christ's followers as being indifferent to animal suffering. Although Paul has been accused of having a callous attitude to animals (see 1 Cor. 9:9–10), it has been pointed out that Paul is here extending the commonplace assumption that of course God is concerned for the oxen – and so should we be – but that God cares even more for us. Dunstan puts it like this: 'St Paul says "Doth God care for the oxen?" – not as expecting the answer "No", but as a rabbinic way of arguing *a fortiori* – "he cares even more for *us*" ' (his emphasis).

Jesus' use of the term 'dogs', as was common in his day, to refer to the Gentiles (Matt. 7:6; 15:21–28), shows us that he did not see animals as equal to humans (dogs were feral, non-domesticated animals in first-century Palestine and not like modern 'pets'). (This is not to deny that affection for animals existed, see e.g. the story of Nathan's lamb, 2 Sam. 12:1–3.) Although this seems a harsh attitude by Christ to the Gentiles (and by extension to dogs), it is clear that God's mercy was being *extended* to the Gentiles (see also Acts 10 and 11). Christ's attitude to animals was that, although they are not equal with human beings, they are included in God's mercy. Indeed, animals are inextricably bound up with the salvation of humankind (Lev. 25:7; Deut. 5:14; Hos. 2:18; Jon. 4:11).

Humanity's dominion over animals

A suggested explanation for the apparent lack of interest in animal welfare among Christians is the notion that animals have been put on earth by God for humanity to do with as they please. However, this is a distortion of true 'dominion theology', which has more to do with careful stewardship and not exploitation of God's creation. Christians should be even more anxious to reflect God's righteous 'servanthood' rule since we have experienced the new creation of redemption (2 Cor. 5:17) that should lead to an attitude of true righteousness and holiness in our role as God's 'vice-regent' of his world (Eph. 4:22–24). We have been given the ministry of reconciliation (2 Cor. 5:18–19), and verses such as Rev. 5:8–10 and 2 Tim. 2:12 seem to imply that God intends a continuation of his plan for us to exercise dominion over his world.

Do animals have rights?

There have been attempts to align the biblical view of animals with 'animal rights' concepts (e.g. by Andrew Linzey, Tom Regan and Stephen H. Webb), although they have also been criticized (e.g. see critiques of Linzey by Dimery and Barclay). In the NT it was taken for granted that humans were 'higher' than animals. Both animals and humans are 'creatures' (*nephesh*) under God, but the NT makes it clear that only humans are made in the 'image of God'. The following hierarchy was thus in the NT writers' minds: God – humans (*nephesh*, with image of God) – living beings (animals and humans = *nephesh*) – plants/inanimate matter.

Although this hierarchy has been misunderstood and abused by those who exploit animals without regard to their welfare, one cannot say that the abuse of animals is because of the hierarchy and that this hierarchy must therefore be wrong. Although many 'animal rights' campaigners would condemn the violence perpetrated by those at the extreme end of the movement, it is clear that at least some are prepared to entertain a 'lower' view of human life compared with animal life in condoning violence against – and even murder of – those who use animals in research.

Additionally some holding an 'animal rights' position fail to address seriously the issue of the 'right' of disease organisms to exist. Perhaps some would agree that diseases such as smallpox or leishmaniasis clearly should be combated, but it is difficult to see where one draws the line. The NT perspective of dominion theology, which places humans as being more important than the creation that surrounds us but that also demands a servanthood *humility, gives us an ethical yardstick with which to measure the control of disease. As John Passmore said, 'Nor should we hesitate about giving precedence to human beings. Schweitzer did so in fact, as Barth pointed out, when he became a doctor.'

Vegetarianism and killing animals for food

Although the Bible does not directly address the subject of animal use for medical, scientific or intensive agricultural purposes, it does deal with the subject of killing animals for food (a detailed study of Jewish slaughter techniques is beyond the scope of this article). For the Jewish people, animals were divided into clean and unclean according to whether they could or could not be eaten (Gen. 8:20; Lev. 7:21; 11; 20:25; Deut. 14:3–20; Acts 10:11–15; 1 Tim. 4:3–5). However, both Jesus (Mark 7:19) and Paul (1 Cor. 6:12) argued that all foods are 'clean' to eat, including meat.

Nevertheless, some Christians argue that Christians should be vegetarian, reflecting God's 'pre-fall ideal' by refraining from eating meat. One Christian writer (Cooper) even used the phrase 'Meat is murder' as the title of a chapter of his book. However, from the following references, we can see that meat-eating was common in NT times (Acts 10 – 11; 15:20; Rom. 14:1–4; 1 Cor. 8; 10:23–33; 1 Tim. 4:3–5), and even Jesus ate meat (he would have done so at the Passover), and it is recorded that he caught, cooked and ate fish (John 21:9; see also Luke 24:41–43). Even the Psalmist recognized predation as something 'good' (Psalm 104:21).

Vivisection

Some Christians argue that since humans are of more value than animals, the use of animals for scientific research is imperative. There are many Christians who are scientists and who use animals in experimentation, and in good conscience they believe it to be God's calling for them. They believe that the biblical concept of the responsible use of the resources God has entrusted to humans can be applied to the use of animals in research to reduce or alleviate disease, pain and suffering. This does not mean that there are easy answers to all the difficult questions concerning whether or not a particular series of experiments should be allowed if they involve an element of pain and suffering for the research animals, but it does mean that a moratorium on animal experimentation is not justifiable on biblical grounds alone. However, it is not easy to balance the need to combat disease with the need to reduce or even eliminate the use of animals in research. Some Christians, however, believe there is a moral duty to develop ways of combating pain and suffering, and if this can be resolved only by the use of animals in research, then there is a biblical duty to do so. At the same time, there is also a moral duty to reassess constantly the methods used and to see if there is any possibility of using alternatives.

Conclusion

Although the issues of animal rights, vegetarianism and vivisection are still controversial amongst Christians, the biblical view is that animals should not be treated with the same rights as humans, although derivative rights based on the hierarchy discussed above can be accorded. This perspective does not mean that the wanton exploitation of animals is allowable, but neither does it mean that animals cannot be used by humans.

The Church of England's General Synod Board for Social Responsibility summarized much of the above in the following statement in 1986: 'The fact that animals may be used in scientific procedures for the benefit of people shows that we believe that human beings have more value than animals. But the fact that we minimize the pain, suffering, distress or lasting harm that animals have to undergo shows that we regard them as having intrinsic value. Within the Christian tradition the relation ship between people and the animals was made clear when Adam was given dominion over the whole animal kingdom and named the animals; but because humans are said to be made in the image of God they must use that God-given dominion in a responsible way.'

Bibliography

O. R. Barclay, 'Animal Rights: A Critique', *Science and Christian Belief* 4.1 (1992), pp. 49–61; R. C. J. Carling *et al.*, 'Animals in Man's Service', *Faith & Thought* 108.3 (1982), pp. 151–161; S. R. L. Clark, *The Moral Status of Animals* (Oxford, 1984); T. Cooper, *Green Christianity: Caring for the Whole Creation* (London, 1990); R. Dimery, 'Critique of "After Noah" by Andrew Linzey and Dan Cohn-Sherbok', <http://www.dimery.com/articles/After_Noah/after_noah.html>; G. R. Dunstan, 'A Limited Dominion', *Conquest* 170 (1980), pp. 1–8; General Synod Board for Social Responsibility, *Our Responsibility for the Living Environment* (London, 1986); C. W. Hume, *The Status of Animals in the Christian Religion* (London, 1957); G. M. Lee, 'Studies in Texts: 1 Corinthians 9:9–10', *Theology*, 81 (1968), pp. 122–123; A. Linzey, *Christianity and the Rights of Animals* (London, 1987); *Animal Gospel: Christian Faith as though Animals Mattered* (London, 1998); J. Passmore, *Man's Responsibility for Nature: Ecological Problems and Western Traditions* (London, 1980).

R. C. J. CARLING

ANNIHILATIONISM, see HELL

ANSELM

Anselm (1033–1109) was born near Aosta, on the frontier with Lombardy. He entered the Benedictine monastery at Bec in 1066, where he came under the influence of Lanfranc, the Italian prior. The scholarship and teaching of Lanfranc had established the abbey of Bec as a centre of learning. Anselm flourished in this environment, so much so that when Lanfranc was appointed abbot of Caen in 1063, Anselm was elected to succeed him as prior. While at Bec, Anselm wrote the *Monologion* (1076), the *Proslogion* (1077–78) and his four philosophical dialogues. In 1093 Anselm became Lanfranc's successor yet again when he was elected Archbishop of Canterbury. His tenure as archbishop was turbulent and difficult due to the antagonistic efforts of the English royalty to diminish ecclesiastical power. Anselm continued to write in spite of the distractions, and it was during this period that he produced *Cur deus homo*, arguably the most important theological treatise of the Middle Ages before the time of *Thomas Aquinas. Anselm died on 21 April 1109.

The relationship between faith and reason had become a central focus of medieval thought. Berengar of Tours, professor of the monastic school of St Martin at Tours, maintained the priority of reason. He admitted the truth of Scripture yet asserted that proper interpretation should be done rationally. Whatever is illogical, including e.g. the doctrine of transubstantiation, is necessarily false. Peter Damian, prior of the hermitage of Fonte-Avellana in Italy, maintained the opposite point of view. He insisted that if something seemed to be irrational, the problem was to be located in human reason or in human grammar which could not fully embrace eternal matters. Lanfranc defended the priority of faith while not discrediting the use of reason. It was left to Anselm to give a more definitive solution to this problem. The main lines of Anselm's work can be seen as the attempt to show that reason and faith lead to the same conclusions. By moving forward these discussions Anselm established his importance during his time and has become known as the father of *scholasticism.

Far from contradicting one another, faith and reason aid each other. Faith receives the teaching of the church, and reason aids one in understanding. The same conclusions come through these different means even though there is a particular ordering. Reason does not establish faith or determine its content, but makes it possible to delight in the comprehension and contemplation of that which is given in Christianity. Anselm thus gave greater weight to *credo ut intelligam* (I believe in order to understand) than to *intelligo ut credam* (I understand in order to believe), and he mirrored the approach of *Augustine on this point.

Anselm's method is 'faith seeking understanding' (*fides quaerens intellectum*). This phrase, which is the alternative title to the *Proslogion* ('An Address'), indicates Anselm's commitment to meditation on God and the nature of being on the basis of faith. This project is open to at least two misunderstandings. Some philosophers have argued that Anselm hoped to replace faith (which is easier) with understanding (which is better). Faith, in this construct, is a lesser source of information, while understanding has the prospect of telling one more about *truth than faith. But it needs to be said that for Anselm and his age, truth was not devoid of its moral consequences. Faith for Anselm indicates the volitional engagement of the hearer. So 'faith seeking understanding' embraces the entirety of life and is not exclusive to the intellect.

Other writers maintain that Anselm's work is essentially theological in character. He begins with faith not with doubt or suspension of belief. On this basis, it has been argued that Anselm sets forward his arguments for God's existence, not to convince non-believers but to aid believers in their comprehension of the faith. This also is a misreading of Anselm's intentions, for the arguments were intended as rational proofs to convince unbelievers even though they started as meditations that originated in faith. Anselm makes this very clear in the first chapter of the *Monologion* where he insists that even someone of moderate intelligence could be convinced of most of the truths regarding God by reason alone without recourse to the Bible.

Anselm's view of faith and reason is the appropriate context in which to understand the *theistic proofs. In the *Monologion*, Anselm's longest work, he demonstrates the principal doctrines of Christianity, principally the idea that there is a supreme being. He begins by asserting that there must be some one thing that is supremely good, through which all good things have their goodness. That good thing must be good in itself and is therefore good *through itself*. This supremely good thing is supreme among all existing things. Anselm proceeds through a series of like arguments reflecting the Christian *Platonism of Augustine.

In the *Proslogion* Anselm seeks one simple argument that will prove that God really exists, that he is the supreme good, who depends on nothing else but on whom all things depend. Anselm argues that God is 'that than which nothing greater can be thought'. Since the idea can be thought it is in the understanding, but God cannot merely remain in the understanding. He exists both in understanding and in reality. Anselm believes this argument gives answer to the one who has said in his heart, 'There is no God.' (Pss. 14:1; 53:1).

Cur deus homo ('Why God Became Man') seeks to show why the Christian account of redemption is reasonable. The work is presented in two parts. The first answers the objections of unbelievers who reject the Christian faith because they regard it as contrary to reason, and the second shows through necessary reasons why it is impossible for anyone to be saved apart from Christ's atoning work.

Bibliography

G. R. Evans, *Anselm* (London, 1989); R. W. Southern, *Saint Anselm: A Portrait in Landscape* (Cambridge, 1990); T. Williams, 'Saint Anselm', in E. N. Zalta (ed.), *The Stanford Encyclopedia of Philosophy* (Spring 2002).

G. L. Isaac

ANTHROPIC PRINCIPLE, see COSMOLOGY

APOCALYPTICISM

In popular *imagination, and fuelled by such cinematic extravaganzas as *Apocalypse Now*, 'apocalyptic' denotes end-of-the-world type chaos, and in particular death, destruction and the dissolution of all things. However, the word 'apocalypse' (Gk, *apokalypsis*) simply means 'revelation' or 'unveiling', and the word 'apocalyptic' frequently calls such imagery to mind largely because of what is unveiled in the final book of the Bible, Revelation. Revelation clearly does concern itself with the fantastic and the end, in a sense, of the world, but it is called 'apocalyptic' fundamentally because the visions given by the angel to John *reveal* not just the future, but rather God's way with the world as it was even then. To a Christian church apparently over-run by the omnipresent Roman Empire, Revelation offers a word of hope and a counter-cultural incentive to resist the prevailing society and values of the day. Many ancient apocalypses survive, notably *4 Ezra* and the *Shepherd* of Hermas, and a consideration of their common characteristics led one group of scholars to the following, highly influential, statement of the defining characteristics of the genre: '*Apocalypse* is a genre of revelatory literature with a narrative framework, in which a *revelation is mediated by an otherworldly being to a human recipient, disclosing a transcendent *reality which is both temporal, insofar as it envisages eschatological salvation, and spatial, insofar as it involves another, supernatural world' (Collins, 'Apocalypse', p. 9).

An older, equally influential characterization, was offered by OT scholar Paul Hanson, who argued that apocalyptic represented a kind of 'collapse of prophecy'. On this view, prophecy was the passionate engagement with the surrounding world which sought to bring about change toward *justice and *shalom*, but when world-weary prophets (or their societies) turned away from such hopes and simply declared judgment on the created order while promising a new divine solution (e.g. Isaiah's new *heaven and new earth), this was 'apocalyptic'. Hanson situated this twofold conflict of views in a class-driven conflict between pro-restorationist priests and apocalyptic visionaries, and it has a certain initial plausibility to it, although the details of his view have found little historical support. Although few would defend this 'collapse of prophecy' model today, it lingers on as perhaps the predominant understanding of biblical apocalyptic at a popular level.

On the distinction between these two basic approaches turns the whole apologetic relevance of apocalyptic. The 'collapse' model inculcates a mentality of withdrawal from 'the world', which is condemned to judgment anyway. Such apocalypticism is marked by its proliferation of end-time charts and road maps for Armageddon. In extreme cases, missionary activity is discouraged on the grounds that the increasing disarray is likely to promote the end of all things. Such views go hand in hand with a dualism of flesh and spirit which relegates matters of importance to a non-physical level. The current ecological crisis stands as a sharp reminder of the unacceptability of trying to pass this off as a form of Christianity consistent with the call to be stewards of creation.

Engaged apocalyptic hope, on the other hand, represents a belief that the created world is a deeper and richer reality than most of us experience most of the time, and suggests that it is precisely the revelation of what is not normally seen that is the pressing task of Christian apologetics in today's world. The task is not to translate the Christian gospel into terms acceptable to modernist and/or rationalist frameworks of justified belief or *truth, but to witness to the broader veiled reality which apocalyptic seeks to open up. In particular, apocalyptic critique such as is found in the books of Daniel and Revelation serves to unmask dominant political interests and ideologies, relativizing them to the true lordship of the God of Israel, fully revealed in *Jesus Christ. This kind of apocalyptic represents a head-on apologetic confrontation with what it brands the idolatrous pseudo-lordships of the forces around us, whether of Caesar, the government, or the economic system. In the light of uncanny parallels between the *pax romana* of Rome in the first century and of supposed super-power 'protectors of freedom' in today's world, a recovery of authentic Christian apocalyptic offers a profound resource for Christian engagement with the world today. It also requires an act of daring and prophetic witness to be willing to challenge the self-sufficient systems and philosophies of contemporary society with theological vision and with apologetic imagination.

Bibliography

J. J. Collins, 'Apocalypse: Morphology of a Genre', *Semeia*, 14 (1979), pp. 1–20; P. D. Hanson, *The Dawn of Apocalyptic* (Philadelphia, 1975); W. Howard-Brook and A. Gwyther, *Unveiling Empire: Reading Revelation Then and Now* (Maryknoll, 1999); H. Peskett, 'Missions and Eschatology', in K. E. Brower amd M. W. Elliott (eds.), 'The Reader Must Understand': Eschatology in Bible and Theology (Leicester, 1997), pp. 301–322.

R. S. BRIGGS

APOCRYPHA/ DEUTEROCANONICAL BOOKS

The additional books and texts from the LXX Greek text included in the OT by the Catholic Church and (with some variation) by the Orthodox Churches are known as the Apocrypha (lit. 'secret writings'). Many prefer the term deuterocanon ('second *canon') to distinguish these books from the protocanon ('first canon') of the Hebrew Scriptures.

Attitudes to the Apocrypha within the early church are inconclusive. Decisions of Councils and citations by Church Fathers do not reflect the existence of a clearly defined list. The Synod of Laodicea (360) favoured a shorter canon, as do also lists in Melito, Cyril of Jerusalem, Epiphanius, and Jerome. However, the Synod of Carthage (397) included the Apocryphal books, which are quoted in many Fathers. It was not until the Council of Trent (1546) that the Roman position was formalized. The Orthodox Churches have yet to decide; they use the books liturgically, but not as a source of dogmatic decision. The Reformers excluded them, although Lutherans and Anglicans recommend them for personal edification.

Advocates of a longer canon argue from the apostles' use of the LXX (which includes the deuterocanon), multiple NT allusions to these books, citations from them in the Church Fathers, *Origen's preference for a 'Christian' over against a 'Jewish' Bible, and especially the long church tradition in favour of inclusion.

Supporters of the shorter list of OT books assume with Jerome that Jesus and the apostles used the Hebrew canon. They hold that: a three-fold division of the OT is reflected in Luke 24:44 and the foreword to Sirach; Matt. 23:35 suggests a canon from Genesis to 2 Chronicles (the last book in the Hebrew Bible); the NT nowhere quotes directly the deuterocanonical books as Scripture; 2 Esdras refers to twenty-four OT books, a number consistent with the ancient practice of grouping together some of the thirty-nine books of the Hebrew canon; and citation by the Church Fathers does not necessarily indicate canonical status.

The Guidelines for Interconfessional Co-operation in Translating the Bible (1968, rev. 1987) between the United Bible Societies and the Vatican made possible the publication of interconfessional Bibles by placing the Apocrypha before the NT.

Bibliography

R. Beckwith, The Old Testament Canon of the New Testament Church (London, 1985); D. G. Dunbar, 'The Biblical Canon', in D. A. Carson and J. D. Woodbridge (eds.), Hermeneutics, Authority and Canon (Downers Grove and Leicester, 1986); S. Meurer (ed.), The Apocrypha in Ecumenical Perspective (Reading and New York, 1991).

F. MACDONALD

APOSTOLIC WITNESS

Christian faith is rooted in the NT documents, which testify to the life, death and resurrection of *Jesus and to the teaching of the earliest Christian leaders concerning him. These documents purport to be written by named Christians or by people whose names were known to their original readers. Theophilus would not have received the Gospel (of Luke) addressed to him and asked, 'Now which of my friends could possibly have written this?' These writers were either apostles (i.e. people directly commissioned by Jesus as leaders in the church) or people closely linked to them. Three problems arise from this:

1. Were the named or assumed writers in fact the actual writers? Or were the documents written by other people at a later date?

2. Can it be maintained that the Gospels contain a reliable account of what Jesus said and did?

3. Is the theology of the NT a faithful development from the earliest apostolic teaching?

Authorship

If any of the documents are not by the named or assumed authors, there are several possibilities. First, they may have been authorized by a person but written by somebody else with that person's consent and *authority, just as somebody today might get a secretary to write a business letter and then sign it as if it were a personal composition. Paul probably dictated the body of his letters word for word to an amanuensis (Rom. 16:22; cf. Gal. 6:11; 2 Thess. 3:17), but sometimes he may have given greater freedom of expression to his helper.

Secondly, they may have been composed by a later writer based on the thoughts of an apostle so that readers might know 'what Paul would have said if he had still been here to say it'. This would have been done quite openly so that the original readers would have known what was happening. Some scholars think that this may have happened with some letters ascribed to Paul (e.g. those to Timothy and Titus are thought to differ sufficiently in expression from Paul's other letters to suggest another writer). Again, there is nothing problematic about this procedure, although at a later stage people supposed that the named author was the actual author.

Thirdly, documents may have been written in the name of apostles at a much later date by people who wished to pass off their own teaching as apostolic. In this case, an element of deception was involved, but some modern scholars argue that this practice was not reprehensible by the standards of the time, and that we need not have qualms about it. Others argue that this procedure is wrong and calls in question the spiritual value of the contents of the documents concerned. Various clear examples of pseudonymity are known from the second century and later; such works were generally produced by heretics and were not accepted by orthodox Christians. Despite frequent claims to the contrary, there are in fact no cases in the NT where pseudonymity has been proved beyond reasonable doubt.

Historical reliability

None of the four *canonical Gospels carries the name of its author; attribution of them rests on confirming or rejecting the ascriptions by second-century Christians. In each case there are scholars who question the traditional ascriptions. There is the greatest confidence regarding the traditional attribution of the Gospels of Mark and Luke. In the case of the Gospels of Matthew and John, however, it is thought by some that while they may well include traditions stemming from these two apostles, the identity of their final authors or editors cannot be known.

The important question is not so much authorship as whether the contents of the Gospels are based on 'apostolic witness'. In other words, do the contents stem from reliable accounts handed down ultimately from persons in a position to know what had happened? Certainly Luke avers that he and other writers wrote on the basis of what had been handed down by 'eye-witnesses and servants of the word' (Luke 1:2). This claim corresponds with what was likely to have happened. In a culture where there was less use of the written word than is the case nowadays, much information was carefully memorized and handed down by word of mouth until it was put in writing. Even after the writing took place, the oral tradition continued, enabling supplementation, correction and confirmation of what had been written. Study of practices in the ancient world, and also in the modern Near East, has shown that the most likely mode of transmission was 'controlled, informal tradition'; this phrase describes how people passed on stories of what had happened with appropriate freedom of formulation ('informal') but in a context where those who told or heard their stories were often in the position to say 'but that is not how we remember it' and to supply the necessary correction ('controlled').

In any case, the timespan was relatively short, and people's memories could have persisted quite accurately over that period. Luke's comment (Luke 1:1–3) suggests that there may have been people in the early church who were particularly entrusted with the transmission of the stories about Jesus. He clearly believed that what he had heard was reliable.

The considerable similarities in content between the Gospels of Matthew, Mark and Luke indicate that they were based not simply on oral materials independently transcribed by each author but rather on common written sources. The most widely held theory is that Matthew and Luke independently made use of what Mark had already written, and that they may also have used a separate source of the teaching of Jesus (the so-called 'Q' source, which is now lost). Theories of this kind are attempts to do justice to the phenomena in the Gospels themselves. They seek to bridge the gap in time between the events recorded and the composition of the Gospels by postulating the existence of earlier sources.

The different Gospels create pictures of Jesus which are essentially similar. Despite individual emphases, distinctive elements and the use of different sources, the depictions of Jesus in these three Gospels are recognizably the same. The Gospel of John stands apart from the others because of its selection of incidents from the life of Jesus and its distinctive account of his teaching, which varies from the fairly uniform material in the other Gospels. Yet there are strong reasons for supposing that it too rests on a core of reliable tradition that is similar in character to that behind the other Gospels.

Theological reliability

The NT documents, and in particular the letters, have been analysed to work out what was the content of Christian teaching in the earliest days of the *Church. From the accounts of the *preaching in Acts and the indications in the letters of what would have been taught to converts, we can reconstruct two types of material.

First, there was the 'gospel', the common outline of the kind of things said by Christian preachers in presenting the message about Jesus to people who were not yet believers. This included an account of the death and resurrection of Jesus supported by material from the OT to show that what had happened to him was in accordance with God's plan and that he could therefore be identified as the promised Messiah; personal testimonies to the fact of Jesus' post-resurrection appearances, which proved he was still alive; a summons to people to accept Jesus as Lord and receive forgiveness for their sins; the promise that the *Holy Spirit would be received by those who believed the good news; and a reference to Jesus' future return to carry out God's final judgment.

This brief set of points formed the basis for the oral preaching of the gospel. This basic outline was expanded and developed in many of the NT writings, but while they may elaborate upon it, the outline controls their teaching despite all the individual differences between them.

The second element in the message of the early Christian preachers was the teaching. It is possible to reconstruct common elements in the kind of teaching that was given to believers and the ways in which they may have expressed themselves in prayer forms, creedal material and so forth. Needless to say, there was considerable scope for individual development in response to the different needs of different situations and in accordance with the varying creativity of Christian preachers and teachers. Nevertheless, there was a core of material that was held in common by early Christians and can be labelled 'apostolic' in this sense. Consequently, we can be sure that the substance of the teaching in the NT documents rests upon the witness of the earliest Christians and is in harmony with it.

The concept of 'apostolic witness' is thus not altogether simple, but there are good grounds for claiming that the NT documents ultimately rest on traditions and testimonies that were in close touch with Jesus and his earliest followers.

Bibliography

K. E. Bailey, 'Informal controlled oral tradition and the Synoptic Gospels', *Themelios*, 20:2, (1995), pp. 4–11; C. L. Blomberg, *The Historical Reliability of John's Gospel* (Leicester and Downers Grove, 2001); *The Historical Reliability of the Gospels* (Leicester and Downers Grove, 1987); C. H. Dodd, *The Apostolic Preaching and its Developments* (London, 1944); B. Gerhardsson, *The Reliability of the Gospel Tradition* (Peabody, 2001).

I. H. MARSHALL

AQUINAS, see THOMAS AQUINAS

ARCHAEOLOGY

Archaeology is the study of the material evidence of humanity's impact on its environment. As such, it is also a tool for the reconstruction of the past. God's dealings with his people Israel, as reported in the OT and NT, took place during specific historical periods and in specific locations. It is therefore reasonable to expect archaeology to throw light on Israel's unfolding history. However, it is a popular misconception that if the Bible is a true record, then archaeology should provide evidence of the events described in it. Biblical narrative and archaeological evidence provide very different kinds of witness to the past and their relationship is complex.

Archaeology as a tool to reconstruct the past

Through archaeology we can retrieve information not expressed in the written record, as well as provide the only information where no written record exists. The archaeological record is objective in the information it gives, as people did not intentionally leave their imprint on the environment. To that extent, this record is an accurate reflection of what humans actually did.

The weakness of archaeology is, however, that it can study only what has survived. A continuous process of decay and human activity in later periods means that evidence of the past gradually disappears. What survives for archaeology to study may be an accurate record, but it is possibly an unrepresentative record of a complex environment. Furthermore, all archaeological remains require interpretation. A lack of objectivity comes in at this stage when, in the process of understanding evidence, people usually begin from some world-view which is not objective.

Some basics of archaeology as a discipline

It is the job of the archaeologist to recover, analyse and understand data. Archaeological data can range from built structures to tools; from concentrations of certain insect remains to changes to the landscape; and from the DNA record to the date at which a pottery vessel was fired. While any find is important in itself, the context of the find is at least as important, and unless we determine this context accurately the data themselves may end up being worthless. It is from the context that we can establish a date and determine why the data are there in the first place.

Once we have retrieved the data, and recorded and conserved them, various specialists can then analyse them, each trying to tease out as much information as possible. With a good understanding of the stratigraphical history of the site, archaeologists can then try to make sense of the information in context. Although there are many points throughout the process where mistakes can occur, it is at the level of interpretation that most mistakes are made.

If the excavators have undertaken and recorded the data extraction and analysis correctly, it is always possible to go back over it and reassess the conclusions reached. However if the data extraction techniques were faulty, it is impossible to go back and check the conclusions because the relevant data has been destroyed. (Archaeology is often referred to as the only discipline which destroys its evidence to understand it.) Archaeology is a relatively new discipline, and in the process of its development many sites were excavated and/or recorded using methods that are unacceptable today. Fortunately, an excavation rarely removes more than a fraction of a site, and new excavations at previously dug sites are often possible (e.g. as currently at Megiddo, Hazor and Jericho).

The specific remit, contribution and limitations of biblical archaeology

Biblical archaeology is a sub-discipline of archaeology that deals, in its broadest sense, with all archaeological evidence that illuminates the Bible. It therefore covers the archaeology not only of Palestine, but of the Ancient Near East in general. In view of the large geographical area and long sweep of history involved, no single person can be an expert in the whole field.

Many who ventured into biblical archaeology during the past century did so from a covert or overt hope of 'proving' the Bible. Until recently biblical archaeologists have on the whole been quite conservative in their tendencies, accepting large parts of the biblical historical narrative more or less at face value.

This has changed dramatically with the recent shift to understanding biblical (especially OT) narrative as 'story' (or the like) rather than *history. As 'story', it is claimed, it needs no correspondence with actual historical events in order to have meaning. From this point of view it is inappropriate to expect convergence between the Bible and archaeological evidence. Furthermore, when reconstructing the history of Israel, archaeology is given priority over the Bible, because it is axiomatic that the Bible does not contain useful historical information.

At the opposite extreme there are still groups (such as the Associates for Biblical Research in the USA) that conduct excavations and publish papers with the aim of supporting the historicity of the Bible, often focusing on areas where negative views have become prevalent (e.g. the exodus and conquest).

The Bible's theological claims are, of course, out of bounds to archaeological evidence. Archaeology may show that Jerusalem escaped devastation during Sennacherib's invasion in 701 BC, but it cannot prove that the angel of the Lord protected it (2 Kgs 19:35). Nevertheless, when archaeology is carried out with the aim of confirming the Bible's historical accuracy, the underlying motive is usually to validate its theological claims as a corollary.

Even at the level of proving or reconstructing specific events, however, archaeology has limitations, e.g. it is often not possible to date the destruction of a city precisely or to say why or by whom it was destroyed. Sennacherib's conquest of Lachish in 701 BC is one of the few instances where the Bible (2 Kgs 18:13–14), extra-biblical written sources and archaeological results complement each other very well. Usually such convergence is difficult to establish.

Archaeology has notoriously failed to produce unambiguous evidence for Israel's conquest of Canaanite cities as recorded in the book of Joshua. As a result, some scholars have concluded that no such conquest occurred. In defence of the biblical account, others have tried to minimize the number of cities that were destroyed and/or to explain away missing evidence; yet others have argued that the majority of scholars are mistaken in dating Israel's entry into Canaan to the thirteenth century BC, and have sought archaeological evidence in an earlier century instead. This unresolved dispute illustrates the complexity of relating a particular biblical narrative with the archaeological record.

Where biblical archaeology has made its most positive contribution is in reconstructing the cultural and historical backgrounds of the Bible. By identifying (albeit provisionally) the settlement patterns, environmental conditions and types of economic and socio-political organization that prevailed within different periods, archaeology has provided contexts against which the words of the prophets, psalmists, evangelists and other biblical authors can be understood much more richly.

Archaeology and apologetics

The contribution of archaeology to Christian apologetics has been mixed. Some claims of archaeological support for the Bible have been ill-advised. There are two main reasons for this. One is that archaeological evidence itself has been wrongly interpreted, leading to some high-profile retractions. The so-called 'Solomon's stables' at Megiddo were subsequently assigned to a later period and are possibly not stables; the same king's 'copper refinery' at Ezion-geber (Tell el-Kheleifeh) has been re-interpreted out of existence (and

Tell el-Kheleifeh is probably not biblical Ezion-geber).

Another reason lies in a failure to appreciate the nature and genre of biblical texts. In the interests of their particular agenda, biblical authors were highly selective and focused on what modern historians would consider marginal, while ignoring major historical processes. Archaeology sometimes highlights this, as in the case of Omri. The Moabite Stone shows that this Israelite king subjugated Moab, and Assyrian texts were still calling the northern kingdom 'Omri-land' when his dynasty was extinct. Yet his significance could never be guessed from the biblical text, which condemns his reign in a few verses (1 Kgs 17:21–28).

Furthermore, biblical writers employed literary conventions that we would not associate with straightforward historiography. Many of these conventions were shared with the rest of the Ancient Near Eastern world. Lawson Younger (*Ancient Conquest Accounts: A Study in Ancient Near Eastern and Biblical History Writing* [Sheffield, 1990]) has shown how an appreciation of Assyrian, Hittite and Egyptian conquest accounts can save us from misunderstanding aspects of Josh. 9 – 12. Biblical narrative can also display a creativity that would otherwise be associated with the writing of fiction.

None of this means that the biblical authors were not concerned with history. They clearly were, for their theological claims are often embedded in historical statements (e.g. Exod. 20:2), but it does suggest they were less interested in an exact correspondence between their narratives and historical events than in bringing out the significance of those events as they perceived them.

All this must be borne in mind when turning to archaeology for light on the biblical text. Archaeology and the Bible may sometimes appear to disagree because they are both only partial (in both senses of the word) witnesses to the past.

When archaeology does provide support for the Bible, that support is often indirect. For example, many details in the description of Solomon's temple can now be paralleled (in terms of architecture and furnishings) by the archaeology of Late Bronze and Iron Age temples from neighbouring regions. The evidence locates Solomon and his temple-building in a specific (though broad) cultural and historical setting. It also undermines the claim that Solomon and his temple were the creation of a post-exilic author, because no writer of that late period could have seen a suitable temple on which to base the detailed description in 1 Kgs 6 – 9. Evidence of this type for the general plausibility of the biblical narratives is plentiful, but it has far less impact on the popular imagination than alleged evidence for a particular event.

Archaeology has often been used defensively in apologetics. This is understandable when it is falsely claimed that some discovery has 'disproved' an aspect of the Bible. But the defensive response has sometimes led to hasty claims in the opposite direction, followed sooner or later by embarrassing retractions. A more responsible use of archaeology will involve a sound grasp of the nature of both archaeological evidence and the biblical text, and a balanced assessment of the ways in which they converge.

J. SODE-WOODHEAD and J. J. BIMSON

ARISTOTLE

Aristotle (384/3 – 348/7 BCE) made his greatest contribution to philosophy in his body of logical writings, later known as the *Organon*. His systematic analysis of the conditions and forms of *reasoning, which includes the development of both the forms of the *syllogism and scientific methodology, goes far beyond anything found in his predecessors. For Aristotle, *logic is an introductory science which is to guide all scientific work. A science is an ordered body of knowledge in which *first principles ground conclusions. Scientific knowledge grasps the cause on which the fact depends. For Jewish, Muslim and Christian thinkers in the Middle Ages and beyond, this conception of science provided the context for determining the nature and method of theology.

For Aristotle there are theoretical and practical sciences. The goal of a theoretical science is knowledge, whereas the goal of a practical science is that which is to be done. Thus, *ethics and politics are practical sciences since their goal is to shape human action through right laws or social context so that the individual may reach the good and be fulfilled (happy). The chief human good consists in contemplation of the highest object, for a complete lifetime, along with virtue, needed external goods and friends.

Aristotle distinguishes three types of theoretical science: physics, which treats things subject to change, mathematics, which deals with unchanging things that do not exist separately but are often considered as separable from matter, and the 'first science' (which Aristotle also calls 'theology'), which considers those things that both exist separately and are unchanging.

With regard to the theoretical sciences Aristotle, in contrast to *Plato, was drawn towards the empirical and scientific. Plato tended to treat material objects as unsuitable for knowledge, but for Aristotle individuals are first substance and they are the focus of natural philosophy. Change requires a subject in which the change occurs. Natural things have within themselves a principle of motion or change. So 'nature' for Aristotle identifies the intrinsic principles that are the source of a thing changing or being at rest.

Aristotle also developed a new conception of soul. Plato conceived of soul and body as separate substances, but Aristotle defines soul as 'the form of a natural body which has life potentially' or 'the first actuality of a natural body which has life potentially'. The human soul is the highest type of soul because it possesses the capacity for knowledge. Before it knows, the soul is like a blank tablet but with the potential for all that is thinkable. Through knowing the mind becomes all things. Because the mind can reach the essential elements of things and mathematical objects, as well as reflect on itself, it must be separate from matter. Aristotle distinguishes between a passive mind that becomes all things and an active mind that makes all things, like light makes potential colours into actual colours. For Aristotle the passive mind is destructible but the active mind is immortal and eternal. Thus, for Aristotle there does not seem to be any personal immortality. This conception of the soul was accepted by *Averroes. By contrast, *Thomas Aquinas used Aristotle's principles to elaborate a psychology that both describes the unity of the human person and defends personal *immortality.

One of the great advances in Aristotle's thought was the distinction of potency and act. Whereas previous thinkers, most notably *Parmenides, had argued that there is only being and non-being, Aristotle insists that objects may also be capable of an act that they are not currently performing. A man who builds is a builder also when he is not building. The same holds with regard to other kinds of change, such as change of place.

Actuality is prior to potentiality in formula, time and substance. 'From the potential the actual is always produced by an actual thing, e.g. man by man.' Since the actual must always be prior to the potential, there arises the question of a series of causes and the need for a first cause. For Aristotle the heavens were unchanging. Not only are the heavenly bodies in motion, but he argues that this motion is eternal. This motion cannot come to be, for that would require a previous change. Hence, there must be something eternal that 'imparts motion' and 'this first mover must be unmoved'.

Since for Aristotle the world is eternal, the question is not whether there is a temporally first cause, but rather a highest cause, a principle of change in the universe as a whole. He asserts that there must be an eternal, unmovable substance, and this substance must be in actuality, for otherwise there would not necessarily be movement. Hence, there must be 'a principle whose very substance is actuality'. Only such a principle can be the source of eternal motion. A thing which is fully actual cannot itself be moved, because it could then be different. So the first mover must move other things not by efficient *causality, but by final causality, by being desired. This principle has the best life, which is thinking, but it cannot receive its object of thought for that would, again, make it receptive or passive. So 'its thinking is a thinking on thinking'. Hence, there is no conception of providence in Aristotle's world.

For Aristotle, the account of the first mover remains closely tied to his system of astronomy and so he suggests that the number of movers be set at forty-nine or fifty-five. This appears to contradict the other arguments for a first mover. Plotinus argued that there must be a first that unites the motions of the spheres. The best known use of Aristotle's arguments are the 'five ways' of Thomas Aquinas who adapted Aristotle's arguments for a first moving cause. For Aquinas, what Christians believe can also be proved, for what is first in each causal order is what Christians call God.

Bibliography

J. L. Ackrill (ed.), *A New Aristotle Reader* (Princeton, 1987); G. E. R. Lloyd, *Aristotle: The Growth and Structure of his Thought* (Cambridge, 1968).

A. G. VOS

ART

Art as a 'religious area'

In the last few decades, the public meaning of 'art', that is to say, of living art, has undergone such a transformation that the more culturally conservative Christians among us, looking in the pigeonholes in which we thought to find 'art', would find them empty. The old classifications have gone, and some of the old *language has flown. But as is so often the case with revolutions, there are ideas to which Christians can relate, if they are prepared to let go of some of their own cultural conditioning and see the freedom of the gospel afresh. There have been changes in three main areas: the public *place* of art, the *ownership* of art and the *meaning* of art.

1. *Place* The museum has been an enduring creation of the *Enlightenment mind, a place where all manner of objects, religious, political, social and secular, could be placed and seen in terms of their common denominator 'the aesthetic'. Under the heading of 'art', their meanings, and to some extent their *power, was bracketed off. Seen as art, they were safe, especially if they were religious. Ironically, museums, having deprived art objects of their function and context, have then had to work enormously hard through explanations and exhibitions to remind people of what that original function and context was.

A recent unexpectedly popular exhibition at the National Gallery called *Seeing Salvation* re-presented some works, long familiar as 'icons of art history' (e.g. Titian's *Noli Me Tangere*), according to their original intention, as functioning, instrumental aids to devotion. In this exhibition, in which the works were permitted to speak their original message (rather than just be 'about art'), people were seen to pray and weep. In some mysterious way, the contextualizing of works of art was no longer academic and detached; the walls of the art-temple had been broken down.

It was another irony of the great temples of art that as repositories of art, they also became its typical location. Effectively this took art out of life into a 'sacred' area where it might also be ignored. Ignoring art has been, very largely, the attitude of the Protestant Christian church since the Enlightenment. While the aesthetic might be seen as good, even good for you in the way that sport is good, the meanings of works of art, as spoken to the world at large, have rarely been part of that 'philosophy' of the world with which Christian apologists have sought to engage. Notable and heroic exceptions in our own day have included G. K. *Chesterton, P. T. *Forsyth, Paul *Tillich, Hans *Rookmaaker and Calvin Seerveld, but for the non-specialist and the non-curious art could be easily bypassed as belonging to its own world.

Now, however, art has come out of the gallery, and not only through ubiquitous posters and art books. Artists themselves have moved their art out into the public arena, through performances and installations and all manner of 'events', which have received a lot of publicity. The gallery itself has been transformed, and is no longer the 'safe place' away from the world but more like an extension of the outside world, in which artists are given space to attempt to challenge or engage viewers. Christians, as ordinary members of the public, may feel as irritated as anyone else by the stunts of publicity-hungry artists, but it is important to realize what is happening. Artists have left behind 'their space' and have invaded 'our space' because they are determined to be heard. They have abandoned the aesthetic, because it too much 'knew its place' and did not appear to challenge anyone. Artists instead have assumed the role of court jesters, speaking the unspeakable, and acting as the conscience of society, exposing the pain which the narcotic of consumerism would suppress. Art is once again in the public space, and it is trying to communicate.

2. *Ownership* Good taste is strongly allied to education and privilege. The classical ideals of harmony and form, exemplified in classical architecture and sculpture, which have been the foundation of Western art, are learnt through training, and familiarization with 'good art' – traditionally through ownership and travel. Even today, certain classes of society are more familiar than others with traditional art, merely through the surroundings of their upbringing. But in the new era of art, the aesthetic has very little place. Balance and harmony have long lost transcendental force; now they are more likely to be seen, like perfect manners, as a social burden. The new art is open to all. Indeed, any attempt to judge it by the canons of taste, so far from being an exercise of privilege, is almost sure to lead to misunderstanding. It is those who are not looking at the new art through the lens of 'fine art' who are most likely to relate to it. The new language of art, although it seems obscure to those insistent on 'understanding it', is a democratic street-culture in which only its simplicity, even at times its banality, is a barrier to understanding. Christians who have a theological investment in an art of beauty may find this new art difficult to handle. It is as well to remember, however, that beauty in the Bible is dynamic, connected to good actions, and that any art that is statically connected with privilege, as a badge of the settled life either spiritually or materially, is liable to invite God's judgment.

3. *Meaning* If the Greek ideas of high ideals and noble birth have at last relaxed their grip, what are we then left with? Art may no longer be a means to 'elevate': neither are the aesthetic virtues still seen as metaphors for virtues in general. The interlinking of standards of beauty and of social standards has long gone. But art is nonetheless religious for that. It may no longer be a religion in terms of its apparent ability to 'improve' people but, nevertheless, it now occupies a religious space without parallel in contemporary *culture.

There are, of course, many places in modern culture where religious questions surface, and an obvious example is *cosmology. But cosmology also has its own – scientific – business to do. With the most recent art, however, we now have the creation of an 'art space' (an empty space designated as having artistic significance, in which any object or event is read 'as art') in which experimental probes into the meaning of reality *are* the business. An arrangement of bricks in the outside world is just that; but inside its own space in a gallery it takes on a presence, even an *authority, where people can engage with it in the sphere of meanings. It is the art space that gives the finite object this power, the power to question or investigate reality or, rather, to be the focus of questioning. And this art space has been thousands of years in development, deriving as it does both from the religious origins of art as a depiction of the unseen world and from art as a 'mirror' by which to understand the world. We come to the picture frame, and now to the nearly empty art space, with an expectancy that some aspect of the world will be reflected or probed. What is reflected is not just bare 'realism', as in a mirror, but an insight into meaning. This is what we look for, because the key to this perplexing life seems, and has always seemed, to lie outside it.

In relation to this art-space, this market place of meanings, the church, which has so long seen itself as the specialist to whom people will turn when they want religion, may seem more concerned to press its own wares than to engage in life's questions. But though the church has been displaced as specialist in the new art-culture, it will not, in principle, be denied a hearing, provided it is willing to join in. An art-space where inquiry happens ought potentially to be a space for *truth.

Engagement as Christians with art

We have, then, a new situation in art. In contrast with the Renaissance, where the church had power and invited the artist to participate, art is now about the business of religion, and the church is the guest. How should the church respond when someone else is making the rules? There are certainly rules, and the chief one puts Christians at a great disadvantage. This is the rule that there are no answers to existential questions, no replies from the other side of the door. The market place dictates that no trader may put others at a disadvantage by claiming finality. What then is the Christian artist to do?

Two common responses should be avoided because they lack integrity. The first is the reactive response, which criticizes the new art as lacking in meaning, humanity, intelligibility or beauty, and does not recognize that there are voices within it that require the courtesy of a hearing. Even more so, if our critique is coming from a commitment to values, then we should show how those values can work artistically today with power and conviction. We cannot simply complain that today is not yesterday.

The second and contrasting response is simply to appease the new art with little attempt at critique. Each innovation inspires some theological rummaging, and reasons are produced for absorbing the latest wonder into the bloodstream of official Christianity. There seems to be a confusion between the desire to respect artists as serious people and an imagined obligation to trust their work as infallible. It is as if St Paul had forgotten that

the Altar to the Unknown God in Athens was not the latest and last word on the subject.

Fortunately, Christians are not bound to the business of approbation or disapproval, nor do they have to engage in the new art as outcasts. Every kind of language is from God, even the confusing tongues of Babel, and there is no reason for Christians not to listen in and learn to speak. But from that point on, their role is not to hide or to conform, since the gospel's effect on art is always to transform.

Some Christian writers have been rather reserved about identifying the Christian presence in art, fearing the corruption that can be visited on art by well-meaning proselytizers. For example, H. R. Rookmaaker, the Dutch art historian who helped free a whole generation from any obligation 'to do evangelistic art', writes, 'Can art be used for Christian purposes? Here I must say emphatically; art must never be used to show the validity of Christianity. Rather the validity of art must be shown through Christianity ... Christian art is nothing special. It is sound, healthy, good art' (*Modern Art*, p. 228). However, Rookmaaker, two pages later, writes, 'Perhaps I was overstating the case when I said that art should never be used to show the validity of Christianity. What I meant was that this is not art's primary function. But if it is going to be used, it ... must do the job well.' Perhaps the mistake here is to think that art can be 'used', apart from what it is in itself, a potential manifestation of God's activity on earth. A parallel instance is to say that Christ's healings were only 'used' to convert, in that they were 'signs' of who he was. It goes against the nature of healing to say that it is a means to some other end.

What is art like, then, if touched by Christ (and his influence spreads far beyond Christians)? Here are a few pointers. 1. Christian communication is intelligible but not exhaustive. *Jesus, God's supreme communication, was as knowable as a flesh and blood man, but also pointed beyond himself to the Father he represented but did not contain. In the same way, Christian art deals with intelligible realities, but is not exhausted by them. The commonplace subject typically is both valued for itself and also points beyond itself. 2. Christian communication serves. God humbled himself to make himself known. Christian artists are not looking to make their viewers run after them, but to bless them with what they see and know.

3. Christian communication is open. The artist is on the same footing as the viewer in relation to the truths shared, just as Jesus the carpenter would have been able to test his own work alongside his clients to see if it was fit for its purpose. Christian art has no private interpretations to which the mind of the artist is key. 4. Christian art, not being a gnostic route to God in which the artist is priest, is grounded in public events in space and time. It need not be about them, but its truth is given and explored in a humble way. Works of *imagination are devised for a world that exists. 5. Christian art has something of God about it. This cannot be forced, and can only result from a real dependence on God, but we can expect character, wisdom, grace and authority – a sense of understanding and a sense of connection.

Since contemporary art characteristically evokes questions rather than presents God-given realities, Christian artists are, it seems, unavoidably involved in a counter-cultural transformation and re-grounding of art. Does this amount to an apologetic?

Christian art from the past nourishes the viewer but seldom seems to challenge present belief. Likewise, a concert audience can listen to Bach profoundly without having their minds changed over the issue of God's existence. Agnosticism is very often the official religion of the cultured. But just as the spiritual void manifested (and sometimes, it seems, carefully orchestrated) in contemporary art seems to speak of God's absence, how much more a Christian presence in art can publicly undermine the boast of human self-sufficiency and demonstrate the abundant life that flows from reconnection with God.

The reformation of art, however, takes time. In any generation, just 'being there' as a faithful witness, doing art well but with little recognition, may be the platform on which others can build. But the collective activity of Christians in an area where people are, so it seems, looking for God, must be powerful. Individual works of art may not persuade, and probably should not be designed to persuade. Since art manifests rather than argues, the witness of Christians in art can be a means of manifesting the grace, life, wisdom and beauty of God, and so be an apologetic that the true apologists can work with.

Bibliography

H. R. Rookmaaker, *Modern Art and the Death of a Culture* (Leicester, 1970); C. Seerveld, *Rainbows for the Fallen World* (Toronto, 1980); David Thistlethwaite, *The Art of God and the Religions of Art* (Carlisle, 1998).

D. E. H. THISTLETHWAITE

ATHANASIUS

Athanasius (c. 297–373), bishop, theologian and apologist, was one of the dominant figures of the fourth century and played a prominent role in defending and explaining key Christian beliefs. His two principal apologetic works are *Against the Nations* and *On the Incarnation*. He also made a detailed defence of Christ's deity in *Against the Arians*.

In *Against the Nations* and *On the Incarnation* Athanasius responds to common Greek religious and philosophical conceptions and presents his understanding of the reasonableness and rationale of the incarnation of the *Logos*. In *On the Incarnation* Athanasius considers three distinct Greek perspectives, those of the Epicureans, Platonists and the Gnostics, and finds each to be defective and opposed to 'the divinely inspired teaching of faith in Christ'. Epicureans argued that the universe was the result of chance and had come into existence on its own. The harmony and order of the universe, Athanasius responds, undercut such a view and point to creation by a reasonable, purposeful God. In the *Timaeus* *Plato taught that God did not create out of nothing, but employed pre-existent matter. As Alvyn Pettersen comments, the god of Plato was 'but a craftsman, unable to make anything unless the raw material to be crafted already exists; and he is dependent upon the pre-existent material, even if that material cannot shape itself and is itself dependent upon the Divine fashioner'. Athanasius insists that God is much more than a fashioner. Rather, God has created all things out of nothing. Finally, Athanasius strongly rejects the Gnostic insistence that matter is inherently evil. Instead, God has used matter to enter the world to redeem it from the distortions and penalties sin entails.

In a wondrous condescension, the uncreated *Logos* has become incarnate in *Jesus Christ. A genuine incarnation deeply troubled Hellenistic philosophers and Arian theologians. In response, Athanasius takes up the common

Greek idea that there is no place in creation where the *Logos* is not present and active and then argues that it is, therefore, neither impossible nor improper for the *Logos* to become incarnate in a particular human body: 'it is not unseemly that the Logos should be in a man and that by him and through him the universe should have light, movement and life ... so he who admits and believes that God's divine Logos is in all and that everything is illumined and moved by him, would not think it unseemly that a human body also should be moved and illumined by him'.

Arius, a presbyter from Alexandria in Egypt, contended that the Father could not share his divine nature with another as he is by definition simple (not made up of parts) and indivisible (incapable of division into parts). Hence, whoever and whatever the Son is, he cannot be eternally God, uncreated and consubstantial with the Father. Athanasius responds by arguing, among other things, that an eternal Father demands an eternal Son. Was God ever without his Word? How could he be? 'Was he, who is light, without radiance? ... God is eternally; then since the Father always is, his brightness exists eternally.' Just as the sun and its light are inseparable, so the Father and the Son are eternally inseparable. To be the sun is to have rays of light. To be the eternal Father is to have an eternal Son.

Not only so, but the church's worship itself points to the deity of the Son. Christian worship makes little sense, is indeed blasphemous, if Christ is only the exalted creature of Arian theology. Yet Christ, Athanasius argues, must be worshipped if the church is to remain true to Scripture. 'The whole earth sings the praises of the Creator and the truth, and blesses him and trembles before him.' Rightly so. But who is this Creator? Does not both Old and New Testament point to the Word, the divine *Logos*, the Word now incarnate in Christ? Thus, Athanasius continued throughout his lifetime to defend the Council of Nicea's decision to describe the Son as *homoousios* or of one essence with the Father. In other words, that while the Father and Son are distinct, they share an essential oneness.

Bibliography

A. Petterson, *Athanasius* (Harrisburg, Pennsylvania, 1995).

C. A. HALL

ATHEISM

Introduction

Atheism is the belief that there are no gods. It is assumed in a variety of philosophies such as, *naturalism, *materialism, *secular humanism and atheistic *existentialism. It is even assumed in various religions such as certain forms of *Buddhism (the Buddha himself was an atheist) and Taoism. The common starting point of each of these philosophies and religions is their denial that any supernatural beings exist. Whatever powers exist in the universe are purely natural and not supernatural.

Western roots

Throughout human history God has been invoked to explain virtually every kind of phenomenon: weather, life, death, victory in war, agricultural prosperity, the motions of the planets and so on. As modern *science progressed, the number of phenomena that seemed to require God to explain them declined. As previously mysterious phenomena succumbed to explanation in terms of nature and its laws, God's explanatory role diminished. For example, as an understanding of the principles of inertia and gravity developed, it was deemed unnecessary to account for the motion of the planets by reference to God. Nonetheless, *Newton claimed that given his understanding of the physical laws of his day, God was needed to enter into the cosmos every now and then to give the planets a boost. Later, however, Pierre Laplace, the premier mathematical astronomer of his day, proclaimed to Napoleon in 1801 that there was no need to bring in God to adjust the cosmic clock as the orbits of planets could be completely accounted for by natural laws. While God was perhaps no longer necessary to explain the order of the planets, he was surely needed to explain the design of the biological world and the unique nature of human beings? This sort of argument was the focus of Darwin's attack. In *Origin of Species*, his theory of natural selection offered an account of the apparent design of the biological world without appeal to a supernatural designer. His *Descent of Man* offered an account of the allegedly unique and otherwise inexplicable status of human beings. By the end of the nineteenth century, God, it seemed, was no longer necessary to explain any significant cosmic or terrestrial phenomena.

What follows about belief in God from his alleged scientific superfluity? Some unbelievers hold that the most reasonable option, lacking a disproof of God's existence, would be *agnosticism in which a person withholds belief in God's existence because of lack of evidence. Nonetheless, many people have taken the alleged absence of evidence for God's existence as grounds for atheism. So the twentieth-century philosopher A. J. Ayer quipped that Darwin made it possible to be an intellectually fulfilled atheist.

Some atheists contend that God's existence can be disproved. This usually finds expression in the so-called problem of *evil, where God and evil are alleged to be logically incompatible. This sort of argument is the only kind that, if successful, would clearly establish God's non-existence; only this sort of argument would clearly ground a principled atheism. Indeed, the existence of evil is the most prominent reason people offer as grounds for their atheism. However, the deductive versions of this argument are demonstratively unsuccessful and the inductive versions are questionable

Not all historical rejections of *theism are grounded in reason, some are more emotional than rational. For example, it is thought that the God of traditional theism providentially orders and righteously judges human lives and could, therefore, be considered a threat to human autonomy. This has motivated some thinkers to revolt against the moral tyranny and domineering sovereignty of God. Also, if there is a God, then humans are not the final arbiters of moral truth and we could not assume a god-like role in the creation of values. In Friedrich *Nietzsche's *Thus Spoke Zarathustra*, Zarathustra exlaims, '*If* there were gods, how could I endure not to be a god! Hence there are no gods.' Jean-Paul *Sartre also seems to reject belief in God because of divine sovereignty's overpowering threat to human freedom. If God sees everything that humans will do, then humans have no choice but to do what God has already foreseen.

Atheists on religion

As a belief in God declined among intellectuals, explanations of religious belief became increasingly naturalistic, that is, without reference to any supernatural forces or entities. Ludwig *Feuerbach developed a 'theology' based on the assumption of naturalism. Believing religion to be 'illusionistic', Feuerbach reduced theology to anthropology, claiming that in the study of religion we learn about human beings, not about some transcendent reality. Humans, he believed, created God in their own image (as a projection of human ideals). Through his alleged unmasking of Christianity, Feuerbach hoped to set human beings on the path of liberation and compassion.

Feuerbach's claim that belief in God is a merely human construct had a huge influence on three monumental atheistic thinkers, Karl Marx, Friedrich Nietzsche and Sigmund *Freud. Supposing God not to exist, these thinkers ask (at least) two questions: What purpose or function does belief in God serve? Is belief in God good or bad?

Through the influence of Feuerbach, Marx came to believe that human beings create religion. He contended that religion is the opium of the masses, a painkiller which treats the symptoms while ignoring the disease, dulling the pain of exploitation but failing to redress the cause of pain and suffering. Religion arises because of legitimate needs but offers a false and illusory remedy. Marx also rejected religious belief because of the social atrocities that have been perpetuated in the name of God. If one could destroy the need for religion by removing economic and social repression, one would thereby eliminate belief in God.

Nietzsche's philosophy begins, first and foremost, with the death of God. With the foundation of theism dislodged, Nietzsche believed that Judeo-Christian *morality would eventually crumble. If there is no God, then where do Christianity, morality and guilt come from? What, if not God, is the source of good and evil? In answering these questions, Nietzsche not only looked at values themselves but also at the value behind the value. What weight, authority or power do values have? Are they life-affirming or life-denying? Are they destructive of what is most fundamentally human or are they creative and satisfying?

Nietzsche's work is a genealogy of morals, what he sometimes calls a 'history of morals', investigating how moralities arise, become approved and maintain their power. How is the history forgotten when moralities are charged with an allegedly trans-historical or transcendental legitimation and power? Nietzsche believed that there are two basic moralities, what he called herd and master moralities. Herd, or slave, morality is that of the weak, the feeble and the enslaved. Herd morality arose in the priestly cultures which denied desire and endorsed the weaknesses of the priest. The priestly morality develops out of fear and hatred of the master class. The impotent, unable to conquer their more worthy and physically powerful foes, sought 'spiritual revenge' by making everything that is opposed to the master class 'good'. Aligning God with their cause, they endorse the eternal damnation of everyone who violates their moral standards. Eternal damnation, the ultimate revenge, shows that Judeo-Christian morality is rooted not in love but in hatred and vengefulness.

Freud, like Nietzsche, looked for the value behind religious belief. Standing behind every human action is our natural *narcissism, the drive for pleasure. Since the unfettered satisfaction of desires would create chaos for human beings, we all join together for a measure of peace and security. But even within civilization our peace and security are threatened, this time by nature. By projecting human qualities and person-like entities onto the forces of nature, we attempt to 'civilize' nature, and we then entreat those various powers as we might entreat persons who would seek to wreak havoc.

The ultimate projection of human properties onto nature is the belief that the ultimate *power is like a father. We wish God into existence, and he 'hears' our prayers, taming nature, helping us accept our fate and rewarding us for our sufferings. Narcissism creates gods as in God all of our desires are satisfied. If we could mature as persons perhaps through psychotherapy, then the need for God would be removed and belief in God would wither away.

The atheist world-view

Atheist philosophers have developed their views about the ultimate nature of *reality into various philosophical systems. How should we understand the nature of the universe without recourse to supernatural powers? First, the atheist must believe that either the universe, or matter and energy, or some other purely natural powers or entities exist eternally. This is because if there were ever a time when there was nothing, then there would be nothing now (because nothing comes from nothing). But something exists now, so there has never been a time at which nothing existed. Since atheists deny the existence of God, then an alternative, such as matter and energy, must exist eternally.

A universe that is nothing but matter and energy in its various manifestations is governed by natural law. Everything that occurs follows the dictates of natural law. The universe, according to the atheist, is closed off to *miracles or perhaps even to free will. Accounts of free will often assume the existence of a part of the human, a soul or spirit, which is not part of the cycle of cause and effect that characterizes the natural world. But if everything is a manifestation of matter and energy as guided by natural law, it is extremely difficult (if not impossible) to develop a robust account of free will. So some atheists deny free will outright and some modify their definition of free will so that it is compatible with human actions being determined (this view is often called 'compatibilism' or 'soft *determinism').

Equally perplexing for the atheist is how to account for the human mind in a way that is sensitive to our characteristic mental life yet consistent with their commitment to matter and energy as the building blocks of reality. The problem for materialist conceptions of the mind is that mental properties (such as the feel of pain or the sensation of redness) seem quite different from physical properties. The subjective qualities of our mental life (our mental 'stuff') seem irreducible to the objective qualities of matter and energy (our brain 'stuff'). Some atheists view this problem as fundamentally irresolvable but others view it as an opportunity for discovery. Indeed, at many major universities vast sums of money are being spent to understand the physical nature of the mind.

Atheists must also develop an understanding of morality which does not appeal to any supernatural realities. Up until the twentieth century, the majority of people believed that morality has something to do with God. It was either the will of God, or it was rooted in our created nature or grounded in God's purposes for human beings. If there is no God, then what is the foundation of morality? One atheistic response to the rejection of the divine foundations of morality is relativism, which claims that there is no single, universal standard of morality that is applicable to all persons in all cultures throughout all of time. Morality is, instead, relative to time, place and circumstance. Nietzsche and Richard *Rorty are relativists.

Not all atheists, however, are relativists. Some atheists have offered their own, non-theistic, foundations for morality. Of the many varieties on offer, let us consider Aristotelianism, social contract theories. Aristotelian approaches to *ethics ground morality in human nature. They approach morality in terms of virtues (strength of character) rather in terms of rules or duties. The virtues, e.g. courage, moderation, wisdom and *justice, are character traits which fulfil our nature as human beings. Vices, such as cowardice, immoderation, foolishness and injustice, are character traits that diminish us as human beings, leaving us to live impoverished lives.

Social contract theorists find inspiration in the ideas of Thomas Hobbes. They contend that right and wrong are nothing more than the agreement among rationally self-interested individuals. According to this view there is no higher moral standard than (rational) human consensus. Taking on the constraints of morality is viewed as rational because of the fear of living among people whose desires are unchecked by morality.

Conclusion

Even if God is not necessary to explain cosmic or biological order, belief in God may be rational for two reasons. First, rational belief in God may not require the support of quasi-scientific arguments (or any arguments at all). Secondly, being able to explain phenomena (e.g. the weather or the orbit of the moon) naturalistically has little logical bearing on whether or not God exists. In addition, there are theistic arguments that attempt to demonstrate the inadequacy of the atheistic contention that the universe may be accounted for along strictly naturalistic lines. Theodicies and defences are attempts to reconcile God's existence with the fact of evil. And theists have developed powerful critiques of atheistic moral visions.

As theists approach atheism, they should consider it with the care with which they would like the atheist to approach theism. The arguments of the atheist should be treated fairly and charitably. The theist should also learn from the atheist wherever appropriate; e.g. there is a great deal to be learned from Marx, Freud and Nietzsche. However, neither willingness to learn nor charity preclude the Christian's forceful yet reasoned response to atheism.

Bibliography

M. Buckley, *At the Origins of Modern Atheism* (New Haven, CT, 1990); A. Flew, *God and Philosophy* (New York, 1966); S. Freud, *The Future of an Illusion* (New York, 1961); M. Martin, *Atheism: A Philosophical Justification* (Philadelphia, 1990); F. Nietzsche, *The Genealogy of Morals* (New York, 1989); M. Westphal, *Suspicion and Faith: The Religious Uses of Modern Atheism* (New York, 1998).

K. J. CLARK

ATHENAGORAS

Athenagoras was an apologist of the middle second century, whose name, evoking Paul's preaching in Athens (Acts 17:16–34), points to his distinctive place in Christian apology. His attractive essay, 'Plea for the Christians' (c. 177) represents a turning-point in early Christian theology, in pioneering the use of philosophical reflection as a basis for apology and notably in developing the Logos ('Word') motif beyond its scriptural use.

Athenagoras objected to the unjust treatment of Christians, accused for their name rather than their deeds, and famously frames the objections made to Christian faith as 'atheism, Thyestian feasts and Oedipean incest'. Christians are not 'atheists', because they worship the one true God ('the God who is'), refusing to worship any creature (God as 'the uncreated one' is distinguished from all else). Athenagoras cites support from the Greek philosophers for such *monotheism and for exposing the absurdities of *polytheism. The one God is known to Christian faith as Father, Son and Holy Spirit, Athenagoras contends, and the notion of Logos as the 'expression' of the Father in the Son and the Spirit as their 'effluence' offers philosophical grounding for this distinctively Christian understanding of God.

That Christians were charged with orgiastic immorality reflects the profound misunderstandings in surrounding society of their worship and relationships. Athenagoras argues that the Christians' life of mutual love is not in the least immoral, but reflects the goodness of the one true God, who lives in the communion of Father, Son and Spirit. He makes a sustained attack on the caprice and immorality of the gods – and their recent invention by humans, who in many cases have turned mere mortals into deities.

Athenagoras makes much of contrasts between Christian and pagan *morality by pointing out that Christians actually practise chastity, whether as virgins or in marriage, and implying that divorce is unknown among them. Christians know that they must give account to their Creator, and so they seek to live in purity and goodness, utterly rejecting murder and cruelty, such as are seen in the games, and not abandoning their children, as the pagans do. Above all, they know that the true end of human beings is to contemplate the love and glory of God, which resurrection in Christ makes possible.

Athenagoras' contribution to Christian apology was to open the way for the integration of biblical and philosophical testimonies to God's truth in Christ, and its implications for authentic living.

Bibliography

L. W. Barnard, *Athenagoras: A Study in Second Century Christian Apologetics*, Théologie Historique 18 (Paris, 1972); M. A. Dawoud, 'Fathers of the School of Alexandria: Athenagoras', *Coptic Church Review* 12.4 (1991).

C. H. SHERLOCK

ATOMISM

Atomism is the belief that the form and qualities of all material objects can be explained by reference to a basic physical unit: the atom. Atomism is frequently associated with *materialism, the belief that all objects can be exhaustively explained by referring only to material causes. Often atomists also became associated with completely naturalistic notions regarding the existence of the cosmos. Such naturalists could postulate eternally existing atoms, sometimes viewed as indestructible, interacting only through physical laws as forming the complete basis for cosmic history.

Atomism has a long history in philosophy. In the middle of the fourth century BC, Leucippus and Democritus became the first atomists. They postulated indivisible atoms that had no other qualities beyond those required by existence, such as weight. All physical qualities were the result of the quantity and combination of atoms. This separates them from later atomists,

such as *Locke, who allowed atoms to have certain primary qualities. These qualities could be combined with those of other atoms to produce new substances and help explain the qualities of the new substance. Even early in its history, atomism came to be associated with *atheism. Epicurus (341–270 BC) and the Epicureans used atomism to dispense with the need for a creator god and a non-material soul. For this reason, early Christians viewed such forms of atomism, best known to them in the writings of Lucretius (94–50 BC), as incompatible with Christianity.

In the early history of *science, atomism was a useful theoretical postulate in the development of modern chemistry and physics. Boyle and Dalton are two examples of scientists who successfully used atomism to advance chemistry and physics. Boyle preferred mechanistic explanations for natural events to more *Platonic explanations, which relied on non-material causation. As a committed Christian, Boyle tried to limit mechanistic explanations in science, but many atomists were not so careful. Atomism remains a useful theoretical way to think about chemical changes. As in ancient times, atomism naturally fits well with non-theistic world-views. Boyle and other early Christian scientists often inadvertently made way for the destruction of the long and fruitful association between Christianity and science. Contemporary popular atheism often assumes a vague atomism as an explanation for the cosmos.

Many atomists were committed to the belief that objects were best explained by reducing them to their component parts. *Philosophically, it is dubious that knowing that the sun is made of hot gas tells the investigator what the star *is*. Apologetically, this form of reductionism can reduce the cosmos to the sum of its parts. Amongst other problems, when applied to human beings, this idea can lead to serious difficulties in *ethics. For Christians, human beings are not just the sum of the chemicals that make them up, nor are the notions 'human' and 'humanity' polite fictions to avoid ethical barbarism. Atomism has few resources to allow for ethically meaningful universal categories.

Despite historical associations, modern physics and atomic theory have moved far beyond historical, philosophical atomism. Science has not found any basic physical particles that can be the foundation for a full explanation of form and substance. However, many people who wish to maintain both *naturalism and materialism in science continue to think of the cosmos as if it can be explained with reference to such actual particles.

Apologetically, traditional atomism is incompatible with traditional Christian ideas such as the existence of a soul with the power to act in the physical world. God himself would have to be material in an atomic theory universally applied. However, this would present fatal difficulties for such important notions as his being omnipresent or omnipotent. A god composed of atoms could not be everywhere, since he would have physical location. This 'atomic' god would also be potentially able to be destroyed since he would be composed of parts. He would also be subject to his own physical laws. As a tentative 'theory of everything' atoms also leave little room for a Creator active in the material world after the creation of the primary atoms and physical laws.

Generally, Christians have responded to atomism by adopting either a Platonic or Aristotelian view of matter. In other words, apologists have asserted some 'form' not reducible to matter that is a necessary part of explanations. Contemporary versions of these ideas, such as modern Thomism, still form viable philosophic options for the Christian. Christians can also demonstrate that science shows that atoms, if viewed as little beads from which the universe is ultimately composed, do not exist. There is no material atom at the bottom of the cosmos. Atomism in forms like those advanced by Boyle can be a helpful thought experiment, but hopefully it will soon be exorcised from the popular mind as a universal explanation for the cosmos.

Bibliography

A. G. M. van Melson, 'Atomism', in P. Edwards (ed.), *The Encyclopedia of Philosophy* (New York, 1972), pp. 193–198; A. A. Long and D. N. Sedley, *The Hellenistic Philosophers* (Cambridge, 1987); N. R. Pearcey and C. Thaxton, *The Soul of Science* (Wheaton, 1994).

J. M. N. REYNOLDS

ATONEMENT

Webster's Dictionary defines atonement in the following ways: 1. (obsolete) reconciliation; 2. the reconciliation of God and man through the sacrificial death of Jesus Christ; 3. reparation for an offence or injury; 4. (Christian Science), the exemplifying of man's oneness with God. Atonement is thus a word that, while it is somewhat uncommon in modern discourse, nevertheless resonates with themes of today's world. We could discuss issues of reconciliation and reparation in areas such as race relations, business and politics.

Images of the atonement can be found in contemporary film, music and art. Recent films such as *The Passion* (2004) and *The Last Temptation of Christ* (1988) have stirred up many deep emotions. Older movies such as Fellini's *La Dolce Vita* (1959) have been similarly controversial. The film opens with a suspended statue of Christ transported by helicopter above Rome. This effigy-like image is crudely juxtaposed with sensuous bodies of bikini-clad women sunbathing on the ground below. Fellini's parody of the ascension expresses his cynicism very powerfully.

Some films are not religious in content but are equally suggestive. *The Graduate* (1967) provides a contemporary view of atonement, or how to be at one with oneself. In it a college graduate's identity crisis is resolved through sex. Other films contain Christ figures that can be useful for apologetics. The Snow Shovel Murderer in *Home Alone* (1990), R. P. Murphy in *One Flew Over the Cuckoo's Nest* (1975), and Jim Casy in *Grapes of Wrath* (1940) could all be used this way. Although contemporary film can provide multiple entry points to engage today's culture, we need to use it judiciously. The apologetic potential of movies may be limited because films from one generation may appear dated in the next.

Contemporary music also offers opportunities to engage in apologetics. Consider Madonna's album *Like a Prayer* (1989) which represents a sexualized Christ. In her album, she enters a church, meets a black statue of *Jesus that comes to life, and subsequently makes love to him.

Contemporary art is similarly provocative. Dali's painting *Christ of St John of the Cross* (1951), often regarded as a reverent depiction of Christ, offers a surrealist rather than a biblical interpretation of the atonement. Serrano's painting *Piss Christ* (1987) is more graphic because it depicts a close-up photograph of the crucifixion submerged in a jar of urine. Serrano succeeded in shocking audiences by making a revered symbol appear obscene and then by calling it art. Da Silva Costa's immense statue of *Christ the Redeemer* (1931) overlooking Rio de Janeiro presents yet another Christ. He appears as a political liberator.

Clearly life today offers many opportunities to engage in discussion about atonement. In this article, we will briefly discuss the biblical view of the atonement, then consider the theory of penal substitution and its detractors, and finally discuss various objections to the atonement from major world-views.

The biblical view

Atonement is derived from the Hebrew verb *kpr* which occurs 102 times in the OT (mostly, but not entirely, in ritual contexts in Exodus, Leviticus and Numbers; cf. 1 Chr. 6:49; 2 Chr. 29:45; Ezek. 43:20). The main idea is of repairing or reconciling the relationship between God and humanity through Israel's sacrificial system. Lev. 16 describes five offerings on the Day of Atonement which atone for the sin of the tabernacle (Lev. 1 – 15) and of the nation (Lev. 17 – 27). A key verse is Lev. 17:11, 'For the life of the creature is in the blood, and I have given it to you to make atonement for yourselves on the altar; it is the blood that makes atonement for one's life.' Atonement here is sacrificial and substitutionary and involves shed blood. Though sin ruins lives, devastates communities, alienates people from God, and deserves his wrath (and ours), atonement covers it all.

Although the word 'atonement' occurs three times in the NT (Rom. 3:25; Heb. 2:17; 9:5), the language is quite varied in this respect. Luke refers to forgiveness (Acts 2:38), the Suffering Servant (Acts 8:32–35), hanging on a tree (Acts 5:30; cf. Deut. 21:22; Gal. 3:13) and a risen Lord (Acts 2:32). John uses sacrificial imagery (John 1:29; 10:11, 15, 17–18; 11:50–52). Paul speaks of redemption (Gal. 3:13–14; Eph. 1:7), propitiation or a sacrifice of atonement (Rom. 3:25), disarming *evil (Col. 2:13–15; cf. 1 John 3:8) and ransom (1 Tim. 2:6; cf. Mark 10:45). Heb. 2:17 identifies Jesus with the high priest, but 1 John 2:2; 4:10 identifies him with OT sacrificial victims. The Gk word the NIV translates as atonement is *hilasterion*, which indicates how God takes the initiative to remove obstacles to his relationship with humanity (Rom. 3:25; Heb. 2:17) and where atonement occurs (Heb. 9:5).

For apologetic purposes, the Gk word *kat-*

allasso (NIV 'reconciled') resonates loudly with the contemporary life (Rom. 5:10–11; 2 Cor. 5:17–18). It describes how hostile relationships are exchanged for friendships. God is the one who initiates reconciliation, and he alone can achieve it (2 Cor. 5:18–19). Human beings respond to God's initiative and can become reconciled to him (Rom. 5:10–11). Contemporary life is filled with broken relationships through divorce, management–labour relations and international hostilities. Each of these areas provide opportunities to discuss the greater reconciliation that God has accomplished through Christ. The fact that God has already pulled down the wall of his own hostility to humanity provides a compelling reason for men and women to pull down their own walls.

Penal substitution theory

This theory emphasizes the effect of the cross on God himself and on humankind. Penal (from Lat. *poena*, 'penalty') refers to the penalty for human rebellion against God. Substitution (from Lat. *substituere*, 'to set up in place of') indicates that one person serves as a representative or substitute for another. On the cross, Jesus stood in our place and bore the penalty for our sin. As our substitute, Jesus offered himself as a sacrifice for sin to satisfy the demands of God's *justice (Rom. 3:25–26), and he also offered forgiveness of sin to the world through faith (Rom. 5:15–16). David Wells distinguishes two key aspects of this view: 'In Pauline thought, man is alienated from God by sin and God is alienated from man by wrath. It is in the substitutionary death of Christ that sin is overcome and wrath averted, so that God can look on man without displeasure and man can look on God without fear. Sin is expiated and God is propitiated' (*The Search for Salvation* [Downers Grove, 1978], p. 29). The Bible describes God's satisfaction for sin through divine substitution (Mark 8:31; 9:12; Luke 24:45–46; John 3:16; Acts 2:23; 3:18; 1 Cor. 15:3). Wayne Grudem (*Systematic Theology* [Leicester and Grand Rapids, 1994], p. 580) explains four ways that the cross meets our needs as sinners: Christ died as a sacrifice for us (Heb. 9:26); Christ died as a propitiation for our sins (1 John 4:10); Christ reconciled us to God (2 Cor. 5:18–19); and Christ redeemed us from the power of sin and *Satan (Mark 10:45; Heb. 2:15).

Contemporary objections to penal substitution

Why is atonement necessary? If human beings are capable of forgiving one another through acts of goodwill, then why is God not able to do the same? Answers to this question today remain frustrating. Consider the analogy of a car crashing into another. The guilty driver could request an act of goodwill from the other. Such an act of forgiveness might appear noble but would fail to deal with the basic problem that someone must pay for the car repairs. Similarly, there is a price to pay for the profound damage between a holy God and sinful humanity (Lev. 19:1–2; Hab. 1:13; Matt. 5:48).

Is it not unjust and abusive to punish an innocent party for the crime of another? William Placher ('Christ Takes Our Place') notes that 'we all bear one another's burdens from time to time, even burdens of sin and guilt. I do something wrong and you forgive me . . . I fall down on the job and you pick up the slack.' So, it is not as unreasonable as it first sounds to let the innocent take the sins of the guilty. The Bible indicates that Jesus voluntarily sacrificed himself (John 15:13; 10:17–18) and that his Father suffered too (Luke 23:44; John 17:21).

How can atonement change a God of wrath into a God of love? This drives a wedge between God's love and his wrath. M. J. Erickson notes that 'by requiring the penalty himself, he demonstrated how great are his holiness and justice. By providing that payment himself, he manifested the extent of his love' (*Christian Theology* [Grand Rapids, 1998], p. 835). God's holiness and his love are fully satisfied through the atonement. Without his love there would have been no atonement in the first place. John Stott's phrase 'divine self-satisfaction through divine self-substitution' captures the heart of the atonement (*The Cross of Christ* [Downers Grove, 1986], p. 159). In other words, self-satisfaction refers to God's justice and holiness, and self-substitution to his love and mercy.

How can one event have universal significance for all time and eternity? One recent suggestion has been that God gains moral authority over sin, temptation and death for all humanity through his own suffering. If suffering then becomes the means by which God has moral authority, then he must be 'lacking in authority' until he suffers (D. A. Carson, *The Gagging of God*, p. 327). V. White takes this view, but fails to handle either the NT's view of Jesus himself as our justification, redemption and propitiation (Mark 10:45; Rom. 3:21–26) or the unfolding drama of God's redemptive purpose throughout all Scripture (*Atonement*, pp. 327–328).

Objections from different world-views

Hinduism

If we accept that Christ suffered for the sins of others (2 Cor. 5:21), then we call into question the *Hindu doctrine of karma, which holds that good deeds create good merit and vice versa. So if Christ had 'good' karma, then his unjust suffering is inexplicable, particularly if he bore the sins of others (1 Pet. 3:18). For many Hindus the cross is not so much a scandal as a fascination. How could Christ take on the suffering of others?

If we accept that Christ rose from the dead (1 Cor. 15:4), then we call into question the Hindu notion of an endless cycle of birth, death and rebirth. His resurrection guarantees a new life and a peace (Rom. 6:4; 5:1) that the Hindu wheel of life cannot offer. David Clark and Norman Geisler summarize the genuine hope the cross offers: 'the hope for genuine personal transformation, social revolution, and cosmic reconciliation comes not from us but from God. Through the cross of Christ, the evil we all experience and long to overcome has already been defeated' (*Apologetics in the New Age: A Christian Critique of Pantheism* [Grand Rapids, 1990], p. 235).

Islam

If Christ died on the cross, then we challenge the *Islamic view that prophets are not defeated by their enemies. Perhaps this explains why the Qur'an claims that Jesus was not crucified (Sura 4:157–158). The crucifixion is also offensive because it appears to question God's sovereignty. If Christ died for the sin of the world (1 Pet. 2:24; 3:18), then we challenge the Muslim rejection of original sin. Another objection for Muslims is that because God is merciful he can forgive without an atonement. This objection, however, misinterprets Jesus' voluntary self-sacrifice (John 10:17–1) and God's holy and just nature which forms the basis for his forgiveness.

Buddhism

Buddhists are taught to revere life in all its forms and so a substitutionary sacrifice is inevitably objectionable to them. Also, it makes no sense to a *Buddhist to talk about sin against a personal God. The way to explain the atonement to Buddhists is in terms of a transfer of merit (*pattidana*). Christ was perfect, therefore he generated an infinite quantity of *kusala* (good deeds), to negate all the *akusala* (evil deeds) of all humanity for all time. And, because Christ was God incarnate, he not only could generate sufficient *kusala*, but he could also transfer its merits to others. This transfer of merits was possible because God had transferred human guilt on to Christ.

Relativism

Atonement is objectionable to relativists because it makes absolute truth-claims about things such as original sin, divine justice and substitutionary sacrifice (Rom. 3:23–26; Heb. 9:26; 10:10). Relativists do not believe in an ethical system that permits judgments but, by definition, must tolerate such absolute claims! Kafka's novel *The Trial* (1925) offers a unique approach to responding to *relativism. A world without moral absolutes still has to confront the issue of guilt and Kafka offers an arresting example of this difficulty. The main character, K, is arrested without reason. Tragically, he feels shame but is unable to identify his guilt. Though psychologists today might suggest that K needs healing rather than forgiveness, Kafka hints indirectly that perhaps forgiveness is K's real need. At the close of the novel, K notices someone at a distance who 'leaned abruptly far forward and stretched out both arms still farther. Who was it? A friend? A good man? Someone who sympathized? Someone who wanted to help?' Is Kafka suggesting that K's guilt should be addressed by a person rather than by the legal system?

Feminism

Feminists would claim that the doctrine of the atonement is unjust because it sanctions submission to evil rather than resistance to sexual and domestic abuse. In response, the Bible shows that in his life Jesus was a liberator for the socially oppressed (Luke 4:18), and in his death he defeated evil (2 Cor. 10:4–5; Col. 2:13–15).

Bibliography

C. Brown, 'The Atonement: Healing in Postmodern Society', *Interpretation* 53.1 (1999); D. Essary, 'A Response to a Gospel Account of Our Father and the Blood Atonement of Jesus as written by Michael Shanbour' (1999), <http://www.tektonics.org/shanbour01.html>; P. Holding, 'A Defense of the Doctrine of Atonement' <http://www.tektonics.org/atonedefense.html>, accessed August 2005; T. Keller, 'Shame and Grace: Scenes of Forgiveness', Tape No. 712 (26 October 1997), <http://www.redeemer.com>; W. Placher, 'Christ Takes Our Place. Rethinking Atonement', *Interpretation* 53.1 (1999); W. Spencer, 'Christ's Sacrifice as Apologetic: An Application of Heb. 10:1–18', *Journal of the Evangelical Theological Society* 40.2 (1997); T. Torrance, 'The Atonement: The Singularity of Christ and the Finality of the Cross: The Atonement and the Moral Order', in N. M. de S. Cameron (ed.) *Universalism and the Doctrine of Hell: Papers Presented at the Fourth Edinburgh Conference in Christian Dogmatics* (Carlisle, 1992); W. A. VanGemeren (ed.), *New International Dictionary of Old Testament Theology and Exegesis* (Grand Rapids, 1997); V. White, *Atonement and Incarnation: An Essay in Universalism and Particularity* (Cambridge, 1991).

J. D. LINNELL

AUGUSTINE

Augustine (354–430), bishop of Hippo (modern Annaba, in Algeria) is the leading Latin theologian of the patristic age, and offered defences of catholic Christianity on a wide range of topics against pagan critics without, and unorthodox Christians within, the church. He was converted to mainstream Christianity in 386, having spent more than nine years as a catechumen of Manichaeism, a sect which, although it claimed to be Christian, was theologically dualist, seeing this world as a mixture of two co-equal kingdoms of good and *evil. From this belief Augustine was liberated by the reading of Neoplatonic philosophy, which convinced him that evil was not something positive but only a corruption of good – total corruption would be non-existence. This meant that God was the sole Creator of the universe, and evil occurred only by his permissive will. With his conversion, Augustine came to regard the teaching of the canonical Scriptures as the principal intellectual and moral *authority for humanity, but he did not reject *Platonic philosophy. He says in his *Confessions* that while the Neoplatonic writings had taught him to seek for *truth beyond material forms, the New Testament both confirmed the truth which Platonists taught and commended divine grace, which teaches *humility. Philosophy had to take second place to revealed truth. Nevertheless, Augustine continued to regard the Platonists with respect and in his work *On Christian Teaching* declared that any truth which was consistent with Christian doctrine should not cause alarm, but be appropriated by Christians as their own rightful property. This meant that there need be, in principle, no clash between faith and reason. Faith depends upon authority, but reason is necessary to determine whether this authority is genuine. The Manichees claimed that they appealed simply to reason and did not impose a blind authority on the believer, but for Augustine the issue was not so simple. Early in his Christian career he had had to establish a ground for belief against the scepticism of the Academic philosophers, who held that, except in mathematics, *certainty was impossible. He was able to do so by appealing to the fact of *doubt: 'A non-existent being cannot be mistaken; if I am mistaken, I therefore am', which anticipates, though apparently did not inspire, *Descartes' argument, 'I think, therefore I am.' However, as a mature Christian thinker, Augustine was always conscious of the need for divine grace for every good action of the human mind, including belief. We are free to act, but only through the power of God: 'God's mercy has gone before, so that you may will; but when you will, it is indeed you who will'. This assertion of the need for grace follows naturally from Augustine's doctrine of creation. He maintained that Gen. 1:2 makes it clear that there cannot be any 'formation' of the world from a pre-existent formless matter, as Platonism holds. Creation is not the imposition of form on the formless, but the spontaneous appearance of beings by the will of God, who is true Being. This necessarily excludes any notion of a natural divinity of the human soul, such as Platonism tended to assume. If the soul is divine, it is by participation in God and not by its own nature. Participation is itself a Platonic concept, which Augustine may have

taken from Plotinus, but he radically Christianizes it by emphasizing that the creation of human beings in God's image and likeness is by the action of the whole *Trinity. We are made children of God by the incarnation, and it is only by the incarnation that we come to the state which Augustine calls deification: 'To make human beings gods, He was made man who was God.'

Creation, for Augustine, is the calling into being from non-existence of concrete realities, wholly subject to the will of God. In this connection, Augustine speaks of *rationes seminales* (the seeds of created things) scattered throughout the universe and capable of development under the directing power of God. This condition enabled Augustine to reconcile the apparently contradictory statements of *Wisdom* (which for Augustine was a canonical book) that God created the world from formless matter (11:17 [18]) and Gen. 1:1 that he created heaven and earth. He says, 'It is not because formless matter is prior in time to things formed from it, since they are both created simultaneously together, both the thing made and what it was made out of, but because that which something is made from is still prior as the source, even if not in time, to what is made from it'. Unformed matter is almost non-being and never exists apart from forms, which forms exist, by participation, in the mind of God. Augustine uses various words for them: *formae, ideae, species, rationes* or *regulae*. The names derive from Platonic philosophy as the models from which existent things are created. They subsist in God's intellect and are eternal, unchangeable and necessary. They have no beginning or end, but are the causes of all things which have a beginning or end; accordingly, they are timeless, and exist in eternity. Augustine's forms resemble those of Plato, but with an essential difference: for him there is no realm of forms in the original Platonic sense. Augustine's ideas do not provide models for a divine artisan to work from; rather they are plans in the mind of God, from which he develops his purposes in the created world of time, preserves and rules all beings in existence, and brings to development the *rationes seminales* which he has scattered throughout the universe.

Inevitably, this raises the problem of divine providence and *predestination. Augustine's God is no absentee landlord of the universe, but an active presence, who acts in the way suitable for a particular time. In that sense what men call *miracles are simply actions of God in a particular set of circumstances. In his works *On True Religion* (389–90) and *On the Usefulness of Belief* (391–2), Augustine had declared that miracles such as Christ performed no longer took place. In his later years, his attitude changed. In 416 the Spanish priest Orosius, returning to Africa from Palestine, brought with him relics of St Stephen the Protomartyr. In the following years, memorial shrines sprang up in Africa at which miraculous cures were effected which Augustine accepted, though he required written evidence to confirm their genuineness. For him, however, the greatest miracle is the world itself and the providence with which God governs it, which is not thwarted by human sin, 'since in his providence and omnipotence God assigns to each individual his own gifts, and knows how to turn to good account the good and evil alike'. Peace is the order of God's universe, and is maintained through all disturbances, until the elect arrive at the heavenly Jerusalem, the city of peace.

God foreknew – or rather, knew from eternity – those who would respond to his call, and prepared their wills to enable them to choose freely. This did not make them any less free, when they chose; but when Adam sinned – by free choice – in Eden, the whole human race, his descendants, mysteriously participated in his sin and deserved eternal damnation. Out of this mass of sin, a few – and Augustine emphasizes how few they are – are elected to salvation which is, martyrdom apart, conveyed by baptism, the sacrament instituted by Christ. This doctrine in Augustine's lifetime shocked Pelagius and his supporters like Julian of Eclanum, who declined to believe in a God who was 'a persecutor of children'. It troubled Augustine himself, but he declined to renounce it, and his doctrine of original sin, which included an original guilt, became characteristic of Western theology during the Middle Ages, was maintained at the Reformation by Catholics and Reformers alike, and still finds supporters.

It is arguable that the climax of Augustine's theology is to be found in his *De Trinitate*, begun in 399 and only completed in the 420s. In this work he seeks to understand the mystery of the Trinity by the image of God in man: memory, understanding and will, three mental qualities which make up one life and one substance. Each contains the whole being and constitutes the whole being; but for the image in man to be perfected, it must participate in the life of God. It is this participation which 'divinizes' the human soul, insofar as a created being can be raised to the ontological status of its Creator.

Bibliography

G. Bonner, *St Augustine of Hippo: Life and Controversies*, 3rd edn (Norwich, 2002); J. Burnaby, *Amor Dei: A Study of St Augustine's Teaching on the Love of God as the Motive of Christian Life* (London, 1938); P. Brown, *Augustine of Hippo. A Biography* (Berkeley, 2000); H. Chadwick, *Augustine* (Oxford, 1991); M. T. Clark, *Augustine* (London, 1994); A. D. Fitzgerald (ed.), *Augustine through the Ages: An Encyclopedia* (Grand Rapids and Cambridge, 1999); É. Gilson, *The Philosophy of St Augustine* (ET London, 1960); S. Lancel, *Saint Augustine* (ET London, 2002); C. Harrison, *Augustine: Christian Truth and Fractured Humanity* (Oxford, 2000); R. A. Markus, *Speculum: History and Society in the Theology of Saint Augustine* (Cambridge, 1989); T. F. Martin, *Our Restless Heart. The Augustinian Tradition* (London, 2003).

G. BONNER

AUTHORITY

The issue of authority, the basis upon which any theological statement can be made, command enforced or action performed, is perhaps the most basic of all in theology.

In the OT, while the Lord frequently speaks and acts directly, both in judgment and deliverance, he also does so through his appointed representatives, the prophets, priests and kings of ancient Israel. These figures acted and were held accountable by God as his anointed agents in the history of redemption, and they find their fulfilment in Christ, who is the definitive locus of God's authority in history, God manifest in the flesh acting to save his people.

While authority in biblical times is more of a given than a problem to the biblical writers, with the close of the apostolic era the issue became acute, with various answers being offered to questions about the *canon and the correct interpretation of the Christian gospel. The early church quickly settled on a threefold approach to authority: apostolic succession, whereby institutional authority resided in particular apostolic sees and was handed down from bishop to bishop; the rule of faith, a brief, anti-gnostic summary of the basic Christian message which appears to have circulated in an oral form throughout the Mediterranean area by the end of the second century; and the canon of Scripture, which took several centuries to reach final form but whose core documents were established at a very early point. Tensions with this approach were evident from the start with, e.g., the problem of the relationship between bishops who conformed in times of persecution and those lay people who stood firm and subsequently enjoyed the same status as martyrs. This culminated in the Donatist controversy, which addressed, among other things, the nature of church authority in relation to the personal godliness of its office bearers.

The strongly ecclesiological conception of authority in the early church had a number of consequences. Ecumenical councils formulated *creeds, particularly in relation to matters of the Trinity and Christology, whose content was assumed to be the correct explication of scriptural teaching and which thus became normative for the Christian church. Ultimately, this ecclesiological tendency bore fruit in the rise to prominence of the Roman see, a development formally linked to Peter's role in founding the church in the city but actually just as dependent upon Rome's secular political pre-eminence. With this development, the Bishop of Rome came to hold particular definitive authority in matters of the interpretation of the faith. This was one point which facilitated the break between the Western and Eastern churches, with the East holding only to the first seven ecumenical councils and rejecting the kind of unique authority claimed by Rome. In addition, through Rome's development of an elaborate sacramental system and overarching emphasis upon the vital unity of the visible church, salvation was effectively denied to all outside of its institutional boundaries. While a number of political crises in the Middle Ages led to a movement to root church *power once more in ecumenical councils, Rome was able to reassert its authority in the fifteenth century.

The Reformation represented a significant crisis in church authority. With their battle cries of grace alone, Scripture alone, Christ alone, the Reformers undermined the sacramental system of the church and rejected Rome's claim to be the final authority in matters of the interpretation of the faith. Their position was, however, more subtle than a superficial reading of their claims might suggest, particularly with regard to tradition. We need to distinguish between types of tradition, the dogmatic tradition of the church based on biblical exegesis (e.g. the ecumenical creeds) and the dogmatic tradition of the church based upon the more independent statements and definitions of the papacy (e.g. dogmas such as the Immaculate Conception). The Reformers, while rejecting the latter, were careful to enter into careful and respectful dialogue with the former, avoiding the anti-historical and anti-traditional excesses implied by modern-day appeals to 'No Creed but the Bible'.

Alongside the Reformers, a number of other groups arose, many of them now bracketed together as Anabaptists. They argued for a more direct, charismatic authority rooted not in notions of the uniqueness and sufficiency of Scripture, but in the direct leading of the Spirit, a position which not infrequently rendered the Bible either redundant or, in extreme cases, actually opposed to current divine leading. In addition, the rise of Socinianism, a precursor of the Unitarian movement, witnessed the development of a strongly literal, anti-metaphysical approach to the interpretation of Scripture. This led to the abandonment of many classic Christian doctrines such as the Trinity and the incarnation and to a consequent reconstruction of notions of atonement and salvation.

In the seventeenth and eighteenth centuries, the traditional understanding of authority came under attack from various sources. *Biblical criticism, ironically fuelled by Protestantism's high regard for the text of Scripture, became in the hands of figures such as Richard Simon and Benedict *Spinoza the means of undermining appeals to the authority of the biblical text. New philosophical ideas (*empiricism, *idealism, *rationalism) all served in their different ways to undermine traditional religious *epistemology. The authority of the institutional church was further undermined not simply by the biblicism of Protestantism but also by the satirical attacks of philosophers such as *Voltaire, which made traditional notions of authority implausible.

Perhaps the most influential thinker of this period was Immanuel *Kant, who overcame the radical scepticism of David *Hume by proposing a distinction between the real world (the noumenal) and the perceived world (the phenomenal) and by relegating religious claims to the realm of *ethics. Kant thus paved the way for a strongly anti-metaphysical approach to theology which also drew attention to the subjective contribution of the knowing subject to knowledge. The effect on traditional theology was devastating, as revealed in Friedrich *Schleiermacher's attempt to reconstruct theology in light of the Kantian critique. For Schleiermacher, Scripture is authoritative, but only because it is an account of a particularly pure form of the human self-consciousness of God. As Ludwig *Feuerbach later argued (providing a springboard for Karl Marx's critique of religion), this made talk about God into little more than talk about human beings. This is surely the great issue raised by Kant and, by and large, accepted by all of liberal thinkers.

In the midst of all this, evangelical Protestantism continued to assert the basic authority of Scripture as being *revelation from God, most influentially in the writings of nineteenth-century Princeton, where the philosophical categories of *Scottish Common Sense Realism were adapted to articulate the notion of scriptural infallibility in an *Enlightenment context. In the case of Presbyterianism and Lutheranism, the churches also maintained a high view of the creeds and confessions of the early church and their specific denominations. Nevertheless, the rise of revivalism and conversionism in the eighteenth and nineteenth centuries also lent a strongly subjective dimension to much discussion of authority. Whereas institutional Protestantism maintained a high view of education and of the teaching offices of the church, revivalism tended to place more authority in those who had had a dramatic experience of conversion. Thus, the same kinds of tension between the authority of institutions and of particular individuals emerged as was found in the early church.

Protestant theology since the nineteenth century has faced a growing number of problems in addition to that posed by Kant. Mainstream liberalism and *neo-orthodoxy have, in their different ways, continued to reject the identification of Scripture with God's word. Liberation theology has raised the legitimate issue of authority in relation not only to orthodoxy but also orthopraxy. Postmodernism emphasizes the importance of *language in the construction of reality while remaining frequently unclear about exactly what is being constructed.

For evangelicals, perhaps the most pressing questions are those of hermeneutics. Marx, *Freud and *Nietzsche all brought into question both the way in which authoritative texts are chosen and read, and also the way in which they are used. This basic hermeneutical problem haunts much modern theology, including that of evangelicals, raising questions of power, manipulation and self-deception in relation to the church's theological enterprise. Indeed, evangelical Christians committed to the notion of sin as a moral problem must also raise such questions about self-interest and self-deception in relation to reading and using Scripture. While there is no easy answer to these challenges, any solution must take into account the following:

1. *Scripture as God's speech.* That which makes Scripture unique is the fact that it is God's speech, and this means that it is utterly trustworthy in what it claims. It must never be read, however, in isolation from an understanding of God himself, for he is the ultimate context for understanding Scripture.

2. *Human beings as sinful and as capable of misreading and misusing the Bible.* Both the finite and sinful nature of human beings imposes a modesty upon our theological enterprise which should make us self-critical about the way in which we construct and use our theology. This is not to say that our theology is not reliable, but it must always be subject to the searching criticism of the word of God.

3. *Human beings as situated in specific times and places.* Following on from the above, we should also be aware of the limitations of our cultural perspectives and therefore be prepared to listen to others. While we should not become so radically particularized in our theology that we can have no conversation with representatives of different traditions, cultures, and communities, we must also beware of imposing a unity upon others which is not strictly the unity of Christ.

4. *The cross of Christ as a paradigm of authority in action.* Finally, we should keep at the centre of our thinking the model of authority presented by Christ, which was one of servanthood, suffering and the way of the cross. Our theology should be developed in a manner which acknowledges this and not as something which enables us to manipulate and control others.

Bibliography

P. T. Forsyth, *The Principle of Authority* (London, 1952); R. A. Muller, *Post Reformation Reformed Dogmatics 2: Holy Scripture* (Grand Rapids, 2003); H. A. Oberman, *The Harvest of Medieval Theology* (Durham, 1983); J. I. Packer, *'Fundamentalism' and the Word of God* (London, 1958); A. C. Thiselton, *Interpreting God and the Postmodern Self* (Edinburgh, 1995); K. Vanhoozer, *First Theology* (Leicester, 2002).

C. R. TRUEMAN

AVERROES

Averroes, or Ibn-Rushd (c. 1126–1198), lived in Spain and was the greatest Muslim philosopher of the Middle Ages. Convinced that *Aristotle was the greatest philosopher, Averroes wrote several commentaries on his works and became known as the 'Commentator'. He replied to Al-Gazel's critique of philosophy in a work entitled *The Destruction of the Destruction*. The philosophical tradition in *Islam declined soon after his death, but his thought was very influential in the Latin West from 1200 to 1650.

Especially influential was Averroes's conception of the relationship of philosophy to religion. According to him, disagreements in philosophy and theology stem from the fact that persons with minds incapable of understanding philosophy study it. The solution is to distinguish types of minds and to limit each o the level of teaching suitable for it. The Koran is miraculous, because it has both an exterior and symbolic meaning for the uninstructed and an interior and hidden meaning for scholars. *Philosophers possess the highest degree of *truth, and they should refrain from communicating philosophical knowledge to persons incapable of grasping it. While philosophy gives complete knowledge, theology provides a dialectical interpretation that is probable, and religion and faith are for those who live by the *imagination and passions.

Averroes's return to a more authentic Aristotelianism led to a view of human nature which asserted that there is only one intellect for all persons. This intellect produces knowledge in individual souls just as the sun produces sight in the eyes through light. An individual merely receives forms. A consequence of this teaching is that there is nothing immortal in the individual, and so individual human *immortality is denied. Averroes also reaffirmed the view that the world is eternal and has no beginning in time.

This complex of teachings, presented as the authentic interpretation of Aristotle, had a profound influence in the Latin West. Averroes's conviction that the philosophy of Aristotle was the highest possible expression of philosophical *truth was taken over in the thirteenth century by Parisian masters in the arts and became known as 'Latin Averroism', and more recently as 'Radical Aristotelianism'. The best known of the early proponents of this view is Siger of Brabant. Although opposed by *Thomas Aquinas and other theologians, these views of Averroes and his Latin followers gave rise, unfortunately, to the popular view that for medieval philosophers, philosophical truth and the philosophy of Aristotle are the same.

Bibliography

R. Arnoaldez, *Averroes: A Rationalist in Islam* (Notre Dame, 2000); O. Leaman, *Averroes and his Philosophy* (Richmond, 1998); F. Van Steenberghen, *Thomas Aquinas and Radical Aristotelianism* (Washington, 1980).

A. G. VOS

BACON, FRANCIS

If we understand Francis Bacon (1561–1626) we have gone a considerable way towards understanding the origins of modernity and the rejection of Christianity in Europe. Lawyer and parliamentarian, a prominent figure in Elizabethan and Stuart public life, Bacon's offices included the Lord Chancellorship of England. Historian and essayist to boot, Bacon's significance derives largely from his proposals for putting scientific work on a sound basis of induction and elevating it to a position of authority as it becomes instrumental in the domination of nature. Behind this lay at least two major concerns. One was with the reconstitution and classification of spheres of knowledge, in opposition to the stifling presence of Aristotelian *metaphysics and the pontificating church. Attempts to describe what goes into our knowledge, and how it is ordered, were common in Bacon's day. But Bacon believed that these could be derived from theory more than from an investigation of what was useful and practical in the way of knowledge, and he worked out his own scheme in accordance with the latter ideal. The other concern was with the replacement of bitter ecclesiastical strife, steeped in bloody arguments about the way to the next world, with peaceable cooperative *science, intent on methodical discoveries for the improvement of life in this world.

Bacon was a fine stylist and shrewd observer of life, but it looks as though, behind the urbane, literary exterior, there was a resolute ambition, sometimes concealed by the need to write carefully in his day. He was determined to launch a holy war, in the name of science, against a Christian religion which had itself engaged in holy wars, both intellectually (against philosophy) and physically (first against Islam and then internally between its own Catholic and Protestant adherents). Bacon has been criticized for lacking appreciation of scientific developments in his own day and lacking understanding of the role of mathematics or personal creativity in the scientific enterprise. He has also been blamed for fostering technological mastery over nature to damaging effect. However, any criticism of Bacon that ignores the scandal of feuding and power-driven religion or fails to ponder seriously his quarrel with medieval metaphysics, misses his true significance. Amongst the factors that complicate an assessment of his legacy is the role of late-Renaissance 'occultic' magic in his concerns.

All these things conspire to make his work, rightly understood, a major gateway into our times. His readable *Essays* and programme for the *Advancement of Learning* should be read alongside not just what is regarded as his most lasting contribution, the *Novum Organon* (1620), but also his posthumously published and fragmentary works, like *New Atlantis* and *An Advertisement Touching on Holy War*. Further, his writings should be read alongside accounts of his life, not in order to gratify a prurient interest in sexual mores and diplomatic intrigue, but so that we do not plot the course of intellectual history independently of the evolution of social life.

Bibliography

S. Gaukroger, *Francis Bacon and the Transformation of Early-Modern Philosophy* (Cambridge, 2001); L. Lampert, *Nietzsche and Modern Times: A Study of Bacon, Descartes and Nietzsche* (New Haven/London, 1993); M. Peltonen (ed.), *The Cambridge Companion to Bacon* (Cambridge, 1996); A. Quinton, *Bacon* (Oxford, 1980).

S. N. WILLIAMS

BAILLIE, JOHN

John Baillie (1886–1960) was Scotland's most prominent theologian during the mid-twentieth century. He held chairs in America (Auburn and Union Theological Seminaries), Canada (Emmanuel College, University of Toronto) and Scotland (University of Edinburgh). He finished his academic career as professor of divinity, New College, Edinburgh (1934–56).

Baillie's *theology resists easy categorization. One way to interpret it is as a form of orthodox liberal Protestantism. Its recourse is typically (directly or indirectly) to a phenomenology of human experience as grounds for knowledge of God, neither to philosophical *rationalism nor biblical *revelation. Likewise, a seemingly universal sense of God's presence, in humans' moral consciousness of value, provides the possibility for second-order theological reflection upon, and language about, *religious experience. He also, however, espouses traditional Christian views on the *Trinity and the person and work of *Jesus – this despite Baillie's rejection of the Chalcedonian formula of two natures in one person.

The phrase 'mediating theology' provides insight into Baillie's theology, his method in particular. Baillie's thought is indeed a dogged effort to reconcile the Christian faith with a vast array of Western intellectual and cultural developments. *Philosophy, philosophical theology, philosophy of religion, theoretical and empirical *psychology, physics – these are but some of the mediating theologian's long-standing dialogue partners.

At no point in the development of his thought does Baillie fully align himself with '*neo-orthodoxy' – even when he comes to *Barth's defence in his early thought. Likewise, it is erroneous to suggest Baillie's having been a 'reformed theologian' in a strictly *Calvinist theological sense, to present Baillie's idea of immediacy as being basically a reissue of Calvin's idea of immediacy (as the product of one of 'Calvin's modern followers'), or to depict Baillie as an apologist concerned to 'interpret [Calvin's] epistemology' in his *Our Knowledge of God*. A straightforward reading of Baillie's *Our Knowledge of God* indicates as much.

Baillie's most renowned apologetic work is in fact his *Our Knowledge of God* (1939), with his posthumously published Gifford Lectures, *The Sense of the Presence of God* (1962), a close second. The former emphasizes that the aim of Christian apologetics is not to demonstrate God's existence but rather to drive the intellectual atheist to a deeper awareness of God and subsequent appropriation of Christ, for God is, through divine action, known intuitively by all persons to exist (this, incidentally, without humans having an inborn-innate disposition to believe in God, cf. Calvin's *sensus divinitatis*). Save that God cannot be exhausted by any number of propositions – discursive operation on both the phenomena of religious experience and divine revelation (which is not primarily propositional in the order of knowledge of God) can never totalize God's being – that the intellectual atheist rejects God with the 'top of the mind', does not logically preclude that the same person has immediate knowledge of God 'in the bottom of the heart' – that is, in one's moral consciousness of value (i.e., moral *realism).

Baillie's concept of knowledge of God as a 'mediated immediacy' is important for understanding his mature thought. Plausibly Baillie's 'most original contribution to the doctrine of knowledge of God' (Fergusson, *Selected Writings*, p. 3), mediated immediacy is 'the cornerstone of Baillie's epistemology of religion and it is [also] crucial for his doctrine of revelation' (Klinefelter, *Scottish Journal of Theology*, 30, p. 409).

Baillie, being a mediating theologian, tended to hang critical thought on the theological and philosophical issues of his day. This preoccupation came with a cost, for he failed to order his thought with a timeless *Summa* or systematic theology. Fortunately, there are inroads for ordering and understanding Baillie's dynamic theological development; Baillie's critical thought tends to gravitate toward the problems of knowledge of God and revelation, for instance. Here is one promising means for diachronically tracing the critical theological development of the 'transatlantic' theologian.

Bibliography

D. A. S. Fergusson (ed.), *Christ, Church and Society: Essays on John Baillie and Donald Baillie* (Edinburgh, 1993); *John and Donald Baillie: Selected Writings* (Edinburgh, 1997); G. M. Newlands, *John and Donald Baillie: Transatlantic Theology*, in J. Francis (ed.), *Religions and Discourse*, vol. 10 (Oxford, 2002).

T. JOHNSON

BARTH, KARL

Karl Barth (1886–1968) was born in Basel, Switzerland and is famous for his opposition to the First World War and his stand later against the Nazis. He is considered by many to be the greatest Protestant theologian of the twentieth century, possibly even since the first generation of Reformers, and a major voice in modern *theology. After studying at the universities of Bern, Berlin, Tübingen and Marburg, he held pastorates in Switzerland (1909–1921) before taking up professorships at the universities of Göttingen, Münster, Bonn (in 1935 he was expelled from Germany by the National Socialist Party for refusing to take the oath of allegiance to Adolf Hitler) and Basel.

Barth was invited to give the Gifford lectures in Aberdeen in 1937. According to the will of their patron, these lectures were to promote the study of natural theology in Scottish universities. Barth, however, criticized this theme and proceeded both to ignore it thereafter and to comment instead on the Scots Confession of 1560. In his view, *natural theology, the attempt to know God apart from *revelation which underpins many 'apologetic strategies', is a theologically mistaken enterprise. In *Jesus Christ we know the trinitarian God as the 'subject' of our knowing (i.e. it is through God's initiating agency that we know). Since God is not an 'object' in the way other things are, God cannot be known in the same way as objects. Therefore, theological rationality remains *relatively* (not absolutely) *independent* of other forms of rationality.

Barth did not draw a contrast between God and the world, faith and reason, in an irrationalist or fideistic manner. His theological account of rationality called into question the legitimacy of first any general view of rationality that does not take seriously the sinful perspectives of our knowing, secondly, any account of knowing that imagines God as an 'object' perceivable through human striving, and thirdly, any focus on the human knowing subject. The thinking that followed from Friedrich *Schleiermacher's theology of religious feeling was guilty of anthropologizing theology and turning God into an unfree object who could be experienced by the human subject. Barth learned from Ludwig Feuerbach that 'one cannot speak of God by speaking of man in a loud voice', although he continued appreciatively to struggle with and learn much from Schleiermacher's work during his academic career.

Barth proposed that 'the best apologetics is a good dogmatics', and maintained that revelation defends itself. Through the agency of the trinitarian God we have come to know God in a life-involving faith. Explaining this faith to others involves describing who Christians believe in, and presumably providing testimony to the possibility of this knowing, so that others may be encouraged to 'see things the way I [or better, 'we', since for Barth knowing is social, and Christian knowing is ecclesial] do'.

Scripture plays an indispensable role in this knowing of God. It witnesses to God's being in Jesus Christ, though that witness is clearer in some parts of the Scriptures than others. This witness is what gives Scripture its *authority, and although that authority is recognized only by the Christian it is nevertheless an 'objective' authority that constitutes it as the second form of the Word of God. It is 'Word of God' in the second place through its testifying to the divine Word spoken from eternity.

The character of Barth's 'faith seeking understanding' (learned largely from *Anselm) suggests further that his approach to theology involves ways of critiquing others thoughtfully and in detail, while humbly acknowledging one's own fragility and constantly testing one's own beliefs. He, however, is not promoting any simple 'internal coherence' defence of Christian belief, one that could perhaps be regarded as immune from critique, like fideism. His true perspective is most evident in his *theological* love of Mozart, his eclectic practice of learning and appreciating insights from, among others, Heidegger and *Sartre, his later reflections on creation's 'little lights' (*Church Dogmatics*, IV.3.1, §69.2), and his earlier claim that 'God may speak to us through Russian communism, through a flute concerto, through a blossoming shrub or through a dead dog. We shall do well to listen to him if he really does so' (*Church Dogmatics*, I.1, 60).

Bibliography

K. Barth, *Church Dogmatics*, 14 vols. (Edinburgh, 1958); K. Barth and E. Brunner, *Natural Theology* (London, 1946); T. J. Gorringe, *Karl Barth: Against Hegemony* (Oxford, 1999); G. Hunsinger, *How to Read Karl Barth: The Shape of His Theology* (New York and Oxford, 1994); B. McCormack, *Barth's Critically Realist Dialectical Theology* (Oxford, 1995); J. Webster, *Barth* (London and New York, 2000).

J. C. McDOWELL

BAUR, FERDINAND CHRISTIAN

Ferdinand Baur (1792–1860) was professor of church history and dogmatics at Tübingen from 1826 until his death, and was one of the most influential scholars of his time. He is generally credited with having founded an approach to the NT which has come to be known as the Tübingen School, and which set the agenda for much, if not most, nineteenth-century discussion of the relationship between *Jesus and the early church. Baur was deeply influenced by *Hegelian philosophy, and believed that the NT revealed a fundamental conflict between *Judaism (the Hegelian 'thesis') and *Hellenism (the Hegelian 'antithesis'), which was eventually subsumed in a new, Hegelian 'synthesis' which Baur called 'early Catholicism'.

In Baur's view, it was Paul who championed Hellenism against Peter's Judaism, and the synthesis can be found mainly in Luke-Acts and John. Using this model as his framework, Baur reconstructed the NT, giving the greatest historical value to the epistles and the least to those books where the eventual synthesis is most apparent. Baur was also the first person to formulate the conflicting notions of 'Christology from above' and 'Christology from below', a duality which was to be very influential in twentieth-century thought. In line with his overall scheme, the more a Christological statement seemed to reflect the 'from above' dimension, the later in date and less historically reliable it was seen to be.

Baur's great strength is that he recognized the need to explain all the NT evidence in any theoretical reconstruction of Christian origins, and in this he has been followed by most scholars ever since. He also underlined the importance of examining each biblical author's intention(s) in writing, and here too his influence has proved to be lasting. More controversially, he regarded the development of Christology as the key to understanding how the NT emerged. Here his views have met with considerable scepticism, and it is now generally admitted that his theological framework was much too schematic and conceptually alien to the outlook of the biblical writers themselves. It was relatively easy for critics like Albrecht *Ritschl to point out that Baur's neat schematizations did not fit the evidence of the texts, which are much more complex than Baur was prepared to accept. On the other hand, for all that Baur's thesis has been shot to pieces on matters of detail, his fundamental conviction that Christianity developed progressively through a series of evolutionary stages is still widely accepted today.

Bibliography

H. Harris, *The Tübingen school* (Oxford, 1975); J. C. O'Neill, *The Bible's Authority: A Portrait Gallery of Thinkers from Lessing to Bultmann* (Edinburgh, 1991); H. Rottmann, 'From Baur to Wrede: The Quest for a Historical Method', *Studies in Religion/Science Religieuses*, 17 (1988), pp. 443–454.

G. L. BRAY

BAVINCK, HERMAN

A Dutch Reformed theologian, Herman Bavinck (1854–1921) was professor of theology at the Theological School at Kampen (1883–1902). He subsequently matriculated to the Free University of Amsterdam (1902–21), where he succeeded A. *Kuyper (1837–1920) in the chair of systematic theology.

Bavinck underscores that Christian apologetics can never establish the *certainty of Christian faith, whilst simultaneously urging the academic theologian to defend the Christian faith in service to the Christian church. This task calls for active engagement with contemporary intellectual currents, an openness to contemporary criticism (e.g. historical,

biblical and literary) and a dogged resolve to contend for a Bible-centred message in the light thereof. Bavinck himself assumes such a posture in much of his thought; e.g. in *The Philosophy of Revelation*, which is the reprint of his Stone Lectures for Princeton Theological Seminary (1908–9).

Bavinck continues to exert a measure of influence on modern Christian thought, especially through his rigorous biblical exegesis, erudition, relentless attention to detail, generally judicious treatment of competing theological positions, and deeply devout expression of Christian piety. Dutch Reformed works of partial indebtedness to Bavinck's thought, such as the well-known dogmatic treatises of L. Berkhof (1873–1957) and G. C. *Berkouwer (1903–96), have contributed to his staying power in such circles. Bavinck summarized his dogmatics in *Our Reasonable Faith*. His stature as a thinker deserves better recognition.

Bibliography

H. Bavinck, *Our Reasonable Faith* (Grand Rapids, 1956); *The Doctrine of God* (vol. 2 of *Gereformeerde Dogmatiek*, trans and ed. by W. Hendriksen; Edinburgh and Carlisle, 1977); *Reformed Dogmatics: Prolegomena* (vol. 1 of *Gereformeerde Dogmatiek*, ed. by J. Bolt, trans. by J. Vriend; Grand Rapids, 2003); *The Philosophy of Revelation* (Grand Rapids, 1979).

T. JOHNSON

BAYLE, PIERRE

Pierre Bayle (1647–1706) abandoned the Protestantism of his birth in 1668 for Catholicism in order to study with the Jesuits at Toulouse, but then seems to have changed back again so as to pursue further studies at Geneva in 1670–4. By 1697 Bayle's *Historical and Critical Dictionary* had been censored by Rotterdam Protestants so he had to hide behind irony at times. E. Labrousse claimed that Bayle had given at least mental assent to the views of the Reformed faith if not heartfelt response.

Positively, Bayle polemicized against Catholic 'superstition' (e.g. the reading of comets to predict the future), which resembled that of pagan antiquity, and intolerance (the two linked by 'fanatical madness'). In this way, *atheism was better than wrong religious belief. Bayle saw contemporary Catholicism as lacking the true inwardness of true spirituality. Given that readings of Scripture could diverge and even go astray, such interpretations had to be subjected to the law of reason. Diversity of opinions was good since many voices were better than one and operated as mutually moderating influences. One should not separate *morality from a belief in God's providence. A love of order corresponding to God is what distinguishes Christian moral living from an 'Epicurean' like *Spinoza, even though many of the latter's principles and virtues were good.

Bayle challenged orthodox Christianity in counting the *Trinity among 'superstitions'. He doubted whether we can know the underlying nature of things, and whether our ideas about right and wrong are anything more than relative. People believe for reasons of interest, not because of reason. Disgrace and love of praise may do more for *morality than conscience or reason. *Predestination would implicate God in knowing about sin and doing nothing, so God's will can only be inscrutable and beyond good and evil. If this means that faith is devoid of intellectual content, then this is the price believers must pay for elevating their faith and its mysteries above reason. Like Spinoza, and ironically like Cardinal Bossuet who emphasized devotional fervour, Bayle had left faith only with obedience; *truth was made the property of philosophy. Perhaps he is most famous for his saying that given the existence of *evil, God cannot be both all-powerful and all-good. The supposed deity and maker of the world was either willing to abolish all evils, but not able; or he was able but not willing. Why did he not prevent someone falling into a ditch rather than sending someone along later to help him out? *Leibniz's rejoinder in his *Theodicy* is that God needed to allow evil for the perfection of the world to involve free will.

Bibliography

E. Labrousse, *Bayle* (Oxford, 1983); R. Popkin, *The History of Scepticism: From Savonarola to Bayle* (New York, 2003).

M. W. ELLIOTT

BEHAVIOURISM, see PSYCHOLOGY

BERGMAN, INGMAR

Ingmar Bergman was born in Sweden in 1918 to a strict protestant minister. He has subsequently become one of the world's most acclaimed filmmakers in part by capturing on film his own struggle between faith and *doubt. Bergman definitely appeals to any serious film student or aficionado. While his films are not easily accessible, they do stir serious conversation and lend themselves readily to discussion.

Through a Glass Darkly (1961), *Winter Light* (1963) and *The Silence* (1964), Bergman's celebrated 'Faith Trilogy', are bleak but brilliantly conceived glimpses into the darkness and despair of doubt and isolation. These might best be saved for a film group rather than a general viewing. In a university setting, *Wild Strawberries* (1959) would offer great opportunities for discussion of life and values as it chronicles the retrospective journey towards death an ageing professor takes on his way to receive an honorary degree. Clearly death and doubt have been Bergman's close companions throughout his career.

Yet it is Bergman's *The Seventh Seal* (1957) that consistently ranks among the most important films ever made, and for good reason. It is required viewing for any serious student of film, and thus it will appeal to a large and diverse audience. The film is an unforgettable parable of death intersecting life in the character of one man, Antonius Block, a medieval knight returning from the Crusades to his native Sweden, now ravaged by the plague. Almost immediately the spectre of death confronts Block, and the two engage in a game of chess, playing for Block's life. Block is not motivated by fear but by the desire to accomplish something meaningful before he dies. Between moves in this death match, Block works to rescue one family (symbolically the Holy Family) from the plague, thus saving them from death's grip as well. Three images from *The Seventh Seal* are not easily shaken: the chess game, the procession of the flagellants and the vision of death dancing across the horizon with his victims in parade behind him.

There is perhaps a more sinister spectre stalking the stark landscape of *The Seventh Seal*: *nihilism. Block has returned from the Crusades doubting the very existence of God and, therefore, the meaning of life. His last quest is a crossroads of sorts as his faith in God is methodically challenged by the cruel reality of death. Block's journey portrays the agony of *agnosticism in the literal face of death. This film is perfect for discussions of *existentialism, nihilism and ontology, not to mention life and death. Simply viewing the chess game itself will lead easily to a discussion of fatalism.

D. S. RUSSELL

BERKELEY, GEORGE

George Berkeley was born in Kilkenny, Ireland, in 1685 and studied at Kilkenny College before entering Trinity College, Dublin. He graduated in 1704 and, after gaining an MA in 1707, he was appointed to a junior fellowship at the College. Berkeley retained his fellowship at Trinity but he went to London in 1713 and made two continental tours before returning to Ireland to take up the position of Dean of Derry in 1724. On his return from a visit to America he became Lord Bishop of Cloyne in 1734. In 1752, having travelled to Oxford to supervise the education of his son, he died and was buried in the chapel of Christ Church.

Berkeley achieved a secure position at the pinnacle of Western philosophy as a result of three publications, *An Essay Towards a New Theory of Vision* (1709), *A Treatise Concerning the Principles of Human Knowledge* (1710) and *Three Dialogues Between Hylas and Philonous* (1713), all of which were produced at an astonishingly early age. In later life he continued to write. He produced *De Motis* in (1721), a further development of his idealist position; he defended, in *Alciphron* (1732), various basic tenets of the Christian faith; and he advocated the virtues of aether, or tar water, in an eccentric work, entitled *Seris* (1744). These later works are not without interest, but they do not in any way match the originality and importance of the writings of Berkeley's youth, and it is upon the central theses of his early work, especially upon the role which they play in the great debate involving *Descartes, *Locke, *Hume and *Kant, that I will now concentrate.

Stated crudely and controversially, Berkeley defended the apparently shocking thesis that there does not exist an external, material world. Berkeley maintained, however, not merely that his immaterialism was consistent with the view of common sense ('the Mob', as he was prone to say!), but that it provided the only coherent way to defend common sense, the existence of God and the findings of the rapidly developing natural sciences. Berkeley's arguments were primarily directed against certain doctrines that had been defended by Descartes and Locke, and it is in the context of that dispute that one can best understand Berkeley's position.

Descartes and Locke maintained that 'the Mind perceives nothing but its own ideas', and that these 'ideas' or 'sensations' or 'perceptions' are caused by external objects which we do not and cannot perceive. Berkeley maintained that an acceptance of these views led to radical scepticism for the following reasons. First, on the accepted view, the mind has no way of knowing anything about material objects themselves; secondly, and here Berkeley was indebted to Malebranche, it is not clear how inert matter can act on minds so as to produce perceptions in them; thirdly, when we talk of objects such as chairs and tables we are talking about things which we experience, not about shadowy, unobservable things and so chairs and tables must be ideas or collections of ideas. Berkeley's immaterialism paved the way for new understandings of the existence of God and the nature of scientific inquiry.

All ideas require a cause, and since ideas of sense are not caused either by ourselves or by material substances, it follows that they must be caused by another spiritual substance. However, not only the occurrence but also the ordering of ideas requires explanation, because our ideas occur in a useful 'train or series'. Our ideas and their ordering are the work of a wise and benevolent God, a 'governing spirit whose will constitutes the Laws of Nature'.

The existence of God also provided an answer to one of the most common sceptical objections to immaterialism, objections which Berkeley immediately anticipated. If *esse est percipi*, then things will cease to exist when we no longer perceive them; and if objects are only collections of ideas, then causal interaction between objects becomes unintelligible, so that we will have to deny, for example, that heat causes metals to expand. Berkeley's replies to these objections were – whatever one's final verdict on them – bold and ingenious. Real things continue to exist when no human is perceiving them because, Berkeley argued, they are perceived continuously by God.

Furthermore, the involuntariness of ideas, their ontological distinctness from minds, and the fact that ideas must exist in some mind entail that they exist in the mind of someone. They exist, Berkeley maintained, in the mind of God, who reveals them to us.

Berkeley's immaterialism also led him to accept a distinctive view of the status of scientific generalizations. Laws of nature do not describe the essential nature of objects, knowledge of which would render the world intelligible. Since there are no essences behind our scientific knowledge, we must conclude that laws of nature are merely analogies which our mind draws between phenomena, and that terms such as 'weight' and 'gravity' are the names of these analogies.

Berkeley's work, however significant in a historical context, has had comparatively little impact on subsequent philosophy of religion. This is not because Berkeley did not sincerely believe in God or in the truths of the Christian religion, or because God did not play a central role in his philosophy. Nor is it, as is sometimes suggested, that Berkeley merely invoked God to solve problems that would otherwise have been insoluble in his philosophical system. It is rather that for Berkeley, as for any other philosopher, the accounts of God's existence and of his nature were determined by the basic philosophical framework within which they occurred. And since Berkeley's immaterialism has not been widely accepted by later generations of philosophers, his account of the philosophical foundations of *theism has had correspondingly little influence.

Bibliography

M. R. Ayers (ed.), *Berkeley: Philosophical Works* (London, 1975); J. Dancy, *Berkeley: An Introduction* (Oxford, 1987); A. C. Grayling, *Berkeley: The Central Arguments* (London, 1986); A. A. Luce and T. E. Jessop (eds.), *Works of G. Berkeley* (London, 1948–51); I. C. Tipton, *Berkeley: The Philosophy of Immaterialism* (London, 1974).

H. BUNTING

BERKOUWER, GERRIT CORNELIUS

Throughout his lengthy career as professor of systematic theology at the Free University of Amsterdam, Gerrit Berkouwer (1903–96)

sought to understand the gospel more deeply. Best known for his multi-volumed *Studies in Dogmatics*, his chief work was in dogmatics rather than apologetics. His writings, however, contain valuable insights relating to the work of apologetics, e.g. 'Apostolicity and Truth' (*The Church*), 'Faith and Criticism' (*Holy Scripture*) and 'The Era of Apologetics' and 'Faith and Reasonableness' (*A Half Century of Theology*).

Distinguishing between an authentic *authority and an unwarranted authoritarianism, Berkouwer affirmed the essential reasonableness of the gospel. The call to faith in Christ is not a call for blind obedience, and believing in Christ does not require a sacrifice of the intellect. He also affirmed the spiritual character of the gospel, distancing himself from the kind of apologetics which tends to place undue emphasis on the capacity of human reason to bring people to faith in Christ. He rejected the idea of faith as a sacrifice of the intellect without ever suggesting that faith is no more than an act of unaided human reason.

Recognizing the value of apologetics without attaching an exaggerated importance to it, Berkouwer emphasized the need for both *humility and courage in the defence of the Christian faith. In humility, apologetics must take care to avoid an unattractively militant approach, but should also resist the temptation to trim the content of the gospel's message in search of relevance and, with courage, should affirm its irreducible content. Emphasizing the gospel's own inherent apologetic significance, Berkouwer was critical of the kind of apologetics which shows little interest in those elements of Christian faith adjudged to be less apologetically relevant.

Bibliography

G. C. Berkouwer, *A Half Century of Theology* (Grand Rapids, 1977), pp. 25–38, 144–178; *Holy Scripture* (Grand Rapids, 1975), pp. 346–366; *The Church* (Grand Rapids, 1976), pp. 232–256; C. M. Cameron, *The Problem of Polarization: An Approach Based on the Writings of G. C. Berkouwer* (Lewiston, Queenston and Lampeter, 1992), pp. 247–284.

C. M. CAMERON

BIBLE, ISLAMIC VIEW OF, see ISLAM

BIBLICAL CRITICISM

Introduction

Christian apologists sometimes find themselves in the unenviable position of defending the use of biblical criticism against its detractors 'inside the camp' and objecting to certain uses of it 'outside the camp'. For the former, the term 'criticism' itself might carry the negative connotations of fault-finding when, in fact, it has to do with careful analysis of the text. Moreover, because biblical criticism has frequently been tied to naturalistic agendas, the importance of its task in tackling the historical and literary elements of Scripture – factors which any attentive reader would seek to endorse – can be missed.

Biblical criticism then and now

It is regularly claimed that the roots of biblical criticism can be traced back to the *Enlightenment in seventeenth-century Europe. Christianity was seen as just one religion alongside others, and to be studied as such. Investigation of the Bible was carried out from a perspective which rejected its infallibility and the possibility of *transcendence, and which sought to uncover the message of *Jesus apart from church dogma. To the contention that biblical criticism is bound irretrievably to such presuppositions, however, three qualifying factors need to be noted.

First, although biblical criticism rose to prominence in the Enlightenment, concern for the 'plain meaning' of the Bible can be traced back to the Reformation and before. With Renaissance humanism came the freedom to translate, print and read classical texts, including the Bible. The emphasis on the 'literal sense' of Scripture by sixteenth-century Reformers led them to draw on the full range of linguistic and historical tools to examine the meaning of the text. It was thus orthodox Protestants (see *Christianity, Protestant) who were at the forefront in the early development of biblical criticism. Even so-called 'pre-critical' scholars were concerned with matters of *history and philology. Some, like *Augustine, who emphasized multiple senses in the text, did not deny the importance, even the priority, of the literal sense.

Secondly, the Enlightenment tradition has itself been called into question. With its reliance on scientific investigation and its alleged lack of presuppositions, it can now be seen that biblical criticism never was the neutral enterprise its advocates claimed it was, but operated as much from a particular perspective as those it disavowed.

Thirdly, in part due to shifts in post-Enlightenment *epistemology, biblical criticism has now broadened its scope to include the entire communicative act involving author, text and reader.

Until the latter part of the twentieth century, biblical criticism was generally understood to refer to that set of interpretive procedures known as the historical-critical method. This required the interpreter to wrestle with features of the text as a historical product of an author, i.e. the history of the text's formation, its sources, its classification into various literary 'forms', the identification of how and why the author has edited traditions together.

Then, from the 1970s onwards, historical criticism came under attack, not least for its neglect of the final form of the text. The Enlightenment arguably led both 'liberal' and 'conservative' scholars astray in seeking meaning *beyond* the text itself. 'Conservatives' sought to demonstrate the historical accuracy of the events depicted in the text, whilst 'liberals' sought the general religious truths the text allegedly illustrated. That both managed, in the process, to 'eclipse' the biblical text itself is the thrust of Hans W. Frei's influential thesis in *The Eclipse of Biblical Narrative: A Study in Eighteenth and Nineteenth Century Hermeneutics* (New Haven, 1974).

Thus came about fresh methods of analysis which focused on the final form of the text itself. Advocates of 'literary' and 'canonical' approaches to Scripture frequently set out their perspectives as an alternative paradigm to historical criticism. Most recently of all, attention has turned to the role of the interpreter, with various 'reader' criticisms highlighting the inevitably subjective dimension of interpretation, as well as calling for committed ideological stances, such as Marxism or feminism, to be applied in the reading of the Bible.

In such a climate, it is hardly surprising that biblical criticism has broadened its boundaries to embrace the worlds of author, text and reader. Furthermore, initial sparring between different approaches (e.g. historical versus literary) has given way to recognition of the need for, and benefits of, integrative work.

Biblical criticism and theological presuppositions

Critical methodologies have clearly led some to question biblical *authority, although that conclusion is not inevitable; methods of biblical criticism can be used from a stance of faith as well as doubt. That approaches sometimes come bundled with the 'theological' presuppositions of *rationalism, *existentialism and postmodernism does not prevent them from being married to faith in God, a commitment to the authority of Scripture and the ongoing formation of the church. Recent years have seen calls for renewed biblical criticism which is open to the transcendent and, within the context of a specifically Christian approach to Scripture, respects the 'otherness' of the text, allowing it to challenge the interpreter's own world-view.

Moreover, if one begins with the presupposition that the Bible is the word of God in the words of human beings, one is obliged to take the human element of Scripture seriously. To denounce the use of critical tools may be to deny the manner in which God has chosen to speak, in texts through words and in history, thus mandating the careful use of a variety of interpretive approaches in understanding his self-disclosure.

Biblical criticism in action

In spite of the proliferation of 'literary', 'rhetorical' and 'readerly' approaches to the Bible in the last quarter of the twentieth century, 'biblical criticism' is still frequently associated with the historical paradigm of interpretation, and with the following methods in particular: textual criticism, which seeks to establish what was the most likely reading among the variants in the many manuscripts of the text; source criticism, associated especially with studies of the *Pentateuch and the Gospels, which tries to determine the sources used by a writer; tradition criticism, which elucidates the history of the traditions that make up texts; form criticism, which distinguishes individual literary 'forms' in the text, classifies them into various groups, and seeks to correlate them with life settings in Israel or the early church; redaction criticism, which identifies how and why an author has edited traditions together; composition criticism, which moves beyond study of editorial changes to look at the overall shape of the final composition; and social-science criticism, which draws on methods used in contemporary *sociology and anthropology for considering the social dynamics of the communities out of which the texts arose.

It is sometimes argued that the use of (e.g.) source, form and redaction criticism necessarily undermines the historical authenticity of (say) the Gospel accounts, but one is not required to adopt that presupposition in using the tools to focus on the possible life-setting of a piece of tradition about Jesus, or the contribution of the evangelist in writing the Gospel. For instance, even before the label 'redaction criticism' was in vogue, a similar approach had been utilized by scholars from different theological perspectives. Ned B. Stonehouse of Westminster Theological Seminary, to take one example, was committed to a high view of Scripture, and so was also dedicated to a careful analysis of the individual Gospel accounts with their distinctive portraits of Christ. He says: 'In particular it has seemed to me that Christians who are assured as to the unity of the witness of the gospels should take greater pains to do justice to the diversity of expression of that witness. It is a thrilling experience to observe this unity ... But that experience is far richer and more satisfying if one has been absorbed and captured by each portrait in turn and has conscientiously been concerned by the minutest differentiating details as well as the total impact of the evangelical witness' (N. B. Stonehouse, *The Witness of Luke to Christ* [London, 1951], p. 6).

Christian interpreters need have no fear from 'critical' approaches to the Bible which show how careful the evangelists have been with traditions about Jesus in their sources, in re-arranging them, and in summarizing events in their own distinctive style in order to proclaim the truth of Christ.

Conclusion

In something of a programmatic statement, N. T. Wright argues for an integration between theology, literature and history in biblical interpretation. His 'creative synthesis' combines 'the pre-modern emphasis on the text as in some sense authoritative, the modern emphasis on the text ... as irreducibly integrated into history, and irreducibly involved with theology, and the postmodern emphasis on the reading of the text' (*New Testament*, pp. 26–27). The circumspect use of critical methodologies by the Christian apologist allows each to be given its proper due, in an approach characterized neither by closed-minded humanism on the one hand nor blinkered fundamentalism on the other hand.

Bibliography

D. A. Black and D. S. Dockery (eds.), *Interpreting the New Testament: Essays on Methods and Issues* (Nashville, 2001); R. A. Harrisville and W. Sundberg, *The Bible in Modern Culture: Baruch Spinoza to Brevard Childs* (Grand Rapids, [2]2002); S. L. McKenzie and S. R. Haynes (eds.), *To Each Its Own Meaning: An Introduction to Biblical Criticisms and their Application* (Louisville, [2]1999); N. T. Wright, *The New Testament and the People of God* (London, 1992).

A. BILLINGTON

BIBLICAL INSPIRATION

A word for all of life

The passionate discussion of the concept of 'biblical inspiration' that has permeated the Christian, and particularly evangelical, community in the last half-century has created an opportunity for reflection on precisely how the Bible functions in the life of the believing *community. The desire of evangelical Christians to link biblical inspiration with the *authority of the Scriptures for all of life is profoundly biblical. Various passages in the OT assert the comprehensive nature of the words which God has spoken to the Israelites. Central to these is Deut. 6:6–10: 'These commandments that I give you today are to be upon your hearts. Impress them on your children. Talk about them when you sit at home and when you walk along the road, when you lie down and when you get up. Tie them as symbols on your hands, and bind them on your foreheads. Write them on the doorframes of your houses and on your gates.' The text is clear. Every moment of every day is supposed to be filled with *torah*, with the story of who God is and what God has done. This story is inside your very being, your *imagination, and you should not be able to help talking about this story to everyone, your children at home and everyone you meet, no matter where you are. When you are awake you tell this story, you even dream in its symbols and metaphors. This story is on your

hand so that you see it enacted in all that you do, and on your forehead so that others see this story in all that you think and say. Even your homes and your life in the public square, in the academy, in scientific endeavour and in historical report are to be shaped by this story.

Although this text applies only to *torah*, 2 Tim. 3:16–17 makes a similarly comprehensive claim in relation to all of what is now our OT. As a result, some have argued that this text is not helpful for a discussion of biblical inspiration because it does not refer to the entire body of Christian Scripture. It is clear, however, that as the writings of the NT were accorded a status similar to that of the OT by the early church, this text was applied by the community to those writings as well. Hence, a dynamic reading of this text in the context of Christian tradition applies it to all those writings that the church confesses to be Scripture.

Paul roots the importance of Scripture for our lives precisely in the inspired, or 'God-breathed', character of Scripture: 'All Scripture is God-breathed and is useful for teaching, rebuking, correcting and training in righteousness, so that the man of God may be thoroughly equipped for every good work' (2 Tim. 3:16–17).

A living word

By describing the Scriptures as 'God-breathed' Paul echoes various OT texts where the breath of God caused life to be present. God breathed the breath of life into the earth-creature in Eden, and Adam became a living being (Gen. 2:7). After describing in rich detail the intricacy of the world that God has created, the psalmist confesses, 'When you send your Spirit, they are created, and you renew the face of the earth' (Ps. 104:30). God's Spirit creates life and renews life. (One needs to note that in Hebrew the word for spirit and breath are the same, *ruah*.) And, of course, in Ezek. 37 it is only when the Spirit of God is breathed into the dry bones of Israel that they live; the breath of God is the Spirit of resurrection.

What this means at the very least is that the Scriptures, being God-breathed, are a living word, a word that brings life, a word that participates in the renewal of creation (see also Isa. 55:10–11; Heb. 4:12). It is worth noting that Paul spends no time trying to describe the process by which the Scriptures are God-breathed or inspired. His focus is rather on the role that such God-breathed texts have in the community. The implications are clear. No matter what we confess about the meaning of inspiration, if the Scriptures are not functioning in our communities in the ways that Paul describes, then our lives deny our confession and the Bible is stifled.

The function of inspiration

So how are the Scriptures to function in our midst, according to 2 Tim. 3:16–17? Paul lists four roles that Scripture plays: teaching, reproof, correction and training in righteousness. The first three of these suggest that the living word of Scripture gives us a new word, it shakes us up, teaching us things we had not dreamed or imagined, reproving us when we have acted in death-dealing ways contrary to its living word, and correcting us when we have allowed our imaginations to become captive to the spirits of our age. This means that the Spirit of God works continually through this text to challenge and transform our communities (cf. Heb. 4:12).

Training in righteousness

Such challenge, moreover, is for the purpose of training us in righteousness. Paul could hardly have chosen a term more laden with meaning. Such meaning becomes even more evident when we acknowledge that *dikaiosynē* (usually translated 'righteousness') can be just as accurately translated 'justice'. Throughout the OT the righteousness of God is concerned precisely with such issues of *justice. When God comes in righteousness the captives will be set free, the oppressed will be liberated and the poor will be lifted up. The prophets continually call for the community to cease their idolatrous oppression of the poor and practise righteousness; and Paul describes the gospel in terms of the righteousness or justice of God, in sharp contrast to the righteousness and justice of the Roman empire (Rom. 1:17).

*Jesus explicitly links the anointing of the Spirit with the practice of such justice or righteousness at his baptism, where he tells John that his baptism is necessary to fulfil all righteousness. Immediately after the baptism, the Spirit of God descends on Jesus like a dove (Matt. 3:14–16). Jesus himself explains the connection between the Spirit and righteousness in Luke 4:18–19, where he says, 'The Spirit of the Lord is on me, because he has anointed me to preach good news to the poor. He has sent me to proclaim freedom for the

prisoners and recovery of sight for the blind, to release the oppressed, to proclaim the year of the Lord's favour.' Not only is Jesus quoting Isa. 61:1–2 here; he is also alluding to texts, such as Isa. 11:1–5, which describe the one upon whom the Spirit of the Lord rests as the one who will judge the poor with righteousness and decide with equity for the meek of the earth, because righteousness, or justice, is the belt around his waist.

The Christian community, which claims to have received this same Spirit at Pentecost, must allow the Scriptures to train it in the practice of such justice, or it denies the presence of the Spirit in both the text and the community. Paul reiterates this point in the next verse: the people of God must be equipped for good work in *everything*. The Greek word *pan* is comprehensive and calls the Christian community to the practice of discipleship in every area of life. This means that the inspired nature of the Bible in relation to geography, *science, *history, education, business and the *arts demands the practice of righteousness in how we plan our life together, in the houses we build and in the shape of our cities; in our scientific endeavours and the purposes for which we do our scientific research; in the way we interpret our history as the story of the privileged and victorious or as the story of 'the least of these'; in the way we educate our children, and whether we allow them to be enculturated by the militaristic consumerism of our *culture; in our business, and where we position profits in relation to the call for justice; in our artistic life and how we offer symbols of hope in the midst of the pain of our culture.

Because the Scriptures are Spirit-inspired, they are one way that the Spirit works in our midst. If the Spirit animates creation, brings life to the dead, enables the proclamation of justice, comforts the oppressed, and reconciles us with God through all of this, then the God-breathed Scriptures function in the same way in our communities: animating our created life, bringing life out of the hopeless death of sin, proclaiming justice and bringing comfort in the face of oppression, and in so doing instructing us for salvation (2 Tim. 3:15).

A prophetic word

Such a view of inspiration reflects the prophetic nature of inspired Scripture. Like the prophets, Scripture calls the community back from unfaithfulness and injustice into a life of justice in relationship with a living and righteous God. In this sense, biblical inspiration is always dynamic, for the Spirit has worked not only through the oral recollection and compilation of the Bible, but also through Scripture's ongoing life in a community that itself has the Spirit living in its midst.

Bibliography

P. J. Achtemeier, *Inspiration and Authority: Nature and Function of Christian Scripture* (Peabody, 1999); J. Begbie, 'Who is This God? Biblical Inspiration Revisited', *Tyndale Bulletin*, 43.2 (1992), pp. 259–282; W. Brueggemann, W. C. Placher and B. K. Blount, *Struggling with Scripture* (Louisville, 2002); C. Gunton, 'All Scripture is Inspired ...?' *Princeton Seminary Bulletin*, 14.3 (1993), pp. 240–253; S. Hauerwas, *Unleashing Scripture: Freeing the Bible from Captivity to America* (Nashville, 1993); R. C. Hill, 'Psalm 45: A Locus Classicus for Patristic Thinking on Inspiration', *Studia Patristica*, 23 (1993), pp. 95–100; I. H. Marshall, *Biblical Inspiration* (Grand Rapids, 1982); J. Muddiman, 'The Holy Spirit and Inspiration', in R. Morgan (ed.), *The Religion of the Incarnation* (Bristol, 1989); J. Perry, 'Discovering the Inerrancy Debate: How Modern Philosophy Shaped the Evangelical View of Scripture', *Journal for Christian Theological Research*, 6.3 (2001); B. Vawter, *Biblical Inspiration* (Philadelphia, 1972); B. J. Walsh, 'Reimaging Biblical Authority', *Christian Scholar's Review*, 26.2 (1996), pp. 206–220; N. T. Wright, 'How Can the Bible be Authoritative?', *Vox Evangelica*, 21 (1991), pp. 7–32.

S. C. KEESMAAT

BIG BANG, see COSMOLOGY

BIOETHICS

Visitors leaving the UK pavilion of the international EXPO 2000 exhibition in Hanover were faced with a photo of Dolly the cloned sheep, symbolizing British achievement. Her creation in 1996 by scientists at the Roslin Institute not only marked a watershed in biology but also created a secular icon for our times. She represents at once the promise and the threat of the rapid developments in biotechnology, both unimagined possibilities and awesome dilemmas. She also reflects the globalization of bioethics in an age of instant worldwide communication. There was an immediate and trans-cultural reaction that reproductive cloning was a technical road from which humanity should refrain on ethical grounds. To go one step further in applying asexual reproduction to humans would violate a moral norm. This and several recent developments in the biological *sciences are posing a deep irony for postmodern culture set on rejecting all universal claims. The popular use of terms like 'playing God' reveal a need to appeal to an absolute in order to express the intuition that we are going too far, too riskily or too fast. Biotechnological advances are raising far-reaching questions about the nature of life which postmodernity is finding itself ill-equipped to deal with.

What is a human being? What limits are there to human genetic capacities in terms of aging and organ replacement? Having over-ridden previous boundaries in reproduction, against what ethical norms do we decide what to do with the new possibilities? As we probe further into the human genome, who has control of genetic information and who should have access to it – wider family members, insurance and drugs companies or employers? Should we select embryos to avoid inherited propensities to terrible diseases or seek to eliminate the diseases by genetically engineering the germline? Should we allow people to enhance human genetic traits? How far should we intervene in nature and into the genetics of other organisms, and for what purposes? Should we allow genetically modified crops or animals? What distinctions ought we to draw among species? Are humans fundamentally different from animals?

Bioethics is providing some of the most significant apologetic opportunities of our times, in two ways. First, people are asking fundamental metaphysical questions with little or no framework around which to form answers. The immediate role of bioethics is to give an informed, sensitive Christian voice in the market place of ideas in which these issues are being debated. It is a place, however, where dogmatic statements of belief are apt to be met by hostility, where we have to earn the right to speak, subtly and not by presuming upon our position. Indeed, the context we speak within may reject any idea of principles and seek to reduce all discourse to matters of efficacy or cost-risk-benefit. In such a debate, the apologist's first task may be to reveal the unspoken principles of the major players in order to clear the ground for proper debate. The second and deeper role of bioethics is for Christians to point beyond the particular issues to the deeper questions of belief and world-view, highlighting some of the drawbacks of contemporary alternative philosophies which these questions reveal.

For example, the ethical imperative of medical research to address human suffering is generally accepted, but its justification is not absolute. It may imply a need to examine deeper issues. Thus, research into embryonic stem cells is justified by prospects of treatments by cell replacement for diabetes, heart failure and Alzheimer's. The projected consequences were argued to override principled ethical concerns about the status of the embryo. Proposals to use pig hearts for human transplant presumed that overcoming organ 'shortages' was more important than other considerations like human-animal interventions. The emerging field of pharmacogenomics – designing *drugs specific to the patient's genetics – epitomizes a trend away from classical medicine as care for the sick in a wider context of life to medicine as a technical fix. In such examples, the justification of novel techniques should not be automatic and unbounded, but needs setting in a wider moral framework. A positivistic, success orientation of biomedical research, especially in the USA, can become dangerously myopic. We should point out that not all diseases will be cured nor all patients. Suffering will always be part of the human condition. No matter how many spare organs or treatments are available, we will all eventually die. Medicine thus needs to recover a proper theology of suffering and of eternity, which presents a vital opportunity for a Christian apologetic.

A second belief is in human progress driven by scientific advance. Through much of the twentieth century this figured as an idol making supreme truth-claims, but as the century closed, it was seen to have feet of clay, after a series of technological and environmental failures and a penetrating postmodern sociological critique. Issues like cloning, sex selection or post-menopausal fertility reveal the inability of the rationale of science to do more than point to the next experiment. In themselves, the biosciences know nothing of

ethical limits nor how to set their discoveries in their wider human context, and often make unspoken value assumptions about progress that Christians would challenge.

The prospect of genetic enhancement of human physical or mental attributes is remote, but it highlights several such issues. To attempt to correct a genetic mutation in the individual patient which causes a severe medical condition like cystic fibrosis is normally viewed as an ethical extension of existing medicine, but what of engineering merely for personal preference? The me-centred ethic of the materialist consumer might ask 'Why not?' But a personal desire to 'hard-wire' whatever genetic advantages I choose into myself or my child would be a luxury only for the rich, which would cut across wider concerns for social responsibility and *justice, equity and love for neighbour. More profoundly it would not improve our human lot if it is based on a false view of humanity and misses the dimension of human moral fallenness. Whatever technical enhancements we might imagine engineering into ourselves, it is an illusion that we have improved humanity while, as Jesus declared, it is what is in our hearts which defiles us. The intrinsic faultline of sin runs through all such human 'improvements'. Even the best repair is only temporary. Deliverance 'from this body of death' requires 'a new heavens and a new earth', the resurrection of the dead, not merely progressive technical improvements. Ideas of improvement are also subverted by the biblical picture of Christ, the perfection of humanity, as the man of sorrows, the shepherd king who though in the form of God became like a servant and was 'made perfect through suffering'. Our calling, man and woman alike, to emulate him 'that Christ may be formed in me' is something very different from changing our genetics.

The controversy over genetically modified food reveals fundamental issues about how far we should intervene in God's creation and shows two prominent and opposing philosophical views. One is unfettered human intervention, treating God's creation as a mere resource and seeing living systems only in terms of their functions for human use, without relation to God, fellow humans or respect for the rest of God's creation. The other is the elevation of nature to an autonomous or quasi-divine status like the earth mother goddess Gaia, which we alter at our peril lest 'she' strike us back. Currently popular notions such as upsetting the 'balance of nature' or harmonizing with energy flows point to neo-pagan or New Age concepts which need to be challenged. In contrast to both, a biblical perspective portrays a creation which is not divine but exists for God first. Humans are called to rule over and work in it, but intervention should be limited under God's laws, humbled by our finiteness and fallenness and moderated by responsibility towards fellow humans and due respect for all that God has created. We seek balance by bringing all these relational factors under God and proceeding, waiting or stopping accordingly.

Finally, the direction of the biotechnology revolution, human and non-human, has become dominated by commercial and political motives. Priorities are not necessarily what meets the most pressing human or environmental needs but what is most likely to deliver profit, jobs, economic growth and a better competitive position over rival companies or nations. Far reaching advances are largely remote from societal values. Questions of justice present opportunities for Christian witness, like whose values are taken into account, who wins or loses, biases to the rich and global considerations. Christians should be careful, however, not simply to jump on secular bandwagons on either side. Campaigning has a tendency to simplify or distort complex issues, demonizing opponents and romanticizing the preferred alternative strategies. Christians are to be truth-tellers but also as wise as serpents in this vital bioethical arena.

Bibliography

D. Bruce and D. Horrocks (eds.), *Modifying Creation* (Carlisle, 2001); D. Cook, *Moral Maze* (London, 2003);

Some useful websites

Society Religion and Technology Project: <http://www.srtp.org.uk>; Centre for Bioethics and Public Policy: <http:// www.cbpp.ac.uk>; Christians in Science: <http://www.cis.org.uk>; Christian Medical Fellowship: <http://www.cmf.org.uk>.

D. BRUCE

BODY PIERCING, see PIERCING

BONAVENTURE

A contemporary of *Thomas Aquinas, Bonaventure (c. 1221–c. 74) lived at a time when *Augustine's great achievement in marrying philosophy and *theology, faith and *reason, Platonism and the Bible, was being seriously challenged for the first time in 800 years. The rediscovery of many of the works of *Aristotle, linked with the development of radical thinking in the newly founded universities, threatened to destroy the synthesis that had given the medieval period a solid foundation on which to build a unified and holistic world-view centred on God and the Christian *revelation, but incorporating also all the best insights of 'the philosophers'.

Confronted with the shaking of established foundations and the challenge of radical new teaching, Christian apologists frequently tend to one of two extremes, choosing to cling firmly to the past, or to embrace the new concepts and reinterpret the Christian world-view accordingly. While Aquinas set himself to do the second, Bonaventure tended towards the first. It was not that he rejected totally the insights of Aristotle and the breath of fresh air the new approach to learning brought, but he felt they were a serious challenge both to a truly God-centred world-view and to the continuing synthesis of theology and philosophy. While the Aristotelians tended to seek an understanding of the world with very limited reference to God, Bonaventure argued for the total dependence of the world upon God: everything emanates from God and returns to God. Where the early stirrings of Renaissance humanism were asserting the autonomy of human reason, Bonaventure argued for the need of God's illumination for us to obtain true knowledge.

Born in Italy and educated in Paris, Bonaventure became a member and eventually minister general of the Franciscan order. By all accounts he had a very attractive personality. A contemporary account stated that 'all who saw him were filled with an immense love for him'. In an age of controversy he saw himself as a bridge builder and mediator.

He wrote widely in the field of philosophical theology and was viewed by many in succeeding centuries as a doctor of the church equal in significance to Aquinas. His theocentricity expressed itself not just in his doctrines but in his own deep relationship with God and in his teachings on mystical union with God through meditation, prayer and contemplation. His attempts to preserve the Augustinian synthesis, however, met with little success, and the future was to lie with the new learning.

Bibliography

E. Gilson, *The Philosophy of St Bonaventure* (Paterson, 1965); P. Rout, *Francis and Bonaventure* (London, 1996).

P. HICKS

BOREDOM

Boredom has been called a disease of our time and a metaphor for the postmodern condition. Paradoxically, in an age in which we are surrounded by ever more sophisticated forms of *entertainment, there is an increase in boredom.

There are two main types of boredom. Temporary boredom is provoked by e.g. the under-stimulation and repetition of a long committee meeting, a tedious lecture or talking to someone who talks only about themselves. Thankfully, for this type of boredom there is usually a remedy. One can leave a boring event or find some temporary distraction to keep one's mind occupied.

A longer term, more permanent boredom results when there is nothing to do that one likes. *Webster's Dictionary* relates boredom to malaise, close to the French word *ennui*, which means 'to annoy'. It is an experience of weariness and dissatisfaction issuing from inactivity or lack of interest and makes life seem futile and meaningless. In this existential type of boredom there is a loss of passion for life and a lack of engagement in anything satisfying. Yet desire is not completely dead because there is still a longing for something more, for something that will not be satisfied by all the available opportunities.

Throughout history people have experienced boredom. The desert fathers and the medieval monks wrote of wrestling with a sense of apathy about life and the things of God, but it was not until the eighteenth century that the word boredom entered the English language and references to it in English literature have multiplied since that time.

There are several possible reasons for this apparent increase in boredom in the last 200 years. Compared with previous generations, people now live longer and have many more leisure hours to fill. Boredom not only arises from under-stimulation but also from the over-stimulation provided by the entertainment and advertising industries, and we may reach a point where we cannot react with much depth to anything anymore. Everything has to be exciting to grab our attention. The media create such expectations for us that ordinary life becomes increasingly boring and we grow more dissatisfied. We also have to contend with a daily diet of advertisements that are designed to make us dissatisfied and bored with what we have and induce us to buy the products that are being advertised. Such saturation with entertainment and disconnection from reality eventually numbs and deadens the sensibilities of our souls. Also, instead of making our own entertainment, we rely on radio, TV, movies, video games and surfing the channels and the web. This stunts our *imagination and creative capacities.

Boredom may also arise from subconscious fears of failure or rejection. Repeated abuse in dysfunctional families may lead to a self-protective numbing of deep emotions and consequent feelings of emptiness and boredom. Similar feelings are common in times of clinical *depression and grief.

The increase in boredom is paralleled by a steady decline in Christian faith. Historically, a Christian view of life gave a motive to endure struggle, difficulty and boredom, and contentment was preached as an important virtue. People felt a responsibility to work hard, to take an interest in and get involved with life, especially with their family and wider social responsibilities. Boredom was seen either as a sin, or a sign of moral weakness or character failure.

Patricia Spacks suggests that boredom is 'a metaphor for the postmodern condition' (*Boredom*, p. 260). If there are no meaningful answers to the big questions of life then where do we find purpose and happiness? The book of Ecclesiastes describes the search for satisfaction in every possible form of activity, work, wealth, pleasure, gardens and beautiful women, ending only with a sense of emptiness and boredom (Eccl. 2:10–11). The writer ultimately learned that it is in the simple things of life that the deepest satisfaction can be found – food, drink, work and family enjoyed in a relationship with God (Eccl. 2:24–25; 3:12–13).

Obviously, some tasks are inherently tedious in a fallen world but boredom can be a healthy challenge to use our creativity in learning to delight in the ordinary things of life. To face the most monotonous parts of life we must remember the big picture that gives meaning to the little things.

God is not bored with his creation. In the Scriptures we read that he feels deeply and passionately about all that he has made. He enjoys the beauty and glory in the creation, and wants us to do that too. And yet God also grieves over the ugliness of sin, and he wants us to work against the evil and brokenness of our world. As we live in a relationship with him, and in the light of what he has told us about the world, our perspective on the often difficult and boring things of life is little by little transformed.

Bibliography

S. D. Healy, *Boredom, Self and Culture* (Toronto, 1984); O. E. Klapp, *Overload and Boredom: Essays on the Quality of Life in the Information Society* (New York, 1986); M. L. Raposa, *Boredom and the Religious Imagination* (Charlottesville, 1999); P. M. Spacks, *Boredom: The Literary History of a State of Mind* (Chicago, 1995); R. D. Winter, *Still Bored in a Culture of Entertainment: Rediscovering Passion and Wonder* (Downers Grove, 2002).

R. D. WINTER

BRUNNER, EMIL

Emil Brunner (1889–1966) was professor of systematic and practical theology in Zurich from 1924 until he retired in 1955. He became a prominent representative of Swiss and German dialectical theology in the 1920s. At that time, he was quite closely associated with Karl *Barth. Brunner became known in the English speaking world earlier than Barth as in the early years he had more contacts with Britain and America and from quite early on many of his books were translated into English. Their ways diverged when Brunner came to emphasize what he described in 1929 as 'the other task of theology' – not only to insist on the transcendent sovereignty of the divine word, but also to reflect on how it was possible for that word to find a 'point of contact' in the people of today's world.

Brunner's controversy with Barth exploded in 1934 when Brunner published *Nature and Grace*. He accused Barth of six exaggerations: that the image of God in humankind is obliterated by sin, and that there is no general *revelation, no grace of creation and preservation, no law of nature, no point of contact for the saving action of God and no continuity between nature and grace. Barth's angry reply in *No! Answer to Emil Brunner* came to Brunner as an unexpected shock. From that time on the two mostly had only strained contact.

Brunner continued to develop his own style of apologetics, which he named eristics – engaging critically with the ideas and assumptions of the modern world in order to challenge them on their own ground and to make the relevance and the challenge of the gospel apparent there. This involved him in an extensive discussion with philosophy of religion and the spiritual and intellectual foundations of human culture and is reflected in a series of books – *The Word and the World* (1931), *God and Man* (1936), *The Philosophy of Religion* (1937), *The Divine-Human Encounter* (1943; later expanded as *Truth as Encounter* [1964]) and *Revelation and Reason* (1947). In 1947 and 1948 Brunner delivered the Gifford Lectures in St Andrews, which were published in two volumes as *Christianity and Civilisation*. In this field he shows a considerable affinity to the work of Reinhold *Niebuhr. Brunner also published widely on dogmatics, *ethics and ecclesiology.

Bibliography

Natural Theology, Comprising 'Nature and Grace' by ... Emil Brunner and the reply 'No!' by ... Karl Barth. ET by Peter Fraenkel. With an Introduction by ... John Baillie (London, 1946); C. W. Kegley (ed.), *The Theology of Emil Brunner* (New York, 1962).

A. I. C. HERON

BUBER, MARTIN

Martin Buber (1878–1965) was born in Vienna into a scholarly Jewish family (his grandfather was the famous Midrash scholar Solomon Buber), but grew up in close contact with Polish Hasidic communities. He was educated in Vienna and German universities, then taught religion and philosophy at Frankfurt University from 1923–33. At the same time, he edited *Der Jude*. During these years he was influenced by the Christian existentialist *Kierkegaard while also beginning to study the Hebrew Scriptures intensely and starting to translate them into modern Hebrew for his students at the Free Jewish Academy. In 1933 he was deprived of his professorship by the Nazis and for the next five years was unemployed. He used this time to help German Jews before himself moving to Israel where he was already teaching at the University of Jerusalem. His move to Jerusalem was the climax of the Zionism which had begun to inspire him when he was still a student in the early 1920s. He remained in Israel until his death in 1965.

Four influences in his background may therefore be noted as determining his approach to apologetics: Hasidism and its pietistic sense of *community and belief in the inate goodness of humanity; *existentialism and its subjective emphasis on loving relationships; Zionism and its strong awareness of Jewishness and the role of Israel and Jerusalem in the purposes of God; the Hebrew Scriptures and a traditional biblical understanding.

I – Thou – It

Buber felt that *Judaism led essentially to the very personal I-Thou relationship with God and other people. Adam and Eve walked in the garden of Eden in the cool of the evening with God. Abraham was known as the friend of God. God spoke personally to the patriarchs and prophets of Israel. This personal relationship between God and humanity should form the model for inter-human relationships also. Being defined as a God of relationships, God may be called the 'Eternal Thou' – his very existence assumes such relationship.

On the other hand, Buber defined the 'It' as the created material world, which is experienced and is essential for human beings but which is in itself inadequate for true human life. Buber noted that human beings cannot exist without the created world of 'It', but real humanness demands more than just living with the 'It'.

So Buber underlined the I-Thou relationship of loving understanding and appreciation of the other, while he saw the I-It relationship as one in which one person uses the other. So proselytism (applying undue moral, emotional or financial pressure to persuade others to convert to one's own faith) is seen as a form of I-It communication. This would not only influence Emil *Brunner, but also the Christian Presence school of Max Warren and John Taylor in which it was said that 'all men [sic] chose either compassion or jabbering'. Thus, John Taylor stated that we must be 'open to all and present with all' in this 'universe of I and Thou'. This approach to mission underlies the ensuing development of Christian apologetics with its emphasis on dialogue rather than the kind of witness that 'targets' people or aims to convert. Such evangelization is pejoratively described as 'proselytism'.

Buber contrasted 'propaganda' with 'education'. In the latter the teacher seeks to unfold what is already within the pupil. This approach is clearly influenced by the Hasidic emphasis on the spark of goodness which already lies within all people and indeed within everything on earth. This is the I-Thou relationship which respects the goodness and truth inherent in our humanness. It is contrasted with I-It propaganda, which seeks to impose the teacher's understanding of truth on the other person and thus presumes the arrogance of an unequal relationship.

Nevertheless, in his writings on the principles of dialogue Buber says that dialogue does not mean a mutual relativization of convictions, but just an acceptance of the other in their humanness as a person. It does not necessarily mean that those involved will have to agree, nor should they have to compromise their beliefs, but they should be willing to listen to each other so that they understand and are enriched by the other. While Buber talks of being enriched 'by the other', this will presumably also include some learning from their faith and beliefs. Apologetics therefore ideally includes both a positive communication of one's own beliefs and also a humble listening to and learning from the other.

Israel as community

With his Hasidic and Zionist influences, Buber believed that the goal of genuine Jewish life, and therefore the witness of Israel, could only be achieved in community. He had observed the influence of the Hasidic communities, but noted the limitation of what they could attain within the gentile society of Poland. Under the power of a gentile government and an alien legal system, the Hasidic communities could not develop the fullness of the theocratic state envisioned in the Hebrew Scriptures. Buber joined with the Zionists, therefore, in their support for the state of Israel. But with his biblical background, he followed a way which was different from the secular Zionists. He longed for Israel to become the godly and ethically upright society which could bring the Law of God to bear on the world and thus 'transform the world'. He observed that already the life of Israel permeated the gentile world, seeing that the best in Christianity, Marxism and humanism all stemmed from Jewish sources. Indeed, Jews like Jesus and Marx have played a leading role in the founding of these various movements.

So Buber saw Jerusalem as 'the gateway of the nations'. He therefore underlined the necessity for Jewish people to seek the salvation of Jerusalem because this would lead to the salvation of the nations. He felt that Israel lay strategically between East and West, and so could be the mediator of God's salvation to all peoples. It could channel oriental mysticism to the West, as was already evident in the development of Western existentialism with its Eastern influence – Buber's early enthusiasm for existentialism is evident here. But it could also funnel Western understandings to the nations of the East. Buber's own wide influence on gentile peoples is a further example of Israel as God's chosen people to mediate divine blessing to the nations.

It is commonly noted that in the Hebrew Scriptures Israel is not called to an outgoing verbal proclamation of God's truth to the surrounding nations. Rather she is called to a centripetal witness which draws the nations to Zion through her holiness in obedience to God's Law. Israel was called to be the honey which attracted the bees, the light which acted as a magnet to the gentile moths. This biblical understanding of Israel's apologetic calling underlies Buber's whole understanding of the role of Israel today.

Buber would, however, have disagreed with D. Kidner, whose understanding of Israel's centripetal mission saw the people of Israel as 'passive and reluctant exhibits'. Likewise, he would not have liked J. Yoder's emphasis on Israel standing still in order to see God's salvation at work. Buber's approach was much more active and dynamic. The people of Israel are called for God's sake actively to affirm the world and themselves in order to transform both. The transformation of ourselves is God's call in order that we may then transform the world.

What then is Buber's approach to apologetics? On the one hand, his Hasidic and existentialist backgrounds draw him to an emphasis on interpersonal relationships which are based on the essential nature of God himself as one who delights to relate to human beings. This emphasis on the I-Thou apologetic of listening and loving in *humility has become his major influence on the history of the development of apologetics. Christians will also take careful note of the influence of the Hebrew Scriptures on his thinking. While they will want to add the NT understanding of witness and mission (going out into the world to preach and teach the good news), his emphasis on the role of the community rather than just the individual believer brings its own challenge. And Jewish Christians may wish to interact with Buber's Zionist emphasis and his understanding of the significance of the State of Israel as God's apologetical instrument. Jewish Christians will also feel a oneness with Buber in his sufferings under Nazism and his agonized reactions to the *Holocaust. In the Bible suffering is a fundamental basis for true witness and therefore for all apologetics.

Bibliography

M. Buber, *I and Thou* (Edinburgh, 1970); *Israel and the World* (New York, 1948); *Kingship of God* (New York, 1990); *On Judaism* (New York, 1972); *On Zion: The History of an Idea* (Edinburgh, 1985); *Tales of the Hasidim* (New York, 1947/48); M. Friedman, *Martin Buber's Life and Work: The Early Years 1878–1923* (London, 1982); *Martin Buber: The Life of Dialogue* (Chicago and London, rev. edn 1976); P. A. Schilpp and M. Friedman (eds.), *The Philosophy of Martin Buber* (London, 1967).

M. GOLDSMITH

BUDDHISM

Buddhism is a term used for a vast body of doctrine, practice and culture which has grown up around the figure of the Buddha. For centuries it has shaped the civilizations of Asia and has recently become popular in the Western world. The person of the Buddha dominates this religious tradition as the pioneer of the 'Middle Way'.

The Buddha

The precise dates of the Buddha's life are uncertain. Many Buddhists consider them to be 566–486 BC, but recent scholars, after re-assessing the evidence, prefer dates of c. 484–404 BC. The child who was to become known as the Buddha was born at Lumbini in modern Nepal. His father was a nobleman of the Sakya clan, and he named his son Siddhattha Gautama. The story is told that a holy man recognized the thirty-two auspicious marks on the child's body that indicated that he would grow up to be either a world ruler or the enlightened one (the Buddha). Gautama's father wanted him to be a great ruler, so he sought to protect his son from the harsh realities of life by providing him a life of luxury. Gautama married a beautiful princess who bore him a son named Radula (meaning 'tie' or 'fetter'). When he was twenty-nine, he was out hunting when he had 'Four Sights'. The first three sightings (of an old man, a desperately ill man and a corpse) raised the question of suffering in the world, and the last (of an ascetic) showed the way to find an answer.

Gautama decided to leave the palace. He spent six years as a wandering ascetic trying some of the methods of religious training available, but he felt that they did not go far enough. He then practised extreme asceticism and fasting, but these did not bring peace of mind. When he accepted food, the five ascetics who had gathered around him left him in disgust. Gautama, however, set out to develop his own spiritual path. After he regained his strength, Gautama sat beneath a large fig tree and resolved to attain enlightenment. *Bodhi* means 'awakened' and later was applied to a species of fig. During his meditation he was tempted by Mara, the Evil One, but he persisted and finally achieved realization of the supreme *truth. The term 'Buddha' literally means an 'Awakened One' or 'Enlightened One'.

The Buddha journeyed to the ancient city of Banaras to find his former disciples and preached his first sermon, the 'Discourse Setting in Motion the Wheel of Truth'. These ascetics are said to have also attained enlightenment, and he commissioned them to preach the message to all beings. For the next forty-five years, the Buddha spent his time in meditation and teaching throughout the kingdoms of the Ganges valley. Many people gave up their ordinary way of life to follow his teaching (*Dharma*) and became part of the monastic *community (*Sangha*). When he was eighty years old, he became sick, entered a deep state of meditation and passed away (*paranirvana*).

The *Dharma*

The Buddha's first sermon expressed the heart of the *dharma* and addressed the problem of suffering. Unlike most religions, his solution did not involve God, but is set out as the 'Four Noble Truths'. These are that all life is suffering; suffering arises from craving; there is release from suffering – *nirvana*; and the way that leads to the end of suffering is the 'Middle Way'.

By claiming that all life is suffering, the Buddha did not mean that it has no pleasure, but that all beings are caught up in the ongoing process of death and rebirth. Everything is impermanent. 'The Middle Way' avoids the extremes of sensual indulgence and physical austerities, and is composed of eight elements: right understanding, right thought, right speech, right action, right livelihood, right effort, right mindfulness and right concentration.

The Buddha shared certain basic ideas with Brahmanism, e.g. *karma*, rebirth, meditation and liberation. Nevertheless, he did not accept their scriptures, the caste system or adopt their sacrifices. He taught that all beings are reborn in one of five (or six) states. The highest is that of the gods (*devas*), the next is human, the next animal, then ghosts, and the lowest that of the hell-beings. The gods are merely exalted beings who live for long periods, have great power and pleasure, but are still caught up in the cycle of rebirth. The Buddha also disputed the prevailing notion that the human soul (*atman*) was eternal and argued that there is no permanent, unchanging substance that could be considered as 'I'. For this reason, the teaching is known as *anatta*, 'non-self'. What is regarded as 'self' is considered a combination of ever-changing physical and mental energies that can be divided into five groups (*skandha*).

This quest for enlightenment commences with a recitation expressing a desire to take refuge in the Buddha, the *Dharma* and the *Sangha*. Most Buddhists then accept the ethical principles of the discipline of which the first five precepts are to abstain from the taking of life, stealing, misconduct in sensual action, false speech and intoxicants.

To join the monastic community one is required to renounce the ordinary way of life and to accept the discipline of the *Sangha*, which is expressed by 227 precepts including five listed above. As monks do not work or grow food, they are dependent upon the lay community for their sustenance. In return the monks teach the *Dharma* and exemplify its teaching.

Buddhist traditions

After the death of the Buddha, the *sangha* initially remained united but finally divided at the Council of Pataliputra. A more reformist group separated from those who preferred to keep the existing code. The great King Asoka, who reigned 268–239 BC was a convert to the teaching around 260 BC. Buddhism was adopted as the state religion, and missionaries were sent to most of the Indian subcontinent and beyond, thus making it a 'world religion'. It was in Sri Lanka that the more conservative Theravada form became dominant and here the teachings of the Buddha were transcribed in the Pali language to form the canon known as the *Tripitaka*. Today the countries of Sri Lanka, Burma (Mayamar), Thailand, Laos and Cambodia continue to follow the Theravada tradition.

Some time between 150 BC and AD 100 a new movement arose as a culmination of the earlier reform developments. This came to be known as Mahayana ('great vehicle') as opposed to Hinayana ('lesser vehicle') as Theravada was called. It emerged from a number of new texts that claimed to be deeper teachings of the Buddha, the most renowned of which are *The Diamond Sutra*, *The Heart Sutra* and *The Lotus Sutra*. Mahayana differed from Theravada in several ways. First, Theravada assumed that there was only one enlightened being in any world cycle – the Buddha – and that he had been a human being. Mahayana had a more exalted view of the nature of the Buddha, and this became expressed as the 'three bodies' doctrine. The first body is the 'transformation body' like that of the person of the Buddha himself. The second body is the 'heavenly body' that may preside over a particular Buddha-realm. And the third and ultimate body is the 'dharma body', which is the absolute essence of the universe.

Secondly, Mahayana offered a new formulation of the path, centred on *bodhisattvas*, enlightened beings, who out of compassion choose not to enter the blissful state of *nirvana* until all sentient beings are delivered. Bodhisattvas, therefore, became important figures of popular devotion, who could bring salvation to those who called upon them. The most important bodhisattvas are Amitaba, Manjusri, Maitreya and Avalokitesvara. Thirdly, a new philosophical outlook developed around the concept of *sunyata* (emptiness). This was expounded by the great philosopher Nagarjuna and is the middle way between affirmations of being and non-being. Mahayana saw the path as not only one for spiritual heroes but also as open to all.

The third major strand of Buddhism is the Tibetan, or Vajrayana ('diamond vehicle') tradition, which arose in India in the sixth century AD. It sought to speed up the long path to enlightenment by methods of practice based on texts called tantras that described complex ritual meditative practices. Mantras are used to aid the visualization of heavenly buddhas and bodhisattvas. The visualized figures may be either male or female and are sometimes portrayed in sexual union. Tantric Buddhism flourished for only a few centuries in India before it was extinguished, but by then it had spread into central Asia, to Mongolia, Siberia and finally Tibet.

Tibetan Buddhism has four main schools. The oldest school is the Nyingma, whose origins can be traced back to the first introduction of Buddhism to Tibet at the end of the eighth century by the scholar Padmasambhava. The second school is Sakya, which emerged in the eleventh century and looks back to the translator Drokmi Shakya Yeshe. The third school is Kagyu, which means 'transmission of the living tradition'. Marpa (AD 1012–96) was instrumental in bringing the Kagyu to Tibet, and his famous disciple was Milarepa (AD 1040–1123). The fourth school is Gelug, founded in the fourteenth century from the tradition of Atisha and Je Tsongkhapa (AD 1357–1410). The Mongols appointed the head of Gelug as their viceroy for Tibet, and he became known as the Dalai Lama ('Ocean of Wisdom'). The Dalai Lama is considered to be a reincarnation of the bodhisattva Avalokitesvara, and each Dalai Lama is said to be the reincarnation of the previous Dalai Lama. When the Dalai Lama dies, a complicated search is undertaken to find the next reincarnation. The current Dalai Lama is the fourteenth embodiment. Similar claims are made for other high lamas. 'Lama' is the Tibetan term for a respected spiritual teacher, equivalent to Sanskrit 'guru'.

Buddhism entered China about AD 50, and the Mahayana teaching fused with Chinese culture to form many schools. The most popular forms were those that focused on particular forms of practice and a particular text. Ch'an (Japanese Zen) uses meditation and gives little attention to texts. Bodhidharma is the legendary founder of Ch'an, and the story is told that when he arrived at a monastery in northern China he spent nine years facing a blank wall as an illustration of his teaching. For Ch'an, the Buddha-nature, or potential to achieve enlightenment, is inherent in everyone but lies dormant because of ignorance. It is awakened not by study of scriptures or practice of ceremonies, but by realizing the buddha-nature within through meditation and probing the mind. This is often achieved by the use of enigmatic questions (*koan*) such as,

'If someone claps his hands, one hears a
    sound at once.
Listen now to the sound of a single hand!'

Buddhism today has the fourth largest number of adherents of any world religion, and its influence spreads far wider with its great impact on Chinese society. It is a vital growing religion with many new movements, and an increasing following in the West.

Buddhism and Christianity

As with Christianity, the human predicament is at the heart of Buddhist teaching, and this has provided an important basis for the Christian-Buddhist encounter. The wisdom literature of the OT uses the Hebrew word *hebel* (usually translated into English as 'vanity') in a way that has similar connotations with the Buddhist term *dukkha*, implying the unsatisfactoriness of life. The writer of Ecclesiastes, like the Buddha, saw desire as the root of the human predicament. The fundamental difference is that Buddhism seeks to eliminate the cause of *dukkha* through the practice of the Middle Way whereas the wisdom literature recognizes the divine. In the frequent use of the expression 'under the sun', the wisdom literature shows the restricted scope of the intellectual inquiry and, therefore, the need to take the transcendent into consideration in the quest for meaning. It is God who is the giver of good gifts, and life will never be meaningful until he is known.

Bibliography

D. Burnett, *The Spirit of Buddhism* (Crowborough, 1996); R. Gethin, *The Foundations of Buddhism* (Oxford, 1998); P. Harvey, *An Introduction to Buddhism: Teaching, History and Practices* (Cambridge, 1992); W. Rahula, *What the Buddha Taught* (Oxford, 1998).

D. BURNETT

BULTMANN, RUDOLF

Rudolf Bultmann (1884–1976) is universally recognized as a giant among twentieth-century NT scholars. His form-critical approach came to dominate the field of NT studies in Germany and has influenced theologians throughout the world. The son of a German Lutheran pastor, Bultmann studied at Tübingen, Berlin and Marburg before becoming Professor of New Testament at Marburg.

Bultmann rejected attempts to reconstruct *Jesus' life, and particularly Jesus' consciousness, with any conclusiveness, and followed his teacher Wilhelm Herrmann's emphasis on the defencelessness of faith. Faith, as the unobjectifiable existential decision of obedience responding to the ever dynamic and always-to-be-renewed encounter with the 'Wholly Other', cannot be secured or suggest that this 'Other' is controllable. Bultmann's distinction between *Historie* (scientific *history reconstructing past events) and *Geschichte* (history in its existential impact on contemporary life) is a way of underlining both that a proper reading of (biblical) texts is to hear the speaking of their subject matter (*Sache*) and that *revelation cannot be 'contained' or 'possessed' by any moment of history.

According to Bultmann, liberal historical critics miss these theological determinations and attempt to secure revelation in historically testable conditions. In so doing, they make the Wholly Other and the confrontation with it in the event of revelation into objects of human conceiving. This undermines God's subjectivity or unpossessable prevenient agency (albeit that this is a 'subjectivity' mediated through the biblical texts).

The proper role of historical criticism is to enable this confrontation, or perhaps ask about *who* is to be discerned through these

125

texts. Bultmann's infamous demythologization of the Gospel records is a way of, first, 'de-objectifying' the naïve theological conceptions of the biblical writers and, secondly, asking what it is that they are trying to say mytho-logically. Myth, Bultmann argues, is a misleading way of describing transcendent forces in objective, quasi-scientific terms. So, the NT is riddled with the myths consist-ent with the first-century world-view of its authors. This world-view is very different from the contemporary one, which assumes, for instance, a closed, causal continuum of events, not repeatedly breached by supernatural agencies, and discounts the notion of miracle as an interruption of the world's causal processes with historical and scientific explanation. Bultmann identifies numerous NT myths, e.g. the three-tier universe as the arena for conflict between the forces of God and *Satan, the Son of God's coming from *heaven and his defeat of Satan's forces, the virgin birth, Christ's bodily resurrection and ascension and his return on the clouds as executor of God's final judgment. To these Bultmann adds the dogmatic theories of the incarnation, *atonement and *Trinity.

Demythologizing replaces these illusory theological objectifications by translating the biblical myths into a more appropriate contem-porary theological idiom. Bultmann represents this in existential, self-involving *language – 'faith' in the cross can realize in human exist-ence a new possibility of forgiveness, freedom and love. In theory, this approach to the biblical record is not a rejection of its *Sache*, or an attempt to strip away externals to get at the heart of its message, but rather consists of trying to discover the original *kerygma* and interpret-ing its expression and mispresentation by the various NT writers. Nevertheless, it remains to be asked whether Bultmann adequately deals with the question of the *Sache*'s own encultura-tion of expression, and whether he does resort in practice to precisely the negation of myth by a discovery of the biblical kernel.

Bultmann takes seriously the impact of the various factors influencing the readers (the pre-suppositions they bring) as well as the authors (their cultural background and belief systems). Consequently, any apologetic that imagines that God's acts can be read off the world, off cultural products, or even off one's experiences misses not only the eventfulness of grace but also the ambiguity of both the world and our readings of its 'meaning'. Moreover, one's set of

pre-understandings, and the questions therein brought to bear on the text, must be malleable when encountered by those texts' *Sache*. There-fore, any apologetic that is not open to the interrogation and transformation of its method is mistaken.

Bibliography

R. Bultmann, *Existence and Faith: Shorter Writings of Rudolf Bultmann* (ed. and trans. S. M. Ogden; London, 1961); *Jesus and the Word* (trans. L. P. Smith and E. H. Lantero; London, 1952); *The New Testament and Mythology and Other Writings* (ed. and trans. S. M. Ogden; London, 1984); D. Fergusson, *Bultmann* (London, 1992).

J. C. McDowell

BUTLER, JOSEPH

Joseph Butler (1692–1752) was, according to Cardinal *Newman, 'the greatest name in the Anglican Church'. As a young man, Butler converted from the dissenting church to the Church of England and, after his degree from Oxford, served as preacher at the Rolls Chapel in London and later as Bishop of Bristol, Dean of St Paul's Cathedral and, finally, Bishop of Durham. Butler is remembered for two import-ant works, *Fifteen Sermons Preached at the Rolls Chapel* (1726) and *The Analogy of Religion, Natural and Revealed, to the Consti-tution of the Course of Nature* (1736).

Butler's *Fifteen Sermons* remains a critical work in moral philosophy. The aim of moral philosophy, as he understands it, is to identify the way of life 'correspondent' to the nature of human beings. Thus, Butler's task is the explora-tion of human nature, and he identifies in us the motivating forces of (in hierarchical order, from that most worthy to be guided to that most worthy of guiding) particular passions, benevolence and cool self-love, all of which are appropriately ruled by the candle of God within us, *conscience. 'Had it strength, as it has right; had it power, as it has manifest authority, it would absolutely govern the world.' The virtuous person follows the natural and fit ordering of his passions in their appropriate strengths towards their appropriate objects, guided by conscience, and the result is an eternal happiness, if not a temporal happiness.

Despite his confidence that acting according to our human natures will lead to happiness,

Butler denies that happiness is the appropriate aim of our actions. Indeed, Butler's criticism of psychological egoism – the view that all human actions are motivated by the desire for our own happiness or pleasure – remains compelling. The fact that the achievement of our aim brings pleasure or happiness is explained by our independently valuing the object of that achievement. As such, happiness is a by-product of our achievement rather than its aim.

Butler's *Analogy* is the most important work in apologetics in eighteenth-century Britain. Taking on the deists, he constructs an argument by *analogy to establish, first, that it is probable that there is an afterlife in which God will reward or punish humans depending upon their performance in their earthly state of 'moral probation'. Given the continuation of consciousness in individuals, despite the corruption and loss of parts of the body, Butler maintains that it is not unreasonable that the entire body be lost, and yet the soul live on. And, since we can observe only an imperfect moral governance in this world in which happiness usually but not necessarily attends virtue, it is reasonable to think that in the soul's continued existence after death the correspondence between happiness and virtue will be exact, as the moral governor of the universe desires it. Secondly, Butler argues that the defects in Christian *revelation alleged by the deists are analogous to the difficulties we find in identifying God's work in nature. Deists who lack no confidence in their reading of nature in a world in which God's workings are hardly transparent should, thus, be *at least as* confident in their reading of the Bible in which the ways of God are made manifest.

Butler acknowledges that his analogical arguments establish only the probability of the truth of Christian revelation. But just as this life is a state of moral probation for humans, so it may also be a state of intellectual probation for finite human beings, those who desire certainty, but can achieve only probability.

Bibliography

C. Cunliffe, *Joseph Butler's Moral and Religious Thought: Tercentenary Essays* (Oxford, 1992); W. E. Gladstone (ed.), *The Works of Joseph Butler*, 3 vols. (London, 1896; repr. Bristol, 1997); E. C. Mossner, *Bishop Butler and the Age of Reason* (New York, 1936).

T. D. KENNEDY

CAIRD, EDWARD

Edward Caird (1835–1908), one of Britain's most notable philosophers of the late nineteenth century, was born at Greenock, Scotland, the younger brother of John Caird. He was educated at Glasgow and Oxford, where he befriended T. H. Green, who was to have a formative and lasting influence on his thought. In 1866 Caird was elected Professor of Moral Philosophy at the University of Glasgow, and in 1893 was appointed Master of Balliol College at Oxford. He was awarded various honours and held numerous lectureships, including two series of Gifford Lectures published as *The Evolution of Religion* (1893) and *The Evolution of Theology in the Greek Philosophy* (1904).

A convinced Hegelian idealist, Caird believed that *truth is to be found always in the most developed forms of thought. Since humanity is understood by Caird as spiritual, spirit is seen to constitute the whole of *reality and to embrace ultimate meaning. Reason is not regarded as independent but as an expression of spirit, and is sufficient for religious knowledge. There is no need for any radically new type of revelation to break into human life, since the supernatural is immanent in mind. Caird argued that an emphasis on feeling or *conscience for the attainment of religious knowledge sets up a false dualism between thought and matter. Hegel overcame this *Kantian dualism by suggesting that the real is taken up in the ideal, so that the freedom of the spirit and the necessities of nature are not irreconcilable, but unified.

Commitment to the sufficiency of reason for the attainment of religious knowledge left Caird unable to affirm much new theology of the liberal Protestant type, since it required a dualism which could lead to scepticism. Nevertheless, some implications of Caird's thought leave his philosophy incompatible with evangelical theology. The problem of *evil is left unresolved, raising serious questions for the significance of the incarnation and crucifixion and for the whole of Christian *ethics. The Creator–creature distinction is blurred, with broad implications for theology and evangelism. Caird's main contribution to apologetics is his contention that reason, as an activity of the spirit, is not to be divorced from faith. However, in successfully refuting this epistemological dualism, Caird expounded instead a dynamic ontological *monism, or oneness of being, which left no room for distinctive revelation.

Bibliography

E. Caird, *Hegel* (London, 1883); H. Jones and J. H. Muirhead, *The Life and Philosophy of Edward Caird* (Glasgow, 1921); A. P. F. Sell, *Philosophical Idealism and Christian Belief* (Cardiff, 1995).

A. M. ROBBINS

CALVIN, JOHN

The contribution of John Calvin (1509–1564) to Christian apologetics may be said to be somewhat oblique, and it is the subject of continuing scholarly debate. Given his reputation as a systematic theologian, he was clearly not an irrationalist, and wherever there is the appearance of contradiction in some theological position Calvin makes efforts to establish logical consistency. Nor is he a fideist, despite the importance he gives to faith. Faith involves belief, and belief requires evidence, importantly for Calvin the self-evidencing character of Scripture.

In the *Institutes*, when dealing with the natural knowledge of God, Calvin appears to attach little if any importance to the proofs of the existence of God. Is this because he thinks that they are impossible, or unnecessary, or is it because *natural theology was not an issue at the Reformation? The closest he comes to medieval apologetics is in *Institutes* 1.8 where he discusses how the Bible's divine character might be given external support. Though his discussion of these 'proofs' is quite lengthy, Calvin believes that they nevertheless have a subordinate role to that of the self-authenticating work of the *Holy Spirit because they can at best change our opinions, never give certainty. Besides these references in the *Institutes*, he also has interesting scattered observations about natural theology elsewhere, e.g. in his comments on Acts 17.

Calvin gives much greater place to the *sensus divinitatis*, an innate sense of the existence of God, than he does to the proofs of natural theology. Claims have been made on Calvin's behalf that this appeal to the *sensus divinitatis* is in effect the claim that the belief that God exists is 'properly basic', i.e. it does not require formal proof but is on a par with other of our

basic beliefs, such as memory beliefs or beliefs arising from immediate perception. Calvin shows little interest in rationality *per se*, and it is likely that his appeal to the *sensus* is his way of underlining the teaching of Paul in Rom. 1 about human accountability. Responsibility, not rationality, appears to be Calvin's chief concern.

Those who have seen Calvin as a proponent of 'negative apologetics' would seem to be closer to his spirit. From his own practice it is clear that his somewhat limited apologetic endeavours were designed to answer objections, particularly logical objections, to Christian claims, and then to let those claims speak for themselves. But the strength and importance of even this limited apologetic strategy has to be qualified by two factors. The first is Calvin's repeated appeal to the principle of divine accommodation in our understanding of the Bible. According to Calvin, as the Bible is not a textbook of astronomy any more than it is of philosophy or medicine, it cannot be expected to 'take sides' in conflicts between *revelation and secular learning. The only exception is where such learning clearly falls within the parameters of scriptural teaching, and one gains the impression that Calvin thinks that these parameters may be fairly narrow. The second factor is Calvin's insistence on the indispensability of the work of the Holy Spirit in illuminating the mind to the saving truth expressed in Scripture and in bringing an individiual to repentance and faith in Christ.

While some in the Calvinist tradition, such as B. B. *Warfield, have seen Calvin's remarks on the natural knowledge of God as evidence of his commitment to full-blown natural theology and a proponent of the *cosmological argument, others have claimed him as a 'presuppositionalist'. If what makes a presuppositionalist is a stress on the importance of premises (starting points in *reasoning), then Calvin might be said to be one. Such an approach is, however, common, by no means exclusively Calvinian. Sometimes the term 'presuppositionalism' is given to the conviction that only by an appeal to the Bible alone can a coherent *epistemology and *metaphysics be established. There is little evidence in Calvin of such an a priori approach. He is much more inductive and guarded in his approach to Scripture, recognizing the presence of *mystery and of our own cognitive limitations, warning against speculation and emphasizing that the purpose of divine revelation in the Bible is overwhelmingly concerned with salvation.

Bibliography

J. Calvin, *Institutes of the Christian Religion* (tr. F. L. Battles; London and Philadelphia, 1961); E. A. Dowey Jr, *The Knowledge of God in Calvin's Theology*, 3rd edn (Grand Rapids, 1994); P. Helm, *John Calvin's Ideas* (Oxford, 2004); R. A. Muller, *The Unaccommodated Calvin* (New York, 2000); A. Plantinga, *Warranted Christian Belief* (Oxford, 2000); B. B. Warfield, 'Calvin's Doctrine of the Knowledge of God', in *Calvin and Calvinism* (New York, 1931).

P. HELM

CANON OF SCRIPTURE

Since the fourth century AD, the term *canon*, meaning 'rule' or 'norm', has been used to describe the books of the OT and NT. Use of this term revealed what Christians had already believed for centuries: that these writings are the final *authority within the church. How did they come to be viewed this way? The process of canonization spanned several centuries and was different for each testament.

The OT canon

Judging from the way NT authors refer to 'Scripture' (John 20:9; Gal. 3:22; 1 Pet. 2:6; 2 Pet. 1:20; cf. 2 Tim. 3:15–16), there appears to have been an accepted set of authoritative texts among Jews at the time of Christ. In fact, throughout the NT most books of the OT are cited in a specific way, denoting their status as authoritative Scripture.

The development of the OT canon was a process. Books were written at different times and came to be recognized as authoritative by a variety of means. It is difficult to say at exactly what point the canon of the OT was firmly settled. Nevertheless, we can say several things.

Since at least 130 BC, we have evidence of a three-fold division of Hebrew Scripture into the Law, the Prophets and the Writings. In a well-known passage about the 'famous men' of Israel, the author of the book of Sirach (Ecclesiasticus) draws from most of the books of what we now call the OT. By doing this he links the books of our OT to the three-fold division of Scripture mentioned in the intro-

duction to Ecclesiasticus. In a similar way, Luke 24:44–45 tells us that *Jesus revealed all that the Scriptures said about him in the Law, the Prophets and the Psalms (probably referring to the 'Writings'). It would seem that Luke's Gospel reflects a tradition of a fairly well-defined, tri-partite canon which had been around for at least 175 years.

Some scholars argue that the canon of the OT was not 'closed' until AD 90, when a council of Jewish leaders met at a city called Jamnia. While these rabbis did debate the place of the Song of Songs and Ecclesiastes in the canon, no record exists of their deliberations, and there is no reason to regard this meeting as a type of 'general council'. Instead, what this minor debate points to is near complete agreement on a canon of the Hebrew Bible (our OT) from well before this time.

We can say with some confidence that the canon of the OT had a clear shape before the time of Jesus – perhaps centuries before. The NT reveals that the earliest church viewed the contents of what became known as the OT with a unified submission to its authority, believing that Jesus himself fulfilled what was promised therein.

The Apocrypha

The books of the *Apocrypha never appear as part of Hebrew Scripture. They do, however, appear alongside the Greek translation of the OT (the Septuagint), and hence in many Bibles today. Segments of the church throughout history have viewed these books as canonical. This is a questionable practice for several reasons. First, these books, though attached to the OT, were never viewed as Scripture by Israel. Secondly, these books were not viewed as Scripture by the earliest church. This is clear because no explicit quotation of an apocryphal book occurs in the NT. Thirdly, the apocryphal books were expressly described as deutero-canonical by a number of influential Church Fathers, including *Athanasius, Jerome, Epiphanius and Cyril. While we may not consider these books to be canonical, they have been used for education and edification throughout the history of the church.

The NT canon

If the OT canon was relatively well established and adopted by the early church, when and how did the church recognize the NT canon?

In both the Eastern and Western churches the canon of Scripture as we know it was firmly fixed by the end of the fourth century. It was born out of three centuries of intense discussion and debate in which it became more and more necessary to articulate the limits of orthodox belief. For the Eastern church this occurred decisively in the thirty-ninth Paschal Letter of Athanasius in AD 367. For the church in the West this same canon was fixed by a church council in Carthage in AD 397.

While it is somewhat anachronistic to speak of a set of specific criteria by which the early church determined canonicity, it is possible to outline several principles which guided the church as it came to recognize certain works as authoritative.

1. *Apostolicity*. For a writing to be considered canonical it had to bear the marks of apostolic authority. In other words, it must have been written by one of the apostles, or otherwise closely connected to an apostle. Because of this, it made sense that older documents had an advantage. In fact, in spite of what some scholars might argue, none of the extra-canonical works known to us today can be dated any earlier than our canonical documents.

2. *Orthodoxy*. Another means of gauging whether or not a piece of writing was authoritative was to look at its theology. If a work proclaimed a different gospel from that which was proclaimed by Jesus and his apostles, then that work was not considered authoritative. This became increasingly important as heretical texts, claiming to speak the truth about Christ, abounded in the second and third centuries.

3. *Catholicity*. Finally, for a writing to be considered canonical it had to have been widely known throughout the church, with near universal acceptance of its authority.

These criteria show that the early church valued eye-witness reporting, theological consistency and widespread acceptance of documents before they were officially recognized as part of the canon. In spite of attempts to denigrate them, these criteria stand up well under inspection. Historical research method indicates that eye-witness testimony corroborated by other eye-*witnesses and quickly accepted by a wide range of people provides superior evidence to relatively late, secondhand accounts which diverge from the standard version.

Recent assaults on the canon

During the twentieth century, discoveries in Egypt and Israel uncovered a number of texts which were either previously unknown or no longer extant. These discoveries led to an enormous increase in our knowledge of early Christianity and *Judaism. They also raised questions as to how and why certain texts had come to be regarded as authoritative while others were forgotten. Ultimately, they precipitated a thoroughgoing critique of the idea of a Christian canon of Scripture. What are the primary criticisms of our notion of the canon? There are many, but it is possible to limit our discussion to three of the most common.

1. Alternative gospel accounts and documents referring to them have recently been discovered. There are over thirty different pieces of 'gospel' writing which purport to describe Jesus' life and ministry. Given the fact that we have so many gospels about Jesus it seems unfair to limit the canonical collection to just four. Why do we insist that the canonical gospels are right and the others wrong?

2. During the first centuries of the church different Church Fathers had different canons. If these important men did not agree on what was canonical, why should we? We need to come to terms with the fact that the canon was not delineated until the late fourth century and that the idea of a canon must have been foreign to the earliest church.

3. Finally, it is time for the church to recognize that the canon was a tool of oppression used to stamp out unpopular voices, limit discussion and legitimize the power of Constantine's empire.

Defending the canon today

These various critiques of the canon are easy to spot both in scholarly and in popular literature. The best-selling novel, *The Da Vinci Code*, by Dan Brown, bases a significant part of its plot on alternative gospel accounts, specifically the Gospels of Philip and Mary. Why do Christians not accept these accounts of Jesus' life as accurate? The main reason is that they were written several centuries after Christ (probably early third century) by a heretical Christian sect called the Gnostics. They were written to justify a set of beliefs that date long after Christ, cannot be traced to the apostles and are clearly a derivation from Christianity.

While those who question the canon of

Scripture point to the diversity of 'canons' in the early church, they generally ignore the astonishing congruence of early views about authoritative texts. To speak of disagreements is to ignore widespread agreement within the church of the second century (compare *Irenaeus with the Muratorian Canon) and the near universal agreement of the fourth century church. To set this feat in perspective one need only bring up the notion of a canon of 'classical Western literature', an idea about which two English professors in the same department cannot agree, much less those debating across cultural and linguistic barriers as did the early church.

One of the hallmarks of postmodern thought is the belief that truth-claims are actually barely concealed claims to *power. Hence, to claim that one text is canonical and another not is to exercise power through the oppression of a different point of view. This belief produces a thoroughgoing sense of suspicion toward all 'winning texts', with the final conclusion that because they are oppressive by virtue of their original use they continue to be oppressive today. With this presupposition in mind it is easy to see why some view the formation of the canon as one of history's most successful power-grabs.

One of the more articulate scholars arguing from this perspective is Bart Ehrman, a professor at the University of North Carolina. His book *Lost Christianities: The Battle for Scripture and the Faiths We Never Knew* (Oxford, 2003) is cogently argued and effective in undermining confidence in the canon.

Ehrman's ultimate goal appears to be to encourage religious tolerance by emphasizing the diversity of early 'Christianities' and the evils of oppression by those wielding 'orthodox' truth-claims. He is interested in promoting not a 'true' alternative Christianity, but a multiplicity of 'Christianities' where each one stands equal and respectful of the others. The result of his work is the barely concealed conclusion that belief in a canon of orthodox Scripture is subscription to an intolerant and oppressive religion.

When addressing this type of critique it is important to remember that literary canons are both common and necessary. Most professions depend upon a body of literature that is authoritative and instructive. If medical doctors were to practise 'unorthodox' medicine, people would die. The simple point is that

a canon is not a tool of oppression by virtue of its existence. It is more often a tool of clarification and the establishment of norms, leading to good professional practice.

Secondly, while we tend to speak of the 'formation' of the canon, it is probably better to speak of the 'recognition' of the canon by the church. Those texts which became known as Scripture were authoritative long before they were canonical. To call something canonical was to recognize the authority it already had. Canonical development was not a power play. It did have ugly moments, but to claim that it was a state-sponsored attempt to silence dissent is to read history through postmodernist spectacles.

Finally, and perhaps most importantly, we must remember that the church was founded on the atoning work of Christ and the gospel that was preached as a result. This gospel was quickly put down in writings that then became authoritative for the church. That we now rely on the canon of Scripture as a final authority within the church is a recognition of God's gracious provision for us, not an oppressive grab for power.

Bibliography

R. T. Beckwith, *The Old Testament Canon of the New Testament Church* (Grand Rapids, 1985); F. F. Bruce, *The Canon of Scripture* (Glasgow and Downers Grove, 1988); P. W. Comfort (ed.), *The Origin of the Bible* (Wheaton, 1992); B. Metzger, *The Canon of the New Testament: Its Origin, Development, and Significance* (Oxford, 1987).

J. W. YATES, III and D. CLOSSON

CAPITALISM

Capitalism has, since its inception, created a conundrum for Christians. It deals with the way in which people in large parts of the world organize the economic structures of and relations in societies since the seventeenth century. Capitalism is an economic system in which private individuals and business firms carry out the bulk of production and exchange of goods and services through a complex network of markets and the prices formed by them.

Although market exchange has existed since antiquity, capitalism as a system is a feature of recent times, preceded by systems based on tradition or command. Like all previous arrangements, capitalism is at bottom a regime of property, *power and privilege, built on rules and patterns of subordination. Under capitalism the economic gains from whatever origin normally accrue to the owners of capital (physical or money) and not to workers, managers, the government or society.

Capitalism has become the most successful system for creating material wealth because of its very productive harnessing of individual freedom to pursue profit-making and create a growth economy. Contrasted to earlier ways, capitalist economies do not use wealth mainly to construct cathedrals, temples or palaces. Instead, wealth provides the instruments (called capital) to expand the process of production. Thus capitalism is essentially a system based on the drive to expand production and wealth, which it does with success.

Capitalism and market economies are often viewed as synonymous. But markets can and do operate without the relentless drive to expand. The private ownership and uncompromising application of capital to increase production, stimulated by increasing market freedom, created the erroneous impression that capitalism and free markets are essentially synonymous.

Capitalism springs from the wrenching economic changes brought by the Industrial Revolution in eighteenth-century England. The major outcome was the explosive growth in industrial output ever since. Fundamental to production growth was increase of the capital stock because it made human labour so much more productive. 'Capital' includes anything that enhances the ability to perform economically useful work – tools, equipment, machines, roads, bridges, ports, knowledge, etc.

The capitalist order has consistently given rise to deep-seated supporting and opposing responses. The supporting arguments are broadly based on the freedom for profit-making enterprise and the historically unique growth in wealth that it caused. The opposing arguments focus on the concomitant gross inequality of outcome, the dehumanization of work, the persistent and widespread poverty, and the increasing pressure on the physical environment.

Basic for a growing capital stock is that part of society's output be channelled away from consumption through saving towards the 'making of capital', including public saving via taxes. Here the main divisive issues about

capitalism arise: who saves, what is sacrificed in the act of saving and who benefits. If only the wealthy save, their sacrifice is almost unnoticeable, but if it includes the poor (as it always does) their pain is much bigger.

Decisions about saving, taxes and public spending are intimately connected to who holds economic and political power and how it is used. It can and has been used to improve the well-being of the majority. Historically, however, capitalist societies have also, particularly in the second half of the twentieth century, used saving to increase the power of a dominant minority, creating not only unheard-of wealth for some but also the increasing subordination and vulnerability of those (the majority) without access to the means of production.

The twentieth century saw enormous increases in production and rising living standards for many. But it also dramatically created a great systems conflict, namely the seventy-two years of struggle between communist, command societies with planned economies, and non-communist, free societies with market economies. From this arose the perception that the only choice is between these two alternatives – with capitalism the victor today. There is an ongoing debate whether history provides only these options or whether some 'third way' can be constructed. The idea of a democratic economy or social democracy is often considered such a possibility.

An important development in the late twentieth century was the dramatic increase in the scope and size of financial activities compared to real (physical) economic activity. Capitalism has become financial capitalism, in the sense that money is mainly used today to make more money directly without simultaneously giving rise to the production of goods or the creation of jobs.

The implication is that the success of capitalist economic activity is no longer measured mainly by how well it provides for human needs, but rather by how much money is generated for holders of shares, stocks and financial resources. This creates powerful incentives for making real production and serving human needs wholly subservient to making money, rather than the other way around.

Capitalism did not emerge and grow merely as the result of organizational or material processes. It arose from a societal culture that put its hopes for material abundance in the free play of selfish economic interests, cogently expressed by the Scottish philosopher Adam Smith. But cultures and societies are fundamentally directed by central, religious motives. These motives embrace hope for the future, faith in God or humanity and love for self or others.

The main motif underlying capitalism is faith in self-made human progress. Since the eighteenth century this has worked itself out in the pursuit of individual economic prosperity, answerable only to itself. The basic issue remains the created meaning of economic life: an opportunity for self-fulfilment and greed, somewhat tempered by values, or careful stewardship of resources to honour God and serve fellow humans.

Capitalist thought and practice has little acknowledgment of the intrinsic connection between everyday economic practice and its ultimate purpose. As in so many other parts of secularized societies, capitalist economic practice is based on a division of life between religious considerations and practical necessity. Compared to earlier periods where economic provisioning and societal well-being were seen as inherently connected – although often uneasily – these two dimensions became separate parts of life under capitalism, governed by different standards and answerable to different authorities.

Capitalism thus radically changed the place assigned to economic goals in society. From a subservient role serving overall human well-being, it made economic pursuits the central consideration in life. Modern societies became essentially economic societies. But changing the role of economic efficiency and growth from an instrument to a pervasive and primary objective now threatens economic fairness, societal coherence, cultural diversity and environmental sustainability.

The central challenge to capitalism is how to restore the necessary cooperation in today's complex global civilization if it persists with its extreme competitive thrust for maximum individual financial gain. Cooperation necessitates agreement about ends and means and must be based on created human nature as a whole, for which economic considerations are imperative but which equally requires the satisfaction of non-economic needs. No increase in material wealth will compensate for arrangements that insult people's self-respect, offend their sense of *justice and impair their freedom.

The Christian tradition contains powerful messages on this point. Nowhere does the Bible contain any statements on economic systems. But it consistently reveals God as the Creator of human life in *community where there is sufficient for the livelihood of everyone. In contrast to today's basic assumption that scarcity prevails and can be softened only by ceaseless material growth – the thrust of both capitalism and *socialism – the biblical message is radically different.

If the righteousness of God is present, there is always enough for livelihood. From the manna to the feeding of the multitude, the biblical story depicts the superabundance of God's provision. To be human and live abundantly is exclusively the gift of God's grace, of which there is no scarcity. But then humans should seek the Creator's will and not fall into economic idolatry.

Capitalism's exclusive focus on individual material advance stands in stark contrast to Christ's command to care for those who are weak and vulnerable, as well as to the Creator's engagement in creating, sustaining and redeeming households. Throughout history, God cares for the households of Israel, the church, nations and the encompassing household of everything created.

The economy of God (Gk: *oikonomia tou theou*) applies to the complete life of the Christian community (Col. 1:25; 1 Cor. 9:17; Eph. 3:2; 1 Tim. 1:4) as well as to God's salvation and maintenance of the household of the creation. Therefore it conflicts with the building of any societal household (economic system) that excludes or marginalizes the poor and oppressed, the uneducated, the less competent, and those without power. True economy is sustainable provisioning for the livelihood of all humans in community.

Bibliography

B. Goudzwaard, *Capitalism and Progress* (Toronto, 1979); R. L. Heilbroner, *The Nature and Logic of Capitalism* (New York, 1985); D. Korten, *When Corporations Rule the World* (Bloomfield, 2001); M. D. Meeks, *God the Economist* (Minneapolis, 1989); A. Storkey, *A Christian Social Perspective* (Leicester, 1979); R. H. Tawney, *Religion and the Rise of Capitalism* (Harmondsworth, 1977).

E. P. Beukes

CAPPADOCIAN FATHERS

The Cappadocian Fathers – Basil of Caesarea (c. 329–379), Gregory of Nazianzus (c. 329–390) and Gregory of Nyssa (c. 335–395) – were bishops during the time of the Arian controversy, and their greatest achievement was their formulation of the doctrine of the *Trinity to counter the heresy.

They were heirs of the *Origenist tradition of the East, which strongly emphasized the distinction of Father, Son and Holy Spirit as three *hypostases* (distinct objective realities). Origenists were suspicious of the Western term *persona*, which seemed to reduce Father, Son and Spirit to mere appearances of the one God (the heresy of Sabellianism or 'modalism'). The Origenist tendency to make the Son and Spirit subordinate to the Father had led to the Arian denial of their true deity, and it was this heresy that Basil opposed. He allied himself with *Athanasius, who had defended the doctrine formulated at Nicea (325), that the Son was 'consubstantial' (*homoousion*, 'of the same being') with the Father and so fully and truly God. 'One *ousia* (being): three *hypostases*', a formula combining the Athanasian and Origenist perspectives, thus became the Eastern equivalent of the Western formula, 'one substance: three Persons'. After Basil's death, Gregory of Nazianzus and Gregory of Nyssa saw the defeat of Arianism at the Council of Constantinople (381) and the Nicene Creed reaffirmed in a new form.

Gregory of Nazianzus, briefly Archbishop of Constantinople, was one of the great orators and poets of his day. Because of his powerful sermons on the Trinity, 'The Five Theological Orations', he was called 'Gregory the Theologian' (or 'Divine'), a title previously given only to the apostle John. Gregory's poetry, written to provide a Christian alternative to the pagan poetry taught in the schools, may be seen as an exercise in apologetics. He published two orations against the apostate Emperor Julian (once his fellow student in Athens) who had tried to revive the ancient Graeco-Roman paganism.

Gregory of Nyssa, Basil's younger brother, had greater philosophical gifts. He continued the fight against the extreme Arianism of Eunomius and adapted the *Platonist assumptions of his culture to develop a Christian view of God and the world. More than most Christian Platonists (such as Origen and *Augustine), he differentiated between the infinite God and (even in the resurrection) the limited creatures of time who will forever advance in their knowledge of him.

Bibliography

A. Meredith, *The Cappadocians* (London, 1995); J. Quasten, *Patrology*, vol. III (Westminster, 1992), pp. 203–296.

T. A. Noble

CAPRA, FRITJOF

Fritjof Capra is a *New Age activist whose writings strive to unite *science and spirituality. Originally a high-energy physicist at the University of Vienna, Capra abandoned scientific research to write and lecture. He is Director of the Centre for Ecoliteracy in Berkeley, California.

In his first book, *The Tao of Physics* (1975), Capra suggests that there are significant parallels between the new concepts of subatomic physics and some of the teachings of the Eastern religions. This theory, now a fundamental belief of New Age spiritualities, has been adapted by many writers of popular science to show that 'modern science proves mysticism'. Capra, however, merely argues that the mystical traditions of the East can accommodate the most advanced scientific theories of the physical universe. In *The Tao of Physics*, Capra defends a holistic world-view which sees a unity in all phenomena, the universe being an interconnected network of dynamic relations. Capra uses Geoffrey Chew's 'bootstrap theory' of physics as an example of holism. Opposing *Descartes' view of the universe as 'mechanistic', the bootstrap theory argues that nature cannot be reduced to fundamental building blocks of matter, but must be understood through self-consistency. The implied corollary of the bootstrap theory is the radical belief that there are no fundamental constants, equations or laws, only a dynamic interrelated web, none of the properties of which is fundamental.

In his second book, *The Turning Point* (1983), Capra rejects several premises of his first book and argues that all disciplines – biology, medicine, psychology and economics – deal with life in the form of living biological and social systems. 'By presenting the new physics as a model for a new medicine ... or social science I had fallen into the very

Cartesian trap I wanted scientists to avoid', he wrote later in *Uncommon Wisdom: Conversations with Remarkable People* (1988). In *The Turning Point* Capra presents physics as part of the broader framework of 'systems theory' advocated by the systems theorist Gregory Bateson and the Nobel Prize winning biochemist Ilya Prigogine. There is a utopian feel to Capra's writing on systems theory. Because he sees the systems view encompassing all *reality (physical, biological, psychological, social and cultural), Capra believes it will lead to a new kind of society in which no social institutions will be superior to others: all will be self-organizing, mutually consistent and cooperative.

Capra explores theological and ecological concerns in several books co-authored in the 1980s and 1990s. In a recent book, *The Hidden Connections* (2003) he continues to integrate the biological, cognitive and social dimensions of life.

Debates in the holistic milieu

Capra's work has been received with enthusiasm by devotees of New Age and alternative spiritualities as well as by activists in the ecology movement. However, some scholars point to problems in his attempt to include the dimension of consciousness in a material universe. Others see difficulties in avoiding the absolute *determinism of the universe implied by the bootstrap theory. The economist E. F. Schumacher criticized Capra's utopian use of systems and bootstrap theory, arguing that science cannot solve social and cultural problems because it cannot entertain the notion of higher and lower levels of being. Both the bootstrap and systems theories accept only one fundamental level of reality and are therefore reductionist. This disagreement reveals the gulf between New Age devotees who have a monistic view of reality and those with a hierarchical view. Capra can be viewed as a pantheist if 'god' is seen as an abstract pattern of relationships. This god is not the ultimate source of all that is, but is the pattern that connects everything.

Christian critique

The Christian can welcome the new interest in spirituality and ultimate questions to which these debates point. The belief that we live in a dynamic, interrelated universe was not new to the writers of the NT documents. The writer to the Hebrews speaks of Christ, through whom God created the world, as 'the radiance of God's glory and the exact representation of his being, sustaining all things by his powerful word' (Heb. 1:3). Christians see a divine unifying pattern sustaining the universe in the God in whom, 'we live and move and have our being' (Acts 17:28). For the Christian, however, he is God, the Creator who cares for all his creation, not the abstract pattern of life. Finally, it is difficult for Christians to ignore the moral dimension of the ecological crisis which has been Capra's concern in recent years. The question remains how humans can know what is right and responsible, yet choose what is harmful to the earth, to themselves and to their descendants.

Bibliography

F. Capra, *The Hidden Connections* (London, 2003); *The Tao of Physics* (London, 3rd edition, 1991); *The Turning Point: Science, Society and the Rising Culture* (London, 1983); W. J. Hanegraaf, *New Age Religion and Western Culture: Esotericism in the Mirror of Secular Thought* (Leiden, New York and Köln, 1996).

R. A. C. Bradby

CARIBBEAN RELIGION, see AFRICAN AMERICAN/CARIBBEAN RELIGION

CARNELL, EDWARD JOHN

Edward John Carnell (1919–67) was Professor of Ethics and Philosophy of Religion at Fuller Theological Seminary in Pasadena, California from 1948 to 1967, where he also served as President (1954–59). He completed the BA degree in philosophy at Wheaton College in 1941, and it was there that he came under the influence of the Christian philosopher Gordon Clark, a committed *Calvinist with a strong interest in apologetics. In 1944 Carnell was awarded the ThB and ThM degrees from Westminster Theological Seminary, with a major in apologetics, under Cornelius Van Til. Determined to further his interest in philosophical apologetics, Carnell completed a ThD degree in *history and philosophy of religion at Harvard Divinity School in 1948, writing his dissertation on Reinhold *Niebuhr. This was later published as *The Theology of Reinhold*

Niebuhr (Grand Rapids, 1951). While at Harvard, Carnell also enrolled in the PhD programme at Boston University, studying under the personalist philosopher E. S. Brightman. He was awarded the PhD for his thesis on Søren *Kierkegaard, later published as *The Burden of Søren Kierkegaard* (Grand Rapids, 1965). While enrolled simultaneously in two doctoral programs, Carnell also wrote and had published an award-winning book, *An Introduction to Christian Apologetics: A Philosophic Defense of the Trinitarian-Theistic Faith*. At the early age of twenty-nine, with two doctoral degrees in hand as well as a published book on Christian apologetics (all completed in less than four years), Carnell was viewed as one of the brightest stars in the newly emerging galaxy of evangelical scholars who were conservative in theology but unhappy about being labelled fundamentalist. In 1948 he accepted an invitation to join the faculty of the newly formed Fuller Theological Seminary, where he served until his untimely death in 1967.

For Carnell, the task of apologetics was twofold. First, it is an attempt to show that Christian faith rests on evidential grounds that satisfied the intellect as well as the heart. Secondly, apologetics demonstrates the truth of Christian faith statements in such a way that unbelief can be shown to be axiologically inconsistent. The rational argument for the truthfulness of Christian belief is grounded on the law of *contradiction. The axiological argument is based on the principle of coherence, where belief is based on the sufficiency of evidence, not the nature of the evidence. This became the central motif of his subsequent works in apologetics, *Christian Commitment: An Apologetic* and *The Kingdom of Love and the Pride of Life* (Grand Rapids, 1960). Carnell argued that there are three types of *truth and thus three ways of knowing. First, there is ontological truth, the truth of what is. The proper method to gain knowledge of this kind of truth is by acquaintance, i.e. direct experience. The second type of truth is propositional truth, and the appropriate means of knowledge is rational inference. Valid inference can be simple or complex, but it always must follow the rules of *logic. The third type of truth is that of one's own moral and spiritual existence as represented by free moral decision. This is the missing link between abstract truth and personal truth. The appropriate method of knowing this kind of truth is moral self-acceptance. Moral self-acceptance is the realization that we are already, by virtue of our very existence as human persons, bound morally and spiritually to each other. While philosophy may be a test for error, it can never provide the kind of evidences that lead to the truth upon which faith must ultimately rest. For Carnell, apologetics seeks to blend the intricate and complex interplay between the so-called subjective and objective aspects of a single structure of *reality. With respect to God, as well as with other persons, the evidences of the moral and spiritual environment are what produce faith, not merely rational argument or empirical fact.

Bibliography

E. J. Carnell, *An Introduction to Christian Apologetics: A Philosophic Defense of the Trinitarian-Theistic Faith* (Grand Rapids, 1948); *Christian Commitment: An Apologetic* (New York, 1957); R. Nelson, *The Making and Unmaking of an Evangelical Mind: The Case of Edward Carnell* (New York, 1988); J. A. Sims, *Edward John Carnell, Defender of the Faith* (Washington, 1979).

R. S. Anderson

CAUSALITY, PRINCIPLE OF

The principle of causality and its relationship to apologetics can be seen to have waxed or waned historically according to the differing emphases in Western philosophical thought. (Related to the use of the principle of causality in apologetics, which cannot be pursued here, is its application to the notion of free will.) Though the principle itself has a long and diverse history in Western thought, its most influential genesis can be traced, not surprisingly, to *Aristotle.

Aristotle's primary concern with respect to causality was metaphysical. Causality, for Aristotle, was intrinsically related to the production, or bringing into being, of essences. Because causality brought about a change in something, Aristotle determined to give an account of that change by way of four categories of causality: material cause – that out of which an effect is produced; formal cause – that by which the essential nature of an effect is determined; efficient cause – that by which the effect is brought into existence; final cause – the end, or *telos*, of the effect.

Of these four causal aspects, it is the third, the efficient cause, that has typically come to be identified with the principle of causality, and which has brought about the most controversy historically in apologetics. Our analysis of the principle of causality, therefore, will have efficient causality as its principal referent.

The principle of causality states that every event must have an adequate antecedent cause. It is this principle that has provided, along with the principle of sufficient reason, the impetus for the historical formulation of (at least some of) the *theistic proofs in apologetics. In *Thomas Aquinas' 'five ways', e.g. the first three seem to be dependent, to a greater or lesser degree, on the principle of causality. The second way is most obviously dependent on this principle: 'The second way is from the nature of the efficient cause. In the world of sense we find there is an order of efficient causes. There is no case known (neither is it, indeed, possible) in which a thing is found to be the efficient cause of itself; for so it would be prior to itself, which is impossible. Now in efficient causes it is not possible to go on to infinity, because in all efficient causes following in order, the first is the cause of the intermediate cause, and the intermediate is the cause of the ultimate cause, whether the intermediate cause be several, or only one. Now to take away the cause is to take away the effect. Therefore, if there be no first cause among efficient causes, there will be no ultimate, nor any intermediate cause. But if in efficient causes it is possible to go on to infinity, there will be no first efficient cause, neither will there be an ultimate effect, nor any intermediate efficient causes; all of which is plainly false. Therefore it is necessary to admit a first efficient cause, to which everyone gives the name of God' (T. Aquinas, *Summa Theologica*, I, 2, 3).

This argument can take, and has taken, various forms. The central thrust of it, however, is found here in Aquinas. Any argument for the existence of God that is based on the principle of causality will attempt to show that the very (empirical) fact that there are effects in this world is sufficient evidence to render necessary the fact that there must be something that is both the ultimate cause of these effects and that is, itself, uncaused. The necessity, it should be noted, centres on a series of premises that seek to show the impossibility of the contrary. First of all, something cannot be the cause of itself. In order for that to be the

case, something would have to exist prior to its own existence, which is impossible. Secondly, there cannot be an infinite regress of causes. Here Aquinas' vocabulary is not *prima facie* clear. What he seems to be saying is that the series of causality must have both a beginning and an (at least temporal) end. His reasoning seems to be that, since it is obvious that we see around us things that are intermediate causes (effects), there must be at some 'point' (not necessarily in time) a first cause. For him, then, it is impossible that, given intermediate causes, there could not be a first cause. Given this argument and the one from efficient causality, it seems Aquinas' notion of impossibility is grounded in the fact that there are things now caused and now moved.

The controversies that surround the principle of causality and its use for theistic proofs stem from various philosophical and theological commitments. Let us first consider the philosophical arguments.

Perhaps the most notorious challenge to the principle of causality came from the Scottish philosopher David *Hume. Hume sought to be as radical an empiricist as possible. Because of this *empiricism, Hume averred that there could be only two kinds of meaningful statements – analytic and synthetic. An analytic statement was one in which the subject was contained in the predicate. A synthetic statement was one which, because the predicate added something to the subject, necessitated empirical verification. Without empirical *verification, a statement was meaningless. The statement that every effect must have an antecedent cause was neither analytic nor empirically verifiable, and so was relegated, by Hume, simply to a connection of *ideas* without real existence. With respect to the notions of cause and effect and a supposed necessary connection, Hume says: 'The mind can never possibly find the effect in the supposed cause, by the most accurate scrutiny and examination. For the effect is totally different from the cause, and consequently can never be discovered in it. Motion in the second Billiard-ball is a quite distinct event from motion in the first; nor is there any thing in the one to suggest the smallest hint of the other.' Hume then concludes: 'But to hasten to a conclusion of this argument ... We have sought in vain for an idea of power or necessary connection in all the sources from which we could suppose it to be derived. It appears that, in single instances of the operation of bodies, we never can, by our utmost scrutiny, discover any thing but one event following another, without being able to comprehend any force or power by which the cause operates, or any connection between it and its supposed effect' (D. Hume, *Enquiry*, Section VII). The best we are able to ascertain, therefore, according to Hume, is that things otherwise not necessarily connected are made to connect in our minds because of custom or habit.

If David Hume's challenge was the most notorious, Immanuel *Kant's was the most influential. While Kant agreed with Hume to a point, he nevertheless sought to show that cause and effect were possible, not because they are empirically verifiable but because our minds are so constructed as to affirm such things. Adding to Hume's analytic/synthetic distinction, Kant sought to show that synthetic *a priori* judgments were possible as well. These judgments employed synthetic *a priori* categories in order to provide statements that were both meaningful and necessary as conditions and pre-conditions of knowledge itself. So, the statement that 'every effect must have an antecedent cause' is a synthetic *a priori* judgment which, *contra* Hume, does have meaning.

For Kant, however, like Hume, these judgments and categories could never leap beyond the range of observation. For Kant, all knowledge does in fact begin with experience (though all knowledge does not arise out of experience). Thus, whatever relevance or necessity the principle of causality may have, it can never be applied or extended to that which is non-observable. It is applicable only to the extent that it is observable. Thus, in agreement with Hume, Kant argued that the principle of causality could never extend beyond the range of observation.

The theological challenges to the principle of causality are not directly about the principle *per se*, but deal rather with the presuppositions behind such a principle with respect to God's relationship to his creation. Though neither Hume nor Kant were successful in their respective attempts to develop a coherent *epistemology, the questions that both of them (and others) were wrestling with were profoundly theological and had deep and serious implications. How, for example, does one apply the notion of causality to God, when causality presupposes a 'moment' of time and God himself is not constrained by, or subject to, such moments? To put the question more

provocatively, just how does one ascribe the same process both to the temporal world and to an eternal God? Is it the case that our predication of, say, fire as the 'cause' of heat and God as the 'cause' of the creation is univocal? If not, is it analogical? If so, are the terms sufficiently similar, in and of themselves, to compel a legitimate comparison?

Though some (like Thomas Aquinas) have determined to use the analogical approach in their employment of the principle of causality, others (like *Calvin) have wanted to press the necessity of God's prior divine condescension in creating and providing for his creation. Given such condescension, biblical *revelation is seen to be the necessary presupposition behind a legitimate use of notions such as causality for a defence of the Christian faith.

Bibliography

W. J. Courtenay, *Covenant and Causality in Medieval Thought: Studies in Philosophy, Theology and Economic Practice* (London, 1984); R. J. Hankinson, *Cause and Explanation in Ancient Greek Thought* (Oxford, 2001); J. R. Lucas, *Space, Time, and Causality: An Essay in Natural Philosophy* (Oxford, 1984); M. Sylwanowicz, *Contingent Causality and the Foundations of Duns Scotus' Metaphysics* (Leiden, 1996).

K. S. OLIPHINT

CELESTINE VISION

The Celestine Prophecy by James Redfield was first published in 1994. The book quickly became an international bestseller and became the best-selling American book in the world in 1995 and 1996. Described by Redfield as 'an adventure parable', it relates the story of the search for an ancient manuscript in the forests of Peru. Within the manuscript are 'nine key insights into life itself – insights each human being is predicted to grasp sequentially, one insight then another, as we move toward a completely spiritual culture on Earth'. In other words, humans are gradually becoming aware of, and practising, certain spiritual insights, which, in turn, are leading to the dawning of a new spiritual era, a 'New Age'.

Born near Birmingham, Alabama, Redfield was brought up in the Methodist Church which, he recalls, was welcoming and friendly. However, it did not provide answers to certain (unspecified) questions he had about spirituality. Hence, over the years, Redfield's spirituality has been shaped by Eastern, psychological, human potential and broadly Christian ideas and themes. However, whilst *The Celestine Prophecy* begins with words from Dan. 12:3–4 and includes several quotations from the Bible (e.g. 'the truth shall set you free'), it both looks to the East for its spirituality and also betrays an underlying antipathy to traditional Christianity. Most of the clergy, for example, are 'bitterly trying to suppress the Manuscript ... because it challenges the completeness of their religion'. In particular, we are told near the end of *The Celestine Prophecy* that the church is concerned about the notion that humans might contribute to their own spiritual evolution: 'The idea of physical evolution is bad enough. But to extend the idea to everyday life, to the individual decisions we make, to history itself. That's unacceptable [to the Church].' Having said that, there is a sense in which Redfield seems to want to retain aspects of the Christian tradition. They are, however, retained on his terms, in that he claims that the Celestine insights clarify the essence of the Christian faith. However, there is a conspicuous lack of clarity concerning what this essence might be and the sense in which these spiritually eclectic insights might clarify it.

The first of the nine insights is particularly important for understanding the Celestine Vision. It is that 'A new spiritual awakening is occurring in human culture, an awakening brought about by a critical mass of individuals who experience their lives as a spiritual unfolding, a journey in which we are led forward by mysterious coincidences.' As the rest of the insights are gradually revealed, the reader is introduced to an essentially Eastern world-view, which is destined to replace the secular and religious world-views that have dominated the West since the Reformation. For example, the third insight insists that 'we live not in a material universe, but in a universe of dynamic energy. Everything extant is a field of sacred energy.' In other words, humans should understand themselves to be interconnected with each other and with an underlying divine energy source (God). As we gradually evolve, acknowledge this fundamental interconnectedness, learn to recognize and build on the many 'coincidences' in life that demonstrate our interconnectedness with each other and 'share energy', humanity will witness 'synchronistic

growth'. According to the ninth insight (entitled 'the emerging culture'), 'Such growth will move humans into higher energy states, ultimately transforming our bodies into spiritual form [*sic*] and uniting this dimension of existence with the after-life dimension, ending the cycle of birth and death.' The transformation to 'spiritual form', to the 'higher energy field', which currently occurs after death, will, in the new spiritual age, be a present reality, thus bringing an end to death.

Following the *Celestine Prophecy*, Redfield has published further books, including *The Tenth Insight: Holding the Vision* (1996), *The Celestine Vision* (1997), and, with Carol Adrienne, 'experiential guides' to *The Celestine Prophecy* and *The Tenth Insight*. He has also identified two more insights which further describe the emerging *culture and how one might contribute to it. In particular, the eleventh insight makes much of the notion of prayer. Whilst this may be understood as a clarification of the Christian understanding, it is more indebted to self-centric human potential thinking than it is to the Christian doctrines of prayer and providence which teach dependence upon and communion with a personal, loving God: 'For centuries, religious scriptures, poems, and philosophies have pointed to a latent *power of mind within all of us that mysteriously helps to affect what occurs in the future. It has been called faith power, positive thinking and the power of prayer ... We are finding that this prayer power is a field of intention, which moves out from us and can be extended and strengthened, especially when we connect with others of a common vision. This is the power through which we hold the vision of a spiritual world and build the energy in ourselves and in others to make this vision a reality.' Working with this understanding of prayer, in October 2001, following the terrorist attacks on the World Trade Center on 11 September 2001, Redfield launched the World Prayer Project.

Finally, it is worth noting that, whilst not specifically supported by Redfield, the ideas informing the *The Celestine Prophecy* have led to the formation of what might be described as a 'new religion' – the New Civilization Network.

Bibliography

J. Redfield, *The Celestine Prophecy* (London, 1994); *The Tenth Insight: Holding the Vision (London, 1996); *The Celestine Vision* (New York, 1997).

C. H. PARTRIDGE

CELSUS

The early attack on Christianity by the pagan polemicist Celsus is known only through the extensive references in *Origen's work *Contra Celsum*, written nearly seventy years after Celsus' death. Scholars have held different views on Celsus, and on where and when he wrote. The conclusion of Henry Chadwick is that Celsus wrote his work, *The True Doctrine*, in either Rome or Alexandria probably around 177–180. Although Origen himself thought that the author of this work was probably to be identified with a certain Epicurean known from other sources, the work itself is more obviously written by a Middle *Platonist who also shows Stoic influences.

Celsus was first and foremost a traditionalist, and his major complaint about the Christians was that they were departing from the ancient Hellenistic tradition of their fathers. Although Jews oddly worshipped only the one highest God, at least they were following their traditions. Christianity, however, was a blasphemous innovation.

Celsus believed that there was an ancient tradition, shared by the wisest and most pious Greeks and barbarians throughout the world, which combined *monotheism and *polytheism. It made no difference whether the Most High was called Zeus or Zen or Adonai or Sabaoth or Amoun, he ruled the world through his lower gods, to be equated with *daemons*. Moses had misled his people that the Most High was the only God, and the Christians had twisted the truth even further when they claimed to worship this one God and yet also worshipped the man, *Jesus.

Celsus had wide knowledge of Christianity and *Judaism, but it was not always accurate. He acknowledged that Christian *ethics were to be respected, but ridiculed the *miracles and Christian teachings on the incarnation and the crucifixion. What he saw as particularly dangerous was that Christianity was not, like all true religion, a civic religion. Christians would not support the emperor or take public office or fight in the army, and this non-cooperation would severely weaken the Empire. As can be seen then, although Celsus'

attack was often bitter and sarcastic, he was not simply a negative or destructive critic of the church. He was motivated by his concern for ancient piety and civic duty.

The relevance of Celsus for today therefore may lie first in those representatives of the ancient religions and civilizations of the East who see Christianity as a Western innovation. He may be seen too as a forerunner of all kinds of syncretism (like that of John *Hick, for example). Those who would require the Christian faith to take the place they would assign to it, muting its claims in order to be subservient to the tolerant civic order, and see the main function of 'religion' as the promotion of the good society, may also be regarded as his heirs.

Bibliography

H. Chadwick, *Origen: Contra Celsum* (Cambridge, 1965).

T. A. NOBLE

CELTIC SPIRITUALITY

The Celtic church, which existed between 300 and 1200 AD, in Scotland, Ireland and Wales, was not an organized ecclesiastical body which ever asserted independence from Rome. However, 'Celtic' was used to describe conservative churches and monastic communities which differed in certain practices from the Roman Church, largely due to their being on the fringes of Christendom, where they were isolated and often out of touch with new developments. The Celtic distinctives were a cause of conflict in the seventh century, culminating in the Synod of Whitby in 664, the agenda of which included disputes about the date of Easter, the tonsure (hair style) of monks and the order for the consecration of bishops. Bede implies that certain doctrinal matters were also controversial but does not specify any alleged unorthodoxy, and it seems that the adherents of the Celtic way were devoted and pious followers of Catholic tradition, while preserving some customs which were different from the Roman Church.

As to spirituality, there was no uniform approach, and to understand it we must turn to sources such as the *Rule of Columcille* (Columba), which was written in Irish and cannot be traced back in manuscripts beyond the ninth century. It is unlikely to have been the work of Columba himself, but may well embody principles which were practised by successive abbots of Iona. It is remarkably severe and austere, advocating eremitic (solitary) and cenobitic (*community) lifestyles, which include willingness to lay down one's life for the faith. The Christian mind should also be prepared for 'white *martyrdom', a form of witness to Christ which was favoured by Irish saints and involved dying to self and all attachments, leaving home and family and going into perpetual exile.

The Iona regime was one of rigorous self-denial: 'Take not of food till thou art hungry. Sleep not till thou feelest desire. Speak not except on business.' The Rule of Columba prescribes three daily activities: reading, work and prayer. Study and scholarship were valued highly in the Iona community, and manual labour was considered essential to the monastic life and compulsory for every member.

In recent times it has been alleged that insight into 'Celtic spirituality' can help to build bridges with '*New Age' thinking in contemporary Western culture. In this way, what is called 'Celtic spirituality' includes an emphasis on *angels, focus on the elements and a denial of a metaphysical divide between physical and spiritual. It is a claim based on traditions which were popularized in the collection of Highland folklore by Alexander Carmichael (1832–1912), *Carmina Gadelica* (Edinburgh, 1900–71). This work seems to reflect traditions of Christian spirituality much later than the time of Columba and the other Celtic saints, and which are considerably less severe and ascetic, as well as being affirmative of the natural world. Recent enthusiasts have made further connections with ecology and feminism, which would never have been on the agenda of Columba and his spiritual successors. This kind of approach has recently been promoted by the pastoral and devotional works of Ray Simpson of the Community of Aidan and Hilda, in which he claims, 'The essence of Celtic spirituality is a heart wide open to God in every person, in all the world. It is to do with crossing frontiers, not erecting barriers. It goes so deep that, without losing what is distinctive, it becomes universal.'

It is very doubtful whether such assertions can legitimately be made, in the light of the above, as Ian Bradley and others have shown, however inspiring and enlightening such contemporary reflections may be. As Bradley notes, 'In our pick-and-mix culture, people are increasingly assembling their own personal spiritual packages in which elements of the Christian tradition are combined with some New Age notions and other bits and pieces ... Celtic poems and prayers ... are the totems of this new privatized religion.' The *Carmina Gadelica* has, in this way, been popularized in recent years, has been helpfully used in private devotions and public worship, and has served as a corrective to some of the anti-physical strands of thought in Western Christianity. But we cannot substantiate claims of any direct line from the Celtic church, and such traditions seem to be medieval in origin. Bradley sees connections, in contrast, between Celtic spirituality and the stark simplicity of Christian life and worship in the Highlands and Islands of Scotland today: 'Instead of the buzz of idle chatter which precedes most church services nowadays, there is an almost palpable stillness as worshippers take their places up to twenty minutes or so before the start of the service, simply to sit in silent prayer and contemplation without any visual or aural distraction, both musical instruments and decoration or ornament of any kind being barred from church buildings. There is a severity here that even Columba might find a shade austere but there is also an atmosphere of profound awe and reverence before the mystery of God.'

Bibliography

I. Bradley, *The Celtic Way* (London, 1993); *Columba: Pilgrim and Penitant* (Glasgow, 1996); D. A. Bray 'Celtic Church, Celtic Saints', K. D. McDonald, 'Alexander Carmichael' in N. M. Cameron (ed.) *Dictionary of Scottish Church History and Theology* (Edinburgh, 1993); R. Simpson, *Exploring Celtic Spirituality* (London, 1995).

G. R. HOUSTON

CERTAINTY

Certainty is a lack of *doubt about some state of affairs, e.g. if one has no doubt that the earth is the third planet from the sun, then one can be said to be certain of that fact. There are degrees of certainty, just as there are degrees of doubt. Absolute certainty is the lack of any doubt at all. Short of that, there are various levels of relative certainty.

Philosophers have sometimes distinguished between the psychological certainty described above and another kind of certainty that is called epistemic, logical or propositional certainty. There is no universally accepted definition of this second kind of certainty, but it is usually thought to have something to do with the justification or warrant for believing a proposition, so that a proposition is epistemically certain if it has a maximal warrant. The nature of a maximal warrant is defined differently in different epistemological systems. *Descartes thought that in order for propositions to be certain, they must be warranted in such a way as to exclude all grounds for doubt. For Chisholm, a proposition is epistemically certain if no proposition has greater warrant than it does. Different philosophers give different weight to *logic, sense experience, intuition, etc. in determining what constitutes adequate warrant.

Epistemic certainty, however it be defined, is not something sharply different from psychological certainty. Whatever level of warrant is required for epistemic certainty, it must be a level that gives us psychological confidence. Indeed, if we are to accept some technical definition of warrant, we also must have psychological confidence that that definition actually represents what we call certainty. So it may be said that epistemic certainty is reducible to psychological certainty. It is also true, however, that we should try to conform our psychological feelings of certainty to objective principles of knowledge, so that our doubts and feelings of certainty are reasonable, rather than arbitrary or pathological. So perhaps it is best to say that psychological and epistemic certainty are mutually dependent. In his *Doctrine of the Knowledge of God*, Frame attempts to describe and defend the mutual reducibility of feelings and knowledge.

Philosophers have also differed on the extent to which they consider certainty to be possible, some being relatively sceptical, others claiming certainty in some measure. Some have distinguished different levels of knowledge and have promoted certainty to the higher levels. For example, *Plato, in the *Republic*, distinguished between conjecture, belief, understanding and direct intuition, conjecture being the most uncertain, and direct intuition (a pure knowledge of the basic Forms of reality) warranting absolute certainty.

Both ancient and modern sceptics have said that it is not possible to be absolutely certain about anything. According to Descartes,

however, we cannot doubt that we are thinking, and from the proposition 'I think' he derived a number of other propositions that he thought were certain, e.g. our existence, the existence of God and so on. Empiricists such as *Locke and *Hume, have argued that we cannot be mistaken about the basic contents of our own minds, about the way things *appear* to us. But in their view, our knowledge of the world beyond our minds is never certain, never more than probable. *Kant added that we can also be certain of those propositions that describe the necessary conditions for knowledge itself, and *Thomas Reid and G. E. Moore argued that certain deliverances of common sense are beyond doubt because they are in some sense the foundation of knowledge, better known than any principles by which they can be challenged.

Ludwig *Wittgenstein distinguished between merely theoretical doubt and real, practical doubt. In everyday life, when we doubt something, there is a way of resolving that doubt, e.g. when we doubt how much money we have in a bank account, we may resolve that doubt by looking at a bank statement. But theoretical or philosophical doubts are doubts for which there is no standard means of resolution. What would it be like, Wittgenstein asks, to doubt that I have two hands and then to try to relieve that doubt? Or how can we address doubts as to whether the world has existed for more than five minutes or whether other people have minds?

The *language of doubt and certainty, Wittgenstein argues, belongs to the context of practical life. When it is removed from that context, it is no longer meaningful, for meaning, to Wittgenstein, is the use of words in their ordinary, practical contexts, in what he calls their 'language game'. To raise such philosophical questions is to question our whole way of life. Thus for Wittgenstein, relative certainty is possible in ordinary life through standard methods, but the traditional philosophical questions are not proper subjects either of doubt or of certainty.

So in the context of ordinary life, Wittgenstein allows for certainty of a relative kind. His argument evidently excludes absolute certainty, but he does recognize that there can be no doubt about some of our beliefs (e.g. that the universe has existed for more than five minutes). He excludes doubt not by proposing an extraordinary way to know about such matters, but rather by removing such questions from the language game in which 'doubt' and 'certainty' have meaning.

Philosophy itself is, however, also a language game, and doubts about the reality of the experienced world have troubled people for many centuries. Philosophers have not hesitated to propose ways of resolving those doubts. So, it may be arbitrary to restrict the meanings of 'doubt' and 'certainty' to the realm of the practical, even given the possibility of a sharp distinction between theoretical and practical. At least it is difficult to distinguish between questions that are improper in Wittgenstein's sense and questions that are merely difficult to answer.

So the questions concerning certainty remain open among secular philosophers. Since Wittgenstein, these questions have been raised in relation to *foundationalism, the view that all human knowledge is based on certain 'basic' propositions. Descartes is the chief example of classical foundationalism because of his view that the basic propositions are absolutely certain. Many recent thinkers have rejected foundationalism in this sense, but Alvin Plantinga and others have developed a revised foundationalism in which the basic propositions are defeasible, capable of being refuted by additional knowledge. In general, then, the philosophical trend today is opposed to the idea of *absolute* certainty; and that opposition is rampant among deconstructionists and postmodernists.

The question also arises in the religious context: can we know God with certainty? Many Bible passages tell us that Christians can, should, and do know God and the truths of *revelation (e.g. Matt. 9:6; 11:27; 13:11; John 7:17; 8:32; 10:4–5; 14:17; 17:3). Such passages present this knowledge not as something tentative but as a firm basis for life and hope. While Scripture uses the language of certainty more sparingly, it is also present. Luke wants his correspondent Theophilus to know the 'certainty' (*asphaleia*) of the things he has been taught (Luke 1:4) and the 'proofs' (*tekmeria*) by which Jesus showed himself alive after his death (Acts 1:3), and he records the centurion at the cross as saying, 'Certainly [*ontos*] this man was innocent' (Luke 23:47, ESV).

The letter to the Hebrews says that God made a promise to Abraham, swearing by himself, for there was no-one greater (Heb.

6:13). So God both made a promise and confirmed it with an oath, 'two unchangeable things in which it is impossible for God to lie' (Heb. 6:18). This is 'an anchor for the soul, firm and secure' (Heb. 6:19). Similarly Paul (2 Tim. 3:16–17) and Peter (2 Pet. 1:19–21) speak of Scripture as God's own words, which provide sure guidance in a world where false teaching abounds. God's special revelation is certain, and we ought to be certain about it.

On the other hand, the Bible presents doubt largely negatively, as a spiritual impediment, an obstacle to doing God's work (Matt. 14:31; 21:21; 28:17; Acts 10:20; 11:12; Rom. 14:23; 1 Tim. 2:8; Jas 1:6). In Matt. 14:31 and Rom. 14:23, doubt is the opposite of faith and, therefore, a sin. Of course, this sin, like other sins, may remain with us through our earthly life, but we should not be complacent about it. Just as the ideal for the Christian life is perfect holiness, so the ideal for the Christian mind is absolute certainty about God's revelation.

We should not conclude that doubt is always sinful. Matt. 14:31 and Rom. 14:23 (and indeed the other verses listed) speak of doubt in the face of clear special revelation. To doubt what God has clearly spoken to us is wrong, but in other situations, it is not wrong to doubt. In many cases, in fact, it is wrong for us to claim knowledge, much less certainty. Indeed, often the best course is to admit our ignorance (e.g. Deut. 29:29; Rom. 11:33–36). Indeed, James tells us, we are always ignorant of the future to some extent and we ought not to pretend we know more about it than we do (Jas 4:13–16). Job's friends were wrong to think that they knew the reasons for his torment, and Job himself had to be humbled as God reminded him of his ignorance (Job 38 – 42).

So, Christian epistemologist Esther Meek points out that the process of knowing during our earthly lives is a quest: following clues, noticing patterns, making commitments, respecting honest doubt. In much of life, she says, confidence, not certainty, should be our goal.

How then can absolute certainty be the appropriate (if ideal) response to God's special revelation, given our finitude and fallibility? How is it possible when we consider the scepticism that pervades secular thought? How is it humanly possible to know anything with certainty?

First, it is impossible to exclude absolute certainty in all cases. Any argument purporting to show that there is no such certainty must admit that it is itself uncertain. Further, any such argument must presuppose that argument itself is a means of finding truth. If people use an argument to test the certainty of propositions, they are claiming certainty, at least for that argument. And they are claiming that by such an argument they can test the legitimacy of claims to certainty. But such a test of certainty, a would-be criterion of certainty, must itself be certain. And an argument that would test absolute certainty must itself be absolutely certain.

In Christian *epistemology, God's word is the ultimate criterion of certainty. What God says *must* be true, for, as the letter to the Hebrews says, it is impossible for God to lie (Heb. 6:18; cf. Titus 1:2; 1 John 2:27). His Word is truth (John 17:17; cf. Pss. 33:4; 119:160). So, God's word is the criterion by which we can measure all other sources of knowledge.

When God promised Abraham a multitude of descendants and an inheritance in the land of Canaan, many things might have caused him to doubt. He had reached the age of one hundred without having any children, and his wife Sarah was far beyond the normal age of childbearing. Furthermore, though he lived in the land of Canaan, he owned no title to any land there. Paul says of him, however, that 'he did not waver through unbelief regarding the promise of God, but was strengthened in his faith and gave glory to God, being fully persuaded that God had power to do what he had promised' (Rom. 4:20–21). God's word, for Abraham, took precedence over all other evidence in forming Abraham's belief. So important is this principle that Paul defines justifying faith in terms of it, 'This is why "it was credited to him as righteousness"' (Rom. 4:22).

Thus, Abraham stands in contrast to Eve, who allowed the evidence of her eyes to take precedence over the command of God (Gen. 3:6). He is one of the heroes of the faith who, according to Heb. 11:13, died in faith, not having received the things promised, but having seen them 'and welcomed them from afar'. They had God's promise, and that was enough to motivate them to endure terrible sufferings and deprivations through their earthly lives.

It is therefore the responsibility of the Christian to regard God's word as absolutely certain and to make that word the criterion of all other sources of knowledge. Our certainty of the truth of God comes ultimately not through rational demonstration or empirical verification, useful as these may often be, but from the *authority of God's own word. God's word does testify to itself, often by means of human testimony and historical evidence (e.g. the 'proofs' of Acts 1:3; the centurion's witness in Luke 23:47; the many *witnesses to the resurrection of Jesus in 1 Cor. 15:1–11), but we should never forget that these evidences come to us with God's own authority. In 1 Cor. 15:11 Paul asks the church to believe the evidence because it is part of the authoritative apostolic preaching.

How does the word of God give us psychological certainty? People sometimes make great intellectual and emotional exertions, trying to force themselves to believe the Bible, but we cannot make ourselves believe. Certainty comes upon us by an act of God, through the testimony of his Spirit (1 Cor. 2:4, 9–16; 1 Thess. 1:5; 2 Thess. 2:14). The Spirit's witness often accompanies a human process of *reasoning, and unless our reason is empowered by the Spirit, it will not give us full assurance. Scripture, however, never rebukes people who honestly seek to think through the questions of faith.

So, certainty comes ultimately through God's word and Spirit. The Lord calls us to build our life and thought on the certainties of his word, so that we 'will never walk in darkness, but will have the light of life' (John 8:12). The process of building, furthermore, is not only academic, but also ethical and spiritual. It is those who are willing to do God's will that know the truth of Jesus' words (John 7:17), and those that love their neighbours who are able to know as they ought to know (1 Cor. 8:1–3).

Secular philosophy rejects absolute certainty, then, because absolute certainty is essentially supernatural and because the secularist is unwilling to accept a supernatural foundation for knowledge. The Christian, however, regards God's word as the ultimate criterion of truth and falsity, right and wrong, and therefore as the standard of certainty. Insofar as we consistently hold the Bible as our standard of certainty, we may and must regard it as itself absolutely certain. So in God's revelation, the Christian has a wonderful treasure, one that saves the soul from sin and the mind from scepticism.

Bibliography

J. M. Frame, *Doctrine of the Knowledge of God* (Phillipsburg, 1987); E. L. Meek, *Longing to Know: The Philosophy of Knowledge for Ordinary People* (Grand Rapids, 2003); A. Plantinga, *Warranted Christian Belief* (New York, 2000); L. Wittgenstein, *On Certainty* (New York, 1972); W. J. Wood, *Epistemology* (Downers Grove, 1998).

J. M. FRAME

CHANCE, see DETERMINISM, CHANCE
AND FREEDOM
CHARISMATIC CHRISTIANITY, see
CHRISTIANITY, PENTECOSTAL AND
CHARISMATIC

CHESTERTON, G. K.

G. K. Chesterton (1874–1936), British writer and apologist, was born in London to a middle-class family. His father inherited Chesterton and Sons, a successful estate agency, and both G. K. and his younger brother were expected to enter the business. From an early age, however, Chesterton found more joy in English literature than business. This love of literature developed despite both his parents' and teachers' initial belief he suffered from mental disabilities because he could not read at age nine.

After attending the Slade School of Art (1893–6), he left higher education to work as a journalist for much of his adult life, contributing approximately 4,000 essays and columns to *The Daily News*, *The Illustrated London News*, his own *G. K.'s Weekly* and other newspapers and magazines. In addition to journalism, he wrote poetry (both nonsense and serious), biographies, plays, short stories, novels, mystery novels, travelogues and works on social theory, religion and politics. His political essays are said to have influenced *Gandhi's vision for an independent India, his novel *The Napoleon of Notting Hill* (1904) inspired Michael Collins to work for Irish independence, and his book *The Everlasting Man* (1925) contributed to C. S. *Lewis' conversion. Between 1900 and 1936 he published roughly 100 books, and his texts reveal personal humility, wit and artful use of *paradox.

In addition to writing, Chesterton was a skilful and popular public debater. He repeatedly faced George Bernard Shaw, his close friend and agnostic, H. G. Wells, Bertrand *Russell and Clarence Darrow. Contemporary reports indicate that audiences frequently agreed Chesterton won these encounters. While his style relied on a relatively meandering form of logic, his popularity is ultimately attributed to his deft mixing of mischievous humour and aggressive argumentation. Ironically, his opponents generally regarded him with deep affection, and Shaw said, 'The world is not thankful enough for Chesterton.'

In 1901 he married Frances Blogg, a devout Roman Catholic, and in 1922 he converted to Roman Catholicism. Chesterton contemplated leaving the Anglican Church much earlier but, as he notes, he was 'much too frightened of that tremendous Reality on the altar'. Frances not only influenced his religious commitments, she also transformed his public image. In addition to being over six feet tall and weighing between 300 and 400 pounds, Chesterton had little 'dress sense'. One of Frances' early tasks was to alter his slovenly appearance. Thus, she began dressing him in a flowing cape and slouch hat, which became his trademark attire.

While he is perhaps best known for his Father Brown murder mysteries (1911–35), one must recall that he was the early twentieth century's foremost apologist. T. S. *Eliot once wrote, Chesterton 'did more than any man in his time ... to maintain the existence of the [Christian] minority in the modern world'. Therefore, his books *Heretics* and *Orthodoxy* are essential reading. In them he argues that Christianity provides the substantial answers to the dilemmas facing society and provides tools for coming to grips with the paradoxes baffling human beings. Additionally, *Orthodoxy* can be described as an intellectual autobiography depicting his own search for meaning and *truth in the modern world.

Besides being an advocate for Christianity, he was an insightful social critic and challenged various social trends of the late Victorian and Edwardian period. Among these were *materialism, scientific *determinism, moral *relativism, *agnosticism, *communism, fascism and eugenics. In *The Flying Inn* (1914) he put forth an analysis of *Nietzsche's philosophy, and in *Eugenics and Other Evils* (1922) and *The Superstition of Divorce* (1920) he defended *marriage and the family against what he viewed as mounting opposition.

Finally, Chesterton wrote a number of literary biographies including texts about Robert Browning (1903), Charles Dickens (1906), George Bernard Shaw (1909) and Robert Louis Stevenson (1927), and lives of Francis of Assisi (1923) and *Thomas Aquinas (1933).

While he is remembered as a prolific writer and skilled apologist, his self-image is different. Frances Chesterton said, 'He considered himself nothing beyond a jolly journalist who wanted to paint the town red.'

Bibliography

G. K. Chesterton, *The Man Who Was Thursday* (1908); *What's Wrong with the World* (1910); *The Man Who Knew Too Much* (1922); *Autobiography* (1936); M. Ffinch, *G. K. Chesterton: A Biography* (San Francisco, 1986); W. Griffin, *G. K. Chesterton: Essential Writings* (Maryknoll, New York, 2003).

J. E. McDERMOND

CHINESE RELIGIONS, see RELIGIONS OF CHINESE AND JAPANESE ORIGIN
CHRIST OF FAITH, see JESUS OF HISTORY AND CHRIST OF FAITH
CHRIST, DEITY OF, see DEITY OF CHRIST

CHRISTIANITY (ORTHODOX)

Historical introduction

The distinctive feature of Orthodox apologetic is the use of the Tradition as a living resource, to be expounded and applied today.

The second-century apologists, such as *Justin Martyr and *Athenagoras, begin the story of Orthodox apologetic. In their work is found the outline of a world-view which is distinctively Christian and yet which also engages, often positively, with surrounding cultures. Their work laid the foundation for later Orthodox approaches.

Following the rise of *Islam, Eastern Christians were forced to defend their belief in the *Trinity and in *Jesus as God incarnate, who died and was resurrected. The most notable apologist during this time was John of Damascus (c. 655/65–c. 750), whose writings remain a basic source for defenders of Orthodoxy. In this period conversions to Christianity from Islam were normally met with severe punishment, and Orthodoxy became a faith practised by ethnic minorities within Islamic society. As a result, the Eastern Christian community tended to withdraw into itself, and for many centuries little practice of apologetics was possible. Also, there is a territorial aspect to Orthodox ecclesiology, in which ethnic identity and religious allegiance are sometimes conflated, so that when non-Orthodox are a tiny minority within a predominantly Orthodox society, there is little incentive to engage in apologetics. These two factors have on occasion led to the church's loss of a sense of its catholicity and of its commission to take the gospel to all peoples, a loss which is still discernible in some Orthodox jurisdictions.

During the seventeenth and eighteenth centuries, Reformation-era theology influenced Orthodox polemicists as they deployed *Roman Catholic arguments against *Protestants and *vice versa*. Inevitably, Eastern theology was subtly influenced (the Orthodox would say distorted) in the process.

The next flowering of Orthodox apologetic came in nineteenth-century Russia, where a number of intellectuals sought to interpret Orthodox teaching in a way which would communicate to the secularized intelligentsia of the period and to apply it to a range of social and philosophical issues. Their creative use of the Tradition carried with it some risk of heresy, evident in the work of thinkers such as Vladimir Solovyov (1853–1900), who has been accused of pantheism. Nevertheless, this renaissance gave birth to a tradition of thought which remains vigorous and fruitful, especially in the West, to where many Russian intellectuals were forced to emigrate after 1917. Influential representatives of this tradition have included Nikolai Berdyaev (1874–1948), Sergius Bulgakov (1871–1944) and Alexander Men (1935–90). A key note is the emphasis on the incarnation as sanctifying the whole created order and making it possible for humanity to achieve union with the divine. Many thinkers have also engaged in extensive critique of Marxist ideology and social theory.

Contemporary Orthodox apologetic

The challenges faced by Orthodox apologists today are numerous: *atheism, *secularism and *materialism, the activities of Western Christian and pseudo-Christian groups in Eastern Europe and, in some areas, the vitality of Islam. Orthodox believers in former Communist countries now face the challenge of articulating a defence of the faith which does not depend for credibility on the church's regaining a privileged position in society over other religious groups. Some are responding to this challenge, but others are more concerned to secure legislation restricting the activities of non-Orthodox groups than to develop a credible defence of Orthodoxy's truth-claims. The church's own failures also present obstacles to be overcome by Orthodox apologetics: compromise and even collusion with anti-Christian governments in the East, and the existence of a plurality of (often inward-looking) Orthodox jurisdictions in the West. These present challenges to the tendency to triumphalism evident in some Orthodox apologetic.

Orthodox apologetic concentrates on such themes as the existence of God and his desire to enter into a relationship with humanity, this being the end for which we were created. The attempt is made to find points of contact in the audience's own culture and world-view. In many ways, this apologetic resembles that of other exponents of 'Great Tradition Christianity', such as C. S. Lewis, who have focused on the fundamental doctrines enshrined in the early *creeds. A noted practitioner of this approach was the Moscow priest Alexander Men. He was of Jewish extraction and scientifically trained, and was able to commend the Christian faith to intellectuals from a wide variety of philosophical and religious backgrounds by virtue of a sound grasp of their cultural context and his presentation of Christianity as the fulfilment of the universal religious quest. As with earlier Russian thinkers, the more traditional Orthodox have been suspicious of his ideas, which may appear just as subversive of a Christian closed society as of a Communist one.

Orthodox apologetic also emphasizes the claim that the Orthodox faith is the authentic apostolic faith. Thus, there can be no full Orthodox apologetic without consideration of the ecclesiological dimension of Christianity. For the Orthodox it can be said that salvation *is* the church, since it is in the church that human beings begin to experience the fellowship with God which will be realized fully in the world to come. Where different Christian traditions co-exist, as in the English-speaking West,

defence of Orthodoxy's claims entails a certain amount of polemic, demonstrating the shortcomings of Catholicism or the various forms of Protestantism. In the West, a well-known, although not representative, contemporary polemicist is the convert Frank Schaeffer. The methodology adopted by some convert apologists betrays the persistence of certain Western styles of apologetic which seek to argue a logical case in such a way as to leave opponents without any ground to stand on. For example, schematic surveys of modern thought may charge Western Christianity with responsibility for the emergence of individualism, liberalism, secularism and materialism, with the apologetic intent being to show that only Orthodoxy has the answers to contemporary social and cultural, as well as spiritual, evils. Such argumentation, with its confrontational tendency and juridical feel, is reinforced in the minds of many by the increasing numbers of Orthodox converts from Western Christian traditions. A considerable proportion of them appear to join Orthodoxy, at least partly, because they find its answers to their religious questions more intellectually convincing than any offered by the traditions from which they come.

While some Orthodox apologists adopt a polemical approach, others prefer to be more dialogical, expounding their faith in more positive terms as the fulfilment of humanity's deepest longings, e.g. Alexander Men and Metropolitan Anthony [Bloom] (1914–2003). The latter's writings have been influential in British church circles in recent decades, and his open apologetic stance is reflected in his diocese's policy regarding ecumenical relationships.

Orthodox apologists agree that rational demonstration alone is inadequate, especially in societies which are leaving behind the rationalistic emphases of modern thought. Indeed, for many such an approach, while it may have a certain *ad hominem* value, is foreign to the ethos of Eastern Christianity. A fundamental reason for this is the apophatic character of Orthodox thought, which stresses that our knowledge of God is a knowledge of one who is utterly beyond human understanding. Rational argument must, therefore, be accompanied by a sense of the transcendent reality of God, experienced through beginning to live the life of an Orthodox Christian, a life which is properly experienced in communion with others.

The apologetic community

The story is told that in 988, Prince Vladimir of Kiev sent emissaries abroad to investigate which religion he should adopt. Finding other options unattractive, they recommended that he espouse Orthodoxy. What convinced them to do so was the liturgy at Hagia Sophia in Constantinople, which struck them as so beautiful and splendid that they did not know whether they were in heaven or on earth. The account encapsulates three important points about Orthodox apologetic. First, beauty has a key role to play: the same God is the source of beauty and *truth. Secondly, that beauty is seen most fully in the context of the worshipping *community as it celebrates the liturgy and thus participates in the union of *heaven and earth. Thirdly, there is a powerful element of *mystery inherent in the experience of a transcendent dimension which such worship provides.

Since the church is to be a demonstration of the reality of God in this way, Orthodox apologetic invites inquirers to participate in the liturgy because, in the final analysis, the faith is something to be experienced rather than defended. It is in this setting that many decide to become Orthodox. In a sense, the whole community joins in the apologetic task, since it functions as a demonstration of the message. A close relationship exists, therefore, between apologetics, evangelism and worship.

Bibliography

E. Roberts and A. Shukman, *Christianity for the Twenty-first Century: The Life and Work of Alexander Men* (London, 1996); F. Schaeffer, *Dancing Alone: The Quest for Orthodox Faith in the Age of False Religion* (Brookline, 1994); N. Zernov, *The Russian Religious Renaissance of the Twentieth Century* (London, 1964).

T. G. GRASS

CHRISTIANITY (PENTECOSTAL AND CHARISMATIC)

When we look at the defence of Christian doctrine, we can do so by exploring the correlation between doctrine and experience. However, we have to ask what we mean by experience, and one way of answering this question is to say that experience is to be found through our five senses of touch, taste, smell, seeing and hearing. In saying this we must be careful to recognize that we can retain memories of experiences, and that these memories may be held in several forms. For instance, memories of music may be best written down in musical notation, memories of places may best be expressed in photographs and memories of emotions may best be expressed in poems and songs.

In looking at Christian doctrine, we are dealing with propositions, or inter-connected statements about Christian beliefs, that hold together logically. So how should we connect these statements about belief with our experiences? This is a much more difficult question to answer than it appears because there is not a direct link between belief and experience. In fact, two people can undergo very similar experiences and emerge with different beliefs. Or, conversely, two people with different beliefs can interpret the same experience differently.

Perhaps the best way to think of the relationship between doctrine and experience is to compare it to that between a map and the land described by the map. You know where you are on the land because you see places in front of you that correspond with the symbols on the map. Similarly, we can say that if our experiences correspond with the words in the Bible, we can understand each better. For instance, if we feel guilty when we do certain things, we relate these feelings to what we read in the Bible about being convicted of sin; if we feel full of happiness after putting our faith in Christ, we can relate these feelings to what we read in the Bible about the joy of salvation, and so on.

Some sectors of the church are more likely to relate *religious experience to doctrine than others. The pentecostal and charismatic movements have emphasized the experiential side of Christianity, but without throwing away the rational and logical side. Pentecostal Christians may differ from others in that they see their own experience of 'baptism in the Spirit' as being similar to that described in Acts 2. Most evangelical Christians will see their experience of the 'new birth' as being similar to that described by Jesus in John 3. There is a logical congruence between evangelicalism and pentecostalism; this is why pentecostals are also evangelical.

This article will therefore consider the experience of the baptism in the *Holy Spirit and its implications, and related issues concerned with divine healing and divine guidance. It will then consider briefly the relationship between rationality and experience before applying the pentecostal and charismatic apologetic to four separate areas of objection to Christianity.

Spirit baptism

Personal subjective accounts of baptism in the Holy Spirit are numerous. In essence, the experience is usually seen as being overwhelming, accompanied by a sense of the presence of Christ and expressed by words of praise to God incomprehensible to the speaker. Five personal consequences of the experience usually follow. First, the Bible is seen to be vindicated in the sense that the text describes experiences 2,000 years ago that the believer feels he or she has now shared. Thus statements about the accuracy of Scripture or its irrelevance are set aside by those whose own deeply felt experience argues against the apparent rationality of sceptics. Secondly, *Jesus is felt to be both close and alive. This is partly the result of the biblical assertions that it is Jesus himself who is the baptizer in the Holy Spirit, i.e. he is the person who administers the experience (Matt. 3:11; Mark 1:8; Luke 3:16; John 1:33). Assertions that Jesus has not risen from the dead or has no *power today depend on the *absence* of a spiritual experience (i.e. the attempt to prove a negative); but this is undermined by the *presence* of a spiritual experience which is interpreted as being possible only because Jesus has risen from the dead. Thirdly, believers feel accepted by Christ as a consequence of the overwhelming experience they have received. This is a renewal and intensification of the original conversion experience. Assertions that their own lives are unimportant or that God is far away are deemed irrelevant because the Acts 2 experience is, among other things, largely an experience understood to be an outpouring of unconditional divine love. Fourthly, Scripture is seen to be inspired. This is not only because of the match between typically described events and personally experienced events, but also because it becomes much easier to understand a theology that speaks of the text as being inspired by the Holy Spirit. The process and mechanics of *revelation become believable. Assertions about the impossibility of revelation are based on too narrow a view of what is or is not believable. Finally, a sense of eschatological

urgency follows from an appreciation of the Acts 2:17 declaration that 'in the last days, God says, I will pour out my Spirit on all people'. In other words, believers come to locate themselves within an unfolding historical plan. Assertions that history is circular or meaningless would have to contradict the sense of a personal life-plan that often accompanies the replay of Acts 2 in the individual's life.

Accompanying signs and miracles

Baptism in the Holy Spirit often leads to a belief that when the gospel is preached it should be accompanied by miraculous signs and wonders to vindicate its authenticity. The long ending of Mark 16 provides a theological rationale for signs and wonders in an evangelistic context, and this rationale is further developed in the book of Acts. It is because prayer in the name of Jesus leads to healing, for instance, that other statements about Christ can be deemed true. Signs and wonders then become a forceful part of the apologetic armoury confronting prejudiced and other religious traditions.

In addition, the propagation of the gospel, when it is accompanied by healing, provides a very practical answer to objections to Christianity on the basis of suffering in the world that has been allowed by a good and all-powerful God. Healing *miracles provide a partial theodicy showing that God does care about seemingly random human suffering. In addition, miracles may be extended to the miracle of prophecy, where prophecy concerns truthful declarations about the future events and not simply statements about current events. To say that God can heal an illness today and that the same God knows the future, and has shown this by the match between OT prophecy and NT fulfilment, is credible since both healing and prophecy presume divine intervention.

Church life

Many of the considerations concerning evangelistic healing also apply to the congregational context of Jas 5, where elders are asked to anoint the sick with oil. Since the oil is normally thought to represent the Holy Spirit, the notion of a congregation as being a place where the Holy Spirit is active and felt can be substantiated. Similarly, when the gifts of the Spirit spoken of in 1 Cor. 12 and 14 (e.g. prophecy or utterances in tongues that are interpreted) are exercised within a thriving congregation, it is much easier to bridge the gap between clergy and laity and to find divine guidance for daily situations. In other words, the notion that the church is a living and active body in touch with Christ moves from the realm of theological theory into practicality. Visitors to such churches may find answers to their own problems (1 Cor. 14:24). In addition, where churches are open to visionary experience, there may be an affinity between this and local non-literary cultures. In parts of the world where dreams are thought to offer an insight into another dimension, visions can bypass intellectual objections to Christianity. For example, there have been cases where Hindus have seen visions of Mary the mother of Jesus or Muslims have felt that Christ spoke to them in a dream.

Application

The particular contribution that the pentecostal and charismatic movements make to apologetics arises from their emphasis upon religious experience. They would argue that experience should not be seen as an alternative to rationality but rather as an accompaniment of it and one based upon the nature of human beings as a psycho-physical unity. Whether experience precedes rationality or follows it, is not the point. What matters is that rationality and experience are harmonious and that it is this harmony which persuades of the truth of Christianity.

The objections to Christianity arising from *Feuerbach's argument that God is simply a projection of human desire (an objection recycled by Marx and adopted by *Freud) are met by the pentecostal and charismatic apologetic in two ways (A. E. McGrath, *Science and Religion: An Introduction* [Oxford, 1999]). First, by simple denial pointing to the deeds of God within their own lives. No projection could heal those who are ill or provide guidance or comfort in the way that matches their experience. Secondly, in relation to the Freudian notion of an unconscious mind from which dreams arise and by which wish-fulfilments are rationalized, the apologetic would point to the notion that the *whole* human being is baptized by the Holy Spirit, not simply the conscious mind. So, if there is an unconscious mind (and this is contestable), it also is accepted and redeemed by Christ and touched by the power of the Holy Spirit.

The objections to Christianity arising from a Darwinian account of the origin of the human race are not met by any original critique within the pentecostal and charismatic community. Nevertheless, the experiential nature of this form of Christianity does make it easier not to adopt literalistic interpretations of the opening chapters of Genesis and thereby to circumvent the most confrontational arguments between creation science and evolutionary theory. *Materialism as a philosophical account of the universe is simply denied.

Regarding other religions, the apologetic, while it would be prepared to accept *common grace on the basis of common humanity, argues for the uniqueness of Christ, particularly on the grounds of his *resurrection, which is seen to be validated by miracles. Attempts to argue that the Holy Spirit may be seen as operative within faiths other than Christianity would be rejected by the vast majority of pentecostals and charismatics, who locate their pneumatology firmly within trinitarian orthodoxy.

In the sense that postmodernism is an assertion that there is no universal *truth and no grand meta-narrative, the apologetic implicitly denies this. By emphasizing religious experience, the apologetic widens the frame of debate since postmodernism is primarily an intellectual Western analysis of the limitations and cultural manifestations of reason. By showing that experience, suitably grounded in Scripture, points to the existence of God and the resurrection of Christ, the apologetic offers an alternative to the view that social and intellectual *history must be seen in terms of a process starting with pre-modernity and moving through *Enlightenment *rationalism to modernity and inexorably, after the exhaustion of modernity within the traumas of the twentieth century, to fragmented but global postmodernity.

Bibliography

S. Burgess and E. van der Maas (eds.), *New International Dictionary of Pentecostal and Charismatic Movements* (Grand Rapids, 2002); S. Coleman, *The Globalisation of Charismatic Christianity: Spreading the Gospel of Prosperity* (Cambridge, 2000); H. Cox, *Fire from Heaven* (London, 1996); D. W. Dayton, *Theological Roots of Pentecostalism* (Metuchen, 1987); M. W. Dempster, B. D. Klaus and D. Petersen (eds.), *The Globalization of Pentecostalism* (Oxford, 1999);

W. J. Hollenweger, *Pentecostalism: Origins and Developments Worldwide* (Peabody, 1997); W. K. Kay, *Pentecostals in Britain* (Carlisle, 2000); V. Synan, *The Holiness-Pentecostal Tradition)* (Grand Rapids, 1997); G. Wacker, *Heaven Below: Early Pentecostals and American Culture* (Cambridge, MA, and London, 2001).

W. K. KAY

CHRISTIANITY (PROTESTANT)

On 31 October 1517 Martin Luther posted ninety-five theses on the door of the castle church in Wittenberg. These theses, criticizing the church's practice of selling indulgences, marked a turning point in the history of the church. They were the culmination of several centuries of growing criticism within the church and threw open the gates to the Reformation which followed.

Almost 500 years later the church around the world continues to be shaped and influenced by the period of the Protestant Reformation, but what distinct contributions has Protestant Christianity made to the apologetic life of the church? In an attempt to discuss this we will look at three of the rallying cries of the Reformation and assess how these different emphases give a distinct shape to Protestant apologetics.

Sola Scriptura

One of the hallmarks of the Reformation was a return to the text of Scripture as the principal *authority for teaching and doctrine in the church. Building on the earlier work of humanist scholars (such as *Erasmus), the Reformers worked to gain a better understanding of the original languages of the Bible. Using this knowledge they then sought to make the Bible more accessible by translating it into the common languages of everyday people. Prior to this, in the West, the Bible appeared almost exclusively in Latin, which was not the language of the common person. By emphasizing the role of 'Scripture alone' the Reformers made several important contributions to our apologetic life.

First, Protestant confidence in the clear meaning of Scripture has enabled generations of apologists to bring their conversation partners directly to Scripture as a first stop in apologetic discussion. While philosophical arguments about issues such as the necessity of the existence of God have their place, a Protestant perspective urges direct interaction with God's inspired word, trusting that the *Holy Spirit can and will act when God's word is read. This approach is exemplified in the work of Cornelius *Van Til, a well-known Reformed apologist.

Secondly, a return to Scripture forces us to deal with the central character of the Bible: *Jesus Christ. The Reformers of the sixteenth century felt the church had become so corrupt that it obscured the gospel of Christ. In order to see Christ clearly they had to reach back into Scripture, beyond the corrupted presentation of the church. Similarly, in contemporary apologetics Christians often find themselves forced to defend the church instead of Christ. This is a distraction from the purpose of apologetics, which is to encourage others to interact with the life and meaning of Jesus himself. By drawing people to Scripture in order to encounter Christ we emphasize that the main issue at stake is the truth about Jesus, not how well the church lives up to its identity as his representative. Furthermore, because the Reformation highlighted the human and fallible nature of the church we are challenged to institutional *humility, recognizing that our witness is both imperfect and culture-bound.

Finally, it was important to the Reformers that people should have Scripture available to them so that they could make their own judgment about the gospel of Christ without being solely dependent on the teaching of the church. The advent of the printing press meant that new translations of the Bible into people's native tongues were widely and cheaply available to the common person. There is a contemporary apologetic corollary to this. In each generation Protestant Christianity attempts to provide a fresh re-telling of the story of Scripture. This does not necessarily mean a new translation of the text into, say, 'modern English'; rather, a Protestant apologetic seeks to allow the Bible to engage with contemporary *culture in a way that is both faithful to God's *revelation in the text and relevant to contemporary culture. This approach recognizes the contribution of the church throughout history, while at the same time realizing that *language, modes of communication and the systems in which Christian thought are placed always need refining. By focusing on 'Scripture alone', a Protestant apologetic must be creative and adaptable, ready to introduce Scripture and its story in a variety of ways.

Sola Gratia

Another of Martin Luther's chief complaints against the church (found most clearly in his commentary on Galatians) was its emphasis on the central role of good works for salvation. The response of the Reformers to this teaching of the church was to emphasize that salvation is by 'grace alone', the free gift of God, and not by works (Eph. 2:8–9). This has a number of consequences for apologetics.

First, if grace is indeed the only way to salvation, then salvation begins and ends with the action of God. If apologetic work is dependent on God's action for a response, then we have to believe that the success or failure of apologetics depends ultimately on God. This should lead us to treat our own efforts with humility, acknowledging our dependence on God and encouraging our reliance on prayer. This should also prevent the church from using coercive methods or manipulation, knowing that no amount of arm-twisting can effect what God alone can do.

Secondly, if grace alone is sufficient for salvation, then good works should be treated as a result, not a requirement, of salvation. Often people will hesitate to believe in Jesus Christ because they feel they are not good enough for God. Alternatively, some may not be willing to change their lifestyle in order to meet what they view as the ethical requirements of becoming a part of the church. Both groups fail to understand that good works are not a requirement for entry, but the natural result of being transformed by the grace of God. Understanding this will affect our apologetics by encouraging us to focus on God's grace and not on people's need to 'clean up their act' before they can become Christians. We must not shy away from articulating the demands of the Christian life, but we should set these in the right context as a natural response to supernatural grace.

Sola fide

A third hallmark of the Reformation was an emphasis on 'faith alone', in the form of trust and reliance, as the basis of one's relationship with God. In an age when attendance at mass, confession and good works seemed to comprise the sum total of one's response to God, the Reformers sought to reassert the importance of personal faith in Christ. While baptism and receiving of communion were important, these outward and visible signs needed to be matched by an inward and spiritual reality, that of faith. This emphasis on the response of faith has several implications for apologetics.

An emphasis on 'faith alone' reminds us that a personal response is necessary, and encourages a focus on the individual. This makes us sensitive towards those with whom we interact and willing to deal with people as individuals. This should also encourage us to be good listeners, seeking to understand the specific spiritual, emotional and intellectual needs of our conversation partners. Finally, this challenges us to be clear and forthright as we explain the need for a personal response to the claims of Christ.

The Protestant idea of 'faith alone' also has the effect of highlighting the relational nature of the Christian life. Emphasis on faith as restored relationship with God leads us to focus our apologetics on encouraging a personal encounter with Christ. This partners with an emphasis on 'Scripture alone' and draws apologetic conversations toward the key moments in Christ's life such as his birth, death and resurrection, highlighting the relationship between these moments in Christ's life and ours. If one purpose of apologetics is to build trust between people and God, this will happen only when people see that God is trustworthy. The Reformers believed that the best way to come to this conviction, and to the faith that results from it, is through God's inspired word.

Conclusion

These Protestant contributions to the apologetic mission of the church can only be understood as a group, because there are pitfalls in emphasizing any one Reformation slogan over the others. A naïve reliance on 'Scripture alone' may turn into a focus on proclamation that lacks sensitivity. A bold belief in 'grace alone' can often turn into a rejection of the need for Christian *ethics, and a conviction that 'faith alone' is all important may lead to hyper-individualism and a failure to appreciate the work of God in his church. These three must be taken together. They ought also to be viewed alongside important contributions made by the Catholic and Eastern Orthodox churches.

These add to the vibrancy of the church's apologetic mission as well as clarifying the distinctly Protestant contribution described above.

Bibliography

O. Chadwick, *The Penguin History of the Church*, vol. 3: *The Reformation* (London, 1990); T. George, *Theology of the Reformers* (Nashville, 1988; Leicester, 1989); D. MacCulloch, *The Reformation: A History* (New York, 2004); A. McGrath, *Reformation Thought: An Introduction* (Oxford, 1999).

J. W. YATES, III

CHRISTIANITY (ROMAN CATHOLIC)

What are the distinctive beliefs of the Roman Catholic Church which may strengthen and which may pose a challenge to the presentation of Christian claims today? Karl Adam offers us a list of distinctives: Christ and the church (body, foundation), the communion of saints, the catholicity of the church, the necessity of the church for salvation, sacramental action and educative purpose. One can see from this that Catholicism is distinct not for its take on the majority of doctrines, but almost only for those which can be seen as relating to ecclesiology and anthropology. Yet it must be remembered that the Roman Catholic Church has often defended the other major doctrines as tenaciously as Eastern and Protestant Orthodoxy (see *Christianity, Orthodox and *Christianity, Protestant).

Although known as the 'Roman' Catholic Church, many prefer to call it simply Catholic in the sense of its universality and its extension through space and time. More controversial is Bossuet's claim, repeated by de Lubac, that Catholic means not so much geographically spread out but universal in touching humankind. This idea of the seed of the church innate in the whole human race goes back to one of the earliest Christian theologians, Justin, and sees Christianity as absorbing the old world, 'baptizing' all that was of value, rather than being corrupted by it. The church is also 'the soul of the world', which means more than just the world's conscience. A feature of Catholic apologetics is a confidence that the Catholic Church promotes a true humanism, to adopt the title of J. Maritain's book, or, with

K. Adam, an affirmation of values, accessibility to all good, union of nature with grace, of art with religion, knowledge with faith and fullness rather than primitive simplicity. The idea that the church is called to speak to the core essence of humanity and to reconcile nations and cultures even today is based on the fact that God has already effected this (Matt. 21:43), but it also hinges on the belief in the eucharist as the sacrament of unity. At the eucharist the church becomes the mystical body by participation in the true body, so that it is more truly *Jesus' body than his own physical body, which was itself a type, a foreshadowing of this mystical one (de Lubac, again following Bossuet). Of course, as a sacrament of unity it cannot create unity when in terms of heart and mind there is disunity, although one could argue that this makes the sacrament more like a symbol. The importance of saints for Catholicism appears in place of martyrdom as a mirror image of the offering of the eucharist. Most saints qualify for their recognition as such ('canonization') through proof of renunciation in this life and through being channels for *miracles after death. The emphasis here on touching flesh and blood illustrates how dominant in Catholicism is the 'incarnational principle', the scandal of becoming flesh, of embodiment, of an emphasis on liturgy which seeks to speak to the senses and move the body (in prostration for prayer, in procession, even in pilgrimage). This leads on to the idea that suffering as a bodily experience has value and is not wholly negative, especially when seen 'in Christ', and resurrection affirms the importance of flesh matter, especially when it has faced death and suffering.

The mission of the church is seen as one of sancifying the world through the sacraments. But is this really possible when, after all, it is the non-physical world of human life that needs God's presence, not the world of bread and ash and water *per se*, for all their efficacy in the lives of Catholics? A *theology of 'blessings' seems more acceptable to the Protestant mind, as it touches on 'real life', the home, work, etc. Similarly, is it possible, or even necessary, for the commemoration of saints' days throughout the year to sancify time?

Another strength of the Catholic Church is its attempt to be clear and proactive. The *Catechism of the Catholic Church* provides a useful summary of doctrine and states that for those individual Christians who do not profess the Catholic faith in its entirety, it is their faith through baptism rather than their ecclesial communities that is recognized as 'Christian'. Yet one can also see a desire to move with the times and embrace the spirit of ecumenism. This was the keynote of the Second Vatican Council (1962–65), with its emphasis on dialogue and taking the world and its questions seriously. According to Karl *Rahner, perhaps the leading theological adviser at the Council, whereas the Catholic Church used to say, 'God speaks, man obeys', now 'we prove that God has spoken, naturally and supernaturally, so all who do not hear are either intellectually inept or morally perverse'.

*Revelation thus needs to be understood as personal and powerful, and as happening in the world, not just in the printed words of councils and learned scholars. Similarly, on the issue of the *canon of Scripture, there is a personal emphasis, with the apostles and leaders of the early church expressing the will of the *Holy Spirit as they wrote and selected what was to be received by the church as Holy Scripture. This may avoid the de-personalizing supernaturalism of verbal inerrancy within the Protestant tradition.

The church as mother is seen as instrumental in salvation, such that full salvation means acknowledging her. So strong is the sacramental theology, that de Lubac, in *The Splendour of the Church*, can write of the church, 'We cannot believe *in* her as we believe in the Author of our Salvation, but we do believe that she is the mother who brings us our regeneration', and the Catechism states that 'all salvation comes from Christ the Head though the Church which is His body'. The church is made first for the sake of humankind, and is perfect even if its individual members err. This means that tradition is seen as the sum of interpretations of Scripture made from earliest times by the mother church, who has gone before us, so that God's original, historical, revelation in Christ is enriched progressively through the ages. One could possibly speak of a re-presentation of revelation in a way similar to that in which Christ's once-for-all sacrifice is re-presented in the mass.

The Catholic Church's keen interest in matters ethical, under the banner of 'moral theology', can seem to verge on legalism, although the 1997 *Joint Roman Catholic–Lutheran Declaration on Justification* asserted that it was not works but 'co-operation as

a middle way' which were required for the fullness of salvation. The combination of prevenient grace and cooperation found in the figure of Mary is probably a good illustration of this. Karl *Barth noticed that, for Catholicism, Mary is a central crucial dogma, 'in relation to which all its cardinal propositions are elucidated'.

The *authority of the Pope in the Council of Cardinals (the Curia), and at times the other bishops, means that some amount of top-down instruction derived from tested theological principles will be administered, even if this looks a bit defensive rather than constructive. This is said to be not so much 'inventing' doctrine as applying that which has already been 'given'. John Paul II claimed that 'our readiness to walk daily with Peter is the test of our openness to Jesus', and while this may seem unequivocal, it corresponds to what Maritain called 'the primacy of the spiritual'. There is thus an unashamed wish to speak with a voice of spiritual authority on the world stage.

In its apologetics, known better since the early twentieth century as 'fundamental theology', Catholic theology poses the question of what 'Jesus' does for our human being and the questions we ask. Fundamental theology thus *responds* to dogmatic theology and its claims about revelation, both in asking questions of it and in taking its message forward. In this, apologists dialogue with believers as much as with unbelievers. Catholic apologetics is about the self-giving of God in Christ *and* the intrinsic credibility of this manifestation that he is by his presence in the world. It makes revelation the first and exclusive object of study – but not just the revelation as *mystery, but also as historical event, which means that it can and must be checked out by reason. There operates a shuttling between the mystery and its historical emergence (e.g. between the 'Christ' and the Jesus of the Gospels) or between the meaning and the uniqueness.

Perhaps the best examples of apologetics are the anthropological foundations presented in the papal documents *Veritatis Splendor* (1993) and *Fides et Ratio* (1998). To consider truth and goodness one must turn to God in Christ crucified and to shun intrinsically evil acts. The second encyclical calls for a revaluation of the metaphysical in philosophy, which should allow itself to be informed by revelation for the sake of the fullness of *truth, and to show how humanity is not autonomous from a Creator.

Bibliography

The Catechism of the Catholic Church (London, 1992); K. Adam, *The Spirit of Catholicism* (New York, 1997); John Paul II, *Crossing the Threshold of Hope* (Knopf, 1994); H. de Lubac, *Catholicism: Christ and the Common Destiny of Man* (San Francisco, 1988); R. McBrien (ed.), *Encyclopedia of Catholicism* (San Francisco, 1995); J. Maritain, *True Humanism* (London, 1938); G. O'Collins and M. Farrugia, *Catholicism: The Story of Catholic Christianity* (Oxford, 2003).

M. W. ELLIOTT

CHRONOLOGY, NEW TESTAMENT, see HISTORICAL DIFFICULTIES IN THE NEW TESTAMENT

CHURCH, EXISTENCE OF THE

The apologetic significance of the existence of the church is clear within the NT itself. The powerful gospel of *Jesus' life, death and resurrection has produced the miracle of faith and the extraordinary phenomenon of gatherings which breach every human barrier in a fellowship of love and service borne of gratitude to God. Christ has made a difference to life now, bringing believers together to hear his word and serve each other. The final gathering around the throne of God and the Lamb is anticipated in human *history in local congregations of faithful men and women.

Such gatherings are not natural, just as the faith that lies at their heart is not natural. In particular, while it is true that the common faith which binds Christians together is never less than rational, it is always more than rational. This faith has its source and focus outside of us, in the gracious activity of God towards us in Christ Jesus (Rom. 3:21–26). Its transformative impact on human lives comes through the *preaching of the gospel of God's grace in Christ (Rom. 1:16–17; 10:14–15). Christian faith is God's gift, not a natural human faculty (Eph. 2:8–9). By his mercy in Christ Jesus, God overcomes our natural state of radical self-centredness and persistent refusal of his right to rule over every facet of our lives. In its place he creates genuine trust and a commitment to love. In this way, each Christian is a testimony to God's power and grace. So too is each gathering of Christians.

The existence of Christian churches cannot be satisfactorily explained by human psychology, culture or even the prevailing political, social and economic environment. All of these have undoubtedly had an impact on the development of churches and associations of churches, often a negative and distorting impact. Indeed, the history of ecclesiastical institutions, both in the West and in the East, has given ample ammunition to those who would attack the faith. However, despite radical institutional failure (e.g. the Crusades, the Inquisition, the doctrinal and moral compromise of denominational leaders) and the continuing reality of human sinfulness alongside the miracle of faith and godliness, it is important to recognize that true churches are extraordinary. Their origin is the proclamation of the gospel of Christ crucified, considered foolish and even scandalous by the intellectual and religious elite of the first century and today. Their determined commitment to 'the faith that was once for all entrusted to the saints' (Jude 3) combined with a confidence that this faith is able to withstand all attempts to discredit it intellectually, defies both the coercion of political and social consensus and the scepticism of modern philosophical hubris.

Christian churches are fellowships of faith where the universal lordship of Christ is recognized. As far as the apostolic teaching of the NT is concerned, Christ's lordship transforms the relationships of those who follow him. In particular this involves a rejection of status (1 Cor 1:26–31; Phlm. 16) and the breach of all barriers which separate human beings. Recognizing that we have a common, immediate access to God in Christ is meant to generate a unity amongst believers that is remarkable in the world. In the churches all are 'one in Christ Jesus' (Gal. 3:28). Holding firmly to the faith necessarily includes a self-sacrificial love which transcends every distinction between believers and is itself a challenge to all surrounding cultures. Embrace of the gospel of Christ and the embrace of others who have been gripped by that gospel are inseparable (1 John 4:19–21). This is in fact a reflection of the teaching of Jesus that 'you have only one Master and you are all brothers' (Matt. 23:8) and 'by this all men will know that you are my disciples, if you love one another' (John 13:35).

The apostle Paul recognized the significance of the existence of Christian churches as itself a testimony to the power and wisdom of God in Christ crucified. Only something supernatural could bring and keep such people together and united in faith and love. The fact that the ancient division of Jews and Gentiles had been broken down at the cross was particularly significant because this division was not just a political or cultural one, it was spiritual as well. God himself had separated Israel from the nations and so created the Jew/Gentile distinction. However, as Paul saw, this was now gone and in the context of explaining this 'mystery' Paul unfolds its apologetic significance. This 'new man out of the two' exists so that 'through the church, the manifold wisdom of God should be made known to the rulers and authorities in the heavenly realms' (Eph. 2:15; 3:10). In other words, the primary audience of this particular testimony is the devil and those allied with him.

However, there is also a human audience to whom the very existence of the churches, fellowships of faith and love, is a testimony of the *truth of the gospel and the glory and mercy of God. Faith in Christ crucified is always remarkable, all the more so in the face of persecution. Genuine love of one another, a love which undermines conventional social divisions and cannot be explained in terms of covert self-interest or the hope of a return – such love is equally remarkable, as Jesus himself made clear. In this vein Paul encouraged the Thessalonian Christians by writing of how their faith had been broadcast throughout Macedonia and Achaia and that their love for one another was clearly something taught by God (1 Thess. 1:9; 4:9). Similarly, he wrote of how the faith of the Roman Christians was 'being reported all over the world' (Rom. 1:8). These things could not occur simply by accident or by human design. Only the work of God in the life of each individual and amongst each gathering could produce such faith and love.

Throughout history appeal has been made to the existence of the church as evidence that Jesus is the Son of God and hence the only Saviour of the world. Yet that appeal has almost always also drawn attention to the character of individual churches. For instance, the counter-cultural make-up of the churches played an important role in the early Christian response to pagan criticism. Men such as *Augustine (later bishop of Hippo) were, in his words, 'driven' to the gospel, not only by the fact that the churches existed but by the way those churches existed. Perhaps in the postmodern and pluralist environment of the early twenty-first century such a double appeal has new power. Contemporary apologists, building upon the sociological insights of Peter Berger, point to the critical role of the churches as 'plausibility structures', social environments which demonstrate rather than simply argue the truth and reality of the Christian gospel. In a world where argument and rationality are suspect, the existence of communities which embody faith, forgiveness and genuine love powerfully commends the Lord they proclaim.

The fragility of the church remains all too obvious. Its failures (historical and contemporary) remain a source of embarrassment and a very effective weapon in the hands of the evil one. Yet what is remarkable is that the gospel continues to deliver on its promise to realize communities of faith whose character mirrors that of the gospel itself: grace, forgiveness, self-sacrificial service and a wholehearted trust in God's mercy and love. It is churches' anchor in the gospel of God's grace to sinners and their character as communities which embody this grace in their internal relations which mark them out as distinct from all other faith communities.

Jesus himself told the apostle Peter 'on this rock I will build my church, and the gates of Hades will not overcome it' (Matt. 16:18). It is Jesus who establishes and builds his church upon the foundation of Peter's confession that he is the Christ. He said he would and he has. And it is Jesus who ensures the continued existence of the church as he said he would. In the light of this great promise the existence of the church is indeed a testimony to God's wisdom, his grace and his victory.

Bibliography

C. H. Dodd, *History and the Gospel* (London, 1938), pp. 149–182; D. Hollinger, 'The Church as Apologetic: A Sociology of Knowledge Perspective', in T. R. Phillips and D. L. Ockholm (eds.), *Christian Apologetics in the Postmodern World* (Downers Grove, 1995), pp. 182–193; H. Küng, *The Church* (New York, 1967), pp. 3–39; P. T. O'Brien, 'The Church as a Heavenly and Eschatological Entity', in D. A. Carson (ed.), *The Church in the Bible and the World (Exeter/Grand Rapids, 1987), pp. 88–119; J. G. Stackhouse, *Humble Apologetics: Defending the Faith Today* (New York, 2002), pp. 114–116; R. L. Wilken, 'Religious Pluralism in Early Christian Thought', *Pro Ecclesia* 1.1 (1992), pp. 89–103.

M. D. THOMPSON

CIRCULAR REASONING, see REASON

CIVIL DISOBEDIENCE

In Rom. 13:1 the apostle Paul writes: 'Everyone must submit himself to the governing authorities, for there is no authority except that which God has established.' Christians, thus, recognize a duty of obedience to political authorities, as they are established by God to restrain evil and to do good. All things being equal, we owe obedience to the laws of a legitimate state. However, as we know from the apostle's own life and his imprisonment in the final years of his life, the decisions of the political authorities are not always just. Sometimes political authorities overstep their bounds. Sometimes, rather than restraining *evil, they are themselves the evildoers.

Thus, Christians recognize the ambiguous moral character and *authority of political agents and organizations intended by God to restrain evil and promote order. These political authorities may satisfy God's intentions for them, or sometimes they may align themselves with the spiritual forces of evil (Eph. 6:12; Rev. 13) and act to thwart God's work in the world. In a fallen and sinful world, even legitimate political authorities may do wrong, may demand of Christians and other citizens that which is rightfully God's, not Caesar's. Christians, understanding their primary citizenship to be in God's kingdom and their fundamental obligations to be to God, not to an earthly state, acknowledge a duty to obey the laws of a state, but not an absolute and unlimited duty of obedience to political authority.

The posture of the Christian towards the state is, then, a watchful subordination – the subordination a recognition of the authority of the state intended by God to rule rightly, the watchfulness a resistance to rendering to Caesar the obedience owed to God alone. As the Reformer, John *Calvin, wrote, 'such

obedience [to rulers] is never to lead us away from obedience to him, to whose will the desires of all kings ought to be subject, to whose decrees all their commands ought to yield, to whose majesty their sceptres ought to be submitted'.

Christians may also recognize that not only they but other individuals who are members of groups demanding some primary allegiance, e.g. adherents of other religions or communities of family, clan, place or ideology, may likewise qualify their obedience to the state. Christians, but not only Christians, may find it morally permissible and, perhaps, morally required to disobey the laws of a state when the laws and policies of a government conflict with the principles or ideals of their primary community. This disobedience is civil disobedience: the intentional, public disobedience of a *law or policy individuals or groups believe to be legitimate but, nevertheless, unjust or immoral or irrational.

Civil disobedience may be placed on a spectrum of practical postures towards a state, one end occupied by the anarchist, who denies the moral authority of all political institutions, or the revolutionary, who denies the legitimacy of some particular political order and who, thus, denies that any obedience is owed to the state. Historically, Christians, like others, have believed that the actions of a state may be such as to undermine its legitimacy and may even require rebellion. The other end of the spectrum is occupied by those who maintain that disobedience to the state is morally impermissible and that political authorities ought never to be disobeyed. This is an untenable position for a Christian, although, regrettably, not without adherents in Christian history. Towards the middle of the spectrum lie political protest and civil disobedience.

In political protest, public attention is drawn to some morally problematic policies or laws of a legitimate state, but no laws are intentionally violated as a part of the protest. Civil disobedience, by contrast, is practised by those who recognize the moral legitimacy of political authorities and yet they maintain that some particular policies or laws require or permit their disobedience. Acts of disobedience may be intended either as the refusals of individuals to do what they believe to be wrong or as a means to reforming the problematic policy or law.

One may, of course, disobey laws knowingly

or unknowingly and, if knowingly, for any number of reasons. One has not engaged in civil disobedience merely by disobeying a law, say, by failing to pay some tax (even if one believes the tax to be unjustified), if the cause of this failure to pay was forgetfulness. Civil disobedience is always intentional, an action aimed at disobedience to laws or policies of an authority. The primary intention or aim is disobedience to what one takes to be immoral or irrational. 'Because of the nature of this law or policy I intend not to obey it,' thinks the civilly disobedient. Although one may hope that a consequence of one's action will be a change in law or policy, the moral permissibility of the disobedience does not depend upon the achievement of any particular consequences.

Civil disobedience is always a public action or set of actions. It is civil both in form and substance. This is to say, the disobedience is directed against the political authority to which one owes obedience, not against some particular individual such as one's pastor. Unlike rebellion, civil disobedience begins from a posture of obedience, recognizing the general legitimacy of the political authority rather than seeking to overthrow it. The disobedience is, as a result, limited, and characteristically non-violent, for overt violence may undermine legitimate authority. The public nature of the disobedience is necessary both to draw attention to the problematic policy or law or to the moral exemption of some from the law or policy, and as an expression of one's willingness to accept punishment for a violation of legitimate authority.

Whether civil disobedience is morally required, or, rather, permissible but not required, depends upon whether the laws or policies of the political authority violate a tenet that is acknowledged as of supreme importance or centrality to Christian faith or whether a policy or law is sufficiently ambiguous as to preclude an easy identification of the law as incompatible with Christian faithfulness. Christians may, for example, believe that it is imprudent but not immoral to drive without a seatbelt and that laws restricting that freedom are, as such, morally problematic. No argument that Christians are required to violate that law is likely to be compelling. By contrast, a law requiring all citizens to bow before an earthly ruler, or political policies endorsing the indiscriminate attack upon innocent persons, at the very least requires disobedience.

Bibliography

J. Calvin, *The Institutes of the Christian Religion*, IV.xx.23–32; J. F. Childress, *Civil Disobedience and Political Obligation* (New Haven, 1971); M. Walzer, *Obligations: Essays on Disobedience, War, and Citizenship* (Cambridge, MA, 1970); J. H. Yoder, *The Politics of Jesus* (Grand Rapids and Carlisle, 1994).

T. D. KENNEDY

CLARKE, SAMUEL

Samuel Clarke (1675–1729) was ordained to the Anglican ministry in 1698. He rapidly ascended in the Church of England, serving as chaplain for John Moore, Bishop of Norwich. He subsequently served in Drayton and St Bennet's, Paul's Wharf, which put him in London circles and resulted in his appointment as Chaplain-in-Ordinary to Queen Anne. In 1709 he was appointed by Moore to be the Rector of St James Westminster (now Piccadilly), where he served for twenty years until his death. Clarke is best remembered for his contributions in philosophy and his work on the *Trinity. The latter topic embroiled him in a rancorous debate which prevented his eventually becoming Archbishop of Canterbury; the former is the focus of this article.

Each age has its particular apologetic challenges. In Clarke's time they were the twin issues of *atheism and deism. The genius of Clarke's work was his ability to synthesize the emerging *Newtonian natural philosophy (*science) with orthodox Christian *theism, thereby producing a formidable apologetic for the existence of God. This apologetic was presented in several different ways, the first of which was his new Latin translation of the French mathematician Rohault's *Traité de physique* [1697], the standard textbook on *cosmology at Cambridge. Over the course of succeeding editions, Clarke added annotations challenging the Cartesian mechanics of the main text with Newton's mathematical demonstrations, thus eventually converting an entire generation of university students from *Descartes to Newtonian natural philosophy.

Clarke's second apologetic venture was the two courses of 'Boyle Lectures' which he gave in 1704 and 1705. The expressed purpose of these lectures was to 'prove the truth of the Christian religion against infidels', and Clarke's first course was entitled 'A Demonstration of the Being and Attributes of God, More Particularly in Answer to Mr. Hobbes, Spinoza and their Followers'. Here Clarke sought to demonstrate in a way 'as near to mathematical, as the nature of such a discourse would allow' the necessity of God's existence and derived attributes. Following Newton's method in science, Clarke started with phenomena and progressed to the agent behind it. Here Clarke laid out in twelve propositions that God must exist eternally as immutable and independent, that he is self-existent and necessary, that although his substance is unknowable his attributes are demonstrable and that he is infinite and omnipresent and one. Clarke went on to argue that God must be intelligent, imbued with liberty and choice, have infinite power and wisdom and possess all goodness. The success of these lectures was such that Clarke was invited the following year to deliver a second set, entitled a 'Discourse Concerning the Unchangeable Obligations of Natural Religion and the Truth and Certainty of the Christian Revelation'. Here Clarke argued, not that natural religion was defective but that it was incomplete, requiring the addition of divine revelation. The deists believed that natural religion alone was sufficient; Clarke argued they were too optimistic in their assessment of humanity. Revelation was required to overcome human moral and noetic corruption. For Clarke, it was not simply more moral information which humanity lacked, but the knowledge of salvation itself, which only revelation could supply. Through revelation we discover how God is to be worshipped, sins expiated and the specific nature of future rewards and punishments. While revelation was an essential addition to reason, it did not contradict it. For Clarke, the congruity of reason and revelation was the foundation of rational religion. In this sense he 'out reasoned' the rationalist deists by showing the eminent reasonability, even necessity, of revelation.

Clarke's third apologetic venture is found in his correspondence (conducted 1715–16, published in 1717) with the continental philosopher Gottfried Wilhelm *Leibniz, who had charged that Newton's science threatened the foundations of natural religion. The thrust of the correspondence can be noted from Clarke's dedication to the Princess of Wales, where he wrote, 'the foundations of natural religion had never been so deeply and so firmly laid, as in the mathematical and experimental philosophy of that great man'. The debate in these letters ranged across a wide spectrum of questions scientific and philosophical, including questions concerning God's relation to the world, the nature of gravity, vacuums, the 'principle of sufficient reason', and the 'identity of indiscernibles'. In all of this, Clarke showed that Newton's science provided a surer foundation to *natural theology than Cartesianism.

Clarke's apologetic, based upon the latest methodology of Newton's physics, proved to have enormous appeal. By using a Newtonian 'mathematical' style and relying primarily (though not exclusively) on the inductive rather than deductive method of *reasoning, Clarke challenged the atheism and deism of his time, revealing the deep deficiencies of both. *Voltaire considered Clarke as first among the English philosophers and credited him with moving him from atheism to theism (though not to Christianity).

Although at the dawn of the third millennium we no longer share the Newtonian world-view, the project of an integrated, reasoned view of reality which embraces God's revelation through both his word (Scripture) and works (nature) remains an urgent task for the church. With the rise in our time of atheistic philosophical *materialism (sometimes called scientific *naturalism) in the West and the influence of monistic pantheism from the East, Clarke's approach and arguments, and particularly his 'Boyle Lectures', are worthy of review for those interested in a reasoned defence of the faith today.

Bibliography

H. G. Alexander, *The Leibniz–Clarke Correspondence* (Manchester and New York, 1956); M. J. Buckley, *At the Origins of Modern Atheism* (New Haven and London, 1987); S. Clarke, *The Works*, 4 vols. (London, 1738); T. C. Pfizenmaier, *The Trinitarian Theology of Dr. Samuel Clarke (1675–1729): Context, Sources and Controversy* (New York and Köln, 1997).

T. C. PFIZENMAIER

CLASSICAL MUSIC, see MUSIC

CLEMENT OF ALEXANDRIA

Titus Flavius Clemens, better known as Clement of Alexandria (c. 140/60–c. 215), was a seeker after truth and after travelling in search of teachers, found satisfaction in Alexandria from the Christian Pantaenus. He became a teacher himself in Alexandria until he left the city in about 202. Clement's principal writings are *Exhortation* (a 'protreptic' to accept Christ), *Instructor* (Christ the 'Pedagogue' teaches morals and manners) and *Miscellanies* (a patchwork of thoughts on true spiritual knowledge).

As a witness to the educated upper classes, Clement set Christian teachings in the context of the philosophical thought of his day, particularly middle *Platonism with elements of Aristotelianism and Stoicism, making abundant quotations from Greek literature. He considered philosophy to be a tutor to bring Greeks to Christ and as God's covenant with them, as the law was his covenant with the Jews. A knowledge of philosophy was useful for Christians, enabling them to expose the errors of philosophers, to help pass from a simple to a more intellectual faith and to make the content of their faith more precise.

In response to the philosophical questions of his time and in opposition to the views of Gnostics and others, Clement developed the basic Christian teachings in relation to God, goodness and *truth. In contrast to polytheism and dualism, God is the transcendent one who created all things out of nothing. God's Word (*Logos*) bridges *transcendence and *immanence and mediates salvation as the harmony of the soul that is united to the Word. Clement reconciles the supreme goodness of God with *evil in the world by distinguishing between what God causes and what happens without his providence, by affirming that God can transform evil into good, by noting God's use of evil as a chastisement and by pointing out that it was free will that introduced evil into the world. The goal for human beings is to be joined to God by participating in his goodness. Christianity is true, but truth includes everything consistent with it. Faith, which is necessary for both salvation and knowledge, is an act of the will as well as a perception of spiritual things.

Clement found symbolic *language useful because it hides the truth from scoffers, requires an oral teaching tradition to interpret it, presents truth in a more impressive way and, by containing more than one meaning, shows the complexity and unity of truth.

Bibliography

J. Bernard, *Die Apologetische Methode bei Klemens von Alexandrien* (Leipzig, 1968); E. F. Osborn, *The Philosophy of Clement of Alexandria* (Cambridge, 1957); A. Van den Hoek, *Clement of Alexandria and his Use of Philo in the* Stromateis (Leiden, 1988).

E. FERGUSON

CLONING, see BIOETHICS

COMMON GRACE

The doctrine of common grace was largely developed by Abraham *Kuyper (1837–1920) as a theological foundation for a view of *history and *culture leading to practical action by Christians in every aspect of creaturely existence. In Kuyper's view, God has two purposes within history: the development of culture by humanity, including the ungodly, by means of common grace, and the salvation of the church by means of special grace. In this view the world exists for the sake of the church, providing a substratum from which God builds his church leading to the renewal of his creation and its fulfilment in Christ. Common grace thus is seen as subordinate to regenerating grace. That God grants gifts and talents to believers and unbelievers alike is not to be understood as grace to the particular apostate individual, but rather is grace for all mankind in Christ, rooted in the Redeemer of the world.

This view has been opposed from within Reformed theology by such as Herman Hoeksema (1886–1964). Hoeksema argued that to espouse common grace was to deny the essential relationship between God and unbelievers, and that by blurring the distinction between church and world it opened up the way to declension within the church.

The proponents of common grace argue that God has not abandoned his creation to suffer the full outworking of the consequences of sinful human rebellion. The physical structures of creation still exist. Also, institutions such as the state, *marriage, the family and culture are sustained by common grace. As well as the restraint of sin there is a positive aspect to common grace. Within human culture there is clear evidence of *justice, goodness, beauty and other admirable qualities. These are present not because fallen humans are inherently good, but because God actively preserves justice, goodness, beauty and the other qualities which enhance the life of his creatures.

God's image in humanity is not effaced entirely by the fall, but rather is distorted. The cultural mandate was not abrogated, and its continuing validity can be seen even in the works of those who openly rebel against God. Great thinkers, artists, scientists and others can bring relative blessing to temporal life. These are traces of grace common to all humanity, and they point to God. Because all of humanity benefits from this grace it is referred to as common grace as distinct from special grace, or the grace of salvation, which changes the hearts of individuals.

Common grace directly answers the question why it is that human beings consciously living in opposition to or denial of God can still do good and produce works of significance and beauty. In doing so, common grace provides a basis for Christian appreciation and interpretation of the *arts.

The doctrine of common grace also gives a basis for validating a position which acknowledges a *common ground of discussion between believers and non-believers, for there is an area of *reality shared by both.

In apologetic methodology common grace and one's understanding of it may alter the apologist's approach. If total depravity is understood as having vitiated our ability to think correctly and apprehend God's existence, then a strictly presuppositionalist approach would be normative.

Common grace does not eliminate the antithesis between the basic motive of the believer and that of the non-believer. The antithesis exists, but whilst in principle it is total, in practice, due to what Klaas Schilder (1890–1952) terms the 'plastic' nature of creation, it is not absolute. When unbelievers speak *truth with accuracy, they can be understood as being inconsistent with their own basic principles. The unbeliever's knowledge may be genuine, although held from a wrong motive.

Bibliography

J. Frame, *Cornelius Van Til: An Analysis of His Thought* (1995); H. Dooyeweerd, *Roots of Western Culture* (Toronto, 1979).

C. CAMPBELL-JACK

COMMON GROUND

'Common ground' can be defined as those areas of like needs, concerns and beliefs between believers and non-believers through which meaningful dialogue can develop and the communication of the gospel can proceed. Like an engineer who builds bridges in order to connect roads and land masses, so Christians construct relational 'bridges' between themselves and non-believers in order to pave the way for a hearing of the gospel. The goal in establishing common ground is to ascertain specific 'truths' embedded in the non-believer's world-view (such as the postmodernist concern for tolerance) that can be employed in constructing a positive argument for the Christian faith. Common ground often helps non-believers begin to trust Christianity – or at least certain aspects of its message – so that a transition from a non-Christian world-view to a Christian world-view might be made.

The problem of common ground

The Bible refers to Christians as Christ's 'ambassadors' (2 Cor. 5:20). This assumes that there is a theological gap between believers and non-believers and that believers have the responsibility to attempt to 'bridge' this gap in various ways. There are at least two potential pitfalls, however, in the development of common ground. First, some circles within the church have traditionally advocated a pietistic view of Christianity. Pietism began in the 1800s but had a certain deficiency. According to Francis *Schaeffer, 'It was "platonic" in that Pietism made a sharp division between the "spiritual" and the "material" world – giving little, or no, importance to the "material" world. The totality of human experience was not afforded a proper place. In particular, it neglected the intellectual dimension of Christianity. Christianity and spirituality were shut up to a small, isolated part of life. The totality of reality was ignored by the pietistic thinking.' Since pietism often results in a 'separatist' stance in relation to the world of human ideas and *culture, it can effectively remove the possibility of establishing common ground with non-believers.

Another problem is that of *fideism, or faith-based belief, and particularly the sort posed by *presuppositional apologetics (i.e. that of Cornelius *Van Til). According to presuppositionalists, believers and non-believers have almost no common cognitive commitments or understandings with respect to spiritual *truth. The *noetic effects of sin have so blinded the mind that God's grace must confront a non-believer and convict the heart of Christian truth. Since the Bible provides the only framework by which non-believers can begin to correctly interpret the evidence of general *revelation, a presupposition of biblical revelation is the only 'common ground' that can lead to fruitful discussion. Presuppositionalism, therefore, provides the apologist with few raw materials (i.e. common beliefs, observable evidence, human experience) for engaging non-believers with positive arguments.

The possibility of common ground

*Thomas Aquinas' 'classical' apologetic, on the other hand, attempted to establish the validity of common ground between religion and philosophy by insisting that God's existence could be demonstrated by reason. According to Aquinas, reason was weakened by the fall but not completely crippled. As a result, non-believers can entertain such rational thought processes as those laid out by the *cosmological or *teleological arguments (which attempt to establish God's existence upon the basis of creation or intelligent design, respectively).

Recent apologetic models attempt to establish an 'audience-sensitive' approach that utilizes several avenues of common ground in the communication of the gospel. David Clark's dialogical apologetics, for example, emphasize that different people rightly come to know Christ in different ways, and thus seek to allow the unique qualities of individuals to guide apologetic practice, rather than an abstract theory about how all human beings know. Common ground can therefore be drawn from various sources – rationality and *logic, human experience, various kinds of evidence – without forgetting the noetic effects of sin that often make the apologetic task much more challenging. In addition, common ground can be drawn from those 'truths' embedded in various *world religions.

The possibility of genuine common ground between Christians and non-believers is established on the presupposition that 'all truth is God's truth'. This means that the truth embedded in a non-believer's culture, religion, or world-view finds its ultimate locus in God, who as Creator of the universe is also the source of all truth. Arthur Holmes proposes, 'If [God] is the eternal and all-wise creator of all things, as Christians affirm, then his creative wisdom is the source and norm of all truth about everything.'

Practical examples of common ground in Scripture

Jesus Christ himself clearly sought common ground with his audience. In John 3, Jesus confronts Nicodemus, a teacher of the law, with some deep theological insights. In John 4, however, he casually converses with the woman at the well about her immoral past and uses the well itself as a simple illustration of the 'living water' he could provide. In each case Jesus showed genuine respect for that person's background and mindset by tailoring the gospel presentation appropriately.

Likewise, the early church sought to establish common ground when communicating the gospel by acknowledging the various experiences of their audiences. In Acts 17, for example, Paul presented the gospel using words and rhetoric customized to the polytheistic, philosophy-oriented Greeks (while he employed different ones with monotheistic, tradition-oriented Jews). At times in the NT we find certain individuals utilizing common cultural heritage to build a natural bridge. Timothy, for example, could easily minister to Greeks because of his Greek heritage. However, common ground is not always so easily attainable, and sometimes must be developed creatively. Paul had Timothy circumcised before they embarked on their missionary trip (Acts 16:1–3), knowing they would come into contact with Jews who saw circumcision as very important.

Particular avenues for establishing common ground

In general, common ground is established on the basis of the 'humanity' experienced by both believers and non-believers. Such a basis allows us to categorize common ground into at least four major areas that are often typical of human experience:

1. Rationality. Postmodernism challenges common ground by adopting a certain form of *relativism, proposing that truth is related

to, or grounded in, specific cultural or community perspectives, which in turn provide alternative ways of interpreting reality. For postmodernists, Christianity usually becomes just another religious preference. In response to relativism, Christians can often establish common ground regarding the notion of truth by calling on the law of non-*contradiction. This law of logic essentially states that no statement can be both true and not true at the same time (e.g. the statements 'he is fifty years old' or 'no-one comes to the Father but through me' cannot be true for some but not true for others). Postmodernists commonly employ this law in the practical affairs of life, for example, in *language (simply by using the word 'is') and when asking directions (when you tell someone to turn left they usually know which way to go). Such principles of thought are consistently employed by all cultures, thus demonstrating that our minds were created by God to function rationally and that such rationality is rooted in God's perfect reason and comprehensive knowledge.

2. Moral *conscience. Closely related to rationality is conscience, which is essentially moral sensibility. J. Budziszewski asserts that 'moral common ground' is established on the idea that 'foundational moral principles are not only right for all, but at some level known to all'. Sometimes called the '*natural law', moral conscience is a critical aspect of the image of God, and is revealed in Paul's statement that the *law is written on the heart (Rom. 2:14–15). Aquinas proclaimed that foundational moral principles are 'the same for all, both as to rectitude and as to knowledge'. C. S. *Lewis argues in *Mere Christianity* that the reality of moral law goes beyond mere social convention: 'We know that men find themselves under a moral law, which they did not make, and cannot quite forget even when they try, and which they know they ought to obey.' Lewis sees a 'law of human nature' in those cries for fairness and *justice heard in everyday conversation: 'How'd you like it if anyone did the same to you?' or 'That's my seat, I was there first.' Indeed all cultures can be shown to hold to certain standards of moral conduct (e.g. 'torturing babies for fun is wrong'), or at least most people agree that they *should* hold to such standards. Christians should point out that cultural relativism actually makes a claim *about* *morality rather than a moral statement *per se*. The fact that different cultures hold to differing

beliefs does not necessarily mean that moral *absolutes do not exist or cannot be known. Once common ground has been established with respect to some basic moral principles and virtues, the relativist's position can be challenged and Christianity can be presented as a superior basis for morality. Not only does Christianity provide a supreme moral law-giver as a basis for the evidence of universal morality and conscience, it also affirms the grace of God in Christ as a path of reconciliation for law-breakers.

3. Religion. Though the Bible clearly states that salvation is found only in Jesus Christ (John 14:6), there are certainly moral and ethical truths in non-Christian religions that can serve as valid stepping-stones toward the Christian faith. *Buddhism's Eightfold Path, for example, appeals to followers to pursue honesty, charity and service, and to abstain from murder and lust. There are also theological truths in other religions that Christians can affirm. Orthodox *Judaism and *Islam share the Christian belief in one God who created all things. Christians and Muslims even share certain beliefs in common concerning the person of Jesus, for example, they both hold that he was a prophet of God and worked many *miracles. Islam, however, denies that Jesus is the Son of God or provides salvation. Christians must acknowledge that, while certain truths can be found in non-Christian religions, they provide no sufficient means for the atonement of sin. The fact that a religious person looks to a 'higher power', holds to ethical principles, and has some conception of sin may at the same time expose their need for the message of Christ's atonement.

4. Human longing. The fact that all humans experience definitive limitations in life (regarding knowledge, strength, abilities etc.) and face the reality of physical death is known as 'the human condition'. Accompanying this is often a longing for some sort of higher purpose and meaning. Ecclesiastes speaks of people having a sense of eternity in their hearts, but without full knowledge of it (Eccl. 3:11). Believers may find common ground with non-believers by appealing to their sense of higher purpose, longing for *transcendence or desire for inner peace not found in the material world. While modern thinkers like Marx and *Freud have proclaimed that such desires are nothing but a product of wishful thinking, Christians must show that the spiritual basis for such longings

lies in the existence of the God who created them. St *Augustine said 'Thou hast made us for thyself, and our hearts are restless until they rest in thee.' Lewis reasons, 'If I find in myself a desire which no experience in this world can satisfy, the most probable explanation is that I was made for another world.'

Procedures for developing common ground

The process of finding and using common ground follows a model of contextualization based upon the incarnation of Jesus Christ. Contextualization involves identifying with others and breaking through barriers in order to establish communication. By taking on human flesh, the holy, infinite God demonstrated a desire to identify with sinful, finite human beings. Christ was then able to break through two kinds of barriers in seeking lost human beings. First, he broke through the cultural barriers that stood between himself (a Jewish male) and others by utilizing the cultural communication patterns found in his present world. Secondly, he broke through the sin barrier between God and human beings by going to the cross and bearing our sin, thus allowing us to be forgiven and come to know God personally.

Christ's contextualization does not end with his death and resurrection but continues through his 'ambassadors', who now contextualize the gospel by finding common ground with non-believers. In order to do this, they must navigate any cultural or intellectual barriers that might prevent them from entering the world of non-believers. This often requires an understanding of the world-views of non-believers and a desire to get involved with their needs and struggles. According to Schaeffer, a foreign missionary 'must learn the language of the thought-forms of the people to whom [he] speaks. So it is with the Christian Church. Its responsibility is not only to hold to the basic, scriptural principles of the Christian faith, but to communicate these unchanging truths "into" the generation in which one is living.' Christians must also show non-believers that Christ has overcome the sin barrier. They do this by sharing the gospel. Their greatest common ground with non-believers, in fact, is that both parties stand as sinners in need of the God's grace offered in Jesus Christ. As it is often said, sharing the gospel with non-believers is as 'one beggar telling another beggar where to find bread'.

In establishing common ground it is also critical that Christians investigate the world-views of our culture. According to David Hesselgrave, 'understanding another person's world view [or belief system] is the starting point for communicating the gospel'. Whether a non-believer seems to hold to the basic tenets of *existentialism, *naturalism, postmodernism, pantheism or a combination of several world-views, Christians will naturally gain credibility and integrity by exploring these beliefs in search of areas of common agreement. An existentialist, for example, is concerned with the development of an authentic existence, which involves making one's own choices and creating one's own destiny. Christians can certainly affirm one aspect of this world-view – the reality of authentic human volition – and can demonstrate that this special capacity is best understood in light of the dignity bestowed to human beings when created in the image of God (Gen. 1:26–28).

World-view dialogue not only establishes particular areas of intellectual agreement, it also exposes specific points of antithesis between Christianity and other world-views. Paul, for example, points out the antithesis between the gospel and the 'different gospel' that some have received (Gal. 1:6–9). The Holy Spirit will often orchestrate well-timed antithesis to open the door for further dialogue. Common ground provides a positive challenge for believers to use their God-given creativity rather than relying on a 'canned' approach to witnessing. As Christ's ambassadors, Christians can utilize their gifts, talents, burdens and abilities as channels for delivering Christ's message within specific contexts. A farmer might teach gardening and incorporate Jesus' parable of the four soils (Mark 4). A panel of Christian doctors might teach a sex education course for students and parents, incorporating physiological, psychological and biblical/moral perspectives. As homemakers, dentists, students, lawyers etc., believers must investigate the prevailing world-views within their respective fields of influence, listen for the specific 'language' employed, and be able to demonstrate how biblical truth provides a credible foundation for their particular field. Non-believers often need to see that biblical truth is relevant in their specific field of interest before they will adopt this foundation for their entire life.

Bibliography

J. Budziszewski, *What We Can't Not Know* (Dallas, 2003); D. K. Clarke, *Dialogical Apologetics* (Grand Rapids, 1993); D. Hesselgrave, *Communicating Christ Cross-Culturally* (Grand Rapids, 1978); A. F. Holmes, *All Truth is God's Truth* (Downers Grove, 1977); C. S. Lewis, *Mere Christianity* (London, 2002); F. A. Schaeffer, *The Complete Works of Francis A. Schaeffer*, 5 vols. (Westchester, 1982).

J. A. STUDEBAKER, JR

COMMUNISM

Communism has offered one of the most vigorous challenges to Christian belief and practice in the twentieth and twenty-first centuries. This is all the more noteworthy in view of the fact that the thought of Karl Marx, which so deeply shaped twentieth-century communism, owes so much to *Judaism and Christianity that it often has been called a 'Christian heresy'. Marxism raises a prophetic voice against the oppression of the poor, identifies a 'chosen people' (the proletariat), and offers a messianic hope for future liberation that is unquestionably biblical in inspiration, although it rejects any role for God in its vision. Marxist communism as a political theory avers that there can be no private ownership of 'the means of production', such as factories and railroads. Rather, society's economic resources belong to the people as a whole. People must contribute to those resources according to their ability and in turn, as Marx famously declared, they are to receive benefits according to need.

It is obvious that this ideal sounds a great deal like the pattern of the early church as described in the book of Acts (Acts 2:42–47; 4:32–37) and as seen elsewhere in the NT's insistence on generosity to the needy and a de-emphasis on social distinctions (1 Cor. 16; Jas 5:1–6). Indeed, the ideal of a social order based on sharing rather than selfishness has had a powerful influence on the Christian tradition, from the Franciscans of the thirteenth century and the early Anabaptists to the Christian Socialists of the nineteenth century and Christian social reformers of today, such as those of the Sojourners community.

Contemporary communism, however, is a decidedly secularist, anti-religious social and political movement that traces its modern lineage to German philosopher and social critic Karl Marx (1818–83). It is from Marx that it inherited its dominant strain of naturalistic, atheistic *materialism. Marx's version of secular *naturalism is known as 'dialectical materialism', and it shares with other versions of naturalism a strong anti-clerical, anti-religious perspective. Marx, descended on both sides from rabbis, was raised and educated in Lutheranism, although the formative influence on his early thought came more from the *Enlightenment than from any religious source. Marx's Enlightenment faith was encouraged both by his father and by his friend and future father-in-law, the Baron von Westphalen.

At the University of Berlin, Marx came to admire the philosopher *Hegel and joined a group called the Young Hegelians or the Hegelian Left. These young theorists radicalized Hegel's ultra-conservative views and idealized the existing Prussian social order as that highest expression of human development to which all previous human *history had led. The Young Hegelians, however, believed that Hegel had shown that history is an ever-evolving process of change, and that philosophical criticism of the existing order is a powerful instrument of social change. Marx would later alter Hegel's view of history by combining it with his own materialistic views to form his 'dialectical materialism', a theory of history which holds that it is a process of economic conflict and class war leading inevitably from feudalism, through *capitalism, and into communism. Marx's thought was also powerfully shaped by the atheistic, materialistic pre-Socratic philosophers of ancient Greece, Democritus and Epicurus, on whom he wrote his dissertation, and by his anti-Christian contemporary Ludwig *Feuerbach, who believed the Christian faith was founded on myth and was merely an expression of human psychological needs.

Marx's extensive writings between 1845 and 1876 culminated in his major work, 'Capital'. The *metaphysics of Marx's communist philosophy is decidedly materialistic, with a particular emphasis on economics. The world consists of the material objects on which equally material human beings act to produce items for human use. In Marx's philosophical anthropology humanity is *homo faber*, man the maker, rather than *Homo sapiens*, man the knower. Human beings are fundamentally transformers of nature, and work is the primary mode of human expression. Central to his thought is the idea that since it is human nature to work, the conditions of human labour will explain history, *culture and the human predicament.

Marx believed that all of human history is a series of clashes between economically antagonistic groups, or classes. This process continues today between the proletariat, or working class, and the bourgeoisie, or capitalist class. In capitalism, workers must sell their working activity, their creative, productive energy, to capitalists simply to survive. Ironically, as the worker succeeds in creating wealth through production, he concentrates wealth and *power in the hands of the capitalist to use against him. The bourgeoisie by its very nature extracts value from the proletariat in a process called expropriation, sapping the proletariat's strength by seizing 'surplus value' from it and creating profit. The more workers produce, the poorer they become economically and spiritually. Human beings become estranged from their fellow human beings, from nature, and from themselves in the fundamentally unfree economic situation in which they must earn their daily bread. Marx insisted, however, that he was not offering a moral critique of this bleak state of affairs, but simply describing it 'scientifically'.

The 'contradictions' of capitalism tend to make it more and more unstable, until in the course of history the proletariat rises up and grasps the means of production. After a foreseeable brutish period of 'raw communism', which Marx in no way celebrates, true communism emerges in which people overcome alienation and realize their true humanity in the brotherhood of a workers' paradise. At this point there is a 'withering' of the state, as it no longer needs its coercive power to enforce compliance with socially desirable goals and activities.

Marx believed that culture, in all its social, intellectual, philosophical, moral and religious dimensions, derives in a deterministic fashion from the economic relationships that underlie it. The most foundational economic reality is the 'economic base', the way that people make a living in a particular area, such as farming, fishing or mining. This base shapes and gives rise to 'relations of production', the fundamental social arrangements by which people organize to do the work of transforming nature to human use, e.g. as agricultural landlords and tenant farmers. These relations give rise to 'social structures', ongoing patterns of human interaction that institutionalize these modes of economic relationship, such as the social hierarchies of Western feudalism. This in turn gives rise to what Marx refers to as a 'superstructure' or 'ideology', which includes the religion, science, ethics and other aspects of cultural life, such as Catholic theology and morality. This superstructure can only be understood as the product of a socio-economic structure and is not to be engaged in dialogue.

Marx's ideology entails that human rights, for example are not timeless moral truths that oblige any societies that would claim to be just, but rather, they are ideas produced by particular economic circumstances. In particular, they gave rise to entrepreneurial individualists in the early days of modern capitalism, by providing a justification for those entrepreneurs to leave the feudal order and set out on their own to seek their own social and economic destiny. When such rights are used today to object to the practices of communist leadership, these objections need not be taken seriously. Such rights, after all, are simply an expression of the ideology of capitalism. In this way, Marx introduces what has since been called a 'hermeneutic of suspicion', which enables opposing positions to be diagnosed and discounted rather than directly engaged and refuted. It is only by changing the economic structure of society that ideological change or any other alterations in the 'superstructure' are to be brought about.

Religion, no less than ethics, philosophy and other aspects of culture, is simply the effect and product of economic factors. Religion in particular arises from societies that are characterized by alienation. Alienation occurs inevitably in capitalism when the worker becomes alienated from his own productive life, being forced to sell it in order to make a living. He then becomes alienated from his fellow workers, from his owner/employer and others. The highest degree of alienation is to imagine that there is a God in whom all the best and finest human features are to be found. Religion is a mere 'opiate' of the workers, not a genuine contact with or description of a supernatural realm. It is a complex web of justifications that render acceptable and bearable current conditions of exploitation and oppression.

In all of Marx's extensive writings, he never

offered a serious treatment of religion, yet he inspired strong anti-religious zeal among his followers that has led to severe persecution of believers in communist lands. Why would a communist feel the need to attack so vigorously a mere 'opiate', which is after all doomed to perish when capitalistic oppression has been vanquished by the revolution? This anomaly is explained by religion's role as part of the ideology of oppressive societies. Religion is not merely to be sneered at or railed against, as it is for other materialist philosophers from ancient Greece to the French Enlightenment; it is also a foe to be combated.

Religion is part of the defence mechanism of capitalism, serving to reinforce oppressive relationships in society and maintain the economic exploitation of workers. Religion, created by alienation, assists the oppressors to maintain their position of privilege over the oppressed by offering both a justification of the existing situation and a palliative to those who might otherwise be motivated to overthrow it. In using his hermeneutic of suspicion, Marx was able to avoid examining theistic philosophical claims or biblical evidence; rather, the falsity of Christian theism and other faiths was assumed, and Marx saw his task simply as finding a plausible account for religion's continued presence and power.

Fundamentally, communism is to be rejected on philosophical, religious and practical grounds. *Philosophically it bears the marks of the more optimistic streams of the secular Enlightenment, disparaging of religion while wildly enthusiastic about human capabilities for self-improvement and self-realization. Today, when support for the Enlightenment is at a low ebb in Western intellectual culture, communism's insistence that human problems can be solved by an application of 'scientific socialism' seems simultaneously comic and tragic as well as hopelessly out of date. Metaphysically, communism is built on a materialist, physicalist philosophy that can neither account for the nature of consciousness of the human person nor provide a foundation for genuine values. Epistemologically, it is guilty of question begging in executing its assault on other viewpoints, such as Christianity, by means of the hermeneutic of suspicion. It is simply illegitimate to assume the falsity of an opposing viewpoint in attempting to refute it. If communism is to offer a critique of Christianity, it must engage and respond to Christianity's truth-claims, its assessment of the human plight and redemption and its ethical implications.

From the standpoint of religion, communism must be rejected because as a deterministic, materialistic system it is fundamentally incompatible with a biblical account of reality. The role of Christianity, in particular Pope John Paul II, in hastening the demise of communism is well understood, but the relationship between Christianity and Marxism is as complex as it is controversial. Some believe that because of Marx's essential atheism, there can be no basis for constructive dialogue between the two. Others argue that Marx's vision of human liberation has a genuine religious dimension, borrowing as it does from the prophetic biblical concern for the poor and oppressed and the hope for an eschatological kingdom. Further, the biblical vision of *shalom* can be discerned in his view of unalienated, free humanity. Liberation theologians press these similarities vigorously, using Marxian analysis of the class struggle to support their biblical challenge to existing socio-economic conditions for the marginalized in the world. While Christians have not needed Marx to notice the plight of the poor, it is doubtless true that Marx and communism have done much to awaken the church from complacent slumbers about the plight of the poor, and to look for ways in which economic systems perpetuate poverty, oppression, and hopelessness. Christians too are concerned for the poor who suffer at the hands of the powerful (Jas 5:1–6).

Communism never addresses the root causes of human alienation, and so its proposed solutions are destined only to exacerbate human problems. Christianity teaches that humanity is deeply flawed by sin and separation from God, and that only God's initiative can begin to remedy these faults. Marx and other communists believe that only structural economic changes are needed for humanity's true creativity and capacity for *community to emerge, a tragic error. The twentieth century shows all too clearly that a wildly optimistic plan for changing humanity without a recognition of the depth of the human predicament can only engender increasing levels of brutal, oppressive, and violent social engineering.

In the practical arena, too, communism must be faulted. The untold millions who have been murdered, and even greater numbers that have been and continue to be brutally oppressed, provide testimony to the failings of this system. Despite their humanitarian aims, communist regimes have had appalling records in human rights and in imprisoning and killing their own people. It is estimated that the Soviet regime killed a staggering 55 million individuals between 1917 and 1987, while China conducted 36 million political murders between 1949 and 1987. The Church's own record over two millennia, while far from spotless, must be seen as relatively mild in comparison to the much more extensive persecution conducted by 'scientific' atheism in a few short decades.

The question has been raised as to whether the oppressive regimes of Soviet and Maoist communism were truly Marxist, that is, true to his vision of human emancipation. How can a theory that sought the liberation of human labour and expression have led to such appallingly oppressive political implications in the real world? Marxist humanism, in particular, has argued that Marx taught that true communism would not even contain the apparatus of the State as we now know it, let alone a totalitarian one. It is debatable whether the totalitarian communist regimes were truly Marxist, but there are certainly elements of the so-called 'dictatorship of the proletariat' in the writings of Marx and his early followers, elements that would be developed by Lenin, Stalin, Mao, Castro and others.

Communism, while not the force it once was, still controls a few countries, such as China, Vietnam, North Korea, Laos and Cuba. In those countries it continues to earn a dubious record in human rights and is under increasing pressure for political and economic reform. Christianity is in some ways more sensitive to social ills because of its encounter with communism, and has retained strength in numbers and influence throughout the world.

Bibliography

F. L. Bender, *The Betrayal of Marx* (New York, 1975); F. L. Bender (ed.), *The Communist Manifesto* (Norton, 1988); K. Bockmuehl, *The Challenge of Marxism: A Christian Response* (Downers Grove, 1980); J. M. Bonino, *Christians and Marxists: The Mutual Challenge to Revolution* (London, 1974); T. Carver (ed.), *The Cambridge Companion to Marx* (Cambridge, 1992); E. Fromm, *Marx's Concept of Man* (New York, 2005); D. R. Janz, *World Christianity and Marxism* (Oxford and New York, 1998); D. Lyon, *Karl Marx: A Christian Assessment of His Life and Thought* (Downers Grove, 1981); K. Marx, *Capital: A Critique of Political Economy* (trans. B. Fowkes; New York, 1977); D. McLennan, *Marxism and Religion* (Basingstoke, 1987); P. Ramsey, *Nine Modern Moralists: Paul Tillich, Karl Marx, H. Richard Niebuhr, Fyodor Dostoevsky, Reinhold Niebuhr, Jacques Maritain, Jean-Paul Sartre, Emil Brunner* (Lanham, MD, 1983); R. Schmitt, K. Lehrer and N. Daniels (eds.), *Introduction to Marx and Engels: A Critical Reconstruction* (Westview, 1997); P. Singer, *Marx: A Very Short Introduction* (Oxford, 2000); D. Turner, *Marxism and Christianity* (Oxford, 1983); M. Westphal, *Suspicion and Faith: The Religious Uses of Modern Atheism* (New York, 1998).

D. B. FLETCHER

COMMUNITY

Stemming from the Lat. *communitas*, from which we get the word 'common', the word 'community' has a very wide range of meanings, from the narrowly descriptive and geographical to the broadly normative and relational. Essentially referring to a group of people living in proximity or sharing some element of their lives together, it has taken on strongly positive connotations of interdependent and supportive co-existence with others. Contemporary phrases such as 'the Gay Community', 'the Global Community' and 'Care in the Community' indicate its complex uses far beyond the traditional 'village community'. Indeed the word is often used to denote a positive social value rather than a social reality.

Since the Industrial Revolution and the early beginnings of modern *urbanization, the break-up of long established rural communities and the gathering together of large numbers of people in new urban centres have left a deep concern in Western culture about the loss of community. Mechanization, high-density architecture, urban anonymity, increased transience and busyness, and the modern mobile workforce increasingly seem to have replaced organic relationships with functional relationships. Attitudes springing from careerism, individualism, consumerism and *materialism have taken their toll on communal identity and inter-dependence. Lately, the high divorce rate and break-up of families have added to the social fragmentation and a loss of the sense of belonging. New communities do, of course, spring up to replace the old, but the overwhelming sentiment for many is that community is something from a kinder, simpler past.

As a result, the twentieth century saw many experiments in community living. These ranged from the small, 'hippie' communes of the 1960s to large movements such as International *Communism with its attempt to establish a political ideology based on community ownership. The almost universal failure of these efforts, often with massively tragic consequences, lay in the romantic idealism and utopian zeal with which they were pursued. Late twentieth-century cynicism can be seen in large part as a response to the failure of these counter-cultural movements to resolve the alienation of modernity.

Nevertheless, community continues to encapsulate a deep hope for many, and never more so than as our culture takes its postmodern turn. Postmodern theory, with its rejection of modernity, its radical critique of *Enlightenment rationalism and its 'decentred' self, has revitalized the concept of community. *Constructivism, perspectivism, contextualization – all now place the principal focus for interpretation, or understanding, on the surrounding subculture, *language-game, 'narrative' tradition or 'community of reference'. The individual 'agent' fades into the collective community which defines it, and *truth increasingly becomes a group construct. Here community is not so much a social goal as an ontological ground. It is the locus for identity, truth and meaning. This is, of course, very useful as a means of avoiding the modern polarities of individual and State and gives something of a theoretical underpinning to 'intermediate' institutions. Here one can readily conceive of society as a 'community of communities'. However, the inability of postmodern theory to ground itself in reality or a transcendent makes it prone to a radical *relativism. As G. E. Veith concludes, 'Postmodernism has the effect of both levelling cultures and exaggerating the differences between them. Postmodernism fragments society into contending and mutually unintelligible cultures and subcultures. Even within a single society, people are segmenting into

self-contained communities and contending interest groups. Christianity itself is ghetto-ised. From Bosnia to American universities, we see the emergence of a new tribalism' (G. E. Veith, *Postmodern Times* [Wheaton, 1994], p. 144).

Perhaps the most recent attempt to give political expression to ideas of community has been the movement of communitarianism. Founded by the American sociologist Amitai Etzioni around the publication of his book *The Spirit of Community*, it has been very influential in political circles on both sides of the Atlantic. As post Cold War politicians sought to find new centrist positions that could supersede the old left-right political divisions, Etzioni's combination of individual freedom and social obligation found a ready audience. In his own words 'The central argument is that a society requires a delicate balance between respect for the individual's rights and needs and interests, and concern for the common good' (in 'Finding the Right Balance', *Third Way* [June, 1997], p. 14). Communitarians believe that in the West the pendulum has swung too far towards individualism. Too many people avoid their communal and civic responsibilities, and moral agreement has collapsed. In response, they advocate a perspective that 'recognises both individual human dignity and the social dimension of human existence'. They believe that 'diverse communities of memory and mutual aid are rich resources of moral voices – voices that ought to be heeded in a society that increasingly threatens to become normless, self-centred and driven by greed, special interests and an unabashed quest for power'.

However, even a thinker as sophisticated as Etzioni has been forced to face the unavoidable Achilles heel of all community-centred philosophy. Etzioni rightly resists the postmodern pull of some communitarianism and recognizes that community as such cannot be a criterion for truth or values and that 'communal values must be judged by external and overriding criteria' ('The Responsive Communitarian Platform', p. 251 in *The Spirit of Community*). Something cannot be endorsed as good simply because a particular community endorses it. An outside source of values is needed to arbitrate between contending communities and to guide the development of a 'good' community. One cannot capitulate to what he calls 'the maze of relativism' (*Golden Rule*, p. 247). Yet, where can appropriate 'external' values be found? In tacit admission of the fact that his earlier formula – 'We ought to teach those values Americans share' ('Platform', p. 3) – was wholly inadequate, Etzioni published *The New Golden Rule*. Here he tried to establish his own version of the Golden Rule – 'Respect and uphold society's moral order as you would have society respect and uphold your autonomy' (*Golden Rule*, p. xviii) – as a paradigm for the good, communitarian society. He also sets out in detail an elaborate system for establishing normative core values but ultimately is forced to take refuge in what he declares are 'self-evident' or 'compelling' moral concepts (*Golden Rule*, pp. 241–242). As a Jew, Etzioni is sensitive to the role that religious *revelation might play in grounding *morality, but his commitment to a broad coalition for the regeneration of civic virtue makes him draw back from the logic of his own arguments. Ultimately, the absence of a transcendent ground makes his system theoretically weak, and his efforts to launch a new virtue-based, community-centred, political ideology (as laudable as it is) in this postmodern 'anti-ideological' era where pragmatic concerns dominate, has meant that his ideas have been prone to providing little more than useful clichés for image conscious politicians.

The Christian, of course, is not at all surprised to find this deep longing for community in the surrounding *culture. Human beings are, after all, created in the image of a triune God who has enjoyed fellowship within himself, among the three persons of the Godhead, for all eternity. Individuals are created for a future, holy and glorious intimacy with God himself, as well as with all God's people. Christian or not, they know deep within the soul, with an undeniable ache, that 'It is not good for the man to be alone' (Gen. 2:18).

Furthermore, the loss of community is also no surprise, though the Christian recognizes that it has far deeper roots than mere social dynamics. Since the fall, all life has been lived in the shadow of death – the ultimate human alienation. Sin, working its corruption from within the self-seeking heart, attacks and destroys first the human-divine bond and then subsequently all human relationships. This social dislocation is mirrored geographically as Adam and Eve's descendants, driven from the Edenic home, must spend their days as sojourners. Even their boldest attempt to build a corporate life, in as much as it centres on their own aspirations, rather than on the purposes of God, is judged at Babel.

Into this, the gospel comes as a message of real hope, not just for individuals but for the life people can enjoy together. However, the Christian hope for community is complex. The Bible offers little direct reflection on community *per se*. *Jesus himself, whilst drawing together an intimate band of disciples, also called them out of their communities of origin for his greater purposes. Biblical ethics, whilst confirming our social obligations, also calls us to look beyond our communities, to love not only our neighbours but also our enemies. Yet the ultimate biblical vision *is* for a redeemed community where 'the dwelling of God is with men' (Rev. 21:3) and where a unity of brotherly love will mark the people of God. The complexities arise because the Bible is clear that such a community experience is only possible 'in Christ' as he is acknowledged as the head, and only fully realized when he returns and brings an end to our temporal existence. As we live 'between the times', however, the hope of the eschatological community of the kingdom is kept vital as we enjoy the creational community of the family and the redemptive community of the church. These temporal institutions are given by God to nourish our community needs and nurture those community values rooted in God's character of love and *justice. They are also beacons of light that help orient and inform the multiple manifestations of our community aspirations that take shape in our particular historical and cultural contexts.

For the Christian apologist, the contemporary longing for community, the perceived loss of community and the secular hope for community, provide many opportunities. The *common ground of our shared humanity and consequently shared desires, offer many fruitful contact points for dialogue as well as much persuasive apologetic material. The human being is not a biological machine; the universe is ultimately personal. People are not 'self-made' but divinely wrought and divinely called. A person is not *homo economicus* but is a fundamentally relational being. The damaging effects of human self-centredness, materialism and individualism have been made manifest and point to the sinful bent of the heart. Furthermore, the tragic failure of so many of humankind's best efforts to establish romantic and utopian ideals points to a massive and fundamental need that our humanistic ambitions cannot overcome. The very real practical need to find a ground for morals and ethics that can guide behaviour within communities and arbitrate between communities, points to the transcendent God who alone secures 'the good'.

Whilst making use of these many opportunities, the Christian apologist will be wary of the lure of communitarian views of truth, now prevalent in our postmodern culture. Whilst coherence is a powerful criterion for truth, the common notion that 'communities of faith' can only make claims within their own tradition is unnecessarily fideistic and concedes far too much to fashionable critical theories. A correspondence criterion for truth is deeply biblical and has an essential role to play in an apologetic that seeks to convince the sceptic that whilst we may live, to a degree, in 'communally constructed' cultures, we also live, inescapably, in a God-sustained reality, accessible, by his grace, to our reason. Similarly, while supporting community-focused efforts, the Christian apologist would make the point that only a God-centred, in contrast to a community-centred, vision can ultimately be realized.

Finally, while pursuing the delicate discernment needed between legitimate longings and foolish ambitions, the Christian apologist who has a heart for this lost and fragmented culture, will always remember the winsome power of what Francis *Schaeffer called the 'final apologetic', that is, the persuasive witness of Christians, fallen yet redeemed, living poorly, yet substantially, in loving Christ-centred fellowship – the Christian community.

Bibliography

R. N. Bellah, R. Madsen, W. M. Sullivan, A. Swidler and S. M. Tipton, *Habits of the Heart: Individualism and Commitment in American Life* (Berkeley, 1985); J. Budziszewski, 'The Problem with Communitarianism', *First Things* (March, 1995), pp. 22–26; A. Etzioni, *The Spirit of Community: Rights, Responsibilities and the Communitarian Agenda* (New York, 1993); *The New Golden Rule: Community and Morality in a Democratic Society* (New York, 1996); R. D. Putnam, *Bowling Alone: The Collapse and Revival of American Community* (New York, 2000);

F. A. Schaeffer, *The Church at the End of the Twentieth Century* (London, 1970).

J. McGregor

CONFUCIANISM, see RELIGIONS OF CHINESE AND JAPANESE ORIGIN

CONSCIENCE

Conscience is an ability of reason to discern between right and wrong, good and bad, in our past, present and intended behaviour. More precisely, it is the acquired habit to use practical reason to apply moral principles to judge our own behaviour. The power of reason is innate to humans and cannot be set aside; the habit of using practical reason to judge well of moral matters is acquired, however, and can be more or less developed.

The English word 'conscience' is derived from the Latin *conscientia*, which, like its Greek equivalent, carries the sense of knowledge that is shared with another or, as humans are reflexive thinkers capable of witnessing their own acts, shared with oneself. Conscience can thus be thought of as the inner or subjective guide to the moral life that allows us to address the question, 'What ought I to do here and now in this concrete situation?'

The judgments of conscience

Following the scholastic tradition, many writers analyze the judgments of conscience in the form of a practical *syllogism. First, there is what *Thomas Aquinas calls 'the habit of first principles', reason's power to grasp fundamental moral truths that supply the syllogism's major premise. These truths, which are to the moral life what axioms are to mathematics, are self-evidently grasped by reason and include propositions such as 'One ought not to cause unnecessary harm', 'Do good and avoid evil', or 'Do as you would be done by'. God has so made humans that the right use of their reason allows them to apprehend and direct their lives in accordance with his objective moral order. For this reason, the apostle Paul tells us that the pagans, who did not benefit from God's revelation to Moses, are nevertheless able to act in accordance with its demands, the moral law being 'written on their hearts' (Rom. 2:14–15). Persons lacking this power of moral judgment must be regarded as defective or broken in some sense. The second aspect of conscience is the application of practical reason to moral matters, which supplies the minor premise by judging that one's present actions fall under a particular first principle. Protestant moralists, with Luther as a notable exception, generally accepted this analysis. Thus, Robert Sanderson (1587–1663), Oxford professor and Bishop of London, defined conscience as 'a faculty or Habit of the Practical Understanding, which enables the Mind of Man, by the use of Reason and Argument, to apply the light which it has to particular Moral Action.'

To portray the judgments of conscience syllogistically may appear to over-intellectualize them. Indeed, the scholastics debated amongst themselves whether in fact conscience belonged to the intellect (the Thomistic view) or to the will (the position of St Bonaventure and the Franciscans), or whether it is a separate faculty altogether. While the majority saw conscience as a function of the intellect, they recognized that one's emotions, appetites and will influence the operations of reason, especially as it touches upon moral matters. Someone may believe that an action is wrong, yet fail to see his own behaviour as exemplifying that wrong. In the Christian tradition, moral maturity requires that we not only arrive at correct judgments about what is good, but that we value and earnestly desire it. So, we are commended to cultivate dispositions to emotions such as hope, compassion, kindness, joy and peaceableness. To identify conscience with the practical reason does not mean that we should regard it as dispassionate or independent of all that makes up our moral character. Moreover, while the deliverances of conscience can arise inferentially from practical syllogisms, they need not. It seems plausible to think that the judgments of conscience are sometimes arrived at non-inferentially, and taken as properly basic. One does not *infer* from the content of one's perceptual consciousness to the belief that one sees a tree; rather, the experience of seeing a tree prompts in one the corresponding belief in an immediate and non-inferential way. Similarly, one might witness a small child being abused, and immediately and non-inferentially see it as wrong.

The functions of conscience

The knowledge of conscience can be applied to our actions in three ways. Conscience 'witnesses' when it judges retrospectively

regarding our past actions; it 'incites' or 'binds' when it urges us towards or away from some possible action; and finally, it functions 'executively' when it not only bears witness to our actions, but also executes its judgment by causing emotions such as guilt, shame, remorse and unease as befit our actions. Some have seen in the work of conscience a tripartite structure, with a legislative function that urges us towards or away from actions, a judicial function that passes judgment on our past actions, and an executive function that 'executes' its judgments in our hearts, either accusing or defending us.

The primacy of conscience

We cannot act contrary to the dictates of a clear conscience without erring, for to do so, says Richard Baxter, is to reject the *authority of God and that wherein we think he commands us. There is a difference, however, between a subjectively certain conscience that neither accuses us nor is plagued by doubt, and a correct conscience whose interior judgments in fact coincide with God's objective moral order. Because one's conscience can be malformed or underdeveloped, the freedom to follow conscience presupposes that we have exercised due care to educate it and to conform its judgments to Scripture and the judgments of morally wise persons. Although a suitably informed conscience can still err, and thereby fail to conform perfectly to God's standard, it does not lose its internal integrity. If our conscience is at variance with Scripture, church tradition, or with the relevant *community of our moral superiors, we must re-examine our conscience, and seek to conform its judgments to those we have reason to think are better informed than we are.

Kinds of conscience

Just as reason can be underdeveloped or ill trained with respect to language or mathematics, so too it can be underdeveloped or malformed in its moral deliberations and judgments. As the writer to the Hebrews says, the morally mature are those 'who have their faculties trained by practice to distinguish good from evil' (Heb. 5:14, RSV). We err in our moral judgments when we fail to apprehend the appropriate *first principles or, having apprehended them, fail to see our present circumstances as falling under them. Our consciences can be underdeveloped and ill-formed, among other ways, by neglect in childhood, by constant exposure to bad examples, by ignorance of the demands of *morality, by low passions that beguile the soul and body, or by repeatedly failing to incline one's will to the voice of conscience. The responsibility that we bear for the state of our conscience is a matter of degree. Conscience errs *invincibly* if the error is one for which we are not culpable and which the reasonable efforts of a prudent person could not overcome. Conscience errs *vincibly* when the mistaken judgment could have been avoided, either by present actions or actions we should have taken in the past.

The NT speaks of a variety of ways in which our consciences can be defective. A conscience is *doubtful* (Rom. 14:22–23) when it judges without having taken appropriate steps to quell doubts that the opposite judgment might be true. The apostle Paul acknowledges that while Christians are free to eat meat offered to idols, those of weak conscience feel defiled in doing so, and he urges those of more mature conscience not to act so as to cause weaker brothers to act from a doubtful conscience (1 Cor. 8:7–13). One's conscience is *corrupted* if one not only acts contrary to godly principles but also is incapable of appreciating what is pure (Titus 1:16). Paul also speaks of those whose conscience is *seared*, by which he means not just hardened through repeated failure to incline to the voice of conscience, but a condition whereby one judges as immoral that which is good and which is given to us by God for our enjoyment (1 Tim. 4:2). The inability to take delight in what is pure and to enjoy God's good gifts to us is related to what moral theologians call a scrupulous conscience. A scrupulous conscience is disposed to feel accused even for sins that have been forgiven, and to seek a level of moral certainty before acting that is not available to us in this life. So we see that among the imperfections of conscience are both the deficiency of dullness and the excess of scrupulosity and an inability to view as morally permissible that which God deems good.

Problems of conscience

Sometimes we confront situations or problems that cause perplexity about what morality or God's will require. May a government agent lie in order to infiltrate a terrorist cell that threatens his country? Not just extraordinary, but ordinary spheres of human action – medicine, the justice system, business, politics, inter-personal relations – can cause a perplexed conscience. Casuistry is the science of dealing with cases of conscience, especially the hard cases and the new or unforeseen circumstances to which our moral principles have not yet been applied. Both Protestant and Catholic traditions cultivated highly refined and detailed systems of casuistry for helping to interpret and apply known moral principles to concrete moral situations.

Cases of perplexity, or a probable conscience as it is sometimes called, arise in two main areas. First, there are the so-called moral dilemmas, where it would seem that sinning is inevitable, that we err no matter what we do. Many moralists, Thomas Aquinas, Robert Sanderson and Immanuel *Kant among them, deny that we can be genuinely bound by competing moral duties of equal force, that one or the other horn of the dilemma is really an imperfect duty, and thus not binding at all. Others, such as Jeremy Taylor, advise that we 'incline to that which hath least danger and least mischief ... No sin is to be chosen when both can be avoided, but when they cannot, the least is to be suffered.'

Secondly, cases of probable conscience arise when we are in doubt about whether in the circumstances in which we find ourselves, we are bound by moral obligation or we retain our liberty. There is agreement in Christian tradition that a doubtful law does not bind the conscience, but disagreement about the degree of doubt we should be willing to accommodate. The view that even if we are slightly uncertain about whether or not we are bound by a moral law, the safest course is always to act as if under moral obligation, is generally rejected as too rigorous. Whereas, to say that if there is the slightest uncertainty, however trivial, then we are not under obligation and should consider ourselves free of moral constraint, is too lax. The Reformers favoured the middle view which says that if the weight of evidence is against our being bound by obligation, then we should give ourselves the benefit of the doubt and incline to liberty. The scholastics, however, argued that if there is reasonable doubt among competent moral judges against one's being morally obliged, then one is not.

Bibliography

R. Baxter, *A Christian Directory* (Ligonier, 1990); K. Kirk, *Conscience and Its Problems:*

An Introduction to Casuistry (London, 1948); D. C. Langston, *Conscience and Other Virtues* (University Park, 2001); C. S. Lewis, *Studies in Words*, 2nd edn (Cambridge, 1967); T. Wood, *English Causuistical Divinity During the Seventeenth Century* (London, 1952).

W. J. WOOD

CONSTRUCTIVISM

The term constructivism appears in many different kinds of discourse. In the philosophy of mathematics, the term refers to the view that mathematical entities exist only as constructed by human activity. This theory opposes the realist position that mathematical entities exist independently of human activity. In art theory, the term refers to a particular stance associated with the Russian sculptor Vladimir Tatlin that artists imitate industrial production, and that art like society needs to be constructed. In educational theory, constructivism is the view that students need to find out knowledge for themselves through practices such as 'self-paced learning' and 'discovery learning'. Piaget, the psychologist, is seen as a pioneer educational constructivist.

In *theology, constructivism is the view that Christian doctrine is of human manufacture as is the putative object of worship, God. The Christian life becomes a very human project of playful self-creation. Theologian and philosopher, Don Cupitt represents this view. In the study of mystical experience, the constructivists argue against the view that there is a core of mystical experience that is found in all the major *world religions. Instead, these constructivists maintain that each claim to a mystical experience is a human construct that is shaped in an integral way by the very *language the subject uses of the experience. On this view, Christian mystical experience is fundamentally different from Hindu mystical experience and so forth. In *ethics, constructivism argues that values are human creations and have no independent existence outside human imagining.

In more general philosophy, constructivism comes down on the anti-realist side of the longstanding debates over the nature of *reality (*metaphysics) and knowing (*epistemology). In historiography, the face of constructivism shows itself in those views that maintain that our writing of the past is an exercise in human creativity which says more about the historian and his or her interests than about the past *per se*. In social theory, the term refers to the view that our reading of reality is of human manufacture or, more radically, that reality as we know it is a human artifact. Even the scientific enterprise is a construct on this view, and Thomas Kuhn has argued that scientific theories are made by scientists and are not simply determined by the natural order in which scientists are placed. This last view is a particularly important one for the Christian apologist both to understand and to address, because this anti-realist way of thinking is a feature of the postmodern stance.

The postmodern view that reality, including human identity, is socially constructed constitutes a powerful challenge to Christian apologetics. According to this view, human nature is a socially manufactured notion that is bound up in the very language we use to articulate a doctrine of it. We are socially and historically located. Meta-narratives or grand narratives that attempt universal explanations of human history, like Marxism, are authoritarian in nature, according to Jean-François *Lyotard, and our viewpoints should instead be local ones or little narratives. To argue differently is to risk exercising a stultifying hegemony over the thoughts and lives of others. Meta-narrative thinking expressed in all-embracing world-views of one kind or another so easily becomes totalizing instruments of oppression which are used by the powerful to suppress certain voices on the margins of society (e.g. women, gays, ethnic minorities).

The apologist should appreciate the strengths of constructivist thinking. The Enlightenment project has failed. We are not Cartesian egos adrift from time and place. We have our histories and our interests. We can fool ourselves, and a claim about *truth can be more about ourselves than reality. The hermeneutic of suspicion does have a point. We can use ideas as instruments of control of others and even of their abuse. Our theology can become ideology. And yet the very fact that we are aware that we are socially and historically particular and that ideas have histories and can be used for *power play is of striking importance. There is something about us that transcends the local and the time bound. We are creatures who not only have reason, interests and passions, but also *imagination. We can indwell other points of view – try them on for size – and then reflect on our own in the light of them without necessarily changing our fundamental commitments. Imagination thus enables us to establish that critical distance that allows the critique of our most cherished ideas as we envisage other possibilities.

The Christian's belief in a Creator and a real creation keeps him or her in the realist camp metaphysically (with regard to what is real) and epistemologically (with regard to what can be known) and ethically (with regard to what is to be valued). Indeed, a robust Christian theism regards creatures as belonging to various kinds (a generic order) and having various purposes in the divine economy (a telic order). But constructivist challenges should keep the Christian from that naïve realism that thinks that seeing is believing. Instead, critical realism, with its awareness of the possibility of mistaken perception and judgment about both the generic and telic, appears far more compatible with the Christian's eschatological location in a fallen world and in the midst of a groaning creation. Moreover, arguably both pure realists and pure anti-realists do not exist. Our realist or anti-realist stances tend to be domain specific as W. P. Alston shows, e.g. someone may be a realist about God and an anti-realist about mathematical objects.

From the Christian perspective, the great problem in postmodern conceptual *relativism with its constructivist implications lies not only in its failure to reckon with human imagination but also in the covert absolutism masked in the postmodern claim. Meta-narratives have always, do now and will continue to oppress. As far as intellectual values are concerned, here then is a claim to an absolute truth about the state of affairs in the world. Moreover, the passion that is expressed in the presentation and defence of postmodern views masks an absolute moral value – the absolute value of personal freedom expressed in one's choices. Still further, the constructivist faces the problem that *ex hypothesi* his or her own view is only an interpretation rather than truth bearing. As *Nietzsche wrote in his notebooks, there are 'no facts ... only interpretations'. Yet postmoderns believe that realists have got the epistemological picture seriously wrong. Conceptual relativism is a self-referentially destructive position.

The Christian apologist, then, will need to be aware of the influence that both modernity and postmodernity have had in shaping contemporary thought. With those still shaped by modernity the appeal to reason, evidence and argument will continue to be essential. Such moderns will not join the people of God until convinced about the truth of what they have to say, and with them the apologist can argue and yet stay relationally connected if the tone of the debate is right. The struggle is over what is true. Postmoderns, on the other hand, will be far more interested in seeing if there is any reality in the lives of those making Christian truth-claims. Attacking the intellectual status of conceptual relativism or various items in postmodern thinking will be seen not as a struggle over ideas but as a personal rejection of the other's freely chosen stance in the world.

With postmoderns the Christian's personal testimony may prove far more important than careful argument. Showing Christian *community will count for more than merely saying Christian words as such people may perhaps join the people of God before joining the God of the people. The attractiveness of Christian community and the love between believers and for the neighbour and stranger will be all the more urgent. Such love has always had deep epistemic significance as the mark of Christians (John 13:35).

The apostolic brief, according to Paul, is to present every person mature in Christ (Col. 1:28). For those shaped by modernity that journey towards maturity might start with embracing Christianity's truth-claims. For postmoderns that journey might start with the attractiveness of Christ. For the Christian apologist the ultimate aim is to see those who come to faith both embrace Christian truth-claims and be attracted to Christ.

Bibliography

W. P. Alston, 'Realism and the Christian Faith', *International Journal for the Philosophy of Religion*, 38 (1995); W. T. Anderson (ed.), *The Truth About The Truth* (New York, 1995); J. Appleby, E. Covington, D. Hoyt, M. Latham and A. Sneider (eds.), *Knowledge and Postmodernism in Historical Perspective* (New York and London, 1996); R. Trigg, *Rationality and Religion* (Oxford, 1998).

G. A. COLE

CONTEMPORARY MUSIC, see MUSIC

CONTRADICTION AND NON-CONTRADICTION

The law of contradiction, also known as the principle of non-contradiction, belongs to the foundations of *logic (the study of correct *reasoning) and *metaphysics (the study of the most general features of *reality). This principle is implicit in all rational thought and communication, and attempts to deny it are self-defeating. Making explicit reference to the principle of non-contradiction can contribute to evaluating truth-claims of any sort, including the claims of the Christian faith.

Context and formulation of the principle

Understanding non-contradiction requires a clear formulation of the principle, which in turn requires placing the principle in its double context of logic and metaphysics.

The three laws of thought

The principle of non-contradiction was identified traditionally as one of the three 'laws of thought', alongside the principle of identity and the principle of excluded middle. All three are expressed in terms of things, properties and propositions, and therefore belong more clearly to metaphysics than to logic. The most helpful way to formulate the three laws is to use the term 'proposition', a word that belongs both to logic and to metaphysics. It belongs to logic since correct reasoning consists of argument forms that may be used to support the claim that given propositions are true (or false); it belongs to metaphysics since it is possible to regard propositions as real features of the world. Using this term, the principle of excluded middle, for instance, can be formulated as: 'Every proposition is either true or not true.'

Logical inconsistency

The principle of non-contradiction belongs to the context of logic, not only because it can be formulated using the term 'proposition', but also because contradiction is a logical concept. In logic, contradiction is a species of the genus 'inconsistency'. The genus has only one other species, called 'contrariety'. Two propositions are inconsistent with one another just when it is necessary that if one is true the other is false. If two propositions contradict each other, then one of them must be true and the other must be false (e.g. 'Bush is president' and 'Bush is not president'). If two propositions are contrary to each other, then at least one of them must be false, but they might both be false (e.g. 'Bush's only car is a Porsche' and 'Bush's only car is a Rolls-Royce'). Either species of inconsistency is a guarantee that at least one false proposition is present.

Formulating the principle of non-contradiction

The following is a broad, metaphysical formulation of the principle: 'No entity, X, can both have a property, P, and lack P at the same time and in the same sense.' A more narrow formulation which fits the principle's logical context is this: 'A proposition cannot be true and false at the same time and in the same sense.' Given that propositions can be regarded as entities (real things), and that truth and falsity are properties of propositions, the narrow formulation is consistent with the broad, metaphysical one.

Rationality and non-contradiction

A rational person is someone who thinks and acts on the basis of correct reasoning. That sounds simple enough, but 'rationality' names a complex concept, for there are many types of rationality with different principles of reasoning for each type. (For a fuller discussion of this, see Cohen, *Companion*, pp. 415–416.)

Non-contradiction implicit in all types of rationality

Adherence to the principle of non-contradiction is not a type of rationality or a principle distinctive to one type of rationality. It is instead implicit in all types of rationality. For instance, consider its presence in the type of rationality sometimes called 'practical reason'. It is rational for an agent to act in ways that will further his or her interests. If it is in the interest of an athlete to win a championship, and if the athlete determines that a certain training regimen is best suited to help him win, then it is rational for him to undertake that regimen. The principle of non-contradiction is implicit in the athlete's reasoning, because he is assuming that 'this training regimen is best' cannot be both true and false at the same time and in the same sense. The same is true for all types of rationality, for each type employs propositions and cannot proceed without presupposing a sharp distinction between each proposition and its contradictory (e.g. 'God exists' and 'God does not exist').

Implications of denying the principle of non-contradiction

To deny the principle of non-contradiction is to allow that a proposition and its contradictory can both be true and false at the same time and in the same sense. It could be true, then, that a certain entity, Fluffy, both is a cat and is not a cat. To allow that Fluffy is 'not a cat' further allows that Fluffy might be anything at all that is not a cat. Fluffy, besides being a cat, could be (at the same time) a dog, a mountain, a human being, and an archangel. In effect, to deny the principle of non-contradiction is tantamount to accepting both species of inconsistency: Fluffy is a cat and not a cat at the same time and in the same sense (contradiction); and Fluffy is a cat and a dog (or anything else that is not a cat) at the same time and in the same sense (contrariety). To deny the principle of non-contradiction is, then, to abandon logical consistency and with it any chance of rational thought and communication. (For another discussion of this, see Nash, *Worldviews*, pp. 81–82.)

Proving the principle of non-contradiction

Given its place in the foundations of logic and metaphysics, the principle of non-contradiction is implicit in all reasoning and therefore in all attempts to prove anything at all. If, then, anyone wishes to prove the principle of non-contradiction, he or she must proceed on the assumption that the principle is true. That would be begging the question, so it is clear that there is no direct way to prove the principle of non-contradiction. But there are indirect arguments for this principle. One of these maintains that the principle of non-contradiction must be true since all significant human action presupposes it. This argument begins by noting that if a proposition and its contradictory can both be true, then there is no real difference between them. For instance, there would be no real difference between 'walking off the cliff' and 'not walking off the cliff'. But of course there is a real and vital difference between these two propositions and the actions they describe, and rational choices by human beings depend upon that difference.

Psychology and non-contradiction

It is rational, then, to accept the principle of non-contradiction, and it is irrational and potentially disastrous to deny it. But is it psychologically possible to deny this principle? Given the fact that the principle of non-contradiction is implicit in all reasoning, it is probably impossible to understand the principle and believe that it is false, or self-consciously and at the same time to believe a proposition and its contradictory ('X is true and X is false').

It is possible, of course, to assert contradictions without believing them, and to believe contradictory propositions without being aware that they are in fact contradictory. In cases of the former sort, the person might be lying, saying something to one person ('I will vote for Smith'), and its contradictory ('I will not vote for Smith') or a contrary ('I will vote for Jones') to another person. The liar does not believe both that he will vote for Smith and that he will not vote for Smith, but he does assert both propositions. In cases of the latter sort, a person might have come to believe a certain proposition (X) at one time, and then later acquired a belief in one of its contraries (say, Y). If this person's set of beliefs is large and complex, he or she might not have noticed that X and Y are logically inconsistent and that there is, therefore, an implicit contradiction among these beliefs. He or she believes X and believes its contrary, Y; if Y is true, then X must be false, so this believer is committed logically both to X and 'not X'. (For a fuller discussion of this issue, see Wolfram, *Philosophical Logic*, pp. 181–182.)

When mentally normal persons learn of contradictions among their beliefs, they reject the contradictions, either suspending judgment ('perhaps X is true and perhaps it is not') or coming down on one side of the issue (say, 'X is true'). For them, the *psychology of belief provides experiential confirmation of the principle of non-contradiction.

Non-contradiction and the evaluation of truth-claims

The principle of non-contradiction supplies a means for evaluating any set of truth-claims. For any set of propositions (A and B and C) to be true, each of its members (A, B and C) must be true. If two or more propositions in the set are logically inconsistent with each other, then at least one member of the set is false and therefore the set itself is false. To determine whether the propositions in a set are logically inconsistent is to apply the principle of non-contradiction to that set, provided that the principle is understood broadly to cover both species of inconsistency. And this understanding is reasonable, since contrary claims imply the presence of contradiction. The application of this (broad) principle to a set of propositions (truth-claims) has only two possible outcomes. First, the set can be shown to be logically consistent, and therefore possibly true (consistency does not guarantee truth). Secondly, and much more significantly, the set can be shown to be logically inconsistent, and therefore *actually false* (inconsistency guarantees falsehood). (For fuller discussions of this issue, see Bradley and Swartz, *Possible Worlds*, pp. 28–30, and Nash, *Worldviews*, pp. 55–57.)

The use of non-contradiction in apologetics

In apologetics the primary use of the principle of non-contradiction is to show that the set of propositions comprising the core beliefs of the Christian faith is logically consistent and therefore possibly true. This cannot be done without first showing that particular Christian beliefs are internally consistent. Richard Swinburne, for instance, argues for the coherence of the theistic concept of God, where 'coherence' is a broad concept that embraces logical consistency and conceivability (see Swinburne, *Coherence*, pp. 11–14). For Swinburne a coherent statement may be false but may be true. If the concept of God is coherent, then it is internally consistent and therefore possibly true. If each core Christian belief is internally consistent, and if all these beliefs form a logically consistent set, then it is possible that the Christian faith is true.

Making a case for the possible truth of the Christian faith falls short of completing the task of apologetics. So to take things further, some apologists combine the principle of non-contradiction with an appeal to the facts of experience to form a test of 'systematic consistency' to argue that the Christian faith is *actually* true (see Carnell, *Introduction*, pp. 56–62, and Craig, *Apologetics*, pp. 22, 196.) They maintain that Christianity is logically consistent and fits all the facts of experience, and therefore it is highly probable that it is true.

Objections to the principle of non-contradiction

Despite its place in the foundations of logic and metaphysics, the principle of non-contradiction has been subjected to vigorous criticism. Chris-

tian thinkers are the source for some of this, but the most radical criticism comes from thinkers influenced by Eastern thought.

Objections from theology

Some Christian theologians have objected to the application of the principle of non-contradiction to thinking and speaking about God. These theologians have not rejected the principle itself, but have insisted that it cannot be used with reference to God, for God (they say) is 'beyond logic' or 'has a logic of his own'. Although this type of objection has a link to the generally accepted proposition that no-one could have exhaustive knowledge of God, it is not entailed by that proposition and it has the consequence of being fatal to all thinking and speaking about God. For if the principle of non-contradiction does not apply to God, then both any assertion about God, and that assertion's contradictory, could be true (e.g. 'God is love' and 'God is not love'). Not only *theology but the whole of Christian faith and life require the principle of non-contradiction to apply to God. (For a helpful discussion of this, with examples from the work of these theologians, see Nash, *Worldviews*, pp. 74–80.)

Objections from Eastern thought

Typically, Eastern thought (e.g. Hindu, Buddhist and Taoist) maintains that reality transcends all distinctions, including the logical distinctions embedded in the principle of non-contradiction. Proponents of Eastern thought respond to the call for logical consistency (*Aristotle's 'X or not X') with a provocative picture of a world in which the concept of logical consistency impedes seeing the world as it really is (the Buddha's 'X *and* not X'). An interesting contemporary application of this Eastern rejection of logical consistency is the development of 'fuzzy logic', which is based on the 'fuzzy principle' that everything is a matter of degree. The fuzzy principle has been put to use in creating powerful new forms of technology that outstrip the performance of older forms based on the black-and-white logic of non-contradiction. Critics of fuzzy logic have said that it is nothing more than an alternative way to express and harness the old concept of probability. Perhaps that criticism is correct. But a more impressive form of criticism is within reach of anyone who reads something by a proponent of fuzzy logic. The reader will discover, in its 'fuzzy' pages, an implicit and pervasive use of the principle of non-contradiction.

Bibliography

R. Bradley and N. Swartz, *Possible Worlds: An Introduction to Logic and Its Philosophy* (Indianapolis, 1979); J. Cargile, 'Classical Logic – Traditional and Modern', in J. H. Fetzer (ed.), *Principles of Philosophical Reasoning* (Totowa, 1984); E. J. Carnell, *An Introduction to Christian Apologetics* (Grand Rapids, 1948); L. J. Cohen, 'Rationality', in J. Dancy and E. Sosa (eds.), *A Companion to Epistemology* (Oxford, 1992); W. L. Craig, *Apologetics: An Introduction* (Chicago, 1984); B. Kosko, *Fuzzy Thinking: The New Science of Fuzzy Logic* (New York, 1993); R. H. Nash, *Worldviews in Conflict: Choosing Christianity in a World of Ideas* (Grand Rapids, 1992); R. Swinburne, *The Coherence of Theism* (Oxford, 1977); S. Wolfram, *Philosophical Logic: An Introduction* (London and New York, 1989).

D. M. CIOCCHI

COSMOLOGICAL ARGUMENT

The cosmological argument is a family of arguments which seek to demonstrate the existence of a 'sufficient reason' or 'first cause' of the existence of the cosmos. They can be grouped into three basic types: the *kalam* cosmological argument for a first cause of the beginning of the universe, the Thomist cosmological argument for a sustaining ground of being of the world, and the *Leibnizian cosmological argument for a sufficient reason why something exists rather than nothing.

A simple statement of a Leibnizian cosmological argument might run as follows: every existing thing has an explanation of its existence, either in the necessity of its own nature or in an external cause; if the universe has an explanation of its existence, that explanation is God; the universe is an existing thing; therefore, the explanation of the existence of the universe is God.

One of the main objections to Leibniz's own formulation of the argument is that it presupposes his principle of sufficient reason that 'no fact can be real or existent, no statement true, unless there be a sufficient reason why it is so and not otherwise'. Many have doubted this principle. Some theists have responded to this objection by agreeing that one must ultimately come to some explanatory stopping point which is a being whose existence is a brute, contingent fact, and that God is a simpler stopping point than the variegated and finite universe. The formulation of the Leibnizian argument given above, however, avoids the objection without retreating to the dubious position that God is a contingent being, as it merely requires any existing *thing* to have an explanation of its existence, either in the necessity of its own nature or in some external cause. This is compatible with there being brute *facts* about the world. What it precludes is that there could be things which just exist inexplicably. This principle seems quite plausible, which is all that is required for a successful argument.

Atheists implicitly endorse the second premise of the argument that 'if the universe has an explanation of its existence that explanation is God'. For they typically assert that, there being no God, it is false that everything has an explanation of its existence because the universe just exists inexplicably. In so saying, the atheist implicitly recognizes that if the universe has an explanation, then God exists as its explanatory ground. Since the universe is obviously an existing thing (especially evident in its very early stages when its density was so extreme), it follows that God exists.

It is open to the atheist to retort that while the universe has an explanation of its existence, that explanation lies not in an external ground but in the necessity of its own nature. In other words, the universe is a metaphysically necessary being. This is an extremely bold suggestion, as we have a strong intuition of the universe's contingency. Still, it would be desirable to have some stronger argument for the universe's contingency than our intuitions alone. Could the Thomist cosmological argument help us here? In *Thomas Aquinas' Aristotelian-inspired metaphysic, every existing finite thing is composed of a nature and an act of being which instantiates that nature. They are, therefore, radically contingent upon a ground of being whose essence is being itself. If successful, the Thomist argument would show that the universe is a contingent entity causally dependent upon a necessary being for its continued existence. The problem with appeal to the Thomist argument, however, is that it is very difficult to show that things are, in fact, contingent in the special sense required by the argument. Certainly, things are naturally contingent in that their continued existence is dependent upon a myriad of factors including temperature, pressure, entropy level and so forth, but this natural contingency does not suffice to establish a metaphysical contingency in the sense that being must continually be added to their natures or they will be spontaneously annihilated.

Can the *kalam* cosmological argument come to our assistance here? It holds that an essential property of a metaphysically necessary and ultimate being is that it be eternal, i.e. without beginning or end. If the universe is not eternal, then it could not be a metaphysically necessary being. But it is precisely the aim of the *kalam* argument to show that the universe is not eternal but had a beginning. It would follow that the universe must therefore be contingent in its existence. More thatn that, the *kalam* argument also shows the universe to be contingent in a very special way: it came into existence out of nothing. The atheist who would answer Leibniz by holding that the existence of the universe is a brute fact, an exception to the principle of sufficient reason, is thus thrust into the very awkward position of maintaining not merely that the universe exists eternally without explanation, but that for no reason at all it magically popped into being out of nothing. This position might make *theism look like a welcome alternative. Thus, the *kalam* argument not only constitutes an independent argument for a transcendent creator but also serves as a valuable supplement to the Leibnizian argument.

The *kalam* cosmological argument may be formulated as follows: whatever begins to exist has a cause; the universe began to exist; therefore, the universe has a cause. Conceptual analysis of what it means to be a cause of the universe then aims to establish some of the theologically significant properties of this being.

The first premise seems obviously true at least, more so than its negation. It is rooted in the metaphysical intuition that something cannot come into being from nothing. Moreover, this premise is constantly confirmed in our experience. The second premise has been supported by both deductive, philosophical arguments and inductive, scientific arguments. Philosophically, various arguments have been offered to show the metaphysical impossibility of an infinite temporal series of past events. For example, the existence of an actually (as opposed to merely potentially) infinite number of things leads to counter-intuituive absurdities and even self-contradictions, e.g. what is infinity minus infinity? Mathematically, inverse operations like subtraction are not defined for infinite quantities because one obtains contradictory answers. For example, if one subtracts all the odd numbers (1, 3, 5 . . .) from all the natural numbers (0, 1, 2, 3 . . .), then an infinite number of numbers is left over (so infinity minus infinity is infinity); but if one subtracts all the numbers greater than 2, one has only three numbers remaining (so infinity minus infinity is three!). It needs to be understood that in both these cases one has subtracted identical quantities from identical quantities and come up with contradictory answers. In fact, one can get any answer one pleases from zero to infinity. This suggests that however fruitful and consistent a concept the actual infinite may be within the universe of discourse created by the axioms and conventions of infinite set theory and transfinite arithmetic, it cannot be transposed into the spatio-temporal world. But since a beginningless series of past events would entail an infinite number of past events, it therefore follows that the series of past events is finite and that the universe began to exist.

Or again, it might be argued that it is impossible to form such an actually infinite collection by adding one member at a time. Sometimes this is described as the impossibility of traversing the infinite. In order for us to have 'arrived' at today, temporal existence has, so to speak, traversed an infinite number of prior events. But before the present event could arrive, the event immediately prior to it would have had to arrive; and before that event could have arrived, the event immediately prior to it would have had to arrive, and so on *ad infinitum*. No event could ever arrive, since there will always be one more event that had to have happened first. Thus, if the series of past events were beginningless, the present event could not have arrived, which is absurd. If one insists that given infinite past time, the present event would have arrived, one is faced with the deeper question of why the present event did not occur yesterday or the day before, since by then an infinite amount of time had already elapsed. In fact, no matter how far back into the past one regresses, it seems that the event in question would have already arrived, which is also absurd.

Scientifically, contemporary interest in the *kalam* cosmological argument arises largely out of the startling empirical evidence of astrophysical cosmology for a beginning of space and time. The standard 'Big Bang' model, which has been the controlling paradigm of contemporary cosmology for the last seventy years, describes a universe which is not eternal in the past, but which came into being a finite time ago. Moreover, the origin it posits is an absolute origin *ex nihilo*. For not only all matter and energy, but space and time themselves come into being at the initial cosmological singularity. Sometimes objectors appeal to non-standard models of the expanding universe in an attempt to avert the absolute beginning predicted by the standard model; but it has been the overwhelming verdict of the scientific community that none of these is more probable than the Big Bang theory. The devil is in the details, and when one examines such senarios closely, one finds that there is no mathematically consistent model which has been so successful in its predictions, or as corroborated by the evidence, as the traditional Big Bang theory. For example, some theories, like the oscillating universe (which expands and re-contracts forever), the chaotic inflationary universe (which continually spawns new universes) or the cyclic ekpyrotic model (which involves periodically colliding three-dimensional membranes in a five-dimensional spacetime), may have a potentially infinite future but turn out to have only a finite past. Vacuum fluctuation universe theories (which postulate an eternal vacuum out of which our universe is born) cannot explain why, if the vacuum was eternal, we do not observe an infinitely old universe. The quantum gravity universe theory propounded by the famous physicist Stephen Hawking, if interpreted realistically, still involves an absolute origin of the universe even if the universe does not begin in a singularity, as it does in the standard Big Bang theory. In sum, according to Hawking, 'Almost everyone now believes that the universe, and *time itself*, had a beginning at the Big Bang' (S. Hawking, *The Nature of Space and Time* [Princeton, 1996], p. 20).

A second scientific consideration concerns the thermodynamic properties of the universe. According to the second law of thermodynamics, processes taking place in a closed system always tend toward a state of equilibrium. Now the universe is, on a naturalistic view, a gigantic closed system, since it is everything there is and there is nothing outside it. What this seems to imply is that, given enough time, the universe and all its processes will run down, and the entire universe will come to a state of heat death. Once the universe reaches this state, no further change is possible.

Now the question that arises is this: if given enough time the universe will reach heat death, then why is it not in a state of heat death now, if it has existed forever, from eternity? If the universe did not begin to exist, then it should now be cold, dark, dilute and dead. Some people have tried to escape this conclusion by adopting an oscillating model of the universe which never reaches a final state of equilibrium. But the thermodynamic properties of this model imply the very beginning of the universe that its proponents sought to avoid. For entropy increases from cycle to cycle in such a model, which has the effect of generating larger and longer oscillations with each successive cycle. Thus, as one traces the oscillations back in time, they become progressively smaller until one reaches a first and smallest oscillation. In fact, it is estimated on the basis of current entropy levels that the universe cannot have gone through more than 100 previous oscillations. The universe appears to have been created a finite time ago, and its energy was somehow simply put in at the creation as an initial condition.

It follows, therefore, that the universe has a cause. Conceptual analysis enables us to recover a number of striking properties which must be possessed by such an ultra-mundane being. For as the cause of space and time, this entity must transcend space and time and therefore exist atemporally and non-spatially, at least without the universe. This transcendent cause must, therefore, be changeless and immaterial, since timelessness entails changelessness, and changelessness implies immateriality. Such a cause must be beginningless and uncaused, at least in the sense of lacking any antecedent causal conditions. This entity must be unimaginably powerful, since it created the universe without any material cause.

Finally, and most remarkably, such a transcendent cause is plausibly to be taken to be personal. Three reasons can be given for this conclusion. First, there are two types of causal explanation: scientific explanations in terms of laws and initial conditions and personal explanations in terms of agents and their volitions. A first state of the universe *cannot* have a scientific explanation, since there is nothing before it, and therefore it can be accounted for only in terms of a personal explanation. Secondly, the personhood of the cause of the universe is implied by its timelessness and immateriality, since the only entities we know of which can possess such properties are either minds or abstract objects. As abstract objects do not stand in causal relations, the transcendent cause of the origin of the universe must be of the order of mind. Thirdly, this same conclusion is also implied by the fact that we have in this case the origin of a temporal effect from a timeless cause. If the cause of the origin of the universe were an impersonal set of conditions, it would be impossible for the cause to exist without its effect. For if the sufficient conditions of the effect are timelessly given, then their effect must be given as well. The only way for the cause to be timeless and changeless but for its effect to originate anew a finite time ago is for the cause to be a personal agent who freely chooses to bring about an effect without antecedent determining conditions. Thus, we are brought, not merely to a transcendent cause of the universe, but to its personal Creator. He is, as Leibniz maintained, the sufficient reason why anything exists rather than nothing.

Bibliography

W. D. Beck, 'The Cosmological Argument: A Current Bibliographical Appraisal', *Philosophia Christi*, 2 (2000), pp. 283–304; D. R. Burrill, *The Cosmological Arguments* (Garden City, 1967); W. L. Craig and Q. Smith, *Theism, Atheism, and Big Bang Cosmology* (Oxford, 1993); S. Wallace (ed.), *Does God Exist?* (Aldershot, 2003).

W. L. CRAIG

COSMOLOGY

It is fundamental to biblical theology that the universe owes its origin and continued existence to the will of God. The God supremely and uniquely revealed in Jesus, is the creator and sustainer of heaven and earth. Christian apologetics has therefore asked how can the scientific and biblical accounts of the origin of the universe be held together, as God is the Lord of both his works and his word. Further, are there insights from the world of *science which point towards the existence of a Creator, or

provide possible bridges for dialogue between those who are not Christians and the Christian faith?

Within the scientific community, it is generally agreed, on the basis of the redshift of galaxies, the observation of the microwave background radiation and the theoretical prediction of the observed hydrogen-to-helium ratio, that the origin of the universe is well described by the model of the hot Big Bang, with the universe expanding from a singularity some twelve billion years ago. Of course, no scientific model is without its problems, and the Big Bang leaves certain questions unanswered, such as the nature of the dark matter which is necessary for galaxy formation. Although the model of the Big Bang has needed some careful refining, it has stood up remarkably well to over thirty years of scrutiny and new observations.

In terms of the biblical account, the fundamental principles of Gen. 1 (which are reflected in many other biblical passages which deal with creation) are that God is the sole and sovereign Creator of all things and the source of order and extravagance in the universe, and that human beings are the highpoint of his creative activity by virtue of his gift of intimate relationship and responsibility.

It is important to note that the Bible is not interested in cosmology for its own sake. The biblical teaching about creation is located in passages which are concerned with other issues such as worship, Christology and salvation. Some knowledge of this Creator God can be seen in his works of creation, but his nature is supremely revealed in *Jesus who is the image of the invisible God and is involved with the Father and the Spirit in the work of creation (Col. 1:15). Christ is the one in whom the universe is created, sustained and finds its ultimate consummation. Therefore, Christians have understood science in Kepler's words of 'thinking God's thoughts after Him' and as being a Christian calling. Indeed, many historians of science point out the positive influence of Christian theology upon the growth of modern science.

Big Bang or Big God?

Although all Christians agree that God is the source and sustainer of the whole universe, there is disagreement on how he creates. A great deal of Christian apologetic effort has been given to reconciling the scientific account of origins with the biblical account, and a diversity of approaches have been offered.

In the nineteenth century, Thomas Chalmers proposed the 'gap theory', which suggested a gap between the first two verses of Gen. 1, the verses referring to a creation and then recreation. Hugh *Miller argued that the 'days' of Gen. 1 represent periods of time. In the twentieth century, P. J. Wiseman suggested that the 'days' of Gen. 1 were not days of creation but days of revelation, that is days when God 'revealed' his creation to Adam. These approaches attempted to reconcile the scientific age of the universe of billions of years with the Genesis chronology, and they still have their adherents today.

More influential within the evangelical community, however, are two competing interpretations. Scientific creationism argues that an acceptance of the Big Bang is incompatible with a Creator God. Proponents of this position point out scientific gaps in the Big Bang model; argue for an age of the universe in thousands rather than billions of years; claim that the early chapters of Genesis are a scientific account of the origin of the universe; and see God as more likely to create in seven days rather than over billions of years.

Within scientific creationism itself there is a diversity of positions. Some suggest that God created the universe to look billions of years old, while in fact its age is only thousands of years. Others suggest that the universe is billions of years old, but the earth was created specially by God a few thousand years ago.

Theistic evolution claims that the early chapters of Genesis are not scientific history but belong to the genre of theological or liturgical literature. The vast amount of scientific evidence for the Big Bang theory and an age of the universe of billions of years are stressed, and God is seen as using the long process of cosmological history to further demonstrate his glory. The scientific model of the Big Bang is therefore to be held together with the theological truth that the whole creation owes its existence to God. Both are needed fully to understand its origin.

There is real diversity on this issue among believers equally committed to the authority of the Bible. There are scientific arguments to be debated, such as the age of the universe, but the issue is one primarily of biblical interpretation. That is, are the early chapters of Genesis meant to be a scientific history of the universe or is their purpose primarily theological? Here apologetics, as always, has to show integrity to our experience of God's world and to the most faithful interpretation of God's Word.

An absence of God?

In recent years, another aspect of apologetics within the area of cosmology has been highlighted. The popularity of Stephen Hawking's *A Brief History of Time* has raised questions to a wider audience about whether science rules out a Creator God.

Hawking has suggested a possible solution to a fundamental problem with the Big Bang, that of 'what happened at the first moment?' Cosmology uses its knowledge of the physical laws to reconstruct a model of what happened in the past. In this it has been extremely successful with our current models describing the universe well back to a time when it was only 10^{-43} second old. At that point current theories break down, due to an inconsistency between general relativity and quantum theory, and therefore a description of the initial conditions of the expansion of the universe is beyond our reach. If science is unable to describe the initial moments of the universe, is this where God comes in?

What Hawking does is to suggest a possible way of uniting quantum theory and gravity (the realm of general relativity) to describe the beginning of the universe. One of the results of this is that he describes how the blue touch paper of the Big Bang lights itself. Hawking is saying that the universe does have a beginning, but it does not need a cause, for Hawking's universe emerges from a fluctuation in a quantum field. No cause as such is necessary.

There are many scientific difficulties with Hawking's theory, and it is not widely accepted. There are other proposals on how to deal with the problem of the laws breaking down. In addition, Hawking actually does not have a full theory; he makes his suggestions on the basis of this is what the theory would look like if he had a full theory. Further, it is difficult to know whether quantum theory can be legitimately applied to the whole universe.

Yet it raises some important theological questions. If Hawking is right, does God become redundant? Is Carl *Sagan right to describe Hawking's book as a book about the 'absence of God'? We need to be clear that Hawking questions the cosmological argument in temporal form. The universe may have a finite age, but it does not follow that one can use a cause/effect argument on the universe to prove a Creator God. This is to be welcomed, for such an attempt to prove God runs into two major problems, the 'god of the gaps' and deism.

The 'god of the gaps' is the temptation that if science has a gap in it then insert God as the explanation. However, as scientific knowledge expanded, the gaps became smaller and smaller and God was pushed out into irrelevancy. The first moment of the universe remains for some as the last big gap, but the God of the Bible does not shelter in gaps. This 'god of the gaps' happens because of the mistake of confusing different types of explanation. Science and *theology can give different but compatible explanations of the same thing. Some atheists, such as the biologist Richard Dawkins, believe that once you have a scientific explanation then that is all you need. Some Christians believe that there are some things in the natural world that science should not explore because they are 'God's work'. Both are wrong. The Bible understands that the whole universe is the result of God's working. He is at much at work at the first 10^{-43} second as at any other time. A scientific description of that moment in time does not invalidate it as being just as much the activity of God as any other event.

Furthermore, such an attempt to prove the existence of God often leads to a picture of God closer to deism than the Bible. Deism is the belief in a god who set the universe off and then went away to have nothing more to do with it and is incompatible with the revelation of God in the Bible. Creation is not a single initial act, but the bringing into being and moment by moment keeping in being of the whole universe (Col. 1:15–17; Heb. 1:3).

Hawking questions a deistic god of the gaps. The biblical understanding of the Creator God is very different, and so Christians need not feel threatened by scientific progress in cosmology.

Pointers to God?

At the same time, such progress in understanding the origin of the universe has raised questions which science itself cannot answer. In this there are opportunities for more constructive Christian apologetics.

Hawking is searching for 'a theory of everything', that is, a theory which explains how the universe develops with time and its initial conditions. Such a theory, if possible, would not explain everything about science. For example, weather forecasting is based on chaotic systems which have virtually nothing to do with the Big Bang. More importantly, a theory of everything leaves a number of other fundamental questions about the universe unanswered. Science is successful because it limits its range of questions. There are many other questions left, questions the Christian apologist might ask.

a. Why the universe?

Hawking himself is quite clear that although his quantum gravity may explain how the universe came into being, it does not explain why. The philosopher *Leibniz asked why is there something rather than nothing? This is not to resurrect the first cause argument, it is to recognize that the purpose and meaning of the universe lie beyond science. The Christian will argue that we find a natural answer in a personal God

b. Where do the scientific laws themselves come from?

If the universe emerges as a quantum fluctuation, we need to ask where quantum theory itself comes from? Where does the pattern of the world come from and how is it maintained? This is not a 'god of the gaps' argument as science itself assumes these laws in order to work. There is a long tradition stretching back to *Newton, who saw the laws of the universe as work of the divine lawgiver. Kepler was 'carried away by unutterable rapture' as the correlation between orbital periods and mean diameters (which showed that the planets moved in elliptical orbits) was disclosed. Once again the Christian will argue the Creator God is the natural answer.

c. Why is the universe intelligible?

Einstein once said that the most incomprehensible thing about the universe is that it is comprehensible. Yet why should this be the case, that the mathematics of our minds resonates with the mathematics of the universe. Some writers, including the former physicist John Polkinghorne, suggest that the natural answer is that there exists a Creator God who is the basis of the order in the universe and the ability of our minds to understand it.

d. What is our significance in the universe?

Recently, there has been a growing appreciation of the anthropic fruitfulness of the universe, i.e. its structure seems to be sensitively tuned to the existence of life. This can be seen in many examples such as the relative strength of the fundamental forces. If they were only slightly different then carbon-based life would not exist in the universe. This has led a number of high profile scientists such as Paul Davies or Sir Fred Hoyle, who have no time for traditional Christian theism, to claim that, 'science offers a surer path to God than religion'.

Davies and Hoyle go too far, but it is fascinating that they find the anthropic arguments so compelling. These insights do not prove God but may point the way towards him. It illustrates a revival of natural *theology, not in the sense of logical proofs but in pointers towards God. This position is consistent with the wisdom literature and other parts of the Bible which encourage Christian thinkers to seek evidence of God in the universe as well as in the Scriptures (e.g. Ps. 19:1; Acts 14:7; 17:22–31; Rom. 1:19–20).

e. Is there a way to know the Creator God?

The astronomer Kepler wrote, 'There is nothing I want to find out and long to know with greater urgency than this. Can I find God, whom I can almost grasp with my own hands, in looking to the Universe, also in myself?'

The Christian apologist will respond to these questions by pointing to Jesus. They are questions which are raised by science but are unable to be answered by it. The physicist Sir Robert Boyd, commenting on whether Hawking's theory would show us the mind of God, wrote that the missing data in Hawking's analysis of the mind of God is the mind of one 'who made Himself of no reputation, Whose love is unconditional and whose Name is above every name'.

With that 'data' the Creator can be known.

Bibliography

J. D. Barrow and F. J. Tipler, *The Anthropic Cosmological Principle* (Oxford, 1986); P. Davies, *God and the New Physics* (Harmondsworth, 1983); S. W. Hawking, *A Brief History of Time* (London, 1988); M. A. Jeeves and R. J. Berry, *Science, Life and Christian Belief* (Leicester, 1998); E. Lucas, *Can We Believe in Genesis Today?* (Leicester, 2001); H. M. Morris and G. E. Parker, *What is Creation Science?* (San Diego, 1982); R. L. Numbers, *The Creationists: The Evolution of Scientific Creationism* (New York, 1992); J. C. Polkinghorne, *Belief in God in an Age of Science* (Yale, 1998); M. Rees, *Just Six Numbers: The Deep Forces that Shape the Universe* (London, 2000); H. Ross, *Beyond the Cosmos* (Colorado Springs, 1999); D. Wilkinson, *God, Time and Stephen Hawking* (Crowborough, 2001).

D. WILKINSON

COUPLAND, DOUGLAS

Douglas Coupland (b. 1961) grew up in Vancouver, Canada, where he continues to reside. Though trained in art and design and a successful sculptor, it is as a writer that he has come to prominence. His first book, the best selling *Generation X: Tales for an Accelerated Culture* (New York, 1991), is a humorous but moving analysis of post-Boomer society. It defined a new demographic and launched his career as a trenchant chronicler of late twentieth-century hyper-modern *culture. Whilst rejecting the role of 'gen-X spokesman', he has nonetheless published a further seven, highly imaginative works of fiction that brilliantly survey our postmodern era. His success arises from his ability to simultaneously deconstruct the superficiality of hi-tech, consumer culture and yet also sympathetically explore the angst of the disaffected and 'denarrated', who find no answers to their deepest longings. The autobiographical nature of his writings lends authenticity, whilst his determination never to abandon hope and to wrestle his readers out of despair is always inspiring.

He has much to offer the Christian apologist. First, his sociological and psychological insights are acute and dramatically expose the bankruptcy of modern/postmodern life and the despair and alienation of those trying to survive it. Secondly, his writings can form the first phase of a Christian apologetic, namely, drawing out the logical consequences of the non-Christian world-view. In Coupland's world, 'life after God' has proved tragically hollow. Thirdly, in his attempts to offer grounds for hope, Coupland finds some intriguing points of connection with this generation. Recurrent themes of loneliness and death, love and rebirth suggest the few remaining shared experiences and yearnings of our fragmented culture. Finally, Coupland winsomely points his audience in the right direction. He avoids the temptation to give in to postmodern *nihilism or to clutch at *New Age mysticism. Rather, in *Life after God* (New York, 1994) he declares, 'My secret is that I need God' (p. 359), and in *Girlfriend in a Coma* (Toronto, 1998) he pleads with his readers to awaken from apathy, 'There *is* the truth. It does exist ... And you're going to have to holler for it, steal for it, beg for it' (p. 268). In his recent *Hey Nostradamus!* (New York, 2003) we find his clearest exploration yet of the possibilities of finding transcendent meaning in theistic religion. Douglas Coupland may not be a prophet of his times, but he has given the Christian community some surprisingly good pre-evangelistic pointers.

Bibliography

D. Coupland, *Generation X: Tales for an Accelerated Culture* (New York, 1991); *Life After God* (New York, 1994); *Girlfriend in a Coma* (Toronto, 1998); *Hey Nostradamus!* (New York, 2003).

J. McGregor

COURSE IN MIRACLES, A

A Course in Miracles consists of almost 1,300 pages of print in three volumes. It began life in the mid-1960s and was published in 1976, following a seven-year maturation period. It consists of the text, a student workbook, which has 365 lessons, and a manual for teachers. Not without stern criticism by Christians and non-Christians alike as being contradictory and self-defeating, the Course continues to enjoy widespread popularity. It boasts of having no human author, and therefore no author appears in the book, only the publisher, the Foundation for Inner Peace. Allegedly, the content came by means of an inner dictation by a 'Voice' (claimed to be Jesus Christ) over a seven-year period.

The recipient of this episodic seven-year dictation (known as channeling) was Helen Schucman, a self-proclaimed atheist and professor of medical psychology at Columbia University's College of Physicians and Surgeons in New York City. At a point of difficulty in her professional relationship with colleague William Thetford, she admitted to him that she was periodically experiencing vivid mental images. He encouraged her to give serious attention to her symbolic dreams, and she began writing down the messages that she received. These would then be typed up by Thetford.

Offered as a course in 'mind training', *A Course in Miracles* combines *psychology, Eastern religions (primarily *Hinduism and *Buddhism) and some Christian terminology. The intent of the Course is to correct the common distorted view of reality in order to bring healing to the brokenness of humanity by teaching correct thinking. According to the Course, all *reality is one, and therefore, one person's healing contributes to the healing of everyone.

Although much of the language of the Course appears Christian, substantively there is little, if anything, that corresponds to historic Christianity. In fact, the Course 'is clearly intended not as a restatement, but as a purification, of traditional Christianity' (R. Perry, p. 6). The purification, however, is actually a redefinition of Christianity. The Course teaches that traditional Christianity has made guilt a part of sin, thus distorting God and limiting inner healing, in that it has 'reinforced our limitations and made God a punisher, instead of a lover' (Perry, p. 6). Accordingly, sin is merely a faulty view of reality, namely that man is limited and lacking which keeps him from realizing his potential. Guilt is negative and, therefore, is not a part of reality. If one thinks in terms of condemnation, it is a dream, and one must be freed from that belief orientation in order to be healed. If one thinks condemnation and fear, one is not really thinking at all. In fact, one is delusional and 'delusional ideas are not real thoughts, although you can believe in them. But you are wrong. The function of thought comes from God and is in God.'

Reality (which the Course calls *Heaven) is pure oneness. 'There are no bodies, no different places, and no separate moments of time. There is only an infinite expanse of unified awareness. In Heaven our seemingly separate identities mingle and merge, uniting to form a single universal Self, which the Course calls Christ' (Perry, p. 21). All that is negative (condemnation and attack) is illusion and includes sickness, hate, pain and guilt. When people see that this is not reality, or love, then they can give up these things because they know they have no value. At that moment, they have no life because the person puts them out of their mind. They only have life when the person gives them life by giving in to the illusion. Sickness is simply an illusion brought about by one's wrong thinking.

Furthermore, the concept of miracle in the Course is not that of Christian teaching, but is couched in psychological nuances where it means a 'divine intervention in our minds which heals our thought-patterns' (Perry, p. 7). A miracle is that which shortens the time involved in the mental healing process. Death and sickness are creations of wrong thinking and can be abolished by correct thinking. The resurrection does not refer to Christ's body being raised from the dead. In fact, it has nothing to do with the body, but rather it is the 'awakening' to the fact we are Sons of God and lack nothing.

According to the Course, *hell is only part of the dream humans have made by focusing on this world, which is merely an illusion. This world is not real because it is that which divides and condemns. Time and space are illusions that divide, they do not unite, and whatever divides is not real. Separation from God is not in the Christian sense of someone being a sinner by transgressing the law of God, but rather it is feeling that one has of lacking something. Any sense of lack is an illusion because each person is a child of God and has everything because each person is 'part of God' (*A Course*, p. 112). When a person realizes this, healing begins and death and negativity disappear.

The purpose of the Course is ostensibly to help people think properly by rejecting all thoughts of disunity and condemnation while facilitating the process of learning their true potential as part of God, for this is all that is real.

Bibliography

P. Miller, *The Complete Story of the Course* (Berkeley, 1997); N. A., *A Course in Miracles* (Glen Allen, 2nd edn, 1976); R. Perry, *An Introduction to a Course in Miracles* (Anaheim, 1987); P. Skutch, *Journey without Distance* (Berkeley and Toronto, 1984).

B. A. LITTLE

CREATION, CREATIONISM, see ORIGINS, THEORIES OF

CREDO QUIA ABSURDUM, see TERTULLIAN
CREDO UT INTELLIGAM, see ANSELM

CREEDS

'Creed' (Lat. *credo*, 'I believe') is the name generally given to short formulaic statements of Christian belief. There have been many creeds in the history of the church, of which three have achieved a semi-canonical status. These are the Apostles' Creed, the Nicene Creed and the Athanasian Creed, all of which have been used for many centuries in public worship. At one time it was believed that these creeds were composed respectively by the apostles, the fathers of the first council of Nicaea (325) and Athanasius of Alexandria (c. 296–373), but it is now universally accepted that this is not the case. It seems that the titles were originally given to the creeds because churchmen of a later generation thought that the texts represented what those people had stood for, and it was their heritage which they wanted to appropriate.

The Apostles' Creed

By far the oldest of the three classical creeds is the Apostles' Creed, though the text as we now have it is the most recent of the three, dating only from the early eighth century. However, it is possible to trace earlier versions of this creed right back to the second century, when a formulaic 'rule of faith' remarkably similar in structure to the later creed is already well attested. It is possible, though not certain, that this creed originated in a baptismal rite, where questions were asked of the candidates and they were expected to reply with their confession of faith, expressed according to a recognized pattern, though not yet fixed in a set form of words. *Tertullian (c. 200) gives us two different versions of the formula, claiming that both are the unalterable rule of faith! He was obviously thinking of the content rather than the wording, and this somewhat loose way of thinking continued for many centuries. In the end, the fixed form which we have today seems to have been adopted by accident as much as by design, being popularized by Charlemagne's theologians and thus transmitted to posterity.

The Apostles' Creed originated either at Rome or in the Latin-speaking church, and there are no real equivalents to it in the Greek world. It was always trinitarian in shape, a fact which may reflect a baptismal origin. Later, a fourth section was added, containing miscellaneous statements of doctrine which are not particularly connected either to one person of the *Trinity or to each other.

The first article deals with the Father, and has developed very little over time. It proclaims that he is the Almighty, the maker of heaven and earth, a statement which reflects second-century anti-Gnostic controversies. The Gnostics tended to believe that the world was created by an inferior deity called the Demiurge rather than by the Father of *Jesus Christ, and it was to counter this error that the first article was devised. Its primitive origin and conservative character can be seen from the fact that the word 'maker' has not been replaced by 'creator', despite the later controversy over whether God made the world out of something already existing or created it out of nothing. It is also noteworthy that the clause was never extended to cover the other two persons, even though the Arian controversy made it desirable to state that they too were almighty and participated fully in the work of creation.

The second article deals with the Son, and is by far the longest of the original three. It is the article which has developed most in the course of time, as the great Christological controversies of the fourth and fifth centuries made it necessary to add further statements and qualifications to the original confession of Christ's divinity. The article follows the historical pattern of Christ's ministry, beginning with his eternal generation in heaven, continuing through the incarnation and concentrating on his crucifixion, resurrection and ascension. These events were chosen because they illustrate the essential theological points that the incarnate Son was fully God and fully man, that he lived and died an authentically human life and death, which can be situated in historical time ('under Pontius Pilate'), and that by his life, death and resurrection he brought God's salvation to human believers. Furthermore, the creed emphasizes that his work is not over; now that he has ascended into heaven, he is seated at God's right hand (i.e. ruling the universe) and that one day he will come back to judge the living and the dead.

The third article of the creed is devoted to the *Holy Spirit and is the least developed of all, again reflecting its early origin. It was not until the fourth century that theologians turned their minds to the Holy Spirit as a distinct person of the Trinity, although he had been part of the confession of faith from the beginning. By that time, this creed had reached a stage of fixity which precluded its adopting this pneumatology, and so it remains extremely reticent on this point.

The final article consists of a miscellaneous set of statements which reflect the controversies of the post-Nicene period. The unity and spiritual character of the church was an issue raised by the Donatists, who adopted a sectarian mentality and, in particular, refused to accept penitent backsliders back into the fellowship of the church. This was because they were unable to accept the possibility that sins committed after baptism might be forgiven, and so belief in the forgiveness of sins was duly added to the creed. The resurrection of the flesh was another issue caused by lingering Platonic elements, which refused to believe that matter could be saved. (The English translation dates from 1542 and puts 'body' instead of 'flesh', which is theologically correct but historically inaccurate.) Finally, belief in eternal life was added, apparently in order to counter the Neoplatonic view that the world would eventually be destroyed in a great conflagration and re-created in an entirely new form, unrelated to our present existence.

Today, the Apostles' Creed is widely used in both Protestant and Roman Catholic churches, where it often forms part of public worship. It is short enough to form the basis for many spiritual meditations and sermon series, with the result that the devotional literature linked to it is enormous and constantly growing.

The Nicene Creed

The second of the three great creeds is the one which is most easily pinned down to its historical context. The first council of Nicaea (325) was called to settle the Arian dispute concerning the nature of Christ's divinity, and it produced a statement of faith setting out the main lines of what it believed was the traditional (and anti-Arian) orthodoxy. However, we now know that this creed is not the one which we use today. The text of our Nicene Creed was officially proclaimed at the council of Chalcedon (451), where it was attributed to the Nicene fathers, though most likely it was composed at or shortly after the first council of Constantinople in 381. That would account for the presence of a long article on the Holy Spirit which owes much to the *theology of Basil of Caesarea (329–79), and most now agree that it cannot be any earlier than this. However, it is not certain that the creed took its final form in 381, and perhaps it was not fixed in its present shape until 451. Even so, the time span is much shorter than that for the Apostles' Creed and the parameters of dating are much clearer.

The Nicene Creed originated in the Greek church, where it remains the only one of the three creeds to find general acceptance and liturgical use. It is now widely adopted in ecumenical circles as the most universal statement of Christian belief, though it remains somewhat less popular in the West than the Apostles' Creed. An important distinguishing feature of it is the use of the plural 'we believe' instead of the singular (as in the Apostles' Creed). This reflects the fact that it originated in a conciliar decision and not in an individual confession of faith such as a baptismal declaration. Modern theologians have sometimes made a great deal of this 'collective' aspect of the creed, and some have even suggested that it reflects a basic difference between Eastern (Greek) and Western (Latin) theology. This is going too far, however, and in most respects the Nicene Creed reflects the same confessional tradition as the Apostles' Creed.

The Nicene Creed contains some specifically anti-Arian statements, such as that the Son is eternally begotten of the Father, and that he is also consubstantial (*homoousios*) with him. But the most striking difference between it and the Apostles' Creed is in the article on the Holy Spirit, where the Nicene text contains a clearly developed pneumatology. This was the result of a series of post-Nicene controversies over the exact status of the Spirit, which were not resolved until 381. Nowadays, the most significant aspect of this article is the ongoing controversy which surrounds the relationship of the Spirit to the other persons of the Godhead. In the original version, the text reads 'who proceeds from the Father', but in sixth-century Spain the anti-Arians added the clause 'and the Son' (*filioque*) to emphasize the complete equality of the first two persons of the Trinity. This addition was canonized in the West by Charlemagne's theologians, but it was not finally accepted at Rome until about 1014. By then it had been noticed in the East and objected to, not only as an unwarranted

addition to the theoretically unalterable text, but (more significantly) as a theological error. A serious controversy over it erupted in the thirteenth century which has never been resolved, despite periodic attempts to find a compromise formula. Today, modern ecumenists prefer the original version, minus the reference to the Son, though most Western churches have been reluctant to drop it, because it would remove a clear statement of the relationship between the Son and the Spirit and leave nothing in its place.

The Athanasian Creed

This is the last, longest and most controversial of the three major creeds. It was probably composed in early sixth-century Gaul (France) and reflects the developed trinitarian theology of *Augustine of Hippo (354–430). There is no connection with the historical *Athanasius, whose name seems to have been adopted because Athanasius was famous as the standard bearer of Nicene orthodoxy. In structure, the Athanasian Creed is very different from either the Apostles' or the Nicene Creeds, and its original purpose seems to have been catechetical rather than confessional in the usual sense. It is very repetitive and clearly designed for memorization, but it is also systematically structured and gives a more complete trinitarian theology than any comparable text. Its use for liturgical purposes has been limited, but it is found in the Anglican *Book of Common Prayer* and may still be recited on special occasions. However, it is not accepted by the Eastern churches, which object to certain aspects of its theology as well as to its false claim to an Athanasian origin.

The creed opens and closes with the notorious 'damnatory clauses', which consign those who refuse to accept its teaching to eternal death. Such illiberalism has been the object of constant attack since the eighteenth century, and is largely responsible for the disappearance of the creed from general use. But, unpleasant as those clauses undoubtedly are, they are consistent with the orthodox Christian belief that heresy is a sin which cuts those who hold it off from the living God.

The creed is divided into roughly equal halves, the first of which is an essay in trinitarianism. The text starts with the premise that there are three persons in one God and goes on to explain what this means in detail. The divine attributes (e.g. infinity, eternity) are shared equally by all three persons, but in such a way that there is only one infinity and one eternity. It then goes on to attribute the names of God (Almighty, Lord, God) to all three persons equally, but once again, in such a way that there can be only one Almighty Lord and God. This belief, says the creed, is imposed on us by the witness of the Scriptures, where the OT (referred to as 'the catholic religion') insists on a strict *monotheism and the NT (called 'the Christian verity') tells us that Father, Son and Holy Spirit are all equally God.

The creed then goes on to explain how the persons are to be distinguished from one another. The Father is unbegotten and uncreated, whereas the Son is begotten, though not created. The Holy Spirit is both unbegotten and uncreated, but he proceeds from the other two – an affirmation of the *filioque* doctrine which makes it clear that Athanasius could not have been its author.

The second half of the creed is Christological and much more like what can be found in the other creeds. The biggest difference is the expanded discussion of the last judgment at Christ's second coming, where it is stated that everyone will rise again and give account of themselves, with the result that those who have done good will be granted eternal life, whereas those who have not will be consigned to eternal hellfire. To modern ears this sounds suspiciously like a doctrine of salvation by works, but the text was composed long before there was any controversy over justification by faith, and it is anachronistic to read it in this way. The Athanasian Creed is composed in a style which is unfamiliar to most people today, but it remains one of the best short statements of orthodox Christian theology and deserves to be more widely known than it presently is.

The creeds today

After a strong tendency, associated with nineteenth-century liberalism, to downplay the importance of the ancient creeds in the life of the church, a renewal of interest in them began in the second half of the twentieth century. This renewal was connected both with the influence of Karl *Barth's *neo-orthodoxy and with the liturgical movement, which advocated the expanded use of the Apostles' and Nicene Creeds in public worship. The Nicene Creed has also benefitted from the ecumenical movement, where it is considered to be the most widely accepted statement of Christian

belief. In the modern church, the creeds continue to provide a brief but comprehensive framework for basic theology. Their trinitarian structure has helped to safeguard the importance of that doctrine, which has also undergone a renaissance in recent years. The balanced emphasis on significant moments in the life of Christ serves as a reminder of the doctrinal importance of his earthly mission and offers a context in which the NT can be read and interpreted. Perhaps most importantly of all, the creeds are succinct enough to be learned by heart, and thus they offer young Christians an excellent introduction to the riches of their faith. In this sense, they continue to fulfil the task for which they were originally designed, and provide a living witness to the communion of the saints of every age.

Bibliography

G. L. Bray, *Creeds, Councils and Christ* (Leicester, 1984); J. N. D. Kelly, *Early Christian Creeds* (London, 1972); *The Athanasian Creed* (London, 1964).

G. L. BRAY

CRITICAL REALISM

While the term 'critical realism' has been used for a variety of epistemologies, they all share two or three common characteristics. Realism affirms that knowledge and belief are transitive: they have objects whose *reality is not dependent on being known or believed. This is in contrast to the phenomenalist claim that all we can know is appearances, and the anti-realist view that theories are subjective constructs without truth-value. Thus, ethical realism opposes the anti-realism of purely subjectivist views of *ethics, alethic realism affirms the objectivity of *truth, and theological realism insists that God is indeed what we confess, e.g. in the Apostles' Creed. But critical realism, in contrast to naive realism, recognizes that things are not always as they appear, and that subjective as well as objective factors affect what we take to be the case. Critical realism avoids settling for unexamined preconceptions as well as for anti-realist scepticism, and it therefore provides a viable alternative to the postmodern *relativism which refuses to acknowledge that truth (as distinct from our knowledge claims) is objective and unchanging.

A major influence in the development of critical realism was the commonsense realism of Thomas *Reid, the eighteenth-century Scottish philosopher. Reid rejected John *Locke's theory of ideas, according to which we have no direct knowledge of extramental objects but only of our own ideas, from which we then have to infer the existence of any external cause. David *Hume had added that causal inferences are logically impossible and so scepticism results. Reid, however, denied that causal arguments are necessary, because our physical senses afford direct awareness of objects, and our God-given belief-forming dispositions give rise to natural beliefs about external things. This 'direct realism' is echoed in twentieth-century realisms.

American critical realism

The first three decades of the twentieth century saw a surge of realist opposition to the idealist philosophies that had dominated late nineteenth-century thought in Britain and America. One of the first was American 'new realism', claiming that causal stimuli produce a direct awareness of physical objects, independently of any intervening ideas. This made it difficult to explain illusion, preceptual error and perceptual relativity. Why do unchanging objects appear differently to different observers or from different perspectives. If mental processes do not affect how things appear, then the relativity must be objectively real, and we should never have erroneous ideas. But if the mind harbours these representations, then we are back to Locke and Hume. This dilemma aroused a group of philosophers calling themselves 'critical realists', following the title of a book published in 1916 by one of their number, Roy Wood Sellars. They emphasized the distinction between knowing that something exists and knowing what it is. Its existence may indeed be directly given by causal stimuli, but not what it is, its essence. The group differed among themselves on this latter question: George Santayana invoked a mental intuition of sense qualities, while others talked of a causal inference in ways still reminiscent of John Locke. But Sellars rejected any curtain of ideas between the knower and the known: it is not just a sense impression that appears in the consciousness, but the object itself appears by means of the sense experience. We interpret such data in the light of past experience and refer the resulting construal

also to the object. Recognizing the role of past experience and the preconceptions it produces, he provides a subjective locus for erroneous ideas but not for the actual appearances. This does not imply an immaterial mind, for Sellars was a materialist, in contrast to Reid with his account of God-given cognitive capacities. This difference is a further example of preconceptions influencing how we construe our experience.

Somewhat different from the American development is the view of British philosopher G. Dawes Hicks, who also called his position 'critical realism'. Like Reid, his contemporary G. E. Moore and the Americans, he insists on starting philosophically where we start in ordinary life, with commonsense belief in the independent existence of physical objects. But his account of the perceptual process is more like *Hegel's than Moore's or Bertrand *Russell's. Rather than regarding perception as constructing objects from sense data, Hicks treats it as a discriminatory process. Physical organisms aroused by their feelings first distinguish what is external to themselves from what is internal, then they distinguish particular objects, and only then do they normally give attention to particular sense qualities. As in other critical realisms, the knower is organically involved with reality, and this is what assures us that things really exist.

The influence of American critical realism was extensive and ongoing. A. N. *Whitehead, for instance, showed Sellars' influence when he linked perception as the 'presentational immediacy' of our ideas to the 'causal efficacy' initiating an experience, by means of 'perception in the mode of symbolic reference'. With the decline of *logical positivism in the 1950s, it became customary to speak of perception in terms of things 'appearing as . . .', indicating a distinction between 'that' and 'what', and a lack of finality about 'what'. Knowing that an object really exists is in some way mediated by what appears, even though appearances sometimes deceive. But it was Sellars' own son, Wilfred Sellars, who developed critical realism in the more rigorous and detailed fashion analytic philosophy required. More recently realists have drawn on *pragmatism in making their case.

The current debate over realism and antirealism has moved from *sense perception to the philosophy of *science, moral philosophy and philosophy of religion. Of particular interest for apologetics is the 'Reformed *epistemology' developed by Alvin Plantinga. Drawing on Thomas Reid, he claims that pertinent experiences lead properly functioning God-given minds to believe, for example, that God really exists, and that such beliefs may have proper warrant. Similarily, William Alston argues in *Perceiving God* (Ithaca and London, 1991) that direct realism is valid not only for sense perception but also for certain kinds of *religious experience. This is not an argument for God's existence, he notes, although his existence is entailed by a realist interpretation of such experiences. Theories of perception also continue to play a part in the philosophy of mind. In *The Evolution of Soul* (Oxford, 1986), Richard Swinburne begins his argument with a consideration of sensations as mental events, not just brain events. Other factors also are invoked, of course, but realistic perception is one of those taken to invalidate a materialistic view of the human person.

Critical realism in science

Until the mid-twentieth century, scientific theories were commonly thought to be objective statements about general empirical laws. But work in the history and sociology of science, most notably Thomas Kuhn's *Structure of Scientific Revolutions* (Chicago, 1962), explored the influence of sociological and other human factors, precipitating fresh disputes about scientific realism and anti-realism. Realists like Ernan McMullin argued that the telling difference between the natural sciences and other societal developments lies in their ongoing testing of theories and their long-term success, while Wilfred Sellars pointed out that good reasons for holding a theory are also good reasons for thinking the entities it postulates exist. This provisional and qualified realism about scientific theories and models, Arthur Peacocke appropriately calls 'critical realism'. It plainly bears on the relationship of religion to science, and raises similar questions about theological theories.

The term 'critical realism' is used in a markedly different way for Roy Bhaskar's alternative to the positivist and the hermeneutical approaches in the human sciences. Positivists want to find general empirical laws in social as well as natural sciences, while the hermeneuticals oppose them because they see radical differences between human and natural science. With Kant's transcendental or critical

*idealism in mind, Bhaskar asks how it is possible for experimental science to discover general laws: he responds that it presupposes a closed system, where particulars are isolated for close study and variables can be effectively controlled. But in the human sciences an open system prevails, where controlled experiments are not as determinative, and actions need to be individually interpreted rather than being subsumed under causal laws. Unlike Kant, however, Bhaskar is a realist, a critical realist who distinguishes between the observable and the actual course of events. Since humans are rooted in the physico-chemical, general laws may still capture general tendencies; but humans are not reducible to the physical-chemical, and so neither the positivist nor the hermeneutical method alone is sufficient. This should be kept in mind in relating the sciences to Christian beliefs about the person and society.

Bibliography

B. Bhaskar, *Reclaiming Reality* (London, 1989); D. Drake (ed.), *Essays in Critical Realism* (New York and London, 1920); A. Peacocke, *Intimations of Reality: Critical Realism in Science and Religion* (Notre Dame, 1984); R. W. Sellars, *The Philosophy of Physical Realism* (New York and London, 1932).

A. F. HOLMES

CRITICISM, see BIBLICAL CRITICISM

CULTURAL APOLOGETICS

Biblical reflection on human nature developed considerably over the centuries during which the original ideas were transmitted verbally, written down, gathered and edited. However, there is a thread running through the unfolding accounts which has relevance to our understanding of human *culture and biblical anthropology. Recent scholarship has validated this approach in a recovery of a biblical theology of covenant, the unfolding account of God's relationship with his people and their responsibilities to him. This is seen as the metanarrative ('big story') which holds the constituent stories together. Of course, the use of Scripture in discussions about culture is not without its problems. Christian realists believe that the Bible is an indispensable way-in to the story of Israel's interaction with God, to the historical figure of *Jesus Christ, and to the experience of the first disciples. We are thus concerned, in reading Scripture, not merely with the events, but with the powerful symbolic images which convey the significance of what happened. This is particularly the case in seeking to glean insight about a biblical understanding of the significance of culture formation.

Hebrew Scriptures

To understand biblical cultural anthropology and provide analytical tools for engaging in Christian cultural apologetics, we must begin with Genesis chapters 1 and 2. Humankind, male and female, is created in the image of God (Gen. 1:27), which means that God, the Father of humankind has imparted characteristics to the race which reflect his own divine nature. As God's vicegerents, they are to have dominion over the plant and animal kingdoms and to be accountable to God as stewards of his domain (1:26). His purpose is that humans may grow as fully as possible into his image in this life. Knowledge is part of that purpose, but limits are set. People have been created to live in harmony with their Maker, and yet this does not mean that they have immediate access to all knowledge. They must rely on God for their understanding of good and *evil. The tree of the knowledge of good and evil contains the only forbidden fruit, which probably signifies that moral knowledge or ethical discernment are not to be autonomous faculties in humankind. People are to know right from wrong as they are taught by God, and to receive the ability to apply their minds to moral problems. Death will ensue if they eat the forbidden fruit, and death means, in essence, separation from God. In other words, people will be de-humanized and will, to some extent, lose their innate moral sense, if they declare unilateral independence of God's will for them (2:9, 17). Ultimately, right and wrong must either be decided by human consensus or by *revelation from God. Either way, some absolute must be referred to in order to make sense of moral affirmations and decisions.

Humankind, according to the biblical account, was originally created as a race of workers and carers (Gen. 2:15) and observers and classifiers (2:20). Here we see the logical priority of *technology over *science as a cultural activity. Our fundamental vocation is to be good stewards of the environment in which we are set, and this knowledge arises out of our daily work. However, the story relates that people chose to disobey God and to seek autonomy rather than theonomy (3:1–9), and that had immediate effects on their knowing (3:10–11). The image of God in humankind was defaced, and human thinking and praxis were corrupted. Yet, in grace, the same God who pronounced judgment gave hope of deliverance (3:15). The fall of humankind into sin did not diminish our calling before God. The primordial paradise may have been lost, but humankind is still accountable for his or her stewardship.

Lynn White famously claimed that the Genesis 1 – 3 'myths' convey a specific set of values focused on the vocation of humankind to 'subdue the earth' (1:28) and that these values have precipitated the contemporary ecological crisis. White's conclusion was that, therefore, we must reject these myths and look for a more constructive source of meaning for creation. However, White's critics argue that he is too rigid in his interpretation of these stories, which can be understood in a quite different way. At any rate, we need to affirm the important place such myths can have in our understanding of the cultural mandate and its relationship to the environment. The crucial issue is White's interpretation of Gen. 1:28, 'God blessed them and said to them, "Be fruitful and increase in number; fill the earth and subdue it. Rule over the fish of the sea and the birds of the air and over every living creature that moves on the ground."' The Hebrew for 'have dominion' can mean 'to rule over' but it can also mean 'to take care of', and it is not necessary to interpret the text in the way White does. The sense of 'dominion' here is not of autonomous exploitation but of having responsibility for something which has been entrusted into one's care. However, while the story may not advocate ruthless exploitation of the environment, it has been misinterpreted by some to provide encouragement for such an approach. In addition, the call to stewardship of earth's resources, which is crucial to the cultural mandate, comes before the account of the fall of humankind into sin. Distortion of the original intention of humanity's dominion is the theological explanation for the kind of exploitation which White rightly condemns. The later stories in Genesis develop this metanarrative after the fall, and we see further evidence of the outworking of the cultural mandate. Adam's son Cain (whose name means 'metalsmith'), the murderer of his brother Abel, builds a 'city' (a village in modern terms) named after his own son Enoch (4:17). *Urbanization precedes nomadism historically as a cultural development, according to the biblical account. Several generations later, Lamech's three sons are noted as the originators of tent-making, animal husbandry (4:20) and portable musical instruments (4:21), all of which became key elements of pastoral-nomadic lifestyles. Yet their cousin Tubal-Cain was a maker of bronze and iron tools (4:22) for agriculture, hunting and construction, no doubt maintaining and developing the more settled domestic lifestyle of his famous forebear. So, from the earliest recorded times, culture is described as a complex phenomenon.

Even after further disaster in the flood, the remnant is commanded to be fruitful (9:1), and fruitfulness implies responsibility (9:5). That is expressed in agriculture (9:20), boat-building (10:5), weapon-making for hunting (10:9) and house-building (10:11). All these craft activities are expressions of humankind's cultural vocation, an outcome of God's image stamped on humanity. Yet the dark side of human nature is never far away, in the story of the Tower of Babel (11:1–9). The ziggurat is a well-known feature of ancient Mesopotamian architecture, often built with mud bricks and tar due to the scarcity of local stone. It is therefore a symbol of the abuse of the cultural mandate; the result of the ingenuity of humankind to cull materials and use them for their own idolatrous purposes of self-aggrandizement (11:4). Excavated inscriptions indicate that these towers were meant to serve as stairways to heaven. They had a purely religious significance, with no practical use apart from religious ritual. They were symbolic of the desire to usurp God's *authority, according to the biblical narrative. They were declarations of independence from the true God, yet expressions of underlying religious needs.

Human culture as described and delimited in the Hebrew Bible may, therefore, be an expression of the sinister side of human nature, yet it is not, by definition, a sinful activity. The cultural skills of craftsmen are exalted in Exod. 31:2–3, when Moses speaks of those who build the Tent of Meeting for the worship of God in the desert: 'See, I have chosen Bezalel ... and I have filled him with the Spirit of God,

with skill, ability and knowledge in all kinds of crafts'. Yet similar skills could be used for the casting of the golden calf (Exod. 32:1 – 33:6), another expression of rebellion. Human cultural-technical skills might glorify God or be used for idolatry. Much later, the prophet Isaiah was to bemoan this recurring failing, but it arose from his convictions about the incomparable *mystery and holiness of God: 'To whom, then, will you compare God? What image will you compare him to? As for an idol, a craftsman casts it, and a goldsmith overlays it with gold and fashions silver chains for it ... "To whom will you compare me? Or who is my equal?" says the Holy One' (Isa. 40:18–19, 25).

Again, cultural activity is seen at its best in the building of the temple under Solomon (1 Kgs 5 – 8), the culmination of which is the King's prayer of dedication (1 Kgs 8:22–61). This was not an attempt to limit God to a house made with human hands (8:27) but a reminder of God's call to be fully committed to his covenant with Israel (8:61). Solomon knew that if the episodes of Babel and the golden calf were repeated, the temple would provide no safe haven for idolatry. It is significant that the temple, as the focal point of the city of Jerusalem, became a symbol of lives lived as good stewards of the gifts of God. It was there that the people celebrated the results of their labours in the annual festivals. It was there that the rebuilding work had to begin after the exile. It was the temple which figured centrally in Ezekiel's vision of the restored people of God (Ezek. 40 – 44). The human skills which arise out of the cultural mandate were represented there. At the temple, the image of God in man as *homo faber* (humankind as tool-makers and users) is celebrated.

Greek New Testament

In the NT, the Greek word *eikon* is used to develop the idea of the image of God in humankind. The word is used in various ways. For example, in Luke 20:24, Jesus draws the disciples' attention to the image of the Roman emperor on a coin. Such an image is no more than a copy or a reflection which is something other than that which it represents. Yet, in Heb. 10:1, we find the writer using *eikon* differently: 'The law is only a shadow of the good things that are coming – not the realities [*eikon*] themselves', i.e. the *eikon* is the reality, the law but a foreshadowing. The law has, therefore, no substantial existence on its own.

Eikon implies the illumination of the inner core and essence of something. In this way, Paul says 'He [Christ] is the image [*eikon*] of the invisible God, the firstborn over all creation' (Col. 1:15). Christ is the *eikon* of the invisible God because he shares in God's real being and hence can be a manifestation of that being. Philip Hughes comments, 'We must understand that the incarnation of the Son is not the identification of us with him who is the Image but his identification with us who are made in the image ... Thus the Son, who is the Image, by becoming man became in the image, without ever ceasing to be the Image.'

Hughes goes on to suggest that the creation of humankind in the image of God is the vital bond between human beings and the Son of God, 'the archetypal Image in which man was formed'. What then are the hallmarks of this *eikon* in humankind? Hughes suggests six qualities of human existence: personality, spirituality, rationality, *morality, authority and creativity. Clearly, it is in this last area that human cultural activity finds its chief locus, although we must not isolate the faculty of creativity from other aspects of the *eikon*, nor should we imagine that cultural activity is anything other than a movement of humans in their wholeness as creatures.

Obviously, human creativity is not to be confused with the divine activity which it reflects. People cannot create something *ex nihilo*, but can bring into fresh relationship and combination only the resources they have at their disposal which are God's gifts. In addition, all people are not equally creative in this sense. Some are more gifted than others and some do not make good use of the gifts they have received. And, of course, our creativity has been marred by the fall, as have all the other faculties noted above. Fallenness affects human creativity because it is an abuse or deprivation of human nature as originally given by God. Evil becomes an actuality when we use our humanness in a manner contrary to its proper nature, suggests Hughes. This is demonstrated in our chronic inability to apply scientific discoveries and technological inventions consistently to the good of all humankind. So often, despite great advances in knowledge and innovatory applications, human complacency and greed have led to disastrous consequences, as we know only too well, for example, in the wake of the nuclear meltdown at Chernobyl, the leaking of toxic gases at Bhopal, the greenhouse effect on global warming, and ozone layer depletion causing ice to melt in the Antarctic. Despite that negative tendency in the race, there is no denigration of human cultural-technical expression in the NT. Paul used illustrations in his teaching which drew on various examples of craft and skill, from armour and weaponry (Eph. 6:10–18), to household articles (2 Tim. 2:20–21), building methods (1 Cor. 3:10–15), pottery (2 Cor. 4:7) and agricultural implements (2 Cor. 6:14). The skills of the builder were also used by Peter to illustrate the building of the Christian church (1 Pet. 1:4–10), and believers were called 'living stones', which was intended as a compliment! In the days before the advent of modern industrial machinery, the shaping and placing of stones was a highly skilled and greatly valued operation.

It is significant that the apostles more often used such practical analogies to apply their message, rather than other cultural vehicles such as poetry or philosophy, although there are some notable exceptions. Paul, the tentmaker and teacher, tended to be very critical of 'mere talkers' (Titus 1:10), yet he knew some of the writings of key indigenous prophets and poets and used his knowledge to good effect. For example, when writing to Titus in Crete, he quoted one of the local prophets (the poet Epimenides, c. 600 BC, who was accredited with having made accurate predictions of the future), who had alleged 'Cretans are always liars, evil brutes, lazy gluttons' (Titus 1:12). Paul apparently agreed with these sentiments, if a little tongue-in-cheek, being only too aware of the implications of such a self-defeating statement! He also referred to cultural sources in Acts 17:28 during his visit to Athens, when he quoted Epimenides again: 'In him [God] we live and move and have our being', and also Aratus (from Paul's native Cilicia, c. 300 BC), who said 'We are his offspring.' This time, it was a very serious and crucial part of his apologetic and evangelistic argument, but it was in a context where Paul was eager, first of all, to make other cultural connections. He spoke of the idolatrous statues which abounded in Athens, and Luke tells us that Paul engaged with the philosophers, who seemed very slow on the uptake despite the fact that they spent their time debating all the latest ideas. Paul had, however, taken careful note of many cultural artefacts which explained the underlying beliefs of his hearers, such as religious objects and inscriptions. Again, in his ethical exhortations in 1 Cor. 15:33, Paul quotes with approval the Greek poet and moralist Menander: 'Bad company corrupts good character'. From all this, as well as from his ongoing commitment to continue his trade as a tent-maker whenever that was advantageous to his mission, we can glean that the apostle Paul took the cultural apologetic task very seriously, as a practical aspect of his obedience to Christ and not merely as an intellectual exercise. He clearly demonstrates developed skills in Hellenistic analytic discourse in Rom. 5 – 8, concluding with the abstract affirmation of his conviction that nothing can separate us from the love of God (Rom. 8:38). Yet Paul can equally show an adeptness at Hebraic holistic thinking, as in 1 Cor. 3 – 4, which was written just a few years earlier, culminating in his key statement, 'The kingdom of God is not a matter of talk but of power' (1 Cor. 4:20).

Another cultural analogy, used more than thirty years after Paul, in letters to key churches in the cities of Asia Minor is surely significant. It is found in the vision of the aged apostle John in his vision of the Holy City of God yet to come: 'I did not see a temple in the city, because the Lord God Almighty and the Lamb are its temple' (Rev. 21:22). This omission is despite the fact that many evidences of cultural expression and technical skill abound in the description of the Holy City, which shone with the glory of God. That glory is not a reprise of the original creation, but a transfiguration of the world as modelled by technological humankind, through faithful obedience to the cultural mandate (Rev. 21:26–27). Of course, the genre of this writing is apocalyptic, and we do well not to read too much into such references. However, in view of the way John's vision of the future is clearly not in tune with the contemporary Greek notions of *history as cyclical, it is surely significant that his vision was not of a return to Eden. According to the biblical vision, the cultural mandate, which leads, among other things, to technological formation and urban development, has eschatological implications. The biblical metanarrative of humankind's cultural quest is clearly world-affirming rather than world-denying. Indeed, the apostle Paul criticized some of those who responded to his initial preaching in Europe who were, shortly after their conversion, opting out of daily work because of their belief that Christ would soon return to earth (2 Thess. 3:10). Their disobedience to the cultural mandate, which implies the value of daily work in this age, and that the fruit of our labour will, in some way, be carried over into the age to come, was a failure to fulfil a key aspect of their humanness.

Human culture as opportunity and threat

Cultural activity is, therefore, to be viewed as both opportunity and threat, as an expression of human nature in God's image, yet subject to the weaknesses caused by the fall. That is because of the reality of human disobedience to God, which has distorted the original perfection of creation, according to the biblical account, on the basis of which we must refer to humans as being in God's image and as sinners at the same time. Humans are neither entirely sinners nor absolutely reflective of the divine nature. The *imago Dei* is neither the indestructible substance of the human being, nor can it be destroyed by human sin. It is to be expected that practitioners of realistic Christian cultural apologetics, therefore, will seek to engage, in a balanced way, with all kinds of culture-formative creativity, not as mere observers but as participants, who share in the human reality of reflecting God's nature and purposefulness, yet are flawed by human sin. Such balance, in the modern world, must reflect the biblical emphasis on craft, skill and praxis, rather than on what Paul calls 'mere talk'. Lesslie *Newbigin based his discussion of gospel and culture on his fundamental premise that 'There can never be a culture-free gospel. Yet the gospel, which is from beginning to the end embodied in culturally conditioned forms, calls into question all cultures, including the one in which it was originally embodied.' Twenty-first-century Christian cultural apologists must take seriously this crucial insight and ensure that their discussion of culture, in the current and future context, is not merely a reactionary intellectual exercise but radically related to contemporary ecumenical missional strategies. They must make connections with postmodern technological society and demonstrate the resultant implications for all kinds of human cultural tradition and the future of the natural and constructed environment, as well as of the entire human race.

Bibliography

G. R. Hunsberger, *Bearing the Witness of the Spirit – Lesslie Newbigin's Theology of Cultural Plurality* (Grand Rapids, 1998); H. R. Van Til, *The Calvinistic Concept of Culture* (Philadelphia, 1972); P. Hughes, *The True Image* (Leicester, 1989); G. Houston, *Virtual Morality: Christian Ethics in the Computer Age* (Leicester, 1998).

G. R. HOUSTON

CULTURE

The term 'culture' has been understood in a variety of ways. In popular usage it is frequently employed to signify specific activities in the realm of the *arts. So used, the word relates to activities which enhance human life through the exercise of the creative abilities of gifted individuals in *music, painting, writing and so on. This elitist definition of culture confines the concept to a particular segment of society and makes possible a distinction between the minority of people who shape culture and the rest who can be classified as mere consumers of culture, or even as 'uncultured' persons.

By contrast, 'culture' has come to be used in the social sciences in a far more comprehensive manner to refer to the beliefs, values, institutions and practices which people have in common within particular societies. This approach can be traced back to the 'father' of modern anthropology, E. B. Tylor, who in 1871 defined civilization as a complex whole including beliefs, customs, art, and other abilities and practices acquired by people as members of a society. According to this use of the term, there can be no such thing as 'uncultured' people, since culture is one of the defining marks of human identity and existence. Even so, agreement on the precise nature and function of human cultures has proved elusive, and by the middle of the twentieth century it was possible to identify almost three hundred definitions of 'culture' within the discipline of social anthropology.

Christian views of culture

The Christian understanding of culture has evolved from the Victorian tendency to classify societies as either 'civilized' or 'uncivilized' to one in which cultural *pluralism is widely recognized as valid and God-given. The earlier, bipolar understanding of cultures dominated Western thinking throughout the colonial era and involved the elevation of one particular civilization above all others. European and North American Christians, shaped by the centuries-long development of a Christendom model of the church and its mission, generally accepted the presuppositions of an age in which it seemed obvious that the peoples of the Western world possessed a historical destiny which required them to share the blessings of 'progress' with the rest of humankind. Such an understanding of culture resulted in an approach to non-Western traditions which seemed to require their *replacement* rather than their preservation or transformation. With the eclipse of cultural modernity and the recognition of the positive elements in other cultures, however, Christians have come to recognize, as the Lausanne Covenant puts it, that the church 'must not be identified with any particular culture, social or political system, or human ideology'.

Historically, the First World War marked a turning point in the understanding of human cultures. J. H. Oldham, who was a key figure at the Edinburgh Missionary Conference in 1910 and shared the confidence of those present concerning the imminent evangelization of the world, revealed a much chastened spirit when, six years later, he wrote that the barbarity witnessed on European soil now compelled Christians to draw a clear distinction between the church and 'what we have been accustomed to speak of as a Christian civilization'. In the following decades the accelerating growth in knowledge of other cultures further eroded the old presuppositions and led to what appeared to be the unavoidable conclusion that the dividing line between good and *evil runs, not between cultures, but rather through the middle of each of them.

For evangelicals, the Lausanne Congress in 1974 placed the issue of culture firmly on the theological and missiological agenda. Christian leaders from the southern hemisphere offered robust challenges to the assumption that the Western church and its missionary representatives had preached a largely culture-free version of the gospel, and insisted that their own cultures had been touched by the grace of God and had positive contributions to make both to the understanding of Christ and to the sum total of human knowledge. Four years later a consultation was convened explicitly to address the questions surrounding the relationship between Christianity and culture, and this resulted in a remarkably sophisticated statement known as the Willowbank Report. Few evangelicals were likely to challenge the conclusion that the gospel 'does not assume the superiority of any culture to another, but evaluates all cultures according to its own criteria of beauty and goodness'.

This was an important statement, since it affirmed the supreme *authority of the *revelation given through the life and work of *Jesus of Nazareth and recognized this as the basis on which all human cultures must be judged. An earlier classic discussion of this matter is found in H. Richard *Niebuhr's much read book, *Christ and Culture* (1951). This identifies a variety of responses in the history of the Christian movement to what the author calls the 'double wrestle' of the church: both with its Lord and with the culture 'with which it lives in symbiosis'. Niebuhr suggests that, historically, the Bible has been read as requiring, at one extreme, outright opposition to converts' cultures, and, at the other extreme, as justifying the co-option of Christ as the guarantor of a dominant civilization. In the one case there is an attempted flight from the world, while in the other the church surrenders to various forms of culture-religion involving ideologies at variance with the biblical revelation. Between these two poles, however, Niebuhr discovered a mediating position in which a non-revolutionary form of Christianity brings about the gradual transformation of cultures. This position, he argued, represents the mature wisdom of the mainstream Christian tradition on this question.

While Niebuhr's analysis remains the indispensable starting point for the modern discussion of the relationship between Christ and culture and retains real explanatory power, the question must be raised whether it takes the radical nature of human wickedness seriously enough and, by the same token, whether it gives proper recognition to the social and cultural implications of the confession that Jesus is Lord. In the earliest Christian centuries this confession did not strike people in the Greco-Roman world as a non-radical middle way; rather, it offered an alternative way of viewing the world and its peoples to that promoted by those with their hands on the levers of *power. At a point in history at which a culture dominated by economic values and corrosive of all truly humanistic ideals is spreading around the globe, such issues require urgent attention. Granted that the beauty and goodness to be found in all human cultures reflect the fact that all people are made in the image of God, what response is required from Christians when, as the result of the reality of the radical evil which is also part of the human condition, cultures degenerate and begin to manifest traits that can only be described as demonic?

The challenge of Western culture

Questions like these have led to a growing concern with the missiological challenge posed by modern Western culture. Lesslie *Newbigin consciously moved this discussion beyond the work of Niebuhr, who, he observed, had no actual experience of seeking to 'transmit the gospel from one culture to a radically different one'. While cross-cultural missionaries had recognized that serious cultural analysis, making critical use of anthropological insights, was a prerequisite for effective Christian witness throughout the southern hemisphere, this concern with culture was noticeable by its absence in the evangelism, theology and even the apologetics done in the Western world. By contrast, Newbigin insisted that the most urgent question confronting the church in the contemporary world concerned 'what would be involved in a genuinely missionary encounter between the gospel and this modern Western culture'. His own subsequent work pointed in the direction of an answer to that crucial question.

It is important to emphasize here that an apologetic which takes the cultural challenge seriously must go beyond the attempt to demonstrate the rational basis of faith. The countering of anti-theistic arguments is not unimportant, and such a task can claim apostolic example and precedent (2 Cor. 10:5). However, the establishing of the authority of Christ as Lord at the heart of culture requires something more than a mere change of ideas. This is precisely why Paul states that the demolition of 'strongholds' involves the use of spiritual weapons able to penetrate to the level of the human affections and *imagination where the battle also needs to be fought and won. In this conflict the sorts of cultural activity mentioned at the beginning of this article, involving the sanctified use of a whole range of artistic gifts, is crucially important in a context in which the Christian imagination is in urgent need of being purified and renewed.

Culture in historical perspective

If an awareness of the true significance of human culture can transform the approach to *theology and evangelism, it may also result in the opening up of quite new perspectives in the study of Christian *history. Andrew Walls has shown how the growth of the Christian movement across time and space can be viewed as a series of transitions through which the message of Christ has penetrated deeply into different cultural areas. In this process the faith has itself grown and developed as Christ has come to be viewed with lenses supplied by successive receptor cultures. Christianity has thus 'developed features which could only have originated in that culture whose impress it has taken within that phase'. Thus, in contrast to other religious traditions, Christianity does not sanctify a single culture, which then becomes the privileged vehicle of faith, but rather insists on the principle of the essential *translatability* of the gospel into ever new cultural and linguistic contexts. Consequently, unlike Islam, for example, Christians have no sacred language of revelation or devotion, and no single geographical centre as a focal point for worship and pilgrimage. Rather, Christ is known and addressed in a multitude of tongues, and the geographical and cultural centre of the movement is forever changing as the missionary Spirit brings new Christian heartlands into existence.

This insight has a number of important implications. In the first place, it suggests that the temptation we noted earlier, to treat one particular culture as providing the context in which the gospel is given definitive expression, actually strikes at the heart of the uniqueness of the Christian religion. This is not to deny that Christ enters into the very depths of those cultures where he is confessed as Lord and deals with the critical questions within them, but there can never be a 'Christian civilization', since at the very point at which people imagine that their wisdom, values and *language have proved capable of expressing the whole meaning of Christ, they are on the verge of losing touch with the deepest truths of the gospel.

Secondly, it is important to notice that, at the start of the twenty-first century, the Christian movement is passing through its latest major cultural transition as the long era of Western dominance comes to a conclusion and is being followed by a new age in which the normative form of the faith will be determined by the spiritual and theological insights emerging from the southern hemisphere, where the majority of believers are now to be found. Such transitions are never easy, especially for people who have only known Christ through the patterns and structures provided by a single, familiar culture. Yet no Christian who is aware of the multicultural vision of the future that runs through the Bible from Genesis to Revelation is likely to be afraid or offended by changes that move us ever closer to the gathering of people 'from every tribe and language and people and nation' before the throne of God.

The Bible and culture

It is possible here only to hint at the resources within Scripture for a Christian understanding of human culture. Clearly, the creation narratives in Genesis are of fundamental importance, not least in the anthropology they reveal, with its central affirmation that all people are made in the 'image of God'. This foundational claim and its development elsewhere in the Bible remain truly revolutionary and is pregnant with hope in cultural contexts in which the most basic questions concerning human identity and purpose go unanswered.

At the conclusion of the primal narratives of Genesis 1 – 11, the neglected 'Table of the Nations' demonstrates the divine concern for peoples in all their cultural and linguistic diversity. At a time when we are being warned of the probability of a 'clash of civilizations', Genesis 10 bears witness against the ethnocentrism that exalts one culture and denigrates all others. On the other hand, the very next chapter (ch. 11) graphically depicts the manner in which fallen humans can use culture as a vehicle for a declaration of independence from the Creator. The builders of Babel manifest a spirit that is, in Derek Kidner's phrase, 'timelessly characteristic' of the world as they 'crowd together to preserve their identity and control their fortunes'.

These contrasting but complementary perspectives on human culture resurface in the New Testament. In Athens, Paul finds himself on the cultural frontier between Jews and Greeks and encounters an ethnocentric dismissal of himself and his people which suggests that the spirit of 'Babel' was alive and well in the ancient world. Acts 17 has rightly been seen as the classic model of Christian apologetics in a cross-cultural setting. The apostle builds his Mars Hill sermon on the theological and anthropological foundations provided by the early Genesis narratives by denying the arrogant Greek claim to linguistic and cultural superiority, while, at the same time, insisting that a variety of cultures is willed by God and fulfils his purpose for the world.

By the end of the Bible, John of Patmos confronts yet another manifestation of the spirit of Babel in the shape of the massively impressive and powerful culture of the Roman Empire. However, the seer has caught a glimpse of another world and of a different kind of ruler, and, having seen reality from the perspective of the throne of God, he sees through the blasphemous claims of Rome and exposes the empire as simply the latest and most terrible manifestation of the human rebellion that goes back to those primal narratives in Genesis. The Apocalypse thus offers perhaps the most significant of all biblical models for the practice of apologetics in a world in thrall to hideous idols. On the one hand, in line with the biblical view of culture, it anticipates the time when the nations of the earth will, in final fulfilment of the ancient promise, bring their 'glory and honour' into the *heavenly city. But, on the other hand, Revelation makes clear that the path that leads to this great end will involve much suffering, so that faithful apologists, as well as prophets and preachers, must be ready for suffering and even for martyrdom. The drafters of the Lausanne Covenant did not exaggerate when they wrote: 'Because man is God's creature, some of his culture is rich in beauty and goodness. Because he has fallen, all of it is tainted with sin and some of it is demonic.'

Bibliography

L. Luzbetak, The Church and Cultures: New Perspectives in Missiological Anthropology (New York, 1990); L. Newbigin, Foolishness to the Greeks: The Gospel and Western Culture (Geneva: 1986); H. R. Niebuhr, Christ and Culture (New York, 1951); G. Stassen, D. M. Yeager and J. H. Yoder, Authentic Transformation: A New Vision of Christ and Culture (Nashville, 1996); A. F. Walls, The Cross-Cultural Process in Christian History (Edinburgh, 2002).

D. W. SMITH

CYBERSPACE

The term cyberspace typically refers to the whole gamut of computer-mediated modes of communication that are permeating and transforming society in numerous ways. The prefix 'cyber' comes from the discipline of cybernetics, the study of self-regulating systems (usually computer systems). Cyberspace is the space or place where humans and computers interact and connect in manifold ways. This neologism was coined by novelist William Gibson after reflecting on a teenager's immersion in a video game. The boy was situated both in literal space (before a screen) and in the virtual space of the computer game. In this sense, one 'enters' cyberspace mentally and imaginatively. To use concepts from philosopher Michael *Polanyi, one's 'focal awareness' is in cyberspace (whether it is a video game, chat room, web page or full-fledged virtual *reality) while one's 'subsidiary awareness' is on the keyboard, the controls or the computer screen. This parallels a surgeon's use of a probe to explore portions of the human body not otherwise accessible and visible, where the 'focal awareness' is on the region made visible by the probe and the 'subsidiary awareness' is on the moving of the probe itself.

The pertinence of cyberspace to apologetics is at least threefold. First, some cyberspace enthusiasts hail cyberspace as a realm of exhilarating freedom where one can leave the body and attain *transcendence through technological means. Some extol virtual-reality technologies as opening up an alternative world free of conventional *morality and the frustrating limits of physical objects (or 'meat space'). Although these technologies are still in their early stages, they allow (or will allow) percipients to immerse themselves in a simulated and convincing cyberspace environment to one degree or another. This is accomplished by means of a body suit equipped with sensory modalities such as sight, sound and touch. One may 'interact' with some wholly computer-generated settings or entities or with other body-suited participants (or some combination thereof). Even beyond this scenario, some have claimed that human consciousness itself can be duplicated through software and loaded directly into cyberspace. This was explored in the horror, science-fiction film, *Lawnmower Man*. This utopian vision represents a kind of techno-gnosticism: one escapes the perils of the living organism (flesh) by immersion into the mechanism of cyberspace (silicon). The 'soul' is freed by being digitized and injected into cyberspace. (Naturally, a crash or corruption of the hardware would insure one's digital oblivion.)

According to a Christian world-view, these large claims – in addition to their technological implausibility – present an unsatisfactory soteriology and include many philosophical conundrums. Whatever benefits cyberspace may offer for the rapid transference of information or for some simulations, it remains a human artifact, not a source of salvation. Redemption is only available from outside the cursed and fallen environs of this world, which is still awaiting its final liberation (Rom. 8:18–25).

On this front, the Christian apologist should marshal two related arguments. First, the physical world, while fallen, should not be fled as inherently *evil. The Scriptures affirm the created goodness of the universe (Gen. 1; 1 Tim. 4:1–4), and the incarnation (John 1:1–3, 14) ratifies that goodness in the person of *Jesus, who is truly human as well as truly divine. The attempt to escape the body into an amoral realm of unlimited potential is both to betray our created purpose as God's image bearers (Gen. 1:26–28) and to replay the ancient error of seeking self-deification when we are but finite and fallen mortals (Gen. 3:5; Ezek. 28:1–10). The second apologetic argument is that, while we are physical creatures who may await a glorious resurrection of the body if we follow the risen Christ (1 Cor. 15), we are not merely physical beings. Jesus and the apostles taught that there is an immaterial element to the human person that interacts with, but is not reducible to, physical states. In addition to the unified biblical witness, contemporary philosophers such as J. P. Moreland and Richard Swinburne have convincingly made this case. If the mind or soul is a substance distinct from the body, the notion of transferring human consciousness (understood as reducible to brain function) into physical software is inherently impossible. This understanding also challenges the claim that sophisticated computers will eventually

attain consciousness. (One philosopher has predicted that computers will so transcend human abilities that they will retain us only as pets.) Matter cannot generate consciousness. Although *artificial* intelligence (AI) is capable of tremendous computational power, it is not sentient.

The second way in which cyberspace is relevant for apologetics is in the role of the Internet as a source of information on diverse religions, world-views and cults. This affords the apologist with both opportunities and dangers. Quality control on the Internet is minimal; anyone with a web page can post anything. In his or her research, the apologist must develop a good sense for what is trustworthy information (such as official web pages for new religious groups) and what is not (hoaxes and amateur apologetics sites). Moreover, one should not substitute on-line research at the expense of pertinent printed materials, such as standard reference works, which have had more editorial filtering and are more legitimate.

Thirdly, as Quentin Schultze has argued convincingly, the conditions of cyberspace, if engaged in uncritically, tend to undermine a life of virtue. With its emphasis on information over wisdom, efficiency over moral character, spin over authenticity, the present over received tradition, and virtual realities over the physical realities that provide the ambiance for communion and *community, cyberspace can pose a threat to the kind of Christian character that is essential to authentic apologetic endeavours. Since winsome apologetics demands both solid arguments and a humble and wise demeanour, apologists will want to be on guard that their cyberspace activities do not short-circuit the fruit of the Spirit in their lives (Gal. 6:16–26). For example, although email makes it easy to engage in heated, rapid and thoughtless disputes (sometimes called 'flame wars'), the representative of Christ must flee such temptations to impatience and anger in order to speak the truth in love (Eph. 4:15; see also 2 Tim. 2:24–26).

Furthermore, many high-powered and popular video games trade on heinous violence (such as shooting innocent elderly people) and graphic sexual scenes. Some 'first-person shooter' games employ the same technologies used in computer simulations by the US military to break down a soldier's reluctance to kill on the battlefield. Evidence indicates that some teenage murderers, influenced by these games, adopted this mentality in their homicides. Since Jesus warned that sins of anger, lust and violence begin in the mind (Matt. 5:21–30), such video game simulations are widely seen as irreconcilable with the life that God blesses. Apologists can recommend wholesome and wise recreations in their place.

Bibliography

D. Groothuis, *The Soul in Cyberspace* (Grand Rapids, 1997; repr. 2001); D. Grossman and G. DeGaetano, *Stop Teaching Our Kids to Kill: A Call to Action Against TV, Movies, and Video Game Violence* (New York, 1999); M. Heim, *Virtual Realism* (New York, 1998); G. Houston, *Virtual Morality* (Leicester, 1998); Q. Schultze, *Habits of the High-Tech Heart: Living Virtuously in the Information Age* (Grand Rapids, 2002).

D. GROOTHUIS

CYNICISM

More than a philosophy, cynicism is the conviction that beneath everything, regardless of its appearance as good, is the more fundamental reality of darkness and *evil and selfishness. Cynicism is suspicious of a hidden agenda lying beneath every public one. To the cynic, marriage seems the mutual exploitation of men and women for their own ends; religion appears as a system designed to protect humans from harsh psychological realities; economics reveals itself as sanctioned selfishness; and democracy appears as the power of the few to buy or coerce the cooperation of the many. Individuals, their words, actions and motivations are as much suspect as are institutions.

David Harvey in his 1989 book *The Condition of Postmodernity* cited *Blue Velvet* as the archetypal film of a new way of looking at the world. The opening sequence of this 1986 film, directed by David Lynch, captures a picture of cynicism – beneath all of the beautiful lawns of 1950s American suburbia lies a land of beetles forever devouring one another.

Frequent confusions

When Christian apologists encounter the cynical mind, they hardly recognize their favourite institutions and cherished beliefs as these are described, and it is too easy for the church in reaction to dismiss the cynic as having a low view of *truth. In fact, we are hearing a powerful and persuasive new story that is making a claim against the Christian message. The cynic says there is no ultimate meaning or purpose or good – and that this is the truth. Most disquieting and confusing of all for Christians is that this is not a matter external to the church; many within the church are suspicious that the cynics are right.

The name 'Cynics' was first given to the disciples of Diogenes of Sinope, a contemporary of Aristotle. His teachings were more a way of life than a system of philosophy, and they therefore were free to influence all other schools of thought. The chief doctrine, shared by this group of diverse individuals, was that virtue – or the life according to nature – was all that mattered. This life according to nature was to live with only the barest essentials and necessities. The Cynics considered all beyond the necessities to be *tuphos*, a Greek word combining the notions of mist and fog, illusion and arrogance. Their simple life was lived as a conscious attempt to find tranquility through detachment; it was a means to protect oneself from the changes and disappointments of fortune. At a time in Greece when the individual identified with the *polis*, the Cynics lived detached lives, refusing to be citizens of any city except the universe. They were fiercely critical of social conventions whenever these complicated the natural life and would point out the hypocrisies in sarcastic diatribes. They were advocates of the utmost freedom of speech and behaviour. For this reason they were called 'Cynics' – or 'dog-men' – for, like dogs, they performed shameful acts in public and violated accepted standards with their natural lifestyle. They saw the conventions of society as threats to an honest life and accepted behaviour and traditional institutions as lies society agreed to believe so that it did not have to face the truth.

The fuel for cynicism

Contemporary cynicism shares many aspects with its ancient form. The engines powering its expression today are at least two. First, is the suspicion of meaninglessness, as discussed above. As long as we had trust in a system, whatever it might be, our greatest fear was to disobey its rules and thereby to reap its condemnation. We were, however, quite willing to risk punishment and a sense of guilt because the system gave us meaning and boundaries, and we trusted in the system's story. Guilt, uncomfortable as it may be, hinted at our significance. Some of the systems that previously gave a sense of purpose were religious belief, national traditions, science, the myth of eventual progress or even Western culture. However, when we stopped believing that any system would fulfil its promises, guilt ceased to be our chief fear and was replaced by the suspicion of meaninglessness.

A second engine for cynicism is the deep experience so many have of disappointment in their relationships, both within the family and with our political and religious leaders. The cynical mind sees through every hero to his or her self-serving motivations. Marketing also plays a role, as each day, in the West, we encounter hundreds of commercial messages appealing to our emotions and making promises of fulfilment, but we have grown used to the truth that, beneath the appeals, the motivation is to sell something for the marketer's profit. No human relationship was ever meant to be the absolute source of hope, because people have always been weak and imperfect and wrongly motivated; but these relationships were meant to be trustworthy enough as an environment that we might learn to handle disappointments and go on to trust the Creator God.

Confronting the cynical mind

There is a very real sense in which the cynics have the story right. In a world subjected to futility through the rebellion of humanity against its Creator, there are beetles beneath all the lawns. Christians, however, are not to be cynics. In Rom. 15:13, Paul declares 'May the God of hope fill you with all joy and peace as you trust in him, so that you may overflow with hope by the power of the Holy Spirit.'

The living God is himself the God of hope. Deeper and more fundamental than our sense of meaninglessness and disappointment is a love and judgment and reconciliation that can bring us through the darkness and back into the real light. There is a joy and a love not dependent upon circumstances, but its source is supernatural. Christians do not pretend that evil things are actually only 'hidden goods' in order to be happy and to escape the infection of cynicism. Optimism is unfounded and ungrounded to truth, but Christian hope has deep roots growing into a conviction about the real nature of our Creator, his universe and its ultimate fate. In the power of the Spirit of God, in spite of our disappointments and the culture of self-protection around us, we may have a hope like his own.

Such hope today is subversive, given the nature of our *culture and the pervasiveness of the cynical mind. When people meet hope embodied in a person, they find it both attractive and repelling. Hope repels because it seems glib, shallow and naïve. It also invites us to the danger of once more being disappointed. Hope does not seem honest to us; it appears to be only a change of perspective, choosing to think optimistically in spite of the evidence. Hope attracts because humans do long for purpose and meaning in the face of reality. Hope is a new thought life, a choosing, a habit that can be cultivated – but it is not only a mental game. In this way it is akin to faith; in fact in Heb. 11:1 the two are related: 'faith is being sure of what we hope for'. The cynical mind is pragmatic and not impressed with a faith that remains abstract mental assent and does not manifest itself in some tangible and embodied manner. Both hope and faith have their mental aspects, but the Bible is appallingly clear that both are expected to be visible in our lives as we go through the world. The church is quite right to protect itself from the notion that we are saved by our works, that we ingratiate ourselves to God by our obedient actions. However, the cynical mind is not impressed when our insistence on this good doctrine causes the church to suppress the equally biblical teaching that real faith always manifests itself. The cynics believe that Christianity is merely a convention, a mental fabrication, and makes no real difference in our situation. Too often, the gospel as expressed has left them unchallenged in their misconception.

Bibliography

D. R. Dudley, *A History of Cynicism* (Chicago, 1937); R. Stivers, *The Culture of Cynicism: American Morality in Decline* (Cambridge, 1994).

W. BRADSHAW

CYPRIAN

Cyprian (c. 200–58) was bishop of Carthage from about 248 until his death, and was one of the most important fathers of the Latin church.

He was a great admirer of *Tertullian (c. 196–212) but very different from him in his own approach to church disputes. Though not a voluminous writer, Cyprian remains a very important source in our attempts to reconstruct church life in the mid-third century because of the survival of a large number of his letters, which give us a clear insight into the inner workings of the Christian community at that time. In the great persecution of 250–51, Cyprian ran away and saved his life, though this apparent cowardice exposed him to great criticism. Later on, when persecution was renewed, Cyprian allowed himself to be captured, and in 258 he was beheaded, the first African bishop to die for his faith.

Cyprian's writings are mainly pastoral and not strictly 'apologetic' in the usual sense of the term. However, he has become famous for his statement that 'outside the church there is no salvation', and his writings have often been cited by Roman Catholic (see *Christianity, Roman Catholic) apologists, who regard them as proof that the Petrine view of the unity of the church was standard Christian teaching in Cyprian's day. This claim has, however, to be weighed against the fact that Cyprian fell out with the then bishop of Rome (Stephen I) and refused to bow to his strictures against the introduction of 'novelties' into church life and worship. It is, therefore, hard to see how Cyprian's Petrine emphasis can be integrated with a view of the supremacy of the bishop of Rome as this came to be understood in later times. Many modern Roman Catholic theologians have preferred to tone down Cyprian's dictum to the point where it almost ceases to have any meaning at all.

Cyprian's teaching is best viewed against the background of contemporary paganism and the disturbing tendency towards syncretism which plagued the church at that time. His undoubted rigorism was theological rather than jurisdictional, and for him the church was defined by its faith more than by its hierarchy.

Bibliography

P. Hinchliff, *Cyprian of Carthage* (London, 1974). Cyprian's works can be found in English translation in E. Wallis, *Library of Ante-Nicene Fathers*, vol. 5 (Edinburgh, 1886).

G. L. BRAY

CYRIL OF ALEXANDRIA

As archbishop of Alexandria from 412 to 444, Cyril was a dominant political figure in both the church and empire. Most of Cyril's polemics were directed against heresy, and he is particularly noted for his contribution to the development of Christology. Following in the Alexandrian tradition of his great predecessor *Athanasius (archbishop, 328–373), Cyril defended the unity of the person of Christ. The rival Antiochene tradition (championed by Nestorius, who had become archbishop of Constantinople) seemed to divide Christ into two distinct agents, the Son or Word of God and the human *Jesus, the Son of Man. Cyril secured the deposition of Nestorius, but then set about achieving some kind of rapprochement. He recognized that the full humanity of Christ must not be compromised and so accepted the Antiochene terminology of the 'two natures'. Cyril's doctrine of the 'hypostatic union', that Christ was one *hypostasis* (*persona* was the Western equivalent) in two 'natures' then became the basis for the church's official doctrine of Christ, agreed at the Council of Chalcedon seven years after Cyril's death.

Cyril also engaged in apologetics against *Judaism and paganism. Although Christianity had become the official religion of the empire, there were still large numbers of pagans and Jews in Alexandria and tension there erupted from time to time into rioting. It is against this background that we must see Cyril's early work, *Adoration in Spirit and in Truth*, which set out to show that the 'types and shadows' of the OT were fulfilled in the New, so that the Christian church, and not Judaism is the heir of the promises of God. Against paganism he published *Against Julian*, probably completed around 439–41. Julian the Apostate, the last pagan Emperor, had published *Against the Galileans* over seventy years before, and although Gregory of Nazianzus had preached two orations against it, Cyril was the first to compose a treatise in reply. He presents Moses as the greatest teacher of wisdom who inspired the Greek philosophers, but who only foreshadowed Christ. Cyril was not particularly well-read in the Greek classics, but he was well-versed in the Bible and church tradition and was a sharp dialectician.

Bibliography

J. Quasten, *Patrology* (Westminster, 1992),

pp. 116–142; N. Russell, *Cyril of Alexandria* (London and New York, 2000).

T. A. NOBLE

DARWIN, DARWINISM, see ORIGINS, THEORIES OF
DAYS OF GENESIS, see HISTORICAL DIFFICULTIES IN THE OLD TESTAMENT

DEAD SEA SCROLLS

Hailed by W. F. Albright as 'the greatest manuscript discovery of modern times', the Dead Sea Scrolls are a collection of documents recovered from caves on the north-west shore of the Dead Sea near to Khirbet Qumran. Following accidental discoveries by Bedouin shepherds in the spring of 1947, planned explorations by Bedouin tribesmen and archaeologists over a number of years brought to light the remains of some 812 texts, stored in eleven caves. On the basis of archaeological and palaeographical evidence, all of the material from the Qumran area was dated before AD 68, with some of the earliest manuscripts originating from the fourth century BC. Documents from other caves located in wadis to the west of the Dead Sea are sometimes included under the general category of Dead Sea Scrolls, but the provenance of these texts differs from that of the material from Qumran.

The discovery of the Dead Sea Scrolls took archaeologists and biblical scholars by surprise. Here was a unique and rich source of material that provided, first, fresh evidence regarding religious thinking in Palestine during the period when Christianity emerged in the first century AD, and, secondly, a wealth of Hebrew manuscripts that bore witness to the text of the OT from about 250 BC to AD 70. In both of these areas the Dead Sea Scrolls have contributed significantly to our knowledge, even if scholarly opinion remains somewhat divided as to how this new evidence should be interpreted.

Although the contents of some of the scrolls, especially those from cave 1, were made known shortly after their discovery, much of the fragmentary material has only recently entered the public domain. While the task of analysing and preparing for publication thousands of fragments of assorted manuscripts was never going to be easy, delays in making the material public provided an ideal environment for all sorts of speculations to be voiced, some especially hostile, regarding the impact of the scrolls upon our understanding of the origins of the Christian faith.

Most scholars strongly favour the idea that the Dead Sea Scrolls once formed the library of a religious community which lived at Qumran from about 125 BC to AD 68. Various factors suggest that this community was linked to the Essenes, a Jewish grouping that was particularly rigorous in its interpretation of the Torah. The Qumran community followed a very disciplined code of behaviour designed to create an environment in which its members could maintain a high degree of ritual purity. Possibly for this reason, women may have been excluded from the community, although some scholars now question to what degree the community was always celibate.

While the Dead Sea Scrolls provide new and interesting material about the Essenes, the fragmentary nature of the evidence means that it is not possible to reconstruct a complete picture of their beliefs and practices. Since the scrolls present a less than uniform picture, some scholars suggest that there must have been some kind of development within the community over the 200 years of its existence, a not unreasonable expectation. Furthermore, the scrolls provide few references or allusions to historical events during the period 150 BC to AD 70.

One difficulty for scholars interested in this period is knowing how far the distinctive practices and views of the Essenes may have influenced the formation of the early Christian church. Speculation that the Dead Sea Scrolls contain allusions to *Jesus Christ, John the Baptist, or even James the brother of Jesus, reflect extreme interpretations and have received little scholarly support. While some scholars draw attention to parallels involving theological vocabulary, doctrinal tenets and organizational practices, such links do not necessarily point to a dependence of one grouping upon the other. Rather, they could be due to the common parentage that both groups have in post-exilic *Judaism.

Prior to the discovery of the Dead Sea Scrolls, the oldest manuscripts of the Hebrew Bible (i.e. the OT) were the Codex Cairensis (AD 895/6), Aleppo Codex (c. AD 925) and Codex Leningradensis (AD 1008/9). Of these, only Leningradensis preserves the whole of the

Hebrew Bible. All three of these medieval codices reflect a common text preserved by Jewish scholars known as Masoretes; this textual tradition is designated the Masoretic Text (MT). Prior to 1947 scholars knew of only one fragment of a Hebrew biblical text that survived from a much earlier period (i.e. the Nash papyrus, dated about 150 BC, which contained a form of the Decalogue and the Shema). Apart from these Hebrew texts, the Codex Vaticanus (fourth century AD) preserved a nearly complete Greek translation of the OT (often known as the Septuagint or LXX). However, the Septuagint was considered to be too much of a paraphrase of the Hebrew text to be particularly useful in the field of textual criticism. The same applied to the Samaritan Pentateuch (SP), a somewhat modified version of the text found in the Masoretic manuscripts.

The discovery in 1947 of two scrolls, one complete and one partial, containing the Hebrew text of Isaiah, was highly significant. It was apparent from the orthography that they pre-dated the MT manuscripts by many centuries. In due course, the remains of over 200 biblical scrolls were recovered from the Qumran caves, providing an important witness to the nature and transmission of the Hebrew Bible in the period from about 250 BC to AD 70.

Given that most of the biblical texts from Qumran have survived only in fragmentary form, the evidence provided by them is not comprehensive. Nevertheless, it soon became clear that the biblical manuscripts were not homogeneous, with some texts corresponding more closely to the LXX or SP than to the 'received' MT. Building on these observations, four alternative views, associated chiefly with F. M. Cross, S. Talmon, E. Tov and E. Ulrich, have been proposed to explain the presence of different text types at Qumran. While the debate among scholars continues, and may well lead to other theories being proposed, two observations are appropriate. First, the Qumran Scrolls bear witness to the fact that the MT of the Hebrew Bible, as found in the medieval codices, closely resembles manuscripts that were in circulation a full millennium earlier. Although our earliest complete copy of the Hebrew Bible is from AD 1008/9, we may with a considerable degree of confidence believe that it accurately reflects the text used centuries earlier. Secondly, the history of the transmission of the Hebrew Bible in its earliest period displays a complexity

that has yet to be fully explained. While different versions of particular books of the Hebrew Bible appear to have been in circulation, our present knowledge does not permit us to describe in detail how these text types were related to each other and how they were viewed within post-exilic Judaism. We do know, however, that beyond AD 70 only one of these text types enjoyed widespread support among Jews (i.e. the text preserved and copied by the Masoretes).

The evidence provided by the Dead Sea Scrolls has also been seen by some scholars as having an important bearing upon our understanding of the process by which the *canon of the Hebrew Bible was formed. It is sometimes suggested that the Qumran community adopted a canon that differed slightly from that used elsewhere. However, such a conclusion is based on limited evidence and relies heavily upon criteria chosen by modern scholars in order to determine which texts enjoyed authoritative or scriptural status at Qumran (e.g. the number of manuscripts found; quotations and allusions; translation into Greek). For example, it has long been observed that the Qumran caves have not produced any fragments of the book of Esther. On this basis, some have argued that Esther was not viewed as canonical at Qumran. Yet, it is equally possible that time and decay may best explain the complete absence of any Esther fragments. For the whole of Chronicles, two fragments, containing only four verses, have been recovered, and no fragments of Nehemiah have yet come to light. It is argued that at least one copy of Nehemiah must have existed at Qumran, since small portions of a single manuscript of Ezra have been found and the books of Ezra and Nehemiah were normally copied on the same scroll. At this stage of research, it has to be said that inferences drawn from the Dead Sea Scrolls concerning the development of the Hebrew canon should be treated with the utmost caution.

Without detracting from the importance of the Dead Sea Scrolls, we need to remember that the largely fragmentary material from Qumran provides at best a partial window on one segment of Jewish society around the time of Jesus. The knowledge that can be gleaned from them is both limited and open to a variety of interpretations. Unfortunately, given the absence of other primary sources for this period, the danger exists that some scholars in their pursuit of definitive answers are tempted to go beyond what may be reasonably deduced from the evidence. For this reason, controversial claims regarding the impact of the Dead Sea Scrolls upon our understanding of the origins of the Christian faith ought to be assessed carefully and cautiously.

Bibliography

P. W. Flint and J. C. VanderKam, *The Dead Sea Scrolls after Fifty Years: A Comprehensive Assessment* (Leiden and Boston, 1998); F. García Martínez and E. J. C. Tigchelaar, *The Dead Sea Scrolls* (Leiden and Grand Rapids, 1997); L. H. Schiffman and J. C. VanderKam, *Encyclopedia of the Dead Sea Scrolls* (Oxford and New York, 2000); R. de Vaux, *Archaeology and the Dead Sea Scrolls* (London, 1973); G. Vermes, *The Complete Dead Sea Scrolls in English* (London, 1997).

T. D. ALEXANDER

DEITY OF CHRIST

The premier OT confession is the monotheistic claim of Deuteronomy 6:4, typically translated: 'Hear, O Israel, the Lord our God is One.' The basic NT confession boldly adds one *Jesus of Nazareth to the monotheistic mix: 'Jesus Christ is Lord' (e.g. Phil. 2:11). This presents two personal foci – Father and Son – for the accolade of 'Lord our God', as seen explicitly in Paul: 'we know that ... "there is no God but one" ... yet for us there is one God, the Father ... and one Lord, Jesus Christ' (1 Cor. 8:4–6, NRSV). The theo-logic of this NT confession led the early church to the doctrine of Christ's deity, his co-equal status and nature with God the Father. This deity claim has since been a fundamental tenet of Christian faith as it is considered essential to the personal identity of the historic Jesus as the eternally (pre-)existent Son of the Father; key accordingly to the more differentiated conception of God as a *Trinity of divine persons; and vital to the depth and dynamic of Christ's mediatorial life and atoning death. After outlining the case for this claim, this article offers some historical perspective on the doctrine of Christ's deity, and concludes by addressing some continuing challenges in articulating the deity of Christ in credible fashion today.

The case for Christ's deity

For those sceptical of God's existence to begin with, the case for Christ's deity is an almost impossible concept, since they are being asked to believe that a historical human person was also divine – very God in very flesh. But even for strict monotheists of Jewish, *Islamic or Christian unitarian or sectarian variety – those who believe that God can only be one identical substantial thing or person – Christ's deity is also very difficult to grasp.

The deity assertion is rooted in the uniqueness of Christ's life, teachings, and death-resurrection as recorded in the NT writings. The NT, by all reasonable estimates, presents a 'realistic narrative' or basic historical portrait of the life of Jesus. In the Gospels we see Jesus of Nazareth as a man on a mission to call his own people to a more faithful practice. Jesus is styled as a new Moses who, aloft the (sermon on the) mountainside, offers a fresh interpretation of Jewish law: 'You have heard that it was said ... But I say to you ...' (Matt. 5–7). The new command he offers, however, is really an old command, the heart of the Law: love of God and of neighbour. Jesus' ministry announces a new season of God's favour, of forgiveness and reconciliation, God with humanity and among human persons. In all this, Jesus is a man with no evident self-interests – politically, socially, economically – apart from the OT vision of a kingdom of righteousness, justice and shalom. He walks his talk in solidarity with the poor, the outcast, 'sinners', and comes into conflict with the powers that be. They crush him. Jesus is crucified as a poor, outcast sinner, sacrificing his life for his gospel of love. By most estimates, Jesus Christ was a great religious teacher, a wise sage and moral example.

But Jesus' teaching went beyond this. In addition to what any human leader would aspire to live and teach, Jesus made claims about himself that overreach the bounds of humanity. In a variety of ways, mostly by title and function, Jesus claimed to be divine.

While Jesus' followers saw in him the anticipated Jewish Messiah (Gk *Christos*), a title not expressly used by Jesus (but never denied and therefore tacitly admitted), this title does not imply divinity. But Jesus' favourite and recurring self-designation as the 'Son of Man' does imply divinity. While this Hebraism can simply mean 'human being' (Ezekiel's self-designation), given intertestamental apocalyptic reflections on Daniel's 'one like a son of man' (7:13), the 'Son of Man' on Jesus' lips refers to the expectation of a pre-existent *heavenly figure who, coming on the clouds, will be the agent of God's final judgment. And this in fact seems to be the principal way in which Jesus interpreted his messianic vocation, as can be seen in Mark 14:61–64, a claim the religious leaders considered blasphemous.

An even more evident association of Christ with deity is found in the title 'Son of God'. Though 'divine sonship' admitted a range of candidates in the OT (*angels, Davidic king, Hebrew nation), in the NT an exclusive claim develops around Christ, one he himself admits (Mark 12:6–7; 13:32; Luke 10:22). This culminates in the Johannine assertion that Jesus is the unique Son, the 'only begotten Son' (John 3:16). That this both distinguishes Christ personally and puts him in the closest possible relationship of deity with God the Father is reinforced by the fact that the best manuscript reading of John 1:18, typically translated 'only begotten Son' is more accurately rendered 'only begotten God'. Within the NT, the relationship between the Son and Father is most fully developed here in John's Gospel, manifesting both personal distinction and divine equality, as seen already in 1:1 (Christ the Word is both 'with God' and 'God'). Whereas the Son as the humanly incarnate 'sent one' is subordinate to God, he is at the same time so united or 'one' with the Father (10:30) that to see him is to see the Father (14:9). In John, Jesus' calling God his own Father and therefore claiming to be the Son of God is considered blasphemy, since he, by all appearances a man, is making himself equal to God (5:18; 10:33; 19:7). Christ's association with the God of Israel is particularly punctuated in John by a series of 'I am' sayings (Gk *ego eimi*), which in essence identify Jesus with the divine name (YHWH) first revealed to Moses at the burning bush: 'I AM WHO I AM' (Exod. 3:14; *ego eimi* in the Septuagint, the Greek version of the Hebrew Scriptures that is overwhelmingly quoted and supposed by NT authors). John frequently uses this formula both absolutely (e.g. 8:58: 'before Abraham was born, *I am*') and with predicates (e.g. 11:25: '*I am* the resurrection and the life'). These reinforce an explicit identification of Jesus with the covenant God of Israel.

Not only by title and intimate association

with God the Father, but also by function, does Jesus lay claim to divinity. For example, Jesus explicitly announces that he is the apocalyptic Judge, the one who will return at the end of days to execute the Day of the Lord (Matt. 25:31–46; Mark 8:38), an activity considered in the Hebrew Scriptures the prerogative of God alone. This reinforces the apocalyptic interpretation of Jesus' most frequent self-assertion as the 'Son of Man' and its implied divinity. Closely related to judgment is Jesus' claim to have the power to forgive sins, which in one episode evokes this response by his detractors: 'He's blaspheming! Who can forgive sins but God alone?' (Mark 2:7b; cf. vv. 1–12) – that is, God the Saviour.

Jesus' claim to deity, to being so one with the Father, occasioned his crucifixion as a religious blasphemer. As C. S. *Lewis observed, this seems to take Jesus out of the sheer category of the wise teacher or moral example, since his claims for himself are astonishingly beyond what any human can honestly assert: I am God, a divine person in the flesh. This occasions a basic dilemma. As an esteemed religious leader, either Jesus is telling the truth and *is* God in the flesh, or he is not telling the truth and *is not* God in the flesh, but then what? A devil, a liar, a lunatic, or some variation thereof? – none of which qualifies him for the title of wise teacher of moral integrity.

The NT church came to the conclusion that Jesus was telling the truth about his divine identity given another unique feature of his life: his *resurrection from the dead (both of which Jesus predicted). This utterly unique event – resurrected never to die again – was considered to be the divine vindication of Jesus' identity and mission. Analogous to the apostle Paul's declaration that if Christ has not been raised from the dead our faith is in vain (1 Cor. 15:14, 17), Christian faith in Christ's deity depends on the reality of the resurrection. While there are many factors to consider in arguing for the veracity of the resurrection, contemporary theologians such as Wolfhart *Pannenberg have emphasized the historical reliability, or non-falsification, of the empty-tomb tradition and the cloud of eyewitnesses to the risen Christ, including the apostle Paul, the prolific NT writer.

Beyond the historical reliability of the resurrection, however, the early Christians were compelled by another force. They believed that they *continued to* encounter the risen Christ in the power of his resurrection. Given their apocalyptic context, Christ's resurrection was understood to be the beginning or first-fruits of the general resurrection of the dead – that expected at the end of days, when God would radically pour out the Spirit to renovate the cosmos. The early Christians believed they anticipated this endgame of salvation, since the very Spirit of Christ's resurrected life was poured out at Pentecost (Acts 2), according believers a new birth (resurrection) into a living hope, a spiritual verve and vitality that nourish faith, hope and love. While intellectual obstacles to Christian faith are important and it is necessary to address them, Christians across the centuries have testified to something like the 'inner testimony of the Holy Spirit', an intuitive sense and experience with the risen Christ in its transforming (resurrecting) effect, as the most compelling reason for belief in Christ's claims. This has led many Christians to be faithful to death – even literally as martyrs (from the Greek for 'witnesses') – for Christ's message of love of God and neighbour. It is the church's experience of the presence of Christ in the *power of his life-affirming and renewing Spirit that has been the most compelling reason for Christian belief. And it is in the light and power of the resurrection that the early Christians 'fleshed out' the deity of Christ in the NT beyond Jesus' own explicit claims.

This accounts for the direct predication of deity to Christ in the NT. Though almost every passage in the discussion of Christ's identity is a matter of interpretive debate, there seem to be three sure NT instances where Christ is called 'God': John 1:1; 20:28; Heb. 1:8–9. To these can be added another five probable instances: John 1:18; Rom. 9:5; Titus 2:13; 2 Pet. 1:1; 1 John 5:20.

It also accounts for the title 'Lord'. Though 'Lord' admits of various senses (sir, master, household lord), as ultimately applied to Jesus in the confession, 'Jesus is Lord', it implies deity, since 'Lord' (Gk *kyrios*) is the word used for the divine name (YHWH) in the Septuagint. To call Christ 'Lord' in the context of worship, therefore, would carry the same connotation as 'God'. This virtual identification of Christ the Lord with the God of Israel brings us back full circle to Deuteronomy 6:4, with its two terms 'Lord' and 'God'. Both are predicated of God the Father, and both are predicated of the Son, including him in the monotheistic confession.

The highest reading of these titles is warranted by the array of divine functions associated with Christ. In addition to Jesus' own claim to be the apocalyptic Judge and Saviour, which the NT further elaborates, Christ is also accorded a role in creation. That God was the Creator distinguished YHWH from all the other so-called gods – those mis-worshipped principalities and powers of creation. Various NT assertions affirm Christ's central role in the world's creation (John 1:3; Col. 1:16; Heb. 1:3), sustenance (Col. 1:17), goal (Eph. 1:9), and re-creation (2 Cor. 5:17). Concerning the last of these, Christ is considered the primary agent of the future resurrection of the dead, an event associated with his second coming in judgment (John 5:25–29). These all place Christ in the closest proximity with the Father, since they are considered acts uniquely divine.

Most telling for the claim of Christ's deity is the fact that he was worshipped together with the Father. All the designations that 'Christ is God', noted above, are probably of liturgical origin, indicating that Christ was worshipped during NT times. This is bolstered by the ascription of doxologies to Christ (Rom. 9:5; 2 Tim. 4:18; 2 Pet. 3:18) and prayers to Christ in his own right (Acts 7:59–60; 1 Cor. 16:22; 2 Cor. 12:8). If worshipped, Christ had to be considered on the divine side of the Creator/creature divide, since to worship him as a creature would constitute both idolatry and *polytheism.

Beyond this general proof-texting, two NT books in particular integrate this variety of evidence for Christ's deity in sustained fashion: The Gospel of John and the book of Revelation. Both elaborate the panoply of titles, functions and worship that accord Jesus Christ divine status with God the Father.

Historical perspective

The NT case for the deity of Christ is strong. It was a reading of its statements, implications and vectors that led the early church to the ecumenical declaration of Nicaea (325), that Jesus Christ was of equal deity with God the Father. From the earliest reflections on the *apostolic witness (NT), there had been two diverging strains of thought about Christ's person. One strain, embraced by all of what we today recognize as church fathers, began its thinking about Christ by affirming his pre-existent divine status. This 'Christology from above' emphasized Christ's deity and his humbling descent to us by means of the *incarnation*. The other strain moves in the opposite direction. Rejecting his pre-existence, Jesus was seen as a naturally born man, a creature, who was later 'adopted' into special relationship with God, thereby achieving a high degree of divinity or God-likeness, but falling short of co-equality with the eternal Father. This 'Christology from below' emphasized Christ's humanity and his ascent to God by means of *adoption*.

The latter was censured at Nicaea. This foundational council was convened by the emperor Constantine to quell the potentially destabilizing Arian controversy over Christ's relation to the Father. Endorsing a concept of deity (God) as indivisible and incommunicable – possessed only by God the Father – Arius held that Christ the Son as a discrete person could not share this same divine nature. Rather, Arius considered Christ the pre-eminent creature, created by the Father's will for the purpose of mediating between the infinite, eternal and unknowable God and the finite, temporal, searching world – a metaphysical bridge between God and humanity. Though the Arians worshipped Christ together with the Father, he was not considered of the same divine status, since 'there was [a time] when he was not'.

Nicaea ruled against Arius by declaring that Jesus the Son was *homoousios* – 'of the same essence' – with God the Father. This established the full deity of Christ as official orthodoxy (right opinion), thereby endorsing an incarnational ('from above') approach against any sheer adoptionism. This declaration paved the way for the doctrine of the Trinity, as the *Holy Spirit's status was clarified after analogy to the Son (as 'another advocate'; cf. John 14 – 16). The so-called Cappadocian settlement of the Trinity (c. 381) defined Father, Son and Spirit as three persons who share the same deity, three persons in one God. The deity of Christ therefore stands or falls with the doctrine of the Trinity. To favour a unitarian conception of God as one person (usually the Father) is to slight the deity of Christ, and typically means advocating an adoptionistic conception of Christ (if indeed he is seen as more than a moral teacher or religious genius).

Trinitarian orthodoxy, which distinguishes Christianity from its monotheistic neighbours *Judaism and Islam, has long held sway in Orthodox, Catholic and most Protestant churches. But the rationalism of the modern period intensified dissent of Nicene orthodoxy.

The Enlightenment, as is well known, posed a rigorous intellectual challenge to traditional Christianity. Its heady confidence in the ability of human reason to map the world and chart the course of life without recourse to traditional authority or supernatural ideas conspired against the doctrine of Christ's deity. A scientific bias against the supernatural, given the assumption of the strict uniformity of nature, dictated that *miracles do not happen. But even if they do, enlightened historical bias dictates that we cannot admit their evidence, since historical truth must be based on analogy with our normal everyday experience. Traditionally, Christ's miracles were cited as telling proof of his own divine power, and therefore of his nature. While this proves a weak argument (because other biblical persons perform miracles), as touches the resurrection the critique went for the jugular of Christian faith, since, we have seen, the resurrection is the surest vindication of who Jesus and the apostolic *witnesses say he is. Much modern historical criticism, reading the Bible like any other book, dissected the real 'Jesus of history' from the mythological 'Christ of faith'. The latter, with its deity claim, was considered a creation of the church, as influenced by Greek philosophy.

Where these Enlightenment trends did not lead to atheism, they reinforced a unitarianism. Deism, for example, the religious philosophy of the Enlightenment, boasted a unitarianism that reduced Christ to a moral teacher and example. So also nineteenth-century Protestant liberalism, the last great attempt to accommodate Christianity to modern culture. Unitarianism lives on today wherever functional or degree Christologies exclude the ontological claim of Christ's full deity.

Continuing challenges

In addition to winning the basic deity of Christ, which the Christian orthodox tradition discerned from the NT witness, there remain three major challenges in making the confession of Christ's deity credible today. These are more 'in-house' challenges, within the context of monotheistic and/or Christian faith.

A first challenge is articulating a credible doctrine of the Trinity, that distinctive understanding of God that arises from the discovery of Christ's deity and finds completion in the Spirit's divine personhood. Historically, the Trinity has also been a problem doctrine, like the incarnation, prone to the *paradox of how three divine persons still equal one God. Many Christians who affirm Christ's deity ultimately deny his personal distinction in God because they have *de facto* a one-person view of God (typically, the Father). Here a more differentiated conception of the Trinity is needed to elucidate the divine distinctions, most evidently revealed in the Father-and-Son relationship in the incarnation. Here a social model for the Trinity is promising, since it purports to maintain the trinitarian distinctions without violating the monotheistic claim that there is one true God.

A second major challenge is not to let Christ's deity overwhelm his real historic humanity. The liability of an incarnational 'Christology from above' is its tendency toward *docetism, the inability to affirm the full humanity of Christ, an equally necessary credal affirmation (Constantinople, 381) and the overwhelming assumption of the synoptic Gospels. Christians of orthodox temper have long been tempted by a docetic image of Christ. Given both a divine and human nature (two-natures Christology), Christ's deity has tended either to smother his humanity, or to split him into two persons – one who does certain things out of his deity (e.g. knows all) and other things out of his humanity (e.g. knows not all). A docetic Christ who floats on the horizon of history is not a credible portrayal of the incarnation. Here a kenotic model of the incarnation proves promising. Inspired in title by Philippians 2:6–7 and context (vv. 6–11), the kenotic theory holds that Christ voluntarily limited or 'emptied' (Gk *kenoō*) himself of his divine powers and prerogatives in the incarnation so as to live a full human life. If viable, a kenotic Christology offers a more coherent model of the incarnation that can overcome tendencies to docetism and duplicity. Among other advantages, it can also capture the truth of both an incarnational Christology ('from above') and the *subordinate* adoptionistic strains of Scripture ('from below'; both seen, e.g. in Phil. 2:6–11).

A last major challenge is to articulate how Christ's deity functions in his mediatorial life and sacrificial death. Here again, docetic perspectives on Christ can overwhelm the place of his humanity, reducing the point of the incarnation to the cross and divorcing Christ's real historical life of struggle and temptation from his atoning death. While there are many valid, complementary perspectives on the life and death of Christ, Christ's deity cannot crowd out his humanity in understanding his saving significance for us.

In the final analysis, the affirmation of Christ's deity has as its greatest challenge the place of his full humanity. But together with the very evident latter, the recognition of Christ's deity asserts a truly amazing thing: that God stoops low for our salvation and in so doing is revealed to be an open and outstretched community of love. Moreover, if true, the deity of Christ also presents the most compelling and concrete case for the existence of God, since he represents a divine community that desires to become known in the simplest, most accessible way – by becoming one of us. While highly circular in argument, this is arguably a most reasonable thing to do if God is relational and has created humanity for the fellowship of love.

T. R. THOMPSON

DEPRESSION

Depression is a widespread phenomenon, which can be both an opportunity and a threat to any reasoned defence of a realistic Christian faith. On the one hand, the sheer weight of numbers of those who are known to suffer from this debilitating set of conditions confirms the appropriateness of a Christian belief in the brokenness of the human race 'Like most other pain, depression is giving a clear message that something is amiss and needing attention' (*New Dictionary of Christian Ethics and Pastoral Theology*, p. 300). We would expect, therefore, to find in the Bible many examples of people who suffered from depressive episodes and experience, while not imagining that the biblical writers necessarily had any explicit interest or objectives similar to those assumed by recent writers on *psychology or psychiatry. On the other hand, there are critics of the Judaeo-Christian tradition who allege that the very presence of such experience in committed believers is a contradiction in terms. If their faith in a loving God is so real and transformational, they argue, how can genuine Christians be subject to depressive episodes or even be chronically depressed? In fact, the titles of two popular Christian books accept this assertion as a valid starting point. In 1973 William Miller asked, *Why Do Christians Break Down?*, and in 2002, in *I'm Not Supposed to Feel Like This*, Chris Williams expressed the distress of many Christians who are suffering from depression. Within the church, therefore, there has often been expressed a conviction that depression should be overcome by committed faith and should not be accepted as part of normal Christian experience. Indeed, pastoral contact with sufferers inevitably involves helping them to cope with the misunderstanding of fellow church members concerning their problems. So there is a need of understanding within Christian congregations, as well as an explanation of our beliefs about the significance of depression in our witness to the wider community.

Here we are using 'Christian', to refer to those who profess to share in the beliefs and lifestyle which *Jesus of Nazareth personified in his life, death and resurrection. That means that we must examine carefully not only what the Gospels and the rest of the NT have to say about depression as a phenomenon among the faithful, but we must also reflect on key examples from the OT, which Christ (Messiah) came to fulfil. The Psalms express so many aspects of spiritual and psychological experience. One of the most searching questions, in the form of an introspective prayer, is repeated three times in Psalms 42 and 43, 'Why are you downcast, O my soul? Why so disturbed within me?' (Pss. 42:5, 11; 43:5). Clearly, the anonymous writer is going through considerable personal anguish. Any sense of the reality of God's presence has vanished, and persistent weeping expresses his sense of desolation and isolation. This feeling of being abandoned is very common in contemporary psychological and psychiatric descriptions of depressive disorders. The psalmist, who probably worked as a priestly assistant in the Jerusalem temple, certainly knew that his depressed state was making him question the very meaning of his existence as well as giving his unnamed opponents ammunition to bring him down. This shows that our contemporary concern that depression may be a stumbling block to Christian witness is not new.

The psalmist feels that hope has departed and he spends time dwelling on the past when he had, so he fondly recalls, joined with God's people at the great religious festivals with joy and thanksgiving. Those who feel that hope has gone often immerse themselves in what has been or might have been. Depression, as it is understood today, certainly may include distortion of memory, and the psalmist had probably forgotten some of the darker times in his past, which seemed to consist solely of brighter days in comparison with his current struggles. However, he had not lost his theological convictions about the nature and purposes of his God, whom he affirms is 'living' (42:2), 'my Saviour and my God' (42:5–6), 'the God of my life' (42:8), 'my Rock' (42:9), 'my stronghold' (43:2), 'my joy and my delight' (43:4). This demonstrates that, in depression, positive spiritual feelings may ebb and flow, and even be swamped by negativity and panic, and yet believers may still affirm the facts of their faith in God, the maker of heaven and earth and in Jesus Christ his only Son our Lord even when a sense of spiritual reality is almost totally absent.

There are several examples of this kind of experience in the stories of the OT, notably from the life of David. Psalm 22 shows him feeling both forsaken by God and yet convinced of God's sovereignty. Psalm 142 demonstrates that, even when David was surrounded by a crowd of his supporters, in his hideaway from the evil and erratic King Saul, he often felt completely bereft of any meaningful human relationship, and his desperate prayer to the Lord is a complaint about his troubles. Similarly, the prophet Elijah, after his great triumph over his religious and political opponents on Mount Carmel, ran away into the desert and slumped into a depression which included a wish to be done with life. Thoughts of suicide and self-harm are not uncommon in the severely depressed individual today. So, from the prophetic, priestly and kingly traditions in the Hebrew Scriptures, we find evidence of the kind of mental and spiritual turmoil which is symptomatic of depression as we now understand this complex phenomenon.

When we come to the NT, there is evidence of theological reflection on the significance of the struggles of Jesus, who came as prophet, priest and king. 'For we do not have a high priest who is unable to sympathise with our weaknesses, but we have one who has been tempted in every way, just as we are – yet was without sin' (Heb. 4:15). Do the Gospels portray him in this light? Could it be that he suffered from depression at times in his life, as part of his Messianic vocation? Might his mental pain prove redemptive for others? There were aspects of the sacrificial death of Christ which were certainly unique and unrepeatable. His cry of dereliction on the cross, 'My God, my God, why have you forsaken me?' (Mark 15:34), was part of his fulfilment of the Messianic hope (cf. Ps. 22:1), which he accomplished through his birth, life, death, resurrection and ascension, claiming as he did to be the unique Son of God, the ultimate Davidic king.

Clearly, it is unlikely that the four authors of the Gospels as we now know them necessarily had any explicitly psychological agenda behind their presentations of the humanity of Christ. But mainstream Christian tradition holds that Luke was also a medical doctor (Col. 4:14), and this has implications for his understanding of Jesus' inner life.

As a doctor, Luke could not have failed to have been influenced by Hippocrates, the so-called 'father of medicine' (b. 460 BC). It was Hippocrates who started the trend of regarding disease as a natural rather than a supernatural phenomenon, and certainly not as a punishment sent by the gods. Writing of epilepsy, then popularly labelled as 'the sacred disease', he said, 'It is not any more sacred than other diseases, but has a natural cause, and its supposed divine origin is due to man's inexperience. Every disease has its own nature, and arises from external causes.' Another probable influence on doctors in NT times was Asclepiades of Bithynia (b. 124 BC). Asclepiades gave particular attention to mental illness, clearly distinguishing hallucinations from delusions, and released sufferers who had been confined in dark cellars by other practitioners and prescribed instead a course of treatment of occupational therapy, soothing music, soporifics (especially wine) and exercises to improve the attention and memory. These two examples demonstrate the inadequacy of the view that mental illness was a category which would not have been understood by NT writers such as Luke, and that they would probably have attributed it to demon-possession.

Luke's interest in the developing mental disposition of Jesus is clearly seen in his account of a key incident which is not recorded in the other Gospels, where the twelve-year-old Jesus is participating in the Passover Feast at Jerusalem, with his parents and a party of family and friends from Nazareth. Luke's conclusion that after his return home, 'Jesus grew in wisdom and stature, and in favour with God and men' (2:52) clearly shows that he was interested in the balanced growth of Jesus into a mature human being, mentally, physically, spiritually and socially. Is there, however, any indication in Luke's Gospel that Jesus displayed symptoms of what we now classify as depression, similar to that experienced, for example, by the writer of Psalms 42 and 43? Certainly, his account of Jesus' personal distress in Gethsemane just before his arrest is compelling, 'And being in anguish, he prayed more earnestly, and his sweat was like drops of blood falling on the ground' (Luke 22:44; cf. Ps. 42:2). Also, Jesus' anger at his disciples' sleeping at their posts on guard duty, despite his repeated exhortation to 'Pray that you will not enter into temptation' (Luke 22:40, 46), expresses his sense of desolation and isolation (cf. Ps. 42:3). This feeling of being utterly abandoned, which is very common in contemporary experience of depression, is reported by Luke, but unlike Matthew and Mark, he does not include the cry of dereliction. It seems that the evident lack of prayerful support by his friends, as well as outright betrayal and denial by two of Jesus' key disciples, was enough for Luke to get over his point that the suffering Messiah was fulfilling the Hebrew Scriptures.

The amazing thing for Luke is that, unlike the ancient heroes of faith, Jesus' mental suffering did not make him question the very meaning of his existence or mission in life, nor did it render his witness incredible. In fact, the contrary is true, as Jesus recognized that his God had allowed his enemies to arrest him on false charges: 'Every day I was with you in the temple courts, and you did not lay a hand on me. But this is your hour – when darkness reigns' (Luke 22:53). Unlike the psalmist, whose lack of hope had led him to dwell on the past and to immerse himself in what might have been (Ps. 42:4), Jesus confronts the darkness, in his appearance before the Jewish council, with his promise that soon the roles will be reversed: 'From now on, the Son of Man will be seated at the right hand of the mighty God' (Luke 22:69). On the way to Golgotha Jesus turned to the crowds who were bewailing his demise and said to the women 'Daughters of Jerusalem, do not weep for me; weep for yourselves and for your children ... For if men do these things when the tree is green, what will happen when it is dry?' (Luke 23:28–31). Like the psalmist, despite the depths into which he had been plunged, Jesus did not lose his theological convictions about the nature and purposes of his God, whom he addressed as 'Father', at the beginning and end of his six-hour ordeal on the cross (Luke (23:34, 46). The intensified experience of depression, which Jesus went through before his death, was understood by Luke to be part of the testing which the writer to the Hebrews asserted was essential to the redemptive suffering of the great high priest who is able to sympathize with every human weakness: 'Because he himself suffered when he was tempted, he is able to help those who are being tempted' (Heb. 2:18; cf. 4:15).

However medical science may explain the causes and cures of depression today, and prescribe psychological therapies and/or medical treatments which may be to the benefit of Christians and non-believers alike, a consistent and realistic Christology must affirm that Jesus the Messiah understands the awful mental pain which depression entails because he has known it personally, and that he can help the sufferer who turns to him in faith and hope. This is good news and no obstacle to the effective promulgation and encouragement of real Christian faith.

Bibliography

J. Dominion, *Depression* (Glasgow, 1976); D. Martyn Lloyd-Jones, *Spiritual Depression* (London, 1965); J. White, *The Masks of Melancholy* (Leicester, 1982); C. Williams, *I'm Not Supposed to Feel Like This* (London, 2002).

G. R. HOUSTON

DERRIDA, JACQUES

Jacques Derrida (b. 1930) began his career as the darling of secular academics, and his turn in recent years to explicitly moral and religious themes has surprised critics and admirers alike. Although Derrida's recent texts are compatible with his previous ones, his early followers saw his practice of 'deconstruction' as allowing not just for relativistic interpretation of texts but *relativism in general. Derrida insists that deconstruction is not a 'method' or 'category', yet has been appropriated as such by many. Simply defined, deconstruction is the 'unbuilding' of a complex structure into its component parts, not so unlike what philosophers call 'analysis'. Both focus on what a text or theory

says, but deconstruction puts particular emphasis on what is left unsaid. Interpreting a text in such a way can be enlightening, but it likewise has the potential for generating interpretations that are peripheral or even contrary to what the text or theory says. So, critics of deconstruction are clearly right that deconstruction has provided an excuse for irresponsible and destructive scholarship.

Yet is deconstruction *itself* the problem? Since Derrida is famous for saying radical things, it might help to examine three of Derrida's more radical claims: 'there has never been any "perception"' (*Speech and Phenomena*, p. 103); 'there is nothing outside of the text' (*Of Grammatology*, p. 158); and there is no 'center which arrests and grounds the play' ('Structure, Sign, and Play in the Discourse of the Human Sciences' in *Writing and Difference*, p. 289).

The first claim is really about Husserl's notion of perception as 'intuitive givenness'. Briefly put, Husserl thinks that perception is when an object is 'present' to my mind. But, if the standard of perception is that an object is *fully* present, human perception never reaches that standard. Secondly, when Derrida says 'there is nothing outside of the text' he has often been read as saying that the world is simply a construct of our minds and so can be constructed as we wish. Yet Derrida's own explanation is that this phrase simply means that there is nothing outside context, and he warns against irresponsible interpretation and upholds its traditional tools, lest interpretation becomes free to say almost anything. In regard to the third claim, rather than suggest that that indeterminate 'free play' replace the traditional metaphysical and epistemological goal of grounding and structuring thought and values, Derrida insists that there is no such possibility as abandoning *metaphysics or even philosophy as it has been traditionally conceived.

Even though there is no simple 'free play', Derrida does believe that all choices (moral, religious or otherwise) are ultimately undecidable. When we make moral decisions or interpret texts, for instance, we can give reasons for our actions or our interpretations, but that justification cannot be like a mathematical calculation. So choices cannot be decided by way of any formula. It is not hard to see how the notion of undecidability could turn out to be an excuse for irresponsibility, but Derrida insists that it simply reflects the limitations of human knowing. *Philosophy has always had the ideal of *adaequatio intellectus ad rei* (lit. 'adequation of intellect and substance', or a one-to-one correspondence between idea and thing known). Derrida seriously questions this ideal, whether for *epistemology, metaphysics, *ethics or religion. In its place Derrida suggests the notion of '*différance*', which might be seen as Derrida's attempt to rethink the ideal of adequation. Human knowing is never 'adequate' in the sense of *adaequatio*, even if perhaps 'adequate' in the sense of being good enough for human activity.

This lack of adequation is clearly seen in Derrida's reflections on *morality. Surprisingly, Derrida maintains that *justice itself cannot be deconstructed. Regarding justice, Derrida attempts to maintain a position between 'essentialism' (i.e. the idea that justice is a 'thing') and what he calls 'irrationalism' (i.e. scepticism or relativism). If one believes in justice, though, the problem is, how do we make it concrete? *Laws and rules are ways of instantiating justice, but Derrida thinks they always fail (no matter how close they come) at doing justice to justice because of lack of adequation. Derrida works out this difficulty in a number of ways. First, doing justice means applying a universal to the particularities of laws and cases. But how can one do right by both the universal of justice and the singular of a specific case? Since each case is unique, no case could ever be 'just another instance' of a particular rule. Somehow, then, one attempts to mediate between the absolute of justice, the law and the specific case. Second, all decisions concerning justice are undecidable, not merely in the sense that there are no moral algorithms but also in the sense that the demands of justice are far more than one can possibly meet. For instance, we all have responsibilities to a whole host of people (and Jesus considerably complicates this last category by implying that *everyone* is my neighbour), but how could we possibly satisfy all of those demands in a perfectly 'just' way? Finally, justice cannot wait. We are always forced to decide before we can be sure that we have all relevant information to hand.

How might all of this apply to religious belief? Derrida recognizes that religious believers (certainly Christians) face a particularly difficult dilemma: we run the risk of forgetting that our descriptions of God fall short of his glory and thus allowing them to become

substitutes for God, but we also run the risk of letting the fear of idolatry silence all talk about God. So what is a believer to do? Here Derrida would suggest the logic of *différance*: whatever we may say about God, he is always different from that saying, not merely in the trivial sense that God and the saying are ontologically different but in the important sense that the saying is truly inadequate to the thing is represents. Using language borrowed from Levinas, we might say that our statements about God bear a 'trace' of God, in the sense that God is made truly present to us but not fully so. Something like this idea of the 'trace' is illustrated by God showing only his back to Moses (Exod. 33:18–23). *Différance* thus characterizes the very nature of faith. If one could spell out *exactly* who God is, *then* one would in effect be turning faith into reason and thus destroying its character *as faith*. The fundamental undecidability of faith is particularly poignant in Abraham's attempted sacrifice of Isaac, for Abraham really does not know how all of this will turn out. In *The Gift of Death*, Derrida reads Abraham's action as a gift, done without calculation or expectation of recompense. It is only *after* demonstrating his faith that Isaac is given back.

As should be clear, there is much in Derrida's thinking that resonates with Christian thought. Rather than being simply antithetical to Christian morality, Derrida's sense of the difficulty of instantiating justice resonates with the hard sayings of Jesus. But there are two cautionary notes that should be added here. First, Derrida clearly goes too far in saying that deconstruction is justice. Deconstruction has proved itself a tool of injustice. It may have good and justified uses, but deconstruction must itself be kept in check. Secondly, one can become so worried by the prospect of doing violence (to God and neighbour) that one is left in inaction or unable to bear witness to the hope that lies within us. To be fair to Derrida, he clearly points out that the demands of morality cannot wait, so it would seem that the demands of belief likewise cannot wait. Yet Derrida seems so reluctant to say much of anything substantive about either his moral views or his 'faith' that both end up having little content. For instance, Derrida is so insistent upon making God so 'wholly other' that there is little room for religious dogma (for what can one say about any God who is wholly other?). True, dogma is dangerous, it can easily end up reflecting us, but it is essential to faith. When we as Christians say we believe, there is something that we believe and there is someone in whom we believe. That belief must always be open to questioning (perhaps we might say deconstruction), for our dogmas can become idols. But the danger from which deconstruction would seek to protect us is one which dogma is also designed to do. The insistence of the early church upon careful formulation of creeds and doctrines was precisely about keeping our image of Jesus pure and unstained, rather than being remade in our image. But, if such is the case, then we are left with the recognition that the church needs both dogma and deconstruction. It is not a question of choosing but of holding them in tension.

Bibliography

B. E. Benson, *Graven Ideologies: Nietzsche, Derrida & Marion on Modern Idolatry* (Downers Grove, 2002); J. D. Caputo, *Deconstruction in a Nutshell* (New York, 1997).

B. E. BENSON

DESCARTES, RENÉ

René Descartes (1596–1650), French philosopher, mathematician and scientist, is often called the father of modern philosophy. He was, however, more than that, for he originated modernity, primarily through the place and role he assigned to human freedom and reason. In his *Meditations* (1641) he argued reason to be absolutely trustworthy, freedom to be boundless, and *truth to be grounded in the human mind rather than in Plato's transcendent forms or Augustine's divine revelation. Descartes believed that humanity is able to walk the path of indefinite progress towards ever increasing well-being so long as it allows itself to be guided solely by its freedom and reason; that their proper joint use creates the *science whose application will ameliorate the human condition.

One of Descartes' contemporaries, the Augustinian Antoine Arnauld, championed Descartes as defender of the faith. In contrast, Blaise Pascal complained, 'I cannot forgive Descartes. In all his philosophy he would have been quite willing to dispense with God. But he could not help granting him a flick of the forefinger to set the world in motion; beyond

this he has no further need of God.' In Holland, where Descartes spent his most productive years and published his works, the Calvinist universities of Utrecht and Leiden prohibited discussion of his work; in Rome the church and in Paris the king placed his works on the Index of Prohibited Books. Pascal, Dutch Calvinists, the Pope, and Louis XIV deplored Descartes' endangering the faith by limiting God and exalting each individual's freedom and reason. Later thinkers, such as those who prepared the intellectual scene for, or were directly involved in, the French Revolution, enthusiastically considered themselves Descartes' heirs because, as D'Alembert wrote, Descartes 'had the courage to show good thinkers how to shake off the yoke of scholasticism, opinion, and authority – in a word, of prejudice and barbarism ... [and] to rise up first against a despotic and arbitrary power'. The French Revolutionaries' grounds for adopting Descartes were the same for which others rejected him, for a limited God is close to irrelevant and, coupled with the egalitarianism implied in the commonly shared powers of reason and freedom, engenders the slogan 'no God, no master'.

Descartes' radical departure from Greek and medieval thinkers concerned both the status of human beings and how they achieve truth and well-being. He considers human beings as thoroughly autonomous, as thinkers who establish truth and achieve goodness unaided by external sources. Such autonomy demands rejection of tradition and a new stance towards 'nature' whose value now becomes instrumental for the achievement of human welfare. The best of tradition is unwarranted truth which, if simply accepted, is prejudice, and is useless for improving the human condition. What is required is utility, and so Descartes writes in the last part of his *Discourse on the Method* (1637) that he developed 'the possibility of gaining knowledge which would be useful in life ... and thus make ourselves, as it were, the lords and masters of nature ... and so enjoy without any trouble the fruits of the earth and ... the maintenance of health'. Human destiny is henceforth seen as in the hands of autonomous individuals.

In the second part of his *Discourse* Descartes articulates the four rules of his method required to develop the sciences whose application will procure this enjoyment of the earth and of health. These are first, to avoid prejudice, i.e., on any issue always let your reason be the final judge. With respect to any matter or question you seek to understand, following reason demands that you, secondly, divide the problem into as many parts as possible and, thirdly, begin with the resulting clear and distinct simplest parts and relate them into more complex knowledge, always taking care that each step in this (re)construction is clear and distinct. Fourthly, when you believe that this (re)construction is complete, review all the steps taken to make certain that nothing relevant was omitted and nothing irrelevant included.

In this articulation of method Descartes, in fact, presents a functional definition of reason, an account of how reason goes about its business in obtaining the foundations for, and developing the contents of, science. Since it is an account which demands that we always reduce whatever is complex to its simplest parts, the method is reductionistic. Reductionism also reveals itself in the criteria of truth, which are 'clarity' and 'distinctness' for, as the forty-fifth principle of Descartes' *Principles of Philosophy* (1644) stipulates, anything is clear only when we are aware of *all* of that which pertains to the item in question, and it is distinct when we are aware of *nothing but* what pertains to that item. In other words, initially knowledge is not a matter of wholeness or of context but a matter of parts or of decontextualization. These criteria function in each of the four rules. Since whatever you initially experience is part of a context and characterized by complexity rather than simplicity, it cannot be clear and distinct to you even if it may be so to others; so your experience always presents you with a problem, with a situation in which you *doubt its truth or value. Such doubt propels the division of the problem until you reach its clear and distinct parts, on the basis of which (re)construction of complexity may commence with each combination characterized by clarity and distinctness. Finally, in the review's insistence that nothing relevant be omitted we meet the criterion of clarity, while distinctness dictates that nothing irrelevant be incorporated.

In his *Meditations* Descartes attempts to demonstrate that reason so defined is absolutely trustworthy. If successful, this demonstration entails that the reductionistic method must be applied to whatever confronts humanity. In this demonstration the idea of God occupies a central role, for it is the hypothesis that God is a deceiver that makes full trust in reason impossible. Moreover, showing that this hypothesis is self-contradictory allows for the proof that God exists and is no deceiver, and this in turn establishes reason's absolute trustworthiness. Some took this part of the argument at face value and pronounced Descartes to be a defender of the faith. Others saw it differently. Since it is the human thinker who sets limits to the omnipotent God's deception, reason proves its power over against an omnipotent God. This power then in principle makes God irrelevant for subsequent human endeavour and so Descartes becomes the champion of an autonomous humanity. The salient aspects of the argument, best presented in the first person singular, are as follows.

Sensory illusions and delusions teach that I cannot always trust my senses, and if they sometimes deceive me they may do so now. Hence, I will not trust my senses to begin with; for all I know, I have no senses, no body, and there is no sense-revealed world. Neither can I begin with trust in applied science, for here reason cooperates with untrustworthy sensation. Can I trust reason working on its own, as in arithmetic? Suppose that God exists, however, not the good God of untrustworthy tradition but (using words from the re-cast argument in the sixth principle of the *Principles of Philosophy*) an 'omnipotent and deceitful' 'creator'. Then I would not be absolutely certain whether even the simple deductions of reason, such as two plus three making five, are in fact true, for this deceiver might make me err about anything. Nevertheless, this omnipotent deceiver cannot make me be wrong about my present knowledge that I exist, for I must exist as a thinking being if he is to be able to deceive me. Thus, even with God against me 'I think therefore I am' is a truth of which I am certain; the most excessive doubt imaginable (occasioned by my hypothesis that God exists and does all he can to deceive me) does not disturb but establishes it. So I adopt it as the firm foundation from which I will demonstrate that God exists and is good, that therefore I can always trust my reason, and that reason can show me to what extent I can – and, for applied science and the possibility of human progress, must – trust sensation.

Descartes holds that, once in our life, we must adopt this path of universal doubt in order to achieve the knowledge that reason is absolutely trustworthy and that sensation is trustworthy to the extent reason validates it.

Human freedom and reason combined halt the greatest doubt one can cast on their reliability as basic tools of human progress. Intended or not, placing the foundation of progress in will and reason makes God irrelevant for progress through science. For this exercise implicitly demonstrates the autonomy of human will and reason as the foundation for the possibility of human well-being. Thinkers like Arnauld would disagree with this interpretation; thinkers like Pascal and D'Alembert would agree – Pascal distressfully, D'Alembert rejoicing.

Bibliography

J. Cottingham, R. Stoothoff and D. Murdoch, *The Philosophical Writings of Descartes*, vols. 1 and 2 (Cambridge, 1985); S. Gaukroger, *Descartes, An Intellectual Biography* (Oxford and New York, 1995); P. A. Schouls, *Descartes and the Enlightenment* (Edinburgh, Kingston and Montreal, 1989); *Descartes and the Possibility of Science* (Ithaca and London, 2000).

P. A. SCHOULS

DETERMINISM, CHANCE AND FREEDOM

Determinists believe that every event (or every event in a certain category) has a cause that makes it happen exactly as it happens. Among the varieties of determinism are the views of (1) *Plato, who holds that one's ethical choices are determined by his view of what is good; (2) B. F. *Skinner, who believes that stimuli, dispositions and motives govern all human behaviour; (3) Democritus, Hobbes, *Spinoza, and many others, who hold that every event in the universe is determined by a physical cause. Of special interest to us are (4) theological determinists, who hold that all events occur exactly as God has foreordained them. These would include *Calvin and others in his tradition. The classic exposition of theological determinism is Jonathan *Edwards' *Freedom of the Will*. Note that it is possible to be a determinist in sense (4) without being a determinist in any of the previous senses. This seems to be the position of the *Westminster Confession of Faith*, which says that 'God did ... ordain whatsoever comes to pass', but also says that man's will 'is neither forced, nor, by any absolute necessity of nature, determined to good, or evil'.

William *James, in his article 'The Dilemma of Determinism', distinguished between 'hard' and 'soft' determinism. In his view, soft determinists hold that all events, including human decisions, are determined, but that some kind of freedom and moral responsibility also exists. Hard determinists hold (what James thought was the more consistent position) that the determination of human decisions requires us to reject the concept of moral responsibility. Other writers, however, have used the hard/soft distinction differently, defining soft determinism as a view that is largely deterministic but that allows for some uncaused or self-caused human choices.

Chance can refer (1) to uncaused events, or (2) to events of which the causes are uncertain and normally uncontrollable. When we throw dice, we often say that the result is 'by chance', but we do not usually mean that the result is uncaused, only that the causes are hard to ascertain or control. Laws of probability enable us to predict the results of such chance events over the long term (e.g. 50% of coin flips come out tails), but not in individual cases. Chance can also be (3) a synonym of fate, conceived as an impersonal force that makes everything happen as it happens. In the first sense, chance is incompatible with determinism. In the second sense, it is compatible with determinism. In the third sense, it presupposes determinism.

Freedom is a more complicated notion. Generally speaking, a person is free when (1) he has the ability to do something, (2) there is some obstacle or barrier that might have prevented him from exercising that ability but is not now preventing him. Someone is 'set free' from prison, e.g. when he can go where he likes without the barriers of prison walls, bars, guards etc. People have political freedom when they are able to publish political opinions, organize political parties, etc. without government interference. So freedom is always both a 'freedom to' and a 'freedom from', freedom to do something and freedom from some obstacle.

On this account, there are many different kinds of freedom, since there are many different things we can be free to do and many obstacles we can be free from. So we speak of economic freedom, political freedom, religious freedom, freedom from illness and many others.

Theologians and apologists are particularly interested in four kinds of freedom – moral freedom, the freedom to act according to our desires, freedom from natural necessity and freedom from all causation. (1) Moral freedom is the ability to do good despite the barrier of our sinful condition. God gives us this freedom by his grace (John 8:32–36; Rom. 6:7, 18–23; 8:2). When Scripture speaks of human freedom, it is almost always in this sense.

(2) The freedom to act according to our own desires. This kind of freedom is sometimes called compatibilism, because it is compatible with determinism. Scripture doesn't describe this capacity as freedom, but it does ascribe this capacity to all human beings. Jesus teaches, for example, that the good person acts out of the desires of his good heart, the wicked person out of his wicked heart (Matt. 12:35). There are times, of course, when we are unable to do what we want to do, at some level of wanting (as Rom. 7:15), but in most of the decisions of life, we do what we want, in the face of potential obstacles.

(3) Freedom from natural necessity, the freedom to act without the constraint of natural causes. This is the freedom mentioned in the earlier reference to the Westminster Confession. Its theological importance is its implication that human choice is not necessarily or always the result of natural causes. Being in the image of God, we have dominion over the earth and in some ways transcend the world process. And we may not excuse our sins by saying that they were forced upon us by heredity or environment.

(4) Freedom from all causation, sometimes called libertarianism, is freedom in the sense that, no matter what I choose to do, I might equally have chosen the opposite. So my choices are not only free from natural causes (as in (3)) but also from divine causation. Indeed, my libertarian choices are also free from myself in a way, for they are not determined by my character, dispositions or desires. These inner motives may influence a free decision in this sense, but they never determine it. So, a libertarian free decision is entirely indeterminate and uncaused. Thus libertarianism is sometimes called incompatibilism, since it is incompatible with determinism.

Libertarianism has been taught by a number of philosophers from ancient Greece (Epicurus) to the present (Alvin Plantinga). It was the position of some Church Fathers including *Justin Martyr and *Tertullian, Pelagius, the opponent of *Augustine, the Jesuit Luis Molina, Fausto and Lelio Socinus, Jacob Arminius, and present-day Arminians, open theists and process theologians.

Libertarians argue that we must have this kind of freedom because our intuition reveals that we have it, and it is necessary for moral responsibility, for we cannot be held responsible for anything we are determined to do.

Opponents of libertarianism, however, reply that (1) human intuition reveals that we choose among various alternatives, but it never reveals to us that any of our choices are absolutely uncaused. Intuition cannot prove a universal negative. (2) Far from teaching that libertarian freedom is essential to moral responsibility, Scripture never mentions libertarian freedom. (3) This doctrine would make it impossible for us to judge anyone's guilt in a court of law. For to prove someone responsible for a crime and therefore guilty, the prosecution would have to take on the impossible burden of proof of showing that the decision of the accused had no cause whatsoever. (4) Law courts, indeed, assume the opposite of libertarianism, namely that people are responsible only for actions that they are sufficiently motivated to perform. If it could be shown that an accused person committed a crime without any sufficient cause or motivation at all, he would most likely be judged insane rather than guilty. (5) Scripture contradicts libertarianism, by ascribing divine causes to human decisions (Exod. 34:24; Isa. 44:28; Dan. 1:9; John 19:24; Acts 13:48; 16:14), even sinful ones (Gen. 45:5–8; Ps. 105:24; Luke 22:22; Acts 2:23–24; 3:18; 4:27–28; Rom. 9:17). In none of these (or many other) cases does divine causation eliminate human responsibility. In fact, these texts often mention human responsibility in the same context. (6) Scripture also contradicts libertarianism by teaching that human decisions are governed by the heart (Luke 6:45) and by teaching that the human heart itself is under God's control (Ps. 33:15; Prov. 21:1). (7) In Scripture, the basis of human responsibility is not libertarian freedom, but (a) God's sovereign right to evaluate the conduct of his creatures (Rom. 9:19–21), and (b) the knowledge (Luke 12:47–48; Rom. 1:18–32) and resources (Matt. 25:14–29) he has given to each person. This shows that in Scripture there is an important relation between responsibility and ability, but the abilities in view here do not include the absolute ability to choose opposite courses of action.

These considerations lead to the conclusion that the Bible teaches theistic determinism, one that is 'soft' in James's sense. It teaches that human beings sometimes have moral freedom, usually have compatibilist freedom, but never have libertarian freedom. Scripture may imply that we have freedom from natural causation as well.

Bibliography

J. M. Frame, *The Doctrine of God* (Phillipsburg, 2002); *No Other God* (Phillipsburg, 2001); J. Edwards, *Freedom of the Will* (New Haven, 1973); W. James, 'The Dilemma of Determinism', in *Essays in Pragmatism* (New York, 1955), pp. 37–64.

J. M. FRAME

DEWEY, JOHN

The American philosopher John Dewey (1859–1952) adopted and developed the *pragmatism of C. S. Peirce and William *James into what he called 'pragmatic instrumentalism', an approach which he applied not just in philosophy but in education and *psychology and in moral and social theory and practice. He had no time for philosophers who spent their energies exploring obscure issues, such as whether or not we can have any true knowledge. Rather, he said, we need to build a philosophy that helps to support and further the tremendous advances in knowledge and practical living that have come through the *sciences. Thoughts or ideas must always be linked inseparably with action. Thinkers and scientists cannot be detached observers; rather, they are always agents whose lives are affected by what they are investigating. Knowledge should never be an end in itself; it is of value only if it enables us to survive or to enrich life. It is thus an 'instrument'; it is functional, never merely factual.

Though he believed in God, Dewey firmly rejected any 'from the top down' type of approach to beliefs or moral or social practices. All solutions, he said, need to be worked out 'from the bottom up' rather than imposed as a doctrinaire principle. Like the other pragmatists, he viewed meaning and *truth wholly in terms of consequent action. The meaning of a concept is made up of the consequences that would result if that concept was valid; its truth is established when the anticipated consequences follow the testing out of various hypotheses that arise from the concept.

Though pragmatism did much to prepare the way for *relativism, Dewey's pragmatic approach to meaning, truth and *morality does not have to entail the rejection of epistemological and moral *absolutes. Dewey certainly did not fall into the common trap of sliding from 'What is true will work' to 'What works is true'. Christian apologists rightly reject the second statement, but frequently use the first as the basis for demonstrating the viability of the Christian world-view. Though they rightly insist on a 'from the top down' way of understanding the world, they can agree with Dewey that the testing of their claims (e.g. that prayer makes a difference) can validly be 'from the bottom up', i.e. the examining of what results from them in specific life situations.

Bibliography

J. E. Tiles, *Dewey* (London, 1988).

P. HICKS

DICTATION THEORY, see BIBLICAL INSPIRATION

DIONYSIUS THE AREOPAGITE

Several works claiming to be written by Dionysius the Areopagite (the Athenian convert of St Paul, Acts 17:34) appeared in the sixth century AD. The unknown author (Pseudo-Dionysius) was an ecclesiastic, probably a Syrian monk, and was strongly influenced by the Neoplatonist philosopher Proclus. He adheres to the Christian doctrines of the *Trinity and the person of Christ, but presents a hierarchical Neoplatonist *cosmology in an attempted synthesis of Christian and Neoplatonist thought.

In this synthesis the deity is above and beyond being or number, transcending all thought and existence, but manifests itself in the Trinity and pours itself out into being and multiplicity. These emanations produce a celestial hierarchy of nine angelic orders (three triads), which is reflected in the hierarchy of the church with its three sacraments (baptism, unction and eucharist), three orders of the clergy (bishops, priests and deacons) and the laity (monks, the 'holy ones' admitted to the sacraments, and catechumens and penitents). The general *Platonist belief that the invisible, spiritual or intelligible world is reflected in the visible, and the more specifically Neoplatonist scheme of the cosmos as a unified whole emanating from the deity are thus given a particular Christian and ecclesiastical form. Pseudo-Dionysius was a highly effective apologist for the Christian church in a Platonist culture. He continued to be influential throughout the Middle Ages and was quoted with great respect by *Thomas Aquinas.

In his approach to the problem of *evil Dionysius addresses one of the classic concerns of Christian apologetics. His Platonism leads him to equate the good with existence and evil with non-existence. A totally evil reality is therefore impossible, for it would simply be non-existent. God is beyond 'form' and 'matter', but within the world, 'form' exists in thought without matter, and at the lower end of the hierarchy of existence, form and matter combine in the physical world. Matter without form would be evil, but matter can have no existence without form, and so evil as such is beyond existence.

The strength of this theodicy is that it rules out any form of Manichean dualism, which makes good and evil equal and opposite powers. Its weakness, however, is its failure to do justice to the reality and offence of evil as actual and malicious cruelty.

Bibliography

D. Rutledge, Cosmic Theology, The Ecclesiastical Hierarchy of Pseudo-Denys: An Introduction (London, 1964); Pseudo-Dionysius: The Complete Works (New York, 1987).

T. A. NOBLE

DISASTERS, see EVIL

DISEASE AND HEALING

The people of Israel were not immune to the diseases which afflicted humankind in the ancient world. They viewed disease, along with other calamities and misfortunes, within the context of their unique covenant relation with God. Disease, sickness, as well as some forms of mental disorders, were not seen as purely random or capricious incidents and experiences resulting from human weakness, misfortune or even a malicious divine power. Rather, they were viewed as being under the *power of Yahweh both to inflict as punishment and to heal. The mortality of human flesh was partly the result of the 'dust' from which it came, but it also represented a divine judgment and inevitable consequence of sin. From this standpoint, sickness and death were viewed as unnatural and a sign of the disorder and chaos into which humanity plunged in falling away from God, a reminder of human weakness and mortality as well as an element and sign of God's judgment. This is reflected in the Psalms, the book of Job and in the Synoptic Gospels.

Disease is the inevitable consequence of human nature fallen from grace and a constant witness to the need for God's redeeming mercy and promise of health. Yahweh alone is the lord of sickness and of healing. *Yahweh rapha* ('the Lord who heals') is one of several covenant titles ascribed to God in the OT (Exod. 15:26). Recovery from illness is something to praise Yahweh for, a signal of his mercy and power to grant life and health (Pss. 30:2, 5, 11; 32:1–11; 103:3; Isa. 53:4). The prophetic voice leads the people towards a future when 'No-one living in Zion will say, "I am ill", and the sins of those who dwell there will be forgiven' (Isa. 33:24).

While there is no clear theology of disease in the OT, the fall of humanity due to the sin of Adam and Eve has long been considered its source. The assumption is that when God declared the original condition of humanity to be 'good' it indicates an absence of all disease and possibility of physical deformity and that Adam and Eve were not subject to mortality or death. Others hold the view that before the fall Adam and Eve were susceptible to disease, but that it was not until after the fall that disease actually occurred. The Bible does suggest that the consequence of sin affected the conditions under which Adam and Eve, and all subsequent humans, experienced their mortal existence here on earth. But it is difficult to insist that all of the organisms within nature which actually cause disease were introduced into nature after the fall. What was lost as a consequence of the fall was the constant life-giving flow of divine healing and support of the human under the conditions of natural mortality. The command of God by which human life is upheld, even in its corruption and disorder, challenges the inevitability and power of sickness in its fatalistic determinism of human existence. Although Scripture does not give us a clear answer as to how disease entered the human condition, it does affirm that all of the diseases that afflict humanity are ultimately to be healed as part of God's covenant love and purpose (Exod. 15:26). The assertion that God's covenant with humanity, first through Israel and finally through *Jesus Christ, will lead to the complete healing and restoration of humanity to wholeness and health is bound to the apologetic significance of God's saving actions as the basis for faith and hope.

The assumption that disease is the direct consequence of an individual's sin lay behind the charge against Job lodged by his friends, who urged him to confess the sin that had resulted in the tragic events which overtook him and the disease which tormented him. David attributed the concealment of his sin as the cause of his own physical and emotional distress (Ps. 32:3–5). When Miriam rebelled against her brother Moses, she was stricken with leprosy as a divine judgment. Moses recognized her sin as the source of her disease, and through his prayer of intercession she was healed and restored (Num. 12:10–16). The connection between sin and disease was assumed as a matter of course even in the time of Jesus. When confronted with a man who had been blind from birth, the disciples wanted to know, 'Who sinned, this man or his parents?' 'Neither this man nor his parents sinned,' replied Jesus, thus challenging the assumed connection between the disease and sin (John 9:1–3).

The NT does not support the assertion that disease and sickness can be understood as the direct cause of sin. While Paul alludes to the fact that certain of the Corinthian Christians had become sick and even died because of their disorderly practice at the Lord's table, we cannot draw from this rather vague warning the conclusion that all disease is caused by sin (1 Cor. 11:30). While there is no direct connection between disease and sin, the NT does report many instances of disease and mental illness caused by demonic oppression. The exorcisms performed by Jesus may be viewed as eschatological signs of the kingdom of God related to his own presence as the Messiah rather than as a diagnostic and therapeutic model for the treatment of disease (Matt. 12:28). Without denying the possibility that some illness and disease may be the result of demonic influence, it is sufficient to remove the effects of *evil without knowing for certain what is the source. The spiritual ministry of pastoral care along with professional therapeutic intervention by persons empowered by the *Holy Spirit can be considered to be forms of 'ordinary exorcism', where healing and wholeness at the physical, mental and emotional level result. 'Extraordinary exorcism' may be considered in extreme cases, but even here, the focus is not on 'demonic warfare' but on the positive effect, as when people so afflicted are found sitting at the feet of Jesus, in their right minds, and fully clothed (Luke 8:35).

Some who argue that the same faith by which one receives forgiveness of sin can be exercised so as to receive miraculous healing base their claim on the theological assertion that healing is in the *atonement of Christ (Baker, *Salvation and Wholeness*). This leads to what has been called the 'faith formula', that if one has enough faith, miraculous healing can be obtained in the same way that we receive forgiveness of sins (Blue, *Authority to Heal*). Failure to obtain healing is then thought to be caused by lack of faith, either in the person who prays to be healed or in the *community of faith, rather than being the fault of God. The implications for those who remain unhealed can be destructive to faith. Others hold that miraculous healing is not part of atonement in the same way as forgiveness of sins is. C. Brown suggests that forgiveness of sin is a 'covenanted mercy' promised to all, while healing is not part of the covenant of forgiveness but is related to the free sovereignty of God (*That You May Believe*).

When the atonement is viewed as completed in the resurrection, both forgiveness of sins and healing are eschatological realities. Present assurance of forgiveness of sins at the final judgment based on the resurrection can be gained in the present through faith as a gift of the Holy Spirit (Rom. 6:23; Eph. 2:8–9). A miraculous healing now is a sign of the future resurrection, and is to be received by the community of faith to strengthen the faith of all in the promise of healing and forgiveness of sins at the end of time. Where healing does not occur as a miraculous release from the power of disease through the prayer of faith, it can be a witness to a faith in God's salvation that can remain strong and vital even through suffering and death. Health is not merely the absence of malfunctions, but the strength of faith to live with them, i.e. the strength to be human (J. Moltmann, *God In Creation: A New Theology of Creation and the Spirit of God* [San Francisco, 1985], pp. 271–273). Healing as a spiritual and personal effect of God's grace may be experienced even where there is no cure. Where physical healing is delayed until the resurrection, God's grace is sufficient (2 Cor. 12:9).

Bibliography

J. P. Baker, *Salvation and Wholeness* (London, 1973); K. Blue, *Authority to Heal* (Downers Grove, 1987); C. Brown, *That You May Believe* (Grand Rapids, 1985); D. R. McConnell, *A Different Gospel – A Historical and Biblical Analysis of the Modern Faith Movement* (Peabody, 1988).

R. S. ANDERSON

DIVINE BIRTH STORIES

Recent challenges to the historicity of the biblical accounts of the virgin birth have been largely based upon the fact that numerous divine birth stories existed in the ancient world. Although Rudolf *Bultmann is the most well-known proponent of this sceptical view, Charles Dupuis in 1796 was the first to propose a parallel between Christian and non-Christian accounts. Dupuis suggested that the biblical accounts borrowed from the stories surrounding the birth of Krishna. The history of religions school that followed in the late-nineteenth and twentieth centuries noted numerous parallels in other stories. Early Christians and NT authors were 'influenced by', 'dependent upon' or they 'borrowed from' these sources as they sought greater definition in their christological formulations in order to demonstrate the supremacy of *Jesus Christ within the broader culture. Another model suggested that Hellenistic divine birth stories made their way into early Christianity via a syncretistic Hellenistic *Judaism.

Examples of divine birth stories may be found within other *world religions and in Egyptian and Graeco-Roman religions and cults. These stories are often associated with great leaders, philosophers and religious thinkers. For example, in ancient Egyptian lore, Amon was thought to have fertilized the mothers of the Pharaohs. Similarly, in Greek mythology, Dionysus was fathered by Zeus, Romulus was thought to be the son of Mars, Alexander the Great was sired by Re, and *Plato and Augustus were considered offspring of Apollo. Divine birth traditions also came to be associated with Buddha and Krishna. In most cases, however, there remains an apparent problem with physicality, and all involved some form of *hieros gamos* (sacred marriage) in which the divine being took on a human or other physical form (e.g. that of a snake) and impregnated a woman by sexual intercourse or other means. Furthermore, the stories often involve acts of seduction, sexual misconduct and even rape. There is no example of a human male impregnating a goddess.

In spite of numerous examples, and their ostensible similarity to the biblical birth narratives, there are significant reasons to reject the assertion that such stories form the basis of the biblical accounts. For all of its considerable learning, the history of religions school has not demonstrated precisely how the stories made their way into the early Christian community. Their use of the language 'borrowing', 'dependence' and 'influence' is frequently ambiguous, imprecise and not supported by accurate data or models. Nor is it certain that such stories would have been known by Greek-speaking Jewish Christians of the first century. Because the literature closest to the NT accounts is found in Judaism itself and not in Hellenistic documents, and because early Christianity was a Jewish movement, the primary influences or parallels ought to be located in Jewish, not Hellenistic, sources. Further, early Christian authors were opposed to the kind of sexual misconduct that underlies many of these pagan stories (cf. Rom. 1:24) and so it is unlikely that they would have been influenced by them. Perhaps most compellingly, there is a substantial difference between the Gospel accounts and the other divine stories: in every other story impregnation occurs as the result of a physical relationship in which the male divine being assumes some physical form. This is clearly not the case in the biblical narratives. Thus, while the proposed parallels contain a glint of similarity, they are in reality superficial and bear little or no resemblance to the actual content of the Gospel accounts.

Bibliography

T. Blosooper, *The Virgin Birth* (Philadelphia, 1967); R. E. Brown, *Birth of the Messiah: A Commentary on the Infancy Narratives in the Gospels of Matthew and Luke* (New York, 1993).

R. BEATON

DIVORCE, see MARRIAGE

DOCETISM

Docetism, the heresy which denies or minimizes the full humanity of Christ, derives its name from the Greek verb *dokeō* ('to seem' or 'to pretend') and noun *dokēsis* ('appearance' or 'phantom'). We may have an early allusion to it in 1 John 4:2–3 and 2 John 7. Ignatius in the early second century warned against those who said *Jesus Christ only *seemed* to suffer and to rise in the flesh, neglected care for the needy and abstained from the church's eucharist because they did not acknowledge it as the flesh of the Saviour.

Docetism took various forms in the second century. Some thought the whole person of Jesus Christ was only a semblance. Marcion, for instance, in his disparagement of the flesh omitted the birth narrative from his edited version of the Gospel of Luke and began it with Christ coming down (from *heaven) to the city of Capernaum (Tertullian, *Against Marcion*, 4.7; *On the Flesh of Christ*, 5–7). Others distinguished the human Jesus from the divine Christ, and it was only the human Jesus who experienced birth, the ordinary functions of life and the suffering of death. This distinction was common among Gnostics. An early version is put forward by Cerinthus, for whom the divine Christ descended upon Jesus at his baptism and left him before the sufferings of crucifixion (Irenaeus, *Against Heresies*, 1.26.1). In the *Apocalypse of Peter* from the *Nag Hammadi codices the 'living Jesus', who is the Saviour, looks on glad and laughing while his fleshly likeness is nailed to the cross. Valentinus took an intermediate view that Christ had a spiritual flesh unlike ours, and thought that the Saviour passed through the womb of Mary in the same way as water flows through a pipe, taking nothing from her who was his means of entrance into the world (Tertullian, *Against Valentinians*, 27; *On the Flesh of Christ*, 10–22). Even orthodox thinkers could feel embarrassment over the heavenly Saviour having fleshly experiences. *Clement of Alexandria affirmed the full humanity of Christ but shared with Valentinus the view that he did not actually need food and drink, going on to explain that he only partook of these things in order to prove his humanity to people (*Miscellanies*, 6.9).

The docetic denial, in whatever form, that the divine Saviour was truly subject to all the experiences of a human person could appeal to Greeks, for whom by definition deity could not suffer. This viewpoint may have supplied the philosophical basis for the rise of Docetism. Docetism could also appeal to Jews, for it avoided the stumbling block of a crucified Messiah. Jewish believers may have been the first to advance the docetic interpretation.

Orthodox Christians responded to the challenge of Docetism by affirming the goodness of creation, including all matter and by claiming that the flesh can be saved. The OT view of a God who fully identifies himself with his people, even in their sufferings, was central to the orthodox response to Docetism. So too was the reality of the incarnation. The orthodox affirmed the salvation of the whole person, body and soul, and this required that the Saviour too partake of the whole nature of those whom he came to save. Thus a whole complex of issues was bound up with the struggle over Docetism: the goodness of God's creation, the incarnation of Christ and the bodily resurrection.

Although an unacceptable option, Docetism was a significant impetus for the affirmation of orthodox Christology that there were two natures, divine and human, in the one person of Jesus Christ. Although the church rejected the early forms of Docetism, tendencies to depreciate Christ's humanity in relation to his divinity recurred in Christian history, as in some forms of Monophysitism (or miaphysitism) and in the view advanced at different times that Christ brought a celestial flesh with him, not a flesh derived from Mary.

Bibliography

A. Grillmeier, *Christ in Christian Tradition*, vol. 1 (Atlanta, 1975); W. R. Schoedel, *Ignatius of Antioch* (Philadelphia, 1985), pp. 20, 90–91, 220–244; M. Slusser, 'Docetism: A Historical Definition', *The Second Century*, 1 (1981), pp. 163–172; E. Yamauchi, 'The Crucifixion and Docetic Christology', *Concordia Theological Quarterly*, 46 (1982), pp. 1–20.

E. FERGUSON

DOOYEWEERD, HERMAN

Herman Dooyeweerd (1894–1977) was the most influential representative of a distinctive school of Christian philosophy that emerged from early twentieth-century Dutch neo-Calvinism. Developing the world-view of the nineteenth-century theologian Abraham *Kuyper, Dooyeweerd's concern was not apologetics as conventionally understood (although he did engage in dialogue with the influential Reformed apologist Cornelius *Van Til). He began his career as a *law professor at the Free University of Amsterdam (founded by Kuyper in 1880) but quickly concluded that to articulate an authentically Calvinian approach to law would require a comprehensive, biblically-rooted philosophical framework which neo-Calvinism still lacked. His life's work was devoted to remedying that deficiency by laying the foundations of such a framework, which he increasingly came to see needed to be ecumenical in appeal. His thought may be compared in scope and depth with the work of Catholic philosophers such as Étienne *Gilson, Jacques Maritain or Bernard Lonergan. A revised and extended version of his three-volume *magnum opus* was translated into English as *A New Critique of Theoretical Thought* (1953–8). The title of the original Dutch version was *De Wijsbegeerte der Wetsidee* (1935), a phrase which has often been rendered as 'the philosophy of the cosmonomic idea', but which literally means 'the philosophy of the law-idea' (where 'law' refers to the divine law for creation).

Although his writings ranged over many disciplines, Dooyeweerd is best known for his penetrating and controversial 'transcendental critique of theoretical thought', developed in vol. 1 of *A New Critique*. Dooyeweerd's aim in proposing such a 'transcendental critique' of Western thought was to demonstrate that underlying every philosophical framework, and in turn every discipline, were powerfully operative fundamental presuppositions driven by 'religious ground motives'. The pervasive and dynamic presence of such presuppositions, however, was systematically denied as a result of *Enlightenment humanism's commitment to the supposed 'neutrality' of rational theorizing, its myopic claim that reason was autonomous with respect to religion. Dooyeweerd called this commitment 'the dogma of the pretended autonomy of theoretical thought'. The proximate aim of his critical philosophical project was to expose the truly *dogmatic* character of this commitment and to press adherents of rival philosophical systems to acknowledge the

deeper religious assumptions on which they – often unwittingly – proceeded. The intention was not merely to expose the fact of deep religious divergence among philosophers, leaving protagonists in a fruitless intellectual stand-off. Rather this proximate aim was preparatory to his larger ambition of creating conditions of genuine intellectual and religious honesty in which meaningful and constructive philosophical dialogue would be more likely to occur, as each participant engaged in the common pursuit of *truth from their own self-conscious standpoint.

The apologetic implications of Dooyeweerd's philosophy have not yet been fully explored or appreciated in the English-speaking world. One reason for this is that his thought reflects a 'Continental' mode of philosophizing with which many Anglo-American philosophers and theologians are unfamiliar and, arguably, of which they are insufficiently appreciative. The writings of Roy Clouser are, however, a valuable attempt to translate Dooyeweerd's ideas critically in the vernacular of Anglo-American analytic philosophy.

Another reason is simply that Dooyeweerd himself wrote no work which fits under the traditional heading of 'apologetics'. Yet some implications are clear. On the one hand, his argument that powerful religious presuppositions guide all theoretical argumentation calls into question a naïve 'evidentialist' apologetic which aspires to prove the truth of Christian faith by drawing deductive or inductive conclusions on the basis of appeals to empirical evidence and also a '*natural theology' which purports to be able to draw rational deductions regarding the existence and nature of God from the design of nature. On the other, it equally challenges an irrationalist '*fideism' which denies any effective role for rational argumentation in the articulation or defence of Christian faith and so risks reducing 'apology' to mere assertion. It is, nonetheless, correct to discern in Dooyeweerd anticipations of certain promising themes in contemporary postmodernism, such as the reaffirmation of 'confession' or 'testimony' as inescapable conditions of thought and *language. Specifically, Dooyeweerd's 'transcendental critique' may be compared to insights of postmodern thinkers close to or within the orthodox Christian tradition, e.g. Michael *Polanyi's claim that all knowledge is 'personal', Alasdair *MacIntyre's proposal that rational inquiry is always 'tradition-constituted' and John Milbank's insistence that *theology must go 'beyond secular reason'.

Contemporary Christian apologists reflecting on how to commend the Christian faith in a postmodern *culture might learn from thinkers such as these, and especially from Dooyeweerd himself, about how to interpret that culture and how to deploy rationality winsomely and effectively within it. Further, Dooyeweerd's profound analysis of 'religion' and 'faith' as universal characteristics of all creatures made in God's image suggests the fruitfulness of his thought for apologetics beyond Western culture.

Bibliography

R. Clouser, *The Myth of Religious Neutrality: An Essay on the Hidden Role of Religious Beliefs in Theories* (Notre Dame, 1991); *Knowing with the Heart: Religious Experience and Belief in God* (Downers Grove, 1999); H. Dooyeweerd, *A New Critique of Theoretical Thought*, 4 vols. (Amsterdam and Philadelphia, 1953–8); *In the Twilight of Western Thought: Studies in the Pretended Autonomy of Philosophical Thought* (Philadelphia, 1960); E. R. Geehan (ed.), *Jerusalem and Athens: Critical Discussions on the Philosophy and Apologetics of Cornelius Van Til* (Nutley, 1977); D. K. Naugle, *Worldview: The History of a Concept* (Grand Rapids, 2002).

J. CHAPLIN

DOSTOEVSKY, FYODOR

Fyodor Dostoevsky (1821–81) is one of the major shapers of the modern *imagination. *Notes from Underground* (1864) provides the prototype of the anti-hero common in twentieth-century literature. Also, as Albert Camus recognized, the history of contemporary *nihilism really begins with Dostoevsky's famous dictum that if there is no God, then everything is permitted. The question of the existence of God lies at the core of his mature novels, *Crime and Punishment* (1865–66), *The Idiot* (1868), *Demons* (1871–72) and *The Brothers Karamazov* (1880). Dostoevsky foresaw that the *Enlightenment optimism about progress and utopianism would devolve into the totalitarian horrors of the twentieth century; a character in *Demons* predicts that in the coming century *atheism would cause 100 million deaths.

Dostoevsky's life was turbulent. At twenty-eight, he was sentenced to death for radical political activities, and only when facing the firing squad was he reprieved and sent to prison. This traumatic event jarred him back to the faith of his Russian Orthodox childhood. Further turmoil resulted from his epilepsy, an unhappy marriage and his compulsive gambling, which left him perpetually in debt. Fellow novelist Ivan Turgenev called him the nastiest Christian he had ever met. After his first wife died, Dostoevsky married his young but sensible stenographer, and his life finally settled into contented regularity.

In *The Brothers Karamazov*, Dostoevsky's capstone novel, the issue of God's existence comes into clearest focus in the inexhaustible legend of the Grand Inquisitor, told by 'my socialist' Ivan to his pious brother Alyosha. In Ivan's 'poem' Christ returns to earth during the sixteenth-century Spanish Inquisition. The Grand Inquisitor, a venerable Roman Catholic cardinal, rebuffs Christ as he wants to rule in Christ's name but not according to Christ's principles. In particular, Christ's principle of freedom is a burden too great for most humans to bear. So the Inquisitor offers selflessly to take the burden of freedom upon himself and provide humans with the security of bread instead. To this utopian scheme Christ offers no reply; he simply kisses the Inquisitor. Dostoevsky believed that none of the detractors of his Christian faith had ever 'even conceived so powerful a rejection of God as exists in the Inquisitor and the preceding chapter'.

Ivan's poem appears in the fifth book of the novel's twelve books. In the sixth, the dying Father Zossima describes monstrous sins, including his own, then delivers rapturous exhortations urging that each person is responsible to show unconditional love towards all. Dostoevsky intended this book to be 'the answer to that whole negative side', but he worried, 'will it be answer enough?' Ivan's argument is unanswerable point by point; hence Christ's silence. Dostoevsky explained to a friend, 'If [book 6] succeeds I shall have done a good deed: I shall compel them to recognize that a pure, ideal Christian is not something abstract but is graphically real, possible, obviously present, and that Christianity is the sole refuge for the Russian land from all its woes.' Only in life itself can one find a theodicy that suffices; thus, some have considered Dostoevsky a Christian existentialist.

Elsewhere, Dostoevsky asserted that the whole novel was his answer to nihilism, and all the Karamazov brothers play roles in fleshing out this answer. Dmitri, the eldest brother, accepts punishment for the parricide which is the central plot event, a murder he contemplated but did not commit. He thereby embodies Father Zossima's principle that all are 'guilty before everyone, for everyone and everything'. Dmitri also exemplifies the Dostoevskian theme of growth through suffering.

Ivan had said he rejected not God but the world as God made it, particularly the suffering of innocent children. Ivan, however, never alleviates anyone's suffering. Instead, he transmits his world-view to Smerdyakov, the illegitimate half-brother, who kills their father, a crime that Ivan had willed but could not commit. When Ivan withholds his approval, Smerdyakov commits suicide. Ivan's subsequent brain fever, displayed in his nightmare about the Devil, makes him unable to tell the court the truth that would spare Dmitri. Nihilism fails in real life.

By contrast, Alyosha, the youngest brother, actually helps children. He transmits Father Zossima's world-view to Kolya, a precocious youth who had initially adopted Ivan's nihilism. This way lies not the Grand Inquisitor's offer of perpetual childhood but Zossima's adult vision that all are responsible for all. Not only the sins of the fathers are visited upon the children; so are the beneficent influences. The final scene features Alyosha with Kolya and other boys in a rhapsodic harmony affirming God's world.

Dostoevsky reinvigorated the religious heritage against which modernity rebelled. The Christian insights conveyed through his narratives are compellingly tailored to address a postmodern world that derogates reason and openly embraces nihilism.

Bibliography

N. Berdyaev, *Dostoevsky* (Cleveland and New York, 1957); A. Camus, *The Rebel* (New York, 1956); F. Dostoevsky, *The Brothers Karamazov* (New York and London, 1976); J. Frank, *Dostoevsky*, 5 vols. (Princeton, 1976–2002); K. Mochulsky, *Dostoevsky* (Princeton, 1967).

E. E. ERICSON

DREAMS, see TRANSCENDENCE, SIGNS OF

DRUGS

Throughout history, drug use and religion have gone hand in hand. Whether it is the peyote cactus of native Americans, the sacred mushrooms of the Aztecs or the ganja (cannabis) of Rastafarians, the ability of drugs to alter perception has led to their use as a means of enlightenment and *transcendence. During the 1960s, LSD became a popular vehicle in Western, industrialized society for the *religious experiences that many people openly sought, and today, even where young people eschew an expressed search for God, there still remains a desire for experiences that are out of the ordinary or insights that enlighten and uplift. This has been a major factor in the widespread use of ecstasy and derivative drugs within the dance culture, most evident in the raves of the 1990s with their emphasis on love, tolerance and sense of *community amongst participants.

When the effects of drugs have worn off, however, what is left? Was the experience real or simply a chemically induced 'feel-good' sensation within the brain? Since many people now question whether there is something tangible that we can call *reality, it is scarcely surprising if drug-induced experiences are deemed equally meaningful and real as those experienced in ordinary 'non-drug' life. Yet to accept chemical experiences as an ultimate reality is to regard human beings as no more than recipients of a range of chemical stimuli. Christians believe that there is a reality that exists independent of our thoughts, views and experiences. The basis for this is God, our creator. Reality is not found in the earthquake, wind and fire of intense drug experiences but in God's word, his providence and his Holy Spirit, active throughout our world and human affairs. Our search for transcendence is our search for God, the ultimate reality, and our hearts will remain restless until we find our rest in him.

For many people in the world today, the use of mood altering drugs is not a search for a higher meaning or greater purpose, but a means of providing different, preferable inner feelings. These may be the confidence, excitement and euphoria of crack cocaine or amphetamine, or simply the physical and emotional analgesia of heroin and tranquillizers, which numb life's pain and unhappiness. Relying upon drugs for solutions, however, denies something vital to our being. The soma of *Huxley's 'Brave New World', a hedonistic tool and an end in itself, really inhibited and controlled, suppressing the truly human qualities of yearning and inquiry and the search for something bigger and greater. Today's soma is alcohol, cannabis, ecstasy, heroin, cocaine or any substance making us feel all right. 'Opium' has become the religion of the people.

Changes induced by drugs are transient and superficial because they do not change us inwardly. They change how we feel, not what we are. Take away the drug and we are more or less back to where we started from. The musician Brian Eno commented upon this, 'I get thoroughly fed up with hearing about people's mystical drug experiences. I don't see the experiences doing anything. I know people who've been having sublime experiences on drugs for years and they're still the same people. It doesn't seem to have affected their behaviour in any way.' It doesn't matter how profound our experiences are if we remain unchanged within.

The quest for meaning and satisfaction is part of human life. Drugs, like so much else, will ultimately disappoint because they are not the answer. As Jesus said, 'Everyone who drinks this water will be thirsty again, but whoever drinks the water I give him will never thirst. Indeed, the water I give him will become in him a spring of water welling up to eternal life' (John 4:13–14).

Bibliography

O. Batchelor, *Use and Misuse* (Leicester, 1999); R. Draper and B. Draper, 'Taboo Technology', *Third Way*, vol. 19, 10, pp. 21–24; M. Gossop, *Living with Drugs* (London, 2000); A. Tyler, *Street Drugs* (London, 1995).

O. BATCHELOR

DUNS SCOTUS, JOHN

John Duns Scotus (1265/66–1308) wrote to instruct believers rather than to convince non-believers; that is, he wrote theology rather than apologetics in the strict sense. Nonetheless, there is much in his work that is of value for a defence of the Christian faith. His elaborate proof of the existence of God still has its defenders. One recent treatment argues that

'Scotus does as well showing the existence of a First Explanatory Being as any philosopher has ever done on any substantive point' (J. F. Ross and T. Bates, in *The Cambridge Companion to Duns Scotus*, p. 225). Like other Christian philosophers and theologians of his day, Scotus does not suppose that every point of Christian belief can be proved in a strictly philosophical way, independently of divine *revelation. But, like *Thomas Aquinas, he is convinced that every point of Christian belief can at least be defended, in the sense that arguments against truths of the faith can be overcome and Christian doctrines can be shown not to involve any incoherence or contradiction. The doctrine of the *Trinity provides a good example of this conviction. Scotus never supposes that one can prove that God is triune, but he does think it is part of the theologian's task to state the doctrine in such a way that it can be shown to be coherent and to defend it from objections that unbelievers have raised against it. Scotus does, however, represent a stage in the progressive loss of confidence on the part of Christian theologians in the ability of unaided human reason to prove truths about God. He thinks it is possible to prove God's existence, for example, but not his omnipotence (in a strict sense of that term). Nor does he think it is possible to prove the *immortality of the soul. The best apologetic can only defend those doctrines against attack. After Scotus, many philosophers would come to doubt whether even God's existence could be demonstrated philosophically.

Bibliography

R. Cross, *John Duns Scotus* (Oxford, 1999); T. Williams (ed.), *The Cambridge Companion to Duns Scotus* (Cambridge, 2003). The online *Stanford Encyclopedia of Philosophy* offers a brief overview of Scotus's philosophy at <http://plato.stanford.edu/entries/duns-scotus>.

T. WILLIAMS

EDWARDS, JONATHAN

Jonathan Edwards (1703–58), Congregationalist minister, Puritan theologian and leader of the First Great Awakening in North America, left no apologetical work to posterity. Yet many of his writings were composed with an eye to addressing the challenges that *Enlightenment 'freethinkers' had raised against orthodox Christian theology. We can discern four strategies he employed when he addressed these challenges.

First, Edwards took an interest in defending Scripture against the work of critics who challenged the traditional understanding of the Bible. In many entries of his private notebook, *Notes on Scripture*, we find him reconciling alleged inconsistencies in the Gospels, addressing scientific and historical questions regarding the early chapters of Genesis, and defending the Mosaic authorship of the *Pentateuch. Here we see Edwards in evidentialist mode, marshalling evidences against particular challenges to the Scriptures. Yet this strategy comprised only one part of his apologetical efforts.

Secondly, Edwards's position on the relationship between reason and *revelation was intended to counter the Enlightenment's exaltation of reason over all other forms of *authority. Edwards had a very high view of humankind's rational powers to apprehend *truth, and in this sense he was a child of the Enlightenment. Yet when he spoke of reason's great potential, he had in mind *sanctified* *reasoning, reason that is illuminated by the *Holy Spirit and wedded to Scripture. Natural, fallen reason, he maintained, is severely limited because of sin: it cannot apprehend the truth of God in Christ. He noted that centuries of philosophical inquiry (by the Greeks, Romans, Chinese) witness to the fact that when left on its own, natural reason leads only to confusion, not to a consensus on the truth. Because of this, Edwards argued that human reason necessarily requires divine revelation to apprehend truth.

Thirdly, Edwards's studies of non-Christian religions were intended to address a certain handicap that, critics maintained, plagued traditional Christianity: the so-called 'scandal of particularity', or the notion that it is unfair for God to limit his salvific activity to a particular body of knowledge (such as the gospel), leaving all others damned. In his private notebooks we find Edwards intrigued by what appeared to be vestiges of special revelation (i.e. the Trinity, the incarnation, original sin) circulating in non-Christian religions. In alignment with a pre-modern apologetical tradition, Edwards reasoned that these truths were relics of an 'ancient theology' (*prisca theologia*) that God deposited early on in the history of the human race (some time around the flood). These truths were subsequently passed down by oral tradition to the developing nations of the world, who corrupted them to fit their own idolatries. The result? Nuggets of religious truth pepper the false and idolatrous beliefs of the world's religions. While such knowledge cannot save apart from faith in Christ, the very presence of such beliefs does mitigate the scandalous nature of Christian particularity: contrary to the opinion of Enlightenment critics, the non-Christian world beyond Western Christendom has always possessed traces of special revelation, traces which it has consistently misunderstood or rejected.

Fourthly, Edwards's well-known theology of spiritual apprehension, summarized in his celebrated sermon 'A Divine and Supernatural Light', can itself be seen as an apologetical strategy. By first emphasizing that a spiritual vision of divine excellency consists in a direct and even self-authenticating experience of God himself and then, secondly, rationally detailing the psychological mechanics of this experience, Edwards offered an interpretation of Christianity that met enlightened sceptics on their own turf. Personal experience and a rigorous application of reason were the foundation of the Enlightenment's critique of conservative Christianity, yet Edwards turned these 'enlightened' intellectual values toward the benefit of Christian orthodoxy. In doing so, his apologetic embodies a unique mixture of evidentialist apologetics, with its stress on rational evidences and objectivity, as well as what would later characterize the romanticist apologetic of *Schleiermacher and Coleridge, with its emphasis on *religious experience and subjectivity.

Each of these strategies was aimed at answering the threat that the Enlightenment posed to Christianity. Together they reveal that Edwards creatively engaged Enlightenment thought only to strengthen further the foundations of his conservative theology.

Bibliography

R. E. Brown, *Jonathan Edwards and the Bible* (Bloomington, 2002); M. McClymond, *Encounters with God: An Approach to the Theology of Jonathan Edwards* (New York, 1998); G. R. McDermott, *Jonathan Edwards Confronts the Gods: Christian Theology, Enlightenment Religion, and Non-Christian Faiths* (New York, 2000); G. R. Marsden, *Jonathan Edwards: A Life* (Yale, 2003).

R. W. CALDWELL

ELIOT, T. S.

T. S. Eliot was the quintessential poet of modernity, reinventing poetry to reflect the bleak disorder of the age and capturing in precise and evocative images the spiritual climate of the twentieth century. Then in 1927, this wildly experimental bane of the conservatives announced, to the astonishment of his bohemian friends, that he had become 'classicist in literature, royalist in politics, and Anglo-Catholic in religion'. Eliot's conversion to Christianity and his subsequent religious poetry, which was still thoroughly modernist in sensibility and style, are thus extraordinarily instructive for those who wish to communicate the faith in a persuasive way to a post-Christian age.

Eliot was born in St Louis, Missouri, in 1888 to a wealthy Unitarian family. As a student at Harvard, Eliot began writing poetry and studying philosophy. A postgraduate scholarship to Oxford, where he planned to finish his projected doctoral dissertation on the idealistic philosophy of F. H. Bradley, brought him to England (where he would later take citizenship) and he fell into the literary circles of the new modernist writers, such as Ezra Pound, Virginia Woolf and James Joyce. As he was shocking the literary establishment with lines about the evening 'spread against the sky/Like a patient etherised upon a table' (the opening lines of 'The Love Song of J. Alfred Prufrock'), Eliot was struggling with ideas that would lead him to Christianity, a conversion, he would insist, that was intellectual before it became spiritual.

One theme of his philosophical studies, his essays about literature and his poetry was 'the disassociation of sensibility', i.e. the distinctly modern (or post-*Enlightenment) split between thinking and feeling, intellect and emotion. The Age of Reason was followed by *Romanticism's Age of Subjectivity, and in the twentieth century, *science and art, *logic and sensation were all flying apart in different directions, both intellectually and artistically and in the fragmented minds of ordinary individuals.

From his studies of Dante, Shakespeare and the metaphysical poets, Eliot noticed that it had not always been this way, that in these writers thought and feeling did not oppose each other, but rather came together. In these poets 'there is a direct sensuous apprehension of thought, or a recreation of thought into feeling'. They 'feel their thought as immediately as the odour of a rose. A thought to Donne was an experience' (*Selected Prose*, pp. 63–64). Eliot came to realize that this unified sensibility, which he attempted to achieve in his own poetry, was related to the Christian faith. Conversely, the loss of that faith – which affirms both objective *truth and personal experience, the abstractions of doctrine and the concrete physicality of creation, incarnation and sacraments – has led not only to the disassociation of sensibility but to the spiritual emptiness of contemporary life.

Eliot employed Christian imagery and Christian themes even in his pre-Christian poems. In 'Gerontion', the old man reflecting an exhausted civilization is devoured by 'Christ the tiger'. In 'The Hollow Men', playing against the emptiness of those with 'headpiece filled with straw', ending not with a bang but a whimper, is a counterpoint from the Lord's Prayer's 'For Thine is the Kingdom'.

In his masterpiece *The Wasteland* Eliot anatomizes the modern condition by employing the myth of the Holy Grail, in which the loss of something holy has turned the once-flowering land into a desert wasteland. He also draws on the recurrent motif – in both *mythology and *theology – of death and rebirth. 'April is the cruelest month' to denizens of the wasteland because they resist the new life that Spring embodies. In its many voices and multiple scenes and characters, the poem depicts a condition in which even what is designed to produce new life – namely, sex – has become something sterile, the pursuit of sensation without love, in which the new life that is occasionally engendered is casually disposed of, with the help of abortificant chemicals.

Even here, though, the Christ of the Grail seems to haunt the wasteland. The characters 'fear the Hanged Man', and the questers stumbling through the desert have the sensation of a 'third who always walks beside you'. The one mood of peace comes in the section 'Death by Water', depicting a merchant who has drowned and whose body rises and falls under the sea. At the end of the poem, it starts to thunder, with rain about to fall on the wasteland. Not too long after writing this poem, Eliot – fresh from the collapse of his marriage and a nervous breakdown – experienced his own death by water. He was baptized in 1927 and confirmed in the Church of England.

Eliot went on to write profound religious verse, still in his trademark modernist style. 'Ash Wednesday' is about both personal repentance, and Christ as the still point of the turning world. (Russell Kirk quotes Eliot's contemporary Rose Macaulay to the effect that this poem turned many of the rising modernist generation to Christianity, instead of to *communism, suggesting that the poem had an impact as apologetics.)

Eliot wrote short poems on biblical subjects ('Journey of the Magi' and 'Simeon's Song') and religious dramas (*The Rock* and *Murder in the Cathedral*). The major work of the latter part of his career was *The Four Quartets*, a difficult, challenging meditation on time and eternity, in which unconventional religious imagery breaks into a distinctly modern consciousness.

Eliot's brand of Christianity, an austere pessimistic strand described as the *via negativa*, was different in tone from the energetic, joyful version of C. S. *Lewis. The two men disliked each other's writing intensely and disagreed about literature on almost every point, though, as Lewis said, they agreed 'about matters of such moment [i.e. their Christian faith] that all literary questions are, by comparison, trivial'. (For an account of their ongoing feud, see Dale, *T. S. Eliot*, pp. 154–155.) The two perhaps represent two different ways of making historic Christianity credible to the contemporary *imagination, or perhaps ways of reaching two different kinds of personalities.

Bibliography

A. S. Dale, *T. S. Eliot: The Philosopher Poet* (Wheaton, 1988); T. S. Eliot, *Collected Poems 1909–1962* (New York, 1963); *Selected Prose* (New York, 1975); L. Gordon, *Eliot's New Life* (New York, 1988); R. Kirk, *Eliot and His Age: T. S. Eliot's Moral Imagination in the Twentieth Century* (LaSalle, 1984); W. Skaff, *The Philosophy of T. S. Eliot* (Philadelphia, 1986).

G. E. VEITH

EMPIRICISM

Empiricism (from Gk *empeiria*, 'experience') is the important epistemological theory that all knowledge ultimately comes through experience. David *Hume (1711–76) wielded his narrow (and unjustifiable) empiricism to the conclusion that human beings are not able to know about *causality, substance, minds or souls, *angels and God. Hume thought humans could not possibly perceive such things, and thus can never be said to know them.

How is one to respond to a narrow empiricist like Hume? One should begin by examining the grounds of the justification for Humean empiricism. One notes quickly that empiricism is not self-justifying in that it cannot validate its own use; for its success depends on certain human processes working together somehow to produce mostly true beliefs. But, as C. S. *Lewis argued, if our thoughts are just movements among the atoms in our brains, why think they are aimed at true belief? Experience as a source of knowledge is only as good as the accuracy and design structure of the mechanisms through which the experience occurs. If our cognitive structures arrived here only through the mechanisms of *naturalism and evolution, how could that causal story possibly account for our cognitive success? One could never erase the *doubt that one's mind was in error on any particular belief produced. But for a properly functioning person, experience does generate mostly true beliefs. The most plausible explanation for our cognitive success, therefore, is design imposed on us from outside. And so to justify empirical knowledge, it seems most plausible to approach empiricism from a theistic background.

It follows that non-theistic empiricisms must be carefully evaluated, for they usually overstep their bounds and propose self-defeating principles, or cannot account for the meaningful knowledge we do have. So, W. K. Clifford (nineteenth century) recommended that no-one should ever believe anything not supported by sufficient evidence (experience). Let us call this principle 'E'. What is the sufficient evidence for E? There cannot be sufficient evidence for E. Thus, it is a philosophical statement going beyond all available evidence. On Clifford's empiricism alone, E is self-defeating (it does not meet its own standard). The downfall of twentieth-century logical positivism (empiricism) hinged on the same self-defeating quality. British positivist A. J. Ayer maintained that a statement is meaningful if, and only if, the statement is analytic (true by definition alone, like 'all black dogs are black') or able to be verified through sense experience. Let us call this principle 'F'. Is F analytically true? No. Is F able to be verified through sense experience? No. Thus, F is self-defeating and steps beyond its bounds unjustifiably. Ayer tried to patch up principle F, leading him to an anaemic empiricism that left out as meaningless some things we know to be meaningful, e.g. general propositions in *science, like 'all ravens are black', and unrepeatable historical truths.

Among Christian apologists the use of experience to justify theistic belief is common, but the types of justification, and where and when justification takes place within an apologetic system, vary. Evidentialists believe the truth of Christianity can be established through the systemization of evidences about the universe, *morality, consciousness, rationality, design, probabilities for life, and Jesus's life, death and resurrection. Evidentialists like Montgomery, McDowell and Habermas argue that if one applies generally accepted principles of historiography and textual criticism to the available evidences, one will find the weight of probability squarely on the side of Christian truth. Presuppositionalists like Van Til are much more concerned with identifying the basis or conditions for making sense of experience before one ever asks where the evidences themselves point regarding Christianity.

A highly significant modern argument for God's existence hinges on the cognitive success of our rationality and our belief-forming mechanisms. How is it that our beliefs picture the world rightly, i.e. that our subjective formation of beliefs usually conforms correctly and accurately with our objective presence in this world? C. S. Lewis and Alvin Plantinga have powerfully argued that *naturalism (the belief that nature is all there is, thus implying evolution is entirely responsible for our cognitive apparatus) is not in itself sufficient to explain the success of the human cognitive enterprise. As Lewis said, the naturalist finds himself hoisted on his own petard: in the very act of explaining that thought is no more than movements among the 'grey matter', he must rely on the orderliness and purposiveness of thought patterns that are clearly aimed at *truth. The naturalist can only say that through time, chance, random mutations and natural selection alone such wonderful structures have been formed and are aimed, somehow, at producing true beliefs. But on naturalism and evolution, thoughts are simply movements of atoms or something caused by those movements, e.g. epiphenomenal happenings in the brain. There is no factor from outside this naturalistic picture to ensure that our internal cognitive structures map correctly to the external world and thus would produce true beliefs about that world (as opposed merely to help us display danger-avoidance behaviour for survival). But, according to Plantinga, *theism has an answer. God creates us in his image, part of which means to be rational persons with cognitive mechanisms producing mostly true beliefs when in the suitable environment.

In many ways, we would know nothing without our experience. Plantinga states that there is even an empirical or phenomenal aspect to our knowledge of necessary and abstract truths such as mathematics and *logic. However, wondering whether our experience produces justified belief, i.e. wondering whether our experience is at base reliable, has an objective and a significant subjective component. Objectively, either it is largely reliable or it is not. If it is not largely reliable, then there is no way out of this predicament. It appears to be largely reliable, and to act otherwise in the community setting is to betray the very assuredness experience gives us. For example, to think it possible that my son is not of human descent, and that he is older than his father, in the ordinary meaning of those terms, is incredible and philosophically untenable, but in some broadly logical sense possible. But the subjective side of the issue intersects at this point with the objective: I am as sure as a knower of most truths I can name that I have a son, and that my son is younger than I am by virtue of my evident and undeniable experiences (e.g. seeing him being born and watching him mature ever since on more or less a daily basis). There is a temporal and spatial continuity to this event of seeing and knowing my son that is objectively and subjectively undeniable. And it was evidently designed that there would be no other reasonable way for me to know these facts than through experience and reflection. There are many conditions for such knowledge (memory, consciousness, reflection, etc.). That these conditions could be doubted, individually or severally, is true, but that it is rational to doubt their truth-conduciveness is not true.

Thus, our attitude as Christians towards the truth of the deliverances of our senses should be thanksgiving. We receive it as an evident gift from God the creator and designer of our senses. God has so designed us that through experience we come to know his world and the things necessary for salvation and life with him. Thomas *Reid remarks that all of the objective components that contribute to our knowing come out of the same shop, i.e. there is an integrity or wholeness in the mechanisms of human cognition that is admirable and wondrous.

It is acceptable to maintain that our considered Christian *epistemology must combine elements of *rationalism and empiricism. In *Critique of Pure Reason* Immanuel *Kant was right when he said that concepts without experiences are empty (useless), and experiences without concepts are blind (undirected). God has so ordered our minds to make sense of our experience. The process of God getting his propositional *revelation to us is largely empirical (transmission of the text, the act of reading). Clearly, however, there are Christian sources of rational beliefs not fully traceable back to experience taken alone (the act of inspiration of Scripture, the act of regeneration, the internal testimony of the *Holy Spirit, mystical experience, *miracles, sense of the divine love, near-death experiences), since God himself is a nonphysical spirit. Even if we look at human epistemology naturalistically (e.g. through the notion of proper function, following Plantinga), it is reasonable to believe that experience is a reliable and justified source of knowledge only if it flowers within a supernaturalistic *metaphysics.

Bibliography

A. J. Ayer, *Language, Truth and Logic* (New York, 1952); D. Hume, *An Inquiry Concerning Human Understanding* (Oxford, 1975); C. S. Lewis, *Miracles* (New York, 1960), chs. 3, 13; A. Plantinga, *Warrant and Proper Function* (New York and Oxford, 1993).

E. N. MARTIN

ENLIGHTENMENT, THE

Like many labels for periods of history, 'the Enlightenment' was introduced by historians to express an estimation of the value of what they identify as an 'era'. Like the term 'Renaissance', but unlike the 'Middle Ages' or the 'Dark Ages', 'the Enlightenment' has stood for a movement in thought and culture that some modern historians have looked upon favourably. They did so because this movement challenged the *authority of religious tradition and celebrated the value, goodness and virtues of human nature, looking to modern *science to secure human progress over ignorance and superstition. The Enlightenment is often delimited from the late 1600s to the end of the 1700s, but there is no universally accepted way to date the period. The closest one can come to a historical summary of Enlightenment thought is Immanuel *Kant's (1724–1804) dictum that 'Enlightenment is man's emergence from his self-imposed immaturity. Immaturity is the inability to use one's understanding without guidance from another. This immaturity is self-imposed when its cause lies not in lack of understanding, but in lack of resolve and courage to use it without guidance from another. Sapere Aude! Have courage to use your own understanding! That is the motto of enlightenment' (Kant, p. 85).

In addition to Kant, key figures who are often seen as champions of the Enlightenment include Michel de Montaigne (1533–92), John *Locke (1632–1704), Baron de Montesquieu (1689–1755), François Marie Arouet de *Voltaire (1694–1778), David *Hume (1711–76), Denis Diderot (1713–84), Adam Smith (1723–90), and Baron de Holbach (1723–89). Sometimes, René *Descartes (1596–1650), Thomas Hobbes (1588–1679) and Benedict de *Spinoza (1632–77) are included as members of this group. Many of these thinkers may be seen from today's perspective as having truly made an enduring, positive impact on European culture and beyond. Certainly their opposition to religious intolerance and persecution is significant and the pursuit of intellectual freedom by opposing excessive censorship is important. Moreover, the Enlightenment ushered in a level of critical reflection on religion which produced masterpieces in both the case for and the case against religious belief. Of the figures named, Locke articulated and defended a vital role for Christianity in culture and politics; Holbach and Diderot wrote polemics against religion, as did Voltaire, though Voltaire's work was often more anti-clerical than anti-theistic. Enlightenment thinkers like Voltaire commended a natural religion that recognized God and an afterlife but shunned special providence, scriptural authority and *miracles. Hume and Kant delivered systematic critical treatments of the classical theistic arguments, though Hume may be interpreted as a deist rather than an atheist, and Kant's critique of *theism needs to be read alongside his *moral argument for Christian faith. Earlier philosophers offered new, 'modern' arguments for theism (Descartes) and non-theistic views of God (Spinoza). During this period we also have positive theistic contributions by Gottfried *Leibniz (1646–1716), Samuel *Clarke (1675–1729), George *Berkeley (1685–1753) Joseph *Butler (1692–1752) and Thomas *Reid (1710–96).

The Enlightenment championed an encyclopedic approach to knowledge. Diderot was a key editor of the *Encyclopédie* (1751–65), which presupposed the ideal of a universal, secular pursuit of knowledge and value. Perhaps the consummate theory emerging from this encyclopedic approach was Adam Smith's 'ideal observer' theory. Smith delimited an ideal moral point of view whereby one may have a sympathetic understanding of all parties involved in moral conflict and then achieve an enlightened judgment over rights and wrongs. There were sharp differences among Enlightenment thinkers on how to ground or justify moral arguments. Smith and Hume saw the basis of *morality in sympathy and benevolent feeling, whereas Kant highlighted practical reason.

The Enlightenment is often credited with either contributing to or at least heralding the American and French Revolutions. The Enlightenment philosophers' commitment to human dignity and freedom resonated with American and French political movements against the concentration of state power in the monarchy. All Enlightenment thinkers listed in this entry opposed political despotism.

Despite its strengths, the Enlightenment had its critics then and subsequently. The idea that each contributor to the Enlightenment was consistently impartial and a humanitarian is ungrounded. Despite his overriding opposition to despotism, Locke thought that *slavery in some of the British American colonies was permissible, and Hume wrote against the claim that blacks are equal in intelligence to whites. Sadly, his racist comments were used by defenders of slavery. Kant was also notorious for his prejudiced view of blacks. The case for the full political, legal, social, educational, scientific and religious equality of men and women was yet to be made. There were some women and men who advocated the full, equally expansive education of women –

mention should be made of Diderot and Lady Damaris Masham – but women's rights to freedom and equality were not widely recognized. After the French Revolution, we have the Napoleonic Wars, and during and after the Enlightenment we see European nations bent on imperial expansion. Many philosophers at the time challenged the high claims being made about the autonomy and power of human reason. Jean-Jacques *Rousseau (1712–78) and Pierre *Bayle (1647–1706) were highly critical, as was Blaise *Pascal (1623–62) before them. Each of these philosophers questioned the impartiality of human reason and opposed what they saw as arrogant claims made on behalf of human autonomy. Edmund Burke (1729–97) was a leading opponent of the Enlightenment ideals of inquiry and reason cut off from tradition. Kant's call to abandon the 'immature' reliance on the guidance of others struck Burke as itself immature and foolhardy rather than courageous. For Burke, we need tradition, *culture and continuity along with freedom to be mature citizens in a republic. G. W. F. *Hegel (1770–1831) offered a brilliant critique of Kant's Enlightenment ideal of reason and moral duty. Hegel held that reason and moral duty make little sense in abstraction and not articulated in the context of communities and living, religious tradition. Late modern philosophers who stand out as critics of Enlightenment humanism include *Kierkegaard (1813–55) and *Nietzsche (1844–1900). They are radically different thinkers, but they unite in challenging our ability to weigh deep matters of morality, reason and science in a dispassionate, impartial state.

Today, the Enlightenment has its defenders (the German philosopher Jürgen Habermas embraces an Enlightenment ideal of a universal, accessible reason) and detractors (Alasdair *MacIntyre and Charles Taylor). According to MacIntyre, proper philosophical *reasoning can and should take place as part of traditions of inquiry. The most widespread criticism of the Enlightenment today is that its upholding of disinterested reason is not itself upheld by disinterested reason. Frederick Beiser puts the problem succinctly: 'The *Aufklärung* [German, 'Enlightenment'] gave reason complete sovereignty because it claimed that reason could criticize all of our beliefs, accepting or rejecting them strictly according to whether there is sufficient eveidence for them … such was the bold programme – and dream – of the

Aufklärung. Tragically, though, it carried the seeds of its own destruction. Simply to state its principle of the sovereignty of reason is to raise grave questions about it. For if reason must criticize everything on heaven and earth, must it not also criticize itself? And, if it does so, how does it prevent its self-criticism from being scepticism? A nightmare looms: that the self-criticism of reason ends in nihilism, doubt about the existence of everything. That fear was the sum and substance of the crisis of the *Aufklärung.*'

Over the past thirty years there has been a movement vaguely referred to as 'post-modernism' that contains many important challenges to the modern, Enlightenment concept of reason. Michel *Foucault (1926–84) undertook a series of studies that unearthed the partial social, political presuppositions behind various Enlightenment projects, from insane asylum to systems of *justice and sex education. The French-Algerian Jacques *Derrida has carried Foucault's work even further, arguing against a stable Enlightenment treatment of meaning. Derrida's work is too dense and complex to yield any easy summary, but he is a useful reference point in the sustained contemporary assault on the Enlightenment.

Two figures who are trenchant critics of modernity but who are more sympathetic to Christian religious tradition are Paul Ricoeur and Hans-Georg Gadamer. Both have argued that religious tradition is a vital source of philosophical wisdom, challenging the ostensible autonomy and maturity of secular culture.

How should Christian apologetics proceed today in light of this vast critical response to the Enlightenment? There are many options. For example, one may accept the Enlightenment ideal about disinterested, free inquiry and argue, as Joseph Butler did in the eighteenth century, that such inquiry vindicates Christianity. The British philosopher Richard Swinburne has continued Butler's project into the twenty-first century, producing an impressive series of books that argue persuasively for theism and the central tenets of Christianity (the *Trinity, incarnation, *atonement, miracles, resurrection, afterlife). An alternative approach, championed today by Alvin Plantinga and Nicholas Wolterstorff, argues that the Enlightenment failed to establish some neutral secular laws of evidence that would either vindicate Christianity (as Swinburne believes) or undermine it (as Michael Martin, a contemporary, pro-Enlightenment atheist believes). Plantinga and Wolterstorff advance a negative apologetic by arguing that none of the Enlightenment objections to Christianity succeeds. Positively, they then argue that Christian belief is reasonable even if alternatives such as *naturalism are reasonable as well.

A final suggestion. Even if a Christian apologist accepts the critique of the Enlightenment launched by Wolterstorff and the thinkers listed above, he or she would do well to take seriously the positive case for Christianity advanced by Swinburne and others. In his most recent work, widely available, Plantinga himself has argued positively for theism based on the nature of reason itself. This is an argument reminiscent of C. S. *Lewis's case for theism in his book *Miracles,* and it challenges atheists and agnostics on neutral ground. That is, the argument has credibility and force, given the Enlightenment ideal of disinterested inquiry.

Bibliography

F. Beiser, 'Post-Kantian Philosophy', in S. Critchley and W. R. Schroeder (eds.), *A Companion to Continental Philosophy* (Oxford, 1998); I. Kant, *Foundations of the Metaphysics of Morals,* and *What is Enlightenment?* (trans. by L. W. Beck; Indianapolis, 1959); A. MacIntyre, *Whose Justice? Which Rationality?* (Notre Dame, 1988); A. Smith, *Three Rival Versions of Moral Enquiry* (Notre Dame, 1990); C. Taliaferro, *Evidence and Faith: Philosophy and Religion since the Seventeenth Century* (Cambridge, 2005); J. W. Yolton (ed.), *The Blackwell Companion to the Enlightenment* (Oxford, 1995).

C. TALIAFERRO

ENVIRONMENTALISM

Christianity challenged

In 1967 the Christian faith was rebuked and challenged by historian Lynn White. In a paper entitled 'The Historical Roots of Our Ecological Crisis' (*Science* [March 1967], pp. 1203–1207), White lambasted the church for its attitude towards the environment. He blamed the biblical commands in Genesis to be fruitful and multiply and to have dominion over the earth for the exploitative nature of the environmental crisis and said that 'Christianity bears a huge burden of guilt'. White was not altogether negative because he drew attention to St Francis and called him the patron saint for ecologists because he 'set up a democracy for all God's creatures'. White challenged Christians to go back and examine the teachings of St Francis.

As the environmental crisis facing today's world has deepened, more and more secular environmentalists and organizations have realized that it is so deep that only ethical and moral stances can hope to address it. There have been many appeals to religions to respond. For example, ecologist Lawrence Hamilton has written, 'It is not ecologists, engineers, economists or earth scientists who will save spaceship earth but poets, priests, artists and philosophers'. Maurice Strong, the organizer of the 1992 Earth Summit in Rio de Janeiro, has said that 'We cannot expect to make the fundamental changes needed in our economic life unless they are based on the highest and best of our moral, spiritual and ethical traditions, a reverence for life, a respect for each other, and a commitment to responsible stewardship of the earth. The transition to a sustainable society must be undergirded by moral, ethical and spiritual revolution which places these values at the center of our individual and societal lives' and that 'We need to re-state and win support for the ethic of living sustainably because it is morally right. Establishment of the ethic needs support of the world's religions because they have spoken for centuries about the individual's duty of care for fellow humans and of reverence for divine creation'.

These quotes and many other statements are a challenge to the church to respond to the environmental crisis.

The environmental crisis

There is no doubt that at the start of the twenty-first century the world faces a grave environmental crisis, as human activity is seriously degrading the environment. Climate is changing because of the fossil fuels we burn and the forests we cut down; species are becoming extinct at an alarming rate; stocks of fish are being severely depleted as we over-fish the oceans; topsoil, upon which agriculture depends, is being eroded and washed away; serious pollution is affecting our air, rivers and oceans; the ozone layer is thinning out, resulting in increased danger from radiation; and population is rising above the carrying capacity of our planet. The predatory lifestyle of the developed world has forced poor nations into serious debt and keeps a third of the world's population in abject poverty. Environmental issues cannot be separated from those of social *justice.

In response to White and other critics, the dominion given to humankind by God is not a licence to destroy and abuse what he has made and declared to be 'very good' (Gen. 1:31). Dominion implies stewardship and not wanton destruction. God is pleased with creation and wishes us to respect it, and this is made plain in many places in the Scriptures, e.g. 'Praise the LORD ... Praise him, sun and moon, praise him, all you shining stars ... for he commanded and they were created ... Praise the LORD from the earth, you great sea creatures and all ocean depths, lightning and hail, snow and clouds, stormy winds that do his bidding' (Ps. 148:1–8).

This and many other Psalms are songs of praise for creation. They celebrate nature and the environment as God's creation but do not advocate the common heresy of worshipping creation instead of the Creator. After Job has been through his trials and the ineffective advice from his friends, God answers him out of a whirlwind. Instead of making a call for repentance or a theological statement, God asks Job the question, 'Where were you when I laid the earth's foundation?' (Job 38:4). He proceeds to point out Job's ignorance of creation and gives him a detailed description of some of the marvels of nature and of the universe (Job 38 – 41). These chapters describe many of the physical and natural features of creation and the lesson in them is that true repentance involves recognition that all we have is lent to us and that all created things belong to God, entrusted to our care, but for our use. Gen. 1:9 indicates this dual role of creation: the trees are for our use, but they are also to be enjoyed. This combination of the economic and the aesthetic means that God's creation has to be cared for and not destroyed. Similarly, the land itself was given to the first people to till (Heb. *abad*) and keep (Heb. *shamar*), i.e. they were to serve and watch over, or preserve, the land. Their stewardship of the land was not to be predatory or destructive. Creation is there to be used and enjoyed, but it is also part of God's revelation: 'I will put in the desert the cedar and the acacia, the myrtle and the olive. I will set pines in the wasteland, the fir and the cypress together, so that people may see and know, may consider and understand, that the hand of the LORD has done this, that the Holy One of Israel has created it' (Isa. 41:19–20).

If this is the purpose of creation, then Christians have a responsibility to preserve it rather than disrupt it. It is not only the trees and the fields that are to be cared for but also the animals – God's covenant with Noah (Gen. 9) is full of references to 'living creatures', and *Jesus said, 'Are not five sparrows sold for two pennies? Yet not one of them is forgotten by God' (Luke 12:6). Jesus, as part of the triune God, was present in creation as 'the image of the invisible God, the firstborn over all creation. For by him all things were created' (Col. 1:15), and he was sent because 'God so loved the world' (John 3:16). God's redemption is not just for humans but for all of creation, and the challenge to all Christians is to be his special stewards and not the agents of destruction. It is a great pity that Christian teaching has neglected creation and been slow to enter into environmentalism. The deepening crisis is causing Christians to re-think these issues, and there are many more Christian organizations involved with the environment and churches encouraging stewardship than a few years ago. As the document produced by the Orthodox Church in 1990 entitled 'Orthodoxy and the Ecological Crisis' states, 'We must attempt to return to a proper relationship with the creator and creation. This may well mean that just as a shepherd will in times of greatest hazard, lay down his life for his flock, so human beings may need to forgo part of their wants and needs in order that the survival of the natural world can be assured. This is a new situation – a new challenge. It calls for humanity to bear some of the pain of creation as well as to enjoy and celebrate it. It calls first and foremost for repentance – but of an order not previously understood by many.'

Bibliography

T. Cooper, *Green Christianity: Caring for the Whole Creation* (London, 1990); F. van Dyke, D. C. Mahan, J. K. Sheldon and R. H. Brand, *Redeeming Creation: The Biblical Basis for Environmental Stewardship* (Downers Grove, 1996); G. T. Prance, *The Earth Under Threat: A Christian Perspective* (Glasgow, 1996); C. Russell, *The Earth, Humanity and God* (London, 1994).

G. T. PRANCE

EPISTEMOLOGY

Introduction

Epistemology, or the theory of knowledge, is the branch of philosophy devoted to the study of human knowledge and related epistemic goods. While epistemologists seek to define the nature and scope of human knowledge, they also inquire into the nature of such intellectual goods as understanding and justified belief, the range and proper function of our cognitive powers, the conceptual and linguistic prerequisites for knowledge, how intellectual virtues promote intellectual flourishing, and related topics. Throughout its history, epistemologists have also sought to combat sceptical arguments that purport to show that we cannot achieve knowledge or justified belief, or at least not to the degree that we ordinarily think.

How do the concerns of epistemologists and ordinary Christian believers intersect? To start, the right use of reason matters to both. Epistemologists and ordinary Christians agree that it is important to superintend our intellectual powers and their right use, for there are better and worse ways we can employ that cluster of cognitive powers we call 'reason'. So epistemologists' efforts to articulate and assess the canons of good intellectual conduct should interest anyone seeking to be intellectually excellent. Epistemology and common sense teach that there are responsible and irresponsible, reliable and unreliable, ways to employ our powers of perception, memory, *a priori* intuition, introspection and *reasoning. Forming visual beliefs while under the influence of hallucinogenic drugs, or forming scientific generalizations on the basis of unrepresentative samples, are obvious examples of the unreliable use of our cognitive powers.

The mind matters for Christians too, for having cognitive powers whereby we discern the difference between *truth and falsehood is one of the ways we bear God's image. Christ himself, of course, commands that we love God with all our heart, soul, strength and mind (Luke 10:27). We may infer from Christ's command that we cannot love God fully without making our intellectual powers a part of our love. Paul, likewise, enjoins us to be 'transformed by the renewing of [our] mind' (Rom. 12:2) and to put on a new nature 'which is being renewed in knowledge in the image of its Creator' (Col. 3:10), and he prays that God may grant us 'the Spirit of wisdom and revelation, so that [we] may know him better' (Eph. 1:17). Unfortunately, persons sometimes fail to exercise due care over their moral and intellectual formation, resulting in what Paul calls persons of 'corrupt' or 'depraved' mind – minds that are 'bereft of truth' or which 'suppress the truth in unrighteousness'. Such persons are described as having 'a veil' that 'covers their hearts' (2 Cor. 3:15), to the effect that their minds are not set upon the things of God, but upon the things of the flesh (Rom. 8:6–7). Our cognitive powers can be disused and abused, so that we undermine our prospect of gaining the truth.

Epistemologists disagree with one another about the nature and proper function of our cognitive powers. *Plato and *Descartes, for instance, famously depreciated the role of *sense perception in acquiring knowledge, going so far as to claim that its deliverances are misleading. Empiricists, by contrast, viewed our sensory faculties as an ultimate basis for knowledge. Thomas *Reid thought the task of acquiring knowledge relied crucially on an innate disposition to accede to the testimony of others, whereas *Locke was generally suspicious of testimony and denied that we possess any such natural disposition. *Thomas Aquinas thought that among reason's powers is *synderēsis*, a capacity of reason to apprehend moral *first principles, an important part of *conscience. Bertrand *Russell, among many others, denied that *synderēsis* is a part of our native cognitive equipment. Recently, Alvin Plantinga's epistemology has revived the notion that humans are endowed with a *sensus divinitatus*, an innate divine sense crucial for experiencing God and apprehending truths pertaining to God. Other epistemologists deny that we have any such divine sense. The disagreements among epistemologists about our knowledge-gathering equipment often reflect deeper disagreements about the nature of persons and the sort of world in which we live. These disagreements, in turn, influence our judgments about our ability to secure religious knowledge.

Justification

Even when epistemologists agree about the nature and scope of our intellectual powers, they often disagree about what standards should regulate their right use, or what conditions we must satisfy to have justified beliefs. Three rival theories, *evidentialism, coherentism and reliabilism, each claiming to give the necessary and sufficient conditions for justification, have dominated recent discussions about justification.

Briefly, coherentism says that we are entitled to accept only beliefs that fit into or cohere with our existing framework of beliefs. This view faces formidable objections, not the least of which is that sets of beliefs may display considerable coherence, yet fly in the face of what we have good reason to think is true. Consider the disordered mind of Don Quixote, whose fanciful constructions seamlessly wove together fact and fiction into a remarkably coherent web of beliefs. Yet we are disinclined to call justified his belief that he jousted with giants, however well it fits into the totality of his beliefs.

Reliabilist theories of justification say that beliefs are justified if and only if they are produced in us by truth-conducive cognitive faculties or processes, i.e. by faculties that statistically yield a high ratio of truths to falsehoods. We need not be aware of how these beliefs were produced in us. A small child, for instance, may have a justified belief that his mother has just entered the room, without having any reflective grasp of how this belief arose or ability to defend its being justified. The child's belief is justified simply in virtue of having been produced by reliable cognitive equipment. One counterintuitive consequence of this view is that I can be justified in a belief even if I think I ought not to hold it. To use an example of Laurence Bonjour's, suppose that clairvoyance is a reliable cognitive faculty, and that it reliably causes one, out of the blue, to believe that the president is in New York City. Suppose also that the person in whom this belief arises denies that anyone has clairvoyance and furthermore doubts the truth about the president being in New York. While this belief formally satisfies reliabilist conditions for justification, many are disinclined to think that one can be justified in holding a belief that one simultaneously doubts is true. Moreover, Christians believe that God sometimes reveals knowledge to us in ways that bypass our native belief-producing equipment. If we make it a necessary condition of justification that a belief arises out of reliable belief-producing processes, we jeopardize our being justified in some of the beliefs God reveals to us.

The nineteenth-century philosopher W. K. Clifford summarized evidentialism thus: 'It is wrong, always and everywhere, for anyone to believe anything upon insufficient evidence.' Stated positively, Clifford proposes that for any belief p, p is justified if and only if it is based on sufficient evidence. Obvious questions confront this proposal. What is evidence? How much is sufficient? In what ways must a target belief be *based on* the evidence? Clearly not all beliefs can require evidential support in the form of additional beliefs to be justifiably believed, for this would lead to an infinite regress. Some beliefs we take as properly basic, i.e. as beliefs to which we are entitled independently of argumentative support. Most of us believe that our sensory faculties reliably convey to us truths about the physical world. While most normal people affirm this, they do not do so on the basis of evidence, for any evidence one offered would be circular in nature. So-called Reformed epistemologists have recently defended the idea that our belief in God can be properly basic. Like our perceptual beliefs, it may be triggered by experiential circumstances but is not based on argument.

Evidentialists also face crucial questions about what kinds of beliefs and experiences count as evidence and how we estimate their probative force. Suppose I am asked why I believe that God exists, and I offer as evidence that I have encountered him in worship. Many philosophers would not count my experience as evidence since it is not publicly accessible and assessable. The claim that all evidence must be publicly accessible is itself controversial, however. Even if we agree about what counts as evidence, we sometimes disagree about how to assess its force. Jurors who listen to the same evidence day after day may nevertheless disagree about whether it is sufficient to show the defendant's guilt.

Virtue epistemology

Christians are not limited to the resources of secular philosophy to draw insight about a well-lived intellectual life, any more than they are limited to such sources in the moral life. In our moral lives, we are guided by Christ's explicit ethical teachings, by his example, by the deliberations of the church, and by reflecting on the life that is made available to us through his Holy Spirit. We receive from these sources direct normative commands, such as to 'love our neighbours as ourselves'. But we also receive insight into how to think about the moral life in less directly normative, more theoretical terms, so much so that a student of moral philosophy can study *ethics from a distinctively Christian perspective. According to this perspective, Christ's life and teachings are rich enough to support our thinking about the moral life, its concepts, ends and notions of human flourishing in a way that makes Christian ethics unlike secular ethics or ethics grounded in any other religious point of view. Analogously, the philosophical subject of epistemology, and not just ethics, can be given distinctively Christian contours.

The notion of intellectual virtues should occupy a prominent (though not exclusive) place in a biblical epistemology. Intellectual virtues are acquired and deeply anchored bases of excellent intellectual functioning, whereby we are able to negotiate gracefully and successfully the various cognitive tasks we face, and to overcome such obstacles as may frustrate our pursuit of intellectual goods. Note the language of the Hebrew wisdom tradition in the opening lines of Proverbs: 'for attaining *wisdom* and *discipline*; for *understanding* words of *insight*; for acquiring a disciplined and prudent life, doing what is right and just and fair; for giving *prudence* to the simple, *knowledge* and *discretion* to the young – let the wise listen and add to their learning, and let the discerning get guidance – for understanding proverbs and parables, the sayings and riddles of the wise. The fear of the LORD is the beginning of knowledge, but fools despise wisdom and discipline.'

The NT too is replete with the language of the wisdom tradition. We are urged not to be children in our thinking, but mature (1 Cor. 14:20). Those aspiring to the office of bishop must display moral and intellectual excellence, holding to the truth as taught, being sensible, apt teachers, and able to confute those who oppose sound doctrine (1 Tim. 3:2; Titus 1:9). The epistles caution us to be on our guard against intellectual vices, settled habits of mind that impede our ability to acquire intellectual goods. Scripture mentions directly, or by implication, a number of intellectual vices, including credulity, crippling *doubt, wilful naïveté, gullibility, folly, obtuseness, disputatiousness and unteachableness.

The Bible offers guidance on how to develop intellectual virtues. First, it teaches that cultivating the virtues is a developmental process that extends through a lifetime. Even Jesus grew in wisdom, and Paul had to learn not to think as a child. Secondly, growth in the virtues is not automatic. Peter urges that we 'make every effort to add to our faith, goodness' (2 Pet. 1:5). To secure wisdom one must conscientiously seek it out. The writer of Proverbs likens wisdom and other intellectual virtues to buried treasure; they must be hunted and dug for. Thirdly, we are not alone in our efforts to become virtuous persons; our careers as moral and intellectual persons develop within the context of a *community: 'As iron sharpens iron, so one man sharpens another' (Prov. 27:17). It is within a community that we learn what intellectual goals are worth pursuing, what goals should be subordinated to others, what practices ought to be avoided, and what resources are available to assist one in moral and intellectual growth. Fourthly, we must work to sustain our gains in the moral and intellectual life, since regression is a real possibility. The writer of Hebrews accuses those to whom the letter is directed of being 'slow to learn' and of needing to be taught 'the elementary truths of God's word *all over again*'.

Scripture also teaches that intellectual virtues must be fostered in conjunction with other human excellences; it offers a holistic picture of persons that intimately connects our having a virtuous mind with our full humanity as knowers. It recognizes the indispensable contribution to cognitive flourishing made by our emotions, bodies, moral character and will. We commonly acknowledge the ways physical or neurological impairment can adversely affect good thinking; less often do we consider how a wayward will bears upon our ability to think well and cultivate intellectual virtue. The will is a complex faculty; in its conative aspect it is the seat of our desires, concerns, attachments and loves, all of which move us to action. In its executive aspect it chooses among the desires that often compete for our attention, and exerts willpower to manage desires we ought not to gratify. The person who cultivates such traits as love of truth, practical wisdom and teachableness must surely care about these qualities and the intellectual goods they help us to obtain. The will must monitor and regulate and suppress desires and disordered affections that frustrate our pursuit of intellectual goods.

The two-way causal connection between right thinking and right *morality is an important motif that runs throughout Scripture and is attested to by common sense. Arrogance, dishonesty, pride, pugnacity and many other manifestations of disordered lives undermine our ability to think well and to pursue the truth. Thus, Paul, in his letter to the Ephesians, commands that we must no longer 'live as the Gentiles do, in the futility of their thinking. They are darkened in their understanding and separated from the life of God because of the ignorance that is in them due to the hardening of their hearts.' On the other hand, persons marked by traits such as charity, compassion, empathy and *justice are more likely to achieve insight and understanding in matters of religion, social justice, interpersonal relations and interpretation (among other areas). Virtue epistemology thus corrects the prevailing idea that the emotions, or properly tutored affections, are merely barriers to good judgment; they are indispensable for some kinds of understanding.

Epistemology and apologetics

Apologetics is often said to have both negative and positive tasks. Negatively, apologetics defends the Christian faith against charges that it is false or that its adherents are unreasonable, or in some way intellectually below par for accepting its claims. Positively, apologists employ reasons and arguments to recommend Christian belief to those who do not already accept it. Epistemology, as a discipline that proposes and evaluates guidelines for reasonableness, is relevant to both tasks.

Consider, as William Alston bids us, the role epistemic standards play in assessing *religious experience. Christians point to religious experiences as initiators and sustainers of faith. Christians often claim to have 'felt that God is comforting them in their grief', or 'to have felt the nearness of God in worship'. Alston says that such experiences provide one with knowledge or justification for God's existence just as experiences of such things as trees, houses and people provide us with knowledge or justified beliefs about the material world. Critics protest that we need independent *verification of God's existence before we accept religious experiences as veridical. Alston points out, however, that such demands are based on a double standard. We do not require independent verification that we are not all deceived about the existence of the material world before accepting perceptual experiences as veridical. To demand this of religious experiences and not material-object experiences is unfairly to apply a double standard.

Many objections to religious belief depend upon controversial epistemic standards. In many cases, apologists would do well to address objections to religious belief not head on, but indirectly, by enquiring about the epistemic standards underlying the objection. If *theism is attacked for lacking sufficient evidence of a commonly accepted sort, theists can either supply the needed evidence, or question whether the demand is itself one they are obliged to meet. If theism is attacked for its lack of unanimity, one can point to other disciplines, such as philosophy, where agreement is not a requirement for rational belief. One can also question the appropriateness of any epistemic standard that makes rough agreement a criterion of justified belief.

Bibliography

J. Dancy and E. Sosa (eds.), *A Companion to Epistemology* (Oxford, 1993); M. DePaul and L. Zagzebski (eds.), *Intellectual Virtue* (Oxford, 2003); P. Moser (ed.), *The Oxford Handbook of Epistemology* (Oxford, 2002); A. Plantinga, *Warranted Christian Belief* (Oxford, 2000); W. J. Wood, *Epistemology: Becoming Intellectually Virtuous* (Leicester and Downers Grove, 1998); L. Zagzebski, *Virtues of the Mind* (Cambridge, 1996).

W. J. WOOD

ERASMUS, DESIDERIUS

Erasmus was born 28 October 1466 or 1469 in Rotterdam in the Netherlands. The name Desiderius was self-given later. He was the son of a Roman Catholic priest and his housekeeper, and this less than noble birth haunted him for the rest of his life. Nevertheless, Erasmus was privileged enough to be well educated. His adult life included a period in a monastery, duty as an ordained priest, theological study at the University of Paris and, finally, a masters and doctorate in theology from the University of Turin.

Erasmus and humanism

Simply put, humanism is the elevation of humanity above divinity. The humanist's quest is to tap into the very best of human potential. This tendency was apparent in Erasmus, as he was less interested in doctrine and more interested in discipline and spiritual exercise. A common thread among humanists is an underestimation of the depth of their own sin and an overestimation of the breadth of their own ability. It is likely that Erasmus was a humanist with some Christian tendencies and a love particularly for the human nature of Christ.

In 1499 Erasmus went to Oxford where he met a diligent lecturer named John Colet. Colet and Erasmus would often challenge each other on theological issues but rarely found resolution because neither had a sufficient grasp of the biblical languages of Hebrew and Greek. Erasmus accused Colet of trying to 'obtain water from a pumice stone', and himself discovered that it was difficult at best to mine theological truth from a text such as Jerome's Latin translation of the Bible (the Vulgate) that was not penned in the original languages. This struggle with Colet thrust Erasmus into the realization that he actually knew very little about true Christianity.

Finally, in 1504 Erasmus published an audacious attack against the Latin Vulgate translation. Erasmus' conclusions were based on the work of a scholar named Lorenzo Valla, who wrote about the discrepancies between the best Greek manuscripts he had access to and what he found in Jerome's Latin. After years of intense Greek study, at the cost of his health and relationships, Erasmus penned his famous version of the Greek New Testament in 1516, using just a few manuscripts. This work had an immediate impact. Melanchthon, Zwingli and Luther used it insistently and semi-authoritatively against many church authorities. Erasmus later issued a second edition in 1519, using ten manuscripts.

In 1533, after labouring over the biblical text for decades, Erasmus stopped trying to harmonize or syncretize Christianity with classical Greek and Roman thought, in which, as a humanist, he had previously trusted. His knowledge of Greek, and the defence and definition that the Greek Scriptures presented of the true faith, finally prevailed. Erasmus died in 1536.

His last words in Latin, translated into English, were, 'O, Jesus, mercy; Lord, deliver me; Lord, be merciful to me!' Then he said in Dutch, 'Beloved God!'

If Erasmus had a flaw, it was his inability to take a stand on issues that mattered. Luther recognized immediately that Erasmus' work would further his own cause, and he tried to meet him. Nevertheless, Erasmus would have nothing to do with Luther, not because he disagreed with him, but because he did not want to be associated with him since he believed that this could have adversely affected his mission to further the practice of learning from the biblical languages.

Perhaps what mattered most to Erasmus was the greatest means to discovering *truth, and not necessarily the truth revealed by those great means. This aspect of Erasmus' life presents an interesting challenge to us today: can we be zealous about the art and science of apologetics while being equally zealous about the truths which it is intended to defend?

Bibliography

J. Huizinga, *Erasmus and the Age of the Reformation* (Mineola, 2001); A. Hyma, *The Life of Desiderius Erasmus* (Assen, 1972); <http://www.utm.edu/research/iep/e/erasmus.html>; <http://www.historyguide.org/intellect/erasmus.html>.

J. A. FORTNA

ERIUGENA

The ninth-century Christian scholar Johannes (800–77) signed himself as 'Eriugena' in one manuscript and thus was referred to as 'the Irishman'. Remarkably for a scholar in Western Europe in the Carolingian era, he had a considerable familiarity with the Greek language, which gave him access to the Greek Christian theological tradition. Eriugena clearly made use of this tradition in his own theological work, combining Christian content within a Neoplatonic philosophical outlook.

Around 847 Eriugena came to France, where he was appointed as head of the palace school during the time of Charles the Bald. He was commissioned to translate the works of Pseudo-*Dionysius into Latin. This translation brought him into prominence in the world of letters and was the occasion for him to become embroiled in a controversy over the doctrine of *predestination. Commissioned to refute the views of a Saxon monk, Gottschalk (806–68), Eriugena rejected any divine predestination to *evil by an appeal to God's unity. The argumentation of *On Divine Predestination* is carried out by close attention to dialectics, the science of disputation. In this treatise, Eriugena claims 'that true philosophy is true religion and conversely that true religion is true philosophy'. The stress on dialectic as the path for attaining *truth is a constant theme in Eriugena's work.

Eriugena's most important writing is the *Periphyseon*, a long dialogue in five books between an anonymous teacher and his student. The dialogue seeks to embrace all knowledge within the *cosmology of procession from and return to the Divine One. Eriugena boldly claims that nature is a term referring to all things that are and all things that are not. Nature can be divided into that which creates and is not created (i.e. God), that which creates and is created (i.e. primary causes or ideas), that which is created and does not create (i.e. temporal effects, created things) and that which is neither created nor creates (i.e. non-being, or nothingness).

Eriugena exerted influence on mysticism through his translation of Pseudo-Dionysius and on *scholasticism through his rigorous use of reason to explicate the coherence of Christianity. His prodigious use of dialetic characterizes his attempts at explaining the coherence of Christianity and the structure of the universe.

Bibliography

D. Moran, 'John Scottus Eriugena', in E. N. Zalta (ed.), *The Stanford Encyclopedia of Philosophy* (Fall 2003); J. J. O'Meara, *Eriugena* (Oxford, 1988); J. Marenbon, *Early Medieval Philosophy 480–1150* (London and Boston, 1983).

G. L. ISAAC

ESCAPISM

Escapism is here understood pejoratively and, therefore, must be distinguished from the idea of rest, leisure or a wholesome variety in one's life and thought. Escapism is an attempt to avoid pain or responsibility that might actually be useful and lead to true knowledge and experience of *reality. Escapism can be a postponing of the inevitable, a form of procrastination; it promises relief or protection and, therefore, appears a reasonable strategy in coping with anxiety or disappointment.

There are several difficulties with the concept of escapism, not least that it can take so many forms that identifying it is confusing. Escape may be found in *sport and *entertainment or a full schedule at work, cultivating personal relationships or refraining from them, travel or the refusal to go anywhere unfamiliar, substance abuse or a craze for fitness, a morose preoccupation with one's self or the refusal to think about one's life. Different people choose different vehicles of escape, and Christians must be very careful and compassionate in judging some activity as escapist in another person. It is useful to remember that many non-Christians consider faith in Christ to be a form of escape from the harsh reality of a meaningless world.

People may not be aware, or they may deny, that something in their life acts as a form of escape. Even when care is taken before making an accusation of escapist behaviour, it may prove very difficult to get someone to agree with the accusation. And there is the added difficulty that escape for some is an effective way of avoiding pain or responsibility. It is naïve for Christians to insist that all non-Christians are secretly unhappy and unfulfilled. Many forms of escape leave a person feeling more alive than the deadened routine of their daily life, and of course Christians indulge in escapist thoughts and actions, too.

It is often difficult to convince people that they are attempting to escape from reality, because to admit something is a form of escape in some situations robs it of its power to relieve pain or to keep real disappointments at a distance. Our role as witnesses to the reality of God is not to convince people of their escapist behaviour but to show them that the discovery and experience of that reality is a far better way of coping with life's fears and difficulties than any escape or form of distraction, whether pleasant or dangerous. To do this successfully we need to know a person well enough to be able to understand what it is they most fear about reality, because it is this fear, combined with their own personality and history, that will explain the form of escape they choose. What the Christian must not do is either deny the existence of pain in the world or be unaware of their own temptation to escapism. The Christian also must not present the good news about *Jesus itself as a form of escape from reality. The gospel does bring ultimate safety and fulfilment, but it does so by a flight into, rather than away from, the ugliness of human nature in a creation alienated from its Creator.

Bibliography

N. Postman, *Amusing Ourselves to Death* (London, 1987); R. Winter, *Still Bored in a Culture of Entertainment* (Downers Grove, 2002).

W. Bradshaw

ETHICS

Everyone faces moral issues, and so ethics are a clear means of engaging in apologetics' discussions. These will focus on the origins and basis, nature and content and the application of ethics. In discussion it is easiest to begin with specific moral issues, and these arise in the media, society and in the lives of individuals. How are any of us to make moral decisions? What criteria of judgment do we use to define what is ethical and to evaluate the options in ethical issues? While there is often a distinct difference between Christian and other ethical systems, there is some *common ground. This is because humanity is created by God and made in his image and *conscience (God's inner law) is written on the hearts and minds of humans (Rom. 2:15). This allows an appeal to shared values, common interests and moral sensitivities. The differences will not simply be in the conclusions reached but often arise from different perceptions of what it means to be responsible and answerable to God, to have a relationship with Christ and to be dependent on the guidance of the *Holy Spirit. These will contrast with an ethic based purely on humanistic grounds.

The basis of ethics is a matter of debate. Human reason, will and emotions are often suggested as the grounds of ethics. Often such ethical systems are reductionistic, fastening on one aspect of human being and failing to do justice to the complexity and holism of humanity. All of these are purely human analyses and see ethics as arising from human nature and reflection. Christians argue that ethics are from God and are a reflection of his nature, will and *revelation. This gives objectivity to ethics in contrast to many subjective accounts. For secular people who argue for objective ethics, the ultimate basis of that must be explored. For those of other religions who accept some notion of the divine basis and revelation of ethics, the nature and content of the divine are the key issue at stake.

Ethics are clearly not just a matter for the individual, nor can they be based simply on personal preference. By nature and definition ethics are social. Ethical standards deal with communities and how people are to treat and deal with each other in their relationships (including animals and the world); individualistic ethics are a misnomer. This leads to a reflection on human nature and our shared ethical values. Society could not operate without some commonly agreed ethical standards. These reflect our common nature and concerns. Again the basis of that nature and concerns may be chance, human development or divine. Comparing and contrasting these bases and weighing their adequacy are important.

It is important to distinguish purely human *law from ethics. We can always ask whether a particular law is ethical or not, and legal standards are separable from ethical norms. Some naturalist ethics suggest that there is a *natural law or some evolution of ethics. Where this comes from and why it is ethical are crucial questions.

Ethical discussion may concentrate on principles, consequences, motives, context or situation and virtues. Various ethical theories proffer a wide range of ethical principles. Usually called deontological, these often express shared values expressed in such systems as the Hippocratic oath. While such common ground is valuable in responding to ethical issues in society, the grounds of these principles will be different. Reflecting on the derivation of principles and how to deal with conflict between competing principles are useful apologetic strategies.

Consequentialist theories, usually called teleological, concentrate on the results and argue that the ends justify the means. *Utilitarianism is classically consequentialist, seeking the greatest happiness of the greatest number. In responding, Christians admit that consequences matter and, indeed, have eternal significance as both a warning and reminder of the importance of what we do and fail to do and the effects. This is very far from suggesting that the end justifies the means, particularly if the means are immoral in themselves. There are some things we would regard as fundamentally wrong in all circumstances, like child abuse. It is extremely hard to know when and how far in the future we need to calculate the consequences. Consequentialism over-optimistically assumes an ability to predict and control consequences both in our own actions and in relation to others.

In making an ethical assessment of an action why someone does something makes a difference. If the intention behing the action was good, that counts for something even if the end result is not what was intended. The road to hell, however, is paved with good intentions, and they are not the only part of ethical evaluation. There is a great variety of possible motivations, and these must be assessed. Human drives and desires motivate actions. There is also the problem of mixed motives, as very few of us have pure motives. Exploration of the motives, their basis and the impact they have on actions all need to be considered. This inevitably relates to an understanding of human nature. Jesus stressed the importance of the inner motivation. Having and nursing feelings of hate and lust are as serious as acting on these motives. The relativist denial of absolute standards of ethics often focuses on the context of ethical reflection and action. Situation ethics argues that we must avoid *legalism and the inconsistency of antinomianism (denial of laws). We must take our ethical standards from the situation. That defines what will count as ethically significant. It is very difficult simply to depend on the situation itself. Joseph Fletcher, author of *Situation Ethics*, argues that love is to be realized in every situation. An emphasis on the importance of context still needs some kind of guiding principle to bring to the situation. What is useful is the stress on applying ethical principles to real people in genuine situations.

This can, however, easily slide into a *relativism which tries to deny ethical *absolutes and yet absolutizes the context and the relative. The status of relativism and the contrary evidence of the universal ethical standards of *truth telling, rules for sexual expression, parent-children relationships, the protection of human life and property undermine strict relativism. There are universal ethical values which are expressed appropriately in different cultures and contexts. This simply shows the importance of applying ethical standards relevantly and does not imply that these are not in some sense absolute. It may be debated whether 'absolute' means always applicable (i.e. requiring justification before departing from it), rather than without exception. A rule will still be a rule even if there is the very occasional, carefully justified exception.

Since Alasdair *MacIntyre's revival of Aristotelian and Thomistic virtue theory, which began with his *After Virtue*, there has been an emphasis on ethics as an expression of certain virtues and characteristics and the development of character in the context of *community. This has captured the imagination of many ethicists and parallels closely Christian teaching on the fruit of the Spirit. The difference will lie in the selection and description of what are the virtues and the motivating and enabling power to live a virtuous life. There may be a false optimism about how realistically human beings can exhibit the virtues and overcome moral weakness and all-too-human desires.

The major challenge in ethical discussion is in the way that people live and the decisions made. There should be a moral difference between Christian and other ways of life. Yet when C. S. Lewis was asked why there were so many good people outside the church, he responded by saying that they were made in the image of their heavenly Father. Similarly, his response to why there were so many bad people inside the church was to say that that was the best place for them to be changed and improved. There is an inevitable and necessary pragmatic test of the transforming power of an ethics. An ethic which does not work in practice and fails to produce good women and men is lacking. This is a crucial test for Christian claims to have a divinely given ethic which enables people to be individually and communally the kind of people we all recognize as good and to transform the world and society. While Christians have no right to impose their ethical values on others, they do have the opportunity and freedom to express and live out these values in ways which challenge society and its values. These values are both good in themselves and good for people. Part of the apologetic task is to engage in ethical debate over issues that face individuals and society. This allows Christians to show the strength and validity of Christian values, as well as recognizing the strengths of other ethical systems and approaches. There will be very different applications and results from Christian ethical reflection. This creates a tension between seeking common ground and building consensus in order to restrain *evil and reinforce what is good and transforming and changing society by being salt and light (Matt. 5:13–16). Evil and bad ethics need to be challenged and refuted. Some ethical systems may be supportive of the values and aims of Christian ethics. To work alongside those with such values does not imply total agreement, but a recognition of common humanity, goals and purposes.

Bibliography
R. Hays, *The Moral Vision of the New Testament* (San Francisco, 1996); G. J. Warnock, *The Object of Morality* (London, 1971).

E. D. Cook

EUSEBIUS OF CAESAREA

Eusebius of Caesarea (c. 260–339) is best known as a biblical exegete and church historian. His *Ecclesiastical History* continues to be an irreplaceable source of information for the history and development of the early church. In Eusebius's apologetic works he responded to a number of common objections against Christian beliefs and practices. These included the claims that Jesus' disciples were uneducated and untrustworthy *witnesses to Jesus' life and accomplishments; Jesus' *miracles were nothing new – there were plenty of other well-known miracle workers in the ancient world; the church encouraged its gullible members to accept Christian teaching on the basis of faith alone and discouraged the use of reason; reliance on prophetic texts such as Daniel was ill-founded as they could be better explained as referring to earlier events and figures in Israel's history; the gospels themselves were unreliable and filled with error and distortion. Eusebius also dealt with issues such as the special place given to the Jews and the nation of Israel and the fate of righteous people who had died before Jesus came.

Eusebius's apologetic response was based largely on his exegesis of the biblical text. He was convinced that the key to understanding the biblical narrative was to be found in its fulfilment in *Jesus Christ, and he emphasized in great detail prophecies predicting the life and teaching of Jesus. Not only did the events of his own day demonstrate to Eusebius that Israel had been set aside and the church raised up, but the lives of Christians themselves demonstrated the truth of the gospel, particularly during times of persecution. Would so many people willingly die for a lie? *History finds its rationale and fulfilment in the incarnate word, a judgment that Eusebius believed would be vindicated at the second coming of Jesus.

Bibliography

T. D. Barnes, *Constantine and Eusebius* (Cambridge, Massachussetts, 1981), pp. 164–188.

C. A. HALL

EVIDENTIALISM

In general terms we may define an evidentialist as someone who holds that beliefs should be supported by evidence. An evidentialist apologetic is one that seeks to persuade people to adopt Christian beliefs by demonstrating the evidence that supports them.

There seems no doubt that we hold many beliefs on the basis of evidence. We believe it is raining because everything looks wet and we can see raindrops falling. But, equally, we believe many things without ever thinking about the evidence. I happily accept that my wife's ancestors were called Lloyd-Evans, even though I have never bothered to research records, examine birth certificates and so on. In this case we might choose to say that I believe in the Lloyd-Evanses because I trust my wife and her family traditions, so my belief is based on faith. An evidentialist, however, would be more inclined to say that though I have not troubled to examine it, evidence is still basic to my belief in the Lloyd-Evanses. I adopt the belief because it is pretty safe to assume the documentary evidence does exist and is dependable, even though I am too lazy to search it out. If I were convinced that there was no evidence for the claim, or that all the evidence showed that her ancestors were Joneses, then I would not believe they were Lloyd-Evanses.

What sort of thing can count as evidence? People adopt all sorts of positions in reply to this. Some would say that the only acceptable evidence for a belief is another belief or set of beliefs. So I believe the water is at 100°C when I see it boiling because I believe water boils at 100°C. This, of course, raises a major philo-sophical problem. If I believe A because of B, it is very reasonable to ask why I believe B. The answer must be a further belief, C (e.g. I believe that scientific text books which say that water boils at 100°C are dependable). And I believe C because of D, and D because of E – and so on. So, some would say, we can never produce acceptable evidence for any belief without going through an unending chain of evidences for supporting beliefs. Clearly, this is something we could never actually do. So, philo-sophically speaking, no belief can ever be justified by another belief. In response we might point out that in real life we never feel we need to provide such total justification. What we actually do is check that the evidence for any given belief plus the beliefs that surround it in our web of beliefs all fit happily together to make a coherent system. If it does, then we are usually happy to take the system and the belief on trust, at any rate until we find some counter evidence that makes us *doubt them.

Others would say that it does not seem realistic to assume that the only form of evidence for a belief is other beliefs. Many would claim that some of their beliefs are based on direct experience, e.g. I believe the water in the river is cold because I have just been swimming in it. Parallel to direct experience is immediate awareness: I know I exist because I am aware of my being. Indeed, some would wriggle out of the infinite regress argument above by seeking to show that a substantial number of our beliefs are ultimately based on immediate awareness or direct experience. But, says the sceptic, since we can sometimes be mistaken about our personal experiences, how do we know which direct experiences and immediately known things are acceptable as evidence for the reality of those things and which are not? Why is it that if someone tells us she has had a direct experience of a tree in the garden we do not bat an eyelid, but if she tells us she has seen a ghost or a hobbit we become suspicious?

A possible answer is that we do a number of things. We assess the evidential strength of any experiential evidence, and in particular, we check to see if there could be other explanations for it. We set it in the context of our general beliefs and other strands of evidence and possible counter evidence, and we check to see if the particular experience is confirmed or disconfirmed by the experience of others who are placed in the same situation. Feeling the icy coldness of the water as I swim in it is pretty strong evidence that the water is cold, though I would have to be careful even about that if, for instance, it could be shown that I am running a fever. What is more, I can see the river is coming straight down from the melting snows, and other swimmers emerge looking blue. But a ghost does not readily fit our accepted set of beliefs. No-one else can see it, and the witness's claim can be countered by showing that what she thought was a white shape hovering in the middle of the dark garden was in fact my swimming towel hanging on the line.

This brings us to the question of how strong the evidence has to be for us to accept it as adequate support for a given belief. There are still some who seem to say that no belief is justified unless its supporting evidence can be shown to demonstrate it conclusively. Here the model is mathematics and the logically watertight 'proofs' of Pythagoras' theorem and the like, where the conclusions seem to follow from the premises without any possibility of uncertainty or doubt. But centuries of sceptical arguments have demonstrated that in the actual world such watertight 'proofs' are very hard to find, if they exist at all. Any piece of evidence, whether prepositional or experiential, can be challenged and doubted, and the possibility that we are dreaming or hallucinating or deceived by an evil spirit can never be totally discounted.

The traditional debates over the proofs for the existence of God have been bedeviled by this demand to provide a total, logically watertight proof that would be such that would compel the sceptic to believe. Such a demand was always unrealistic, and those who, to this day, reject the various arguments for the existence of God on the grounds that they do not provide this kind of proof are being very unfair. By those criteria, they would have to reject the existence of other minds.

So if we are going to hold a belief, whether about the world or about God, on the basis of evidence, we will have to settle for less than total indubitable evidential proof. Just how much evidence we will need to persuade us to accept a specific belief depends on several factors. The first is its fit or coherence with our other beliefs. If it is a belief that fits well with our general web of beliefs we will probably not even bother to ask for evidence, even though we will assume the evidence is there. If

our atlas (which we have always found to be reliable) tells us that Little Nodding is three miles north of Great Nodding, we will probably believe it without having to go and pace the distance out. But if it is a strange new idea – that hobbits have colonized my garden – then we will require much more evidence.

The second factor is the type of evidence offered. If we are reading an ancient Athenian writer and come across a description of the buildings on the Acropolis we will be very inclined to accept what he says as good evidence for the architecture of ancient Athens. But we would be much slower to accept the same writer's description of the origin of the universe as an accurate cosmogony.

A third factor arises from the type of people we are. We may be particularly sceptical, or we may be very trusting, or we may be simply naïve. Our personalities are going to affect the amount of evidence needed to convince us. We may be scientifically or logically minded, needing to have everything set out in clear arguments before we are convinced; or we may function intuitively, adopting beliefs without needing to work things carefully through. It has generally been assumed that being sceptical is somehow intellectually superior to being trusting, and that to think things through logically is a more dependable procedure than believing something by direct experience or intuition. These assumptions are part of the legacy of the *Enlightenment, and though they have shown their usefulness in the development of the scientific world-view, there is no reason why we should have to apply them strictly in all areas of life.

No Christian apologist can function without the use of evidence. Not all have agreed, however, on what types of evidence are valid for Christians to use. Some would be prepared to use any type of evidence to bolster their argument: with the scientist they would use scientific evidence; with the philosopher, philosophical; with the New Age person, the sense of the spiritual – seeking by all possible means to convince some. Others, emphasizing that it is the work of the *Holy Spirit to do the convincing, would limit themselves to evidence that is more clearly his specific work: the witness and trustworthiness of the Scriptures, the evidence of the presence of God in Christian individuals, and the personal experience of the Spirit's work.

In this context, during the last few decades,

there has been a vigorous rejection of evidentialism by writers from a Calvinistic Reformed background, partly at least influenced by the writings of Cornelius *Van Til. These so-called 'Reformed epistemologists' are not claiming that all evidence is irrelevant; indeed, many of them would be happy to accept, for instance, that the existence of the universe is evidence for the existence of a Creator. The form of evidentialism they are rejecting is what they call the 'classical' form, which makes the strong claim that we may not accept a belief, specifically a belief in God's existence, unless we have sufficient rational evidence to support that belief. The Reformed epistemologists point out that many of our beliefs, such as our awareness of objects we perceive or of other minds, are not supported by sufficient rational evidence, but are nevertheless valid. In fact, they are 'properly basic', in that we accept them as starting points or presuppositions rather than as conclusions of rational arguments. The existence of God, say the Reformed epistemologists, comes into this category. It is properly basic, and we may validly take it as our starting point.

Some would use the insights of Reformed epistemology to assert that all use of evidence in support of the claims of Christianity is invalid. At best the apologist may demonstrate the inadequacy of alternative world-views, without taking the additional step of demonstrating the adequacy of the Christian world-view. To attempt this would not only be attempting the impossible, it would be usurping the work of the Holy Spirit. Others welcome the freedom Reformed epistemology offers to accept that we do not need to feel that it is improper or intellectually dishonest to make God the foundation of our world-view, but they would still allow a valid place for evidences in their apologetic.

It is tempting for those accepting the insights of Reformed epistemology to conclude that since belief in God is properly basic, there can be nothing tentative or hypothetical about it, and it can be held with total confidence and *certainty. No counter evidence will ever be able to shake it. It would seem wiser to assert that we can be certain about something, but still concede that it is conceivable that we could be shown to be wrong – though we are still sure we never will be shown to be wrong. My belief in the reality of the outside world provides a useful parallel. I take that belief as properly basic, I am totally convinced and

certain that the world around me really exists. But I do accept that it is conceivable that if I were to discover a huge amount of evidence to the contrary I would be foolish to hang on to that belief. I am, of course, sure that no such amount of counter evidence will turn up, but that is not to deny its philosophical possibility. I may wake up some time and find I have dreamt the whole thing. While I am confident that my belief in God is as validly properly basic as my belief in the real existence of the world around me, I have a shrewd suspicion that believers in the Great Pumpkin are on much more shaky ground and as time goes by they will find that the counter evidence to their belief is very considerable and in due course it ought to be allowed to challenge that belief.

There is a theological factor which predisposes some to a strong Reformed epistemological and so anti-evidentialist position. This is the belief that fallen and unregenerate men and women are not only unable to grasp any *truth about God, but because their minds are corrupt and they are self-deceived they will always pervert the truth. It is thus a waste of time or even counterproductive to present them with evidences for Christian truth. Moreover, offering evidences, some would say, is an invitation to unregenerate people actually to sit in judgment over God. We are allowing them to judge whether or not God exists, whether the Bible is true, and so on, and this is spiritually offensive. So, far from allowing people to adopt such a position, we should present the truth of God to them without any supporting evidence and allow it, through the work of the Holy Spirit, to stand in judgment and conviction over them.

Those who reject this approach would point out that, though fallen, unregenerate human minds can still think true thoughts and weigh up the validity of evidence. This may be because their fallenness has not obliterated the image of God in them, or it may be that the Spirit is in fact at work, enlightening their minds and enabling them to accept the evidence and come to a knowledge of the truth.

Bibliography

K. J. Clark, *Return to Reason: A Critique of Enlightenment Evidentialism and a Defense of Reason and Belief in God* (Grand Rapids, 1990); A. Plantinga and N. Wolterstorff (eds.), *Faith and Rationality: Reason and Belief in God* (Notre Dame, 1983); P. S.

Williams, *The Case for God* (Crowborough, 1999).

P. HICKS

EVIL

'Why do I suffer? This is the rock of atheism.' Georg Büchner's metaphor is enough to suggest how imperatively Christian apologetics is called to face the age-long 'problem of evil'. In Gordon Graham's more academic style: 'The existence of evil, both moral and natural, forms the basis for one of the oldest and most persistently troubling arguments against Judeo-Christianity' (*Evil and Christian Ethics*, p. 98).

The core difficulty lies in the combination of three tenets: the reality of evil, divine goodness (benevolence) and divine omnipotence (sovereignty). Many critics asssume that they contradict one another, but Graham has rigour on his side when he observes, 'Plainly this is not so. There is no contradiction between the propositions *as they stand*', if one does not presuppose what must be established. Yet, holding them together appears an arduous task.

Since *Leibniz (1710), attempts at a solution have been called theodicies ('justifications of God'). Some writers distinguish between theodicy, a theory that claims to tell the actual reason of evil, and defence, something that offers a posssible explanation only. The following presentation offers comments on the notions involved and on criteria that may apply, and surveys main apologetic strategies.

The exact meaning of terms

What does one mean by 'evil'? *Augustine, following Plotinus, argued that the question 'What is evil?' takes precedence over 'Whence?' and 'Why?' Calling 'metaphysical evil' the fact that creatures are unequal and therefore 'imperfect' raises the question of value judgments. If a man lacks the elephant's strength or the eagle's sight, why should this be termed 'evil'? The absence of a quality qualifies as evil if it *ought to be* there. 'Moral evil' is the clear form of evil, wickedness, selfishness, treachery, cowardice, wilful departure from the good, but it is truly clear only in a biblical perspective, with God's preceptive will as standard. What is the moral status of 'utility', or even of 'happiness', to which evil is opposed in other views?

Considering unnecessary lack of intensity (triviality) as a main form of evil (in process theodicy) is not a self-evident axiom. Modern sensibility, in contrast with ancient and biblical thought, sees the supreme form of evil in pain, and moral evil in causing pain. This cannot go unexamined. As to 'natural evil', boundaries are far from settled. Swinburne locates 'bad desires' under that head, which Christian tradition considered 'moral'. The suffering of animals has grown into a major preoccupation, whereas it had little place in older reflections. To steer a safe course amid such uncertainty, the apologist, while guided by special *revelation, can refer to the basic sense of evil as the unjustified reality, what is there and should not be there, the correlate of shame and indignation.

Divine benevolence seems easier to delimit. However, many forget what 'divine' entails: it is predicated of God analogically, in a way that safeguards *transcendence. Affirming it in no way allows us to submit the Lord's mysterious ways to our ideas of benevolence and our sense of suffering.

Omnipotence is a slippery notion. It is fertile soil for sophistic *paradoxes (can God create a ball too big for him to move?). While few wish to affirm that God could make square circles, there may be dangers hiding under too quick and 'obvious' a denial (the law of non-contradiction above God himself?). More deeply, the ambiguity of the possible comes into play: 'possible' may refer to the positive attribute of power (Ps. 115:3), or to the ontological category of the virtual, between existence and pure non-existence. What is possible in the latter sense does not exist, and yet it is handled as if it did, in some weaker way: it is not nothing. This Greek concept raises problems for *monotheism (is 'possibility' an ontological partner for God, 'in the beginning'?) and it fosters equivocation. It plays a major role in many theodicies, with abundant talk of 'possible worlds' (from Leibniz onwards) – and few face the challenge of elucidation.

Courts of appeal

Apologetic considerations on evil, as elsewhere, are likely to persuade people if they connect with experience. But the *noetic effects of sin and the sway of lies in public opinion (see Eph. 4:17–19; 2 Thess. 2:10–12) distort the lessons of experience. This is probably truest in the case of evil, the most sensitive issue.

Hence the need to 'catch' experience in its native or nascent state, 'raw' experience, before it is suppressed and twisted by theoretical elaboration (Rom. 1:18–32). As suggested above, a simple phenomenology may help, aiming at the 'originary' experience of evil through its correlates of shame and indignation, adding the resources of common language, characteristic metaphors, symbols and stories.

The role of reason is debated, especially since many charge traditional teaching with *contradiction. How could we waive the challenge and vocation of giving a valid answer to those requesting the *logos* of our conviction (1 Pet. 3:15)? Reason we must. Three warnings, however, are relevant. First, a heavy technical apparatus may add little substance to an argument (Feinberg, *Many Faces*, pp. 65–66, observes that Plantinga's development 'merely reasserts' his passionate conviction that prior determination is incompatible with freedom). Secondly, a mechanical sort of reasoning that applies to the divine–human relationship what is valid among creatures, and disregards the uniqueness of the Creator–creature, Absolute–relative, bond, is no use of reason, but an abuse. When 'God' is named as if the referent were one item among many, one has fallen prey to *un*reason. Thirdly, reason cannot pronounce without criteria, presuppositions, a 'fiduciary framework' (*Polanyi): one 'reasoner' deems consistent what another considers contradictory. One should be on the alert, also, when 'innocent' ways of putting the problem beg important questions, such as 'God created a world containing evil'. The wording suggests that evil is implied in creation as such, a thought orthodoxy opposes, and, with the word 'containing', a status for evil comparable to that of the other 'contents', with a similar comprehension by reason – a denial of its radical otherness.

Scripture does not, yet, carry authority for the addressee of apologetic discourses, but it remains the norm for apologists if they are to defend the Christian message. No apology may count as adequate which violates the analogy of faith. Scripture itself is not devoid of apologetic hints and intentions. On the subject of evil, some may be detected in wisdom literature, and also the early chapters of Genesis.

Strategic choices

Attempts to solve or relieve the tension between the three tenets of tradition fall under four types. They range from versions that minimize the evilness of evil to some that maximize it. The following exposition sketches them in that order. The same writer may combine two types or more.

The first strategic type, and the one that most thinkers in Christian history have settled for, is of evil drained of its evilness and revealed, when all things are considered, as, paradoxically, a good in disguise. This explanation easily agrees with God's goodness and power. Augustine offers a perfect formulation of it when he says, 'To a learned person, it is clear that what causes offence in a part [of the whole] does so only because the whole is not seen (*quia non videtur totum*), with which that part wonderfully agrees' (*De Ordine*, II.xix.51).

Extreme forms of this argument that leave little to evil beyond subjective illusion (*Spinoza, Mary Baker Eddy) lie outside the pale of Christian thought, and the optimism of Leibniz and *Teilhard de Chardin sounds too massive to most people, but the moderate Augustinian-Thomistic version, with its view of evil as deprivation and linked to the 'non-being' from which creatures were drawn (*ex nihilo*), has held sway in the greater part of Christendom. Modern treatments such as Hicks's or Swinburne's (which also use the second strategy) are less concerned with *metaphysics and more with empirical evidence. Paul Helm's *Calvinistic proposal shows restraint, but he nevertheless suggests 'that those events which involved sin and suffering ... were permitted by [God], or ordained by him, in order that the "eternal glory that far outweighs them all" should come to pass', and he appropriates the *felix culpa* of Roman liturgy (*Providence*, pp. 204, 214).

One distinguishes two lines of argument, that evil is a *necessary* component of the overall harmony of the world, and that evil is the 'ransom' of a *greater good*. Both are found in Augustine, who claims that evil can be compared with solecisms that poets call 'tropes' and contribute to poetical delight, and that without the presence of hangmen and prostitutes, things would be worse. More generally, Augustine argues that the wicked increase the merits of the good. Swinburne, less attracted by aesthetic justifications, labours to find a greater-good counterpart for all evils, especially natural: he justifies the pain of 'the victims of carnivorous dinosaurs millions of years ago' by the compassion the thought produces in us and says that 'the world is better for there being such concern' (*Existence*, p. 241).

This strategy appeals to rational wishes and habits of 'comprehension' and on the experience of evaluations changed by broadening perspectives. It exploits the central Christian conviction that God draws benefits from evil deeds (from Gen. 50:20 to the cross), so that 'all shall be well and all mannner of things shall be well'. Are not the horrendous character of evil (as such) and the command to *abhor* evil (Rom. 12:9), somewhat muted? Scripture does not make God's victory over evil the reason for his originally permitting it, and never dares to say *felix culpa*.

The second strategy, the 'free-will defence', has been popular in modern times, but many find it in Augustine's *De Libero Arbitrio*. Plantinga stands out as an influential champion. The presence of evil is reconciled with God's power and goodness by claiming that it originates from the creature's free will. This exonerates God, who, when he conferred freedom (the ability either to choose good or to choose evil), took the risk of evil, which became actual in our world by human, not divine, decision. This rational solution allows for a greater emphasis on the evilness of evil, but at the cost of a reduced version of divine 'omnipotence'. God *could not* create a free agent without the real possibility of evil; God does not control this agent's decisions (the former is regarded as simply non-contradiction, the latter as *self*-limitation). Usually, the risk of creating freedom is justified by the excellency of freedom. The free will defence is a special 'greater good' one, and according to Swinburne, the goodness of free choice offered to people is 'evident', including 'the opportunity to harm each other' (*Existence*, p. 224).

There are a whole gamut of different versions of this strategy, from Berdyaev's quasi gnostic, uncreated freedom, and the finite god of process theology, the denial of God's infallible foreknowledge of human decisions in 'open theism', to the equivocal position of theists who affirm God's sovereign control and yet appear to entertain an indeterministic view of freedom.

Natural evil raises a problem. Traditionally, it is viewed as the consequence of moral evil, following the hints of Gen. 3. This position is tenable if one excludes from the category of genuine evil animal pain and death (with Ps.

104; Job 38ff.). For Plantinga, it follows from the first free-will fall of *Satan (God, Freedom and Evil*, pp. 58f.). Swinburne argues that 'natural evil provides opportunities for especially valuable kinds of emotional response and free choice' (*Existence*, p. 240).

The strategy rebuts the idea of God the 'author of sin': all Christians concur (certainly Augustine's concern). Many today welcome its concept of freedom, though others will point to its frailty when confronted with empirical evidence of conditioning and determination (psychological, sociological, etc.). The same difficulty arises with biblical teachings on the 'bondage of the will' and, above all, the total dependence of created being on God's sovereign rule.

The third strategy, further from common sense, emphasizes the evilness of evil – at first sight. Evil is depicted in tragic tones, but a reversal from No to Yes (dialectical) ascribes to its very opposition to the good most beneficial effects. Thus is progress made possible, and so the victory of the good. It is often located within deity or is construed as a moment of God: the depth of divine benevolence harbours a strain of darkness.

With binary dialectics, the emphasis falls on the way contrast enhances the glory of goodness (J. Boehme) and on God/Being overcoming Evil/the-Negative/Non-Being (e.g. Paul *Tillich). With *Hegel and his followers, the antithesis begets the synthesis, the full bloom of reconciliation, in the becoming of God. Though he tries to escape Hegel's rationalism, Moltmann in *The Crucified God* pursues that theodicy line.

This strategy exploits the message of the cross as the heinous crime through which God does away with evil, provides *atonement and ushers in the kingdom. But it uses it as a symbol, irrespective of its biblical interpretation. Pan(en)theistic leanings further diverge from orthodox Christianity.

The final strategy is that of evil as radical otherness. *Kant affirmed the failure of all the theodicies he had ever met, and several writers quoted above confess an ultimate 'inscrutable' residue. This strategy, instead of reducing the evilness of evil, the range of omnipotence, or the purity of goodness, rather sharpens the difficulty of thinking of all three together. Though it involves no contradiction, God's sovereign and determinative permission of evil remains the 'opaque' *mystery, the 'thorn in the flesh of reason'. No rational comprehension of the problem of evil can be reached (see Job and Rom. 9:19–29), so 'perhaps "no answer" is, in the end, *the* answer' (S. E. Balantine, 'For No Reason', p. 367).

What others consider a weakness reveals itself as a strength and a mark of truth, once the failure of 'solutions' has been exposed. The uniqueness of the opaque mystery signals the *otherness* of evil, radical disorder, alien to the 'very good' creation of God (Gen. 1:31). The vocation of reason is the discernment of creational harmony, it is made for things that go together, and any attempts to 'comprehend' evil with the rest amount to denying its evilness.

This strategy adheres to the basic experience of evil, that it is 'unjustifiable'. It provides a foundation for the assurance of hope – the practical answer to the existential question 'How long?' – and it humbles reason before God, rather than enthroning it supreme (theodicy turned arrogance is 'the sin par excellence' according to Hille, p. 62).

Bibliography

S. E. Balantine, 'For No Reason', *Interpretation*, 57 (2003), pp. 349–369; H. A. G. Blocher, *Evil and the Cross* (ET, Leicester and Downers Grove, 1994; repr. Vancouver, 2003); G. A. Boyd, *Is God to Blame?* (Downers Grove, 2003); S. T. Davis (ed.), *Encountering Evil: Live Options in Theodicy* (Louisville, 2001); J. S. Feinberg, *The Many Faces of Evil: Theological Systems and the Problem of Evil* (Grand Rapids, 1994); P. Geach, *Providence and Evil* (Cambridge, 1977); G. Graham, *Evil and Christian Ethics* (Cambridge, 2001); P. Helm, *The Providence of God* (Leicester, 1993); J. Hick, *Evil and the God of Love* (London, 1966); R. Hille, 'Das Theodizeeproblem im Kontext neuzeitlicher Religionskritik und biblisch-theologischer Antworten', *Jahrbuch für evangelikale Theologie* 15 (2001), pp. 51–68 (ET, *Evangelical Review of Theology*, 28 [2004], pp. 21–37); J. J. Johnson, 'Should the Holocaust Force Us to Rethink our View of God and Evil?', *Tyndale Bulletin*, 52 (2001), pp. 117–128; Ch. Journet, *The Meaning of Evil* (ET, New York, 1963); J. Moltmann, *The Crucified God* (ET, London, 1974); A. C. Plantinga, *God, Freedom and Evil* (New York, 1974); J. G. Stackhouse, Jr, *Can God Be Trusted? Faith and the Challenge of Evil* (Oxford and New York, 1998); R. Swinburne, *The Existence of God* (Oxford, 2004); *Providence and the Problem of Evil* (Oxford, 1998); J. W. Wenham, *The Goodness of God* (Leicester and Downers Grove, 1974).

H. A. G. BLOCHER

EVOLUTION, see ORIGINS, THEORIES OF

EXCLUSIVISM

Exclusivism has generally become shorthand for describing a Christian response to other religions, but it is fundamentally an aspect of logic. The logical principles of non-*contradiction and excluded middle help ensure that the things we say are not absurd. As William A. Christian has written, 'two assertions are in opposition if it would be absurd to take both what is said in one and what is said in the other as true', and in this sense, *truth is exclusive. One cannot make any truth-claim without, simultaneously, excluding contrary claims.

In the area of religion one might consider the historical belief of most Christians that the person Jesus of Nazareth died through the wounds inflicted by crucifixion. This claim is contradicted by the counter-claim many Muslims make that the one crucified only looked like the prophet Jesus (based on Surah 4:156). These two claims are contradictory, and one cannot hold both to be true at the same time. They are 'exclusive' claims in the sense that they exclude their rivals. In this sense all religions have some exclusive beliefs, as holding to certain doctrines excludes rival religious doctrines.

With regard to Christianity, the core belief is in *Jesus Christ as the unique saviour (John 14:6; Acts 4:12). This claim has its roots in the OT conviction that loyalty to Yahweh excluded loyalty to any other god (Exod. 20:2–3). There is a profound exclusiveness in the Israelite worship of Yahweh: 'I am the first and I am the last; apart from me there is no God' (Isa. 44:6). It is because Yahweh really is the true God that all other 'gods' are idols. The NT gospel is thus universal in its scope (Col. 1:19–20) and exclusive of all other purported gospels (Gal. 1:8). If Jesus is truly God, then he is the God of the whole universe and not simply a god of Christians. It is important to stress here that this is a logical point and nothing to do with racism or intolerance. As a matter of coherence, the Christian who claims that salvation is only possible through the God revealed in the Bible must reject the alternative claims of other religious communities when those claims contradict Christian belief. Exclusivism is not unique to Christianity as there are exclusivist forms of all the major religious traditions. In a sustained account of the Dalai Lama's Buddhism, Gavin D'Costa describes him as 'a rigorous exclusivist' for he clearly holds that buddhist practice is a pre-condition to attaining *śūnyata* (emptiness), and that both can only be attained within Buddhism. The value of other traditions is that they lead one nearer to the goal, but can never attain it in their own right. The Buddhist claim that a particular religious practice is essential to ultimate salvation (however defined) must be exclusive of the alternatives (*The Meeting of Religions and the Trinity*, p. 90). However, the term exclusivism has come to be used particularly with regard to the relationship between Christianity and other *world religions.

Exclusivism and the world's religions

Christian responses to other religions have been categorized in three ways: exclusivism, inclusivism and *pluralism.

Exclusivism is broadly defined as the view that true knowledge of God is mediated exclusively through Christ and the church. This has been the mainstream position of Christianity for most of its history. The traditional Roman Catholic dogma that outside the church there is no salvation is taken as representative of exclusivism. However, it has been pointed out that this dogma was originally formulated to describe the predicament of heretics and apostates who had been excommunicated from the church rather than adherents of non-Christian religions. Among Protestants, Karl *Barth is considered one of the most sophisticated contemporary exclusivist theologians. Evangelical theology is generally described as exclusivist.

Inclusivism holds that though Christ is the focus of God's *revelation to humanity, this knowledge is also mediated through other religions. While Christ is still acknowledged as saviour, he is also thought of as present in saving grace among these religions. Roman Catholicism, since the second Vatican council, has promoted various forms of inclusivism, and Karl *Rahner is a key exponent. Among contemporary evangelicals there is a growing enthusiasm for inclusivism, and this is evident in the work of theologians Clark Pinnock and John Sanders.

Pluralism holds that Christ is neither unique nor superior to other religious leaders and teachers. God reveals himself through all of the major world religions and is at work in them drawing people to himself. An ancient Eastern parable of ten blindfolded men and an elephant is often used to present the pluralist case. Each man feels a different part of the elephant and comes up with a different idea about what it is they have encountered. One man thinks it a snake, another thinks it a spear, and so on. The analogy implies that the religions have no more than a partial grasp of ultimate reality and that apparent contradictions will be reconciled through a deeper awareness perhaps only achieved beyond death. John *Hick has developed a highly influential defence of pluralism.

Many theologians are now uncomfortable with the narrow categories underpinning this threefold classification. Some have sought to clarify exclusivism with the term 'restrictivism', a way of restricting salvation to those who consciously profess faith in Christ. Others have preferred the term 'particularism' as being less emotionally charged. The very word 'exclusivist' can be misunderstood as an elitist view of Christianity which sits uneasily with a gospel in which all are one in Christ Jesus (Gal. 3:28).

There is a basic ambiguity with the position of exclusivism in this threefold typology. The term may refer to the doctrine of salvation or to the doctrine of divine revelation. It is possible to be exclusivist in regard to one of these without being exclusivist on the other. We will consider exclusivism in relation to these two doctrines.

Exclusivism and salvation

Restrictivism is a subset of exclusivism. It holds that only those who explicitly belong to the covenant community of God can be saved. This includes Israelites under the old covenant and Christian believers under the new covenant. The children of believers also, including those dying in infancy, are taken to belong to the covenant community. Because salvation is exclusively through faith in God's Messiah, those who have not heard or who have rejected the gospel are eternally lost. Though there is a strong *logic to this position, it provokes a number of objections of which we shall consider four. While not all exclusivists are restrictivists, even they must often respond to similar objections.

How do we know who belongs to the covenant community? Given a distinction between the church visible and the church invisible, it is no simple matter to determine who is who. It is pointed out that there are those in the church who do not belong to God, and those who belong to God who are not in the church. Exclusivism only applies to the church invisible, and a judgment on who is part of that invisible church is one that only God can finally make.

What about believers who do not belong to the covenant community? This includes those before the Abrahamic covenant (such as Noah), those who entered the covenant community from outside (such as Rahab), and those who do not seem to fit anywhere (such as Job and Melchizedek). The first two groups are the least troubling, as there were covenants prior to the Abrahamic, including one with Adam and one with Noah. Of the second group, those outside the Israelite race, the key is not that they came from pagan backgrounds but that they became part of the Israelite nation. Rahab and Ruth are both honoured gentile converts, being ancestors of the mother of Jesus. The existence of the third group, those who had an experience of God but never became part of the covenant community, suggests God is able and willing to work in surprising ways outside of his visible people. The Ninevites are another example of this. They repented in response to the preaching of Jonah, and God had mercy upon their city. They were certainly responding to a knowledge of the true God given through Jonah, but they did not join the covenant community with its worship and traditions.

How does one deal with special cases? Special cases include the severely mentally handicapped and those dying in infancy. Of the latter much may be made of the rather ambiguous words of David (2 Sam. 12:23). Even the most hardline restrictivist would tend to consider this an unknown area and assume that God is able to work directly on the human heart in such circumstances. B. B. Warfield suggested that most Reformed thinking would hold that all those dying in infancy are saved.

Is there a moral problem with the mass of humanity facing condemnation? Describing the millions who have lived outside of the reach of the missionary movement, John Hick asks incredulously, 'can one really, simply on the basis of the fact that they did not hear the Christian gospel, declare that all these millions of men and women deserved to go to eternal hell? Is this not *a priori* dogmatism of the most blindly insensitive kind?' (*The Rainbow of Faiths* [London, 1995], p. 84). It is this question more than any other that drives many Christians to abandon exclusivism in favour of some form of inclusivism. The objection, however, is faulty. The Christian claim is that people are condemned not for failing to respond to the gospel, but for their rebellion against God. Condemnation is primarily God's judgment on human sin, not on a failure to turn to Christ. Continuing this line of thought, God would remain just if he were to condemn the entire human race without exception. God's moral purity would not be impugned even if no-one were saved. Salvation is an expression of God's mercy, not a demand of his *justice. Furthermore, it is hard to apply the moral category to God. We are not morally superior to God, and it is our moral judgment that is lacking rather than his. Therefore, it is better to say with Abraham, 'Will not the Judge of all the earth do right?' (Gen. 18:25). Of course, God will deal fairly with all people, and the Christian takes comfort in the fact that one who is infinitely wise and merciful will take the position of Judge.

Rather than adopting inclusivism, many evangelicals have offered various modifications of exclusivism. Essentially, these distinguish between what is necessary for salvation (the atoning work of Christ) and what we need to know in order to appropriate that salvation. Norman Anderson held that while preaching the gospel is the ordinary way in which people come to a saving knowledge of Christ, 'God *can*, and sometimes does, work directly in men's hearts to convict them of sin and prompt them to throw themselves on his mercy' (*Christianity and World Religions* [Leicester, 1984], p. 175).

The key feature of exclusivism is that salvation is not thought of as being mediated through the world's religions or any being other than Christ. If a non-Christian is saved, it would be in spite of their religious context rather than because of it. This clearly distinguishes the position from inclusivism. Christ is a saviour who excludes all other pretenders to that role.

Exclusivism and revelation

Most Christians would accept that non-Christians have access to certain truths. We all agree on how to repair cars, measure distances to the stars and use mobile phones. We may also agree on certain moral principles and how best to order society. Exclusivism really applies to the primary religious doctrines about God, humanity and salvation.

Karl Barth's exclusivism rests on his claim that revelation is opposed to religion. Religion is an idolatrous human construct, the sinful human attempt to know God apart from his revelation. Revelation is God's free act of grace in Christ. Therefore, the true knowledge of God is only possible through Christ. Religion, even in the form of Christianity, is an example of idolatry apart from this grace in Christ. Jesus Christ is the criterion by which all claims to religious knowledge must be judged. Apart from him all religion, including Christian *theology, is unbelief. This is a strong view of exclusive revelation. However, in preserving the absolute sovereignty of God over revelation, Barth would not be drawn, even when pressed, on whether all humanity were elect in Christ. Certainly this form of exclusivism is compatible with *universalism. The example of Barth demonstrates the weakness of the threefold typology we have considered. Some theologians do not fit neatly into it.

There are several lines of biblical teaching that suggest a broader exclusivist understanding of revelation. God has not exclusively revealed himself through his word. General revelation describes a source of the knowledge of God mediated through creation and conscience (Rom. 1:18 – 2:16). Unless one has a very low view of *common grace, there is much in the world that may be attributed to the general presence and activity of God in creation. Furthermore, men and women were created in the image of God. Though this image has been distorted since the fall, it remains a part of human nature, giving at least some partial sense of divine reality. There is also the demonic dimension to human existence, which explains cruel and aggressive forms of religion. All these strands of biblical teaching point to a knowledge of God outside Christianity, however muddled, vague and incomplete it may be.

Some exclusivists find a basis in this doctrine of general revelation to acknowledge various truths about God found in other religions. However, this acknowledgment must also be handled with care. The fact that non-Christians believe in God does not mean they are necessarily talking about the same 'God'. They may define this term so differently that it would be superficial to suggest that they have discovered truths about the Christian God. Nonetheless, the doctrine of general revelation provides a positive basis for apologetics among other religions. Apart from a living relationship with Christ, this knowledge from general revelation has no saving value within an exclusivist framework. However, it does provide a point of contact for apologetic encounter. Among all people Christians may expect there to be some sense of the existence of God and the reality of a supernatural realm.

Bibliography

N. Anderson, *Christianity and the World Religions* (Leicester, 1984); G. D'Costa, *The Meeting of Religions and the Trinity* (Edinburgh, 2000); H. Netland, *Dissonant Voices: Religious Pluralism and the Question of Truth* (Leicester and Grand Rapids, 1991); A. Race, *Christians and Religious Pluralism* (London, [2]1993); J. Sanders, *No Other Name: An Investigation into the Destiny of the Unevangelised* (Grand Rapids, 1992); D. Strange, *The Possibility of Salvation among the Unevangelised: An Analysis of Inclusivism in Recent Evangelical Theology* (Carlisle, 2002); T. L. Tiessen, *Who Can Be Saved?*, (Leicester and Grand Rapids, 2004).

C. SINKINSON

EXISTENTIALISM

Existentialism covers a wide variety of subjects and people, from *Sartre and Camus to *Dostoevsky and *Nietzsche, but concentrates on human existence and the human situation. It is a reaction against *rationalism and *romanticism. There are key central themes at the heart of the various expressions of existentialism in philosophy, literature, poetry and drama. Anxiety, dread and death, being and existence, absurdity and meaninglessness, the individual and choice are presented, often indirectly, and form the basis for interaction and apologetic response.

Positive engagement

There is *common ground in the importance of these themes, even if Christians analyse them differently and come to different conclusions. Likewise, it is vital to stress that the existentialist refuses to be abstract and remote, but insists on active engagement and taking everything seriously, especially the reality of the here and now. By focusing on the extreme moments of fear, suffering, guilt and death, the existentialist reminds us of the dark, painful and negative aspects of life. But these are balanced by many positive experiences, and the existentialist's emphasis on extremes is unhealthy. Even to recognize extremes implies some notion of the ordinary and regular. Those experiences are more central to human being than simply the negative. Our grasp of sin and *evil needs to be matched with the hope of the good aspects of humanity and the possibility of hope and improvement.

In depicting the absurdity and meaninglessness of life, a clear picture of life without God is given. The issues then are whether or not there is a God, what his nature is and whether he has revealed himself to humanity. A clear choice exists between living in the light of God or living on our own as isolated individuals.

The difference between authentic and inauthentic existence reminds us that human beings can seek to escape from *reality and use all kinds of tools to protect themselves. While that analysis is helpful, it needs to be set in the context of a balanced view of time, temporality and an holistic view of humanity. The past, present and future cannot be reduced simply to the existential moment. The Christian idea of hope for the future is a useful corrective.

Life is a serious business, and we need to live out the *truth of what we believe. Life may be hard, but that does not mean it is without hope or that we are thrown back on our own resources. Christians must try to live out the gospel they proclaim. The choices we make are meant to affect every aspect of how we live and act in the world. The danger is that we isolate the choice from the rest of the person and the rest of society.

Christian critique

The main apologetic response to existentialism must be that it is ultimately reductionistic. It reduces the moments of pain, suffering, dread and death from the sum and mixture of positive and negative experience. It treats the exceptional and occasional as if that was the normal and everyday. It takes the exception and neglects its dependence on the regular pattern of life even to make sense. The very statement of existentialism as the only response to the absurdity and meaninglessness of the world and everything needs to be challenged. It is contradictory to make a statement that 'everything is meaningless' and claim that it is meaningful. If that statement is also meaningless, then existentialism is itself meaningless. We need to enquire whether or not it is an accurate account of the world.

Humanity seeks to understand the world, and science shows the remarkable success of grasping and manipulating reality. Our ability to know the truth about human existence and the world shows that truth is not just about inner perception, but is a balance of engagement with the objective and the subjective. Our capacity to make sense of the world is matched by the fact that the world makes sense.

Truth is not an isolated, do-it-yourself activity but depends on the wisdom of, and interaction with, others. The world is not absurd but intelligible, and we have the intelligence to understand and even control much of the world. We are not at its mercy, nor are we consumed with absurdity. Human science, literature and wisdom enable us to function successfully in our world.

The existentialist seems to be dualistic and then opts for the inner and subjective rather than the outer, objective aspect. In reality we are an amalgam of subjectivity and objectivity, the inner and the outer, and these are aspects of the one unified person which all of us are in ourselves. In the same way, we are not simply isolated individuals trying to make sense of and cope with the world on our own. We are complex, unitary people with many different aspects of our beings. The existentialist emphasis on the will and choice needs to be set alongside our dependence on our rational, emotional and spiritual natures. Underlying this is a disagreement about the nature of humanity. Christians cannot accept the picture of isolated individualism either as an account of the human being of a person or of a community. We are integrated people whose minds, bodies, emotions, wills and spirit interact with each other.

Such reductionism fails to do justice to the complexity of human being. We are born into a social context of family and society. We are educated in a social and cultural context, and learn from others. They help shape who we are from the family to the peer group, the cradle to the grave. The influence and role of society and *community is crucial in defining who we are, even if it is in reaction against what we have been taught and experienced.

Given that there is no meaning in any one thing or in everything all together, then the only way to make sense of *morality is by focusing on individual choice and the exercise of the will. However, there is such an emphasis on the will in existentialism, that it is as if the choices we make are not subject to our reason. We think about them and gather information to make good choices. Likewise, we feel deeply about many of our choices, and those emotions are an important part of what leads us in making particular choices. We are an amalgam of reason, will and emotions.

The existentialist emphasis on choice is centred in the moral choices we make. It does not not seem to matter what we choose but what does matter is that we choose, and in making such choices to commit the whole of our being to fulfilling the aim and consequences of those choices. If this only meant being serious about the choices we make then there would be little unease, but this is rather an account of the nature of morality. Morality is not merely a function of human will. Moral philosophers have argued about every aspect of morality, but few suggest that the will alone is what makes morality moral. Even if it were, that would only tell us about the process of making moral choices and nothing about the nature and content of morality. It would be flawed on both counts. The will must be rational and consistent in order for there to be a morality which can make sense at all. The exercise of that will requires some moral standards by which to judge the goodness and badness of choices, actions and the consequences of choices. Most of us believe that some choices are evil. The idea of the weakness of the will acknowledges that human wills can be affected by desires and temptations which are not just the will itself, but part of the whole person as he or she struggles to make good moral choices and to do what is right.

The existentialist goes further than this in describing morality. It is not simply a matter of nothing but human choices, but can be seen as a result of the death of God. If God is dead then everything is permitted, suggests Dostoevesky, as a way of showing the necessity for God. Nietzsche argued that we have killed God and so now must be worthy to take responsibility of living in the world without God. This is a stark contrast to the Christian recognition that God is the author of morality and what we count as moral is a revelation in line with God's nature. His standards are given to humanity and are not simply good in themselves but also good for people.

Christians will argue that God is far from dead and that his standards, whether in the Ten Commandments or in the Sermon on the Mount, embody the very highest moral ideals for humanity. The life of *Jesus shows how it is possible for a human being to live out those moral standards. Interestingly, few existentialists will deny that Jesus embodies perfect humanity in the choices that he made. But Jesus never pretended that he could live morally without the help, guidance and sustaining of God and the *Holy Spirit.

In apologetic approach to existentialism, the nature of human experience, truth, meaning, authenticity and choice must all be addressed. The ultimate conflict will be over competing views of human nature and the essentially complex nature of individual being in the context of community. It will also drive people back to reflect on the reality of God and of his revealed moral standards and where the awareness of morality, and the possibility of living morally, really arise and can be fulfilled.

Bibliography

E. D. Cook, *Blind Alley Beliefs* (Downers Grove, 1996); W. Kaufmann, *Existentialism: From Dostoevsky to Sartre* (New York, 1988); Reissue edition (February 1988).

E. D. COOK

EXPERIENTIAL APOLOGETICS

Experiential apologetics is defence of the faith, or parts of it, that is in some way based on experience. 'Defence of the faith' is taken broadly to include not only arguments for the truth of *theism or Christianity, but also arguments for the rationality of, justification of or warrant for theistic or Christian belief. What is meant by 'based on experience'? We talk in two ways of statements' being based on experience. When we describe how a meal tastes, we are making a statement *about* an experience. When we say something like, 'I know from experience that two people cannot easily fit in a phone box but I know by repute that subatomic particles exist', experience is the *mode* of knowledge behind the statement.

Apologetics based on experience as the mode of knowledge

This applies to, for instance, arguments for the proposition that God exists, or for the truth of some other part of Christian belief that contains premises that are justified from experience; in other words, premises that the apologist claims to know from experience. This contrasts with, for example, arguments that contain premises that are justified from *authority, such as the authority of the Bible; in other words, premises that the apologist claims to know because he or she knows that the Bible affirms them. So, on this definition, the *ontological argument for the existence of God, i.e. the argument that the nature of the mere concept of God implies the existence of God himself, would not be an instance of experiential apologetics, since none of its premises is known from experience. On the other hand, the *teleological argument for the existence of God, i.e. the argument that the order that we experience all around us in the world is evidence of a designer, *is* an argument based on experience. The advantage of apologetics based on common experience in this way is that the premises are often such as will be believed by the reasonable unbeliever, whereas it is often more difficult to get the sceptic to admit that the Bible is authoritative. The premises of the ontological argument are similarly acceptable to an unbeliever, but in this case the argument is more difficult and has always been more an argument of philosophers than one that has convinced a large part of the public. Certainly, many great apologists for theism and Christianity, such as William *Paley, were enamoured of arguments that relied for their premises on propositions that were verifiable in the common experience of all or most of humanity.

'Experience' is usually taken by philosophers to mean sense experience – in other words, the experience given to us by our five physical senses, with perhaps the addition of introspection (the ability to know what we are thinking or feeling) or proprioception (the alleged ability to know where the parts of one's

body are without having to use any of the five physical senses). Indirect arguments for the existence of God have been deduced by extrapolating from the evidence afforded in this way, e.g. the 'Five Ways' of *Thomas Aquinas. Arguments of this sort have become slightly unfashionable over recent years, partly owing to doubts about their logical cogency, and partly owing to doubts as to whether they are necessary. Despite the efforts of many prominent Christian philosophers, such as Richard Swinburne, to recast the arguments as inductive rather than deductive and to mount a cumulative case involving many arguments, apologists for *atheism reply that the hypothesis that an infinite number of universes exist accounts just as well as the hypothesis that God exists for the order and other puzzling features that we see in our universe. As to the necessity of such arguments, philosophers have recently claimed that there is no good reason to believe that arguments are necessary for religious belief. The claim that everything needs to be based on evidence is self-refuting, the claim that *religious* beliefs (but not others) need to be based on evidence is arbitrary, and beliefs based on evidence are (it is claimed) weak and tentative.

On the other hand, direct arguments for the existence of God have been furnished from alleged direct experience of God. Most believers would agree that we cannot physically experience God today using our five physical senses, but could one say that those who saw, heard and touched *Jesus, God incarnate, had a physical encounter with God, or at least something divine? But here we run into complications. We need to remember that because God is spirit (John 4:24), he is invisible, inaudible and intangible. So, it was possible to see, hear and touch Jesus's *body* when he was on earth, but not his *spirit*. The same distinction would apply today to those claiming to have seen Jesus, and to the many alleged theophanies and Christophanies that occurred before the incarnation proper.

Direct arguments for the existence of God are more usually based on what one might call 'spiritual' experiences of God. Typically, mystics do not claim *physically* to have seen, heard or touched God, but rather *spiritually* to have seen, heard or touched him. Other mystics claiming to have experiential awareness of God eschew such terms as 'spiritual sight' and 'spiritual ears', and describe their awareness of God in terms of introspection or proprioception or as being similar to none of the modalities of physical experience. It might be thought that this phenomenon – 'spiritual' experience of God – is too rare to be worth considering, but this would be a mistake. Societies such as the Alister Hardy Trust have collected thousands of testimonies to spiritual experiences of this kind, and one survey indicated that '75% of Christians take themselves to have been at some time aware of the presence of God' (Alston, *Perceiving God*, p. 36). Indeed, if we take 'experience' sufficiently broadly, we may say that everybody should spiritually hear God speaking to him or her through the words of the Bible. Alvin Plantinga has proposed in *Warranted Christian Belief* that we take 'experience' so broadly as to include doxastic experience, i.e. the experience that certain propositions seem true or false. Here again, we may say that everybody should have this kind of experience, and Christianity should seem true to everyone. Whether it should seem true to everyone without additional reasons or argument of some kind is the topic of fierce debate. This has been fuelled by Plantinga's claim in *Warranted Christian Belief* that theistic and Christian belief do not need to be, and indeed *should* not be, based on (just) evidence or argument; mere doxastic experience is sufficient. Note that the content of the experience does not feature here as a premise in the argument: the claim is that one is directly warranted in believing in God or Christianity in virtue of one's religious or doxastic experience. Apologetically, one could claim that the inquirer should seek the experience and then believe on the basis of that, rather than seek an argument or evidence. Or one could claim that the inquirer should believe on the basis of the testimony of the person who has had the experience. Thus, Richard Swinburne in his *The Existence of God* puts forward two principles: the principle of credulity, that what one seems to perceive is probably so (p. 254), and the principle of testimony, that the experiences of others are probably as they report them (p. 272). If one has an experience of God, then, it is at least warranted, and perhaps obligatory, for one to believe that God exists, and if one tells others it is at least warranted, and perhaps obligatory, for them also to believe that God exists.

There may be a problem with regard to conflicting experience. Could not the atheist defeat theistic experiential apologetics by merely pointing to his or her own *absence* of experience of God? In fact, this would not pose a problem for the theist, as the absence of an experience proves nothing unless one has positive reasons for expecting the experience. The atheist might, however, claim not to have had the absence of an experience of God, but to have had an experience of the absence of God. This also will not avail, for what is an experience of an absence? An absence is nothing, and one cannot have an experience of nothing. Therefore, the experiential apologist for theism need not fear such a response from the atheist. More worrying is the challenge of contrary religious experiences. For example, the Christian experiential apologist may well claim that his or her experience of Christ warrants him or her in believing in the *deity of Christ. How does this square with the Muslim or Jewish experiential apologist who claims that he or she has had an experience of the undifferentiated nature of the Godhead and that this experience warrants his or her denial of the doctrine of the *Trinity? If the Muslim or Jew shares his or her alleged experience with the Christian, then the principle of credulity will clash with the principle of testimony. The former will suggest that the Christian should trust in his or her own experience and not the report of the Muslim or Jew; the latter will suggest that the Christian should trust the report of the Muslim or Jew and not his or her own experience. How does one resolve this clash? It seems that, other things being equal, the principle of credulity should take precedence over the principle of testimony. One should trust one's own experiences more than the reports of the experiences of others, since such reports could be deliberately deceptive, or relate to an illusory experience or mistaken reports of a genuine experience. Beliefs founded on one's own experiences cannot be wrong in the first of these ways. This rule, however, will lead the Muslim or Jew to trust his or her own experience rather than the Christian's report, and it will not help a third party listening to two conflicting reports. Here the Christian must either, on the one hand, argue that the conflicting Jewish or Muslim experience is illusory or misreported or, on the other hand, seek to bolster the reports of his or her own experience by other means. Experiential apologetics has its limits, like apologetics of other sorts.

Apologetics based on arguments concerned with experience

Now let us turn to apologetics based on experience in the sense of arguments for the proposition that God exists or for some other part of Christianity that has premises that are *about* or *concerned with* experience. Some philosophers (e.g. Richard Swinburne in his *The Existence of God*) have argued that the very existence of conscious experience is best explained by the existence of God. John Locke argues from the proposition that there is conscious experience to the proposition that there is an eternal cogitative being, which he identifies with God. This is quite different from arguing directly for the conclusion that God exists, claiming that one knows that this is true through one's religious experiences. In apologetics of *that* sort, the experience is the mode of knowledge of the proposition that God exists; in apologetics of *this* sort, one argues that the existence of God furnishes the best explanation for the existence of these experiences. Here the atheist will try to come up with some purely naturalistic explanation for the occurrence of these experiences in psychological, sociological or neurological terms. The theistic apologist will have to try to show that the atheist's account is inferior to his or her own.

Experience can feature in other ways as the content of arguments for the proposition that God exists. One of the most startlingly original is that of Robert Merrihew Adams, who argues that the existence of God is the best explanation of the correlation between certain stimuli such as seeing a banana and certain experiences such as the experience of seeing something yellow. He argues that this correlation could never be explained by science and that, therefore, one must turn to God for an explanation.

The term 'experiential apologetics' is used in many different ways, and some of these ways are less fashionable now than they used to be. However, some forms of experiential apologetics, particularly the direct argument for the truth of Christianity from religious experience, are not only helpful but in fact offer the best mode of defending the Christian faith against the contemporary sceptic.

Bibliography

R. M. Adams, 'Flavors, Colors, and God', in R. M. Adams, *The Virtue of Faith* (New York, 1987); W. P. Alston, *Perceiving God* (Ithaca and London, 1991); J. Locke, *An Essay Concerning Human Understanding* (London and New York, [2]1964); W. Paley, *Natural Theology* (London, [9]1805); A. Plantinga, *Warranted Christian Belief* (Oxford and New York, 2000); R. Stark and C. Y. Glock, *American Piety: The Nature of Religious Commitment* (Berkeley and Los Angeles, 1968); R. G. Swinburne, *The Existence of God* (Oxford and New York, [2]1993).

D. J. HILL

EXTRA-TERRESTRIAL LIFE

While early Christians do not appear to have been concerned about the subject of extra-terrestrial life, thinkers during the Middle Ages offered their opinions. *Thomas Aquinas (1224–74) seems to have believed that the existence of life on other worlds might disrupt the unity of God's creation. Nicholas of Cusa (1401–64), on the other hand, suggested that God might have created life elsewhere. Giordano Bruno (1548–1600) was burned at the stake, possibly in part because of his belief in other worlds. Later, eighteenth-century political and deistic writer Thomas Paine (1737–1809) tried to show the incompatibility of Christianity with the idea of extra-terrestrial life, supposing that a plurality of worlds would undermine the Christian faith. In contrast, C. S. *Lewis (1898–1963) wrote extensively about the subject through the medium of science-fiction, placing Christianity within a larger cosmic framework.

Though Scripture is written for the inhabitants of earth, the existence of extra-terrestrial beings is nowhere denied. Given the fact that there is at least one other 'race' of non-earthly beings, namely *angels, it is possible that other life-forms populate the universe, the discovery of which would warrant serious analysis by theologians and apologists. Recognizing the theological implications, William Derham, as long ago as 1715, coined the term 'astrotheology'. More recently, Ted Peters has spoken of 'exo-theology' and Steven J. Dick of 'cosmotheology' as terms for theology that pertains to extra-terrestrials.

Presuppositions

A Christian perspective on extra-terrestrial life must begin with certain assumptions, the foremost of which is the belief that there is a God and that he has spoken. Special *revelation (located in the Christian Scriptures and supremely manifested in God's unique Son) provides the primary basis for a Christian world-view. General revelation (via extra-biblical avenues such as nature) supplies additional insights into God's creation.

Together, these form the starting point for addressing the subject of extra-terrestrial intelligence (ETI) as it pertains to such themes as creation, anthropology, incarnation and redemption.

Key themes

Creation. God is the maker and sustainer of the universe (Col. 1:15–17). The constellations and the galaxies are his handiwork (Gen. 1:1; Neh. 9:6; Amos 5:8). Thus, the presence of extra-terrestrial beings would supply further examples of his creative genius. While no-one can imagine the impact of extra-terrestrial contact, and though the specific mode of divine revelation to these creatures is difficult to predict, they would be accountable to the only true God (Heb. 4:13).

Anthropology. A related issue concerns humanity's place in a universe containing other intelligent life-forms. Both dignity and depravity mark the human condition. Scripture portrays human beings, made in God's image, as the apex of his creative activity (Gen. 1:26–31). However, humanity is also in a fallen state (Gen. 3:6–7), having violated the Creator's will and so experiencing the noetic consequences of sin (Rom. 3:9–18). Whether creatures from other worlds, if they exist, might be in a similar state is beyond current knowledge. Presumably, they would carry the Creator's imprint, and certainly their existence would not detract from the status of human beings, who are recipients of God's favour. Any potential communication with extra-terrestrials would thus include a healthy belief in God's gracious disposition toward humanity, while avoiding 'earth chauvinism' through the recognition that God has been at work in other segments of the cosmos.

Incarnation and redemption. In God's timing (Gal. 4:4) the Son of God, without forfeiting his divine nature, took on the nature of humanity (John 1:14). *Jesus entered this world in order to rescue human beings through his death (1 John 4:10), and he was raised from the grave as a declaration of his successful mission and a validation of his claims (Rom.

1:4). Assuming such fundamental features of the gospel as the uniqueness of Jesus, certain extra-terrestrial scenarios strain the imagination and stretch our theological creativity. If a race of non-human creatures required redemption, might God's Son have became incarnate on other worlds? Does the once-for-all character of Jesus' death (Heb. 9:12, 26, 28) limit its application to the inhabitants of this planet (cf. Col. 1:15–20)? Whatever the precise *modus operandi* – and many would maintain that the spiritual rescue of extra-terrestrial beings would require that God become one of them (Gal. 4:4–5; Heb. 2:14–18) – Jesus alone is God-incarnate, perfectly revealing the very nature and character of God. Though the redemption of other life-forms is conceivable, evangelicals do well to guard against anything that minimizes the manifestation of God on earth. While not necessarily linked to Jesus' earthly *atonement, it is well in keeping with biblical theology to imagine that any type of extra-terrestrial salvation would be tied to the second person of the Trinity, the one described as 'the image of the invisible God, the firstborn over all creation' (Col. 1:15).

The resiliency of the Christian faith

Christians have a long history of responding to complicated issues. In the early days of the church, the place of the Gentiles in God's economy was disputed and eventually settled (Acts 11:1–18). The Copernican revolution ultimately caused the church to reconsider its assumptions regarding geocentrism. More recently, scientific claims of an ancient earth have spawned a discussion about the best way to interpret the relevant biblical data. Though Christians have often resisted change, 'the faith' itself (Jude 3) is amazingly resilient and adaptable to the challenges of history.

Given the complexity of these issues, definitive answers regarding the theological and practical implications of ETI are at best speculative. Thus, Christians who choose to study this subject in a serious and theologically informed manner must take God's truth seriously (2 Tim. 2:15), treat his creation respectfully (Ps. 8:3–4) and honour his Son supremely (Rom. 11:36) as the sole Creator-Redeemer.

Bibliography

S. Dick (ed.), *Many Worlds: The New Universe, Extraterrestrial Life and The Theological*

Implications (Philadelphia and London, 2000); J. R. Lewis (ed.), *The Gods Have Landed: New Religions From Other Worlds* (Albany, 1995).

C. C. DICELLO

FAITH AND REASON, see THEOLOGICAL METHOD
FALSIFICATION, see VERIFICATION/ FALSIFICATION, PRINCIPLES OF

FANTASY

In its most general and enduring sense, fantasy is an essential feature of human mental life. Just as thinking is a power and product of the intellect, fantasy is a power and product of our imaginative faculty. The free play of fantasy is the mark of *imagination at work, just as thought displays the reason in action.

Fantasy has interested psychiatrists, e.g. Melanie Klein, because of the way it shapes our very perception of the world and our relationships. For this reason alone fantasy is of importance to Christian apologetics.

Fantasy is also, however, a mode of art, requiring skill and knowledge. It is a dimension of a number of literary and oral genres, such as science fiction, heroic romance (the type to which J. R. R. Tolkien's *The Lord of the Rings* belongs), allegory, apocalyptic (as in the biblical book of Revelation), and the faery story. In this mode, fantasy draws attention to its fictional and poetic nature, and so has to be well-crafted to achieve its effects, such as our 'willing suspense of disbelief'.

A dominant type of fantasy is Christian fantasy, the best-known twentieth-century practitioners of which are *Tolkien (1892–1973) and C. S. *Lewis (1898–1963). The former is known primarily for his *The Lord of the Rings* (1954–5) and the latter for *The Chronicles of Narnia* (1950–6). In fact, Tolkien remains in the vanguard of the entire modern fantasy genre. Without his writings we would not have large sections of bookshops devoted to 'Fantasy and Science Fiction'. He created an adult readership for fantasy in the last century, in a period when faery stories had been relegated to children's literature. In this endeavour he enlisted the help of his close friend C. S. Lewis, who sub-titled his anti-modernist science-fiction novel, *That Hideous Strength*, 'A Modern Fairy Tale for Grown-Ups'. Popular writers such as J. K. Rowling, Terry Pratchett, Stephen Lawhead and Ursula LeGuin owe a debt to Lewis and Tolkien. The cultural relevance of Christian fantasy in the twenty-first century is dramatically evidenced in the globally popular film sequence of *The Lord of the Rings* by Peter Jackson (2001–3) and the series of films of *The Chronicles of Narnia* (2005 onwards).

Christian fantasy has a long and varied history. It is defined by Colin Manlove as 'a fiction dealing with the Christian supernatural, often in an imaginary world'. It draws upon the imaginative richness of the Bible, with its integrated and organic picture of both the seen and the unseen world. There are visions in Scripture of heaven and God, fantastic beasts and dragons. There are also a talking snake and ass, in a realistic setting. The literary origins of Christian fantasy are perhaps the Arthurian stories of the Middle Ages. Its history includes Dante's fourteenth-century *The Divine Comedy*, the poignant Middle-English poem *Pearl*, Spenser's *The Faerie Queene*, Marlowe's *Dr Faustus*, Bunyan's *The Pilgrim's Progress*, and George *MacDonald's *Phantastes* and *Lilith*.

In the period of modernity, the Christian presuppositions of Western civilization have of course disappeared – we live in a post-Christian world (as argued by Francis *Schaeffer, C. S. Lewis, and many others). This has made the apologetic task of the writer of Christian fantasy much more difficult. In the medieval period, it was believed that Eden lay far off in the east; today paradise has to be located in an alternative or secondary world. Writers such as Tolkien and C. S. Lewis wrestled with the artistic problem of portraying Christian meanings in contemporary fantasy.

Their strategy focused on the very notion of story, which they saw as the child of myth. Indeed, Tolkien's thinking about the relation between myth and fact helped to persuade his friend C. S. Lewis of the truth of Christian claims. Lewis previously had been an atheist of many years' standing. The Gospels, Tolkien argued, require and in fact demand both our imaginative and our reasoned response. They focus and bring to fruition insights into the nature of reality and God to be found in human storytelling, myths and persistent archetypes. Symbolic stories essentially shape our very perception of reality; the Gospels do this in an ultimate way, by capturing our imaginations as well as by their truth-claims.

It follows, if Tolkien and Lewis are correct, that stories have a deep structure, which cannot be reduced to a naturalistic analysis of narrative. Stories embody a multi-faceted reference that is like reality itself. Lewis and Tolkien, in this view of story, were rehabilitating older ideas which had been marginalized by the *Enlightenment and then modernism. As Derek Brewer observes, in his *Symbolic Stories*, 'The concept of the story as a rich and complex entity has not been accepted by literary intellectuals for several centuries.' Through the writings of Tolkien, Lewis and other contemporary storytellers, Christian and otherwise, this illiberal denial of the multi-levels of story is weakening. Furthermore, by entering the world of a story, a reader is able to experience a different, felt consciousness, which provides a perspective on his or her world which may be revisionist or critical. A story is eminently able to be subversive, transcending the barriers and blindspots of the modern world. Storytelling – as in C. S. Lewis and Tolkien – gives a unique and evident opportunity for powerful and popular Christian communication.

Bibliography

D. Brewer, *Symbolic Stories* (Woodbridge and Totowa, 1980); C. Duriez, *Tolkien and C. S. Lewis* (New York, 2003); C. S. Lewis, *Of This and Other Worlds* (London, 1982); C. Manlove, *Christian Fantasy* (Basingstoke and London, 1992); J. Segal, *Ideas in Psychoanalysis: Phantasy* (Duxford, 2000); J. R. R. Tolkien, 'On Fairy Stories', in *The Monsters and the Critics and Other Essays* (London, 1983).

C. DURIEZ

FARRER, AUSTIN MARSDEN

Austin Farrer (1904–68) was trained in philosophy but saw himself first of all as a pastor, in an Anglo-Catholic mould of credal orthodoxy. The child of a Baptist minister, he was ordained into the Anglican Church in 1929, and served as a chaplain and fellow of several Oxford colleges. There some considered him one of the most brilliant of its thinkers at the time. (He was a Gifford and Bampton lecturer

and a Fellow of the British Academy.) Bishop Richard Harries saw Austin Farrer as displaying an intellectual, imaginative and spiritual unity, combining these talents in his 'sheer brilliance of intellect, ... the quality of his imagination and ... the depth of his spirituality'. His thinking was done on his knees.

Farrer was born in London on 1 October 1904 and went up to Balliol College, Oxford, as a Classical Scholar in 1923, studying Classics, Philosophy, Ancient History and Theology. After his ordination he served at All Saints', Dewsbury. In 1931 he returned to Oxford, where he was Chaplain and Tutor at St Edmund Hall until 1935, Fellow and Chaplain of Trinity College until 1960, and then Warden of Keble College until his unexpected death on 29 December 1968.

Austin Farrer's larger metaphysical interests led him to reject the fragmentation of the Gospels that had occurred under modern biblical criticism. He dismissed the 'Q' hypothesis, arguing rather that Luke skilfully revised Mark and Matthew according to his purpose, and that Mark pioneered the gospel genre. These interests also led to some first-rate explorations of *theism (e.g. in *Finite and Infinite*, 1943) in which existence has a positive and actively operational rather than passive character. He reframed the neo-Thomist model of divine action, defending double agency, or 'downward *causality', in which a causal hierarchy is posited. Furthermore, like his friend C. S. *Lewis, Farrer was in the forefront of thinking on the nature of metaphor and symbol, as in his study of the book of *Revelation, *A Rebirth of Images* (1949). Images, he believed, capture the multi-referential character of *reality itself in a way that scientific propositions cannot: 'There is a current and exceedingly stupid doctrine that symbol evokes emotion, and exact prose states reality. Nothing could be further from the truth: exact prose abstracts from reality, symbol presents it. And for that very reason, symbols have some of the many-sidedness of wild nature.'

Bibliography

P. Curtis, *A Hawk among Sparrows* (London, 1985); A. Farrer, 'The Christian Apologist', in J. Gibb (ed.), *Light on C. S. Lewis* (London, 1965); *The Freedom of the Will* (London, 1957); R. Harries, 'We Know on our Knees', in B. Hebblethwaite and E. Henderson (eds.), *Divine Action: Studies*

Inspired by the Philosophical Theology of Austin Farrer (Edinburgh, 1990).

C. DURIEZ

FEMINISM, see GENDER

FEUERBACH, LUDWIG ANDREAS

The Enlightenment's attack on the ancient regime yielded the devastation and disorientation of the French Revolution and the Napoleonic Wars. In turn this led to an age of ideologies which ranged from extreme reactionary to revolutionary. This was a desperate search for a totality perspective – or grand historical narrative – that could bring, or bring back, ordered progress to the peoples of Europe.

In Germany, *Hegel (1170–1831) saw his philosophy as the final dialectical synthesis of Western thought and cultural ideals – pagan Graeco-Roman, Christian and modern humanist. Here was a 'realized eschatology' in which the divine world-spirit had finally realized itself in and through the self-consciousness of humanity, and specifically in the form of Hegelian philosophy and the Prussian monarchy.

Yet this final synthesis had hardly been announced before diverse and vehement reactions set in, which sought to re-interpret it as merely a new thesis to be negated *en route* to the genuinely final synthesis. The very allegiances that Hegel had sought to synthesize felt themselves deeply compromised and betrayed. Neo-pagan (Buddhistic pessimist *Schopenhauer), Christian (*Kierkegaard) and humanist (Bauer, Feuerbach, Stirner, Marx and Engels) each delivered their distinctive anathemas against the Hegelian dialectic. And each proposed a new dialectical schema expressive of their diverse world-views.

Late in his life, Feuerbach summed up his own development in these terms: 'God was his first, reason his second, and man his last thought.' Disillusioned with theology at Heidelberg, Feuerbach became a disciple of the philosopher Hegel in Berlin. But there he came to suspect that Hegel's synthesis, though subversively relativizing the Christian faith, still residually served as the last refuge for theology. At least, the Hegelian right believed that Hegel was presenting the ultimate rational apologetic – even for the Trinity and incarnation. So both God and Hegelian reason were to be negated.

For Feuerbach humankind is not the creature of God, existing for the manifestation of his glory; nor is it the unwitting instrument for the self-realization of the rational world-spirit. All there really is is humankind and nature. Consequently, both God and the (ersatz God) world-spirit are the projections of the real flesh-and-blood human species, but these theistic and idealistic illusions are not to be dismissed as mere superstitions. For Feuerbach these projections play a crucial role in the dialectical unfolding of *history leading to the full self-realization of humanity. The 'logic' is that these projections are a necessary stage of human self-consciousness, necessary for humanity to be able to see itself, albeit initially, as a projection. At this point, God is enriched with wonderful attributes at humanity's expense because the attributes of God are really the attributes of humanity. The next dialectical step is for humanity to re-appropriate its own self-alienated and projected attributes that came to constitute the Christian God and the Hegelian Absolute.

Feuerbach certainly is an atheist with respect to the God and Father of Jesus Christ, but he believes fervently in the divinity of humankind. This is the true gospel, the real, hidden 'essence of Christianity'. Indeed, he maintains that within the Christian theological tradition, the move from medieval theology's concern for God-in-himself was significantly replaced by Christology (God-for-us), the human face of God, during the Reformation. Then followed the subjectivism of modern theology, in which the attributes of God had to be understood in terms of human experience, e.g. Schliermacher's 'sense of absolute dependence' that replaced any ontological claims about creaturely dependence on the Creator. The final disclosure or destination is the replacement of even such an attenuated theology with anthropology. God (and reason) are dead; long live humanity!

Just as subjectivistic liberal theology was vulnerable to Feuerbach's anthropological transformation, so was theological anthropology itself. The way in which the biblical data (heart, body, image of God, etc.) are forced into alien categories, mostly Neoplatonic in origin, leaves the human identity and calling deeply ambiguous. Feuerbach, in the conclusion of his Heidelberg lectures (1848), declared that his principal aim was to change 'the friends of God into the friends of man, believers into thinkers, worshippers into workers, candidates for the other world into students of this world, Christians, who on their own confession are half-animal and half-angel, into men – whole men'. To these proposals he had earlier added, '...theologians into anthropologians ... religious and political footmen of a celestial and terrestrial monarchy and aristocracy into free, self-reliant citizens of the earth'.

Feuerbach's new secular and romantic religion of humanity strikingly had a great deal in common with the contemporary, but independent, vision of Auguste Comte in France. It was to have wide and varied impact upon many – including Marx and Engels, Schopenhauer, Wagner, *Nietzsche, *Freud and *Buber.

Bibliography

K. Barth, *Protestant Thought from Rousseau to Ritschl* (New York, 1969); H. Dooyeweerd, *Roots of Western Culture: Pagan, Secular and Christian Options* (Toronto, 1979); L. Feuerbach, *The Essence of Christianity* (trans. G. Eliot; New York, 1957); *Principles of the Philosophy of the Future* (trans. M. H. Vogel; Indianapolis, New York and Kansas City, 1966); K. Lowith, *From Hegel to Nietzsche: the Revolution in Nineteenth Century Thought* (New York, 1967).

R. A. RUSSELL

FIDEISM

Fideism is the view that religious commitment is based primarily upon the intuitive apprehension of God by faith (Lat.: *fides*, trust), rather than rational arguments (moderate fideism) or contrary to rational arguments (extreme fideism). Paul appears to be advocating the latter in 1 Corinthians 1:20–21. Although all people have an intuitive awareness of an omnipotent, moral Creator arising from their perception of nature (Acts 14:15–17; 17:24–29; Rom. 1:19–20, 32; 2:14–15), their thinking about God is perverted and darkened by human sinfulness (Rom. 1:21 – 3:20; Eph. 2:3; 4:17–19). Knowledge of God comes through the faith that is implanted in the human heart by the *Holy Spirit (1 Cor. 2:1–4, 12–14; Eph. 1:17–18; 3:16–19). This is not, however, an irrational faith, but is based on the historicity and significance of Christ's life, death and resurrection (Acts 13:26–37; 17:31; 26:22–23; 1 Cor. 15:12–20).

*Justin Martyr (d. c. 165), *Clement of Alexandria (c. 150 – c. 215) and *Origen (c. 185 – c. 254) believed that Platonic philosophical truths could be a pathway to faith in Christ. But Tertullian (c. 160–220) advocated an extreme fideism: 'For philosophy is the material of the world's wisdom, the rash interpreter of the nature and the dispensation of God ... We want no curious disputation after possessing Christ Jesus, no inquisition after enjoying the Gospel! With our faith, we desire no further belief. For this is our pre-eminent faith, that there is nothing we ought to believe besides.'

Martin Luther (1483–1546) contrasted the God of wrath, known as remote and fearful by sinners, with the God of mercy revealed by grace to believers by the crucified Christ. In relation to God, however, fallen reason has a fatal tendency to pride itself in its own achievements, refuses to accept its creaturely status, and sets itself up as the final judge of everything, including God's Word. Whereas 'reason knows that there is a God' and has the moral law inscribed upon it, it partakes of the flesh, and is controlled by the devil. Fallen reason seduces believers into thinking that they are self-sufficient and so they judge the things of God in terms of their own self-orientated naturalistic perspectives. But 'all God's works and words are against reason'. 'Reason despises faith' and is 'the greatest whore the devil has'. Faith overcomes the impotence of fallen human reason and does not presuppose it or complement it, although redeemed reason has a subordinate role of explaining Scripture and doctrines.

John *Calvin (1509–64) closely followed the Pauline perspective in holding that an awareness of God, a 'seed' of knowledge of the deity, has been implanted in the human heart so that humans are guilty in failing to submit to the will of their Maker. But sinful human beings suppress this and turn to idolatry. The god created by the 'empty speculations' of fallen reason is thus 'a figment and dream', 'a dead and empty idol' that has nothing to do with the true God. Calvin was deeply aware of the noetic effects of sin, the suppression by fallen human beings of their innate knowledge of God so that their understanding is darkened. For Calvin, the Bible is the self-authenticating Word of God inasmusch as God speaks through it and reason cannot demonstrate this truth to unbelievers.

'The highest proof of Scripture derives in general from the fact that God in person speaks in it. The apostles and prophets do not boast either of their keenness or of anything that obtains credit for them as they speak; nor do they dwell upon rational proofs.'

Blaise *Pascal (1623–62) had a powerful experience of God on 23 November 1654. His brief account, written at the time, says: 'Fire. "God of Abraham, God of Isaac, God of Jacob," not of philosophers and scholars. Certainty, certainty, heartfelt joy, peace. God of Jesus Christ … He can only be found by ways taught in the Gospels …' Pascal sought to construct a persuasive apologetic in conformity with his fideism. The limitations of human knowing and the ambiguity of nature negate the possibility of deriving God's existence. 'If there is a God he is infinitely beyond our comprehension, since, being indivisible and without limits, he bears no relation to us. We are therefore incapable of knowing either what he is or whether he is … Reason cannot decide this question.' 'It is the heart which perceives God and not the reason.' 'The heart has its reasons of which reason knows nothing.'

Søren *Kierkegaard (1813–55) reacted against the superficiality of conventional church-going Christianity and against *Hegel's version of Christianity by exalting the *paradoxical, the irrational and the absurd. Kierkegaard opposed the intrusion of reason into the domain of faith, which by its nature must transcend all reason. God is infinite, whereas reason can grasp only what is finite. The Christian 'believes against the understanding' and 'also uses understanding to make sure that he believes against the understanding'. 'The real task is not to understand Christianity but *to understand that one cannot understand it.* That is the sacred cause of faith, and reflection is sanctified by being used for it.' God is not an object of knowledge to which we assent, nor a reality we merely contemplate. God is a totally transcendent, infinite, indescribable Person who evokes repentance, worship and unconditional commitment of our total being. To philosophize about God is a way of avoiding the unreserved personal commitment by which alone the living God can be known. If we are to find God, we must do so with no reservation, by surrendering ourselves with infinite passion, taking a leap of faith into the dark unknown, contrary to all natural reason.

Karl *Barth (1886–1968) consistently maintained that God is known only by self-authenticating *revelation imparted through the Word of God. There is an absolute disjunction between the holy and infinite God and even the best in finite and sinful human beings, such that all *natural theology is to be repudiated. Barth does acknowledge that there is an objective revelation of God in nature. But human beings are so depraved in their sin that they do not respond to it. Far from using this awareness of God's eternal power and deity as a bridge to God, human beings in their sin use it as a barricade against submission to him. They become religious within the terms of their own self-orientation, self-sufficiency, self-justification and self-preservation. They worship gods of their own making, and this results in the degradation of their moral life. In their present sinful state they cannot construct a true natural theology. They can only promote idols like the 'God of the philosophers', who is an abstract idea, not the Lord of glory to be worshipped and obeyed.

The later Ludwig *Wittgenstein (1889–1951) held that meaningful discourse is a series of *language games (e.g. recounting an accident, making a joke, giving a command), whose rules are derived from the usage to which the language is put in relation to the realities apprehended by the speaker. Just as different games and sports have rules that constitute their meaning, although the rules are not explicitly visible to those watching the game or sport, so different forms of discourse have underlying rules that impart meaning to the discourse. The rules of a language game constitute its associated 'form of life', i.e., the mode of living that apprehends the reality to which the language game refers. The religious language game is meaningful to believers and conveys the reality of God for them. But this language game is meaningless to sceptics, for the same words connote an entirely different meaning for them. Religious beliefs are visions that determine the way religious believers live, and they govern the way they talk about their faith. Those who try to engage in a scientific type of apologetic are in fact 'unreasonable', i.e., not being true to the real nature of religion. Religious beliefs are neither true nor false, as they do not bear on the factual world, and they are subject to neither *verification nor falsification. Norman Malcolm (1911–90), Peter Winch (b. 1926), D. Z. Phillips (b. 1934) and W. D. Hudson (b. 1940) have adopted

Wittgenstein's approach to religious language. There is no Archimedean point in terms of which a philosopher can criticize religious discourse, for it has its own specific criteria of intelligibility and *reality. *Theology is the 'grammar' of religious discourse; i.e., the set of doctrines which believers hold determines for them what it is meaningful for them to say.

For Cornelius *Van Til (1895–1987), the minds of non-Christians are so darkened by sin that rational appeal to them by means of theistic arguments is futile. Unbelievers falsely suppose that their rationality is the ultimate power by which the truth about God may be determined. They fail to allow for the ultimacy of God, the primacy of the self-attesting Christ revealed through Scripture, and the finitude and dependency on God of their created intellects. Van Til seeks to make explicit the contrasting presuppositions that lie behind the thinking of Christians and non-Christians. Christians seek to understand their world in self-conscious subjection to the plan of the self-attesting Christ of Scripture. Both the uniformity of nature and the diversity of facts have at their foundation the all-embracing will of God. But, by contrast, non-Christians presuppose a dialectic between chance and regularity, the former accounting for the origin of matter and life, the latter accounting for the current success of the scientific enterprise. Non-Christians argue that the chance character of observed facts, along with the inexorable regularity of natural processes, rules out the possibility of God and his intervention in the world. But if pure chance and irrational matter are seen to be the source of human rationality and a world amenable to scientific investigation, then this explanation is itself self-contradictory and no explanation at all. The only 'proof' of Christianity is a transcendental one: the fact of human rationality is possible only because it has a rational Creator. Only by presupposing Christianity is rational argumentation about ultimate reality, or anything else, rationally possible at all.

The Calvinist philosophers Alvin Plantinga (b. 1932), Nicholas Wolterstorff (b. 1932) and William P. Alston (b. 1921) have proposed that, for Christians, belief in God is not primarily a derived belief dependent on other beliefs, but arises from a direct apprehension of God, which may or may not be confirmed by other beliefs. This belief in God is a 'basic belief' which can be associated with other basic beliefs, such as those produced by the perception of physical objects, knowledge of other persons, self-evident truths, etc. Such basic beliefs form a framework for our understanding of reality, by which we conduct our lives. Acquired beliefs are derived from our basic beliefs in conjunction with our experience and thought. This approach is known as 'Reformed epistemology' and is a type of moderate fideism.

As a basic belief, belief in God's existence has no need of rational support, just as direct perceptual claims usually have no need of additional confirmation, except in situations in which one's perceptions could be confused. Indeed, many Christians hold fast to belief in God without seeking further rational justification of their belief. This is a challenge to evidentialists, who maintain that it is rational to believe something only if one has adequate evidence and/or arguments for one's belief. But belief in God is advocated as valid regardless of evidence or arguments for his existence. Reformed *epistemology is also a challenge to strong *foundationalism, which is one variety of *evidentialism and holds that a belief is rational only if it is self-evident or incorrigible (e.g. a direct perception), or is derived from self-evident or incorrigible beliefs using acceptable methods of logical inference. But belief in God arising from the immediate awareness of him does not fit the categories of being self-evident or incorrigible. Philosophers, like other people, hold prior pre-philosophical commitments regarding religion that are likely to determine their conclusions about it. It does seem to be the case that believers are convinced of God's reality because of an assurance implanted in them by the Holy Spirit. Support for this belief from the historical records of the Bible or from arguments for the existence of God are only supplementary to this. In this sense the evangelical Christian faith does seem to be an example of a moderate fideism.

Bibliography

S. B. Cowan (ed.), *Five Views on Apologetics* (Grand Rapids, 2000); N. Geisler, *Christian Apologetics*, ch. 3, 'Fideism' (Grand Rapids, 1976); D. Z. Phillips, *Faith and Philosophical Enquiry* (London, 1970); R. Trigg, *Rationality and Religion: Does Faith Need Reason?*, chs. 6, 7, 9 (Oxford, 1998).

J. W. WARD

FINE ARTS, see ARTS
FIORENZA, ELISABETH SCHÜSSLER, see
SCHÜSSLER FIORENZA, ELISABETH

FIRST PRINCIPLES

A principle was defined in scholastic philosophy as 'that from which anything proceeds in any way whatever'. Thus defined, a principle can be either an element of *reality or a first or axiomatic premise in a chain of *reasoning. It can, that is to say, be a principle of reality or a principle of knowledge. To begin, like *Descartes, with the subject-orientated question 'What can I know?' is to begin with principles of knowledge or *science. It is however clear that knowledge is ordered towards *truth, which is in the mind when the mind holds things to be as they really are. From this it follows that principles of being come before principles of knowledge or science. They are more purely and hence 'more principally' principles.

On a Christian scheme, as in any of the monotheistic religions, the first principle of all things has to be God. It is what we call God, in fact. In a sense, God is the only principle, something especially emphasized in Islam but moderated in Christianity by the stress on the dignity of creation as having its own principles (such as the Greek philosophers sought to find out) and by the affirmation of certain necessary relations and hence principles within the deity itself. Thus, all things are made through or by 'the Word', that one word uttered and loved by the Father and one with himself in nature and infinitude. Christianity agrees with atheist philosophers, such as J. E. McTaggart, who argue that there cannot be a solitary divine person. Thus, the relation of Father and Son (Word), once revealed, is a first, necessary principle of *theology and no mere afterthought. Without it one holds a distorted picture of God unless one leaves an opening for such relations at least. The *Trinity of persons, anyhow, in the Christian (Augustinian) tradition is nothing other than the set (in itself a simple unity) of these necessary relations themselves, of which our human and mental spiritual processes offer a finite likeness within unlikeness. Theologians confine themselves to showing, where they can, that the ensuing *paradoxes do not commit believers to flat *contradictions.

The debate on the first principles of knowledge, in particular the principle of non-contradiction, takes its rise, in the West at least, from *Aristotle's *Metaphysics* (Book IV), although this nexus of *logic and *metaphysics together is treated in *Plato too, of course, and he in turn took his cue from the ground-assertion of *Parmenides of Elea (whom Plato accordingly calls a 'giant') that 'being alone is'. The Presocratics of Ionia had earlier sought to identify first principles of reality. In fact, Aristotle is concerned to show that the first principle of knowledge depends upon the stability amid change (the reality of which Parmenides had denied) of material substance. Hence, he says, being is substance. Thus, by contrast, for a Heracleitean or *Hegelian, who deny such a stability of substance, contradictions in reality (Marx) taken up as dialectic in thought are in order.

The early Christian thinkers were fully aware of this twofold way in which there can be a first principle. We find it in *Augustine and *Anselm, and so it is taken up into *Thomas Aquinas' discussion of Anselm's *ontological argument for God's existence, a convenient focus for us here. We may note too that for Aquinas there will also be a parallel set of first principles of *practical* reasoning, corresponding to laws of behaviour, as found in the OT, though we should not forget that the parallel is only partial. In reality moral or practical thinking is just one department of reasoning in general, depending as it does on logical reasoning *about* behaviour of the same type as obtains in science generally. The real first principles are principles of reality, of being, from which, in a delimited field, the principles of behaviour arise. So, if there were, as *Hume and others have argued, a 'naturalistic fallacy' in reasoning from 'is' to 'ought', then this, as the use of quotation marks suggests, would be a purely logical truth about the terms used. Any laws of nature, human or other, in which considerations of obligation might be enshrined, would still arise directly from how things are. This is the force of the ancient directive to 'know thyself', *conscience arising directly from such real knowledge.

In discussing Anselm, Aquinas notes that the first principle of actual reality must consist in a necessary identity of essence and act (or existence, the primal act of being) which is God. This, for Anselm, was an aspect of God's self-evidence, as first principle therefore of both systematic speculation (i.e. thought) and of reality. Aquinas begins by discussing merely the notion of self-evidence. Propositions self-evident in themselves are not always self-evident to us. He is not thinking here necessarily of principles of reasoning. God is himself the first principle of any theology. Hence, for Aquinas, the question as to God's real existence is the first question theology must face in order to exist as a science. It is only in this context that the first principles of reasoning (at the heart of Aristotle's philosophical enquiries) are discussed but as being merely typical examples of what might be self-evident.

Anyone committed to God must posit this otherwise surprising class of self-evident principles not evident to us, though absolutely prime in themselves. Thus Aquinas does not treat principles of reasoning or logic as anything unique. From his theologian's point of view they are on a par with other self-evident propositions, such as that bodies occupy space.

Aquinas treats Anselm's argument as a kind of meta-argument to show that argument is not needed, since the mere idea of God implies his necessary existence. To show Anselm's error, as he considers it, he distinguishes between an order of *causality in reality and our ordered knowledge of causality, which begins with knowledge of effects (of causes), the so-called a posteriori. Aquinas' own arguments for God's existence are a posteriori in this sense, while Anselm's is a priori, prior to experience of these effects. Aquinas proceeds from what is more knowable to us to what is more knowable in itself, from first principles of knowledge (even these, Aristotle had argued, are known from experience) to the first principle of being – in other words, the infinite being, God.

Aquinas agrees with Anselm that God's existence must be self-evident in itself, if God is infinite. But it is not thus evident to us. Some first principles are evident only to 'the learned'. The predicate of a self-evident proposition has to 'form part of what the subject means', as in 'Life is existence', though this self-evident proposition is by no means a first principle. For it would be self-evident even if nothing were alive. Similarly human beings are self-evidently animals since being an animal is 'part of the meaning' of being human. It would not follow that everyone knows this. *Descartes, for example, established *certainty about a thinking subject's existence before any knowledge of human beings as animals or as being embodied. Cartesian certainty, based on the theory of the natural light of reason, parallels

Aquinas' category of what is evident to us. Descartes ignores the complementary category of the objectively 'self-evident', which is absorbed in his system into that of the certain, i.e. what the subject cannot *doubt.

It was perhaps evident to Descartes 'what it is to be' human. It was not evident to him that there are humans, or that he himself was a human being (and not just a mind, say). Nor does Aquinas claim to know this in claiming that 'animal' is part of the meaning of 'human', as he goes on to say that 'existing' is part of the meaning of 'God'. This is what makes God a necessary being. But this is only so if God exists in the first place, he argues against Anselm. It belongs to God's notion that he exists necessarily, but not that it is necessary that he exists.

As far as first principles of thinking or of logic are concerned, within the field of Christian apologetics we have the celebrated argument of C. S. *Lewis (Miracles, 1947) against *naturalism, understanding naturalism as the view that nature forms a closed deterministic system excluding the free play of thought needed for the making of true judgments. This implies, says Lewis, that no claim, no judgment, can consistently be made as to the truth of naturalism. It would be, as Bernard Lonergan also pointed out in his book Insight (1957), a 'contradiction in performance'. These arguments are in fact variations upon an original argument of Augustine's concerning truth in the mind as proof of the presence of a necessary being.

Lewis's argument has survived the criticism made against its formulation by G. E. M. Anscombe in 1947, herself a Christian thinker who later claimed (in her 'Modern Moral Philosophy', Philosophy, 1958), along with Lewis in his Mere Christianity, that acknowledgment of moral imperatives as first practical principles committed one logically to the reality of a divine law-giver. It is regularly discussed in philosophical controversy while its premises are increasingly defended, as against dogmatic naturalism, by philosophers not especially connected to Christian apologetics (John Searle, Re-Discovery of the Mind; Thomas Nagel, The Last Word; J. Kim, Supervenience and Mind). Acceptance of Lewis's argument, however, might seem to commit believers to an unnecessary dualism, difficult to sustain in the face of the increasingly unified evolutionary view of humankind. This is because Lewis starts out, with the more extreme naturalists, with a view of nature as blind and deterministic. In our time, however, it is easy, or easier, to feel that he need not have conceded so much to the materialists. Nature need not be seen as so blind. God, if he exists at all, is present in each part of it as it unfolds first into life, then into an ever greater complexity of life, becoming conscious of itself in the human mind and still pressing onwards. This is the vision of *Teilhard de Chardin (*The Phenomenon of Man*, 1959) and, suitably interpreted, of Hegel, though Hegel personally denied evolution.

On such a view, the validity of our reasoning processes, our first principles, will depend upon a general recognition of nature as an intelligent being's creation. Philosophical theology can maybe show that this being is infinite and omniscient and eternal, hence unchanging. Such an infinite being's omniscience can take in the real role of chance, which we now acknowledge, in our physics for example, just as it can take in human free choices, their freedom being simply the aspect under which he creatively knows them, as Aquinas argued. It is a profound conception, which gave rise to a centuries-long dispute in Counter-Reformation times between Dominicans and Jesuits.

According to Christian belief, God set a guarantee upon our thought processes by becoming a man himself and even presenting arguments in his time on earth. Whether such a guarantee can be found independently in a 'natural theology' is a difficult question. The claim that the universe has become conscious of itself in us is rather ambitious. Within the theory it might only seem certain that intellect has developed, pragmatically, to help us to survive. However, one can disarm that argument by according to truth itself a survival value. Thus, sensations which do not mislead but are of the reality are needed to preserve the animal's life (transcendental identity of truth and being), and human knowledge is founded upon sensation. One might claim, further, that with the advent of intellect, the vital thrust called evolution now transcends the biological in favour of a unification in love, freedom and knowledge, called by Teilhard the noosphere (after the biosphere). In this way the absoluteness of our first principles does indeed bear a relation to our standing in the line of evolutionary progress. The immense time taken, similarly, is to be seen as the piece by piece unfolding of an eternal divine utterance, while our at least partial knowledge of this shows us to be in the divine image in a unique way, this again vindicating the absoluteness of the first principles of reasoning, but above all of the principle of freedom as needed for any thinking and judging.

Indeed, in a theological variant which has gained increasing ground, from the time of Nicolas of Cusa at least, such freedom is presented as a first principle, not simply as a mode of action or judging consequent upon spiritual being but as itself the principle of principles, the truly first. Thus Berdyaev states, in his *The Destiny of Man*, 'God is not being. God is freedom.' Such had been implicit in Hegel's theology, where divine thinking and divine creation are not significantly differentiated, and the idea goes back at least to Jakob Boehme and even Eckhart. These thinkers and mystics state or imply that God has no full reality apart from his relatedness to creation, a view creating problems for traditional Christianity, but which many think to resolve by developing the idea of a necessity of love which does not limit divine freedom. God was intrinsically bound to create, but not as if compelled from outside.

These views on the divine nature are not entirely new. A basis for much of them can be found in Plotinus and Neo-platonism generally, inasmuch as Plotinus posits the first principle as something above and beyond being. One can relate this to a development within philosophy, by Richard Sylvan and others, called 'sistology', taking much of its inspiration from Alexius Meinong, according to which our prejudice in favour of the existent should be disregarded. We should instead treat all our conceptions equally. The scholastic variant upon this was the doctrine of beings of reason, which preserves the primacy of being in name alone, critics say, since human ideas, of possible beings for instance, are precisely understood as lacking real being. For Anselm, however, once again, the idea of God as infinite, the greatest possible being, must itself as an idea include (necessary) existence.

For when we return to thinking about God, we have to concede that the distinction between idea and reality is difficult to maintain. Each of the divine ideas, Aquinas asserts (and he takes up the doctrine as first developed by Augustine in an explicitly Neo-platonic context), is necessarily identical with the divine nature and being, since God is incomposite, simple. He has no real relation with anything outside himself. So if we accept this, God knows each of us not as we are in our worldly reality, but in his own eternal idea of us. Such an idea, it follows, is more real than 'worldly reality'. Thus, Aquinas teaches as a basic principle that although our relation to God is real, God's relation to us is not a real relation for or within God. We are simply not on the same divine or infinite level. We can recall here Paul's words, 'In God we live and move and have our being'. Others, such as Hegel, have been accused, even against their own protests, of pantheism for making similar statements (See G. van Riet, 'The Problem of God in Hegel', *Philosophy Today*, XI [Summer 1967]). Yet the orthodox John of the Cross flatly called God 'the All'.

Bibliography

G. E. M. Anscombe, 'A Reply to Mr C. S. Lewis's Argument that "Naturalism" is Self-Refuting', *Socratic Digest* 4 (Oxford, 1948); N. Berdyaer, *The Destiny of Man* (London, 1931); C. S. Lewis, *Miracles* (London, 1947); B. Lonergan, *Insight* (London, 1957); G. van Riet, 'The Problem of God in Hegel', *Philosophy Today* (Ohio, Summer 1967); P. Teilhard de Chardin, *The Phenomenon of Man* (London, 1959); S. Theron, *Philosophy or Dialectic* (Frankfurt, 1994).

S. THERON

FLEW, ANTONY

Antony Flew (b. 1923) is a British philosopher and apologist for *atheism, the son of the distinguished Methodist theologian R. N. Flew. He has held a number of senior academic posts, including chairs of philosophy at the universities of Keele and Reading. His editing (with A. C. MacIntyre) of the collection *New Essays in Philosophical Theology* (1955) was a major step in reviving interest in theological matters among English-speaking philosophers in the analytic tradition.

Flew insists that the burden of proof lies with theists; so in this sense, though not in any stronger one, there is a 'presumption of atheism'. He calls this 'negative atheism', as opposed to that which positively asserts the non-existence of God, and against which there would presumably be an equal presumption. In his 1966 book *God and Philosophy* (p. 69) he

used a much stronger 'presumption', which he called 'Stratonician', to the effect that 'whatever characteristics we think ourselves able to discern in the universe as a whole are the underivative characteristics of the universe itself'. This would rule out any kind of *natural theology from the start. However, he would not now insist on this stronger form.

As for traditional *theistic proofs, Flew points out that there is no one 'cosmological argument' for the reality of God; there have been many, most of them now obsolete. The one perhaps most forcibly advocated today (e.g. by Richard Swinburne), that we can look for a cause of the world as a whole, he rejects on lines derived from *Hume, that if every item in a collection is explained, there is no need for a further explanation of the collection as a whole. (This is true if the explanation[s] are in terms of items outside the collection – which is exactly what theists maintain – but hardly if all are explained solely in terms of one another.) Flew agrees that argument from design (or better, as he says, *to* design) has been considerably strengthened by recent arguments from 'fine tuning', but he agrees with *Kant that this is 'much too weak to prove the existence of an infinite, omniscient and omnipotent God'.

In a contribution to the *New Essays* Flew issued a celebrated challenge to believers: 'What would have to occur or to have occurred to constitute for you a disproof of the love of, or of the existence of, God?' The point is that 'if there is nothing which a putative assertion denies, then there is nothing that it asserts either: and so it is not really an assertion'. In the subsequent debate, Flew conceded that theists, when confronted with apparent evidence against *theism (notably the existence of *evil), usually seek explanations for it; but he believed that eventually they would be forced instead to qualify their assertions until they asserted nothing. Although normally adept at finding embarrassing quotations from Christian writers past and present, he seems not to have been very successful in finding many which resort to such qualifications; still less, as he admits, to the alternative refuge he suggested, George Orwell's concept of 'Doublethink'.

As regards the traditional 'problem of evil', Flew rejects the 'free-will defence' on two grounds. He is a compatibilist, i.e. he thinks that free will, in the ordinary untechnical sense, is quite compatible with scientific *determinism, and that 'libertarian' freewill, which is not, is not needed for responsibility or genuine choice. (He is equally opposed to those who believe psychological and social sciences have shown that responsibility and choice are nonexistent.) Hence God could have created a world of free agents and yet without sin. Secondly, he holds (perhaps rather inconsistently) that God, in creating sinners and sustaining them in existence, must be seen as a 'manipulator', and held responsible for their actions, even those which are free in the ordinary untechnical sense.

Flew has also written studies of Hume, guides to clear thinking, and attacks on left-wing political views. He has recently modified his views in the light of problems over the origin of life, and would now call himself a deist.

Bibliography

A. Flew, *The Logic of Mortality* (Oxford, 1987; reissued as *Merely Mortal?* [New York, 2000]); *God and Philosophy* (London, 1966; reissued as *God: A Philosophical Critique* [La Salle, 1984]); *The Presumption of Atheism* (London, 1976; reissued as *God, Freedom and Immortality* [Buffalo, 1984]); *Atheistic Humanism* (Buffalo, 1993); A. Flew and A. C. MacIntyre (eds.), *New Essays in Philosophical Theology* (London, 1955).

R. L. STURCH

FLINT, ROBERT

Robert Flint (1838–1910), Scottish philosopher, theologian, minister and apologist, was born at Dumfries, the son of a farm overseer. He left Glasgow University in 1859 and served as a missionary and minister in Glasgow, Aberdeen and Kilconquhar before his appointment to the Chair of Moral Philosophy and Political Economy at St Andrews. He moved to Edinburgh as Professor of Divinity in 1876. Flint produced arguably the most notable Baird Lectures, later published as *Theism* and *Anti-Theistic Theories*, and extended his influence as Croall Lecturer at Edinburgh in 1877–78 and Stone Lecturer at Princeton in 1880. Flint acquired deep learning across many disciplines and wrote significant works in philosophy, history and theology.

As a philosopher of religion, Flint intended to lay out a rational and natural basis for theistic belief. Though he believed the resulting knowledge was incomplete for salvation without *revelation, he nevertheless attempted to use the cumulative force of the traditional cosmological, teleological and ontological proofs to demonstrate the compelling evidence for the existence of God. His concern was to preserve for faith a reasonable ground for belief, without which Christianity would be intellectually deprived. He criticized those who were happy to reject the role of reason as an inappropriate tool for the strengthening of religious belief, and thus set himself apart from many thinkers of his day with a preference for an *a posteriori* apologetic. Despite his reliance on this older methodology, Flint welcomed advances in *science and was not afraid of evolutionary theories, since he believed they favoured, rather than discouraged, a *teleological argument, with respect to natural order and progress. Nevertheless, he resisted the fashionable philosophies that emphasized feeling and *conscience, in the contemporary trend towards various forms of *Kantian and *Hegelian *idealism.

Flint's work offers evidence for the fact that not all philosophers in the late nineteenth century were antagonistic to the intellectual credibility of Christian belief. Although his work may be found wanting, especially with respect to the role of revelation in the awakening of distinctive faith, he offers encouragement to those who do not favour a complete rejection of the role of reason and *natural law in Christian theology and apologetics.

Bibliography

R. Flint, *Theism* (London, 1878); *Agnosticism* (London, 1903); D. Macmillan, *The Life of Robert Flint* (London, 1914); A. P. F. Sell, *Defending and Declaring the Faith* (Exeter and Colorado Springs, 1987).

A. M. ROBBINS

FORM CRITICISM, see BIBLICAL CRITICISM

FORSYTH, PETER TAYLOR

Peter Forsyth (1848–1921) started as a theological liberal but became an ardent apologist for evangelical theology following a personal experience of the holiness and grace of God.

He wrote widely on cultural, social and moral issues, but his most significant works were theological.

Key to Forsyth's apologetic was what he called 'the effectual primacy of the given'. If we start with human concepts, as the liberal theologians do, we will never get beyond them, but the essence of Christianity is that we are not restricted to human concepts. There is a 'given', a *revelation. An objectively real God has come to us, and because he is active in the world we can experience him, not so much through our intellects as in our wills, as we encounter his holiness and his grace. Though the Scriptures are a key aspect of God's revelation, revelation is much more than the Scriptures. Revelation is not just words or truth about God, but God himself, Christ the Word, Christ the *Truth. Even experience is inadequate if it is *experience* of God, rather than experience of *God*.

Forsyth sought to defend his distinctive brand of evangelical theology not just against the dominant liberalism of his day but also against those evangelicals who were retreating into obscurantism or depending on a predominately rationalist approach. A Scottish Congregationalist with roots in the Anabaptist tradition, Forsyth was educated in the post-*Kantian school and influenced by Albert *Ritschl, but he rejected both obscurantism and the dogmatism of the rationalists. For him the heart of Christianity was the action of a holy and gracious God, not a set of carefully defined doctrines. 'Christianity does not peddle ideas; it does things.' God's supreme act is his 'self-communication in *Jesus Christ for man's redemption'.

In *The Justification of God: Lectures for War-Time on a Christian Theodicy* (1916), Forsyth rejected philosophical theodicies, considering it far too hubristic of us to seek to justify God. Rather, God has justified himself, and instead of human theories we have the action of God in the Christ of history. God justifies himself on the cross where 'the Father suffered in His Son even more than the Son did ... The last theodicy is a gift of God ... Christ is the theodicy of God and the justifier both of God and the ungodly. The supreme theodicy is atonement.'

Christocentric and theocentric but with a broad vision of how Christianity impacts every area of life, Forsyth demonstrated the relevance of the evangelical world-view for all the major issues of his time. There is much we can learn from him today.

Bibliography

T. Hart (ed.), *Justice, the True and Only Mercy* (Edinburgh, 1995).

P. HICKS

FOUCAULT, MICHEL

Defining Michel Foucault (1926–84) proves problematic for many reasons. His writings cover an encyclopedic array of topics and cross disciplines such as philosophy, history, medicine and sociology. Not only was Foucault unsystematic but he pushed the boundaries of both scholarship and personal behaviour. That Foucault was openly gay and died of AIDS has prompted some (unwisely) to dismiss his thought. But Foucault's premature death also cut short the trajectory of his thinking, one ultimately directed towards concern with the cultivation of the self.

Unlike Kant, who sought to establish the universal and necessary limits of thought, Foucault investigates the historical and contingent contours of thought and how those change over time. For example, in *Madness and Civilization* (1961) Foucault shows both that our contemporary conception of 'madness' differs markedly from that of previous ages and that our conception cannot be shown to be superior. Thus the question running throughout Foucault's thought is: 'why do we think the way that we do and how might we overcome the limitations of that thinking?' rather than 'what is the correct way to think?'.

Foucault's earlier thought can be termed 'archaeological' in nature. In *The Birth of the Clinic* (1963) Foucault is less concerned with the actual practice of modern medicine than with the basic conceptual and linguistic systems undergirding it. *The Order of Things* (1966) delineates the 'epistemes' (i.e. linguistic systems) lying beneath the thought of different eras and shows a marked discontinuity between the modern disciplines and the classical ones they replaced. *The Archaeology of Knowledge* (1969) was Foucault's attempt to explain this methodology. In the 1970s, Foucault (influenced by *Nietzsche) turns to a 'genealogical' method focusing on the singular, contingent, even conflicting, elements that bring about changes in thought. For example, in

Discipline and Punish (1975), Foucault demonstrates that disciplinary practices (not just of prisons but also of armies, factories and schools) were connected to the rise of the social sciences. Yet rather than replacing archaeology, Foucault uses genealogy as a supplement.

Whereas philosophers have generally treated knowledge as independent of politics and use, Foucault emphasizes the close relation between knowledge and *power. Not only does possession of knowledge provide power to the possessor, but those with power are usually the ones who determine the contours of knowledge and thus what is to be valued. In the essay 'The Discourse on Language' (1971), an excellent entrée into his thought, Foucault shows how discourse is controlled by prohibition, by the ways in which it draws boundaries around itself (and thus excludes others), by its reigning conceptions of truth and falsity, by what count as authoritative texts and acceptable commentaries on those texts, and by the bodies that both define knowledge and promulgate that knowledge in a systematic way that includes some and excludes others.

Foucault has often been criticized for having no 'objective' place to stand in order to criticize historical and present practices. Yet his work clearly can be read as a critique of society as it functions. How can these two aspects be put together? While Foucault's critique could be read as simply inconsistent, it can also be described as immanent critique. On Foucault's account, no-one is ultimately able to step outside *history and its modes of thought, yet one can still oppose one mode of thought to another. Such a point has deeply influenced the thought of Richard *Rorty. Although Foucault is often read as a relativist (whether moral or metaphysical), he never makes such explicit claims. Instead, his work shows how our moral and metaphysical assumptions have been shaped historically. Thus, there is room in Foucault's thought for a weaker conception of objectivity or objective *truth.

That Foucault seems convinced that some ways of thinking and being are superior to others is evident throughout his writings, but it is particularly evident in the project that consumed the last years of his life, the three-volume *History of Sexuality*. The third of these texts, *The Care of the Self* (1974), turns to the personal cultivation advocated by ancient Greek philosophy and Christianity. There Foucault focuses on the 'practices of the self'

or 'spiritual exercises' found in Stoic philosophy and Christianity as ways of developing one's true self. Unfortunately, it was precisely at this point in his development that Foucault's life was cut short.

Foucault's methodology of examining how institutions and ideas develop over time has greatly affected the human sciences, even the study of church history. As is common in the tradition of French *agnosticism/*atheism, Foucault nowhere provides a refutation of Christianity. He simply assumes that it is not a 'live' option. Since Foucault likewise never provides anything like a philosophical system, no simple apologetic to his thought is possible. One might, of course, criticize Foucault for at least implying that there is power play behind everything and exercising a marked 'hermeneutics of suspicion'. Yet, while that criticism has some validity, it cuts both ways. Christians can easily employ Foucaultian analysis to argue that there has been a power play behind secular thought in modernity. So Foucault's methodology can be used for a variety of purposes.

Bibliography

P. Rabinow (ed.), *The Foucault Reader* (New York, 1984).

B. E. Benson

FOUNDATIONALISM

Foundationalism is a view about how a person's beliefs must be structured if they are to be rational. An understanding of foundationalism is useful for considering the differences between the apologetics of theistic evidentialists and the negative apologetics of Reformed epistemologists. In order to explain these two approaches to apologetics and how they are connected with foundationalism, we must first take a careful look at what foundationalism is.

1. Defining foundationalism

Crucial to understanding foundationalism is a clear grasp of two distinctions: that between rational beliefs and irrational beliefs and that between basic beliefs and non-basic beliefs. To say a belief is rational is to evaluate the way it was formed, saying that it is held in a way that is sensible or reasonable or warranted or justified. To say it is irrational is just to say it is not rational.

The distinction between basic beliefs and non-basic beliefs is a psychological, not an evaluative, distinction. It has to do with how beliefs are formed, not whether they are rational. A basic belief is a non-inferential belief, one that is not formed by inference from other beliefs. For example, when a person stubs her toe and is in extreme pain, she forms the belief that she is in pain. That belief is not inferred from or based on any other belief, but is based on the experience of the pain. By contrast, a *non-basic* belief is an inferential belief, one that is inferred from other beliefs one has. If one wants to figure out what 7×46 equals, one typically will come first to believe that $7 \times 40 = 280$, that $7 \times 6 = 42$ and that $280 + 42 = 322$. Then one infers from those beliefs the further belief that $7 \times 46 = 322$. Since that last belief is inferred from other beliefs, it is a non-basic belief.

Putting these distinctions together, we get four kinds of belief: two kinds of basic belief (rational and irrational) and two kinds of non-basic belief (rational and irrational). Foundationalism has mostly to do with rational basic beliefs, often called '*properly* basic beliefs'. Some beliefs that are formed without inference seem to be entirely appropriate, as in the example above about pain. These sorts of beliefs seem to be examples of properly basic beliefs. But other basic beliefs seem to be irrational. For example, if a gambler is having bad luck at a casino and then believes on a whim, without any inference from other beliefs, that their luck is about to improve, this belief seems to be irrational. The beliefs of both the gambler and the person who is in pain are basic since neither is an inferential belief. But the pain belief seems to be a properly basic belief whereas the gambler's belief does not.

Employing the distinctions above, we can define foundationalism as the view that if a person's beliefs are rational they must include a foundation of properly basic beliefs and, if there are any rational non-basic beliefs, they will be based on inferences from, or chains of inference tracing back to, the properly basic beliefs which form the foundation.

2. Alternatives to foundationalism

A good way to gain a better grasp of foundationalism is to understand the alternatives to it. The best way to clarify what these alternatives are is to consider a famous argument, originally found in the works of *Aristotle,

for the conclusion that there can be properly basic beliefs. The strategy employed in the Aristotelian argument is to show that the denial of this conclusion leads to absurd results and, thereby, to show that the conclusion itself is true.

The denial of the conclusion that there can be properly basic beliefs is the claim, which we can call 'inferentialism', that a belief can be rational only if it is inferred from another belief. The Aristotelian argument begins by distinguishing two versions of inferentialism, a more plausible version and a less plausible version. The more plausible version says that a belief can be made rational by inference from another belief only if that other belief is itself rational. The less plausible version says a belief can be made rational by inference from another belief even if that other belief is itself irrational. Now consider what follows if a belief can be rational only if it is inferred from another rational belief. For the other belief to be rational, it too must be inferred from another rational belief, and so on. Thus, if the more plausible version of inferentialism were true, a belief could be rational only if it were based on either an infinite chain of *reasoning or a circular chain of reasoning.

Keeping these things in mind, we can summarize the Aristotelian argument succinctly as follows. If there could not be any properly basic beliefs, then inferentialism is true. But if inferentialism is true, we are forced to choose between four unacceptable alternatives. According to the more plausible version of inferentialism, a belief can be rational only if it is inferred from another *rational* belief. But if that is true, then, as was indicated above, rational beliefs are either impossible or based upon an infinite chain or a circular chain of reasoning. If, in order to avoid these three results, one tries to adhere to inferentialism while rejecting the more plausible version of it, one is forced to accept the less plausible version of inferentialism which says that a belief can be made rational by inference from an irrational belief.

The only way to avoid all four of these alternatives is to reject inferentialism in any form and admit that there can be properly basic beliefs. And avoiding these four alternatives is a desirable goal. After all, no-one thinks that rational beliefs can be based on circular reasoning or irrational beliefs. And it is highly implausible to think that rational beliefs are literally impossible rather than merely difficult to come by. It is equally absurd to think that our beliefs can be based on infinite chains of inference – we just are not capable of such lengthy reasoning. Moreover, an infinite chain of reasoning cannot, by itself, make a belief rational without some original rationality to be transferred along the chain. Since each of these alternatives to foundationalism is so unattractive, the Aristotelian argument concludes that there can be properly basic beliefs.

Of the four alternatives to foundationalism mentioned above, the second one – which permits circular reasoning – deserves special attention. That alternative is often referred to as 'coherentism', and in the literature on foundationalism one often reads that coherentism is the main alternative to foundationalism (the other three alternatives are simply not taken very seriously). Unfortunately, this gives rise to an important confusion. The problem is that there is more than one view that goes by the name 'coherentism', and most of them side with foundationalism in rejecting circular reasoning. The result is that the most common forms of coherentism do not endorse the second alternative above. In fact, the most common forms of coherentism do not reject foundationalism as defined above. For this reason, it is misleading to characterize foundationalism and coherentism as competing views. (See ch. 4 of A. Plantinga, *Warrant: The Current Debate* [New York, 1993] for further discussion of these issues and an account of how the most plausible forms of coherentism are compatible with foundationalism.)

This argument for foundationalism seems to be irresistible. Nonetheless, one often finds discussions in the literature on this topic that are unfriendly to foundationalism. Some even say that foundationalism is widely rejected. How can this be if the above account is correct? The answer is quite simple. The term 'foundationalism' is often used to refer to one particular version of foundationalism, a version that was for a time the most prominent, though it has since fallen on hard times. This once popular version of foundationalism is often called 'Cartesian foundationalism' because *Descartes is considered to be its most prominent proponent. When people proclaim that foundationalism is widely rejected, they have in mind Cartesian foundationalism (a view discussed in greater detail below).

3. Varieties of foundationalism

Now that we know what foundationalism is, we can consider how various versions of foundationalism differ from one another. This will prove to be helpful when we turn to an examination of the connection between foundationalism and apologetics. Perhaps the most useful way to distinguish versions of foundationalism from one another is to look at their views on what is required for a belief to be rational. Because foundationalists typically think there are both properly basic beliefs and rational non-basic beliefs, a foundationalist account of what is required for rational belief will have two clauses: one saying what is required for a basic belief to be rational and another saying what is required for a non-basic belief to be rational. The first clause is the more interesting one. It identifies the conditions for proper basicality (i.e. the conditions a basic belief must satisfy if it is to be rational). Here is where all the most important distinctions arise between different versions of foundationalism.

Consider for example what the conditions of proper basicality are according to Cartesian foundationalism. It says that to be properly basic, a belief must be absolutely certain and impossible to *doubt under any circumstances. The only basic beliefs of ours that seem to have a chance of passing this test are introspective beliefs about our own mental states – beliefs concerning how we feel or what we are thinking. According to Cartesian foundationalism, those beliefs (along with some simple logical and mathematical beliefs) are the only ones that make it into the foundation. No other beliefs can be rational unless they are non-basic beliefs that are properly built on that foundation via the right sort of inference.

The reason Cartesian foundationalism has become so unpopular is that its proponents have tried and failed to identify good inferences that enable our memory or perceptual beliefs to be properly built upon the meagre foundation of introspective beliefs. There just do not seem to be any successful arguments starting solely with premises about our own mental states and yielding the conclusion that there is a physical world around us and that we and it have a past. So we are forced to either reject Cartesian foundationalism or accept its consequence that none of our beliefs about the world around us or about our past is rational. The unattractiveness of that sceptical result has been one of the main reasons for the demise of Cartesian foundationalism.

There have been two main sorts of reaction to the demise of Cartesian foundationalism. One is the postmodern disillusionment with Descartes's exaltation of reason and his quest for certainty. The other, which will be our focus here, is the reaction of most professional philosophers who work in the field of *epistemology. They consider themselves to be less optimistic than Descartes and less pessimistic than postmodernists about the power of reason alone. They think that the problem with Cartesian foundationalism is that its conditions of proper basicality are too strict. In place of those conditions many alternatives have been proposed, typically designed to allow perceptual and memory beliefs into the foundations. With such beliefs included among the properly basic beliefs, it is easy to see why our beliefs about the world around us and about the past are rational despite the fact that we lack any convincing arguments for them based solely on our introspective beliefs. In short, this reaction to Cartesian foundationalism consists of rejecting Descartes's conditions of proper basicality while endorsing foundationalism of a different sort – one that relaxes the conditions of proper basicality so that perceptual and memory beliefs count as properly basic.

4. Foundationalism and apologetics

We can now turn to the connection between foundationalism and Christian apologetics. One popular position held by Christian apologists, both historically and today, is theistic evidentialism. According to this view, belief in God is rational only if it is properly inferred from other beliefs, i.e. only if it is the conclusion of some good theistic argument. In order to show that theistic belief is rational in this way, theistic evidentialists have devised various sorts of arguments for God's existence (ranging from deductive 'proofs' to more probabilistic or best-explanation type arguments). However, another approach to Christian apologetics – one that focuses more on a good defence than on a strong offence – is Reformed epistemology, so called because of its connection with the Reformed tradition, grounded in the writings of John *Calvin. According to Reformed epistemologists, belief in God can be properly basic, i.e. it can be rational even if not inferred from other beliefs by any theistic argument whatsoever.

This gives us two responses to atheistic evidentialists, who argue as follows that belief in God is irrational: (i) belief in God is rational only if properly inferred from other beliefs via good theistic arguments; (ii) there are no good theistic arguments; therefore, (iii) belief in God is irrational. The theistic evidentialist's response is to accept (i) and to try to show, by producing good theistic arguments, that (ii) is mistaken. The Reformed epistemologist's response is to reject (i) by saying that we have no good reason to think that belief in God cannot be rational without argument. Just as the Cartesian foundationalists were mistaken to think perceptual and memory beliefs are not properly basic, so also theistic and atheistic evidentialists are mistaken to think theistic belief is not properly basic. (Reformed epistemologists may or may not accept (ii); some of them accept it and some join theistic evidentialists in rejecting it.) Thus, the *theistic evidentialist's apologetic is a positive one in the sense that it offers arguments for theism. But the Reformed epistemologist's apologetic is a negative one in the sense that it challenges the atheistic evidentialist's assumption that belief in God cannot be properly basic.

Both the theistic evidentialist and the Reformed epistemologist are foundationalists. The difference is that the Reformed epistemologist's conditions for proper basicality are more liberal than the theistic evidentialist's. For, according to the theistic evidentialist, belief in God is *not* properly basic whereas according to the Reformed epistemologist it is.

Bibliography

R. Audi, 'Contemporary Foundationalism', in L. Pojman (ed.), *Theory of Knowledge* (Belmont, 1999), pp. 204–211; R. Fumerton, 'Theories of Justification', in P. Moser (ed.), *The Oxford Handbook of Epistemology* (New York, 2002), pp. 204–233; A. Plantinga, 'Reason and Belief in God', in A. Plantinga and N. Wolterstorff (eds.), *Faith and Rationality* (Notre Dame, 1983), pp. 16–93.

M. A. BERGMANN

FOX, MATTHEW

Matthew Fox (b. 1940), a Roman Catholic priest expelled from the Dominican Order in 1994 for disobedience, and now ordained in the US Episcopal Church, is the founder and director of the Institute (now University) in Culture and Creation Spirituality in Oakland, California. Fox rejects the traditional Christian interpretation of sin as arising from disobedience and alienation from God in favour of an incompleteness coming from immaturity and disconnectedness to creation. Instead of original sin, he advocates 'original blessing', which he claims to be the oldest Bible doctrine. His alternative to conventional Christian doctrine (which he calls 'fall/redemption spirituality') is 'creation-centred spirituality', exemplified for him in the medieval mysticism of Hildegard of Bingen, *Thomas Aquinas and Meister Eckhart. Fox shares with *New Age and feminist writers an abhorrence of dualism and transcendentalism, and generally encourages New Agers, albeit criticizing their lack of historical perspective. More confusingly, Fox is often linked to Celtic Christianity because of the Celtic emphasis of worshipping God through (although not *in*) nature.

Fox's approach attracts many Christians who are searching for a 'creation-friendly' spirituality and liturgy. He is correct in recognizing defects in some streams of Chrisitanity where the doctrine of creation tends to be ignored or redemption is limited to human salvation. His answer is to play down the fall and its consequences, and this leads him to undervalue the need for redemption.

Following classical mysticism, Fox proposes four 'paths' towards God. In the *via positiva* we befriend awe and wonder by celebrating creation and regard earthiness as good (Gen. 1; Job 38 – 39; Rom. 8; Heb. 1:1–3); in the *via negativa* we welcome silence and befriend loss and let go before God (Hab. 3:17–18; Luke 9:23; Gal. 2:20); in the *via creativa* we co-create with God through the fruit and gifts of the Spirit (Gen. 2:20; Exod. 31:3; Luke 19:12–26; Heb. 6:10); and in the *via transformativa* we and the whole of creation are being transformed (Rom. 8:21; 12:2; Eph. 1:10; Col. 1:20; 1 Pet. 1).

The paths remind us of the goodness of God's creation, the 'original blessing' of Gen. 1. Fox is right to affirm this. Where he errs is in treating 'fall-redemption' and 'creation spirituality' as opposites. Sadly, conventional Christian teaching also often fails in not giving a proper biblical emphasis to the three elements of creation, fall and redemption. The implications of Col. 1:20 are too often ignored: God chose through his Son 'to reconcile to himself all things, whether things on earth or things in heaven, by making peace through his blood shed on the cross'. If we ignore the significance of 'all things' and limit salvation to humans alone, we are failing to understand the authority of the cosmic Christ and allowing the defective teachings of creation spirituality to spread. Real creation spirituality is described in Rom. 8:19–22, where those who have been redeemed (Rom. 5:1–4) can – and have responsibility to – heal a creation which will continue to suffer as long as we do not fulfil our proper role as stewards or creation caretakers.

Bibliography

I. Bradley, *Celtic Christianity: Making Myths and Chasing Dreams* (Edinburgh, 1999); M. Brearley, 'Matthew Fox and the Cosmic Christ', *Anvil*, 9 (1992), pp. 39–54; M. Fox, *Original Blessing: A Primer in Creation Spirituality* (Santa Fe, 1983).

R. J. BERRY

FRAZER, SIR JAMES GEORGE

James Frazer (1854–1941), the accidental grandfather of ethnology and modern social anthropology, was born in Glasgow, where his father was an evangelical Presbyterian minister. He attended the universities of Glasgow and Cambridge before reading law at the Middle Temple. Knighted in 1914, he received numerous honorary degrees and other awards for his academic work including election as a Fellow of the Royal Society (1920). Trained as a classical scholar, he translated and produced critical editions of various Greek works. A Fellow of Trinity College, Cambridge, he became the non-stipendiary professor of social anthropology at the University of Liverpool in 1907, although he soon abandoned this position.

An avowed rationalist, Frazer achieved fame through the publication of *The Golden Bough*, which first appeared in 1890 and later as a twelve-volume work between 1911 and 1915. In it he sought to demonstrate the comparative nature of world *mythology while exposing underlying themes that formed the basis of Christian teachings about the resurrection and virgin birth of Christ. His other important works included *Totemism* (1887) and *The Magical Origin of Kings* (1920). Central to his work is the still influential theory that magic and religion are forms of bad *science.

Although often called an anthropologist, he never undertook fieldwork and relied entirely on written sources for his highly creative studies that drew upon numerous folklore traditions without regard for the social and historical context of the stories themselves. Consequently, he is often dubbed an 'armchair anthropologist'. Actually, he was a brilliant amateur folklorist whose academic work is steeped in the nineteenth century folklore tradition stemming from German *Romanticism. Writers like James MacPherson (1738–96), the author of the fraudulent *Works of Ossian* (1765), and the Brothers Grimm (Jacob Ludwig Karl, 1785–1863, and Wilhelm Karl, 1786–1859) of fairy-tale fame, also clearly influenced his approach to folk tales. Frazer's comparative method and clear anti-Christian bias applies a rationalist grid to such stories similar to the one used by Tom Paine (1737–1809) to debunk the Bible in his classic work *The Age of Reason* (1794–96).

Frazer's clear intent was to destroy Christianity and other religions by reducing sacred stories to archetypal myths common to all *cultures. In this way he sought to undermine the historical claims of particular religions while finding the roots of faith in the psychological make-up of humans. Later, Sigmund *Freud (1856–1940) and Carl Gustav *Jung (1875–1961) developed various aspects of Frazer's approach. Although he had very little actual impact on the development of anthropology as a discipline, Frazer had an enormous influence on writers and literary figures including Kipling, T. S. *Eliot and a host of others. Nevertheless, Ronald Hutton appears to be correct when he observes that Frazer's work actually encouraged the growth of new religions, particularly modern witchcraft and neo-paganism, something that would have horrified the man himself.

Bibliography

R. Ackerman, *J. G. Frazer, His Life and Work* (Cambridge, 1990); *J. G. Frazer and the Cambridge Ritualists* (New York, 1991); R. Fraser, *Sir James Frazer and the Literary Imagination* (Basingstoke, 1990); J. Frazer, *Totemism* (Edinburgh, 1887); *The Golden Bough* (London, 1890); *The Magical Origin of Kings* (London, 1920); R. Hutton, *The Triumph of the Moon* (London, 2000).

I. HEXHAM

FREE WILL, see DETERMINISM, CHANCE AND FREEDOM

FREUD, SIGMUND

Sigmund Freud (1856–1939) was an Austrian neurologist and psychiatrist and the founder of psychoanalysis. Born in Freiberg, Freud began his training as a neurological researcher and later received his medical degree from the University of Vienna. Following his appointment by the university as a lecturer in neuropathology in 1885, he learned the technique of hypnosis from the French neurologist Jean Charcot and began using hypnotherapy to treat patients suffering from hysteria.

Theory of psychoanalysis

Working with the Viennese physician Joseph Breuer, Freud substituted the technique of 'free association' in place of hypnosis, and began to develop the basic tenets and methods of what he called 'psychoanalysis'. Far more than just a new approach to treatment, psychoanalysis constituted 'a comprehensive and exhaustive system of personality, psychopathology and psychotherapy'. Its most basic assumption was that 'all human behavior is determined by psychic energy and early childhood experiences'. Unresolved conflicts, retained as inaccessible, 'unconscious' experiences, inevitably become 'the primary determinant of psychic life' (Jones and Butman, *Modern Psychotherapies*, pp. 89, 66–67).

The goal of psychoanalysis is 'abreaction' or 'catharsis' of formative, painful childhood experiences by 'making the unconscious conscious' through free association, dream analysis, interpretation and analysis of the 'transference neurosis' or relationship with one's analyst. Successful working through of these conflicts results in decreased anxiety, a reduction of 'neurotic' symptoms and greater integration within the personality.

Theory of religion

Freud held that religion in all its forms represents 'the universal obsessional neurosis of humanity'. Its source is the overwhelming, primitive terror of living without the infantile security and love of one's physical parents. The intolerable anxiety of authentic human existence triggers the defensive function of 'wish fulfilment', which drives human beings to construct an illusory, divine 'father figure'.

The projection of this imaginary divinity acts as a defence against childish helplessness by providing eternal security and the promise of fulfilment of unmet needs and longings.

Christian critique

Paul Vitz notes that Freud had no adult *religious experience himself, and 'not one of Freud's major published cases dealt with a patient who was a believing Christian or Jew'. Accordingly, Freud's analysis of secular religious practice devoid of true religious experience should neither surprise nor alarm genuine Christians, precisely because Freud never saw or experienced *genuine* belief. While his critique of 'secular religion' may be quite accurate in the absence of authentic faith, Freud's error was to apply his findings universally to all religion.

Freud's own childhood experiences may also have affected his theory of religion. The analyst Ana-Maria Rizzuto demonstrates that Freud's early losses, including that of his beloved Catholic nanny, could well have made it psychically impossible for him to believe in any form of divine providence. Rizutto also feels that Freud's unconscious religious biases skewed his otherwise firm commitment to cold objectivity. As Nicholi notes, Freud's observations about religion and philosophy 'are not characterized by the objective, dispassionate tone of the clinician or scientist' (Nicholi, *The Question of God*, p. 53). This position is further supported by Nicholi's detailed exploration of the biographies of Freud and C. S. *Lewis.

Freud's selective knowledge of the Bible and theology was another factor. After his own exhaustive study of the Bible, C. S. Lewis addressed Freud's 'wish fulfilment' theory of religion by countering that 'the biblical world-view involves a great deal of despair and pain and is certainly not anything one would *wish* for' (Nicholi, *The Question of God*, p. 45; italics his).

Finally, Freud's theory of religion is also weakened by its naturalist, materialist, reductionist and deterministic assumptions, leaving him vulnerable to a wide variety of presuppositional critiques. For example, if the existence of a personal, loving God has been ruled out *a priori*, there is no room to explore the possibility that our hearts and souls are actually designed to be in a relationship with God. It may be that the Augustinian model of

the psyche is more accurate in this respect than Freud's, but simply asserting that all such human longings represent illusory projections is untenable.

Bibliography

S. Freud, *The Essentials of Psychoanalysis: The Definitive Collection of Sigmund Freud's Writing* (London, 1998); P. Gay, *The Freud Reader* (New York, 1989); S. L. Jones and R. E. Butman, *Modern Psychotherapies: A Comprehensive Christian Appraisal* (Downers Grove, 1991); A. M. Nicholi, *The Question of God: C. S. Lewis and Sigmund Freud Debate God, Love, Sex, and the Meaning of Life* (New York, 2002); A. Rizzuto, *Why Did Freud Reject God? A Psychodynamic Interpretation* (Boston, 1998); P. Vitz, *Sigmund Freud's Christian Unconscious* (New York, 1988).

H. R. BERCOVICI

GANDHI, MOHANDAS KARAMCHAND

Gandhi (1869–1948) is generally recognized as the spiritual architect of Indian independence. Though popularly revered as *Mahatma* ('Great Soul'), Gandhi repudiated honorific titles and memorials, preferring that his followers adopt his ideal of a non-violent society. He was born in Porbandar in the *Vaishya* (merchant/trader) caste and was a devout Hindu with distinctive social and political emphases. Radhakrishnan claimed that 'he was the first in human history to extend the principle of non-violence [*ahimsa*] from the individual to the social and political plane.' Accordingly, his initiatives were expressions of his ideal of a predominantly non-violent world in which unequal status would be obliterated. His use of sources as diverse as Tolstoy and Ruskin gave his views eclectic appeal. Gandhi advanced his reforms as organizer of non-violent campaigns, such as his Dandi March in 1930 to protest against Britain's Salt Act, as well as his efforts on behalf of Indian self-government. He was assassinated on 30 January 1948 by a member of the Brahman caste who feared his uncompromising tolerance of all people.

Gandhi's beliefs centred in his self-denying quest for *truth (satya)* that could only be discovered by experimentation in social relationships. For him, truth is God that can be known by love (motive), prompting non-violent reverence of all beings (method). If we love truth 'perfectly', we will love everyone, and humanity's welfare (*sarvodaya*) will be our goal. The 'realities' of life are actually illusory. God alone exists as a pervasive, indefinable power. As such, he is the impersonal law of life that is a living 'light' in this violent world. This divine power in all people was the basis of Gandhi's optimism about the ultimate outcome of struggles for *justice through *history. God is also 'a million other things that human ingenuity can name', since he is known pluralistically as the many rays of the single sun. He is goodness without special *revelation, 'all things to all men'. Everyone should worship God according to his own faith, living peaceably with all religions.

Gandhi called his approach *satragrapha* (the way of the truth-force), a 'direct corollary' of non-violence that should be expressed by civil resistance. He viewed injustices as breaches of integrity that undermined human dignity and freedom from misery. His quest was based on an instinctive trust in 'the inner voice of conscience' for guidance and courage. A morally informed *conscience is universal, the 'soul-force within every person' that potentially allows everyone to attain self-realization (*moksha*) and a vision for non-violence. Though he rejected the injustices of caste, he affirmed the 'law of *varna*', which acknowledged diverse abilities and occupations without loss of equality in personhood. His trust in conscience informed by justice overshadowed any appeal to past wrongs or future goals. His 'experiments in truth' required a mastery of fear in inevitable struggles, a simple lifestyle for identification with the poor masses and unwavering non-violence for social change. He believed that the *power of non-violent non-cooperation would force governments to reconsider exploitative policies. Since he believed that one's behaviour is more important than reason, he imaged himself as a humble visionary whose unwavering quest was his virtue. In his words, 'My life is my message'.

Gandhi's writings are laced with biblical language like 'kingdom of God', 'straight and narrow path' and 'gospel'. However, differences between *Hinduism and Christianity are so pronounced that meaningful dialogue can seem futile. Truth in Christianity is not based on 'experimentation in social relationships' but rather on mighty acts of a living God that reveal the history of salvation through the redemptive accomplishments of the Messiah.

The Christian Saviour is the second person of the triune God, whose finished work of salvation is antithetical to an impersonal, polytheistic, inclusivistic divine law of life and love. Gandhi's faith in a universally informed conscience to overcome injustices by non-violence seems naïve, when compared with 'the way, the truth, and the life' who died violently so that ideals of justice and righteousness could ultimately prevail.

A Christian's dialogue with a Gandhian-type of Hindu, pragmatic and committed, will require a bridge that is based on *Jesus' ideals and virtues: the Christ of peace, simplicity and love as reflected, for example, in his Sermon on the Mount. Gandhi viewed Christ as a great teacher of non-violent ideals in company with other religious leaders, and he drew freely from diverse religious traditions to try to unite his fragmented nation. His hope was in the perfectibility of humanity, thus 'salvation' was social transformation that used a variety of means toward the greater goal of peace. We must understand that Gandhi used parts of these traditions that were consonant with his vision rather than embracing biblical principles as coherent parts of a single religion.

One problem with Christianity, for Ghandi, was that Christ's ethos of simplicity and love was grounded in biblical revelation. His lifestyle of simplicity reflected his commitment to the fulfilment of 'the Law and the Prophets' and the loving commitment of 'our Father' in heaven (Matt. 5:17–18; 6:25–34). His assurance of peace (John 14:27) is connected to the *Holy Spirit's work in the church as Paraclete. Thus, an ethos of simplicity, love and peace flows from the distinctiveness of biblical revelation, salvation and *Trinity.

A second problem was that Gandhi viewed Western Christendom as only nominally Christian. As Western values have conflicted with religious ideals, so Christians have been following anti-Christ in their profiteering. Christ was an advocate of peace and meekness, while his 'followers' have tended to measure moral progress by their material possessions. This is a reminder that the church must be humble about its own shortcomings. Only when Christians embrace their Master's example can they hope to establish a 'theology in relationships' for meaningful communication (Ariarajah, ch. 7).

Bibliography

W. Ariarajah, *Hindus and Christians: A Century of Protestant Ecumenical Thought* (Grand Rapids, 1991); Y. Chadha, *Gandhi: A Life* (New York and Toronto, 1997); M. K. Gandhi, *An Autobiography or The Story of My Experiments with Truth* (Ahmedabad, 1990); K. Kripalani, *All Men Are Brothers: Life and Thoughts of Mahatma Gandhi as Told in His Own Words* (Ahmedabad, 1960); B. R. Nanda, *Mahatma Gandhi* (London, 1958); S. Radhakrishnan (ed.), *Mahatma Gandhi: Essays and Reflections* (Allahabad, 1944); J. Tewari, *Sabarmati to Dandi* (Delhi, 1995); <www.mkgandhi.org>.

L. BURNS

GENDER

The word 'gender' commonly refers to cultural norms and expectations about women's and men's roles and behaviour, while the word 'sex' denotes their biological and physiological distinctives. Gender includes intangibles like self-image, as well as observable phenomena such as dress and language, and is especially used in connection with the roles that societies assign to men and women in family life, in the world of work and in recreation. In most societies people do not examine or question the assumptions about gender that they have internalized.

During the last half-century in the Western world, however, there has been an extensive debate on the issue of gender, and in particular on the relationship between sex and gender, namely the extent to which biological and psychological differences mandate specific gender roles for women and men.

Paradoxically, on the threshold of this debate, the generation after the Second World War saw a reversion to traditionalist gender norms, running counter to a trend towards women's emancipation in the public arena over the previous century or so. From the 1830s through the 1920s women in the West had progressively gained access to formal education, the learned professions and the political franchise. And during the Second World War, millions of women had served in industry and in non-combatant military roles. After 1945, however, the victorious Allied governments were obliged to provide employment for returning servicemen, and used the media to persuade women to return to purely domestic roles. Likewise the 'baby boom' kept Western women at home and occupied for the next two decades. The ideology of the period taught that sex dictated differential gender norms, while it discouraged reflection on this radical disjunction between women's and men's roles, their distinct identities and their separate worlds.

The early 1960s saw an explosive reaction and a movement for women's liberation from their confinement to the sphere of home and children. Early voices such as Betty Friedan and Germaine Greer rebutted the notion that sex determines gender, arguing against any essential differences between men and women that would bar the latter from full participation in education, government and employment. This egalitarian feminism typically supported measures such as *abortion and free child-care with a view to liberating women from their erstwhile domestic confinement. From the 1970s onwards, a second current of socialist feminism critiqued their sisters' eagerness for entry into the world of work, even as women's access to leadership in business and the professions expanded. Socialist feminists like Juliet Mitchell argued that industrial *capitalism was terminally sick, based as it was on the oppression of whole classes, including naive women. Token admission of women to boardrooms merely enmeshed them further, and the egalitarian appeal to individual rights should give way to a deeper critique of the whole capitalist system. Then from the 1980s on, a third current of feminism gathered force. Represented by Shulamith Firestone, Susan Brownmiller and others, this variant pressed an even more radical critique of human societies, and it returned to a view of gender that stressed difference over equality – even daring to suggest a new biological essentialism. Women's reproductive biology meant that from time immemorial, men (even well-disposed men) have owned and exploited women's *sexuality. The problem is, therefore, deeper than women's exclusion from paid employment, or their subjection to the institutions of modern capitalism. Patriarchy is the problem, and women need to find significant ways to separate themselves from men, their control and their oppression. Women need space to live in ways that are appropriate specifically to them. In the 1980s and 1990s, linguistic and philosophical studies (e.g. by

Deborah Tannen, Carol Gilligan) supported this new emphasis on difference, while not following the radically separatist inferences of Firestone and Brownmiller.

Despite the differences amongst egalitarian, socialist and radical feminists, they all agreed that normative values like *justice do exist, and that women can tell a 'meta-narrative' to explain their current oppression and to identify their future prospects. In this sense these currents of feminism were arguably 'modern'. However, from the 1980s onwards, a complex ideology of postmodernism rejected any fixed points in human life, any binding norms, any meta-narratives that offered to explain *history. Indeed, with its assertion that human consciousness is the only *reality, postmodernism threatened to collapse into madness. Its implications for the sex/gender conversation were predictable. Postmodernist sociologists like Anthony Giddens in Britain argued that sex itself was plastic and mutable. Sex-change operations and proliferating homosexual and bisexual behaviour now meant that individuals must explore and invent their own sexuality. If sex is up for grabs, obviously gender must be even more negotiable. *Chacun à son goût* and *de gustibus non disputandum* were the only guidelines. Postmodernism offered no coherent account of anything, let alone sex and gender, and its wholesale *relativism undercut its own truth-claims.

Varieties of modernist feminism continue to win many adherents in the West, however, despite the strength of postmodernist views in academia and the media. Christians owe modernist feminism a thoughtful response. Feminism appeals to values like justice that Christians also affirm. Yet Christians have been vulnerable to charges of injustice, for they have so often assumed unreflectively that both the Bible and biology mandate the subordination of women to men. In the early twenty-first century evangelical Christians have adopted four different responses to the challenges posed by modernist feminism.

One response is a sophisticated and well-informed essentialism. This approach takes full account of all the research in the past half-century that has studied male and female biology, physiology, *psychology and social behaviour. It recognizes the wide areas of similarity between the sexes in ability, intelligence and skill, and the fact that generalizations about differences between women and men

have to do with statistical averages and not absolute dichotomies. Nevertheless, this approach argues that physiological, hormonal and other differences do produce distinct differences between the sexes in psychology and social behaviour. Therefore, it recommends that human societies recognize and build on these sexual distinctives and develop gender-norms and practices that celebrate women's and men's respective strengths. This essentialist school tends to favour male headship in the home and in the church, based on an assessment of men's greater aptitude for leadership, and on a reading of the Bible from this point of view. The patriarchal nuclear family is the normative model. Stephen Clark's excellent *Man and Woman in Christ* pioneered this argument from a Roman Catholic perspective, while John Piper and Wayne Grudem edited the thoughtful *Recovering Biblical Manhood and Womanhood* in the Reformed tradition.

A second response has been a biblical egalitarianism, typified by the work of psychologist Mary Stewart van Leeuwen. This school appeals to the same body of scientific research as the first, but denies that the verifiable psychological and sociological differences between the sexes should mandate specific gender roles – though such cultural conventions may be useful so long as they do not stifle individual gifts. Differences in dress are harmless and may be charming. Differences in *power are another matter. Patriarchy is a consequence of the fall, and Pentecost marks the emancipation of women's gifts (including the vocation to leadership) from the curse in Gen. 3:16. The great commission of Matt. 28:19–20 is God's mandate for all Christians, and on the mission field women and men are equally called, severally gifted and all eligible for the charism of leadership. This viewpoint then acknowledges the legitimacy of feminism's critique of patriarchy, and argues that the overall trajectory of the biblical story supports and affirms its aspirations.

A third approach acknowledges the physiological and psychological differences between women and men and recognizes the aptness of distinct gender roles. It emphasizes, however, that over a whole lifespan, individual women and men may work to incorporate certain contra-sexual elements that they have necessarily denied in their earlier lives. Hence, both the assertions of the essentialists and those of the egalitarians find a place in a larger story that includes both difference and reunion, the latter symbolized by the *marriage and the lamb and the bride in *Revelation*. This perspective finds support amongst Christian *Jungians such as Ann Belford Ulanov and also from lifespan developmental psychologist Robert Kegan.

Finally, some Christian theologians like Elaine Storkey argue that while egalitarian, socialist and radical feminism have run into error and exaggeration from a biblical point of view, nevertheless they all make points with which Christians can agree. Storkey writes that the Bible presents a rich and balanced picture of sex and gender, interweaving the four themes of difference, similarity, complementarity and union. We must live in the tension between these four equally biblical themes, trusting that the end and goal of human history is the reconciliation of all things, women and men included.

Bibliography

S. B. Clark, *Man and Woman in Christ* (Ann Arbor, 1980); A. Giddens, *The Transformation of Intimacy: Sexuality, Love and Eroticism in Modern Societies* (Stanford, 1992); R. Kegan, *In Over Our Heads: The Mental Demands of Modern Life* (Cambridge, MA, 1994); J. Piper and W. Grudem, *Recovering Biblical Manhood and Womanhood: A Response to Evangelical Feminism* (Wheaton, 1991); E. Storkey, *Origins of Difference: The Gender Debate Revisited* (Grand Rapids, 2001); A. B. Ulanov, *The Feminine in Jungian Psychology and in Christian Theology* (Evanston, 1971); M. S. Van Leeuwen, *Gender and Grace: Love, Work and Parenting in a Changing World* (Downers Grove, 1990).

L. P. FAIRFIELD

GENEALOGIES, BIBLICAL, see
HISTORICAL DIFFICULTIES IN THE OLD
TESTAMENT
GENERAL REVELATION, see
REVELATION

GILSON, ETIENNE HENRI

Etienne Gilson (1884–1978), a French Catholic philosopher, had a career on both sides of the Atlantic. He lectured at the Collège de France (elected a member of the Académie Française, 1947) as well as the Toronto (Pontifical) Institute of Mediaeval Studies, which he had founded in 1929. His Gifford Lectures (two series, 1931–1932) on *The Spirit of Medieval Philosophy* added international fame to his academic authority as *the* expert on thinkers and schools of thought during the Middle Ages, and as a leading exponent of *Thomism. His published works fall into three categories: (a) historical studies, distinguished by unmatched mastery of primary sources and exact scholarship (on *Augustine, *Bonaventura, *Thomas Aquinas, *Duns Scotus etc.); (b) expositions of the metaphysical core of Thomism as he re-discovered it, often targeted at a wider readership; (c) essays on related 'culture' topics, such as fine *arts and *music, painting, literature and the phenomenon of human *language.

Though remembered as a historian, Gilson did not deny the apologetic import of his work. Of relevance to apologetics is, first, the view of 'Christian philosophy' that he championed in the midst of lively controversy. While he maintained that the proof of philosophical propositions is purely rational (faith is no part of their 'texture'), he emphasized the major role of Christian motifs in the historical genesis of an original philosophy that may therefore be called 'Christian'. Faith is not an intrinsic part of philosophy, but neither is it irrelevant to it. It has enormously enriched rational thought, and its intellectual fruitfulness may be offered as an apologetic consideration.

Gilson's historiography demonstrates that fruitfulness, which is also seen in personal experience. As a Bergsonian doctoral student, he first read Aquinas on the advice of a Jewish scholar, L. Lévy-Bruhl, to unearth the roots of *Descartes' key concepts. He discovered a treasure of original thinking which uniquely illuminates subsequent philosophy.

Christian influence, Gilson insisted, made possible the distinction between essence and existence (unknown to *Aristotle), a major philosophical breakthrough, with existence having primacy in (*not* above) being. Being is then understood as act, with full verbal force (*esse*). Apologetic value attaches to that 'metaphysics of the Exodus' (Exod. 3:13) inasmuch as it corresponds to contemporary emphasis on existence.

Bibliography

E. Gilson, *The Spirit of Medieval Philosophy* (ET London and New York, 1934); *God and*

Philosophy (Newhaven, 1969); *Christian Philosophy. An Introduction* (ET Toronto, 1993); A. C. Pegis (ed.), *A Gilson Reader. Selected Writings of Etienne Gilson* (Garden City, 1957).

H. A. G. BLOCHER

GLOBALIZATION

Globalization is one of the leading religious, cultural, socio-economic and political issues of the twenty-first century. But the range of opinions regarding what it means is vast. Some dismiss the debate as 'globalony', claiming that 'globalization' is a vacuous term encompassing every social phenomenon but offering little insight into the contemporary human condition. The prevalence, however, of the term 'globalization' reflects a widespread perception that in every area of life, from the cultural to the criminal, from the financial to the environmental, there is a broadening, deepening and speeding up of worldwide interconnectedness. The sense is of a world being recast, through the impact of economic and technological developments, into a shared social and cultural space.

This article outlines some of globalization's key features and lays the basis for the development of a Christian perspective in the doctrine of creation. Most literature on globalization takes an unashamedly secular, anthropological approach. The spiritual and religious dimensions of globalization are, however, of crucial importance. This is partly why attempting to define globalization is like 'trying to nail a blancmange to the wall' (U. Beck, *What is Globalization?*, p. 20). Clarification is best achieved through description rather than through definition. Globalization can be described by means of three schools of opinion and a fundamental paradox.

Three schools

Globalists argue that the emerging single global economy, transcending and integrating major economic regions, marks the beginnings of a radically new era. In this new, borderless world, national governments are relegated to little more than bystanders to global capital flows. As people become less constrained by the disciplines of the state and more by the global market, the end of the welfare state and of social democracy is fast approaching.

Demythologizers deny the revolutionary character of globalization, insisting that similar processes of have occurred in the past. National governments, they point out, maintain the power to regulate international economic activity and are both the originators and sustainers of economic liberalization. Globalization is therefore a myth. Rather than integrating with each other, the world's political-economic systems are breaking up into regional civilizational blocks with their own religious, cultural and ethnic rivalries.

Restructuralists argue that globalization is transforming and restructuring the economic and political power of nation states. They reject both the globalists' rhetoric about the end of the nation state and the demythologizers' claim that 'nothing much has changed'. Instead, they assert that, through a burgeoning of complex transnational networks, a new kind of sovereignty is displacing traditional patterns of statehood. Authority in society is becoming increasingly diffused among public and private agencies at local, national, regional and global levels.

In making sense of these conflicting accounts of globalization, traditional political or ideological positions are of little value. The three schools do not neatly correspond to traditional ideological positions or world-views. Socialist, liberal and conservative perspectives can be found among each of them. Globalists, for instance, include not only neo-liberals, who welcome the triumph of individual autonomy and the market principle over state power, but also neo-Marxists, for whom contemporary globalization represents oppressive global *capitalism. Opinion among members of the same ideological groupings is often sharply divided, therefore, regarding the benefits and dangers of globalization. Globalization is a process, or set of processes, riddled with paradox.

Interconnectedness and fragmentation

One of the key paradoxes is that of interconnectedness and fragmentation. Globalization emerges from all three of the above accounts as a process of greater interconnectedness – even if such integration is more evident in certain regions than in others. What is generally overlooked by commentators, however, is that globalization also involves fragmentation. This paradox reflects two important factors that also contain the dynamic of paradox.

Globalization and localization

It is often argued that globalization is chiefly about the extension of Western (principally American) *power across the world. Some, indeed, reject the term 'globalization', insisting on 'Americanization' as a more accurate term. But while the USA plays a key role in shaping globalization processes, it is also deeply affected by the impact of globalization – symbolized most notably in the tragic terrorist attacks of 11 September 2001. Globalization cannot, in fact, be detached from local circumstances. Although it involves increasing physical mobility, its key cultural impact is the transformation of localities. The paradox of interconnectedness and fragmentation is partly revealed, therefore, in the fact that globalization involves a process of localization.

Globalization and (post)modernity

The same paradox also reflects the fact that globalization embodies both modernity's emphasis on universality and postmodernity's emphasis on plurality. At the heart of the world-view of modernity lies a belief in the universal rule of reason that will replace ignorance and tradition with truth and objectivity. This is reflected in the way globalization is often heralded as an entirely benign process of interconnectedness and integration, facilitated through the extension of Western culture.

The irony of the present situation is that confidence in the quest for the universal coexists with a growing scepticism about the validity of this quest. As a consequence, the universal is being replaced by the much less well-defined concept of the global. This concept, sometimes referred to as 'globality', lacks a grand scheme based on deeply held convictions and high ideals. It is about people all over the world being able to eat the same kind of hamburgers, drink the same kind of soft drink, watch the same television programmes and use the same software packages, not about their sharing common values. It thus reflects the scepticism towards 'meta-narratives' (grand narratives that seek to explain reality) that characterizes postmodernity. The ascendant ideologies of neo-liberalism and consumerism may seem exceptions to this trend. In their contemporary forms, however, they tend to appear as ideologies in denial. They are propounded as the only systems that work, and it is 'what works'

(however narrowly defined) that is accorded special status in the postmodern world-view.

An important social consequence of this loss of meta-narratives is not only cultural homogenization but also, paradoxically, cultural fragmentation. The postmodern world-view, emboldened through the rise of consumerism and made eminently transportable through the revolution in electronic media, inevitably encourages the spread of individualism and the consequent atomization of society. This leads to the opposite of universalism: plurality. This is the acceptance, in theory at least, of all forms of belief and lifestyle as equally valid. The emergent 'pick-'n'-mix culture' is one in which local forms of religion, *morality and *culture are relativized and repackaged as consumer choices. An example is the use of spiritual and ethnic imagery by Nike and the Body Shop.

Globalization is therefore an expression both of modernity and of postmodernity. It is modern in its universalist pretensions, and postmodern in its fragmentation and *pluralism. This highlights the limited value of 'definitions' of globalization. These almost invariably involve notions of interconnectedness and integration. While this is understandable, there is a danger that such terms are taken to represent an organic, holistic development. Though much benefit can be gained as the world is brought closer together, the cultural homogenization of globalization does not imply social cohesion. It often means the multiplication of worlds, any of which individuals can choose to inhabit, either simultaneously or consecutively. Fragmentation is the inevitable consequence of the kind of individualism that is underpinned by a rationalist and functionalist view of the world, which was heralded in modernity but is maintained in postmodernity.

In sum, globalization can best be understood as a set of transforming processes, driven ostensibly by economic and technological impulses but manifesting deep religious dimensions. Its impact, likewise, is not merely economic but encompasses virtually every sphere of life, including politics, culture, education, religion, *marriage and the family. Its processes generate networks of interaction that transcend previous boundaries between these spheres. Indeed, the intensification and institutionalization of global interconnectedness through new global and regional infrastructures of control and communication are unprecedented. As such, globalization marks a new era in human affairs. The paradoxes ensure that it is highly uneven in its embrace and impact; it excludes as well as includes, divides as well as unites. For some it means a shrinking world that is put at their fingertips. For others it means that opportunities and influence recede ever further into the distance. Largely as a result of this, globalization is becoming an increasingly controversial political, social, economic, ethical and religious issue. The debate is gathering momentum, with protagonists on both sides unwilling to admit to its paradoxes and ambiguities. A Christian response needs to insist that globalization is not a neutral or merely factual phenomenon. It is also a spiritual one. Globalization is infused with beliefs, many of them stemming from the Christian-infused culture that gave rise to capitalism, others springing from the values and assumptions of *modernism and postmodernism. This is important to recognize, for it is the only way to ensure that a Christian perspective is properly theological rather than merely economic or ethical.

What does globalization look like in the light of creation? More specifically, what are the economic implications of three key aspects of the creation story: namely, having dominion; the creation of human beings in the image of God; and the setting of certain limits in the created order?

Having dominion

We read in Genesis 1:26 that the first human beings are to 'have dominion' over the rest of creation. This passage has often been interpreted in an anthropocentric way to legitimize the exploitation of the earth's resources in the service of humanity. When the first two chapters of Genesis are taken together, however, it is clear that 'having dominion' encompasses the horticultural terms to 'till' and to 'keep' (Gen. 2:15). This suggests that the relationship human beings are to have with the natural world is to be one of nurture and care. This is best expressed in the notion of stewardship, which provides the basis for a truly theocentric, ecological theology.

It also goes to the very heart of the original meaning of the term 'economics', derived from the Gk term *oikonomia*. This is the responsible and careful administration of the household (*oikos*) of creation for the good of all. This vision of economics took a severe blow under the impact of the dualistic world-view of the *Enlightenment. As a result, modern economics

often left *ethics out of its equations, preferring to see itself as a rational and objective *science free from the partiality of moral commitment.

Made in the image of God

Christians conclude from their reading of the OT and NT that God is a Trinity of persons-in-relation. It follows that, if human beings are made in the image of God, what is essential to human existence is being-in-relationship. In other words, human beings find their true identity in relationships that are characterized by intimacy and self-giving.

This insight questions the way in which human beings are perceived by some of the more vociferous and ideological defenders of economic globalization, which tends to be in terms of autonomous individuals. As such, they are free from all obligation except that of serving their own self-interest within a competitive struggle for economic prowess.

The values of autonomy and competition can also be traced back to the Enlightenment, and find expression in the notions of 'the survival of the fittest', from evolutionary theory, and of 'economic man' in classical and neo-classical economics. They have a dubious record, including monopolies of power, war, human degradation and environmental destruction.

Limits

Human beings, we read, were forbidden to eat the fruit from the tree of the knowledge of good and evil (Gen. 2:17; 3:1–3). They were also told to refrain from work on the Sabbath because God rested from his work of creation on the seventh day (Exod. 20:8–11). Here, then, we have the notion of rest from economic activity, which implies the value of restraint. While both growth and choice are integral to the flourishing of the contemporary global economy, the assumption needs to be challenged that these are, or should be, unlimited. Within a world in which both society and the environment are bound by certain irremovable limits, the unfettered pursuit of growth and choice as overriding objectives comes at a heavy social and environmental cost.

Grounded in a divinely created world that is marked by the fall but transformed by redemption, globalization has great potential to be a means of spiritual and material blessing to the peoples of the world. A Christian world-view and the actions it inspires can help to fulfil this potential.

Bibliography

Z. Bauman, *Globalization: The Human Consequences* (Oxford, 1998); U. Beck, *What is Globalization?* (Cambridge, 2000); J. Bhagwati, *In Defence of Globalization* (Oxford, 2004); F. Catherwood, *The Creation of Wealth* (Wheaton, 2002); U. Duchrow and F. J. Hinkelammert, *Property for People, Not Profit: Alternatives to the Global Tyranny of Capital* (London, 2004); J. H. Dunning, *Making Globalization Good: The Moral Challenges of Global Capitalism* (Oxford, 2003); K. A. Eldred and T. Yamamori (eds.), *On Kingdom Business: Transforming Missions Through Entrepreneurial Strategies* (Wheaton, 2003); A. Giddens, *Runaway World: How Globalization is Reshaping Our Lives* (London, 1999); T. Gorringe, *Fair Shares: Ethics and the Global Economy* (London, 1999); B. Goudzwaard, *Globalization and the Kingdom of God* (Grand Rapids, 2001); D. Held, A. McGrew *et al.*, *Global Transformations* (Cambridge, 1999); P. S. Heslam, *Globalization: Unravelling the New Capitalism* (Cambridge, 2002); *The Role of Business in Making Poverty History* (Cambridge, 2005); P. S. Heslam (ed.), *Globalization and the Good* (London, 2004); S. Rundle and T. Steffen, *Great Commission Companies: The Emerging Role of Business in Missions* (Downers Grove, 2003); P. Singer, *One World: The Ethics of Globalization* (New Haven, 2002); M. L. Stackhouse (ed.), *God and Globalization*, 3 vols. (Harrisburg, 2000–); M. Wolf, *Why Globalization Works* (New Haven, 2004).

P. S. HESLAM

GNOSTICISM

Gnosticism refers to a body of related teachings, both ancient and modern, stressing the acquisition of *gnosis* (Gk 'knowledge'), or secret, inner, esoteric knowledge. The knowledge sought is not strictly intellectual, but mystical; not merely a detached knowledge of or about something, but a knowing by experience or participation. This gnosis is the knowledge of ultimate reality, particularly one's divine essence and origin. Gnosis reveals the spark of divinity within, which Gnostics think is obscured by ignorance, convention and mere conventional (or exoteric) religiosity.

Gnosis is not the possession of the masses, but of only the few.

Until recently, the teachings of an obscure sect called the Gnostics was primarily the concern of the specialized scholar or the occultist, who explored their arcane origins and influence. Yet Gnosticism has more recently influenced a revised portrait of *Jesus as an illumined illuminator who serves as a guide for others' awakening. This concept is often invoked by *New Age proponents, who deny biblical Christology. The Swiss psychiatrist Carl *Jung, a constant source of inspiration for the New Age (or 'New Spirituality' movement), did much to introduce Gnosticism to the modern world by viewing it as kind of ancient depth *psychology and as superior psychologically to orthodox Christianity. A variety of esoterically oriented groups have roots in Gnostic soil. These include theosophy and its various and varying spin-offs, such as Rudolph Steiner's anthroposophy, Alice Bailey's Arcane School, the I Am movement, the Church Universal and Triumphant (Elizabeth Clare Prophet), the Rosicrucians, followers of G. I. Gurdjieff, and the channeller J. Z. Knight's Ramtha group. These organizations share an emphasis on esoteric teaching, the hidden divinity of humanity and contact with non-material higher beings called masters or adepts. Recently, noted literary critic Harold Bloom has written a book defending his own version of Gnosticism called *Omens of Millennium*.

Although Gnosticism has long been known through the writings of the Church Fathers as an early Christian heresy, in 1945 a collection of mostly Gnostic writings were uncovered in *Nag Hammadi, Egypt, which gave scholars a cornucopia of primary sources not previously available. Fifty-two texts were recovered, dating from approximately AD 350. Although many of the documents had been referred to and denounced in the writings of early church theologians such as *Justin Martyr and *Irenaeus (particularly in *Against Heresies*), most of the texts themselves were thought to have vanished. So, as Elaine Pagels put it, 'Now for the first time ... the heretics can speak for themselves'. Her central thesis is that Gnosticism should be considered at least as legitimate as orthodox Christianity.

The gnostic world-view

Although its exact historical origins are

shrouded in mystery and controversy, Gnosticism presents a distinctive spectrum of beliefs, and a central philosophical core is discernible. Gnosticism teaches that something is desperately wrong with the universe and delineates the means to explain and rectify the situation. The cosmos is not good; nor was it created by an all-good God. Rather, a lesser god, or demiurge (as he is sometimes called), fashioned the world in ignorance. The *Gospel of Philip* says, 'The world came about through a mistake. For he who created it wanted to create it imperishable and immortal. He fell short of attaining his desire.' The origin of the demiurge, or offending creator, is variously explained. But the upshot is that some precosmic disruption in the chain of beings emanating from the unknowable Father God resulted in the production of a substandard deity. The result was a material cosmos soaked with ignorance, pain, decay and death. This deity, nevertheless, despotically demands worship and even pretentiously proclaims his supremacy as the one true God. Gnostics typically demote the God of the Hebrew Scriptures to the level of his demiurge, and display an anti-Jewish cast in general.

This creator god is not the ultimate *reality but, rather, a degeneration of the unknown and unknowable fullness of Being (or *pleroma*). Yet human beings, or at least some of them, are in the position potentially to transcend their imposed limitations. Locked within the material shell of the human race is the spark of this highest spiritual reality, which the creator accidentally infused into humanity at their creation. This is akin to a drunken jeweller who accidentally mixes gold dust into junk metal. Spirit is good and desirable; matter is *evil and detestable. As contemporary Gnostic Harold Bloom puts it, 'You yourself ... come to see that originally our deepest self was no part of the Creation-Fall, but goes back to an archaic time before time, when the deepest self was part of the fullness that was God.'

If this inner spark is fanned into flame, it can liberate humans from the world of matter and the demands of its confused and overbearing creator. What has devolved from perfection can ultimately evolve or ascend back into perfection through a process of self-discovery. This escape of the divine spark from its incarceration in the material can even be understood as the salvation of the deity itself, who wrestles free from ignorance and the domination of dark forces to ascend to the highest level.

Into this basic structure enters the idea of Jesus as a mystical redeemer of those trapped in materiality. He descends from the spiritual realm with a message of self-redemption. The body of gnostic literature, which is wider than the Nag Hammadi texts, represents various views of this redeemer figure. There are, in fact, differing schools of Gnosticism with differing views of Christ. Nevertheless, a basic image emerges.

Christ comes from the higher levels of intermediary beings (called aeons) as a revealer, an emissary from error-free environs. He is not the personal agent of the divinity who is revealed in the OT, but has descended from a more exalted level to be a catalyst for igniting the gnosis latent within the ignorant, giving metaphysical aid to underachieving deities (humans). Gnostics deny that Christ died on the cross to atone for sin, since that would entangle the spiritual Christ far too intimately with the degradations of mere matter and would entail that the basic human problem is ethical (sin), not metaphysical (materiality). Similarly, gnostic accounts of Jesus' resurrection differ significantly from NT records. A resurrection is affirmed, but the risen Jesus is disclosed through spiritual visions rather than physical circumstances.

The Christian world-view in relation to Gnosticism

Before exposing Gnosticism to logical and historical criticism it is incumbent to compare its essential world-view with that of Christian *theism. Scripture reveals that an all-good and omnipotent God created the heavens and the earth and found it to be 'good' (Gen. 1). Humans were created in God's image and likeness and pronounced 'very good'. The original creation is God-given; it is not the result of an incompetent deity. Nor do humans possess a spark of the divine. They are finite creatures under divine jurisdiction. The evils of the world were brought about through human rebellion against God (Gen. 3; Rom. 3), and while the created goodness of the world and humanity remains, it is effaced by the corrosive and comprehensive effects of sin (Rom. 8:19–23).

Despite humans' alienation from their Creator, God acted in many ways to seek out his erring mortals (Heb. 1:1–3). He made himself generally known through creation and conscience (Ps. 19:1–6; Rom. 1 – 2) and specifically revealed himself through his interaction with the Jewish nation (Rom. 3:1–2). This culminated in the promised coming of the Messiah, who lived a perfect life, demonstrated his credentials as the Son of God, died on the cross to reconcile humans to an holy God, and rose physically from the dead on the third day to defeat sin, Satan and death. Christ offers spiritual liberation not through the cultivation of an inward gnosis, but through faith in his work of loving and just redemption (Eph. 2:1–8; Titus 3:5–7).

The gospel is to be proclaimed to all people; it is not reserved for an esoteric inner circle (Matt. 28:18–20). Christ bodily ascended to heaven from whence he will come again at the end of the age in judgment and restoration (Acts 1:6–9; Phil. 3:20). In the meantime, God works out his plan of the ages for the spiritual and material universe (Rom. 8). The culmination of history will involve the physical resurrection of the just and the unjust (Dan. 12:2; Matt. 25:46).

An apologetic encounter with Gnosticism

An apologetic encounter with Gnosticism must challenge its claim to present a truer account of Christ than that given in the Gospels. It should also address whether or not the gnostic world-view is logically superior to Christian theism.

The *Gospel of Thomas* has generated the most scholarly and popular attention and probably has the best historical credentials of the Nag Hammadi materials. The liberal Jesus Seminar refers to it as 'the fifth Gospel'. Some scholars argue that it is as reliable if not more reliable than the *canonical Gospels, although no scholars believe that the apostle Thomas wrote it. The sayings of Jesus are given minimal narrative setting, generally lack a thematic arrangement, and tend to have a cryptic, epigrammatic flavour. Although Thomas does not articulate a full-blown gnostic system, some of the teachings fit the gnostic pattern. Other sayings closely parallel or duplicate material found in the synoptic Gospels.

The earliest references to the *Gospel of Thomas* in ancient literature come from Hippolytus and *Origen in the third century. These very late references are unlike the plentiful early references to the four Gospels, which date as far back as the early second century. Such a long

silence would be unlikely if Thomas were indeed a first-century document. Furthermore, Thomas quotes sayings paralleled in every Gospel and in every putative Gospel source, which strongly suggests that Thomas is dependent on these previous sources. For these and other reasons, many scholars contend that Thomas dates after the canonical Gospels, and that it is not an original source for material on Jesus but a reworking of earlier accounts. The other gnostic texts date well into the second or third centuries and are clearly dependent on a pre-existent Jesus tradition, which, like Thomas, they reinterpret according to a gnostic world-view.

When compared to the historicity of the Gospels (and the rest of the NT), the gnostic materials (they are not true 'gospels' because they fall outside of that genre) fail on three counts. First, unlike the NT, they lack any credible manuscript tradition, so no-one can verify that they have been accurately transmitted over time. Secondly, the authorship of these documents is unknown. While the traditional authorship of the Gospels has been questioned, there is far more evidence for their being written by eyewitnesses or by those who consulted eyewitnesses than can be ascribed to any gnostic document (see Luke 1:1–4). Thirdly, the earliest gnostic document (probably Thomas) dates from into the second century, while it is widely held that the NT Gospels were written before the end of the first century and maybe before 70. They are, therefore, far closer in time to the events they describe and more likely to be accurate. Philip Jenkins persuasively argues in his book *The Hidden Gospels* that much of the contemporary interest in gnostic 'hidden gospels' is more a matter of ideological interest in overthrowing orthodoxy than of pure scholarship, since the evidence for the alternative sources is quite weak in relation to the canonical Gospels.

But beyond the nature of these documents, what about the gnostic world-view in general? Many gnostic treatises speak of the ultimate reality or godhead as beyond intellectual comprehension. In the *Gospel of the Egyptians* the ultimate reality is said to be the 'unrevealable, unmarked, ageless, unproclaimable Father'. The text speaks of giving praise to 'the great invisible Spirit' who is 'the silence of silent silence'. At this point the divide between the NT and the gnostic documents could not be greater. The incarnation means that God communicated himself in person through life and language (John 1:14). Jesus declares, 'Anyone who has seen me has seen the Father' (John 14:9), and John speaks of 'That which was from the beginning', and says, 'The life appeared; we have seen it and testify to it, and we proclaim to you the eternal life, which was with the Father and has appeared to us' (1 John 1:1–3).

If God is utterly beyond any descriptions, we could then say absolutely nothing about God. To have a theology of any kind – gnostic or orthodox – we must use words to describe God positively. By definition, the gnostic writers can say nothing meaningful of 'the silence of the silent silence', but they speak nevertheless. However, no-one can utter the unutterable, either to affirm what it takes to be true (Gnosticism) or to deny what it takes to be false (Christianity) because the denial of the Christian world-view would have to be based on the knowledge of the alternative gnostic conception of ultimate reality. Yet this is exactly what Gnostics rule out in principle. Paradoxically, Gnostics ('the knowers') can know nothing in this regard – a point highlighted by *Irenaeus.

Gnosticism and the contemporary mind

Despite its appeal to many today, we find traditionally gnostic elements that clash with contemporary sensibilities. First, Pagels and Jung put the Gnostics in a positive psychological light while sidestepping their elaborate *metaphysics. However, the gnostic outlook is just as much theological and cosmological as it is psychological. Most modern Gnostics reinterpret gnostic literature in a psychological fashion in order to remove any objectionable pre-scientific claims, which are taken to be mythical and not literal. Nevertheless, the gnostic message is all of a piece; the psychology should not be artificially divorced from the total world-view, which, most will grant is highly mythological.

Secondly, the gnostic rejection of matter as illusory or evil is at odds with sentiments regarding the value of nature and the need for an ecological awareness. The documents reveal no love for 'Mother Earth' or for the human *body.

Thirdly, Pagels to the contrary, the Gnostics were not feminists, nor did they view women as equals in any sense. Gnostic groups did sometimes allow for women's participation in religious activities, and several of the emanational beings were seen as feminine. Although Gnosticism uses feminine religious symbolism, this does not guarantee the exaltation of the feminine. The conclusion of the *Gospel of Thomas* has Jesus say that women must be made male to enter the Kingdom of God, a saying with no parallel in the teachings of Jesus recorded in the Gospels. Philip Jenkins's comment is apt, 'Though women play so crucial a role in Gnostic texts, the religious system as a whole had nothing good to say of women.' Women were held in low esteem because of their close connection with physical procreation, which the dualistic Gnostics detested.

Gnosticism remains a perennially seductive outlook. However, in light of the evidence, it must be suggested that its appeal owes more to an enticing sense of esoteric superiority than it does to either logic or to history.

Bibliography

H. Bloom, *Omens of Millennium: The Gnosis of Angels, Dreams, and Resurrection* (New York, 1996); D. Groothuis, *Jesus in an Age of Controversy* (Eugene, 1996; repr. 2002); Irenaeus, *Against Heresies*; P. Jenkins, *The Hidden Gospels: How the Search for Jesus Lost Its Way* (New York, 2001); E. Pagels, *The Gnostic Gospels* (New York, 1979); J. M. Robinson (ed.), *The Nag Hammadi Library* (San Francisco, 1988).

D. GROOTHUIS

GREENE, GRAHAM

Graham Greene (1904–91), British writer, was born in Berkhamsted, Hertfordshire, the fourth of six children. School bullying contributed to Greene's unhappy childhood and his repeated suicide attempts during adolescence. At the age of fifteen his parents sent him to Kenneth Richmond, an analyst who, in Greene's words, moved him from 'irrational melancholia' to 'normal unhappiness'.

Greene studied modern history at Oxford, receiving his BA in 1925, and converted to Roman Catholicism (see *Christianity, Roman Catholic) in 1926. As an adult, Greene sought to avoid boredom by travelling to countries experiencing both social repression and upheaval. These experiences served as material for many of his works.

Although he wrote as a dramatist, essayist, and journalist, Greene is best known for his novels. In 1932 *Stamboul Train* brought him public popularity, and *The Power and the Glory* (1940) is frequently hailed as the greatest Roman Catholic novel ever written. Its reception, however, reveals the controversy surrounding both Greene's life and work. The novel won the *Hawthornden Prize* in 1941 but was soundly condemned by the Vatican.

While Greene preferred to be viewed as a writer who happened to be a Roman Catholic, many of his works employ Roman Catholicism as the primary framework. Moreover, under the influence of Cardinal *Newman, Greene argued that he must write about both good and *evil. Having experienced much of the twentieth century's chaos first hand, Greene possessed a unique ability to describe graphically evil's seductive power. His characters wrestle with political, religious and social stress in the face of omnipresent evil. Additionally, in his novels a Catholic priest often has the final word in an attempt to re-establish a sensible perspective.

Having suggested a positive influence by the Roman Catholic Church, one must also note Greene argued it was the storyteller's role 'to act as the devil's advocate' (DeVitis, p. 10). In particular, he addressed the issue that twentieth-century events might lead some to conclude the 'world was governed by a God who seems unreasonable, hostile and often indifferent' (DeVitis, p. 13). Thus, Greene explores how flawed humans cope in a seemingly abandoned world.

Bibliography

G. Greene, *Brighton Rock* (London, 1938); *The Heart of the Matter* (London, 1948); *The End of the Affair* (London, 1951); *The Quiet American* (London, 1955); *The Comedians* (London, 1966); A. DeVitis, *Graham Greene* (Boston, 1986); M. Shelden, *Graham Greene: The Enemy Within* (New York, 1994); N. Sherry, *The Life of Graham Greene* (New York, 1989).

J. E. MᶜDERMOND

GREGORY PALAMAS

Gregory Palamas (c. 1296–1359), archbishop of Thessalonica, enunciated a distinction between the 'essence' and the 'energies' of God which became an accepted part of Eastern Orthodox theology (see *Christianity, Orthodox).

The distinction has some basis in the *Cappadocian Fathers and was developed by Palamas in order to explain how human beings can know the inaccessible God who is beyond knowledge. His main contribution to Christian apologetics is in this theological *epistemology.

The thought of Palamas was developed in controversy with a fellow monk, Barlaam of Calabria, who was influenced by the Greek philosophical traditions, both Aristotelianism and Neoplatonism. Since (following *Aristotle) any rational demonstration required logic working from the experience of the senses, then knowledge of God could come only through divine illumination to the mind. But Barlaam taught that such illumination allowed us only to make negative statements about God, that is, to say what God was *not*. We could not say anything positive. Barlaam also attacked the 'hesychasts', monks who used specific bodily postures as methods of meditative contemplation (*hesychia*) and who believed that the 'pure in heart' may see God even while in the body.

Palamas by contrast took a more negative view of the pagan Greek philosophers. *Truth was hidden from the wise and revealed to babes (Matt. 11:25), and human wisdom was shown to be folly (Rom. 1:21–23; 1 Cor. 1:18–25). Illumination from God could not be received by the natural powers of the human intellect, but only by a real participation in the divine presence. The divine essence was beyond the human mind, but beyond the 'cloud' on Sinai, Moses had a vision of God. This spiritual sense presupposed a purification of the mind and body and a surpassing by grace of merely human possibilities. In the resulting synergy between divine grace and human effort it was possible to reach out in love and so encounter God. This experience of the infinite God in his 'uncreated energies' was an eternal advance 'from glory to glory'. In opposition then to the intellectualist philosophical view of Barlaam, Palamas based this view of 'deification' on the incarnation of the Word. Knowledge of God was not a matter of merely intellectual illumination, but a transfiguring of the human flesh by the uncreated divine light.

Bibliography

V. Lossky, *The Vision of God* (London, 1963); J. Meyendorff, *A Study of Gregory Palamas* (London, 1964).

T. A. NOBLE

GROTIUS, HUGO

Huigh de Groot (1583–1645) was born in Delft, Netherlands. A child prodigy, he matriculated at the recently founded University of Leiden in 1594, and in 1598 received his Doctor of Laws degree from the University of Orleans while on a diplomatic mission to France. Called to the bar in 1599, he continued to rise, becoming Attorney-General and First Public Comptroller in 1607. By 1617 he was an important member of Prince Maurits van Nassau's Committee of Counsellors and a supporter of the prime minister, Johan van Oldenbarnevelt. In 1608 he married Marie van Reigersbergh, by whom he had eight children. In 1618 he was arrested on account of his opposition to Prince Maurits's Calvinist policies and calling of the Synod of Dort. After a political trial, he was imprisoned for life at Loevestein castle. However, with assistance from his enterprising wife, he escaped in a case of books in March 1622, spending (with one short exception) the rest of his life in exile in Paris, much of it as the Swedish ambassador to France. In 1645 he suffered shipwreck crossing the Baltic, dying shortly afterwards in Rostock, Germany. His wife continued to campaign to clear his name, ultimately successfully when an annexe to the Peace of Westphalia in 1648 nullified his condemnation as a traitor.

Pious and thoughtful, Grotius read voraciously and wrote prolifically all his life, taking extensive notes and quotations as he went. His work displayed the legal training of an advocate, being both systematic and apologetic in tone. It has been observed that both the rough drafts of his works, to be found in his notes, and subsequent lifetime editions hardly change in their basic structure; the effect of ever-wider reading simply being to annotate and amplify. He wrote widely – poetry, history, law and theology – but is best known today for his contribution to political thought, developing and applying state sovereignty theory to international law in his *On the Laws of War and Peace* (1625). He is also significant as standing on the cusp of medieval and modern notions of *natural law. There is still controversy over the exact relationship between his *theism and his theory of natural rights.

Grotius's theological work, which included a catechism, works on church government, soteriology and a commentary on the Old and New Testaments, has been largely ignored in the twentieth century. But interest was stimulated again by the discovery in 1984 by G. H. M. Posthumus Meyjes of a copy of his earliest theological work, *Meletius, or a Letter on the Points of Agreement between Christians* (1611). The early sections of *Meletius* can be regarded as an embryonic version of his principal apologetic work, *On the Truth of the Christian Religion*. This first appeared as a Dutch poem written in captivity in early 1620. It was published in 1622 with a Latin translation, and subsequent editions appeared from 1627.

De Veritate Religionis Christianae comprises six books. Book I defends the existence and properties of God, the eternal life of souls and the need to seek true religion to gain eternal bliss. Book II argues that Christianity is the true religion on the grounds of the factual basis of *Jesus' life, *miracles, death and resurrection and the ethical superiority of the Bible. Book III defends the reliability of the Bible on grounds of its authenticity and credibility. Books IV to VI refute paganism, *Judaism and *Islam respectively. Jan Paul Heering has demonstrated that *De Veritate* is largely derivative of the works of earlier apologists. The arguments of Books I and V are taken from Philippe Duplessis Mornay, Book VI from Juan-Luis Vives, while Books II and III are drawn (under the cover of a pseudonymous attribution) from the heretic Faustus Socinus. What Grotius added was his customary structural rigour, a refusal to be drawn on doctrinal disputes internal to Christianity, and a focus on the practical and ethical outworking of the Christian faith.

De Veritate met some initial hostility on account of its refusal to defend doctrines such as the *Trinity and the deity of Jesus Christ, but in spite of this, and a more general concern about Grotius' Arminian soteriology and Erastian ecclesiology, it was phenomenally successful, especially in England during the eighteenth and early nineteenth centuries. It has been estimated that after 1645 there were 144 Latin and translated editions of the work, and it remains a masterpiece of Christian humanist classicism.

Bibliography

E. Dumbauld, *The Life and Legal Writings of Hugo Grotius* (Oklahoma, 1969); C. Gellinek, *Hugo Grotius* (Boston, 1983); S. M. Knight, *The Life and Works of Hugo Grotius* (London, 1925); J. Lagrée, 'Grotius:

Natural Law and Natural Religion', *International Archives of the History of Ideas*, vol. 180 (2001), pp. 17–40; H. J. M. Nellen and E. Rabbie (eds.), *Hugo Grotius – Theologian: Essays in Honour of G. H. M. Posthumus Meyjes, Studies in the History of Christian Thought*, vol. 55 (Leiden, 1994); D. Nobbs, *Theocracy and Toleration: A Study of the Disputes in Dutch Calvinism from 1600 to 1650* (Cambridge, 1938), pp. 59–91.

J. RIVERS

GUINNESS, OS

Os Guinness (Ian Oswald Guinness) is a speaker and writer, cultural analyst and Christian apologist, who is Senior Fellow at The Trinity Forum, Washington, DC. The foundation of this Forum was inspired by the example of William Wilberforce and the sociological insights of Peter L. Berger. Os Guinness's pedigree includes a number of years as a young associate of Francis *Schaeffer at the L'Abri community in Switzerland, and his childhood in China, the son of medical missionaries Henry and Mary.

He was born in China in 1941, the great-grandson of Henry Grattan Guinness. As a toddler he was hung in a basket on a pole as his family desperately fled thousands of miles overland from the Japanese. His two infant brothers are buried in China. With the defeat of Japan, the Guinnesses returned to China until finally being forced to leave in 1951. They returned to England, where Os Guinness continued his education. He graduated in Divinity in 1966, and later, by then a veteran writer and speaker, gained a social science DPhil at Oriel College, Oxford. Not long afterwards, in 1984, he made his home in the United States.

The subject of Os Guinness's research in social science reflected his increasing concern with social meaning, and its importance for contemporary apologetics. It formed the basis of one of his seminal books, *The Gravedigger File* (1983). This book shares the inverse perspective of C. S. *Lewis's *The Screwtape Letters*, in giving the enemy's portrayal of its strategy. Whereas Lewis's book concerned hell's attempt to damn an individual, Guinness's counter-epistles are preoccupied with the likely fate of the Western church in a post-Christian culture. In his Afterword to the book he presents a central question of apologetics

today: 'How will people be turned ... not only from secularism but from the post-Christian religious alternatives as well? How do we speak to an age made spiritually deaf by its scepticism and morally colour-blind by its relativism?'

Os Guinness's writings consistently wrestle with apologetics, evangelical strategy and faithful Christian living, and accurately and attentively read the signs of our times. They include *The Dust of Death* (1973; new edn 1994), *Doubt* (1975), *The Call* (1998), *Long Journey Home* (2001) and *Time for Truth* (2002). Guinness aims to bridge the gulf between academic and popular knowledge, and to perceive the meanings of *culture as well as the significance of the history of ideas. He also attempts to practise, not just theorize about, *truth. While his books can sometimes make demanding reading, they are eminently quotable – a proverbial effect that is fascinating and remarkable. Ultimately he praises the seeming folly of Christ: 'If we intend to change our culture, we must become, like Christ, fool-bearers and fool-makers in our world' – a strategy of cultural subversion. 'Allegiance to Christ', Os Guinness writes, 'relativizes all other allegiances and perspectives' – it is a 'third way'.

C. DURIEZ

HARNACK, ADOLF VON

Adolf von Harnack (1851–1930) was the leading representative of liberal Protestantism in Germany in the early years of the twentieth century, and is still regarded today as its classical exponent. Harnack was professor at Leipzig, Giessen and Marburg before going to Berlin in 1888, where he remained until his retirement in 1921. He was knighted for his support of Germany's war effort in 1914, an aberration which disgusted Karl *Barth, one of his former pupils, and helped propel him into a lifelong opposition to the kind of liberalism which Harnack represented.

Harnack's reputation rests mainly on his magisterial *History of Dogma* (1886–9) and his famous series of lectures in 1900 on *The Essence of Christianity*. In these works he defined and defended his view of Christianity, which is now accepted as the standard exposition of nineteenth-century liberalism. Harnack believed that the doctrinal framework of Christianity which we now regard as traditional orthodoxy was a corruption imposed on the church by the invasion of alien Hellenistic concepts. Primitive Christianity, according to him, was a spiritual religion without any sort of dogma, in which the cardinal principle was 'love'. The first churches contained people of many different origins and viewpoints, but there was no such thing as 'heresy' until a particular group took over the leadership and began to impose its own rigidities on the others, often driving them out of the main body of the church.

Harnack owed much to F. C. *Baur and the Tübingen school but ignored their *Hegelianism in favour of a total commitment to the scientific *rationalism which had come to dominate most European thought by 1900. He always believed that his work was fundamentally evangelistic, in the sense that he was trying to reformulate Christianity in a way which would make it acceptable to contemporary enlightened opinion.

It was a point of view which was bound to clash with the growing awareness that *Jesus could not be neatly packaged as a nineteenth-century liberal, but it was not until after 1918 that Harnack's world collapsed around him, both politically and intellectually. He remained opposed to Barthian *neo-orthodoxy, but his influence declined sharply in his later years. Nevertheless, his works are still read, and they continue to exert a greater influence than many scholars are willing to admit. The main reason for this is that Harnack was radically committed to historicity and insisted that scientific principles must prevail over philosophical theories in NT study. To that extent, even his fiercest critics have benefited from his work.

Bibliography

W. Pauck, *Harnack and Troeltsch* (New York, 1968); M. Rumscheldt (ed.), *Adolf von Harnack: Liberal Theology at its Height* (London, 1989).

S. N. WILLIAMS

HEALING, see DISEASE AND HEALING

HEAVEN

If there is one thing that the general public associates with the Christian faith, it is usually the idea of going to heaven. Friendly debates about Christianity often revolve around questions such as whether life after death exists, how one qualifies to go to heaven, whether people of different religious beliefs are all destined for heaven, and whether heaven is the only destination for all those who have died. Very rarely today, however, do people think or talk much about what heaven itself is like. This is particularly true in parts of the world where death has become less visible and is less frequently untimely, in those communities that benefit most from advanced medicine, political stability, good nutrition, safe travel, elderly-care facilities and the like.

Yet Christianity's unique picture of heaven is fundamental to the faith. In fact, Paul wrote, 'If only for this life we have hope in Christ, we are to be pitied more than all men' (1 Cor. 15:19). In other words, if the Christian understanding of life after death is not accurate, then the Christian life is a pitiful one. Christianity without heaven is not a good moral code, a path to security and happiness in life, a helpful social construct, or an effective way to make the world a better place – but is rather a sham. Eternal life is the piece without which everything else in the Christian faith falls apart.

So, what is this eternal destination that proves to be such an essential component of the Christian faith? The Bible uses the term 'heaven' in many different ways, but in Christian theology the term generally refers to the future destiny of Christians. The Bible says a great deal about the future life of those who trust and follow Jesus. For them, life after death has several specific characteristics.

Heaven is personal

Many Eastern and mystical religions teach that each soul is destined to be re-absorbed into a cosmic unity, like a drop which falls into an ocean and becomes an indistinguishable part of it. The Bible, on the other hand, says that people will retain their individuality in heaven. Christians will spend eternity with each other and with the Lord (1 Thess. 4:17), who will relate to them as distinct individuals (Rev. 2:17). People will not only be 'themselves' in heaven, they will be more themselves than ever before. For they will be purified and transformed; their sin, weakness, fear and personal baggage will be removed to reveal their genuine, perfect selves, as they were created to be (1 Cor. 15:42–49).

Heaven will involve reunion with people whom we have known and loved on earth (Luke 16:9; 1 Thess. 2:19). While many popular treatments of heaven include the idea of reunion after death, they generally miss out on several of the Christian aspects of it, including the fact that the most exciting reunion will be with *Jesus himself (Phil. 1:23; 1 Thess. 4:17). Jesus' reunion with his friends will be so precious, loving and personal, in fact, that he compares it to a wedding ceremony. In first-century Israel, an engaged man would often set to work building an extension on to his father's house for his new family to live in. When he had completed this additional room, or rooms, he would go to collect his betrothed from her family's house and take her home to be with him. Jesus uses this custom to describe his own preparation for and reunion with his people, his beloved friends (John 14:2–3; cf. Rev. 19:7). Those in heaven will also be united not only with people whom they knew in this life, but with all of God's people throughout history, from all over the world (Rev. 5:9; 7:9). They will have new friends and family, as well as old, awaiting them in heaven. Relationships will not simply be restored to the state in which people experienced them on earth, but will be transformed, as individuals will be transformed (Heb. 12:23; Rev. 21:3–4). Life in eternity will not be a return to some sort of 'good ol' days', but an experience of days that are far, far better.

The Bible's description of eternal life as a personal reality makes sense of our human experience of death. Views of the world that treat death as the end of personal existence fall down at this point. Some argue that death is just part of the circle of life; thus, when you die, you rot. Others see death as the point of entry into some great, impersonal life force. But neither of these views explains the universal reaction of grief with which humans respond to the death of those they love. On an emotional level, humans protest against the reality and acceptability of death. Something in us finds it inherently wrong. We do not easily accept death as a natural, impersonal part of life. Neither can we celebrate it unequivocally as reunion with a cosmic life force. Human grief points to a fundamental expectation and desire for personal life to continue uninterrupted.

Heaven is material

The Bible presents the stunning notion that God's eternal kingdom will ultimately be located here on earth (Isa. 65:17; 2 Pet. 3:13; Rev. 5:9–10). This vision of the future stands in marked contrast to that presented by any other world religion. Eastern religions tend to view the present world as an illusion, from which the soul will ultimately be detached. So people's thoughts, not their bodies, are the only real things about them. Many Western religions, on the other hand, have traditionally seen the physical world as real, but essentially negative and limiting. Life after death is therefore pictured as an ethereal spirit-world where the soul is liberated from the body. Christianity, however, views the physical world as both real and good – created by God and destined for restoration.

The book of Revelation describes Jesus' second coming to earth, when he will judge and recreate the world. It portrays Jesus as coming down from heaven to earth, at which point God's home will be with his people (Rev. 21:2–3). The biblical picture of the future is of heaven coming down to earth – of heaven and earth merging. In 1 Thess. 4:17, Paul says that Christians who are still alive when Jesus returns will 'meet' him in the air. The word he uses for this meeting is related to an ancient diplomatic custom in which emissaries would come out of a city to welcome a dignitary as he entered their city. So when Christians 'meet' Jesus in the air, they will not stay there, but will welcome him and join his entourage as he enters the world.

When Jesus comes again, the world will not stay the same but will be renewed. Some Christians believe that it will be completely destroyed before it is remade (cf. Rev. 21:1; 2 Pet. 3:10), while others understand the process as one of purification, or purging (Rom. 8:19–21). In any case, the new earth will be the place where God lives together with his people. It will be a world set right, the world as it was meant to be, a world where, in the words of J. R. R. *Tolkien's Samwise Gamgee, 'everything sad [is] going to come untrue'. This new world will continue to be physical. People in this world will have bodies like the one Jesus had after his resurrection (Phil. 3:21); they will walk, eat and drink (Matt. 26:29; John 21:4–15; Rev. 3:4; 19:9). Thus, the ultimate home of Christians is in a renewed earth.

One might ask what happens to Christians between the time they die and the day of Jesus' return to earth. Some believe that they immediately go to be with the Lord in his heavenly dwelling, where they enjoy his company and await the resurrection of their bodies and the restoration of the world (cf. 2 Cor. 5:8; Phil. 1:23). Others hold that they simply enter some state of 'soul sleep', where they unconsciously rest until the Lord's return. In either case, their ultimate destiny is clear: they will live for ever with God and with his people on a renewed earth.

The eternal nature of this world makes sense of our human desire to work for *justice and peace on earth. If the world is simply an illusion, or if it is a hopeless physical prison to be survived and then escaped, then why spend time and energy addressing its inequalities, oppression and environmental problems? Christians' understanding of the physical world as an eternal, good reality explains the human desire to work for its long-term good.

Heaven is active

Some traditional representations of heaven make it seem incredibly dull. Visions of clouds, harps, and endless choral singing leave many people feeling less than excited about an eternity full of such activity. But the Bible's picture of heaven is quite different. Two particular aspects of life in heaven rule out the possibility of *boredom. First, heaven will be a place of partying. At the heart of the festivity will be a huge wedding banquet – a reception to end all receptions – with amazing food, fine wine, wonderful company and lots to celebrate (Isa. 25:6; Matt. 26:29; Luke 22:30; Rev. 19:9). *Music and dancing are likely to be part of the celebration as well (Luke 15:25; Pss. 149:3; 150:4).

Secondly, heaven will be a place of purpose. Believers will have positions of responsibility that include administration (Luke 12:44), leadership (2 Tim. 2:12; Rev. 20:6) and the execution of justice (Matt. 19:28; Luke 22:30; 1 Cor. 6:3). They will rule as humans were commissioned to do at the beginning of the world (Gen. 1:28). Jesus taught that people's faithfulness in small things during this lifetime qualifies and prepares them to take charge of greater things in heaven (Matt. 25:21–23; cf. Rev. 22:3). It is often difficult for us to appreciate the idea of having responsibility in heaven. We are so accustomed to experiencing work under the curse (Gen. 3:17–19) that we struggle to conceive of work without drudgery, frustration and stress. But humans' reign in heaven, like that of the Pevensie children in C. S. *Lewis' *Chronicles of Narnia*, will be a glorious adventure rather than a chore. Ruling with Christ will not interfere with resting from labour (Rev. 14:13).

The Christian picture of heaven as active makes sense of the way that humans experience work. When pursued in balance with other things, work often provides a sense of purpose, direction and focus for one's time and energy. For example, students who spend long summers without working often find themselves so bored that they are eager to return to college. Similarly, countless celebrities could testify to the lack of satisfaction in a life of constant leisure, and as a result, many fill their time with charity work, sponsorship or voluntary projects. The Christian picture of heaven accords with the human experience of work at its best as a constructive thing.

Heaven is certain

The NT often speaks of Christians' 'hope' in God's ultimate future for them. This word might be better translated into English as 'expectation' or 'anticipation', since from the Bible's perspective there is no element of uncertainty involved. Christian assurance regarding the reality of heaven is directly related to the resurrection of Jesus. His historical, physical resurrection from the dead is an indication that death, now defeated, no longer has the last word. Jesus' followers spoke of him as 'the firstborn from the dead' (Col. 1:18; Rev. 1:5; cf. Rom. 6:4–5). In other words, he was the first of many who will be able to walk through death and come out the other side, unharmed and transformed. Christians, by their association with Jesus, are assured the same victory over death that he had. Jesus' resurrection is a preview of the eternal life that his followers will enjoy, and the gift of his *Holy Spirit is a down-payment on this promise of heaven (2 Cor. 1:22; 5:5; Eph. 1:14). If heaven is 'pie in the sky', then it is a pie of which humankind has already had a piece. And this taste is what makes people hungry for the rest of it.

Thus, unlike other visions of the afterlife, the Christian one is inextricably tied to human *history. It is an extension of concrete human experience in the world. It is grounded in physical reality and not just philosophical preference or spiritual conjecture.

Heaven does not require us to deny grief

The Christian understanding of heaven, however, does not make it illegitimate or unnecessary to grieve about death. Death was not part of God's original design, but entered the world as a result of human rebellion against him. Jesus' response to death included both sadness and anger, and it is legitimate for the Christian to experience the same (John 11:33–38). But understanding heaven gives Christians the ability to grieve *with hope* (cf. 1 Thess. 4:13). They hold on to to the promise that one day death itself will be destroyed, suffering will be swallowed up, disease will be eradicated, violence will be brought to a final end, the world will be put right, and they will spend eternity with the Lord and with each other (Rev. 21:4; cf. Isa. 11:6–9). Christians are certain that death is not the end for them, and this expectation enables them to cope with death now in a way that is honest but not despairing.

The Christian hope at death makes sense of human discomfort with the state of the world. People find the world – with its grief, violence, broken relationships, uncertainties and frustrations – somewhat strange and disappointing. This unease with the world as it stands points to our innate expectation that it is not the end. C. S. Lewis points out that even people's attitudes to time attest to their fundamental nature as eternal creatures: 'We are so little reconciled to time that we are even astonished at it. "How he's grown!" we exclaim, "How time flies!" as though the universal form of our experience were again and again a novelty. It is as strange as if a fish were repeatedly surprised at the wetness of water. And that would be strange indeed; unless of course the fish were destined to become, one day, a land animal' (C. S. Lewis, *Reflections on the Psalms* [New York, 1958], p. 138). We find the world unsatisfactory because we were not designed to live in it as it is. The hope of heaven explains our discomfort with the present state of the world.

Bibliography

Dr T. Keller, Sermon Series on Christian Hope, March–May, 2004. Available from <http://www.redeemer.com/store/catalog/>; P. Kreeft, 'What Will Heaven Be Like?', in D. Neff (ed.), *Tough Questions Christians Ask* (Colorado Springs, 1989); J. W. Sire, *The Universe Next Door* (Downers Grove and Leicester, 1997); N. T. Wright, *New Heavens, New Earth: The Biblical Picture of Christian Hope* (Cambridge, 1999).

S. G. LEBHAR

HEDONISM

Hedonism is the view in ethical theory that pleasure (Gk, *hedon*) is the only intrinsic good and/or that pleasure is what every moral agent ought to pursue. According to hedonism, the good life consists in maximizing pleasure and minimizing pain.

Hedonism in history and ethics

Aristippus of Cyrene (c. 435–366 BC) is regarded as the father of hedonism, though Epicurus (342–270 BC) is the philosopher most often associated with it. In his *Letter to Menoeceus* he wrote, 'For it is to obtain this end that we always act, namely, to avoid pain and fear ... And for this cause we call pleasure the beginning and end of the blessed life.' In modern philosophy, hedonism formed the basis for the ethical theories of Jeremy Bentham (1748–1832) and J. S. *Mill (1806–73). They formulated the earliest versions of *utilitarianism according to which an action is right if, and only if, it brings about the most pleasure for the most people. Some versions of ethical egoism (the view that one's only obligation is to pursue self-interest) are also based on hedonistic principles.

We must distinguish three types of hedonism. First, there is psychological hedonism, which is the view that human beings are psychologically determined to pursue pleasure. Secondly, there is ethical hedonism, which holds that moral agents ought to seek pleasure, the pursuit of pleasure being our ultimate obligation. Thirdly, there is value hedonism, according to which experiences of pleasure are the only intrinsic goods, all other goods being merely instrumental to achieving pleasure.

An evaluation of hedonism

Hedonism has had many able defenders and has exerted considerable influence in ethical theory. Nevertheless, all three kinds of hedonism are subject to strong criticisms. There is no doubt that people are motivated by the desire for pleasure. The question, however, is whether pleasure is the only thing we seek or value. It would seem that people are often motivated by other things, such as knowledge, beauty, friendship and achievement. The hedonist claims that we pursue such things because of the pleasure we derive from them. Yet Joseph *Butler argued that we pursue things like knowledge and friendship because we find them intrinsically valuable and only derive pleasure from them as a consequence of obtaining them. In other words, we get pleasure from things like knowledge and friendship, but that is not why we pursue them. Imagine, for example, that one is offered the option of being attached to a machine that constantly provides one with a lifetime of pleasant sensations, though at the cost of never accomplishing anything in the real world. Intuitively, few would choose to be attached to this 'pleasure machine'. This shows that people desire and value other things besides pleasure, contrary to both psychological and value hedonism.

An objection that undermines both psychological and ethical hedonism is the hedonistic *paradox. It would seem that those people who are most intent on gaining pleasure are the ones least likely to find it. As Qoheleth said of his own experience, 'I denied myself nothing my eyes desired; I refused my heart no pleasure … Yet … everything was meaningless, a chasing after the wind' (Eccl. 2:10–11). The pursuit of pleasure for pleasure's sake often ends in dissatisfaction, while those who pursue other worthwhile goals with no conscious desire for pleasure, tend to be deeply satisfied. It follows that the psychological hedonist can seldom fulfil his or her desires and that the ethical hedonist ought not to be a hedonist. These paradoxical facts suggest that psychological and ethical hedonism are false.

Both ethical and value hedonism assume that pleasure is always good. But it is arguable that there are some intrinsically bad pleasures such as that taken by some in the sadistic treatment of others. Moreover, these hedonisms contradict some of our strongest moral intuitions. For example, we believe that torturing children for the fun of it is morally wrong. Yet, if torturing children brings me pleasure (and little or no pain), then ethical and value hedonism suggest that I ought to do it.

Some hedonists attempt to avoid these problems by distinguishing between the *quantity* and the *quality* of pleasure. If all that concerns the hedonist is maximizing the quantity of pleasure, then he falls victim to the above criticisms. However, pleasures may differ with respect to their quality, some types of pleasure being qualitatively better than others. As J. S. Mill declared, 'It is better to be a human dissatisfied than a pig satisfied' (*Utilitarianism*, p. 348). On this view, what people value is not simply a maximum quantity of pleasurable sensations, but the highest quality of pleasure, the kind of which humans are uniquely capable. The sadistic pleasure derived from torturing children or the raw sensations of the pleasure machine, on this view, would be inferior to pleasure derived from more noble activities such as art, philosophy, athletics, etc. And what we ought to do is maximize pleasures of the nobler kind.

It is not clear, however, that the qualitative hedonist truly escapes the problems. Imagine another pleasure machine, which provides not simply raw sensations but gives people false memories and sensory experiences, fooling them into thinking that they have achieved many things which supply high quality pleasures – e.g. friendships, knowledge and artistic accomplishments. Would people choose to participate in this illusion or would they prefer to have real friendships and real accomplishments? Our intuitions indicate the latter.

Moreover, in order to make the distinction between quantity and quality of pleasure, the qualitative hedonist introduces into hedonism a principle of value other than pleasure. What determines the difference between different qualities of pleasure? It cannot be pleasure itself, but some non-pleasurable property that superior pleasures have and inferior pleasures lack.

Christianity and hedonism

The Bible does appeal to pleasure to motivate worship of God. The psalmist, for example, longs to be in God's presence where there are 'joy' and 'eternal pleasures' (Ps. 16:11). And Christians are called to sacrificial living with the promise of eternal reward (Matt. 6:19–20; Luke 12:33).

Nonetheless, the Bible does not endorse a hedonistic ethical theory. Rather, Scripture presents God as the highest good (Pss. 34:8; 148:13; Rev. 4:121), contrary to value hedonism. Moreover, the supreme obligation is not to seek pleasure, but God's glory (1 Cor. 10:31), contrary to ethical hedonism. Of course, we are indeed called to 'Delight [ourselves] in the LORD' (Ps. 37:4), but the pleasure found in God cannot be what we value most or ought most to seek without becoming a form of idolatry.

Bibliography

Epicurus, *Letter to Menoeceus*, in S. M. Cahn and P. Markie (eds.), *Ethics: History, Theory, and Contemporary Issues* (Oxford, 2002), pp. 184–186; W. Frankena, *Ethics* (Englewood Cliffs, 1973), pp. 79–92; D. M. Haybron, 'Happiness and Pleasure', *Philosophy and Phenomenalogical Research* 62:3 (2001), pp. 501–528; J. S. Mill, *Utilitarianism*, in S. M. Cahn and P. Markie (eds.), *Ethics: History, Theory, and Contemporary Issues* (Oxford, 2002), pp. 343–377; J. Piper, *Desiring God: Meditations of a Christian Hedonist* (Sisters, 1996); L. P. Pojman, *Ethics: Discovering Right and Wrong* (Belmont, 1995), pp. 66–68, 82–91.

S. B. COWAN

HEGEL, GEORG WILHELM FRIEDRICH

Georg Wilhelm Friedrich Hegel (1770–1831) is one of the more influential thinkers of modern times. Marx's dialectical *materialism and *Kierkegaard's *existentialism contain weighty reactions to Hegel; much of twentieth-century continental theology and philosophy are unintelligible without understanding him; the analytic philosophy of the English-speaking world in the twentieth century studiously rejected him. It has been said that Hegel stands at the end of every road traversed by thinkers trying to come to grips with modernity. Yet even sympathetic commentators admit that his philosophical prose can be convoluted to the point of being impenetrable and that this precludes definitive interpretation of his thought.

Before his appointment to a chair of philosophy in Berlin in 1818, where he remained until his death, Hegel held a variety of positions outside, as well as inside, universities, including in Jena, Nuremberg and Heidelberg. He lived in a time of vital transition on social, political and intellectual fronts: it seemed that the French Revolution was marking the birth of modern Europe and *Kant's philosophy the death of traditional *metaphysics. Hegel sought to understand modernity in its unity and in all its comprehensive ramifications and to ground human understanding on a philosophically

rigorous analysis of modern consciousness. That meant grasping the movement of world *history. Tracing the story of civilizations through their Oriental, Graeco-Roman, early-Christian and modern course, Hegel argued that the history of the world consisted in the progress of the consciousness of freedom. The principle of freedom, which the human spirit comes to actualize, comes to light in Christianity, and the development of Christianity until Hegel's own day is essentially the development of this principle. But freedom is not sheer subjective self-determination. It is a profoundly rational principle, the intellectual and spiritual discernment of the rationality of the essential world order and of our consciousness of it.

History is the sphere of the development of *Geist*, a word alternatively translated as 'mind' or 'spirit' even in the title of what is probably his greatest work, the *Phänomenologie des Geistes* (Phenomenology of Spirit [Mind]). That Hegel held the inner reality of the world to consist in the developing self-consciousness of Mind or Spirit seems clear. What is less clear is how to interpret this in relation to the traditional Christian ideas of God and humanity. Hegel saw himself as a Christian philosopher. Religious language and imagery express ideas that philosophy must conceptualize rationally; philosophy is a translation of religious belief. Hegel has been read as an orthodox Lutheran, a pantheist and an atheist, to mention only three options. The case for his orthodoxy appears impossibly hard to sustain, unless orthodoxy itself is interpreted in an unacceptably broad way. His thought is perhaps akin to panentheism: Hegel held that deity and humanity share a fundamental identity, yet a description of humanity or the material world does not exhaust what can be said about deity. God is self-unfolding Spirit; history is its course.

Battle has raged over the interpretation of Hegel's political philosophy in its relation to twentieth-century totalitarianism. Some hold that his glorification of the Prussian State set the precedent for Hitler, subsuming individual freedom entirely under allegiance to the political order which, under Prussian hegemony, evolved into a unified Germany later in the nineteenth century. However, there is a strong case for maintaining that this is unfair to Hegel. His correlation of freedom and rationality militates against the notion of absolute State sovereignty. Still, we might allow for more or less conservative or liberal interpretations of Hegel's social and political thought. Attempting to understand it in the light of history shows the importance of the role of speculative philosophical thought in modern culture. Hegel's philosophy was indeed encyclopaedic in its scope, the *Encyclopaedia of the Philosophical Sciences* being one of the four major volumes that he published during his lifetime.

Generally speaking, Hegel's thought presents us with at least two challenges. One is to comprehend our historical times, a task Hegel undertook with exemplary dedication. The other is to ask how far the meaning of religious vocabulary can be preserved by a philosophical redescription and what transformation of biblical ideas is consistent with authentic Christianity. These questions are abstractly posed, but their concrete handling by Hegel and successors has proved both vital for modern theology, and, arguably, fatal, despite the undoubted intellectual power of Hegel's contribution.

Bibliography

F. C. Beiser (ed.), *The Cambridge Companion to Hegel* (Cambridge, 1993); S. Houlgate, *Freedom, Truth and History: An Introduction to Hegel's Philosophy* (London, 1991); T. Pinkard, *Hegel: A Biography* (Cambridge, 2000).

S. N. WILLIAMS

HELL

The Christian doctrine of hell has fallen on hard times, and in recent years has also become a scandal or embarrassment to a large number of Christians. In Western culture, people are not as willing as they once were to accept on faith the actions of authority when they consider them arbitrary or cruel. This cultural tendency has affected many Christians. Those grieving the loss of loved ones who died without acknowledging Jesus may react especially strongly against the doctrine of hell. Even after the emotions have subsided, many find themselves unwilling to accept traditional forms of the doctrine.

Many others, Christian and non-Christian, who do not wrestle with the doctrine on such a personal level still raise objections against it. Some people believe that the ability of humans to make choices and develop character continues after bodily death. They object to the forms of the Christian doctrine of hell that teach that the condition and fate of individuals is fixed after death. Others object to forms of the doctrine that teach eternal torment of the damned, believing that eternal punishments for finite crimes are inherently unjust. Some find the entire concept of retributive justice immoral for an all-powerful being. They argue that humans have had recourse to retributive *justice because we are limited in our ability to prevent injustice by more humane means, but God is not subject to these limitations and could use an alternative, less aversive, method of eliminating human *evil.

Throughout the history of Christianity, several views have emerged from those seeking to be faithful to the biblical text. The development of each of these views has been motivated, to some extent, by the desire to find a satisfactory answer to some of the objections raised against the doctrine of hell. The two most crucial issues regarding the fate of the condemned in hell centre on the nature and the duration of the punishment. Are the biblical images of hell meant to be taken literally or figuratively? Do the damned suffer endlessly, or will those confined to hell eventually cease to exist (annihilationism)?

Those who espouse a literal interpretation understand the biblical teaching on hell to be depicting a place of material fire where the unrepentant will suffer conscious, eternal torment. In hell the flesh of the damned will burn perpetually and be eaten eternally by worms in deep darkness; they will wail in agony, horror and grief. According to this view, God inflicts these bodily torments on the damned in rightful judgment in light of his holiness and justice. Proponents of this view note that *Jesus spoke more on the subject of hell than any other biblical person and point to passages such as Matt. 5:22; 10:28; 13:42, 50; 18:9; 22:13; 25:41; Mark 9:47–48; 2 Thess. 1:9 and Jude 7, 14 to support their literal interpretation. They argue that human objections to the justice of eternal, bodily torments are vitiated by self-interest and contempt for God. In fact, given the many injustices that go uncorrected in life and the tendency of human beings to engage in more extreme forms of injustice when they believe they can get away with it, God can be just and good only if he engages in thorough and forceful posthumous judgment. Furthermore, rebellion against an

301

infinitely worthy being deserves nothing less than infinitely prolonged torment. That we find this verdict so objectionable only reveals the depths of our arrogance.

The literal interpretation has been the majority view in Christian tradition, receiving the explicit endorsement of Church Fathers such as *Tertullian and *Augustine and the eighteenth-century Protestant theologian Jonathan *Edwards. Traditional interpretation plays an important role (more for Roman Catholics than for Protestants) but is not the final arbiter in determining issues of interpretation.

Proponents of a second view (including the sixteenth-century Reformer John *Calvin, F. F. Bruce and Billy Graham) suggest that while hell is a place of endless conscious suffering, the precise nature of that suffering is unknown. They argue that hell is a real place, but caution that interpreting the symbols of hell in a literalistic fashion is misguided and fails to do justice to the true significance of the scriptural assertions. The biblical images of hell were intended to convey more the seriousness of impending judgment and the attending horrors of hell rather than the precise nature of the penalties. Adherents of a metaphorical view of hell note the discrepancy between the image of a 'lake of fire' (Rev. 19:20; 20:10–15; 21:8) and the image of utter darkness (Matt. 8:12; 22:13; 25:30; cf. Jude 7, 14). The incompatibility of these images, they argue, suggests that they are not to be taken literally, but are intended to point to realities more horrific than either image can convey on its own. Especially in portions of Scripture dealing with eschatology, powerful, culturally relevant images that were understandable to the original hearers are used to symbolize realities that are beyond present human experience. What is important, they note, is that the images point to the sobering reality of hell as a place of conscious, perpetual torment where the impenitent are cast from God's presence for ever.

Despite their differing approaches to the interpretation of the biblical images of hell, both of the aforementioned views affirm that there is unending, conscious suffering of some sort. Whether or not the fire, worm, gnashing of teeth and darkness are literal, the consignment of the unrepentant to a place and condition forever removed from the presence of God remains dreadfully miserable. Proponents point to passages such as Matt. 25:46, where the contrasted destinies of both the righteous and impenitent are described with the same word, 'eternal'.

Some literalists charge that the metaphorical interpretation attempts to 'soften' the doctrine of hell beyond what the Bible warrants. Adherents of the metaphorical view, however, tend not to argue that the reality of hell will be less awful than the biblical images suggest. Instead, some argue that the sufferings of the damned are to a great extent self-inflicted. In this view, hell is a monument to human freedom. For those who resist God to the bitter end, God says in effect, 'Your will be done.' That this leads to eternal torment is a consequence of God's determination to isolate the damned from the rest of creation, which deprives them of access to anything good, so that their presence and activity can no longer cause harm. According to some proponents of this view, it answers the charge that the punishments of hell are arbitrarily cruel by showing that they are a natural consequence of rejection of God.

A third view, referred to as annihilationism (also known as 'conditional immortality'), rejects the idea that the biblical doctrine of hell involves the endless, conscious suffering of the wicked. Proponents of this view argue that the biblical symbols of hell point to the dissolution or extinction of the impenitent rather than to everlasting torment. Hell is the 'second death' mentioned in Revelation 2:11; 20:6, 14. After an unspecified period of retributional suffering, the wicked are destroyed and simply cease to exist.

According to annihilationists, the Hellenistic concept of the *immortality of the soul has crept into Christian anthropology and given illegitimate sanction to the idea that the soul must exist for ever. Rather, the biblical view is that the soul as well as the body is mortal and so, annihilationists contend, there is no need to posit an eternal abode for the impenitent. Eternal life is the gift of God given to all who are in Christ. Those who are not to be found in Christ on the judgment day will simply cease to exist at some point. There is no agreement as to when the extinction of the unrepentant will occur. Some suggest on the judgment day itself, others after an unknown period of conscious torment in hell (to allow for the gradations of punishment and suffering alluded to in passages such as Matt. 11:24; Luke 12:47–48; Rev. 20:11–12).

According to annihilationists, what is eternal about hell is not the conscious suffering of the unrepentant, but rather the irreversible future extinction of the impenitent. So, for example, in Isa. 66:24 (see also Mark 9:48) it is the worm gnawing on rotting, dead flesh, and the unquenchable fire, that are described as eternal, not the consciousness of those who are punished. Proponents recognize that Rev. 20:10 offers what appears to be at first blush an irrefutable challenge to their view, but argue that the larger apocalyptic context of the verse allows for a symbolic interpretation. In the parable of the sheep and goats where Jesus declares, 'Then they will go away to eternal punishment, but the righteous to eternal life' (Matt. 25:46), annihilationists argue that in light of the larger biblical teaching on the nature and duration of hell, one can interpret 'eternal punishment' as referring to the irreversible destruction of the impenitent, rather than the duration of the torment of immortal wicked souls. The continued existence of the rising smoke, lake of fire, and undying worm do not conflict with the annihilationist's insistence on cosmological harmony in the new *heavens and new earth because they serve as perpetual monuments to God's justice.

Annihilationists further argue that terms such as 'second death' (Rev. 20:14; 21:8) and 'destruction' (2 Thess. 1:8–9; 2 Pet. 2:1–3; 3:6–7) suggest a future extinction of the wicked by the wrath of God rather than unending conscious torment (see also Ps. 37:2, 9–10, 20, 38; Mal. 4:1–2; 1 Cor. 3:17; Phil. 3:19). At some future point 'the wicked will be no more' (Ps. 37:10) because 'the wages of sin is death' (Rom. 6:23). The punishment of hell is spoken of as eternal precisely because the consequences of God's judgment on the impenitent (death and destruction), rather than their continued existence in torment, are irreversible.

One of the major objectives of proponents of this view is to answer the objection that eternal, conscious torment is unjust. They argue that everlasting punishment for finite sins committed in time is disproportionate and violates the principle of fitting the punishment to the crime (Exod. 21:23–25; Lev. 24:18–22; Deut. 19:21). In fact, proponents of annihilationism often argue inferentially on the basis of theological, judicial and moral consistency. They argue that the concept of God torturing sinners for ever does not cohere with the biblical portrayal of his love and mercy, most clearly exemplified in the life of

Jesus. A place like hell cannot continue to exist for ever in light of the biblical teaching that at the second coming and ensuing final judgment there will finally be a resolution to the conflict between good and evil with the formation of a new heaven and earth (Rom. 8:19–23; 2 Pet. 3:10–13). If everything is to be renewed (Rev. 21:5), there cannot be some dark pocket of unending torment and rebellion against God, led by the devil and his minions, coexisting with this new order.

The impulse to mitigate everlasting punishment is understandable, and has an impressive pedigree in the history of Christianity, including Clement, *Origen, C. S. *Lewis, Philip E. Hughes and John Stott. Some of these have argued for the annihilation of the condemned in hell at some point, others for some sort of remedial process or 'second chance' after death (leading, as in the case of Origen, to the espousal of *universalism).

The official Roman Catholic (see *Christianity, Roman Catholic) doctrine of purgatory is also partly based on the idea that eternal torment is a disproportionate punishment for many sinners. Purgatory is an interim state after death for Christians to complete the process of sanctification. In the Catholic scheme of salvation, the number of Christians who are holy enough to experience full fellowship with God immediately after death is relatively small. The doctrine of purgatory provides a way for the vast majority of the Christian populace, whose lives exhibit neither the extent of evil deserving of eternal torments nor the extent of good deserving of immediate entrance into heaven, to be counted among the saved.

Proponents of a literal hell often argue that both a metaphorical view of hell and annihilationism 'soften' the biblical teaching on hell, taking the 'hell out of hell' so to speak. Some argue that this robs the doctrine of its potential as a moral deterrent against sin as well as a central theological motivation for evangelism and missions. In response, those espousing a metaphorical interpretation of hell as well as annihilationists point out that whether hell is unending torment (of one sort or the other) or the end of one's existence, both are grim realities in light of the biblical teaching that humankind was made in God's image to worship him and enjoy him for ever.

It is important to stress that the aforementioned opinions regarding the nature and duration of the punishment of the impenitent after death differ on matters pertaining to the interpretation of Scripture. Proponents of all three views claim adherents who hold to a high view of Scripture, find some degree of support for their interpretations throughout church history, and understand hell to be a sobering possibility due to the freedom of humans to reject God's love. The fundamental issue is one of correct biblical interpretation, not biblical authority. More precisely, the issue centres around how the biblical passages on hell are to be properly interpreted. At issue is not whether or not we find the biblical doctrine repugnant to our enlightened, modern minds, but what it is that the Bible actually teaches. Especially when dealing with eschatology, we need to affirm what can be positively affirmed, but hold our positions regarding details tentatively and humbly, acknowledging the divine *mystery of eternity from our time-oriented perspective. Whether hell is a literal blazing inferno, a place of ceaseless, self-inflicted anguish, or a hideous grave marker, its horrors ought to spur believers on into holy living based on gratitude and a renewed evangelistic and missionary zeal to share with the lost the eternal blessings to be found in Christ alone. At this juncture in redemptive history, we simply do not possess the categories by which to fully understand the mysteries involved, for 'now we see but a poor reflection as in a mirror' (1 Cor. 13:12). We possess only analogies to teach the mysterious horrors of hell, but the reality of hell, banishment from God's presence by those created in his image and designed for fellowship with him, is sobering no matter how dimly and incompletely we understand it.

Bibliography

W. Crockett (ed.), *Four Views On Hell* (Grand Rapids, 1996).

E. MOORE

HENRY, CARL F. H.

Carl Henry is often described as twentieth-century America's premier evangelical theologian. Much of this reputation was earned by his role as leader of a post-fundamentalist movement that arose in the 1940s to make an intellectual case for Christianity. From his earliest books, his twelve years as editor-in-chief of the journal, *Christianity Today*, his oversight of a series of works on evangelical

apologetics to his magisterial six-volume *God, Revelation and Authority*, a 'neo-evangelical' reasoned defence of Christian faith was his priority.

Henry's concern for the rationality of faith is related both to the anti-intellectual tendencies he perceived in influential mainstream theologies of the day, and to the piety of contemporary evangelicalism. On the one hand, he excoriated *neo-orthodoxy's 'paradoxes' and anti-apologetic dogmatics, as represented pre-eminently by Karl *Barth, with an ancestry traced through *Kierkegaard back to *Tertullian. On the other hand, he sought to stretch the popular revivalism of the times to include rational warrants for, and the intellectual exposition of, the gospel.

For Henry, the centrality of reason in matters of faith is grounded in the very being of God, the eternal *Logos* who, in turn, grants rational capacities to humans in the *imago Dei*. The fall has distorted our capacity to discern definitively the divine evidences given in creation, hence the need for the enfleshment of the *Logos* in *Jesus Christ and divine disclosure of saving *truth through an inerrant Scripture, the written Word of God. Thus the invitation to 'come now, let us argue it out' (Isa. 1:18, NRSV) and the mandate to give 'a reason of the hope that is in you' (1 Pet. 3:15, KJV).

Dogmatically, the *Logos*/logic interface means *revelation is delivered in the intelligible propositions of Scripture, to be ordered according to the dictates of a Spirit-guided reason. Apologetically, it means that the Christian faith is intrinsically rational, following the laws of *logic derived from the divine *Logos*. Alternative interpretations of *reality are false as they do not have their source in that *Logos*. Because the fall has damaged but not destroyed the rational dimension of the *imago Dei*, exponents of other world-views can be shown their violation of the universal laws of logic, one aspect of the apologetic task. The other is the demonstration of the superior rationality of the Christian faith itself. Defence of the faith, therefore, requires both the exposure of the errors of other world-views and a critique of inadequate Christian theologies.

Two laws of logic are given pride of place: consistency and coherence. While often used synonymously in apologetics, Henry distinguishes them: 'logical consistency is a negative test of truth and coherence is a subordinate test' (*God, Revelation and Authority*, vol. I,

p. 232). A point of view cannot be true if it entails a logical contradiction. Thus the fallacy of *relativism is exposed as inconsistent when it espouses its own theory as an absolute. A point of view cannot be true if it is incoherent, failing to do justice to all the facts of both life and thought in a unified way. Thus the fallacy of Marxism is exposed when it cannot account for the sin that infects every presumed historical advance. Alternatively, patient investigation will show that the Christian faith is both self-consistent and coherent internally and externally.

Henry differentiates his view from other evangelical apologists that he believes either overvalue or undervalue reason. On the one hand, as a moderate presuppositionalist, he holds that all *reasoning proceeds from axioms of faith, and that Christian faith, finally, is the fruit of the *Holy Spirit's converting grace, not argument or evidence. On the other, he spent a lifetime showing that reason has a role in clearing the ground for faith, and that Christian truth-claims must be subjected to the tests of consistency and coherence.

Henry is criticized by some in a succeeding generation of evangelicals for a *rationalism that itself bears the marks of modernity, and that does not speak to the sceptical postmodern mindset. However, Henry was a pioneer in the twentieth-century break-out of evangelicalism from its intellectual ghetto, a prober of alternative world-views without evangelical peer who prepared the way for those who want to take their own adventurous steps in cultural engagement.

Bibliography

C. F. H. Henry, *God, Revelation and Authority*, 6 vols. (Waco, 1976–1983).

G. FACKRE

HERBERT, EDWARD

Edward Herbert (Baron Herbert of Cherbury, 1583–1648), soldier and diplomat, historian and poet, is commonly known as the 'father of English deism' and wrote *De Veritate* (1624, enlarged 1645), which discussed the meaning and attainment of *truth. Rejecting the sceptics that regarded truth as unobtainable and the metaphysicians who thought that all truth is attainable, Herbert argued that certain 'common notions' have universal application

and can form the basis for arriving at assured truths. God has imparted to every person numerous faculties for cognition of, and interaction with, the world. These faculties could be grouped under four heads: 'natural instinct' (the light of nature, the Platonic reason that includes cognition and understanding) that dominates the other faculties; internal apprehension (*conscience and will); external apprehension (sensation); and discursive thought (in *logic and reflection). Correct use of these faculties is grounded in the 'common notions', which are *universals by which certain truths may be obtained. Whereas appeal to *history, tradition or faith can at best yield only probability, the 'common notions', recognized universally by rational people, are sure foundations by which reason and experience can arrive at truth, demonstrable by its harmony, uniformity and universality. Herbert regarded his rationalist programme as the bulwark against what he saw as the ignorant, the headstrong, overweening *authority, superstition, fanatics, enthusiasts, Puritan bibliolatry and Catholic arrogance.

In the expanded edition of 1645 Herbert expressed his deistic beliefs. Disavowing doubtful claims built upon the supposed sacred authority of priests and preachers, an infallible church or the *religious experiences of faith, one must rather investigate the origins of religions and test them by means of the 'common notions'. In *De Veritate* and *De Religione Gentilium* (published posthumously in 1663) Herbert specified the 'common notions' or universal truths characteristic of all valid religions: there is one supreme God; he ought to be worshipped; virtue and piety are the chief part of divine worship; we ought to be sorry for our sins and repent of them; and divine *justice and goodness dispenses rewards and punishments according to merit, both in this life and the next.

Herbert did not suggest that these commonly accepted truths are sufficient for an actual religion but he proposed them in order to promote a toleration of different forms of Christianity. He was not opposed to the value of religious experiences and did not exclude divine providences in the life of a believer, but he had no significant place for the Incarnation in his system. Although conservative Christians will not be sympathetic to Herbert's minimizing of the fundamental role of divine revelation in the Christian life, it can be considered whether 'common notions' (widely held beliefs) can be a point of contact for communicating Christian truth. One might point to the uniformity, rationality and beauty of nature that can be apprehended by scientific endeavour (John Polkinghorne), or to the commonality of moral awareness (H. P. Owen), or to the existential *Angst* (dread) in the face of the apparent meaningless of modern life and the threat of death (*Kierkegaard). Whilst this approach may be of help to those committed to modernity's search for truth, it may not succeed with the postmodernist mindset that denies the possibility of transcendent truth valid for all cultures.

Bibliography

E. Herbert, *De Veritate* (Bristol, 1937); H. R. Hutcheson (ed. and trans.), *Lord Herbert of Cherbury's De Religione Laici* (New Haven, 1944); R. D. Bedford, *The Defence of Truth: Herbert of Cherbury and the Seventeenth Century* (Manchester, 1979); H. R. Hutcheson, 'Lord Herbert and the Deists', *Journal of Philosophy*, vol. 43 (1946), pp. 219–221.

J. W. WARD

HEROISM

A hero is distinguishable from two other kinds of notable people, a talent and a celebrity. A talent is someone with a skill. A celebrity is someone who is well-known. A hero could be either, but is more importantly someone who inspires aspiration in some significant way. We want to be like him or her. A hero's life expands our *imagination and motivation about what is possible in our own lives. In biblical terms, it is someone who embodies the glory, honour or greatness that we should imitate. In the Bible the opposite of heroism is shame and dishonour, negative heroism. As the attractiveness of a hero inspires aspiration, so the humiliation of shame provokes aversion.

Challenge for apologetics

Heroism becomes an issue for apologetics when a culture's heroes, or lack of them, conflict with biblical virtues. In a fallen world, some peoples' heroes will be pseudo-heroes, and other people will deny that human greatness exists at all. There will be a powerful pressure to dismiss or scorn faith in Christ because it appears unheroic, even shameful.

To the person whose heroes are 'big-time sinners', faith in Christ will seem weak and wimpish. To the person whose heroes embody relativistic openness and non-judgmentalism, faith in Christ will seem intolerant and arrogant. To the cynic who claims to reject the very possibility of heroism, faith in Christ will seem naïve and unsophisticated.

The importance of heroes lies in the power of their stories over the imagination. Heroism sometimes even leads people to reject what they know to be true at a conceptual level. Herod Antipas felt the need to be heroic in front of all his friends, in the Roman heroic model of supreme *power and wealth. This desire for heroism overpowered the moral convictions which had led him to protect John the Baptist up until that time, and Herod, though deeply upset, had John killed (Mark 6:17–29).

Negative apologetics

A biblical apologetic has a ready response to the pseudo-heroes of both ancient and modern cultures. Since the theatre of heroism is not primarily conceptual but imaginative and narrative, biblical writers do not lecture us. Instead, they engage our imaginations, disenchanting us with pseudo-heroes such as 'the fool', a figure who appears throughout the book of Proverbs. He is graphically represented as a loser, a blind guide whose initial glamour ends in humiliation. Today's heroic values of heavy drinking, greed, investment capital, violence, sexual conquest and *cynicism are all there – and exposed as losers in the battle for status in the human imagination.

Many modern popular heroes are heroic for non-moral or immoral reasons. They are heroes of youth, beauty, money and power. The context for heroic action for many young people is limited to sex, popularity and shopping. We must press the question whether stretching towards these pseudo-heroic virtues ends by expanding or shrinking the human spirit.

Public heroes are often heroic for their stage or film personas, which could never exist in the real world. Their heroism is out of reach. They do not enlarge us, but encourage only psychic hitchhiking and heroism of compensation. They inspire daydreaming about what our lives would be like if only we were like them, a daydreaming which ends in self-disgust and a sense of being poor, ugly, dull and helpless.

Positive apologetics

*Jesus is the only unqualified hero. His followers, having received salvation by God's grace, are called to imitate him, not in everything that he did but in his quality of life. By contrast to other world-views, Christian heroism is not one-dimensional, with a single basic heroic virtue such as bravery. We are told explicitly to imitate Jesus in the full breadth of his excellence – in *humility, love, service, forgiveness, unjust suffering and courage.

The apostle Paul wrote, 'Follow my example, as I follow the example of Christ' (1 Cor. 11:1). Although Jesus is the only complete hero, other people can be partial or qualified heroes to the extent that they are Christlike. No-one today will be Christlike in all virtues, or even in one virtue all the time. We may, nonetheless, be surrounded by wonderful visual aids of Christlikeness in the lives of those near us. Virtues of Christlikeness are not inaccessible to us as is the heroism of professional sports, entertainment and eternal youth.

The Christian can be sure of three things. First, that we are accepted by God not because of any heroism of our own, since we fall far short of his glory, but by his grace through faith in Christ. Secondly, that by the same grace of God, we can be transformed into the image of Christ 'with ever-increasing glory', beginning in this life (2 Cor. 3:18). Thirdly, that there will be an ultimate redemption of the imagination when fools will no longer be praised as heroes, and true heroism will be recognized as excellent (Isa. 32:5).

Bibliography

L. Braudy, *The Frenzy of Renown* (New York, 1986); R. Browne and M. Fishwick, *The Hero in Transition* (Bowling Green, Ohio, 1983); P. Gibbon, *A Call to Heroism* (New York, 2002); R. Keyes, *True Heroism* (Colorado Springs, 1995); O. Klapp, *Heroes, Villains and Fools* (Englewood Cliffs, 1962); J. Lawrence and R. Jewett, *The Myth of the American Hero* (Grand Rapids, 2002).

R. KEYES

HICK, JOHN

One of the most influential philosophers and theologians of the twentieth century, John Hick began his academic career in the 1950s as an able defender of orthodox Christian theism. But by the 1980s he had become a formidable critic of traditional Christian beliefs, and his unorthodox views helped to set the agenda for Christian apologetics. Hick was born in England in 1922 and was educated at the universities of Edinburgh, Oxford and Cambridge. The author of over two hundred books and scholarly articles, Hick taught philosophy of religion at major universities for four decades, retiring in 1992. His writings focus upon religious *epistemology, theodicy, Christology and religious *pluralism.

The legacy of *logical positivism, with its demand that statements about God be verifiable or falsifiable by empirical experience if they are to be accepted as 'cognitively meaningful', was still strong in the 1950s and 60s. Hick responded to positivism by arguing that the statement 'God exists' is cognitively meaningful since there are conceivable states of affairs (perhaps not in this life but in a life to come) that would remove all grounds for rationally doubting its truth, and thus it is in principle verifiable.

In *Faith and Knowledge* (1966) Hick rejected traditional attempts to demonstrate the truth of Christian *theism through *natural theology, arguing that the theistic arguments were inconclusive. The universe is religiously ambiguous and can be interpreted rationally in either religious or non-religious terms. Nevertheless, Hick argued, it can be entirely reasonable for the Christian who has experiences which he or she takes to be experiences of God to believe in God. This shift away from the agenda of natural theology to the more modest task of showing the rationality of belief in God based upon one's experiences was increasingly adopted by apologists in the 1980s and 1990s.

In *Evil and the God of Love* (1966) Hick developed a 'soul making' theodicy, which holds that God's purpose in creation is to bring human beings progressively to spiritual maturity, and that genuine challenges from *evil must be part of the process. Hick also claimed that, given the reality of evil, traditional Christian theism can only be accepted if we embrace soteriological *universalism, so that all people ultimately will be redeemed.

During the 1960s and early 1970s Hick became increasingly uncomfortable with the orthodox teachings on the incarnation and the deity of *Jesus Christ and much more accepting of other religions. *God and the Universe of*

Faiths (1973) put forward a more pluralistic way of understanding Christianity and other religions. The implications of this for Christology became clear in the controversial collection of essays edited by Hick, *The Myth of God Incarnate* (1977). The orthodox doctrine of Jesus Christ as literally both God and man, the unique incarnation of God, was rejected in favour of a view of the incarnation as an elaborate myth or metaphor suggesting God's special presence and activity in Jesus of Nazareth. In *An Interpretation of Religion* (1989), arguably the most sophisticated defence of religious pluralism, Hick argued that 'the great world faiths embody different perceptions and conceptions of, and correspondingly different responses to, the Real [the religious ultimate] from within the major variant ways of being human'. The various religions, then, are the product of the Real revealing itself to humankind and humankind in turn responding in historically and culturally conditioned ways to the Real. Jesus Christ is just one among many religious figures throughout history in whom appropriate responses to the Real are manifest.

The religious pluralism of Hick, which captures nicely the ethos of the times, presents a formidable challenge to traditional Christian faith. An adequate apologetic response to Hick's pluralism must address the problematic assumptions in religious epistemology and NT scholarship upon which it is based, internal inconsistencies within the model itself and its inability to account for the radical differences in truth-claims among the religions.

Bibliography

P. Badham (ed.), *A John Hick Reader* (Philadelphia, 1990); H. Hewitt (ed.), *Problems in the Philosophy of Religion: Critical Studies of the Work of John Hick* (New York, 1991); H. A. Netland, *Encountering Religious Pluralism* (Downers Grove, 2001); A. Sharma (ed.), *God, Truth and Reality: Essays in Honour of John Hick* (London and New York, 1993).

H. A. NETLAND

HINDUISM

The term 'Hinduism' is a useful shorthand for the religious beliefs and practices of most of the people of India. The Muslims who invaded India called it the land of the Hindus (Hindustan), or the land of the River Indus. Other scholars suggest that 'Hinduism' was invented later by Europeans as an umbrella-term for the complex diversity of religions found among the peoples of the sub-continent. Hindus themselves prefer the term *sanatana dharma* ('everlasting law', 'eternal teaching') which indicates the eternal and revelatory nature of Hindu beliefs. *Dharma* has many translations, but most suggest a comprehensive ordering of life according to principles and practices appropriate for one's age and station in life. Also important is the law of *karma* (cause and effect) which carries the consequence of a person's good and bad deeds through a succession of lives. A Hindu strives to live appropriately in order to achieve a better rebirth or release (*moksha*) from the cycle of rebirth (*samsara*).

Hinduism is one of the world's more popular religions. At the beginning of the twenty-first century, it could claim more than 1 billion adherents, which means that at least one sixth of the world's population is Hindu. More than 80% of Indians are Hindus, but it is also a worldwide faith, with perhaps 30 million Hindus living outside of India. Not traditionally a missionary religion, it has spread through the world as Hindus have travelled and emigrated. However, since the Hindu reformer Vivekananda made a missionary journey to the USA at the end of the nineteenth century and founded the Ramakrishna Mission, various missionary *gurus* have travelled to the West bringing a form of Hindu belief. In response, many from traditionally Christian countries have turned to Hinduism out of disillusionment with their own religious and philosophical traditions.

In the last decades of the twentieth century and the beginning of the twenty-first century, Yogic, Tantric and Vedantic practices have become well-known in the West through the popularity of alternative (or *New Age) spiritualities and therapies. In addition, some authentic forms of Hinduism have won substantial numbers of Western adherents. For example, ISKCON (The International Society for Krishna Consciousness), popularly known as the Hare Krishna movement, teaches a faithful version of Bengal Vaishnavism.

Historical development

Hinduism claims to be the world's oldest surviving religion. Its development has been traced back to at least 3000 BC. Scholars point to its unfolding through various stages: first there was the famous Indus valley civilization; then came the highly developed Dravidian culture and the Aryan invasion when the Vedas (*shruti*, revealed literature) were collected; finally there was the modern period (from AD 1500 onwards) when colonialism and the presence of Christian missionaries in India brought much interaction between Hinduism and Christianity. While Hinduism is seen to have unfolded through these stages, some beliefs and practices from earliest times still continue today. The eclectic genius of Hinduism means that it has been able to assimilate seemingly contradictory and alien beliefs within a broad unity.

Principal beliefs and practices

A Hindu has been defined as one born into the caste system and one who accepts the Vedas as scripture. The Vedas (primary or *shruti* scriptures) are believed to be eternal truth revealed to sages (*rishis*) and written down after a period of oral transmission. Also important are later 'remembered' (secondary or *smriti*) scriptures. These include the epics *Mahabharata* (containing the *Bhagavad Gita*) and *Ramayana*, which have perhaps had the greatest influence on the Hindu population at large.

Hinduism recognizes three ways to God. The first, the way of *karma* (works), originally associated with sacrifices prescribed by the Vedas and performed by Brahmin priests, became in later periods a metaphor for ethical living. The second path, *jnana* (the way of knowledge), is associated with the *Upanishads* (speculative Hindu texts expounding philosophical and religious ideas) and the idealistic philosophy which sees the indescribable, transcendent Brahma as identical with the human soul (*atman*). The path of knowledge leads to the realization that one's true self is identical with Brahma. This realization of fusion with Brahma brings liberation from the cycle of rebirth. The first two paths were open only to those of high caste. The third path, that of *bhakti* (devotion) was open to all. It requires an incarnation (*avatara*) of God sent to help the earth through a difficult or evil period. In *bhakti*, the devotee appeals for God's mercy and enters into a relationship of love and devotion to an *avatara*. The best known incarnation is Lord Krishna, who appears in the *Bhagavad Gita*.

Points of contact with Christianity

Theism and monotheism

It may surprise some Christians to know that *theism dominates Indian religion. The bewildering proliferation of gods and goddesses in common stereotypes of Hinduism is usually understood as one God manifest in many forms commanding personal allegiance from the devotee. Likewise, the threefold manifestation of God in Hinduism, that of Brahma as creator, Vishnu as preserver and Shiva as destroyer illustrates a cyclical view of life (as opposed to the Christian linear view of *history) and is understood as one God manifested in endless recurrences.

A creator god

In Hinduism, God (manifested as Brahma) has the power to bring things into appearance. Like Christians, Hindus believe that God is the creator of all that is, and that God pervades all creation. The Hindu belief in the interconnectedness of all things means that everything is considered sacred.

Scripture

Hindus have a great respect for their own scriptures and also for the Christian scriptures. The Christian concept of the *logos*, the Word of God, and the importance of God speaking, finds apparent parallels with the Sanskrit concept of creative speech (*vak*), which goes back to the Vedas. Even for devotees of the philosophical and idealistic *Advaita Vedanta*, it is a word of scripture, often 'That thou art', which brings consciousness of oneness with Brahma and liberation from the cycle of rebirth. Vedantins hold that scriptural *revelation is the only reliable *authority for knowledge of God, and scripture is the final criterion for mystical experience. The tradition of theologian-grammarians, most famously Bhartrhari (c. AD 480), taught that communication is possible because *language and meaning are grounded in divine consciousness. In this belief, Christians and Hindus may be closer to one another than to those postmodern thinkers who deny the possibility of a stable *reality behind verbal interpretations. At the popular level, even more important than the philosophical texts, are the great Hindu epics, the *Ramayana* and the *Mahabharata*. The best-known and loved section of the *Mahabharata*, the *Bhagavad Gita* lies at the heart of Hindu spirituality. Like Christians, Hindus understand God through the interpretation of narrative texts.

A concept of grace

Vaishnavism, arguably the largest branch of Hinduism, has a strong emphasis on *bhakti* (devotion in response to God's love and grace). This emphasis on a personal relationship of love between the worshipper and God has initial parallels with the NT image of Christ's love for the church as his bride. Vaishnavas also emphasize purity, holiness and service to the community as a response to God's love.

Ethical concerns

The all-encompassing concept of *dharma* shows that Hindus understand that it is not simply what one believes that is important, but even more the way one lives. This view can be appreciated by Christians, who understand the importance of the link between faith and works which witness to one's faith in Christ.

Christian distinctions

At the turn of the millennium, various stereotypes of Hinduism have become integrated into Western cultural discourses. Contemporary alternative spiritualities and the increasingly popular New Age self-help therapies have brought aspects of Hindu belief and practice into the marketplace as a practical resource for all. Christians may find intriguing the many and surprising connections between Hindu and Christian belief and practice. They may be moved to awe by the *Advaita* vision of Brahman as the transcendent, mysterious one who is beyond all finite understanding and human description. They may warm to *bhakti* ideas of devotion and self-surrender to a personal God (or *avatara*) who reciprocates with love and grace. However, there are at least three important areas of difference between the Christian and Hindu vision.

First, in the person of *Jesus, Christians do not see one of several *avataras* unveiling new insights into humanity's already existing relationship with God, but the full and final revelation of God. In his life, death and resurrection, Christ is seen to break the relentless power of the law of *karma* and anything else that enslaves people, thus establishing the possibility of an altogether new relationship between God and humankind (cf. Col. 2:13–

15). Secondly, it can be argued that the Christian vision of creation and the material world is different from the Hindu understanding of the world as being in some way merely an appearance or illusion (*maya*). God's creation of the world was pronounced 'good' in the Genesis creation account. Human redemption is referred to, along with the redemption or renewal of the whole creation, in the NT (e.g. Rom. 8:19–22). Thirdly, in the Christian vision, the final goal of the spiritual journey is seen to be not an individual soul's liberation from the cycle of rebirth, but a new life in relationship with God, in relationship with a new *community, the body of Christ, and in relationship with those in the wider world whom Jesus taught his followers to love as neighbours.

Conclusion

Relations between Christians and Hindus have been, for the most part, friendly. The memory of colonialism and its perceived connection to Christian faith may seem less important to the rising generation. Nevertheless, Ram Gidoomal reminds Christians of two important points. First, Hindus remember the impact of other religions and their attempt to convert them in the past. Secondly, Hindus feel distress when people leave Hinduism because they are seen to be betraying their family and culture. Christians engaged in dialogue with those of the Hindu faith would do well to remember the advice in 1 Pet. 3:15, written to Christians living in a pluralist society, 'Always be prepared to give an answer to everyone who asks you to give the reason for the hope that you have. But do this with gentleness and respect.'

Bibliography

D. G. Burnett, *The Spirit of Hinduism: A Christian Perspective on Hindu Thought* (Tunbridge Wells, 1992); R. Gidoomal and R. Thomson, *A Way of Life: Introducing Hinduism* (London, 1997); S. Kulandran, *Grace in Christianity and Hinduism* (London, 1964); G. Parrinder, *Avatar and Incarnation* (Oxford, 1997).

R. A. C. BRADBY

HISTORICAL APOLOGETICS

Like many terms in contemporary parlance, 'historical apologetics' is used in a variety of ways, one of which parallels the term 'historical theology'. Just as historical theology involves the study of the practice of *theology throughout history, historical apologetics is the study of apologetics in church history. Historical apologetics is also used generally, referring to any defence of the historicity of events essential to Christianity, such as the resurrection, and so nearly every apologetic for Christianity will include historical apologetics. This article, however, will consider the term in a narrower sense, as the apologetic method the defining characteristic of which is the primary reliance on historical evidences to demonstrate the truthfulness of the Christian world-view. Contemporary exponents of this method are Gary Habermas and John Warwick Montgomery.

Historical apologetics as an apologetic method

While apologetic debates in the not-so-distant past reflected an assumption that there were clear dividing lines between apologetic methodologies, today it is commonly acknowledged that there are many grey areas and points of overlap. Historical apologetics is best understood as a species of the broad and diverse category of evidentialist apologetics – a category united by a common emphasis on the value of evidential argumentation in apologetics. As befitting its evidentialist heritage, historical apologetics shares this emphasis but is distinctive in its emphasis on the primacy of historical argumentation.

One important difference between historical apologetics and other apologetic methods concerns how historical evidences and arguments are used. Presuppositional apologists argue that the epistemic impact of evidence, historical or otherwise, is determined by the presuppositions central to one's world-view. Consequently, historical arguments for the truthfulness of the central claims of Christianity will be persuasive only to one who accepts the presuppositions of the Christian world-view. While historical apologists acknowledge the potency of presuppositions, they claim that a valid argument for the historicity of some aspect of Christianity can, in principle, transcend world-view boundaries.

A second difference between historical apologetics and other apologetic systems concerns how historical arguments are related to other kinds of arguments. Classical apologists, for example, acknowledge the value of historical arguments but insist that their value is contingent on the success of theistic arguments. They claim that it is problematic to speak of an event such as the resurrection as being an 'act of God' without first establishing that God exists and can 'act' in the way required. While historical apologists do not deny the usefulness of theistic arguments, their claim is that historical arguments can, on their own, in principle, establish the existence of God.

Thus far, historical apologetics has been described in rather generic terms – an apologetic system in which historical arguments play a fundamental role. But how does historical apologetics work practically? A variety of approaches are discernible.

One common method calls attention to fulfilled prophecy. For example, it is claimed that the probability that all the biblical prophecies regarding the Messiah would be fulfilled in a single person (*Jesus) *without supernatural design* is infinitesimally small. Another method builds a case for Christianity by appealing to well-supported, generally acknowledged facts about the life of Jesus.

And another concentrates on arguing for the general historical trustworthiness of the biblical text. It does this first by claiming that the authorship and dating of the text suggest that particular biblical authors were in a position to know the accuracy of material they present. Secondly, the historicity of specific texts is defended, the most important of which concern the life and teachings of Jesus Christ. This is done by appealing to both internal and external evidences – features internal to the text indicative of authenticity as well as archaeological findings and extra-biblical texts that corroborate events described in Scripture. Finally, historical apologists argue for the supernatural cause of the events described in the Bible, the existence of a theistic God and the truth of the central lines of Christian *theism.

Numerous objections to historical apologetics have been put forward. The most basic challenge is that *history itself cannot be known. A second, more specific, challenge concerns whether putatively miraculous events can be the object of historical knowledge. The final set of objections are epistemological in nature and concern whether historical evidences can accomplish the task of demonstrating the truthfulness of Christianity.

1. The subjectivity of history

The most general objection to the apologetic usefulness of historical evidences is that history itself is irreducibly subjective. On this view, there can be no objective account of history because history is fundamentally shaped by the perspectives, biases and values of the historian. Of course, it is undeniable that the recording of historical events is coloured by the historian's perspective. Even if the historian's goal is merely to describe a historical event, their background information, intended audience and values will inevitably influence their description. Most clearly, a historian's perspective can be discerned in what is not said, what is not investigated and in sources that are not consulted.

Does this lead to historical *relativism, a position which would certainly invalidate the practice of historical apologetics? It does not. First, taken in their most extreme form, the claims of the historical relativist are self-referentially incoherent. If all historical claims are invalid *because they are tainted by the subjective perspective of the historian*, then certainly the claims of the historical relativist are also invalid because they too are subjective, tainted by their (relativistic) perspective. A thoroughgoing historical relativism is no more defensible than naive historical *objectivism. Further, the fact that we can distinguish good history from bad means that historical accounts are not all equally invalidated by the historian's perspective. For example, while Tacitus certainly reflected a pro-imperial perspective, he is widely acknowledged to be a careful and accurate historian. *Josephus, likewise, is viewed as a careful recorder of events. Finally, the very fact that historical accounts are constantly being reinvestigated and rewritten entails the belief that we can get closer to the truth and present a more accurate account of what happened.

2. Miracles in history

A second challenge to historical apologetics grants that historical evidences can be used but argues that miraculous events cannot be investigated by history. Even among those who accept that *miracles are possible, some argue that miracle-claims cannot be the subject of historical research since, by definition, the agent to which a miracle is ascribed is a non-empirical, supernatural being.

Despite its surface clarity, it is not clear how this objection should be understood. Is the objection that historians cannot investigate the putatively miraculous events *at all*? This is clearly false. Historians can investigate the facts surrounding an alleged miracle without taking a stand on its supernatural origin. The resurrection of Jesus, for example, is associated with historical phenomena that are in principle verifiable, i.e. Jesus' existence, teaching and death.

Perhaps the objection is that investigating the *cause* of a miraculous event is beyond the province of the historian. But this matter concerns not only historical method, but also the philosophy of history. To be successful, the historical apologist must articulate a philosophy of history that is compatible with Christian theism and combat philosophies of history driven by a competing world-view. Take, for example, the Jesus Seminar's effort to propose a non-traditional perspective on the historical Jesus. Their voting method (the infamous coloured beads) is based on an understanding of what a historically reliable text would look like, an understanding expressed by their 'authenticity criteria'. But these authenticity criteria presuppose a philosophy of history that effectively rules out the miraculous as a viable possibility. Consequently, the possibility of the miraculous is a topic dealt with most effectively not at the level of authenticity criteria, but at the level of philosophy of history.

3. Epistemological challenges

A final challenge to historical apologetics is epistemological in nature. The essence of this objection is that historical evidences cannot accomplish the task envisioned by the historical apologist – they cannot comprise a good reason to accept the central claims of Christianity. The objection is that the historical evidences championed by the historical apologist do not in fact lead to the conclusion that the Christian God exists, and therefore they are insufficient to ground knowledge of the truth of the central claims of Christianity.

It is important to note that while the previous two objections entail (or at least imply) a denial of Christian theism, this challenge does not. A Christian might raise this objection against the historical apologist's use of historical evidences and in doing so object not to the historicity of the underlying events, but to the *epistemology assumed by the historical apologist's use of evidence.

A number of arguments have been offered to show the epistemological insufficiency of historical evidences. The first is what might be called *the problem of dwindling probabilities*. The essence of this objection is that historical arguments rest on a sequence of propositions where each proposition in the sequence provides grounding for the next. When considering the probability of the biblical account of the resurrection, the relevant sequence of propositions includes at least the following: Jesus existed – Jesus was arrested – Jesus was crucified and died – Jesus was buried in Joseph of Arimathea's tomb – After three days the tomb was found to be empty – Jesus appeared to his disciples in bodily form. Of course, the actual sequence of propositions is much longer and more complex. Equally certain is the utter implausibility of attaching any meaningful numeric values to probabilities of these propositions. But, for the purpose of illustration, suppose each of the propositions has a high probability of ·9. The problem is that the probability that Jesus was resurrected is not determined by averaging the propositions, but by multiplying them. The result is ·53, just a little better probability than the flip of a coin. Of course, the problem of dwindling probabilities is a problem for all varieties of apologists and for most religious traditions. But it is particularly problematic for the historical apologist who relies primarily on historical evidences.

Are matters really so bleak for the historical apologist? If the historical case for the resurrection rests on a single sequence of propositions, then the outlook is bleak indeed. But what if multiple sequences of propositions, each evidentially supportive of the resurrection, were proposed? In such a case, even though the probability of a conjunction or sequence of propositions is low, the probability of multiple conjunctions can still be relatively high. Ironically, the law that decreases the probability of a conjunction of propositions also increases the probability of a disjunction.

A second argument against the epistemological sufficiency of historical evidences is conceptually related to the first. This might be called *the problem of prior probabilities*. While the historical apologist believes that a putatively miraculous historical event can lend support to the belief that the Christian God exists, the historical apologist is only justified in deeming

a particular event to be miraculous if they have good reasons to believe the cause of the miracle – the Christian God – exists. It makes very little sense to speak about, say, the resurrection as an act of God without first establishing (or at least arguing for) the existence of a God who can perform actions like the resurrection. In other words, the probability that an event is miraculous, an act of God, is dependent upon the prior probability of God's existence.

This fact places the historical apologist in something of a predicament. If the historical evidence by itself is insufficient to demonstrate that a particular event is indeed miraculous, then either the distinctive aspect of this apologetic methodology – the primacy of historical as opposed to philosophical evidences – is undercut or the historical apologist's case is greatly weakened. However, because miracles play such an important role in historical apologetics, the most reasonable approach is to include non-historical arguments. This is why most contemporary historical apologists are not (what might be called) *pure* historical apologists – they use philosophical and even experiential evidences to augment their historical case. Habermas and Montgomery, for example, are better labelled as eclectic historical apologists.

A final philosophical objection to historical apologetics concerns the proper epistemic response to a successful historical argument. Suppose a set of historical evidences shows that the resurrection is probable. According to Alvin Plantinga, in such a case the proper epistemic response is not full-fledged belief, but something weaker, sometimes called 'acceptance'. When the meteorologist says the chance of rain tomorrow is 90%, one does not *believe* 'It will rain tomorrow'. They might accept the rationality of so believing or believe 'It would be prudent to bring an umbrella'. But these are different from believing the truth of the proposition 'It will rain'. Similarly, since historical arguments are inherently probabilistic, the proper conclusion would seem to be 'x is probable', not 'x is true'. The problem is that most accounts of knowledge, in addition to truth and either justification or warrant, require full-fledged belief. Knowing seems incompatible with mere acceptance.

The historical apologist can counter this argument in one of two ways. First, since it seems the historical apologist might use non-historical arguments (and thereby be an eclectic historical apologist), it is possible to answer this objection by augmenting historical evidence with an experiential component. While the historical evidences alone can only render the resurrection highly probable, the experience of the risen Jesus could provide a higher degree of conviction. A second response to Plantinga's objection is to argue that 'probable' belief is epistemically sufficient. Habermas, for example, agrees that providing apodictic *certainty is clearly impossible. The goal of the historical apologist is to show that a miracle (such as the resurrection) is highly probable *and* to argue that the evidence excludes viable rational or factual *doubt.

Ultimately, many (if not all) of the objections to historical apologetics as an apologetic method reflect contentious debates over the nature of belief, rationality, knowledge and history. Since these disagreements are not likely to be resolved anytime soon, the debate over the utility of historical apologetics will also continue.

Bibliography

J. Colwell, 'The Historical Argument for the Christian Faith: A Response to Alvin Plantinga', *International Journal for Philosophy of Religion*, 53 (2003), pp. 147–161; S. B. Cowan (ed.), *Five Views on Apologetics* (Grand Rapids, 2000); A. Dulles, *Theological Resources: A History of Apologetics* (London, 1971); R. D. Geivett and G. R. Habermas (eds.), *In Defense of Miracles* (Downers Grove, 1997); G. R. Habermas, *The History of Jesus, Ancient Evidence for the Life of Christ* (Nashville, 1984); T. L. Miethe and G. R. Habermas, *Why Believe? God Exists! Rethinking the Case for God and Christianity* (Joplin, 1993); J. W. Montgomery, *Christianity and History* (Minneapolis, 1986); *The Shape of the Past* (Edmonton, 1975).

J. BEILBY

HISTORICAL DIFFICULTIES IN THE NEW TESTAMENT

Readers of the NT may have problems believing that what is recounted as history actually happened just as it is described.

Examples of difficulties

Such difficulties may be of various kinds:

1. Contradictions between two or more accounts in Scripture of what are purportedly the same events. For example, in Luke 24 the ascension appears to have taken place immediately after the resurrection, but in Acts 1 it happened forty days later, and the accounts of the meeting of Paul and the apostles in Acts 15 and Gal. 2 differ considerably.

2. Contradictions between the scriptural account and the evidence from other archaeological or literary sources. For example, the census of Quirinius (Luke 2:1) took place well after the death of Herod, and the order of events in Acts 5:36–37 (Theudas and Judas) and in *Josephus is different.

3. Insufficient external evidence to substantiate the scriptural account of an event. For example, the alleged custom of the governor releasing a prisoner at Passover time is otherwise unattested (Mark 15:6; Luke 23:25).

4. The scriptural account contains impossible or unlikely events. These difficulties may be connected with natural or supernatural events. For example, the number of soldiers who accompanied Paul from Jerusalem to Caesarea seems disproportionately high (Acts 23:23). Of course, *miracles in general fall into this category.

5. It is not possible to see how the author could have known what had happened. For example, in Acts 26:30–32 Luke relates what was said behind closed doors as if an observer had been present.

6. It may be easier to account for the contents of a narrative in terms of literary considerations. For example, it is often argued that various features of the Pentecost story are literary motifs rather than actual events (Acts 2:3).

Categories of problems

Whatever their nature, historical difficulties may cause problems for the readers of the NT, because they call into question the historicity of the narratives in which they occur. Where the difficulties are comparatively minor and merely affect details of the narrative and not the basic account (e.g. differences in the names or number of people present on a particular occasion) there is no need to dismiss the whole account as fictitious. However, the discrepancies may be on such a scale that they raise substantial doubts as to whether the incident happened in the way that it is described, or indeed whether it happened at all. This may relate to a single incident or a series of incidents and cast doubts on the historicity of a person's life story.

The existence of difficulties of this kind also raises questions as to the historical reliability of the author, such as: Did he have reliable sources? Was he capable of evaluating the sources? Was he attempting to be reliable? It may even cause us to ask whether what we have before us is a narrative of what happened or a work of deliberate fiction and invention.

While questions of this kind, regarding the historicity of the events described and the reliability of the author, arise with any text that purports to record what happened, in the case of Scripture there is a further implication. According to the doctrine of the inspiration of Scripture, the writings (or the writers) of the NT were inspired by the Holy Spirit, and so they will be free from error. Does this include historical errors and inaccuracies? Would the established existence of even a single, incontrovertible error be sufficient to cast doubt on the doctrine of *biblical inspiration?

Analysing the difficulties

If we were dealing with 'ordinary' writers as opposed to 'inspired' writers, there would be no great problem, in principle, with recognizing their fallibility and taking it into account in evaluating the historicity of their accounts. Nobody is worried by minor errors in a historical work, and we learn to make due allowance for them, but major errors, or errors at key points, are a different matter. Similarly, when we come to Scripture, it would make no real difference to the story in Acts if there were minor inaccuracies in (let us say) the itinerary of Paul, but there would be serious consequences if the evidence for the resurrection of *Jesus could be shown to be unreliable.

A distinction must be drawn between historical accuracy and infallibility. Historians deal in probabilities and improbabilities, not in certainties, and therefore all that a historian can do is to state to an appropriate degree of probability whether a purported difficulty is real or otherwise, or whether a historical account is accurate or otherwise. No historian can prove absolutely whether an account is historical or otherwise. It is always possible that new evidence or a new interpretation of the evidence may be produced. The explanations given by historians are consequently always provisional. It follows from this that the historical infallibility or fallibility of

Scripture is something that cannot be proved absolutely. Acceptance of historical infallibility is a matter of faith, i.e. it is a decision that rests on something other than historical evidence. Certainly, there are considerations that may make it appear very reasonable or very unlikely, but the task of apologetics remains on the level of establishing the probabilities of the situation.

Two kinds of difficulties arise when we come to the supernatural. There is the problem of events taking place that are by ordinary standards incredible (such as a miraculous healing) and cases where the cause of an event is understood as divine (e.g. when the death of Herod is attributed to God in Acts 12:23).

In the case of extraordinary events there are two considerations. The first is that acceptance or rejection of a miraculous event rests in part upon whether the critic has a world-view that allows for the miraculous or not. If he or she does not, then all stories of miracles will be held to be fictitious or based on a mistaken understanding (i.e. either the alleged healing did not occur or it can be accounted for in some non-miraculous way). If he or she does accept the possibility of miracles, then the account may be accepted if the evidence is otherwise satisfactory.

Secondly, even if a historian considers it appropriate to allow the miraculous as part of his or her world-view as a historian, in any given instance it will still be incumbent upon him or her to ask whether the 'miraculous' explanation is more probable than some other kind of explanation. A decision on the likelihood of the miracle must be made, but it will not be dependent on a biased decision that the category of the miraculous is unacceptable.

In the case of how to 'explain' an ordinary event, it is again a question of whether a 'religious' account is acceptable, and much the same considerations apply as in the former case. To say that God struck Herod Agrippa down (Acts 12:23) is perfectly compatible with giving a 'natural' interpretation of his fatal illness, but whether it is an appropriate verdict would appear to be beyond the competence of a historian to decide.

Problems also arise with accounts that on the face of it are historical. According to some contemporary scholars, the Acts of the Apostles should be understood as historical fiction rather than as history. The early church, on this view, created an entertaining story of its beginnings, based, to be sure, on history, but taking great liberties with the story in order to make it both interesting and edifying.

Here again we have a situation where the historical difficulties are swept away by the claim that what we are reading is fiction rather than history (even if there is a modicum of history at the root of it). In this case, the question to be tackled is the broader one of whether the evidence is being correctly read. In the case of Acts it can be strongly maintained that Luke declares his intention of writing history, that the onus of proof is on those who would dispute this, that the alleged evidences of fiction rather than history are inconclusive and that the account can be understood as historical. To affirm that Acts is a historical work, of course, means that the historical difficulties found by critics are still there and have to be dealt with.

When we come to the area of historical errors, it is important to consider just what we would count as such. Inexactness is not necessarily error, and in many situations approximations are acceptable. A historian may recount what was said by somebody without striving for the precise wording, and may use abbreviation or paraphrase. This is particularly obvious in the parallel accounts of sayings of Jesus in the Gospels.

In this connection reference must be made to the problem of harmonization. A traditional method of dealing with different versions of a saying of Jesus is to add together the various forms so that each individual version can be seen as a selection out of a longer version of what Jesus said. Stories of incidents may be dealt with in the same way. This procedure is very risky (the *reductio ad absurdum* is in the reconstruction of Peter's denial, according to which he actually denies Jesus six times, but each of the Gospels records only a [different] selection of three of the occasions). Not all harmonization is so obviously flawed as this example, and there are certainly cases where it is an appropriate procedure, but often it makes better sense to recognize that the evangelists edited their accounts for their own purposes. In other words, some apparent historical discrepancies between parallel accounts are to be ascribed to the freedom of editors rather than to actual historical differences. A conspicuous example in Acts is the fact that the three accounts of Paul's conversion vary among themselves, but the fact that they are all the

product of one author shows that he did not regard them as discrepant. Luke was too careful a writer for us to say that he simply did not notice the differences.

We should remember that discrepancies between biblical and non-biblical sources are not always due to error in the biblical version. Josephus was not always correct, but had his own biases, misinformation and carelessness. Also, new discoveries have been shown to confirm the biblical narrative or resolve apparent contradictions between narratives; e.g. from W. M. Ramsay to C. J. Hemer evidence has been compiled that eases many of the problems with the background and setting of the story in Acts.

A particular problem for the Gospels is the way in which scholars have tended to lose Jesus behind a web of developing traditions of what he said and did, and attempt to reconstruct the way in which the traditions changed and evolved in transmission. Here there is the danger of thinking that if we can give an explanation of why a writer may have said something in a particular way, this is sufficient to show that he invented it rather than that he recorded it in that way because that is how it actually happened. In such cases, there has to be painstaking examination of the evidence. It can, however, safely be said that to a very considerable extent equally competent scholars have been able to demonstrate good grounds for arguing that the accounts in the Gospels give a substantially reliable account of what Jesus actually said and did.

We can see now that the types of problem outlined at the very beginning of this article do not negate the historical reliability of the NT documents in which they are found: Luke could have condensed his narrative in one account for literary reasons and expanded it in another (1); Gamaliel may have got the order of incidents wrong but this is not a mistake that affects the force of his argument (2); fresh evidence or new interpretation may yet surface to deal with the problem of Quirinius (e.g. should we translate 'the census before Quirinius was governor'?) and the Passover release (opinions differ on whether a Mishnah regulation reflects it) (3); a force of 300 men is perhaps not excessive if an ambush of forty terrorists was expected (4); there is nothing wrong with Luke using his skill and knowledge to reconstruct the gist of what was said behind closed doors in the palace (5);

nor is it impossible that there are elements of symbolism in the way that a narrative is told, and frankly the historicity of the descent of the Spirit is far more important than whether there were literal tongues of fire on the heads of the disciples (6). We do well with *Calvin to recollect that the Holy Spirit was not too worried over trifling matters.

Bibliography

F. F. Bruce, *The New Testament Documents: Are They Reliable?* (London, 1943); C. L. Blomberg, *The Historical Reliability of the Gospels* (Leicester and Downers Grove, 1987); C. J. Hemer, *The Book of Acts in the Setting of Hellenistic History* (Tübingen, 1989); V. P. Long, *The Art of Biblical History* (Grand Rapids, 1994; repr. in M. Silva [ed.], *Foundations of Contemporary Interpretation* [Leicester and Grand Rapids, 1997]).

I. H. MARSHALL

HISTORICAL DIFFICULTIES IN THE OLD TESTAMENT

Literary-critical studies of the historical narratives of the OT, and historical-critical studies utilizing other historical sources, have revealed various discrepancies which, in the view of some scholars, cast serious doubts on the historicity of the biblical accounts. Such scholars tend to see the OT narratives as late and tendentious, and their value for a modern, critical *history of ancient Israel as consisting only in the information they contain regarding their authors and what may be deduced from them concerning the circumstances and interests of their day.

For some, the OT is simply a source of religious ideas, to be either moralized or spiritualized. The OT, however, does not merely present us with religious ideas, any more than it just records events. It presents us with theological history, combining both the record of events and the theological interpretation of those events, expressed in terms of the outworking of God's redemptive purposes for his people in history. This being the case, Christian faith, as V. P. Long remarks, 'can never entirely insulate itself from the findings of historical study'. He goes on to point out what is at stake in the debate regarding biblical history: 'Faith does not require that the factuality of the biblical events be proven (such proof

is, at any rate, seldom possible). On the other hand, should it be conclusively shown that the core events of redemptive history did not happen, not only would the veracity of the Bible be seriously undermined, but the fall of historicity would inevitably bring down Christian faith with it.'

A supposed lack of literary congruence or coherence in OT texts is sometimes taken as grounds for questioning the historicity of the events they record, e.g. the account of Saul's rise to power in 1 Sam. 8 – 12 seems to contain discrepant attitudes towards the monarchy and multiple and contradictory accounts of Saul's accession to the throne of Israel, which supposedly prevent us from taking it seriously as history. Difficulties of this kind, however, can often be resolved by careful and patient exegesis of the text. Long's detailed treatment of this particular passage (*The Art of Biblical History*, ch. 6) offers an exegesis which reconciles the discrepant attitudes towards the monarchy and argues successfully for the literary coherence of its multiple accession accounts.

Difficulties at the literary-exegetical level can also arise when different biblical writers appear to offer divergent accounts of the same story. All history writing takes place inevitably from a particular standpoint in time and, consciously or unconsciously, reflects the writer's own ideology and/or purpose in writing. For example, Samuel–Kings addresses the exiles and interprets to them the reason for the disastrous fall of Jerusalem and their exile to Babylon. The Chronicler, however, addresses those who had returned to the land after the exile, and assures them of God's covenant-faithfulness and his continuing care and concern for them as his people. These differences of standpoint in time, audience addressed and theological purpose largely account for the different selection and treatment of material in the two accounts. Long explains the relation thus: 'The Chronicler is not only himself acquainted with Samuel–Kings but apparently assumes a similar acquaintance on the part of his audience. This frees him to present his didactic history in creative ways, sometimes making explicit what may have been only implicit in his sources.'

Historical difficulties of a different kind occur when there are conflicts between the biblical text and other external literary sources, e.g. in chronological or numerical matters. The nature of this extra-biblical material, its date and its reliability all need to be subjected to careful historical investigation and assessment. For example, the annals of the Assyrian kings, considered a significant historical source in reconstructing the history of Assyria and its adjacent lands, are themselves not lacking in ideology, but served a clear propaganda purpose in their day. We should bear this in mind when we are comparing their account with that recorded in the book of Kings. As Iain Provan points out, 'There are, in fact, no grounds for granting the Assyrian sources any epistemological primacy in principle in our striving for knowledge about Israel's past.'

The same need for careful investigation and evaluation is true also in dealing with archaeological material, and the limitations of this type of evidence need to be borne in mind. By its very nature archaeology is able to give only a partial picture and one that is open to a variety of interpretations. Provan reminds us that 'archaeological remains ... are of themselves mute. They do not speak for themselves: they have no story to tell, and no truth to communicate. It is archaeologists who speak about them, testifying to what it is that they have found and placing the finds within an interpretive framework that bestows upon them meaning and significance.' However, 'The whole business of correlating archaeological finds with the specifics of the past as described by texts is, in fact, fraught with difficulty. Interpretation inevitably abounds as to what has been in fact found.' Long, too, notes that most of what archaeology unearths illuminates 'life conditions in general and not specific events'. Scholars who reject the historicity of the biblical accounts of early Israel on archaeological grounds frequently do so on the principle that 'absence of evidence is evidence of absence'. But Provan observes: 'The absence of evidence on the ground for events described by a text cannot necessarily be interpreted as evidence of the absence of those events, even if a site has been correctly identified.'

In the middle years of the last century, biblical archaeologists like G. E. Wright, W. F. Albright and J. Bright held a generally positive view of the historical reliability of the OT accounts of the Patriarchs, the exodus and Israel's entry into the land of Canaan and subsequent history. They regarded the findings of archaeology, or 'biblical archaeology' as it

was then commonly called, as broadly substantiating the biblical account of Israel's history. In the last third of the century, however, many of their conclusions were called into question on archaeological grounds. Scholars such as T. L. Thompson and N. P. Lemche, of the so-called 'Copenhagen School', and P. R. Davies and K. W. Whitelam of the University of Sheffield, propounded instead a radical, more sceptical view of the OT's historical trustworthiness. According to these scholars, the OT historical records are late productions, written for ideological reasons, and are, therefore, to be regarded as mostly fictional. Lemche thus wrote: 'We decline to be led by the biblical account [of early Israel] and instead regard it, like other legendary materials, as essentially ahistorical, that is, as a source which only exceptionally can be verified by other information.' Further, he considered that 'the traditional materials about David cannot be regarded as an attempt to write history, as such. Rather, they represent an ideological programmatic composition which defends the assumption of power by the Davidic dynasty.' And Thompson avers confidently, 'There is no more "ancient Israel". History no longer has room for it. This we do know.'

According to these historians, the biblical evidence must be assessed, not on its own terms, but only in relation to the corpus of historical knowledge established independently of it. Thompson asserts that 'a valid history of Israel's origins must be written within a historical geography of Palestine, based primarily on Palestinian archaeology and ancient Near Eastern studies ... Israel's own origin tradition is radically irrelevant to writing such a history'. Thus, Israel's own historical testimony is regarded as, at best, attesting only to the personal interests or political agenda of the writers, not to the true 'facts' of the matter, the 'real' history. This has been described as 'the hermeneutics of suspicion'.

Provan has argued forcefully, against this prejudicial dismissal of the evidential value of the OT historiography, that the biblical evidence must be counted as forming part of the corpus of historical knowledge, except for cases where it can be shown to be unhistorical. J. K. Hoffmeier, likewise, concurs that there has been too much condescension and suspicion of biblical documents during the past couple of decades by historians and biblical scholars who have treated the Bible more critically than other ancient literature. The OT should be viewed as a generally credible witness, whose testimony, while open to questioning, is to be accepted as true unless it can be shown to be in error. Much other valuable, detailed work has also been produced in response to the scepticism of the revisionists. A helpful discussion of the evidence relating to the patriarchal period, which takes into account the criticisms of Thompson and J. van Seters, may be found in M. J. Selman, 'Comparative Customs and the Patriarchal Age' and D. J. Wiseman, 'Abraham Reassessed', in A. R. Millard and D. J. Wiseman (eds.), *Essays on the Patriarchal Narratives* (Leicester, 1980).

W. G. Dever, in *What Did the Biblical Writers Know and When Did They Know It? What Archaeology Can tell Us About the Reality of Ancient Israel* (Grand Rapids and Cambridge, 2001), has also argued on archaeological grounds against the revisionists. He claims that the 'convergences' between the biblical texts and the archaeological and other extra-biblical evidences support the view that the biblical writers are recording real history, both in outline and in many points of detail, and that they must have had access to historical memories if not historical texts. He notes also, on the basis of these convergences, that if the biblical texts purporting to tell of pre-exilic times were written in the Persian or Greek period (as the revisionists claim), then their authors have made a remarkably successful and accurate job of archaizing their accounts. For Dever, 'While the Hebrew Bible in its present, heavily edited form cannot be taken at face value as history in the modern sense, it nevertheless contains much history.' For his part, he has little doubt that ancient Israel really existed, from at least the thirteenth to the seventh century BC.

K. A. Kitchen argues that there is genuine evidence of Israelite/Jewish culture from 2000 to 400 BC in the biblical texts, and he supports this with an impressive array of circumstantial evidence from Egyptian and other ancient materials confirming the credibility of the biblical history. J. K. Hoffmeier, in *Israel in Egypt: The Evidence for the Authenticity of the Exodus Tradition* (Oxford, 1996), similarly, has argued that 'in the absence of direct archaeological or historical evidence, one can make a case for the plausibility of the biblical reports based on the supporting evidence'. His extraordinarily detailed discussion of almost every aspect of Israel's presence in Egypt and of the geography and topography of the exodus is a *tour de force*, which draws on a wide range of Egyptian sources – archaeological, geographical, textual and pictorial – to make that case very convincingly.

The sceptics' approach to the evidence is rooted in the *rationalism of the *Enlightenment. Their philosophical/epistemological presuppositions are evident, for instance, when they dismiss any biblical text containing reference to divine, miraculous intervention as having no evidential value in an inquiry into the 'real' history of Israel. The rationalism in Enlightenment thinking, which stems from the old classical *foundationalism, applied to the area of biblical studies, resulted in a divorce between history and *theology and a profound scepticism regarding the historicity of the biblical narratives. This tide of scepticism receded only for a while under the short-lived impact of discoveries made in the field of biblical archaeology. After this interlude, in which the moderating influence of the 'Wright-Albright-Bright' school achieved something of a consensus, P. R. Davies describes a 'paradigm shift', which has recently taken place in scholarly approaches to ancient Israel. 'We are enjoying', he writes, 'a climate in which a non-theological paradigm is beginning to claim a place alongside the long-dominant theological one. The new paradigm emerges by the simple effort of demonstrating that the old paradigm is a paradigm, sustained by consent and claiming a truth for itself to which it is not entitled.' But Davies' new paradigm, for which he implicitly claims a truth to which it supposedly is entitled, is at heart simply a return to the old rationalism.

Certainly, there are historical problems with the OT text that have not yet been successfully resolved. That such difficulties remain, both in interpreting the biblical texts as literature and in understanding them in relation to other evidences, is perhaps inevitable, given the span of history covered, the complexity of the evidence and the distance from us in time of the events concerned. This fact, however, should not be taken as grounds for doubting the reliability of the OT's witness, but should be used as a spur to further study and investigation of the text, both internally and in relation to the external evidences, from the standpoint of '*faith* seeking understanding'.

Bibliography

C. Bartholomew, C. S. Evans, M. Healy and M. Rae (eds.), 'Behind the Text': History and Biblical Interpretation (Grand Rapids and Carlisle, 2003); K. A. Kitchen, On the Reliability of the Old Testament (Grand Rapids, 2003); V. P. Long, The Art of Biblical History (Leicester, 1994; repr. in M. Silva [ed.], Foundations of Contemporary Interpretation [Grand Rapids, 1996]); V. P. Long, G. J. Wenham and D. W. Baker (eds.), Windows into Old Testament History: Evidence, Argument, and the Crisis of 'Biblical History' (Grand Rapids, 2002).

E. ROWLANDS

HISTORICAL JESUS, see JESUS, HISTORICAL

HISTORY

Christianity is a historical religion in the sense that its claims rest on events that took place in the past. The redemption of the world was achieved not through some process beyond time but through the work of *Jesus Christ, God manifest in the flesh, who lived at a specific time in history. Faith in him therefore entails beliefs about the incarnation, about the events of his life and about the accessibility of the past. Christians have always wished to repudiate the contention of the German *Enlightenment theorist G. E. *Lessing that contingent truths of history can never be the proofs of necessary truths of reason. The Bible, furthermore, presents the historical process as a grand panorama extending from creation to final judgment. God operates in and over the decisions of human beings to work out his purposes. His providence includes a general dimension, through which he directs the overall pattern of history, and a particular aspect, by which he intervenes at specific junctures in order to bring judgment on sin and mercy to sinners. Although the extent to which these junctures outside biblical times are discernible has not been agreed among Christians, the reality of providential rule has often been defended. *Augustine's classic theology of history The City of God is a vindication of divine support for the community of believers against their opponents in every age; and the English Methodist historian Sir Herbert Butterfield demonstrated the legitimacy of interpreting the past in providential terms in his Christianity and History (London, 1949). Specific Christian beliefs have also given rise to bodies of literature evaluating their historical plausibility. The resurrection has been a focus of debate, with orthodox believers contending for its historicity on the a priori grounds of the possibility of miracle and the empirical grounds of the circumstantial evidence.

The credibility of the Bible has been endlessly discussed since the eighteenth century, with its champions arguing that it faithfully reflects developments of the times that can be established from independent sources. And the record of the Christian church has been subjected to rigorous scrutiny, with its defenders claiming that notwithstanding the crimes committed in its name that testify to human fallenness, the divine origin of the church is evident because it has done more good than bad for the welfare of humanity. History continues to be the arena of much Christian apologetic.

Objectivity

The issue of the objectivity of the discipline of history has frequently arisen in broader debate. Critics of the Christian faith – and theologians too – have commonly supposed that professional historians would have used more demanding standards of evidence than were assumed by credulous believers, whether in biblical times or afterwards. They go on to assert that Christian beliefs are indefensible by proper canons of historical analysis. That stance, however, is often built on the premise that the discipline of history has an agreed method that enables the researcher to achieve something approaching *certainty about the past. On this understanding, history is a science, treating human beings as no different from nature as an object of investigation. By identifying causes and effects, it is capable of arriving at truths that are hardly less final than those so successfully established by the natural sciences. History, on this view, is a social science, seeking to establish the general laws that govern human behaviour. All that is required is a rigorous exclusion of any bias that might contaminate the judgment of the historian in evaluating the evidence. Objectivity, which is sometimes understood as excluding religious belief, is the condition of attaining a valid account of the past.

Such an estimate of the historian's task, however, is partisan, an expression of a point of view that is sometimes called positivism. The positivist school of history, rooted in the Enlightenment of the eighteenth century, has been challenged by theorists of history writing from a different perspective that owes more to subsequent developments associated with philosophical *idealism. It argues that since human beings are unique in possessing ideas, they have to be studied in a different way from natural phenomena. Their behaviour is charged with intention and so cannot be reduced to a matter of causes and effects. The purpose of the historian is not to establish regularities but to understand the complex interplay of intention and outcome in human affairs. Hence, history is not a science but, as some have claimed, an aesthetic enterprise, appreciating the uniqueness of individuals and the diversity of their situations. R. G. Collingwood's *The Idea of History* (Oxford, 1946) is a classic exposition of this point of view. Although the distinct philosophical standpoint of idealism has to be allowed for as much as that of its opponents, its case against the positivists shows at least that their assumptions deserve to be challenged. Their supposition that there is a single technique, the method of science, by which historians may uncover the truth about the past is unjustified. Historians will write accounts of the past that reflect their own personalities, for their minds are active in evaluating the evidence before them. Thus the gospel writers, however unscientific, were presenting legitimate historical accounts of the figure of Jesus. They cannot be ruled out of court on the grounds of their lack of objectivity.

Postmodernism

The most pressing intellectual challenge to Christian beliefs about history in the twenty-first century comes, however, not from positivism but from postmodernism. That school of thought must be seen as a stance rejecting the assumption that meaning is uncomplicated. There is no intrinsic bond, it holds, between *language and the things it describes. Discourse is of fundamental importance, but the words of which it is composed have no more than an arbitrary connection with what they signify. Authors cannot stamp an intended meaning on the texts that they compose. Hence, in history, accounts of the past cannot recover the reality of what once took place. Sources have no fixed meaning, but can be interpreted in a wide variety of ways. History, according to one of the leading French postmodernist theorists Roland Barthes, is 'a parade of signifiers masquerading as a collection of facts'. The best way of gaining an appreciation of the past is to have more than one interpretation of any phenomenon. Ultimately it is impossible to set a boundary between history and fiction, for the two merge into one another. There can be no set of criteria for determining what is true knowledge of the past, and the exercise of trying to identify such criteria is dismissed as the fruitless enterprise of '*foundationalism'. When history began to be swayed by postmodernist assumptions in the late twentieth century, it took what has been called a 'linguistic turn', shifting from the traditional study of events to the examination of the language used both in the past and by historians. These developments were expressed in an early and highly sophisticated form by Hayden White in his *Metahistory* (Baltimore, 1974).

This new attitude to history has provoked responses that have ranged between enthusiastic welcome and angry rebuttal. An analysis based on a Christian point of view might propose that the best way of appreciating the significance of the postmodernist phenomenon is to trace it back to its intellectual roots in the thought of *Nietzsche, *Freud and other theorists of around the close of the nineteenth century. The analysis might go on to suggest that an evaluation of postmodernist history in Christian terms might applaud its self-critical approach to questions of method but propose a higher estimate of the link between words and things in a universe ordered by God. It might wish to imitate the postmodernist concern for the close scrutiny of discourse but insist that texts can express the intention of their authors. And it might accept the postmodernist contention that rules of evidence are subject to change over time and so do not guarantee the attainment of truth but, nevertheless, hold that evidence can sufficiently discipline our accounts to enable them to convey authentic knowledge of the past. For these reasons, it might be suggested, the Christian church may still have confidence that its Scriptures can be read in accordance with the wishes of their human authors as revealing the reality of God's dealings with his world.

Bibliography

D. W. Bebbington, *Patterns in History* (Vancouver, 2000); R. J. Evans, *In Defence of History* (London, 1997); D. P. Fuller, *Easter Faith and History* (London, 1968); V. A. Harvey, *The Historian and the Believer* (London, 1967).

D. W. BEBBINGTON

HODGE, CHARLES

Charles Hodge (1797–1878) was arguably the most influential of nineteenth-century American theologians. Firmly in the *Calvinistic-Presbyterian tradition, he sought to defend evangelical orthodoxy against what he saw as dangers arising both from the excesses of revivalism and from the errors of post-Kantian liberal theology. His works included commentaries, sermons, numerous articles on theological and philosophical themes, popular apologetics, and his *magnum opus*, the massive, three-volume *Systematic Theology*.

Faced with the anti-intellectualism of the revivalists and the insistence of many post-Kantians that theology had nothing to do with the sphere of 'ordinary reason', Hodge defended the reasonableness of the Christian revelation and the role of the mind in receiving God's truth. Perhaps because his stance gave rise to the strongly rationalistic apologetic of the later Princeton school, Hodge has been accused of excessive *rationalism. In fact, he was careful to insist on a holistic approach to apologetics. Both the 'head' and the 'heart', intellect and feelings, thought and will, are involved in the receiving of God's truth. Any act of knowing involves the whole person, the 'understanding, heart, conscience, and experience'; 'neither the cognition without the feeling, nor the feeling without the cognition' (*Princeton Review* 23 [1851], p. 343).

Hodge held that no intellectual grasp of a theological truth was valid without the accompanying work of the *Holy Spirit (*Systematic Theology*, 2.660). Human persons cannot be divided into separate faculties, allowing the religious part to operate independently of the intellect. Nor can knowledge itself be divided, allowing Christian beliefs to operate independently of 'scientific truth'. Hodge, therefore, saw no conflict between God's revelation and scientific truth. Where *science and revealed Christianity appear to disagree, a resolution must be sought either by rejecting the unproved theories of the scientists (which are, after all, 'constantly changing') or, where theories are well established, by revising the interpretation of Scripture (as happened in the case of Copernicus). Since the same God is the author of creation and of revelation, Hodge was confident that all conflict could ultimately be resolved (*Systematic Theology*, 1.55–59).

Hodge did much to defend evangelical orthodoxy against encroaching liberalism. Despite a different context, his insistence on a holistic approach to our reception and defence of Christian truth sounds a note that needs to be heard today.

Bibliography

P. Hicks, *The Philosophy of Charles Hodge* (Lewiston, 1997); C. Hodge, *Systematic Theology* (New York and London, 1871–73).

P. HICKS

HOLOCAUST

The term holocaust is derived from the Greek (*holokaustos*) for a completely burned offering (e.g. the LXX of Lev. 6:23). According to Yehuda Bauer, the word first came into use in the English language between 1957 and 1959 to describe the extermination of six million European Jews under the Nazi regime from 1941 to 1945 in a concerted attempt at the destruction of an entire race. The name of one of the death camps in which this programme of genocide was carried out, Auschwitz, is often used as a symbol of the total horror of Hitler's 'Final Solution' (*Die Endlosung*).

Another term, used particularly by Jewish writers, to designate the mass murders of this period is the Hebrew word *shoah*. According to Uriel Tal (cited in Rubenstein and Roth, p. 6), it was first used by Polish Jews as early as 1940 to describe their plight under Hitler. The word, however, has its roots in the Hebrew Bible, being found in Job (30:14 'ruins', NIV), the Psalms, and Isaiah (10:3 'disaster', NIV). It can refer both to the destruction of Israel at the hands of surrounding nations and to the distress and desolation experienced by an individual. However, as Holocaust is more commonly used in English, it will be employed throughout the remainder of this article. By extension of meaning the term is now often applied to the mass destruction of large groups of human beings as, for example, in Cambodia, during the Pol Pot regime (see W. Shawcross, *The Quality of Mercy – Cambodia, Holocaust and Modern Conscience* [London, 1985]).

It should not be forgotten that many others besides Jews perished in the death camps, frequently under the all-embracing designation *untermenschen* ('subhuman') – the mentally and physically handicapped, homosexuals and lesbians, Sinti and Roma ('Gypsies'), Arab or Afro-Germans, Jehovah Witnesses, and Soviet prisoners of war. Though the number of non-Jews who perished was not nearly on the same scale as that of the Jewish victims, it was not inconsiderable – probably more than a million at least.

During the 1930s the Nazi regime acted to exclude from society members of three designated groups – the handicapped, Jews and Gypsies. The Government enacted a series of laws that targeted and penalized these groups. Under these laws the handicapped were forcibly sterilized and often dispatched by so-called 'euthanasia'. Jews were forced out of the professions and their businesses were attacked. Gypsies were incarcerated in so-called Gypsy camps. With some notable exceptions the major churches, Protestant and Catholic, acquiesced in the killing of the mentally and physically disabled. Euthanasia thus served as a model for the Final Solution which, when Hitler gave the order, issued in the destruction of the Jews on a mass scale. (For treatments of pre-Holocaust euthanasia in Germany see Burleigh in Cesarani, ch. 2).

Interpretations of the Holocaust

How the Holocaust is to be understood has been, and continues to be, the subject of a lively debate that shows no sign of ending.

Some scholars adopt an historical approach as they seek to understand how the Final Solution came about, how it was implemented, and how its Jewish victims experienced it. Representative of this approach are Raul Hilberg's *The Destruction of European Jews* (New York, 1985) and Martin Gilbert's *The Holocaust: The Jewish Tragedy* (London, 1986). The latter work by means of massive documentation builds up an overwhelming picture of the horror of the Holocaust. Such studies, emphasizing as they do the politics, economics and social changes that helped to shape the Holocaust, are essential to any sound approach to it.

Other scholars focus upon Jewish-Christian relationships in the story of the Holocaust. They see its prehistory as rooted in the prevailing anti-Semitism of such 'Christian' nations as Germany and Poland, fostered by the notorious anti-Jewish utterances of Martin Luther and expressed in the enforced conversions encouraged by the Catholic Church (see Robert Browning's poem 'Holy Cross Day'). The Holocaust is seen as the appalling culmination of the long tradition of Christian anti-Semitism, as for example in Franklin H. Littell's *The Crucifixion of the Jews* (New York, 1975). The Roman Catholic theologian Rosemary Radford Ruether in her *Faith and Fratricide: The Theological Roots of Anti-Semitism* (Seabury, 1974) goes even further. She charges that the NT itself, particularly the Gospel of John, exhibits an anti-*Judaism that constantly finds expression in anti-Semitism. Though her arguments are by no means universally accepted, they have provoked an intense debate (for a brief rebuttal see Keith, pp. 34–55).

Issues raised by the Holocaust

For many scholars the Holocaust raises profound philosophical and theological issues, which purely historical approaches leave out of account. The testimony of survivors raises such issues. Some became convinced atheists for whom the absence of God during their suffering was the evidence of his non-existence. Others, such as Hugo Gryn, viewed the Holocaust as an unprecedented explosion of *evil over good: 'It was a denial of God. It was a denial of man. It was the destruction of the world in miniature form' (quoted in Gilbert, p. 826).

From a more philosophical standpoint some have argued that the Holocaust is 'uniquely unique' (Roy Eckhardt). It marks such a break in human *history that history can no longer be understood as linear or continuous, or as a progression from lower to higher forms of civilization. Thus, the Jewish theologian Arthur A. Cohen applies Rudolf Otto's term *tremendum* to the Holocaust in order to emphasize its vastness and terror.

This approach raises problems. First, if the employment of historical method brings out the Holocaust's uniqueness, the most that can be claimed is that it is unique in history *thus far*, not that it can be removed from the realm of history. Secondly, some Jewish scholars argue, with justification, that the claim that the Holocaust is unique has been used since the 1967 war to deflect any criticism of Israel's treatment of Palestinian Jews. Thus Norman G. Finkelstein, whose parents were survivors of the death camps, argues that 'it has been used to justify criminal policies of the Israeli state and US support for these policies' (pp. 7–8). Thirdly, in the light of the biblical teaching that humans have a staggering capacity for evil, it would be foolhardy to believe that something like the Holocaust could never happen again.

For many thinkers the terrible events of the Holocaust prompt the question 'Where was God?' Some, such as Richard Rubenstein, declare that 'After Auschwitz it is impossible to believe in God.' Others, such as Arthur Cohen, argue that it is no longer possible to believe in the omnipotent God of traditional theology. Yet others, such as Jürgen Moltmann maintain that to theologize after Auschwitz is a futile exercise: God was not absent but participating in the sufferings of the victims because he is the crucified God, not the impassible God of traditional Christian theology. Attractive though Moltmann's thesis is, it is not without problems, especially in view of Christian complicity in the Nazi programme of extermination. Yet the issue of theodicy will not go away. It remains to haunt the minds of thinkers – Christian or otherwise.

In the light of the Holocaust it is inevitable that the evangelization of Jewish people should be called into question. From the Jewish side it is sometimes claimed that to work for the conversion of Jews to Christ is a form of genocide, a crime against the Jewish race. No-one was more proud of his Jewish heritage than the apostle Paul (Rom. 9:4–5; 11:1), yet he could write 'my heart's desire and prayer to God for the Israelites is that they may be saved' (Rom. 10:1). To exclude Jews from the mission of the church to spread the gospel of Christ is in fact to be guilty of a form of anti-Semitism as it effectively shuts them out from the blessings of the gospel. But having said this, all Jewish evangelism today must be undertaken in deep penitence, with great sensitivity to Jewish culture and with a readiness to accept that church life be incarnated in distinctively Jewish forms interpreted in the light of the gospel.

There are other issues raised by the Holocaust that require mention. First, there is the power of propaganda, forever associated with the name of Hitler's minister, Joseph Goebbels. Of its subtlety we need to be constantly aware. Then there is the practice of scapegoating a group of people like the Jews, holding them responsible for the economic and social ills of a nation. Scapegoating has not disappeared with the closure of the death camps. It is all too alive today.

To categorize Jews as subhuman made it easier for the Nazis to exterminate them. Is the description of the human foetus as 'just a bunch of cells' but not having truly human status, so far removed from this? And can it ever be permissible to describe someone in a comatose state as a 'vegetable'?

Bibliography

M. Burleigh, *Ethics and Extermination – Reflections on Nazi Genocide* (Cambridge, 1997); D. Cesarani (ed.), *The Final Solution – Origins and Implementation* (London, 1994); N. G. Finkelstein, *The Holocaust Industry – Reflections on the Exploitation of Jewish Suffering* (London and New York, 2000); M. Gilbert, *The Holocaust – The Jewish Tragedy* (London, 1987); G. Keith, *Hated Without A Cause? – A Survey of Anti-Semitism* (Carlisle, 1997); R. L. Rubenstein and J. K. Roth, *Approaches to Auschwitz – The Legacy of the Holocaust* (Atlanta and London, 1987).

D. P. KINGDON

HOLY SPIRIT IN APOLOGETICS

In Christian *theology the Holy Spirit is the third person of the triune Godhead. As the Niceno-Constantinopolitan Creed of AD 325/ 381 states, 'We believe in the Holy Spirit, the Lord, the giver of life, who proceeds from the Father and the Son. With the Father and the Son is worshipped and glorified.' The doctrine of the *Trinity is grounded on the biblical *revelation (e.g. Matt. 28:18–20; 2 Cor. 13:14), and any understanding of the divine Spirit's role in apologetics needs to appeal to the foundational documents of the faith. Scripture reveals the Spirit to be the effective agent of God's ongoing engagement with creation (Gen. 1:2; Pss. 33:6; 104:30). The Spirit, in particular, plays a crucial role in making the character, ways and plans of God known to the creatures made in the divine image. God makes himself known by word and Spirit both in the OT and in the NT (Num. 11:25; Luke 1:67). There should be no surprise then at the idea that the Spirit is integral to the communication and defence of the gospel.

In the witness of the Fourth Gospel, the Spirit is another like *Jesus, who continues Christ's mission to the world, *witnesses to the *truth about Jesus and puts the world on trial for its unbelief (John 14 – 16). He is the agent of conviction who convinces the world of its sin, of Christ's righteousness and of judgment (John 16:7–11). He convicts or convinces the world of sin because human unbelief in Jesus is blameworthy, of righteousness because Jesus returns to the Father and is thus vindicated, and of judgment because the prince of the world stands condemned. The Greek word translated 'convince' or 'convict' may also be translated as 'expose'. If it is taken in this sense then Jesus is saying that the object of the Spirit's work in this context is the disciples. The Spirit, as the advocate of Jesus, will show the disciples where the world has been wrong about Jesus.

Whichever the correct translation, Jesus made it clear that the disciples were also to bear witness to him and that as they did so the Spirit would testify along with them (John 15:26–27). Thus the disciples too continue the mission of Jesus. He sends them as he himself was sent (John 20:19–23). At the very least this means in the context of the Fourth Gospel that the disciples would have the Spirit's presence and *power for the mission just as Jesus did.

The communication of the gospel or good news about Jesus Christ is the first order priority according to the NT witness. So much so that the oral gospel is over and over again referred to as the 'word of God' (1 Thess. 2:13; 1 Pet. 1:22–25). The early Christians first spoke of what had happened amongst them, the coming of Jesus, his death, resurrection and expected return, and they shared this with both Jew and Gentile and invited their hearers to repentance and faith. They were not, however, alone in this task, for the promised presence of the Holy Spirit was with them, as the Acts shows in numerous places (Acts 1:4; 2:1–4; 5:32).

Sharing these facts about Jesus soon begged the important question of why the hearers should believe the report. In the NT, apology is a second order activity that arises from the first order one of sharing the good news. In Peter's language, they needed to be ready to give a defence of the hope that was in them (1 Pet. 3:15). This hope was based on the resurrection of Christ from the dead (1 Pet. 1:3–5. In the Gospels Jesus had promised his disciples the Spirit's presence with them during persecution, when the difficult questions would be put to them (Mark 13:11). The witness of Stephen, full of the Spirit, in Acts 6 – 7 provides a case in point.

The Creator God delights to work through what he has made. He uses creatures to affect other creatures. In the OT God used a strong east wind to drive the waters back so that Israel might safely escape the pursuing Egyptians (Exod. 14:21). In our era he uses our proclamation of the good news whether in formal meeting or informal conversation to make known his saving work in Christ. He uses our arguments to convince others of the plausibility of that news (a possibly true claim) and credibility of that news (a worthy of belief claim). *Pascal captured the dialectic well when he wrote that God puts his grace into our hearts sometimes using proof to do so. The Creator and Redeemer uses creaturely means – like proclamation, witness and argument – to achieve his ends. The apostle Paul's argument for the resurrection in 1 Cor. 15 illustrates the point. Some in Corinth had their doubts and so Paul presents a cumulative case of many strands: the gospel of resurrection was part of the apostolic tradition that had been delivered to the Corinthians (v. 3); the resurrection was according to the OT (vv. 3–4); many had seen the risen Christ including Paul himself (vv. 5–8); and if the resurrection had not happened then Paul had been misrepresenting God in his proclamation (vv. 12–20). This chapter is full of argument and the appeal to discursive reason with its ability to mount and demolish arguments, and yet earlier Paul had made it clear that without the Spirit no-one will welcome the truth of God (1 Cor. 2:6–16).

The Spirit does not bestow the human brain with extra cells so that we can understand propositions that before we could not. We may meet non-believers who can repeat accurately the content of the Christian gospel. Although Jesus told Nicodemus he needed to be born again, he also expected Nicodemus as a teacher of Israel to have understood what he was talking about (John 3:7, 10). Rather the Spirit changes our affections. We now welcome the word that formerly we did not.

The Spirit is the great persuader. His ministry does not make our arguments any more logically certain. Logical certainty is about the way the steps in an argument validly hang together from premise to conclusion. It concerns the relationship of proposition to proposition. The Spirit, however, is the agent of certitude. Certitude, as John Henry *Newman argued, has to do with the relationship between our minds and those propositions. Our attitude to those arguments changes. Hostility becomes sympathy becomes embrace. We now have a confidence in those arguments, and they have a cogency for us that they did not have before. B. B. *Warfield put it well in saying that the Spirit works 'a new ability of the heart to respond to the grounds of faith, sufficient in themselves, already present to the understanding'. The Christian apologist should avoid the Cartesian trap of thinking that we appeal to what are, in effect, disembodied intellects. We are embodied persons who reason and have passions. Pascal is again instructive when he suggests that 'the heart has reasons that reason knows nothing of'. The Spirit by definition knows how we are made and works accordingly.

The Spirit also does another important work in believers. He is the agent of boldness. When Christ's claim over human life is disputed, then the Christian needs boldness to proclaim him and defend that claim. This boldness shows itself in the courage to state the truth about Christ and to defend that truth in the face of opposition. In the book of Acts that boldness was especially to be seen in the context of the Jewish leadership's opposition to the gospel. The early Christians prayed for a boldness to bear witness to Christ after Peter's arrest and subsequent miraculous release (Acts 4:23–31), and the answer came in terms of the Spirit's fullness. Paul similarly needed boldness in facing down the opposition to his apostleship that was being fostered by some at Corinth. The boldness he wrote of was that which takes every thought captive to Christ and which demolishes opposing arguments (2 Cor. 10:1–6). Importantly, Paul was aware that the task of disputation was not merely a matter of human will opposing human will. The struggle has a supernatural dimension, the implication being that the Spirit is involved as well.

The classic discussion of the role of the Holy Spirit in persuading us of the truth of God is found in *Calvin's magisterial *Institutes of the Christian Religion*. In Book 1 and Chapter 7 of that seminal work he deals with the Roman Catholic challenge that the believer needs the church to decide the meaning of Scripture. He counters with the notion of the Spirit's internal testimony that Scripture is the word of God. Indeed he maintains that 'we ought to seek our conviction in a higher place than human reasons, judgements, or conjectures, that is, in the secret testimony of the Spirit'. This internal testimony shows itself in our experience as a persuasion. That persuasion is stronger than reason itself. Yet importantly, Calvin contends that 'the best reason agrees' with the believer's convictions. If the discussion had stopped there, one might have thought that Calvin was a mere fideist. But in the very next chapter he deals with the enthusiast's claim that an appeal to the Spirit is all that is needed. Not so according to Calvin because 'as far as reason goes' there are arguments that serve as secondary helps to our weakness in believing the Scripture as truly the word of God and in establishing the credibility of Scripture as a divine book. He parades a variety of them from fulfilled biblical prophecy to the willingness of the apostles to die for the faith. Calvin displays an awareness that the Spirit uses means to ends, and thus argument has a role in Christian apology. Calvin's discussion also exhibits a feature of the Scripture record itself. At times apology is necessary within the church, e.g. Paul had to apologize for his apostleship before the Corinthians, and Calvin before the Roman Church and the Spirit-centred enthusiasts.

Amongst recent apologists with a high view of Scripture as God's written word there are a variety of approaches to the question of the Spirit's role in apology. William Lane Craig (a classical apologist) argues that the witness of the Holy Spirit is self-authenticating and provides the Christian with an immediate apprehension of the truth of the gospel. Argument is not then the basis of belief, rather it is the Spirit's witness. Argument, however, constitutes 'a welcome and provisional confirmation of [the believer's] properly basic and warranted belief in Christian theism'. Reformed epistemologist and apologist Kelly James Clark holds to a similar view, though he would prefer to use different terms to those of Craig. An evidentialist apologist Gary R. Habermas maintains that 'the Holy Spirit may work through the use of apologetics (just as he does through preaching or witnessing), not only in bringing unbelievers to himself (Acts

17:1–4) but also in providing full assurance to believers (perhaps apart from evidences) that they are the children of God (Rom. 8:16).' Paul D. Feinberg takes a cumulative case approach to the apologetic task. On his view, the Holy Spirit provides two categories of witness, one subjective and the other objective. The internal witness of the Spirit convicts and convinces unbelievers of their unbelief, appeals to the *conscience and helps believers understand God's truth. The Spirit provides believers with their certitude about God's truth. This is the subjective track of the Spirit. The external witness of the Spirit works through the theistic arguments, *religious experience, the moral and revelation. This is the objective pathway of the Spirit. The presuppositionalist approach is exemplified by John M. Frame. According to him, the Spirit 'makes us believe what is true'. Indeed, the Spirit 'creates faith in the heart ... And that faith may or may not arise through an argumentative process'. Frame is a strong believer in the witness of the Spirit, and that witness is to the gospel message and the truth of the word. All of these apologetic thinkers argue for a vital role for the Holy Spirit in Christian apology.

According to Jesus in his dialogue with Nicodemus, the Spirit is like the wind in his activity (John 3:8). There is mystery. To move then from the scattered references in Scripture to a systematic statement of the Spirit's role in apology is not an easy task. However, at least this can be said. There is no knowledge of God without the Spirit's work, and there is no effective, life-transforming change in fallen human persons without the Spirit's ministry (1 Cor. 2:14–16). The gospel may be preached and defended and people believe in a sense and yet they may not have that real connection with God that is eternal life. Put another way, people may change their views of God but not actually put their trust in God. This is humbling for the Christian apologist who may be tempted to think that to have won the argument is to have won the audience. The human problematic of sin goes far deeper. As Luther colourfully said we are bent in on ourselves. Without the Spirit there is no effective straightening out either ontologically or epistemologically for fallen humankind.

Bibliography

J. Calvin, *Institutes of the Christian Religion*, trans. F. L. Battles (London and Philadelphia, 1961); D. K. Clark, 'Narrative Theology and Apologetics', *Journal of the Evangelical Society*, 36/4 (December 1993), pp. 499–515; S. B. Cowan (ed.), *Five Views On Apologetics* (Grand Rapids, 2000); B. Pascal, *Pensées*, trans. A. J. Krailsheimer (Harmondsworth, 1972).

G. A. COLE

HOMOSEXUALITY

This article details philosophical and socio-scientific arguments against endorsing homosexual unions.

A nature argument for structural prerequisites

The problem of confusing generic love with sexual intimacy

The basis for maintaining an other-sex prerequisite for valid sexual unions may start with the principle that sexual intimacy cannot be simply equated with love. *Jesus, for example, made it clear that he had a sexual ethic distinct from his love ethic by not collapsing his sexual *ethics into the commandment to love one's neighbour as oneself. Although he expanded the meaning of 'neighbour' to embrace everyone with whom one might come into contact at a moment of great need, he narrowed the number of people with whom one might have sexual relations to one person per lifetime. Had the principle of love been an adequate criterion for determining sexual norms, Jesus would have commanded his followers to have sexual relations with everyone as an expression of love. It is not that Jesus viewed love as undesirable in a sexual union; one is to love one's spouse in the deepest sense as one's own 'flesh' and 'body'. However, the generic principle of love does not say everything that needs to be said about sexual unions. Indeed, sometimes what holds true for generic love is utterly untrue of sexual love, as with the demand to expand love's net to include everyone.

Modern secular societies retain the notion that sexual relationships must meet special structural criteria; that is, objective facets of congruity or complementarity that are grounded in nature or physical makeup and transcend positive dispositions of the heart or mind and even positive behaviours. These include considerations of consanguinity, number, age and species. It is not necessary to prove measurable harm to all participants in all circumstances in order to establish absolute prohibitions or at least to withhold societal approval universally. It is sufficient to combine an intuitive nature argument with the scientific evidence of a disproportionately high rate of problems attending that genre of relationships. Traditionally, sex or *gender has also been viewed as a structural criterion for valid sexual unions. Indeed, it has a just claim to being a foundational criterion, the basis or analogical model for others.

Foundational linkage between heterosexuality and monogamy

The principle of monogamy, restricting a sexual relationship to two people at a time, is predicated on the twoness of the sexes. Because there are essentially two and only two sexes, the presence of a male and female in a sexual relationship is necessary and sufficient for reconstituting a sexual whole, so far as the number of people in the union is concerned. A third party is neither needed nor desirable. Jesus recognized the significance of sexual duality for marital monogamy and indissolubility when he cited Genesis 1:27 and 2:24 back to back as normative and prescriptive for human sexual behaviour: 'For this reason', namely, because God 'made them *male and female*', 'a man ... will be joined to his woman, and *the two* will become one flesh' (Mark 10:6–8). He implicitly extended the logic of the twoness of the sexes, which had always been incumbent on women, to men as well, closing a loophole that Moses had granted due to human 'hardness of heart' by appeal to the beginning of creation. It is difficult to see how a society can long maintain a strong monogamy standard apart from such a two-sex requirement, particularly where patrilineal concerns have receded in significance.

If society repeals a male–female prerequisite, there no longer remains any logical or nature-based reason for society to withhold approval from multiple-partner sexual unions. If someone argues that a person can truly love only one other person at a time, another can counter that parents have no difficulty loving all their children equally intensely and fully. If someone contends that multiple-partner unions are not a necessity of sexual life in the way that same-sex partnerships are for homosexually oriented people, another can respond that there are surely at least as many people (especially men) who experience a dissatisfaction with monogamy that is as intense, and as 'hard-wired', as any dissatisfaction with other-sex partners experienced by homosexual people. Finally, if someone makes the point that multiple-partner unions are less stable configurations than monogamous unions, another could retort that homosexual unions on the whole have shown themselves to be even less stable and, at least as regards male homosexual activity, characterized by more partners than traditional polygamous arrangements. In the end, only an insistence on the male–female dimension of sexuality enables a consistent stance to be taken against various 'plural' unions.

The existence of 'intersexed' (hermaphroditic) people does not significantly undermine the binary model of sexual relations, since this phenomenon involves overlapping features of the two existing sexes. Moreover, extreme sexual ambiguity is very rare. Usually an allegedly intersexed person has a genital abnormality that does not significantly straddle the sexes. The category of the 'intersexed' no more justifies an elimination of a binary model for human sexuality than some fuzziness around the edges of defining 'close blood relations' and 'children' justifies the elimination of standards against incest and paedophilia. Of course, too, homosexual people who seek to discard a binary model for sexual relations do not claim, for the most part, to be other than male or female. Thus they, at least, remain logically and naturally bound to a binary model for partner selection.

Analogical linkage between homosexuality and incest

Opposition to incest is based on a principle analogous to that for opposition to homosexual intimacy. Incest is wrong in all circumstances because it entails the sexual union of people who are structurally too much alike on a familial level – what Leviticus calls intercourse with the 'flesh of one's flesh' (Lev. 18:6). There is a certain narcissistic, inward bent to incestuous unions. By the same token, and on a deeper level, homosexual activity entails the union of people who are structurally too much alike on a sexual level, lacking a critical element of complementary sexual difference. If, out of a desire to affirm homosexual unions, society dismisses the principle that human sexual bonds require a certain degree of complementary difference, rejecting the twin extremes of too much and too little structural likeness, then society will have no reasonable grounds for rejecting incest or even worse extremes.

That reasonable grounds for rejection are lacking apart from some notion of structural complementarity is evident from the fact that society has not, and probably cannot, prove that every adult incestuous union, much less every adult polyamorous or polygamous bond, necessarily produces scientifically measurable harm to all participants. Universal *measurable* harm cannot even be demonstrated for children who have sexual intercourse with adults.

The point of these linkages

The point is not primarily to argue that approval of homosexual behaviour will inevitably lead to a slippery-slope approval of polyamory, incest and worse. To be sure, though, over time such a development probably will occur, initially as regards increasing openness to multiple-partner unions. Nor is the point that all those endorsing homosexual practice consciously promote polyamorous or incestuous behaviour (though some homosexual apologists have already begun to consider the legitimacy of 'polyfidelity'). But the arguments currently being made for accepting committed homosexual unions obviously have application well beyond the issue of homosexuality and can lead to unintended results. Nor is the preceding discussion operating on the common assumption that adult consensual forms of polyamory or incest are worse structural violations than homosexual intercourse. On the contrary, the latter is a more foundational violation.

The point is rather twofold. First, there is a need for multiple levels of structural correspondence between sexual partners. It is not enough to emphasize the presence of love and commitment in a sexual bond and the absence of scientifically measurable harm or exploitation in all bonds of a given type, especially when evidence exists for a disproportionately high (though not universal) rate of negative effects. Second, if committed multiple-partner unions and incestuous unions are unacceptable, then committed homosexual unions should be even more problematic; for the twoness of human sexual relations, on which a prohibition of polygamy is based, is predicated on the deep structure of two sexes, and the structural requirement of complementary difference, on which a prohibition of incest is based, is more

keenly disclosed in sexual differentiation than in blood unrelatedness.

The nature argument in story form: Genesis 1 – 2

The point made above is illustrated in the story of human origins in Genesis 2:21–24, where the precipitating act for sexual intimacy is solely the differentiation of the one original human into two sexes. Irrespective of the extent to which this story is taken symbolically or literally, it communicates that man and woman are each other's sexual counterparts, two halves of a single sexual whole. The Hebrew word often translated 'rib' (*tsela*), denoting what is extracted from the *adam* (earthling, human) to form woman, is better understood as 'side'. This also accords with its thirty-six other occurrences in the OT and some later ancient Jewish interpretation. Speaking allegorically about the creation of woman in Genesis 2:21–24, Philo of Alexandria (first century AD) states: 'Love ... brings together and fits into one the divided halves, as it were, of a single living creature' (*On Creation* 152). 'And which side did he take? For we may assume that only two are indicated ... Did he take the left or the right?' (*Allegorical Interpretation* 2.19–21; compare the rabbinic text *Genesis Rabbah* 8:1, where a division of the earth creature front and back, rather than left and right, is proposed). The image of one flesh becoming two sexes grounds the principle of two sexes becoming one flesh. The only way to restore the original sexual unity is to reunite (not just unite) the primordial constituent parts, man and woman.

Given this, it is contextually invalid to cite God's declaration in Genesis 2:18, 'It is not good for the man to be alone', as a biblical warrant for homosexual unions. Genesis 2:21–24 depicts a conditional opportunity for sexual intimacy that must meet certain structural prerequisites consistent with embodied existence as designed by God. The story requires sexual complements, not just generic sexual partners. A woman, not another man, supplies what is missing from male sexuality, and vice versa.

The core problem: sexual narcissism and/ or sexual self-deception

Dissolving a two-sex prerequisite for valid sexual unions strikes at the heart of whether there should be *any* requirement of deep structural compatibility between prospective sexual partners that takes its cue from the material structures of creation and transcends the issue of personal affections. For at the heart of all sexual practice is the sex (gender) of the participants. Because there are two sexes and because the two sexes are structurally complementary at many levels, a given individual, by virtue of belonging to only one of these two sexes, interacts sexually as only one, incomplete, part of a two-part sexual whole. On the crucial level of sex (gender), one's structural complement can only be a person of the other sex.

The problem with any attempted homosexual bond is not merely that it is sexually incomplete but that it is also, by definition, sexually narcissistic or at least sexually self-deceptive. Most people are capable of intuiting that there is something developmentally wrong about being erotically aroused by what one already is as a sexual being and shares in common with a partner of the same sex. The modern word 'homosexual' (from the Greek homoios, 'like' or 'same') underscores this self-evident desire for the essential sexual self shared in common with one's partner. This, incidentally, is why the argument by Paul and others that homosexual practice is 'contrary to nature' is such an effective critique.

If one is conscious of being strongly aroused by the distinctive features of one's own sex, it is a case of sexual *narcissism. If one is not conscious of the fact that one is aroused by sameness but thinks instead that joining oneself to another of the same sex completes one's maleness or femaleness, it is a case of sexual self-deception, for God bestows maleness or femaleness as an already intact structure. What one brings to the sexual table, so to speak, is one's God-given sex (gender). One's true sexual identity may be in need of affirmation, but it is not in need of structural supplementation. What one lacks sexually is the sex that one is not, not the sex that one already is.

In this connection, it is interesting that research indicates that homosexual men, even those who bear effeminate traits, usually desire very 'masculine' men as their sex partners. Undoubtedly many desire what they see as lacking in themselves: a strong masculine quality. Such a desire is really a form of self-delusion. They are already men, already masculine. They are masculine by virtue of their sex, not by virtue of possessing a social construct of masculinity that may or may not reflect true masculinity. They need not seek completion in a sexual same. Rather, they must come to terms with their essential masculinity.

When one perceives union with a sexual same as an avenue for completion of the sexual self, the integrity of one's sex is implicitly denied. In a sexual bond between people of the same sex, the extremes of one's sex are not moderated and true gaps are not filled. It is this reality that incidentally contributes in a significant way to the disproportionately high rate of problems associated with homosexual practice.

A consideration of counterarguments

Doesn't homosexual orientation validate homosexual behaviour?

The presence of a pre-existing, biologically based 'orientation' contributes nothing to the question of validity, since people can be strongly oriented to a number of structural incongruities or unacceptable behaviours; for example, polyamory and paedophilia, alcoholism, greed and self-centredness. The existence of a homosexual orientation might affect the pastoral response, inculcating greater sensitivity, patience and compassion as one recognizes the persistent character of sexual urges and the need for long-term oversight if effective management of these urges is to be achieved. Yet it should not change the evaluation of homosexual practice as structurally narcissistic, self-deceptive and dysfunctional. Biological causation cannot determine *morality because all behaviour is biologically caused.

Isn't long-term commitment a solution to the primary problem?

Making a homosexual union long-term and committed does not materially improve the quality of the sexual bond. Rather, it merely regularizes with a particular person the problematic dimensions of that bond. Most people recognize that a long-term monogamous and caring incestuous union such as between a man and his sister does not transform the relationship as a whole into a positive good, even when children are not produced from the union. Obviously, the incest is still present. Most people would readily recognize the flaw in viewing 'polyfidelity', commitment to multiple sexual partners at a time, as a preferred and thus viable alternative to promiscuous behaviour by people wired for polyamory. The violation of a monogamy standard remains, irrespective of whether one manifests fidelity to all one's sexual partners. By analogy, a faithful homosexual union does not resolve the root problem of homosexual practice. Homosexual behaviour is wrong, in the first instance, not because of a lack of longevity or monogamy, but rather because of its same-sex erotic quality. Longevity and monogamy are solutions to the problems of short-term sexual unions and polyamorous behaviour respectively, not to the problem of treating a sexual same as the appropriate counterpart to the sexual self.

Isn't the sex of the partners secondary to self-constructed sexuality?

The argument that 'gender' is constructed by self or society and bears little connection to a person's biological sex contradicts another staple premise of homosex-advocacy groups; namely, that the overwhelming majority of male homosexuals and many female homosexuals claim to be exclusively attracted, or virtually so, to members of the same sex. For if sexual differentiation were not a significant feature of sexuality, then a male who claimed exclusive sexual attraction to other males could find sexual satisfaction with a gender-nonconforming woman possessing a strong masculine affect. Similarly, a woman who claimed exclusive sexual attraction for females would really be content with relating sexually to a gender-nonconforming, effeminate male. As it is, the very assertion of an exclusive homosexual orientation amounts to an admission that the two sexes are such significantly distinctive and essential categories of being that, for the vast preponderance of people in modern Western society, they transcend any other meaning imputed to gender by individuals or groups. In short, the binary character of bodily sexual differentiation is central to sexual self-definition, with the result that even those who attempt to deny this reality usually end up affirming it in their normal behaviour.

Isn't an other-sex prerequisite a superficial obsession with 'plumbing'?

The attempt to distinguish between a superficial 'plumbing' argument (i.e. a fixation on distinctive anatomical features), which opponents of homosexual practice allegedly hold, and a full-orbed conception of sexual bonding as intimacy, which proponents of committed homosexual unions espouse, is convoluted at several points.

First, the so-called 'plumbing' of the sexes is indeed a key determinant for partner selection among homosexuals, as it is among heterosexuals. Not surprisingly, the correlation between distinctive anatomy and arousal plays a particularly significant role among males, who, owing in part to high levels of the main sex hormone, tend to be more visually stimulated and genitally focused than women.

Secondly, the argument being made here is not restricted to 'plumbing', but rather sees essential maleness and femaleness in more holistic terms. The anatomical complementarity of men and women is both part of, and emblematic or symbolic of, a broad array of sexual differences that make up the entire package of maleness and of femaleness. These differences involve anatomy, physiology, sexual stimulation traits and relational expectations, among other facets. Homosexual males are obviously aroused by whatever they perceive to be the distinctive sexual features of other males, females by whatever they perceive as essential femaleness. Sexual arousal for what one is and shares as a sexual being is posed here as the root problem with a homoerotic inclination.

Thirdly, no critique is being offered here of non-sexual intimacy between members of the same sex. Intimate, non-erotic, same-sex friendships are healthy and appropriate. It is only when an erotic or sexual dimension is introduced into the equation of same-sex relationships that the dynamics change significantly. A sexual relationship is not just intimacy in depth. If it were, then sexual relationships with close blood relations, children, large numbers of people, and perhaps even animals would be good things. A sexual relationship involves a structural merging with another into what Jesus aptly described, based on Genesis 2:24, as being no longer two, but one flesh. This is in fact what the copulative act both symbolizes and partly effects, underscoring the obvious character of men and women as complementary sexual counterparts.

Finally, if someone were to retort that the distinction between non-sexual intimacy and sexual intimacy is often difficult to figure out, another could respond that the distinction is really quite clear. People know the difference as regards relations with children, close blood relations, people other than their spouse, co-workers and fellow church members. So it should not be difficult to recognize the distinction in same-sex relationships.

Doesn't speaking of two halves of a sexual whole mean that single people are less than whole?

To assert that male and female are two incomplete parts of a sexual whole is not the same as saying that all people must marry if they are to be whole people. It is to say, rather, that *if* a person chooses to engage in sexual activity, that person does so always and only in his or her particularity as one incomplete part of a two-faceted sexual whole. Since there are in fact two sexes, the assertion that a single-sex union does not constitute a holistic joining of the sexes is axiomatic. Moreover, Jesus and Paul did indeed view the single state as a form of deprivation, though recognizing the value of a sexually unattached life for the advancement of God's kingdom (Matt. 19:10–12; 1 Cor. 7:7–8, 25–40). They also recognized a distinction, as people do today, between forgoing a valid sexual union, which is an experience of deprivation but no sin, and wilfully entering into a structurally incompatible union, which is sin.

Bibliography

J. Budziszewski, *What We Can't Not Know: A Guide* (Dallas, 2003), pp. 87–94; *Written on the Heart: The Case for Natural Law* (Downers Grove, 1997), pp. 177–219; R. A. J. Gagnon, *The Bible and Homosexual Practice: Texts and Hermeneutics* (Nashville, 2001; online notes and many other articles at <http://www.robgagnon.net>); R. A. J. Gagnon and D. O. Via, *Homosexuality and the Bible: Two Views* (Minneapolis, 2003); T. K. Hubbard, *Homosexuality in Greece and Rome: A Sourcebook of Basic Documents* (Berkeley and London, 2003); S. L. Jones and M. A. Yarhouse, *Homosexuality: The Use of Scientific Research in the Church's Moral Debate* (Downers Grove, 2000); T. E. Schmidt, *Straight and Narrow? Compassion and Clarity in the Homosexuality Debate* (Downers Grove, 1995); W. J. Webb, *Slaves, Women, and Homosexuals* (Downers Grove, 2001).

R. A. J. GAGNON

HOOKER, RICHARD

Richard Hooker (1554–1600) was the leading apologist and principal defender of the Elizabethan Settlement against criticisms from Puritans and presbyterians, both inside and outside the Church of England, that episcopacy, royal supremacy and ceremonial had hindered a truly scriptural reformation in the national church. Educated at Corpus Christi College, Oxford, where he became a fellow in 1577, Hooker was appointed the Master of the Temple at the Inns of Court in 1585. Here he became embroiled in controversy with its Reader, the Puritan Walter Travers, when he taught that it was God's will that all men be saved, that assurance of salvation is not immediately self-evident and that some Roman Catholics are saved. Hooker was subsequently appointed to livings in Boscombe and Bishopsbourne. From 1591 he was employed in writing his *magnum opus, Of the Laws of Ecclesiastical Polity*. Books I–IV were published in 1593, Book V in 1597 and Books VI–VIII posthumously.

Well versed in Aristotelianism and medieval *Thomism and holding that there was no fundamental dichotomy between nature and grace, Hooker began with an exposition of divine laws evident in nature and *revelation in order to show that the Church of England was the valid successor of the unreformed medieval church and in conformity with God's laws and the laws of the state. Whereas the Puritans maintained that the Scriptures were apprehended by the believer as the self-authenticating Word of God, because of the inner witness of the Spirit, Hooker saw the danger that this opened the door to the subjective 'private interpretations' of the Anabaptists and argued that the divine *authority of the Scriptures was bestowed by the church. The true interpretation of the Scriptures was to be determined by one's God-given reason in the light of the church tradition proceeding from the early Fathers.

Hooker propounded a defence of religious symbols, ornate church buildings, the forms of worship of the Book of Common Prayer and the episcopacy to answer Puritan advocacy of presbyterian church government and the exclusion of anything not sanctioned in Scripture. Whereas the Puritans believed that the NT enjoined presbyterian church polity, Hooker argued that it specified no particular pattern and episcopacy conformed to tradition and reason. Hooker contrasted the Puritan over-emphasis on *preaching with the efficacy of an intercessory priesthood and the salvific power of the sacraments by which we participate in

Christ. Underlying his polemic against presbyterianism was his rejection of the *Calvinistic doctrines of total depravity and unconditional double *predestination in the belief that election was conditioned by God's foreknowledge of people's response to divine grace. Moreover, Christ's *atonement availed for everyone, not just the elect, and God desired everyone to know his love and be saved. In accordance with this, the visible church, inevitably a mixed multitude, was not to be defined by those who claimed to be the elect but by all who would receive the sacraments and profess the Christian faith.

Hooker's *Laws* had lasting influence on Anglican theology and were required reading for theological students into the nineteenth century.

Bibliography

R. K. Faulkner, *Richard Hooker and the Politics of Christian England* (Berkeley, 1981); W. S. Hill (ed.), *The Works of Richard Hooker*, 6 vols. (Cambridge, Mass. and Binghamton, 1977–93); *Studies in Richard Hooker: Essays Preliminary to an Edition of His Works* (Cleveland, 1972); P. Lake, *Anglicans and Puritans? Presbyterianism and English Conformist Thought from Whitgift to Hooker* (London, 1988); P. Munz, *The Place of Hooker in the History of Thought* (London, 1952).

J. W. WARD

HUMAN BODY, THE

Being embodied is a basic reality of human living, embracing several theological dimensions.

Human embodiment in creation

The Scripture's opening chapter states that human beings are created in the 'image of God' (Gen. 1:27). The text links this with being 'male and female' and the call to 'be fruitful and multiply' – a strongly bodily emphasis, affirming our reproductive capacity as a fundamental dimension of human existence. Likewise, the second creation account describes the first human as *ha'adam* ('earthling') fashioned from *ha'adamah* ('earth') (Gen. 2:7), charged to 'work and take care of' the garden of Eden (Gen. 2:15). Readers thus meet, in their first engagement with the biblical narrative, a firm affirmation of the bodily character of human life – seen by God as 'very good' (Gen. 1:31).

These chapters emphasize the diversity of human embodiment, most notably in our being made individually as male *or* female, corporately male *and* female, but also in the emergence of skills and *culture (Gen. 4:20–22). Yet they also imply a rejection of false dualisms – separating different aspects of human life into opposed tendencies (e.g. body/soul or mind/matter). The Greek philosophical tradition made a clear distinction between soul and body, the latter being either despised (due to the limitations of time and place which it places on human existence) or glorified (especially the male body, in war and the sports derived from it).

The Christian theological tradition has often employed such distinctions, but as a way of bearing witness to the diverse strands of personal human existence. Straightforward observation tells us that a dead body has 'lost' something – life, spirit, soul or whatever – and on occasion it is important to focus on one aspect of human existence (e.g. surgeons must concentrate only on the body before them). Christian faith accepts such distinctions, but refuses to allow them to divide human life, affirming that God's work in creation and recreation extends to every aspect of human existence, however we may speak of it (cf. 1 Thess. 5:23).

Many feminists view Christian faith as contributing to dualism between male and female, derived from a split between the mind (associated with masculinity) and body (associated with femininity), the former being favoured over the latter. Christian faith, it is contended, thus supports patriarchy at the personal level. In response, Christian theology attests the importance of seeing human life as a whole (both personal and communal), affirming the motifs of connectedness and inclusiveness associated with feminism. Further, feminist reflection opens up new vistas of understanding of the distinctive bodily experiences of women and men. For example, the ways in which menstruation and circumcision are re-appraised in the NT is being appreciated anew in biblical exegesis (cf. Gen. 17:9–15 with Gal. 5:1–6; and Lev. 15:22 with Mark 5:25–34). In welcoming feminist affirmations about human existence, however, Christian faith maintains a 'dualism' between Creator and creature, and a distinction between male and female.

The humanity of Jesus Christ

*Jesus Christ is presented in uncompromisingly bodily terms in the NT, including the particularity of his life as a male, a Jew and a rabbi. Jesus was circumcised (Luke 2:21), grew in physical as well as other ways (Luke 2:51), knew hunger and thirst (Luke 4:2; John 4:7), touched and was touched (Matt. 8:3; 9:29; 1 John 1:1), was kissed (Luke 22:47–48), wept (John 11:35), ate and drank (Luke 22:14–20) and so on. As Paul puts it, he came 'according to the flesh' (Rom. 1:3) and was 'born of a woman' (Gal. 4:4), the virgin Mary.

Early in the Christian church, this bodily nature of Christ was questioned – how could God be so closely associated with a body without being soiled? The apostolic witnesses insist on Christ's physical reality, even after he was raised (cf. Luke 24:22), a stress which gave rise to the language of incarnation (Lat. *carnis*, 'flesh'; cf. John 1:14). The tendency to see Jesus as only seemingly human gave the name *docetism (Greek *dokeo*, 'to seem') to the earliest heresy, already rejected in the NT (so 1 John 1:1). As the *Cappadocian Fathers of the fourth century would argue, if Christ did not take on our full, embodied human nature, then we could not be wholly healed.

More positively, the wide range of Jesus' human experiences offers Christian disciples a pattern for human living in 'imitation of Christ'. The OT Scriptures affirm how good it is to be embodied, e.g. God has given us 'food from the earth', 'wine that gladdens the human heart', 'oil to make the face shine', and bread that sustains the heart' (Ps. 104:14–15). The NT depicts Jesus as frequently present at feasts, to the point where he was accused of being a drunkard (Luke 7:34), and his saving death is framed by the Passover and resurrection meals.

Paul affirms this positive attitude: 'everything created by God is good, and nothing is to be rejected if it is received with thanksgiving, because it is consecrated by the word of God and prayer' (1 Tim. 4:4). On the other hand, abuse of the body through excessive imbibing of wine is not only folly (so Prov. 20:1) but spiritual disobedience (Eph. 5:18). Abuse of the body through *drugs (including wine) has been prevalent in human history, most often flourishing where there is poverty or oppression, or where human self-image is poor. Christian faith affirms that such abuse of the body cannot be attributed to the individual abuser alone, but calls for shifts in values and priorities in society as a whole, values which Christians are called to embody and model as members together of 'the body of Christ' (a most significant metaphor in this regard).

The body of the Holy Spirit

The first Christians described their experience of the risen Christ as one of knowing the presence of the *Holy Spirit (cf. Rom. 5:5). Such an emphasis on 'spiritual' life might appear to undermine the importance of the human body, but the contrary is the case. Paul speaks of our bodies as 'God's temple' (1 Cor. 3:16), teaching that we are to 'honour God with your body' (1 Cor. 6:20), not least in our eating and sexual conduct. The contrast he draws in Rom. 8 between 'living according to the Spirit' and 'living according to the sinful nature' is not between spirit and matter, but between obedience and disobedience in our mortal bodies, to which God will give life, not repudiate.

From early days, tendencies towards false asceticism have arisen, in which 'spiritual' health is equated with denial of the body (cf. Col. 2:23; 1 Tim. 4:1–4). Such trends distort our *sexuality, result in exaggerated stress on what is *not* eaten or drunk, and so denigrate healthy patterns of living. On the other hand, the Scriptures face the reality that we are open to bodily temptations, so that self-discipline is a vital element of Christian life (cf. Matt. 5:29; 1 Cor. 9:25–26).

In some societies the body has been pierced or disfigured as an expression of spirituality. Conversely, fascination with maintaining 'the body beautiful' has prevailed in every generation (and evaluated women primarily in terms of their attractiveness to men). From a Christian perspective, such attitudes reflect the extremes of hatred or idolatry of the body. In contrast, the Scriptures affirm that seeing our bodies as temples of the Holy Spirit leads us both to respect and accept them, rejecting both bodily mutilation (cf. Deut. 14:1; Lev. 19:28) and self-idolatry (1 Pet. 3:1–5). Christian faith affirms that it is good to be embodied, so that neither self-hatred nor false pride are to form part of truly human living according to the spirit of Christ.

The resurrection body

The scriptural emphasis on the importance of the body concerns not only our present existence, but our future transformed nature. The

Christian hope is not in the first place for the survival of some 'spiritual' or 'religious' part of us – the *immortality of a natural soul. Rather, it consists of the total transformation, through death, of the whole person in Christ: what Paul describes as resurrection to a 'spiritual body' (1 Cor. 15:44).

Human embodiment is thus not to be seen as a tragic, restrictive reality, but the welcome condition of our living not only in this age but in the age to come. The NT sees our being made in the image of God not so much as a past reality now marred (true though this is), but even more as a future hope towards which, by the Spirit, we are growing in Christ. As John puts it, 'we are children of God, and what we will be has not yet been made known. But we know that when he appears we shall be like him, for we shall see him as he is' (1 John 3:2). The full humanity of the risen Christ signifies the new humanity into which we are growing (Eph. 4:13; 1 Cor. 15:47) and now beginning to experience through the Holy Spirit as members of the earthly body of Christ, Mary being the classic exemplar.

Such an eschatological view of the body is of great comfort as we consider our human frailty and disability. The human bodies in which we presently live may be diseased, crippled or maimed, making living difficult. We may be blessed with health, beauty and vitality, open to the temptations of pride and *power. Christian faith speaks to every situation of our bodily living of the hope of resurrection in Christ, not as isolated individuals, but as persons living in relationship with God and one another, looking for the transformation of all things, even through death and judgment, the new *heavens and earth (2 Pet. 3:10–13).

Bibliography

D. Hall, *Imaging God* (Grand Rapids, 1986); J. Nelson, *Embodiment* (London, 1989); C. H. Sherlock, *The Doctrine of Humanity* (Leicester, 1996); M. S. van Leeuwen (ed.), *After Eden* (Grand Rapids, 1993); N. Wolf, *The Beauty Myth* (New York, 1991).

C. H. SHERLOCK

HUME, DAVID

David Hume was born on 26 April 1711 in Edinburgh. After studying at Edinburgh University, he took jobs in Bristol and in France.

The bad reception of his first book, *A Treatise of Human Nature* (1739–40), did not prevent him publishing *An Enquiry Concerning Human Understanding* in 1748. This contained the notorious section on *miracles. *An Enquiry Concerning the Principles of Morals* was published in 1751, and Hume later took this to have been his best book. It was followed by *The Natural History of Religion* (1757), and various non-philosophical works such as his *Political Discourses* (1752) and his *History of England* (1754–62). Having retired from his civil-service position to revise *Dialogues Concerning Natural Religion* for posthumous publication, Hume died on 25 August 1776. He apparently faced death with atheistic equanimity, which provoked the admiration of Adam Smith but the bafflement of Boswell and the scepticism of Dr Johnson.

Influence on apologetics

Hume has had a considerable impact on apologetics in two ways. First, he has cast *doubt on the effectiveness of traditional arguments for the existence of God. Secondly, he has cast doubt on the reasonableness of Christianity, particularly as regards belief in miracles. Although the dialogue form of some, and the ironical tone that pervades all, of his philosophical works mean that Hume's view does not usually lie on their surface, it is usually possible to reconstruct his view with reasonable confidence. *Dialogues Concerning Natural Religion* purports to record a sequence of debates held among three characters: Cleanthes, Philo, and Demea. Cleanthes is portrayed as a supporter of natural religion, claiming that the argument from design should persuade any reasonable person. Demea, an agnostic concerning the nature of God, thinks that one should instead rely on the a priori proof of the *ontological argument. Philo, Hume's mouthpiece and a sceptic concerning the existence of God, attempts to punch holes in the others' arguments and to use the existence of *evil to buttress a sceptical position.

Hume's second blow to Christian apologetics is summed up in the famous words: 'the Christian Religion not only was at first attended with miracles, but even at this day cannot be believed by any reasonable person without one. Mere reason is insufficient to convince us of its veracity: and whoever is moved by *Faith* to assent to it, is conscious of a continued miracle in his own person, which subverts all the principles of his understanding, and gives him a determination to believe what is most contrary to custom and experience.' The particular attack on belief in a miracle, which is defined as 'a violation of the laws of nature', is based on his principle that a wise person 'proportions his belief to the evidence' and the view that 'no testimony is sufficient to establish a miracle, unless the testimony be of such a kind, that its falsehood would be more miraculous, than the fact, which it endeavours to establish'.

Apologists have tried to meet Hume's objections either directly by trying to show that the evidence for God's existence and the occurrence of miracles is compelling, or indirectly by claiming that Hume's probabilistic arguments are not relevant to Christian belief. Hume's influence, which first aroused *Kant from 'his dogmatic slumbers', still lives on, however.

Bibliography

T. L. Beauchamp (ed.), *An Enquiry Concerning the Principles of Morals*, vol. 1 (Oxford, 1998); *An Enquiry Concerning Human Understanding*, vol. 2 (Oxford, 2000); T. L. Beauchamp, D. F. Norton and M. A. Stewart (eds.) *The Clarendon Edition of the Works of David Hume*, (Oxford, 1998 onwards); J. Earman, *Hume's Abject Failure: The Argument Against Miracles* (Oxford, 2000); A. Flew (ed.), *Writings on Religion* (La Salle, 1992); J. C. A. Gaskin, *Hume's Philosophy of Religion* (Basingstoke, [2]1988); J. C. A. Gaskin (ed.), *Dialogues Concerning Natural Religion and The Natural History of Religion*, (Oxford, 1993); P. H. Nidditch (ed.), *A Treatise of Human Nature* (Oxford, [2]1978); E. C. Mossner, *The Life of David Hume* (Oxford, [2]1980); D. F. Norton (ed.), *The Cambridge Companion to Hume* (Cambridge, 1993).

D. J. HILL

HUMILITY

John *Calvin's *Institutes of the Christian Religion* was first written as an apologetic to defend the young Protestant movement before the king of France. He echoes *Augustine as he declares: 'As the orator when asked, "What is the first precept in eloquence?" answered Delivery: What is the second: Delivery: What is the third: Delivery: so, if you ask me in regard to the precepts of the Christian religion, I will answer, first, second, and third, Humility'.

Apologetics – the defending and commending of our faith – likewise must be humble. It must be humble for several reasons, but chief among these is that God himself comes to us in humility, seeking our love and drawing us to him. Apologetics, therefore, must be humble in at least three respects: it must be epistemologically humble, rhetorically humble, and spiritually humble.

Epistemologically humble

Given Christian doctrine regarding the finitude and fallenness of human beings, and of our thinking in particular, we must be careful not to claim too much for what we believe. We recognize that all human thought is partial, distorted, and usually deployed in the interest of a personal agenda. Thus, our stance is not one of *certainty, but of commitment: We are as committed as we can be to what we are convinced is real, and especially to the One whom we love, worship, and obey as the Way, the Truth, and the Life.

In apologetics, therefore, we gladly offer what, and whom, we believe we have found to be true to our neighbours in the hope that they also will recognize it, and him, as true. We recognize that there are good reasons for them not to believe, even as we recognize that there can be good reasons for our own *doubts. Indeed, we can recognize that God may have given *them* some things to teach *us* even as we maintain our fidelity to the supreme blessing of the gospel of Jesus Christ. We recognize, ultimately, that to truly believe, to truly commit oneself to God, is itself a gift that God alone bestows.

Rhetorically humble

Given these epistemological realities, apologetics should forego the triumphalist accents that bespeak a certainty that our own theology claims we cannot have. John *Locke, not known for his philosophical or rhetorical modesty, addresses his audience thus: 'What from [the Bible], by an attentive and unbiased search, I have received, reader, I here deliver to thee. If by this my labor thou receivest any light or confirmation in the truth, join with me in thanks to the Father of lights, for his condescension to our understandings. If, upon a fair and unprejudiced examination, thou findest I have mistaken the sense and tenor of the gospel, I beseech thee as a true Christian, in the spirit of the gospel (which is that of charity) and in the words of sobriety, set me right in the doctrine of salvation.'

We should adopt the voice of a friend who thinks he has found something worth sharing, but recognizes that not everyone will agree on its value. Indeed, we should adopt the voice of the friend who wants to stay friendly with our neighbours whether or not they agree with us. To put it more sharply, we should sound like we really do respect the intelligence, and spiritual interest, and moral integrity of our neighbours. We should act as if we see the image of God in them.

We are *not* prophets infallibly inspired by God, let alone the One who could speak 'with authority'. We are merely the messengers of that One. Messengers who earnestly mean well, but who forget this bit of the message or never really understood that bit, who never entirely live up to their own good news and who recognize the ambiguities in the world that make the message hard to believe. We should therefore be messengers who can sympathize with neighbours who are not ready to believe everything we are telling them.

Spiritually humble

Apologists who remain faithful to basic Christian teaching acknowledge that it is God who does the crucial work of drawing our neighbours towards his light, giving them eyes to see it and hearts to want it, and then 'shedding this light abroad' in their hearts as they enjoy spiritual renewal.

C. S. *Lewis, perhaps the twentieth century's greatest apologist, warns us of a dual danger: we can simultaneously congratulate ourselves for our brilliant argument (and self-congratulation is never a spiritually healthy thing) and, ironically, we can also imperil our own faith by reducing its basis to that particular argument.

The apostle Paul himself, a skilful debater who was happy to wrangle with rabbis and philosophers alike, recognized the perils of linking faith improperly with clever argument: 'When I came to you, brothers, I did not come with eloquence or superior wisdom as I proclaimed to you the testimony about God. For I resolved to know nothing while I was with you except Jesus Christ and him crucified. And I came to you in weakness and in fear, and with much trembling. My message and my preaching were not with wise and persuasive words, but with a demonstration of the Spirit's power, so that your faith might not rest on men's wisdom, but on God's power' (1 Cor. 2:1–5).

So if we are so modest about apologetics, why engage in it at all? The apostles, and the great Christian apologists through the ages, commended the faith to others because they believed that God had given them the privilege of hearing and embracing the good news. They believed that they knew some things that other people did not, and that those things were good for their neighbours to hear. Above all, they believed that they had met Jesus Christ, and that he had commissioned them to make disciples of all nations (Matt. 28:19).

We can make the same claim today, with the same confidence, the same enthusiasm and the same humility. Therefore, as *Thomas Aquinas put it, 'In the name of the divine Mercy, I have the confidence to embark upon the work of a wise man, even though this may surpass my powers, and I have set myself the task of making known, as far as my limited powers will allow, the truth that the Catholic faith professes, and of setting aside the errors that are opposed to it.'

If Calvin, Locke, Lewis and Aquinas – let alone the apostle Paul himself – commend the virtue of humility to apologists, we do well to heed them.

J. G. Stackhouse, Jr

HUXLEY, ALDOUS LEONARD

In his best-known book, *Brave New World* (1932), Aldous Huxley (1894–1963) warned against the danger of a possible future society depriving individuals of their freedom in the name of *science and technology. He returned to this theme in *Brave New World Revisited* (1958), a set of essays on real-life problems, in which he expresses the fear that some of his earlier prophecies may be coming true much sooner than he imagined. Huxley's interest in science continued throughout his life, and his final book was entitled *Literature and Science* (1963). Other fears about the world's future are expressed in a satire about the world after an atomic war – *Ape and Essence* (1948) – and an early essay on ecology. His concern with freedom led him, in later life, to move in the directions of mysticism, *drugs and the occult. After moving to southern California in 1947, he became associated with the Ramakrishna Mission in Hollywood.

Huxley searched for a drug that would allow an escape from the self yet, if taken with caution, would be physically and socially harmless, and he became famous in the 1950s, for his interest in the psychedelic or mind-expanding drugs, mescalin and LSD. He described his supervised experiments with mescalin in *The Doors of Perception* (1954). Huxley did not encourage free experimentation with drugs, warning against this in an appendix to *The Devils of Loudun* (1952), a psychological study of an episode in French history. In *Heaven and Hell* (1956), he compared the ecstatic and depressed states produced by mescalin with accounts of *heaven and *hell given by mystics. He also pursued various occult studies. His novel, *Island* (1962), reflects his interest in mysticism and drugs and is linked to *Brave New World* by the theme of freedom. In *Brave New World*, Huxley deplored the use of soma, a drug which produced an artificial happiness that made the people content with a lack of freedom. In *Island*, he approved of a perfected version of LSD which the people used for religious purposes. Huxley was a significant influence on Timothy *Leary (1920–96), widely known in the 1960s as an 'LSD guru', and on the 'drug culture' in general, with its associated problems of increased crime.

The Christian apologist can learn from Huxley's protest against the undermining of individual freedom. Examining Huxley's own search for freedom, we must emphasize that true freedom is found in Christ (John 8:36; Gal. 5:1). In Huxley's writings, there is a restless awareness of a transcendent dimension that cannot be captured by a world-view that is limited by the perspectives of science and technology. This persistent longing for an 'out of this world' dimension led Huxley in the directions of mysticism, drugs and the occult. His wide-ranging search for *transcendence may be seen by the Christian apologist as evidence of a divine dimension – God has 'set eternity in the hearts of men' (Eccles. 3:11). In Huxley's writings, the search for transcendence is unending and ultimately unfulfilled – always seeking and never finding. In Christ, we see something very different – the *revelation of the transcendent God who came 'among us' to 'seek and to save the lost' (John 1:1, 14; Luke 19:10). Knowing Christ as 'the truth'

in which we can confidently trust, we will be saved from following the way taken by Huxley, the way of being 'blown here and there by every wind of doctrine', the way which speaks of 'freedom' while leading us to become 'slaves of depravity' (John 14:6; Eph. 4:14; 2 Pet. 2:19).

C. M. CAMERON

HUXLEY, JULIAN

Julian Huxley (1887–1975) was the grandson of Thomas Henry Huxley ('Darwin's Bulldog' and coiner of the term 'agnostic') and great-grandson, on his mother's side, of Dr Arnold, the reforming headmaster of Rugby School. Julian Huxley was a zoologist, but his lasting contributions have been in bringing together ideas from different disciplines rather than in exhaustive studies of a particular topic. He can be regarded as the founder of both evolutionary embryology and ethology but is best known for his formulation of the neo-Darwinian synthesis in *Evolution: The Modern Synthesis* (1942), which integrated genetics and palaeontology in a convincing manner. In later life he was influential in *science popularization and policy-making; he was the first secretary-general of UNESCO.

Huxley epitomizes scientific humanism. He had no doubts that humans have developed from 'lower' animals but believed that they are now in a 'psycho-social' phase of evolution, replacing and transcending Darwinian adaptation. He regarded the direction of this specifically human stage as determined by 'the line of evolutionary progress ... increase of control, independence, internal coordination, knowledge, means of coordinating knowledge, of elaborateness and intensity of feeling'. Huxley did not believe that there was any purpose or direction in evolution, but saw progress as we make 'correct' decisions. It was this that led him to write an adulatory introduction to the English translation of *Teilhard de Chardin's *The Phenomenon of Man* (1959). The biological bases for this approach have been pursued more recently in sociobiology (see H. Cronin, *The Ant and the Peacock* [1991] and E. O. Wilson, *Consilience* [1998]). His espousal of evolutionary *ethics falls into the naturalistic fallacy ('that which is, is morally right') but is positively and persuasively contra-indicated by there being no evidence whatsoever that moral decision-making has improved in any way throughout history or prehistory.

Julian disagreed with the views of his grandfather, who saw human progress as occurring only when we successfully oppose our innate tendencies of cruelty, selfishness, greed, etc. The older Huxley wrote, 'It is the secret of the superiority of the best theological teachers to the majority of their opponents that they substantially recognize the reality of things, however strange the forms in which they clothe their conceptions. The doctrines of predestination; of original sin; of the innate depravity of man; of the primacy of Satan in this world ... faulty as they are, appear to me to be vastly nearer the truth than the "liberal" popular illusions that babies are all born good and that the example of a corrupt society is responsible for their failure to remain so; that it is given to everybody to reach the ethical ideal if he will only try; that all partial evil is universal good; and other optimistic figments, such as that which represents "Providence" under the guise of a paternal philanthropist, and bids us believe that everything will come right (according to our notions) at last'.

Notwithstanding, both Huxleys saw a need to account for the deficiencies of human nature and wanted to avoid the dualistic assumption (as they saw it) of a soul implanted into a physical body. Their problem disappears once we reject the Greek notion of body and soul as separate entities and embrace the biblical concept that we are unitary beings, albeit distinguished from non-humans by incorporating 'God's image' – even if we do not yet understand how this happens.

Bibliography

J. S. Huxley (ed.), *The Humanist Frame* (London, 1961); T. H. and J. S. Huxley, *Evolution and Ethics 1893–1943* (London, 1947); M. Keynes and G. A. Harrison (eds.), *Evolutionary Studies. A Centenary Celebration of the Life of Julian Huxley* (London, 1989); M. Ruse, *Evolutionary Naturalism* (London, 1995).

R. J. BERRY

IDEALISM

Like many terms, philosophers use 'idealism' in a range of ways. What is common to them all is the primacy of the mind. An idealist holds that *reality is in some way dependent on the mind.

Most of us would accept that all our access to reality, and so all our awareness and knowledge of the external world, is dependent on the functioning of our mind. Without a mind we can have no knowledge of anything. This applies even to those who think of 'mind' in very materialistic terms, and hold, e.g. that only matter exists. When pushed, such people would probably concede that 'believing that only matter exists' is itself, in some sense at least, a *mental* act.

Historic philosophical idealism, however, has tended to make stronger claims, such as that the external world is dependent on mind for its reality. This mind might be that of the individual thinker ('If I don't observe it or think it, then it doesn't exist') or something larger such as the sum total of all human minds, or some sort of cosmic mind located within the universe, or a divine mind located beyond the universe. These claims were contested by the traditional scientific world-view, which, for the most part, depended upon the ontological independence of the world around us and the assumption that chairs and tables and distant galaxies continue to exist even when nobody is thinking about them or is even aware of their existence.

Though popular in many forms in the nineteenth century, idealism was attacked fiercely through much of the twentieth century, typically on the basis that what we call the workings of our minds are nothing but the operation of our physical brains and nervous systems according to predetermined physical laws. Minds, therefore, are dependent on matter for their existence and so matter cannot be dependent on mind. This view was typified by Bertrand *Russell, who reacted against the idealist philosophy that was prevalent in his youth and stressed the objectivity of logic and science.

The old question, 'Which is primary, matter or mind? Is mind dependent on matter, or is matter dependent on mind?' tended to be looked on in the twentieth century as a chicken and egg question. Chicken and egg questions, we were told, are not to be answered but simply dismissed. The question of the primacy or otherwise of mind only applies if we clearly distinguish two types of entity, mental entities and other non-mental (generally 'material') entities. But, we were told, it is a mistake to draw a clear line between what is mental and what is non-mental. To do so is to make the mistake of dualism, frequently, though probably unfairly, blamed on *Descartes. Dualism divides the world into two, the mental and the non-mental. But the world is one. There is only one sort of thing. We are not bodies and minds. We are psychosomatic unities. My inner thoughts or experiences are not some sort of independent existences inside of me; they are to be identified with things in the world such as chemical changes in my brain or physical objects outside of me.

However, as the twentieth century wore on, the objectivity of both *logic and scientific fact were increasingly called into question, until it was almost universally conceded that all our *reasoning and all our observing are at the very least overlaid with subjective features. No two people ever view the same chair in exactly the same way. This is not just because they look at it from different angles or because one is slightly colour-blind. It is also because they each bring different concepts of 'chairhood' to their viewing, concepts that have been formed by a whole range of experiences unique to them and which control the way they see or think of the chair. It may even be, if we extrapolate from the claims of subnuclear physicists, that our very viewing of the chair in some way 'physically' affects what it is.

These considerations, linked in with the awareness mentioned above that to believe even 'only matter exists' is primarily to perform a mental or personal act, have brought the issues that shaped idealist philosophies once more to the fore. In many ways postmodern approaches have moved back to something similar to the idealist position, though often without using the concept of mind. The key to reality, they would say, is in the observing or thinking subject, not in the observed or thought object. The reality of the external world is, for the postmodernists, dependent on their subjective experience. If they do not smell the rose, it has no smell. If they don't believe something, it is not true.

Idealism from Plato to New Age

*Plato has often been viewed as an idealist in that he gave primacy to his 'Forms' or 'Ideas'. Though his idealism is very different from that of *Berkeley and his successors, Plato did make

the Forms the basis for both the existence and the intelligibility of the objects around us in the world. While these objects are changing and impermanent, the Forms are reliable and eternal, thus guaranteeing reality and stability to the universe. It was his theory of Forms that saved Plato, and much of subsequent Western thought, from the conclusion, reached by many Eastern thinkers, that since the objects around us are changing and impermanent, everything in the universe is ultimately unreal.

Plato equated the real with the good, and subsequent Platonism tended to view the objects in the world around as both less real and less good than the world of Ideas or Forms. From this came the cleavage between the mental or spiritual, which is good and eternal, and the material, which tends towards *evil. God thus cannot be material, nor can he be directly involved with matter. His essence and his activity are thought, and the material world is the product of his thought, not the work of his hands.

*Augustine, who laid the foundation for eight hundred years of medieval Christian thought, was profoundly influenced by Platonism and accepted the primacy of the mental over the material. Before anything in the universe existed, the immaterial God was. By his thought he brought into being the created order, which continues to exist only because he holds it in being.

The philosophy of *Aristotle has traditionally been contrasted with that of Plato in that he emphasized the reality of the objects in the world around us over against Plato's stress on the reality of the Forms. Though this is an oversimplification, it was the Aristotelian tradition, when it came into ascendancy in Western thought in the thirteenth century, that laid the foundation for the 'scientific' worldview that located reality in the world around us and saw the task of the human mind as to grasp and accurately define what is thus to be accepted as the given.

No philosopher throughout the modern period doubted the validity of the scientific enterprise. But it raised one serious problem which would not go away. However much we believe that the external world is the real, the fact remains that all I can know about the external world is my experience of it, and there is always the possibility that my experience of it may be false. Indeed, every now and then I have deceptive experiences, as when a stick half-immersed in water looks bent, so I can never be sure that any experience is reliable. As a result, if I have an experience of a tree, there is no way of knowing that there really is a tree there. I cannot grasp the reality of the tree, I can only grasp the reality of my 'tree-experience'. Even if lots of other people confirm my experience of the tree with similar experiences, I am no further forward, for all I have then is a 'tree-experience' plus a second experience of lots of people who claim to experience the tree. I cannot get any further than my own experiences. The tree itself is for ever out of my reach.

Various responses were made to this problem. The only one that was at all successful was to ignore it and simply assume the reliable correlation of our mental processes with external reality. Berkeley grasped the nettle by urging the strongly idealist response that the mental is primary, and it is the act of perception that gives the object of perception its reality. But he used the mind of the omniscient Creator God to undergird his argument and to supply the ultimate basis for the existence of all external things. Only what is perceived can exist, and God is all perceiving.

Subsequent idealists, notably the post-*Kantian tradition culminating in *Hegel and the neo-Hegelians, were not willing to use God as Berkeley had done, and yet in most cases found themselves bringing in some parallel concept to save themselves from solipsism, that is, from seeing each individual locked exclusively into his or her set of experiences, with no way of finding universal reality or truth. This concept took various forms, ranging from a sort of cosmic consciousness (familiar today in various pantheistic and *New Age approaches), through to a transcendent Absolute, which at times began to look rather like the Christian God shorn of most of his personal attributes.

Christianity and idealism

There is much in Christianity which sits happily with an idealist approach. Certainly, *materialism, which historically has been the most strident alternative to idealism, is as dismissive of the 'spiritual' as it is of the 'mental', and so would seem to be a less acceptable alternative to Christians. And it is tempting to use the conclusions of Berkeley and the Hegelians and even the cosmic idealists to bolster arguments for the existence of God. After all, they have admitted they are unable to

devise a philosophy that covers the data of the world and human life without postulating the existence of a consciousness or mind that is somehow transcendent, and the Christian God would seem to fill the bill just as well, if not better, than Absolute Spirit, or the like. Further, as Christians, we do not believe that matter is primary; for us God is primary.

We need to be careful, however, as it is one thing to produce a Christian apologetic aimed specifically at those who accept an idealist position, using idealist concepts in so doing; this would be parallel to using the fact that Jesus had no fixed abode to commend him to someone sleeping rough on the streets. It is quite a different thing to tie a Christian philosophy or apologetic into an idealistic world-view. There are several good reasons why we should not do so.

First, biblical Christianity does not set the mental or spiritual over against the material in the way that the Platonic tradition did. The doctrines of creation, incarnation and the resurrection of the body make it hard for us to assert the clear priority of one over the other.

Secondly, it would seem quite unbiblical to argue that the nature of God is primarily mind or thought. The neoplatonists may have conceived of him as 'pure thought', but the Bible picture is much richer, including love and personal involvement and will and action and plenty more.

Thirdly, it would seem unwise for a contemporary apologetic to conceive of God as primarily mind and thus as essentially or typically engaged in rational thought. The collapse of the confidence in reason that was the hallmark of the modern period has allowed our current generation to adopt a much more holistic way of viewing human persons than merely as rational animals. Rationality, though a part of us, is not our essence. We relate, choose, suffer, experience, love, feel, intuit and so on, as well as reason. We operate in the moral and spiritual and axiological spheres as well as in the rational. We are bodies as well as minds. Such a view of the human person seems wholly in keeping with the biblical picture. So, given our claim that we have been created by God in his image, it is surely important to present a rich and holistic picture of the nature of God, rather than stressing one aspect at the cost of all the rest. Perhaps, in the Age of Reason it was right for Christian apologists to

341

focus on a God of reason, just as they sought to defend the reasonableness of the Christian revelation. But we are no longer in an age of reason, and we are able to present a much more holistic concept of God, one which in fact more readily answers the needs of a post-modern age.

Modern idealism was adopted as a fall-back position in the face of the failure to provide a definitive rational basis for the reality of the world around us. If I cannot be sure this is a real table before me, then I have to retreat to saying the only reality I can be sure about is my mental or subjective awareness of a table. But we do not have to take that step. Instead, we can point out that the demand for a rational demonstration of the validity of my experience of the world was a mistaken one. I do not need a rational demonstration of the existence of this table to be quite certain that it is real. Indeed, I live all my life encountering any number of things in the external world without ever doubting their reality or feeling the need to provide a 100% rational justification for believing in them. I am, and they are. I accept them, generally without question, and get on with living. This is not to say that my accept-ance of them is irrational or contrary to reason; if I encounter something that is contrary to reason, like water running uphill, then I will certainly stop and ask questions. For the most part, however, I accept them on trust and do not need proof of their reality to accept them. They are part of the world, part of life, and life is more than providing rational proofs.

There is a close parallel, of course, between the demand for conclusive proof of the reality of objects in the external world and the demand for conclusive proof of the existence of God. Both were asking for the impossible, and both were unnecessary. We believe in the world because we live in it. Indeed, the only satisfactory way we can live in the world is by accepting its real existence. The case with belief in God is not very different.

Bibliography

F. H. Bradley, *Appearance and Reality* (Oxford, 1893); N. Rescher, *Conceptual Idealism* (Oxford, 1973); A. P. F. Sell, *Philosophical Idealism and Christian Belief* (Cardiff, 1995); G. Vesey (ed.), *Idealism, Past and Present* (Cambridge, 1982).

P. HICKS

IGNATIUS LOYOLA

Ignatius Loyola (1491–1556) was the founder of the Society of Jesus (Jesuits). Born Iñigo López de Loyola to Basque nobility, he became a courtier and then a soldier for King Ferdinand. Convalescing from severe leg wounds in 1521, he read the lives of *Jesus and the saints and resolved to become a knight of Christ bringing souls to God. After his recovery he retreated to an austere life of prayer guided by Dominicans at Manresa and then visited Jerusalem in 1523. He and a band of spiritual companions studied in Paris and in 1534 vowed poverty, chastity and service to God. Pope Paul III formally approved the order in 1540, and Ignatius became superior general until his death. The order was intended to strengthen the church, partly in response to Protestantism and the new humanism. Its ideal was to be that all things are done 'for the greater glory of God'. Ignatius was canonized in 1622.

Ignatius' *Book of Spiritual Exercises* conveys the essentials of his spirituality by guiding a four-week retreat aimed at strengthening the soul in knowledge and love of Christ's person. The first week emphasizes how sin separates from God; the second poses Christ over sin as the fundamental option; the third effects deeper conversion through meditation on the passion; and the fourth confirms conversion in Christ by meditating on the resurrection and the joys of *heaven. However, the broader legacy of Ignatius continues through world-wide Jesuit commitment to Christian edu-cation, evangelization and social *justice, and current world membership stands at more than 20,000.

Bibliography

Ignatius Loyola, *Autobiography of St Ignatius Loyola* (trans. J. O'Callaghan; New York, 1993); *The Constitutions of the Society of Jesus and their Complementary Norms* (trans. J. McCarthy; St Louis, 1996); *Letters of St Ignatius of Loyola* (trans. W. Young; Chicago, 1959); *The Spiritual Exercises of St Ignatius of Loyola* (trans. L. Puhl; New York and London, 2000); R. Jonanthan, *Companion to the Spiritual Exercises* (London, 1965); D. Lonsdale, *Eyes to Hear: An Introduction to Ignatian Spirituality* (New York, 2000); P. Mariani, *Thirty Days: On Retreat With the Exercises of St Ignatius* (New York and London, 2002); W. Meissner, *Ignatius of*

Loyola: The Psychology of a Saint (New Haven and London, 1992).

P. WEIGEL

IMAGINATION

The role of the human imagination in the perception of *reality and in the construction of what anthropologists call a 'world-view' is closely related to ways of knowing that transcend rational thought, such as dreams, visions and intuitive knowledge. For the biblical authors the absence of vision results in sterility and death, while one of the defining marks of the activity of the *Holy Spirit is found in the fact that 'young men will see visions' and older people 'will dream dreams' (Joel 2:28; Acts 2:17).

Imagination in the Bible

The visions of an Isaiah or a Micah provide access to a world which stands in sharp contrast to that within which the prophets conduct their ministries, but so real is this imagined and future world, in which the peoples turn towards God, hunger for his truth and, as a result, 'beat their swords into ploughshares' (Isa. 2:4), that those who read the resultant prophecies are exhorted to 'walk in the light of the LORD' in the present (v. 5). That is to say, while the imagined world remains distant in time from the empirical realities of the present, it becomes the focus of faith and hope in such a way as to determine both individual *ethics and social possibilities.

The same thing can be said concerning the visions seen by John of Patmos, who is lifted 'in the Spirit' to a realm in which the values governing empirical society are completely subverted. John is shown a 'door standing open in heaven', which acts as both an exit from the madness of the Roman world and an entrance into a transcendent realm in which all reality is viewed from the perspective of the throne of God. When the seer returns to the mundane reality of a world in thrall to idols, he does so in possession of a *revelation that enables him to view the existing political and socio-economic order in a new and critical light. In fact, the book of Revelation is a key text with regard to the place of the imaginative faculty in Christian experience, and it offers us an important model for the use of the imagination in mission and apologetics. Confronted by a world in which Roman definitions of reality were supported by imperial propaganda and by the highly visible symbols of state power and success which dominated urban landscapes, the visions of the Apocalypse make possible the purging and renewal of the Christian imagination.

It is important to notice, however, that in the Bible the turn to the imagination is neither an escape into the realm of fantasy nor a route to the kind of false comfort which led Karl Marx to attack religion as a mere 'opiate of the people'. Contrary to much popular usage, the term 'imagination' is not used here to signify things that are 'unreal'; rather, it denotes a faculty which provides access to aspects of reality ignored and suppressed within modes of thought confined within strictly materialistic frames of reference. The prophetic and apocalyptic visions of the Bible break open readers' existing worlds, opening them up to a transcendent and theistic perspective from which the mundane order of things can be viewed in a new and critical light. The visions of the book of Revelation are thus highly contextual and extremely subversive, because, seen through the lenses provided by such visionary experiences, the glory that was Rome becomes a tarnished and squalid thing, founded on obscene violence and maintained through the enslavement and dehumanization of thousands of people whose very bodies and souls were traded like mere commodities (18:13).

The relevance of this to the task of Christian apologetics in the era of contemporary globalization is obvious. Bombarded, like John of Patmos, by images and symbols promoting a radically materialistic view of human existence and purpose, we dare not ignore his recognition of the vital importance of visions, symbols and imagery in the task of mission. Indeed, the much needed renewal of Christian *preaching and teaching can come about only as the pulpit becomes a place for the kind of 'imaginative speech' that nurtures an alternative *community with the courage and freedom 'to act in a different vision and a different perception of reality' (W. Brueggemann).

The loss of imagination in Western culture

Regrettably, under the impact of the *Enlightenment, which gave priority to human reason as a privileged source of knowledge, Western

Christianity has tended to downplay alternative ways of knowing such as those described above. Although the early evangelicals recognized the fundamental importance of an experiential knowledge of God and nurtured their piety both on the biblical narratives and on the dreams recorded by the Bedford tinker John Bunyan, the nineteenth century witnessed a discernible shift towards a much more cerebral form of faith and a growing suspicion of claims to have experienced direct encounters with the divine. Writing to his wife in 1825, Edward Irving reflects both the growing dominance of this kind of dogmatic orthodoxy and his own reaction against it: 'I was an idolater of the understanding and its clear conceptions; of the spirit, the paralysed, dull, and benighted spirit, with its mysterious dawnings of infinite and everlasting truth, I was no better than a blasphemer.' The protest here was against what was perceived to be a form of syncretism by means of which Christianity entered into an uncritical alliance with the *culture of modernity, so compromising its own transcendent vision and offering a halo of sanctity to a world-view in which the Holy Spirit could be declared redundant. In such a setting, apologetics became focused on the rational defence of Christian doctrine, and the role of the imagination was largely overlooked.

Two things have radically changed the situation and created a context in which there is an urgent need for the Christian imagination to be given its rightful place in the life and witness of the church. First, the astounding success of the modern missionary movement has resulted in an encounter with other cultures which have been shaped by world-views in which transcendent, spiritual phenomena are treated as an integral part of reality. Indeed, by virtue of the fact that they have found themselves at the meeting point of two very different worlds, Western missionaries have frequently become uncomfortably aware of the poverty of their received theology and spirituality when these have been put to the test at the frontiers of cross-cultural mission. Whether in Asia (where the Indian Christian mystic Sadhu Sundar Singh observed that Europeans seemed to privilege scientific knowledge while almost entirely neglecting the spiritual world) or among the millions of primal peoples (such as aboriginals who understood their whole existence in relation to the 'Dreamtime'), the inadequacies of a theology accommodated to the Enlightenment became obvious. One anthropological study of Australian aboriginal experience bears the suggestive title *White Man Got No Dreaming*. At the same time, converts to Christ from such cultures soon spotted the importance and pastoral significance of those elements in the biblical narrative that were neglected by the missionaries and began developing local Christian responses to the questions arising in those contexts. No-one who has viewed aboriginal Christian art, with its extraordinarily complex and expressive symbolism, can doubt that much was lost when the human imaginative faculty became marginalized in the Western tradition.

Secondly, in the era of postmodernity the dangers of a one-sided stress on human rationality have become clear within the Western world itself. In a book (*The Western Dreaming*, 2001) with the subtitle *The Western World is Dying for Want of a Story*, sociologist John Carroll describes the cultural malaise of those societies which struggle 'to live in a present without vision of any future'. However, it is one thing to recognize the serious shortcomings of modernity, with its well-documented tendency to erode the meaning of human existence, and quite another thing to discover a way out of the present morass. The problem is that we have exhausted the spiritual capital acquired from the past and lost contact with the sources from which visionary and creative powers might be renewed. The evidence for this claim is to be found in the *arts, where a contemporary cultural critic observes that 'the great music from earlier centuries expressing the hope of human progress now sounds like the music of our lost hopes and illusions, reaching us like the last light from extinguished stars' (M. Ignatieff). Similar evidence can easily be cited from the fine arts, and from literature, where the inspiration to tell hope-filled stories seems largely confined to authors from non-Western contexts.

Imagination and apologetics today

Given the context we have described, it would seem that this particular juncture in human cultural history offers an extraordinary opportunity to Christians who are able to rise to the challenge of recovering the biblical vision of the future of the world and then retelling that story in imaginative ways so that it connects with the concerns of postmodern society. It should not be forgotten that Isaiah's vision of a new world, in which the arms industry will become redundant, emerged from a context in which the religious and ethical situation of empirical Jerusalem seemed to be utterly hopeless, while the radiant dream of John of Patmos of the holy city, where God will live among people in the most intimate fellowship, was given to him in a Roman penal colony where all the outward indicators suggested that such hope was a symptom of dangerous delusion. The parallels with our times might suggest that we stand on the cusp of a period in which the Christian imagination can be recovered, and in which the ancient promises articulated by poets and prophets might be recast in *language and forms which would clothe them with renewed power to bring hope to a despairing age.

What, therefore, would be involved in purifying and renewing the Christian imagination today? First, biblical history suggests that the worship of Israel and the church has done one of two things: either it has legitimated and sanctified an understanding of human life that originates outside the prophetic tradition, or it has inspired and nurtured a radically different vision, one which has involved the denial of the claim, made by successive empires, that there simply is no alternative to the way things are in the world. When their worship has been inspired by the biblical vision of the future, the people of God have recognized that their affirmation of the sovereignty and glory of the Lord involved a denial of the claims of false gods. Such worship is far from being a neutral, innocuous activity, but is instead dynamic, world-transformative and even dangerous. Those who hold the reins of power and control the means of communication and propaganda do not take kindly to a religion that breaks out from the confines of the private world, spreading an alternative story and literally constructing a new, hope-filled world through its praises. The time is ripe for Christian leaders and teachers to recover their nerve, to return to the vision of the coming kingdom embedded within the Bible, and to strive to connect that hope with present reality through the deployment of imaginative language and imagery.

Secondly, the task of imaginative apologetics is too important and challenging to be left to religious professionals; it demands the recognition and encouragement of Christians who possess creative and artistic gifts. This is not to suggest that art, *music or literature should be placed at the service of evangelism, but rather that talented writers, painters or composers must use their imaginative gifts within the framework of a broader understanding of the Christian mission. This will involve the recognition that '*signals of transcendence' may often be seen far beyond the walls of the church. George Steiner describes gifted composers as custodians of 'felt intimations of open horizons', and suggests that they are uniquely able to provide 'well-springs of recuperation and self-surpassing for the constricted and worn humanity'. Western theology has some way to go in recognizing the crucial importance of the arts in nurturing and communicating the Christian vision of the world in postmodern society.

Finally, there is an urgent need to overcome the false dichotomies between the mind and the spirit, or between *theology conceived of as a largely intellectual pursuit or as involving mystical experience. John of Patmos again serves as a model for us in this regard because, when following him through the door that stands open in *heaven, we do not pass from the real to the illusory; on the contrary, we enter a transcendent realm in which, before the heavenly throne, the whole of reality becomes grounded in the revelation of the eternal purpose of the Saviour God. In truth, imaginative apologetics can be done effectively only by men and women who have glimpsed this ultimate reality and found it so utterly transforming that movement through that doorway in worship and prayer has become a settled pattern of their lives.

Bibliography

W. Brueggemann, *Hopeful Imagination: Prophetic Voices in Exile* (Philadelphia, 1986); J. Dillenberger, *A Theology of the Artistic Sensibilities: The Visual Arts and the Church* (London, 1987); G. Howes, 'Theology and Art', in D. Ford (ed.), *The Modern Theologians: An Introduction to Christian Theology in the Twentieth Century* (Oxford, 1997), pp. 669–685; G. van der Leeuw, *Sacred and Profane Beauty: The Holy in Art* (New York, 1963); H. R. Rookmaaker, *The Creative Gift: The Arts and the Christian Life* (Leicester, 1989); G. Steiner, *Real Presences* (London, 1991).

D. W. SMITH

IMMANENCE

The concept of immanence (Lat. *immanentia*, 'indwelling') has been applied in modern philosophical theology to the view that there is something in the natural order which points beyond itself to a transcendent reality, which Christians call God. The concept of immanence can be traced back to the origins of the Judeo-Christian religious tradition, but the word itself is generally reserved for a certain kind of post-*Enlightenment thinking about the relationship between God and the world, and particularly about the possibility of divine action in human affairs.

Antecedents

In looking for the origin of the concept of immanence, we may begin with the biblical affirmation that human beings are created in the image and likeness of God (Gen. 1:26–27). For centuries this image was identified with the human soul or *conscience, allowing theologians to suppose that there is something intrinsic to human nature which speaks to us about the reality of God. This belief can also be supported from certain NT passages, such as Paul's affirmation that the Gentiles act according to God's law because they have it written on their hearts (Rom. 2:14). In later Christian writings, similar ideas recur from time to time and their cumulative impact may be said to constitute a recognizable tradition of thought on this subject. For example, *Tertullian believed that the human soul was 'naturally Christian' and *Augustine affirmed that our hearts are restless, until they find their rest in God. Statements of this kind presuppose that all human beings, whether they have had access to divine *revelation or not, feel in themselves a deep inner longing which propels them in the direction of God their Creator.

It is also true, however, that the same ancient tradition insisted that no-one can know God unless God first reveals himself to that person, and that everyone is blind to divine truth from birth because we have all inherited the effects of Adam's original sin. Whatever the longings of the human heart may be, they can only be satisfied as and when the transcendent Creator acts in the world to redeem sinners from the effects of that sin which has cut us off from enjoying fellowship with him.

Modern thought

The modern concept of divine immanence derives from this earlier form of *natural theology but differs significantly from it because it discounts the traditional view that Adam's sin cut the human race off from God and attempts to bridge the gulf between human nature and divine grace which is often perceived as the legacy of medieval theology. Proponents of immanentist theory claim that medieval theology, and especially that of *Thomas Aquinas (1226–74), envisioned a universe which was fundamentally separated into two realms. These realms overlapped to some extent but were nevertheless substantially different from one another. The realm of nature could be examined and known by the use of human reason, but that of grace required divine revelation, given in the Bible and interpreted by the church, for it to be understood. That a realm of divine grace existed was proved by the occurrence of *miracles, which defied the laws of nature and could be explained only by reference to a supernatural order. This way of thinking began to break down in the eighteenth century when rationalist principles were systematically applied to the concept of miracle. Philosophers like David *Hume (1711–75) argued that events which had traditionally been placed in that category were either fictitious or else crude attempts to explain complex natural phenomena. Very often, the 'miracle' was in the eye of the beholder, who would interpret a natural event in a way which demanded divine intervention. Traditional apologetics, of the kind advocated by François Turretin (1623–87), attempted to argue that God could not be made the object of scientific investigation and that his activities had to be measured by his own explanation of them – by revelation, in other words, which comes to us as a divinely appointed *authority.

Arguments of this kind were naturally rejected by the rationalists, who could find no objective reason for accepting the truth-claims of any revelation, and so some would-be defenders of Christianity concluded that they would have to develop a new form of apologetic. This is the point at which the modern notion of divine immanence came to be formulated.

Immanence, as the concept was developed by Immanuel *Kant (1720–1804) and his followers, rested on the fundamental belief that there is such a thing as the human mind. We may accept (as all the eighteenth-century rationalists did) that this mind is a part of nature and not something which has been imposed on it from the outside. But if the mind and human reason are natural, then nature itself must be grounded in mind, since otherwise we would not possess such a faculty, nor would it be of any use to us in determining the character of the universe in which we live. In other words, the greater the congruence between human thought processes and objectively observable *reality, the more it is necessary to assume that that reality is itself connected to a higher reason which makes such congruence possible. If this is true, then we can say that the existence of the human mind (which many of the ancients had identified as the image of God in man) necessitates the existence of a supreme mind which possesses all the qualities of the human mind, including individual consciousness, or personhood. If this is the case, then we can say that God has structured the universe in such a way as to make it logically necessary for us to acknowledge his existence. This belief is what is now understood as the doctrine, or concept, of immanence.

The heyday of immanentist theory was the late nineteenth and early twentieth century, when it attracted a number of intelligent people who were looking for a new, more credible philosophical theology than the one offered by scholasticism and its descendants, including traditional Protestant orthodoxy. It was highly influential in the movement known as Catholic modernism, which the Vatican condemned, not least for that reason. It also appealed to a number of Protestant thinkers, particularly in the English-speaking world which was slow to lose the optimism of Enlightenment thought. One of its last, but also one of its ablest defenders was William *Temple, whose Gifford Lectures of 1932–4 remain a classic exposition of it. More recent philosophical theologians recognize the issues with which immanentism tried to deal, and occasionally they express a certain sympathy with it, but as a coherent apologetic for the Christian faith it is no longer widely accepted as credible. It seems likely that a new formulation of the age-old problem will have to be found which can answer the objections which the original immanentists made against traditional Christian orthodoxy, without falling into the traps which defenders of the latter have been all too easily able to point out.

Advantages and disadvantages

From the standpoint of its advocates, the advantages of a doctrine of divine immanence are overwhelming. It enables them to overcome the scholastic nature grace duality by claiming that there is really no such thing as the 'supernatural', since the natural order itself points to the transcendent and cannot be made intelligible without it. There is therefore no ground for saying that reason stands in opposition to faith, since the right exercise of reason will inevitably lead to the acceptance of the transcendental dimension which has traditionally been regarded as faith's preserve. At the same time, ancient authorities like the Bible, while (it is argued) no longer defensible in terms of revelation, can be upheld as authentic witnesses to this universal reality as it has been experienced by spiritually-minded people in every age. According to this view, however, the Bible's claim to be a revelation of the divine cannot be regarded as exclusive of other such claims. What is true of the Christian Scriptures must also be true of any other form of religious expression, since immanence is a universal phenomenon, and all religions bear witness to it.

Critics of immanentism come from two very different stables – the rationalist and the traditionally orthodox Christian. The former regard it as merely another attempt to demonstrate the undemonstrable, and generally reject the whole notion of *transcendence. The latter offer a more sustained critique, which can be summarized as follows. First, immanentism set out to make Christianity credible to rationalists, and it has obviously failed to achieve this aim. This is not because its method is faulty or implausible in itself, but because one has to be a believer first if immanentism is to have any appeal, or even make sense. If that is the case, then it is self-defeating because it is trying to offer rational proof for something which has already been accepted on other grounds. Secondly, immanentism restructures the beliefs which it is trying to defend in such a way as to destroy their inner coherence. For example, Christianity is not simply a doctrine of transcendence clothed in the language of first-century Judaism and packaged for Graeco-Roman consumption, it is a belief in such things as evil, disobedience and sin, which have led the human race to a destruction from which only a dying and rising Saviour God can deliver it.

This belief demands a certain *exclusivism – Jesus is the only Saviour of the world – which is fundamentally at odds with the immanentist principle. Thirdly, opponents claim that the immanentist theory is basically one of minds talking to themselves, since belief in a transcendent supreme mind is not the same thing as having contact with it. Revelation is necessary if such contact is to take place. In short, immanentism is an attempt to find a rationally plausible apologetic for pre-existing faith, and as such it may help some believers to remain such, even in the face of scientific *rationalism. But it cannot persuade unbelievers of the truth of Christianity, both because of its own inherent weaknesses and because such persuasion is beyond the competence of reason to provide.

Bibliography

B. P. Bowne, *The Immanence of God* (New York, 1905); G. Daly, *Transcendence and Immanence: A Study in Catholic Modernism and Integralism* (Oxford, 1980); W. Temple, *Nature, Man and God* (London, 1934); K. Ward, *Divine Action* (London, 1990).

G. L. BRAY

IMMORTALITY

Does the Bible teach that human beings are immortal? Today, a negative answer is often given to this question on the grounds that God alone is immortal (1 Tim. 6:16) and the immortality of the soul is a *Platonic doctrine falsely read into the Bible. However wide this opinion is held, it is false and to see why, three kinds of immortality must be distinguished. Something is *supremely immortal* if it exists in all possible worlds and does not depend on anything else for its existence. Something is *strongly immortal* if it exists in all possible worlds and depends on something else for its existence that has the property of necessarily sustaining it. Something is *weakly immortal* if it does not exist in all possible worlds, but in those worlds in which it does exist, once it comes to be, it will never cease to be. Only God is supremely immortal, *universals and other abstract objects are strongly immortal, and the human person is weakly immortal.

Disembodied intermediate state

Throughout history, Christianity has correctly been understood to teach that the human soul, while not by nature immortal, nevertheless, never ceases to be after it is created. Upon death this soul enters a disembodied intermediate state, however incomplete and unnatural this state may be, and, eventually, is reunited with a resurrected body.

There are three chief rivals to the classic disembodied intermediate state position. The 're-creation' position claims that at death the person ceases to exist and is recreated *ex nihilo* at the final resurrection. Biblical statements to the effect that one is immediately with Christ at death are construed in terms of phenomenological *language. However, clear biblical statements that to die is to be with Christ (Phil. 1:23) should be interpreted according to their plain sense. Moreover, the reality and activity of those in the intermediate state is often described in Scripture (Isa. 14:9–10; Heb. 12:23; Rev. 6:9–11). Further, the appearance in Scripture of deceased people is best taken as temporary embodiment and not as a temporary creation *ex nihilo* of human beings (Matt. 17:3). Finally, the OT warnings against necromancy (communicating with the dead; cf. 1 Sam. 28) presuppose a conscious intermediate state.

The 'temporary tabernacle' view holds that in the intermediate state a person either has or is some physical object, for example, an entire intermediate state body or some surviving micro-part of the earthly body. For at least two reasons, this view is strained. First, Scripture teaches that the intermediate state is disembodied (2. Cor. 5:1–10), and those in that state are described as active spirits with the same language and imagery as are used to describe God and *angels, both of which are pure spirits (Heb. 12:23; Rev. 6:9–11). Since inter-testamental *Judaism depicted the intermediate state as disembodied (1 Enoch 22; 2 Esdras 7), NT descriptions should be interpreted against that background with an unmet burden of proof on those advocating a bodily intermediate state.

Finally, there is the 'soul sleep' view, according to which persons in the intermediate state are unconscious. This position falls victim to several points: numerous texts clearly describe a conscious intermediate state (Luke 23:43, 2 Cor. 5:1–10); death is described as gain for believers precisely because the next moment involves conscious enjoyment of Christ (Phil 1:23); the claim in 1 Thess. 5:10 that Christ died so that whether awake or asleep, we may live together with him makes no sense if being asleep means being unconscious; in ancient cultures, being asleep was used to describe the dead as they appear to those remaining, and those cultures also affirmed the conscious existence of the dead in another realm.

The traditional position entails some form of substance dualism in at least the sense that a person can retain identity as a conscious, immaterial spirit while the body is left behind. Dualism is currently unpopular, but it is most likely the biblical view, and no good arguments exist that show it is false. Some claim that dualism is a Greek idea falsely read into the Bible, that Hebraic holism is the scriptural view, not Greek dualism, and that dualism implies that the body is either evil or of little value. None of these assertions is true. There were Greek physicalists as well as dualists. Although the terms have a wide field of meaning, the Bible's employment of 'spirit' and 'soul' in clearly dualist ways and in a manner precisely analogous to their use in describing God and angels shows that dualism is the biblical view and not merely a Greek notion. Further, while the Bible emphasizes functional holism, this is consistent with ontological dualism. In general, entities can function holistically, while having a diversity of parts. Finally, the difference between body and soul carries no implication whatever about the value of the body.

The case for life after death

The case for immortality consists in empirical and non-empirical arguments. The two empirical arguments are near-death experiences and the resurrection of *Jesus. The non-empirical arguments divide into theistic dependent and independent ones. The former assume the existence of the God of traditional theism and therewith argue for immortality. So understood, the case is beyond reasonable doubt. Three such theistic dependent arguments are especially important. The first is two-pronged and argues from the image of God and the love of God. Given that humans have tremendous value as image-bearers, and given that God is a preserver of tremendously high value, then God is a preserver of persons. Moreover, given that God loves his image-bearers and aims to bring them to full maturity and fellowship with himself, he will sustain humans to continue this purpose. The second argument, from divine *justice, asserts that in this life good and evil,

rewards and punishments, are not evenly distributed. If God is infinitely just, he must rectify these inequities, and an afterlife is thus required. Finally, there is the argument from biblical *revelation. It can be established that the Bible is the truthful word of God, and it affirms life after death. To be an argument, rational considerations must be marshaled on behalf of the Bible's divine status. This cannot be affirmed fideistically.

Two non-theistic dependent arguments exist for immortality. The first is the argument from desire (advanced by *Thomas Aquinas and C. S. *Lewis) and states that the desire for life after death is a natural desire; every natural desire corresponds to some real state of affairs that can fulfil it; therefore, the desire for life after death corresponds to some real state of affairs – namely life after death – that fulfils it. Critics claim that the desire for immortality is nothing but an expression of ethical egoism, that people do not universally desire it and, even when they do, it is a learned not a natural desire, and that even if it is a natural desire, sometimes such desires are frustrated. While adequate responses exist for these rebuttals, they weaken the force of the argument, though it is hard to say precisely how much.

The second argument claims that property and substance dualism are true and this supports belief in life after death in two ways. First, it makes disembodied existence and personal identity in the afterlife intelligible, and secondly it provides evidence for the existence of God and against *naturalism because naturalism requires the emergence of mental entities from pure matter (naturalistic depictions of matter do not attribute to it mental potentiality). This is a case of something coming into existence from nothing, and the reality of finite mental entities is best explained by the existence of a primitive, brute mind. This, in turn, provides grounds for reintroducing the theistic dependent arguments for life after death.

The argument for property dualism claims that, however much mental and physical states are causally related, they are not the same. Consciousness, consisting of various sensations, emotions, thoughts, beliefs, acts of will, is constituted by distinctively mental properties and can in no way be described using physical predicates. Once one gets an accurate description of consciousness, it becomes clear that mental states are not identical to physical states. Mental states are characterized by their intrinsic, subjective, inner, private, qualitative feel, made present to a subject by first person introspection. Mental states like pain have an intrinsic, raw conscious feel. There is a 'what-it-is-like' aspect to pain. Most, if not all, mental states have intentionality, i.e. they are of or about things, but this is not a physical attribute and no purely physical state has intentionality. Mental states are inner, private, and known by first person, direct introspection. Any way one has of knowing about a physical property of a physical entity is available to everyone else, including ways of knowing about the physical attributes in one's brain. But a subject has a way of knowing about his mental properties/states not available to others – through introspection.

Some sensations are vague, e.g. a sensation of an object may be fuzzy or vague, but no physical state is vague. Some sensations are pleasurable or unpleasurable, but nothing physical has these properties. A cut in the knee is, strictly speaking, not unpleasurable. It is the pain event caused by the cut that is unpleasurable. Mental states can have the property of familiarity (e.g. when a desk looks familiar to someone), but familiarity is not a feature of a physical state. Since mental states have these features and physical states do not, they are not identical.

The case for substance dualism is rooted in the claim that in first person introspective knowledge, we are aware of our own egos as immaterial centres of consciousness. This awareness is what grounds our intuition that when one has an arm cut off or loses memories, one does not become only part of a person, that various bodily or psychological criteria for personal identity are neither necessary nor sufficient for sameness of person, that libertarian freedom of the will is true and is most reasonably grounded in an immaterial, substantial self, and that even if false, disembodied existence is at least metaphysically possible which it could not be if human persons were identical to their bodies.

Further, the unity of conscious experience provides evidence for a substantial, immaterial ego. Consider one's awareness of a complex fact, say one's own visual field consisting of awareness of several objects at once, including a number of different surface areas of each object. Now one may claim that such a unified awareness of one's visual field consists in the fact that there are a number of different physical parts each of which is aware only of part of and not the whole of the complex fact. However, this will not work, because it cannot account for the fact that there is a single, unitary awareness of the entire visual field. Only a single, uncomposed mental substance can account for the unity of one's visual field or, indeed, the unity of consciousness in general.

While these two arguments provide some grounds for belief in an afterlife, it must be admitted that they are far from conclusive. At the end of the day, the justification of belief in life after death is largely theistic dependent, though the empirical arguments (at least evidence from near-death experiences, since it is a matter of dispute whether historical arguments for Jesus' resurrection presuppose theism) and the non-theistic arguments provide some presumption in its favour.

Annihilationism

Recently, some have argued for conditional immortality for the unsaved on scriptural and moral grounds. Scripturally, it is claimed that the biblical fires of *hell are literal and that flames destroy whatever they burn. Morally, it is claimed that infinite punishment is disproportionate to a finite life of sin. Thus, everlasting punishment in extinction is morally preferable to everlasting punishment.

The argument from Scripture is weak. Texts whose explicit intent is to teach the extent of the afterlife overtly compare the everlasting conscious life of the saved and the unsaved (Dan. 12:2; Matt. 25:41, 46). Moreover, the flames in hell are most likely figures of speech for judgment (cf. 2 Thess. 1:8; Heb. 12:29). Otherwise, contradictions about hell obtain (e.g. it is dark yet filled with flames).

The moral argument fails as well. For one thing, the severity of a crime is not a function of the time it takes to commit it. Thus, rejection of the mercy of an infinite God could quite appropriately warrant an unending, conscious separation from God. Further, everlasting hell is morally superior to annihilation. Advocates for the sanctity of life eschew active euthanasia while advocates for the quality of life embrace it. The former reject it because on the sanctity of life view, one gets one's value, not from the quality of one's life, but the sheer fact that one exists in God's image. The latter accept it because the value of human life accrues from the quality of life. Thus, the sanctity of life position has a higher, not a lower moral regard for the dignity of human life. Now the traditional and annihilationist views about hell are expressions, respectively, of sanctity and quality of life ethical standpoints. After all, the only grounds God would have for annihilating someone would be the low quality of life in hell. If a person will not accept salvation and if God will not extinguish someone made in his image, then his only alternative is 'quarantine' and that is what hell is. Thus, the traditional view, being a sanctity and not a quality of life position, is morally superior to annihilationism.

Bibliography

J. W. Cooper, *Body, Soul and Life Everlasting* (Grand Rapids, 1989); S. T. Davis (ed.), *Death and Afterlife* (New York, 1989); G. Habermas and J. P. Moreland, *Beyond Death* (Wheaton, 1998); J. P. Moreland and S. B. Rae, *Body and Soul* (Downers Grove, 2000).

J. P. MORELAND

INDETERMINACY, see DETERMINISM, CHANCE AND FREEDOM
INDIGENOUS RELIGION, see PAGAN AND INDIGENOUS RELIGION

INDUCTIVE METHOD

There is a radical difference between the method of deduction and the method of induction. In deduction we remain within the data given. In induction we go outside or beyond the data. Take the statements: swan 1 is white; swan 2 is white; swan 3 is white; swan 4 is white; swan 5 is white. Deduction can conclude, 'Swan 5 is the same colour as swan 1', or that 'there are at least five white swans'. These conclusions seem to be indubitable, given the truth of the original five statements. Induction would conclude, 'Swan 6 will be white', or 'All swans are white.' These conclusions can be questioned. They do not have the logical force of the deductive conclusions. They go beyond the information we have and include an element of conjecture.

Most people feel that though the conclusions of the inductive method can never carry the logical force of the conclusions of the deductive method, we can still use it as a very reliable tool. Granted, they say, observing five white swans tells us nothing about the colour of swan 6. But if we observe 1,000 swans and all of them are white, we are pretty safe in assuming swan 1,001 will be white. Logically, of course, this is fallacious. If we have a bag containing marbles which may be black or white, the chances that any specific marble we take out will be black are 50:50. The fact that the first thousand or even million marbles we take from the bag are black will not change this probability for marble 1,001 or 1,000,001.

Despite the attempts of early Enlightenment philosophers such as *Descartes to build a world-view based on deduction, it is now universally recognized that almost all our understanding of the world around us is based on induction. In particular, the inductive method underlies the whole of the scientific world-view. *Science depends totally on the extrapolation of general principles (once called 'laws') from a limited number of observed instances. Water on this occasion boils at 100°C; water on the next occasion boils at 100°C; and the next; and the next ... therefore all water boils at 100°C.

Aware of the inconclusiveness of inductive *reasoning, philosophers of science have tried to set in place safeguards which they hope will increase, if not ensure, its reliability. Right at the start of the modern scientific enterprise, Francis *Bacon, a younger contemporary of Descartes, made two proposals which he felt would make the inductive method a more dependable tool. In the first place, we should be painstaking and scrupulously honest in our initial collecting of data; the more careful and thorough we are, and the more we are willing to examine apparent counter-instances, the more reliable our extrapolations will be. Secondly, we should use our observations to form a preliminary hypothesis which can then be tested by carefully planned experiments. Bacon believed that if the hypothesis passed these tests, then it was effectively established as a 'law'.

These safeguards appeared to work well. Isaac *Newton used this inductive method to establish his 'laws', from which, in turn, deductive predictions could be made. When the prediction of the return of Halley's Comet in 1758 was gloriously fulfilled, many assumed that the total dependability of the inductive method was finally established: careful research, exhaustive testing and elimination of alternative hypotheses could give us sure and certain *truth.

Despite, however, the huge success of the inductive scientific method, this assumption was not justified. David *Hume demonstrated this in his sceptical attack on the concept of *causality, where he said that however often event B follows event A, we can never prove that A causes B. Outside of the world of deduction, in the actual world of ordinary life and science where we proceed inductively, we always have to make inferences and guesses that introduce an element of uncertainty. Not even the most meticulous observations and thorough testing and confirmation of a hypothesis can remove this element. A notorious illustration of this arises from the discovery of the planet Neptune in 1846. Astronomers, using Newton's 'laws', observed certain anomalies in the behaviour of the planet Uranus and formed the hypothesis that they must be caused by the existence of a hitherto unknown planet, which was duly discovered and named Neptune. This confirmation of a hypothesis was universally acclaimed as the final vindication of both Newtonian physics and the inductive method. But in our post-Einstein age, we now know that this was an unjustified conclusion; the confidence in both Newtonian physics and the inductive method was misplaced.

The middle of the twentieth century saw two epoch-making books showing the limitations of the inductive method. In *The Logic of Scientific Discovery* (1959), Karl *Popper showed not only that no scientific theory can ever be conclusively established but also that, however large a number of confirmations of a scientific hypothesis we may have, the probability of that hypothesis being correct is not increased one bit. Not even repeated confirmations can make the truth of a hypothesis more likely. The most we can do by our testing is conclusively falsify a hypothesis; we can never conclusively verify it.

In *The Structure of Scientific Revolutions* (1962), Thomas Kuhn showed that science neither establishes definitive facts about the world around us nor proceeds in the coherent rational and methodical way that has generally been supposed. What in fact happens is that a community of scientists who have been trained to see the world in a particular way, and thus to practise science according to their belief system or '*paradigm', work at fitting all the data from their observations and experiments into that paradigm. Some do not fit well, so these become the challenges and puzzles on which they concentrate. The resolving of these problems or anomalies is seen as success and progress. Paradigms continue to be used unquestioningly until the number of unsolved problems begins to mount up. This precipitates a crisis; some of the scientists begin to realize that the paradigm is at fault and search for a new one. One is found and adopted, not because it can be shown to be true, or even because logical arguments can be adduced to show its superiority over any other one, but because it answers some of the problems inherent in the old paradigm. But while it may provide better answers to the current problems than the old one, the new paradigm will also bring with it a new crop of problems. So the change is not necessarily for the better. In fact, from the nature of the case, said Kuhn, there is no rational way of relating one paradigm to another to see which one is best. They are 'incommensurable'. We should not think in terms of science gradually getting nearer and nearer to the ultimate goal of a 'full, objective, true account of nature'. Rather, we should see it as 'evolution-towards-what-we-wish-to-know'. Paul Feyerabend went beyond Kuhn in his scepticism about the rationality of the scientific method. In contrast to the traditional concept of orderly rational progress, the story of science, he said, is one of 'epistemological anarchism'. Historically, so far from advancing in a rational manner, the dominating factors in the story of science have been non-rational elements like politics, rhetoric and propaganda. There is no rational justification, said Feyerabend, for adopting the scientific world-view over any other, such as that of voodoo.

Although popular thought continues to retain a huge confidence in the inductive method as still almost universally used by science, the Christian apologist can welcome the less dogmatic approach that philosophers of science are now adopting. No longer is it a matter of 'proved scientific fact' to be set over against unprovable religious beliefs held by faith. Both the scientific world-view and the Christian world-view require steps of 'faith', the accepting of beliefs which cannot be ultimately rationally proved.

Equally, of course, Christian apologists need to be aware of the limits of inductive arguing when they make use of it. They may with justification claim that, say, the positive results that flow from people being converted to Christianity are best explained by assuming that Christianity is true; they may not say that they conclusively prove its truth.

Bibliography

T. Kuhn, *The Structure of Scientific Revolutions* (Chicago, 1996); K. Popper, *The Logic of Scientific Discovery* (London, 1968).

P. HICKS

INFINITE SERIES

Concept and distinctions

An infinite series is a series without a beginning term, an ending term, or both. Mathematician and logician Georg Cantor defined it more precisely as a series that has the same number of terms as one of its sub-series, e.g. the series 1, 2, 3 ... (the series of natural numbers) has a subseries 2, 4, 6 ... (the series of even numbers). However, there are just as many even numbers as there are natural numbers, paradoxical as that may sound. That *paradox identifies the series as infinite.

Among infinite series, we may distinguish between *actual* and *potential* infinites. The set of natural numbers is an actual infinite: that set actually contains an infinite number of members. A potential infinite, however, is a series that approaches an infinite number but never reaches that point, as when we try to list all the natural numbers one by one, or when we divide an object by half, and then by half again and so on. In those cases we never reach an ending point, a last member of the series. We never reach a number that we could call infinity.

Apologetic importance

Some forms of the *cosmological argument for the existence of God deny the existence of certain kinds of infinite series. *Thomas Aquinas, in the first three of his 'five ways', denied that chains of causes (causes of motion, being, and necessity, respectively) can go back forever. He argued that every causal chain has a beginning: a first mover, a first cause of being, and a first necessary being, namely God. The *kalam* argument of Al-Ghazali, recently expounded by William Lane Craig, denies that there can be an actually infinite

series of events succeeding one another in time. Therefore, the universe had a beginning, which must be explained by a divine cause. Craig argues, first, that there cannot be an actually infinite collection of *things* (though there can be actually infinite sets of numbers) and, secondly, that even if such a collection were possible, it could not be achieved by adding one member after another, as must happen in a temporal succession of events.

To show that there cannot be an actually infinite collection of things, Craig refers to the three paradoxes noted by Cantor that in an infinite series, the whole is equivalent to some of its parts; one can add members to an infinite set without increasing the number of members in the set – the number remains at infinity; one can remove members from the set without decreasing its membership. Such is the case in the abstract world of numbers, but, Craig says, it would be impossible to have a set of concrete objects or a series of events that had these properties. He borrows the illustration of 'Hilbert's Hotel' from George Gamow that if a hotel had an infinite number of rooms filled with guests, additional guests could check in without anyone moving out, and the number of guests would be the same as before. The sign could read, 'No vacancy – guests welcome' (*Reasonable Faith*, p. 96).

Craig then argues that even if we grant the possibility of an actually infinite collection of things, we cannot form such a collection by adding one member after another. It is impossible, e.g. to count an infinite collection one by one for 'No matter how many numbers you count, you can always add one more before arriving at infinity' (*Reasonable Faith*, p. 98). The same must be said of an infinite series of events in time. If the process of nature and history extends infinitely far into the past, then it is an infinite succession of events, and that succession has proceeded one by one, ending precisely at the present moment. But why did it end now, rather than yesterday, or a thousand years ago? For on this hypothesis yesterday was also the end of an infinite chain of events, and so was the moment a thousand years before the present one. But, in fact, there can be no end at all, for an infinite series never ends. So, Craig concludes, the series of past events is finite. Therefore, the universe had a beginning, and therefore a cause, because 'whatever begins to exist has a cause' (*Reasonable Faith*, p. 92).

Evaluation

Certainly, it is difficult to conceive of an actually infinite collection of things. Hilbert's Hotel is counter-intuitive, but many find the Cantor paradoxes themselves hard to believe at first hearing. After we learn to work with infinite sets of numbers, we tend to accept the Cantor definitions as a matter of course. We have not, however, encountered infinite sets of material objects. If we ever do, however, might we not eventually get used to the strange properties of such sets? Here, images are important. The idea of an infinite hotel is somewhat ridiculous, as is, say, the idea of a hotel with the hiccups. But how about the idea of an infinitely extended chain of beads? Might we not one day get used to the idea of adding or subtracting beads without changing the number in the infinite collection? Part of the problem is that when we try to picture in our minds an infinite hotel, we tend to think of it as a finite hotel with very odd properties – people being squeezed into it without others being squeezed out. But if the hotel were truly infinite, those properties would not be odd, but expected, hard as it may be to imagine these properties in a mental picture. It is also hard to imagine such properties in a series of numbers, but Cantor proved that they exist.

Similarly, the notion of an infinite series of events continuing through time is hard to comprehend, but is it impossible? It may indeed be impossible to count through an infinite series and end with a final number. If time itself were subjective, however, rather than objective, then an infinite set of past events might exist simultaneously (like the series 1, 2, 3 ...), rather than existing by a temporal process of addition. The same would be the case if time were an objective dimension of n-dimensional space, and all events of past, present, and future, could be viewed together by a being of a higher dimension. And if we could go backwards in time from the present, then we could visit yesterday, the day before yesterday, and the day before that, much as we now move from today, to tomorrow, to the day after. In that case, we would perceive the days of past history much as we now perceive the days of the future: as a potential infinity, rather than an actual infinity.

Of course, these three suppositions are contrary to Craig's own theory of time. (See his *Time and Eternity: Exploring God's Relationship to Time* [Wheaton, 2001].) These considerations do not challenge the consistency of Craig's view, but they do indicate that our present questions about infinite series do not have obvious answers. Indeed, they are linked to other issues that deserve book-length treatment.

Thomas Aquinas would object to the supposition that even a potentially infinite series of natural events in the past is insufficient to account for the world as we know it. For on this supposition, each event is caused by a previous one, and no event actually begins the series. Therefore, no event (or group of events, by the same logic) serves as the cause of the rest. So the universe is uncaused, unexplained. Aquinas believes the universe must have a cause, so the chain of causal explanation cannot be infinite, even potentially infinite.

Aquinas argues that the universe has a cause and, therefore, there cannot be an infinite series of causes. Craig argues the reverse that there cannot be an infinite series of causes and, therefore, the universe must have one cause. I confess that I find Aquinas more persuasive as it seems more obvious to me that the universe requires a cause than that an infinite series of events is impossible. But even Aquinas' view requires assumptions, namely that nothing exists or happens without a sufficient cause, and that causes (including the cause of the universe) are accessible to human reason. Many sceptics of the past and present would not grant those assumptions.

These arguments suggest that our concepts of cause, reason and infinite series depend on world-views and on ontological and epistemological assumptions. They are insufficient in themselves to serve as grounds for world-views. Christian theists will think differently from sceptics about these matters. Their Christian theism will govern their concepts of cause, reason and infinity, rather than the reverse.

Bibliography

G. Cantor, *Contributions to the Foundations of the Theory of Transfinite Numbers* (ET, Chicago, 1915); W. L. Craig, *The Kalam Cosmological Argument* (New York, 1979); *Reasonable Faith* (Wheaton, 1994); G. Gamow, *One, Two Three, Infinity* (London, 1946).

J. M. FRAME

INFORMATION THEORY

Information Theory (IT) was first formally developed by Claude Shannon ('A Mathematical Theory of Communication', *Bell System Technical Journal*, vol. 27, pp. 379–423, 623–656 [July and October, 1948]). As an engineer at Bell Labs, he sought to provide a precise scientific theory for communication systems. Thus, 'information' is a quantitative notion, concerned solely with the transfer of data from one source to another. Shannon realized such information could be measured in bits, most conveniently using logarithms to base 2, thereby allowing for both simplicity and additivity. According to IT, the information a process communicates is simply a measure of the extent to which it reduces the original number of possibilities. If some process s (e.g. an election) results in the reduction of candidates from 4 to 1, the information the election produces, $I(s)$, is given by the formula, $I(s) = \log_2 4 = 2$, called the *entropy* of the source. If the various possibilities are not equally probable, one signifies the probability of some event i as $p(s_i)$, and then the amount of information produced by s_i equals $\log_2 1/p(s_i) = -\log_2 p(s_i)$, called the 'surprisal' of (s_i). Thus, the average information of a source where different events have different surprisals is the sum of the product of each probability [$p(s_i)$] times the surprisal of each s_i [$I(s_i)$]. The 'noise' produced by any communication is simply the difference between the information generated at the source [$I(s)$] and the information received at the end of the process [$I(r)$]. That difference will be due to sources other than s. The 'equivocation' of s is the information available at s that does reach r. Given any transfer of information, $I(s) \geq I(r)$, for the information available from s at r is $I(s)$ minus the 'noise'.

Two facts should be noted. First, IT is a purely formal theory for measuring the quantity of data transferred from a source to a receiver. It does not, therefore, either decipher or measure the cognitive or semantic content of a message. A message with just 1 bit of information could communicate more content than one with 16 bits of information if the single bit coded greater content than the 16 bits. IT measures signal quantity and the degree to which that quantity is received. Information in the everyday and the usual philosophical sense connotes meaning, and a great deal of meaning can be communicated by a small amount of IT information, while a large amount of IT information might well contain very little cognitive information. Secondly, IT is not an account of causality. It may well be that any causal interaction transfers information from one state to another, but causes are not identical with the information so transferred. Moreover, while any transfer of information will require some causal interaction between transmitter and receiver, those interactions are not identical with the information they transfer.

Its formal, quantitative nature has prompted biologists, physicists and cognitive scientists, among others, to create IT models to explain physical processes. Philosopher Fred Dretske (*Knowledge and the Flow of Information* [Cambridge, MA, 1981]) for example, employed IT to account for intentional notions such as belief and knowledge on purely naturalistic grounds. Biologists and cognitive scientists have also used IT to model evolution, perception and other cognitive processes. The fact that DNA contains a code by which genes 'direct' the development of organisms, and the fact that computer models can represent cognitive processes which themselves carry information, make it natural to try to explain these in terms of information transfer. Meanwhile, Christian apologist William Dembski has argued that IT provides irrefutable evidence that purely naturalistic evolution cannot adequately account for the development of new biological forms.

The use of IT in areas of *science other than communication theory is of interest to the Christian apologist insofar as it creates a perspective from which to analyse and criticize *naturalism. To the extent that naturalistic proposals such as Dretske's are found wanting by the scientific and philosophical communities, the likelihood increases that human life cannot be fully explained naturalistically. Dembski, however, employs IT to present a positive case against naturalism, which is that it cannot in principle account for the evolutionary development of the world.

Dembski's basic thesis is that evolution requires the increase of information as organisms become more complex, but IT demonstrates that naturalistic processes alone cannot account for those increases. Hence, evolution – which Dembski, unlike young-earth creationists, does not dispute *per se* – requires informational input from some other kind of source. Since the required input is information, the source must be intelligent, for non-intelligent natural processes can transfer but cannot create information. While this intelligence need not be supernatural, lurking in the background is the reasonable premise that an infinite regress of merely contingent intelligent causes cannot offer a satisfactory explanation. Eventually, the cause of informational increase must come from a source having intelligence. Although not a proof of Christian *theism, clearly Dembski's argument, if sound, makes it a most reasonable hypothesis, thereby bridging the gap between science and theology/philosophy by science.

Dembski's argument assumes that the laws of IT hold for the transmission of biological information. Every organism develops as it does because of the information contained in its genes, and the origin of that information must be accounted for. Once a particular kind of animal exists, it can pass its 'information' on to the next generation, but any new development of forms requires additional information. The information carried by DNA, he argues, is contingent, complex specified information (CSI). It is contingent because the laws of nature did not create it necessarily, i.e. it might not have been. Complexity is a measure of the 'distance' information has from randomness; the more complex the information, the less likely it is that it results from chance. The complexity of a string of alphabet blocks expressing a proposition, for example, makes it unlikely that the string is merely the product of a child's aimless play. Specification refers to a pattern's independence from the event it describes, e.g. a blueprint specifies a structure, and from it one can construct the building.

Dembski argues first that complex specified information cannot be generated by chance. Randomness can create contingency, but not CSI. Secondly, neither physical laws nor their combination with chance can increase CSI. *Ex nihilo, nihilo fit.* His 'law of conservation of information' follows: natural causes are incapable of generating CSI. Thus, naturalism cannot account for the increase of CSI necessary for the development of new life forms, while the intelligent-design hypothesis can. Consequently, the existence of CSI, given IT, entails that any adequate scientific explanation of life's development in general and of human life in particular will include intelligent design.

Three foundational issues confront this argument. First, are IT principles literally applicable to biological processes? Perhaps biology can be modelled by IT, but does not literally instantiate it. The real causes of an organism's development, and so of evolutionary history in general, would then be not information, but physical causes. Limiting the possibilities of evolutionary development by appeal to IT may simply be mistaking a useful model for reality. IT is a theory about the quantitative transmission of information, not a set of laws which constrain biological interactions and developments.

Secondly, the success of this argument will depend upon the success scientists have in accounting for the 'increase' in information over evolutionary history. Just as the physical law of entropy does not exclude localized increases in energy, so might natural laws not prohibit the increase of information under specified conditions. Clearly, if increased information is literally the vehicle by which evolutionary development takes place, and evolution tracks increased complexity, without a naturalistic mechanism for such increase, naturalism is untenable. Science, however, is in the business of uncovering such mechanisms. Moreover, some scientists see no difficulty in the idea that nature does mindlessly what we do intentionally. 'Intelligent design and natural selection produce similar results. One justification for this view is that programmes designed by humans to produce a result are similar to, and may be indistinguishable from, programmes generated by mindless selection' (J. Maynard Smith, 'The Concept of Information in Biology', *Philosophy of Science*, vol. 67.2 [June, 2000], pp. 177–194).

Lastly, it is not incontestable that the 'design hypothesis' is a purely scientific hypothesis. Granted that we do, on the one hand, make judgments about design and randomness (e.g. in personal situations), and about intent and accident (e.g. in a court of law) on the other hand, in these situations we have our own experience by which to judge whether an event was designed or coincidental or whether an act was deliberate or accidental. But what warrants such judgments in science? Science *per se* does not entail design, for it deals only with quantifiable causes and processes. Inferring design requires philosophical input, and so is essentially dependent upon one's philosophical and theological assumptions. It may well be a compelling philosophical conclusion, but not a scientific one.

Bibliography

W. Dembski, *The Design Inference* (Cambridge, 1998); *Intelligent Design* (Downers Grove, 1999).

T. J. BURKE, JR

INNER LIGHT

The concept of the inner light has a rich and variegated history. Rooted in Quaker thought and experience, the inner light has most recently manifested itself in the *New Age movement. The Society of the Inner Light (UK), founded by Dion Fortune, stands as an example. The basic notion entails two primary elements: a radical subjectivism of religious or spiritual experience and a belief that the divine dwells in all human beings and can be reached or experienced through the inner light.

The Quakers, known as the Society of Friends, are also known, though not as familiarly, as the Children of Light, emphasizing what some have referred to as Quakerism's distinctive belief, rooted in the teachings of its founder, George Fox (1624–91). The thought of Thomas Muenzer (1490–1534) and Caspar Schwenkfeld von Ossig (1489–1561) served as a precursor to Quaker thought, the latter holding to the primacy of the 'internal living word' and a radical mysticism and spiritualism. For Fox, the inner light was in fact God manifesting himself within the human's inner being; it was direct and experiential. The purpose of the Quaker church service was to allow all members to experience the inner light and to share the *revelation with others. Though George Fox initially taught that the inner light was of the same voice as Scripture, he also warned his followers against what he termed 'the idolatry of the Bible'. This tension eventually relaxed in favour of the Spirit over the Word, of the living, on-going revelation over the recorded revelation in the Bible.

This further led to the eclipse of Scripture as the basis for Quakerism's beliefs, as evidenced in William Penn (1644–1718), who rejected the doctrines of the Trinity and atonement and advocated the universalism of the inner light. This resulted in a quite subjective approach to religion, equating religious truth with the individual's experience. It also concomitantly spurred religious tolerance and *pluralism, the roots of Penn's 'Holy Experiment' in the colony of Pennsylvania. Finally, it fostered an intense mysticism, downplaying doctrine and eschewing formal beliefs or systems or even formal visible church practices. All of these qualities conspire to make the concept of the inner light an attractive force and useful tool in the hands of its New Age practitioners.

In contemporary usage, the concept functions as the point of connection between the individual, physical being and the world of the divine or spiritual being. This is evidenced in the teachings of The Society of the Inner Light, based in the UK, which views the inner light as a 'divine spark' that enables recipients to live to their highest potential, move from the 'Lesser Mysteries' to the 'Greater Mysteries' and live on the inner planes or the 'worlds behind appearances'. Numerous other centres or cultic groups from the mundane to the bizarre take the name of the inner light. The term also appears in book titles, such as Debbie Mandel's *Turn on Your Inner Light: Fitness for Body, Mind and Soul*. Various emphases on meditation, especially Buddhist ones, also use the concept of the inner light, employing it synonymously with Kabbalistic language, the principle of *chakra* and the language of the inner self. In all of these manifestations, the concept is a quite subjective guide to one's life, which enlightens and empowers through connection with the spiritual or divine.

The main problem with the concept of the inner light is that it reduces all religious belief to the subjective and experiential, allowing for no means to adjudicate between conflicting religions and disallowing the presentation of a compelling case to either accept or reject religious claims. This problem, however, also accounts for its appeal in a pluralistic age, as the inner light is by definition pluralistic and reflects extreme tolerance. Further appeal for the inner light comes in its emphasis on lively experience or spirituality, especially alluring in a materialistic or technological culture. The inner light, however, is no substitute for the orthodox view of the *Holy Spirit's work in conjunction with Scripture, understood as the experience of the Holy Spirit working through Scripture, and the indwelling presence of the Spirit in the life of the believer.

Bibliography

T. D. Hamm, 'The Problem of the Inner Light in Nineteenth-Century Quakerism', in

M. L. Birkel and J. W. Newman (eds.), *The Lamb's War: Quaker Essays to Honor Hugh Barbour* (Richmond, 1992), pp. 101–117.

S. J. NICHOLS

INSPIRATION, see BIBLICAL INSPIRATION
INTELLIGENT DESIGN, see ORIGINS, THEORIES OF

IRENAEUS

Irenaeus (c. 130–c. 202) grew up in Asia Minor, where he heard Polycarp teach, and after going to the West, he became bishop of Lyons in 177. He worked for peace in the disputes over practices within the church, but he took a strong stand against Marcionites and Gnostics, whose teachings challenged fundamental Christian doctrines. His *Demonstration of the Apostolic Preaching* is a catechetical work containing apologetic elements. *Against Heresies*, in five books, outlines gnostic systems, particularly that version of Valentinianism expounded by Ptolemy, and refutes them from logic and Scripture.

In his surviving writings, Irenaeus is a defender of the orthodox faith against the major doctrinal errors of his time. The apologists had already made use of philosophy in addressing outsiders; Irenaeus went further by employing it to refute ideas arising from those bearing the Christian name. He found the implications of the gnostic blending of Christianity, philosophy, pagan *mythology and religion and Jewish speculations to be destructive of the doctrines of creation, incarnation and resurrection.

Irenaeus argues that the correct meaning of Scripture is in accord with the 'canon [or rule] of truth', a summary of apostolic teaching, itself derived from Scripture. In doing so, he emphasizes the fundamental unities: of God (the one God is the Creator of all and Father of Christ), of the Lord *Jesus Christ (the *Logos* become flesh), of the divine plan of salvation (the harmony of God's progressive *revelation in the biblical covenants), of human nature (flesh and soul receiving the divine Spirit), of Scripture (the harmony of Old and New Testaments), and of the church (preserving and proclaiming the apostolic tradition). His key ideas are summed up in his frequently recurring words: 'one and the same God', 'economy' (God's arrangements to bring humanity from infancy to maturity), 'recapitulation' (Christ as the new Adam summing up human nature and the history of redemption), and 'participation' (sharing in Christ through his Spirit effects unity with God).

Irenaeus learned as thoroughly as he could the teaching of his opponents and answered them with logical and historical arguments and especially with basic doctrinal and scriptural ideas.

Bibliography

Works ed. and tr. (Fr.) by A. Rousseau, L. Doutreleau, *et al.*, in *Sources Chrétiennes* (Paris), vols. 100 (1965), 152, 153 (1969), 210, 211 (1974), 263, 264 (1979), 293, 294 (1982); M. A. Donovan, *One Right Reading? A Guide to Irenaeus* (Collegeville, 1997); E. Ferguson, 'Irenaeus' *Proof of the Apostolic Preaching* and Early Catechetical Instruction', *Studia Patristica*, 18.3 (1989), pp. 119–140; E. F. Osborn, *Irenaeus of Lyons* (Cambridge, 2001).

E. FERGUSON

ISLAM

Islam: an eschatological religion

Islam was founded by the prophet Muhammad, who was born in Mecca in 570 and who died in Medina in 632. Chronologically, the latest of the world monotheistic religions, Islam is seen by Muslims as the eschatological, or final, religion. The Qur'an acknowledges that God had revealed the *tawrat* (Torah) to Moses, the *zabur* (Psalms?) to David, the *injil* (Gospel) to *Jesus (3:3). Consequently, Jews and Christians are presented as 'the People of the Book', *ahl al-kitab*. This favourable designation highlights what Jews, Christians and Muslims have in common: each community received a Holy Scripture. The Qur'an being God's last Word, the Muslim community forms 'the People of the Book' par excellence. Thus Islamic theology identifies *Judaism, Christianity and Islam as God-given religions, *al-adyan al-samawiyya* ('The heavenly religions').

Islam: a missionary religion

From an Islamic point of view, Judaism and Christianity were saving religions up until the rise of Islam. Since then, Islam has been, and will always be, the only valid religion (3:19). In other words, the status of Judaism and Christianity in Islam is that of outdated religions. Their respective teachings are imperfect for opposite reasons. Jewish law is deemed too earthly, its moral standards are too lax, and its penal code is too strict. Christian doctrine, by contrast, is otherworldly, its ethical values are idealistic, and its penal code is too lenient. Islamic law is a well-balanced law in all respects, holding the middle ground between Judaism and Christianity (3:110). The Muslim community believes in all prophets, discriminating against no-one (3:84), unlike the Christian community, who do not accept Muhammad as prophet, and the Jewish community, who reject both Jesus and Muhammad.

Furthermore, Muslim theologians see Judaism and Christianity as corrupted religions. Their doctrines no longer reflect God's *revelation to Moses and Jesus. Islam, they argue, is the only religion that has preserved God's revelation in its truthfulness. Islam is also a universal religion destined to all nations (21:107). Muhammad, God's final prophet (33:40), was sent to convey God's message to 'the People of the Book' and to the Gentiles (3:20). Thus Islam is by definition a missionary religion.

Mission, apologetics, polemics

Muslims have the duty to invite everyone to embrace Islam 'by way of wisdom and good exhortation' (16:125). This general command about da'wah, or Islamic mission, applies to Jews and Christians in particular: 'Do not argue with the People of the Book but in the best possible way, except in the case of those among them who have been unjust' (29:46; cf. 3:64).

The ambivalence of Qur'anic teaching about Christianity and Christians is such that Muslim people and Islamic regimes have referred to different Qur'anic texts to justify different approaches to Christians. These attitudes range from tolerance and respect (Senegal) to apologetics (see U. Aziz-Us-Samad) to polemics (see A. Deedat) to opposition and even persecution (Saudi Arabia). Needless to say, these various attitudes are based on various Qur'anic interpretations which themselves are determined by the historical context, local and international, in which the Muslim and the Christian communities relate to each other.

Theological issues

It has been noted that Islam considers Christianity as a divine religion but a religion which has been corrupted. Thus Islamic theology has raised very serious criticisms against Christian doctrine. We need now to look at some of these criticisms and to offer a brief response.

1. The reliability of the Scriptures

The Qur'an claims that the coming of Muhammad has been prophesied in the Torah and the Gospel (7:157) and by Jesus himself (61:6). Jews and Christians have denied this allegation. Muslim theologians have drawn the conclusion that 'the People of the Book' must have altered their Scriptures: the relevant texts have been either changed or misinterpreted. Indeed, the Qur'an accuses 'the People of the Book' of falsifying the Scriptures (2:75; 4:46; 5:13, 41). Evidence for textual falsification includes the following: the Torah ascribes major sins to prophets, e.g. Noah, Abraham, Lot, David (prophets are seen as sinless in Islam); the four Gospels have replaced 'the Gospel of Jesus'; contradictions between parallel texts in the Gospels (e.g. Jesus' genealogies in Matthew and Luke); the authors of many biblical writings are either unknown or ordinary men (not prophets).

Christian response:
i. The Qur'an makes no reference at all to the Bible to back its claims about Muhammad.
ii. The Qur'an describes the existing Torah and Gospel as 'light and guidance for humankind' (5:46; 6:91). If they had been corrupted, they would not have been described in these terms.
iii. The Qur'an says that God watches over his Word to protect it from corruption (6:34; 15:9). God himself would be untruthful if he let his Word become unreliable.
iv. What the concept of revelation means in Christianity is not the same as in Islam. Unlike the Qur'an, the Bible is both God's Word and a human text.
v. Many so-called inconsistencies will disappear if the intended meaning of the relevant texts is understood correctly. A literal or rationalistic interpretation is not necessarily the right one.
vi. Textual evidence about the Bible, i.e. manuscripts, clearly indicates that its text

has been handed down accurately. Differences between the manuscripts do not affect the reliability of the Scriptures by any means.

vii. Some texts in the Bible (and in the Qur'an) do raise difficulties. Perhaps these problems are due to our ignorance. *Humility and trusting in God's Word should characterize the believers' attitude towards their Holy Scriptures.

2. The Trinity

The Qur'an rejects the doctrine of the *Trinity (4:171; 5:73) as it seems to represent a most serious threat to God's oneness (112:1–4). Muslim theologians argue that either God is one or he is three, he cannot be both. The word 'trinity', they say, is not even in the Bible. It is a blasphemy to call Mary 'the Mother of God'. In fact the doctrine of the Trinity has been made up by the early church.

Christian response:
i. Christians believe as firmly as Muslims that there is one and only one God.
ii. What the Qur'an rejects is the triad God-Mary-Jesus (5:116), not the biblical and Christian Trinity Father-Son-Holy Spirit.
iii. The word 'trinity' is not in the New Testament because it is a theological word, but what it refers to is there. The word *tawhid* which Muslim theologians use for God's oneness is not found in the Qur'an either. Does this mean that the doctrine about God's oneness is alien to the Qur'an?
iv. God is one *substance*, three *persons*. He is not one and three from the same point of view. This distinction is to some extent comparable to the difference between one humanity and many human beings.
v. An alternative way of defining the Trinitarian God consists in describing the Father as God, the Son as the Word of God, and the *Holy Spirit as the Spirit of God. The Bible and the Qur'an present Jesus as the Word of God, *kalimat Allah* (1 John 1:1, 14; Qur'an 3:39, 45; 4:171). Both of them refer to the Holy Spirit, *ruh al-qudus*, in connection with Jesus' mission (John 14:26; Qur'an 2:87, 253; 5:110).
vi. In Christianity as well as in Islam faith is primarily defined as trusting in God, *al-tasdiq bi Allah*, and in his Word. Because God is our Creator, we should expect him

to be beyond our human understanding. The doctrine of the Trinity remains 'a *mystery', i.e. a belief which, although based on God's Word, is too high for us to grasp rationally.

vii. The title 'Mother of God' is not meant to deify Mary (who is no more than a human being) but to point out Jesus' divinity. We may consider it theologically sound but it is certainly unhelpful and misleading in an Islamic context.

3. Jesus' divinity

Islam holds Jesus as one of God's greatest prophets. He was born of the Virgin Mary (21:91) but this fact does not imply that he is the Son of God. Like Adam, he was directly created by God (3:59). The Qur'an denies explicitly that Jesus is the Son of God (9:30), for 'God begets not, nor is He begotten' (112:3). To say that God has a Son means that he has a female partner (6:101).

Muslim scholars have rejected the doctrine about Jesus' sonship for three main reasons:

i. God is one (112:1). Either God is one and Jesus cannot be his Son, or Jesus is God's Son and God is not one.
ii. God is the supreme Lord (1:2). It is unfitting for God to humble himself and become a human being.
iii. God is transcendent (42:11). The Creator is far above his creation. It is unthinkable that he should 'enter' the created world and become part of it.

Muslim authors observe that Jesus never claims in the Gospels that he is God. It is Christians who have made him into a god. If Jesus is to be called 'Son of God', this can only be done allegorically, in a way similar to Adam (Luke 3:38), *angels (Job 1:6), Israel (Deut. 14:1), Solomon (2 Sam. 7:14) and Jesus' disciples (Luke 6:35).

Christian response:
i. What the Qur'an seems (rightly) to deny is a temporal and physical conception of Jesus' sonship. God has no partner whatsoever. Jesus is not the Son of God because he was miraculously conceived in the virgin Mary's womb. He is co-eternal with God the Father, as God's Word (i.e. the Qur'an) is co-eternal with God in Islam. His conception is not only miraculous but

unique. Isaac, Samuel and John the Baptist (*Yahya* in the Qur'an) all had human parents. Adam was the first human being and therefore the way he was created cannot be compared with the way Jesus was conceived in his mother's womb.

ii. God is eternal and he derives his existence from no-one but himself. In this sense, 'God begets not, nor is He begotten' (112:3). This Qur'anic text (and many others) is not about Christian beliefs but Arab polytheists who worshipped God and his alleged daughters (17:40).

iii. Jesus is the *only* Son of God (John 1:14; 3:16). This title is to be understood neither literally nor metaphorically, but spiritually. It denotes Jesus' unique relationship with God. Those who have special relationships with God are called God's sons and/or daughters in a way similar (not identical) to Jesus' relationship with the Father.

iv. It is true that Jesus does not say 'I am God' in the Gospels. The reason behind this is that he did not want to be mistaken by the Jewish people. They would have thought he was challenging God's oneness and would have accused him of blasphemy. However, his claims and acts clearly pointed to his divine status. One of his claims was that he had the *authority to forgive people's sins (cf. Qur'an 3:135). In fact he did grant forgiveness of sins to several people including a paralysed man, whom he then healed so as to show that he had the right to do what he did (Mark 2:1–11).

v. God is one. As sinful creatures we are unable to know God through our mind. The only way to know him is through his self-disclosure. God's revelation must override human rationality. Did not God summon Muhammad to submit to him even if he was to reveal himself in a totally unexpected way: 'Say: "If the Ever-Merciful [God] had a Son, I would be the very first to worship [him]"' (43:81)?

vi. God is the Lord, hence he is sovereign. Has he not the right to do what he pleases? Who are we to say that it is unworthy of him to lower himself and to become like one of us? Through Jesus Christ God revealed himself as the Servant King. This teaches us what true lordship and authority consist of. Do we not long for our leaders to use their power to serve their people instead of lording it over them?

vii. God is transcendent. The Bible also teaches us that human beings are unique creatures in that God made us in his own image (Gen. 1:26–27). Thus the very special nature of humankind provided the framework for the incarnation of God's Son.

4. Jesus' death

The Qur'an denies the claim made by the Jewish people that they crucified Jesus. Muslims explain that what really happened was that God stepped in when Jesus was about to be arrested. He lifted him up to himself (4:157–159). Muslim commentators argue that God made someone look like Jesus (Judas Iscariot? Simon of Cyrene? Barabbas?), and this person was crucified instead of him. Jesus will come back from heaven before the end time. Jews will then believe that he was God's messenger sent to them and Christians that he was not the Son of God. Both will see that he was not crucified at the end of his first mission. Jesus will defeat the Anti-Christ and implement Islamic law worldwide. Having completed his second mission he will die a natural death and will be buried by Muslims next to Muhammad in Medina.

Muslim theologians contend that the Christian doctrine about Jesus' atoning death is unwarranted. God is sovereign and he does not need a sacrifice to forgive our sins (4:48). Christian doctrine, they say, undermines personal responsibility (6:164). It has never been preached by Jesus and was made up by Paul who was not even one of Jesus' twelve disciples.

Christian response:

i. The Qur'an denies the crucifixion of Jesus in one single text whereas the four Gospels report the event with such detail and a realism that only eyewitnesses could relate.

ii. Muslim commentators are aware that the way the Qur'anic text has been understood by most Muslims raises some serious questions. One of them is that God appears to have deceived the Jewish people as well as Jesus' disciples, who wrongly believed that Jesus was crucified. There is a need for an alternative interpretation which is consistent with God's truthfulness.

iii. God vindicated Jesus, not through stopping his enemies from putting him to death, but through raising him from the dead (Acts 2:22–24).

iv. Jesus died on the cross in fulfilment of God's purpose which was to save humankind from sin, death and *evil (Acts 2:23). This purpose was revealed hundreds of years before the event took place (Isa. 52:13 – 53:12).

v. Jesus was fully aware that his distinctive mission would not be fulfilled without his death on the cross (John 12:27–28). He told his disciples about his forthcoming death long before it happened (Matt. 16:21–23). He himself presented his death as an atoning sacrifice for the redemption of the world (Mark 10:45).

vi. God is just and 'he does not leave the guilty unpunished' (Exod. 34:7). Jesus offered his life as a sin sacrifice so that God may forgive our sins without compromising his justice.

vii. God's forgiveness is not granted automatically to everyone. People still need to respond positively to God's offer. Our responsibility is fully engaged as we decide whether or not to accept what he has done for us in Christ.

5. Muhammad's prophethood

Muslims believe that Muhammad is the greatest and last prophet (33:40). Jews and Christians should accept him as such. God entrusted him with the Qur'an which confirms the Torah and the Gospel (2:91). The case for Muhammad's prophethood includes the following four proofs:

i. Biblical prophecies. Muhammad was foretold in the Torah and the Gospel (7:157) and by Jesus himself (61:1). The prophecies about the 'New Moses' (Deut. 18:15, 17–18), the Lord's Servant (Isa. 42:1–4) and the Paraclete (John 14:16) are all about him.

ii. The Qur'an miracle. Muhammad produced many miracles, the greatest one is the Qur'an itself. The Qur'an is miraculous in that its literary form is not just perfect but supernatural (17:88). Its Arabic is an integral part of the revelation, which is why it is God's Word only in that language. The fact that Muhammad was illiterate (7:157) enhances the miraculous character of the Qur'an.

iii. The content of the Qur'an. Islamic law is perfect in all its aspects (religious, legal,

penal, etc.). It combines mercy and *justice, forgiveness and punishment; it provides guidance for this life and for the afterlife. This perfection is lacking in Jewish law (which is little concerned with eternal life) and Christian teaching (which has no political agenda).

iv. Islam's political and military success. Muhammad's triumph over his enemies represents God's seal of approval upon his mission. Within less than a century of his death, Muslim armies conquered vast territories stretching from Spain in the west to the Indian subcontinent in the east.

Christian response:

i. Biblical prophecies, which allegedly point to Muhammad, are applied to Jesus in the New Testament. Jesus considers himself as the 'New Moses' (John 5:46; cf. John 1:45; Acts 3:20–22) and the Lord's Servant (Luke 22:37; cf. Matt. 8:16–17). As for the Paraclete, Jesus speaks plainly about him as the Holy Spirit. He said that he would come in Jerusalem within 'a few days' of his departure (Acts 1:4–5). The Holy Spirit did come upon the disciples ten days after Jesus ascended to heaven (Acts 2:2–4).

ii. The Qur'an excepted, Muhammad's *miracles are reported in the Hadith compilations (written in the third century of the Islamic era). The reliability of the relevant accounts has not been established beyond any reasonable doubt. Even if they were, they would still not form compelling evidence for Muhammad's prophethood. From a Christian perspective, miracles certainly represent an important criterion for assessing a person's claims to prophethood. However, this criterion is neither necessary nor sufficient (Deut. 13:1–4). John the Baptist was a great prophet yet he performed no miracles (Matt. 11:11; John 10:41). Jesus tells us not to give too much credit to signs and wonders as some false prophets are able to perform spectacular miracles (Matt. 24:24).

iii. The Arabic perfection of the Qur'an is a debatable issue even among Arab and Muslim scholars. The quality of its literary style is a subjective matter which can only be appreciated by Arabic-literate people. This raises the question about the universal destination of the Qur'an. Is it compatible with the fact that when translated it has no longer the status of God's Word?

iv. The illiteracy of Muhammad is also open to debate. The *ummi* prophet (5:157) does not necessarily mean the 'illiterate' prophet. It has been translated (in French) as the 'Gentile' prophet by the highly respected Muslim scholar Muhammad Hamidullah. The word *ummi* is found in four other Qur'anic verses. In 2:78 it describes some Jews as ignorant of their own Scriptures. In 3:20 it refers to the 'Gentiles' (or 'Nations') who, unlike 'the People of the Book', have no Holy Scriptures. In 3:75 and 62:2 the same word is applied to Arabs as a whole, identifying them as a people without Holy Scriptures, that is until they received the Qur'an.

v. As a monotheistic message, the Qur'an confirms the teaching of the Torah and the gospel. But it does not confirm the core of the gospel which is about the loving and saving God – not just the merciful and forgiving God as in Islam. Because God is not the redeeming God, Jesus Christ is not the crucified and risen Saviour either. The failure to recognize God's fuller revelation in Christ causes Christians to doubt and indeed to challenge the alleged perfection of Islam's message.

vi. Success does not represent, from a Christian perspective, a guarantee of divine approval. If we were to judge Judaism, Christianity and Islam by their worldly success, none of them would pass the test. Our world seems to be dominated by non-monotheistic religions and by secular ideologies. The Qur'an itself admits that many prophets were killed by their enemies (2:61, 91; cf. Heb. 11:37–40). Were they unsuccessful? People must be judged rather by their faithfulness to God which can actually lead to an apparent failure. Jesus' death on the cross seemed at first a complete failure even to his own disciples (Luke 24:20–21). In fact it was his greatest achievement. God confirmed Jesus' victory over evil and death by raising him from the dead and honouring him in a way he did for no other prophet.

vii. Because of the fundamental disagreement between Islam and Christianity over Jesus' mission and person, it is impossible for Christians to accept Muhammad as *the* prophet. However, some Christians (W. M. Watt) are happy to consider him as *a* prophet as a way of acknowledging that Islam is a monotheistic and Abrahamic religion. Christians who take this view point out that the Qur'an refutes, not Christian doctrines (e.g. the Trinity, Jesus' divinity), but false ideas of them. This distinction is certainly a valid one but it is also clear that Islamic theology, founded on the Qur'anic message, has denied the orthodox and biblical teaching. Unless we consider that Muslim theologians have been misguided in their interpretation of the Qur'anic text, it is difficult to avoid the conclusion that the Qur'anic message contradicts the gospel, if not plainly, at least potentially. In a paradoxical way, Islam brings Muslims closer to God and yet prevents them from knowing him in his perfect revelation in Jesus Christ. This has led some Christians to consider Muhammad as a false prophet. This judgment is based exclusively on the negative aspect of Islamic teaching, especially its denial of the gospel truths. It reinforces the prejudices that many Christians have already against Islam and Muslims. It is unlikely to help Christians to relate lovingly to Muslims and to share the gospel with them.

Muhammad was certainly a great religious reformer and an outstanding political and social leader. Instead of dismissing Islam's message altogether, Christians need to relate the gospel to this message and to do it in all fairness. This requires engaging in serious study of Islam and in personal relationships with Muslims. It also requires avoiding two opposite misreadings of the Qur'an: Christianizing its meaning by reading Christian truths into it, or demonizing its content by considering its truths as deceitful tactics. A Christian approach to Islam is not straightforward. Christians dealing with the Qur'an need to keep in mind that it is the Scripture of the Muslim community. They can challenge Muslims in their understanding of it, but they need to recognize that Muslim scholars are ultimately the authoritative interpreters of its message.

The aim of Christian–Muslim apologetics is to highlight the uniqueness of Jesus Christ. The way he revealed God to us does not undermine what Muslims know about him (e.g. his oneness, mercy, justice, *transcendence, sovereignty). The opposite is true: by revealing God as the Saviour he fully disclosed the glory of our Creator.

Finally, Christians (particularly in the West) need to realize that the crusades (11th–13th centuries) had a long-lasting negative impact on Christian–Muslim relationships. The crusading mentality has not entirely disappeared. Many Christians today see Muslims as *the* enemy; they engage Islam in 'a war of words', or polemics (the Greek word *polemos* means 'war'). Present-day crusaders attack Islam, its prophet and its Scriptures instead of explaining the gospel peacefully to Muslims. This confrontational approach is incompatible with 'the gospel of peace' (Eph. 6:15) and does not honour 'the Prince of peace' (Isa. 9:6). Muslims will respond to God's love in Jesus Christ only when we see them as our neighbours and love them as such.

Bibliography

M. Ata ur-Rahim, *Jesus: A Prophet of Islam* (London, 1977); U. Aziz-Us-Samad, *A Comparative Study of Christianity and Islam* (Karachi, 1970); K. Cragg, *Muhammad and the Christian: A Question of Response* (London, 1982); A. Deedat, *The Choice. Islam and Christianity*, 2 vols. (Birmingham, 1995); J.-M. Gaudeul, *Encounters and Clashes. Islam and Christianity in History*, 2 vols. (Rome, 1990); G. Moshay, *Who is this Allah?* (Ibadan, Nigeria, 1990); C. Moucarry, *Faith to Faith. Christianity and Islam in Dialogue* (Leicester, 2001); W. M. Watt, *Muslim–Christian Encounters: Perceptions and Misperceptions* (London, 1991).

Websites

<http://www.al-islam.com>;<http://www.answering-islam.org.uk>; <http://www.debate.org.uk>; <http://www.divineislam.co.uk>; <http://www.islaam.org.uk>; <http://www.islamicity.com>; <http://www.islamic-knowledge.com>; <http://www.islamtoday.net>; <http://www.quran.org.uk>.

C. MOUCARRY

JAINISM

The Jain world-view

Originating in India in pre-Christian times, Jainism is a religious faith distinct from both Brahminism and *Buddhism. According to Jain *cosmology, the world is eternal and uncreated, and there is no supreme being or creator God. The occupied universe consists of upper, middle and lower worlds surrounded by an infinity of empty space. At the apex of the upper world, in the supreme *heaven, are the perfected beings (*siddhas*), who have attained liberation (*moksha*). Human beings live in the middle world of the inhabited universe. In the upper world are fourteen heavens graded according to their perfection, and in the lower world there are seven *hells of increasing misery. Only from the middle world of human existence can souls achieve liberation. However, humans are not the only ones to have souls; all animate forms of life with one or more senses have souls.

The universe contains two eternal realities, *jiva* (sentient) and *ajiva* (non-sentient). *Jivas* are embodied souls, which are eternal. The body inhabited by the *jiva* is determined by its *karma* in previous lives. This results in a hierarchy of being, which includes human, animal and plant life, but ranges far wider to include celestial and hellish beings. The ultimate aim of *jivas* is to achieve liberation and attain to the abode of the *siddhas* and *tirthankaras* (pathfinders). *Ajiva* consists of everything in the universe that is insentient, including all matter and the principles of space, time, motion and rest.

Time is seen as cyclical like an ever-revolving wheel. Each cycle consists of six ascending phases and six descending or degenerating phases. According to Jain belief, the universe is now in the fifth phase of the degenerative cycle. In the current cycle of time, Jains believe there have been twenty-four *tirthankaras*, who help souls (*jivas*) to cross the ocean of bondage to rebirth (*samsara*). The last of these to gain liberation in this era is known as Mahavira (great hero). This title was given to Vardhamana (599–527 BC) for achieving enlightenment without assistance from any other being. He achieved enlightenment, or a state of complete omniscience (*kevalajnana*), after twelve years of intense ascetic practices.

Jains believe, as do Hindus and Buddhists, in the principles of *karma* and rebirth and in *moksha* as the goal of release from the cycle of birth, death and rebirth. According to Jainism, the path to liberation passed on by Mahavira consists in a process of renunciation, which can only be pursued to its final stages by monks and nuns, because it involves a rigorous regime of bodily mortification and ascetic practices based on *ahimsa* or non-violence towards all living things, including plant and insect life. The goal of Jainism, however, is not extinction or total dissolution of the individual, but liberation for the soul, which retains its individuality in a timeless state of infinite bliss. Each individual has to achieve his or her own salvation and be purged of the effects of deeds done in previous lives. There is no external God to assist, because there is no creator and sustainer of the world.

There is, however, a trend toward *theism within Jainism, which involves seeing the *tirthankaras* as manifestations of a supreme deity with the ability to intervene in human life and give devotees their assistance. This leads to *bhakti* style worship, where God is the focus of devotion. It is not surprising that Jains who worship in this way find no conflict in going to Hindu or Sikh temples, indeed the pressure for this theistic trend comes from Hindu influence.

Ahimsa or non-violence is the central ethical teaching of Jainism. Because there are souls (*jivas*) in every living thing, harm to all forms of life must be avoided. This affects not only the Jain diet, which must be strictly vegetarian, but also the employment that a Jain takes up.

The challenge of Jainism

Mahavira, like Buddha, made a profound impact on his contemporaries. The fact that his example and ideas are still followed by Jains today is a tribute to his legacy. Like Buddhism, Jainism attacked the ritualism of the priestly classes and departed from *Hinduism in denying the existence of a supreme being, but unlike Buddhism it retained a belief in *atman*, the eternal soul present in all living beings.

Jain intellectuals think of themselves as modern and progressive, in touch with scientific and rational thought and therefore well adapted to the West. Prominent among the key ideas of this modernist stance are *vegetarianism and the importance of a balanced diet for mental health, non-violence, ecology, animal welfare and meditation as opposed to ritual.

Jainism is well placed to influence the West with its highly developed exposition of ecology, animal welfare and non-violence. It teaches that the major principle of ecology is the mutual interdependence of all living things and the material universe, and it opposes the destruction of natural resources through industrialization. With its emphasis on conserving and recycling, Jainism fits in well with current concerns.

Critique of Jainism

Jainism has connections with both Hinduism and Buddhism and shares some of the strengths and weaknesses of both these traditions, in particular transmigration, *karma* and their view of time.

A Christian will appreciate the overriding concern of Mahavira to achieve liberation, but will question why liberated souls are placed at the apex of the cosmos to the exclusion of any supreme being. The absence of a creator is matched by the lack of *revelation, and there is complete dependence on the tradition passed on by Mahavira and his claim to omniscience. This claim looks misguided in the light of the vast array of scientific knowledge which has been amassed in recent centuries, as well as other forms of knowledge.

The fact that no Jain has claimed to have attained final liberation since Mahavira did so more than 2,500 years ago only serves to underline the Christian belief that it is impossible to obtain salvation without God's intervention. Human beings cannot purify themselves and rise to the heights of omniscience. That is why humanity does need a divine saviour. Jainism appears to offer no hope of liberation for centuries to come, until the next cosmic cycle begins.

Despite its fine views on ecology, Jainism cannot square its strict application of *ahimsa* to all forms of life with modern industrial society. In fact, no civilized society can practise this strict code of non-violence because it is incompatible with even the most elementary forms of agriculture. Hence, only Jain monks and nuns have attempted to practise the asceticism the faith requires.

A Christian response

There are points of contact between Jainism and Christianity. Most obviously, the burning desire for liberation and for the attainment of the heavenly realm of perfection is an aspiration Christians can identify with. The human predicament is underlined by the acknowledgment that salvation can only be attained by human beings. We can also appreciate the role of the *tirthankaras*, as spiritual pioneers on behalf of mankind and the discipline of Jain monks and nuns in giving themselves to fasting and meditation. In a world of violence, both against humanity and the created order, we need the call to *ahimsa* and the focus on ecology.

If we are to commend the gospel of Christ to Jains, we will have to find points of contact within the Jain tradition. For example, starting from *ahimsa*, we can show that *Jesus was the supreme apostle of non-violence, who was willing to sacrifice his life for the sake of every living soul. Also, starting from the trend towards theism preferred by many ordinary Jain worshippers, we can point to Christ as the revealer of the supreme reality, the divine *tirthankara* who took human form not for his own liberation but for the liberation of human souls. Finally, we have much in common with the a-theistic *sthanakvasi* tradition, for these Jains worship in a plain hall devoid of idols, images and icons. The only furniture is a table, on which their scriptures are displayed. Meditation on the parables of Jesus would be one way of introducing them to the world saviour.

Bibliography

P. Dundas, *The Jains* (London, 1992); K. Oldfield, *Jainism, the Path of Purity and Peace* (Derby, 1989); N. Shah, *Jainism, the World of Conquerors* (Brighton and Portland, 1998); S. Stevenson, *The Heart of Jainism* (Oxford, 1915).

B. J. M. SCOTT

JAMES, WILLIAM

Harvard philosopher William James (1842–1910) is considered the founder of *pragmatism, the distinctive American philosophy. In *Pragmatism* (1907), James contends that human inquiry unavoidably reflects our temperament, needs, concerns, fears, hopes and passions. The centrality of temperament and inclination in intellectual disputes is rooted in 'the underdetermination of theory by data'. Underdetermination holds that for any given set of data, there are many hypotheses which adequately account for the data but which are incompatible with one another. When such theories are in competition, no appeal to the evidence could determine the winner. In order to decide which to accept, we must bring all that we are as human beings to bear on these matters; this means that rational choice must involve passions, intellect, reason and even 'dumb conviction'. In addition, James rejects the traditional conception of *truth that claims that a belief is true if it corresponds to reality. James contends that the idea of beliefs (statements) corresponding to reality (facts) has no real meaning. For the pragmatist, beliefs are true if they prove useful to us in the practice of our lives.

Although many later pragmatists would be atheists, James used the pragmatic approach to philosophy to defend, at nearly every turn, the rationality of religious belief. His two most influential books in defence of religious belief are *The Will to Believe and Other Essays in Popular Philosophy* (1897) and *The Varieties of Religious Experience* (1902). In *The Will to Believe* James defends religious belief against the increasingly strident criticism of *Enlightenment evidentialism. By the time of James, belief in God had been denigrated due to an alleged lack of evidence. James courageously criticized Enlightenment evidentialism and defended the right to believe in God.

James argued that while it is perfectly rational for the scientist to hold up his or her scientific beliefs to the demand for evidence, the universal demand for evidence is simply not tenable. In certain cases one is forced to make a decision in the absence of adequate evidence. To believe in God or not is one of those forced choices and the stakes are so high that, even in the absence of evidence, each person has a right to believe in God based on an assessment of the benefits and costs of belief or unbelief. Each person may legitimately bring passion to bear on the question of belief in God. In so doing, a person helps create the kind of *reality that the person seeks and desires involving a personal relationship with God.

Bibliography

W. James, *Pragmatism* (Indianapolis and Cambridge, 1981); *The Will to Believe and Other Essays* (New York, 1985); *The Varieties of Religious Experience* (New York, 1997).

K. J. CLARK

JAPANESE RELIGIONS, see RELIGIONS OF CHINESE AND JAPANESE ORIGIN

JASPERS, KARL

Karl Jaspers (1883–1969), originally a psychiatrist, became a leading German existentialist philosopher. He defined three areas of philosophical concern: scientific knowledge, existence and *transcendence.

In the world of scientific knowledge we can find a degree of truth, but it is only relative and does little to answer the basic questions of life. For Jaspers, as for all existentialists, existence is not something we can examine objectively but something we have to experience or live. It is the individual existing and finding authenticity in *community with others. We can exist inauthentically, being simply 'there', or we can be committed to authentic existence, exercising our true freedom, realizing our being, using our freedom creatively to make authentic choices and thus opening ourselves up to reality. In particular, existence confronts us with *paradox and mystery, with chance and anxiety and with 'limit situations' like guilt and death, which both expose our humanness and give us the opportunity to become more authentic persons through the choices and responses we make.

We can, however, never stop with mere existence; our very incompleteness leads us to what is beyond us, to Being or the transcendent, the third area of philosophical concern. Transcendence is beyond our grasp, and yet we 'existentially' encounter it, especially through 'ciphers' (symbols, such as a face, which point beyond themselves to the transcendent) and 'myths', which are not to be viewed as mere fictions but which reliably express elements of the transcendent.

In contrast to, say, *Freud or *Sartre, Jaspers accepted religion as the symbolic expression of our encounter with the transcendent and so with God, but he refused to accept the dogmatic or doctrinal formulations of Christian theology. Perhaps there were two elements that were foundational to this refusal. The first was Jaspers' concept of Being, which was something very different from a personal God who is able to express himself and his truth through incarnation and *revelation. The second was his locating of meaning and *truth primarily in humanity, in our existence, in the social community and in our ciphers and myths. Mainstream Christianity, by contrast, locates meaning and truth primarily in God, who thus is able to 'authorize' concepts and stories which we then can accept as true and meaningful.

Bibliography

K. Jaspers and R. Bultmann, *Myth and Christianity* (New York, 1958).

P. HICKS

JAZZ, see MUSIC

JESUS, HISTORICAL

Jesus as a figure in history

Jesus of Nazareth lived about 5 BC to AD 30 (the exact dates remain disputed) in the Roman province of Judea. That he existed as a figure in *history is almost universally admitted by atheist and believer alike, however much they may differ over his character and significance. In modern Western scholarship G. A. Wells (*The Historical Evidence for Jesus* [New York, 1992]) remains a lone voice in arguing persistently that there was no historical Jesus, but that Paul's development of a Jesus myth demanded the invention of a fictional earthly 'history'.

How can we know about Jesus?

Evidence from non-Christian sources

There are very few references to Jesus in non-Christian writings of the first two centuries AD which have any claim to be regarded as independent evidence. The Roman historian Tacitus about AD 115 has a brief paragraph (Tacitus, *Annals* 15.44) mentioning the execution of Christus by order of Pontius Pilatus, but this occurs merely as an explanation of who 'Christians' are, and need be no more than a reflection of what Christians themselves were known to say about their own origins. Other Roman writers refer occasionally to Christians, but give no information about the founder of the movement.

There is a brief section about Jesus in *Josephus' account of Jewish history (Josephus, *Antiquities* 18.63–64), written towards the end of the first century, but most scholars agree that the text as we have it is a Christian adaptation of whatever, if anything, Josephus himself wrote. The balance of probability is that Josephus did mention Jesus as a popular teacher and miracle-worker who was crucified by Pilatus at the instigation of 'the leading men among us' and who gave rise to the 'Christian' sect, but his original wording, which may have been much less complimentary than the preserved text, cannot now be reconstructed with confidence.

Rabbinic writings contain a few brief and generally very obscure references to Jesus, the most significant of which (Babylonian Talmud, *Sanhedrin* 43a) mentions his execution on Passover Eve as one who 'practised magic and led Israel astray'. Several supposed rabbinic references to Jesus are uncertain because they use a pseudonym. It is clear that followers of Jesus were a recurrent problem to the Rabbis, but their writings tell us almost nothing about the founder of the movement.

So we may conclude from non-Christian sources that Jesus existed, was executed, and gave rise to the Christian movement, but that is about all. From the perspective of 2000 years of Christian history it seems surprising that Jesus left so little mark at the time in the (admittedly very limited) records which survive from his world. But historical realism must recognize that a few years' itinerant ministry in a distant province by a Jewish workman-turned-preacher was hardly the stuff of imperial headlines. It was only after the movement he started began to attract a significant following and come to the notice of the authorities that Christians and their Jesus might expect to be noticed in non-Christian records, and that is exactly what we find.

Christian evidence outside the New Testament

Numerous Christian writings from about the middle of the second century purport to give accounts of Jesus; they are often referred to rather misleadingly as 'the apocryphal gospels'. Prominent among the earlier examples are the *Gospel of Thomas* (a collection of 114 purported sayings of Jesus), fragments of a *Gospel of Peter*, which describe Jesus' death and resurrection in less restrained terms than the NT Gospels, and the *Protevangelium of James*, which describes the events leading up to and surrounding Jesus' birth and is the source of much later elaboration of the Christmas story and of the life of Mary. There are also numerous references to and quotations from other early 'gospels', now lost, in the works of early Christian Fathers. Most of the later apocryphal gospels contain little or no narrative, but consist almost entirely of alleged teaching of Jesus, much of which is of a recognizably gnostic character in contrast with the teaching found in the NT Gospels. (A wide range of surviving 'apocryphal gospels' may be found in E. Hennecke, *New Testament Apocrypha*, vol. 1 [ET London, 1963].)

There is no reason in principle why some of the sayings and incidents found only in these later gospels (notably some of the sayings in the *Gospel of Thomas*) may not go back to the historical Jesus, and several recent attempts to reconstruct 'the real Jesus' as someone very different from the Jesus we find in the NT have been based on such second-century evidence. But the problem is to discern which may be genuine among the large amount of material which is clearly legendary or reflects later Christian and especially gnostic ideas. The considerable interval between the first-century Gospels of the NT and these later works suggests caution, and the scholarly majority has felt it wiser to take the earlier evidence as the basis for historical reconstruction.

The apocryphal gospels and patristic quotations may then offer some interesting supplements to what we already know from the NT Gospels, but cannot be used to support a significant reinterpretation of the Jesus of history.

The evidence of the New Testament

All this means that for specific information about the life and teaching of Jesus we are almost entirely dependent on the first-century Christian writings which we know as the NT, and more particularly the four canonical Gospels, since in the rest of the NT there are surprisingly few direct references to what Jesus said and did beyond the brief summaries of his life which occur in the sermons recorded in Acts.

It is rare to have multiple accounts of a single historical figure preserved from the ancient world. One of the NT Gospels (John) is clearly independent in both style and content, while the other three reflect different developments of what is largely a common tradition. While many would date all the Gospels within thirty or forty years of Jesus' death, others believe Matthew, Luke and John to be a decade or two later than this. Most agree, however, that Mark was written within a generation of the events.

Much can happen in a generation, of course, and it used to be fashionable to argue that the oral tradition of Jesus' words and deeds during that period would have been subject to such drastic recasting and expansion that we should regard the Gospels as evidence for the faith of the first-century church rather than for the facts of Jesus' life. Nowadays such a view is regarded as extreme. Scholars have noted both the general reliability of oral tradition in the ancient world, especially among the Jews, and also the possibility of written records earlier than our Gospels but now lost (such as Luke apparently had access to, Luke 1:1). It has been noted that while the Synoptic Gospels provide ample evidence of variation in detail and in the colouring of accounts, their presentation of the essential story-content is impressively parallel, while there is substantially less variation in the wording of the preserved sayings of Jesus than in narrative detail. Even the Gospel of John, long regarded as late and unreliable, is now more widely acknowledged to be based on independent historical tradition, however much coloured by the author's richly theological understanding of the significance of Jesus as 'the Word made flesh'.

Thus, while scholars still vary considerably in the degree of their 'scepticism' or 'conservatism', there is now more general agreement that our canonical Gospels may be taken as a proper historical basis for understanding Jesus of Nazareth. Due allowance must be made for the individual interests and sources of information of each of the Gospel writers, and for the different situations to which their writings were addressed, but taking their different accounts together we have an impressively consistent account, in all essentials, of the life and teaching of Jesus.

The evidence of archaeology and of the historical background

Archaeology has, not surprisingly, discovered no object or writing which is specifically linked with the story of Jesus (the Turin shroud is now generally regarded as medieval in origin). What it does is to add its testimony to that of ancient literature in illuminating in remarkable ways the places Jesus went and the society in which he lived, not only in its material aspects but in its values, religion and politics.

Thus, while archaeology cannot directly confirm the Gospel records of what Jesus did and said, it can and does bring them to life. One of the most stimulating aspects of the study of Jesus in the late twentieth century has been a remarkable deepening of our awareness of the world of first-century Palestine, which enables us to gain new insight into Jesus' ministry and teaching and the way people reacted to him. The result is that he appears more clearly as a man of his own times, but also as one who constantly challenged the status quo and proved an enigma to his contemporaries.

What do we know about Jesus?

What the Gospels tell us

The Gospels are not arranged as chronological accounts of Jesus' life on a year by year basis, and attempts to derive such an outline from them have not been successful. There is in the Synoptic Gospels a basic story outline, beginning (in Matthew and Luke) with Jesus' birth and infancy, and going on to John the Baptist and Jesus' baptism and temptation. Then an extended period of public ministry in Galilee leads on to a single catastrophic visit to Jerusalem, within which there is a common sequence of confrontation, arrest, trial, crucifixion and resurrection. But within this very broad schema the various stories and sayings are contained more in the manner of an anthology than of a consecutive chronicle, and the Gospels are by no means unanimous in the order they follow.

Even the broad common outline of the Synoptics is not adopted by John, who begins (like Mark) in the context of the ministry of John the Baptist, and thereafter has Jesus moving freely between Galilee and Jerusalem, with the focus more on the latter even before the final visit. Only after Jesus' arrest does John fall more nearly in line with the Synoptic narrative sequence, though his lengthy account of the last supper (13 – 17) has no parallel in them.

It seems then that what we are offered is not a chronological biography of the type that might be written today, but four different (though in the case of three, broadly convergent) anthologies of stories and sayings of Jesus within only the broadest overall narrative framework. The writers have preserved a rich variety of traditions which enable us to see what sort of person Jesus was, what sort of things he did, and the main emphases of his teaching, and have put them together into flowing narratives which carry the reader

369

irresistibly forward towards the cross and resurrection. On the way, a multi-faceted portrait of Jesus emerges, powerful and often surprising, but ultimately satisfying in its inner coherence.

Jesus in his historical context

Jesus was a first-century Galilean Jew. He thus inherited his nation's privilege of being the chosen people of Yahweh, their heritage of prophets, kings and wise men, and the ancient religious system focused in the great temple at Jerusalem. But he was born into a period of political oppression under the power of Rome, and of eager looking forward to the time when God would intervene to restore his people's fortune. When he began to preach the coming of the 'kingdom of God' it was inevitable that he would be heard as one of those nationalist leaders whose religio-political message so often stirred up agitation against the Romans during the first century. Much of the story of the Gospels is of Jesus' attempt to disentangle his message of God's coming salvation from the revolutionary implications which the crowds, and sometimes even his own disciples, persistently read into it, and it was as a rebel against Rome that he was eventually crucified, however unfairly.

He was hailed as a prophet and eagerly followed as a miracle-worker (an attribute which he shared with a number of Jewish holy men of the period), while his spectacular exorcisms marked him out as a man of exceptional spiritual power. He called people to follow him in creating an alternative society of love and holiness. He soon ran into trouble with the religious establishment, however, because of his bold reinterpretations of OT laws and his concern for the outcast of society which led him to infringe their strict code of ceremonial purity. At the same time his uncompromising call to repentance in view of God's coming reign (continuing the same radical line of preaching which had taken John the Baptist to his death) alienated the comfortable classes, and when he predicted the fall of Jerusalem and the destruction of its temple he had gone too far for most patriotic Jews. But by the time his enemies engineered his execution, he had already established and trained a group of disciples, and his own amazing return from the tomb made the movement unstoppable.

The Gospels, read in the light of what we know of the society of the time, reveal the gradually dawning awareness of Jesus' disciples and others that they were in the presence of more than a conventional prophet and reformer, a process which continued beyond his lifetime into the fully developed doctrine of the incarnate Son of God who gave his life for the salvation of his people and rose from death to take his seat of final authority at God's right hand.

It is this startling Galilean figure, in all his historical particularity, who is the essential basis for all subsequent Christian *preaching and belief. The more we discover of the historical dimension, the richer and firmer that foundation becomes.

Bibliography

M. Bockmuehl, *This Jesus: Martyr, Lord, Messiah* (Edinburgh, 1994); R. T. France, *The Evidence for Jesus* (London, 1986); J. P. Meier, *A Marginal Jew: Rethinking the Historical Jesus* (New York, 1991, 1994); E. P. Sanders, *The Historical Figure of Jesus* (London and New York, 1993); G. Theissen, *The Shadow of the Galilean* (London, 1987); B. Witherington, *Jesus the Sage: The Pilgrimage of Wisdom* (Minneapolis, 1994).

R. T. FRANCE

JESUS OF HISTORY AND CHRIST OF FAITH, THE

The NT understanding of Jesus develops from that of the historical figure of a Galilean worker-turned-preacher who fell foul of the Jerusalem authorities to that of an incarnate Son of God who gave his life for the salvation of his people. (See *Jesus, historical.) As Christian faith has become more elaborate, and more distant from its origins, the issue of how these two are to be related has become more significant.

For most of Christian *history the question was seldom raised or even noticed. The 'Christ of faith' was the unquestioned starting-point, and the Gospel stories were read in the light of the full-blown Christology of incarnation. There was little interest in how the human historical figure of Jesus of Nazareth would have been perceived by his own contemporaries, nor was this thought to have significant implications for Christian faith.

It was only with the *Enlightenment in the eighteenth century that Western scholarship began to take a critical interest in the historical basis of Christian faith, and the suggestion began to be entertained that the 'real' Jesus of history might have been a different figure from the Christ of faith, with a different agenda which might sit uncomfortably alongside traditional Christianity. Gradually it began to be noticed how each *culture and each generation has tended to refashion Jesus to fit their own world-view and their own religious needs.

This is not purely a matter of academic sophistication. Popular Christianity too has always been more strongly moulded than it has recognized by the culture within which it lives, and its image of Jesus and his salvation has changed accordingly. The unquestioned presuppositions of one age or one culture become the heresy of the next. In the modern world, with its increased awareness of the broad range of differing cultures around the world, it has become increasingly obvious that the Jesus of, say, Latin American liberation theology is very different from the Jesus of comfortable middle America or the Jesus of Orthodox mysticism is very different from the Jesus of Black Pentecostalism. The question becomes increasingly urgent how these various images of Jesus relate to the historical Galilean preacher, and whether it matters that the two should be related. What is the practical value of the frequent assertion that Christianity is a faith rooted in history?

The 'Quest of the Historical Jesus'

This was the title of the English translation (1910) of an influential book by Albert *Schweitzer (published in German in 1906) which catalogued, and in effect put an end to, over a century of attempts to get back to the 'real Jesus' (almost entirely within German scholarship), which had begun with the groundbreaking work of Hermann Samuel Reimarus 'On the Purpose of Jesus and his Disciples' (published anonymously after his death by G. E. *Lessing in 1778 and often known as the 'Wolfenbüttel Fragments'). Reimarus presented Jesus as a Jewish nationalistic leader who had no thought of founding a new religion; it was his disciples who promoted him as a spiritual redeemer, after stealing his body and proclaiming his resurrection. Reimarus promoted a 'rational religion' based on deism.

Other 'rational' accounts of Jesus soon followed, the most influential being that of David Friedrich *Strauss (1835–36), made available to the British public by George Eliot's translation, in which Strauss used the category of 'myth' to explain the miraculous element in the Gospel accounts. J. R. Seeley's *Ecce Homo* (1865), while not so radical, caused much discussion by its move away from a theological to a more human, historical portrait of Jesus, but other Victorian British writers such as F. W. Farrar (*Life of Christ*, 1874) attempted to combine critical scholarship with a more traditional piety and respect for the historical worth of the Gospels.

These varied approaches all shared the conviction that by a proper application of critical inquiry it was possible to reconstruct a genuinely 'historical' account of Jesus. What Schweitzer did was to call into question the supposed 'objectivity' of their authors and of the methods used. In particular he highlighted the tendency of nineteenth-century authors to reconstruct Jesus as a liberal like themselves, instead of the deluded Jewish fanatic Schweitzer himself believed Jesus to have been. The problem is summed up in the famous verdict of George Tyrrell on Adolf von *Harnack's *Das Wesen des Christentums* (1900): 'The Christ that Harnack sees, looking back through nineteen centuries of Catholic darkness, is only the reflection of a liberal Protestant face, seen at the bottom of a deep well.'

The quest abandoned and resumed

Schweitzer's powerful invective combined with the historically sceptical stance of the new discipline of form criticism to put an effective stop to most scholarly attempts to rediscover the 'historical Jesus' until after the middle of the twentieth century. NT scholarship was dominated by Rudolf Bultmann's view that: 'We can now know almost nothing concerning the life and personality of Jesus, since the early Christian sources show no interest in either, are moreover fragmentary and often legendary, and other sources about Jesus do not exist' (*Jesus and the Word* [1934], p. 8). The writing of 'lives of Jesus' continued only in circles detached from mainstream NT scholarship.

In the 1950s, however, some of Bultmann's followers (led by E. Käsemann and E. Fuchs) began to develop what came to be known as 'the New Quest', not now attempting detailed reconstruction of the course of events but rather, in the words of G. Bornkamm, the first to produce a full study of Jesus from within the Bultmann school, to 'compile the main historically indisputable traits, and to present the rough outlines of Jesus' person and history' (*Jesus of Nazareth* [1960], p. 53). This more modest and impressionistic approach within German scholarship was balanced by a more robust resistance among British scholars to radical form criticism, notably in the works of Vincent Taylor, T. W. Manson and C. H. Dodd. Taylor's *The Life and Ministry of Jesus* (1954) attempted a more detailed chronological reconstruction based on Mark's Gospel, while Dodd's *The Founder of Christianity* (1970) summed up with deceptive simplicity the results of the more positive approach to the historicity of the Gospels which was now beginning to come back into fashion.

The 'Third Quest'

N. T. Wright, in his revised edition of Stephen Neill's *The Interpretation of the NT, 1861–1986*, coined the title the 'Third Quest' to designate a variety of more recent approaches to the Jesus of history (since roughly the early 1970s) which represent a decisive move away from earlier historical scepticism. What characterizes these varied studies is a more consistent attempt to set the records of Jesus in the context of our rapidly expanding knowledge of the world, especially the Jewish world, of the first century.

Of course, there was previous knowledge of Jewish history and literature, but what has happened is a growing interaction of NT scholars with specialists in ancient history and Judaism, which has forced NT scholarship out of its previously rather introverted perspective. The result is that, while there is perhaps less agreement than ever over the various portraits of Jesus that emerge, those that are proposed are more securely located in the wider world of first-century Palestine. The reason why the resultant portraits do not agree is largely that there is now such a remarkable richness of historical material available, offering a wide range of different social types and movements of thought against which Jesus of Nazareth may plausibly be understood.

A harbinger of this approach was the work of Joachim Jeremias, who maintained against the prevailing climate in German scholarship a commitment to historical investigation of the Gospels in the light of his extensive study of first-century Judaism and of the Aramaic language. His culminating work, *New Testament Theology, Part One: The Proclamation of Jesus*

(1971; subsequent parts were never written), confidently expounds the teaching of the historical Jesus on the basis of its context in first-century Judaism and of Jeremias' reconstruction of Jesus' original Aramaic sayings, and defends the methodological presupposition that 'in the Synoptic Tradition it is the inauthenticity, and not the authenticity, of the sayings of Jesus that must be demonstrated'.

The more recognizably 'Jewish' Jesus who emerges from the various 'Third Quest' studies takes many forms. There is the politically motivated Zealot Jesus of S. G. F. Brandon, the magician Jesus of Morton Smith, the charismatic Galilean holy man of Geza Vermes, the Cynic preacher of Gerald Downing, the 'savvy and courageous Jewish Mediterranean peasant' of John Dominic Crossan and many others. But what most such studies have in common is the recognition that Jesus cannot be isolated from the political and ideological currents of his day, and that it must be possible to discern from the Gospels how he responded to them and how other Jews at the time would have understood his stance.

For E. P. Sanders (*Jesus and Judaism* [1985] and subsequent studies) Jesus was essentially an orthodox and law-abiding Pharisee, who ran into trouble because of his unconventional openness to 'sinners' and especially his unpopular crusade against the Jerusalem temple. His view is in many ways parallel to that of several Jewish writers (notably G. Vermes, *Jesus the Jew* [1973]) who have attempted to reclaim Jesus as a faithful Jewish teacher and have attributed the invention of Christianity to his misguided followers.

Marcus Borg (*Conflict, Holiness and Politics in the Teachings of Jesus* [1974]) takes the hopes of Israel as the central issue for understanding Jesus, but locates Jesus' contribution in his insistence that the holiness of God's people means not a judgmental separation from others but an imitation of the mercy of God, a view which put him on a collision course with popular nationalism.

N. T. Wright (*Jesus and the Victory of God* [1996]) argues that Jesus proclaimed the coming of the 'return from exile' which the exilic prophets had preached but which many believed had never yet been enjoyed despite their physical return to Palestine, since they remained in political subjection. He called the people not, however, to armed rebellion but to repentance and to a new concept of what it meant to be the people of God, especially questioning the traditional canons of keeping the Mosaic law. When the religious establishment rejected his call, he predicted that God would vindicate him by destroying the temple, and in the events of AD 70 the Son of Man was vindicated.

Many other contributions could be listed. It soon becomes clear that within the overall agenda of making sense of Jesus in his historical Jewish context there is an endless variety of emphases which may be selected, some complementary, others (notably those of Brandon and Borg) totally incompatible. The debate will continue, but at least it now seems to be firmly grounded in the historical realism which reads Jesus as a man of his times.

One remarkable product of this movement is the 'historical novel' by Gerd Theissen, *The Shadow of the Galilean* (1987), which harvests a vast range of historical scholarship to provide a vivid account of life in occupied Palestine and of the various currents in contemporary Judaism, so that the reader can locate Jesus (who remains 'off stage' throughout the novel) within them.

The historical Jesus and contemporary faith

As the 'Third Quest' throws light on Jesus in his historical context, there is a danger that he will therefore be explained away as merely a man of his times, one who fits into first-century Jewish society, whether as conformist or as rebel, so comfortably that one wonders why Christianity ever arose. The more he merges into his background the more difficult it may become to recognize in him the Christ of faith.

But historical realism does not demand that Jesus be seen as just like everyone else at the time. It is as he is seen against that background that his uniqueness can emerge, that he can be perceived, in the words of Eduard Schweizer, as 'the man who fits no formula'. The study of the Jesus of history, then, while it may not by itself reveal all the features of the Christ of faith, can both provide the essential basis for our awareness of the latter and, by highlighting the humanity of Jesus, make him the more accessible as the object of our faith.

Scholarly discussion has spawned a variety of more popular attempts in books and films which have offered 'alternative' views of Jesus. One such TV series, *Jesus – The Evidence* (1984), memorably summed up its message in the image of a traditional bust of Jesus which was exploded into fragments on screen, after which pieces of mosaic were assembled instead into a dark and disturbing face, tantalizingly incomplete. Many such popularizing reconstructions have been deliberately shocking, usually drawing on the more radical extremists on the fringes of the 'Third Quest', and few have enjoyed the endorsement of mainstream scholarship.

One unfortunate effect of such revisionist productions has been to strengthen resistance among ordinary Christians against any suggestion that we may have something to learn from the study of Jesus in history. Yet popular Christianity remains prone to the tendency, usually unconscious, to assimilate Jesus to the values and expectations of our own culture, and so to distance the Christ of faith from the Jesus of history. There remains an important task for responsible NT scholarship to harvest and communicate the sound results of historical research in such a way that ordinary Christians can recognize Jesus more readily as a man who connected with the real issues of his own world.

Such a historical awareness is an important control on the subjectivity of faith which can otherwise subtly replace the testimony of the Gospels with the predilections of the individual worshipper or indeed of the whole culturally-conditioned worshipping community. If Christianity is a historical religion it cannot afford to lose touch with the Jesus of history.

Bibliography
G. W. Dawes, *The Historical Jesus Quest: Landmarks in the Search for the Jesus of History* (Louisville, 2000); L. T. Johnson, *The Real Jesus* (San Francisco, 1995); W. S. Kissinger, *The Lives of Jesus: A History and Bibliography* (New York, 1985); N. T. Wright, *Jesus and the Victory of God* (London, 1996).

R. T. FRANCE

JOSEPHUS

Flavius Josephus was born in AD 37 and died some time after 100. He was a Jewish historian, who took part in the revolt against the Romans (66–74), and his writings are our most important extra-biblical source for first-century Palestine.

At the outbreak of the revolt, Josephus was appointed commander of Galilee. At the siege of Jotapata (67) he surrendered to Vespasian, whom he hailed as the next emperor. He received the honorary name 'Flavius' after Vespasian's family name, but was regarded as a traitor by his Jewish compatriots.

Josephus wrote an autobiography (*Vita*) and an apology for *Judaism (*Contra Apion*), but his two most important works are his riveting eyewitness account of the revolt (*The Jewish War*) and his history of the Jews (*The Antiquities*). Writing for a Roman audience, his paraphrase of the Hebrew Scriptures is embellished for greater effect and omits questionable accounts (see E. Yamauchi, 'Josephus and the Scriptures', *Fides et Historia* 13 [1980], pp. 42–63; L. H. Feldman, *Josephus's Interpretation of the Bible* [Berkeley, 1998]).

Josephus is important for NT studies because the information he provides both substantiates and supplements the biblical accounts. For example, he mentions that the death of Herod the Great took place at the time of an eclipse, and this helps to establish that the birth of *Jesus must have taken place before 4 BC. He gives us the name of Herodias' daughter who demanded the head of John the Baptist as Salome (*Antiquities* XVIII 136; see H. Hoehner, *Herod Antipas* [Cambridge, 1972]) and he mentions the death of 'the brother of Jesus who was called Christ' under Ananus in AD 62 (*Antiquities* XX.200; see J. S. McLaren, 'Ananus, James, and Earliest Christianity', *JTS*, 52.1 [2001], pp. 1–25).

The so-called *Testimonium Flavianum* (*Antiquities* XVIII.63–64) is one of the most important extra-biblical witnesses we have to Jesus. The Greek text as we have it was cited by the fourth-century church historian *Eusebius. Today, there is a consensus among scholars that the passage as a whole is genuine, though there have been some Christian interpolations (see R. E. Van Voorst, *Jesus Outside the New Testament* [Grand Rapids, 2000]; J. C. Paget, 'Some Observations on Josephus and Christianity', *JTS*, 52.2 [2001], pp. 539–624).

Bibliography

P. L. Maier (tr.), *Josephus: The Essential Writings* (Grand Rapids, 1988); S. Mason, *Josephus and the New Testament* (Peabody, 1992); T. Rejak, *Josephus, the Historian and His Society* (Philadelphia, 1984); C. L. Rogers, Jr, *The Topical Josephus* (Grand Rapids, 1992).

E. M. YAMAUCHI

JUDAISM

Introduction

Certainly the oldest, and perhaps the greatest, apologetic challenge is the presentation of the gospel to the Jewish people. Both today and throughout Christian history, the resounding 'No' to *Jesus has been a major defining feature of the Jewish people, in their historical development, religious thought and contemporary existence. Christian anti-Judaism, the 'teaching of contempt', has compounded the effect of this miscommunication, and a number of significant issues must be faced for an apologetic to be found that is relevant for the twenty-first century. This article will aim to set the contemporary situation of the Jewish people and Judaism today in historical and theological context, then identify and respond to particular issues involved in Jewish apologetics, and finally note the key concerns for Jewish apologetics in the future.

Judaism and Jewish identity

Judaism, the religion of the Jewish people, includes the totality of Jewish life and thought. As a religious civilization, Judaism embraces the historic and cultural experience of the Jewish people from earliest times to the present, so that today Jewish identity cannot be described as a purely religious phenomenon, but is best understood as shaped by a variety of historical, sociological and theological factors. Whilst the Christian apologist needs to understand the theological basis on which Jewish rejection of Jesus and Christianity is constructed, it is necessary to consider the theological debate as just one aspect, and a minor one at that, of the more important questions for the Jewish people of the nature of Jewish existence, identity and survival.

The terms 'Hebrew', 'Israelite' and 'Jew' come from the Jewish Scriptures, which Christians call the OT. The first Jew, Abraham, is called into covenant relationship with Yahweh, and receives the promise of offspring, land and blessing (Gen. 12:1–3). The universality of the Abrahamic covenant is understood differently by the two faith traditions of Judaism and Christianity. For Christians the NT shows how the Gentiles are included in the promises to Abraham through faith in Christ (Rom. 4; Gal. 3), but for Jews the 'scandal of particularity' of God's election of the descendants of Abraham forms the basis for the future development of Israel as a distinct entity, both ethnic and religious. Israel itself has a missionary mandate, to be a light to the nations and a priestly people bearing witness to God as Creator and Redeemer (Exod. 19:4–6).

The primary model of redemption in Judaism is the exodus, accompanied by the giving of the Torah to Moses on Mount Sinai. The Hebrews were redeemed from slavery in Egypt and called into a covenant relationship with God at Sinai that embraced personal and social *ethics, civil and criminal *law, and corporate and personal holiness. The covenant *community was called to the missionary task of being a light to the nations and a priestly people, mediating between God and the other nations. The mission of Israel today is defined in this way, as a function of the Jewish people's demonstration of the ethics and practical holiness that come from observance of the Torah. For most Jewish groups (with the exception of the Reform movement in the USA) active proselytism is unnecessary, and non-Jews (Gentiles) are merely expected to live up to basic moral standards, summarized in seven basic principles known as the Noachide Commandments. These include prohibitions on idolatry, blasphemy, bloodshed, sexual sins, theft, eating from a living animal and the requirement to establish courts of *justice.

Biblical Israel's identity developed in reaction and response to the idolatry and *polytheism of her neighbours. Failure to live according to the covenant led to the destruction of the Northern Kingdom (722 BC). Judah, the remaining tribe, gave its name to the Southern Kingdom. After the Babylonian exile (586 BC) and return, the term 'Jew' (Yehudi) came to refer to subjects of the Babylonian/Persian province of Judah. 'Judaism' is generally considered to have begun in exile, and the religious system survived and was transformed through the institution of the synagogue as a centre for study, prayer and community. Also during the exile, the five books of Moses were codified as the written Torah (torah she-biktav). To them were added, after the return, the Prophets (Neviim) and

Writings (Ketuvim). Eventually, the vast body of oral law (torah she b'al peh), interpretations of the written Torah, were committed to writing as the Mishnah (lit. 'repetition') and the Gemara (lit. 'completion') in AD 200 and 500 respectively. These two make up the Talmud (lit. 'teaching'). The Talmud exists in two forms, the Babylonian Talmud, the larger and later compilation and the one which is accorded greater authority, and the Jerusalem Talmud, which reflects earlier tradition more closely associated with the land. The Jewish thought expressed in these writings forms the backdrop to the life of Jesus and the earliest beginnings of the church and therefore for apologetic purposes a working knowledge of these materials is necessary.

The Judaism of the inter-testamental and NT period developed in several ways, leading to a bewildering variety of expressions of belief and practice. In response to the influence of *Hellenism the Maccabean revolt (164 BC) led to the reconsecration of the temple and the establishment of the Hasmonean dynasty. Apocalyptic literature and eschatology saw the pressures of survival in such a hostile political climate in otherworldly terms of imminent and miraculous restoration through Messianic figures. The Essenes of Qumran evidenced in the *Dead Sea Scrolls their disenchantment with the corruption of the Jerusalem temple and the politically compromised Sadducean establishment. The Pharisees, a lay movement also concerned for cultic purity, brought a reforming zeal to the Sanhedrin, the administrative authority under Roman jurisdiction, and articulated new formulations of the Torah that would eventually be codified in the Mishnah. Within such diversity the sect of the Nazarenes was initially no less recognizably 'Jewish' than other groups, although the distinctiveness of their belief in a resurrected Messiah would by the time of the fourth century be seen as incompatible with Jewish identity.

This diversity of faith and practice formed the background to the NT period, a time when the majority of Jewish people lived outside Israel in the Diaspora. After the destruction of the temple (AD 70), the successors of the Pharisees, the Rabbis, had a normative influence on later belief and practice, whilst other groups such as the Karaites, Essenes, Sadducees and Nazarenes (Jewish Christians) were marginalized. The parting of the ways between Jews and Christians began to occur from the time of the NT onwards, with the insertion into the liturgy of the synagogue of the euphemistically entitled 'Blessing of Heretics' (*Birkat Haminim*), and, from the Christian side, anathemas on those who continued to observe Jewish practices. The religion was reformulated so that the Jewish people could survive as a minority group without immediate need of statehood or sovereignty and the symbols of land, temple and Messiah. The term 'Judaism' (*Ioudaismos*), found in the NT and inter-testamental literature, expressed the struggle for self-definition of Israel in the Diaspora and in response to Hellenism.

In the medieval period the strategies for survival developed in the frequently hostile environments created by *Islam and Christianity. The Crusades are but one example of the behaviour of the Christian community at that time, and it continues to this day to act as a strong disincentive to consider the claims of Christ. Renewed interest in conversion led to public disputations over messianic prophecies, such as that between Nachmanides and Pablo Christiani in Barcelona in 1263. Such encounters led to the development of sophisticated argumentation and a growing mutual study of the belief systems of Judaism and Christianity. These, however, were generally held under duress and with an agenda of forced conversion or penalties for non-acceptance, and so they failed to achieve their object of effectively sharing the Christian faith, and simply galvanized an informed negative response from the Jewish participants. The development of Jewish mysticism (the *Kabbalah*) and ongoing Messianic expectation (e.g. the false Messiah Shabbetai Zevi in 1665) continued to focus Jewish expectation of ultimate redemption without the need for Jesus.

In the period of emancipation (1700–1900) the influence of *rationalism and humanism encouraged Jewish people out of the ghettos into wider European society. Within Judaism the parallel movement of *Haskalah* (Enlightenment) allowed Jewish communities to develop their own institutions of learning and communal activity in response to religious orthodoxy and emerging liberalism and nationalism. Secular thought was influenced by Jewish thinkers such as *Spinoza, Marx, *Freud and Einstein, whose own Jewish backgrounds affected their contribution, and whose secularized explorations of mysticism, eschatology and *cosmology have re-drawn the map of modernity's consciousness.

The pogroms of Eastern Europe at the end of the nineteenth century led to increased emigration and the assimilation of Jews fleeing persecution into the West, especially America. This period also saw the birth of Zionism and the beginnings of settlement in Palestine. After the Second World War, and in the aftermath of the *Holocaust, the State of Israel was established in 1948. A successful apologetic must seek to answer the theodic demands of Holocaust theology, whilst also seeking to articulate a continuing theological significance for the Jewish people which does not ignore the contemporary issue of the land of Israel with its two competing nationalisms and the trauma of successive wars in the Middle East.

As a result of these demographic and ideological changes, the forms of Judaism of the twentieth and twenty-first centuries display a theological and cultural *pluralism. Religious expression includes Orthodox, Reform, Liberal and Reconstructionist Judaism (the latter expressions blending humanist and secular expressions of Jewishness with elements of tradition). Zionism has become the major expression of Jewish identity for a majority in Israel and the Diaspora who are disenchanted with religious faith but wish to express solidarity with the Jewish people. Post-Holocaust disillusionment and postmodern suspicion with the Zionist project has led to a longing among some for a just peace with the Palestinians, and to a reaction against the religious Zionism which gives ideological support to the expansionist claims of right-wing Israeli politics.

It remains to be seen how postmodernity has affected the Jewish people. Certainly, key postmodern thinkers have made no secret of their Jewish origins, and have influenced many in the Jewish community. To some extent the Jewish world anticipated the trends of postmodernity, especially the issues of *globalization and identity. Orthodox Jewish thought has grappled with the challenge of articulating traditional religion and a biblical worldview in the midst of religious pluralism and secular society, and Conservative and Reform Jewish thinkers have also addressed issues of Jewish identity in postmodern times. Messianic Jewish thinkers have only recently begun to note the change in the intellectual and cultural climate.

Jewish belief

Judaism has always avoided credal formulation, preferring to stress orthopraxy over orthodoxy. Nevertheless, the ethical and religious values of rabbinic Judaism can be summarized in the Ten Commandments and the Thirteen Principles of Faith of Moses *Maimonides (1135–1204). The latter combine a biblical *theism with Aristotelian thought. The identity markers of Sabbath observance and food laws (kashrut) are important distinctives of Jewish life, as are the celebration of the festivals (especially Passover, New Year and the Day of Atonement) and the events of the Jewish life-cycle (circumcision, bar/bat mitzvah, *marriage, mourning).

Jewish thought (the term 'theology' is seen as a Christian imposition on what is generally holistic and pragmatic rather than systematic and abstract) revolves around the core themes of God, Israel and Torah, as summarized in the Shema, the confession of faith of Deut. 6:4. A further central topic is that of the land, Eretz Israel. Whilst much of Jewish life and religion developed in the Diaspora, the ultimate 'teleological justification' of such existence was predicated on an eventual return to Israel, traditionally ushered in by the arrival of the Messiah. Secular Zionism saw this hope realized through this-worldly means and developed its own human response in political activity to fulfil the programme proposed by Theodore Herzl in 1896. The combination of secular and religious messianism realized in the re-establishment of the State in 1948 still provides significant parameters to Jewish identity and belief. Christian witness in such a context must avoid the extremes of wholesale embracing of the politics of Zionism, which some conveniently fit into the Christian eschatological schemes of dispensational premillennialism, and the insensitivity to the rationale that still motivates the need for defence, security and peace for Israelis. It is projected that by the year 2020 the majority of world Jewry will be living in the land, and no workable solution is at present in view that will construct a peace that brings both security to Israel and justice to the Palestinians.

The question to which Christian apologetics must provide an appealing and convincing answer is the nature and identity of the Messiah. Maimonides maintained belief in the future expectation of the Messiah. He viewed Christianity as an acceptable form of *monotheism, provided it was not espoused by Jewish people, for whom it would constitute idolatry and apostasy.

That Christians have accepted the claims of Jesus to be the Messiah has led Jewish people to seek a peaceful co-existence whilst avoiding debate on what for many is a peripheral issue. This 'two-covenant theology' has also been developed by some Christians involved in Jewish–Christian relations, arguing the views developed by Franz Rosenzweig that Jewish and Christians have parallel paths to salvation, and that 'conversion' takes place within each religion, rather than by transfer from one to the other.

The Jewish reclamation of Jesus over the past two centuries has led to an increasing appreciation of the Jewishness of Jesus and of the context of his teaching and movement. A steady flow of books and studies demonstrates the increasing popular interest in Yeshua (Jesus), and today perhaps more than at any other time in Jewish history Jewish people have been willing to recognize Einstein's 'luminous figure of the Nazarene'. In doing so, however, they stop short of a full exploration of the message of the NT and as a result Jesus is often re-cast in response to the needs for an idealized figure that addresses the agendas of the various strands of Judaism. Reconstructed 'Lives of Jesus' do not include a full awareness of Jesus' Messiahship and divine nature. It is only through the loving witness of Christians and a willingness to search the Scriptures without presuppositions that a full appreciation of Jesus' death and resurrection, as well as his life and moral teaching, can emerge.

The Jewish apologetics of today concentrates on providing appropriate contemporary responses to questions that originated in NT times about the nature of God, the Messiah and Jesus, and has evolved over the centuries through polemic and debate. The historicity of the resurrection and the fulfilment of Messianic prophecy must be addressed with an understanding of the matrix of various ancient and contemporary Jewish views. The place of Israel as the people of God, and to a lesser extent the place of the land of Israel, are also involved in the discussion. Perhaps most needed of all is for Christians to learn to overcome the barriers of misunderstanding, exacerbated by the 'teaching of contempt' which held that the Jews deserved persecution as they were responsible for the death of Christ, by showing practical love and genuine involvement with Jewish people.

The argument of many Jewish people that Christianity is anti-Semitic is hard to answer in the light of the anti-Judaism of the early Church Fathers, the later writings of Martin Luther and the perpetration of the Holocaust in a nominally Christian country. A number of distinctions can be made between anti-Judaism as the theological denigration of Jews and Judaism and anti-Semitism as the practical outworking of policies directed against Jews, but for most Jewish people this are hardly persuasive. The NT is seen by many as containing the roots of Christian anti-Judaism, and a close reading of the texts in their Jewish context is necessary to show what is in fact the opposite: that the first followers of Jesus, all of them Jewish, saw themselves as part of their own community and claimed that true membership of Israel involved recognition of Israel's Messiah; that Jesus and his Jewish disciples would never have advocated the things that have been done in his name; and that the message of the gospel is not the same as the conduct of its later 'defenders' in the Crusades and Inquisition. But the issue that is at the heart of the objection can be answered satisfactorily only through a realization of the fundamental truth of the claims of Jesus and a recognition that it is perfectly compatible with Jewish identity to accept them, despite the prejudices and misperceptions of the past.

Whilst those engaged in Jewish apologetics need to have studied well the historical and theological objections to belief in Jesus, it is the social objections of the cost of discipleship and possible rejection from the community that are the hardest to address. The label *meshumad* (lit. 'destroyed' but signifying 'traitor' or 'apostate') carries the same stigma as it did when the writer of Hebrews urged fellow Jewish Christians to stand 'outside the camp' (Heb. 13:13). The emergence of a community of testimony in recent decades in the shape of the Messianic Jewish movement of an estimated 100,000 Jewish believers in Jesus, many worshipping in Messianic Jewish congregations, has therefore contributed significantly to openness to, and interest in, the claims of Jesus.

Bibliography

D. Berger, *The Jewish–Christian Debate in the High Middle Ages* (New York, 1979); M. L. Brown, *Answering Jewish Objections to Jesus*, 2 vols. (1999, 2000); C. Chapman, *Whose Promised Land?* (Oxford, 1989); D. Cohn-Sherbok, *Messianic Judaism* (London, 2000); D. Hagner, *The Jewish Reclamation of Jesus* (Grand Rapids, 1984); R. Harvey, 'What Shapes Jewish Identity?' in *Lausanne Consultation on Jewish Evangelism Conference Proceedings* (New York and Denmark 1999), vol. 2/5, pp. 72–85; P. Johnson, *History of the Jews* (London, 1993); J. Neusner, *Messiah in Context* (Philadelphia, 1984); W. Riggans, *Yeshua Ben David* (Crowborough, 1995); G. Scholem, *The Messianic Idea in Judaism* (New York, 1971); T. Zaretsky (ed.), *Jewish Evangelism: A Call to the Church* (Lausanne, 2005).

R. HARVEY

JUNG, CARL GUSTAV

Swiss psychiatrist and founder of analytical *psychology, Carl Jung (1875–1961) and his writings have stimulated an often polarized debate among Christian apologists. Dubbed 'the Apostle to the Gentiles' by *Freud, Jung's life-long enquiries into the depths of the human psyche have stirred accusations of occultist and charlatan on the one hand, and inspirational guru and wise old man on the other. Describing his psychology as 'the work', Jung, reflecting in his later years, declared this work to be an expression of his inner development. That inner journey was heavily influenced by the dual themes of his family background. This included the analytical, empirical tradition of his paternal grandfather, a German physician and rector of Basel University, and the strongly intuitive spiritualism of his mother and her relatives. Jung saw his engagement with psychiatry as a unitary force in bringing together the disparate strands of 'nature' and 'spirit', of his 'No. 1' personality, rational and scientific, and his 'No. 2' personality, irrational and prescient. It is the duality of these themes that preoccupies much of the debate about Jung among Christians: one camp celebrating his rationale and his exploration of symbol and the mystery of human nature, the other inveighing against his dabbling with psychic phenomena and engagement with a range of esoteric beliefs.

The contemporary debate between Christianity and Jung's methodology has certain parallels in the dialogue between the early church and *Gnosticism. As Anthony Stevens puts it, Jung was 'a lifelong gnostic – one dedicated to knowing and experiencing the reality of the spirit' (A. Stevens, *On Jung* [Harmondsworth, 1991], p. 141). Jung's gnostic tendency is seen in his engagement with *theology and psychology at a syncretistic level as he plumbed the depths of the human psyche through an inductive process based on experience, intuition, active *imagination and dream interpretation. In the manner of early Gnosticism he tapped a wide range of streams of consciousness so that he could ask, 'What then is so special about Christ? ... Why not another model – Paul or Buddha or Confucius or Zoroaster?' (C. G. Jung, *The Zofingia Lectures, Collected Works*, para. 251). In this enterprise Jung was not averse to simple eclecticism, borrowing from other belief-systems that which accorded with his own presuppositions. As Sudhir Kakar points out, Jung's stance towards Indian religious thought and psychological understanding was an ambivalent one that both idealized the Indian psyche and plundered its beliefs of those 'parallels that confirmed his own theories' (*Culture and Psyche: Selected Essays* [Delhi, 1997], p. 28).

Christian apologists need to engage with Jungian thought, seeking discernment amidst the sometimes self-contradictory complexities of his theorizing. Particular discrimination is needed in the debates about selfhood and the Godhead; the connection, if any, between the Jungian concept of 'the shadow' and human sinfulness; the contribution Jung has made, albeit limited by his patriarchal background, in questioning stereotypical views of maleness and femaleness; and the notion of 'archetypes', entities that rise up from the collective unconscious and, Jung argued, may need to be confronted imaginatively for psychological growth. Much less controversially the Myers-Briggs Type Indicator, constructed on the bedrock of Jung's theory of personality, has entered many Christian contexts as a useful adjunct in counselling, self-assesment and group dynamics.

Bibliography

Collected Works, 20 vols. (London, New York and Princeton, 1953–1978); R. F. Hurding, *Pathways to Wholeness: Pastoral Care in a Postmodern Age* (London, 1998); R. L. Moore and D. J. Meckel (eds.), *Jung and Christianity in Dialogue* (Mahwah, 1990); R. Noll, *The Jung Cult: Origins of a Charismatic Movement* (Glasgow, 1996); D. S. Wehr, *Jung and Feminism: Liberating Archetypes* (London, 1988).

R. F. HURDING

JUSTICE

Justice has many definitions depending on the context in which the word is being used. It is often roughly understood as fairness, indicating some measure of equality between people. When justice is described as punitive, it is usually referring to the administration of *law in a society, and to bringing criminals to make some sort of reparation for breaking the law and/or causing injury to another party. More often, in ethical and theological study, justice is used as the organizing concept for discussion of fair distribution of resources for well-being amongst members of a particular society, or in wider humanity. It may refer to distribution of wealth in particular, but also involves issues like *power, freedom, peace and the environment. Essentially, justice involves discussion of the quality of relations between people and groups of people, and the resources they share for life.

Historical-philosophical perspective

Interpretations of these considerations have varied significantly. For some, justice is deontological, entailing rules to be followed in order for justice to be demonstrated. For others, it is teleological, a goal to be achieved. For *Aristotle, and in some ways for *Plato before him, justice was a matter of virtue that enabled just practices and the just state to cohere. For some, it is about changing laws and structures; for others, it is a matter of personal transformation. Plato recognized the intrinsic connectedness between the two.

Immanuel *Kant believed justice to be ontological and a matter of ethical principles. If certain categorical imperatives were followed, then justice would result. These imperatives included doing only that which one would wish to be a universal law, treating people as ends and never as means, and living as though life were directed towards a kingdom of ends. Those who emphasize human rights and dignity as the basis for justice follow a deontological approach.

By contrast, the utilitarian approach emphasizes results rather than rules or rights. For moral philosophers like John Stuart Mill and Jeremy Bentham, justice is a matter of achieving the greatest happiness for the greatest number of people. This does not necessarily aim to achieve equality between all people in a given society. Rather, the overall utility is reflective of an average utility of a group of people. There may be a certain degree of inequality between people, but what is important is that the average happiness represents the highest possible average.

In contemporary secular approaches, there is often an emphasis on the conditions necessary for justice to flourish. For John Rawls, justice is a matter of securing the conditions for equal liberty and equal rights. Influenced by the social-contract ideas of *Locke and *Rousseau, Rawls proposed a theory of justice based not on utility, but on fairness. Fairness is achieved by offering the conditions by which all people have equal freedom and right to participate in society and its instruments. State intervention may be required to protect liberty and to ensure that liberties do not lead to a level of inequality that compromises self-evident rights.

An entitlement view of justice highlights the tensions between equality and freedom. Entitlement views stress that conditions of liberty are essential in any exchange of goods. So long as the exchange is just, then whatever the outcome, justice is served. Entitlement approaches stress a diminished role for the state, as justice is not connected to equality or distribution.

Twentieth-century *theology wrestled extensively with the concept of justice. At the beginning of the century, it was the social gospel that brought the issue to the attention of the church, emphasizing the nature of justice as love. Walter Rauschenbusch believed that love could be directly applied to society, and when that happened, justice would be realized. Justice for him was about distribution of wealth and freedom from oppression and victimization. It was important for theology to start from the conditions of suffering in life and build its understanding of the world from there, in light of relevant biblical material. Justice demanded that the structures of society be transformed to reflect Christian values of love, and he stressed in particular the need for reform in the business community. Changing laws to protect the vulnerable was crucial, and he was willing to join with any movement for reform as a symbol of God at work in the world, whether it was Christian or not. He believed that only when the structures were changed would individuals experience the reality of justice.

Many others were not so convinced that the church would be able to usher in the kingdom of God and bring about his justice. A generation after Rauschenbusch, Reinhold Niebuhr wrote that Christian love could not be applied directly to society. Rather, justice as a concept represented love as applied to social existence, but it was always short of perfection. The efforts of humanity to realize love were under the judgment of Christ's perfect love, and that sense of judgment on human pretensions to love was what allowed a measure of justice to be achieved. In this sense, justice will be an ongoing process of uncovering sinful pretensions to power. Justice is divisible in that greater and lesser forms of justice will be achieved in society. The challenge will remain to attempt to see better forms of justice realized.

Many grew frustrated with this limited sense of what might be achieved by humanity with respect to justice in the world. Reflecting the common good, Roman Catholic social teaching has been positive in its statements, focusing on God's intentions for his creation as determinative of justice. Out of this seedbed, movements of liberation stressed the demand for justice for the oppressed as a theological *a priori* that needed to be realized in practice and not relegated to the realm of theory. Stressing God's preferential option for the poor, liberationists such as Gustavo Gutiérrez believe that identification with the oppressed is part of the soteriological concern of the Christian faith. For many, justice is not simply a concept to strive after, but one to be realized by bringing in the kingdom of God through identification with the crucified Christ. Influenced by Jürgen Moltmann, other leaders of the movement stress the eschatological significance of making real in the present the future that is anticipated, bringing hope to hopeless situations.

Much recent theology has moved away from transformative participation in the structures of society as a means of achieving justice. For such leaders and thinkers, personal character and the witnessing *community embody justice in a way that can never be realized by society. For some, this means that the church should strive to embody structures of justice as an alternative community, while for others it means that personal transformation must precede any attempts to point governments to true justice in Christ.

Biblical perspective

A biblical view of justice defines the theological content of the concept. In the OT justice is closely connected to righteousness and is a corollary of being in a right standing before God. The vertical relationship of the faithful to God is what is credited as righteousness, and righteousness must be worked out horizontally, in the context of relationships between people, as justice. The two are connected in the creation narrative, through the fall and the giving of the law. At creation, as affirmed throughout the OT, God's intention for his creation was wholeness – *shalom*. Human sin diminished *shalom*, and the unfolding salvation history is an account of God's attempts to restore his people to a place of wholeness. *Shalom* is not possible without justice, emerging from righteousness. Therefore God reveals an ongoing concern for justice between the members of his creation. In an attempt to restore the wholeness lost in the fall, God gives his people the law, which spells out how they can live in *shalom*. The first four commandments given to Moses at Sinai relate to the importance of being rightly related to God (righteousness); the rest work out the implications of that relationship in social life, indicating how humans ought to behave in relation to one another (justice).

More directly, as part of the levitical code, and recorded as early as Exod. 23, the Israelites were exhorted not to deny justice to the poor. The alien and the orphan are given special mention in Deut. 24. Leaders were consistently charged with the administration of justice. This notion is affirmed consistently in Yahweh's instructions to his people, and the principle of jubilee was instilled as a measure to prevent the development of inequality, need and oppression over generations. In the Psalms, it continues as an important theme, intimately connected with God's character, and his desire for his people. The Lord decrees justice (Ps. 7), loves righteousness and justice (Pss. 11; 33), is known by his justice (Ps. 9) and gives justice to the oppressed (Ps. 103); the Lord secures justice (Ps. 140), and those who maintain justice are blessed (Ps. 106). The major prophets are preoccupied with justice as recognition dawned that God desired justice rather than a demonstration of empty ritual. In Isaiah, particularly from the perspective of the exile, the prophet seeks after justice, and those who deny justice to the innocent and oppressed are severely criticized and are subject to judgment. Isa. 58 offers a description of real religion, which points to enacting justice as preferable to liturgical ritual, as an indication of the righteousness of the faithful. This same view is reinforced by the minor prophets, who warn against the trappings of religion without justice (Amos 5:18–24; Mic. 6:6–8).

In the NT the theme of justice continues and is highlighted from the outset in Mary's song of Luke 1. Peace and wholeness are again affirmed as God's intention for his people; poverty and oppression deny *shalom*. The promised Messiah will lift up the humble and lay low the proud. In Luke 4, *Jesus affirms his mission as being intimately connected with justice as he proclaims himself the fulfilment of Isaiah's prophecy. Jesus' confrontation with those who were denying justice to the poor, and his own association with those in need of justice, are notable. Even the more doctrinal books of the NT convey a concern that weaker members of the community are not to be neglected. In the letter of James, the matter comes again to the fore as directives against preferential treatment and as a matter of working out faith in relationship with others. In Revelation, there is an undercurrent of encouragement and assurance to those who are marginalized from participation in the marketplace, as the ultimate downfall of injustice is declared.

Apologetic challenge and theological response

An apologetic challenge to Christians comes in the forms of oppression and injustice that militate against the witness to God's goodness. Any injustice that prevents people from experiencing *shalom* detracts from the witness of the church, which proclaims the reign and rule of God. The need for the church to engage issues of justice is not merely one of practical obedience, but in itself serves the apologetic task. Yet, while Christians pursue justice in the world, significant misunderstandings between them may be avoided by acknowledging the coherence of the biblical view of justice.

Christian anthropology and a doctrine of creation establish the dignity of human life, as it reflects the image of God. It is clear through the creation account that God desires all life to flourish, and he provided the means by which creation could be properly sustained. Human sin allows people to despise the provision God has made for them, as they accumulate wealth for themselves in greed. This leads to inequalities in the distribution of wealth and power. In situations where the balance of wealth or power is tipped strongly in one direction, injustice will result as humans are prevented from enjoying the measure of *shalom* that was intended for them at creation. Resetting the balance is the ongoing concern of the Christian disciple.

In his life and teaching, Jesus announced the presence of the kingdom of God, where justice stands in opposition to the values of earthly kingdoms and powers. Jesus' own identification with oppression, to the point of his own death, ushers in final justice for humanity. Through his cross, Jesus affirms justice, and rebaptizes it in the context of love. The resurrection vindicates those who suffer and cry out for justice. The justice that Jesus offers differs in kind from the justice sought by humanity. Jesus' cross provides restorative justice, where those who were alienated from God and deserving of his retribution were brought back into the wholeness of relationship with God and one another. Jesus Christ offers a challenge to those who would believe in him to pick up their cross daily and follow him. Believers should reflect his concern for justice, embracing the command to love as he loved us.

God's justice, though final, is in many ways realized only in potential. Clearly, justice is still demanded in many lives and communities today. An eschatological vision assures those who seek justice that the risen and ascended Lord is with them through his Holy Spirit; and in that vision, they may find hope for the present. This takes on tangible expression in the lives of those who seek to identify with and encourage those who are in need of justice, wherever they are in the world today. As a community in Christ, we are to bear witness to his final justice, which disarms and stands in judgment over the principalities and powers of this world.

Justice for the Christian is both personal and structural. It is concerned with the transformation of people and powers, individuals and groups. It will involve both charity and empowerment, as Christians seek to restore dignity to people and not dependence. It is deontological, as the demand for justice comes first from God and has been met in Christ. But it is teleological in the sense that God's kingdom is not yet fulfilled. Commitment to effect justice in this lifetime may sometimes falter and yield few results, but that does not negate the attempt, as our efforts witness to the *shalom* of the world to come. God has entrusted certain tasks to his people, but ultimately it is he who will bring visible, final justice to his world.

Bibliography

K. Lebacqz, *Six Theories of Justice* (Minneapolis, 1986); R. Niebuhr, *Love and Justice* (Louisville, 1957); A. M. Robbins, *Methods in the Madness* (Carlisle, 2004); N. Wolterstorff, *Until Justice and Peace Embrace* (Grand Rapids, 1983); J. H. Yoder, *The Politics of Jesus* (Grand Rapids, 1994).

A. M. ROBBINS

JUSTIN MARTYR

Justin Martyr (c. 100–65) was born in Samaria to a Greek family which had settled there. He became a leading apologist for the Christian faith at a time when it was still a little-known minority cult, and his intimate knowledge of Palestine and familiarity with *Judaism was unusual in the Gentile world, though too much should not be made of this. He remained a Greek writing for other Greeks, hoping to win them over to the teachings of Christ, which he had himself discovered in his search for truth.

Justin was converted sometime in early manhood and made his living as an itinerant teacher for many years. At some point during the reign of the Emperor Antoninus Pius (138–61) he made his way to Rome, where he founded a school whose most famous pupil was Tatian, later to become himself a somewhat eccentric apologist for Christianity. Justin was beheaded for his faith along with six others, when Junius Rusticus was prefect of Rome (163–7).

Justin was a prolific writer, but only three of his works have come down to us. Two of these are apologies designed for his fellow Gentiles, and the other is his *Dialogue with Trypho*. Trypho is most probably to be identified as Tarphon, a Jewish rabbi who seems to have lived at Ephesus and who is mentioned in the Mishnah.

In his first apology, which Justin addressed to the emperor, he attacked the illicit way in which the Roman state persecuted Christians, merely on the strength of the name. Christian refusal to worship the pagan deities was not atheism but common sense, and Christians were preserved from wrongdoing by their own moral standards, which were inherent in their beliefs about divine rewards and punishments. From defending his position against pagan attacks, Justin turns to a presentation of the truth of the Christian faith. Most important for him was the fact that the life and career of *Jesus Christ, the Son of God, was clearly foretold in the Jewish Scriptures, which philosophers like *Plato had read and adapted to their own ends. Justin concludes his presentation by demanding fair treatment for Christians based on an imperial rescript issued by Hadrian in 125, which gave strict guidelines for trying them in the courts.

The second apology was apparently provoked by the unjust execution of three Christians and concentrates exclusively on the phenomenon of persecution. Even while proclaiming its fundamental injustice, Justin points out that persecution is an opportunity for Christians to demonstrate the truth of their faith and to show the world that they are not afraid of death, which is the gateway to eternal life. The emphasis on Christian behaviour in times of trial suggests that this work was written not for pagans but for Christians, to strengthen them as they faced *martyrdom for their beliefs.

The *Dialogue with Trypho* is incomplete but is the most interesting of Justin's works. In it he outlines the Christian approach to the OT and does his best to show how it is the preparation for the coming of Christ. In many respects it appears that Justin and Trypho were in fundamental agreement about the nature of biblical interpretation. The main difference between them is that Trypho could not accept that the ancient prophecies had been fulfilled in the life, death and resurrection of Jesus Christ. It has also been noticed that Justin emphasizes those OT passages which speak of the rejection of Israel and the subsequent ingathering of the Gentiles, though this emphasis should not be interpreted as a sign of anti-Semitism in the modern sense. It seems, in fact, that Justin and Trypho were on good terms with one another, and the dialogue is remarkably friendly, if inconclusive. Justin came away convinced, but Trypho was not converted, an outcome which reflects the historical reality quite accurately, whether or not the dialogue itself ever took place.

Bibliography

K. O. Bullock, *The Writings of Justin Martyr* (Nashville, 1998); L. W. Barnard, *Justin Martyr, His Life and Thought* (Cambridge, 1967); A. J. Bellinzoni, *The Sayings of Jesus in the Writings of Justin Martyr* (Leiden, 1967); W. A. Shotwell, *The Biblical Exegesis of Justin Martyr* (London, 1965).

G. L. BRAY

KABIR

An Indian mystic with a genius for poetic expression, Kabir was brought up in a Muslim weaver community. His dates are uncertain, but he lived in the fifteenth century some time between 1398 and 1518, mostly in Benares (modern Varanasi). He regarded traditional forms of religion, both Hindu and Muslim, as worthless, and rejected the Hindu practices of caste, idol worship, asceticism and Brahmanic ritual. He was equally dismissive of the *Islamic routine of daily prayers.

Despite being born as a Muslim and being influenced to some extent by Sufi ideas, Kabir's world-view was Hindu. It is not surprising that Hindus claim him as one of their own, but Kabir does not fit easily into any sect of *Hinduism or any religion. Sikhs honour him, and Muslims believe he was buried with Islamic rites.

Kabir's teaching is not systematic but it is wide-ranging. The goal of existence is loving union with the Supreme Being, who is to be found within. This union is sometimes described in the language of *advaita*: 'The one who knows the Self has no more to know.' More frequently God is described in personal terms and may be addressed by any name, whether Muslim or Hindu, such as Ram or Allah. Human beings are lost. 'All men are deceived, blind and misled' and their only hope is to escape from rebirth by means of *bhakti*, which is the only religious path worth following. Love for God is the essence of *bhakti*, but this is no easy way. The path is almost impossible to find and follow. Though man must strive for salvation (*moksha*), he can reach the goal only by the mercy of God.

Clearly there are many insights in Kabir's thought which Christians can identify with. These include his passionate love for God and longing for union with him, his acknowledgment of the *evil tendency of human nature and his appreciation of the mercy and love of God.

Kabir was, however, handicapped by ignorance of the *revelation of the God who descends to save fallen humanity. For him God could be found only at the end of a desperate search by the very few. He rejected the Hindu idea of *avatar*, but did not know of the altogether different incarnate Christ. He rejected the traditional Muslim view of God as an infinitely distant sovereign, but did not know of the God who takes the initiative to reveal himself to sinners. Consequently, Kabir speaks of the grace of God not as a wonder freely given but as a favour awarded to those who have sacrificed their lives to attain it.

Bibliography

F. E. Keay, *Kabir and His Followers* (Calcutta, 1931); C. Vaudeville, *A Weaver Named Kabir* (Oxford, 1993); G. H. Westcott, *Kabir and the Kabir Panth* (Calcutta, 1943).

B. J. M. SCOTT

KALAM COSMOLOGICAL ARGUMENT, see COSMOLOGICAL ARGUMENT

KANT, IMMANUEL

Immanuel Kant (1724–1804), marks a watershed in Western philosophy. His writings have left a lasting imprint extending as far as the criticism of art and literature. We can clarify Kant's significance under four aspects: as epitome of the intellectual world of his day, as agent of the 'Copernican revolution', as pace-setter for his immediate disciples, and as originator of a long-range legacy.

Kant's world

Perhaps too much has been made out of the fact that Kant spent his entire life in Königsberg, East Prussia, leading a regular and disciplined life. He was far from insular in his thinking and maintained a lively – and at times precarious – relationship with the political institutions of his day. Kant's thoughts flowed within the intellectual stream of the *Enlightenment, which was characterized, at least in part, by its celebration of human autonomy. Furthermore, Kant was swept up in the excitement surrounding the rise of modern *science, particularly Isaac *Newton's discovery of the laws of motion.

Kant initially operated within the rationalistic system of Christian Wolff (1679–1754), who attempted to ground knowledge in indubitable principles. However, as Kant himself attested, the writings of the empiricist sceptic David *Hume (1711–76) catalyzed him into a whole new way of thinking. It is important to observe here that Kant was interacting with two reductionistic extremes: a *rationalism that sought to give *metaphysics absolute *certainty and an *empiricism that declared metaphysics to be impossible.

Kant's 'Copernican revolution'

No one was more convinced of the revolutionary nature of Kant's thought than Kant himself. He believed that he had achieved a revolution in philosophy akin to that of Copernicus, who had asserted that the earth revolves around the sun rather than the sun around the earth. Kant declared that knowledge is not the mind's passive reception of orderly truth from outside of itself, but the active work of the mind in formulating the very truths it is assimilating. As an analogy, let us imagine that Kant's predecessors held variations on the idea that the mind receives certain previously canned goods and stacks them on permanent shelves. For Kant, the mind receives unrecognizable raw materials, turns them into various goods, cans them and stacks them on shelves it has simultaneously made. Just so, says Kant, the mind receives inchoate unprocessed sensory data, shapes them, packages them and lines them up according to categories produced by the mind itself. More specifically, as the mind receives unprocessed sensory intuitions, it first imposes the forms of space and time on them and then makes sense of them by means of logical categories of judgment, which are grounded in the mind's own pure concepts of understanding. The result, according to Kant, is knowledge.

Note three important facts about Kant's innovation. First, its revolutionary character is due largely to its context in modern philosophy with its extremely passive approach to knowledge. In previous ages, philosophers had already recognized that knowledge involved some active engagement of the mind with the object of knowledge, as seen, e.g. in *Aristotle's notion of the agent intellect.

Secondly, we must recognize that Kant did not claim that the human mind creates its own knowledge *ex nihilo*. Kant held fast to the notion that outside of the mind there is an external *reality. This 'thing' provides the initial content, which then becomes subjected to the mind's formative actions.

A third crucial observation has to do with the *logic of Kant's analysis. In contrast to Hume, Kant did not begin with a method for knowledge and then see what, if anything, we can possibly know. Kant decided in advance *that* we know and then set out to discover *how* we know. Thus, for example, Kant began with the assumption of the reality of causality – which Hume could not establish – and then asked how it is that the mind could ascertain causal relations.

Still, arising out of Kant's transcendental method was his own form of scepticism. Kant set out to find an underpinning for the knowledge that he was sure we had, and the outcome of his search were the concepts of the mind, such as *causality, that made such knowledge possible. However, Kant did not permit us to take the further step to treat these concepts as though they were also items of knowledge. That would lead to contradictions and was, therefore, strictly prohibited. In Kant's terminology, the regulative concepts of the mind are considered to be *synthetic a priori*, which means that they contribute content (*synthetic*), but are derived from within the mind (*a priori*). Kant expressed the divorce between the accessible and inaccessible aspects of knowledge with the terms *the phenomenal* and *the noumenal*, the latter of which includes both the thing-in-itself and the concepts within the mind.

This elimination of metaphysics also barred the possibility of a rational defence for religion. For Kant, God's existence is not an inescapable truth, but a hypothesis that provides significance for moral actions by stipulating a 'highest good' (*summum bonum*).

Kant's ethics

If one begins with the idea that human minds construct their own phenomenal worlds, how can one possibly have a viable moral philosophy that carries validity from individual to individual? Again, Kant's approach to this issue is transcendental: given genuine ethical decisions, how are they possible? Kant's earlier conclusions prevented him from appealing to any external metaphysical realities, not even God, but he could draw on human reason. An ethical decision must be rational, and so a person confronted with a moral dilemma must look for a rational solution. For example, could it be legitimate for a man to lie about his financial situation in order to receive a desperately-needed loan of money? Kant says no, for by lying the man would be contradicting his own will. He would be free to lie and, thereby, to improve his present state temporarily, but in doing so he would also legitimize the use of lying for the sake of one's personal convenience. But surely, the person does not intend for all lies of convenience to be acceptable, beginning with his proposed new creditor; he continues to expect all other people to keep telling him the truth. Thus, Kant says, the man can will the lie (of the moment), but he cannot will lying to be universal practice. And this recognition becomes the cornerstone of Kant's 'categorical imperative' for *ethics, which we can paraphrase as 'Always act in such a way that, whatever choice you make, you are willing to let that choice become a universal obligation'.

Kant's immediate influence

A number of Kant's contemporaries bought into his 'Copernican revolution' and appropriated his transcendental method. Among his early disciples were Fichte, Schelling and *Hegel, each of whom published significant works during Kant's own lifetime. However, these German idealists unanimously rejected the notion that knowledge began with an unknowable thing-in-itself outside of the mind and located the origin of all knowledge within some form of absolutized self-consciousness.

Kant's long-range influence

In addition to the more technical philosophical heritage that Kant left behind, he was also responsible for a broader legacy of subjectivity. It was he who first opened the door to the notion that to find knowledge we need to look inside the mind, not out to the world. There is no question that this open door made possible the subsequent arrival of phenomenology, *existentialism and postmodern relativistic philosophies.

Bibliography

I. Kant, *Critique of Pure Reason* (ET New York, 1965); *Foundations of the Metaphysics of Morals* (ET Chicago, 1950); W. S. Körner, *Kant* (Baltimore, 1955).

W. CORDUAN

KEMPIS, THOMAS A, see THOMAS A KEMPIS

KIERKEGAARD, SØREN

Søren Kierkegaard (1813–55) was a Danish Christian writer whose authorship resists easy classification. Many of his books have a highly literary character and can almost be seen as novels, whilst others are highly philosophical and/or theological in character, and many have an 'upbuilding' or edifying character. Often all of these qualities are present in the same work. Kierkegaard's influence on secular European thought as the so-called 'father of *existentialism' has been profound. However, many of those who have appropriated some of his insights, such as Heidegger and Camus, have detached them from Kierkegaard's own deep Christian faith, leading to results he surely would have repudiated. Ironically, Kierkegaard's association with these secular philosophers has sometimes led those in the church to treat him with suspicion.

Kierkegaard's father was a pietistic Lutheran who struggled with guilt and depression all his life, and who brought the young Søren up in a strict Christian home. As a young man, Søren rebelled against his father and Christianity, but was reconciled to both prior to his father's death, though he continued the struggles of his father and in some strange way saw his own problems as bound up with his father's. He completed the university course that qualified him to become a pastor, but never accepted an official position, though he preached occasionally in various churches in Copenhagen. He fell in love with a young woman, Regine Olsen, became engaged to her, but quickly decided that the engagement had been a mistake. His own feelings of guilt and depression made it impossible for him to marry, and he came to believe that God was calling him to give up Regine. He broke the engagement and created a public scandal, but continued to love Regine

deeply for the rest of his life. Kierkegaard began to write a series of books, initially designed in part to communicate his true motives to Regine, who had married someone else, but which from the beginning had broader purposes as well.

The interpretation of Kierkegaard's writings is made difficult by the fact that many of his books were attributed to pseudonyms such as 'Johannes de Silentio' and 'Vigilius Haufniensis'. Kierkegaard himself explains that this was not done for the sake of anonymity, but in the service of what he calls 'indirect communication'. According to this view, moral and religious truths must be personally appropriated to be understood, and a writer who understands this ought to write in such a way as to encourage such subjective grappling with the ideas. We might think of Kierkegaard's pseudonymous authorship as something like a long novel, in which the pseudonymous authors are like characters with their own perspectives on human existence and how it should be lived. Kierkegaard thought that readers who encounter such characters would be forced to think for themselves about the issues they raise. A good example is found in the infamous 'Diary of a Seducer' that concludes the first volume of *Either/Or*. The Seducer is clearly intended as a demonic figure, but the reader must see this for himself or herself. No warning lecture is attached, and the author does not make things easy by having the Seducer go insane or commit suicide. Obviously, if a reader confuses the voice of the Seducer with Kierkegaard himself, the misinterpretation will be disastrous.

In these pseudonymous writings Kierkegaard explores the meaning of human existence, confronting both Romantics, who exalted a life of individual feeling and experience, and Rationalists, who identified a full human life with intelligence or knowledge. For Kierkegaard existence is essentially the task of becoming a self, and he believed that one could not become one's true self without a relation to the God who has created human persons. Christianity is essentially an answer to the question of existence; someone who does not understand the question will not understand the answer. These explorations of existence are addressed primarily to non-Christians. At the same time Kierkegaard wrote a series of 'Upbuilding Discourses' to accompany these aesthetic writings.

Kierkegaard describes himself as a kind of missionary, called to the task of 'reintroducing Christianity into Christendom' (see *The Point of View for My Work as an Author*, trans. H. V. Hong and E. H. Hong [Princeton, 1998], pp. 123–124). As he saw it, Christianity in Denmark had become virtually indistinguishable from being a proper Dane. Everyone was a Christian, unless they happened to be Jewish, just by virtue of being born in Denmark and being baptized. Though Kierkegaard did not oppose infant baptism, he did strenuously oppose the idea that one could be a Christian without a passionate faith in Christ. Genuine faith is something that God himself must create in the individual, though he also saw faith as something the individual must freely affirm. To be a genuine Christian one must be a follower of Christ, an imitator. To be sure, when we try to imitate Christ we will inevitably fail and we must take refuge in Christ as the one who atones for sin. But when we are thus strengthened by Christ's atonement, we must renew our efforts at following him.

Being a genuine disciple of Christ will always involve opposition from 'the world'. Christ's followers are called to love their neighbours as themselves, and all human beings are our neighbours. The world may give lip service to caring for others, but in reality all who follow the radical example of *Jesus can expect contempt and even persecution from the world. The identification of Christianity with human culture in the form of 'Christendom' is a betrayal of the radical demand of the gospel.

Philosophically, Kierkegaard is best known as a great opponent of *Hegel. The Hegelians claimed to have developed a Christian philosophy that vindicated the truth of Christianity as one of the three great expressions, along with art and philosophy, of 'Absolute Spirit'. On the Hegelian view, as Kierkegaard interpreted it, the truth contained in Christianity was essentially that the human race is the embodiment of the divine or God or Absolute Spirit. There is a fundamental unity of the human and the divine. The same truth that Christianity expresses in the form of religious stories for Hegel is expressed more adequately by philosophy.

For Kierkegaard, the truth of Christianity cannot be reduced to any philosophical formula, Hegelian or otherwise. Rather, the central truth of Christianity is the incarnation of God in Jesus. This incarnation is a reality, not a doctrine to be speculatively understood. It is in fact a *paradox to human reason, something that can only be believed in faith. Far from showing the unity of the human and the divine, the incarnation is made necessary by human sinfulness, which separates us from God. Christianity is thus a revealed religion, whose truth must be grasped through faith, and whose truth is equally accessible to the educated and the uneducated, the intelligent and the simple. Apologetic attempts to prove that Jesus was God or to show the probability of the incarnation are rejected on the grounds that New Testament Christianity must always be presented in such a way that 'the possibility of offence' is preserved. Anyone who pridefully believes that human reason is sufficient to gain ultimate truth cannot help but be offended by the claims of Christ.

At the end of Kierkegaard's life he made a public attack on the state church as a falsification of New Testament Christianity, conducted in newspapers and in a periodical that he began and financed called *The Moment*. He collapsed on the street while carrying the tenth and final planned issue to the printer, and died shortly thereafter. He had exhausted his inherited fortune and willed his few remaining goods to Regine, who declined the honour. These late writings had a profound impact on the development of the free church movement in Scandinavia. His works as a whole continue to have a major impact on contemporary philosophy and theology.

C. S. EVANS

KIESLOWSKI, KRZYSZTOF

Polish director Krzysztof Kieslowski (1941–96) is best known for his 1994 trilogy, *Three Colours: Red, White, and Blue*. These acclaimed films were designed to be visual commentaries on contemporary Europe in the hues of the classic French virtues, liberty, equality and fraternity. Kieslowski strips away conventional cinematic techniques and uses nearly every aspect of film-making to expose the substance of his subjects. They are on display, caught in the act of being human.

Of the three films, *Blue* is the most relevant to our purposes here. Julie, the wife of an accomplished composer, is faced with the death of her husband and daughter in a car crash. The poignant turn in *Blue*, which thematically represents liberty, is Julie's inability to cope with the loss of her family, the cruellest kind of liberty, an unwanted freedom. Julie retreats into near total isolation, effectively isolating the audience with her to witness her changing emotions and to share her inmost, heart-wrenching thoughts. *Blue* is a powerful film to engage an audience with the issues of death, regret and survival.

Central to the plot of *Red* is the theme of fraternity realized in the motif of communication. A well-known fashion model becomes acquainted with a retired judge who is in the habit of tapping his neighbour's phone calls. Thus the worlds of explicit and illicit communication are brought into dialogue, exposing the palpable lack of genuine communication in the world. This film would work well in a discussion of *ethics, especially the ethics of the mass media and communication in the world of the Internet. One could also contrast the issue of *revelation (both common and specific) with what passes for communication in our age.

Along with these films, we must note Kieslowski's ten-part television mini-series, *Dekalog* (1987), now available on DVD. In ten one-hour episodes, Kieslowski dramatizes each of the Ten Commandments with vignettes from the lives of various residents of the same apartment building in Warsaw. Each episode is charged with enough emotion and memorable characters to fuel a lively discussion long after the film ends. Perhaps the most accessible episode is the very first, in which a father relies solely on a computer to guide his adoring son, with tragic consequences. This would likely be a disturbing and provocative film to show to any group of computer-dependent people. The most powerful episode is *A Short Film about Killing* and would lend itself to a discussion of the death penalty. Obviously this series would do well in a Bible study or other group studying the Decalogue, but individual episodes or scenes could be used as well.

Bibliography

G. Andrew, *'Three Colours' Trilogy* (London, 1998); A. Insdorf, *Double Lives, Second Chances: The Cinema of Krzysztof Kieslowski* (New York, 1999); D. Stok (ed.), *Kieslowski on Kieslowski* (London, 1995); S. Zizek (ed.), *The Fright of Real Tears* (Bloomington, 2001).

D. S. Russell

KOYAMA, KOSUKE

As a Japanese Christian, Kosuke Koyama (b. 1929) saw the need to adjust Christian theology in order to relate to Mahayana *Buddhism, Shintoism, Confucianism and traditional Japanese religion. He became a missionary to Thailand, where he encountered Theravada/Hinayana Buddhism with its apparent eternally repeated cycle of birth, growth, decay, death, birth. Koyama had been influenced by K. Kitamori's *Theology of the Pain of God* with its emphasis on the formula L + W = P (love and wrath together producing pain in the heart of God), but he now searched for a theology which would break into Buddhism's continual circle in which the once-for-all incarnation, death and resurrection of Jesus could play no part.

To communicate effectively in Thailand Koyama developed his skills in pictorial forms of expression rather than the traditional academic vocabulary of theological study. Thus the titles of his books vividly describe their theological content, e.g. *Three Mile an Hour God* reveals the patiently slow-moving God who travels by buffalo cart rather than by jet and *No Handle on the Cross* develops the theme that the cross of Christ cannot be tamed and domesticated by human formulations. Koyama's best-known work *Waterbuffalo Theology* struggles with how to relate to Thai Buddhism, while *Mount Fuji and Mount Sinai* shows his own pilgrimage to such a contextualized theology.

In relating to Thai culture, Koyama felt the key issue to be that God is outside of and irrelevant to human *history. Even 'the pepper' of the colonial gun-boat may prove positive in breaking violently into the Buddhist circle of *apatheia*. Koyama believed that Thai *apatheia* stemmed from the Buddhist doctrine of *Anatta* (non-being) and asked the question, 'How indeed can "no-self" be perturbed?' Spiritual imperturbability is every Thai monk's ideal, but life within history inevitably includes perturbation. Somewhat unrealistically Koyama also felt the cycle of nature in Thailand with its total predictability was a mirror of the Buddhist circle of death and rebirth.

Koyama stresses that the God of righteousness is perturbed by human sin. Although he underlines Luther's *opus proprium* of God's mercy, he also stresses particularly the *opus alienum* of God's wrath as the attribute which cannot be tamed or domesticated. He fears that without this emphasis God and the Christian faith may be 'captivated in an ontological cage'. Biblically God is an independent personal power who acts of his own volition in history. While God's love may easily lead to the taming of God, his wrath has 'a unique power to historicize God' and is 'the critical expression of "God in history" '. In his wrath God descends from the 'incomparably high beyond' to stage an assault on human 'ontocratic complacency'.

Bibliography

D. T. Irwin and A. E. Akinade, *The Agitated Mind of God – The Theology of Kosuke Koyama* (New York, 1996); K. Kitamori, *Theology of the Pain of God* (London, 1991); K. Koyama, *Mount Fuji and Mount Sinai: A Pilgrimage in Theology* (London, 1984); *No Handle on the Cross: An Asian Meditation on the Crucified Mind* (London, 1976); *Theology in Context: Six Reflections on God's Word and Man's Life in God* (Madras, 1975); *Three Mile an Hour God* (London, 1979); *Waterbuffalo Theology* (London, 1974); C. Michalson, *Japanese Contributions to Christian Theology* (Philadelphia, n.d.); M. Morse, *Kosuke Koyama, a Model for Intercultural Theology* (Frankfurt am Main, 1991); S. Choan-Seng, *Doing Theology Today* (Madras, 1976).

M. GOLDSMITH

KUYPER, ABRAHAM

Abraham Kuyper (1837–1920), the Dutch Reformed theologian, politician, journalist, social reformer and prime minister, is one of the most significant shapers of contemporary evangelical thought. This is largely due to the ongoing impact of the Stone Lectures which he delivered at Princeton Theological seminary in 1898 (published under the title *Lectures on Calvinism*). In these lectures Kuyper sketched out the contours of a Christian world-view relevant to every sphere of life, including *science, education, the *arts and politics. It is a vision that has helped preserve the evangelical mainstream from the worst ravages of fundamentalism and anti-intellectualism. This is reflected in the work of British theologians influenced by the Kuyperian tradition, including N. T. Wright, Oliver O'Donovan, Alister McGrath, Graham Cray, Jeremy Begbie, Elaine

Storkey and Lesslie *Newbigin. Kuyper's impact on the English-speaking world would, however, almost certainly have been less significant without the advocacy of Benjamin Breckinridge *Warfield, an eminent member of the Princeton faculty at the time of his Stone Lectures.

Warfield's enthusiasm for, and propagation of, Kuyper's work may seem odd in view of the fact that these two theologians represent different standpoints regarding the relationship between faith and reason and can even be said to represent two different camps within evangelical scholarship. Due to the importance of this division to the field of apologetics, this article will seek to elucidate Kuyper's ideas by contrasting them with those of Warfield.

Warfield engaged in apologetics and endorsed its use with unrivalled vigour, tending in doing so towards the post-Reformation scholastic view that reason was a prerequisite to faith. He argued that human reason compelled people to believe the Bible because of evidential or logical proofs of its divine character. The Scriptures had therefore to be vindicated as a technically reliable guide to science and history before a person could trust in them. Kuyper, on the other hand, shunned apologetics, maintaining that the *Holy Spirit moved people to accept the authority of the Scriptures because of the message of salvation they contained. The function of Scripture was, in fact, soteriological: it brought people to salvation. Kuyper appealed to *Calvin's *testimonium Spiritus Sancti* in his rejection of reasoned argument in the effort to affirm the authority of the Scriptures; the Holy Spirit, who indwelt the believer, bore witness to their truth. Thus he declared at the start of his Stone Lectures, in words that were no doubt aimed directly at Warfield and his colleagues: 'In this struggle [between the world-views of Christianity and modernism], Apologetics have advanced us not one single step. Apologists have invariably begun by abandoning the assailed breastwork, in order to entrench themselves cowardly in a ravelin behind it.' The point reached its intended target as Warfield later wrote in criticism of Kuyper and his associates that apologetics had a primary part to play in evangelism. He confessed to finding the Kuyperian aversion to apologetics 'a standing matter of surprise'. Kuyper's functional view of the Bible differed markedly, therefore, from Warfield's rational or 'philosophical' approach, even though the dogmatic positions maintained by Kuyper and Warfield on the authority and inspiration of Scripture bore striking similarities.

The divergence between Kuyper and Warfield on the relationship between faith and reason also manifested itself in their respective approaches to science or 'scholarship' (*Wissenschaft*). Although Kuyper's ideas ran counter to the dominant agnostic trend in science, he refused to cultivate antipathy for science or any belief in a conflict between science and faith; love for science and the absence of any dualistic withdrawal from science were marks of authentic Christianity. There existed, however, a fundamental conflict between Christian and non-Christian presuppositions, manifesting itself in a sharp division between those scientists who believed the cosmos to be in an abnormal (fallen) state and those who believed it to be in a normal (unfallen) state. Whereas if there had been no fall, Kuyper argued, human consciousness would have operated in the same way for all people, the intervention of sin and the need for regeneration had resulted in two kinds of consciousness, that of the regenerate and that of the unregenerate, the former of which held to the abnormal state of things and the latter to the normal. Now, if human consciousness is the starting-point of all knowledge, it must also be the starting-point from which all science proceeds, and due to the twofold division in consciousness, the science of normalists and the abnormalists must be fundamentally different from each other. The 'two kinds of people' that existed by reason of the divine act of regeneration represented an irreconcilable division in human consciousness and therefore inevitably produced 'two kinds of science'. Warfield regarded this argument as seriously misguided. He saw no reason to challenge the prevailing scientific consensus that science was an objective, unified and cumulative enterprise of the whole of humanity, regenerate and unregenerate alike.

The epistemological question that divided Warfield and Kuyper was whether or not the acquisition of knowledge was exactly the same in principle for the regenerate and the unregenerate mind. Kuyper, who was influenced by the Idealist tradition, conceived of knowledge in terms of the organic relationships it involved between creator, cosmos and the knowing subject. For this reason, all human knowledge presupposed certain givens about the way the universe was held together;

knowledge independent of religiously held presuppositions simply did not exist. Warfield, in contrast, was schooled in the *Baconian tradition with its insistence that knowledge was gained by considering the evidence and reaching conclusions based on that evidence. Accordingly, human knowledge was independent of the belief system held by the investigating subject. Warfield's argument suited his context in the United States, a country that was founded on principles derived chiefly from the moderate Enlightenment, but it differed markedly from Kuyper's fiercely critical attitude to the *Enlightenment, which in the Netherlands presented itself as a much greater threat to orthodox Christian belief than in the United States.

Bibliography

A. Kuyper, *Lectures on Calvinism* (Grand Rapids, 1931); *Principles of Sacred Theology* (Grand Rapids, 1980); *The Problem of Poverty* (Washington and Grand Rapids, 1991); *The Work of the Holy Spirit* (Grand Rapids, 1975); J. Bolt (ed.), *A Free Church and a Holy Nation: Abraham Kuyper's American Public Theology* (Grand Rapids, 2001); J. D. Bratt (ed.), *Abraham Kuyper: A Centennial Reader* (Grand Rapids and Carlisle, 1998); H. A. Harris, *Fundamentalism and Evangelicals* (Oxford, 1998); P. Heslam, *Creating a Christian Worldview: Abraham Kuyper's Lectures on Calvinism* (Grand Rapids and Carlisle, 1998); C. van der Kooi and J. de Bruijn (eds.), *Kuyper Reconsidered: Aspects of his Life and Work* (Amsterdam, 1999); L. E. Lugo (ed.), *Religion, Pluralism and Public Life: Abraham Kuyper's Legacy for the Twenty-First Century* (Grand Rapids, 2000).

P. S. HESLAM

LANGUAGE AND LITERARY THEORIES

Language is at the heart of what Christianity claims to be true of God and of humankind. The God of the Bible is a speaking God. God's ultimate *revelation of himself, in *Jesus Christ, is described in the Bible as the incarnation of 'the Word' (John 1:14). The fundamental means by which he chooses to relate to us is a covenant (i.e. a promise) – and a promise is a complicated kind of action which can be performed only by means of language. God, therefore, chooses to relate to us linguistically, not bypassing language. He also calls on human beings to express their love for him in the ways they speak (use language) with one another (e.g. Eph. 4:25, 29; 5:4; Jas 3:1–12). Christianity is, therefore, touched by, and has a particular contribution to make to, general discussions of language.

Christianity is also fundamentally interested in literature, because the Bible, God's written Word, is in literary form. The Bible might conceivably have been made up of a simple series of unrelated short sayings, or given by God ready formed, bypassing the literary artistry of human authors, but it was not. Instead, God has chosen to speak to us through the literary skills of human writers who produced law, history, prophecy, parable, apocalyptic, gospels, letters, etc. Each of these is a complex literary form (also called a literary genre) in its own right. The particular blend of literary genres which go to form the *canon of Scripture leaves us with a very literary and very complex Word. Much that is important in Christianity hinges on what we think the Bible is and how we should interpret it. Christianity is therefore affected by, and has much to contribute to, literary theory.

Language and the world: reference and meaning

Various views of how language functions in relation to the world have been expressed over the centuries. One ancient and fundamental view of the function of language is that it is descriptive: it exists to refer to and picture objects in the world. This view is expressed in different ways by ancient writers, both Christian (*Augustine) and secular (*Plato). More recent writers added the notion that language refers to thoughts as well as to objects in the world, while retaining the same basic view (the early work of the twentieth-century philosopher Ludwig *Wittgenstein is a notable example). This 'picture theory' of language accords well with the way language is used in Gen. 2:19, where Adam gives a name to each animal by which it will be called. Yet there is more to the Christian conception of language than this. God's words, even when expressed in human language, are active and dynamic, not just referential and expressive (Heb. 4:12), and through God's words we come to relate to him, not just understand him.

A second view, expressed more recently in the second half of the twentieth century, especially in post-structuralism and deconstruction, is of language as inventive of the world. The argument is not the silly one that the world does not exist, but instead that it is we who give meaning to the world by making judgments and distinctions, which we express linguistically. Since the meanings which we give to the world in this way are conventional and cultural, they are at heart, it is claimed, arbitrary, and do not and cannot reflect 'how the world really is'. Key writers who express this view of language are Jacques *Derrida, Michel *Foucault, Roland Barthes and Richard *Rorty. This is an attack on the very roots of Christianity, as Barthes acknowledges: 'to refuse to fix meaning is, in the end, to refuse God'.

The Christian response is that language and the world can indeed be said to be inherently meaningful only if there is a Creator God who has created a meaningful world. To say that meaning is fixed is not, however, the same as saying that we have understood a particular text perfectly (there is always more to discover), but to deny that there is a meaning out there to be discovered is to say that all we can ever know is ourselves and the communities of which we form a part. Moreover, since God has spoken to our world through the Word Jesus Christ, and since we as linguistic beings are made in the image of this linguistic God, then God and his speaking activity provide the firm basis on which we can say that language refers meaningfully to the world.

A third view of language's relation to the world is of language as inter-personal action. This view was expressed particularly clearly in the twentieth century in the 'ordinary language' philosophy of Wittgenstein (his later writings), J. L. Austin, John Searle and others. The basic claim is that language is to be understood by how it is used. Language does not just refer to the world, but is a means by which people perform actions (e.g. uttering the words 'I promise ...' itself simply performs the action of making a promise). In this view, language sometimes acts to reflect the world (e.g. stating a fact), but sometimes acts to change states of affairs in the world (e.g. when the foreman of a jury utters the word 'Guilty'). This view of language fits very well with that of Christianity. God both speaks to us descriptively about himself, us and the world, and he also acts to change the world by establishing a relationship with human beings by speaking to us the words of a covenant promise, such that for us to respond to those words is to respond to him.

But what kind of act are literary texts performing? The philosopher Paul Ricoeur regards literary texts as projecting a 'world', i.e. proposing a way of looking at things, for the reader to consider and respond to. The Bible can helpfully be thought of in this way. It does not so much argue for the existence of God as propose that we look at the world a different way, through a variety of literary perspectives.

Language and the self: human identity

What we think about language is intimately related to what we think about human identity. For the last few centuries until recently, the predominant Western (modernist) view was that the self is an autonomous thinking subject, who is a (self-)sufficient ground of meaning and *truth. Language is the vehicle by which such an autonomous mind communicates its thoughts to other minds. Postmodernity and Christianity are equally opposed to this view.

Postmodernity's different view of the self derives significantly from Ferdinand de Saussure's influential work of linguistics, *A Course in General Linguistics* (1916). Saussure argued that words derive their meaning not by virtue of their referring to objects in the world or to thoughts, but because of their difference from other words. Thus the English word 'tree' means what it means because of its difference both from similar sounding words (three, the, tea, etc.) and also because it is not 'plant' or 'shrub'. Meaning is therefore a result of difference, not reference. Postmodern thinkers, most originally Derrida, applied this linguistic insight to the whole of reality, thereby treating everything in the world as if it derived its meaning and identity in the same way as words in a system of language. (Derrida coined a new French word for this, *différance*). When human beings are viewed in this light, we cease to be autonomous, and become the products of the (linguistic) system of judgments and distinctions which form the particular *culture into which we are born. We do not speak with our own autonomous voices, but can speak only the languages we inherit. Human identity is therefore also never fixed: unlike God, who can say of himself 'I AM WHO I AM' (Exod. 3:14), our identity is constantly in flux, formed by our cultures and our experiences.

Christianity agrees with postmodernity that the modernist view of the self is unsustainable. It requires the human self to have God-like autonomy, but such autonomy is unattainable, and the desire for it is the primordial human sin (Gen. 3:4–5). We cannot simply say of ourselves, with God, 'I am who I am', because our identity is partly formed by the narrative of our lives and experiences, and by our interaction with other people. However, Christianity disagrees that the only alternative is a deeply fractured notion of selfhood. Our identity is founded not in ourselves but in the creating and sustaining God to whom we owe our continued existence, and whose own call on our lives is the ground of our identity. God began the restoration of humankind by calling to them to come into his presence (Gen. 3:8–9), and he furthers it by calling humans into a fully restored relationship with him (Rom. 8:30). Moreover, we develop our own identity by the linguistic actions we perform. To a significant extent I am constituted as the person who has made promises to other people (as husband, mother, friend etc.). Christianity judges modernity to have fatally treated human identity as quasi-divine, and postmodernity to have dissolved human identity into nothing more meaningful than an item of vocabulary in a linguistic system. As an alternative, Christianity proposes that human identity is grounded in our creation by God and his call on us, and that this best explains our experience of feeling that we have an identity, but that we cannot make sense of ourselves in isolation from the rest of the world.

Language and other people: ethics

How should we treat the authors of texts and the speakers of language? The predominant modernist approach was to treat the text as a window into the mind or psyche of the author, the aim of interpretation being, according to *Schleiermacher, 'to understand the text as well as and then even better than its author'. This has been widely criticized as overly 'psychologist', for it supposes that a text can allow us to peer into the mind of another person.

Postmodernity has often been accused of being uninterested in *ethics, but more recent writers have worked hard to show that this is not the case. Some postmodern interpretations of texts, it is true, seem to play with the text simply for the writer's own amusement, with little concern for how they are treating the author of the text. Others, though, desire not to see meaning pinned down because they are attempting to leave interpretation open for other voices, often suppressed voices, to have their say. Postmoderns, assuming that all that we take to be 'natural' is in fact arbitrary and conventional, want us not to decide too quickly that texts mean what we conventionally think they mean, and so to leave the meaning of texts open in order that the 'other' may speak through them. This grand ethical aim, though, often overrides the question of how individual authors are to be treated.

By contrast, the Bible's fundamental view of language, including literary language, is that it is a means by which persons perform communicative actions, e.g. God creates by speaking (Gen. 1:3), and his Word performs what he intends for it (Isa. 55:10–11). For a human being to respond in faith towards Christ he must respond in faith towards Christ's words (John 15:10), and we demonstrate the reality of our love for God by the way we act towards one another through what we say (Jas 3:1–12). Persons are therefore intimately related to the words by which they act in the world. To respond ethically to another's language or text must therefore mean not, in the first instance, psycho-analysing that person, or playing with their text, but respecting the otherness of the author as a person. The interpreter is ethically bound to try to understand what act that person has performed in the text which he or she has authored. We may conclude that we cannot discern the nature of that act – or, having discerned it, we may decide to resist it – but our first duty is to listen for it. This is an ethical application to interpreters of Christ's teaching about love for one's neighbour.

Literary theories

Literary theories are inevitably theological. What one does with a text is the practical outcome of what one thinks about human identity, the nature of language, and the grounds for meaning and truth. These are inescapably theological questions.

Literary theories are commonly divided into three categories, according to their main focus of interest. Some theories focus on the author. This was typical of Romantic hermeneutics of the eighteenth and nineteenth centuries, and was defended into the twentieth century (notably by E. Hirsch). Author-centred theories have often, as was noted above, used the text as a window into the psyche of the author. A number of Christian writers (notably A. Thiselton, K. Vanhoozer and N. Wolterstorff) have recently revived the author as the ground of meaning, using explicitly biblical and theological concepts of language and personhood to focus on the author as a person who performs communicative actions through his or her text.

A second group of theories has focused on the text itself. This was typical of a number of theories popular in the mid-twentieth century. First, New Criticism was an influential literary movement which thought of texts (primarily poems) as self-sufficient meaningful objects whose literary art was to be studied as one might gaze at an artefact or at a religious icon. Secondly, structuralist approaches to literature try to discern how texts express the supposed permanent structures (often in the form of opposing pairs such as light/dark, good/bad) of the mind and *reality. Both fit well with Christianity's ethical imperative to attempt to understand the text on its own terms, but both ignore the extent to which the author is my 'neighbour' who asks to be heard as a person who has spoken and acted.

A final group of literary theories focuses on the role of the reader. Some reader-focused theories have analysed how literary texts engage readers by leaving gaps which the reader must fill, rightly acknowledging that readers are active participants in the reading process, not passive observers. This leads readers to face up to their own preconceptions, just as Christianity calls us to acknowledge our limited knowledge and perspective as creatures (e.g. 1 Cor. 13:12). Other reader-focused theorists, by contrast (e.g. Stanley Fish), have argued that readers create meaning, rather than discovering it in texts, leaving it unclear whether we can truly know anything but ourselves. Christianity offers a quite different view of the world. Meaning is to be discovered in the world and in texts, because at the heart of human identity is the image of a speaking/acting God, and at the root of language is a God who has spoken/acted in the world to make himself known as the source of meaning and truth.

Bibliography

R. Lundin et al., *The Promise of Hermeneutics* (Grand Rapids, 1999); L. Ryken,

Windows to the World: Literature in Christian Perspective (Eugene, 2000); A. Thiselton, *Interpreting God and the Postmodern Self: On Meaning, Manipulation and Promise* (Edinburgh, 1995); K. Vanhoozer, *Is There a Meaning in This Text? The Bible, the Reader and the Morality of Literary Knowledge* (Leicester, 1998); N. Wolterstorff, *Divine Discourse: Philosophical Reflections on the Claim that God Speaks* (Cambridge, 1995).

T. J. WARD

LAPIDE, PINCHAS

Pinchas Lapide (1922–97), an Orthodox Jew who defended the *resurrection of *Jesus, was an Israeli diplomat and scholar who engaged in dialogue and debate with leading Christian theologians.

As an academic, Lapide produced significant studies on the history of the papacy in relation to the Jews; the use of Hebrew in the church; early translations of the NT into Hebrew; and the teaching of the NT in the Israeli school system. It was, however, in the field of Jewish–Christian relations that he enjoyed notoriety as an Orthodox Jew willing to advocate controversial positions which appeared to support the doctrines of the incarnation and resurrection of Jesus.

Lapide was part of the 'Jewish reclamation of Jesus' (*Heimholung*) movement led by scholars such as Joseph Klausner, Geza Vermes and Shalom Ben-Chorim, which rediscovered the Jewishness of Jesus and had considerable influence on NT studies. 'The rabbi from Nazareth' found a welcome place in Lapide's broad-minded outlook, and he was well placed to popularize Jewish understandings sympathetic to Christianity through his speaking and writing. Based in Italy and Germany, he engaged in dialogue with Hans Küng, Jürgen Moltmann and other leading continental theologians.

Lapide's views came to international attention with the English translation of *Auferstehung: Ein Jüdisches Glaubenserlebnis* (1983), which was reported in *Time* magazine. Here he took liberal theologians to task for being 'ashamed of the material facticity of the resurrection', arguing that the raising of Jesus from the dead after his crucifixion was the most likely explanation for the transformation of the disciples and the birth of the church, and was fully consistent with contemporary

pharisaic beliefs. However, he stopped short of accepting the Messiahship of Jesus, choosing to see the events of the first Easter as the 'gateway to the Messianic event' that would be universally accepted only at some future time, a traditional but inconsistent Jewish view advocated by the leading medieval Jewish authority, *Maimonides.

Whilst not an original scholar in his own work on Jesus, he adopted the views of many in the 'third quest for the historical Jesus' (Marcus Borg, N. T. Wright). Privately (in conversation with this author) he was supportive of the growing number of messianic Jews (Jews who affirm the messiahship and resurrection of Jesus) but was not willing to state this publicly.

Bibliography

P. Lapide, *The Resurrection of Jesus* (Minneapolis, 1983; London, 1984); H. Küng and P. Lapide, *Brother or Lord?: A Jew and a Christian Talk Together about Jesus* (London, 1977); D. A. Hagner, *The Jewish Reclamation of Jesus: An Analysis and Critique of Modern Jewish Study of Jesus* (Eugene, 1997).

R. HARVEY

LAW

Introduction

Secular law offers considerable apologetic resources. Both law and Christianity are concerned to establish correct accounts of past events, both are concerned with the interpretation of authoritative texts, both are oriented towards the question of what one ought or ought not to do, and if one focuses specifically on apologetics, both are set in a context of argument, persuasion and decision. It is, therefore, hardly surprising that early modern Christian apologetics should have been dominated by a work of the great Dutch lawyer, Hugo *Grotius (1583–1645) and that many Christian apologists since should have had a legal background.

Grotius' *De Veritate Religionis Christianae* (1619) contained, in embryonic form, three broad groups of argument from law to the truth of Christianity. First, there are arguments from the divine nature of law to the existence of God. Secondly, there are arguments from the reasonableness of legal methods to the reliability of the

Bible, in particular to gospel accounts of Jesus Christ. Finally, there are arguments from the attractiveness of Christian legal principles to the truth of the Christian religion.

Arguments from the divine nature of law

Like his medieval predecessors, *Thomas Aquinas (1225–74) assumed that all law shared a single divine essence. There was a set of necessary connections binding the eternal law, which exists in the mind of God, to human law, by way of revealed divine law and *natural law accessible to all reasonable human beings. Such 'natural law theories' should be distinguished from 'legal positivist', or 'legal realist' theories, which in spite of their internal differences both accept that law can be understood entirely in terms of human acts of will or desire. Individual law-makers may use law to implement a certain *morality or religion, but there is no necessary connection between such non-legal factors and the legal quality of what they produce. Bad law is as much law as good law.

Modern natural law theories are generally concerned to establish the connection between law and *ethics rather than the connection between law and God. There are a number of ways in which this can be done. For example, in *Natural Law and Natural Rights* (1980), which is the most successful modern restatement of the Thomist tradition, John Finnis argues that the process by which we identify certain social phenomena as 'legal' is necessarily an ethical one. He goes on to argue that ethics is based on a number of objective basic goods, such as life, knowledge, play, friendship, religion, aesthetic experience and practical reasonableness. Law can only be satisfactorily understood as a collective attempt to coordinate action such that everyone may participate in these basic goods. But there are other ways of making the connection between law and ethics as well, including the argument that the process of judicial reasoning necessarily requires the judge to make moral judgments in the course of stating the law, and the argument that legal obligations can only have binding force if they are viewed as a species of moral obligation.

Arguments that there are necessary connections between law and ethics are open to a range of different ethical theories. For example, modern Kantians might argue that law and ethics are founded on human dignity and natural rights, rather than basic goods.

From an apologetic perspective this debate is secondary, because whatever ethical theory one adopts, one must go on to show that this theory presupposes the existence of God. Finnis argues that positing the existence of God is a necessary further explanation for his theory of the good. The difficulty is that this runs up against the argument that further explanation is redundant. If there really are knowable objective basic goods, or if human beings really do have dignity (defined as a naturally knowable quality giving rise to ethical consequences), then the further hypothesis that there is also another being (God) whose character is in conformity with these things or, more significantly, who willed such things into existence, adds a level of complexity without *explaining* anything. It seems to make the universe unnecessarily complicated.

If that last argument is valid, the obvious response is to avoid any suggestion that a non-theistic ethic is possible. Both Phillip E. Johnson and John Warwick Montgomery have argued that the assertions of rights and *authority underlying law are simply power-claims incapable of creating obligations unless a theistic account of the world is correct. The difference between these arguments and that of John Finnis lies in epistemological pessimism about natural reason. Natural reason can indicate that law needs a foundation of objective ethical validity if its intrinsic claim to authority is to be justified, and natural reason can also indicate that non-theistic attempts to ground objective ethical validity (whether neo-Thomist or Kantian) fail. But this simply clears a path for the revelation of truth about God in Christ, which satisfies all our ethical needs.

In view of the difficulties in arguing from law to God via ethics, it is worth considering whether one could avoid the detour. For example, Charles Taliaferro (*Contemporary Philosophy of Religion* [1998], pp. 75–78, 81) has suggested that *Anselm's conception of divine omnipotence could fruitfully be applied to the debate about the nature of legal sovereignty. In order to be intelligible, an act must have a motive. A motive implies a conception of a good to be achieved. Thus, in Anselm's view, divine omnipotence is not pure unbounded will (the *power to do anything), but will directed to the divine conception of the good. In the context of law, Lon Fuller (*The Morality of Law* [1973]) similarly argued that law must be understood as a purposive enterprise which necessarily commits the sovereign law-maker to certain canons of law-making, which can appropriately be qualified as 'good'. On the other hand, positivists and realists are surely right that in human law-making there is a creative, and hence potentially destructive, moment which distinguishes it from morality. The point is that law cannot be conceived either as pure unbounded will or as pure reason. Ideal law presupposes a perfect compatibility between will and reason, in which everything that is reasonable (good) is willed, and everything willed is reasonable (good). Although human law *can* be used for all sorts of extraneous ends, its existence is justified only to the extent that it 'seeks' or 'points' towards this ideal. That search for justification will make sense only if there is a point at which the ideal exists. But this can be found only in the creative activity of God himself, so the necessarily assumed goal of law is the law-making activity of God himself.

Arguments from the reasonableness of legal methods

At the heart of the apologetic enterprise lies a defence of the reliability of gospel accounts of the life, death and resurrection of Jesus, and the need for the individual to respond appropriately. Legal methods involve the weighing of evidence, the evaluation of arguments and the interpretation of texts to reach practical conclusions about what ought to be done. Several writers have thus chosen an overtly legal approach to their apologetic, as is apparent even from the titles of well-known works such as *The Evidence for the Resurrection* (Sir Norman Anderson) and *Evidence that Demands a Verdict* (Josh McDowell). Likewise, Frank Morison's classic *Who Moved the Stone?* is self-consciously set in a legal idiom, leading many to assume erroneously that its author was a lawyer. Of course, adopting legal methods is not an infallible route to Christian conviction, but these and many other books are reflections of the assertion attributed to the English judge Lord Darling (1849–1936) that 'there exists such overwhelming evidence, positive and negative, factual and circumstantial, that no intelligent jury in the world can fail to bring in a verdict that the resurrection story is true'. Although this approach has usually been applied to the Gospel accounts, it can also be put to good use more generally in defence of a

biblical world-view, as for instance in Phillip E. Johnson's *Darwin on Trial* (1991).

The use of legal methods in apologetics has a long history. One classic defence of the Gospels by way of the law of evidence was mounted by Simon Greenleaf in his 1846 work, *An Examination of the Testimony of the Four Evangelists by the Rules of Evidence Administered in Courts of Justice with an Account of the Trial of Jesus*. Respected as a lawyer on both sides of the Atlantic, Greenleaf was professor of law at Harvard University and author of a leading text on the law of evidence. In an extended introduction, Greenleaf identified five rules of evidence which he applied to the Gospel accounts, concluding that they were utterly reliable. The rules are worth reproducing, since they (or similar ones) can be found underlying other evidentialist apologetics with a legal flavour.

1. Every document, apparently ancient, coming from the proper repository or custody, and bearing on its face no evident marks of forgery, the law presumes to be genuine and devolves on the opposing party the burden of proving it to be otherwise.

2. In trials of fact, by oral testimony, the proper inquiry is not whether it is possible that the testimony may be false, but whether there is sufficient probability that it is true.

3. A proposition of fact is proved, when its truth is established by competent and satisfactory evidence.

4. In the absence of circumstances which generate suspicion, every witness is to be presumed credible, until the contrary is shown; the burden of impeaching his credibility lying on the objector.

5. The credit due to the testimony of *witnesses depends upon, firstly, their honesty; secondly, their ability; thirdly, their number and the consistency of their testimony; fourthly, the conformity of their testimony with experience; and fifthly, the coincidence of their testimony with collateral circumstances.

Legal methods are particularly valuable because they have been developed in a context in which the stakes for participants are very high, and yet which do not and cannot require standards of proof normal in the natural sciences. Law provides the most rigorous context in which the question of whether a single event occurred is tested. At the same time, those standards which are routinely applied when life, liberty and property are at stake are not nearly as sceptical as some modern biblical scholars. The levels of consistency between the Gospels and extra-biblical accounts (read as straightforward descriptions of events) are astonishing from a legal perspective. As far as the documents themselves are concerned, lawyers and classicists combine to remind the sceptics that if we know nothing about Jesus then we know nothing about anything in the distant past.

Arguments from the attractiveness of Christian legal principles

Finally, there are arguments from the attractiveness, or evident *justice, of Christian legal principles to the truth of Christianity. Often, these arguments are historical, seeking to show the influence of particular Christian people or ideas on law. Well-known law reformers consciously motivated by their Christian faith include William *Wilberforce (slavery), the seventh Earl of Shaftesbury (employment conditions), John Howard and Elizabeth Fry (prison conditions), and Seebohm Rowntree (urban poverty). Moving away from broad questions of legal policy to the development of the common law, one familiar example of the beneficial influence of faith on law is provided by Lord Atkin's judgment in *Donoghue v Stevenson* (1932), in which he used Christ's command that one should love one's neighbour as oneself to help formulate the modern general principle of civil liability for negligence under English law.

In 1989, Lord Denning (Master of the Rolls 1962–81) wrote a booklet for the Lawyers' Christian Fellowship setting out a number of ways in which he thought that English law had been beneficially affected by Christianity. These included a belief in the importance of *truth, requirements of good faith in statutory interpretation and contractual obligations, the development of the law of negligence, basic presuppositions of criminal law, such as the requirement to demonstrate that the accused had a 'guilty mind', the principle of government under law, the rise of social welfare legislation and the centrality of a Christian conception of *marriage

However, apart from some very clear instances in which Christians have consciously brought about beneficial legal change as suggested above, arguments based on historical cause and effect in the realm of ideas are hard to maintain with complete conviction. It may

generally be better to recast such arguments as setting out systematic links between modern conceptions of justice and Christianity instead. These arguments then form a direct counterpart to natural law arguments. For whereas natural law arguments seek to show that some conception of justice and God must be held by all reasonable human beings, arguments from the attractiveness of Christian legal principles depend for their force on the suggestion that particular principles of justice are *not* naturally knowable. People committed to these more particular principles of justice then have to show why they are committed to them in the absence of a richer supporting metaphysical framework such as Christianity.

The basic contours of this apologetic strategy can only be sketched here by way of an example. Modern conceptions of religious liberty as a political and legal principle depend on some fairly specific ideas about the nature of religion, its importance, its relevance to human affairs and the importance of separating religious from political processes. These ideas grew historically in a culture saturated with Christianity and can be defended on the basis of the truth of Christianity. It is far from clear that they make sense within the context of other world-views, whether theistic or not. In general, the 'secular' values of liberal democracy may be more deeply and exclusively Christian than is commonly perceived. And the increasing value-pluralism of Western cultures, while posing a challenge to liberal democracy, also makes this type of apologetic particularly appropriate.

Law, faith and postmodernity

Legal theory, like any other discipline in the humanities, has not remained untouched by postmodernism. There is a set of theses which is now taken almost for granted by a section of the academic legal community: legal texts have no meaning except those imposed upon them by the interpretative communities in which they are read; law is capable of diametrically opposed interpretations and hence radically indeterminate; accounts of past events are deeply flawed and historical 'truth' inaccessible; appeals to justice are more or less explicit bids for power.

But if legal theory has been as subject as any other discipline in the humanities to the postmodern suspicion that all is meaningless, the practice of law has remained untouched. As intellectuals, lawyers may claim to have given up believing in truth or justice, but as professionals they continue to make judgments as to which version of events is more or less plausible and whose behaviour is more or less reprehensible. Judgments of more or less cannot be made in the absence of a standard, and it is this practical necessity for lawyers to behave as if there were such a thing as truth and justice which provides the chink in the postmodern armour. The claim of the Christian apologist is that we all face a similar practical necessity to live as if the claims of Jesus Christ were true. It is in the experience of living this 'necessary fiction' that we discover that by faith we can reach beyond our limited reason to truth itself.

Bibliography

N. Anderson, *Jesus Christ: The Witness of History* (Leicester, 1985); R. Clifford, *Leading Lawyers Look at the Resurrection* (Oxford, 1991); J. Finnis, *Natural Law and Natural Rights* (Oxford, 1980); Lord Hailsham, *The Door Wherein I Went* (London, 1975); P. E. Johnson, 'The Modernist Impasse in Law' in D. A. Carson and J. D. Woodbridge (eds.), *God and Culture* (Carlisle, 1993); J. W. Montgomery, *Human Rights and Human Dignity* (Edmonton, 1995); F. Morison, *Who Moved the Stone?* (Bromley, 1983).

A. J. RIVERS

LEARY, TIMOTHY

Timothy Leary (1920–96), born in Springfield, Massachusetts, the son of Irish Catholics, was one of the leading intellectuals within the American counter-culture movement of the 1960s and '70s and is perhaps best known for his exhortation to 'turn on, tune in and drop out'. Never afraid to challenge the existing order, even from an early age, it was Leary's experimentation with hallucinogenic *drugs that really brought him into confrontation with the establishment. A clinical psychologist by training, he became somewhat disillusioned by the ineffectiveness of his profession, particularly psychotherapy, and this, coupled with personal tragedy when his wife committed suicide whilst suffering from post-natal depression, led him to search more widely and deeply for answers to the workings of the human mind and the nature of our existence.

Leary discovered the effects of hallucinogenic drugs in 1960 whilst on a trip to Mexico. His initial interest was in their clinical value, something that at the time was not particularly off-beat – use of LSD was still legal, and during the 1950s the drug had been widely trialled as a therapeutic tool, treating individuals with severe alcohol problems. Leary himself used psilocybin on prisoners and effectively reduced re-conviction rates. His views, however, increasingly departed from those held by colleagues within experimental and mainstream *psychology and he became convinced that psilocybin, LSD and peyote could provide spiritual enlightenment and *transcendence – a short cut to the experiences that mystics have had for centuries. 'If you are serious about your religion', he told a group of Lutheran students, 'you must learn how to use psycho-chemicals. Pursuing the religious life today without using psychedelic drugs is like studying astronomy with the naked eye.'

It is not possible to reconcile Leary's beliefs with a Christian viewpoint. Accepting the Bible as God's word, the truth revealed to us, provides us with our reference point, not personal experiences dependent upon chemical inducement. Christians cannot accept that God and his work in our lives are simply constructs of the mind which can be manipulated and changed at will or shaped by drugs. This makes God into a creation of human beings, whereas God created and formed us and the world in which we live. He has existed eternally – 'In the beginning God was.' Many religions have been based upon visions and ecstatic experiences, but drugs which induce these offer a promise that they cannot fulfil. They change our perceptions but not our inner selves. As Jesus said, it is 'out of a person's heart that evil thoughts come' and drugs cannot change this sinful human core. Only the acceptance of Jesus, his forgiveness and the working of God's Spirit in our lives can change us.

Though Christians would profoundly disagree with Leary's beliefs, his willingness to sacrifice his career, freedom, possessions and family at various times in his life for the sake of his beliefs is perhaps the greatest challenge his life presents today. For the pearl of great price we should give up everything, including our carefully constructed Christian comfort zones. True discipleship is to follow Jesus whatever the cost.

Bibliography

O. Batchelor, *Use and Misuse* (Leicester, 1999); S. Turner, *Hungry for Heaven* (London, 1988); T. Leary website: <http://www.leary.com>.

O. BATCHELOR

LEGALISM AND MORALISM

Legalism and moralism may each be seen as distortions of important aspects of the Christian faith, attitudes which are parasitic on the proper estimate of the place of the moral *law in the Christian life. These distortions may be due either to unintentional misunderstanding or to deliberate endeavours to caricature the faith. For law and *morality each have an important place in the Christian faith and in the life of the Christian, coming together in the idea of the moral law of God. A delight in the moral law of God is an important part of the Christian life, and is to be viewed as a consequence of union with Christ. According to that law certain types of action are required, others are forbidden, while others are permitted. And in the teaching of Jesus on the law (for example in the Sermon on the Mount) and in the NT more generally, particular emphasis is placed on its 'inwardness', on the place of desire, motivation and intention in action.

As a consequence of the fact that certain types of action are neither commanded nor forbidden but are permitted, the idea of Christian liberty, of actions and activities which are neither forbidden nor commanded by the law of God, is also of importance. (Liberty, though a term hallowed by use, is a somewhat unfortunate term here in view of the emphasis that the NT places on all proper attitudes to the law of God being aspects of the liberating activity of Christ and of his Spirit.)

Moralistic and legalistic attitudes thus arise when the saving work of Christ does not take centre stage, or when its significance is reduced or misinterpreted, or when the boundaries of Christian liberty are not properly observed.

Legalism

Legalism is usually taken to mean an insistence on the letter of the law as against its spirit, the failure to recognize hard cases and to temper the specifics of the law by considerations of equity. In a more precise theological sense, it is taken to refer to a way of gaining acceptance with God which depends on the keeping of his law as against relying on Christ for forgiveness and righteousness. Such a reliance on Christ, and the contrasting moralism, in turn give rise to two contrasting kinds of obedience: 'legal obedience' (that which arises merely from the obligatoriness of the moral law) and 'evangelical obedience' (that which arises from gratitude to God for his free grace in Christ). Sometimes the reaction against legalism can move in the direction of antinomianism, and Paul's saying 'the letter kills, but the Spirit gives life' (2 Cor. 3:6) has been used as a warrant for this move. Paul is not, however, making an absolute or principled contrast of law *against* spirit, but drawing attention to two contrasting ways of endeavouring to keep the law, the 'legal' and the 'spiritual'. A legalistic attitude must in turn be distinguished from the conviction of sin, the recognition of an *in*ability to keep the law of God and the consequent recognition of guilt before God.

Moralism

Moralism is an attitude to the particularities of events and circumstances, including those of everyday life and of those represented in history or fiction, together with the particularities of the Christian faith and of the biblical narratives and parables. The moralizer sees these particularities mainly or exclusively as vehicles for drawing general moral lessons or as exemplifying moral ideals or aspirations in the manner of Aesop's fables. So moralism is a way of treating some datum of fact or fiction which sees the chief purpose of that fact or fiction as not only the setting forth of some moral ideal but also as providing sources of moral motivation. Thus the parables of Jesus can be seen as efforts to promote perseverance (as in the parable of the lost coin) or enterprise in commerce (as in the parable of the talents). Their theological significance as parables of the kingdom of God is missed, because the 'kingdom of God' has come to represent simply a set of moral or social ideals. More significantly, the life of Jesus Christ himself is seen simply as that of an unparalleled moral teacher whose career ended in tragedy. So that as far as the interpretation of biblical materials is concerned, moralism tends to be strongly reductionist, eliminating or downplaying their theological and supernatural aspects.

The influence of moralism and legalism

The contrast or conflict between moralism and evangelicalism reaches back into the patristic period and particularly to *Augustine's conflict with Pelagius. Medieval views of human merit, the idea of the possibility of performing works of supererogation, undoubtedly resulted in producing a religion that largely consisted in moral endeavour. Some have rightly discerned a shift to moralism in English theology at the end of the seventeenth century, motivated, it would seem, by a fear of antinomianism and of civil disorder. In modern Christian thought, particularly Protestant thought, moralism has taken its inspiration from Immanuel *Kant's notion of 'moral religion', a religion of pure reason independent of the particularities of history. This understanding of religion regards Jesus as an inspirational moral teacher rather than a divine-human Saviour, and sees the religious life in almost exclusively moral terms, as the fulfilling of the moral law for its own sake. Such moralism usually presupposes an exaggerated human ability to keep the law of God unaided (though not in Kant's own case) and strongly tends, when advocated in a Christian context, to favour exemplarist views of the person and work of Christ.

Quite apart from the question of whether moralistic attitudes do justice to the theological or religious intent of the particularities on which they are often made to rest, moralism has often had a repressive and stultifying effect on personal growth and formation, and it can hinder the development of moral objectivity and distance and even give rise to superstitious observances and to a warped sense of guilt. In theory, moralism can of course take various forms, depending on the content of the favoured morality. For example, it can have either a legalistic or an antinomian flavour – Christ can be seen exclusively as the upholder of the law or a giver of a new law, or as the liberator from all law. But historically, moralism tends to have been identified with an exclusive focus on the moral law, not with its dismissal or reduction.

Obstacles in apologetics

Insofar as there is a popular or general preconception that the Christian faith is simply a version of legalism or moralism (and there often is) such preconceptions are serious obstacles to the fair and accurate presentation and reception of that message. In the modern era in the West there has often been a deliberate effort by Christianity's opponents to present it in such legalistic or moralistic terms, and then to reject it as narrow and dehumanizing. In the rhetoric of such accusations, the terms legalism and moralism may come to have a strong emotive significance. Sometimes these representations are, alas, based in fact, as in certain Victorian and Edwardian attitudes to Christianity and when religion is seen simply or chiefly as a series of prohibitions against certain kinds of action or activity. But at other times attempts to represent the Christian faith as such as moralistic or legalistic are the result of deliberate caricature.

It should be clear from the foregoing that moralistic or legalistic attitudes are endemic in our present mindset. They are ever ready to assert, or re-assert, themselves and need very little encouragement to do so. But it is plain that these frames of mind are distortions of the Christian faith and may in turn lead to further distortions. The response to them must lie in vigilance to maintain the truly evangelical character of the Christian message, that it is the good news of the provision of a Saviour for the lost, to uphold the centrality of the moral law of God in Christian intention and action, and to jealously guard the boundaries of Christian liberty.

Bibliography

C. F. Allison, *The Rise of Moralism* (London, 1966); P. Byrne, *The Moral Interpretation of Religion*, (Edinburgh, 1998); E. F. Kevan, *The Grace of Law: A Study in Puritan Theology* (Grand Rapids, 1976).

P. HELM

LEIBNIZ, GOTTFRIED WILHELM VON

Leibniz (1646–1716) was a German mathematician and philosopher, whose importance in the field of apologetics is twofold. He gave versions of the ontological and *cosmological arguments for the existence of God which were for a long time standard, and he gave a famous resolution of the 'problem of *evil' (a 'theodicy', to use his name for it).

He saw that the *ontological argument could prove at best that if a perfect being was possible, then there was one; it therefore required proof that such a perfect being was possible. A perfection is a property which can have a superlative (unlike, say, length, which can always be added to) and which does not exclude other perfections (in the way that, say, blueness excludes redness). Since all perfections are compossible, the idea of a perfect God is a possible one, and since existence (or necessary existence; Leibniz uses both expressions) is a perfection, God is real.

He based his cosmological argument on the principle of 'sufficient reason'; there must be a reason for any *truth. Even an infinite collection of contingent things would lack sufficient reason for its existence; it must be grounded in a necessary truth, external to it, which is its own sufficient reason, and this is the existence of God.

Leibniz added a proof based in his own *metaphysics. In this all substances are 'windowless' and do not interact. Since, however, they exist in harmony with one another, there must be a supreme intelligence which brings this about – God.

His theodicy pictured God as considering an infinite array of possible worlds he might create. Being perfect goodness, God would create the best of these. (This is 'the whole temporal succession of existing things', and it is quite possibile that it has not yet reached its perfection.) The evils in it contribute to the goodness of the whole, and to eliminate one would produce greater evil instead. Leibniz does not use the usual 'free will' theodicy; we act in accordance with our natures (a form of freedom), but God decides which human natures to create as part of the best possible world.

Modern discussions of the ontological and cosmological arguments could be said to presuppose Leibniz's work as a foundation, and his notion of 'possible worlds' has become increasingly popular as a tool not only in apologetics but also in many other fields of philosophy.

Bibliography

Not all Leibniz' writings are available in English. *Leibniz: Philosophical Writings*, trans. Mary Morris, Introduction by C. R. Morris (London, 1934, 1956). N. Jolly (ed.), *Cambridge Companion to Leibniz* (Cambridge, 1995), chs. 10 – 11; D. Rutherford, *Leibniz and the Rational Order of Nature* (Cambridge, 1995); R. Saw, *Leibniz* (Harmondsworth, 1954).

R. L. STURCH

LESSING, GOTTHOLD EPHRAIM

Often elusive, sometimes intriguing, Gotthold Ephraim Lessing (1729–81) was a major force in the German *Enlightenment of the eighteenth century. He was a pioneer in modern German drama, and his reputation rests on far more than his specifically religious thought. Disagreement persists on the real nature of his religious convictions. Undoubtedly, he repudiated theological orthodoxy and encouraged the growth of theological radicalism, but his positive views never found expression in a transparent or comprehensive statement of belief. Lessing pictures God offering us the choice between *truth and the search for truth, and he chooses the latter, but such is his suggestive literary style that we should be wary of concluding dogmatically from this that, in religion, Lessing preferred to travel than to arrive. There is some evidence that his theological resting place was in the pantheistic system of the seventeenth-century Jewish philosopher, *Spinoza (1632–77).

Lessing addressed with perspicacious force the matter of Christianity and *history. As librarian in Wolfenbüttel, he published the famous or notorious *Fragments* of a work by the deist, Reimarus (1694–1768), who strongly challenged the integrity of the Gospel accounts of the life and ministry of Jesus. But while Lessing doubtless supported the development of historical criticism of Scripture, he was not necessarily a typical rationalist in his approach to the Bible. In relation to its historical accounts, he was preoccupied not just with the question of what degree of *certainty we can have concerning alleged events, but also with the logic of basing one's life on contingent occurrences in history, things which could not give proofs of necessary truths of reason. In his celebrated *Concluding Unscientific Postscript* (1846), the Danish author *Kierkegaard deemed important and took up the gauntlet thrown down by Lessing: how can an historical occurrence be a point of departure for eternal happiness? The 'problem of faith and history' in modern Christian thought has various dimensions; Lessing spotted many of them and recognized the significance of the challenge therein posed to Christian self-understanding. But he did not always make clear distinctions, and this lies behind different ways of understanding what is called 'Lessing's ditch'. This can be either (a) about the impossibility of arriving at the certainty of faith on the basis of the uncertainties of historical knowledge or (b) about the difference between an historical truth about a known past event and a rational, religious truth, about universal reality. (This is the subject of a fine study by G. E. Michalson, *Lessing's 'Ugly Ditch': A Study of Theology and History* [Pennsylvania State University, 1985]).

Lessing looked forward to the education of the human race, a divine *revelation (whatever exactly that meant) that was progressive. For now, the proof of the truth of a religion lay in the spirit and power of its love. In his challenge to the church to demonstrate the veracity of its claims in this way, as in his remarks on faith and history, Lessing presents us with inescapable issues which remain surprisingly relevant today.

Bibliography

H. E. Allison, *Lessing and the Enlightenment* (Ann Arbor, 1966); H. Chadwick (ed.), *Lessing's Theological Writings* (London, 1956); H. Thielicke, *Modern Faith and Thought* (Grand Rapids, 1990); L. P. Wessell, *Lessing's Theology: A Reinterpretation* (The Hague, 1977).

S. N. WILLIAMS

LEWIS, C. S.

Screwtape, Puddleglum the Marshwiggle, Elwin Ransom the Cambridge don, Aslan the talking lion and creator of Narnia, Sarah Smith of Golder's Green, Mr Sensible, Redival of ancient Glome, Jane and Mark Studdock of the English Midlands – these are just a few of the inventions of Clive Staples Lewis (1898–1963). From his teeming mind and *imagination sprang stories and powerful rhetoric aimed at persuading people of the truth of Christian faith. For many years an atheist, 'Jack' Lewis (for so he preferred to be called) did not become a believer in Christ until over half way through his life. Not only have his books steadily taken on a global popularity, but he was reluctantly one of the first major media evangelists, with huge audiences for his wartime BBC radio broadcasts. And the media have not ignored him since. There have been two film versions of *Shadowlands*, the story of his love and marriage to a New York poet and novelist, Joy Davidman Gresham, and a major film of

The Lion, the Witch, and the Wardrobe. Along with John Stott, J. I. Packer and Francis *Schaeffer, C. S. Lewis has been a major shaper of American evangelicalism. He has also had a powerful impact on Roman Catholics, Russian and Eastern Orthodox believers and many unable to accept his Christian faith, such as the critic Ken Tynan.

C. S. Lewis was born in Belfast in 1892, where he had a happy childhood. He grew to love the countryside of County Down, which in later years inspired the geography of Narnia. His life changed dramatically when his mother died in 1908, and he was sent off to England to a small school run by a headmaster on the verge of insanity. Later he was tutored for Oxford entrance by an Ulsterman who taught him to think rigorously. His Oxford studies were interrupted by action in the First World War, in which he was wounded. After graduation with a triple first-class degree Lewis taught philosophy for a year at Oxford before gaining a Fellowship in English at Magdalen College, where he remained until 1954, when, with J. R. R. *Tolkien's persuasion, he accepted the newly established Chair of Medieval and Renaissance Literature at Cambridge. Over twenty years earlier, Tolkien had persuaded Lewis, with help from a mutual friend, H. V. D. 'Hugo' Dyson, to accept the claims of Christian faith. Lewis remained at Cambridge until early retirement through ill health in 1963, although he continued to live in Oxford and to meet with the Inklings, a circle of literary friends founded in 1933.

There were many facets to Lewis. He made an enduring contribution to children's literature with his Narnian Chronicles (1950–56). He was a major literary scholar, with works such as *The Allegory of Love* (1936), *English Literature in the Sixteenth Century* (1954) and *An Experiment in Criticism* (1961), all of which are still in print. He was an outstanding apologist of Christian faith, making the cover of *Time* magazine ('Don v. Devil') as early as 1947. His *Mere Christianity* alone has been cited in the testimonies of many as a major influence in their conversions to Christ. He was a significant science-fiction author, respected by practitioners such as Arthur C. Clarke and Brian Aldiss. He was a novelist – his *Till We Have Faces* has affinities with his friend Tolkien's work, in exploring insights into the nature of God and *reality within the confines of the pre-Christian imagination. He was a thinker who, early in his academic career, was part of a discussion group with young Oxford philosophers that also included Gilbert Ryle. He was a popular theologian, able to convey biblical themes convincingly with wit, imagination and clarity. His theology is embedded in his fictional works like *The Pilgrim's Regress* (1933), *The Screwtape Letters* (1942), The Narnian Chronicles, and his science-fiction trilogy (1938–45). It is also found in his *Mere Christianity* (1952), *Miracles* (1947; revised ed. 1960), *Reflections on the Psalms* (1958), *Letters to Malcolm* (on prayer, 1964) and *The Problem of Pain* (1940). He was also a poet and a notable letter writer.

These varied facets of Lewis constantly interrelate in an organic way. In the Narnian story *The Silver Chair*, for instance, there is a familiar incident which reveals this powerful integration. This is the part of the story where the Queen of Underland tries to persuade Prince Rilian, Puddleglum and the children that Narnia does not really exist. She tries to enchant them, suggesting that their idea of a sun in the sky is really based on their experience of lamps in Underland. Lewis is here alluding to an important phase of Western intellectual tradition in which a Christian understanding was literally turned upside down in favour of a materialist view and faith in God, the afterlife and similar beliefs was presented as mere projection of our deepest human wishes. Lewis' ability to incarnate a defence of Christian faith successfully into a well-told and globally attractive children's story was just one mark of his increasing maturity as an effective Christian writer with mainstream appeal.

Lewis saw apologetics as part of a coherent and consistent Christian world-view. In all the variety of his imaginative and discursive writings this unified viewpoint is expressed. For him the apologist's role is a humble one, but nevertheless vital to the proclamation of the gospel to modern people. The apologist helps to create favourable conditions for the reception of the gospel, making way for 'the Evangelist, the man on fire, the man who infects'. The apologist helps 'the spread of an intellectual (and imaginative) climate favourable to Christianity'. His advocacy and practice of complementary roles for imagination and reason is Lewis's great contribution to apologetics in an age of modernity. Austin *Farrer commented: 'He provided a positive exhibition of the force of

Christian ideas, morally, imaginatively, and rationally. The strength of his appeal ... lies in the many-sidedness of his work. Christian theism ... commends itself as fact, not theory, by the sheer multiplicity of its bearings.'

Bibliography

R. L. Green and W. Hooper, *C. S. Lewis: A Biography*, 3rd edn (London, 2002); A. N. Wilson, *C. S. Lewis: A Biography* (London, 1990); G. Sayer, *Jack* (London, 1988); C. Duriez, *The C. S. Lewis Encyclopedia: A Comprehensive Guide to His Life, Thought and Writings* (London, 2002); *Tolkien and C. S. Lewis* (New York, 2003).

C. DURIEZ

LITERARY THEORIES, see LANGUAGE AND LITERARY THEORIES

LOCKE, JOHN

John Locke (1632–1704), English philosopher, was the first of the great British empiricists. He was educated at Westminster School and Christ Church, Oxford, of which he was a Student from 1659 to 1684. He trained in medicine, though he never became a professional physician. His political ideas, expressed in his *Two Treatises of Government* (1690), were important factors in the framing of the constitution of the United States.

Locke's most important philosophical work, the *Essay Concerning Human Understanding* (published in 1690, though begun nearly twenty years earlier), is mainly about the nature and sources of our knowledge, though it also includes an implicit *metaphysics. This metaphysics is basically dualist: the material world is as *science describes it, the immaterial world consists of minds whose 'ideas' (mainly sense-impressions) are the source of our knowledge.

Locke distinguishes between knowledge, which is awareness of facts, and assent (or belief), which is taking something to be a fact, and this distinction is important in the parts of the *Essay* concerned with faith. Faith is assent to a proposition on the *authority of God, and is therefore less than knowledge (though a *truth may be accepted both on authority and by reason). Relying on a very inadequate form of *cosmological argument, Locke contends that the existence of God may be known, not merely apprehended by faith. This knowledge, however, is very limited, and so *revelation is also necessary.

Revelation justifies belief and, indeed, outweighs even the probable dictates of reason, though it will not contradict those that are certain. But we may only believe, not know, that God has actually revealed some proposition, and 'inner experience' is insufficient grounds for such belief. Rather, the authority of *Jesus and of Scripture generally, is demonstrated by the *miracles that support it, especially those of Jesus himself.

Locke's later work *The Reasonableness of Christianity* (1693) may be reckoned 'apologetics', and was directed against those who complained that Christianity was too complex and subtle. Since the fall, he urged, humankind has lost bliss and immortality, and no-one can earn these by works, since all are sinners. God has therefore given us a 'law of faith', whereby he accepts as righteousness a firm belief in what he may require us to believe, without doubting his promises. The content of this belief may vary; with Abraham, for example, it was belief that God would give him a son and innumerable descendants (Gen. 15:6). Since the coming of Christ, however, the contents of this belief are that Jesus is the Messiah, the Son of God (John 20:30–31). This was what Jesus himself preached, as did his apostles, and acceptance of it, along with repentance, is all that is required for salvation. The epistles, of course, do contain much more teaching than this (and Locke wrote 'Notes' on several of them), but they were intended for people who were already Christians and designed to take them deeper, not to offer them salvation for the first time. Though certainly we must not deny their teachings, people can be saved through faith and remain ignorant of what the epistles teach.

This minimalist version of Christianity led to Locke's being accused of Socinianism (the ideas associated with Faustus Socinus [1539–1604], who denied the divinity of Christ, the Trinity and anything more than an exemplary form of atonement). Locke denied that his book justified this charge, but Socinians could undoubtedly have accepted nearly all of it without difficulty.

Locke is generally acknowledged as the father of British empiricist philosophy, and he has also been seen by some as a forerunner of deism. His emphasis on miracle and revelation indicates that he was certainly not an intentional deist, but the later deists could well be seen as simply taking further his views on the supremacy of reason and his minimizing of the need for doctrine.

Bibliography

J. Locke, *Essay Concerning Human Understanding*, abridg. and ed. by A. D. Woozley (London, 1964); *Treatises of Government*, repr. in 'Everyman' series (London, 1975); *The Reasonableness of Christianity*, abridg. and ed. by I. T. Ramsey (London, 1958); R. I. Aaron, *John Locke* (Oxford, [2]1955); M. Jinkins, 'Elements of Federal Theology in the Religious Thought of John Locke', *Evangelical Quarterly*, vol. 66 (1994), pp. 123–141; N. Wolterstorff, 'Locke's Philosophy of Religion', in V. Chappell (ed.), *The Cambridge Companion to Locke* (Cambridge, 1994), pp. 172–199.

R. L. STURCH

LOGIC

Logic is the science of valid inference and proof, and it affects every aspect of communication and argument. There are many forms of logic, and modern logics are highly complex and mathematical. Logic deals with both formal and informal modes of *reasoning. It rests on the structures and principles of thinking and sound argumentation. Apologetics is based on formal and informal reasoning and argument and will ask what is the basis and justification of logic and what does it tell us about reason, *language and the world in contrast to Christian perspectives.

Everyone wants to present good arguments rather than bad, so there is a shared concern for correct reasoning. This may deal with both the form and the content of arguments. Thus logic is concerned with *truth and validity. An argument can be valid without actually being true. Truth depends on the truth of the premises; validity depends on the inferences made from the premises in arriving at the conclusion. Christians must be concerned to have both valid and true arguments. However, the basis and nature of the logic involved must be a matter of debate. The question 'Is logic logical?' highlights the problem of assumptions and ultimate presuppositions. Are the laws of logic expressions of some natural, ideal standards in a *Platonic sense or simply a set of assumptions made by humanity in order to reason and argue? The creation of truth tables as a means of checking the validity of arguments seems to point to an assertion of particular standards as tools to order discussion and thinking. In contrast, the laws of non-*contradiction and the excluded middle seem to derive from universal, fundamental ideals.

The Christian suggests that God is the source of order and looks to the OT Hebraic idea of *Logos* and the NT expression of *Logos* as both indicating the originator of order, sense and meaning in the world. This is both an epistemological (about knowing) and an ontological (about being) expression of the origin and continuing grounding of the order of the world and of our reasoning as resting and existing in God and his will. We can make sense of the world because the world makes sense and both the intelligibility of the world and the intelligence of humanity derive from God. Either logical laws rest on some expression of ultimate *reality or they are simply heuristic, human constructs. It will never be enough to settle simply for the validity of arguments. Christians are committed to truth and believe that both truth and validity are founded in God himself.

Apologetics uses many different forms of argument. All share a deep concern for the understanding, presentation and assessment of evidence as well as inference from what is known and accepted to what is unknown. Paul in addressing the Areopagus in Athens (Acts 17) clearly used the evidence of nature, religion, history and what poets and philosophers had said in order to present a case for the living God and the reality of judgment and the resurrection.

Philosophers of religion like Alvin Plantinga and Richard Swinburne have made excellent use of tight, logical, formal argumentation to make the case for the validity of belief in God and the propriety of religious beliefs. This has given great confidence to Christian philosophers and a means of detailed argument in relation to God's existence and the status of, and grounds for, religious beliefs. There are more informal arguments presented by Christian apologists which, while lacking the technical exactitude of formal logic, still have a valid logic of their own. There may be a fundamental sense of logic which concerns the general rules necessary for use of reason and

language at all. There may be another sense of logic which deals with different expressions and applications of different logical systems in different linguistic and mathematical contexts. Assertions and arguments are woven together as part of the fabric of discussion. Language itself is the key means of articulating a position, presenting support, assessing truth and falsity, adequacy and inadequacy and arriving at valid and acceptable conclusions. We need to be aware that often there are unexpressed and assumed premises in any argument and these need to be clarified and recognized. The implications of claims and evidence need to be clarified. When we make statements certain things are assumed, claimed and implied. The development of conversation and argument depends on those involved being able to deal properly with assumptions, implications and the move from what is being stated or assumed to what may be concluded.

Behind informal logic is a recognition that meaning, sense and reference are complex and contextual. Different logical systems offer differing accounts of the nature and relationship of truth with meaning, sense and reference but that means we must ensure that we look at meaning clearly in context and allow for the wide variety of expressions which are part of human communication and argumentation. What is in fact warranted by the evidence and statements made and how good that warrant is are necessary parts of good argument. Logic is part and parcel of justifying what is believed and expressed as true. It is a tool for everyone, especially Christians.

Logic distinguishes between deductive and inductive forms of arguments. Deduction rests on a closed relationship between premises and conclusions so that one clearly does or does not follow from the other according to accepted criteria. We only arrive in the conclusion at what is already implicit in the premises. This only tells us what we know already. In contrast, induction is the method of *science and exploration where we move from evidence to new conclusions which were unknown before. Deduction is often the method of *theology and doctrine, deriving from Scripture and the nature of God what may be asserted validly in creeds and doctrinal statements. Induction is more the method of apologetics, looking at evidence from the world, science, human experience and human understanding and drawing conclusions about the nature and existence of God and responses to particular questions, doubts or attacks on Christianity.

Inductive logic is always subject to Bertrand *Russell's example of the limits of induction. If a chicken is fed every day for a year at the same time, then it is reasonable to expect that on any particular day it will be fed at that time. One day it has its neck wrung. This is a fatal objection to imagining that the mere accumulation of evidence can produce absolute *certainty. This cuts both ways for the Christian apologist. It allows the recognition that alternative views and counter arguments based on evidence may be countered and the apologist is no worse off than the attacker. But they are no better off either, as counter evidence may undercut what seems to have been established.

There is no absolute certainty in expressions of faith, whether they are in science or theology. All human statements and evidence are subject to interpretation, revision and new evidence. The laws of logic are accepted as given and allow a framework for thought, communication and argument. The themes discussed and the evidence presented using these laws are fallible and not absolutely grounded. Distinguishing the two levels is crucial.

Using logic assumes certain things about reason, language and the world. Reason and reasoning are attempts to make order where there is either chaos or an order to be grasped and followed. Reason either rests on its own *authority or on some other ground. Christians claim that reason rests on the God who created an ordered world and gave humanity the sense with which to understand it. Ultimately, all exercise of reason depends on the Creator, thus Christians have nothing to fear from the proper use of reason and the search for truth. Indeed, some will claim that it is only in relationship to God that a proper and full understanding of logic can be achieved.

Logic reveals the general features of the structure of language. Semantics are part and parcel of logic, because logical thought has to be expressed in words, statements and propositions. The form and content must be evaluated. It is vital to draw some careful logical distinctions between what has sense, but no reference, like the present king of France or mythological beings, and claims that the term 'God' both is coherent and refers to reality. Apologetic argument will look to establish not only meaningfulness but also truth. Understanding the variety of linguistic contexts and usages is important in logical analysis.

Logical forms and thought raise questions about the fundamental nature of the world and of human being. Christians will want to ground these in the nature and will of God. John's Gospel emphasizes that *Jesus, the *Logos*, is the ground of all being, order and understanding. This is reinforced in Col. 1, where Paul expresses the way in which in Christ everything holds together in existence and in its order and purpose. These expressions challenge any view of logic which claims a free-standing, autonomous status for human logic.

Bibliography

J. P. Moreland and W. L. Craig, *Philosophical Foundations for a Christian Worldview* (Leicester, 1996); N. Geisler and R. Brooks, *Come Let Us Reason* (Grand Rapids, 1990).

E. D. COOK

LOGICAL POSITIVISM

The logical positivists were a group of scientists, mathematicians and philosophers that met in Vienna from 1924 to 1936 under the leadership of the philosopher Moritz Schlick (1882–1936). The group included Gustav Bergmann, Rudolph Carnap, Herbert Feigl, Phillipp Frank, Kurt Gödel, Hans Hahn, Karl Menger, Otto Neurath and Friedrich Waismann. They were in contact with Karl *Popper (1902–94) and Ludwig *Wittgenstein (1889–1951) and were influenced by the latter's *Tractatus Logico-Philosophicus* (1922), although Wittgenstein himself had come to doubt the rigid doctrines on the nature of meaningful *language that he had expressed in that work. The young A. J. Ayer (1910–89) visited the group and popularized its ideas among Anglo-American philosophers in his influential *Language, Truth and Logic* (1936). Schlick was killed by a deranged student, and the group was dispersed mainly to America because of the rise of Naziism. In the light of the difficulty of substantiating the logical viability of the verifiability principle (the key idea of the movement), despite repeated attempts at reformulation, a number of their adherents, such as Bergmann, Carnap, Feigl and Neurath, moved to the more flexible position of logical *empiricism, which was held by sympathetic contemporaries such as Carl Hempel, Hans Reichenbach and

Richard von Mises, originally based in Berlin and also later in America. Although the logical positivists failed to justify their claims, they have had a long-standing influence on Anglo-American analytic philosophy in the demand that meaningful propositions about *reality must be grounded in empirical observations, and in casting doubt on the validity of religious claims, such as 'God is omnipotent', because God, by definition, cannot be the object of empirical observation.

The logical positivists wanted to draw a clear line of demarcation between justifiable language about reality and spurious and empty claims about it. They saw the scientific method, particularly as evident in physics, as the ideal model for gaining knowledge, an approach commonly called 'scientism'. They were reductionist in believing that all the *sciences could be unified by being reduced to the concepts of physics. They also held to the then common *foundationalism that maintained that all valid knowledge claims were based on observations. In opposition to the prevailing *Idealism (e.g. neo-Kantianism), to the gross claims of fascism and *communism, and to differing ethical and religious beliefs, they sought to dismiss metaphysical assertions as lacking significant reference and therefore meaningless.

Their approach had been foreshadowed by David *Hume (1711–76), who had argued that all meaningful utterances were either propositions about the logical relations of ideas or statements based on sensual awareness. The claims of transcendent *metaphysics in *theology or in philosophy should be committed, he said in the last line of his *Enquiry Concerning Human Understanding* (1748), 'to the flames, for it can contain nothing but sophistry and illusion'. The great philosopher *Kant (1724–1804) had also argued in his *Critique of Pure Reason* (1781) that a transcendent metaphysics was not possible for human beings, whose knowledge was inevitably limited by the forms of the human cognitive apparatus, which could gain access to external reality only through the five senses. But it was the philosophy of science of Ernst Mach (1838–1916) that particularly influenced the logical positivists. For him, all valid science was reducible to propositions that were justified by observational statements ('positivism'). But the logical positivists differed from him in wanting to provide clear, logically based criteria for this claim.

The logical positivists identified two types of meaningful propositions: first, analytic propositions, such as those of mathematics and scientific theorizing, whose truth could be demonstrated by logic and the meaning of their concepts; and secondly, synthetic propositions that referred to the external world and those truths could be demonstrated by physical observations. Kant, however, while he accepted these two categories, also maintained that a third category, comprising synthetic a priori propositions, was valid, namely, general truths about physical reality, such as 'Every event has a cause', that are not derivable from logic or discrete observations alone. Some modern philosophers, such as W. V. Quine (1908–), have denied that there is a rigid demarcation in meaningful language between analytic and synthetic propositions.

The linchpin of the logical positivists was what they called the verifiability principle, which was first formulated by Waismann in 1930 in these words: 'Anyone uttering a sentence must know in which conditions he calls the statement true or false; if he is unable to state this, then he does not know what he has said. A statement that cannot be verified conclusively is not verifiable at all; it is just devoid of any meaning.' This strong version of the verifiability principle asserted that a putative proposition about reality could be meaningful only if it was logically possible to confirm it directly or indirectly by empirical observation. Schlick summed it up in the well-known aphorism: 'The meaning of a proposition is the method of its verification.' In other words, the meaning of a proposition is logically identical to what is involved in demonstrating its truth. The meaning of an analytic proposition was determined by examining the logical consistency of its concepts and by its logical relation to other propositions. The meaning of a synthetic proposition was established by stating the procedures that are needed for its confirmation by observation. The logical positivists were adamant that traditional metaphysics and religious doctrines, such as 'God created the world', were to be rejected as meaningless, as there was in principle no empirical observation that could justify them. Such propositions were otiose, like 'Fairies help the flowers to grow', as there were no referents for them. For Schlick, *ethics could be reduced to a naturalistic version of *utilitarianism, whereas for Carnap and Ayer, ethical assertions were not assertions at all, but emotive expressions of approval or repugnance.

It soon became clear that the strong version of the verifiability principle was self-refuting. It was not a self-evident truth, a statement whose truth could be determined by the meaning of its terms. Nor was it an empirical proposition, whose truth could be confirmed by observation. To counter this major objection Carnap suggested that the verifiability principle was an 'explication' that helped to discriminate between science and metaphysics. But this then ceased to imply an all-encompassing veto on metaphysics and religion. Carnap went on to reconstruct the *verification principle in the terms of the confirmability of significant propositions, and moved into a less intolerant logical empiricism. Ayer also sought to reconstruct the verifiability principle in order to meet with objections to the strong version. He allowed that no proposition can be conclusively verified or refuted by observational experience; but a valid proposition must have *some* empirical justification. This then, however, allowed many of the rejected metaphysical and religious claims to be meaningful. Ayer tried further formulations of the verifiability principle, but these all failed to logically exclude such statements.

Other difficulties were found with the principle. To what kind of statements does it apply, given that propositions by convention are either true or false, not meaningless? Does the criterion determine the meaning of a statement, or merely that it is meaning*ful*? Are there not many serious scientific claims (e.g. the universality of gravitational force, the existence of black holes, etc.) that cannot be conclusively verified? How certain can one be of an observational experience? Is not an experience a subjective awareness that is not open to public examination? Is it not now clear that science itself is built on non-empirical assumptions (e.g. the continuity and rationality of nature; the capacity of human understanding to penetrate the structures of nature)? Do not these very assumptions have metaphysical and religious implications? And has it not become clear that science progresses through a series of paradigm shifts (as Thomas Kuhn [1922–96] showed in his book *The Structure of Scientific Revolutions*, 1962), which create new visions of the nature of reality, which in turn dictate the kinds of experiment that are undertaken and the interpretation of their results? Finally, the logical

positivists assumed that the conditions for meaning were identical to the conditions for *truth. But we are often able to understand statements without knowing the conditions under which they would be true.

Religious believers offered three main responses to the verification principle. First, some accepted its dismissal of the meaningfulness of religious doctrines. Richard Braithwaite (1900–90) held that they had to be reinterpreted in terms of dispositions to appropriate forms of behaviour. Thus, belief in a God of love is reducible to the intention to behave in a loving way towards other human beings. But it is evident that religious believers hold that their doctrines reflect independent truths about divine reality. A second approach accepted that there was some validity in the verifiability principle. John *Hick (1922–) maintained that belief in a God was in principle verifiable in terms of a post-death beatific vision of him. This led to the rejoinder that such a criterion was of little use in the present life, and, even if some such vision occurred after death, there would still be the difficulty of confirming that one was experiencing a pure, immaterial, uncreated, infinite spirit by finite and unknown cognitive powers.

A third, wider response saw the verifiability principle as far too narrow and dislocated from everyday life, in which people hold unverified beliefs but find daily living and conversation with others reasonably meaningful. This approach adopted the later Wittgenstein's understanding of everyday conversations as a series of 'language games', in which the meaning and validity of claims made were justified by the 'rules' (subconsciously held beliefs and convictions) of the 'games'. Each game had its appropriate 'form of life', a mode of personal commitment, and the religious form of life was as valid as any other. The 'truths' of religious faith were perfectly meaningful for believers, and indeed constituted convictions by which they lived and understood the world around them. Whereas this approach overcame the scientism and narrow empiricism of the logical positivists and empiricists, it allowed an unrestrained *relativism and failed to give any assurance to unbelievers of the truth of religious claims.

Karl Popper responded to the failure of the logical positivists to provide a watertight version of the verifiability principle by proposing his falsification principle: a putative statement is meaningful only if it is logically possible to falsify it. 'Diamonds exist under the surface of the moon' is a meaningful statement, as it is possible *in principle*, if not in fact, to falsify it. But the metaphysical claim that 'Reality is all one' is not meaningful, as it is not in principle falsifiable. Popper advanced his falsifiability principle partly because he wanted to show that Freudianism and Marxism were pseudo-sciences, and to have a means of distinguishing a valid science from a spurious form such as astrology. Antony *Flew took up Popper's falsifiability principle to attack religious beliefs as meaningless, because whenever empirical evidence (e.g. pain, premature death) count against belief in an all-loving omnipotent God, believers restate the nature of their claims by introducing further qualifications (e.g. 'God's love is inscrutable') and refuse to give them up. For believers these claims are not falsifiable, and therefore for Flew they must be dismissed as meaningless. Their plausibility is undermined by counter-evidence, and they die 'the death of a thousand qualifications'. But Christians can respond by saying that their faith is falsifiable in principle, for possible falsifying conditions can be defined: if God had not become incarnate in *Jesus, if life were entirely irremediably evil, if there were never an occasion when suffering improved someone's character, then the Christian faith would be falsified. With respect to the verification principle, finally left by the logical empiricists in the form of the statement that some empirical observations are needed for maintaining the meaningfulness of putative claims, Christians can point to the eyewitness reports behind the Gospels (Luke 1:1–4; John 20:30; 21:24), the conformity of the NT to what is known of the Roman Empire in the first century AD, and the visibility and tangibility of the risen Christ, who appeared to many people (1 Cor. 15:5–6). Jesus said, 'Look at my hands and my feet. It is I myself! Touch me and see; a ghost does not have flesh and bones, as you see I have' (Luke 24:39; cf. John 20:27). The truth of the Christian faith is confirmed to believers by the inner witness of the *Holy Spirit (John 15:26; 16:14–15; 1 Cor. 2:12–13) and by the new dimensions of God's presence in their lives (2 Cor. 3:17–18; Gal. 5:22–23; Eph. 1:17–19). The logical positivists and empiricists had no awareness of God's capacity to make himself known to individuals by the action of his Holy Spirit.

Bibliography

R. W. Ashby, 'Verifiability Principle', in P. Edwards (ed.), *The Encyclopedia of Philosophy*, vol. 8 (New York and London, 1967); A. J. Ayer, *Language, Truth and Logic* (Harmondsworth, 2nd edn, 1946); G. Bergmann, *The Metaphysics of Logical Positivism* (Madison, 2nd edn, 1967); F. Copleston, *Contemporary Philosophy: Studies of Logical Positivism and Existentialism* (London, 2nd edn, 1972); C. J. Misak, *Verificationism: Its History and Prospects* (London, 1995); J. Passmore, 'Logical Positivism', in P. Edwards (ed.), *The Encyclopedia of Philosophy*, vol. 5 (New York and London, 1967); C. Ray, 'Logical Positivism', in W. H. Newton-Smith (ed.), *A Companion to the Philosophy of Science* (Oxford, 2000); W. C. Salmon, 'Logical Empiricism', in W. H. Newton-Smith (ed.), *A Companion to the Philosophy of Science* (Oxford, 2000); D. R. Stiver, *The Philosophy of Religious Language: Sign, Symbol, and Story* (Oxford, 1996).

J. W. WARD

LOMBARD, PETER

Peter Lombard (c. 1095–1169), a theologian of north Italian origin, became archbishop of Paris in 1159 and was the author of the most widely used theological textbook in the Middle Ages. Although he wrote a commentary on the Psalms and a gloss on the Pauline epistles, the only work of his which has made any lasting impression is his renowned *Book of Sentences*, which he completed shortly before becoming archbishop. His aim was to compile theological extracts from the Church Fathers and the leading authorities of his own time and to arrange them in a systematic way, so that students could learn the basic principles of Christian theology. The first of the four books deals with the *Trinity, the second with the creation, the third with the incarnation and the last with the sacraments, which Lombard defined as being seven in number.

Peter Lombard's genius lay in his ability to synthesize his material, which he did with outstanding success. He avoided falling into extremes of interpretation and adopted the question and answer method which was becoming popular as a teaching tool in the nascent universities of his time. He is justly regarded as the father of medieval sacrament-alism, regarding the sacraments as signs of God's real presence in the world. For him, they necessarily had far more than a merely symbolic significance; they were the true link between *heaven and earth, the ongoing form of the incarnation of Christ and, therefore, the effectual means by which we can receive divine grace.

Lombard's willingness to make use of suspect authors like Peter *Abelard in the *Sentences* caused controversy after his death, and there were always points of theology which were regarded as open to dispute and described as such in later commentaries. Nevertheless, the *Sentences* were decreed to be orthodox at the fourth Lateran council in 1215, and seven years later Alexander of Hales introduced it as the standard text in his theological lectures in Paris. It retained its prominent position until the sixteenth century and even later, when it was finally displaced by *Calvin's *Institutes* on the Protestant side and *Thomas Aquinas' *Summa Theologiae* on the Catholic one. As a result, there were hundreds of commentaries on it produced in the Middle Ages, and their study is a discipline all its own.

In modern times, Lombard has been little read, and his work is now the preserve of medieval specialists in a way that the writings of *Anselm or Aquinas, for example, are not. There is still no translation of the *Sentences* into English, and the theological manual used by Luther and Calvin when they were students remains a closed book to their modern followers.

Bibliography

G. R. Evans, *Mediaeval Commentaries on the Sentences of Peter Lombard* (Leiden, 2001); E. F. Rogers, *Peter Lombard and the Sacrificial System* (Merrick, 1917; repr. 1976).

G. L. BRAY

LYOTARD, JEAN-FRANÇOIS

Jean-François Lyotard (1924–98) was a French philosopher best known for his definition of postmodernism, which he summarized as 'incredulity toward meta-narratives'.

Lyotard began his career as a Marxist, but after the failure of the Paris uprising in May 1968 he began to question Marxism, and with it the potential of any such purport-edly universal discourse to account for the complexity of human drives and relationships. From this point, Lyotard warned increasingly against the tendency of overarching 'grand stories', or 'meta-narratives', to function in a totalizing manner, associating them with the suspect myths of a modern age marked by various forms of tyranny. In *Discours, Figure* (1971), he applied this critique to structuralism, attacking its notion that a common 'grammar' underlies different *languages and *cultures, and that this is isomorphic with the mind.

Lyotard developed this postmodern, post-structuralist approach in *Libidinal Economy* (1974). Here he construed from *Freud an emphasis on the 'libidinal intensities' at work in society – i.e. on the contingent 'swarms' of events and feelings which characterize human experience. Such events and feelings, he claimed, resist final integration and explanation. Something is always 'deferred' after they have been institutionalized, and it is this deferral which fosters diversity, experimentation and change within cultures.

From a Christian standpoint, it is telling that Lyotard described his thinking at this stage as 'pagan'. If narratives are semantically unstable – if they do not always 'conform to their object' – then, as with *pagan gods, 'no-one has the last word, and there is no *coup de grace*'. In short, the God worshipped by Christians as Lord of heaven and earth is recast as one voice among many in an infinitely open-ended conversation. However, whereas Lyotard saw such indeterminacy as liberating, classical Christian understanding could point to its more baleful consequences. If the relationship of language to God and the world is as arbitrary as Lyotard suggests, then not only theological *truth, but objective truth as such, is impossible or at least incommunicable. Lyotard's perspectivism is relativistic with respect to both *epistemology and *ethics. He may seek to unmask the totalizing pretensions of meta-narrative, but in doing so he still reduces language to an instrument of power; it is just that the *power is seen as more properly localized and individualized. Yet on Lyotard's own terms, there can be no clear moral grounds for preferring 'little stories' to 'grand stories', since *morality itself is plural and perspectival rather than objective and universal. Thus he totalizes difference, even as he denies all totalization.

While celebrating paganism, Lyotard did at least recognize the ethical problems which attend it. In particular, he saw that it challenged established models of *justice. In *Just Gaming* (1979) and *The Differend* (1983), he suggested that in contemporary pagan society one must continue to make judgments, but without criteria. Rather, justice must be worked out pragmatically, case by case. Such discourse pragmatics might invoke past narratives as precedents, but might just as readily narrate new norms. There can be no one fundamental concept of justice, only a multiplicity of justices. Again here, one is left questioning the basis on which Nazi justice might be rejected in favour of justice as dispensed by, say, the European Court of Human Rights – or, indeed, whether Lyotard sees human rights themselves as anything more than rhetorical tropes.

Lyotard's use of the phrase 'incredulity toward meta-narratives' to describe the postmodern condition appeared in a 1979 report on the latter commissioned by the Quebec government. The main concern of this report was the status of knowledge in an increasingly computerized and consumerized post-industrial world. Whereas the modern era had been driven by meta-narratives of moral progress and the totalization of knowledge, Lyotard argued that Western society in particular had entered a new phase, in which the availability of vast electronic databases would change the way such knowledge gets legitimated. Rather than being proved against fixed standards of truth, knowledge would function as a contingent commodity – information – whose validity would be established not denotatively but performatively, i.e. according to the dynamics of power, wealth and need which bear on its exchange in any specific context. For Lyotard, this might especially compromise scientific discourse, which in modernity had been legitimated by cosmic 'laws', but which in postmodernity might derive legitimation purely from its usefulness to global corporations.

Sociologically, Lyotard's predictions about the commercialization of *science in *The Postmodern Condition* now look prophetic. Yet once again they lack any coherent ethical basis, and on this and other key points it is hard to reconcile his work with Christian orthodoxy. In particular, his critique of meta-narrative springs from a strong anti-essentialism, which implicitly denies both the independent existence and the universal *authority of God. Lyotard did grow more amenable to religious discourse in his later years, writing extensively about the interplay between God's presence and absence, his word and his silence, in biblical and devotional texts. Although he related this to the more general indeterminacy of language and meaning, the fact that Lyotard applied such indeterminacy to all narratives led him to view theological discourse as neither more nor less legitimate than scientific or artistic discourse. Like them, he suggested, it is self-legitimating. Indeed, Lyotard was drawn to the pure prescriptions of the Torah on the basis that they do not succumb to ontological *verification, and cannot be deduced. Rather, he stressed, they are legitimated simply inasmuch as they command obligation, and are obeyed.

There are echoes in all this of presuppositionalist apologetics, which, as distinct from evidentialist methods developed in modernity, rejects the need to prove theological claims in terms of other meta-narratives, such as those of *logic or reason. Indeed, Christians might welcome this approach for its apparent willingness to let Scripture speak for itself. More fundamentally, however, they must part company with Lyotard as they maintain that there *is* a divine meta-narrative, and that this meta-narrative is not *ipso facto* malign. Indeed, far from being driven by a bid for power, it has as its heart an act of radical renunciation and self-sacrifice – the atoning death of Christ on the cross. To hold this atonement as objectively true is to challenge Lyotard's identification of meta-narrative with totalization and tyranny, since the meta-narrative in this case turns precisely on the divestment of cosmic dominion, authority and might (Phil. 2:5–8).

Bibliography

A. Benjamin (ed.), *The Lyotard Reader* (Oxford, 1989); J.-F. Lyotard, *The Postmodern Condition: A Report on Knowledge* (trans. G. Bennington and B. Massumi; Manchester, 1984); *The Differend: Phrases in Dispute* (trans. G. Van Den Abbeele; Minneapolis, 1988); S. Malpas, *Jean-François Lyotard* (London, 2003).

D. H. K. Hilborn

McCOSH, JAMES

James McCosh (1811–94) served for sixteen years as a parish minister at Arbroath and Brechin, before he moved from his native Scotland in 1851 to take up the Chair of Logic at Queen's University, Belfast. This appointment arose out of his growing reputation as a natural theologian, achieved as a result of the publication of his book, *The Method of Divine Government, Physical and Moral* in 1850. He moved to the USA in 1868 when he was appointed by Princeton College to the dual position of professor of philosophy and the president of the college. In 1888 he resigned from the presidency, continuing as professor of philosophy until his death. He was an enthusiastic supporter of the *Scottish Common Sense Philosophy – 'the principles of common sense' – propounded by Thomas *Reid (1710–96) in opposition to the scepticism of David *Hume (1711–86). Though lacking in originality, his vigorous writings on this subject, e.g. *Intuitions of the Mind* (1860), *The Scottish Philosophy* (1874), have exerted a significant influence on the theological development of 'old Princeton and Westminster'. Different conclusions have been reached concerning the extent to which old Princeton and Westminster theology is built on Scottish Common Sense Philosophy. Vander Stelt draws a close connection between the two, while Calhoun does not. In his defence of theistic evolution, e.g. *The Typical Forms and Special Ends of Creation* (1855) and *The Supernatural in Relation to the Natural* (1862), McCosh adopted a view which was extremely uncommon among orthodox evangelicals of his day. Those who share his outlook will regard his work as apologetically significant. He also engaged in the kind of apologetics which argues for the Christian faith by challenging the validity of alternative philosophies. In these controversial writings, e.g. *An Examination of Mr. J. S. Mill's Philosophy* (1866) and *Christianity and Positivism* (1871), he often advanced rather superficial criticisms which were based on a failure to achieve an adequate understanding of the views he attacked.

Bibliography

D. B. Calhoun, *Princeton Seminary: The Majestic Testimony (1869–1929)* (Edinburgh, 1996); J. C. Vander Stelt, *Philosophy and Scripture: A Study in Old Princeton and Westminster Theology* (Marlton, 1978).

C. M. Cameron

MACDONALD, GEORGE

George MacDonald (1824–1905), born in Huntly, was one of Scotland's most important Christian writers of the nineteenth century. His biggest impact on twentieth-century literature came through C. S. *Lewis, who stated, 'I have never concealed the fact that I regarded him as my master; indeed I fancy I have never written a book in which I did not quote from him.' MacDonald also served as the narrator's guide through heaven in Lewis' *The Great Divorce*.

Works

MacDonald wrote fifty-three books: thirty-five works of fiction, including stories for children, some of which have never been out of print, such as *At the Back of the North Wind*, *The Princess and the Goblin*, and *The Princess and Curdie*, two collections of short stories, three literary books, five volumes of sermons, six volumes of poetry, and two *fantasy stories for adults, *Phantastes* at the start of his career (1858) and *Lilith* near the end (1895). These fantasies, considered by many to be his most compelling works, inspired H. G. Wells, J. R. R. *Tolkien and Madeleine L'Engle, to name a few. In *Phantastes* and *Lilith*, MacDonald uses a journey motif in which allegory and deep symbolism clothe his essential ideas about the nature of God, the importance of repentance and dying to self, the beauty of Christian death and the hope of resurrection.

Controversy

One controversial aspect of MacDonald's writing is his suggestion of *universalism. MacDonald's own almost-saintly father had given him a sense of a father's love that was so great towards his children that MacDonald believed God would be unable to allow anyone to suffer for long. C. S. Lewis comments, 'I dare not say that he is never in error; but to speak plainly I know hardly any other writer who seems to be closer, or more continually close, to the Spirit of Christ Himself.'

An ordained Congregationalist minister, MacDonald was forced to give up his pulpit because of his universalistic views and his opinion that animals go to *heaven, and he subsequently earned his living writing books and lecturing. He visited America and was so well received that he was offered a preaching position in New York City paying $20,000, a fortune for the time, which he declined. He drew great strength from his wife, Louisa and their eleven children. Troubled by poor health for most of his life, he died in England in 1905.

Recent revival of interest

MacDonald was extremely popular in his day and was even considered for the post of Poet Laureate after the death of Tennyson. However, by the middle of the twentieth century MacDonald was being overlooked by most readers. A MacDonald revival began in 1982, when Wheaton College professor Rolland Hein published some of MacDonald's *Unspoken Sermons* series under the title *The Harmony Within*. Also in the 1980s, Canadians Dan and Elizabeth Hamilton and American Michael Phillips edited MacDonald's novels, condensing some of his typically Victorian long sermonizing sections and 'translating' the more difficult portions of his Scottish dialect into simpler language for audiences unwilling to tackle the original versions. In the 1990s, Johannesen Printing and Publishing and Sonrise Books reprinted each MacDonald volume as it was originally published, making his unedited works easily accessible.

At the beginning of the twenty-first century, MacDonald criticism is flourishing. *Jungian and feminist critics, those interested in Scottish novels, those exploring Victorian ideas of *science and those pondering MacDonald's impact on twentieth-century authors are considering his works and his dynamic faith, which was the keystone of all his writings and his life. His son Greville wrote, '[His] books will assuredly be read yet again when the world has grown wise enough to appreciate their writer's singleness of vision and the open road between him and God' (Phillips, p. 347).

Bibliography

C. S. Lewis, *George MacDonald: An Anthology* (New York, 1947); M. Phillips, *Discovering the Character of God* (Minneapolis, 1989).

J. C. ZELLMANN

MACHEN, J. GRESHAM

J. Gresham Machen (1881–1937), NT scholar and Presbyterian clergyman who taught at Princeton and Westminster seminaries, was born and raised in a devout Presbyterian home in Baltimore. He attended The Johns Hopkins University, where he studied classical Greek, before attending Princeton Seminary from 1902 to 1905. After a year of graduate study in Germany at Marburg and Göttingen Universities, Machen returned to Princeton Seminary, where he taught New Testament until 1929.

Machen gained notoriety for his critique of liberal Protestantism, most clearly expressed in *Christianity and Liberalism* (1923), in which he argued that liberal religion and Christianity were completely incompatible. Before he became prominent in the fundamentalist controversy, Machen gained a reputation as a first-rate conservative biblical scholar. In his first book, *The Origin of Paul's Religion* (1921), he interacted with the latest European scholarship in defending the historic Christian view that the apostle's teaching and faith were not the product of Greek religions or Jewish sects but were rooted in the life and work of Christ. Machen drew upon his work on Paul to argue against liberalism that Christianity, from its origins, was a doctrinal religion in which sin and grace were paramount, not a faith that appealed to human goodness. During the 1920s Machen continued to work in NT studies and produced *The Virgin Birth of Christ* (1930), a work he considered his *magnum opus*. Machen surveyed the biblical evidence for the virgin birth and, as in the book on Paul, he interacted with the scholarly literature. His work was a scholarly attempt to defend traditional Christian teaching about Christ's birth.

Church controversy, however, prompted Machen to leave Princeton for Westminster Seminary in 1929, and his involvement in the struggles of the Presbyterian Church in the United States ended his scholarly work. He continued to teach at Westminster, but in 1935 he was suspended from the ministry of the Presbyterian Church, and eventually the work of establishing the Orthodox Presbyterian Church (founded in 1936) occupied most of his energies.

Machen's work represented the characteristic approach of Princeton's tradition of biblical scholarship. Abreast of the latest scholarship, attentive to the humanness of Scripture and committed to the Bible as God's word, Machen's study of the NT functioned as a form of apologetics in which he defended the Bible's trustworthiness and message from critical academics. Machen thus stood in a tradition of theological learning that stretched from Charles *Hodge through Benjamin B. *Warfield and William Henry Green to Robert Dick Wilson, scholars who defended the Reformed faith and responded to the higher critics' objections through their study of Scripture.

Bibliography

D. G. Hart, *Defending the Faith: J. Gresham Machen and the Crisis of Conservative Protestantism in Modern America* (Baltimore, 1994); B. J. Longfield, *The Presbyterian Controversy: Fundamentalists, Modernists and Moderates* (New York, 1991); R. A. Harrisville and W. Sundberg, *The Bible in Modern Culture: Theology and Historical-Critical Method from Spinoza to Käsemann* (Grand Rapids, 1995).

D. G. HART

MACINTYRE, ALASDAIR

Alasdair MacIntyre (b. 1929) is one of the most important philosophers of our time. A prolific author, MacIntyre's writings blur disciplinary boundaries, though his main fields of interest are moral philosophy and the social sciences. MacIntyre's intellectual pursuits are as varied as his own life has been: from early studies for the Presbyterian ministry, to the British New Left of the 1960s, to professor at the University of Notre Dame in the USA. Though his first book, published when he was twenty-three years old, was on Marxism and Christianity, soon thereafter he ceased to be committed to both. His influential paper 'Notes from the Moral Wilderness' (1958–9) reflects his ambivalent mood at the time and also prefigures the later and better-known Aristotelianism of *After Virtue* (1981). In the period between *After Virtue* and *Whose Justice? Which Rationality?* (1988), MacIntyre shifted once again, this time by enclosing his Aristotelianism within a wider embrace of *Thomism. In embracing philosophical Thomism, MacIntyre also recommitted himself to the Christian faith and became a Roman Catholic (see *Christianity, Roman Catholic). This is important in light of the link between MacIntyre's conception of Protestantism (see *Christianity, Protestant) as modern, schismatic and anti-traditional and his philosophical critique of modernity, the *Enlightenment and the contemporary crisis of the liberal democratic culture.

Though MacIntyre has not written explicitly on the subject of Christian apologetics, his writings, nonetheless, bear highly important implications for this area. In fact, Stanley Hauerwas and Charles Pinches, in their book *Christians Among the Virtues* (1997), suggest that MacIntyre is engaged in what may be classified as Christian apologetics. As they see it, MacIntyre believes that the Christian faith, if conceived as a 'traditioned' account of *morality, can provide answers to questions that are dialectically problematic given the Greek inheritance. In other words, MacIntyre's Thomistic appropriation of Aristotelian virtue *ethics may be profitably viewed as an argument for the rational superiority of Thomism, a move which thereby resolves the difficulties plaguing not only the Greeks but also much modern moral philosophy (both continental and Anglo-American).

A centrepiece of MacIntyre's writings is what has been called his 'interminably long history of ethics'. Ever since the publication of *A Short History of Ethics* (1966), MacIntyre's ongoing project has been the interpretation of the history of moral philosophy from antiquity to modernity. Part of MacIntyre's argument is that every such interpretation always proceeds from a particular vantage-point. This is controversial, especially because MacIntyre identifies a number of such rival vantage-points, what he calls 'traditions of inquiry'. Since he is particularly critical of the Enlightenment and its offshoot in a form of moral theorizing which repudiates tradition and *authority, he is sometimes interpreted as espousing a form of moral *relativism, but, arguably, this misrepresents his position. While MacIntyre certainly relativizes the role of reason, his central point is to conceive of the relation between rationality on the one hand and tradition and authority on the other, not as antithetical, but as complementary. On this score, his conception of tradition may be compared with Hans-Georg Gadamer's notion of 'prejudice'. For both, human rationality is constituted by tradition and *history, so that deference to the authority of tradition is not a form of superstition (as Enlightenment thinkers held), but rather a very precondition for rational inquiry.

Perhaps the most fertile and most problematic aspect of MacIntyre's thought for Christian apologetics is his conception of the relation between faith and reason, rhetoric and dialectics, or Christianity and Greek ethics. John Milbank perceives a tension here. On the one hand, MacIntyre's philosophical perspective on Christianity affirms the rhetorical character of the Christian texts, and then attempts to secure their validity by a universal method, namely dialectics. On the other hand, his theological perspective proposes a mode of discourse involving the imaginative explication of Christian texts and pointing beyond dialectics. The tension exists partly because MacIntyre believes that *Thomas Aquinas has been able to achieve a perfect synthesis of Greek and Christian conceptions of virtues which hitherto were seen as incompatible.

This area of MacIntyre's thought is the most suggestive for Christian apologetics because it brings to light the complexity and ambiguity of the relation between faith and reason. On the one hand, MacIntyre is apprehensive about privileging the faith element because it may eclipse the role of rational argument, so reducing Christian faith to mere fideistic assertion. On the other, his tradition-constituted conception of rational inquiry forcefully points to the inescapability of pre-rational presuppositions as the very conditions for rational reflection. Knowledge cannot be based on certitudes self-evident to reason or logically demonstrable by reason; as many have argued, the notion that a *foundation for* reason can be found *within* reason itself is self-defeating.

MacIntyre is also well known for his controversial thesis that moral debates within contemporary liberal democratic culture suffer from 'interminability'. For example, debates over *abortion, distributive *justice and the legitimacy of warfare are inconclusive because consensus is impossible in our morally heterogeneous society. Our moral discourse is impoverished, and the language of political consensus is platitudinous and superficial, merely masking the reality of deep moral disagreement. To remedy the situation, MacIntyre proposes a re-examination of our moral heritage and the resuscitation and nurture of those forms of social life that stand some chance of resisting the managerial bureaucracy of the modern nation state and the institutions of

advanced *capitalism. This pessimistic analysis has been contested. If, however, there is any truth in it, and if it is conjoined with MacIntyre's general view that ideas and beliefs are always socially situated, then an implication is that, where Christian communities function as forms of social resistance, the intellectual plausibility of the Christian faith will be enhanced.

Bibliography

K. Knight (ed.), *The MacIntyre Reader* (Notre Dame, 1998); A. MacIntyre, *After Virtue* (Notre Dame, 1984); *Dependent Rational Animals* (Open Court, 1999); *A Short History of Ethics* (Notre Dame, 1998); *Three Rival Versions of Moral Inquiry* (Notre Dame, 1993); *Whose Justice? Which Rationality?* (Notre Dame, 1988).

S. GASSANOV

MAHAYANA, BUDDHISM, see BUDDHISM

MAIMON, MOSES BEN

Moses ben Maimon (also known by the Gk form of his name, Maimonides, and by the acronym Rambam) was born in Córdoba, Spain, in 1135, and is, arguably, the greatest of post-biblical Jewish religious scholars. Accounts of Christian thought often omit mention of him, but the history of Christian thought itself bears his imprint, especially through *Thomas Aquinas and *Thomism.

Persecuted by the ruling Almohad Muslims, Maimonides' family first fled Córdoba for Almería, and finally left Spain altogether for the more tolerant Egypt. They eventually settled in Fostat (Old Cairo) in 1169. From his youth, Maimonides steadily gained exceptional stature as a teacher, philosopher and physician, and by the mid-1180s, he was Sultan Saladin's physician and nagid (head) of Egypt's Jews.

While still in Spain, Maimonides had concluded that, while the Talmud stimulates (sometimes useful) discussion, the Mishnah, more importantly, elicits moral decision, which necessarily requires free moral agency. In 1168 he presented his understanding in a commentary on the Mishnah. Vigorous response ensued. Opponents, especially traditionalists, chided him for seldom referencing sources. Supporters lauded his use of the newly rediscovered *Aristotle and his insistence that they evaluate ideas on their own merits, including both rational coherence and tradition in the process, rather than appealing simply to the reputation of an author. Attaining to *truth, he said, requires thinking, the free use of the intellect in pursuit of moral meaning. Faithful thinking constitutes holiness. Love of thinking, of pursuing knowledge of God, expresses love for God.

The responses to the commentary compelled Maimonides to examine his ideas in the light of traditional Jewish understandings of the relationship between Torah and Mishnah. So in 1178 he presented his Mishnah Torah. Torah, the Word of God, he said, rules absolutely in matters concerning the knowledge of God, but Torah requires exegesis, for which Aristotelian philosophy is a uniquely suitable tool. Further, philosophy (primarily Aristotelianism) may witness independently to the truth of Torah, and apologists should demonstrate the harmony between the two. Methodologically, this requires maintenance of the integrity and authority of each. Resolving dissonance may require allegorizing, but allegorizing must not undermine reason, for reason must first receive divine *revelation.

According to Maimonides, Aristotle erred in holding that matter is eternal, that the human is but an expression of material nature (and therefore is not a free moral agent), and that the human soul is not immortal. Three revealed biblical assertions, therefore, limit Aristotelianism's usefulness to apologetics and adequate theology. First, the God of the Patriarchs created the heavens and the earth – in time and out of nothing. Secondly, God created humans to relate specially to him, graciously granting them free will, which entails moral responsibility. Thirdly, God offers *immortality to those who do justly.

Maimonides' *Guide for the Perplexed* appeared in 1190. Here, he addressed mature scholars who struggled with establishing a proper relationship between faith and reason. This task, said Maimonides, is not an end, but a means to knowing God. Metaphorically, the ideal is a morganatic marriage of prophetic illumination (via knowledge of Torah) and philosophical insight, each in full rigour and integrity. Engagement in this enterprise engenders and requires perfection of mind, character and *imagination.

Maimonides wrote primarily to edify fellow Jews, some of them hypercritical. Some Christian schoolmen, however, especially Thomists, seeking to synthesize all knowledge under the aegis of biblical faith, found in Maimonides a useful methodological model, which fully utilized Aristotle, even, ironically, to the point of rejecting on Aristotle's own grounds the Stagirite's own notions of the eternality of matter, the materiality of the human being (to the exclusion of the soul in any sense consonant with Scripture or Christian tradition), his denial of genuine human moral freedom (and hence moral responsibility), and his denial of human immortality.

Bibliography

I. Arbel, *Maimonides: A Spiritual Biography* (New York, 2001); A. J. Heschel, *Maimonides: A Biography* (ET, New York, 1982).

P. M. BASSETT

MARRIAGE

The Christian apologetic of marriage has a threefold character: (1) We must give reasons for marriage to be defined as it is (see below), that the public, lifelong faithfulness of one man and one woman is the only moral context for sexual intimacy. (2) We must give an account of the ends or purposes for which (we claim) marriage has been ordained in creation; that is, we must answer the question, 'What *good* (*bonum*) does marriage serve?' Traditionally, this has been answered in terms of the good of children, the good of the marriage relationship itself, and the good of preserving sexual and social order. All these may be considered under the governing ethic of the service of God in his world. (3) Finally, we will also want to show how marriage itself can be an apologetic for the living God and for Christ. The faithful love of husband for wife is to image the faithful love of God for his people, and that of Christ for his church; and the faithful love of wife for husband is to image the answering love of redeemed humankind for its God and Christ (e.g. Eph. 5:22–33). The experience of faithful love in marriage serves as a pointer that such a faithful love undergirds the whole of human life and indeed the created order.

In Western societies, marriage is no longer overwhelmingly accepted as the one proper context for sex. It is threatened both by the acceptance of sex outside marriage and by the growing practice of unmarried cohabitation, either as a prolonged preliminary to marriage or as an alternative social and sexual arrangement.

How may the Christian definition be commended? Five lines of argument may be suggested, none reliant on the presupposition of a shared submission to scriptural authority.

1. The longing for permanence. Embedded within every serious sexual relationship is the longing for permanence. The lyrics of love songs evidence this; no lover sings, 'I love you passionately *but only for a while.*' Human beings are persons with a history and a future, not free-floating individuals in free-floating pinpoints of time. At a deeply instinctive human level we perceive that a sexual relationship *ought* to last, and that if it breaks it introduces a fracture line into two human histories. Christians believe that this perception is rooted in the faithful love of one creator God for his own people – indeed, more deeply, with his one created order. The love of husband and wife in marriage images the love of God for his people and their answering love to him. This longing for permanence accords with the Christian doctrine of marriage as a pledge of faithfulness for life.

2. Disapproval of infidelity. There is a near-universal abhorrence of infidelity. Although marital unfaithfulness may be glamorized in some contexts (especially novels and films), social studies consistently show that in real life we recognize that it is wrong and shameful to cheat on a sexual partner, whether we are married or not. To do this compromises our integrity. This abhorrence accords with the Christian doctrine of publicly pledged fidelity.

3. The damaging effects of sexual disorder have been well documented in many social studies. Sexual chaos damages the health of both men and women, disadvantages them economically, harms their children and has a significant impact on housing needs (the proportion of single-occupant housing in the UK has multiplied by about 2.5 since 1961, and broken relationships account for much of this). The sexual liberation that accompanied 'the Great Disruption' (Fukuyama) from the 1960s onwards has had seriously negative effects upon social capital. It has also, paradoxically, shown that marriage, far from being solely in the interests of the male, serves to protect women from abuse and exploitation. In particular, there is a growing body of statistical evidence to show that unmarried cohabitation is significantly less stable than marriage.

4. The weakness of rampant individualism. Marriage is a necessary counterbalance to the rampant individualism that is damaging Western societies. Marriage ties a man and a woman into a wide social ecology; it makes of them a social as well as a sexual unit, and offers to that unit vital networks of wider social support, with protection for the weak and sanctions against the strong who abuse their *power in the break-up of a marriage.

5. The health-giving effect of an outward-looking ethic. A Christian understanding of marriage will emphasize the obligations that a couple have to serve the wider social order of a *community or society; this obligation is the focused expression for a particular couple of the common obligation of all human beings to serve the creator God in his world. These outward-looking obligations turn a couple beyond themselves (or their nuclear family) outwards in service. Paradoxically, such an outward-looking ethos serves to protect a marriage against the self-destructive effect of a purely relational intimacy. This latter inevitably leads to disillusion.

Each of these five arguments may be developed and incorporated into a Christian apologetic of marriage.

Bibliography

<http://www.marriage.rutgers.edu>; <http://www.statistics.gov.uk>; C. Ash, *Marriage: Sex in the Service of God* (Leicester, 2003); G. W. Bromiley, *God and Marriage* (Grand Rapids, 1980); D. Dormor, *The Relationship Revolution* (London, 1992); F. McAllister (ed.), *Marital Breakdown and the Health of the Nation* (London, 1995); P. Morgan, *Marriage-Lite: The Rise of Cohabitation and its Consequences* (London, 2000); P. Taylor, *For Better or Worse: Marriage and Cohabitation Compared* (London, 1998); H. Thielicke, *The Ethics of Sex* (ET, London, 1979).

C. ASH

MARTYRDOM

Biblical and historical precedents

Martyrdom and persecution have been a reality in the life of the Christian churches from the beginning. The biblical story considers the exodus from Egypt, a story of God's redemption of a group of slaves from their suffering under tyrannical rule, as a seminal event in the life of God's people, Israel. The central episode of the Christian story is the passion of *Jesus of Nazareth, the story of the plot against him, his arrest on trumped-up charges, his 'trial' in a succession of unjust hearings, his torture and death on a cross, the ultimate symbol of the power of Rome over its enemies. The pattern of Jesus' persecution and martyrdom (although Christians would consider the death of Jesus as much more than the term 'martyr' would imply) is reproduced in the lives of his followers. Following Jesus (and aware of his warning that those who hated him would also hate them, John 15:18), persecution and martyrdom soon became a reality of the life of the early church. Acts records that Stephen was the first 'martyr' (lit. a 'witness', in this case one who is willing to bear witness to Jesus even to the point of death), the first Christian put to death for believing in Jesus (Acts 7:54–60). Several NT books seem to have been written in order to strengthen Christian groups threatened with, or suffering under, persecution or martyrdom (e.g. Matt. 5:10–12; Luke 21:12–19; Heb. 12; Jas 1:2, 12; 1 Pet. 4:12–19; Rev. 6:9–11).

The example of patient perseverance under suffering was often a catalyst which led outsiders to faith in Christ, so that the North African theologian *Tertullian (c. 160–c. 225) could declare that 'the blood of the martyrs is the seed of the church'. This has proved true on more than one occasion, e.g. the origins of Christianity in Uganda are often traced back to a group of young Protestant and Catholic converts put to death under the 'Kabaka' in 1886.

It might be asked, then, whether Christians should seek persecution and martyrdom. The answer is that although martyrs have often been held in high esteem because of their faithfulness, seeking martyrdom is not a virtue in mainline Christian thought. Pragmatically, it did not always prove to be the case that martyrdom led to church growth: the intense persecution of the churches of North Africa and Nubia led to the demise and eventual extinction of these churches. Theologically, Christians have a high view of creation – 'God hates nothing that he has made' as one ancient prayer puts it – and Christians have no right to seek to end their own lives, even by

martyrdom. Biblical Christianity is not world-hating or world-denying but asserts that this world was created and redeemed by a God who loved it (John 3:16) and its destiny is not annihilation but renewal (see Rom. 8; 1 Cor. 15; Rev. 21). Christian martyrs also differ from, for example, *Islamic martyrs, and there is no Christian justification for martyrdom which involves inflicting violence on others in the course of taking one's own life for the sake of the cause. The Bible advocates love for enemies, not hatred (Matt. 5:44).

The modern situation

It may be a surprise for some that the modern period has proved to be the age with the largest number of Christian martyrs. In the contemporary world Christianity is often portrayed as a religion of 'the West', as European, intolerant, complicit with colonialism and, when present outside of Europe and North America, an offshoot of white hegemony sustained by Westernized elites or by people duped or bribed into accepting Christianity. Added to this characterization of Christianity as eurocentric is the suggestion that persecuted Christians are somehow psychological misfits who thirst for martyrdom. Both of these claims are mistaken.

Christians are not predominantly white: some two-thirds of nominal and four-fifths of active Christians live outside the West. More people attend worship in China, even illegally, than in all of western Europe combined. Christianity may now be the largest third-world religion. The average Christian is more likely to be a Chinese peasant, an Indian *dalit* ('untouchable': most Christians in India are *dalits*) or a Sudanese pastoralist than a Westerner. The average Anglican, for example, is a twenty-six year old Nigerian mother of four. The church's non-Western character has persisted for two millennia: the gospel was in Africa before Europe, India before England and China before America.

While there is no denying that there are persecutions in the name of Christ (such as by Serbians in Bosnia, or Russians in Chechnya), the overwhelming reality is that the church itself is heavily persecuted. In fact, it is the most widely persecuted religious body in the world. At the beginning of the third millennium, Christian communities in the countries and areas where such persecution occurs number about 230 million, while hundreds of millions more suffer from discrimination. These communities do not thirst for victimhood, they have it thrust upon them since their Christian witness, however passive, is a challenge and a threat to dominant powers.

In the remaining countries that call themselves communist or post-communist, there may be relative freedom to worship in state-controlled religious bodies, but all other religious expression is suppressed. In China, the Roman Catholic Church is illegal since it accepts an external authority, the Pope. Its priests and bishops have been imprisoned, while several hundred leaders of the Protestant underground church have been jailed and sent to labour camps. A similar pattern holds in Laos, Vietnam, Cuba, Turkmenistan and Uzbekistan. Reliable information on North Korea is scarce but it appears that almost every free Christian expression is viciously repressed, and large numbers of Christians have been sent to labour camps and prisons.

In South Asia, many Hindus and Buddhists identify their country with their religion, so that religious minorities, such as Christians, are often treated as second-class citizens and subjected to communal violent attack. In India, conversion laws are used to target Christians, and the number of religiously motivated attacks, particularly on clergy and other religious workers, has risen to several hundred a year. In Nepal and Bhutan, Christians suffer discrimination and arrest. In Sri Lanka, radical Buddhist monks often attack churches. In Myanmar (Burma), the regime in power wraps itself in a cloak of Buddhism and continues a war against the largely Christian eastern ethnic groups, a war that has destroyed whole villages and killed tens of thousands.

Growing Islamic extremism is producing intensifying attacks on Christians from Morocco to the southern Philippines (terrorists such as Osama bin Laden say explicitly that their war is against Christians and Jews, rather than the 'West' *per se*). In Saudi Arabia, private worship services are raided by the religious police, and worshippers are often imprisoned. There, and in some other Gulf states, in Mauritania, Iran, the Comoros Islands and Sudan, the legal code requires that any Muslim convert to Christianity be executed. In many other places, family members or vigilantes do the killing. In Sudan, the Khartoum regime has sought to impose its form of Islam on the largely Christian and animist south, and two million people have died of war-related causes. There has been widespread *slavery and forced conversion to Islam. In Egypt, the southern Philippines, Turkey, Bangladesh, Iran and Pakistan, the threat to Christians also comes from radical groups or mob violence. In north and central Nigeria, over 10,000 people have died in conflict over the introduction of Islamic law. In eastern Indonesia, Islamist militias such as Laskar Jihad have massacred thousands of Christians.

The reasons for such persecution, and the reasons for its growth, are many and complex, but one major factor is that, again contrary to many Western prejudices, the Christian church is now a major factor in creating free societies and democracies. Most of the world's genuinely free countries have a Christian background, and recent studies show that, even where the church is not politically active, it is a force for political freedom. Simply by claiming the right to hold its own beliefs free from external control, it claims that there must be space in society free from state direction. Simply by claiming that God's *authority is beyond Caesar's, it asserts that the state cannot be the ultimate authority. This is a challenge to every authoritarian regime.

Currently, the Christian church is a largely non-Western, non-white movement that is a major force for freedom both within and outside its own membership, and for which it suffers significant, unsought-for persecution and martyrdom.

Bibliography

D. Barrett, G. Kurian and T. Johnson, *World Christian Encyclopaedia*, 2nd edn, 2 vols. (Oxford and New York, 2001); S. Cunningham, *'Through Many Tribulations': The Theology of Persecution in Luke-Acts* (Sheffield, 1997); J. F. Faupel, *African Holocaust: The Story of the Ugandan Martyrs* (Nairobi, 1962); P. Jenkins, *The Next Christendom* (Oxford and New York, 2002); P. Marshall, *Their Blood Cries Out* (Dallas, 1997); *Religious Freedom in the World: A Global Report on Freedom and Persecution* (Nashville, 2000); J. S. Pobee, *Persecution and Martyrdom in the Theology of Paul* (Sheffield, 1985).

G. LeMarquand and P. Marshall

MARXISM, see COMMUNISM

MASS CULTURE
*Culture is a complex concept, which involves historical, sociological, political and artistic aspects. However, it may be defined simply as the way of life of a people. It is inevitably a social concept, and intrinsically reflects anthropological and aesthetic elements. Culture thus represents the collective achievements of humanity in general, and encompasses those symboling activities of society that form and express its values or sense of meaning. Culture is the social context in which we live our lives, including the invisible aspects, such as customs, ethical values and shared meaning, together with the visible symbols that express such values.

Mass culture is a relatively recent phenomenon, which highlights the globalized nature of culture in the contemporary world, made possible through the development of mass media (communication systems which transmit messages around the world, quickly and simultaneously), particularly *television, film, the internet and advertising in many forms. Mass culture embodies those signifying practices that are shared across localized cultures, creating symbols that are recognized by large numbers of people across boundaries of traditional culture.

Mass culture, at least in its contemporary guise, emerged through the turn of the twentieth century out of debate over its role as the antithesis of 'high' culture. High culture, within modernity, was connected to the historical avant garde, and an accompanying desire to preserve aesthetic purity and resist cultural 'contamination'. In the post-Second World War period, culture became a key participant in commodity production, and is now itself a commodity, as part of the 'culture industry'. Dependent on technologies of mass production that create a homogenization of difference, culture in the postmodern world becomes classless, in the sense that consumerism is classless. We may be tempted to think that mass culture is exclusive to those who have sufficient resources to participate in the consumer economy, but even those who are marginalized from actually generating the culture still share in its values, as those values are promoted by industry and adopted at least in potential.

In the postmodern world, mass culture is still seen sometimes in opposition to the values of high art and high culture, representing the lowest common denominator. In art, it is represented as a taste for the kitsch – things that in themselves lack meaning or aesthetic merit. They are symbols of the souvenirs of rapidly increasing numbers of people moving quickly up the social strata. Indeed, social philosopher Jean Baudrillard describes mass culture as 'lowest common culture'. He suggests that, unlike 'high' culture *per se*, mass culture precludes symboling or didactic activity, as that would inhibit participation. For Baudrillard, mass culture boils down to making a purchase. However, for others, mass culture is not a distraction from meaning, but rather a place where meaning is to be found.

Development of mass culture through the mass media
The development of mass culture is dependent on the development and growth of the mass media. The development of mass media must be traced back to the fifteenth century and the advent of Gutenberg's printing press. Many of the issues that define mass culture today have their origins in that period of history.

Financiers of early printing presses, including John Fust, who invested in Gutenberg's Bible production, immediately grasped the opportunity to make money from the process. The shift from painstaking copying of manuscripts to quick, relatively easy production of books was culturally revolutionary. Many thought that some supernatural power had intervened to bring about the appearance of so many printed texts in such a short time. Not surprisingly, the powerful guilds of copyists attributed it to demonic influences, in order to challenge the credibility of those trying to recover their investments by selling Bibles at the universities. It is impossible to turn history backwards on *technology, and a mass print culture developed that eventually changed the way that society operated, and the ways that people would learn and think.

Elizabeth Eisenstein has pointed to some of the features of print culture that initiated such changes. Increased input and altered intake gave people a chance to compare texts, which increased reading, literacy and knowledge. Standardization of texts led to standardization and codification in many fields of knowledge. Rationalizing, codifying and cataloguing of data enable the body of knowledge to grow. Print culture allowed for revisions, corrections and improvements to texts, and this accelerated the rate of knowledge. It also inhibited memory and fostered an individualized culture, as people could trade public hearing for private reading. Moreover, it fostered a drive for fame through personal celebrity, as people could extend their popularity through publishing pamphlets, plays and books of all kinds.

The dissemination of information meant that there was now the possibility of influencing large numbers of people without initiating a public gathering. The promotion of ideas through pamphlets fostered competitions to sway public opinion. A period of debate over censorship ensued, which raised debate over issues of freedom and *authority. In 1644 John Milton's *Areopagitica* championed the case for liberty of unlicensed printing. Directing his case to Parliament, he argued that authors and publishers should be free from external constraint and able to write, print and disseminate their views without fear of persecution and control. Liberty for the individual conscience was his ultimate goal. Before the advent of the printing press, such ideas would not have been comprehensible. Within a few years, the cumulative rate of change would increase through the influence of the printing press and the first developments of mass culture.

By the beginning of the twentieth century, the printing press had changed Western society drastically. But culture would soon be transformed almost beyond recognition as technology escalated at a phenomenal pace, bringing to birth mass culture as it is known today. Print culture gave way to the development of the electric media as film, the telegraph, radio and the telephone brought communications to a new level of immediacy. Gathering around the radio in the evenings, entire families, communities and nations began to share together moments of *entertainment history, advertising and unfolding news events. Radio brought to every home the propinquity of shared experience, which could be surpassed only by the advent of television in the middle of the century. At the cinema, newsreels delivered major world events to local communities. Film further offered *escapism from the troubles of life as the entertainment industry made its mark on Western culture. It would later become a fulcrum for reflection on culture, *ethics and meaning.

Television did more to influence the development and direction of mass culture than any other medium in the twentieth century. More accessible than cinema, and more riveting than radio, television with its visual image has changed the way that culture functions, much as the printing press did five hundred years earlier. Because it is available to anyone with even a primitive power supply, broadcasters send images around the world and into space, transmitting and reflecting the values of a people. With it, television advertising transmits consumer values to those who are able to afford them, or at least aspire to them. Wherever television goes, new markets open up. Local cultures are overwhelmed by the products, lifestyles and values of the characters on the screen.

Moreover, increased mobility has led to the formation of diverse multicultural communities in many places. A globalized cultural blend, dominated by the values of the marketplace, has grown into a mass culture, despite some localized resistance and fragmented impetus towards reforming national identities. Notwithstanding the efforts of anti-*globalization movements, the symbols of Coca-Cola and the golden arches are amongst the most universally recognized emblems in the world.

In the contemporary world, a new revolution is at once fostering the globalization of mass culture and militating against it. The influence of digital technology, particularly through the internet, but increasingly through digital television, radio and mobile telephones, allows for increased cultural participation for any who have the resources to become connected. Interactivity, customized choice and networking have become the watchwords of the age. Immediacy, access to information rather than developing knowledge, and an increased emphasis on the image over the word are all trends that began with television but are reinforced in a digital age. Immateriality and temporality are also marks of digital media. *Reality in a digital mass culture is transient; *truth is subjective and created. Just as the printing press brought about irreversible change, so the digital revolution is initiating significant shifts in global culture; the way we interact with the mass media structures how we learn, what we learn and our apprehension of reality.

Mass culture and apologetics

Mass media, mass marketing and their creation of mass culture have provided varied opportunities for apologetics in recent decades. The mid to late 1900s witnessed the development of mass evangelism and the use of all types of mass media for sharing the gospel message locally and globally. First on radio, and then through television, ministries sprang up to take advantage of the huge audiences promised through the use of modern media. Billy Graham is perhaps the best-known amongst Christian leaders who sought to use the mass media to the best advantage for the sake of spreading the news of Christ. Embracing radio, television and print media, Graham's organization was able to reach mass audiences with evangelistic crusades and other ministries. Engaging the resources of mass culture is an important aspect of Christian communication in the modern and postmodern worlds. In North America, television evangelists of diverse backgrounds and affiliations have sprung up, which has, in a few instances, gone some way towards discrediting the faith as the consumerist pressures of celebrity and financial gain take their toll. The use of mass media with integrity is a significant challenge for those who seek to access mass culture for Christian ministry.

In Britain, the existence of publicly funded television and an established church has served to restrict access to broadcasting and mass media for religious purposes. Licensing restrictions have prevented the proliferation of radio and television ministries that is seen in the United States, though more recent days have witnessed growth in Christian radio broadcasting. Nevertheless, single-faith broadcasting is largely discouraged in multi-faith Britain. Such issues of control are becoming largely redundant in a world of internet, digital and other satellite communications. No form of effective control has been found to restrict religious or any other activity on the internet and in digital broadcasting. Everything religious is to be found there, from virtual church to alternative worship experiences. Rather than supporting the development of shared values, the internet is a forum of self-expression and eternal searching, with little expectation of finding single solutions to the basic problems of human existence. Nevertheless, some Christians have grasped the significance of being a ministry presence in *cyberspace, and are creating methods of using that tool to meet the needs of individuals who may be searching for more than a website.

Christians have varied in their attitudes towards the use of advertising to promote the gospel. Some suggest that to participate in advertising is to promote the gospel as a consumer product, and so have resisted methods of advertising faith as a consumer item. Others acknowledge that in a mass culture, advertising is the accepted and most effective form of communication, and seek to use it to the church's advantage. The Alpha programme is just one example of the church engaging the new media and forging a presence in mass culture, through brand development.

Mass culture also provides opportunities for apologetic engagement that cuts across the diversity of communities and local cultures. Recognizing the postmodern condition of mass culture means that we must engage its icons. As high culture was once regarded as the realm for seeking and reflecting on meaning, so mass culture serves that function in contemporary culture. Theological reflection on television shows like *The Simpsons* and in the cinema provides the opportunity to offer a Christian perspective on issues, ideas and values that are pervasive in culture. In this sense, Christians identify with the mass culture of which we are part.

The question remains as to whether it is possible for Christians to identify so closely with mass culture that any sense of distinctiveness is lost. Certainly some would highlight the limits of accessing truth that is not culturally conditioned. If all truth is mediated truth, then we should not seek to be separate from mass culture, but should be alert to signifiers of God within mass culture. This creates a mandate to use mass culture as a vehicle for presenting and understanding God at work in the world. Others suggest that since mass culture is based on consumer values, commodifying everything within its realm, Christians ought to resist mass culture. Resistance may range from critical engagement and transformation to an active 'Christ against culture' stance, which provides an alternative witness to the values of God's kingdom.

When Christians become indistinguishable from the culture around them, their apologetic witness is disempowered. If a Christian life is based on the same acquisition of goods as the rest of the world, only with Christian slogans and lyrics, are we providing a credible witness to Christ? Are we building communities that welcome all kinds of people, regardless of whether they stand at the centre or on the margins of mass culture? Or do we allow mass culture to define our popular leaders within a cult of celebrity? Are we engaging mass culture for the purposes of propagating the message of the gospel or are we using engagement to mask our own level of comfort with our cultural skin? Are we happy to use the mass culture for the marketing of Christian books, programmes and personalities? Or does the church need to demonstrate relationships of integrity that are not simply links in the consumerist chain?

These are challenging questions that demand apologetic engagement. The increased sense of alienation and loss of meaning in contemporary culture is not surprising when the values of consumer culture are reflected in icons and symbols of unfulfilled desire. In order to self-perpetuate and to generate the economy, such desire must remain unfulfilled in mass culture. But if members of the church are willing to wrestle with such questions, they may find that their prophetic and apologetic voices connect with culture in ways that bring Christ's transforming grace to fulfil the desire of hearts that are conditioned by the values of mass culture.

Bibliography

C. Bartholomew and T. Moritz (eds.), *Christ and Consumerism* (Carlisle, 2000); J. Baudrillard, *The Consumer Society* (London, 1998); T. Eagleton, *The Idea of Culture* (Oxford, 2000); A. Huyssen, *After the Great Divide* (Basingstoke, 1986).

A. M. ROBBINS

MATERIALISM (ETHICAL)

Materialism is the view that the gaining and possession of material things is the highest goal in life. A desire to acquire material goods is considered by some to be part of human nature. Human beings appear to love things. In all cultures we observe that people like to buy, exchange and collect things. The belief that the accumulation of material goods brings ultimate happiness drives many individuals to formulate their life's goals, plans and desires purely in terms of acquiring goods. In some instances this is taken to the point where they live for material things and even define themselves and their lives according to what they own. When this desire to accumulate material goods is joined by greater prosperity, it enables the person to acquire goods beyond those required for their basic needs. Add to this the availability of attractive new goods, marketing and the desire to emulate members of a higher social group, and you have a consumer society. Such conditions emerged in late seventeenth and early eighteenth-century Western Europe and are generally held to be the beginnings of what we call the materialist society.

This was also the period when modern *science was beginning to take root and, along with it, views about human nature. Thomas Hobbes (1588–1679) thought that people were driven by two motives: the fear of death and of other people and the *evil they may do, and the desire for pleasure and glory. Hobbes also held that children are born concerned only with themselves, and although they can be trained and educated to be concerned for others, they rarely are. Thus, from Hobbes, we conclude that people have concern primarily for themselves and can never be secure enough or have enough. People always desire more, and what they desire is predicated upon what others have or want. To satisfy this desire people must always be striving to outdo others who are seen as competitors. Hobbes was a philosophical materialist, so when he describes human nature in this way he is really saying that you cannot be a person and act in any other way. People are machines, they may influence the forces acting on them, but they cannot influence themselves.

In addition to this, the rise of science and this materialistic view of the universe may have, in a different way, contributed to the notion that happiness can be obtained through the amassing of material goods and wealth. If all that can be known is material, then traditional moral norms cannot be known to be real. Moral norms, after all, are not material things. Hence, it is difficult to see how science is able to test or even confirm the existence of such immaterial things. Moreover, if science is to be the accepted method to tell us what is real, then we can only conclude that any talk of moral *absolutes is meaningless.

Hobbes and his contemporaries were not the first to formulate a materialistic view of the universe. The atomist Epicurus held that the universe was just matter and void and, like Hobbes, believed that the greatest fear for humans was death. Epicurus added that we also fear the punishment that we face after death for the wrongs that we commit in this life. As Epicurus' philosophy is therapeutic, he consoles us by denying that there is any life after death. If we are only atoms, then at death we will be annihilated and unable to face any ultimate judgment. This thesis establishes a vast gulf between Epicureanism and matter–spirit dualistic doctrines such as Christianity, Platonism and Cartesianism.

This view also opens the way for happiness, or the good life, to be sought purely by seeking after the pleasures of this life rather than the rewards or punishment of an after-life. If a better material life is what gives the agent the greatest pleasure then seeking after material goods or wealth becomes the ultimate aim. Even though materialism and consumerism have gained in momentum, this type of lifestyle has prompted serious doubts about its promise to deliver happiness.

Henry David Thoreau (1817–62) noted that most people spent their lives superficially by seeking after wealth and following custom. His claim was that the pursuit of more goods had forced Americans to labour unceasingly and thus, ironically, lessened their quality of life. His adopted style of living showed that to maintain oneself on this earth should not be a hardship but a pastime.

Georg W. F. *Hegel (1770–1831) also realized quite early on the way that the consumer society was heading. In a section of *The Philosophy of Right* he argues that what the English call comfort is something inexhaustible and illimitable, and that the need for greater comfort is not created by those who experience it directly but by those who hope to make a profit from its emergence.

What is wrong then with adopting a materialistic life that most people seem to enjoy? Materialism is hard to argue against, for many people outwardly appear to enjoy its initial reward of an accumulation of goods. How can we protest against a lifestyle that delivers a better material life?

Recent research seems to indicate that even though cultures have become more affluent, people have not become happier. Americans earn at least twice as much in dollars as they did in 1957, yet surveys from the National Research Center show a decline in those who declare themselves as 'very happy'. Other research shows that the pursuit of materialistic goals may actually be undermining our well-being. Our needs for security and safety, relationships with others, self-esteem and autonomy are generally unsatisfied when materialistic values are held strongly. Additionally, our desire for goods easily becomes addictive. It appears that as we get used to accumulating these goods that are not basic needs, we no longer consider them additional 'luxuries' but view them as necessities. Few people in the industrialized nations would deem, for example, items such as cars, washing machines, microwave ovens and televisions as luxury items but basic essentials for living a happy life. Also, we seem to want more because we become disappointed with consumption of the same things. And because our materialistic lives prevent those basic needs of security, relationships, self-esteem and autonomy from being met, we feel an additional emptiness which we then try to fill by consuming even more. Thus, we find ourselves addicted to, and in pursuit of ever new and more exciting goods and experiences, the very things that caused us to feel dissatisfied in the first place.

What is the Christian view of materialism? It is clear from 1 Tim. 5:8 that some attention must be given to material things in order to provide for your own household. However, Eph. 4:28 adds that the labour of one's hands is also to be used to give to those that are in need. This passage charges us to provide for the needy and not to amass material wealth or goods for ourselves. It should also be noted that it is the *love* of money, and not money itself, that is described as the root of all evil (1 Tim. 6:10). Thus, although some attention needs to be paid to material things this does not imply that we must be materialistic.

Christ's teachings in Luke give an account of the positions of the poor and the rich in God's eyes: 'Blessed are you who are poor, for yours is the kingdom of God ... But woe to you who are rich, for you have already received your comfort' (Luke 6:20, 24). In Matthew's Gospel Christ warns us, 'Do not store up for yourselves treasures on earth, where moth and rust destroy ... But store up for yourselves treasures in *heaven, where moth and rust do not destroy' (Matt. 6:19–20). He also warns against accumulating wealth and not being 'rich towards God' (Luke 12:21). It appears that it is not material goods, wealth or the wealthy that God condemns, but rather a preoccupation with material goods that excludes the worship of God. This is confirmed by Christ's statement that 'No-one can serve two masters. Either he will hate the one and love the other, or he will be devoted to the one and despise the other. You cannot serve both God and money' (Matt. 6:24). It seems clear from these and numerous other scriptures that those who have material wealth or possessions are under obligation to assist those who have less.

However, there are very few people who seek to gain material wealth or possessions with the intention of helping others. They hold to the ethical doctrine, if it can be called that, that consideration of oneself is the only goal or aim in life. Concern only for your own needs is egoism and is thus contrary to the teachings of Christ and the message of loving your neighbour as yourself. The Christian tradition offers a life where true fulfilment is found only through losing self and in sharing and giving within a communal society.

Bibliography

T. Kasser, *The High Price of Materialism* (Massachusetts and London, 2002); B. Schwartz, *The Costs of Living: How Market Freedom Erodes the Best Things in Life* (New York and London, 1994); P. N. Stearns, *Consumerism in World History: The Global Transformation of Desire* (London and New York, 2001).

S. DUFFIN

MATERIALISM (PHILOSOPHICAL/METAPHYSICAL)

In simplest terms, materialism (or physicalism) is the philosophical doctrine that on the ultimate level of *reality, when one gets to the bottom of existence, all is matter. The exact content of the view depends upon what one takes matter to be and upon what characteristics and capabilities one takes matter to have. Classical materialists saw matter as consisting of tiny unalterable bits of substance which interacted in purely mechanical ways to constitute all objects and events in the cosmos – including us. Contemporary materialists see matter as the strange, nearly unpicturable waves, energies and fields of contemporary physics, which interact in the utterly non-intuitive ways postulated by quantum mechanics. But whatever matter is taken to be, philosophical materialism rules out the ultimate, fundamental existence of a mental or spiritual reality independent of matter.

Materialism derives its plausibility and attractiveness from several sources. First, by promising a single, unifying explanatory principle, it offers conceptual elegance. Secondly, the ever expanding success of the purely physical *sciences looks to many like an affirmation that all is indeed ultimately physical. (Scientism – the view that science is the *only* route to genuine knowledge and/or is in principle a reliable route to all knowledge – combined with the popular contention that science deals only with material [physical] reality, strongly suggests materialism and is frequently allied with it.) Thirdly, materialism offers a freedom from ultimate accountability. If there is no spiritual realm, then there is no supreme being to demand and enforce such accountability. Fourthly, if all is material, then while there may be beings more advanced than are we, they too are finite products of natural processes, having no profoundly different status than do we. Consequently, even if we turn out not to be the top of the cosmic heap, at least there will be nothing else to which we rightly owe reverence, worship and submission.

This all-encompassing philosophical materialism has been challenged from a number of standpoints. Such materialism conflicts with key religious doctrines – the existence of a transcendent God, for instance – and some argue that it undermines any objective *morality as well. Philosophically, some have argued that matter is capable neither of eternal existence on its own nor of emergence from non-existence, and that thus the very existence of matter itself demonstrates that matter cannot be the whole story of reality. It has also often been argued that even within nature we find things and processes – such as life, consciousness and evidences of deliberate design – which even if they themselves were wholly material could not be fully explained without ultimate reference to things lying beyond the material realm. Ironically, although materialism has often been thought to be the 'scientific' position, cases against materialism have themselves recently acquired a scientific flavour, e.g. recent arguments concerning both cosmological fine tuning and biological design. And many philosophers of science contend that by its very nature, science is not capable of either generating or dealing with all *truth – much less capable of establishing a sweeping philosophical materialism.

Material subdomains

Most who reject a sweeping philosophical materialism endorse some type of metaphysical dualism – the position that both a material and an immaterial realm exist. Such dualism, of course, leaves open the possibility that while reality itself is not wholly material, some subdomains of reality might be. (Most of those who reject materialism would, nonetheless, insist that, say, stars or automobiles are wholly physical objects.) Historically, some Christians, while denying that the material realm is all that exists, nevertheless took nature to be a wholly material realm, governed by natural laws, and argued that it was to be investigated and explained in terms of purely material concepts. Many contemporary Christians, while also denying that the material realm is all that exists, nonetheless accept methodological naturalism or methodological materialism – the view that proper scientific method can employ only material concepts, procedures and theories. Although methodological naturalism has recently become controversial, the truly fiery disputes rage over whether human beings fall into a 'wholly material' subdomain of reality.

Anthropological materialism or physicalism

This is the view that humans are fundamentally material beings, and comes in a variety of forms, of which I will mention only a few. For instance, behaviourism alleges that references to thought, intent, and other 'mental' processes do not refer to immaterial 'mental' phenomena but are ultimately just shorthand ways of referring to observable physical behavioural tendencies – much as references to an 'average person' do not refer to a real entity – a person – but are just shorthand ways of referring to distributions of characteristics in a population. Identity theory points to neurophysiological activity and events in the brain, and says that is what thoughts, thinking and consciousness *are*. A particular network of brain connections being active is not something which either merely accompanies, causes or results from a fear of large spiders – that neural activity *is* the fear. According to functionalism, neurophysiological states are properly classified as mental not because they have special 'mental' characteristics, but because of the causal roles they play in inner and outer human activity. In all three views, although properties and processes such as consciousness or thinking may be very special and complex, they are nonetheless completely describable in terms of physical structures, components and processes. Nothing, on this view, would preclude future development of a conscious computer.

Most materialist philosophers believe that matter is the only substance – the only kind of stuff – that exists. Some materialists, however, argue that contrary to the three views just mentioned, genuinely mental properties cannot be exhaustively understood in terms just of complexes of physical properties, structures and processes. However, the argument continues, some material entities having very special structures can have not only physical properties (such as mass, colour, shape) but can also have genuinely non-physical mental characteristics. On this view (known as property dualism), thinking, consciousness and similar properties are special, genuinely mental properties, but the objects which have those properties (brains) are physical things – there are no independently existing immaterial human minds (no such immaterial things).

Anthropological materialism has struck most people (and most philosophers) as not only contrary to common sense but as having insurmountable difficulties (both philosophical and theological). Philosophically, to many it has seemed indisputable that minds (or souls) are things that reason, have beliefs and have consciousness, and equally indisputable that purely material explanations are inadequate. Consciousness and thoughts, it is argued, have directly experienced qualities – mental *feels* – which no purely physical object, no matter how complex, could have or could produce. Indeed, it is argued, thoughts are usually *about* something, and it does not even make sense to think of a flow of electrons, changing concentrations of neurotransmitters, neuron activity, ion exchanges or other such physical brain processes as being *about* something – much less consciously about it.

Furthermore, materialist conceptions of humans have been criticized as being deterministic and as eroding processes of reason. If matter is governed by laws and humans are ultimately material, it is difficult to see what genuine human free will could be. And if thought itself is just physical/chemical interactions, then beliefs arise ultimately not from rational deliberation, but from unguided physical processes in one's brain, determined ultimately by random events resulting from the explosion of this particular cosmos out of the Big Bang.

Anthropological materialism is not without responses, but even if it can survive other objections, there remains one which many see as insurmountable. Most religions teach that there is another life after this one – that the self, the person, the soul does not die when the physical body does. But if human persons are ultimately just physical (or physical-dependent), then death of the physical body will necessarily constitute eternal extinction of the person. If so, then anthropological materialism, like philosophical materialism, is inconsistent with most religions.

Anthropological substance dualism

This is the view that there are two realms – a material and an immaterial – and that human beings (at least in this life) are unions of body and mind, flesh and spirit, dust and soul, and are thus firmly anchored in both realms.

Dualists differ over which realm (if either) is more fundamental. Among those seeing matter as ultimate, emergentists take minds and consciousness to emerge out of special types of purely physical complexity, just as fluidity emerges out of suitable collections of water molecules (none of which individually exhibits fluidity). Epiphenomenalists see minds and consciousness as by-products of physical brain processes. On most views of this sort, immaterial minds may actually exist, but they are wholly dependent upon the material in that if all material objects ceased to exist, all minds and consciousness would cease to exist as well.

Most Christians, on the other hand, take the immaterial, spiritual realm as ultimate, seeing the material realm as depending for its existence upon God's creative activity. Substance dualism of this latter type has historically been the most popular position. It fits commonsense conceptions of human beings, accords well with our internal experience of our self and our mental life, coheres with the way most Christians read Scripture, and provides an intuitively attractive explanation of survival of bodily death and life after death.

But anthropological dualism has its own difficulties. Dualists have been unable to say much about the exact nature of the postulated immaterial mind – except that it is immaterial and thinks. How something immaterial might be better able to support consciousness, thinking

and similar processes than can something material is almost never addressed and may upon scrutiny turn out to be just as puzzling as the idea of something purely material being able to think. (On the other hand, most people believe that dogs are conscious, feel fear and so forth, despite being completely material.) Furthermore, despite centuries of effort, dualists have made little apparent progress explaining how such profoundly different things as immaterial minds and material bodies can interact with each other – the traditional mind/body problem. (That problem is not universally thought to be as devastating as it once was, however.)

Christian anthropological materialism

Seeing the difficulties with dualism, and convinced that some of the difficulties facing anthropological materialism may yield to scientific investigation, some Christian thinkers are now trying to reconcile anthropological materialism with religious orthodoxy. The difficulties are daunting, but perhaps not completely insurmountable. For instance, a number of physicalist possibilities concerning life after death are currently being explored. Although involving philosophical difficulties, one intuitively plausible proposal is that God created each of us once and, being omnipotent, can create (or re-create) each of us again after death for an eternal afterlife.

Conclusion

While philosophical materialism is clearly inconsistent with *theism, methodological and anthropological materialism, although controversial, may not be in irremediable conflict with basic theistic or Christian tenets. These issues are all areas of ongoing investigation among Christian thinkers.

Bibliography

W. Hasker, *Metaphysics: Constructing a Worldview* (Downers Grove, 1983); *The Emergent Self* (Ithaca, 1999); J. P. Moreland and S. B. Rae, *Body and Soul: Human Nature and the Crisis in Ethics* (Downers Grove, 2000); P. van Inwagen, *Metaphysics* (Boulder, 1993).

D. RATZSCH

MESSIANIC JUDAISM, see JUDAISM

METAPHYSICS

Metaphysics is the branch of philosophy which seeks to work out the most basic structure of *reality by means of systematic and critical thought. The British metaphysician F. H. Bradley defined it as 'the study of *first principles or ultimate truths'. To this he added 'the effort to comprehend the universe, not simply piecemeal or in fragments, but as a whole'. The use of the word 'metaphysics' has frequently been restricted to systems which do seek to comprehend the whole of reality. A complete metaphysical system would show the nature and relationships of God, matter, mind, science and ethics – perhaps more. Metaphysical positions and arguments can, however, be advanced simply in respect of certain parts or aspects of the universe, e.g. the *idealism of *Berkeley is certainly 'metaphysics' although it deals only with questions about the nature (or reality) of matter.

The actual word 'metaphysics' derives from a book by *Aristotle which in his collected works came after (Gk, *meta*) his writings on physics. Aristotle may be seen as one of those metaphysicians who sought to make explicit the patterns of our normal thought about the world and articulate our experience of it. Other metaphysicians, perhaps the majority, have thought that these patterns were in some way defective and have tried to find better ones, seeking to reason their way to that which lies behind our experience.

We should note that many philosophers have criticized the idea of metaphysics, if it is taken as a way of getting to an ultimate reality beyond that of experience. This was true e.g. of Immanuel *Kant, who argued that the 'categories' which make experience possible, such as cause, substance and unity, are not part of reality in itself, but only conditions of our experiencing it. Hence they cannot be used to go beyond experience to God, the soul or the world as a whole. The logical positivists of the twentieth century were even more hostile, claiming that metaphysical assertions were devoid of any real meaning as there was no way to test their truth. Such extreme positions are probably less widely held today than they once were, though there are still some who regard at least metaphysical *systems*, as opposed to particular arguments or positions, with scepticism.

Metaphysics is clearly likely to have implications for religion, *theology and apologetics.

The most obvious area is that of '*natural theology'. If there is a god, there cannot be a more basic first principle or ultimate truth than his existence, and many metaphysicians have thought they could prove this, or have incorporated the existence of God into their system. But many other concepts in common use among Christians may also have metaphysical implications, such as 'soul', 'creation', 'miracle', 'heaven', 'revelation' and the like. To employ these involves commitment, explicit or implicit, to views about the basic structure of reality.

The relationship between Christianity and metaphysics has, however, varied enormously. There have been metaphysicians who saw themselves as above all serving God and his church; many of the great medieval thinkers like *Thomas Aquinas or St *Bonaventura would come in this class. Others, though believers, worked to some extent independently of their beliefs. They thought of themselves as primarily philosophers, though, being Christians, they believed a true philosophy would provide room for the faith. *Descartes, *Leibniz, *Locke and Berkeley might serve as examples. Yet others were actively hostile to religion, like David *Hume in the eighteenth century or Bertrand *Russell in the twentieth. Finally, there have been metaphysicians who saw their metaphysics as *replacing* Christianity with something better. *Hegel would be an example and so would *Spinoza (though in his case it was Judaism as much as Christianity that he thought needed to be superseded).

Conversely, there have been Christian thinkers who saw metaphysics as an ally, and others who saw it as an irrelevance, or even an enemy. Aquinas can be seen as an example of the former approach. He took over the philosophy of Aristotle, then recently rediscovered, and in effect integrated it into Christian thought both to defend the faith and to help Christians understand the contents of that faith. (His two most famous works, the *Summa contra Gentiles* and the *Summa Theologiae*, might serve respectively as examples of these two approaches.) Similarly, in the eighteenth century Jonathan *Edwards incorporated a good deal of John Locke's thought into his own. In the nineteenth century there were a number of Christian Hegelians, some fairly orthodox, such as H. L. Martensen in Denmark (at least in his earlier writings) and John Caird in Scotland. There were also thinkers in the Hegelian tradition who were bitterly opposed to Christianity, such as D. F. *Strauss and Ludwig *Feuerbach. More recently the 'process philosophy' of Alfred North *Whitehead has been taken up by a number of 'process theologians'.

This kind of approach can have considerable apologetic value among those who share metaphysical views. It is less likely to impress the ordinary doubter or enquirer, except perhaps in so far as they may have been affected by a prevailing philosophical tendency. And it has an obvious drawback, in that if the metaphysics used is rejected (or simply goes out of fashion) the Christian version shares its fate. As a result, it has happened that much which was valuable in the thought of metaphysical Christian thinkers gets lost, or needs to be sorted out by later generations from among what seems to them unnecessary lumber.

An example of this is Aquinas' celebrated 'five ways' of proving the reality of God which are embedded in his *Summae*. One of these ways, the argument from the existence of motion to that of a prime mover, was taken almost word for word from Aristotle's *Physics* and depends heavily on Aristotle's theory of motion, which few would accept today. The other four ways, however, are not so dependent on Aristotelian metaphysics, and can more easily be debated in their own right, as can many of Aquinas' other arguments and theories. But they have to be detached from Aquinas' system for this to be done, and as a result we do not perceive them in quite the way Aquinas himself would have perceived them. The problem is even greater with Hegelian and process theologians, where it is harder to detach particular parts of the system.

At the opposite extreme, some Christian thinkers have wanted to reject metaphysics completely. The Bible, after all, makes no mention of it and on the contrary insists that human wisdom is incapable of knowing God (1 Cor. 1 and 2 are of course the classic passages here). Moreover, even among those philosophers who wish to do metaphysics there is no general agreement. Natural theology, the aspect of metaphysics apparently most relevant to Christianity (and especially apologetics), is thus (it is claimed) warranted neither by Scripture nor by reason. Some, such as Karl *Barth, have even seen it as an implicit *rejection* of the biblical faith. There can be no knowledge of God except through Jesus Christ as he is revealed to us in Scripture, and to claim

that there is is to set oneself above God's *revelation.

Defenders of Christian metaphysics may reply that there is a world of difference between knowing intellectually that there is a God and knowing this God as our Father and Lord; it is the latter that depends upon the revelation in Christ. They point to passages like Acts 14:17 and 17:22–31 or Rom. 1:18–20, and argue that often the only way to meet opponents of Christianity is to show that even on their own terms they are in the wrong – which will require metaphysical arguments, even if not a metaphysical system. For instance, surely Christians will hold that materialist metaphysical positions which deny the existence of anything except matter are certainly false and can be argued against. Again, even if philosophical arguing for the reality of God is abandoned, the *language of religion and theology calls for metaphysical thought. Much of the metaphorical language so often used to describe the God of the Bible, like 'transcendent' 'creative' and 'omnipotent', can only be understood in metaphysical terms. Christian opponents of metaphysics, however, might answer that, for them, such terms must derive their meaning from the Bible and not from any preconceived philosophy. Yet, to quote Leonard Hodgson, 'the prophet's proclamation inevitably becomes a matter of study for the philosophical inquirers; it can only be tested by asking whether it can assimilate and interpret without distorting them all the observed facts of existence.'

It should be remembered, too, that metaphysics and Christianity come into contact in areas other than debates over proving the reality of God, e.g. in the long tradition in Christian thought of seeing body and spirit as two distinct kinds of thing (dualism), which are united during a human life but can exist separately, the latter perhaps for ever. But once again it has been argued by some theologians that this is unbiblical, that our hope is for the resurrection of the body, not the immortality of the soul, and many philosophers are highly critical of dualism. They hold there are certainly 'mental' expressions and descriptions, but these describe the whole person (or possibly aspects of the brain), not a mysterious substance whose relationship to the body is very hard to state. Now this debate is clearly of importance to Christian apologists, and it is equally clearly a metaphysical one, and the metaphysician may legitimately claim to be heard in it. Of course, it does also bring in questions of biblical interpretation, such as whether the absence of dualist language in the OT is simply a matter of lack of sophistication, and whether it is continued in the New.

Yet again, there has been much debate among Christians about the extent, if any, to which the human will can properly be described as 'free'. But this is also of great interest to the metaphysician. It is perhaps true to say as a generalization that the more systematic metaphysicians have denied free will or asserted it only in a very restricted sense, and that most metaphysicians who have defended 'libertarian' free will have not been system-builders. But the debate has been prolonged and has greatly affected the theological debate as well. Indeed, much of the latter has been conducted in philosophical terms. A good example of this is Jonathan Edwards' defence of Calvinism in *A Careful and Strict Inquiry into the Freedom of the Will*, which is not a survey of the biblical evidence but a discussion of philosophical arguments about the meaning of free will and about its reality.

While it is therefore risky for apologists to commit themselves to one particular metaphysical system, even one which they believe to be correct, it is clearly advisable for them to be acquainted with metaphysical ideas and arguments and to be ready to use them if they are to give a reason for the hope that is in them.

Bibliography

A. J. Ayer, 'The Claims of Metaphysics', in *The Central Questions of Philosophy* (London, 1973); C. D. Broad, 'Critical and Speculative Philosophy', in J. H. Muirhead (ed.), *Contemporary British Philosophy* (London, 1924); W. Hasker, *Metaphysics: Constructing a World View* (Downers Grove and Leicester, 1983); L. Hodgson, 'Faith and Philosophy' in *The Grace of God in Faith and Philosophy* (London, 1936); D. F. Pears (ed.), *The Nature of Metaphysics* (London, 1957); R. Taylor, *Metaphysics* (Englewood Cliffs, 1974); W. H. Walsh, *Metaphysics* (London, 1963).

R. L. STURCH

MILL, JOHN STUART

John Stuart Mill (1806–73) is the most important and influential of nineteenth-century British philosophers and a founding father, along with Jeremy Bentham (1748–1832), of classical *utilitarianism. Mill remains an important influence in moral theory, political theory and, to some extent, in religious thought.

Mill's most important work is *Utilitarianism* (London, 1863). A philosophical hedonist, Mill argues that pleasure alone is desired for its own sake and that all else is desired or avoided either for the pleasure or the absence of pain or as a means to achieving pleasure or avoiding pain. Good actions are those bringing about a greater amount of pleasure and/or a lesser amount of pain for all those affected. Mill endorses Bentham's 'greatest happiness principle', our duty is to do what will bring about the greatest good, in terms of pleasure, for all. Radically impartialist, Mill argues that our duties extend to all sentient creatures. Partiality to one's family or friends is morally justified only insofar as pleasure for all is thereby maximized.

Although he retains the consequentialist and impartialist aspects of Bentham's utilitarianism, Mill significantly alters Bentham's *hedonism in his claim that the quality of pleasure is as important as its quantity. Mill distinguishes between 'higher', or mental, pleasures and 'lower', sensual pleasures, which are qualitatively inferior to mental pleasures. All things being equal, we should prefer qualitatively superior pleasures for ourselves and for others.

Mill's *On Liberty* (London, 1859) is a classic articulation of the liberal principle of freedom. Defending the freedom of minorities against the 'tyranny of the majority', Mill objects to unwarranted extensions of the coercive *power of State and Society. A good Society will permit as much freedom as possible, interfering with the actions of individuals only when such interference is necessary to prevent direct and immediate harm to others. Individuals are more likely to flourish when they are unafraid of the interference of the State and other persons. Since majority opinion is often as coercive as physical interference, that, too, must be guarded against.

Mill's *Three Essays on Religion* (1874) was published posthumously. The first, 'Nature', critiques theories that derive moral norms from nature. 'Utility of Religion' argues that while religious faith offers some benefits, it is unnecessary for motivating or justifying *morality. 'Theism' presents Mill's rejection of classical theism with his conclusion that God is not all-powerful.

Mill's criticisms of religion, although creating a stir at the time, have had far less influence than his moral and political ideas. The continuing influence of his moral thought is perhaps most evident in the philosopher Peter Singer (with whom Mill himself would have significant disagreements), who maintains that a reverence for human life is morally akin to *racism, arbitrarily privileging as it does one species. Better, he argues, to give equal consideration to any creature's capacity to suffer.

Christians who would engage Mill and his followers might appeal to our intuitions and the biblical teaching that humans possess a value incommensurate with other species, and not just because of our higher aptitude for pleasure and pain. Furthermore, Mill's consequentialism fails to recognize this inviolability of each individual. Nor do Mill's views comport well with the richness and complexity of our lives, in which attachments to others are not deemed worthy merely as a means of maximizing pleasure. Also, liberty is a nebulous good when enjoyed in the absence of those other goods – God, *community, knowledge, etc. – without which no person can flourish.

Bibliography

J. S. Mill, *Essays on Ethics, Religion and Society, Collected Works of John Stuart Mill*, vol. X (Toronto and London, 1969); A. Millar, 'Mill on Religion', in J. Skorupski (ed.), *The Cambridge Companion to Mill* (Cambridge and New York, 1997); A. P. F. Sell, *Mill and Religion: Contemporary Responses to Three Essays on Religion* (London, 1997).

T. D. KENNEDY

MILLER, HUGH

Hugh Miller (1802–56) was a Scottish geologist and ecclesciastical polemicist. Despite no formal training in geology, he had a great amount of experience in the field, particularly in the Devonian rocks of the Black Isle in Scotland, where he was born. His initial interest in geology was stimulated by his work as a quarryman after leaving school in Cromarty. His books were popular at the time, not least because whilst a geologist, he was a fervent believer in the Bible, and extensively involved its interpretation in his discussions about geology.

Miller took up geology at the time when the old biblical chronology of creation seemed to be coming under assault from the increasingly confident physical *sciences. Throughout his life he struggled with the interpretation of the Genesis account of creation. The six days of creation he interpreted as six geological epochs. Each epoch was detailed from his vast knowledge of geologic and fossil formations. Miller rejected the idea of a global Noachian flood, believing the evidence to be completely inconsistent with the interpretation of the earth's geology as the product of a global flood. Miller concluded that the flood was of only local extent, probably somewhere in the Middle East or Central Asia.

To those who argued that the geological evidence took no account of the miraculous, Miller replied that 'the expedient of having recourse to supposititious miracle in order to get over a difficulty insurmountable on every natural principle, is not of the nature of argument, but simply an evidence of the want of it. Argument is at an end when supposititious miracle is introduced.'

In 1839 Miller moved south to Edinburgh and become editor of *The Witness*, a newspaper established to champion the evangelical party in their struggle with the moderates in the Church of Scotland. A sharp polemicist prior to the Disruption of 1843, Miller became a leading figure in the Free Church of Scotland after it. He wrote hundreds of articles on many subjects, attacking social injustices such as child labour and the Highland Clearances. His bestselling introduction to geology, *The Old Red Sandstone*, was published in 1841 and was followed by *Footprints of the Creator* and the posthumously published *The Testimony of The Rocks*, in which he tried to reconcile his religious beliefs with the scientific evidence of his studies.

Miller died at his own hand as a result of long but episodic mental illness, perhaps aggravated by the stress of writing his final work.

C. CAMPBELL-JACK

MIRACLES, EXTRA-BIBLICAL

Almost everyone believes in miracles. But definitions of what a miracle is vary widely. One person would define a miracle as something that causes wonder, the meaning of the Latin *miraculum*. So, say, the birth of a baby is a miracle. There is nothing 'unscientific' about miracles, except, perhaps, inasmuch as we are transported from cold 'scientific' objectivity to awe and wonder and even reverence. A second person would define a miracle as a supernatural event. It has no 'natural', that is, 'scientific', explanation. The 'laws of nature' are 'suspended' or 'violated'. Something outside of nature interrupts the course of nature.

A third definition of a miracle is an act of God which does not run counter to the 'laws of nature' but is special because of its context. Prayer, for example, is offered for someone dying of cancer. The cancer goes into remission and the person lives. Medical science can claim that the remission is part of the 'natural' process; those who prayed can claim it is the work of God.

A fourth definition could be that a miracle is a special event which has religious significance. We are told that random events, inexplicable to the scientist, occur at the subnuclear level. These are not to be seen as miracles, since they seem meaningless, but a special event which demonstrates the love or truth or goodness of God would rightly be called a miracle.

Fifthly, some would say that everything is a miracle. All that happens is God's action. Gravity, say, happens because God makes it happen. For the most part God works in regular and predictable ways, which we observe and assume to be 'laws of nature', but he is entirely free to work in unexpected ways, which we then label as special miracles.

All of these definitions have helpful insights, and, given the wide range of types of miracle, it may be wisest to allow that they all have a place in building up our understanding of the concept. Though we may wish to retain a strong element of the supernatural in any concept of miracle, it does not seem necessary to insist that every miracle must entail a strict violation of a natural law. This is illustrated by R. F. Holland's story of the mother who cries to God for a miracle when she sees her child stuck on the level crossing and hears the train approaching round the corner. The train shudders to a halt within inches of the child, not because the driver has seen him on the line, but because he was taken ill a quarter of a mile back and the train's automatic emergency braking system came into play. The mother rightly thanks God for a miracle, even though there is a perfectly 'natural' explanation for the train stopping.

The debate over miracles is at root a clash of rival world-views. Those whose world-view has no room for the supernatural will resist any concept of miracle that involves supernatural intervention, and will seek to find alternative explanations for anything that does look miraculous. Those whose world-view includes the supernatural will, generally speaking, have no problem with the miraculous. If, they would say, there is a God, if he made the world in the first place, if he upholds all things by the word of his *power, if he loves his creation and is concerned for his creatures, if his might and wisdom are infinite, then it is not at all surprising that on occasion evidences of his special activity should be seen in the world.

Miracles have traditionally been used in Christian apologetics to provide evidences for the existence of God and the authenticity of his *revelation in Christ and the Bible. Despite the philosophical weakness of an argument that says 'Your prayer has been answered, therefore God must exist', there can be no doubt that when an individual does experience a spectacular event in answer to prayer, he or she will be very inclined to accept it as evidence for the existence of God and thus a validation of the claims of Christianity. More recently, the value has been recognized of presenting this argument in the broader presuppositional perspective: 'We may view the world in one of two ways. Either it is the fixed machine of the naturalistic "scientific" world-view, or it is the handiwork of a living active present personal God. Given the occurrence of a miracle, which of these two world-views is most likely to be the right one?'

Both these approaches carry with them the risk that their use may be counterproductive. If a miraculous answer to prayer is evidence for the existence of God, then, some would say, an unanswered prayer is evidence that God does not exist. If the presence of miracles confirms a supernaturalistic world-view, the absence of miracles (and most would admit they are few and far between) can be seen to disconfirm it. Apologists need therefore to state their case with care. Sweeping statements like 'God answers prayer' or 'God heals today' need suitable qualification. Too many people have 'lost their faith' because such claims appear to have been falsified.

Besides using miracles to convince people of the truth of Christianity, Christian apologists need to defend the concept of miracle against the attacks that have been made on it. The most common attack is that miracles are inconsistent with a truly scientific world-view. In response, the apologist can point out that the inconsistency only applies in the case of one specific scientific world-view, the 'clockwork universe' mechanistic view that claims that everything that occurs happens according to rigid scientific laws which totally control everything. Most contemporary scientists have a much less deterministic understanding of the world. Radical changes in many areas, especially quantum physics and in the philosophy of *science, have taken away the old inflexibility and replaced it with a much more 'open texture'. Many scientists believe in miracles and find no contradiction between that belief and their scientific world-view.

A traditional attack on the concept of miracles, going back to David *Hume, claims that the evidence for a miracle will always be small compared with the evidence that miracles do not happen, and since we should proportion our beliefs according to the evidence, we are never justified in believing a miracle has happened. Both parts of this argument are open to challenge. Granted, if one blind person miraculously sees, and a million blind people continue to be blind, the evidence in general seems strong that blind people do not become sighted. But as far as concerns the one person who sees the evidence is by no means small, it is totally overwhelming. And in practice it is very questionable that we do, or even should, proportion our beliefs according to the evidence. It is now recognized that we hold our beliefs for all sorts of reasons, and comparatively rarely do we balance up the sum of evidences for and against any specific belief. Rather, for example, we hold a belief because it is part of a package of beliefs, and the overall package appears to us to be the most satisfactory on offer.

A third line of attack challenges the value of miracles as evidence for the truth of Christianity, since other religions also claim miracles. In response the Christian apologist can point out that the Christian world-view readily accepts the existence and miraculous influence of other supernatural powers besides God. Most Christians would also be ready to allow that in his grace God does not limit his miraculous workings to Christians. And, again, though the supernatural effects worked by a West African juju practitioner may have no evidential value for the Christian God, a miracle that occurs in a specifically Christian context, in answer to

Christians praying, and demonstrating the love and goodness that are the heart of Christianity, will be accepted by most people as positive evidence for the truth of the Christian world-view.

Bibliography

R. D. Geivett and G. R. Habermas, *In Defence of Miracles: A Comprehensive Case for God's Action in History* (Leicester, 1997).

P. HICKS

MIRACLES IN SCRIPTURE

Miracles and apologetics

Alongside the appeal to prophecy, miracles in Scripture have always had a prominent role in Christian apologetics. However, they have not always been regarded positively. As Colin Brown states, 'Miracle was once the foundations of all apologetics, then it became an apologetic crutch, and today it is not infrequently regarded as a cross for apologetics to bear.'

The appeal to miracles has been met with scepticism from earliest times (some of the Athenians scoffed at Paul's mention of resurrection, Acts 17:32). In the middle of the first century, thinkers such as Pliny the Elder argued that 'not even for God are all things possible'. God 'cannot, even if he wishes, commit suicide nor bestow eternity on mortals or recall the deceased, nor cause a man that has lived not to have lived or one that has held high office not to have held it, and that he has no power over what is past, save to forget it.'

Miracles and the Christian gospel

Arising in the wake of a 'recalling of the deceased', the Christian proclamation is miraculous at its core. The apostolic preaching recalled *Jesus' marvellous deeds (Acts 2:22; 10:38) and repeatedly testified to his resurrection from the dead (e.g. Acts 2:24; 4:33; 10:40). What Pliny deemed impossible had occurred in human history, and now the risen Christ promises to bestow eternity on mortals as well (see 2 Tim. 1:10; cf. Acts 4:2; 23:6; 24:15–21; 25:19; 26:6–8, 23).

God working marvellous deeds should have been no surprise to the Jewish people (cf. Acts 26:8), for the OT bore eloquent testimony to God's miraculous activity and promised a future age in which miracles would occur (e.g. Isa. 35:5–6; 61:1–4). The Jewish people waited for a Messiah to arrive, performing these mighty works (cf. Matt. 11:2–4; Luke 7:18–23). Jesus' wonderful deeds attested to the fact that this age had arrived.

Apologetic issues raised by the miraculous

Since the gospel is miraculous at its core, various questions may have to be answered in its defence.

The problem of definition

Since any definition should arise empirically, i.e. from the events themselves, it is simplest to begin with the observation that miracles are noteworthy events that appear to be out of the ordinary and create wonder and amazement. This definition allows for the possibility of such wonders being performed by others, such as false prophets (Deut. 13; Mark 13:22), and it also allows for 'negative' miracles (e.g. Mark 11:12–14, 20–21; Acts 5:1–11; 13:11).

Did the miracles in the Gospels really happen?

The normal rules of evidence seem to indicate quite clearly that Jesus did many marvellous deeds that provoked wonder in those who observed them. The Gospel records show us that Jesus' *power to heal drew huge crowds, and the very public nature of the miracles could be taken as an indication of their authenticity (e.g. Acts 2:22; 26:26; 1 Cor. 15:3–11). The NT is based on the testimony of eyewitnesses (Mark 3:13–19; Luke 24:48; Acts 10:39–42) who, after Jesus' *resurrection, spoke about the marvellous powers he had displayed beforehand. Each Gospel contains numerous reports and descriptions of Jesus' various miracles, culminating in his resurrection. Matthew and Luke, each in his own way, also proclaim a great miracle at the beginning of Jesus' life, namely his virginal conception (Matt. 1:18–25; Luke 1:26–56; cf. John 8:41). On the standard critical understanding of the Gospels' composition, six independent sources (Mark, Q, M, L, John, apostolic preaching) attest to Jesus' miracles. Furthermore, sources outside of the NT, such as *Josephus and the Talmud, also clearly affirm the fact that Jesus did some amazing things. On the historical 'criterion of multiple attestation', the miracles are well supported.

How could they happen?

The Bible itself does not often provide information about how miracles occurred. Some may be explained phenomenologically, i.e. from the point of view of how it seemed to the observer. This may be the case, for example, for Joshua's long day (Josh. 10:12–14) or for Philip's journey to Azotus (Acts 8:40), but, then again, these may be instances of something that is simply inexplicable.

Naturalistic explanations are sometimes possible, and even occasionally are supplied by the biblical account (e.g. Exod. 14:21). Some miracles can be understood as an acceleration of natural processes, but this kind of explanation is not possible for all miracles. Sometimes Jesus appears to use 'magical' means (e.g. Mark 7:31–37). If the world contains secret powers that can be unlocked by those with greater insight, why should the Son of God not know about such things?

Are they unique?

Stories of great wonders and miracles have survived from elsewhere in the ancient world. The prophets Elijah and Elisha performed healings through divine power; first-century Gentiles attributed miracles of healing to the Greek god Asclepius and the Egyptian god Sarapis; and Apollonius of Tyana was a first-century wise man later reputed to be a healer. Rabbi Hanina ben Dosa, who lived in the first century, was known as a man who could predict the outcome of his prayers for healing, and also much later gained a reputation for actually doing marvellous deeds.

Exorcisms were a different matter. Although the idea of demon 'possession' (and so exorcism) does not seem to have been a feature of the Greek world prior to the time of the NT, Ancient Near Eastern materials indicate a familiarity with the notion. The NT itself knows of Jewish exorcists operating both inside (Mark 9:38–39; Matt. 12:27) and outside (Acts 19:13–16) the Jewish homeland.

People of the first century would have had a sense of the 'ordinary', which would then have alerted them to the extraordinary, and one of the reasons for the success of the early Christian movement was probably the fact that the stories of Jesus' miracles were sufficiently like the stories of miracles in the pagan world to earn them a hearing.

However, if Jesus' miracles were not unique, what made him so special? History clearly demonstrates that Jesus *was* regarded as special and that his wonder-working was an integral part of the remarkable impact that he had on this world.

To come at it from another angle, as citizens of the Graeco-Roman world, the NT writers themselves would have been aware of other miracle stories and yet they show very little interest in them. Other miracle workers appear at the edges of the NT story (Matt. 12:27; Mark 9:38–39; 13:22; Luke 11:19; Acts 19:13–16), but, in spite of such things occurring, the crowds can still recognize that something genuinely new was happening in Jesus' miracles (Matt. 9:33; Mark 1:27). What is this newness that was detected?

Attempts to differentiate biblical miracles, as 'signs', from mere pagan 'wonders', fail when the usage of the various terms is carefully assessed. Jesus most certainly stands out because of the sheer number of miracles attributed to him, and in their variety. It is also clear that his miracle-working drew huge crowds, large enough to be a factor in the call for his execution. These points should not be underplayed in the discussion of what made him remarkable. It is also possible to identify other unique features in the character of Jesus' wonder-working, and when other miracles are dealt with individually, the parallels with Jesus' miracles are not as close as when they are referred to *en masse*.

The basic difference lies in the connection between Jesus' miracles and the kingdom of God. The NT does not deal with Jesus' miracles in isolation from his teaching and other activities, or from the OT prophetic material which he fulfilled.

Isaiah promised an age of miracles (Isa. 35:5–6), associated with the Servant of the Lord (61:1–4), whose ministry would issue in a whole new era for Israel and for the world (Isa. 55 – 66). Daniel spoke of this as the kingdom of God, when all ungodly human power would be removed and one like a Son of Man would reign for ever (Dan. 2:44; 7:13–14). When Jesus acted as the Servant (Matt. 12:15–21), through performing miracles, this signalled that the kingdom of God was about to arrive (Matt. 12:28). When he rose from the dead and was exalted to the right hand of God as the Son of Man, he was installed as king in God's kingdom (Matt. 28:18).

Do miracles suspend the laws of nature?

The philosophical definition of a miracle as a 'suspension of the laws of nature' immediately raises a variety of problems. In the first century, Pliny declared that the things that are impossible for God to do (see above) 'demonstrate the power of nature, and prove that it is this that we mean by the word "God"'. For Pliny, as for many moderns, nature was the 'given', so powerful that it could not be overturned.

In the biblical world-view, nature is not autonomous, for the Creator is always active, sustaining and ruling over his creation. From a human point of view, his order can be discerned in what we might call 'laws of nature', which are provisional, descriptive and subject to the limitations of our time (e.g. human flight was once deemed impossible).

God's marvels are objectively present all around us, even if his role in them is ignored by sinful humanity (Rom. 1:20), and he is active in the ordinary course of events. This means, in one sense, that everything is 'miraculous', because everything is capable of provoking wonder at God's almighty power. However, against this backdrop of God's all-pervasive sovereignty, he still works extraordinary events that produce awe, wonder and excitement. Rather than being a suspension of some autonomous law, these are occasional, startling displays of the same almighty power with which God upholds the universe. By creating awe and wonder, these unusual events point human beings to the fact that God is Lord over the usual course of events. They show that behind 'nature' lies 'grace'.

The grace of God is supremely disclosed in his self-*revelation in human *history. When he revealed his name to Moses, he said, 'I AM WHO I AM', or, better, 'I WILL BE WHO I WILL BE' (Exod. 3:14). This was a promise that God would gradually disclose himself to human beings. Extraordinary events in the Scriptures tend to cluster around a new stage in God's self-disclosure (the exodus, the beginning of the prophetic period with Elijah and Elisha, the coming of Christ, the expansion of the gospel into new territories). As noted in the discussion on God and nature, any extraordinary event in human history wrought by God displays the almighty power that is normally operative behind ordinary historical processes and events. The climax of God's self-revelation in history was in the incarnation (John 1:14, 18; Heb. 1:1–3).

Should we expect miracles to continue?

The continuance of Jesus' miracles was a key factor in the progress of the gospel recorded in Acts. Such things were recognized as the 'signs' of an apostle (2 Cor. 12:12), part of the first generation of gospel preaching (Heb. 2:4).

There are also hints that the miraculous continued into the life of the early church (cf. 1 Cor. 12:28; Jas 5:13–18). Some Church Fathers placed a great deal of emphasis on miracles occurring in their day, thinking as we can tend to do today that contemporary miracles endorse the reality of the biblical miracles.

The temptation to forge too close a relationship between any contemporary miracles and those of Christ, however, should be resisted. In the freedom of God, he can continue to act in extraordinary ways for ill (1 Cor. 11:30) or for good (Jas 5), although he does not promise to do so. Such occasions are dramatic reminders of who is sovereign in this world, in both the extraordinary and the ordinary course of events. As the activity of God is discerned behind all of life, so believers can bear testimony to a continuity between the God of their present experience and the God who became flesh in the Lord Jesus Christ. Contemporary miracles should not be permitted to eclipse the specialness of that time.

What did the miracles mean?

What his contemporaries noted as 'powers', Jesus called 'signs'. What did they signify?

Jesus has been accused of being a magician (Mark 3:22; 6:14; cf. Justin, *Dialogue*, 69; Origen, *Against Celsus*, 1.6, 28; Babylonian Talmud tractate *Sanhedrin*, 43a; Suetonius; Lucian, *Passing of Peregrinus*, 13), but his failure to use magical techniques, the variety and number of his miracles, and the wider character of his ministry show that he was much more than a magician. On the analogy of Elijah and Elisha, the wonders Jesus performed could signal that God was with him as a prophet (cf. Mark 6:15; Luke 7:16), but, acting and speaking on his own authority, he was much more than a prophet.

Drawing on prophecy, the Gospels depict Jesus as the long-awaited Christ, the Servant of the Lord who comes to bring in the kingdom of God. His coming amongst Israel manifested many wonderful signs, as promised, and these signs brought renovation to Israel as a foretaste of the cosmic renovation that was soon to come. They also showed that the Messiah, 'the Son of God' (cf. Ps. 2:7), was 'God the Son'. His Father had shown him what to do (John 5:19) and had committed to him divine prerogatives (John 5:21–29).

In the long run, Jesus' miracles show that 'God became flesh'. They are signs of the freedom and sovereignty of God. Some miracles, in particular, are special demonstrations of his divinity (e.g. walking on the sea, raising the dead, bread in the desert). These tend to be the ones in which Jesus takes the initiative, as if his self-disclosure as the great 'I AM' (see Mark 6:50 and John's 'I am' sayings) was of paramount importance. This is endorsed by his resurrection and exaltation, in which he is declared to be the Son of God (Rom. 1:4), installed as Lord (Acts 2:36), and given the name above all names (Phil. 2:11).

The miracle of grace

This miracle of grace is at the core of the Christian proclamation. God became flesh and dwelt amongst us poor sinners. The miracles of the OT anticipate, and the miracles of the NT endorse, this event. The nature of this event is consistent with the virgin birth at its beginning, the wonders performed as its result, and the resurrection at its historical end.

The incarnation is the final great self-revelation of God in human history. It led to the cross, where the miracle of grace is so clearly displayed for those with eyes to see (Phil. 2:5–8). As Jesus hung on the cross, the Jewish leaders recognized that he had performed many miracles (Mark 15:31) and called for a final miracle by which he would avoid death (Mark 15:32). He did not accede to their wishes and died the death of a cursed man. Ironically, however, this was in order to secure the biggest miracle of all, for at the cross, God supremely displays the miracle of grace.

This also has its counterpart in the human heart. The Spirit of God brings about a deep conviction that the gospel word is, in fact, the word of God (1 Thess. 1:5; 2:13). It may be foolishness to those who do not understand, but the cross is the power of God for those being saved (1 Cor. 1:18–25). God's grace is discovered in this weakness, rather than simply in great displays of power. Thus, conversion is the greatest of all miracles (John 5:20–21).

If this miracle of grace in the believer is accorded the wonder that it truly deserves, then the other 'lesser' miracles can be understood in its light. The extraordinary events which we see displayed in the Scriptures as the almighty God acts in out-of-the-ordinary fashion are consistent with the miracle of conversion, bringing new life out of the old. As Jesus temporarily restores life to those who suffered under the various versions of human suffering, we catch a glimpse of that life to come in the restoration of all things.

The miracles display God's commitment to save human beings. In this fallen world, human beings live under the shadow of death, manifested in all kinds of suffering. Jesus' miracles show that God is opposed to this state of affairs. In this way, these signs of divine reality are a picture and a foretaste of future reality in the kingdom of God (cf. Rev. 21:1–4).

Bibliography

P. W. Barnett, *Is the New Testament History?* (Sydney, 1986), ch. 9; K. Barth, *Church Dogmatics* (Edinburgh, 1958), IV/2, pp. 212–247; C. Brown, *Miracles and the Critical Mind* (Grand Rapids and Exeter, 1984); W. Cotter, *Miracles in Greco-Roman Antiquity: A Sourcebook* (London, 1999); J. P. Meier, *A Marginal Jew: Rethinking the Historical Jesus* (New York, 1994), vol. 2, pp. 509–971; Y. Zakovitch, 'Miracle (OT)', and H. Remus, 'Miracle (NT)', *Anchor Bible Dictionary*, vol. 4, pp. 845–869.

P. G. BOLT

MITCHELL, JOHN CAMERON

John Cameron Mitchell (b. 1963) wrote, directed and starred in *Hedwig and the Angry Inch* (2001), a film that might too easily be dismissed as a 'gender-bending' musical in the tradition of *The Rocky Horror Picture Show*. Much to the contrary, *Hedwig* is a profound tale of a young man who seeks freedom but finds only confusion and rejection. When his sex change operation is botched, Hansel becomes Hedwig and masquerades as a woman. Caught in limbo between the sexes, Hedwig seeks companionship and answers, only to be abandoned by those who promise to rescue her.

The film captures some of the schizophrenic androgyny that is so much a part of post-modern sexuality. In an almost worshipful climax, Hedwig becomes whole again, reunited with his true self, and the story is ultimately hopeful. Helped along by a powerful and even catchy rock score, *Hedwig* asks some pretty big questions about *sexuality, personal identity and role-playing.

Of special interest to theologians would be the song *The Origin of Love*, which remythologizes the creation myth in *Plato's *Symposium*. This myth becomes thematic to the film and should serve as a strong example of how such stories, when cast in a contemporary context, can capture imaginations and even devotees in a unique and powerful fashion.

D. S. RUSSELL

MODERNISM/MODERNITY

The term 'modern', used in connection with 'modernism' and 'modernity', refers to whatever is characteristic of the Western intellectual tradition during the 'modern period' (the period following the Reformation era). It should not to be confused with 'whatever is most recent'. Modernism refers to a framework of ideas that define Western intellectual culture during the modern period. Modernity is often used as a synonym for modernism, but it may also refer to the ethos of modernism wherever and whenever that ethos is manifested, even if the modern period as such has come to an end.

In philosophy, the post-Reformation period begins with the work of French philosopher, René *Descartes (1596–1650). It happens that Descartes is also the most widely recognized emblem of all that is thought to be characteristic of modernity. Heir to the waning *scholasticism of the late medieval period, and troubled by internecine squabbles among religious authorities during the Reformation and Counter-Reformation periods, Descartes was especially interested in the possibility of putting all knowledge on a firm foundation. He was a man of unusual genius, with a penchant for charting new territory in the realm of ideas. Two of his ideas, regarding the problem of scepticism, and scientific investigation, reflect centrepieces in the modernist ethos. Both emerge in his masterpiece *Meditations on First Philosophy* (1641).

Descartes gave the problem of scepticism unusually trenchant formulation. Yet he showed the greatest optimism about the possibility of defeating the most penetrating of sceptical arguments. He did this while assuming that the *truth of a belief must be certain in order to count as knowledge. His creative and controversial solution to the problem of scepticism attempted to ground all knowledge in a foundational judgment that is indubitable and from which a substantial edifice of knowledge can be constructed. While he did not achieve the consensus he hoped for, he did effectively change the direction of philosophy by placing the issue of knowledge and justified belief in the centre of debate.

Also, Descartes set the scientific enterprise on a new course by arguing against the Aristotelian science of scholasticism and charting new methods of investigation. His attempted demonstration of the existence of the external world resulted in a novel conception of physical *reality. He concluded that the essence of physical things in the external world is extension. This just means that physical things take up space for a time and can therefore be understood using geometry and the mathematical *sciences. They can be measured in terms of space and time. This was the foundation of a new scientific programme that Descartes helped to launch. This programme is commonly called 'modern scientific practice'.

The idiosyncrasies of Cartesian physics would eventually be replaced by the 'classical dynamics' of Isaac *Newton. Descartes, however, had convinced many that a science of the physical world is possible because it has an intelligible structure that God has ordained the human mind to understand. The general idea that the physical world could be understood in terms that are mathematical would last throughout the modern period. Science had been given a method.

During this period, an assortment of empirical observations flooded from the laboratories of practising scientists. Methodology was refined, especially in appreciation of the work of Francis *Bacon (1561–1626), who systematized the method of induction that is so crucial to the scientific enterprise. To some, it began to seem that a complete science of the universe was within arm's reach. A new consensus could be achieved, as scientists worked together to understand the world. This consensus would be possible because the principles of rationality were beginning to be well defined. The foundations of knowledge provided the basis for scientific inquiry, and the new empirical methods of observation, together with the *logic of induction, would carry this inquiry forward. And it would do so without displaying the factionalism of disputatious theologians.

Descartes was a sincere Christian, and so were many of the leading lights of the modern era leading up to and including Immanuel *Kant. For Descartes, confidence in the possibility of knowledge and in the intelligibility of the physical world must be grounded in the solid conviction that God exists and that God is omnipotent, omniscient and morally perfect. Nevertheless, he and others who came after him felt that science ought to proceed without interference from ecclesiastical authorities, some of whom would disavow the scientific method.

Ecclesiastical authorities, for their part, were challenged to entrust the knowledge tradition about the physical world to those whose methods did not depend in any crucial way on the principles of revealed theology. Some feared that God would be lost in the shuffle to erect the envisioned edifice of knowledge. There were also concerns that the knowledge of God would be pre-empted by a secular form of knowledge. Others were more accommodating. They recalled a long tradition of ''*natural theology' that might be brought up to date in light of all the new knowledge that was being produced. Thus, natural theology and revealed theology could serve as partners in the knowledge enterprise for the glory of God, who is a providential Creator.

There was, then, an attempt to regard the new science as a complement to traditional theology. During this period, an optimistic programme of natural theology was cobbled together combining the materials of science and the elements of Christian tradition. An especially prominent point of contact was emphasized by proponents of the design argument for the existence of God. Landmark works in Christian apologetics were produced under the inspiration of this noble ideal. Early on, Bishop Joseph *Butler (1692–1752) composed *The Analogy of Religion* (1736). Decades later, William Paley (1743–1805) brought out two influential works, *Evidences of Christianity* (1794) and *Natural Theology* (1802).

British philosophers John *Locke (1632–1704), Bishop George *Berkeley (1685–1753) and Thomas Reid (1710–96) all layered arguments for *theism and evidences for Christianity into their systematic work in philosophy. The brilliant continental philosopher, Gottfried *Leibniz (1646–1716), who wrote commentaries on Descartes and Locke, composed *The Theodicy* (1710), his only philosophical work to be published during his lifetime. *The Theodicy* was an elaborate defence of theism against the argument from *evil. Samuel *Clarke (1675–1729), in his Boyle lectures of 1704 and 1705, offered his own version of natural theology, but managed to raise considerable doubt about his orthodoxy.

The more animated religious believers in opposition to this whole endeavour retreated to a *fideism that they sought to clarify and justify in theological terms. There were also detractors who went in the other direction. Some luminaries – many of them *philosophes* of the '*Enlightenment' period who contributed articles to the *Encyclopédie* (published 1751–72) – did 'apostatize'. They became deists, who considered God to be remote from the concerns of human creatures and irrelevant to the business of understanding the world and constructing meaningful and moral lives within the world. Or, worse, they became atheists, overtly denying the existence of God, who seemed not to have anything to do that would justify his existence. And, of course, many clerics declared that there was no difference between deism and *atheism.

Descartes's young contemporary Baruch *Spinoza (1632–77) was a subtle metaphysician of pantheistic persuasion who offered what is really the first modern critical study of the Bible, *Tractatus Theologico-Politicus* (1670, published anonymously). *Voltaire (1694–1778) mocked Leibniz's theodicy without providing an alternative defence of God's goodness in his entertaining work *Candide* (1759). About the same time that Paley produced his work on Christian evidences, American politico Thomas Paine (1737–1809) was publishing his deistical work *The Age of Reason*.

The most celebrated critic of 'natural religion' was David *Hume (1711–76). In his *Dialogues Concerning Natural Religion* (published posthumously in 1779), Hume attacked the popular argument from design and formulated an enduring version of the argument from evil against theism. But Hume was sceptical about a good many things besides God's existence, including the existence of an external world and of a unified and enduring self. So his reputation as a 'modernist' is a mixed bag.

It is generally agreed that the modern period came to a close with Immanuel Kant (1724–1804). Kant, who began as a thoroughgoing rationalist, was awakened by Hume from his 'dogmatic slumbers', and sought to revolutionize the tradition regarding human knowledge. In his *Critique of Pure Reason* (1781) Kant set forth, in obscure German prose, his two-world theory. The *noumenal* world is the world as it is in itself, prior to experience and the human effort to understand reality. The *phenomenal* world is the world of experience, constructed by the mind as it organizes the data of experience. Kant concluded that the *noumenal* world was cognitively inaccessible, very much the opposite of Descartes's epistemological vision. Kant did argue for the existence of God, but his argument depends on the original, elaborate and controversial moral theory he developed. Ten years before he died, Kant produced a work called *Religion within the Limits of Reason Alone* (1793), in which he paved the way for nineteenth-century Protestant liberalism.

Needless to say, the much-anticipated consensus regarding the nature and content of knowledge was so long and hard in coming that it never really happened. Increasingly, the critical apparatus under construction throughout this period was thought to pose a particular challenge to the concept of divine *revelation and the *authority of Scripture. During the nineteenth century, the energy and optimism of modernism settled into a more qualified and somewhat fragmented enthusiasm for reason. On the heels of the Kantian revolution, German scholars interjected a fascination with the *metaphysics and *epistemology of a resurgent idealism. With new intellectual trends in the making, the prodigious activity of Christian apologists from the previous century lost traction, while scholarly criticism of the Bible blossomed. Remnants of modernity mutated into the hyper-rationalism of some intellectuals (e.g. the German and British Idealists) and into the radical subjectivism of others (e.g. Friedrich *Schleiermacher).

The stage was set for a dramatic, but short-lived, insurgency of modernity in its most pretentious guise – the *logical positivism of the early twentieth century (beginning in the 1920s and already in decline in the 1940s). The logical positivists endorsed a particularly severe form of epistemological foundationalism that was intimately connected with their central principle, the so-called 'verifiability criterion of meaning'. This principle assumed that philosophy is reducible to the meaning of sentences, and asserted that meaningful sentences are either tautologous or empirically verifiable. On this criterion, the statements used to express truths of religion and *morality are literally meaningless, and so do not express truths at all. The entire movement of positivism was overshadowed by ongoing developments in theoretical physics (e.g. the role of 'unobservables') and the pesky threat of self-refutation – its own criterion of meaning was neither tautologous nor empirically verifiable.

The spirit of modernity, as it continues to be called (most often by its detractors), endures. At its best, it is more modulated and less pretentious. It acknowledges the finitude and fallibility of cognition. It recognizes the influence of *culture and experience in the knowledge enterprise. It heeds counsel to nurture the intellectual virtues without which cognition would succumb to the instincts of pride and self-preservation and deliver a limp surrogate for the truth. Yet it presses on with the expectation that knowledge of the truth about the things that matter most is still possible. It proceeds with the conviction that human persons are by nature evidence-gatherers. It reposes, still, in the belief that the weighing of evidence is repaid with some closure in the quest for truth. And traditional work in Christian apologetics continues within the framework of a more modest foundationalism and a fallibilist conception of *evidentialism.

The same spirit that animates the ongoing enterprise of Christian apologetics threatens, as always, to break out again into unrestrained pretence. Scientific and philosophical *naturalism is dominated by this propensity. Modernism degenerates into a specious 'scientism' that dogmatically asserts that the knowable is limited to what can be found out by the methods of science. Vigorous programmes of natural theology are being developed to meet this challenge.

Some Christian intellectuals have responded with a plea to forsake the effort to ground belief in evidence and reason. Others seem confident that the intellectual culture has already turned the corner and, without regret, sidled away from the run-down neighbourhood of modernity. As always, however, there is no consensus about these things. The long-standing tension between those who yield to the blandishments of reason and evidence, and those who flee to the welcoming arms of 'postmodernism', is bound to continue for the foreseeable future.

R. D. Geivett

MOLINISM

Molinism is the term now commonly associated with the picture of divine providence fashioned by Luis de Molina, a sixteenth-century Spanish Jesuit. Molina argued that it is only by postulating what he called 'middle knowledge' that we can reconcile divine providence with human freedom.

The traditional Christian notion of providence maintains that the world is as it is because of God's nature and will. As a free and omnipotent Creator, God has complete freedom to decide which beings to create and into which situations those beings will be placed. As a perfect Creator, God manifests his love by willing what is good for his creation and directing his creatures toward the ends he ordains for them. And as an all-knowing Creator, God has full and detailed knowledge about every event (past, present and future) in his world. God, then, is in total control; our world is the creative product of its omnipotent, omnibenevolent, omniscient sovereign.

This conception of providence, though, seems to conflict with the affirmation of human freedom, at least if such freedom is understood in the way that seems philosophically most plausible. We usually think of free agents as those who are genuinely responsible for their own actions and who could have done other than they do. Nothing over which they lack control – no prior conditions and causal laws, and no other agent – determines what they do when they act freely. This seems to pose at least two problems if God is indeed provident in the strong traditional sense outlined above. First, if God is omniscient, he knows what we will do long before we do it. But then, how can we do anything other than what it is God knows? And secondly, if God is truly in control of his world, it seems that all events – including free creaturely actions – are ultimately up to him, not up to us. So if he is truly sovereign, we are not truly free.

Molina argued that such problems can be resolved only if we postulate a special type of divine knowledge. God must have not only natural knowledge (knowledge of necessary truths beyond his control) and free knowledge (knowledge of contingent truths under his control), but also middle knowledge (knowledge of contingent truths beyond his control). Most important among the contents of his middle knowledge would be what contemporary Molinists call 'counterfactuals of creaturely freedom' – conditionals that state, for any being God might have created and any situation in which it might have been created and left free, what that being would freely do if placed in that situation. So long as God knows but does not control such counterfactuals, his providence and our freedom can be reconciled.

An example here might help. Suppose the following were true: If God were to create Cuthbert in situation C, Cuthbert would freely decide to purchase an iguana. Since God is omniscient, he would always have known this proposition, even prior to his making any decision about creating Cuthbert. But because the conditional proposition describes a free action, and because Cuthbert, not God, decides what Cuthbert freely does, God knows but does not determine the truth of this conditional; hence, it is indeed part of his middle knowledge.

Now suppose that God, knowing this counterfactual of creaturely freedom, decides that his providential ends can be achieved by creating Cuthbert and arranging for him to be in situation C. Once he decides to create Cuthbert in C, God knows that Cuthbert will in fact freely decide to purchase an iguana. God has this knowledge immediately upon selecting his own creative action; he need not wait for Cuthbert to act (or even to exist) in order to know what Cuthbert will do. So middle knowledge provides God with complete foreknowledge concerning free creaturely actions such as Cuthbert's. And since that middle knowledge is always available to God, it also provides him with significant control over his world. Cuthbert, for example, decides to buy the iguana only because God put him in a situation where God knew Cuthbert would so decide. Had God willed for Cuthbert to act otherwise, he might well have seen (again via middle knowledge) that situations that would culminate in different free actions were indeed available. Hence, both divine foreknowledge and divine control are compatible with genuine human freedom so long as God possesses middle knowledge.

Though Molina's position elicited intense debates when first proposed, it was largely forgotten in Anglo-American circles until it was inadvertently resurrected by Alvin Plantinga's presentations of the free will defence (as a response to the problem of evil) in the 1970s. Since then, controversy concerning the Molinist approach has raged almost continuously. Anti-Molinists have developed elaborate arguments to show that there can be no middle knowledge because the truths supposedly known thereby would lack adequate metaphysical grounds. Molinists have offered equally elegant responses to this so-called 'grounding' objection, and have attempted to spell out how Molinism can be fruitfully applied to particular Christian topics (e.g. prophecy, petitionary prayer, biblical inspiration and the incarnation). They have also insisted that the Molinist account of providence fares particularly well when compared to its chief rivals – a Thomist (or Calvinist) picture that rejects our ordinary sense of freedom, and the so-called 'open theist' alternative that jettisons central elements (e.g. divine foreknowledge of free actions) of the traditional picture of providence.

No consensus has formed among Christian philosophers and theologians on which of these views is to be preferred. But it is increasingly recognized that Molina was probably correct in arguing that the everyday notion of freedom and the traditional picture of providence can both be maintained only by making room for middle knowledge.

Bibliography

T. P. Flint, *Divine Providence: The Molinist Account* (Ithaca and London, 1998); W. Hasker, *God, Time, and Knowledge* (Ithaca and London, 1989); L. de Molina, *On Divine Foreknowledge: Part IV of the 'Concordia'*, trans. by A. Freddoso (Ithaca and London, 1988); W. L. Craig, *The Only Wise God: The Compatibility of Divine Foreknowledge and Human Freedom* (Eugene, 2000).

T. P. FLINT

MONISM

Underlying much of Western as well as Eastern philosophy is the question of whether everything is basically one or many. If it is all one unchanging whole, then why does it appear to be many? But if it is ultimately many different things, then why do they seem such an ordered whole? The questions multiply. In this apparent world of change is ordered oneness permanent, eternal? Is it perhaps divine? It satisfies our minds, so could ordered oneness also satisfy our lives? In effect the whole range of philosophical inquiry spills out of the question about one or many.

Monism is the theory that *reality is all one rather than many: either all of one kind as in materialistic philosophies (qualitative monism) or numerically all one being as in pantheism (quantitative monism). Both sorts of monism have appeared throughout history. The earliest known Greek philosophies were materialistic, reducing everything to physical elements, and analogous views persisted throughout modern times and continue today. *Plato opposed *materialism because it had difficulty accounting both for the orderedness of nature and for human reason and moral ideals. In Hellenistic times neoplatonic idealists argued that both physical and immaterial things participate in different degrees in an eternal and immaterial 'One', the source of all being and goodness. Similarly the modern materialism occasioned by the rise of modern science was contested by new forms of *idealism that took natural processes to be functions of an all-embracing mind. With the emergence of energistic and particle physics, the term '*naturalism' is often preferred: things may not be composed of matter but, the naturalist claims, everything is explicable in terms of nature's processes.

The problem with both naturalism and idealism is that explaining everything by just the one kind of process tends to be reductionistic, that is, qualitative monism fails to explain adequately both the physical and the mental, reducing the one to nothing but the other. Thus, every sort of mental process, including imagination, creativity, abstraction, valuing, purposing, belief and choice, is typically traced to physical causes alone, and no immaterial soul exists. One alternative might be a neutral monism that invokes a hypothetical third kind of thing as the one reality underlying both the mental and the physical, but then the problem is to identify what it is. Dualistic alternatives, of course, have to explain the mind-body relationship. Some Christian thinkers like the eighteenth-century bishop George *Berkeley have therefore opted for idealism, and others favour a non-reductive naturalism, while most continue to prefer some form of dualism.

Quantitative monism faces an analogous problem: how to explain the very many different things that appear to exist. The early Greek *Parmenides took all change and plurality to be illusion and logically absurd for, since being either is or is not, 'becoming' is not even a logical possibility. His pupil Zeno constructed a variety of famous paradoxes to prove the point, paradoxes that continued to puzzle philosophers and mathematicians well into the twentieth century. Neoplatonism was a quantitative as well as a qualitative monism, and it explained change and plurality as various emanations from the one source of all being. Nature flows out of that source, rather than being created from nothing as Christian theology asserts. In the seventeenth century Benedict *Spinoza went further and identified nature with God himself in pantheistic fashion, using the term 'God' for its active attributes and 'nature' for the passive. Particular people and things do not exist as individual entities but are finite modes of the infinite Being, causally determined by nature's purposeless driving energy. The nineteenth-century German idealists were mostly quantitative monists too. *Schleiermacher, for instance, took religious experience to reveal the ultimate oneness of the universe and God, and *Hegel viewed all of history as the progressive actualization of God as infinite spirit. This was the source of liberalism's immanentistic theology, which supposed divine revelation to arise within the human spirit rather than occurring by the mighty acts of a transcendent God. Eastern religion also is sometimes pantheistic, and similar strains are evident in the *New Age spirituality that regards Nature as divine or locates God within one's inner self. The same basic problem surfaces in all these cases, namely how one reality can have so many different and often contradictory appearances.

These monistic philosophies, if not overtly pantheistic like Spinoza, are panentheistic: they see the creation as somehow immanent within God but not the entirety of God. What is at stake in both kinds of view is the God-creation distinction with its far-reaching implications. If everything is an indivisible whole, do different individuals even exist? Could individuality have any meaning or value? If everything is causally determined by its place in the whole, what do we say about freedom and responsibility? If this world with its horrendous *evils is divine, is there evil in

God? And what basis do we then have for distinguishing good and evil? If evil is a necessary ingredient of the whole, what progress towards the good is even possible? If God is inseparable from nature, is he really free to act? Does he care? Is he a distinct personal being or just some unknowable ground of all being, the One?

In contrast to all this, the traditional Judaeo-Christian doctrine of creation *ex nihilo* affirms that God in his goodness freely brought worlds into being and sustains them by his ever-present activity, yet he so transcends this world that he remains free to overcome evil and achieve the good he still intends. Monism denies that this is even possible, for God cannot act, but Christian *theism ascribes the ordered unity monism sees to a God who acts, and affirms the possibility of individual lives being reordered and made whole by his love.

Bibliography

L. Gilkey, *Maker of Heaven and Earth* (New York, 1959); D. R. Groothuis, *Unmasking the New Age* (Downers Grove, 1986); H. R. Mackintosh, *Types of Modern Theology* (London, 1937).

A. F. HOLMES

MONOTHEISM

Monotheism is the view that there is only one God and, as such, can be compared with *polytheism (belief in multiple gods) as well as its cousin henotheism/monolatry (the worship of one god while accepting that other gods exist).

Monotheism in world religions

Monotheism is found in three great *world religions, namely, *Judaism, *Islam and Christianity. The monotheism of Islam and Christianity is, of course, derived historically from Judaism. In all three of these faiths, the one God is understood as the Creator of everything that exists other than himself. God thus transcends the created order. This further contrasts monotheism with pantheism, which denies any sharp distinction between God and the world, holding that everything is God or an aspect of God. In monotheism, God is sovereign over his creation and, though he is transcendent, he also acts providentially and miraculously in the course of human history.

God is also all-powerful or omnipotent, as well as omniscient, knowing infallibly all truths, past, present and future. Moreover, the God of monotheistic faiths is thoroughly righteous and holy, and acts with benevolent mercy at least towards his chosen people.

Three other religions are sometimes classified as monotheistic. *Zoroastrianism, the religion of ancient Persia and still followed by some today, asserts the existence of a supremely good god who will triumph over evil at the end of history. It departs, however, from true monotheism by postulating the existence of an evil god or force that is as eternal and uncreated as the good god. At most, Zoroastrianism claims that monotheism will be the final state of things, but its world-view is essentially dualistic, not monotheistic.

Vaita *Hinduism and *Sikhism are also superficially monotheistic. Though many Hindus are pantheistic, the Vaita (dualistic) schools, founded by Ramanuja (1017–1137) and Madhva (1199–1278), affirm the existence of one, personal god. However, they deny the doctrine of creation *ex nihilo*, and thus god's sovereignty and independence. Sikhism also affirms the existence of only one god, but this god is not personal and can be known only in mystical experience.

The origin of monotheism

In the nineteenth and early twentieth centuries, many anthropologists and scholars of religion came to hold the view that monotheism was the final stage in an evolutionary development of religion. This development began with animism (the worship of nature or ancestor spirits), and progressed through polytheism and henotheism, until the single god worshipped by a particular group was asserted to be the one and only God.

This evolutionary model of religion has been largely discredited, however, due to two factors. On the one hand, it was discovered that rather than consolidating the attributes and functions of various deities into one god, polytheistic societies actually tend to multiply deities (witness the one million-plus gods of Hinduism). On the other hand, it has been demonstrated by W. Schmidt (*The Origin and Growth of Religion*) and others that in animistic and polytheistic cultures – the most primitive on the evolutionary model – there is universally a belief in a 'high god' who, though distant and seldom worshipped, is held to be the omnipotent creator of all. Winfried Corduan (*Neighboring Faiths*, p. 33) remarks that 'in almost all traditional contexts – in Africa, America, Australia, Asia or Europe – we find belief in a God located in the sky (or on a high mountain) and almost always referred to with masculine languange. This God creates the world ... [and] he provides standards of behaviour ... Particularly in later cultures, he stands apart from the routine worship of gods and spirits. There is a memory of a time when this God was worshipped regularly, but something intervened. Many (but not all) cultures that refer to this interruption explain that it happened because this God did not receive the obedience due him.'

All of this points to the conclusion that human history began with an original monotheism, and that animism, polytheism, etc. are departures from that initial faith. This conclusion points to a significant argument for the actual truth of monotheism. If we may assume that the world has some sort of supernatural origin, that there is a god or gods of some kind, then the fact that human beings started off as monotheists is most easily explainable if in fact monotheism is true. We may surmise that God, as the creator of humankind, made himself known to his creatures at the beginning so that this initial divine self-revelation was the cause of original monotheism. Later, for various reasons, human beings exchanged their true knowledge of God for a lie (Rom. 1:25).

A philosophical defence of monotheism

The fact that human history begins with a monotheistic faith provides an indication that monotheism may be true. However, there are other arguments that, taken together with original monotheism, provide a stronger cumulative case for the truth of monotheism.

The argument from perfection

We may conceive of God as an absolutely perfect being. As *Anselm, the medieval theologian, claimed, God is 'that than which a greater cannot be conceived'. As a perfect being, God will possess all perfections in the maximum degree. He will, that is, possess such attributes as having *power, having knowledge and having goodness. He will also possess these attributes maximally, thus possessing maximal or perfect power, knowledge and goodness. It is arguable as well that a perfect being will be

immutable and eternal. He would exist necessarily (i.e. not contingently), since the capacity for non-existence is an imperfection, and he would be an immaterial spirit since material beings are subject to change.

The question arises as to whether or not there can exist more than one perfect being. It would seem that there cannot. Suppose, for the sake of argument, that there were two perfect beings. Two such beings would both possess all perfections to the the maximum degree. They would, that is, be exactly alike. But, if they are exactly alike, on what basis can we say that there are *two* such beings? Two distinct beings must differ with regard to at least one property. If 'two' perfect beings do not differ in some way, then we are really talking about only one being.

It might be replied that two perfect beings may not differ with regard to their essential properties, but perhaps they might differ with regard to accidental properties. For example, suppose that a particular perfect being has the accidental property of being the creator of a planet that contained no living things, and another perfect being has the property of being the creator of a planet containing many other living things. In such case, the first perfect being would differ from the second with respect to at least one property. This response fails, however, because prior to creating these planets, the two beings would not differ, and thus at least one of them would not exist.

The argument from omnipotence

An argument for the oneness of God can be formulated on the assumption that God is omnipotent. Let us define a being as omnipotent if and only if it can do anything that is logically possible for an absolutely perfect being. This definition allows that God cannot do that which is logically impossible *per se*, such as make a square circle. It also allows that God cannot do things which may be logically possible in general (e.g. tell a lie or swim), but which would obviously not be possible for a being that has other attributes which we normally attribute to God (e.g. moral perfection and immateriality). Yet, it also captures our intuitions to the effect that an omnipotent being would have the greatest possible scope of power.

Given this definition, however, it is clear that there could not be more than one omnipotent being. The power of any alleged two omnipotent beings would cancel each other out. That is, the power of one would pose a necessary limitation on that of the other such that neither being would be omnipotent according to our definition. Take, for example, some action logically possible for a perfect being (say, creating the earth), and let us suppose that one omnipotent perfect being desires to perform that action. If there were another perfect being equally powerful, he could evidently thwart the desire of the first being.

It will not do to respond, as some have, that two omnipotent beings could exist if they had necessarily harmonious wills (such that they never disagreed and thus never acted to thwart each other's exercise of power). For even if they did have necessarily harmonious wills, it would still be the case that each being lacked omnipotence as defined above, i.e. there would be actions logically possible for a perfect being that neither being could do. By way of explanation, consider that it is logically possible that there is only one omnipotent perfect being. In such a case, we can imagine a possible world in which one existing omnipotent being did some logically possible action x. Imagine another possible world in which a second omnipotent perfect being exists alongside the first and in which this second being desires to do not-x. In this world the first perfect being would not be able to do x because his will would be necessarily harmonious with the second being's, and they would together will to do not-x in that world.

The argument from Ockham's razor

When there is more than one competing explanation for some phenomenon, the principle of rationality known as Ockham's razor requires that, all other things being equal, the simplest explanation is to be preferred. Another way of stating the principle is that one should not multiply explanatory entities beyond those required to explain the phenomenon in question. God's existence is often invoked as an explanatory hypothesis to account for numerous empirical phenomena such as the existence and orderliness of the cosmos or the existence of objective *morality. In so far, then, as the existence of one God (one with sufficient power and knowledge) will suffice to explain these and other phenomena, Ockham's razor requires that we postulate the existence of no more than one God.

The argument from revelation

The unmistakable teaching of the Bible is that there is only one God. The *Shema* of Deuteronomy declares, 'Hear, O Israel: The LORD our God, the LORD is one. Love the LORD your God with all your heart and with all your soul and with all your strength' (Deut. 6:4–5). The God of the Scriptures is the great 'I AM' (Exod. 3:14), which directly implies that other divine claimants 'are not'. In Isaiah, the God of the Bible is emphatic: 'there is no God apart from me' (Isa. 45:22). In the NT Jesus quotes the *Shema* (Mark 12:29–31), and Paul claims that 'there is no God but one' (1 Cor. 8:4).

The Bible claims to be a special *revelation from the God who created the heavens and the earth (1 Tim. 3:16). If this claim can be authenticated, then we have direct evidence for monotheism. A thorough defence of the divine inspiration of the Bible lies outside the scope of this article, yet Christian apologists have argued that the predictive prophecies of the OT, the *miracles of the apostles and especially the *resurrection of Jesus provide sufficient evidence for the Bible's divine origin and thus for its monotheistic teachings.

This conclusion seems even stronger if we combine it with the original monotheism demonstrated above. If human beings began their history as monotheists but then evolved into paganism, then we might very well expect that God (if he exists) would at some time reveal himself to his creatures in order to correct their error. We have reason, then, to look for evidence of a special revelation from a monotheistic God. Such evidence might very well come in the form of prophetic messages authenticated by miraculous signs such as those recorded in the Bible. Of course, the Christian faith is not the only religion that claims that God has revealed himself in history. Both Judaism and Islam claim to be divinely revealed faiths. The Christian apologist argues, however, that the miraculous authentication of the Bible (as opposed to, say, the Qur'an) is superior to that for any other putative revelation.

It should be noted that the above arguments for monotheism are based on three assumptions. First, these arguments presuppose that the term 'God' refers to a being that is worthy of worship and unqualified allegiance. Since people throughout all of human history have devoted themselves to the worship of whatever they have called 'god', this presupposition may be taken for granted. Moreover, these arguments assume that God – whoever he is and whatever he is like – is the Creator and sustainer of the universe. In so far as God's existence is necessary to provide a sufficient explanation for the existence of the universe, this assumption too may be seen as eminently plausible.

The third presupposition of these arguments is that neither polytheism nor pantheism (monotheism's major competitors) can adequately support the first two assumptions. Though polytheists and pantheists do worship their respective 'gods', they can provide no rational account of why such worship is appropriate. The gods of polytheism are powerful and intelligent, and they may in some sense be partly responsible for the origin of the cosmos, but they are nonetheless finite and fallible. They cannot command our absolute devotion on any principle other than 'might makes right', but, of course, might does not make right. Neither can the finite gods of polytheism explain the existence of the cosmos, since their own existence is in need of a sufficient explanation.

The pantheistic deity is not a person but an impersonal force. Such a force may inspire a degree of wonder, but it is not at all clear why it deserves worship. Regarding the existence of the cosmos, pantheists leave it completely unexplained. Some go so far as to say that the physical world is an illusion created by ignorance, while others claim that it has existed eternally as an unexplainable brute fact.

So, given that God is worthy of our worship and is the Father of creation, and that polytheism and pantheism cannot justify these beliefs, the above arguments make a strong cumulative case for monotheism.

Bibliography

W. Corduan, *Neighboring Faiths: A Christian Introduction to World Religions* (Downers Grove, 1998), pp. 19–35; D. S. Dockery, 'Monotheism in the Scriptures', *Biblical Illustrator*, 17.4 (1991), pp. 27–30; N. L. Geisler, 'Primitive Monotheism', *Christian Apologetics Journal*, 1.1 (1998), pp. 1–5; N. L. Geisler and W. D. Watkins, *Worlds Apart: A Handbook on World Views* (Grand Rapids, 1989); T. V. Morris, *Our Idea of God: An Introduction to Philosophical Theology* (Downers Grove, 1997); W. Schmidt, *The Origin and Growth of Religion: Facts and Theories* (ET, London, 1931); Thomas Aquinas, *Summa Theologica* (Westminster, 1981).

S. B. COWAN

MORAL ARGUMENT FOR GOD

The traditional arguments for the existence of God are ontological (based on the nature of God's being), cosmological (based on order in the world) or teleological (based on purpose in the world). The moral argument for God was first propounded by Immanuel *Kant after he presented what he regarded as fatal flaws in the alternative proofs of God's existence. Kant still believed in God and argued that God's existence is a necessary postulate, even if it cannot be logically and rationally proved. Kant argues that all human beings seek their greatest good. That greatest good is happiness, which can only be properly based on duty. All of us should try to attain that greatest good. Morally we ought to do this and 'ought' implies 'can'. If there is a moral obligation to do something (an ought) then we must have the capacity so to do or else there is no moral sense in the idea that this is a duty. According to Kant, we can only make sense of *morality and duty if we make certain assumptions. These are that we have freedom, that there is a God and that there is *immortality in a future life, where the greatest good can be achieved, because it is clearly not fulfilled in this world.

Kant's threefold claim is that for morality to make sense we must postulate freedom, life after death and the existence of God. We must assume freedom to choose to do or not to do an action, otherwise it makes no sense to hold someone responsible and to praise or blame them for what is done. If we are predetermined or simply victims of *determinism, we have no choice, and morality makes no sense. This life is clearly unfair in that the good are not always rewarded and *evil is not always punished. For the world and human affairs to be ultimately moral then there must be a time after death when the greatest good is achieved and when goodness and evil reap their just rewards. Kant interpreted morality as a set of moral laws or imperatives. These were both categorical and hypothetical. 'Treat people as ends in themselves and not as means in themselves' and 'Do to others what you would wish them to do to you' are moral rules and laws. They must come from somewhere and have some moral basis.

They are laws and that requires a lawgiver. God is the lawgiver and so we must presume and postulate that he exists, otherwise the whole moral edifice would collapse in nonsense. For Kant, this moral argument 'proves', as far as is possible, that God exists. Without the idea of God, human freedom and immortality, morality would make no sense, for there would be no lawgiver and no reason to obey our moral duty.

This moral argument for God spawned many variations on the theme. Some are more robust than others in claiming that the existence of God can be proved. F. R. *Tennant and A. E. Taylor stress the remarkable congruity of moral judgments across cultures and history. This suggests that moral order is objectively part of *reality. Moral standards are seen as binding us objectively. They argue that we cannot judge what is better or worse unless we have some objective standard to which we can appeal. All of this points to divine activity in setting these moral standards.

This is critiqued on the grounds that God is not the only hypothesis. Human needs or desires might be the basis of such morality. The advantage of that would be to avoid the problem of divine agency and causation. A further problem with the God hypothesis is that there is no empirical *verification or falsification so the proposition cannot be confirmed or denied. While the moral argument for God's existence can make sense of moral demands, it may in fact make the inexplicable intelligible. Existentialists would deny that there is a moral *law and would claim that morally the world is irrational and meaningless. All humanity can do is to create its own morality.

Austin *Farrer finds the moral argument for God morally persuasive. Christianity offers a unique means of enabling us to love the neighbour who is unlovable. The moral argument makes Christianity plausible and impressive in its transforming power. Most Christians add that Christianity also makes truth-claims about the moral nature of the world's reality and human reality. C. S. *Lewis offered a variation of the moral argument, arguing that the moral law is necessary to make sense of our moral disagreements and moral criticism of each other. Without some absolute standard by which to judge, these moral aspects would make no sense. We need a basis for keeping our promises. The fact that we make excuses when we behave immorally and break the moral law in a perverse way proves that there is a moral law and that human beings have moral awareness. This is usually interpreted as *conscience, and following Paul's account in Rom. 1 – 3, that is interpreted as God's moral law written on the hearts and minds of each human individual. Humanity itself cannot be the source of morality as we are not perfect. We need a source which is all good, and God alone is that source.

In making apologetic use of the moral argument for God's existence we must consider alternative explanations for the existence of morality, the nature of the moral law, the idea of God as the lawgiver, the nature and basis of moral *authority, postulates and faith. Apologists have often seized on the moral argument as an answer to the apologetic search for a successful proof of God. It avoids the major problem of the traditional proofs which at best prove the existence of a first cause, prime mover, necessary being – all of whom seem very far from the living God of Abraham, Isaac and Jacob and the New Testament. It also offers an account of God as a person of the highest moral stature – the very ground of all goodness. It is a clear step away from the theoretical and deals with the practical realm of our human moral situation.

The apologist must deal with alternative explanations of the source of morality. It is not just a natural human instinct. If that were so, the stronger instinct would always win. We do not always act from instinct. Morality is often in conflict with our instinctual drives, and we control and overcome them to do what is right. Our instincts are not always good or morally correct. The capacity to act selflessly certainly does not seem purely instinctive. Social convention is not an adequate account of the basis of morality. We are able to go against social convention as in conscientious objection in war. The very judgment that we recognize as social and moral progress shows that we are not simply victims of our social conventions, but are able to distance ourselves from and reflect morally on them. These imply that there are some basic moral laws which we recognize and to which we refer.

While some argue that the moral law and the *natural law are the same, it is clear that there is some difference in that natural laws are descriptive and moral laws are prescriptive. We can always ask whether or not natural laws are morally good.

The main move in the twentieth century was to base morality on some feature of humanity. This might be reason, the emotions or the will. Morality was seen as a purely human function and therefore subjective rather than objective. In fact, morality might be an objective feature of human being, but the stress is often on the subjectivity of morality, implying that we could easily have other moral laws and standards than the ones we actually have. The fact that we cannot easily get rid of moral standards whenever we feel like it suggests that it is not simply our human creation. It rather seems that morality is impressed on us from some external source beyond our human control. In dealing with the various schools of moral philosophy, it is often necessary to recognize that they are right in what they affirm, e.g. that will, emotions and reason matter. They are also guilty of a reductionism which seeks to make their emphasis the total explanation of morality, rather than allowing that morality is a complex, multi-layered reality.

There is also an argument that in fact the reality of *evil and injustice in the world counts against any divine ground of morality. However, the sense of falling short of what is good reveals that there is some prior sense of goodness and morality. Some perfect standard is assumed and necessary if we are to make sense of what is less than good.

In making the moral argument for God's existence one key step is the idea of the moral law. Morality is presented as a series of commands. It would make limited sense to suggest that the moral law is nothing more than a series of self-commands. Though there are occasions when we have to 'order' ourselves to do what is right. The fear is that the idea of law is in itself insufficient to explain the varied nature of moral deliberation and judgment.

What is rather being recognized is that there seems to be a universality to moral standards and a remarkable consensus about what counts as good and bad in moral terms. That consensus requires some explanation, and so the competing views must be assessed. The hypothesis that God is the author and source of morality certainly requires such an assessment.

The problem is whether reducing the nature of God to that of a moral lawgiver really captures the essence of who God is. In the NT, when Christ gave commands, e.g. to stretch out a withered hand or to get up and walk, he also gave the power to obey the command. Part of the theological debate is whether God is only a lawgiver and whether he commands what is impossible for humanity and how fair that is. The stress of the moral argument is that if the claims of morality are absolute and universal, then there must be some absolute and all-encompassing basis and that is God. It is as if God has to exist to make sense of the reality of moral experience.

There are two broad explanations of the ground of morality. Either it is simply grounded on humanity or it has a divine origin. We all agree that there is morality and that we need to find some kind of basis for that. Of course, *existentialism argues that there is no basis, so human beings make morality. This provides a basis. It also shows the heart of the issue is not so much the origin but where the authority rests in moral standards and laws.

This can lead to an important philosophical discussion. Does God command what is good because it is already recognized as good or is it good simply because God has commanded it? The critic argues that Christians, if they are morally aware and sensible, need to ask whether the laws and commands of God are good in themselves before they commit to following God's moral laws. That would require an awareness of moral standards independent from God. Thus morality is grounded not on God but on some prior notions. The real issue here is the source of moral authority. The individual or community may come up with their moral standards and then will judge everything and everyone else in light of those standards. Moral authority then rests in the individual or the human community. In contrast moral authority rests in the God who reveals moral standards. This is summed up in the story of Abraham's willingness to sacrifice Isaac when God commanded him. *Kierkegaard stressed that this 'suspension of the teleological' highlights where ultimate moral authority rests. Human beings are unwilling to accede to external authority. This independence, or what Christians would call sinful wilfulness, stands in sharp contrast to the accepting of the authority of God. This drives us back to ask what it is about God and God's *revelation that makes us exercise the step of faith in trusting his authority. It is clear that when *Jesus taught, he taught as one who had authority. There was a clear sense that this was no ordinary human teacher but someone who expressed and embodied divine truth. For Christians, the real ground of moral authority rests in the life, example and teaching of Jesus. Experiencing the reality of Christ and his authority calls us in question and replaces our self-confidence with trust and faith in Christ.

Kant argued that we need to postulate the reality of human freedom, immortality and the existence of God to make sense of morality. This has interesting parallels with the practice in science of forming an hypothesis and conducting experiments in light of it. When scientists talk of the structure of reality consisting of atoms, electrons, neutrons or sub-atomic particles they are really offering postulates which are pragmatically useful and necessary to make sense of the world. Scientists recognize that they cannot prove the reality of these constructs but they are heuristic tools to enable us to deal with the world. While it is tempting to follow that line with the moral argument, there must be a point where the Christian claim of truth limits how far we can use the parallel.

Likewise it is unclear that 'ought implies can' in every case. We can easily be confronted with a command or demand which we cannot actually fulfil, but that does not change the reality of the demand. Theologians argue that we are unable to obey all that God requires of us, but that does not undermine the reality of the requirement. Duty is still duty even if we cannot fulfil it. It requires a step of faith in the ultimate victory of good to believe that there will be a final balancing of good and evil beyond the here and now. Faith rather than simple rationality seems necessary for such a belief.

The moral argument does not offer us a full and final proof of the existence of God. If it did it would prove too much, for then faith would be redundant and everyone would be irrational not to believe in God. The evidence is open to differing interpretations and requires faith.

Moral questions confront everyone. The ground of our morality is a natural and fruitful way of opening up apologetic discussion. The moral argument for God may not finally prove God's existence, but it does create an opportunity to confront the questions of what authority we live by and where we find a basis for morality. The final judgment will be between a simply human or divine authority.

Bibliography

I. Kant, *Critique of Practical Reason* (Indianapolis, 1996); C. S. Lewis, *Mere Christianity* (New York, 2001).

E. D. COOK

MORAL DIFFICULTIES IN SCRIPTURE

General considerations

Moral difficulties arise in Scripture whenever there is a dissonance between the biblical ethic and our own moral understanding. The construction of a biblical ethic is itself far from straightforward, and four relevant problems should be noted.

First, there are conceptual problems. At times the Bible thinks in alien categories. For example, OT law uses oppositions such as 'clean' and 'unclean' (Lev. 11 – 15), and this fact can be used to deny Scripture's moral relevance. But the difficulty can be overstated, for there are continuities as well, not least in the ideas of God, his character and his relationship to his faithful people. Once ethics is located in that context, the possibility of moral relevance is established.

The problem of normative force raises the difficulty that it is not always clear what Scripture is presenting as ethically desirable. Some instances are completely clear: there is no doubt that David's unconventional behaviour in worshipping before the ark of the covenant (2 Sam. 6) is approved and his adultery with Bathsheba is not (2 Sam. 11 – 12). Many other cases, however, are harder to discern. When the psalmist calls for the destruction of Babylonian children (Ps. 137:9), is this simply an affirmation of the value of honesty about real feelings of vengeance before God, a delight in the *justice of God which is pictured symbolically, or an approval of what we can only see as cruelty? Just what was so pleasing about Samson (cf. Heb. 11:32)? There is no general solution to such difficulties, and no substitute for careful contextual exegesis.

Then there are problems of situation. At one point *Jesus commands his followers to evangelize in a spirit of absolute poverty (Luke 10:4); later on he rescinds, or at least modifies, that command (Luke 22:35–36). To one church Paul appears to enjoin silence on women (1 Tim. 2:11–12); in another context he refers to women praying and prophesying (1 Cor. 11:5). Proverbs gives contradictory advice (cf. Prov. 26:4–5). There is no real difficulty in the idea that different situations require different responses; the difficulty is knowing how situation-specific the injunction is. The Ten Commandments have often been taken to express universal moral propositions, but it is far from clear that the text warrants this (Deut. 5:6, 15–16), and in practice moral theologians rework them into more general underlying moral principles. This process of unearthing the underlying principles should take account of the whole witness of Scripture in constructing a coherent biblical ethic. If the problem of normative force requires depth of study, the problem of situation requires breadth.

Finally, there are problems of progression. Few would want to support a crude distinction between OT and NT. Nevertheless, in constructing a biblical ethic, some element of progression has to be recognized. There is movement from Exodus to Deuteronomy, from pre- to post-exilic, from Gospel to epistle. Just how much real development there is in this depends, for example, on how far one considers the ethical dimensions of Christ's 'fulfilment' of the law (Matt. 5:17) to be already latent in it or developed out of it, a point on which scholars will no doubt continue to disagree.

The other side of any moral difficulty is a discrepancy with our own sense of what really is good and *evil. It would be a mistake to absolutize our moral sense: older attempts to grapple with moral difficulties in Scripture betray the fact that the points of tension, and indeed the very interpretations of Scripture themselves, vary with shifts in conventional *morality. Not many today will share the difficulties some Puritan commentators had with the Song of Songs; we get exercised instead by the Pauline view of gender. So there is an element of fashion about moral difficulties in Scripture. Openness and perseverance in the struggle towards a 'reflective equilibrium' between Scripture and our moral sense is the characteristic attitude of those committed to its authority.

Moral difficulties with theism

Any theistic faith faces three closely related moral problems: the problem of evil, the problem of suffering and the problem of human moral responsibility. The three problems are related by reference to the belief that God is good and omnipotent. If God is good and omnipotent, why was evil ever allowed to come into existence in the first place, why are people permitted to suffer unjustly and how can individual human beings be held morally responsible for their actions?

Philosophers of religion have made various suggestions which go some way to reducing the extent of the difficulty, but it is probably wise to accept that there is no perfect theoretical solution. Instead one can point out that *atheism faces parallel difficulties. In a materialist universe it is hard to explain why the concept of evil is coherent at all, why suffering matters morally and how human action is neither random nor completely locked into determined chains of cause and effect.

The Bible affirms all aspects of the problem: God is perfectly good (Mark 10:18) and completely sovereign over human affairs (Matt. 10:29–30), yet evil is real (Eph. 6:12), human suffering is deeply problematic (John 11:35) and human beings are responsible to God and each other for the harm they cause (Rom. 2:5–8). It also acknowledges the experiential difficulties associated with evil and suffering, explored at length in the wisdom literature. It is better to live with the tensions than to seek a resolution which is ultimately false to some aspect of our understanding and experience. What is distinctive about the Bible's accounts of these difficulties is that God is deeply implicated in their solution. We can live with the problem of evil because ultimately it requires another *mystery – the death of God's Son – to resolve (Phil. 2:6–8).

The judgment of God

The Bible consistently affirms that God has the power to create and destroy human life (Matt. 10:28). Examples include the destruction of the world by flood (Gen. 7:21–23), Sodom and Gomorrah (Gen. 18:16 – 19:29), the plague on the Egyptian firstborn (Exod. 12:29), the plague after the golden calf (Exod. 32:35), Nadab and Abihu (Lev. 10:1–2), the death of those who craved quail (Num. 11:33), the Korahite rebellion (Num. 16), the plague on those who slept with Moabite women (Num. 25), the men of Beth Shemesh who looked in the ark (1 Sam. 6:19–20), Uzzah (2 Sam. 6:6–7), the plague caused by David's census (1 Chr. 21), the boys who taunted Elisha (2 Kgs

2:23–24), the annihilation of Sennacherib's army (2 Chr. 32:21), Ananias and Sapphira (Acts 5:1–11), Herod (Acts 12:21–23), the world at the end of time (2 Pet. 3:7) and the final judgment (Rev. 20:15). All are deliberate acts of divine intervention.

Difficulties arise in three respects: the apparent triviality of the wrong (e.g. the boys' taunting of Elisha), the extent of the punishment (as in the traditional doctrine of *hell) and the notion of collective punishment present in some cases (as in the death of 70,000 Israelites for David's sin of numbering).

Careful exegesis can go some way to reducing these difficulties. The 'boys' who mocked Elisha may well have been a mob of young men with more in mind than rude words. The ultimate fate of those who consistently refuse God's offer of forgiveness and reconciliation is clearly pictured symbolically, and theologians continue to debate the possibility of ultimate annihilation. Collective aspects of punishment are complex. One has to recognize both a line of thought that ties the fate of peoples to their leaders and the fact that notions of collective guilt are often, and increasingly, muted (Gen. 18:22–33; Jer. 31:29–30; Ezek. 18; Rom. 2:6–11).

In seeking to understand the appropriateness of divine retribution in the particular case, it is important not to overlook the general message, which is the moral significance of death. The normality of even 'natural death' can never quite remove the sense of moral outrage that all death provokes. Human death – spiritual and physical – is the appropriate divine response to human sin (Gen. 2:17; Rom. 5:12–14). The delay in execution is already a sign of God's mercy and an opportunity to seek the remedy he offers (Luke 13:1–5; Rom. 2:4; 2 Pet. 3:9).

War, crime and proportionality

If there is one group of moral difficulties in Scripture most often raised, it is the apparent approval of disproportionate responses to war and crime. The total destruction of the indigenous tribes of the Promised Land, starting with Sihon and Og (Num. 21), the Midianites (Num. 31) and Jericho (Josh. 6:21), are the most notorious incidents, but the list continues with the death of the Amalekites (1 Sam. 15), the 20,000 men of Seir (2 Chr. 25:11–12) and the slaughter of 75,000 in 'self-defence' recorded in Esther (Esth. 9:16). On a smaller scale one can note the mayhem committed by the Levites in the aftermath of the golden-calf incident (Exod. 32:27–28), a whole series of assassinations (e.g. Judg. 4:12–30; 1 Kgs 2:13–46) and the slaughter of Ahab's family by Jehu (2 Kgs 10:1–17).

Apparent disproportionality in war is matched by apparent disproportionality in punishment. The death penalty was prescribed for non-accidental killing (Exod. 21:12–14), striking or cursing parents (Exod. 21:15, 18), kidnapping (Exod. 21:16), failing to restrain a dangerous animal (Exod. 21:29), contempt of court and false testimony (Deut. 17:12; 19:16–19), Sabbath-breaking (Exod. 31:14), priestly drunkenness, sacrilege and false prophecy (Lev. 10:8–9; Num. 4:15; Deut. 18:20), witchcraft, idolatry, apostasy and blasphemy (Exod. 22:18, 20; Lev. 20:2; 24:15–16), adultery, incest, homosexual acts, bestiality and other sexual offences (Exod. 22:19; Lev. 20:10–16). The Sabbath-breaker was stoned (Num. 15:36) and Achan and his family executed (Josh. 7:25), and Elijah managed to dispatch 850 prophets of Baal and Asherah (1 Kgs 18:40).

It is probable that the wars of occupation have to be seen as unique acts of God's judgment (cf. Gen. 15:16) from which Israel was not exempt (Deut. 28:15–68); full discussion is beyond the scope of this article. But it is not clear that all this has to be justified in detail. The difficulty – if there is one – is that God works in cultures as cruel and violent as the Ancient Near East; there is still relative good and evil even there. And some reflection on the horrendous practices of surrounding cultures will go a considerable way to mitigating the apparent disproportionality of Israel and exposing its relative humaneness. Of course, the non-coercive character of the kingdom of Christ is one of the clearest points of progression from OT to NT.

Lies and deception

At several points in the OT, people deceive others and are approved of. The clearest example is that of the Hebrew midwives, who not only lie to Pharoah to save the lives of newborn Hebrew boys, but are commended and blessed by God for doing so (Exod. 2:15–21). One might also note Jacob's dealings with Laban (Gen. 29 – 31), Rahab and the spies (Josh. 2; cf. Matt. 1:5), Michal's attempts to mislead Saul's men to save David's life (1 Sam. 19:11–16), and David's own feigned madness and campaign of deception at the court of King Achish (1 Sam. 21:13; 27:8–12). Likewise 2 Sam. 17 records the successful concealment of Ahimaaz and Jonathan from Absalom's men, and 2 Kgs 10 tells of Jehu's deceitful slaughter of the priests of Baal. If these events are ambiguous in their approval, Elisha's trap for the Arameans is not (2 Kgs 6:8–23). Elisha lies to the soldiers, calls on God to blind them and successfully leads them into the hands of the king of Israel in Samaria, albeit to a great feast! The NT contains no such incidents, although the escape of Paul from Damascus (2 Cor. 11:32–33) and Jesus' own escape from the people of Nazareth (Luke 4:28–30) are worth noting. Did the latter involve similar 'induced blindness'?

These incidents cause difficulty for an absolutist approach to truth-telling, and earlier ages spent considerable effort in explaining them away in order to maintain the proposition that one should never lie. Eventually such explanations have to rely on divine intervention to block the inevitable consequences of truth-telling. The better view, however, is that truth is not owed to an enemy, a category which embraces at least those who unjustly threaten the lives of others. Indeed, the 2 Kgs 6 incident and Jesus at Nazareth suggest a connection between human acts of deceit to save life and God's judicial blinding of those who persistently reject him (cf. Luke 8:10).

Prophetic acts and symbolic language

Prophecy is primarily about providing God's perspective on human affairs. In their struggle to get the message across to an unwilling audience, the prophets at times resorted to behaviour and *language that was unconventional, even bordering on the immoral. Hosea was commanded to marry 'an adulterous wife' (Hos. 1:2) and Ezekiel's strange acts (Ezek. 4:1 – 5:4) may have contributed to the early death of his own wife (Ezek. 24:15–24). In each case, the emotional turmoil involved served a higher purpose of portraying the passion of God for his people. Similarly, Ezekiel's language in chapters 16 and 23 transgresses the bounds of decency, although modern insensibilities may find less to cavil at than an earlier generation.

Other, rather harder, instances can also be seen as pushing the bounds of morality in the service of truth. The weird behaviour of the prophets recounted in 1 Kgs 13 and 20 can be seen in this light, as can – outstandingly

– God's call to Abraham to sacrifice Isaac (Gen. 22:1–19). The few points at which Jesus' behaviour seems odd to modern eyes – the cleansing of the temple (John 2:12–25), the destruction of the Gerasene swine (Mark 5:1–20) and the cursing of the fig-tree (Matt. 21:18–20) – serve to highlight important truths about God's ways with people. The violent language of the Apocalypse (e.g. Rev. 14:18–20), as well as Jude and 2 Pet. 2, makes powerful points symbolically and causes real moral difficulty only to the literally minded.

Do such prophetic acts and words have general normative force? If they do, one must note that the immorality they express and condone is relatively minor. It is not insignificant that Abraham did not actually sacrifice Isaac, and although we cannot be precisely sure of the extent of his prophetic insight (cf. Heb. 11:17–19), the text hints that he did not expect his son to die (Gen. 22:5, 8). At the very least, these incidents are useful reminders that propriety is not always appropriate.

Family, gender and sexuality

Traditional Christian teaching about *marriage and family is under considerable social pressure today at two points in particular: the notion that *gender roles are in some important way distinctive and the idea that appropriate sexual relationships are always heterosexual. Both pressures arise from a loss of commitment to the notion of a necessary 'otherness' in sexual relations. Furthermore, the casualization and even commercialization of sexual relations is widely tolerated. Of course, considerable amounts have been written reassessing biblical teaching in this area. The only point to note here is the consistency of the biblical witness to the value of marriage as lifelong monogamous heterosexual union, both as a principle of social ordering and as a metaphor of God's relationship to his people (Hos. 2:2 – 3:3; Ezek. 16:1–14; Matt. 19:4–6; Eph. 5:25–32; Rev. 21:2).

From an apologetic perspective it is helpful to remember that the biblical ethic can be seen as morally problematic in different ways. The teaching of Christ and the apostles relativizing marriage and the family in order to affirm the value of celibate singleness (Matt. 10:37; 12:46–50) presented a considerable challenge to conventional rabbinic morality. Polygamous societies struggle with monogamy; societies in which the intergenerational bond (e.g. mother-son) remains primary even after marriage struggle with the element of rupture and re-establishment. In all likelihood the growing casual unisexism of the Western world will seem as problematic to future generations, as indeed it does currently to much of the rest of the world. Evidence of the enormous physical and emotional costs it brings in its wake is not hard to find.

Slaves and animals

Concerns are commonly expressed about the Bible's attitude to slaves and animals. Why was Paul not more outspoken about the institution of *slavery? How could God permit the widespread destruction of animal life attendant upon the sacrificial system (1 Kgs 8:63)?

Careful exegesis can go a long way to unearthing what the Bible actually has to teach in such matters. The Hebrew institution of slavery is more akin to medium-term bonded servitude, and the 'slave' had a number of important rights (e.g. Deut. 15:12–18). Slavery is a symbol of oppression by sin from which Christ came to release us (Luke 4:18–19). Even Paul, for all his acceptance of Roman slavery – and its collapse as an institution would have risked widespread destitution and death – encouraged slaves to seek their liberty within the law (1 Cor. 7:21) and condemned slave-trading (1 Tim. 1:10). As for animals, the writer to the Hebrews made the obvious point that God cannot take delight in the destruction of what he created (Heb. 10:8; see also Exod. 20:10; Deut. 25:4; Prov. 12:10). A more careful articulation of the concept of stewardship (Gen. 1:28) can avoid charges of environmental exploitation. For all that, the Bible is clear that humans matter more than animals. We might usefully reflect on the standards of our own society, which kills foetuses but not foxes and which spends more money on pampering pets than on preventing starvation and disease among countless fellow human beings.

Conclusion: God in the dock?

C. S. *Lewis once wrote: 'The ancient man approached God ... as the accused person approaches his judge. For the modern man the roles are reversed. He is the judge: God is in the dock. He is quite a kindly judge: if God should have a reasonable defence for being the god who permits war, poverty and disease, he is ready to listen to it. The trial may even end in God's acquittal. But the important thing is that man is on the bench and God in the dock.'

We will not learn from Scripture unless we first understand it, but the process of understanding can easily put God in the dock. The difficulties we find in Scripture remind us of the need for both humility and perseverance in 'correctly handling the word of truth' (2 Tim. 2:15). By contrast, a recovery of a proper sense of wonder at the moral excellence of Scripture will help us to keep the difficulties we find in perspective.

Bibliography

H. E. Guillebaud, *Some Moral Difficulties of the Bible* (London, 1949); J. Rivers, 'The Moral Authority of Scripture', *Cambridge Papers*, vol. 3, no. 3 (Cambridge, 2004); W. J. Webb, *Slaves, Women and Homosexuals* (Downers Grove, 2001); J. W. Wenham, *The Enigma of Evil: Can We Believe in the Goodness of God?* (Guildford, 1974); C. J. H. Wright, *Living as the People of God* (Leicester, 2004).

J. RIVERS

MORALISM, see LEGALISM AND MORALISM

MORALITY

Morality is a concept basic to human existence, and has been contemplated by philosophers since ancient times. 'We are discussing no small matter, but how we ought to live,' *Plato reported of *Socrates in the *Republic* of 390 BC. Morality is a matter of behaviour, action, pursuit of the good and right living, and deals with the realm of values. To the philosophers, morality is a matter of achieving some sort of systematic understanding of values and right action, or the effort to guide human conduct by reason. For Christians, morality may include any or all of these concepts, as an attempt is made to understand how humans ought to behave, and what sort of attitude they should have towards themselves, others and God. There has been much discussion over whether morality for the Christian has any common ground with the morality of human beings generally.

The way that these issues are addressed may depend on the general understanding of what constitutes morality. Is morality a matter of conformity to laws and rules (deontological absolutism), of behaviour arising from right motive or good character (virtue *ethics), or of behaviour that achieves a good outcome for the greatest number possible (eudemonism/ *utilitarianism)? We may well support the inclusion of all of these aspects in a complete understanding of morality, particularly from a Christian point of view. However, various emphases in the history of moral philosophy and Christian ethics have not always achieved such a balance.

The nature of morality

Diverse tensions exist between various Christian understandings of the nature of morality. Not everyone answers the basic questions in the same way. Is morality natural or reasonable, and is it present in all human beings? Are *moral values universal or culturally relative? Moreover, is morality dependent upon a special *revelation of God in Christ? If so, then how do we understand the morality of those who do not share Christian faith?

The association between the goodness of God and human goodness is essential to an appreciation of the influence of religion on morality. As Christian morality is inevitably linked to a Christian world-view, an understanding of God and his relationship to his creation will determine much of the nature and content of morality. For example, some suggest that the good is an autonomous characteristic that is independent of both God and humanity: God wills the good because it is good. Others argue that the good is very much dependent on the nature and will of God: something is good because God wills it, not because it possesses some innate quality of goodness.

While we may wish to affirm aspects of both, Christians and others are still left with the quandary of how to discover what the good entails. In Greek philosophy, the pursuit of morality was characterized by reason and the cultivation of virtues to counter human vices. For Plato, this meant using reason to apprehend the true and eternal good, while for *Aristotle, it was a matter of discovering what virtues were consistent with human nature and potential. The Stoics emphasized a morality of reason that transcended circumstance, while the Epicureans placed great value on the pursuit of physical pleasure. These early tensions between natural and ideal morality,

and between reason and experience, characterize many of the debates in moral philosophy today. Not surprisingly, they are also reflected in discussions of Christian morality.

For *Augustine, and later for *Thomas Aquinas, morality required an engagement of faithful reason. In Aristotelian fashion, they contended that there are certain observable ends towards which humans are directed by nature. Observation of nature leads to the development of particular ideas of morality to which humans ought to conform. For Augustine, love was the ultimate ethical category, which gave direction and proportion to all other actions: 'Love, and do what you will,' he exhorted. By contrast, Aquinas directed his natural understanding towards the development of virtues, which the scholastic thinkers later attempted to apply in detailed form to particular situations through the painstaking form of casuistry. For some scholars, morality provided reasonable evidence of the imprint of God on humanity and lent reasoned support to *theistic proofs.

Immanuel *Kant pushed the role of reason further. Suggesting that reason was an imperfect tool for apprehending God, he indicated that it could be useful for apprehending modes of human behaviour, though he later raised doubts about the validity of moral knowledge as well. He devised several categorical imperatives, which he believed could guide the reason into knowledge of the good, and appropriation of the good in human behaviour. The first categorical imperative stated, 'Do only that which you would wish to become a universal law'; but he soon felt that it was insufficient on its own. He added several others that indicated the importance of using other people as ends and never as means, and focused on good consequences as well as right actions. The *conscience was an important moral consideration for Kant, as he was a critical idealist who believed, to some degree, in the immanent mind of God in humanity. Duty was also an important focus of social morality. The social impetus and requirement of moral obligation not only offered Kant evidence for a universal ethic but pointed to the very existence of God.

Is the universality of morality, as posited by Kant, evidence for the existence of God? Some would argue yes, despite some cultural exceptions to the universality of certain values such as prohibitions against murder. Others accuse those who believe in the universality of moral values of committing the naturalistic fallacy. The naturalistic fallacy has been the topic of much ethical debate, suggesting that it is false to derive an ethical obligation from a statement of fact or observable natural phenomenon. The debate often revolves around the nature of the divine–human relationship, where moral obligations are said to derive from the fact of God's fatherhood. Others have argued against this, suggesting that the fact of donating genetic material is insufficient to establish a relationship of duty or obligation from child to parent. They would assert that obligation arises from the quality of the relationship, rather than its fact.

Personal morality

Theologically, revelation must be held together with reason in any consideration of morality. Karl *Barth pushed this idea to the extreme, indicating that an action based on anything other than the revealed Word in *Jesus Christ constituted empty religion and rebellion against God. Others, however, wanted to allow for general revelation, and the idea that actions – even of non-Christians – could be evaluated in categories relative to the good. They pointed to moral obligations arising from humanity's created nature and to the existence of the image of God in all humanity as a point of commonality between Christians and non-Christians. Potential to know and achieve the good is necessary in order to maintain moral responsibility.

Many Christians, however, believe that the condition of sin inhibits humanity's ability to perceive and pursue the good (the 'noetic effect' of sin). The sinful condition separates humanity from God, but acts of sin committed freely constitute active rebellion against him. Morality in this sense is more than an attitude or world-view; it is also a matter of action. Although there is a human predisposition to sin, Reinhold Niebuhr posited the 'impossible possibility' – the idea that humans could conceivably resist sin, thus maintaining their moral responsibility.

Special revelation reinforces obligation and responsibility to God, as he has made his nature and will evident through grace. The Christian responds in gratitude to God for his divine gift. Moreover, the believer is morally reoriented, having a cleansed conscience and a new eschatological motive. Empowered by the Spirit, the believer is yet still morally responsible, and the possibility of sin is ever present.

The knowledge of God's gift in Christ reinforces the cost of achieving the good.

Public morality

Considering the moral responsibility of humanity, and the special revelation of the moral standard of the cross, should Christians expect their morality to prevail in the public square? Philosopher J. S. *Mill championed the notion that the morality of a particular group should not be imposed upon society. Rather, the only moral imposition should be that which prevents harm. The question of what constitutes harm, and whose morality defines that concept, is debated to the present day. Moreover, not all accept Mill's basic premise about the degree of liberty that should be permitted in a society. Christians have pursued diverse approaches to this question historically and in recent times.

Culture wars

For some, morality is a matter of cultural conflict. Predominantly an American approach, the idea of the *culture war suggests that Christian morality will find itself in strident conflict against the values of secular society. Advocates of the culture war support the antagonistic position of Christians in the public square, as they attempt to legitimize Christian moral interests for society as a whole. Often, it involves challenging laws that appear to counter the claims of the gospel, and enacting laws that embody them. Such a counter-cultural approach may not reflect the variety of moral positions that Christians may actually hold on a given issue. It may also seem strident, literal and legalistic. Yet, there have been times in history when faithfulness to Christian belief and doctrine meant conflict with society on the matter of morality.

Social gospel

The social-gospel attitude has led many Christians to seek moral alliances with those of similar mind on given issues. Regardless of their faith perspective, the cooperation of others on matters of justice, for example, is seen as evidence of God-consciousness at work in his creation, revealing the kingdom of God. In this sense, morality is seen as a matter of corporate 'enlightenment', and the provision of moral resources to engage actions that will bring about human fulfilment. Moral values are shared amongst those of diverse faith commitments, and none.

Liberation

Liberation ethics emphasize God's preferential option for the poor, and insist on identification with the oppressed as evidence of Christian conviction. As in the social-gospel approach, shared convictions and actions to bring about change are at least as important as sharing doctrinal belief. Morality is more a matter of *praxis* than *dogma*. Therefore Christian convictions must be lived out, and they may well find commonality with others who are involved in the same action, though they may not share a common belief.

Study dialogue

In the post-Second World War period, there was a clear emphasis on the importance of Christians studying matters of public policy, in order to reflect biblically and ecumenically upon them. For some, it is still an important approach to public morality. Advocates of this approach will be clear about the distinctiveness of Christian moral teaching, but will be open to engage in conversation with other groups in society in order to find ways of living out morality that benefit everyone.

Moral formation

An emphasis on the development of character, especially within the context of a faith *community, is the concern of moral-formation advocates. The basic contention is that morality is not a matter of making decisions, but rather of developing virtues through enacting corporate practices within the life of the church. Human beings will always act in accordance with their character, and so rather than emphasize participation in the public square, or recommend policies to non-believers, advocates of this position believe that the church simply needs to be a living witness to an alternative moral reality of peace.

It may be argued that the preferred approach to public morality may well be determined by context; for example, under conditions of oppression, approaches that depend on principles of an open society may not be relevant. Generally, however, in a democratic society, Christians have the same opportunities, responsibilities and obligations as others to encourage the adoption of policies that will benefit them as members of society. Christians are not to be surprised that public morality does not necessarily represent their values, nor should they expect a Christian point of view to prevail in the public square. On the other hand, they should be encouraged to remember that there is no such thing as a value-free society, or value-neutral policy. In every policy decision, some kind of morality is reflected. Christians in democratic countries should not hesitate to inform the moral content of policy decisions or to challenge those that they believe to be contrary to their morality. Moreover, Christians involved in such activities are obliged to articulate their morality in ways that are accessible to those who do not necessarily share their religious commitments.

The distinctiveness of Christian morality

Although a certain commonality may exist between Christian and natural morality, as affirmed through a doctrine of creation, there is a distinction when Christians consider the challenge and claims of Christ on their lives. Christian belief informs a world-view through which believers understand and fashion their morality, and it may differ radically from secular morality. The Pauline corpus emphasises this, as Paul consistently highlights the ethical implications of doctrinal belief and teaching. Action must grow out of belief: *if* this is what Christ has done, Paul exhorts, *then* this is how we should live. The life of faith is lived in such a way that provides apologetic evidence of the character of the God whom Christians serve.

The distinctiveness of Christian morality need not isolate Christians from moral discussion with people of other faiths or none. Christians have sometimes been accused of having an ambivalent attitude towards moral philosophy. Yet even a basic familiarity with the field of Christian ethics, in both contemporary and historical contexts, reveals the influence of moral philosophy and the apologetic potential of dialogue between the two.

N. H. G. Robinson noted that there are at least four points of common interest between Christian ethics and moral philosophy, which offer opportunity for such a dialogue. He indicated the possibility of morality (freedom and responsibility), the purity of morality, the objectivity of morality, and the coherency of the moral claim, as points where Christians and moral philosophers may find dialogue mutually edifying. Recent shifts in moral philosophy have had repercussions for Christian ethics in significant ways that suggest that the relationship is closer than Christians may sometimes be willing to admit. To consider Christian ethics within the wider framework of morality is itself an apologetic challenge.

Bibliography

A. MacIntyre, *A Short History of Ethics* (London, 1998); J. Rachels, *The Elements of Moral Philosophy* (London and New York, 2002); A. M. Robbins, *Methods in the Madness* (Carlisle, 2004); N. H. G. Robinson, *The Groundwork of Christian Ethics* (London, 1971).

A. M. ROBBINS

MORAL VALUES, OBJECTIVITY OF

Moral values comprise the ethical code by which humans measure their behaviour. Objectivity refers to the degree to which such values stand outside of the realm of individual and cultural experience, to be discovered and manifested free from subjective interpretation. The objectivity of moral values, perhaps once taken for granted, has fallen on hard times in recent days.

Early in the history of moral philosophy, reason and virtue were considered as universal instruments to discern moral values. For *Plato, moral values stood beyond the realm of experience and desires, as ideals that could be approximated through virtue. His student *Aristotle opted for a more teleological approach, suggesting that the proper exercise of natural reason is the end towards which humans are directed. Moral virtue is achieved in so far as the precepts of reason are obeyed. In the first instance, moral values are embodied in ideals; in the second, they conform to reason.

For many in the Christian era, moral value became embodied in God's absolute commands for obedience. The objectivity of moral values, at least from a human perspective, was provided by God's authority to command, and by his character, as he desires the good for his creation. Such *absolutes stand outside subjective contexts. Yet the way humans grasp and apply absolutes in diverse contexts remains complex and varied. For example, Plato's division between the natural realm of desires and the ideal realm of virtues became reflected in *Augustine's theological approach to moral values. Aristotle's approach, of bringing *morality in line with obedience to a reasonable

good, prevailed with *Thomas Aquinas. In both cases, reason and values correspond, to some degree, with moral reality.

The crisis of correspondence between reason and reality began in the modern period with David *Hume. Hume indicated that the only certainties that are verifiable by sensory experience are those related to analytical truths. Beyond that, no knowledge can be certain. Immanuel *Kant attempted to overcome this scepticism by appealing to reason, while acknowledging that reason was reliable because of its universality rather than because of any inherent quality of verifiable *truth. Reason was the tool by which Kant sought to understand and apply objective morality, which applied as categorical imperatives to all of humanity.

For Kant, moral values are to be found beyond the realm of nature, in a presupposed category of perceptions. As we are unable to know things in themselves, and know only our perceptions of things, we must learn to distinguish between inclination and duty. Duty challenges the subjectivity of our inclinations or desires, as we obey only those laws that we would wish to become universal laws. Though Kant's approach presupposes God, he is not interested in dictated values, or in values that represent some utilitarian outcome. His are reasoned values that are to be enacted rationally in every place and for all time. Accordingly, individuals are inescapably their own moral authorities.

Even the *utilitarianism of Jeremy Bentham and John Stuart Mill, and the social contract of Jean-Jacques *Rousseau, offered some degree of moral objectivity. For the utilitarians, moral values are embodied in those actions that bring about the greatest average utility or happiness for a group of people. For social-contract theorists, moral values are more pessimistically represented in those things that harness *evil and allow the common good to flourish. However, even such non-absolutist views give rise to inevitable questions about who decides what the good entails, and how we are to meditate between competing versions of what constitutes the good. Challenges to the objectivity of moral values have been many.

Challenges to objectivity

Cultural relativism

Unlike scepticism, which posits that there are no moral values, cultural *relativism suggests that moral values exist but are far from universal or absolute. Anthropological studies throughout the early twentieth century demonstrated that not all cultures share the same values. This discovery threw the matter of objectivity of values into renewed crisis. Social scientists verified that some cultures value truth-telling while others admire deceit. Some revere the elderly while others consider them to be a drain on scarce resources. Some value compassion and mercy while others are more fatalistic about matters of life and death. Some value sexual monogamy and others tolerate sexual promiscuity. In early anthropological studies, such moral variety was explained simply by distinguishing cultures as civilized, or uncivilized. The moral values of various cultures were dismissed as 'primitive' if they did not correspond to the values held by the Western world.

It did not take long, however, for people to recognize that such dismissive attitudes did not do justice to the moral variety that existed between cultures. Dismissing other cultures as 'primitive' was itself a culture-bound judgment. Some began to posit that moral values were really a matter of cultural practice. There could be no such thing as universal morality or absolute moral rules. Moral values were held to be nothing more than codes embodied in particular cultures and passed down through generations with adaptations as necessary.

James Rachels has responded to the challenge of cultural relativity by suggesting that simply describing ethical practices may detract from understanding the actual moral values of a culture. For example, the culture that abandons its elderly may not necessarily value human life less than another; rather, it may understand such behaviour as the best means of preserving life according to available resources. Nevertheless, many still conclude that, because of our limited perspectives, one culture could no longer judge the moral code of another except by its own cultural standards. Cultural relativity called into question the ability of moral reason to access reality objectively, beyond well-conditioned parameters.

Science and subjectivity

Other contemporary challenges to objectivity emerge from an epistemological distinction between fact and opinion. *Science, operating according to coherent structures and observable phenomena, is often seen to deal with the realm of fact. Other types of knowledge reflect beliefs and preferences. The realm of moral values, standing outside the scientific enterprise, cannot be objective in the same sense that science is objective.

However, work by Michael *Polanyi and Thomas Kuhn challenged the understanding of science as establishing objective fact. They showed that scientists work in accordance with preconceived ideas, just as non-scientists do. Such preconceived ideas function coherently as world-views, indicating less objectivity in the scientific enterprise than is usually assumed. The concepts of true and false are measured as such only against various other assumptions and value commitments to what is true and what is false.

Some scholars would wish to move beyond the point of sheer relativism in science and in other types of knowledge. Polanyi, for example, does not necessarily deny that there is a 'real' to which we wish to refer in our knowledge. Certainly, 'we know more than we can tell'. He suggests we must recover for our knowledge a sense of belief, as all knowledge is belief, a gift of grace, in the tradition of Augustine. It is also personal, based on our own sense of experiencing and knowing; yet it is not completely subjective, and offers some sense of connecting with objective reality.

Polanyi offers a challenge to some contemporary scholars who prefer to follow the analytical philosophers into an analysis of *language that leaves little opportunity to engage with objective reality. For them, all of reality is shaped by and composed of language, which is therefore completely relative, both to each culture and even to each individual. Beyond this, there is no knowledge of what is real, and therefore no objective moral values.

Situationism and pragmatism

As a proponent of 'the new morality' in the 1960s, Joseph Fletcher pursued a form of *pragmatism with respect to moral values. Suggesting that *legalism, antinomianism and even absolute relativism are untenable, he indicated a way forward that took love as the moral absolute and pragmatism as a method of applying love in various situations. He acknowledged a form of relativism, indicating that relativism implies a norm or absolute, as moral values are enacted 'relative' to the norm of love. Focused on contexts and outcomes, moral values will be determined by the situations to which love is applied.

Moreover, Richard *Rorty has suggested that the words 'objective values' themselves constitute an absurdity. Values by definition imply subjectivity, as they reflect little more than personal preferences and culturally conditioned ideals. Consequently, our understanding of 'truth' should not be thought of as 'objective'. Rorty would like us to move beyond the divide between fact and value, or knowledge and opinion, indicating that they are far closer together than we usually admit. Moral values will then reflect what it is useful to do in a given context, and will have no inherent universal or objective quality.

Under contemporary intellectual conditions, pragmatist and contextual approaches have grown increasingly popular. Postmodern philosophy has reinforced epistemological scepticism, and even some Christians find it difficult to discuss moral values outside a subjective, narrative and ruggedly contextual framework. For some, there is growing scepticism that reasoned absolutes can be apprehended by a humanity that is so deeply conditioned by language and *culture. An increasing anthropological awareness has led many to conclude that moral values are culturally relative, and therefore are not absolutes at all, but pretensions to *power of one cultural group over another. Objective moral absolutes as such do not exist. There are merely moral relativities.

Meeting the challenges

Although it may be right to critique claims to knowledge unfettered by any cultural, contextual or otherwise subjective criteria, such critiques need not destroy confidence in the reasonableness of morality. Reason may be insufficient to establish the objectivity of moral values, but that is not to say that they are therefore unreasonable, completely contextual or a simple matter of cultural preference.

Pragmatists such as Rorty encourage us to surrender the quest for correspondence with truth or reality, and simply indicate that one vocabulary offers more help than another in a given situation, or for a particular purpose. But it is still not clear what makes one vocabulary more helpful or successful, and how that is appraised. Every form of rationality, even pragmatism, needs criteria that extend beyond individual or cultural preference. Christian moral values wish, not simply to describe, but to explain something about the God we worship and our relationship with him.

God has revealed himself to humanity, and in his *revelation we may understand something of the good that lies outside our subjective experience. Theologically, Karl *Barth saw the God of revelation as 'subjective' in the *Kierkegaardian sense that humans encounter God, not as the object of their rational mind, but as the subject who reveals. This recalls for us our limits in attempting to 'objectivize' God and the good, as creations of our machinations. It also reinforces a source of moral value that lies beyond our experience. Because of our sinful pretensions, humans need a critique of our moral positions that comes from beyond our potentially narrow subjective viewpoints.

It cannot be denied that different moral codes characterize diverse cultures of the world. However, adhering to moral relativism would prevent us from criticizing not only the moral code of other cultures but also our own. There is, within the band of relativism, no clear means of determining better and worse codes of behaviour, and therefore no means for improving the moral values even within a particular culture.

Yet the challenge of relativism reminds us of the potential we do have for absolutizing mere human inclinations or preferences. We may mistakenly turn our ideas of how things ought to be done into objective absolutes by which we judge the behaviour of others. Such absolutism may easily turn into a legalistic or moralistic system of exclusion, judgment and oppression. This is exacerbated when biblical texts or religious beliefs are brought in to justify a particular position that may rightly be described as cultural.

Cultural absolutism demonstrates the potential dangers of an ethic that is neither realist nor contextual. The *realism of moral values indicates that there are moral absolutes that exist independently of our apprehension of them. The reality of context challenges us to do our best to apprehend biblical commands and to apply them in ways that are consistent with the character of God and with the quality of our relationship with him. *Humility in the appropriation and application of moral values militates against inclinations to render our contexts absolute.

Kierkegaard reminds us of the 'teleological suspension of the ethical', that is, the need for objective ethical principles to be tempered by the existential parameters of the religious life. Legalism is to be avoided, without retreating to

459

complete ethical subjectivity. Love again enters the picture as an absolute moral value, but one that is recognized as both relevant to and transcendent over our respective contexts. As Paul Ramsey, echoing Augustine, indicated, 'The commands of love are as stringent as the needs of the world are urgent: sensing this, let any man *then* do as he pleases.'

Bibliography

D. Bloesch *Freedom for Obedience* (Eugene, 2002); J. Fletcher, *Situation Ethics* (London, 1966); A. MacIntyre, *A Short History of Ethics* (London, [2]1998); D. Naugle, *Worldview* (Grand Rapids, 2002); J. Rachels, *The Elements of Moral Philosophy* (London and New York, 2002).

A. M. ROBBINS

MUGGERIDGE, (THOMAS) MALCOLM

Malcolm Muggeridge (1903–90) was a journalist, controversialist, media personality, essayist and novelist. Brought up an ardent socialist, Fabian and admirer of Beatrice and Sidney Webb, he graduated from Cambridge and taught at a Christian college in India until 1927, when he married Kitty Dobbs, a relative of the Webbs. There were infidelities on both sides, but the marriage endured until Malcolm's death. They moved to Moscow, where Malcolm worked as correspondent for the *Manchester Guardian*, but returned, deeply disillusioned with the Soviet experiment, in 1933. During the war Malcolm served with the Intelligence Corps.

In the 1950s he became a notorious anti-establishment figure. He was a controversial editor of *Punch* (1953–7) and an early contributor to BBC radio, including *Any Questions*, and to *Panorama* (1953–60). His views forced his resignation from *Punch* and estrangement with the BBC, but a new regime at Broadcasting House welcomed him back in 1960. A founding father of the new political satire, he briefly edited *Private Eye* in 1964.

The Muggeridges moved to the country and adopted an ascetic lifestyle. A neighbour and Cambridge friend Alec Vidler influenced Muggeridge to re-examine his youthful interest in Christianity, which, though he was often abrasively critical of its followers, he had often publicly admired as a moral code. He became Rector of Edinburgh University in 1967, dramatically resigning in 1968 over plans to give students the contraceptive pill. This, and his rigorous TV interviews, confirmed his growing reputation as a moralist and media pundit. He declared himself a Christian, associated himself with such causes as the Festival of Light and Mary Whitehouse's campaigns, and in 1982 was received into the Catholic Church, to which he was drawn by its strong ethical stance and the example of Mother Teresa, whom he greatly admired.

Muggeridge saw God as a wise omnipotent and the benign playwright of the human drama. To attempt to influence God's will was impertinent and impracticable; 'When the author steps on to the stage, the play is over'. His favourite prayer was 'Thy will be done', and his usual counsel, 'Wait upon God'. The incarnation became for him the focus of God's supreme understanding of humanity. This embraced God's (and his own) ridiculing of human folly. However, all who knew the Muggeridges spoke of their kindness and compassion. He and Kitty embraced a sacramental view of daily life, influenced by Henri de Caussade (whose *Sacrament of the Present Moment* Kitty translated).

Muggeridge was famously negative about the media that he had served for most of his life. He was at his best as a moral pundit, judging human achievement as he felt God might judge it, and as an accomplished mocker of the ungodly.

While his targets did not much change on his conversion, the personal change was profound. As A. J. P. Taylor once commented, 'The greatest change in him was his discovery of God and Jesus Christ ... I cannot explain or even describe what happened to Malcolm'.

Bibliography

R. Ingrams, *Muggeridge: The Biography* (1995); M. Muggeridge, *Christ and the Media* (1976).

D. PORTER

MUHAMMAD, see ISLAM

MUSIC

Music is organized sound, produced by human beings. It takes its place among the range of cultural activities which constitute human vocation, and has several connections with apologetics. Some would dispute music's ability to articulate a world-view, arguing that art is 'for art's sake'. Admittedly, some music interpretations simplistically turn a composition into a philosophical statement, but, since music is a cultural activity, and since music-makers are God's image-bearers who operate within a world-view, then there must be a relation between the particular sphere of music and the larger meaningful context in which we live.

Deciding what sort of world-view is being articulated through the *language of music entails an understanding of the nature and character of a world-view. Music not only comes in a cultural context, but it is itself a cultural expression. For one thing, it is an expression of human ideas. Paul Henry Lang's massive work entitled *Music in Western Civilization* (New York, 1941) represents a high watermark in historical musicology, showing the complex interrelationship between music and the intellectual climate of the West.

Since those earlier days, musicology has vastly expanded its field, first, by recognizing a variety of types of music outside of 'art music', such as jazz, rock, folk and so forth. Secondly, while music history had focused primarily on the West, disciplines such as ethnomusicology have opened up studies to world music, with its extraordinary diversity of styles and practices. Thirdly, understanding music as a cultural phenomenon has meant recognition of a plethora of other features, such as contractual, artistic, economic, sponsored, religious, and numerous others. When these are properly measured we may begin to understand a people-group through the lens of its music.

Each people-group exhibits different values through the music it produces. For example, in the West, which is characterized by secularization, *entertainment occupies a central place. At the same time, despite, or perhaps because of, secularization, there is strong evidence of a longing for transcendence. The sudden popularity of John Tavener's *Song for Athene*, played at Princess Diana's funeral service, the enormous success of the avowedly Christian rock group U2, and the top-selling recordings of Gregorian chant are among the musical witnesses to this hunger for eternity. Rock historian Steve Turner argues that much of rock and roll music represents a sort of search for redemption, which is epitomized by the Bob Dylan song, *Knocking on Heaven's Door* and U2's *Joshua Tree* album.

Since the 1950s it has increasingly been recognized that *culture is dynamic, not static. Therefore, there is in each society a relation of music to continuity and change, tradition and adaptation, the clash of two cultures etc. When one society encounters another, accommodation, resistance, combinations and recombinations are all to be found. Music is a useful index to this complex process, which, in turn, tells us much about the society. Music can help us understand the religious priorities of an urbanizing society. Consider the case of Malaysian Islam in Singapore. Since the 1959 grant of self-government, then independence in 1965, Singapore's political leaders have been busy industrializing, consolidating and urbanizing. The 'resettlement project', ratified in 1967, meant the gradual dissolution of the rural population and the construction of new satellite towns and high-rise apartments, surrounded by highways and other carriers of modernity. This created a problem for the Malay, whose religion, Islam, had been socially structured in a homogenous way, so that the amplified, quasi-musical call to prayer, known as the *adhan*, was heard and heeded by everyone in the village. At first, in the new setting, the *adhan* was heard by everyone in the area surrounding the prayer tower, but soon this exclusive, sacred, acoustical environment was threatened. An anti-noise campaign was fought in 1974, led by those outside of Islam who felt that the call to prayer was intrusive. After angry polemics a compromise was reached, whereupon not only would the decibel level of the *adhan* be greatly reduced, but it would be broadcast over the radio. This 'privatizing' of a musical call led to certain changes in the Muslim experience. It helped create a new sense of *community, albeit an invisible one and gave women greater access to Islam than previously. In short, it produced the opposite of the secularization that various critics of technology and modernization often predict.

Music can articulate specific human qualities. Because it is invisible, music can speak from the heart and speak to the heart. Because it is temporal it can tell us things in a way that is significant and expressive beyond the capacity of words. Music helps us understand certain theological verities in a unique way.

Jeremy Begbie suggests that in Western music the way different parts are layered tells us something about how two biblical truths that are independent can yet be simultaneous as well. For example, Jesus' teaching on the Mount of Olives (Matt. 24) describes the end of the world in terms both of the fall of Jerusalem and the parousia at the end of time. The two are not mutually exclusive. Polyphonic music helps us hear that prophetic overlay. Further, if nearness and delay are part of the way we should understand the history of redemption's final phase, then music's ability to take us to various peaks and cadences within a larger pattern helps us sense the biblical approach to history. Music's very rationality challenges the assumptions that time must be conceived in one-level linear terms.

Music carries with it the concerns and aspirations of the human spirit. It can convey the reality of suffering, as well as the certainty of hope; for example, the history of African-American music reveals much about a particular people's experience of affliction, and the ways in which hope and renewal emerged from oppressive circumstances.

The relationship of music to apologetics raises the question of beauty. Is music a sort of *cosmological argument? Does music's aesthetic quality prove the existence of a supreme being full of glory? The ancient world thought there was such a connection. *Plato argues in *Timaeus* that music, especially inaudible sounds, is given by God (through the Muses) in order to harmonize our souls and bring them into conformity with heavenly realities. Immanuel *Kant considered 'the art of tone' to be a universal language, directing our souls upwards through obedience to various objective rules. But the Bible does not warrant this sort of mimesis. It speaks instead of a much broader aesthetic, based more on ethics than timeless rules. Music celebrates redemption and victory (Exod. 15:2; Ps. 95:1–2; Rom. 15:9), but it can also become noise and confusion (Exod. 32:17–18; Amos 5:23; 1 Cor. 14:7–8). It is better to consider music as faithful, or unfaithful, to the truth as it is revealed in redemptive history, than as an earthly replica of universal harmony.

There is great *power in music. Where does it come from? Is it from psycho-accoustical forces imbedded in the musical substance? Some worry that rock concerts can violate the conscience. More likely, music's power comes from a combination of elements working together. Music is able to speak of truth and falsehood in many ways, and especially in performance is a sort of 'conversation' with God and with his world. While music is not altogether a language, it does operate as language does, convincing, distracting, suggesting an idea to its listeners.

This raises the question of ethical integrity in the use of music. Sometimes the sounds of music may appeal to an audience for reasons quite in contrast with the message. Some (though by no means all) of the Contemporary Christian genre is lacking in the narrative of deep-misery-to-deep-joy that characterizes the gospel message. Individual musicians have confessed to selling out to a ready-made market, rather than taking the risk of exploring more authentic, faithful styles. It does not have to be this way. Should not music be congruent with the message?

Finally, the proper use of music is an important part of missiology. There has been an emerging recognition of the need to work with local music and not simply impose the music of the original culture. Ethnomusicologists Thomas Avery and Roberta King have pioneered taking music from particular people-groups and reworking it into appropriate means for heralding the Christian message. Through her work with the Senufo, the Cebaara and the Nyarafolo of the Ivory Coast, as well as her extensive knowledge of African cultures, Roberta King has produced guides for promoting Christian music in African expression. Particularly helpful is her discussion of form in African music, and the ways to appropriate it for gospel purposes. Ultimately, then, the nature and use of music is related to the world-view within which it functions.

Bibliography

J. Begbie, *Theology, Music and Time* (Cambridge, 2000); H. Brand and A. Chaplin, *Art and Soul: Signposts for Christians in the Arts* (Carlisle, 2001); W. Edgar, *Taking Note of Music* (London, 1986); R. R. King, *A Time to Sing: A Manual for the African Church* (Nairobi, 1999); I. Monson, *Saying Something: Jazz Improvisation and Interaction* (Chicago, 1996); B. Nettl, *The Study of Ethnomusicology: Twenty-Nine Issues and Concepts* (Urbana, 1983); C. Seerveld, *Bearing Fresh Olive Leaves: Alternative Steps in Understanding Art* (Carlisle, 2000); J. M. Spencer, *Blues* and *Evil* (Knoxville, 1993); W. Wioria, *The Four Ages of Music* (New York, 1965).

W. Edgar

MYSTERY

Any attempt to defend the Christian faith needs to take into account the fact that religions in general and Christianity in particular include a certain amount of mystery. Even though an apologist should be able to explicate the content beliefs of Christianity to his or her contemporary audience, there is a wall of hiddenness beyond which human knowledge is not able to penetrate. Consequently, someone wishing to convince an unbeliever of the truth of Christianity simply by demonstrating that the Christian faith is 100% intelligible to human reason would be bound to founder sooner or later. This article will describe this concept of mystery in terms of its classical and biblical origin, its use in a subjectivized theory of religion, and its application to logical *paradoxes. The central point is that 'mystery' should never be an escape hatch for overworked or underprepared apologists at the end of their arguments.

Classical origin

The term 'mystery' goes back to the *mystery religions of ancient Greek culture. Etymologically, the term was derived from the word *myein*, which initially meant 'to close the eyes or mouth', in other words, to conceal something. Thus a *mysterion* was something hidden, some deep spiritual realities, unknown to the ordinary mortal human being, but accessible to the initiated. Note the pattern indicated here. The so-called mysteries were not considered to be impenetrable in their entirety; otherwise there would have been no point in promoting the cult. The spiritual elite could gain insight into the mysteries and, by being reborn, enter into a new spiritual life.

'Mystery' in the Old Testament and Septuagint

Given the concept's origin in classical pagan culture, it is not surprising that it does not play a role in the OT, which was composed earlier. Not everything about God is knowable, but those things that are hidden are concealed from all human beings and not reserved for disclosure to the spiritually privileged. Nevertheless,

the ancient translators of the OT into Greek – the Septuagint (LXX) – used the word *mysterion* in the book of Daniel (e.g. Dan. 2:17). The dream of the king was a 'mystery' to Daniel – until God revealed it to him.

'Mystery' in Paul

The idea of a mystery as something formerly hidden but presently revealed also governs the use of this term by the apostle Paul in the NT. In the fifteen most prominent uses of the word 'mystery', five deal directly with the inclusion of Gentiles in the people of God (Rom. 11:25; Eph. 3:3–9), one refers to the translation of our bodies at the second coming (1 Cor. 15:51), four occur alongside various allusions to union with Christ (Eph. 1:9; 5:32; Col. 1:26–27), one associates the term with godliness as displayed in Christ's incarnation (1 Tim. 3:16), two refer to Christ himself (Col. 2:2; 4:3), and two denote the content of Paul's gospel (Rom. 16:25; Eph. 6:19). All of them are situated in the realm of what was once hidden and is now disclosed. None of them claim that there is something unknown, let alone intrinsically unknowable, which a Christian is obligated to believe.

Subjectivity as mystery

During the twentieth century, the word 'mystery' was applied to subjective *religious experience. This usage and its framework were made famous by Rudolf Otto, who contended that in order to understand the true nature of religion, one needs to understand the non-rational side just as much as the rational. This non-rational dimension of religion shows itself when a person encounters the 'numinous', a term coined by Otto derived from the Lat. *numen* (the 'sacred').

The essence of the numinous is a feeling, not a concept or an idea. Consequently, Otto said that 'it cannot be strictly defined' and it cannot 'be taught, it can only be evoked, awakened in the mind'. It is something that can only be experienced, and discussion of it can only consist of rough approximations. The most important attribute of the numinous is that it evokes in us a feeling of mystery, what Otto called the *mysterium tremendum et fascinosum*.

Religious believers encountering the Holy will confront a mystery, says Otto. They will learn not just about another objective reality, but will learn something that is 'wholly other', a dimension that does not fit into any pre-conceived sets of concepts. There is a dark, impenetrable character to the numinous, which seals it off from any brazen attempts by the human mind to grasp it. Consequently, the person's first response is going to be one of awe, a holy fear that leads human beings to be aware of their inadequacy and sinfulness, such as the horrified confession of unclean lips by Isaiah (Isa. 6:5). This is the *tremendum* aspect of the *mysterium*, which is followed by the *fascinosum*. As much as individuals may be repelled by the numinous, it also fulfils a deeply felt need for them. The same Peter who said, 'Go away from me, Lord; for I am a sinful man' (Luke 5:8) also said, 'Lord, you know that I love you' (John 21:6). We see then that for Otto the core religious experience, and thus of religion itself, is a mystery that both repels and attracts.

Now the question becomes for us how constitutive this *mysterium* is for all of religion, including Christianity. In other words: descriptively, do all religions demonstrate such a *mysterium* at their core, and, prescriptively, must they do so? Clearly, Otto's own dogmatism notwithstanding, it is physically impossible to answer the question of whether the *mysterium* is a universal phenomenon in all religions for all people at all times since this would require an empirical survey impossible to carry out. And if that is so, then it is certainly wrongheaded even to pretend to claim that it is necessary with credibility. However, this response can be too facile, since a good case can be made that we have yet to find true religious experience apart from the *mysterium*, and that, consequently, such notion of a universal experience may remain as a hypothesis so far unfalsified.

Otto himself, representative of many modern writers on the subject, was not willing to let matters rest there. Despite his insistence that the rational and the non-rational must be considered together, he allowed the reality of non-rational subjective feelings ultimately to swallow up the rational concepts derived from *revelation and tradition. If feelings are at the core of religion, then revelation cannot be, and vice versa, and feelings won out for him. And so, despite his own best intentions, Otto let the subjective mystery become the only item that counts with finality in his analysis of religion.

Surely, however, we need not let the matter rest with such a reductionism. There is nothing inherently problematic with the idea that on the subjective side of our Christian experience we encounter feelings similar to those described by the *mysterium tremendum et fascinosum*. Nevertheless, that possibility would not imply that, therefore, on objective consideration the realities of faith are beyond knowledge. If I may risk an analogy here, obviously, the rapture and excitement of two people engaged in marital consummation cannot possibly be captured in words, while at the same time, a physiologist may be able to provide an accurate biochemical account of the event. Neither dimension rules out the other. In short, a profound religious experience may carry a non-rational element of mystery, but we should not infer from this fact that therefore the realities encountered are not rationally accessible from another perspective.

Paradox as mystery

Another prominent notion of mystery is based on the idea of paradoxes within Christian thought. In order to clarify this idea sympathetically, let us suggest a distinction between a *contradiction, an inconsistency and a paradox. Two statements are contradictory if one of them must be true and the other one false, such as 'no-one has ever seen God' and 'at least one person has seen God'. It is not just that they cannot both be true; if one is false, the other one must be true, or vice versa. An inconsistency occurs if there are two statements that cannot both be true, though they could both be false. For example, neither of the two statements, 'all human beings will go to heaven', and 'no human beings will go to heaven', need be true, but they clearly cannot both be true. They could both be false, but not both true. We will now assume that Christianity is neither contradictory nor inconsistent, but bring in the idea of paradox/antinomy. A paradox is an apparent contradiction that is capable of resolution, whereas an antimony can by its very nature never be cleared up. However, this distinction can only be made as a kind of pre-judgment on whatever issue is in view. After all, puzzles do not come prelabelled. One person's antinomy may be another person's paradox. Aside from rhetorical purposes, it is probably best to treat the two terms as synonymous.

A paradox is a conundrum, the mutual exclusion of some statements from each other once we have applied certain rules to them. For example, the statements, 'God exists as an omnipotent and omnibenevolent being', and

'Evil is real', are neither contradictory nor inconsistent until we apply another statement, such as 'The existence of an omnipotent and omnibenevolent being and the reality of evil are incompatible.' At that point, it would appear that one would have to sacrifice either the first or the second statement in order to avoid an inconsistency.

Similarly, there is no logical problem with the statements 'There is only one God' and 'Jesus is God'. In fact, we can add 'The Father is God', and 'The Spirit is God', without engendering any difficulties. But if we add another statement, 'The three persons of God are eternally distinct from each other', then we seem to be getting caught in inconsistency. Thus, there seem to be genuine paradoxes within Christianity.

Now, the problem with true logical paradoxes is that they are intractable. Take Bertrand *Russell's famous paradox, which asks us to establish the set of all sets that are not members of themselves and asks whether this set is a member of itself. If it is not, then it is; but if it is, then it cannot contain itself. A popular illustration, due to Russell himself, is the statement, 'The barber in our town shaves only those people who do not shave themselves. Who shaves the barber?' If he does so himself, then he does not, but if he does not, then he does. The problem is not just logical in the purest sense; it is aggravated by the fact that any attempt to solve it must step outside of *logic and invent some rule to disallow the paradox. Russell himself proposed a theory of 'ramified types' according to which no higher-order set can be a member of a lower-order set, and so no set can be a member of itself. This is reasonable – but it is arbitrary. Furthermore, Gödel eventually showed (with his 'incompleteness theorem') that it does not even work.

Some people have argued that the mystery of Christianity lies in its paradoxes. According to them, Christianity does generate inconsistencies, and not only do we need to learn to tolerate them, but it is incumbent upon us to accept them. Vladimir Lossky, for example, an Eastern Orthodox theologian of the twentieth century, argued that the doctrine of the *Trinity contained apparent contradictions, and he went so far as to state that it is wrong to attempt to resolve them. True piety, he counselled, demands that we submit to the logical problems in faith and not try to discover some way out of them. Thus the mystery of Chris-

tianity consists in its logical contradictions, but these must be embraced in unquestioning faith.

Other writers have demurred and challenged the idea that such logical paradoxes are a part of Christianity. Paul *Tillich complained that the original intent of the doctrine of the Trinity has been reinterpreted from being a symbolization of God's self-manifestation to 'an impenetrable mystery, put on the altar to be adored', to the point of 'the glorification of an absurdity in numbers'. Such an approach, said Tillich, loses track of both the nature of revelation and the theological task. Let us take a cue from this observation and look a little more closely at what is involved in these apparent paradoxes.

Take the puzzle brought on by the existence of God in the face of the reality of *evil. We said that there is no paradox here until we have also established that God and evil are incompatible. However, we could modify our statement to that effect by saying, 'The existence of God and the reality of evil are incompatible unless there is good reason to believe that God has a higher purpose for allowing evil.' As quickly as that, the logical inconsistency is gone. Now, one might wish to jump in quickly and ask, 'What purpose could God conceivably have for allowing evil?', and perhaps we might be totally stumped for an answer. Then there still is a mystery (God's purpose), but it is not a logical paradox. The mystery lies in a lack of information on my part, not in an apparent contradiction.

With regard to the Trinity, we need to keep in mind that the whole idea behind the articulation of the doctrine was an attempt to avoid the logical inconsistency between asserting that there is only one God and that there are three gods. The early theologians put together the classical statements as a model in order to make as much sense as possible out of the biblical data. They saw that the best way to bring the relevant scriptures together was with a model in which God is 'one' in one category ('substance') and 'three' in another category ('persons'), so that you do not have 'one' and 'three' of the same kind. But the model itself was not revealed, and so one should not capitulate to the model as a divinely revealed mystery, because it is a human formulation, not a revealed datum. Now, of course, a question remains, and it is again a question of content, not of logic: how can it be that one

465

substance can be eternally in three persons? Ultimately, we do not know, and so there is a mystery, but the mystery is brought about by our lack of knowledge, not by a logical paradox.

Mystery as limit of knowledge

This, then, is the simple and prosaic role that mystery plays in Christian apologetics. It is not the appeal to subjective experience when rational thought has failed. It is not the glorification of certain logical paradoxes. It is the fact, plain and simple, that there is a genuine limit to our knowledge. Some things we may never know, others may become clearer gradually. Some of what we casually call 'mystery' might just disappear if we do a little more homework. There is no promise in the NT that all knowledge will be revealed to us, but we are told that we will some day have a direct encounter with the one who does hold all knowledge. 'Now I know in part; then I shall know fully, even as I am fully known' (1 Cor. 13:12). 'But we know that when he appears, we shall be like him, for we shall see him as he is' (1 John 3:2).

Bibliography

V. Lossky, *The Mystical Theology of the Eastern Church* (Cambridge, 1944); M. K. Munitz, *The Mystery of Existence* (New York, 1965); R. Otto, *The Idea of the Holy* (ET, London and New York, 1931); P. Tillich, *Systematic Theology* (3 vols., Chicago, 1951–1963).

W. CORDUAN

MYSTERY RELIGIONS

Mystery religions in the Roman world existed alongside the more formal cults, such as the patron (Olympian) deities of cities in the Greek East, or the Capitoline deities found in the Western provinces and in Roman colonies of the Greek East. Mystery religions were not open in the way that a civic cult was open to all members of a city's citizen body. There would be a series of initiation ceremonies that would not be public knowledge.

Although Christianity could be seen in the ancient world as distinct from the central pagan cults, the public proclamation of the central Christian truths by preaching made it distinctly different from other *mystery cults of the

Roman Empire. The increasing habit of recording dedications in pagan sanctuaries, especially from the second century AD, means that it is not always possible to make a synchronous comparison between early Christianity and mystery cults.

Mystery religions from the Aegean world

Eleusis

One of the most important mystery cults in the Greek East was based at Eleusis, within the territory of the city of Athens. The focus was on the cult of Demeter and Persephone (also known as Kore, 'the girl'). This cult can be traced back to the archaic period. Its origins are outlined in the Homeric Hymn to Demeter, which explains the way that Persephone had to spend part of the year in the Underworld with Hades. From the late sixth century BC the sanctuary attracted a series of monumental buildings. One of the most important was the large Telesterion, apparently built as part of the Athenian building programme under Pericles. This hall, partly cut into the hillside, had steps round the edges which allowed initiates to stand and watch the mysteries which were focused on the Anaktoron, a rectangular room in the centre of the Telesterion.

The sanctuary remained extremely popular in the Roman period. A monumental gateway was given to the sanctuary c. 50 BC by Claudius Appius Pulcher, the Roman governor of Cilicia, and decorated with a pair of colossal caryatids. It was completed in 48 BC, and the name of the benefactor was inscribed in Latin rather than in Greek. Several emperors, notably the philhellene Hadrian and Marcus Aurelius, became initiates of the cult. Though the cult was originally for Greeks, during the Roman period it was opened to Roman citizens. The second-century AD travel writer Pausanias, though describing many of the monuments of Attica in detail, failed to discuss the cult in any detail, presumably because he too was an initiate.

The sanctuary had close links with the city of Athens. The city of Eleusinion was located on the northern slopes of the acropolis, just above the south-east corner of the agora, the political heart of the ancient city. From this urban sanctuary the 'Sacred Way' left the city through the Dipylon Gate and thence to Eleusis. This became the official route for the ceremonies relating to the cult.

The initiation process was extended and carried over two main festivals. The first, in the spring, during the Athenian month of Anthesterion, was when those wishing to be initiated were prepared by the priests of the cult. The second stage was in the autumn, in the month of Boedromion.

The Great Gods from Samothrace

An important mystery cult developed on the island of Samothrace in the Northern Aegean. It seems to have attracted worshippers from the sixth century BC onwards. Among the deities worshipped were the heroic Kabeiroi. The cult was patronized by the Macedonian royal family and developed under the Ptolemies. Excavations have revealed remains of the buildings associated with the initiation into the cult, such as a rectangular hall. The language of the cult ('the Great Gods') was conveniently ambiguous so as to include Egyptian deities. Thus a Greek could see the Great Gods as referring to Greek deities or to the Egyptian deities, such as Isis and Serapis, who would require initiation ceremonies. An inscription from the Ptolemaic base of Methana in the Peloponnese, which gives thanks to the 'Great Gods' for a safe arrival of the base's administrator and staff, is suitably ambiguous to address the needs of both Greeks and Egyptians in the service of the Ptolemies.

Dionysos

The Olympian god Dionysos had female followers or Bacchae. Women could be initiated to the cult, and concerns about propriety led to Roman legislation. A significant portrayal of the cult and its initiation formed the decoration of the walls of a large villa just outside the walls of Pompeii. The scenes appear to represent the initiation of a woman which includes the reading of ritual from a scroll, a sacrifice, the unveiling of sacred objects, and whipping of the new initiate. A precise interpretation of the iconography is probably not achievable, given the secrecy surrounding the rites.

Mystery religions from Anatolia

Cybele

The cult of Cybele had its origins in Phrygia in central Anatolia. Cybele was sometimes known as 'the Great Mother'. Her male companion was Attis. As the Roman Empire started to expand in the Eastern Mediterranean, the cult of Cybele was transferred to the city of Rome, though it was also found in many cities of the Eastern Mediterranean. Dedications from the cult were found at Moschato in Attica, and a cult of Cybele was recorded at Corinth by Pausanias. Male followers of the cult were known as the Galli. One of the common characteristics was self-castration so that they could serve the goddess. By the Late Roman period the cult had features that were shared with Mithraism, notably the *taurobolium* or slaughter of the bull.

Mystery religions from Egypt

Isis

The cult of Isis had its origins in Egypt; however, the cult became established across the Greek East, and thence to Rome and Western provinces. One reason for its spread into the Aegean may have been the Ptolemaic territories. The cult at Methana (renamed Arsinoe by the Ptolemies) in the Peloponnese is mentioned by Pausanias and by a Roman period inscription, where Isis is linked with Sarapis.

The cult of Isis became popular in the Greek East. At Athens there are numerous representations of women with knotted dress and holding a sistrum, often on funerary stelai of the Roman period. This distinctive costume is indicative of priestesses of the cult of the goddess. A cult of Isis, Serapis and Anubis has been identified in the private estate of the great second-century AD benefactor, Herodes Atticus, at Marathon in South-eastern Attica. The cult was also found in Italy. The sanctuary at Pompeii was devastated by the earthquake of AD 62, but quickly rebuilt. Its privacy was preserved by the construction of a thick wall. The sanctuary made provision of a large hall presumably for communal dining.

One of the most important ancient descriptions of the cult of Isis is derived from the work of Apuleius. This fictional work centres on the important sanctuary of Isis at Cenchreae, the harbour of Corinth which faces the Saronic Gulf. Apuleius described what was involved in the initiation for the cult. One emphasis seems to have been the links between the sailing season and the worship of the goddess.

Egyptian cults, especially of Isis and Serapis, are noted at several locations on Southern Crete. One explanation has been that the grain ships plying between Alexandria and Ostia (the port of Rome) brought the cult with them.

Mithras

The cult of Mithras had its origins in the East, and was noted among the pirates of Cilicia (Southern Turkey) in the first century BC. It became particularly popular among soldiers which is why many of the temples (mithraea) associated with the cult have been found in frontier provinces such as Germany and Britain. It is noticeable that the cult is rarely found in the Greek East. An exception is the sacred cave constructed on the island of Andros by members of the Praetorian Guard who would appear to have been stationed on the island to guard political exiles. Much of the evidence for the cult comes from the second and third centuries AD. The cult included seven stages of initiation, outlined by Jerome. Visual evidence for the grades has been found in the floor mosaic of the mithraeum of Felicissimus at Ostia, the harbour of Rome, as well as in the wall paintings from the temple beneath the church of Santa Prisca in Rome. The focus of the cult was the killing of the bull, celebrated in the iconography of the mithraea.

Bibliography

D. Engels, *Roman Corinth: An Alternative Model for the Classical City* (Chicago, 1990); H.-J. Klauck, *The Religious Context of Early Christianity: A Guide to Graeco-Roman Religions* (Edinburgh, 2000); B. M. Metzger, 'A Classified Bibliography of the Greco-Roman Mystery Religions 1924–1973 with a Supplement 1974–77', *Aufstieg und Niedergang der Romischen Welt*, 2.17.3 (1984), pp. 1259–1423; N. Reed, 'The Mithraeum on Andros', *Zeitschrift für Papyrologie und Epigraphik*, 18 (1975), pp. 207–211; I. F. Sanders, *Roman Crete: An Archaeological Survey and Gazetteer of Late Hellenistic, Roman and Early Byzantine Crete* (Warminster, 1982).

D. W. J. GILL

MYSTICISM, see RELIGIOUS EXPERIENCE AND MYSTICISM

MYTHOLOGY AND THE NEW TESTAMENT

'Myth' is a particularly slippery term. Originally it referred to 'stories' rather than 'historical reports', and was used for stories which were not true. Stories involving supernatural actors, the gods and other semi-divine beings, who appeared on earth or were described as if they behaved in certain respects like human beings, were termed 'myths'. Some stories of this kind were recognized as being told not merely for their entertainment value but because they accomplished particular functions. The most common of these were aetiological myths, which explained how things came to be the way they were. Where historical or scientific information was unavailable, people might tell stories that 'explained' how things came to be, such as the origins of the world and the people in it.

The stories in the early chapters of Genesis serve the function of explaining that the universe is not something that has always been there but had an origin, and that origin lay in God. They also explain that, if the universe is imperfect, this is not because God made it so, but because somehow it has been corrupted by another agency. The account of the 'fall' of Adam and Eve depicts in story form the fallen, rebellious character of human beings right from the beginning. Thus, the Genesis stories assert the original goodness of the creation along with its rebellion against God. Such stories can be classified as 'valid' myths, in that they present in pictorial form truths about the universe and human nature, as opposed to 'invalid' myths, which offer pictures that are not a true representation of *reality. Clearly a story can function in this kind of way whether or not it is historical. The Genesis stories can be historical while retaining this mythical function. Nevertheless, in general, 'myth' is a category that is not historical.

With regard to the NT, the controversy is centred on a famous essay by Rudolf *Bultmann in which he argued that much of the NT story is told in a way that is mythical, i.e. not historical. It depicts supernatural actors appearing in human *history and performing supernatural actions such as raising people from the dead, effecting instantaneous cures of illness and disability and having knowledge of events that cannot be known by ordinary means. Bultmann held the belief, which he attributed to modern people, that only what is scientifically possible can happen. Supernatural events cannot happen, and therefore all accounts of such events must be dismissed as unhistorical. Consequently, these accounts must be regarded as mythical, and of the same character as the Greek myths about gods and goddesses.

Up to this point Bultmann was not saying anything novel. In the nineteenth century David *Strauss had argued that the accounts of *Jesus in the Gospels are not historical but strictly mythical, the work of Christian *imagination. Up to the time of Bultmann the typical response to these stories was simply to dismiss them as unhistorical and not to enquire any further into them, beyond offering 'rational' explanations where these were possible (such as cases of psychological explanations of apparent cures of paralysis and the like). The significance of Strauss was that he held that there were no such rational stories lying behind the Gospel narrative that had then been transformed into unhistorical accounts of *miracles. They were purely mythical and thus of no value.

Bultmann, however, took a different route. He argued that in the Gospels, theological truths were being conveyed in the style of the time by the telling of mythical stories. It was necessary and possible to 'demythologize' these narratives by recognizing the mythical nature of the appropriate elements within them and the fact that things did not in reality happen in this way. But the mythical stories were in fact conveying a valid message that could be expressed otherwise in a non-mythical manner, and therefore the result of 'demythologization' was not to leave us with nothing, but rather to leave us with truths that could be re-expressed in a manner more appropriate in a contemporary framework of thought. Bultmann thought he had found the modern equivalent in the philosophical categories of Martin Heidegger, who employed the ideas of authentic and inauthentic existence to describe the possibilities open to humanity. Where Jesus spoke of the inbreaking of the kingdom of God and the resurrection from the dead, Bultmann spoke of the promise of authentic existence, life in its fullness, to people who were living an existence that fell short of its possibilities. This could seem to be a secularization of Christian theology, making it say no more than a non-Christian philosopher, who rightly recognized that there are two ways of living. However, Bultmann insisted that the transition from inauthentic existence to authentic was possible only through Jesus Christ, who confronted people with the possibility of authentic existence and challenged them to respond to his offer of the latter.

It should be noted that Bultmann was motivated by the positive desire to present the gospel to modern people in a way that would be effective for them. He thought that the mythical elements in the NT constituted a barrier or obstacle that prevented people from recognizing the *truth and the appeal of the gospel, and he genuinely believed that the essential substance of the gospel was preserved through the translation from the mythical to the philosophical vehicle of thought. He could, therefore, be regarded as carrying out a helpful apologetic activity by ridding the NT presentation of features that were a barrier to belief. He was trying to take away what he regarded as unnecessary obstacles to belief, while nevertheless preserving the real 'offence' of the gospel in its challenge to human self-centredness and sin.

In the 1970s the question of mythology came to life again through the work of John *Hick and his colleagues in a book, *The Myth of God Incarnate*. They contended that the biblical picture of God (or, rather, the Son of God) becoming a human being was an example of the mythical *language about divine beings which had fallen under Bultmann's axe. This language was a mythical way of expressing the fact that Jesus was the figure of supreme significance for the destiny of human beings, someone with what might be called transcendent significance, but he was not literally a human being who was somehow joined to a divine being. The book was clearer in its demolition of traditional views than in its presentation of a plausible alternative, and it is unlikely that the contributors could have agreed with one another on what to put in its place.

Some sixty years after Bultmann's original presentation, it is clear that demythologization is unnecessary and reductionist. Bultmann worked on the assumption that all talk of God and divine beings in human language is inevitably mythical and is to be rejected. In doing so, he failed to recognize that if we are to talk about God at all, we cannot avoid using human language. He also accepted the 'scientific' postulate that 'miracles are impossible', which begs the question completely. It is very questionable, moreover, whether Bultmann's version of the gospel is any more intelligible to people than the biblical version and whether the translation in fact preserves all the essential features of the original.

It is equally questionable whether the programme of Hick and his colleagues is viable. It has proved to be impossible to construct a version of Christian belief in which Jesus does not have transcendent significance which goes beyond saying things like 'Jesus is the man of universal destiny.' Most of NT theology has to be rejected if Hick and his colleagues are to be consistent. It is important, however, to make a clear distinction here. It is one thing for people to deny that Jesus was God incarnate, and hence to deny the basis of the Christian faith, which they are entitled to do if they so wish. It is quite another thing to think that a Christian can deny the concept of incarnation and find some acceptable alternative way of expressing the content of Christian faith. There is no adequate substitute for the Christian for the belief that 'God was in Christ.' Hick's demythologizing programme may think that it has merely drained away the bath water; unfortunately the baby slipped away at the same time.

Bibliography

H. W. Bartsch (ed.), *Kerygma and Myth*, 2 vols. (London, 1953, 1962); D. Cairns, *A Gospel without Myth?* (London, 1960); J. Hick (ed.), *The Myth of God Incarnate* (London, 1977); I. H. Marshall, 'God Incarnate: Myth or What?', in *Jesus the Saviour* (London and Downers Grove, 1990), pp. 181–196.

I. H. MARSHALL

NAG HAMMADI GOSPELS

In 1945 a group of fifty-two papyrus texts written in Coptic were found near Nag Hammadi, Egypt. These texts, produced in the fourth century AD, were translations from Greek texts, mostly written in the second and early third centuries. The Nag Hammadi texts are the single most important find of primary writings that are for the most part representative of the ancient gnostic movements, primarily found in the early church and attacked by the Fathers as heresies. The Nag Hammadi texts are contained in thirteen codices (books), and the individual writings are known as tractates. The collection is often designated by the symbol CG (Cairo Gnosticus), since all the manuscripts are now in the Coptic Museum in Cairo.

The fifty-two Nag Hammadi texts contain six internal duplicates, thus forty-six texts are represented, six of which were already known

to exist. Thus, the Nag Hammadi find yielded forty new, primarily gnostic, texts. Four of the tractates designate themselves as Gospels: *The Gospel of Truth* (two copies: CG I, 3; XII, 2); *The Gospel of Thomas* (CG II, 2; previously known Greek fragments [*Oxyrhynchus Papyri* 1, 654 and 655] are now known to be part of this text); *The Gospel of Philip* (CG II, 3); and *The Gospel of the Egyptians* (two copies: CG III, 2; IV, 2). None of these gospels is actually very similar to the form and structure of the *canonical Gospels.

The Gospel of Truth opens with the words, 'The gospel of truth is joy for those who have received from the Father of truth the grace of knowing him.' The term 'gospel' in this text is used in the Pauline sense to mean the message about *Jesus Christ. This document is probably from the Valentinian school of *Gnosticism (named after Valentinus, a mid-second-century AD gnostic teacher) and is a theological reflection or homily on the saving work of Jesus Christ. *Irenaeus, in the context of his defence of the four canonical Gospels, polemicizes against a *Gospel of Truth*, presumably this very work (*Adversus Haereses*, 3.11.9).

The Gospel of Thomas, the most discussed work from Nag Hammadi, consists of 114 sayings of the risen Jesus without any narrative framework or stories. Approximately one half of these sayings have a significant parallel in the canonical synoptic Gospels. In some ways, *The Gospel of Thomas* is similar to what traditionally has been posited as Q (the alleged source of sayings of Jesus common to Matthew and Luke). There are major scholarly debates over at least two issues: to what extent are the sayings of Jesus dependent on or independent of the canonical Gospels; and to what extent is *The Gospel of Thomas* a gnostic text. It is more likely that *The Gospel of Thomas* is a second-century gnosticizing composition which, however, probably contains independent (and even genuine) Jesus tradition. This is, however, virtually impossible to identify.

The Gospel of Philip is primarily a Valentinian gnostic theological reflection on the sacraments (baptism, anointing, eucharist, redemption, bridal chamber). It has no narrative framework, but appears to be a compilation of data from various sources. It does contain a few stories about Jesus (none paralled in the canonical Gospels) and seventeen sayings of Jesus, nine of which are related to canonical Gospel sayings.

The Gospel of the Egyptians, which calls itself as well 'The Holy Book of the Great Invisible Spirit', represents Sethian gnosticism, a second-century AD gnostic movement and group of texts in which Seth is revered as the progenitor of the 'immovable race' and as a redeemer and revealer figure. It describes the emanations in the *pleroma* (the Greek word for 'fullness', which in gnostic thought refers to the perfect realm of heavenly beings), culminating with the great Seth as the saviour of the true (gnostic) race. (This is not the work of the same name mentioned by Clement of Alexandria and other Church Fathers.)

Although not self-designated as gospels, three other Nag Hammadi texts should be noted here, since they all have the risen Jesus speaking with some of his disciples. *The Apocryphon of James* (CG I, 2) has the risen Jesus speaking with Peter and James, and some of the sayings have similarities to those in the canonical Gospels. *The Apocryphon of John* (CG II, 1; III, 1; IV, 1; also previously known in the Codex Berolinensis 8502, 2) has the risen Jesus speaking with John. *The Dialogue of the Saviour* (CG III, 5) has the Saviour or Lord (who is not explicitly called Jesus) speaking with Judas, Mary and Matthew, and some of the sayings are similar to those in the canonical Gospels, especially John, and in *The Gospel of Thomas*.

Also to be noted here is *The Gospel of Mary*, which is found in the Codex Berolinensis 8502, 1. This codex was discovered in the late nineteenth century and contains four works. Two are found in the Nag Hammadi texts (*The Apocryphon of John* and *The Sophia of Jesus Christ*) and one is closely related to a Nag Hammadi text (*The Act of Peter*; cf. CG VI, 1: *The Act of Peter and the Twelve Apostles*). Thus, *The Gospel of Mary* may be considered as a Gospel closely related to the Nag Hammadi Gospels. This very fragmentary Gospel, also now known from at least two ancient Greek fragments (*Oxyrhynchus Papyrus 3525*; *John Rylands Papyrus 463*), is a dialogue between the risen Saviour and Peter, Andrew, Levi and Mary Magdalene, in which she is the most important disciple. Mary Magdalene is also a key disciple in *The Dialogue of the Saviour*, *The Gospel of Philip* and *The Gospel of Thomas* 114. Assuming that *The Gospel of Thomas* and *The Gospel of Philip* were composed in the second century, their use of 'gospel' to refer to a literary composition about Jesus is significant evidence for the development of this term (*Justin Martyr in his *First Apology* and *Dialogue with Trypho* from about AD 150 is the earliest datable evidence for this use of the term 'gospel'). The term 'gospel' is also used in *The Gospel of Truth* (CG I, 3, 48, 6–10) to refer, presumably, to one of the canonical Gospels' account of the transfiguration.

These non-canonical gospels discovered at Nag Hammadi are significant for what they reveal about second-century AD gnostic thought and the development of gospel traditions in the early church. They were not ever part of the NT canon, because of the absolute priority of the four canonical Gospels, whose earlier dates and perceived inherent authentic claims to *authority made it impossible for subsequent gospels to enter into the canonical process. The majority church of the second century AD would have also seen these Nag Hammadi Gospels to be theologically deficient or deviant. It is important for Christian apologetics to know and understand the nature of early gospel traditions and gospels and the history of the development of the NT canon.

Bibliography

E. de Boer, *The Gospel of Mary: Beyond a Gnostic and Biblical Mary Magdalene* (New York and London, 2004); K. L. King, *The Gospel of Mary of Magdala: Jesus and the First Woman Apostle* (Santa Rosa, CA, 2003); A. H. B. Logan, 'The Gnostic Gospels', in J. Barton (ed.), *The Biblical World*, 2 vols. (London and New York, 2002), pp. 305–322; *Gnostic Truth and Christian Heresy: A Study in the History of Gnosticism* (Edinburgh, 1996); A. Marjanen, *The Woman Jesus Loved: Mary Magdalene in the Nag Hammadi Library and Related Documents*, Nag Hammadi and Manichaean Studies, 40 (Leiden, 1996); M. W. Meyer, *The Gospels of Mary: The Secret Tradition of Mary Magdalene, the Companion of Jesus* (San Francisco, 2004); E. H. Pagels, *The Gnostic Gospels* (New York, 1979); P. Perkins, *Gnosticism and the New Testament* (Minneapolis, 1993); J. M. Robinson, *The Nag Hammadi Library in English*, 3rd ed. (San Francisco, 1988); D. M. Scholer, 'Gnosis, Gnosticism', in R. P. Martin and P. H. Davids (eds.), *Dictionary of the Later New Testament and Its Developments* (Downers Grove and Leicester, 1997), pp. 400–412; D. M. Scholer, *Nag Hammadi Bibliography 1948–1969*, Nag

Hammadi and Manichaean Studies, 1 (Leiden, 1971); *Nag Hammadi Bibliography 1970–1994*, Nag Hammadi and Manichaean Studies, 32 (Leiden, 1997).

D. M. SCHOLER

NARCISSISM

Narcissism takes its name from the legendary figure Narcissus, who fell in love with his own reflection in a woodland pool and pined away in unrequited love, and has come to refer to self-love. It involves a vain and grandiose self-centredness, and auto-eroticism, *hedonism, vanity, exhibitionism and arrogant ingratitude are commonly considered to be elements. The late twentieth century has been characterized as the age of narcissism because of its hedonistic self-centred focus.

Developmentally, object-relational theorists such as Klein and Mahler describe the first few months of postnatal development as characterized by primary narcissism. According to their theory, 'good enough' mothering helps the infant to bridge the initially split-off perceptions of 'good self, bad self' and 'good other, bad other' into more realistic whole objects or experiences that acknowledge the complexity of self and other as both good and bad. In this way they allow room for the glorious image of God in each of us to exist in tension with our fallenness and sin.

Narcissism is a feature of many mental disorders, and all humans exhibit some narcissism although socialization curbs it to some degree, but in its full form narcissism is thought of as a personality disorder. The addition of narcissistic personality disorder to the diagnostic system in 1980 reflects the growing interest in this condition. Statistically, it is difficult to distinguish narcissistic personality disorder from other personality disorders, but the most distinctive features include vanity, exhibitionism and a heightened sense of self-importance.

The word 'narcissism' does not appear in the Bible, and is seldom found in Christian theology, but the idea is present nonetheless. Jesus' two great commands are to love God with our whole being and to love our neighbour as we love ourselves. These commands directly confront narcissism by calling us to its opposite. Loving ourselves is taken as a given here. It is neither repudiated nor encouraged.

Rather, our attitudes towards God and others are called to be in balance with our attitudes towards ourselves. This theme is echoed in the epistles (e.g. Rom. 12:3, 16; Gal. 6:3–5).

We are warned that in the last days people will become lovers of themselves rather than lovers of God. Pride, a synonym for narcissism, has long been considered one of the seven deadly sins. The Bible repeatedly warns against pride (e.g. Prov. 16:18; Jas 4:6) and to a lesser degree arrogance (Prov. 8:13; Jer. 48:26). Christians are called to esteem others more highly than themselves (Phil. 2:3–4) and to serve others in love (Gal. 5:13). Thus, Christians are warned to avoid narcissism and called to manifest its opposite.

Efforts to treat this personality disorder have generally been unpromising. Dialectical behaviour therapy, developed by Marsha Linehan in 1993 for the treatment of borderline personality disorder has shown some promise. Elements of DBT include developing awareness of thoughts, feelings, physical sensations, and behaviours, building distress tolerance, learning how to regulate emotion, learning self-management and gaining interpersonal effectiveness. Recently it has been extended to other personality disorders including narcissistic personality disorder with some evidence that it may be effective.

A couple of additional strategies may hold promise. The first is empathy training. It has been proposed that as we understand our own pain – rejection, loneliness, physical injury and so on – we can gain insight into others' experiences of pain and become less self-centred. Secondly, Kirwan proposed that an important therapeutic strategy is encouraging acts of service to others. Paradoxically, serving others is not so much something we do for God as something God does for us – as we engage in service for others we are transformed, becoming more like God. In part it combats our inherent narcissism. Thirdly, Scripture calls upon us to be transformed by renewing our minds (Rom. 12:2) and bringing every thought captive in obedience to Christ (2 Cor. 5:10). Memorizing and meditating on verses such as Phil. 2:3–13 ('consider others better than yourselves') and using constructive self-talk may help transform self-centred attitudes. Thus a variety of cognitive-behavioural strategies can be employed to combat narcissism if the individual is motivated to change her life.

Bibliography

M. Linehan, *Cognitive Behavioral Treatment of Borderline Personality Disorder* (New York, 1993).

R. K. BUFFORD

NATIVE AMERICAN RELIGION, see PAGAN AND INDIGENOUS RELIGION

NATURAL LAW

1. Introduction

According to age-old Christian understanding summarized by *Thomas Aquinas' *Summa Theologica*, certain foundational principles of *morality are 'the same for all, both as to rectitude and as to knowledge' – they are not only right for all but at some level known to all. Along with their first few rings of implications, these principles are called natural law.

Natural law is 'law' because it has the properties of all *law. Its precepts are not arbitrary whims, but rules that the mind can grasp as right; they serve not special interests, but the common good; their legislator is not a private person, but the public *authority of the universe; and they are not secret rules, for God has so designed creation that every rational being knows them.

In turn, natural law is 'natural' because it is built into the design of created human nature and woven into the fabric of the normal human mind. Another reason is that we rightly take it to be about what really is. A rule like the prohibition of murder reflects not a mere illusion or projection, but genuine knowledge. It expresses the actual moral character of a certain kind of act.

2. The relation of natural to biblical law

Although natural law is different from biblical law, the distinction does not imply opposition, but reflects two different ways in which God makes his moral requirements known. The former is 'general *revelation', given by God to all human beings; the latter, 'special revelation', given by God to the community of faith. These two modes of revelation partially overlap, and the Decalogue is an equally good summary of both. Where they do not overlap, each illuminates the other. Natural law contains certain moral principles which the Bible presupposes but does not make explicit, such as the norm 'give to each what is due to him'. Biblical law makes many remote implications of natural law clearer than they would have been through human reasoning alone. Moreover, it addresses the means of salvation, which reason by itself could never have known. By showing us our shortcomings, natural law might be said to prepare Gentiles for the gospel in roughly the way that the law of Moses prepared the Hebrew people (Gal. 3:23–24).

3. How natural law is known

Natural law theories differ little regarding the contents of natural law. Their disagreements concern mainly how it is known, how God imparts it to our intellects. Four general ways have been proposed. Following Paul's remark that God has not left himself without witness among the nations (Acts 14:17), herein these four ways will be called the four 'witnesses': deep *conscience, designedness in general, the particulars of our own design and natural consequences.

Mainstream natural law tradition affirms all four witnesses. Each witness is also confirmed by Scripture, as shown below. However, theories of natural law differ in the emphasis they give to each witness. Thomas Hobbes focused exclusively on natural consequences. In ways that are often overlooked, John *Locke relied on the two witnesses of design. The 'new' natural law theory of Germain G. Grisez, John Finnis and Joseph M. Boyle explores the structure of deep conscience.

a. The witness of deep conscience

Paul called attention to the witness of conscience when he wrote, 'Indeed, when Gentiles, who do not have the law [of Moses], do by nature things required by the law, they are a law for themselves, even though they do not have the law, since they show that the requirements of the law are written on their hearts, their consciences also bearing witness' (Rom. 2:14–15). However, the term 'conscience' may be used in two different senses. Medieval philosophers and theologians distinguished these senses by the terms *conscientia* and *synderesis*, but we may call them 'surface conscience' and 'deep conscience'.

Deep conscience is that feature of the created human intellect which is designed by God to

473

bear witness to his most basic moral requirements. This 'law written on the heart' cannot
be reprogrammed. It is not innate, for we are
not born knowing it. However, it is *per se nota*,
'known in itself'. This fact does not deprive
moral teaching of its function. Rightly understood, however, moral teaching does not
'pump in' the basic distinctions between good
and *evil, right and wrong (which would be
impossible), but elicit, sharpen and reinforce
our latent knowledge, embed it in practices and
virtues and protect it from misapplication.

Surface conscience is the application of
moral knowledge to the individual case. We
may also think of it as conscious moral belief,
especially about the details of moral law.
Although surface conscience is derived from
deep conscience, this fact must not be understood to mean that it is always derived correctly
and honestly. Indeed, surface conscience can go
deeply wrong, either through ignorance of fact,
error in reasoning or obstinate self-deception.
Thus, when natural law thinkers speak of
the 'formation of conscience', they mean the
formation of surface conscience.

b. The witness of designedness in general
The second witness is the manifest designedness of things. Paul indicates that this fact is
plain even to the wicked, 'For since the creation of the world God's invisible qualities –
his eternal power and divine nature – have
been clearly seen, being understood from what
has been made, so that men are without
excuse' (Rom. 1:20). His complaint is not that
such people ought to recognize the one God,
but that they do recognize him and pretend to
themselves that they do not. They are not
ignorant of the truth, but 'suppress' it (Rom.
1:18).

What has this to do with the knowledge of
natural law? In the first place, the designedness
of things draws attention to our duty, indeed,
our longing (Eccl. 3:11), to reverence the God
who designed us. But the witness of design has
another role as well, for it is pivotal to the
integrity of other witnesses. If George Gaylord
Simpson had been right when he wrote that
'man is the result of a purposeless and natural
process that did not have us in mind', then
deep conscience would 'witness' not to the
purposes of the designer but to the accidents
of natural selection and would be just another
meaningless part in the works. What holds for
deep conscience holds equally for the other

witnesses: apart from design, there would be
no reason to take any of them seriously. Not
only would natural law be deprived of its
lawfulness, but if we could somehow change
our nature, there would be no reason to hold
back.

c. The witness of our own design
After designedness in general comes the more
particular witness of our own design, the
features of created human nature. Consider
the complementarity of the sexes, alluded to
by Paul in Rom. 1:26–27. Not only are male
and female different, but their differences
correspond: to their union, the woman brings
something which is lacking in the man, and the
man brings something which is lacking in
the woman. Complementarity holds not only
physically but in every dimension of their
being. It is the foundation of the procreative
partnership we call *marriage, which in turn is
the foundation of the family, because father
and mother must cooperate not only for the
conception of the children, but also for their
nurture. It is also the foundation of erotic
transcendence, because within this partnership
the gift of self is offered to someone who is not
a mere reflection, a looking-glass idol of self,
but truly 'other'.

In recent years, scholars of the family have
rediscovered the peculiar appropriateness of
marriage and family. Sociologists McLanahan
and Sandefur write 'If we were asked to design
a system for making sure that children's basic
needs were met, we would probably come up
with something quite similar to the two-parent
ideal.' According to the natural law tradition,
the reason why marriage and family look
designed is that they are. For this reason they
are natural institutions, and the rules necessary
to their flourishing, like conjugal faithfulness,
are part of the natural law. Similar inferences
can be drawn from other features of our
species design.

d. The witness of natural consequences
Thomas Aquinas says law is a kind of discipline that compels through fear of punishment.
Although he offers this comment in a discussion of human law, it applies to natural law as
well, for the witness of natural consequences is
the way natural law 'kicks back' after violation. As Paul puts it, 'God cannot be mocked.
A man reaps what he sows' (Gal. 6:7).

Taking bad consequences seriously does not

imply the sort of *ethics called 'consequential-ist'. Consequentialists merely want to avoid negative consequences, they do not regard them as an index to the purposes of the designer. If someone invented a pill that made it possible to commit immorality without the usual consequences, consequentialists would say 'Now everything is permitted.' Natural law thinkers would say they had missed the point.

A good illustration of the witness of natural consequences is what happens when we violate the precept that sex must be contained within marriage. One immediate consequence is injury to the procreative good, because the woman may get pregnant but have nobody to help raise the child. Another is injury to the unitive good, because the man and woman forfeit the chance for that total self-giving which can develop only in a secure and exclusive relationship. Longer-term consequences include poverty, because single women must provide for their children by themselves; adolescent violence, because male children grow up without a father's influence; sexually transmitted disease, because formerly rare infections spread rapidly through sexual contact; child abuse, because live-in boyfriends tend to resent their girlfriends' babies and girlfriends may resent babies which their boyfriends did not father; and *abortion, because children are increasingly regarded as a burden rather than a joy. The longer people persist in violating the natural law, the heavier the penalties for violation. Provided they do not refuse the lesson, eventually even the dullest among us may put the clues together and solve the puzzle. Over the course of its history a culture may have to re-learn the timeless truths many times over. It may of course refuse to learn them and disintegrate.

Over and above the other consequences of violating natural law are the noetic consequences, the workings of guilty knowledge. Deep conscience operates in three different modes. In the cautionary mode, it alerts us to the peril of moral wrong and generates an inhibition against committing it. In the accusatory mode, it indicts us for wrong we have already done, and in the avenging mode, it punishes the soul who does wrong but who refuses to heed the indictment. The most well-known signal of deep conscience in the accusatory mode is the feeling of remorse. However, no-one always feels remorse for doing wrong and some people never do. Yet even when remorse is absent, the subconscious knowledge of guilt generates unavoidable needs for confession, atonement, reconciliation and justification. These needs can be truly satisfied only by 'a broken spirit and contrite heart' (Ps. 51:17). If we refuse to repent, however, we futilely try to appease the furies by other means. We may compulsively rationalize, confess every detail of our sins except the fact that they were wrong, or pay pain after pain, price after price, in a cycle which has no end because we refuse to pay the one price demanded.

5. The significance of natural law for apologetics

Through natural law, biblical principles like 'worship only God', 'honour your father and mother' and 'do not murder' are at least dimly known even where the Bible has not reached. As a general standard of morality which is not only right for everyone but at some level known to everyone, the natural law has profound importance for apologetics because it provides a point of contact between Christians and nonbelievers. If no such point existed, conversation with them could never begin.

A natural law apologetic begins by calling the attention of listeners to things that they already know. Paul proceeds in this manner when he reminds the Athenians of their altar 'To An Unknown God', bringing to the surface their cloudy awareness that despite their hundreds of idols, they have not found true deity. Then he 'connects the dots': 'Now what you worship as something unknown I am going to proclaim to you' (Acts 17:23). Notice that although Paul makes use of the witness of design, he does not say 'let me tell you about the witness of design'. There is no need.

Paul's hope was to persuade his listeners of the truth of the gospel. However, natural law also provides a basis for the effort to persuade unconverted people of moral truths short of the gospel, so that we can share a decent society. As in Paul's case, one begins with what the listeners already dimly know. In defending the natural institution of marriage, for example, one does not begin by saying 'According to the theory of natural law, men and women are complementary.' One simply calls attention to the fact that they are complementary.

If we do think of natural law as *common ground, however, we must understand it as slippery common ground. Though in some fashion, people already know the foundational principles of natural law, it does not follow that they are aware of knowing it. They may even be in rebellion against knowing it, desperately trying to convince themselves that they do not know what they really do. The difference between a naïve and a sophisticated natural law apologetic is that the former ignores this difficulty, while the latter anticipates it – it dissipates smokescreens and gets behind self-deceptions. For example, many women who are considering an abortion argue to themselves that they are boxed in by circumstances and say things like 'I know abortion is wrong, but I just can't have a baby right now.' From the perspective of natural law, a counsellor might simply ask, 'What do you call what's in you?' No matter what her conscious views about abortion, almost every pregnant woman immediately replies 'I call it a baby.' And in that case one can say without offence, 'Then it sounds like you already have a baby. The question isn't whether to have one, but what you're going to do with the one you've got.'

From this point of view, natural law apologetics will sometimes resemble dredging. It digs up suppressed facts and suppressed moral knowledge and brings them to the surface, so that they can be applied properly to the case at hand.

Bibliography

T. Aquinas, *Summa Theologica*, I-II.90–97; J. Budziszewski, *What We Can't Not Know: A Guide* (Dallas, 2003); R. P. George, *The Clash of Orthodoxies: Law, Religion, and Morality in Crisis* (Wilmington, 2001); R. Hittinger, *The First Grace: Rediscovering the Natural Law in a Post-Christian World* (Wilmington, 2003).

J. BUDZISZEWSKI

NATURAL THEOLOGY

Natural theology is the study of what can be known about God independently of special *revelation, i.e. independently of God's revelation of himself in Christ, the Scriptures and the prophetic word. The phrase 'what can be known about God' can be taken in two senses: what all normal human beings would know about God, were it not for the effects of sin and the fall, and what all human beings still know

about God in their fallen condition. Natural theology is best understood as addressing what can be known of God in the first of these two senses, according to humankind's original, unfallen capacities. However, Paul's argument in Rom. 1:18–20 sets a limit to the possible effects of the fall on these capacities. In order for sinful humans to be 'without excuse', it is essential that God's existence and divine qualities still be made 'plain' to them in what has been created, despite the damage their cognitive capacities may have suffered as a result of the fall. Paul lays the blame for unbelief squarely on our misuse of those capacities to 'suppress the truth by wickedness', and not on any defects within the capacities themselves. We could not be held accountable for unbelief or idolatry had the fall effectively erased our knowledge of the one God to whom we owe our exclusive worship.

The scope of natural theology is, by common agreement among Christian theologians, quite limited. It is generally accepted that such facts about God as the trinity, the incarnation, the vicarious atonement, salvation by grace through faith and the efficacy of the sacraments lie beyond the bounds of natural theology. Most would agree with Luther that the natural knowledge of God is not a saving knowledge; it is a knowledge of God as Creator and Judge, but not as merciful Saviour. In fact, if this distinction between a natural knowledge and a saving knowledge of God is not respected, natural theology can become a threat to Christian *theology, closing off the very possibility of a revelation of God that surpasses the bounds of natural theology. It is this threat, evident in deism, in the moralism of *Kant and the historicism of *Hegel and in the subjectivism of liberal theology, that prompted the reaction against natural theology on the part of Søren *Kierkegaard and Karl *Barth.

Worries about the dangers of natural theology from the perspective of Christian faith have a long history, reaching as far back as *Tertullian, who asked, 'What has Jerusalem to do with Athens?' It includes Blaise *Pascal, who denied that the God of the philosophers is the God of Abraham, Isaac, and Jacob, and Karl Barth, who labelled the God of natural theology an 'idol', not to be confused with the God who speaks to us through his word. These worries are legitimate, since we must always be on guard against any natural theology that arrogantly oversteps its bounds and seeks to supplant the revelation of God in Christ. However, we must not overreact, since Christian theology cannot do without natural theology. If natural theology is empty, then sin is not universal, since sin is intentional rebellion against God, and one cannot rebel against that which is wholly unknown. The universality of natural theology is thus a necessary presupposition of the universality of Christ's mission.

There are two forms of the natural knowledge of God – basic knowledge and knowledge by inference. The first form is sometimes called our natural sense of divinity (*sensus divinitatis*) and is most conspicuous in Augustinian and *Calvinist theologies. The second relies upon 'proofs' or arguments for God's existence, such as *Thomas Aquinas's famous Five Ways.

It is important to distinguish between the claim that we have a basic, non-inferential knowledge of God and the thesis of *fideism, that we have, by nature, no knowledge of God whatsoever. The so-called Reformed *epistemology of Alvin Plantinga and Nicholas Wolterstorff centres on the defence of the claim that our knowledge of God is, or can be, properly basic, i.e. that we can know that God exists without proof or evidence. Reformed epistemologists agree that our observations of nature and our experiences of *conscience can play a causal role in providing us with knowledge of God. In other words, our experience of the beauty and order of nature can be an occasion or a trigger that is a necessary condition for our knowledge of God's existence. However, they deny that we must reason from facts about nature or our conscience to the conclusion that God exists. Instead, they argue that we typically respond to these experiences by simply believing, without argument or inference, that God exists and that these acts of natural, spontaneous belief can constitute genuine knowledge of God.

Reformed epistemologists need not deny that knowledge by inference of God's existence is possible or that arguments for God's existence have some value. Conversely, Thomists need not deny that basic knowledge of God is possible. In the *Summa Theologica*, Aquinas argues that our knowledge of God cannot be basic, but he could be interpreted as arguing that the scientific knowledge of God requires proofs, i.e. that we cannot acquire a conception of God (as absolute, unconditioned being) that is adequate for *metaphysics apart from explicit arguments. Aquinas clearly recognizes that most human beings justifiably believe in God without the benefit of such arguments. A basic knowledge of God is sufficient to make us accountable before God, but perhaps not sufficient to make us expert metaphysicians.

Natural theology can be further subdivided into first and second orders. First-order natural theology is a branch of metaphysics: the study of God himself insofar as he is knowable apart from special revelation. Second-order natural theology is a branch of epistemology: the study of human ways of knowing God apart from special revelation. As Etienne *Gilson, Alvin Plantinga and others have convincingly argued, we should not think of epistemology as a kind of indubitable super-*science that must be completed before any other inquiry can begin. Instead, the study of human knowledge is just one facet of our study of the natural world. Theists and atheists recognize different bodies of data concerning what is and is not known about God, and so the epistemological theories they arrive at will be correspondingly different.

The apostle Paul teaches us that non-believers 'suppress' the truth about God (Rom. 1:18), and so Christians should not be unnerved by the fact that they and non-believers have profound disagreements about the epistemology of religion. First-order natural theologians should not be unnerved that many greet their conclusions with scepticism, even with scoffing, and second-order natural theologians need not shrink from the conclusion that all know of God's existence, even if many deny that they have such knowledge.

Natural theology is not primarily an apologetic or evangelistic enterprise, although its results may be relevant to apologetics or evangelism. Natural theology is a science, and so natural theologians must not be diffident about affirming the facts of the matter, even if some non-believers find some of these affirmations offensive. Apologists and evangelists are well advised to use the materials of natural theology with discretion and sensitivity. Natural theology may affirm that God's existence is evident to all and that unbelief is irrational, but this may not be the most prudent thing to say in an evangelistic or pre-evangelistic setting. Wise apologists understate the conclusions of natural theology, always striving to claim less and prove more.

There are five forms of argument for God's existence: ontological, cosmological, teleological, moral and epistemological. In addition, natural theologians must provide an adequate response to the problem of *evil, either by offering a theodicy, or by providing grounds for affirming God's goodness and righteousness in the absence of a theodicy (what Plantinga has called a 'defense').

Some philosophers, including David *Hume, have argued that the project of natural theology is doomed from the start, since one cannot infer an infinite cause from finite effects. However, this overlooks two facts. First, that we prefer simpler explanations to more complex ones, and the existence of an infinite God is a simpler hypothesis than the existence of a finite creator (as Richard Swinburne has argued), and, secondly, that the analysis of causation that forms part of the *cosmological argument supports the conclusion that an uncaused First Cause must be infinite.

Others have charged natural theology with the 'God of the gaps' fallacy, an illegitimate appeal to our ignorance of the natural causes of phenomena. These critics complain that it is unreasonable to posit a supernatural cause of what we cannot explain naturally, since the search for natural causes is an ongoing and always incomplete project. However, natural theology, when it is done well, is based upon what we know, not on what we do not know. Just as we know that the methods of alchemy cannot turn lead into gold and that the methods of ancient geometry cannot square the circle, we know that certain kinds of complex biological entities or cosmic fine-tuning cannot be produced by blind and unintelligent forces.

Another common objection to natural theology is that it fails to respect the separate, complementary roles of science and theology. Scientific knowledge cannot lead to theological conclusions, it is claimed, because science is concerned exclusively with what happens in the natural world, and theology is concerned exclusively with the meaning or ultimate purpose of those events. This view is often associated with a position of 'methodological *naturalism', the principle that scientific theories must always be limited to the positing of finite, natural causes. However, this dichotomy between two supposedly isolated forms of knowledge is ultimately untenable. In both science and theology, we seek to explain events by finding an adequate causal explanation. We must always be free to follow the evidence wherever it leads, and we must not hobble either science or theology by rigid, dogmatic restrictions on what they may or may not consider as possible explanations.

Bibliography

K. Barth, *Church Dogmatics* (Edinburgh, 1949); D. Hume, *Dialogues Concerning Natural Religion* (Indianapolis, 1970); W. Paley, *Natural Theology* (New York, 1839); A. Plantinga, *Warranted Christian Belief* (New York, 2000); R. Swinburne, *The Existence of God* (Oxford, 1979); Thomas Aquinas, *Summa Contra Gentiles* (London, 1923).

R. C. KOONS

NATURALISM

The term 'naturalism' can be used in various ways. Here it is used in the sense of the metaphysical doctrine that contradicts the beliefs of Christianity and of other theistic religions like Judaism and Islam. In this sense naturalism is the view that nothing exists except nature, the natural world. Nature itself can be delimited in more than one way; for present purposes we may identify it with the physical universe. To hold that the physical universe is all that exists directly contradicts the existence of God, a purely spiritual, infinite, omnipotent, omniscient, and perfectly good personal agent on whose creative activity everything other than himself depends for its existence at every moment. Of equal concern for Christianity, this also implies a denial of the doctrine of divine providence, that God takes an active part in the governance of the universe and from time to time brings about results that are other than what they would have been had only natural causes been involved. These include recoveries from illness, outcomes of battles, communications to certain individuals, calls to particular vocations, not to mention the birth, ministry, death and resurrection of Jesus Christ. Divine providence is also denied by deism, the view that God simply originates his creation and then leaves it to its own devices, governed by the laws he has given it, but Christianity and other theistic religions view God as much more active than this in his creation.

The chief reason for the widespread advocacy of naturalism on the current scene is the enormous success of natural *science from the seventeenth century onwards. A trenchant presentation of this line of thought is given by the distinguished biologist, Julian *Huxley: 'the god hypothesis ... appears to have reached the limits of its usefulness as an interpretation of the universe and of human destiny ... it is no longer adequate to deal with the phenomena, as disclosed by the advance of knowledge and discovery. The idea of miraculous intervention has grown progressively less and less tenable, until it has now become repugnant ... to a growing body of those educated in the scientific tradition ... the advance of knowledge is making the god hypothesis untenable for an increasing number of people' (Huxley, *Religion*, pp. 62, 185–86).

We can distinguish two lines of argument in this passage. The more obvious one is the argument from science against *theism. Science, with its purely naturalistic explanations of a wide range of phenomena, does a much better job of making sense of the universe than theism does. Secondly, Huxley makes it explicit that this is also an argument *for* naturalism. He supposes that since theism is the only serious competitor to naturalism, if science has ruled out theism then that amounts to supporting naturalism.

This way of claiming a scientific support for naturalism depends on very questionable assumptions. First, it assumes that theistic religion and science are trying to do the same job. Since science does that job better, it displaces its competition. It is a great mistake, however, to think of Christianity – or even theism in general – as primarily concerned with giving explanations of natural phenomena of the scientific sort (aimed at prediction and control), and hence as being in competition with science in that area. In assuming that this is the basic purpose of religion, Huxley vastly overemphasizes those cases in which phenomena, such as mental diseases, were once explained in terms of the direct action of God and are now ascribed to this-worldly causes. Rather than being primarily concerned with explaining natural phenomena, Christianity and other theistic religions have arisen because people have felt the presence and activity of God in their lives and have responded in a variety of ways – awe, reverence, worship, prayer, obedience (and disobedience) and devotion – all of which play an orienting role in their lives, enabling them to see those lives as falling within a scheme that gives them

meaning. It is true that Christianity has become involved in what are properly scientific concerns, e.g. the geocentric picture of the universe, the origin of species, and this has brought it into conflict with scientific results. But these involvements are peripheral to the central concerns of religion. They can be, and have been, abandoned without sacrificing anything essential to Christianity.

Suppose we waive this objection and agree that science's success in greatly extending the area of naturalistic explanations (including areas previously claimed by theistic religion) is, so far as it goes, a black mark against theism, but that hardly suffices to give decisive support to naturalism. Naturalism is a metaphysical view that the physical universe is all there is, but science by its job description is restricted to exploring the constituents of the physical universe and regular patterns in their behaviour. Because of that restriction, it can have nothing to say about whether there is anything other than that universe. The results of scientific observations, experiments, and theorizing could not possibly imply either that there is or is not something more. That is outside its province. Therefore, no matter how much knowledge science gives us of the internal constitution of the physical universe, it cannot tell us whether the 'something more' to which theistic religion is committed exists. If a scientist like Huxley undertakes to do this, he is not engaging in scientific investigation but rather in philosophical speculation. The idea that the results of science support a naturalistic rather than a theistic world-view is based on a misunderstanding of the nature of science.

Thus far the criticism has been of Huxley's appeal to the results of science to oppose Christianity's foundational belief in the existence of God. But what about Christianity's other commitment to God's direct action in the natural world? Is there more of a case for the idea that science lends support to the naturalistic position on this?

The aspect of naturalism that conflicts with divine action in the world is the view that the physical universe is a closed causal system. Any causes of what happens in the universe are themselves within that universe, and there can be no causal influence from outside.

There are two ways in which science might be thought to support this component of naturalism. First, in the last few centuries more and more has been discovered about the natural causes of phenomena, including diseases, biological reproduction and inheritance, atomic and sub-atomic processes and chemical interactions. The idea is that the more such discoveries are made the more likely it is that it will be shown that everything in the universe depends only on causal factors from within nature.

Although these developments are impressive, they fall far short of showing that every natural occurrence depends solely on natural factors. All this evidence is equally compatible with the view that natural causal determination holds only some of the time and even when it does, only approximately so. Scientists have observed only a tiny sample of natural happenings, and it is, therefore, rash to make an unrestricted generalization from this evidence. As for the second point, our observations are always subject to a margin of error. Indeed, we often exploit this fact to correct observations into a good fit with deterministic laws. Thus the results of science can reasonably be taken to suggest, at most, a close approximation to purely natural causation rather than the full-blown article.

The second scientific support for causal closedness comes from the alleged fact that science *assumes* it. If scientists did not assume that everything has natural causes, why would they devote so much time and energy to looking for them? But a closer look at the situation reveals that the only thing a scientist is committed to assuming is that there is a *good chance* that the *phenomena he is investigating* depend on natural causation *to a significant degree*. These three qualifications mark three ways in which the scientist need not be assuming a completely closed natural order and need only assume a significant probability for the particular area of investigation; and even there need assume only a chance of complete closure.

Up to this point we have been considering what might be called a *metaphysical* support for naturalism from science, ways in which science is thought to indicate that the physical universe is all there is to *reality and, even if it is not, it is closed to influences from without. But there is also an alleged *epistemological* route from science to naturalism. It involves confronting claims for the existence of something other than the physical universe, with statements beginning 'There is no scientific proof for ...' and continuing with, e.g. various Christian doctrines – the existence of God, divine providence, the divinity of Christ, the resurrection of the body and so on. Even if these claims are justified, there is the question of what significance this absence has. Why is this not just one example of the way in which the methods of one domain fail to answer questions in another? Historical research does not tell us what basic physical particles there are. What goes on in a chemical laboratory does not indicate how best to organize the economy.

Here the naturalist who depends on this last argument will say, 'Science is the only source of truth. Only the scientific method can provide us with knowledge of objective reality.' But when we ask for the grounds for these claims, the only thing on offer is the fact that science has done very well at its chosen tasks. This may be agreed, but why suppose on that basis that scientific method is the only way of getting truth about anything? Is this not an arbitrary partiality? It is as if one who recognizes the stupendous musical achievements of J. S. Bach thereby concludes that he has completely exhausted the resources of musical expression, leaving no room for a Mozart, a Beethoven, a Wagner. Or, a closer analogy, it is as if one who is dazzled by the heights to which modern mathematics has ascended should conclude that only pure mathematics can give us knowledge, thereby ruling any empirical evidence out of court.

The upshot of the above is that Christianity has nothing to fear from naturalism, if the only basis for that position is found in the natural sciences. And without that support there is little to be said in defence of naturalism.

Bibliography

O. K. Bouwsma, 'Naturalism', in *Philosophical Essays* (Lincoln, 1965); Y. H. Krikorian (ed.), *Naturalism and the Human Spirit* (New York, 1944); J. Huxley, *Religion without Revelation* (New York, 1957); S. J. Wagner and R. Warner (eds.), *Naturalism: A Critical Appraisal* (Notre Dame, 1993); S. Weinberg, *Dreams of a Final Theory* (New York, 1992).

W. P. ALSTON

NEO-IDEALISM, see IDEALISM

NEO-ORTHODOXY

Historical usage

Neo-orthodoxy is a term used to denote the theological 'movement' associated with the names of Karl *Barth, Emil *Brunner, Rudolf *Bultmann and Friedrich Gogarten, which developed in continental Europe in the late 1920s and early 1930s. The term is to be understood in a relatively broad sense insofar as it is a collective term used by commentators on the significance of the movement, rather than one used by those so described. The journal *Zwischen den Zeiten*, published between 1922 and 1933, may be said to be representative of those associated with neo-orthodoxy.

The roots of neo-orthodoxy are linked to the publication of the second edition of Barth's *The Epistle to the Romans* in 1922 (ET, London, 1933). In this work, Barth signals a decisive break from the tradition of liberal theology, as exemplified in the work of Adolf von *Harnack, and a move towards a theology of the word of God on the basis of his self-revelation. Barth may be understood as continuing, albeit with considerable qualification and without explicit acknowledgment, the theological inheritance of Wilhelm Herrmann.

By the early 1930s, however, neo-orthodoxy began to fragment as the theological paths pursued by those involved took radically different directions. For example, Gogarten's endorsement of the German Christian Movement and the latter's accommodation with National Socialism under Hitler led to a break between him and Barth and the cessation of the journal. In like fashion, Barth's contribution to the *Barmen Declaration* (1934) signalled his rejection of the possibility of such an accommodation.

Within the English-speaking world, the greatest impact of neo-orthodoxy is linked to the divergence between Barth and Brunner on the possibility of a renewed *natural theology, as advocated by Brunner. Although the actual disagreement occurred in 1934, it was the 1946 publication of the English translation of the two points of view, under the title *Natural Theology*, that gave renewed life to the debate. Thus, in *Nature and Grace*, Brunner argued that there continued to exist a point of contact between a fallen humanity and God on the basis of the image of God, and that this point of contact enabled a fallen humanity to be addressed by the gospel of Jesus Christ. Brunner may be understood as contending, as a consequence of this, that the point of contact should shape our understanding of the nature of theology. Thus, the task of *theology is to enable the realization of the potential inherent in the point of contact. In similar fashion, the task of Christian proclamation is founded on the basis that such a point of contact exists. Further, we should note that central to Brunner's position is his belief that his theology stands in continuity with that of the Reformers such as *Calvin. The claims made by Brunner must, therefore, be understood as having a particular significance in the field of historical theology, as well as their direct theological significance. Barth famously issued a *Nein!* to Brunner's position in the publication of *No! Answer to Brunner*, which rejected the basis of such a point of contact and affirmed the impossibility of beginning a theology, properly understood, from here. According to Barth, it is God alone who creates the possibility of *revelation through the self-giving of Jesus Christ, and there is no other point from which the tasks of theology and proclamation may begin. Thus, we note that, for Barth, the possibility of an apologetics grounded on a general revelation of God in nature is ruled out in principle. In like fashion, we note Barth's rejection of Brunner's identification of his theology with that of Calvin and the Reformers and his contention that he more faithfully reflects their position.

Theological usage

As indicated, the term neo-orthodoxy is one that has a relatively broad meaning. However, we may usefully distinguish a theological use of the term from the historical usage, and this may enable us to clarify the relationship between neo-orthodoxy and the task of apologetics. In making this distinction, we should note that the tendency to read Barth as representing neo-orthodoxy is a phenomenon particularly associated with English-speaking interpreters of Barth, as opposed to continental European interpreters. This tendency has been helpfully corrected by B. L. McCormack's *Karl Barth's Critically Realistic Dialectical Theology: Its Genesis and Development 1909–36* (Oxford and New York, 1995).

We have already noted Barth's rejection of natural theology and we may identify the precise theological justification for this in his rejection of the concept of an *analogia entis*, i.e. an analogy between the reality of God's being and our existence as human beings, such that it is impossible to construct an apologetic route from our experience of the conditions of human existence to the reality of God's being. To attempt to do so would be to make a categorical error, insofar as our starting point would be an anthropological, as opposed to a theological or Christological, one.

Instead of such a starting point, Barth contends that we must begin at the only point from which a theology, properly understood, can begin. That is, it must begin from a hearing of the word of God that is received in faith, which leads to our understanding the reality of our human situation in the light of what Christ has done for us. Thus, we note again that the apologetic route to a knowledge of God, by *analogy drawn from our human situation, is excluded in principle.

In contrast to this analogy, Barth contends that 'God is known only by God' (*Church Dogmatics* II, 1, p. 179), such that he may speak of an *analogia fidei* in which our knowledge of God is grounded in the gracious act of God in Christ as received by faith. Thus, the *analogia fidei* replaces the apologetic appeal to the *analogia entis*.

Barth's understanding of the *analogia fidei* has been developed by T. F. Torrance to explicate our scientific knowledge of the created order in terms of such knowledge being grounded in the act and being of the Creator. Thus, the creation is to be understood in terms of its relationship to the covenant brought into being by the act of the triune God. In so doing, Torrance develops Barth's thought and offers an approach to the knowledge of God that is, in principle, consonant with the self-revelation of God.

Bibliography

K. Barth, *Church Dogmatics* (ET, Edinburgh, 1936–75); K. Barth and E. Brunner, *Natural Theology* (ET, London, 1946); G. W. Bromiley, *Introduction to the Theology of Karl Barth* (Edinburgh, 1979); T. F. Torrance, *Theological Science* (London, 1969).

J. L. McPAKE

NEO-THOMISM, see THOMISM

NEW AGE

The expression 'New Age' came to prominence in the mid-1980s, since when it has been used as a designation for the alternative spiritualities and life-styles that first emerged in the 1960s. The media generally use 'New Age' in a negative way, depicting it as an exploitational commercial enterprise, which is why those who would once have happily embraced the label now distance themselves from it, insisting that this is a serious spiritual pathway more adequately described as 'New Spirituality'.

The terminology of a 'new age' originated in an astrological tradition which understands human *history as a series of seven different ages, beginning 14,000 years ago with the age of Leo, followed in turn by the ages of Cancer (approx. 8000–6000 BC), Gemini (approx. 6000–4000 BC), Taurus (approx 4000–2000 BC), Aries (the 'age of the Father', approx. 2000 BC–0) and Pisces (the 'age of the Son', approx. 0–2000 AD). The final stage, which on this analysis is now emerging, is the age of Aquarius, supposedly a time of ultimate enlightenment and transformation (the 'age of the Spirit').

To reduce the phenomenon of New Age to such curiosities misses its major significance on the spiritual landscape of contemporary culture. It is better understood as a part of the cultural change that is leading to the emergence of postmodernity. Though Christians are likely to pay more attention to the so-called philosophers of the postmodern era (e.g. *Derrida, *Lyotard, *Foucault), the popular postmodernity that has given rise to New Spirituality depends less on philosophical insights than on the experiences of ordinary people as they struggle to make sense of everyday life. There is growing awareness of the enormity of the changes that have occurred in the past fifty years or so. Nothing at all now works in the way it once did, including such everyday things as cooking, laundry, transportation and communication, as well as the institutions of government, education and finance. Included in this is the church, which while it provided spiritual meaning to previous generations, no longer seems to connect with today's concerns (not least because patterns of family life have also changed beyond recognition). Alongside that, there has been an opening up of Western society, with increasing understanding of other cultures and different ways of being spiritual. Some of these pre-date the inherited Judeo-Christian tradition, and often appear to be less individualistic and have a more holistic vision. When those factors are combined with our evident sense of lostness – increasingly articulated as a desire to recover the 'spiritual' – we have the matrix which has created New Spirituality and within which it flourishes.

At the heart of this spirituality, therefore, is a dissatisfaction with the world-view of modernity, indeed with the entire fabric of Western civilization. Despite its many achievements, that way of understanding the world and our place in it is increasingly coming to be regarded as neither conceptually meaningful nor practically useful. Behind this is not so much a rejection of scientific theory (we still happily espouse the rationalized systems characteristic of modernity), but a new sensitivity to the actual facts of history. By the 1960s the proliferation of nuclear devices was threatening world stability, and the terrifying possibilities of *technology without boundaries became increasingly real. This concern was then supplemented by the growing awareness of how Western lifestyles were damaging the environment and depleting our natural resources, and a greater understanding of the high price paid by people of other cultures, who had suffered under the imposition of our Western civilization. It was inevitable that serious questions would be asked about the ideology which had brought us to this situation – questions which appear even more urgent in the light of recent events, such as the calamity of 9/11, the growing AIDS crisis in Africa, or the impatience of Western politicians with the Islamic world. The influence of a dualistic world-view, which validated all this by distinguishing spirit from matter, body from soul, people from nature, men from women, and Westerners from the rest of the world guaranteed that any discussion of these matters would have an overtly spiritual dimension. This is where the holistic approach of the New Spirituality comes in, by highlighting what look like valuable insights from other cultures and reinstating aspects of Western spirituality that have either been marginalized or forgotten.

In the past, people looked to the church as their spiritual guardian, but that is no longer the case in Britain, and northern Europe generally. Although the situation in the USA is different, the same signs of impatience with traditional Christian churches can be documented there too. That is not to say that Christian concepts are entirely absent from New Spirituality, but they tend to be adopted randomly. So, for example, medieval mystics like Hildegaard of Bingen or Julian of Norwich are far more likely to be esteemed than John *Calvin or Karl *Barth. Other major strands feeding into the New Spirituality include insights from major non-Western faiths, especially *Buddhism, together with a whole variety of diverse concerns such as Wicca, channelling, auras, eco-villages, tarot, healing therapies of every conceivable sort, and much more besides. People educated in the traditional Western paradigm are likely to assume that there must be some common core that unites these disparate concerns. But for a world-view that begins with radical questioning of that paradigm, one obvious way to correct the perceived deficiencies is to prioritize almost anything that is 'other' in order to identify new and better ways. It is this 'otherness' that provides coherence to such an apparently amorphous collection of 'alternative' ways of doing things. They are not conventional, many of them are of non-Western origin, and those that are not come from the margins of Western culture rather than the centre.

Not everyone is interested in all this, and many people still profess no interest in spirituality of any kind. But Christians should not underestimate the importance of the New Spirituality. Insofar as there is a dominant spiritual outlook in our culture, this is it. In addition, many of its prime movers are people who have either been members of churches or are the sort of people who in a previous generation would have been lay leaders in local congregations. Not surprisingly, Christians have adopted a variety of attitudes towards all this. Particularly in the USA, the New Spirituality has been viewed as a demonic threat to be vigorously opposed, and even on occasion regarded as a world-wide conspiracy bent on destroying everything (the church included). At the opposite end of the spectrum, some have embraced it rather uncritically, on the understandable assumption that anything spiritual must be better than the materialist attitude that has dominated Western culture for so long. Then there are those who see the New Spirituality as evidence of a genuine search for meaning and purpose, and who actively engage with it, recognizing that much of its critique of Western culture – and of the church – is correct, while insisting that the gospel challenges all our accepted notions (traditional Christian ones included). There is a growing trend, particularly in the UK and Australia, for Christians to engage with New Spirituality in a missional context by taking stands at Mind, Body and Spirit fairs and similar events.

Any meaningful Christian apologetic in this context must begin with a recognition that the situation today is very similar to that the apostles and the early church faced. The difference being that we also have two thousand years of Christian history to be accountable for, not all of which has commended the gospel. Acknowledging the mistakes of the past might be a necessary prelude to creative engagement with the present and the future. One biblical passage that is especially relevant to such engagement is the story of Paul in Athens (Acts 17:16–34). Throughout Acts, Luke offers models for evangelism with different people groups, and here it is people who are disillusioned with the religious *status quo* (in their case traditional Greek values and belief systems) and who are searching for a new spirituality that will match the needs of the hour. This is exactly where today's spiritual searchers are located.

Significantly, Luke mentions Paul's insecurity and fear as he encountered the 'supermarket' of faiths, but even in this seemingly alien place there was an expectation that God would already be at work (the *Missio Dei*). The Bible offers no support to a theology that would declare some places no-go areas for God. Engagement with New Spirituality will be more challenging than many Christians realize. It is the equivalent of learning a new language in order to contextualize the gospel in another *culture, and will therefore take time, and considerable personal openness to hear what others are actually saying.

Who are these 'others'? The key questions with which the contemporary spiritual search engages are the classic issues of human identity and purpose: who am I, where did I come from, what does my life mean, and how can I make a useful contribution to the life of this world? Far from being an intrinsically self-centred narcissistic movement, this is in fact a response to the failure of modernist culture to

deliver on its promises, and it represents a genuine search for a new world-view that will chart a safer course for the future of the planet and all its people. The search is for spiritual tools that will overcome our hurts, empower us to realize our hopes, and to make the world a better place. Within this frame of reference, the unifying theme is the desire for empowerment that will enable people to fulfil their own potential and serve others, which is remarkably similar to Jesus' recommendation to 'love your neighbour as you love yourself' (Mark 12:31). Paul recognized the importance of making connections like that, and in Athens did so via the 'altar to an unknown god'.

Effective mission within New Spirituality is probably a specialist ministry to which not every Christian will be called. There are, however, some matters that we could pay attention to so that, like the waiting father in Jesus' parable, we are ready to welcome home the wanderers (Luke 15:11–32).

We need to recognize that, under the influence of an excessively cognitive culture, we have paid less attention to human pain than we should have done. The search for healing – of emotions and relationships as well as bodies – is very genuine, and invites us to reconsider what the *community of faith might look like if it were to follow Jesus' advice about the holistic nature of discipleship (Mark 12:29–30).

Alongside this, we need to revisit some key biblical beliefs, most notably to articulate a theology of creation and incarnation that will take seriously the conviction that people – as people – are 'in God's image' (Gen. 1:26–27). Who we think people are has a profound effect on the way we seek to connect with them. Church life should reflect this high value that God places on persons. Church should be a place where people are empowered to become whom God wants them to be, not a place where the human spirit is crushed. This will be a particular challenge for those Christians who continue to pursue a dualistic vision in which, for example, women and men are not treated with equal regard, or there are strict hierarchical distinctions between clergy and laity. There is also a need for a more serious engagement with environmental issues.

We need to recover confidence in the *missio Dei* as the context in which to tell the story of Jesus, alongside our own stories of faith. A transformational story has its own challenge.

Though many Christians accept Lyotard's claim that no-one nowadays wants a meta-narrative, there is little hard evidence from popular culture to support that. On the contrary, people are desperately seeking a new meta-narrative that will be worthy of carrying them through to the future – one that, unlike the oppressive and exploitation meta-narrative of the past, will be liberating and empowering.

We also need to give serious thought to the nature of 'truth'. *Truth as relationship has a different agenda than truth as only proposition, and it calls for different ways of exploring and expressing it.

Bibliography

R. Clifford and P. Johnson, *Jesus and the Gods of the New Age* (Oxford, 2001); I. Hexham, S. Rost and J. Morehead (eds.), *Encountering New Religious Movements: A Holistic Evangelical Approach* (Grand Rapids, 2004); G. Johnston, *Preaching to a Postmodern World* (Grand Rapids, 2001); D. Kemp, *New Age: A Guide* (Edinburgh, 2003).

J. W. DRANE

NEWBIGIN, LESSLIE

Lesslie Newbigin's approach to apologetics reflects an outworking of core theological convictions in response to his analysis of contemporary culture. He argues that 'Enlightenment' thinking still pervades Western culture – not least in its continuing elevation of the role of reason in the search for *truth. As a result there is a general belief that certain propositions may be accepted as 'fact', whilst others are simply 'opinions'. As professions of religious faith are firmly perceived to fall within the latter category, the church has repeatedly faced the apologetic temptation to defend the gospel on the basis of prevailing cultural assumptions about 'truth'. Too many apologetic approaches in the West have suffered as a result, argues Newbigin, being characterized by the attempt to defend Christianity on grounds of its supposed 'reasonableness'.

Tracing this style of rationalistic apologetics back through the scientific revolution of the sixteenth and seventeenth centuries (and the attempt by *Descartes to defend the Christian faith against the growing scepticism of his time), Newbigin focuses upon the work of

*Thomas Aquinas in the thirteenth century as a key turning point. In the *Summa Theologica* Aquinas offered proofs for the existence of God which rested on grounds of reason rather than those of *revelation, initiating a crucial shift from the approach of *Augustine (summed up by the phrase *credo ut intelligam* – 'I believe in order to know') to one based on the more rationalist philosophy of Aristotle. Newbigin describes the implications of this shift as the 'fatal flaw' of apologetics during the last 300 years.

Newbigin's approach, therefore, aims to ground apologetics in the *authority of divine revelation rather than upon the spurious foundation of reason. After all, the heart of the gospel message is inherently *un*-reasonable to the natural human mind. As the Christian faith revolves around a man crucified on a cross, it is clear that no amount of brilliant argument can make this sound 'reasonable' to the inhabitants of a post-*Enlightenment culture. Whenever the gospel is defended on grounds of its supposed reasonableness, therefore, Newbigin argues that the resulting apologetic strategies frequently reveal a greater debt to Enlightenment *rationalism than to biblical faith.

By contrast, Newbigin argues that revelation must itself constitute the foundation of the apologetic enterprise, there being no sufficient grounds on which to defend the gospel except those offered by the gospel itself. This insistence upon revelation as the only foundation for apologetics lies at the heart of Newbigin's approach, and represents both a reversal of the Enlightenment's dislocation of revelation by reason, as well as an outworking of Augustine's insistence that faith remains the prerequisite for true understanding.

Newbigin does not draw out the practical implications of such an approach in detail, preferring rather to lay out repeatedly the presuppositional framework outlined above. Nonetheless, three inter-related perspectives emerge from his writings on the practice of apologetics. First, in the light of his insistence that apologetic strategies be founded upon revelation, Newbigin emphasizes that the 'proper form of apologetics is the preaching of the gospel itself'. This he often describes in terms of the need to re-tell the Bible's 'story' – a story which finds its climax in the incarnation, death and resurrection of *Jesus Christ as God's supreme self-revelation. Secondly, Newbigin insists that despite its cultural unacceptability,

Christian claims about truth based upon God's revelation of himself are in fact similar to all claims to truth – namely that each rests upon 'faith commitments' which cannot be proved. Thirdly, therefore, he insists that the trustworthiness of the gospel reveals itself in the course of faithful Christian living. For it is through being tested in the course of life's experiences, as well as through dialogue with others, that Christian faith shows itself more reliable than its rivals in making sense of human existence.

Newbigin's writings are therefore an encouragement to Christians to bear witness to the gospel as 'public truth', and a reassurance that they may do so with a 'proper confidence'.

Bibliography

J. E. L. Newbigin, 'Way Out West: The Gospel in a Post-Enlightenment World', *Touchstone*, 5.3 (1992), pp. 22–24; 'Religious Pluralism: A Missiological Approach', *Studia Missionalia*, 42 (1993), pp. 227–244; *Proper Confidence: Faith, Doubt and Certainty in Christian Discipleship* (London and Grand Rapids, 1995).

P. D. A. WESTON

NEWMAN, JOHN HENRY

The philosophical work of John Henry Newman (1801–90), Anglican, Tractarian leader, later Roman Catholic Cardinal, contextual theologian, educator and churchman, has been largely ignored. The prominence of his thought in education, doctrinal development, lay involvement in the church and spiritual autobiography may have contributed to this oversight. Newman, however, formulated a philosophical defence of the rationality of Christian belief in the *University Sermons* (1872) and the *Grammar of Assent* (1870). The *University Sermons* offer a preliminary exploration of the conditions under which Christian belief is rationally acceptable, unpacking the role of implicit and explicit modalities of *reasoning in the life of faith and showing how antecedent probabilities shape the process of belief-formation. The *Grammar of Assent* provides a fuller response to the question of how Christians can be certain of theological claims for which they lack demonstrative proof and for which they lack comprehensive understanding. Newman appeals to a cumulative

process of reasoning in which the illative sense, a non-rule-governed process of reasoning, determines how various probabilities converge towards a certain conclusion and form the best possible explanation.

Newman's proposal takes *empiricism seriously and explores the conditions under which both Christians and others form and sustain their beliefs within real-world environments. It also rejects the extremes of *fideism (Christian belief is strictly a matter of faith) and *evidentialism (Christian belief is rationally acceptable if and only if it can be supported by the preponderance of evidence). The formation of beliefs is a dynamic process expressed in implicit (spontaneous process of belief-formation) and explicit (retrospective analysis of beliefs) modalities of reasoning. The key here is to distinguish between the formation of Christians and the justification of Christian belief.

The implications of Newman's proposal are profound. Belief-formation reflects a holistic process, involving cognitive, affective and moral dimensions of the human person. The stress here is on the integration of subjective and objective dimensions of Christian belief. The case for Christianity is not exhausted by inductive and deductive arguments; rather judgment plays an indispensable role in assessing the cumulative nature of belief-formation. Such a move, for example, shows up in the work of Basil Mitchell. Moreover, reducing human cognition to one modality of reasoning contributes to truncated versions of rationality. Consequently, Newman deems the task of apologetics (explicit reasoning) as a part of the church's ministry, but it should not be construed as a precondition for Christian belief.

Bibliography

F. D. Aquino, *Communities of Informed Judgment: Newman's Illative Sense and Accounts of Rationality* (Washington, DC, 2004); M. J. Ferreira, *Doubt and Religious Commitment: The Role of the Will in Newman's Thought* (Oxford, 1980); *Scepticism and Reasonable Doubt: The British Naturalist Tradition in Wilkins, Hume, Reid and Newman* (Oxford, 1986); W. R. Fey, *Faith and Doubt: The Unfolding of Newman's Thought on Certainty* (Shepherdstown, 1976); T. Merrigan, *Clear Heads and Holy Hearts: The Religious and Theological Ideal of John

Henry Newman (Louvain, 1991); B. Mitchell, *The Justification of Religious Belief* (New York, 1973); *Faith and Criticism* (Oxford, 1994); J. H. Newman, *An Essay in Aid of a Grammar of Assent* (Oxford, 1985); *Fifteen Sermons Preached before the University of Oxford* (Notre Dame, 1996); W. J. Wainwright, *Reason and the Heart: A Prolegomenon to a Critique of Passional Reason* (Ithaca, 1995).

F. D. AQUINO

NEW TESTAMENT APOLOGETICS

After having answered many challenges and objections during his ministry, and just before going to his death, *Jesus warned that in the last days his disciples would also be required to give a defence (*apologia*) in a variety of contexts (Mark 13:9–13; cf. Luke 12:11; 21:14). In the days immediately following, Jesus alone survived the pressure of the times to offer a defence before the Jewish and Roman leaders. Nevertheless, the requirement to stand unashamedly for the gospel, despite threat to life and safety, is part of the 'taking up the cross' (Mark 8:34) that is to characterize Christian discipleship.

According to Alexander, one of the 'primary difficulties in exploring apologetic within the New Testament' is the 'wide range and fuzzy definition of the term "apologetic"' ('Acts as Apologetic', p. 16). An *apologia* was a speech offered in a legal setting in defence against some kind of charge (*katagoria*). It was a particular form of rhetoric, the 'art of persuasion', answering the charges of a hostile opponent, before one who can arbitrate (who is not connected to the apologist or his group), in the context of a larger audience to whom appeal can also be made.

In the ancient world apologies were offered on behalf of individuals and of groups. Probably the most famous ancient example of an apology for an individual was that of Socrates, which survives in the versions of Plato and Xenocrates. In the second century AD, Apuleius also wrote an apology against the charge of using magic to win the hand of an older, wealthy widow. In the NT, the apostle Paul offered his apology to the Jerusalem crowd (Acts 22:1) and, according to standard Roman legal procedures, before Roman and Jewish officials (see Acts 22 – 26). In his letters he also mounted a defence against those who criticized his apostleship (1 Cor. 9:3; 2 Cor. 12:19), and he regarded his various stints in prison as opportunities for an apology for the gospel of Christ (Phil. 1:7, 16; 2 Tim. 4:16–17).

Embattled minority groups may also resort to apologies to the larger, hostile host society. Jewish diaspora literature has often been regarded as apologetic although, as it was written to fellow Jews rather than to pagans, it is not technically apologetic literature. When Christianity became the dominant force in society in the fourth century, pagans also began to use the device of apology. Probably the most famous apologies in defence of a group were those written in defence of Christianity from the second to the third century. Apologists such as Quadratus, Aristo, Aristides, *Athenagoras, Tatian, *Justin Martyr, Melito, Theophilus, Minucius Felix and *Tertullian defended Christianity against such charges as sedition and immorality. They commended Christianity as the final and true religion that not only fulfilled the OT but also gave the answers to the questions and concerns being asked by the pagans. Many of their arguments were anticipated by the NT writers.

To what extent is the NT itself written as an apology? The new movement centred on Jesus arose in a context that demanded an apology, and Jesus' warning of the need for a defence was reiterated at the commissioning of Paul (Acts 9:15–16; 22:14–15; 26:16–18). Ordinary Christians are also urged to be prepared to defend the hope within (1 Pet. 3:15), and the Philippians were commended for their eagerness to share in Paul's defence of the gospel (Phil. 1:7, 16). As the gospel was preached to an ever-increasing audience, the early church met opposition of many kinds – religious, cultural and political – which required a defence. Apology was required against four different types of attack – from Jews, from paganism, from the Roman imperial system and from internal disagreements and challenges.

To the Jews, the crucifixion of Christ was a stumbling block that required a defence. Apostolic preaching argued that Jesus was the Christ, appealing to his *miracles and to fulfilled prophecy and centring on the resurrection of Christ. But how could the Messiah have been crucified? The risen Jesus had already had to explain this scandal to the apostles themselves (Luke 24:27). Once they knew that his suffering was according to the Scriptures, their preaching turned the fact that a crucified man was cursed (Deut. 21:23) into an asset (Acts 5:30; 10:34), by the realization that, as the Servant of the Lord (Isaiah 53) he gave his life for many, becoming a curse for them (cf. Gal. 3:13). The appeal to prophecy is a hallmark of the NT writings and continued on into the second-century apologists. It had appeal not just for the Jews but also for the Gentiles, who were interested in the antiquity of ideas and in prophecies made by sacred books.

Israel's unbelief, which emerged during Jesus' ministry, was also a difficulty that needed to be addressed. Perhaps strangely, their unbelief even became a proof for Jesus being the Messiah, for it was a continuation of the same hardness of heart that was apparent in their history. Manifested by a focus on the externals, rather than a heart obedience to God's word, this hardness meant that Israel had always rejected God's word and his messengers. Will they now reject the new thing that God has done in Jesus, making the old order of *Judaism redundant? Stephen (Acts 7) used these kind of arguments, as did Paul, the Gospel writers and the author of the letter to the Hebrews. Paul also explained the unbelief of Israel as a necessary part of God's plan to save the world (Rom. 9 – 11). The influx of the Gentiles was designed to provoke Israel to jealousy, so that there would also be a steady stream of Jews turning to their Messiah (Rom. 11:26, 'And so all Israel will be saved').

The cross of Christ was also a stumbling-block for the Greeks, not simply for the pragmatic reason that a dead person cannot deliver others but because the Gentile world also regarded a crucified man as being under a curse. Paul certainly shows an awareness of this difficulty (e.g. 1 Cor. 1:18–25). In the book of Acts, however, when engaging with pagans, Paul exposes the weaknesses of idolatry (as the OT and the Jewish writings such as Aristeas and Wisdom had already done). Paul's brief speech in Lystra (Acts 14:8–18) has been regarded as an apology to unsophisticated pagans, and that before the Areopagus (17:16–34) as an apology to sophisticated pagans. In both, he aims to help his hearers turn from idolatry, arguing for the existence of the living God from the good things they had received at his hands. Some later apologists point to such speeches as the justification for a kind of ''*natural theology'

which appeals to points of contact in pagan experience. In this stream, the apologists such as Lactantius, who sought to build on the insights of the Greeks, were favoured by Christian humanists such as *Erasmus and were attractive to later apologists. Understandably, apologists such as Tatian and Tertullian, who rejected the idea that the Greeks had any insight, were less attractive. It is questionable, however, whether Paul used natural theology in Acts 14 and 17 at all. Instead, he is simply proclaiming the gospel, which exposes the weaknesses of the Greek world-view. Before the Areopagus, he concludes with a reference to something that no natural theology would ever reveal, that God had appointed a judgment day and furnished proof through raising the future judge from the dead. In response, God now invites all people to repent in this time of grace when he has overlooked the previous times of ignorance. In his letters, Paul continues to proclaim the liberation that Christ brings to the idolater, enslaved to all kinds of rules, regulations and rituals, from a life characterized by futility, hardness of heart and immorality (cf. Eph. 4:17–19).

The Romans, too, would have been scandalized by the cross. Luke, especially, places Christ and Christianity on the stage of world history dominated by the Caesars (Luke 2:1; 3:1; Acts 26:26). Jesus' response to the tribute question (Mark 12:14) would have been useful for those wishing to show that, with regard to taxation, there was no problem being a Christian and a citizen of Rome (cf. Rom. 13:1–7; 1 Pet. 2:13, 17). A bigger problem for Christianity was that it began with a founder who had been executed – even crucified – as a criminal according to Roman law. In addition, Christianity was accused of creating disorder wherever it went (cf. Acts 17:6). Against these charges, Luke-Acts shows that the condemnation of Jesus was a miscarriage of justice and that even the Roman officials involved declared him to be innocent. The book of Acts shows that the disorder surrounding the early church arose from Jewish jealousy, rather than anything politically subversive.

Luke's writings have been a particular focus of attention when discussing this apologetic 'front'. 'Luke must be recognized as the pioneer in that type of apologetic which is addressed to the secular authorities in order to establish the law-abiding character of Christianity' (Bruce, *Defence*, p. 60). Despite significant disagreement about the exact apologetic situation addressed, Acts is the NT book that has most persistently been called 'apologetic', going back to at least 1721 when Heumann suggested it was an *apologia* in defence of Christianity to the pagan official Theophilus.

As time went on, the apostles faced the necessity of defending themselves and their message against Christian deviations. In the early days, this was a persistent *legalism from Jewish sources (Acts 15:1), which Paul strongly answered in Galatians. Later, he defended the gospel against an asceticism with the flavour of an early gnosticism (Colossians; cf. 1 Tim. 4). Jude has been identified as a defence against an antinomian pre-gnosticism, and the epistles of John against a form of *Docetism. Hebrews and John have been called 'the final outcome of the New Testament considered as an apologetic', since they present the gospel as the final *revelation of God, making Christianity unique and exclusive, 'the absolute religion'.

This defence against internal attacks on Christianity, which has sometimes been distinguished from apologetic and called 'polemic', should probably be excluded from a discussion of NT apologetic. There is some justification for dealing with internal conflict as apologetic, since Paul mounted his own defence against those who criticized his apostleship (1 Cor. 9:3; 2 Cor. 12:19), and the Corinthians, in turn, spoke in their own defence against Paul's painful letter (2 Cor. 7:11). However, if these were truly internal disputes, then they are not proper 'apologies', which were addressed to outsiders on behalf of the group. In addition, since in dealing with false teaching, the NT writers do not engage directly with the false teachers, but address the churches who were being influenced by them, this also removes this material from the rhetorical setting of apology. The NT does counsel various strategies for dealing with internal opponents, such as gentle correction (2 Tim. 2:25), merciful caution (Jude 23) or downright avoidance (2 Tim. 3:5; 4:15). But the rhetorical setting of the material is a warning from one member of the group (the NT writer) to other members of the group (the recipients) about a third party coming from outside. The 'genre' of this material is therefore neither apologetic, nor even polemic, but pastoral.

Discussed along the lines set by the four types of opposition, apologetic has been described as the cradle in which Christianity was developed. Scott argued that NT Christianity, having no fixity, developed as it defended itself against these four opponents. Droge shares this understanding: 'In the first century, Christianity lacked a uniform church structure and theology. Instead Christian communities tended to be shaped theologically and organizationally by their respective founders. Relations among these groups often ranged from close co-operation to competition and outright hostility' (Droge, p. 305). Thus, Galatians is 'the first systematic apology for Christianity, not to outsiders but to Christians themselves' (Droge, p. 305). For sceptical NT criticism, discerning apologetic motives behind the NT writings questioned the authenticity of much of what was written. So, e.g. *Bultmann classifed the empty tomb story as an 'apologetic legend', written by the early church to support the message of resurrection. Thus the 'facts' were created to suit the apologetic interest of the early church.

With respect to apologetics towards Christian deviations, Bruce noted that 'The presentation of the gospel in all its fullness and depth is the best defence against pseudo-Christianity. So evidently the apostles and other first-century Christians believed' (Bruce, pp. 86–87). In fact, the proclamation of the gospel in all its fullness seems to be the task which occupied the NT writers, and any apologetic motive or strategy in the NT writings must be inferred. The major task of the NT writings is the proclamation of the gospel and the explanation of its implications. Any 'apologetic' or 'polemic' that can be identified is subservient to this primary task. However much the NT displays a sensitivity to its various audiences, its message did not arise from those audiences but from the events of God's self-revelation in Jesus Christ. The NT arose not primarily out of the need to *defend* Christianity but out of the urgent need to *proclaim* the message about Christ's life, death and resurrection and his invitation to life in the new covenant. Since the message turns on the resurrection of Jesus Christ, it includes the 'defence' which appeals to the word of the human *witnesses of that event (e.g. Acts 10:39–42; 1 Cor. 15:1–11). The apology for the hope that is within us (1 Pet. 3:15), is another way of referring to the promises of the gospel. The proclamation of the gospel gives rise to the need for apology, and the apologetic situation, in turn, becomes an opportunity for further proclamation. Even Paul's defence of himself was a defence of the gospel (Phil 1:7; 2 Tim. 4:16). When he appeared to be defending himself, he was actually speaking for the edification of his hearers (2 Cor. 12:19). Each need for an apology gave him new audiences with which to share the good news of Christ and his resurrection, a further defence and confirmation of the gospel (Phil. 1:16).

One of the advantages of understanding NT apologetics is for the instructional value for those called to give a defence at the current time. First, the defence of the gospel is a secondary activity that arises as a result of the primary activity of the proclamation of the gospel. This is never done in a condescending manner, but always, according to Karl Barth, 'as poor sinners alongside other poor sinners', commending the grace of God in Christ. Secondly, the proclamation and its defence centres upon Jesus as the Christ, the Word made flesh, the divine Son of God. The proclamation is as complex as Jesus himself, but includes the following four elements. 1. Jesus' person and work are explained against the backdrop of OT texts. This proof from prophecy is applied to all aspects of Jesus' life, but especially his resurrection and installation as Lord. 2. The miracles of Jesus, and especially the resurrection, attested to God being with him, to him being the Christ, to him being the divine Son of God. 3. The scandal of the cross is explained by reference to Jesus' innocence, his role as the Servant (cf. Isa. 53), and his death as a curse for others (Deut. 21:23). 4. Because the events of Jesus' life, death and resurrection were the fulfilment of God's revelation in human *history, Jesus is the unique name by which all people must be saved (Acts 4:12). This is never stated defensively, but is a positive statement of Christ's lordship and a positive invitation to all people everywhere to find the grace of God in Christ.

Bibliography

F. F. Bruce, *The Defence of the Gospel in the New Testament* (Grand Rapids, 1959; rev. 1977); A. J. Droge, 'Apologetics, NT', *Anchor Bible Dictionary* (New York, 1992), I, pp. 302–307; M. Edwards, M. Goodman and S. Price (eds.), *Apologetics in the Roman Empire: Pagans, Jews, and Christians* (Oxford, 1999); B. Lindars, *New Testament Apologetic: The Doctrinal Significance of the Old Testament Quotations* (London, 1961); E. F. Scott, *The Apologetic of the New Testament* (London, 1907).

P. G. BOLT

NEW TESTAMENT MANUSCRIPTS

Every translation of the NT is based on 'manuscripts' (from the Lat., meaning 'written by hand'), which are hand-written copies made by scribes. Each manuscript differs to a lesser or greater extent from every other manuscript, and these variations ('variants') clearly cause some concern to Christians who wish to know what the Bible says. The task of classifying and evaluating these manuscripts is known as 'textual criticism'. At several places in the NT, the original text is disputed. This article will explain some reasons for textual variants, outline some basic principles required for treating the NT manuscripts and then will examine several contested texts.

Principles

How should Christians respond to the simple fact that there are many extant manuscripts and that they do not agree with each other? As a fundamental principle, a decision on the true reading of the NT can be reached only after careful consideration of the available witnesses with respect to external evidence (date, provenance, number of manuscripts, etc.) and internal evidence (possible reasons for scribes to introduce variant readings, style, etc.). While this will not, in practice, be required of every interpreter of the Bible, it is important that our decisions are based on careful work with the available manuscripts, whether our own work or that of other reliable scholars. Any approach to the question which confers special privilege on one manuscript for purely theological reasons is to be rejected. This is primarily because Scripture (which must be our sole *authority) does not ascribe such priority to any manuscript. Any approach which does not take multiple factors into account follows too simplistic an approach which simply accepts the reading of the majority of manuscripts or the earliest manuscript without taking the whole range of relevant issues into account.

To reject a variant, even one which has been found in Bibles for many years, is not necessarily to reject the divinely breathed-out character of Scripture. Rather, it is to recognize that no translation or edition of the NT is perfect, and to claim that the evidence which divine providence has made available to us suggests that the variant in question was never a part of the divinely breathed-out text.

Reasons for textual variants

When we consider the nature of the textual variants, we need to ask what led a scribe to change what someone else had written. We may follow Metzger's excellent discussion and class them as 'unintentional changes' and 'intentional changes'.

Unintentional changes

These may arise for various reasons. Sometimes a scribe's poor eyesight or poor concentration led to his reading two individual letters as if they were one different letter. (The scribe's task was made all the more difficult when some theologically important words were abbreviated in such a way that two abbreviations, or an abbreviation and another regular word, could appear very similar.) On other occasions, when two lines of text ended with the same words in the same form (*homoioteleuton*), the scribe's eye skipped from the first line to the second line, thus omitting the text in between. If a scribe was copying from dictation, he might confuse two words which look different but sound alike. The list of possible mishaps goes on, but in many of these cases the mistake will stand out because it makes no sense or because it is highly unlikely, and there will be little difficulty in tracing the original reading. For example, one scribe so muddled Luke's genealogy that he made God the son of Aram.

Intentional changes

The greatest risk to the accurate transmission of the NT text, according to Metzger, was from 'scribes who thought'. These scribes made various deliberate changes to their manuscripts. Some attempted to correct what they regarded as faulty grammar or spelling, or added words which, they thought, were implied in what was written. Others harmonized passages (for example, Luke's version of the Lord's Prayer was made to conform to Matthew's version) or tried to resolve historical or geographical difficulties. Sometimes if a scribe found himself looking at two documents which offered him two different alternative readings, he might decide to reject neither but

instead to conflate both of them into one entirely new reading. Even more intrusive were those scribes who modified their sources so as to make or correct a doctrinal point. These variants are more likely to make some sense in their context. Yet even in these cases of deliberate alteration, the majority of cases may be decided by comparison of the many available manuscripts and the use of the criteria employed by textual critics. Only a small proportion of these variants causes thorny problems.

Reasons for confidence in the accuracy of manuscript tradition

There is no doubt that the extant manuscripts vary one from another and thus it is inevitable that all contain changes from the original reading of the autographs, although it may be difficult to ascertain which accurately represent the original text and which vary from it. No benefit is gained by claiming that any one extant manuscript is 'without error'. It is important to stress, however, that 'the vast majority of all changes found in our New Testament manuscripts are careless mistakes that are easily recognised and corrected' (Ehrman, p. 443), particularly errors in spelling and word order. That is, they are frequently unintentional changes and largely have no bearing on the meaning of the text. Other changes may have been intentional, made by scribes who believed they were acting in the interests of orthodoxy (Ehrman, p. 446), although we have no access to the intentions of the scribes to confirm this view. Even in these cases, comparison of the readings of several manuscripts frequently provides a ready explanation for the diverse readings and a fairly clear indication of which is most likely to be original.

Contested cases

I will now examine two specific cases of significant textual variants. These are selected partly because they are well known and frequently discussed among Christians who might not otherwise deal much with the issues of textual criticism, partly because they illustrate the impact that text-critical decisions have on Christian faith and partly because they receive attention in Metzger's *Textual Commentary*, where interested readers may find fuller discussion. The contested texts are Mark 1:1 and Mark 16:9–20.

Mark 1:1

Many English translations will indicate, either by brackets or a footnote, that there is some doubt over whether the words 'the Son of God' at this point are original or not. The words are omitted by the original hand of the important codex (a manuscript in 'book' form) Sinaiticus, which dates from the third century. Yet, several factors suggest that the words are original. First, there is strong external evidence for including the words; they are present in, for example, the usually reliable Codex Vaticanus. Secondly, it is possible that a scribe's eye accidentally skipped over the abbreviated forms of these significant terms when copying the manuscript. Thirdly, the phrase 'Son of God' is found in the confession of the centurion in Mark 15:39. If the phrase is original to Mark 1:1, then the two occurrences form an 'inclusio' or literary bracket indicating completion of Mark's case concerning Jesus. This is lost if the phrase is not original. It should be said that there is no doubt as to whether the words of the centurion are original, so that even if the words in 1:1 are not, Mark still conveys the rich theological declaration by another means and no doctrinal foundation is lost.

Mark 16:9–20

The traditional (longer) ending of Mark's Gospel is well attested in a variety of manuscripts, including ancient ones. It is, however, not present in two important early manuscripts, and is, in Metzger's judgment, to be rejected on the basis (particularly) of internal evidence (vocabulary, style etc.), i.e. on the strength of the noticeable change in writing style. Such use of internal evidence is controversial and interpreters disagree. The editors of the standard Greek editions regard this passage as the work of someone other than the evangelist but include the passage in double square brackets out of deference to the historical association of the passage with Scripture (which might be regarded as a somewhat indecisive policy). My own cautious view is that it did not form part of Mark's work. However, once again, no significant doctrine is affected by this decision. (For example, the testimony to the ascension is not lost but is found in Luke's Gospel and Acts.)

Conclusions

Having examined the contested cases above, it should be clear that there is simply no possibility of having *absolute* certainty regarding the original readings in every disputed case. It is virtually inevitable that no matter how carefully a view is argued from the available evidence, someone will argue precisely the opposite view from the same body of evidence! Yet there are good grounds for retaining confidence in the accuracy of our NT translations. First, the numerous manuscripts which have been preserved until the present day provide scholars with an unparalleled body of evidence upon which to base their judgments. Secondly, while different from each other in some (often very minor) respects, the extant manuscripts present a remarkably consistent testimony to the original text of the NT. Thirdly, no variant readings require modification of a fundamental point of Christian doctrine or ethics.

While 'absolute certainty' is not available to us, the number and broad agreement of the extant manuscripts give us strong grounds for the view that we can know with great confidence the text of the original autographs.

Bibliography

D. A. Black (ed.), *Rethinking New Testament Textual Criticism* (Grand Rapids, 2002); D. A. Carson, *The King James Version Debate* (Grand Rapids, 1978); B. D. Ehrman, *The New Testament: A Historical Introduction to the Early Christian Writings* (Oxford, 2000); B. D. Ehrman and M. W. Holmes, *The Text of the New Testament in Contemporary Research* (Grand Rapids, 1995); B. M. Metzger, *The Text of the New Testament* (Oxford, 1968); *A Textual Commentary on the Greek New Testament* (Stuttgart, 1975).

A. I. WILSON

NEWTON, ISAAC

Isaac Newton (1642–1727) was born in Woolsthrope near Grantham in Lincolnshire. He received his bachelor's and master's degrees from Cambridge University, where he was appointed to the Lucasian Chair of Mathematics in 1669. He is renowned for his contributions in mathematics, with the invention of the calculus, and in physics, with his publication of *Opticks* (1704) and his magisterial *Philosophie Naturalis Principia Mathematica* (1686), in which he demonstrated the law of universal gravitation, forever changing the course of modern *science. Newton was appointed as Master of the Royal Mint in 1696 and elected President of the Royal Society in 1703, holding that office until his death. Newton's interests spanned a wide range beyond mathematics and science, including alchemy, biblical chronology and prophecy, church history and theology. His scientific endeavours provided a major contribution to the Christian apologetics of his time.

The platform of Christian apologetics in late seventeenth- and early eighteenth-century England was erected upon the pillars of the 'two books': the book of God's works (nature) and the book of God's word (*revelation). Newton's major contribution was the way in which his revolutionary mechanics of the universe bolstered the teleological (design) argument, thereby apparently binding the two books into one apparently seamless volume.

Newton understood that his *Principia Mathematica* (1686), with its overthrow of the Cartesian *cosmology, would contribute to the rational defence of the existence of God. In 1692 he wrote to Richard Bentley, 'When I wrote my treatise about our Systeme, I had an eye upon such Principles as might work with considering men for the beliefs of a Deity and nothing can rejoyce me more then to find it useful for that purpose.' Newton had a role in launching the Boyle Lectures, whose expressed purpose was to defend the Christian faith, and he believed that the right understanding of the mechanics of the universe naturally led to belief in a Creator. In his *Opticks*, he wrote that the role of science was to examine natural phenomena and deduce causes from effects until we arrive at the first cause, which 'certainly is not Mechanical' but one 'very well skilled in Mechanics and Geometry'. For Newton, the crucial attribute of God was dominion. In the General Scholium of his *Principia* he wrote, 'This most beautiful system of the sun, planets, and comets, could only proceed from the counsel and dominion of an intelligent and powerful being ... This Being governs all things, not as the soul of the world, but as Lord over all; and on account of his dominion he is wont to be called *Lord God παντακράτωρ*, or *Universal Ruler*.' Newton believed that God's dominion was manifested in the coordinated design of his laws and creatures, and asks rhetorically, 'Was the Eye contrived without skill in Opticks, and the ear without knowledge of Sounds? ... does it not appear from Phaenomena that there is a Being incorporeal,

living, intelligent, omnipresent?'. Here we see Newton's position in the design or 'watchmaker' argument which travelled down through *Paley, *Hume, Darwin, Dawkins, Behe and Miller. 'Did blind chance know that there was light, and what was its refraction, and fit the eyes of all creatures, after the most curious manner, to make use of it?' For Newton, the conclusion was inescapable. 'Atheism is so senseless and odious to mankind, that it never had many professors ... Whence arises this uniformity in all their [creatures] outward shapes but from the counsel and contrivance of an author?'

Newton's work was first used to support biblical *theism but was later turned against it. The best apologetic deployment of Newton's work was by Samuel *Clarke (1675–1729) in his two courses of Boyle Lectures. The purpose of these lectures was to defeat *atheism and deism. Clarke also helped establish the Newtonian basis through his translation of Rohault's *Traité de Physique*, the standard Cartesian textbook, which Clarke subverted with Newtonian annotations. Finally, Clarke's correspondence with *Leibniz established Newtonian mechanics, which required God's continual preservation of the creation through special providence, specifically in regards to 'the very nature of gravitational attraction', as the only adequate apologetic against the 'materialism and fate' of deism. By the middle of the eighteenth century, *Voltaire and others took up deism and, with a twist, sought to support it with Newtonian mechanics. For this reason, some scholars have erroneously concluded Newton himself was a deist. In fact, Newton believed in divine creation, miracles as a necessary exercise of God's special providence to sustain the universe, and that the world would end and be renewed through apocalyptic cataclysm, all directed by the divine will. Newton explored the full spectrum of scientific and theological disciplines searching for what is today called the unified theory; the theory of everything, which would unlock the mystery of God's will. He not only read the 'two books', thoroughly, but provided a paradigm for seeing how they were seamlessly bound in the dominion of the divine will; a paradigm to which, only now, are we returning.

Bibliography

D. Brewster, *Memoirs of the Life, Writings and Discoveries of Sir Isaac Newton*

(Edinburgh, 1855); M. Buckley, *At the Origins of Modern Atheism* (New Haven, 1987); S. Clarke, *Works* (London, 1738); I. Newton, *Principia Mathematica* (Mottes trans. London, 1803); J. Thrower, *Western Atheism: A Short History* (New York, 2000).

T. C. PFIZENMAIER

NIEBUHR, H. RICHARD

Helmut Richard Niebuhr (1894–1962), like his better-known theologian and ethicist brother Reinhold and Christian educator sister Hulda, was born into a German-American family. His father had been an immigrant to the United States, and became a pastor in the German Evangelical Synod of North America. His mother was the daughter of an immigrant pastor who had been sent to the United States by a European missionary society. Richard and Reinhold followed this family tradition and became pastors and teachers in the Evangelical Synod.

Early in their ministries, the brothers struggled to help their denomination break away from its German heritage and join what they regarded as the modern American cultural mainstream. Both Niebuhrs are often listed among the most important neo-orthodox theologians of twentieth-century Europe and North America, seeking to shift the liberal focus of religion from humanity back to God.

Helmut taught in the Synod's seminary and served briefly as the president of the Synod's college. He also served on a committee whose work led to the union of the Evangelical Synod with the German Reformed Church. When he became a professor of Christian *ethics at Yale Divinity School he shed his German given name and became known as Richard.

His first book, *The Social Sources of Denominationalism* (1929), showed how differences among divided churches were neither as theological nor as high-minded as partisans led their faithful to believe. His next book, co-authored with Wilhelm Pauck and William Miller, *The Church Against the World* (1935), refocused the problem of how to be 'the church in the world' to an honest assessment of 'the world in the church'. *The Kingdom of God in America* (1937) traced the theological themes of North American Protestantism (see *Christianity, Protestant). In it is Richard's most quoted phrase, a critique of liberal Protestantism: 'A

God without wrath brought men without sin into a kingdom without judgment through the ministrations of a Christ without a cross.' Later books included his theology of *history, *The Meaning of Revelation* (1941); his classic statement of a Christian *sociology of history and most important book, *Christ and Culture* (1951); and a critique of nationalism and other idolatries, *Radical Monotheism and Western Culture* (1960). *The Responsible Self* (1962), based on his Yale lectures in ethics, was published after his death.

While brother Reinhold's interest was the transformation of society, Richard devoted his life to theological reflections on the relationship between the church and the world. His biographer Jon Diefenthaler wrote that he 'was a man for whom the vocation of churchman remained central throughout his life'. He taught that Christ turned persons and societies away from self to God, but always within the framework of *culture: 'We are in history as a fish is in water.' Within this cultural context, however, the 'continuing imperative' of the church was reformation. He wrote, 'I still believe that reformation is a permanent movement, that *metanoia* is the continuous demand made on us in historical life.' The Christian life was a permanent revolution of the heart and mind.

At the peak of his career, following the publication of his most important book, Richard postponed all other scholarly research to direct an intensive study of theological education in North America. One of the three published results of this investigation was the book, *The Purpose of the Church and Its Ministry* (1956). Reflecting his ongoing though critical appreciation for the North American social-gospel movement, he defined the mission of the church as the 'increase among men of the love of God and neighbor'.

J. HELT

NIEBUHR, REINHOLD

Reinhold Niebuhr (1892–1971) was a comparative rarity: a theologian who could command the public interest and respect of non-Christian as well as Christian citizens. He did not, however, regard himself as a theologian, certainly not in the usual sense that might better fit his famous younger brother, H. Richard *Niebuhr. His emphasis was practical in that he addressed contemporary social and political issues from a Christian perspective, rather than directing his attention to doctrinal questions in their own right. His major work, *The Nature and Destiny of Man* (published in two volumes during the Second World War), however, shows considerable theological acumen, especially in its investigation of the nature of human sin.

Born in Missouri, Niebuhr took up a pastorate in Detroit after completing his theological studies. The industrial milieu of the city signally helped to form his social conscience and convictions, and from his base there he launched out on a travelling and speaking ministry in the United States which eventually extended to Europe. In 1928 he went to teach ethics and philosophy of religion at Union Seminary in New York, where he remained until his retirement in 1960. An energetic political activist, as well as teacher and speaker, Niebuhr gained a reputation for *socialism, but he was an independent thinker within that broad context. This independence characterized his theology, too; labels such as 'neo-orthodox' or 'liberal' fail to capture one or another feature of his thought. Niebuhr described reality as he saw it, dismissing firmly superficial analyses of the human or social condition that implicitly denied its many paradoxes.

A certain type of *realism was probably the most distinctive feature of Niebuhr's thought. Applied to social teaching, this meant that Niebuhr was opposed to an optimistic, idealistic social gospel. His thought has been regarded as a negative constraint on socially revolutionary action by some sympathetic to liberation theology, which emerged towards the end of Niebuhr's life. Niebuhr's early writings draw distinctions between the *ethics that apply to individuals and the ethics that apply to groups, and between love and *justice. The love which Jesus reveals and embodies is not directly applicable to group behaviour and public policy in society, for it concerns interpersonal relationships of the kind where self-sacrifice and forgiveness are appropriate. In the wider sphere, our quest must be for justice. But Niebuhr does not make the distinction absolute: love can temper and moderate justice in the wider sphere, and justice itself is not a single, monochrome idea. To appreciate the various nuances of this, *The Nature and Destiny of Man* must be read alongside earlier works, like the famous *Moral Man and Immoral Society* or *An Interpretation of Christian Ethics*.

Niebuhr, who was willing to style himself an 'apologist' since he sought to commend Christian perspectives in the public place, is in some respects enduringly important. Changes in society and politics obviously make some of his writing rather dated. He too often evacuates Christian doctrine of its proper content (e.g. when he mythologizes eschatology) or neglects it (e.g. in the area of ecclesiology). But his instinct for realism and penetrating observations should always command the attention of anyone seriously seeking to formulate a Christian philosophy of society and politics.

Bibliography

R. Fox, *Reinhold Niebuhr: A Biography* (New York, 1985); R. McAfee Brown (ed.), *The Essential Reinhold Niebuhr* (New Haven, 1986); L. Rasmussen (ed.), *Reinhold Niebuhr: Theologian of Public Life – Selected Writings* (London, 1989); R. Song, *Christianity and Liberal Society* (Oxford, 1997).

S. N. WILLIAMS

NIETZSCHE, FRIEDRICH

The son of a Lutheran pastor, Friedrich Nietzsche (1844–1900) abandoned Christianity as a university student and gradually became sceptical about all accepted theories and beliefs, whether religious, ethical, scientific or philosophical. The concept of God, he declared, is hostile to life, a sign of weakness and decadence, for it directs us towards an unreal supernatural world. Christianity in particular produces conformity and obedience, a slave mentality, submissive and tortured in conscience. So the greatest event of modern times was the realization, as he put it, that God is dead, unworthy of belief, and the decay of belief opens the way for our creative energies to develop fully.

But Nietzsche's is not an evidential scepticism. His reasons for disbelief are psychological rather than scientific, historical or philosophical. Like *Freud and Marx, he deliberately attempts to unmask the hidden motives that make us project our subconscious desires onto the world of experience, for he is convinced that this is what shapes behaviour and beliefs. So his work *On the Genealogy of Morals* claims that Christianity began as a popular uprising against the Jewish religion by the underprivileged, by publicans and sinners, by women and the sick. OT characters had the strength and courage to accept suffering and death, but NT hopes of healing and of life after death and a kingdom of God reveal a resentment of this world. These are signs of weakness. Nietzsche's key concept, what he calls 'ressentiment', is that the weak work out their resentments by subverting the values of the strong: they weaken a master by making him depend on his servants, they bless the meek and have them inherit the earth, they invent 'conscience' to repress human nature, and they make Christian love a *power play of the weak. Christianity opts for God over nature, for heaven over earth, for soul over body, and for a self-flagellating conscience over virile passion.

This 'hermeneutic of suspicion', which interprets what people say and do in terms of subconscious desires, underlies much of postmodern subjectivism and *relativism with its scepticism about *truth claims generally. Merold Westphal points out that the focus on hidden motives should be a stimulus to self-examination, for it reminds us of the capacity for self-deception that Christian theology ascribes to original sin. But Nietzsche's conclusion that suspect motives falsify Christian beliefs, like the possible counter-claim that Nietzsche's own suspected motives falsify his disbelief, simply ignores the fact that a belief may be true despite the motivation involved. Neither truth nor falsity follows from such suspicions; rather they call for a more careful examination of the belief involved, whether the claims of Christ and historic Christian theology or Nietzsche's own constructive proposals.

In *Beyond Good and Evil*, however, he proposes that behind all *logic, *language and truth stand value judgments, and behind value judgments the psychological demand for a certain kind of life. This is the case not only with religious beliefs but with scientific and philosophical theories as well. Logical arguments and verbal formulations simply conspire to create the ordered world their advocates want: the traditional arguments for God's existence, for instance, depend on philosophical premises that are psychologically driven, as is the *science to which those premises refer, and the laws of logic to which the arguments appeal. So while philosophers have argued for the existence of God, they are no different from the Jewish priests who created a moral world

order by affirming that God willed once and for all what humans are to do and not do. They both made a fictitious world the 'real' world, and made nothing into 'God'. Now God is dead, exposed for the nothing he is, and that ordered world no longer exists, life has no inherent order or purpose, no value or meaning. Every ordered world will likewise fail, for they are all in the end alike, just psychological projections of our frustrated hopes. The outcome is *nihilism, the end of all meaning to life, and the contrast with the Christian message could hardly be greater.

Life requires a balance, Nietzsche proposes, between the Apollonian type and the Dionysian passion, a balance which was precluded by Christianity's siding with the weak. So he vests his hopes in the strong-willed who have the courage to live in such a barren void. Now God is dead, he cries in *Thus Spake Zarathustra*, we must be the meaning of the earth! He exalts the strength that can embrace suffering and shout a hearty 'Yes!' to nature, a kind of superior person (*Übermensch*) willing to challenge this wasteland even through endless recurrences of life and death. He develops the vitalist hypothesis that a creative force animates the whole range of nature, and this hidden drive is what lies behind the irrepressible vitality of the strong as well as the ressentiment of the weak.

We can appreciate Nietzsche's suspicion of *Enlightenment claims about 'reason alone' and the finality of science. Such a rationalistic approach to knowledge and to life was plainly reductionistic. But he is guilty of a similar reductionism when he reduces religious and moral beliefs to nothing but psychological reactions. If we take this at face value, as some radical postmodernists might, then the resultant scepticism will have no limits: it extends to Nietzsche's own psychological explanations and to the very possibility of any valid knowledge at all. However, the view of language and logic it entails seems plainly exaggerated. Language is not always nor just a means to reshaping the world for our own ends, for it has other and more cognitive functions that are not always nor altogether self-serving. Granted all we say and do may to some degree be self-referential, it is not thereby devoid of all objective reference and truth value. We may see through a glass darkly and know in part, but we do still see and know. Christian theology grounds that knowledge in the self-revelation of God in his creation and incarnation, a

God who endowed us with the capacity for understanding and love. On the other hand, Nietzsche's psychological egoism is a large part of his problem: by reducing human interests and motives to nothing but veiled self-interest, he cannot take seriously either the objective pursuit of truth for its own sake or any altruistic and irenic moral concern. To the psychological egoist, objective knowledge and an ethic of love are nothing but power plays.

In the end, then, we are faced with a choice between two alternatives: a reductionist *naturalism with an ethical egoism and Christian *theism with its ethic of love. Both might be subjected to a hermeneutic of suspicion, but Nietzsche thinks the choice boils down to a pragmatic weighing of consequences, which turns out to be an instinctual response, a psychologically driven moment of truth that decides who are the weak and the strong rather than whether naturalism or Christian theism is itself more likely to be true. The Christianity he criticizes sounds more effeminate and more Victorian than it is biblical, for the poor and oppressed are equally the concern of both Old and New Testaments, as is the call for mercy and love. Similarly, courage and strength of will in the Old is readily matched in the New, for Christ willingly embraced suffering and death, as did those martyred for his sake. Nor is Christianity otherworldly: the medievals strove to balance contemplative and active lives; Luther saw justification freeing us for earthly tasks; and creative Christian energies are evident in every area of culture. Above all, Christianity offers hope, not just for the weak but also for the strong with courage enough to recognize their weaknesses and failing. The choice then lies between this and the arrogant Promethean desire to master one's own fate in rebelling against God.

Bibliography

W. Kaufmann (ed.), *The Portable Nietzsche* (New York, 1954); F. Nietzsche, *On the Genealogy of Morals* (New York, 1967); *The Anti-Christ* (New York, 1918); M. Westphal, *Suspicion and Faith* (Grand Rapids, 1993).

A. F. HOLMES

NIHILISM

This article is concerned with value-nihilism rather than with the metaphysical denial that there is anything at all. Metaphysical nihilism implies value nihilism. Value nihilism does not imply metaphysical nihilism. Most forms of nihilism relate themselves to an evaluation of freedom, even where forms of despair predominate, issuing politically into anarchism or collectivism, as among the nineteenth-century Russian nihilists. The term was popularized through Turgenev's novel *Fathers and Sons*, finding its classical literary representation, however, in Dostoyevsky's *The Possessed*. The idea is to destroy all that exists before, possibly, building something new. One thus declares everything actual worthless, though a certain moral earnestness can remain. Dostoyevsky's character Kirilov, for example, promises to commit suicide whenever 'the movement' shall require it.

There is a certain ancestry in *Descartes' *Meditations*. Descartes wills to *doubt where possible every present belief as a means to new certainties. This leads to a sceptical problem through *Hume to *Kant from which *Hegelian *monism might seem to offer only an equivocal salvation. Nihilism thus became one of the main modern options, whatever it was in the ancient world.

A main figure in the rise of conscious nihilism was Friedrich *Nietzsche (1844–1900), in whom we see the Janus-type nature of nihilism, its double aspect as a doctrine both of despair and of salvation, or of the latter through the former. This indicates a somewhat complex relation to Christianity. Nietzsche is often regarded as ferociously anti-Christian and hostile to existing moral standards in particular. His thought is taken as confirming Ivan's dictum in Dostoyevsky's *The Brothers Karamazov* that 'If God does not exist then everything is permitted'. Yet one should note that although he was a value-nihilist in the sense of holding a non-cognitivist view of *ethics (i.e. ethical principles are not fixed intellectual truths), he despised and rejected the above dictum as being the ultimate consequence of a servile attitude to *morality and life, requiring divine guarantees for one's convictions and lacking any will to give life a new meaning after the collapse of the 'Christian-Platonic' view of it. He called rather for the creative choice of other, new values to which we might commit ourselves. Therefore, it is possible to interpret Nietzsche as a reforming prophet or philosopher *within* the Christian tradition, as many since have done. His preaching of a coming, superior type of humanity recalls at least by analogy the Pauline stress on 'the new man'. There is a type of Messianism here, as in Marx, with clear roots in the Judaeo-Christian tradition.

This type of value-nihilism, anyhow, being a judgment upon *existing* values, carries over into the twentieth-century existentialism of M. Heidegger, J.-P. *Sartre and others. There are also Christian existentialist philosophers such as G. Marcel or P. *Tillich, while many others have adopted the characteristic doctrines and attitudes without the label (H. Küng, K. *Rahner). One denies that there is any human nature or essence upon which moral *law could be based. 'Man is what he makes himself and nothing else,' Sartre proclaimed (*Existentialism is a Humanism*). Sartre, however, also denies the determinist theories of psychology as part of his championship of human freedom – a clear value for him, like authenticity, but one he bases upon the denial of God. Either God exists or man does.

There are clear Christian parallels to this phenomenon of modern times, supporting the contention that value-nihilism typically depends upon other values perceived, rightly or wrongly, as superior. Thus Hans Küng declares that there is 'no natural law' and Bruno Schüller (in *Die Begründung sittlicher Urteile*, a textbook of moral theology for seminarians), following R. M. Hare's ethical philosophy of universal prescriptivism, insists that the moral teaching found in the Pauline epistles is mere *paranese*, a Greek term for exhortation, urging behaviour that will hold the community together and not a laying down of moral law, since Christ, Paul emphasizes, has freed us from law. Similarly Herbert McCabe argued (*Law, Love and Language*) that *natural law was too static a doctrine of humanity for Christianity, since Christian proclamation should herald a new humanity. He compared Christian ethics, apart from the single 'commandment' (an analogical term) of love, to practical directives during a revolutionary struggle, often dictated by circumstances. Thus murderers are declared in the gospel to lack eternal life not because they have violated the value of human life but because they are seen as haters of their brothers, not living by love.

The doctrine of natural law was classically formulated by *Thomas Aquinas. He identified it with the 'law written on the heart' of which St Paul speaks in Rom. 1. This in turn is

identified with the Mosaic Ten Commandments, treated by Aquinas as 'divine law' revealed by God, even though we have it within us already. This is part of an analogical treatment of law including also the eternal law, one with God under the aspect of governor of creation (an Augustinian concept) and 'human' law, or that positive legislation which is law as normally understood. These connections enable Aquinas to declare that any legislation contradicting natural law is invalid, an argument taken over by those prosecuting Nazi judges as criminals at the end of the Second World War.

Most important, however, though treated regrettably briefly by Aquinas, is the late development or fulfilment of divine, revealed law (the 'old law') in the 'new law' of the gospel which is charity, not the command of it but charity itself. For this, says Aquinas, is not a written law at all but a principle of life poured into the heart of the believer. It is thus more like a law of nature as understood by natural scientists and no longer a prescription at all, described rather as an empowerment for life and happiness. Luke's Gospel ends with the promise that the disciples will be 'clothed with power from on high' (Luke 24:49).

This is only analogically law. It is a value in a quite other sense, the 'highest development of morality', wrote Martin Grabmann (*Thomas von Aquin* [Munich 1959], p. 159). Kant or *Kierkegaard seem to neglect this when they wonder how love can be commanded and try in consequence to reduce Christian charity to a moral attitude of good will rather than a remaking of the whole man in the likeness of Christ. This tendency to reduce the message is called by Nicholas Berdyaev sociomorphism (*Slavery and Freedom* [New York, 1944]), transferring human legal arrangements to the divinity. In fact the 'new wine' or grace is able to remodel and refine the whole human being, as illustrated in the treatment of the virtues set forth in Aquinas' *magnum opus*.

Thus, the theologians mentioned go behind the long Roman legal tradition with its own specific interpretation of Christianity against which the nineteenth-century nihilists reacted, as does also E. Schillebeeckx in his study, *Jesus* (London, 1979). They show how in the Gospels *Jesus was regarded by the conservative religious authorities as destroying and denying law – much, in fact, as Nietzsche was at first regarded, though we now appreciate better that it was the particular form of Christianity which Nietzsche encountered socially against which he revolted, much as did Kierkegaard in Denmark in his *Attack upon Christendom.*

When Jesus told people their sins were forgiven this was seen by the Pharisees as negative, a lack of respect for divine law: 'Who can forgive sins but God alone?' This model presupposes that God has given inflexible laws. But in fact Jesus was elevating just, mutual forgiveness to the highest of laws, just as God sends his rain on the just and the unjust. The reference is not exclusively to some *Anselmian quasi-legal theory of atonement. Jesus is not simply claiming *authority for himself. Again, Nietzsche too compared forgiveness to 'a rainbow after long storms', remarking that this is how members of one family or brothers treat one another. He seems scarcely to notice his Christian roots here.

The idea of a value is closely linked to that of transcendent law and so from a Christian point of view as well as in general philosophy it can well be accorded a questionable aspect, sound as the basic notion may be. Thus G. Marcel remarks that value found no place in the work of the older metaphysicians, including that of Christians, saying that mention of it is often a sign of a certain devaluation of *reality (*Les hommes contre l'humain* [Paris 1951], p. 127). The Christians stressed the *being* of God, rather than an eternal realm of values, as the source of their ethical judgments. The happiness that had appeared in the world, not Stoic moralism, was to be the foundation of behaviour. Christian thinkers accordingly developed the doctrine of the transcendental predicates in their *metaphysics, whereby being alone (*esse*) was real, whereas truth and goodness were mere 'beings of reason' in reality identical with *esse* as presented to intellect and will respectively.

Thus there is a certain value-nihilism even in the old natural law doctrine, in that it subordinates value to being and to the actual nature and inclinations of humankind, rather than idealizing some putatively transcendent moral realm. Happiness is seen as the highest value in the good life, a view compatible with the Christian tradition that certain forms of behaviour invariably imperil the attainment of happiness, particularly lovelessness.

A genuine and complete value-nihilism denies the goodness of being and creation. Its practical expression is a readiness either to commit suicide or annihilate the world. In transcending natural law Christianity dramatizes nihilism as an option, the proverbial 'anti-Christ'.

Bibliography

C. S. Lewis, *The Abolition of Man* (London, 1943); H. de Lubac, *The Drama of Atheistic Humanism* (New York, 1963); H. McCabe, *Law, Love and Language* (London, 1968); S. Theron, *Natural Law Reconsidered* (Frankfurt am Main, 2002).

S. THERON

NOAH'S FLOOD, see ORIGINS, THEORIES OF

THE NOETIC EFFECTS OF SIN

The word 'noetic' refers to the effects of sin on the mind (Gk, *nous*, 'the mind or understanding'). The doctrine acknowledges that the fall has affected the human intellect as well as the will, other faculties and the body. It wants to do justice to the biblical concept of a 'depraved mind' (Rom. 1:28) and to account for Jesus' proclamation that 'you have seen me and still you do not believe' (John 6:36). This has significant implications for apologetics. Among other matters, it affects apologetic method. If reason is flawed by sin, to what extent may we engage in arguments which make use of logic, proof or evidence? What is the role of grace in relation to appeals to the understanding?

While most theologians admit that sin distorts human thinking, they differ widely on the degree and extent of that distortion. *Augustine recognized two causes for reason's weakness. First, because reason is finite. The pure light of God's presence is obscured by our being mere images of God, with a rationality that is 'weak'. Secondly, because of the effects of sin, pride thwarts reason from attaining its object, making the mind unfit to receive the knowledge of God unless healing faith enters.

The scholastic tradition in medieval Christianity recognized certain limitations in human reason but tended to accept the Aristotelian ideal of the primacy of the intellect. For *Thomas Aquinas, reason is subject to weakness and can be used incorrectly. At the same time it could be trusted to discover certain truths without the corrective intervention of revelation. In the *Summa Contra Gentiles* Aquinas argues that human reason is endowed in such a way that without faith it can recognize certain properties about God, such as his existence, his unity and his goodness. Faith confirms reason's views, and it is only by faith that we can know the higher truths about God, such as his triune nature and his plan of redemption in Christ. Human reason, however, can be trusted to know a large range of doctrines without redemptive revelation.

With the Protestant Reformation came a more comprehensive view of the noetic effects of sin. Luther viewed fallen persons as virtually impotent and human reason as treacherous. Yet redemption could alter its role as 'Prior to faith and a knowledge of God, reason is darkness, but in believers it is an excellent instrument.' With *Calvin, we have a significant step away from the medieval view. Calvin's chief concern was the knowledge of God and so his emphasis was on the contrast between the glory of God revealed in the creation and the folly of human ignorance of that glory. In an extended treatment on human sinfulness in the *Institutes of the Christian Religion*, Calvin makes numerous comments about the incapacity of unaided reason to know God in any kind of positive way. In that context, he concludes that 'the reason of our mind, wherever it may turn, is miserably subject to vanity'. This does not mean for him that unbelievers are incapable of reaching any *truth or of advancing the sciences, but that without the Word of God and the discernment of the *Holy Spirit, the mind cannot 'direct us aright'.

Calvin's heirs include Abraham *Kuyper, who insisted that there were two kinds of science, based on the regenerate or unregenerate consciousness of the thinker. Cornelius *Van Til argued that while the mechanical capacities of reason were not affected by the fall, nevertheless sinful creatures cannot orient their logical faculties properly, making reason incapable of knowing anything truly without the corrective actions of divine grace. Only a 'transcendental method' which seeks to 'think God's thoughts after him' can rescue reason from the dual temptations of univocalism (thinking as God thinks) and equivocation (only approximating the truth). John Frame has developed the idea that human reason is always ethically conditioned, either by way of

sympathetic friendship with God, or unsympathetic enmity with God. Nicholas Wolterstorff has criticized *foundationalism, especially its exponent John *Locke because it fails properly to account for the religious basis of human knowledge and thus the possibility of a sinful prejudice.

At the same time, the heirs of the Thomistic view have maintained that the fall has not affected the use of reason in such a way as to render its capacity to discover certain basic truths about the claims of the Creator and Redeemer invalid. Chief among them are the authors of *Classical Apologetics* (1984), R. C. Sproul, John Gerstner and Arthur Lindsley. They argue that sin does not affect the reliability of the mind in apprehending true knowledge, but only the will's influence on the mind. Thus for them, the noetic influence is indirect, allowing for the validity of *natural theology and the classical proofs for God's existence. Various types of *evidentialism claim that honest historical investigation will yield the certainty of Christianity's veracity. Wolfhart *Pannenberg posits that historical research done with integrity will always lead to the facts of salvation history. The issue here is how sin affects even the most basic operations of the mind which enable it to look at logical proofs and historical evidences.

In recent times, the preconditions for knowledge have been more deeply appreciated than hitherto. The so-called postmodern condition asks that we fully take into account the desire for *power that informs our understanding. Christians have learned from this mood. Stephen K. Moroney has suggested the addition of a psychological and social dimension to the noetic effects of sin. Merold Westphal asks that we be willing to exercise the hermeneutics of suspicion on atheism itself, turning the tables on the usual view that believers are the only ones duped by religious prejudice. Yet the challenge is to keep alive the objective reality of revealed truth, while at the same time fully recognizing the distortions of the mind in apprehending this truth.

Bibliography

D. J. Hoitenga, Jr, *Faith and Reason from Plato to Plantinga* (Albany, 1991); S. K. Moroney, *The Noetic Effects of Sin* (Oxford, 2000).

W. EDGAR

NOSTRADAMUS

Nostradamus (1503–66) is the latinized name of the French physician and astrologer Michel de Nostredame. He was of Jewish origin, but his parents became Christians while he was a boy. He qualified in medicine at Montpellier University, practised chiefly at the town of Salon, and eventually became physician in ordinary to the French court, but he was, and is, best known for his 'prophecies'. Many such have circulated under his name, including many forgeries, but the main authentic work is a collection of ten 'Centuries' (i.e. sets of a hundred – in this case, of verse quatrains), mostly in French but with a few in Provencal and one in Latin. Only part of this body of material was published in Nostradamus's lifetime. The prophecies are very hard to understand, with few explicit dates and many ambiguities and anagrams, as well as a cryptic style. A few certainly appear remarkably prescient, seeming to foretell, for instance, the execution of Charles I (IX.49), the fall of the Shah of Iran (I.70), and the Great Fire of London (I.51). Others can be made out to be predictive, with the aid of hindsight and much ingenuity, often by reading new meanings into his words, e.g. taking 'Armorique' (Brittany) to refer to America or 'Hister' (the Danube) to Hitler. Others, however, are simply wrong, such as the prediction of the coming to earth of a 'King of Terror' in July 1999 (X.72), or of a calamitous war followed by a long peace, apparently in June 2002 (VI.24).

Although Nostradamus practised as an astrologer, he dismisses astrology with contempt in one passage (VI.100) and seems to claim in the opening quatrains of the *Centuries* that his predictions were based on trance experiences. This affords what is probably his only relevance to apologetics: if he could obtain genuine information about the future, and this was not by any natural means (counting astrology here as 'natural'), perhaps this opens the door to recognition of the supernatural in other contexts too. However, a more likely view is that his 'predictions', with a few lucky exceptions, are the creation of wishful thinking on the part of commentators.

Bibliography

E. Cheetham (trans. and ed.), *The Prophecies of Nostradamus* (London, 1973); J. Laver, *Nostradamus, or the Future Foretold* (London, 1942; repr. Maidstone, 1993).

R. L. STURCH

OBJECTIVISM

Objectivism about a certain thing is the doctrine that that thing is objectively real (or, indeed, objectively unreal); objectivism about a certain sentence is the doctrine that that sentence expresses an objective *truth or an objective falsehood. 'Objective' here is usually explained as meaning *mind-independent*, i.e. something is objectively real (or unreal) if and only if its reality (or unreality) is not due to its being thought real (or unreal), and a proposition is an objective truth (or falsehood) if and only if its truth (or falsity) is not due to its being thought true (or false). It is tempting to try to define objectivism about an object as the doctrine that that object is real (or unreal) whether or not it is thought to be real (or unreal), and objectivism about the proposition expressed by a sentence as the doctrine that that proposition is true (or false) whether or not it is thought to be true (or false). This will not do, however, since nothing is real (or unreal) without God's thinking it so, and no proposition is true (or false) without God's thinking it so. Some Christians, it must be admitted, do think that the world around us exists only because God is thinking that it does. Such Christians are not objectivists. It is orthodox to hold that the world exists only because God sustains it in being, but God thinks that the world exists because it does, not *vice versa*. Similarly, God thinks a proposition true because it is and not *vice versa*.

One may be an objectivist about things and sentences of many different kinds. So, an objectivist about beauty will insist that a sentence asserting of something that it is beautiful or that it is not beautiful will express a truth or falsehood, and that the truth or falsehood of what is expressed will not be due to its being thought true or false; a subjectivist about beauty will think that the proposition's truth or falsity is due in some way to what people think. An objectivist about God will hold that God is real and that his reality is not due to what anyone thinks; a subjectivist about God will hold that God's reality is in some way due to what we think, e.g. because God is nothing other than a projection of our desires. But, clearly, one may be an objectivist about beauty but not about God, or *vice versa*.

The remainder of this article lists the various ideas opposed to objectivism.

Non-cognitivism: emotivism

Non-cognitivism about a sentence is the view that the sentence expresses no proposition that has a truth-value, i.e. the sentence expresses neither a truth nor a falsehood. A famous variety of non-cognitivism is emotivism, the doctrine held by many of the Vienna school and by A. J. Ayer. Emotivism about a sentence is the view that the sentence expresses only emotional content, i.e. it expresses no cognitive factual content that is true or false. Ayer held this view about all sentences involving words like 'God', 'divine', 'beautiful', 'ugly', 'moral', 'wicked' and so on. In other words, Ayer thought that, far from expressing an objective truth, theological, aesthetic, and ethical sentences were nonsensical, expressing emotion in the same way as 'Boo!' and 'Hooray!' express nothing but emotion.

Non-cognitivism: formalism

This variety of non-cognitivism treats the sentence in question as a merely formal entity with no substance, i.e. as having shape but no true or false content. This view is most frequently found opposed to objectivism in mathematics, where the objectivist holds that there are mathematical truths and that their truth is not due to what is thought or can be proved. The formalist holds that mathematical sentences express neither truths nor falsehoods, but, rather, are like records of the moves in a chess game, where there are certain rules that dictate which moves may follow which other moves, yet where it is ridiculous to say that a certain move is true or is false.

Error theory

To hold an error theory about a sentence is to hold the view that that sentence is in error, i.e. expresses a falsehood. Oxford philosopher John Mackie held this view about all attributions of beauty, ugliness, moral goodness, moral badness and divinity. He thought that, for example, 'the *Mona Lisa* is beautiful', 'the *Mona Lisa* is ugly' and 'the *Mona Lisa* is aesthetically indifferent' were all false, as were 'murder is good', 'murder is bad' and 'murder

is morally indifferent'. Indeed, he thought that these were all necessarily false, i.e. that they could not have been true.

Eliminativism

One way of developing an error theory is into eliminativism. This is the view not just that the sentence is in error, i.e. expresses a falsehood, but that the sentence should, accordingly, not be used. For example, eliminativists about the mind say that the word 'mind' refers to a non-physical thinking substance, and that since science has shown that there is no such substance, all sentences expressing attributions of properties to such a substance, such as 'My mind is made up', express falsehoods and, accordingly, should not be used. Rather, we should talk about the brain and its neural properties. Objectivists about the mind, of course, reject this demand and practice.

Fictionalism

Another way of developing an error theory is into fictionalism. This is the view that, while the sentence is, strictly speaking, in error, i.e. it expresses a falsehood, it does not follow that the sentence should not be used. After all, writers of fiction use sentences that they know, strictly speaking, express falsehoods, and nobody censures them for this practice. Certain fictions can be very useful. So, the fictionalist claims that while, for example, sentences expressing ascriptions of properties to a mind may, strictly speaking, express falsehoods, they are still very useful, and we can distinguish between those that are totally in error, i.e. that express falsehoods strictly speaking and also according to the fiction, and those that are only partially in error, i.e. that express falsehoods strictly speaking but not according to the fiction. 'Sherlock Holmes lived at 221B Baker Street' expresses a falsehood strictly speaking, since Sherlock Holmes did not exist, but expresses a truth according to the fiction of Sir Arthur Conan Doyle. 'Sherlock Holmes lived at 222B Baker Street', however, expresses a falsehood both strictly speaking and according to the fiction. In the same way, 'My mind is made up' can express, according to the fictionalist, a truth according to the fiction that we have minds, even if, strictly speaking, it expresses a falsehood. Objectivists about minds, of course, by contrast, claim that 'my mind is made up' can express a literal truth too.

Subjectivism

To hold a subjectivist view about a sentence is to hold the view that that sentence reports an experience of a subject. So, a subjectivist, about the sentence 'the *Mona Lisa* is beautiful' will typically think that the sentence reports an experience of the utterer, i.e. that it is equivalent to something like 'I like the *Mona Lisa*'. Alternatively, the subjectivist may think that the sentence reports experiences of those in the utterer's community, i.e. that it is equivalent to something like 'twenty-first-century Westerners like the *Mona Lisa*'. Note that this is different from emotivism, according to which theory the sentences in question merely express, rather than report, the feelings of the utterers in question.

Relativism

To hold a relativistic view about a proposition is to hold that its truth or its falsity is relative to something. An innocuous (if false) form of *relativism is temporal relativism: the view that a proposition is not timelessly true or timelessly false but, for every moment of time, either true at that moment or false at that moment. So, it is possible, on this view, for a proposition, e.g. the proposition that today is Wednesday, to be true today and false tomorrow. A less common form of relativism is topical relativism, i.e. the view that a proposition is not spacelessly true or spacelessly false, but, for every place, either true at that place or false at that place. So it is possible, on this view, for a proposition, e.g. the proposition that John is here, to be true here and false somewhere else. Perhaps the most popular, and most pernicious, form of relativism is personal relativism, i.e. the view that a proposition is not impersonally true or impersonally false, but, for every person, either true for that person or false for that person. So it is possible, on this view, for a proposition, e.g. the proposition that I am Daniel Hill, to be true for me and false for you. The propositions I have mentioned as examples have all been *indexical* propositions, that is, propositions expressed using words such as 'now', 'here' and 'I'. Most relativists, however, extend this doctrine from relativism about indexical propositions to relativism about every proposition, i.e. global or universal relativism. So, on this view, all propositions from 'the *Mona Lisa* is beautiful' or 'murder is wrong' to 'God exists', 'grass is green', or 'two and two make four' are all relative to times, places, or persons (or all three). The most common form is personal relativism. This has been a thorn in the side of Christian apologetics, for it meets every argument for Christianity with the retort 'That may be true for you, but not for me'. It might be thought that if one could get the relativist to agree that the premises of the argument are true for him or her, then he or she ought to agree that the conclusion is true for him or her too. A thoroughgoing relativist, however, may merely reply, 'That argument is valid for you, but not for me'. What can one say in response? The objectivist often claims that relativism is self-defeating in that the relativist must admit, it is argued, that at least one truth is *not* relative, viz. the 'truth' that every truth is relative. The objectivist then charges the relativist with self-contradiction, since he or she holds both that every truth is relative and that one truth is not relative. In fact, this is not a successful response to the relativist, since a consistent relativist will hold that the truth that every truth is relative is itself relative. The objectivist may now reply that, in this case, the proposition that every truth is relative must be false relative to something, and, hence, that there is indeed at least one objective truth. This attempted refutation of relativism also fails, for there is no reason why the relativist should admit that, if the proposition that every truth is relative is itself relative, it is false in relation to something. For example, the temporal relativist will maintain that every truth is true relative to some or other moment of time. The temporal objectivist may object that in that case, the very proposition that every truth is true relative to some or other moment of time is itself true relative to some or other moment of time. The temporal relativist should concede this, and, if the objectivist makes the false move of claiming that in that case the proposition that every truth is true relative to some or other moment of time is false relative to some or other moment of time, the relativist should simply deny that this follows, maintaining rather that it is true relative to every moment of time that every truth is true relative to some or other moment of time. This may be false, but the relativist cannot be charged with self-contradiction. Clearly, the same goes with 'place' or 'person' instead of 'moment of time', since we are here concerned with the mere form of the argument.

A better way with the relativist is to ask precisely what it means for something to be true for one person but not for another, or true in one place but not another. Relativists are usually unable to give any satisfactory characterization of their views. Most relativists are also unhappy with uses that relativism may be put to, and a way to test this is to strike the relativist on the nose and then refuse to apologize, claiming that one's action was right for oneself even if wrong for the relativist. This claim may be false, but the relativist will be unable to refute it.

An argument that is often levelled against objectivism is that 'one cannot step out of one's own situation'. This confuses belief and truth: beliefs are person-relative in that a belief exists because a believer holds it, whereas a truth is not true because a believer thinks it so. Even if each of one's beliefs is conditioned by one's situation, it does not follow that each of one's beliefs is not true. Another argument levelled against objectivism is the argument that we can never be certain about anything. This confuses *certainty and truth, for one can certainly have a true belief without being certain about it, as in a lucky guess. A third argument is that one can never know the whole truth. The relativist propounding this argument is at a loss to explain why not knowing the whole truth implies not knowing anything. The Christian apologist will readily admit (perhaps basing this admission on 1 Cor. 13:12b) that he or she does not know everything, but will typically insist that he or she nevertheless knows something, e.g. that his or her Redeemer lives (Job 19:25a). Perhaps most irritating of all is the frequent accusation that the claim that what one says is objectively true is 'arrogant'. This is misguided. Arrogance is an unwarranted belief in one's own excellence, but the Christian typically insists that he or she did not work out (and could not have worked out) what he or she believes for him or herself; rather, he or she needed it to be revealed by God to him or her. The Christian is thus merely passing on what he or she has learnt from another source, and nobody can seriously suggest that God is arrogant for claiming that what he says is objective truth. Nor does a claim to objective truth betoken a closed mind. It is perfectly possible to think that a certain proposition is objectively true and yet to be quite prepared to change one's mind. Indeed, it is perfectly possible to be quite tentative and hesitant in one's belief that a certain proposition is objectively true.

While it may be possible to be a Christian without being an objectivist, it cannot reasonably be denied that Christian apologetics has historically depended on objectivism and been hindered by those that refuse to accept objectivism.

Bibliography

M. A. E. Dummett, *Truth and Other Enigmas* (London, 1963).

D. J. HILL

OCKHAM, WILLIAM OF

William of Ockham (c. 1288–1347), an English Franciscan friar, is frequently credited with the foundation of a new, 'nominalist' school of philosophy or 'modern way' (*via moderna*), which is usually thought to have dominated the universities of Oxford and Paris for the rest of the fourteenth century. Modern scholarship has uncovered a more nuanced picture, in which Ockham appears as one (though perhaps the most influential) of several thinkers who were moving in a broadly 'nominalist' direction, and whose influence never went unchallenged, particularly at Oxford.

Ockham excelled at linguistic philosophy, and his logical works have added significantly to the modern *logic of terms. It is this aspect of his writing that has appealed to modern secular philosophers, who have claimed him as one of their own in many respects. The connections are undoubtedly real, but Ockham's views cannot be pressed in an exclusively secularist direction without serious distortion. At heart he remained a medieval Christian who wanted to expound the true nature of God and creation. To do this, he gave priority to concretely existing things (like 'man') and regarded abstractions (like 'humanity') as derivative from them. In other words, it is the actual qualities of existing human beings that shape our understanding of the species as a whole, not some idealized abstraction that we then see replicated (more or less accurately) in existing people. It is in this light that we must understand his famous 'razor' principle, which says that the fewer presuppositions and arguments needed to explain a phenomenon, the better.

When applied to an analysis of the universe, Ockham's razor has far-reaching implications. He disliked the view that there was such a thing as natural 'goodness' that must necessarily exist. He believed that God is the only necessary being, absolutely self-sufficient, independent and good, but he argued that this is because of what God actually is, not because of some inner logical necessity that makes it impossible for him to be anything else. God is therefore not constrained by the absolutes of his own nature, and is free to disregard his own 'laws', so that he can achieve his ends even by a more complicated route than Ockham's razor would normally allow. God can also 'contradict' himself without being inconsistent, of which the most famous example is the salvation of the human race, where he reached out to achieve by grace and mercy something that the logic of his justice could never permit.

Since God is the only necessary being, moreover, all created things might have been different; there is no inherent necessity for them to be as they are. So whatever God produces by secondary causes, he can also produce immediately.

Ockham saw God's grace as the work of his love, rather than the product of some inevitable necessity, and therefore conceived of *predestination in personal, not abstract, terms. His thought stands at the beginning of a movement away from medieval *scholasticism towards modern *empiricism, and to that extent he can be regarded as a harbinger of both Protestantism and modernity, even though he cannot be fully identified with either.

For Ockham there is little that can be demonstrated about God through natural reason. The only argument for the existence of God he accepted was one based on the impossibility of an *infinite series of causes, and he did not think it possible to show that there is only one God. Persuasive arguments can be made for God's eternity, for example, but these do not amount to demonstrations.

Ockham also sought to broaden the base of *authority in the church. He was convinced that the pope had fallen into doctrinal error and should be removed, and argued for the limiting of his power by a General Council. He did not go as far as his contemporary Marsilius of Padua, however, in the direction of favouring lay authorities over against the papacy. Instead, he insisted on a clear distinction between the spiritual and temporal powers: the former is directly from God; the latter is from God through the consent of the people.

Bibliography

M. McCord Adams, *William Ockham*, 2 vols. (Notre Dame, 1987); P. V. Spade (ed.), *The Cambridge Companion to Ockham* (Cambridge, 1999); William of Ockham, *Opera Politica*, ed. by H. S. Offler *et al.*, 4 vols. (Manchester and Oxford, 1956–97); *Opera philosophica et theologica*, ed. by G. Gál *et al.*, 17 vols. (New York, 1967–88)

G. L. BRAY and A. VOS

O'CONNOR, FLANNERY

Flannery O'Connor is recognized as one of the best American authors of the latter half of the twentieth century. Her fiction is provocative and haunting, an unsettling combination of comedy and violence. The world of her stories is one of circus freaks, serial killers, sidewalk preachers, racist hypocrites, and religious con artists. And yet, for all of her unconventional style, her sometimes shocking subject matter, and her critical acclaim, she was a devout, rigorously orthodox Christian whose purpose was overtly evangelistic.

O'Connor was born in 1925 in Savannah, Georgia, and grew up in Milledgeville, a small, rural community in the deep South. Her family were Roman Catholics in the heart of the fundamentalist Bible Belt. She moved north, to the University of Iowa for its distinguished 'writing workshop' programme and to New York for an artists' colony. In 1950, she was struck with lupus, a debilitating, painful, crippling disease that had killed her father, and went back to Milledgeville and the care of her family. All the while, she was writing short stories, novellas, essays, and good-natured letters to a wide range of friends and correspondents, even as her health deteriorated. She died in 1964, at the age of 39.

Her approach to apologetics was well described by Robert Drake: 'Her overriding strategy is always to shock, embarrass, even outrage rationalist readers'. If your audience shares your beliefs, O'Connor said, you can speak to it in a normal way. When it does not, she wrote, 'then you have to make your vision apparent by shock – to the hard of hearing you shout, and for the almost blind you draw large and startling figures'.

When she writes about baptism, she depicts a drowning. When she explores the notion that human beings are temples of the *Holy Spirit, she writes about a circus sideshow hermaphrodite. Moments of grace come as a woman is being gored by a bull or shot by an escaped convict or having a corrupt Bible salesman run off with her wooden leg.

In her short novel *The Violent Bear It Away*, a modern psychologist and a fundamentalist preacher battle for the soul of a young boy, who struggles to get away from them both. The world-views clash, particularly over the different ways of looking at the psychologist's little boy, who is mentally handicapped. The story turns into a modern-day tale of Jonah, the reluctant prophet, as the central character finds he cannot escape from the grace of God.

'I see from the standpoint of Christian orthodoxy,' O'Connor wrote. 'This means for me the meaning of life is centred in our Redemption by Christ and that what I see in the world I see in its relation to that. I don't think that this is a position that can be taken halfway or one that is particularly easy in these times to make transparent in fiction.'

Bibliography

J. P. Baumgaertner, *Flannery O'Connor: A Proper Scaring* (Wheaton, 1988); R. Drake, *Flannery O'Connor: A Critical Essay* (Grand Rapids, 1966); H. Fickett and D. R. Gilbert, *Flannery O'Connor: Images of Grace* (Grand Rapids, 1986); K. Feeley, *Flannery O'Connor: Voice of the Peacock* (New York, 1982); F. O'Connor, *Collected Works* (New York, 1988); B. A. Ragen, *A Wreck on the Road to Damascus: Innocence, Guilt, & Conversion in Flannery O'Connor* (Chicago, 1989).

G. E. VEITH

OLD TESTAMENT AND CHRIST

1. Christological Old Testament interpretation

'Christ in all the Scriptures', the title of a book first published in 1907 and still in print in the early twenty-first century, has often been the motto of a conservative exegesis of the OT. This approach apparently has a good foundation and a long pedigree, but it also has significant problems.

According to the Gospels, *Jesus frequently applied OT texts to his own ministry, and after his resurrection he explained to his disciples 'what was said in all the Scriptures concerning himself' (Luke 24:27). The apostles continued to apply OT texts to Christ, as in Peter's Pentecost sermon (Acts 2), his first letter (1 Pet. 1:10–12) and the many Pauline and other epistles.

However, the Church Fathers faced many attacks on the Christian use of the OT: Jews denied its fulfilment in Christ, Gentiles (e.g. *Celsus) thought it immoral and contradictory, and Gnostics saw in it an inferior God. Marcion in particular forced the orthodox church to substantiate the OT as a Christian book, and the easiest way for them to do so seemed to be by *typology and allegory. Accordingly, the treasure hidden in the OT field was Christ; any significant reference to wood was taken to symbolize the cross (e.g. tree of life, Noah's ark, Moses' rod, Elisha's stick), any significant mention of water symbolized baptism and so on. This approach can be seen partially in *Justin Martyr and *Irenaeus, and more fully in the Greek-influenced Alexandrian school of Clement and *Origen.

By contrast, the Antiochene school to the north-east developed a more historical interpretation of the OT. Diodore presented his approach (which he called *theoria*) as a middle road between excessive allegory and 'Jewish' literalism; Theodore of Mopsuestia attacked Origen's allegorization; and John Chrysostom insisted, 'We must mark the mind of the writer.'

Unfortunately, the Alexandrian school exercised the greater influence on Western Christendom, and it was its fourfold interpretation of the OT, first associated with John Cassian, which dominated the Middle Ages despite occasional protest. In this approach every text is thought to have different levels of meaning: literal (historical), allegorical (prefiguring Christ), tropological (moral guidance) and anagogical (future hope). For instance, any reference to Jerusalem could be interpreted as, respectively: the historical city, the church of Christ, the individual Christian soul and the heavenly city.

The leading Reformers sought a more authentic approach to the OT, albeit along different lines. Luther roundly rejected allegory in theory, though he found it hard to break with it in practice. He developed what he called a 'literal-prophetic' interpretation of the OT, claiming that it spoke continually of Christ through both direct prediction and indirect permeation of the gospel. By contrast, for *Calvin the OT testified to God's word and activity, which could be profitably studied without necessary reference to Christ. These two approaches to the OT, Christocentric and Theocentric respectively, represent the twin focal points of most subsequent conservative OT interpretation. (See Greidanus for an historical survey.)

Conservative Christians have often argued that there were many precise predictions of Christ from very early times. For instance, W. Kaiser (*The Messiah in the Old Testament*, 1995) sees six in the *Pentateuch, three in Samuel, four in Job, thirteen in the Psalms, and thirty-nine in the Prophets. But many of these are not as clear as he asserts, particularly the earlier texts. In the Pentateuch, for instance, Gen. 3:15 is imprecise, since 'offspring' can be used collectively; Gen. 9:27b probably indicates not God but Japheth living with Shem (so most versions and commentators); Gen. 12:1–3 predicts blessing through Abraham and his offspring (again collective use); Gen. 49:10 and Num. 24:17–18 envisage David rather than Jesus; and Deut. 18:18 simply mentions a future prophet. Christians may wish to read these six texts Christologically, but in none of them was a reference to Christ originally obvious. Further, this tendency to count and list texts betrays a rather static view of Israelite faith and a non-contextual approach to the OT.

By contrast, much biblical scholarship in the last two centuries has strongly questioned the traditional Christological reading of the OT, along the following lines. Most relevant texts are seen to address the immediate situation and to refer to a current or imminent human king, not to a distant time and a superhuman deliverer. Indeed, the Israelites had no term for such a figure, since 'anointed one' ('messiah') never has this meaning in the OT. Further, the post-exilic community in Jerusalem apparently accepted the lack of restored independence and kingship and accommodated themselves to this pragmatically. Messianic expectations only arose in the late post-exilic period, fuelled by the second-century BC Maccabbean revolt and its aftermath. This is attested in various inter-testamental writings, which re-interpret OT texts in ways similar to the NT.

Evangelical scholars today largely agree with this more historical reading of the OT, but they also argue for a legitimate Christological reading, as follows. Some prophetic texts are clearly predictive (e.g. Mic. 5:2), even if they were initially applied to the historic kingship. Others obviously address their immediate context (e.g. Isa. 7:14, Immanuel), yet their theological motifs surpass it and later find a richer fulfilment. Extravagant descriptions of the king in royal psalms and prophetic oracles may well have raised hopes of a truly righteous monarch well before the exile, and the later recitation of these psalms by faithful Israelites would have maintained this hope despite political subservience. When the Davidic kingship failed to be reinstated after the exile, and particularly when national survival itself was threatened in the second century BC, such hope rekindled into fervent if diverse expectation of a divinely appointed deliverer and national restoration. Further, various OT themes not linked to messianic expectation before Jesus' ministry can nonetheless be linked to him in hindsight, e.g. sin and death, priesthood and sacrifice, blessing to the nations, the suffering servant. Thus various texts and themes within the OT can be legitimately applied to Christ, whatever their original understanding. Historical and apologetic interpretations need not be opposed. (For introductory and scholarly discussion, see respectively Motyer and Satterthwaite.)

Some biblical scholars have argued recently that messianic expectation was not only a very late development (first century BC), it was also partial, diverse and diffuse, and there was no widespread or generally accepted messianic paradigm at the time of Jesus. However, while accepting the diversity of expectations, others reply that there were elements of messianism significantly earlier (e.g. LXX, *Dead Sea Scrolls) and that the differences were minor variations within a generally coherent eschatological whole.

2. Relevant Old Testament concepts

a. Messiah

The term 'messiah' comes from a Hebrew root, which occurs some 130 times in the OT mainly as the verb 'to anoint' (*māsaḥ*) and the noun 'anointed one' (*māšîaḥ*). People and objects were anointed with oil to consecrate them for specific purposes. Anointing was a widespread custom in the Ancient Near East, and was used of suzerain (i.e. supreme) kings, vassal kings, priests, even stone monuments. In the OT it is used of kings (mainly), priests (occasionally) and prophets (once), also of pillars (Gen. 31:13) and temple vessels (Exod. 40:9–11). The noun 'anointed one' indicates someone appointed to a significant office. It is used mostly of the reigning Israelite or Judean king (though once of Cyrus the Persian, Isa. 45:1) and also of priests. It refers to a distinctive future figure in only one passage (Dan. 9:25–27), without elaboration of his character or role.

The LXX translated these Heb. words by their obvious Gk equivalents *chrio* and *christos*, which had similar secular meanings. It was the emerging church, as reflected in the NT, which first treated *christos* as a proper name. (The NT also occasionally uses the Gk form *messias*, e.g. John 1:41; 4:25.) The concept of a future figure anointed by God to deliver Israel clearly developed from the term *māšîaḥ*, though it also incorporates other themes.

There are three important sets of OT texts which are relevant here. The first is in historical narrative, where Saul and David are frequently called *māšîaḥ* (1, 2 Sam.), though the term is not used in the institution of the Davidic covenant (2 Sam. 7). Here David is promised a descendant on the throne in perpetuity, as indeed occurred almost throughout the Judean monarchy. The exile suspended its fulfilment, though even then Jehoiachin retained certain privileges (2 Kgs 25:27–30). After the exile, his grandson Zerubbabel led the returnees (Ezra 2:2) and was portrayed in quasi-royal terms by contemporary prophets (Hag. 2:23; Zech. 4:1–14). However, the monarchy was never re-established, and in the course of time restoration hopes were gradually transmuted from an immediate monarch to an eschatological 'anointed one'.

The second set of texts occur in the many psalms which portray the king in grandiose language, e.g. as God's son (Pss. 2:7; 89:27), the most excellent of men (Ps. 45:2), righteous, eternal, all-powerful (Ps. 72), possibly even divine (Ps. 45:6, though this phrase is better translated 'God has enthroned you'). For most commentators, these psalms applied originally to the reigning king, using hyperbolic language typical of ancient courts. Only after the exile were they reapplied to a future 'anointed one', thus contributing to the growing messianic expectation of the late post-exilic era.

Thirdly, several prophetic passages portray a coming ruler in extravagant terms similar to the royal psalms (e.g. Isa. 9:2–7; 11:1–5; 32:1–2; Mic. 5:1–6). Like the psalmists, the prophets may have originally envisaged fulfilment by a new Davidic king in immediate succession to the current one. When later kings, even the great reformers Hezekiah and Josiah, repeatedly failed to match expectations, these passages were reinterpreted eschatologically.

The NT appropriation of this theme is complex. On the one hand, throughout his ministry Jesus was cautious about being labelled as 'messiah' since the term was commonly understood to mean a political king and liberator. Thus, when demons 'knew he was the Christ' he demanded their silence (Luke 4:41; cf. also Mark 1:25, 34; 3:12); when Peter acknowledged him as *christos* he immediately reinterpreted the concept (Matt. 16:16, 21); and he referred to himself as 'anointed' only once (Luke 4:18).

On the other hand, Jesus and later his apostles obviously understood that he was the long-awaited messiah, as shown in several ways. Jesus' true kingship was proclaimed in the annunciation (Luke 1:32), regularly implied in his teaching about God's kingdom, and affirmed by the early church (Acts 2:30). Jesus' self-designation as anointed (Luke 4:18) was clearly programmatic, in his applying the spiritual anointing of Isa. 61 to his earthly ministry. Peter talked similarly after Pentecost of God anointing Jesus (Acts 4:27; 10:38). Believers increasingly used *christos* as a title of Jesus, as they came to understand the true nature of his mission. Now that the term was redefined in the light of Jesus' death and resurrection, it could be used freely and confidently.

b. Prophet

According to Deut. 18:14–22, God would raise up a prophet like Moses who would speak in his name and whose predictions would come true, in contrast with other prophets. The Israelites should listen to him and do what he commanded, rather than practise divination like the nations they would dispossess. This seems to envisage a single, perhaps immediate prophetic leader succeeding Moses. It also implicitly sets a paradigm for true prophecy in Israel. Nevertheless, it is not cited elsewhere in the OT in predictive or paradigmatic senses.

In later *Judaism this text was interpreted

eschatologically, but not messianically, both at Qumran (1Q5 9:11, 'the Prophet and the Messiahs of Aaron and Israel'; 4Q175, *Testimonia*) and by Jesus' contemporaries (John 1:25). But for Peter at Pentecost, it clearly points to Christ (Acts 3:22–23). Appropriately so, since Moses initiated God's first kingdom on earth and Jesus founded another.

c. Priest

As already noted, OT priests were regularly anointed. In the pre-monarchical period Aaron and his sons were anointed, and after the collapse of the monarchy the post-exilic high priests were anointed and increasingly gathered political authority to themselves in the absence of a king. It was probably this latter role, coupled with Zechariah's oracles (Zech. 3 – 4) which led to later expectation of an authoritative priestly messiah.

However, the portrayal of Christ as high priest in Hebrews picks up a quite different aspect of priesthood, not his religious and political authority but his principal duty of presenting acceptable sacrifice to God. This bypasses historical development and contemporary expectation to return to the theological foundation of priesthood and to re-apply it radically but appropriately to Jesus.

d. Suffering Servant

The concept of a leader suffering with and for his people goes back to Moses (cf. Exod. 32:31). But it was exhibited more in the prophetic ministries of Hosea and Jeremiah, both of whom in different contexts experienced something of God's heartbreak and their people's punishment. It is seen most clearly in the enigmatic servant figure of Isa. 42 – 53, who fulfils God's purpose for Israel and beyond, meets suffering and death, yet somehow will 'see his offspring and prolong his days' (53:10). This intriguing portrayal has several discordant elements: a figure who is both active and passive, silent but sovereign, identified with though still distinct from Israel, honoured yet humiliated. Not surprisingly, it was never seen as messianic until the key to the puzzle was revealed in Jesus of Nazareth.

Similarly, the concept of vicarious death for sin was undeveloped in Judaism, and never linked to that of the messiah. But this was explained by Jesus, fulfilled in his death and understood by his disciples, then the Suffering Servant's obscure act became plain as 'he makes his life a guilt offering' (*'āšām*, Isa. 53:10, cf. Lev. 5:6). This, the most startling element of the Servant's role, thus falls into place.

e. Other OT references

The same benefit of hindsight which applies the concepts of high priesthood and Suffering Servant to Jesus can be used elsewhere in interpreting the OT. Israelite readers could only have referred the 'he/it' of Gen. 3:15b ('he/it will crush your head') to Eve's offspring in general, or to Abraham and Israel in particular. We can now see it as fulfilled in Jesus' atoning death, a concept previously incomprehensible. The heroes/deliverers of the book of Judges prefigure Christ, not in any moral sense (far from it!), but in being used by God to rescue his people, however temporarily. Job repeatedly pleaded for a superhuman figure to present his case to God (Job 9:33–34; 16:19–21) and to play a crucial part in his vindication, whether he envisaged this after death or, more likely, before it (Job 19:25). Unlike him, we can now see this yearning answered in Christ.

3. Conclusion

The OT is not primarily about Christ. It is a collection of material about the relationship of the nation of Israel to their God Yahweh: their patriarchal origins, exodus from Egypt, laws and customs, settlement in Canaan, turbulent history, exile and return, prophetic oracles, prayers to God and reflections on life. Scattered verses envisage an ideal leader and an idyllic future, but as king after king failed to match these expectations, and especially as the monarchy was suspended and not restored, these hopes were transferred to a future figure, whom we can now identify as Jesus of Nazareth, the 'anointed one' *par excellence*. Other non-eschatological OT concepts were also given new significance by Jesus' ministry. The OT is essentially about God's salvation of and relationship with his people, which finds its culmination in Jesus. It leads historically and theologically to Christ, but it is not all about him. Calvin's approach is sounder than Luther's.

This has several implications for apologetics. God's *revelation is progressive, and the OT should not be combed simply for encrypted predictions. Prophecy was complex, and many oracles had immediate significance yet also hinted at the larger pattern of divine activity. We must resist a simplistic choice between one or other interpretation. Even in OT times, some texts were reinterpreted and invested with new significance, without denying the original meaning. Most importantly, we can and must distinguish between an Israelite understanding of their Scriptures and a Christian rereading of the same texts in the light of Christ.

Freed from the straitjacket of Christological interpretation of every detail, the OT can again be seen as pertinent to some of the compelling issues of our day: creation and environmental responsibility, *justice and social responsibility, *history and political responsibility, and above all the engagement of a just and merciful God with a fallen world and a delivered people.

Bibliography

S. Greidanus, *Preaching Christ from the Old Testament* (Grand Rapids, 1999); R. S. Hess and M. D. Carroll R. (eds.), *Israel's Messiah in the Bible and the Dead Sea Scrolls* (Grand Rapids, 2003); A. Motyer, *Look to the Rock* (Leicester, 1996); P. E. Satterthwaite *et al.* (eds.), *The Lord's Anointed* (Carlisle, 1995).

P. S. JOHNSTON

OLD TESTAMENT MANUSCRIPTS

Introduction

Although there is an impressive range of manuscript evidence for the text of the OT, it is immediately apparent that no ancient manuscripts are identical. There are diverse textual traditions, and such variant traditions (at least prior to the destruction of the temple in AD 70) seemed to be allowed to exist side by side with little attempt to reconcile them. This raises issues concerning the degree to which the text of the OT as we have it is a faithful reflection of what was originally written, and, since we are unable to reconstruct the original text, the extent to which the Bible *as we now have it* can be understood to be the inspired word of God.

Hebrew texts of the Bible were generally copied on to leather or papyrus scrolls. Each scroll would contain one or occasionally two books of the OT, or more if the books were short, as is the case of the twelve 'minor prophets', which were all fitted on to one scroll. Each book would have been copied separately and thus had separate histories of copying and corruption. Only when the codex, parchment pages sewn together in book form, began to be used for Hebrew texts around AD 700 did the independence of the transmission history of each book cease.

Masoretic Text

The Hebrew text of the OT books was originally written with only consonants. This text is called the consonantal text and is evidenced for instance in the *Dead Sea Scrolls. From around AD 500, Jewish scribes, referred to as the Masoretes, added vowel signs above, below and within the consonants in order to specify how the words were to be pronounced. They also added accents and marginal notes to aid the accurate transmission of the text. The resultant text is referred to as the 'Masoretic Text' (MT).

Apart from the Dead Sea Scrolls and Samaritan Pentateuch (see below), all the substantial surviving Hebrew manuscripts of OT books belong to the Masoretic group of manuscripts. These represent a strikingly uniform group of medieval manuscripts dating from the ninth century AD onwards. The consonantal precursor to the MT is called the proto-Masoretic Text. The close similarity between proto-MT and the consonants of the MT comes as no surprise since the Jewish copyists in the early centuries AD exercised extraordinary care in copying the text to avoid the risk of adding corruptions. This care in transmission was not, however, the rule prior to AD 70, since a much greater diversity of texts is present among the Dead Sea Scrolls, and a greater carelessness and need for subsequent scribal corrections are apparent in those scrolls. It is the MT which provides the basis for most modern translations, adjusted at points in the light of evidence from other witnesses, especially the Septuagint (LXX) and the Dead Sea Scrolls.

The fact that the original manuscripts were consonantal suggests that it is best to see the consonants alone as inspired, rather than the vowels. If this is the case, there is some ambiguity in some places (especially in poetic passages) between alternative words which fit the consonants and context. Nevertheless, the strong correlation between the vowels of the MT and the readings implied by the LXX translation suggests that the vocalizations were reliably preserved by oral tradition, at least from the third century BC, when much of the LXX was translated. This suggests that the vowels of the MT, whilst not 'inspired', should nevertheless be taken seriously.

Translations

The Hebrew text was translated into a number of other languages in the ancient world in order to make it accessible to speakers of those languages. The earliest, and most important from our point of view, was the Septuagint, which was a translation into Greek probably undertaken in Egypt over an extended period of time but primarily in the third and early second centuries BC. The LXX is represented by an extensive and very complex range of manuscript witnesses and even translations of the LXX into other languages. There are problems of reconstructing, on the basis of the Greek text, the Hebrew text from which it was translated and of knowing which 'differences' between the Greek and Hebrew reflect real textual differences as opposed to differences that result from the process of translation. Nevertheless, the LXX represents a very important witness to early Hebrew texts which differed from the proto-MT. The fact that some Dead Sea Scrolls reflect a Hebrew text similar to the LXX's underlying text indicates that the differences between the Hebrew and Greek texts cannot be ascribed purely to translation.

Other ancient translations of importance as witnesses to the ancient Hebrew text are the Old Latin, Latin Vulgate, Syriac Peshitta and Aramaic Targums. Although useful, the traditions of all of these are complex and suffer from significant limitations for reconstructing ancient Hebrew readings. The Old Latin is only attested in small fragments and in some ancient scriptural quotations. The Aramaic Targums incorporate significant elements of interpretation/expansion as well as pure translation, so that variants will often reflect the process of 'translation' rather than reflecting a variant Hebrew text. The Vulgate, Syriac and Targums mostly reflect the state of the text after the period when the proto-MT had become dominant (around AD 70), although they may preserve some more ancient translation elements. This means that they are most valuable where they agree together with other ancient witnesses (LXX, Dead Sea Scrolls or Samaritan Pentateuch), since this may indicate

that the MT tradition has itself been subject to corruption at that point.

Samaritan Pentateuch

The Samaritan Pentateuch, although preserved only in manuscripts from the twelfth century AD onwards, represents an early and independent tradition of the Pentateuch latterly preserved by the Samaritan community. Its underlying text is reflected in some Dead Sea Scrolls and is a significant witness to an early textual tradition.

Dead Sea Scrolls

The Dead Sea scrolls, found in a range of caves in the vicinity of the Dead Sea from 1947, are a key witness to the ancient text of the OT. Around 200 of the 900 Dead Sea scrolls are manuscripts of biblical books, mostly extremely fragmentary, with only one near complete scroll (the Isaiah scroll). There is a much greater textual diversity among these scrolls than would later exist between Masoretic manuscripts. Indeed, although the majority reflect the proto-MT text (i.e. a text to which the later MT was closely related), there are other scrolls that reflect a text related to the Hebrew text which underlay the LXX or the Samaritan Pentateuch. The proportion of scrolls reflecting these traditions, calculated from the statistics of Emanuel Tov, is 45% proto-MT, 3% related to the LXX, 6.5% (of Pentateuch scrolls) related to the Samaritan Pentateuch and 45% non-aligned. It may be that the non-aligned proportion is significantly overstated, so that the proto-MT-related proportion is significantly higher than indicated in these statistics. In any case, the tradition which the later MT was to reflect was the dominant tradition even at this early stage (pre-AD 70).

Diversity

The presence of precursors to the Samaritan Pentateuch and the LXX, as well as non-aligned texts, alongside proto-MT texts among the Dead Sea Scrolls shows that a diversity of textual traditions existed during the period when these were copied (c. 250 BC – AD 73). Indeed, different traditions of some books (such as Jeremiah, Samuel and Exodus) existed side by side or were used for purposes of quotation without any attempt to correct towards one text. The scrolls found at Masada (up to AD 73) and at, for instance, Wadi Murabba'at (up to AD 135), are by contrast uniformly proto-MT. The transition from diverse texts existing side by side to dominance of the proto-MT around AD 70 is also evidenced by efforts to revise the LXX tradition towards the MT, and by the fact that most of the later versions tend to follow the MT against the LXX and (in the Pentateuch) against the Samaritan Pentateuch, as well as by the later survival of only Masoretic Hebrew manuscripts. Whether this standardization of the text was because the MT was the text of the Pharisees, who were the group surviving the devastation of the nation after AD 70, or was the result of choices or text-critical activity perhaps associated with the temple in order to isolate preferred texts for each OT book, is still debated, although the former option is usually preferred. The fact that at least two ancient non-Masoretic traditions (Samaritan Pentateuch and LXX) have been preserved outside of Qumran confirms that the diversity of traditions pre-AD 70 was not limited merely to the community at Qumran.

Quest for the original text

Textual criticism (sometimes called text criticism) is the means by which the various readings found in extant manuscripts are compared in order to identify the earliest reading and so to move as near as possible to the original text for each book of the Bible. The primary methods of textual criticism involve assessing the value of each of the available manuscripts or witnesses (antiquity, frequency of errors and textual tradition are significant criteria here), and assessing which reading (extant or reconstructed) could explain how each of the extant readings could have arisen from it either intentionally or accidentally during the process of copying.

The original text is either the text as it left the pen of the original author (if no subsequent editorial activity is allowed for), or the text at the end of the literary development phase. There is a question as to whether there was ever a single original text of a book, or whether there were merely parallel traditions with a mixture of literary and textual developments variously represented in each, which could have arisen if the process of textual corruption and development had started prior to the completion of the literary development phase. This debate becomes significant if it is the 'text as originally given' which is inspired by God, since such a doctrine appears to require a single original text

which one can aim to reconstruct. Nevertheless, even if there is an overlap between literary and textual-development phases (and it is not clear that this is the case), it is possible to seek to identify the textual corruptions from the extant textual witnesses, and thus to move as near as possible a putative original text – an original which closely reflects (but is not identical to) actual texts that were in parallel existence at an early stage.

A reliable text?

Careful text-critical work can give rise to a text which is a good approximation to the 'original text', or at least to the text that existed in the fourth or third centuries BC, but it can never be possible to reconstruct the original exactly. Examples of such corruptions within the text of the MT include 'Let not the archer draw his bow' (Jer. 51:3), where the repetition of 'draw' is a common type of copying error which is 'corrected' by translators, and the correct age of Ahaziah at his accession (22 in 2 Kgs 8:26, and 42 in 2 Chr. 22:2). Moreover, since each book was transmitted separately, the quality of each textual tradition of the OT is not uniform. For instance, the MT of the books of Samuel is generally seen as less well-preserved than the MT of other books. The recognition that all texts (Masoretic or otherwise) contain corruptions which have arisen in the process of copying gives rise to an issue of how we can trust the biblical accounts *as we have them*, if we know that these are not identical to the original. The issue becomes more trenchant when it is remembered that most Christians throughout the centuries have had to make do with translations of variable quality and which have not benefited from modern text-critical labours, i.e. that their Bibles were a less good approximation to the original text.

Despite the huge periods of time across which the text of OT books has been transmitted by copying, with all the risks of corruption and supplementation of the text which are associated with this, and despite the clear presence of copying errors, it is striking how similar the surviving witnesses to the text are to each other. *Biblia Hebraica Stuttgartensia*, the standard critical edition of the Hebrew OT, notes on average only one textual note per ten words (and most of these are insignificant), so that at least 90% of the text is substantially unquestioned. Waltke claims that 'even if we accepted the earlier and/or other literary editions of portions of the OT, no doctrinal statement within the Protestant tradition would be affected'.

Some seek to reduce the gap yet further by declaring a text (the MT) or a translation (usually the KJV) to have been particularly well-preserved by the providence of God. Whilst the MT is both ancient and (generally) well preserved, it is best not to see it as intrinsically better throughout than all the other texts, but to weigh each reading in the light of all the key witnesses. The KJV, contrary to the arguments of some, is *not* based on the best manuscripts and its usage does not reduce the gap between inspired original and the text as we have it, not least because it is based on a relatively narrow set of Hebrew manuscripts and is substantially based on the MT, which itself is not perfect. Moreover, to assert the KJV as *the* appropriate translation provides no solution for those prior to its creation in the seventeenth century or whose first language was/is not English.

Clearly God *could* have so superintended the copying of the Scriptures that all manuscripts were identical, and so superintended the process of translations that (insofar as it is possible with a translation) the translation was a perfect rendering of the text into the target language. But all manuscripts (at least before the printing press was invented) differed from each other and all translations differ from each other too, so that it is clear that God did not ensure that all manuscripts and translations were identical. An alternative 'solution' to the gap between original Scriptures and extant text must be found.

The best option here seems to be to note that the Bible is much larger than might be required if one were wishing to provide a body of doctrines, examples and prayers for use by believers. In short, it is repetitive, with doctrines or perspectives of significance being reflected many times. This means that, even if you were working with a poor manuscript copy of a poor translation of a corrupt Hebrew manuscript, the text you are working from will still be sufficiently close to the original that doctrines or perspectives that are reflected in the original Scriptures a number of times will not be lost. Although one or perhaps even two references may be corrupted, there will be sufficient surviving references to ensure that important perspectives remain clear. So long as doctrines and actions are not based on single references, especially where these are in places where there are text-critical uncertainties or where the perspective appears not to fit well with the wider perspectives of the Bible, then the reader is safe. The alternative, which is building major doctrines on single scriptures, is the stuff of cults!

Bibliography

D. A. Carson, *The King James Version Debate: A Plea for Realism* (Grand Rapids, 1979); E. Tov, 'Textual Criticism (OT)', in D. N. Freedman (ed.), *Anchor Bible Dictionary* vol. 5, pp. 393–412 (New York, 1992); *Textual Criticism of the Hebrew Bible* (Minneapolis and Assen, 2001); E. Ulrich, *The Dead Sea Scrolls and the Origins of the Bible* (Grand Rapids, 1999); B. K. Waltke, 'How We Got the Hebrew Bible: The Text and Canon of the Old Testament', in P. W. Flint (ed.), *The Bible at Qumran: Text, Shape, and Interpretation* (Grand Rapids, 2001), pp. 27–50.

E. D. HERBERT

ONTOLOGICAL ARGUMENT

The most influential formulation of the ontological argument (though he did not use the term 'ontological') is found in the first three chapters of the *Proslogium* of *Anselm of Canterbury (1033–1109). Anselm had earlier written a *Monologium* in which he considered many arguments for God's existence, but then, he says, 'I began to ask myself whether there might be found a single argument which would require no other for its proof than itself alone; and alone would suffice to demonstrate that God truly exists ... and whatever we believe regarding the divine being.' He says that he made an extensive search for such an argument, and, when he was almost ready to discontinue his quest, that argument 'began to force itself on me, with a kind of importunity'.

The *Proslogium*, unlike the *Monologium*, is a prayer. In the first chapter, Anselm invokes God's presence, confessing God's incomprehensibility and his own sin. He concludes with these famous words, 'I do not endeavor, O Lord, to penetrate thy sublimity, for in no wise do I compare my understanding with that; but I long to understand in some degree thy truth, which my heart believes and loves. For I do not seek to understand that I may believe, but I believe in order to understand [*credo ut intelligam*]. For this also I believe – that unless I believed, I should not understand.'

The second chapter begins the argument that seemed to force itself on Anselm. In accord with the resolution of his prayer, that he seeks to believe in order to understand, he begins with a Christian belief: 'And, indeed, we believe that thou art a being than which no greater can be conceived.'

Now Anselm recognizes that some do not believe in such a God, like the fool in Ps. 14:1 who 'says in his heart, "There is no God."' Nevertheless, this fool at least understands the words 'a being than which no greater can be conceived', so we may say that in a sense this being 'exists in the [fool's] understanding'. If, however, it exists in the fool's understanding alone and not in *reality, then we can imagine a greater being, namely one that exists, not only in the understanding but in reality. So then, the being in the fool's understanding is not really a being 'than which no greater can be conceived'. So a being that truly meets Anselm's definition of God, 'a being than which no greater can be conceived', must exist not only in the understanding, but also in reality. Therefore God must exist, by virtue of his very definition.

In Chapter 3, Anselm draws the further implication that this God 'cannot be conceived not to exist'. That is, if God can be conceived not to exist, it would be possible for us to conceive of a still greater God, one that cannot be conceived not to exist. So God not only exists; he exists *necessarily*, as some later philosophers and theologians would put it. He does not just happen to exist; he must exist. Once we know the meaning of God, as Anselm has defined it, we *cannot* conceive of him not existing. For it is greater, better, for him to exist than not to exist, and to exist necessarily rather than contingently. Then through the rest of the book, Anselm seeks to prove the traditional attributes of God using the same method: God is 'just, truthful, blessed, and whatever it is better to be than not to be'.

We can simplify Anselm's argument, for ease of reference: God has all perfections; existence is a perfection; therefore, God exists. At first glance, many immediately suspect a fallacy. Can it really be this easy to prove the existence of God? It has not been easy, however, for philosophers and theologians to show where the fallacy is located, if indeed there is one.

Anselm's contemporary Gaunilo, *Thomas Aquinas, David *Hume, Immanuel *Kant, J. L. Mackie and others have all rejected the argument, but many philosophers down to the present have accepted versions of it, including *Descartes, *Spinoza, *Leibniz, *Hegel and his followers, and twentieth-century thinkers Charles Hartshorne, Norman Malcolm and Alvin Plantinga.

The *Proslogium* includes an Appendix 'In Behalf of the Fool' by the monk Gaunilo, with a response by Anselm. Gaunilo points out that it is doubtful that we can even conceive of God in our minds according to Anselm's definition, for who can conceive of a being than which no greater can exist? And if we can reason from concept to reality as Anselm does, we could as easily prove the existence of a perfect island. 'For if it does not exist, any land which really exists will be more excellent than it.'

Anselm answers Gaunilo at considerable length. Although Gaunilo speaks 'In Behalf of the Fool', Anselm knows he is 'by no means a fool, and is a Catholic'. So, he says, 'I think it sufficient that I answer the Catholic.' In response to Gaunilo's first point, Anselm replies that Gaunilo, being a Catholic, cannot deny that God is conceivable, for he himself conceives of God. Anselm rather brushes off Gaunilo's analogous proof of a perfect island, but his basic reply is that such an island could not fit his definition of God, 'that than which no greater can be conceived'. Only one being meets the terms of that definition, namely the God of Christianity. The rest of Anselm's reply discusses various senses of 'conceiving', 'understanding', 'existing' and relations among these concepts.

Immanuel Kant thought that Anselm misunderstood the nature of existence by treating it as a perfection of God. In Kant's view, existence is not a perfection, or even a property. It is not, indeed, a 'real' predicate, though it can occupy the predicate position in a sentence like 'God exists'. For existence, Kant said, does not add anything to our concept of something. If you conceive of a nondescript car and add to it the colour blue, your concept changes. If, however, you conceive of a car and then conceive that same car as existing, nothing changes, for it is, after all, the same car. As Kant puts it, 'a hundred real dollars do not contain a penny more than a hundred possible dollars'. So Kant thinks Anselm has erred by making existence one of God's attributes or properties.

However, Kant admits that his financial position is better with real dollars than with possible ones. And we know that a real car is different from an imaginary one, and that a real unicorn, if it existed, would be different from an imaginary one. The real car may look the same as the one in our head, but it is certainly something different. Existence is, therefore, different from other properties and predicates in some ways, but not in the sense that it makes no difference to the objects that have it. Thus it seems that Kant's objection to the ontological argument fails, though it has generated and continues to generate much discussion.

The most common objection to the argument, voiced by Aquinas and followed by many others, is that concepts in the mind imply only mental existence, never existence in reality. There can be no 'leap' from mind to reality. This argument invokes our intuition that we can think of many things, like unicorns and leprechauns, that do not exist in reality, and it is hard to conceive of anything in such mental concepts that in itself could prove that these objects exist in the real world. Anselm, however, does not say that it is generally valid to infer realities from concepts. For him, this inference is valid in only one case, the case of God. It is not valid for our concepts of unicorns or perfect islands, only for that being than which no greater can be conceived.

Now if it is *never* possible to argue from the contents of the mind to the nature of reality, then we are in a bad way. In one sense, the contents of our minds (including the experience of our senses, our rational reflection, our memories, imaginations and concepts) are all we are directly acquainted with. If we are never able to reason from any of these to conclusions about the real world, then we cannot know the real world at all; we are shut up to scepticism. Empiricists, rationalists, idealists and others propose various ways of drawing this inference. (Insofar as Kant denied its possibility, he implicated himself in the charge of scepticism.) The inference must, however, be drawn.

Anselm's own inference may owe something to *Plato, for whom objects of our experience are reflections of more perfect objects, Forms or Ideas. We have a concept of goodness, for example, though nothing in our experience is perfectly good. Therefore, Plato believed, there

must be a Perfect Good in the real world, which serves as a model, criterion or standard of goodness. Although we may well reject Plato's idea that we know the Perfect Good from having experienced it in a past life, it still makes sense to assert that the highest criteria of truth, beauty and goodness must exist in reality, not only in our minds. Else we could not measure these qualities except by a subjective (and therefore arbitrary) standard. If goodness, truth and beauty exist, there must be an objective standard by which to measure them.

To say with Anselm that God is 'that than which no greater can be conceived' is to identify God as the highest perfection, the standard and exemplar of all greatness and, therefore, of all goodness, truth and beauty, and whatever other perfections there may be. Without such a standard or exemplar, there could be no goodness, truth or beauty in the world, i.e. the world would be a chaos. So there is a kinship between the ontological argument and the *transcendental argument. Both argue that if God exists only in our minds, there is no truth or meaning, indeed, no being at all. The greatness of God, therefore, must necessarily exist.

The ontological argument, therefore, expresses for Anselm the heart of the Christian world-view. God is the source of all value, so his existence must be presupposed if we are to accept the existence of anything else. It is not surprising, then, that this argument arises in answer to prayer and is expressed in the language of prayer, and it is not surprising that when Gaunilo raises objections Anselm responds, not to the fool, but to the Catholic. As he says in his Preface, he is not trying to understand in order to believe, but to believe in order to understand. When he discovers in a deeper way who the God of the Bible really is, 'that than which no greater can be conceived', he sees an important reason why he *must* exist.

The trouble with the argument is that people with other world-views try to use it too. The God proved by Spinoza's version of the argument is very different from Anselm's, a God identical with nature, *Deus sive Natura*. The same may be said of the Absolute of Hegel and the process God of Hartshorne. In part the differences lie in the fact that different world-views differ as to what is great or perfect. For Anselm, it is a perfection for God to create all things from nothing, but not for Spinoza. For

Anselm, it is a perfection for God to be passionless, but not for Hartshorne. The ontological argument necessarily presupposes a system of values. For Anselm, that system comes from his understanding of the Christian faith. In that sense, the argument presupposes the Christian *revelation, which, again, should not be surprising in view of Anselm's prayers and the *credo ut intelligam*.

As Thomas Aquinas says, not everybody would acknowledge God to be 'that than which no greater can be conceived', for some, he says, have thought that God has a body. Nor would some acknowledge that existence is a perfection, even given that it is a 'real predicate'. To many Buddhists, for example, annihilation is preferable to existence.

So the cogency of the ontological argument as an apologetic for the Christian faith depends on the cogency of the biblical system of values, its notion of perfection. It is not a religiously neutral argument, but one that immediately assumes the truth it seeks to validate. Presuppositional apologists frankly acknowledge and defend that kind of circularity in apologetics. Others may reject the ontological argument for this reason, but they must ask whether other arguments are not circular in similar ways. Does the *cosmological argument not presuppose a causal order such as we find in Scripture, but not in David Hume? Does the *teleological argument work unless it understands purpose to be personal, rather than impersonal?

Bibliography

K. Barth, *Anselm: Fides Quaerens Intellectum* (Richmond, 1960); S. N. Deane (ed.), *St. Anselm: Basic Writings* (La Salle, 1962); J. M. Frame, *Apologetics to the Glory of God* (Phillipsburg, 1994); I. Kant, *Critique of Pure Reason*, abridged and ed. by N. Kemp Smith (New York, 1958); A. C. Pegis (ed.), *Introduction to Saint Thomas Aquinas* (New York, 1948); A. Plantinga, *God, Freedom and Evil* (New York, 1973).

J. M. FRAME

ORIGEN

Origen (c. 185–c. 253) was born to Christian parents in Alexandria. A precocious youth, he supported the family as a teacher after his father's martyrdom. Bishop Demetrius put him in charge of catechetical instruction in the church, but later difficulties with the bishop caused Origen to move in the early 230s to Caesarea in Palestine, where he had earlier received ordination as a presbyter. He travelled extensively and enjoyed great fame as a teacher and preacher. One of Origen's students paid tribute to his educational approach, saying his instruction covered a full university curriculum, he encouraged the reading of all philosophers except atheists, and he taught above all by example. Injuries inflicted in the persecution under Decius resulted in his death not long afterwards.

Origen was the greatest intellect and most prolific writer of the early church before *Augustine. Many of his works show apologetic concerns. He laid a scholarly basis for his own biblical studies and for conversations with Jews by compiling the *Hexapla*, a remarkable philological achievement for the study of the text of the Old Testament. His *On First Principles*, the first attempt at a Christian theology based on the rule of faith and Scripture, included in its concerns a refutation of heretical ideas. The treatise *On Prayer*, important for spirituality, answers philosophical problems associated with prayer and providence. The surviving portion of his major scientific commentary on the Gospel of John includes a response to Heracleon, a member of the school of Valentinus.

Origen produced the greatest Greek apology for Christianity, *Against Celsus*. *Celsus was a Middle *Platonist philosopher who wrote the *True Word* as a refutation of Christianity. Unlike most pagan intellectuals in the second century who began to take notice of Christianity, he read the Christian Scriptures and engaged the thought of its defenders. Origen's method was to quote short passages from Celsus and after each offer his reply. Celsus's charges against Christianity included the following points: Christianity could not be true because it appeared so late in history; it is a superstition that takes the attitude, 'believe, do not think'; it appeals to low-class, uneducated people; Christians break the order of society by abandoning traditional customs and religion; the Scriptures tell unworthy stories and have a mean style; Christians are themselves divided; the incarnation is philosophically unacceptable; the *miracles of Jesus were done by magic; the resurrection is ridiculous.

Origen replied in the following ways: Christianity came in the fullness of time, when the unity and peace of the Roman world prepared for it; faith is valuable for those who cannot philosophize, and all human life depends on faith, but the church contained intellectuals as well as common people; Christ called sinners because all people are sinners; Christians blessed society by preaching and living by the truth; the Scriptures are superior to Greek myths, have helped more people than philosophy has, and have moved many to faith. Against Celsus' attack, Origen especially defended miracles and prophecy as evidences for Christianity's truth. He argued that the miracles happened because even uneducated Christians continued to exorcize demons in Jesus' name, miracles gave help to the church in its infancy but were now no longer needed, and they fulfilled prophecy. That the incarnation and resurrection were not invented and that the prophecies were indeed fulfilled were proved by the fact that uneducated disciples gave their lives for the message. The miracles of Jesus were different from magic because they had a moral quality about them and resulted in the improvement of human beings. Indeed, Origen made much of the point that Christianity produced improved moral lives and could not have accomplished this by deceit. The success of Christianity against all opposition can only be explained by divine power.

Origen had a great influence on the development of Christian doctrine and spirituality. Misunderstandings of his views, however, led to his condemnation as a heretic in the sixth century. His view of the resurrection body as spiritually transformed was not thought to give enough place to a resurrection of the flesh, and his position on the pre-existence of souls was considered too philosophical and without biblical basis. His speculation on universal salvation (even of the devil) was only one option he considered and one he elsewhere denied. Nonetheless, Origen remains a model of the pious intellectual who places learning at the service of the church.

Bibliography

H. Chadwick (tr.), *Against Celsus* (Cambridge, 1953); 'The Evidences of Christianity in the Apologetic of Origen', *Studia Patristica*, 2 (1957), pp. 331–339; H. Crouzel, *Origen* (San Francisco, 1989); J. Daniélou, *Origen* (New York, 1955).

E. FERGUSON

ORIGINS, THEORIES OF

Biblical interpretations of origins (of matter, life or humankind) have to confront secular knowledge of the world and its creatures – including ourselves. They have been challenged both by Christians wanting a range of literal interpretations and by others (Christians and non-Christians) claiming that the biblical narratives have no relation to a scientific understanding of origins. Either extreme is unnecessary: we can accept the truth of the scriptural record whilst also acknowledging that God has worked through processes which are in principle discoverable and which are wholly consistent with the biblical *revelation. The problem is to separate fact from assumption (or 'myth').

Probably all cultures have their own stories of origin, most of them describing arguments between gods, with our present world emerging as a counter in the supernatural strife of these deities. Throughout the Ancient Near East there was a conception of a primary watery emptiness and darkness, with creation as a divine act *ex nihilo* and humans made for the service of gods. The OT account is distinct in its clarity and *monotheism; there are no struggles between deities or attempts to exalt any special group. The contrasts between Gen. 1 and all the known extra-biblical cosmogonies are more striking than the resemblances.

Two points should be stressed in the Bible accounts of creation. First, they are not scientific accounts, but are concerned with theological truths. This is not to impute factual inaccuracy, but to recognize that the Bible frequently uses phenomenalistic *language in relation to natural processes. Francis *Schaeffer in *Genesis in Space and Time* (London, 1973), pp. 35–36 warned, 'We must remember the purpose of the Bible: it is God's message to fallen men ... The Bible is *not* a scientific textbook if by that one means that its purpose is to give us exhaustive truth or that scientific fact is its central theme and purpose.' Galileo (*Letter to the Grand Duchess Christina*, 1615) put it, 'the Bible teaches us how to go to heaven, not how the heavens go'.

The emphasis in the first two chapters of Genesis is on change, not an unalterable state. This is most obvious in Gen. 1, where we begin with chaos and travel through to humankind. Indeed, the Bible as a whole starts in a garden and ends in a city, taking us through wilderness to the Promised Land, and from sin to salvation. The repeated judgment that creation at the beginning was 'good' or 'very good' is a statement of the worth and praiseworthiness of creation in all its parts and does not necessarily imply perfection in an absolute sense. Likewise the statement in Gen. 2:1 that 'the heavens and the earth were completed' could be taken as indicating an end to God's creating work, but in view of his active sustaining of all he has made (Col. 1:17) and in the context of the establishment of the Sabbath, it is better to interpret it as a declaration of achievement, the artist admiring his handiwork.

The age of the earth

Judaism dates creation at 3761 BC; writing in the eighth century AD, the Venerable Bede put it at 3952 BC; but the most frequently quoted date is 4004 BC, calculated by Archbishop *Ussher of Armagh in 1650 and still printed in some Bibles above the text of Gen. 1. These dates are largely derived from the genealogies in Gen. 5 and 11.

In the eighteenth and early nineteenth centuries, evidence began to accumulate that the earth was much older than had been hitherto assumed. On the basis of the rate of cooling from the earth's apparent origin from the sun, Isaac *Newton (1642–77) arrived at a figure of 50,000 years, but he thought he must have calculated incorrectly because of the generally accepted biblical dating. The Comte de Buffon (1707–88) published an age of 74,832 years from experiments on the cooling of spheres, although he privately believed the earth was much older. However, studies of sedimentation rates in the formation of rocks, the growing awareness of biological extinctions and the use of fossils to characterize strata forced an acceptance that the original creation was very much earlier than 6,000 years ago, even if the climax of creation (i.e. humankind) could still be dated from that time. These assumptions about dating did not rise from doubts about the authenticity or *authority of the Bible, but they required that the traditional interpretation of Scripture be examined. For example, the most obvious understanding of the 'days' of creation in Gen. 1 is that they represent literal twenty-four hour periods, but it is also possible that they may be more general expressions of the passing of time; periods of re-creation after an original period of chaos (this was the argument of

Thomas Chambers [1780–1847] taken up in the 'Scofield references'); days of revelation to the inspired author; or a literary framework to provide for the establishment of the Sabbath (see H. Blocher, *In the Beginning* [Leicester, 1984], pp. 39–59). It is now clear from a number of independent and convergent measures (notably radioactive decay rates in rock) that the earth is about 4,700 million (4.7 billion) years old.

Our knowledge of the age of the earth comes from extra-biblical sources, but it has had a profound effect on our theological understanding of origins. Although it is theoretically possible that God could have created the world 'as if' it was already old (an idea mooted by Philip Gosse in *Omphalos* [London, 1857]), this would imply that God was a deceiver. On the other hand, the likelihood that geological and biological change has taken place since the original creation reveals 'the Achilles heel of natural theology. It would be possible for a creator to design a perfect organism in a static world of short duration. However, how could species have remained perfectly adapted to their environment if this environment was constantly changing?' (E. Mayr, *The Growth of Biological Thought* [Cambridge, MA, 1982], p. 349). It is worth noting that B. B. *Warfield, upholder of biblical inerrancy, held that 'The question of the antiquity of man has of itself no theological significance ... The Bible does not assign a brief span to human history; this is only done by a particular mode of interpreting the biblical data, which is found on examination to rest on no solid basis' ('On the Antiquity and the Unity of the Human Race' [1911], reprinted in M. Noll and D. Livingstone, *B. B. Warfield: Evolution, Science and Scripture* [Grand Rapids, 2000], p. 271).

Current understanding

The discovery that the universe is expanding has led to a scientific consensus that it had a beginning (or 'Big Bang') around 10–20 billion years ago, a date derived from calculations on its rate of expansion, the radioactive dating of meteorites, the age of globular clusters of stars and the decay of radioactive elements. Cosmologists are confident of tracing back the history of the universe until 10^{-43} seconds after its assumed beginning, but the very earliest moments cannot be known from our present scientific understanding because the density of the universe approaches infinity as its volume nears zero; at this point the existing laws of physics break down. Intuitively, one feels there must have been a beginning or 'singularity', but we cannot be certain. The Cambridge cosmologist Steven Hawking has argued that the universe may have arisen from a quantum fluctuation in a finite expanding region. However, the debates about the first 10^{-43} seconds do not remove the need for an 'originator' (Wilkinson, *Big Bang* [Mill Hill, 2001]).

Studies of the physical constants (gravity, etc.) involved in cosmological processes reveal that if they vary only infinitesimally, the universe either falls in upon itself (a Big Crunch) or expands too explosively to form stars. This extraordinarily fine tuning has been called the Anthropic Principle; our very existence depends upon it (J. Barrow and F. Tippler, *The Anthropic Cosmological Principle* [Oxford, 1986]). Some have claimed that this is a modern version of the argument for God's existence from design (e.g. H. Montefiore, *The Probability of God* [London, 1985]).

We now know in detail the molecular biology of life. Its essential characteristics are self-replication and mutation (i.e. the ability to change, allowing new forms to arise). Speculations in the 1920s about the origin of life (by J. B. S. Haldane and A. I. Oparin) suggested chemical reactions taking place in an organically rich soup. Stanley Miller (1953) produced complex carbon compounds (including ten of the twenty naturally occurring amino acids) by passing a strong electrical current (mimicking lightning) through a culture of water, hydrogen, methane and ammonia. Although the actual history of life on earth is completely unknown, there seems no serious reason to doubt that it could have arisen from apparently 'natural' causes. The oft-quoted calculation of Fred Hoyle that the chance of life originating by the random shuffling of molecules is about 1 in $10^{40,000}$, as 'ridiculous and improbable as the proposition that a tornado blowing through a junk yard may assemble a Boeing 747' is wrong. Hoyle based his claim on a complex biochemical system originating at a particular place and time, whereas the proper assumptions are of a much simpler system being formed at any place on earth within a period of a billion years or so.

The earliest forms of life upon earth would have been primitive micro-organisms. The oldest unequivocal fossils (of single-celled organisms) occur in rocks c. 2.2 billion years old. For a long time, the first complex fossil biotas known were from the Cambrian, about 540 million years ago. We now know of several 'Edicaran faunas' from pre-Cambrian rocks (around 600 million years ago), including some multicellular forms apparently antecedent to later groups, and also a range of Cambrian faunas (notably from the Burgess Shale in the Rockies) containing fossils not represented by modern animals (see D. Briggs and P. Crowther [eds.], *Palaeobiology* [Oxford, 1990]). In addition, hundreds of linking or intermediate forms ('missing links') have been described. It is not true that all modern animal groups appear suddenly at the beginning of the Cambrian, nor that no 'missing link' has ever been found.

Evolution

The theological objections to the *fact* of evolution depend on a deist idea of God remote from his creation. Aubrey Moore (in C. Gore [ed.], *Lux Mundi* [London, 1889], pp. 99–100) commented that in the mid-nineteenth century, 'God was "throned in magnificent inactivity in a remote corner of the universe" ... Science had pushed the deist's God farther and farther away, and at the moment when it seemed as if He would be thrust out altogether, Darwinism appeared and, under the guise of a foe, did the work of a friend. It has conferred upon philosophy and religion an inestimable benefit by showing us that we must choose between two alternatives ... We must frankly return to the Christian view of direct Divine agency, the immanence of Divine power in nature from end to end, the belief in a God in Whom not only we, but all things have their being; or we must banish Him altogether.'

The Origin of Species was published in 1859, and by 1880 the bulk of scientific and theological opinion had accepted that evolution had occurred. Its rapid acceptance came from Darwin's discovery of a mechanism for adaptation (i.e. the fitting of animals and plants to their environment, previously explainable only by the 'special creation' of every species), the rational cohesion that evolution gave to biogeography, and a simple basis for the existence of 'vestigial' organs and for classification. Legitimate scientific debates about the mechanism(s) of evolution have continued, although there is no dissent about the main mechanisms involved, including the fact that natural selection is apparently the only way of producing adaptation (apart from special creation). It should be noted that Darwinian evolution is not dependent on chance: adaptation is a determinative process, and chance only enters in the occurrence of the variation upon which selection acts.

It has been assumed from early Christian times that God created *ex nihilo* and that creation is distinct from God. This means that creation is not intrinsically sacred. This affirmation is important in the face of claims that Christian *theology has 'de-sacralized' and therefore reified God's work. The critical point to accept is the repeated identification of God as the Creator of all things (e.g. Gen. 1:1; Ps. 24:1–2; John 1:1–3; Heb. 1:2), recognizing that nowhere are we told the mechanism he used in creating. Indeed Heb. 11:3 is explicit that it is *by faith* that 'we understand that the universe was formed at God's command'. This is wholly in accord with our recognition of God's work in the world (in the lives of individual believers, in answered prayer, etc.); we fall into a major logical error if we assume that creation by known mechanisms (such as evolution by natural selection) is 'nothing but' the operation of blind forces, or that knowing the natural cause of an event inevitably excludes any divine or supernatural control of it. This error is widespread and is the fallacy in the ontological reductionism of Richard Dawkins (*The Blind Watchmaker* [London, 1986]) and Peter Atkins (*Creation Regained* [San Francisco, 1992]). An associated danger is to deny that a loving God would not use a mechanism like evolution, which involves death and 'waste', for his purpose, since this extrapolates improperly our human assumptions about God's ways of working. This objection is discussed in detail by Michael Ruse (*Can a Darwinian be a Christian?* [Cambridge, 2001]).

A distinction should be made between Darwinian evolution and Darwin*ism* (or evolutionism), since it highlights the dangers of 'social Darwinism', an illegitimate extension of Darwin's ideas into social questions, largely by his contemporary, Herbert Spencer (1820–1903). It is 'Spencerism' and not 'Darwinism' that is the alleged justification for *laissez-faire* economics, fascism, despotic capitalism etc. Attacks by Christians on 'evolutionary *naturalism' are really criticisms of Spencerism, but the debate tends to be confused by the protagonists using 'Darwinian' or 'Darwinism'

when evolution is meant, and improperly treating evolution and evolutionism as the same thing.

It can be difficult to separate legitimate criticisms of evolutionary processes from wholly spurious ones. For example, a book by Michael Denton (*Evolution: A Theory in Crisis* [Bethesda, 1986]) is frequently cited by anti-evolutionists as supporting their beliefs. Denton was horrified to discover this. He responded, 'I reject completely the special creationist world view ... I see the entire course of evolution as driven entirely by natural processes and *natural law' (in P. Johnson and D. Lamoureux [eds.], *Darwinism Defeated?* [Vancouver, 1999], p. 142). Attempts to argue that evolution requires additional inputs besides natural processes are misplaced. They have received widespread currency through the powerful advocacy of an American lawyer, Phillip Johnson, and are frequently linked to the claims of Michael Behe (*Darwin's Black Box* [New York, 1996]) that some structures (like cilia) and processes (like blood clotting) are 'irreducibly complex' (an assumption faced and discussed by Darwin himself in the *Origin*) and by the notion of 'intelligent design' associated particularly with the writings of William Dembski (see his edited volume *Mere Creation* [Downers' Grove, 1998]). There is nothing new in such assertions: R. A. Fisher (1890–1962) called them 'difficulties less of the reason than of the imagination' ('Retrospect of Criticisms of the Theory of Natural Selection', in J. Huxley, A. Hardy and E. B. Ford [eds.], *Evolution as a Process* [London, 1954], p. 89). Evolutionary biology is not intrinsically atheistic. The issues have been examined in detail by Robert Pennock and Michael Ruse (see Bibliography).

Modern day 'creationism' has only tenuous links with the arguments leading up to and following the publication of *The Origin of Species*. The main begetter of current creationism was a Seventh-day Adventist and high school teacher George McCready Price (1870–1963), who sought to re-instate Noah's flood as a worldwide catastrophe that reshaped the earth's surface. His literalist interpretations of the Genesis creation narratives provided the stimulus for anti-evolution legislation (largely in the USA) and various legal battles (most notoriously the Scopes prosecution in 1925 and a 1981 Arkansas trial of an Act requiring 'equal time' in the school curriculum for 'creation *science' and 'evolution science'). Price's thesis resurfaced in *The Genesis Flood* (Philadelphia, 1961) by John Whitcomb and Henry Morris. Later in life, Price renounced his belief in a 'young Earth', accepting that the universe was created about 2,000 million years ago. In passing, it is worth noting that at least half of the authors of the series of pamphlets on the 'fundamentals' of Protestant Christianity as defined by the General Assembly of the American Presbyterian Church in 1910 (which formed the basis of 'fundamentalism') were entirely happy with scientific evolution. For example, James *Orr argued that 'the first chapter of Genesis is a sublime poem ... which science does nothing to subvert', and American evangelist R. A. Torrey declared that one could, 'believe thoroughly in the absolute authority of the Bible and still be an evolutionist of a certain type'.

Human beings

The Bible distinguishes humankind from all other animals as being in the 'image' of God (Gen. 1:26–27). Theologians are united in agreeing that this likeness is not anatomical or genetical. C. D. F. Moule concluded, 'The most satisfying of the many interpretations ... is that which sees it as basically responsibility (Ecclus. 17:1–4)' (*Man and Nature in the New Testament* [London, 1964], p. 5).

Was Adam a historical person? The Genesis text can certainly be read as God creating a human 'type' as distinct from a person. However, Paul's comparison between the first man and the man Jesus Christ (Rom. 5:12–17; 1 Cor. 15:21–22) seems to demand their historical equivalence as individuals. The Adam described in Genesis is a Neolithic farmer, placed in a garden to care for it, with one son who was a shepherd, another who lived in a town, and a near-descendant (Tubal-Cain) who 'forged all kinds of tools out of bronze and iron' (Gen. 4:22). If we are to interpret these statements literally, this would mean that Adam and Eve lived 10–20,000 years ago and hence could not be the genetical progenitors of the whole human race. The species *Homo sapiens* was distributed in the Americas, Japan and the Far East thousands of years before the 'Neolithic Revolution' began in the fertile crescent of the Ancient Near East. But there is no reason why Adam and Eve could not be the spiritual ancestors of all humankind, since God's image is his supernatural imprimatur of human-ness

and is not transmitted through normal reproduction like a physical trait.

If God intervened in history in impressing his image on a living human, so that *Homo sapiens* became, as it were, *Homo divinus* (the Heb. word used for human creation is *bara*, implying a specific act of God; in contrast the word commonly used for God's work in Gen. 1 [*asah*] implies the moulding of pre-existing material, as when a potter shapes a pot from clay), he could then have extended his 'bara-act' to all members of the species alive at the time. The 'death' which Adam and Eve suffered the day they sinned (Gen. 2:17) was primarily separation from God (Eph. 2:1); they survived as individuals and had all their children following their expulsion from Eden.

The idea that God extended his image to include all mankind and that the death resulting from the fall is spiritual are interpretations which make sense of the biblical record. They are interpretations which take the Bible text seriously whilst accepting the possibility that we are physically (though not spiritually) descended from the apes (we share 98.4% of our DNA with chimpanzees). This differs from the conventional scientific story only – but significantly – in insisting that we are 'more than' mere apes – we are creatures specially created by God according to his own will. We need not dissent from or deny the likelihood that we are part of a human lineage which began in Africa. And from the apologetic point of view, we can also insist that we have traits given to us by God which affect our behaviour and relationships and which have to be taken into account if we are fully to understand the human condition.

Bibliography

E. Lucas, *Can We Believe Genesis Today?* (Leicester, 2001); R. Numbers, *The Creationists* (New York, 1992); R. Pennock, *Tower of Babel: The Evidence Against the New Creationism* (Cambridge, MA, 1999); M. Ruse, *Can a Darwinian be a Christian?* (Cambridge, 2001); D. Wilkinson, *God, the Big Bang and Stephen Hawking* (Mill Hill, 2001).

R. J. Berry

ORR, JAMES

James Orr (1844–1913) born in Glasgow, was the son of an engineer, and was orphaned at an early age. He was encouraged to prepare for the ministry and graduated from the University of Glasgow, receiving a BD, and later a DD by examination. He exercised brief ministries with Glasgow City Mission and at Irvine, before settling into a long-term ministry at Hawick. In 1891 Orr was appointed to the Chair of Church History at the Divinity Hall of the United Presbyterian Church in Edinburgh, and later to the Chair of Apologetic and Systematic Theology at the United Free Church College in Glasgow. He held numerous lectureships, both in Britain and in the United States, where he was popularly received as a thoughtful defender of orthodox theology. His many published works reveal a passionate pastoral concern and a sharp philosophical acumen, drawn from a biblical, evangelical perspective. They range from the award-winning *The Problem of the Old Testament* (1906) and academic lecture series such as *The Christian View of God and the World* (1893) and *The Progress of Dogma* (1901), to the more popular apologetic works, *The Bible on Trial* (1907) and *The Faith of a Modern Christian* (1910). He served as editor of the *International Standard Bible Encyclopaedia* (1914) and was a contributor to *The Fundamentals* (1910–15). Although he presented a formidable challenge to his intellectual opponents, especially in his critique of *Ritschlian theology, he was nevertheless charitable in tone and tolerant in spirit.

Orr desired to identify, and be faithful to, those aspects of doctrine that were unchanging, even as they required fresh expression for the specific challenges of a new era. He perceived Christian doctrine as an organism, and believed there were important consequences for all of theology if any particular doctrines were altered beyond historically orthodox recognition. Orr believed that God's existence was a necessary postulate for all of Christian thought, and thus preserved the role of the supernatural in his apologetic method. However, he was keen also to uphold the place of reason in theology and belief. Under certain conditions, he insisted, reason may be a trustworthy guide towards *truth, and he defended the *authority of the Bible, the virgin birth of Christ and the resurrection against contemporary opposition to the reasonableness of Christian faith, while critically engaging realist, idealist and moral philosophies.

Orr's method of proposing the postulate, examining opposition and reaffirming the

postulate in light of any necessary qualifications yielded a vibrant and ordered apologetic. His devotion to the continuity of doctrine, engagement of contemporary challenges to faith and commitment to the scrutiny and employment of reason by *revelation suggests a continuing relevance, and challenge, for evangelical apologetic theology today.

Bibliography

J. Orr, *The Christian View of God and the World* (Edinburgh, 1893); *The Ritschlian Theology and the Evangelical Faith* (London, 1898); G. G. Scorgie, *A Call for Continuity: The Theological Contribution of James Orr* (Macon, 1988); A. P. F. Sell, *Defending and Declaring the Faith* (Exeter and Colorado Springs, 1987).

A. M. ROBBINS

ORTHODOX CHRISTIANITY, see CHRISTIANITY, ORTHODOX

PACIFISM AND WAR

The word 'pacifism' derives from the Latin word for 'peace' and has been associated historically with the position of refusing to participate in war. Christian pacifists base their position on Matt. 5:9, but one need not be a Christian to be a pacifist, as Buddhists and the followers of *Gandhi's approach illustrate. Most forms of pacifism, however, include labouring for the abolition of strife in general and are based on the person and teaching of Christ. Pacifism includes a wide gamut of variations extending from the personal level, which even the just war theory advocates, to the public position that no wars are to be undertaken whatsoever. As such, pacifism contains no one authoritative position. A recent study identified nearly thirty distinct versions of the belief (Yoder, *Nevertheless*, p. 12), the common denominator being opposition to war in all its forms.

Pacifism became the majority opinion of Christians during the first three centuries of the church, represented by a host of early theologians including Ignatius, Clement of Rome, Polycarp, *Athenagoras, *Clement of Alexandria, *Justin Martyr, *Irenaeus, *Cyprian and *Origen. *Tertullian summed up the consensus with his statement that 'Christ in disarming Peter (in the Garden of Gethsemane) disarmed every soldier'. Early Christians characterized their pacifism as *patientia*, or a steadfast longsuffering in resisting *evil without doing violence to the evildoers. One looks in vain for an opposing view during this period. Given the ambivalent stance of Scripture concerning war (cf. Deut. 20; Ps. 144:1–2; Joel 3:9–10; Luke 3:14; 14:31; 22:36–38), it is thought that the relative dominance of pacifism in the early church was based on three premises: the rejection of violence as incompatible with Christ's teachings (Matt. 5:39, 44); the pervasive paganism in the existing Roman military; and the requirement of unquestioning loyalty from soldiers, which was seen as incongruent with loyalty to Christ. After the nominal acceptance of Christianity by the Roman State under the Emperor Constantine and his successors, pacifism remained popular though increasingly challenged by the emerging just war theory. Now advocates of war participation could argue that a Christianized Rome could bear the sword and thus harmonize OT state-oriented war passages with the NT's personal non-violent mandates.

During the Middle Ages, pacifism was largely in retreat, with the rise of the idea of crusade. It did remain strong in the new, poverty-based religious initiatives of the twelfth and thirteenth centuries such as the Waldensians and the Franciscans. In the Reformation the quiet wing of the Anabaptist movement made pacifism a salient feature of their theology, holding that it was requisite for all who are regenerate in Christ. In the seventeenth century, the Society of Friends embraced pacifism in an even more stringent way, calling on all, regenerate or not, to renounce war. Modern-day Christian pacifism has best been represented by these two traditions, with the Mennonites and Quakers heading the list of 'peace churches'. In the last half of the twentieth century a variant of pacifism emerged which held that the advent of weapons of mass destruction, whether nuclear, biological or chemical, made justified warfare impossible. Nicknamed 'nuclear pacifists', these advocates of non-violence argue that the weapons systems of today, by their indiscriminate slaughter of innocents, have nullified the just war theory. Whether pacifism regains its dominant position among the Christian faithful remains to be seen, but the healthy interchange of ideas between those who envision permissible war and those who do not can but improve the chances that war will not be waged without

serious review and may act as a limiting agent on what St *Augustine called the *libido dominandi*, or 'lust to dominate', which is at the heart of human strife. In the light of recent events, such interchange seems even more urgent.

Bibliography

R. H. Bainton, *Christian Attitudes toward War and Peace* (Nashville, 1960); O. R. Barclay (ed.), *Pacifism and War* (Leicester, 1984); J. Driver, *How Christians Made Peace with War: Early Christian Understandings of War* (Scottdale, 1988); J. C. Wenger, *Pacifism and Biblical Nonresistance* (Scottdale, 1968); J. H. Yoder, *Nevertheless: The Varieties and Shortcomings of Religious Pacifism* (Scottdale, 1992).

B. W. REYNOLDS

PAGAN AND INDIGENOUS RELIGIONS

The word 'pagan' (derived from the Lat. *pagus*, lit. 'from the countryside' or 'rural') has, over the years, been used pejoratively by Christians to mean 'uncivilized', 'non-Christian', and even 'satanic'. Indeed, the term 'pagan' was first used in a general religious sense by the early Christians to describe the non-Christian gentile religions. Although some Christians still use the term 'pagan' in a pejorative sense, it is now generally used to refer to a broad range of nature-venerating religious traditions. Although the term 'neo-paganism' is sometimes used by academics and even by some devotees, particularly in the USA (e.g. the Church of All Worlds), practitioners generally prefer to refer to themselves as 'Pagans'.

There are fundamental discontinuities between indigenous religions and contemporary Western Paganism. That said, because many contemporary Pagans do seek to learn from indigenous cultures, there are also some (often tenuous) continuities between the two forms of religion. Hence, for example, although the shamanism practised in the West is distinct from that practised by the Tungus people of Siberia (from whom the term originates), or the Inuit (Eskimos), there are attempts being made to understand and follow indigenous shamanism in a Western context. However, although claims by Westerners to practice indigenous religion should be treated with respect and sensitivity, they should also be treated with caution. Western Pagans often have selective and eclectic belief systems that may have more in common with certain *New Age spiritualities than they have with contemporary indigenous or ancient pre-Christian religions.

Indigenous religions

From the Arctic to Australia, from Siberia to the Pacific Islands, from South East Asia to sub-Saharan Africa, indigenous religions can be found in small-scale societies. Although a range of terms have been used, 'indigenous' is preferred to, for example, 'primitive', 'traditional', 'non-/pre-literate' and the more acceptable 'primal'. The reason for this preference is simply that the earlier terms tend to be misleading in that they suggest simplicity, undeveloped antiquity, the archaic and, in some cases, homogeneity. In fact, these religions are often developed, highly complex, distinctive, literate and sometimes technologically aware. Nowadays, some indigenous religionists write books and make use of the Internet.

Principal beliefs and practices

Although it would be misleading to generalize about indigenous religions and, ideally, each indigenous religion should be studied alone in its context, there are certain common themes that can be identified, for example, the fundamental continuities between the sacred and the secular. Although particular sacred spaces are recognized (e.g. temples, shrines, rocks, trees, mountains), generally speaking, the environment and the whole of individual and communal life are invested with religious significance.

Also, as in some forms of contemporary Paganism, humans are believed to be outnumbered by numerous demons, deities, ancestor spirits and non-human persons. Transcending all these is often a supreme or high god, sometimes understood to be distant and relatively uninvolved in everyday affairs. In some religions this deity can be directly related to; in others, intermediaries (e.g. shamans, priests) are required or prayers are directed to lesser deities and spirits, who may then intercede with the supreme being or there is a combination of both. However, not all in the spirit world is personal. For example, many indigenous peoples recognize the presence of a spiritual power or energy, sometimes termed

mana, which flows through the natural world, is concentrated in sacred places, amulets and charms and can be manipulated for personal ends.

Although not all indigenous world-views are inherently 'green', there is often a profound understanding of a spiritual relationship between humanity and nature, a relationship which is often evocatively described and explained in myths. (All indigenous cultures have cosmologies or stories which explain how the world began and the place of humans within it.) Because each plant, rock, stream, and mountain is thought to be infused with spiritual energy or attached to a spiritual being, the natural world is accorded great reverence. This, of course, has immense religious implications, and walking through a river or sitting on a particular stone can be spiritually meaningful. Similarly, activities such as hunting are commonly saturated with religious significance and involve complex relationships between the hunter and the hunted. Consequently, hunts are never carried out recreationally.

Contemporary Paganism

Principal beliefs and practices

From a Christian apologetic perspective, and bearing in mind certain erroneous Christian presuppositions, it is important to understand that, although it is always difficult to generalize about such diverse and eclectic spiritualities, Paganism should not be understood as a synonym for *Satanism. For many Pagans such an association is offensive, being understood as one of the many ways Christians have historically sought to demonize indigenous, nature-venerating religions. Most contemporary Pagans will insist that, because Satan does not feature in the Pagan world-view, and because Satanists work with a perverted understanding of the Christian world-view, Satanists are not Pagans, but rather Christian heretics. Indeed, many Pagans will actively distance themselves from Satanists and Satanism. The Paganism–Satanist confusion, which probably stretches back to the Christian denunciation of Pagans as 'devil worshippers', has been exacerbated in recent years by misrepresentations in films, horror novels and popular books dealing with the occult. Moreover, because Satanists themselves will use the names of pagan gods (as well as the names of the gods of other faiths, e.g. Kali) to refer to Satan and the demonic pantheon, some have wrongly concluded that when Pagans refer to gods such as Hecate, Lilith, Pan and Set they are actually worshipping Satan. This, however, is not the case. The cosmology of Paganism 'has no room for a battle between forces of "good" and "evil" fought over the "souls" of humans who might be enticed towards heaven or hell' (Graham Harvey).

Many Pagans reject not only the concept of Satan, but also the Christian understanding of God. Indeed, in common with some forms of eco-feminist spirituality, there is a general opposition to patriarchal *monotheisms and the depiction of God as solely male. Although Pagans do claim to seek a balance, and although many will teach that the masculine and the feminine are of equal importance, the emphasis is often placed very firmly on 'the Great Goddess' and the feminine. A variety of names are used, e.g. Isis, Diana, Astarte, Cerridwen, Sekhmet, Kali, Innanna, Hecate, the Lady. Similarly, the god too is referred to using a variety of names, e.g. Anubis, Bacchus, Pan, Zeus, Apollo, Odin, Herne, Cernunnos, the Lord.

In a similar way to indigenous religions, there is often a pantheistic deification of nature in Paganism. An implication of this is the belief that humans are in some sense to be considered divine. That said, Pagans are usually more panentheistic than pantheistic in that they do recognize that, although inextricable, there is a conceptual distinction between the divine and the natural world.

Also important for Pagans are natural cycles, bodily, lunar and solar. For example, lunar cycles and seasonal festivals order the lives of most Pagans. In the Pagan calendar ('the wheel of the year') there are eight major festivals: Samhain, Midwinter (also Yule or Winter Solstice), Imbolc (also Oimelc or Candlemas), Spring Equinox, Beltane, Midsummer (also Summer Solstice), Lammas (or Lughnasadh), Autumn Equinox.

Finally, it is important to grasp the plurality within Paganism. Although there are many forms of Paganism, and although there are solitary and private practitioners, arguably there are three principal traditions. Perhaps the largest and most influential of these is Wicca (also called the Old Religion, Witchcraft, Wisecraft or simply the Craft). Needless to say, the popular, media-perpetuated image of the witch (e.g. the spooky old hags portrayed

in Shakespeare's *Macbeth*) is inaccurate. As with all Pagans, Wiccans are often normal, unassuming people with ordinary lives. Most Wiccans meet regularly in small groups or 'covens' of like-minded people for social, religious and educational purposes. During these meetings, and also on their own, they sometimes seek to practise magic, of which there are two forms, 'natural magic' and 'high magic'. High magic (often spelled 'magick') involves initiation and rituals, and aims at personal transformation through contact with the divine. Natural magic, on the other hand, is more materialistic in that, by means of herbs, crystals or other natural materials, it aims to harness what are believed to be natural (or sometimes supernatural) forces in order to effect changes in the physical world, from healing sick minds and bodies to influencing the weather. Both types of magic, it is usually stressed, should be directed toward good and healthy ends. Needless to say, although some people become Wiccans out of a spiritual concern for the environment, or because they seek a radically feminist spirituality, or because they are attracted by non-dogmatic faith, many are drawn by the desire to practise magic(k). This is enormously attractive, not only because of the sense of *power that it brings, but also because, particularly in high magick, there is a gnostic-like sense of being initiated into a secret tradition with secret knowledge and secret symbols. A person becomes one of the privileged few.

A second contemporary Pagan tradition is Druidry. Although Druidry was clearly a pre-Christian Celtic religion, the continuity between this ancient faith, of which little is known, and contemporary Druidry is questionable. Moreover, Christians should understand that the history of contemporary Druidry, which stretches back to the eighteenth-century revival of the tradition, is not the history of a Pagan tradition as such, in that many of the early modern Druids considered themselves and their beliefs to be fully compatible with traditional Christianity. Many continued to worship as Christians and hold offices in their local churches. Indeed, although Pagans have been involved in Druidry for many years, and increasingly so since the 1960s, explicitly Pagan Druid orders did not emerge until the late 1970s.

More structured than Wicca, individual Druid groups belong to a particular Druid

Order, which is overseen by an elected 'Arch-druid' (different orders use different titles). In Britain these orders usually belong to the umbrella organization, the Council of British Druid Orders. Although no such council exists in the USA, there are two main bodies to which most Druids belong, Ar nDraiocht Fein and Keltria.

Although there is no Druid orthodoxy as such, generally speaking, contemporary Pagan Druids (there are still many Druids who very clearly identify themselves as Christian and not Pagan) have what might be described as a neo-Celtic Pagan faith, in that it is an eclectic mixture of general Pagan beliefs constructed around what is known of Celtic belief and culture. Celtic gods and goddesses are wor-shipped and prehistoric sites are revered as sacred spaces (e.g. Stonehenge and Avebury).

Finally, within contemporary Paganism there is a tradition often referred to simply as the 'Northern Tradition'. Northern Tradition Pagans often prefer the appellative 'Heathen' rather than 'Pagan'. 'Heathen' means roughly the same as 'Pagan', but is derived from Ger-manic languages rather than Latin. It is also a term that has been used pejoratively by Chris-tians. The Northern Tradition/Heathenism draws inspiration principally from Anglo-Saxon, Norse and Icelandic pre-Christian mythology, religion and culture. There are believed to be nine worlds, of which ours is the middle (*Midgard*/Middle Earth). These worlds are connected by *Yggdrasil* (the World Tree) and are populated by different beings (deities, humans, giants, dwarves, elves etc.), some of which can travel between worlds. Two distinct groups of deities are recognized, namely, the *Æsir* and the *Vanir*. The *Æsir*, the sky gods and goddesses of Norse myth-ology, are the sovereign deities of warfare and magic, and the most important and popular deity of the *Æsir* is Odin. Indeed, some Heathens prefer to be called Odinists. That said, because many worship other deities as well as Odin, sometimes the name *Ásatrú* ('loyalty to the *Æsir*') is preferred. The deities of the earth associated with agriculture and fertility make up the *Vanir*.

One of the most well-known aspects of Heathenism, one which has been popularized by New Agers as a form of fortune-telling, is the use of runes. Runes are symbols (often painted on small, smooth stones) which for Heathens are more than simply tools for fortune-telling in the modern sense of that term. That is to say, using the runes is more about seeking spiritual guidance, achieving wholeness, communicating with non-human beings and listening to the deities, and less about finding out what a person's future might hold. The chanting of runes is common during Heathen rituals.

Meeting Pagans

As most readers will not encounter indigenous cultures, what follows are some general points to be borne in mind by Christians interested in discussion with contemporary Pagans.

Pagans believe different (sometimes very different) things about the world. Hence, dialogue (particularly listening) is important if one is to grasp the world-view of a Pagan. Books provide only a general overview of Pagan beliefs, some of which some Pagans will reject.

Effective communication is severely miti-gated by incorrect presuppositions, unhelpful suspicion and offensive caricature. Although there is much within Paganism that is clearly non-Christian (sometimes explicitly anti-Christian), it is important that confrontation is avoided and sensitivity employed. Most Pagans are suspicious of Christians, feel misrepresented by the media and misunderstood by the major-ity of Westerners. Their self-perception is often one of a persecuted minority. Indeed, because of an often romanticized history of persecution by Christians (including the destruction of Pagan and indigenous sacred sites, the burning of witches and the eradication of pre-Christian religions, not to mention more recent mission-ary activity amongst contemporary indigenous peoples), many Pagans will identify them-selves as those in opposition to institutional Christianity.

As we have seen, not only do many Pagans deny the existence of Satan or ontological *evil, but they also reject the Christian concept of sin, believing it to inform an unhealthy attitude towards the natural world. In particular, there is no understanding within Paganism of the natural world needing to be redeemed and of humanity looking forward to a new *heaven and earth in which there will be no more dying. For Pagans (as well as for indigenous religions), life and death, spring and autumn, growth and decay, the hunter and the hunted are key aspects of the healthy circle of life. Pagans feel at home in a world of birth, sex and death and explicitly do not seek salvation from it. Indeed, Pagan spirituality is not so much about salvation, as it is about understanding and celebrating one's place in the natural world. Hence, Christian concepts of sin and salvation, and related ideas regarding death as the final enemy, are vigorously opposed. This means that any fruitful engagement will require a good understanding of both of these issues and also of Christian theology. That said, because a sophisticated understanding of evil has been developed by Christian theologians, and because a cogent understanding of sin and evil is relatively undeveloped within much contemporary Paganism, it is an area that should be explored. Not only that, but more importantly, Christianity is a religion of great hope which squarely faces moral and natural evil.

Bearing in mind the above point, another fruitful area for dialogue with Pagans would be attitudes to the environment. Again, it is important to understand that dialogue is about listening as well as speaking. Many Pagans have carefully thought through views about the natural world from which Christians can learn. As an ecological faith tradition, Paganism seeks to break down hierarchies, learn from indigenous religions and develop attitudes to the natural world which are felt by many to be healthy. In an eco-conscious culture, in which many are highly critical of Christianity's alleged involvement in the modern eco-crisis, a non-Christian, eco-conscious spirituality is understandably attractive. Because there is often a great deal of misunderstanding about Christian attitudes to the natural world, it is, however, crucial that intelligent theologies of nature and creation are discussed.

It is also helpful to correct any erroneous negative understandings held about Christian attitudes to the sexual and the body. Pagans celebrate their *sexuality and many rituals contain sexual symbolism. This does not mean that they are sexually deviant in any way, but simply that they want to develop what they understand to be a healthy and natural view of the body and sexuality. Again, those entering into dialogue with Pagans should make themselves aware of the positive and affirming Christian theologies of sexuality.

Regardless of whether this is always the case or not (and sometimes it is not), Paganism certainly advertises itself as being ethically and doctrinally non-dogmatic. In a culture which is uncomfortable with exclusive *truth claims, such as those made by Christ and Christianity, it is not difficult to see the attraction of a religion which demands only a reverence for 'the life force', an honouring of 'the divine' (however that might be understood) and the single ethical injunction, 'if it harms none do what thou wilt'. However, avoidance of epistemological issues raised by questions of truth and the lack of a developed ethical framework call for critical scrutiny.

Systematic argument (such as that characteristic of much Christian apologetics) is usually the wrong way to approach indigenous and Pagan religionists. Their world-views are often expressed in stories and art, not rational, doctrinal statements. Hence, the sharing of personal and biblical narratives will often be more meaningful.

The appeal of ancient, secret/occult knowledge, power and ritual is perennial. For damaged and insecure people living in an individualistic and selfish culture that engenders feelings of powerlessness and insignificance, the attraction of a small, closely-knit group of people who claim to have access to such ancient power and knowledge is hard to underestimate. Hence, for a few people attracted to the occult subculture, again it is not theological argument that is required, but rather simple and genuine pastoral concern. A caring church, a trusting relationship, an awareness of one's personal significance to Christ will mean a great deal more that philosophic engagement.

Bibliography

M. Adler, *Drawing Down the Moon* (Harmondsworth, 1997); G. Harvey, *Listening People, Speaking Earth: Contemporary Paganism* (London, 1997); *Indigenous Religions: A Companion* (London and New York, 2000); R. Hutton, *The Triumph of the Moon: A History of Modern Pagan Witchcraft* (Oxford, 1999); T. M. Luhrmann, *Persuasions of the Witch's Craft: Ritual Magic in Contemporary England* (Cambridge, MA, 1989); J. Pearson (ed.), *Belief Beyond Boundaries: Wicca, Celtic Spirituality and the New Age* (Aldershot, 2002); S. L. Reid and S. T. Rabinovitch, 'Witches, Wiccans, and Neo-Pagans: A Review of Current Academic Treatments of Neo-Paganism', in J. R. Lewis (ed.), *Oxford Handbook of New Religious Movements* (New York, 2004); J. Pearson, R. H. Roberts and G. Samuel (eds.),

Nature Religion Today: Paganism in the Modern World (Edinburgh, 1998); C. H. Partridge, 'Pagan Fundamentalism?', in C. H. Partridge (ed.), *Fundamentalisms* (Carlisle, 2001).

C. H. PARTRIDGE

PAGLIA, CAMILLE

Camille Paglia (b. 1947), professor of humanities at the University of the Arts in Philadelphia, burst on the academic and cultural scene in 1990 following the publication of *Sexual Personae: Art and Decadence from Nefertiti to Emily Dickinson* (London and New Haven, 1990). Media attention was drawn by her book's contrarian positions on *gender and sexuality, which Paglia first introduced to a popular audience in a *New York Times* editorial on 14 December 1990. Here she proclaimed pop-icon Madonna 'a real feminist' who has 'taught young women to be fully female and sexual while still exercising control over their lives'. While Christian apologists may reject some of her positions on social issues, her arguments remain an important touchstone for contemporary debate.

Sexual Personae refers to recurrent personality types, or 'masks' that comprise the continuity in Western art, life and thought. These projections are a result of the fundamental human struggle between the rational and the primal urges (or Apollonian and Dionysian), which she traces from antiquity (Nefertiti) through the Renaissance and Romantic movements (Emily Dickinson). In this panorama, sex and nature are seen as 'brutal pagan forces'; Paglia boldly bases sex differences upon biological bases. Man is not free, but in biological chains. Paglia's own feminism is a celebration of woman's life-giving *power over man; the womb is every man's source, which condemns him to 'life-long sexual anxiety'. Rationality and physical achievement are male-orientated attempts to overcome this anxiety. The Judaeo-Christian tradition is an Apollonian 'sky cult', positing order in the face of the uncontrollable power of nature. Volume II of this magnum opus promised a similar reading of contemporary popular culture, but it remains unpublished. Since 1990, Paglia has produced primarily essays, which have been collected in *Sex, Art, and American Culture* (New York, 1992) and *Vamps and Tramps* (New York, 1994).

As 'an atheist who worships only nature', Paglia explicitly opposes the Christian doctrine of creation, relegating the Creator God to a *Freudian projection. Yet she places a premium on the study of comparative religion as *culture, which separates her from the prevailing *secularism and the academy. By celebrating popular culture primarily in terms of Dionysian *pagan religion, Paglia throws a stark and unintentionally biblical light on the antithesis between the believer and her own world, an antithesis too often missing from Christian apologetics.

B. J. LEE

PALAMAS, see GREGORY PALAMAS

PALEY, WILLIAM

William Paley (1743–1805), in the latitudinarian tradition that stemmed from the seventeenth-century Anglican theologians known as the Cambridge Platonists, who emphasized reason as the arbiter of true religion, and apparently holding to a covert unitarianism, is renowned for his *teleological argument for the existence of God based on the analogy of a watch. He was educated at Christ's College, Cambridge, and became a fellow there in 1766, leaving in 1775 to follow a number of appointments in the diocese of Carlisle, eventually becoming archdeacon there. Although not an original thinker, he wrote three major works to oppose scepticism to the Christian faith stemming from the *Enlightenment.

In *Principles of Moral and Political Philosophy* (1785) Paley espoused a utilitarian *morality reinforced by divine sanction, anticipating some of the arguments of Jeremy Bentham (1748–1832). In 1794 he published *A View of the Evidences of Christianity* in which he defended the historicity of the New Testament on the grounds that the apostles endured great hardship because of the veracity of what they preached, and the miracles of Christ are confirmations of divine revelation through him. This work became required reading for entrance to Cambridge University during the nineteenth century.

Paley's classic version of the argument from design appears in *Natural Theology, or Evidence of the Existence and Attributes of the Deity Collected from the Appearances of*

Nature (1802). If one were to wander across a heath and come across a stone and a watch, one would inevitably infer that the stone was a natural object, but the intricacies of the watch would leave one in no doubt that it was the product of design and artifice, even if one had never seen a watch. Likewise, the complexities of the human anatomy, as in the organs, muscles and eyes, can leave no doubt but that these are the product of a cosmic designer.

However, twenty-three years earlier, David *Hume had already subjected such arguments to devastating critique in his *Dialogues Concerning Natural Religion*, asking: why not take a vegetable, which grows of itself, as an appropriate analogy of the universe, instead of a watch? Indeed, any universe would have regular interactions that would give the misleading impression of design. At best, this imperfect world could suggest only an imperfect deity, or, perhaps, a number of deities.

Paley partly answered such criticisms by maintaining that the unity of nature gives grounds for affirming a single Creator. But Darwin's theory of evolution was the death knell for his theory, for it proffered a purely natural explanation of complex organisms in terms of improvements that aided survival of the fittest and it evacuated nature of teleology.

Paley's argument might be updated by extending into the domain of embryological development the kind of teleological argument that is based on the strong anthropic cosmological principle, namely, that the fine-tuning of the physical constants required for a universe that can produce and support life implies a divine designer who predetermined the values of these constants. Likewise, the fine-tuning of the characteristics of complex molecules (e.g. DNA, RNA, haemoglobin) and biological systems (e.g. the switching on and off of genes) necessary for the origination and growth of complex organs in the embryological development of a huge variety of animals and insects must presuppose a God who fine-tuned these characteristics and their correlated interactions. If we further allow that the evolutionary process has produced human beings with a rationality and moral awareness that are not reducible to material processes or psychological and sociological conditioning, then we can say that human purposiveness presupposes a divinely ordained teleology that pervades all biological growth and evolution itself.

Bibliography

A. Chalmers, *The Works of William Paley* (London, 1819); M. L. Clark, *Paley: Evidences for the Man* (Toronto, 1974); D. L. Mahieu, *The Mind of William Paley: A Philosopher and His Age* (Lincoln, NE, 1976).

J. W. WARD

PANNENBERG, WOLFHART

Wolfhart Pannenberg is a German theologian with an ambiguous role in apologetics. On the one hand, he is a leading defender of classical Christian faith; on the other, he is not willing to relegate the task of arguing for the truth to apologetics as a separate field of theological/philosophical studies but regards it as the goal of all work in systematic *theology.

In Pannenberg's opinion, the truth of the Christian message cannot be presupposed, either on the basis of the Scripture-principle (which was destroyed by the Enlightenment) or by appeal to church authority or personal piety. The main goal of theological work is to establish the truth with the help of rational argumentation and appeal to *history. Pannenberg advocates the coherence theory of truth in which all parts need to be related to the whole; the triune God is the centre, and all other topics need to be related to him. Thus, Pannenberg has also engaged in dialogue extensively with both the natural and social sciences.

For him, theology is a public discipline and a scientific enterprise. This comes to focus also in his distinctive view of '*revelation as history'. God's self-revelation does not happen as divine speech, as in classical theology, but evolves out of historical happenings in universal history – rather than only in salvation history – and is open to all who 'have eyes to see'.

Theology and Christian faith cannot, however, reach final certitude until the eschaton, when the idea of the God of the Bible is shown to be the one that best illumines the world experience. How then can any Christian be certain of his or her faith? Here the central role of the resurrection of Christ comes to focus. If Christ's resurrection can be shown to be an historical event (and Pannenberg believes it can, following the criteria of critical historical inquiry, in this case based on the traditions of the empty tomb and eyewitness reports), then it can provide a 'proleptic' insight into the coming eschatological validation.

While evangelicals have hailed Pannenberg's defence of classical doctrines such as the resurrection and his appeal to the public *truth of Christian claims, they have also been troubled by his less than orthodox view of Scripture, underemphasis on the cross, and seemingly overrationalistic approach to theology and faith.

Bibliography

S. Grenz, *Reason and Hope: Systematic Theology of Wolfhart Pannenberg* (Oxford, 1990); W. Pannenberg, *Systematic Theology*, vol. 1 (Grand Rapids, 1991).

V.-M. KÄRKKÄINEN

PARABLES OF JESUS, see NEW TESTAMENT APOLOGETICS

PARADIGM

A paradigm case is one that is ideal or clear. So, for example, celery is a paradigm vegetable, whereas rhubarb is not, for it is sometimes considered a fruit. In philosophy, the appeal to a paradigm case to define a term is in contrast to a conceptual analysis of the term. In a conceptual analysis a term is defined by identifying the necessary and sufficient conditions for the term's application. A philosopher may forgo this method in defining consciousness, for example, and substitute for conceptual analysis some paradigm cases of consciousness (feeling pain, fearing a danger, thinking about mathematics). Definition by paradigm is often preferred when terms resist close analysis due to borderline cases, in which it is unclear whether the term applies.

Paradigm case arguments are sometimes brought against forms of scepticism. It has been argued that if the term 'knowledge' is meaningful, then there must be some genuine instances in which the term is properly applied. Sceptics who claim not to know anything must (if they are using the term 'know' meaningfully) grant that there are at least possible cases in which the term applies, and thus cases in which they or someone else can have *bona fide* knowledge. O. K. Bouwsma uses paradigm case arguments, as does Hilary Putnam. (For a critical discussion see D. W. Hamlyn.)

Another use of the term 'paradigm' stems directly from the now classic work, *The Structure of Scientific Revolutions* by Thomas Kuhn. In this book the history of *science is delimited as a series of revolutionary achievements, e.g. Aristotelian dynamics, Ptolemaic astronomy, Newton's *Principia* and *Opticks* and so on. Each achievement revolutionized the science of that era, displacing an older model of the cosmos and scientific practice. Older scientific models have been overcome because they were unable to solve problems which were found to be intractable. Classical physics, with its atomic theory, faced problems with photoelectric effects that could not be resolved in its own terms, whereas there was a resolution in the alternative terms and science introduced by Einstein. The new paradigm often involves a profound shift in the identity of key problems and modes of explanation. In Kuhn's scheme, shifts from one paradigm to another are not a matter of scientists re-describing and re-explaining facts that are neutral between dominant theories. Rather, it is a revolutionary matter by which one comes to see the world and one's science in radically different terms.

In a theological context, each use of the term 'paradigm' is possible. Kuhn's treatment of the history of science can be used to map shifts in religious perspectives (a move from atheism to theism or Hinduism to Buddhism). Some versions of an *ontological argument for God's existence may be articulated in terms of paradigm case arguments. Such arguments may also be used against the charge that theism is incoherent. (This objection is less common now than in the 1960s, but it still has some role in the philosophy of religion literature.) The fact that there is paradigmatic theistic *language places a burden of proof on critics who charge it with incoherence. Finally, some philosophical theologies prefer to demarcate divine attributes, not in terms of analyses, but in terms of ideal cases. (See Peter Geach's alternative, non-analytic approach to omnipotence.)

Bibliography

O. K. Bouwsma, *Philosophical Essays* (Lincoln, NE, 1965); P. Geach, 'Omnipotence', *Philosophy*, 43 (April, 1973), pp. 7–20; D. W. Hamlyn, *The Theory of Knowledge* (New York, 1970); H. Putnam, *Reason, Truth and History* (Cambridge, 1981).

C. TALIAFERRO

PARADOX

'Paradox' is derived from two words that literally mean *against opinion*. The *Oxford English Dictionary* (1989; vol. 11, p. 185) identifies several meanings for 'paradox'. It may refer to: (1) claims contrary to common opinion, often suggesting that the statement is incredible, absurd or fantastic, but sometimes with a favourable connotation as a correction for ignorance; (2) a statement that seems self-contradictory, but which is actually well founded; (3) a statement that involves a genuine *contradiction; (4) in *logic, a conclusion based on acceptable premises and sound *reasoning that nonetheless is self-contradictory. These inconsistent uses of the term pose practical problems for communication, as the intended meaning may not always be apparent.

For philosophers, paradox has a special place in the context of logic and the basic principles of thinking they have held for centuries. Three principles of thinking are commonly given: the principle of identity: if anything is A it is A; the principle of non-contradiction: nothing can be both A and not A; and the principle of excluded middle: anything must be either A or not A.

Although discussion of paradoxes can be traced back to Greek philosophy, serious concern about paradoxes emerged among philosophers only at the beginning of the twentieth century. During the period from 1897 to 1906, several important paradoxes were discovered. With the report of *Russell's paradox in 1902, it immediately became apparent that Russell's paradox posed significant challenges to mathematics and logic as then conceived.

Two major classes of paradoxes are: (1) set and property paradoxes, including logical paradoxes dealing with sets and cardinal numbers, such as Russell's paradox, and semantic paradoxes, such as the Liar paradox; and (2) epistemic paradoxes, including the Lottery, Preface, and Surprise Examination paradoxes.

The Liar paradox, attributed to Eubilides, asks whether the claim 'I am lying' is a true statement. The problem with this statement is that it is false if it is true, and true if it is false. It has been proposed that it is absurd, that it addresses a non-existent event, that it is self-destructive and self-defeating, and that it cannot be considered a *truth claim at all. Alternatively, we may consider the claim a meta-claim; that is, it involves statements at another level of language or analysis, rather than being a simple truth claim. Similar considerations apply to the other paradoxes.

Russell's paradox revolves around the question whether a set of all sets contains itself as a member. The Preface paradox reflects the common practice of text prefaces to state that any errors in the text are the responsibility of the author despite the author's belief that all errors were corrected in the editing process. Thus the book is (presumably) error-free but (presumably) contains errors due the author's shortcomings.

For *Kierkegaard, God, as 'Wholly Other', is a paradox. By this he means that God is beyond human reason and thus cannot be known by rational means.

*Kant proposed that the categories of reasoning cannot be applied to reality. For example, the paradox of First Cause exposes this antinomy. If we assume that everything must have a cause, then there must be a first cause. But the first cause, too, must have a cause. As a solution to this paradox, Christians have proposed that God is self-existent.

Similar to paradox, *dialectic* is a central feature of *Buddhism and *Hinduism. For these religious world-views, the quest for knowledge involves an ongoing process of thesis and antithesis from which emerges a synthesis of the competing views. In response to synthesis, a new antithesis emerges, and the dialectic process continues until particularity is superseded by the universal oneness of experiencing the unity of all that exists.

Closely related to the Buddhist position is the thesis that every argument must have its counter-argument. Every issue has two sides. This leads to the paradox of human reason, the notion that therefore we must *doubt the truth of all positions.

A striking twentieth-century development was that 'paradoxes have repeatedly been turned into theorems' (Craig [ed.], *Routledge Encyclopedia of Philosophy*, vol. 7, p. 219). According to Craig, the Zermelo-Fraenkel axioms regarding the hierarchical organization of sets have come to be generally accepted by mathematicians as the preferred solution to the logical paradoxes. But no generally accepted solution has yet emerged for the semantic paradoxes.

Another major development that occurred during the second half of the twentieth century was the development of *paraconsistent logic*. Paraconsistent logic at least partially rejects the principle of non-contradiction. Traditionally, it has been held that rejecting this principle requires accepting that everything is true. But paraconsistent logic contends that one can accept inconsistency without agreeing that everything must be accepted.

Paraconsistent logic allows for situations in which our information is inconsistent but we wish to draw conclusions nonetheless. Examples include court decisions when witnesses disagree, competing scientific theories (such as wave and corpuscular theories of light), and using inconsistent information in computerized databases. The term *dialetheia* is used in referring to such inconsistencies. It has been proposed that Russell's paradox, the Liar paradox and moral dilemmas are examples of dialetheias.

In 1998, Graham Priest proposed that paraconsistent logic violates the principle of non-contradiction, much as intuitionist logic violates the law of excluded middle. To address this problem it has been suggested that both the conflicting principles may be true 'in some possible world', or that they can be 'both true and false'. In summary, Priest concludes that the viability of paraconsistent logic presents a significant challenge to consistency as a cornerstone of contemporary philosophy.

Paradox has important practical implications and important implications for Christians. *Science involves several paradoxes – competing theories (above), for example. Another paradox is that of freedom and *determinism – or *causality and choice. Subjective/participant and objective/observer perspectives on the same events are also paradoxical; the actor observes his or her choices, while the observer attends to the events that cause those choices. Commonality and uniqueness form another paradox; each person or event shares both qualities in common with other persons or events and unique attributes. Finally, science uses measurement to discover the properties of events, yet measurement changes whatever we measure.

Christian beliefs involving paradox include (1) the belief that God is one yet God is three persons; (2) tensions between law and grace or *justice and mercy; (3) the view that humans make responsible choices for which God will judge them, yet God knows the end from the beginning; (4) the view that human knowing is fallen and imperfect, yet all stand guilty before God because they suppress the truth and practise *evil (Rom. 1:20–21). Also, Christians believe that God is utterly holy and cannot abide sin, thus his judgment rightly falls on all persons; yet in his mercy God himself paid the penalty for sin. It has been proposed that the Beatitudes are paradoxical, since Christians commonly profess to believe them yet seldom practise them.

Moreland and Craig describe two ethical paradoxes associated with ethical egoism: the paradox of *hedonism, and the paradox of egoism. Hedonism involves seeking one's own happiness. Yet it has been observed that those who seek happiness commonly fail to find it, while those who pursue other goals, such as justice or social service, often find personal happiness as 'a byproduct of a life well lived and of doing what is right' (*Philosophical Foundations*, p. 427). Similarly, ethical egoism involves looking out for one's own best interests. Moreland and Craig propose that a number of common virtues, such as self-sacrifice, altruism, deep love and genuine friendship, are incompatible with seeking one's own best interests. Serving others, for example, is not compatible with egoism, since it requires putting their interests above one's own. Thus, paradoxically, seeking one's own happiness or best interests ultimately fails as a fully satisfying approach to life.

Paradox also has important implications for the relationship between science and Christian beliefs. Many Christians view scientific and divine causality as paradoxical. In general terms, if we believe that the earth was created and is sustained moment by moment by God's divine power, then we may conclude that all events that happen on the earth are ultimately a result of God's action, and hence have underlying divine causality. At the same time, we can also talk meaningfully about natural (or 'creational') causes. Thus conception may be understood both as the result of the human acts that bring together egg and sperm, initiating a set of biological processes, and as a consequence of God's divine activity in creating and sustaining these processes.

This paradoxical view has important practical implications. For example, a Christian faced with cancer, diabetes or a broken bone may both pray for God's healing and seek medical or surgical intervention. When healing occurs, the Christian may respond with gratefulness both to God and to his or her physician for their respective roles in the process. An interesting anomaly, however, is that many Christians remain reluctant to seek medical or scientific help for schizophrenia or other mental disorders.

A special form of paradox sometimes accounts for the fact that science and Christian beliefs appear to be contradictory. Several possibilities must be considered when theological conclusions and scientific conclusions appear to be in conflict. First, our scientific conclusions may be wrong. Secondly, our theological conclusions may be wrong. Thirdly, and theoretically more troubling, both scientific and religious conclusions could be wrong (though we may never know it in this life). Finally, it is possible that neither the scientific principle nor the theological principle is wrong, although they appear to be in conflict. This could occur (1) in instances where their perspectives are different, (2) where different aspects of the same phenomenon are under consideration by the two disciplines, or (3) where each addresses one side of a paradox. For example, *theology often emphasizes the subject perspective and choice while science normally emphasizes the observer perspective and causality. Similarly, enduring earthly hardship for spiritual rewards, especially heavenly ones, does not seem to make sense psychologically to some, but the capacity for delayed gratification generally is considered a hallmark of psychosocial maturity.

In summary, the term 'paradox' is troublesome because it is used inconsistently. Paradoxes have become important in logic, mathematics, philosophy and science since the twentieth century. Paraconsistent logic has been proposed as one solution to some of the practical challenges, but has in turn posed a challenge to the fundamental principles of knowing commonly held in modern philosophy. Finally, paradox plays an important role in Christian beliefs and in the relationship between Christian beliefs and modern science.

Bibliography

E. Craig (ed.), *Routledge Encyclopedia of Philosophy* (New York, 1998); J. P. Moreland and W. L. Craig, *Philosophical Foundations for a Christian Worldview* (Downers Grove, 2003); J. A. Simpson and E. S. C. Weiner, *The Oxford English Dictionary* (Oxford, 2nd edn, 1989).

R. K. Bufford

PARMENIDES

Parmenides of Elea, born around 515 BC, is generally regarded as the most important and influential of the Presocratic philosophers. His most famous students are Melissus and Zeno.

Parmenides' philosophical views were articulated in a single hexameter poem, large fragments of which have been preserved through the writings of other philosophers. He held that whatever exists must be ungenerated, indestructible and otherwise wholly unchanging. His defence of this view rests on the idea that non-existence is unintelligible. It is impossible to talk about, or to think about, what does not exist, presumably because what does not exist is simply not available to be an object of thought or discourse. Thus, non-existence claims (e.g. 'Socrates does not exist') can never be true. But if non-existence claims cannot be true, then generation, destruction and other changes are impossible. If, for example, Socrates is generated, then there must have been a time at which 'Socrates does not exist' was true. Likewise if Socrates is destroyed. If Socrates undergoes change (say, from being short to being tall), then there must have been a time at which 'Socrates' tallness does not exist' was true. But, again, according to Parmenides, none of these sorts of non-existence claims can be true. So nothing can undergo generation, destruction or change. On the traditional interpretation of Parmenides' work, he also held that there exists exactly one thing. That view was clearly held by Parmenides' pupil Melissus, but many scholars now doubt that Parmenides himself held it.

Parmenides' views about *reality exerted a strong influence on subsequent Greek philosophy. Though few apart from Parmenides' immediate disciples were able to tolerate the idea that there exists exactly one thing, many philosophers – among them, Anaxagoras, Empedocles, Democritus and *Plato – accepted, in one way or another, Parmenides' view that fundamental reality must be ungenerated, indestructible and (at least intrinsically) unchanging. Parmenides is also sometimes credited with influencing Christian *theology, particularly in providing the most important motivation for the controversial view that God is absolutely simple and unchanging.

Bibliography

J. Barnes, *The Presocratic Philosophers* (London, 1993); P. Curd, *The Legacy of Parmenides* (Princeton, 1998); G. S. Kirk, J. E. Raven and M. Schofield (eds.), *The Presocratic Philosophers* (Cambridge, [2]1990); A. A. Long, *The Cambridge Companion to Early Greek Philosophy* (Cambridge, 1999).

M. C. REA

PASCAL, BLAISE

Blaise Pascal (1623–62) was an eminently brilliant French mathematician, scientist, polemicist and philosopher, whose contribution to apologetics is often sadly underrated for several reasons. Pascal did not leave us a finished system of thought. He never completed his proposed apologetics book, *An Apology for the Christian Religion*, although he left nearly a thousand fragments sketching the approach he would take. This collection, *Pensées* (or Thoughts), was published posthumously and is fragmentary and susceptible to several interpretations. The fear of misinterpretation has deterred some from mining the treasury for apologetic gold. Some have judged Pascal to be a fideist, who disparaged rationality as an aid to Christian faith. Pascal's famous line, 'The heart has reasons which reason knows nothing of', is often taken to dismiss any objective apologetic. But Pascal was speaking here of intuition as a way of knowing; he was not rejecting reason as a means of coming to know religious truth.

One should be undaunted by these concerns because the *Pensées*, though unfinished and sometimes enigmatic, can be deciphered and profitably applied to contemporary apologetics. A close reading of the *Pensées* and Pascal's other work does not reveal a fideistic approach, but a rich and multifaceted apologetic method that attempts to divide clearly what can be known through human philosophizing from knowledge that requires divine *revelation.

Pascal's rejection of *natural theology, which he shares with *Kierkegaard, leads some to think he is rejecting apologetics altogether. Pascal broke from the tradition of medieval philosophy in refusing to first argue for a generic *theism on the basis of cosmological and design arguments before making the case for Christianity proper through historical evidences. He made much of the cognitive defacement wrought by the fall, which cripples the creature's ability to reason his way to the Creator. In the problematic prologue to the famous wager argument in the *Pensées*, Pascal seems to say that it is impossible for a finite being to prove the existence of an infinite being. In other places, Pascal does not question the intellectual efficacy of these proofs (to establish *monotheism) as much as he does their spiritual adequacy. Fearing deism, Pascal believed that 'metaphysical proofs' only establish 'the God of the philosophers' and not the God of biblical revelation, with its insistence on original sin, the incarnation, salvation and the need to 'seek God'. Even a successful natural theology would be defective in several ways. First, Pascal claims the Bible itself offers no specimen of natural theology, so it is not biblically warranted for us to do so. Secondly, the God of natural theology is abstract and abstruse, not personal and incarnational. Thirdly, success at natural theology would engender intellectual pride, which is antithetical to humble faith.

None of these arguments against natural theology seem decisive, although they may remind us of its limits. If an apologist over-emphasizes the *noetic effects of sin, he or she runs the risk of abolishing apologetics. The effect of sin on the mind may make the task of natural theology more difficult and its rewards less than impeccable, but it does not rule out the enterprise *a priori*. The question of whether a finite being can give good arguments for the reality of an infinite being needs to be tested by appeal to developed arguments, not by a mere assertion to the contrary. Pascal's concerns about the 'thinness' of natural theology can be rebutted by arguing that a robust monotheism opens the door to the strong possibility of Christian theism. The philosophical rehabilitation of theistic arguments by Christian philosophers who use them for overtly apologetic purposes (as do William Lane Craig and J. P. Moreland) further counts against Pascal's worries.

Despite Pascal's disavowal of natural theology, he articulates a fertile apologetic approach consisting of several distinctive features. Pascal's apologetic method seems to be neither presuppositional, inductive or deductive. Instead, he builds a cumulative case of many strands and argues that the Christian account or explanation of *reality is superior to that of contemporary alternatives, such as *Judaism, radical scepticism, deism, *atheism, scientism and *Islam. Since Pascal did not complete his apologetic project, this cumulative and comparative method was not fully applied, but the rudiments remain and may be built upon by apologists today. Pascal used several arguments from traditional apologetics, such as the argument from the Bible's predicative prophecy fulfilled in the *history of the Jews and supremely in *Jesus as the promised Messiah, the salutary effects of Christianity on the pagan nations, the uniqueness of the Jews, the credibility of the resurrection and the evidence from *religious experience. From the latter comes the oft-quoted notion of 'the God-shaped vacuum, which only God can fill'. These are Pascal's specific words, 'What else does this craving, and this helplessness, proclaim but that there was once in man a true happiness, of which all that now remains is the empty print and trace? This he tries in vain to fill with everything around him, seeking in things that are not there the help he cannot find in those that are, though none can help, since this infinite abyss can be filled only with an infinite and immutable object; in other words by God himself.'

Pascal's most discussed contribution to apologetics arguably lies in his anthropological argument, although he is most famous for 'Pascal's wager'. The former has not received the careful attention it deserves and the latter is typically abstracted from the rest of Pascal's apologetic approach, thus eviscerating its force. Both errors unjustly hamstring Pascal's prowess as a philosopher and apologist.

Pascal registered uncommon insights into the vicissitudes of the human condition – its misery and its greatness, its genius and its stupidity, its beauty and its ugliness, its knowledge and its ignorance. He captures this in a famous aphorism, 'What sort of freak then is man! How novel, how monstrous, how chaotic, how paradoxical, how prodigious! Judge of all things, feeble earthworm, repository of truth, sink of doubt and error, the glory and refuse of the universe!'

These 'contrarities', he thought, cried out for an explanation. We are neither angels nor beasts, nor can we make much sense of ourselves when left to our own unaided rational resources. Pascal says, 'Man's greatness and wretchedness are so evident that the true religion must necessarily teach us that there is in man some great principle of greatness and some great principle of wretchedness,' and that 'All these examples of wretchedness prove his greatness. It is the wretchedness of a great lord, the wretchedness of a dispossessed king'. After surveying the human scene and fostering a desire to resolve this conundrum, Pascal argues that the source of greatness is our divine origin. The root of wretchedness is the fall of humans into sin and its consequences. This explanation, he claims, is unique to Christianity, and it illuminates the human horizon with a divine glow otherwise unavailable. Other world-views either exalt greatness at the expense of wretchedness (the pantheism of the Stoics) or exalt wretchedness at the expense of greatness (the scepticism of Montaigne). Pascal prefers this anthropological argument to natural theology because it trades on distinctively Christian – and not merely theistic – assumptions, such as the doctrines of humans created in God's image and original sin.

Furthermore, if humanity languishes east of Eden, its restoration is found only in Jesus Christ, the divine mediator. There is a natural and strong link between the anthropological argument and the message of salvation. Fallen beings need a redeemer, and Scripture offers us Jesus Christ as the Redeemer. As Pascal put it, 'Not only do we only know God through Jesus Christ, but we only know ourselves through Jesus Christ; we only know life and death through Jesus Christ.'

Pascal realized that even his best arguments may not convince a hardened sceptic. Therefore, he devised an approach that would encourage belief on the basis of prudential considerations, not merely by appeal to evidence. This is found primarily in his wager fragment, which is full of interpretive and philosophical challenges. The wager is not a theistic argument, but a proposal for the development of rational religious belief. It is divided into four main sections: a prologue stipulating that proof of God is not available; an explanation of the risks and rewards of belief or unbelief in God (*heaven or the loss of it); encouragement to engage in religious practices in the hope that one will become a believer; and a coda where the apologist speaks of the theological seriousness of his argument. There is a flow to the argument, however many mysteries remain within it. Pascal claims that even though philosophical proof for God is not possible, one should believe in God since, if God exists, one would be far better off believing in him (since this is a necessary condition for heaven) than disbelieving in him (which means the loss of heaven). In light of this, Pascal urges his interlocutor to engage in a devotional experiment that may generate theist belief and salvation.

Any fruitful use of the wager should come to terms with four recurring criticisms. First, if the prologue means that we can know nothing of God, all bets are off, since we would not know anything about the God on whom we are urged to wager. This understanding appears forced. Read in the light of the rest of the *Pensées*, the prologue seems to be ruling out philosophical *certainty about God's existence *based on theoretical reason*, not any possible knowledge of God. Secondly, the wager appeals to crass self-interest and is not genuine Christian faith. Pascal, however, did not see the wager as the last word in producing faith but rather as encouraging the unbeliever to pursue faith based on prudential considerations. A more mature faith, as Pascal knew, moves beyond this. Jesus himself was not above warning people of the realities of heaven and *hell (Matt. 25:31–46). Thirdly, Pascal wrongly limited the choices to the Christian God, *agnosticism or atheism. There are many other religions to consider. However, Pascal gives arguments for the rationality of Christianity throughout the *Pensées*. These arguments, if successful (and they may be successful without being 'proofs'), count against the claims of other world-views. A contemporary Pascalian can further consider the evidential and prudential pertinence of religions Pascal did not specifically address, such as *Hinduism and *Buddhism. Fourthly, the wager recommends mere religious brainwashing that lacks any positive epistemic status. But the wager speaks of the evidence of 'Scripture and the rest' and can be combined with Pascal's other apologetic arguments. The religious experiment need not be viewed as acquiring belief through mere habituation. Certain patterns of action and reflection may open one up to new truths not otherwise knowable. This is probably what Pascal had in mind.

Bibliography

D. Groothuis, *On Pascal* (Belmont, 2003); P. Kreeft, *Christianity for Modern Pagans: Pascal's Pensées Edited, Outlined and Explained* (St Louis, 1993); T. Morris, *Making Sense of It All: Pascal and the Meaning of Life* (Grand Rapids, 1992); B. Pascal, *Pensées*, trans. A. J. Krailsheimer (New York, 1966).

D. GROOTHUIS

PASSOLINI, PIER PAOLO

Passolini (1922–75) is the kind of film director that stirs deep emotion in people, from humour to rage to revulsion. A self-avowed Marxist and open homosexual, Passolini often used his films as a vehicle for his socio-political views. While his best-known films are his bawdy, riotous retellings of classic literature, one stands apart: *The Gospel According to St. Matthew* (1964). While one might expect Passolini's treatment of the life of Christ to be politically charged or somehow deviant, this film is remarkably understated and even reverent. Rather than well-known, professional actors, Passolini populated his production with local Italian citizens (including his own mother), a choice that adds a raw, realistic tenor to the film. Judas is not easily singled out from among the disciples as in so many other adaptations, where his glowering face or sinister appearance readily gives him away. Even *Jesus himself is not a striking, doe-eyed model but rather a gruff pedestrian character.

Many film fans who scorn Hollywood productions of the life of Christ consider this film to be in an altogether different category. Most of the dialogue and plot are drawn, as the title suggests, from Matthew's account rather than a Hollywood script doctor. The scenery, costumes and cinematography (shot in stark black and white) are so unlike most Hollywood productions that the film cannot help but seem a fresh and refreshing work. This presentation of the life of Christ, especially coming from such a controversial director, might attract an audience unlikely to sit through a conventional version.

Bibliography

P. Rumble, *Pier Paolo Pasolini: Contemporary Perspectives* (Toronto, 1994); M. S. Viano, *A Certain Realism: Toward a Use of Pasolini's Film Theory and Practice* (Berkeley, 1993).

D. S. RUSSELL

PAUL, APOLOGETICS OF, see NEW
TESTAMENT APOLOGETICS

PENTATEUCH, THE AUTHORSHIP OF THE

Context

For most of Christian history it was taken for granted that Moses wrote the Pentateuch, and this view, shared by Jewish writers, finds expression in the NT in texts such as John 5:46. By and large, early opponents of Christianity did not challenge this assumption, focusing their fire on ideas and laws in the Pentateuch that they found distasteful.

From the seventeenth century onwards, however, the picture changes. The Reformation had made the truth and *authority of the Bible central to Christian thinking, so it was almost inevitable that the *Enlightenment, which insisted on the supremacy of human reason and denied that God intervened in the world by miracle or revelation, would challenge the truth of Scripture. Though most effort was dedicated to challenging the reliability of the NT, the OT also came under criticism. Writers like *Spinoza, Hobbes and the English deists argued that the Pentateuch was written much later than Moses and, therefore, that its history was untrustworthy and so its theological ideas were not to be trusted either.

The debate about the composition of the Pentateuch that was kindled in the Enlightenment has continued to rage in scholarly circles ever since. It would be untrue to claim that all those who have accepted that the Pentateuch was not written by Moses also deny its inspiration and authority. Many believing scholars have come to hold that the Pentateuch was at least edited a long time after Moses and that this does not compromise the theological or moral claims of the Pentateuch. Nevertheless, even today apologetic concerns are often not far below the surface of the current debates. Conservatives, whether Christians or Jews, tend to advocate an early date for the composition of the Pentateuch, associating it with Moses as closely as possible and believing that this enhances the credibility of its *theology. Radicals, on the other hand, argue for a date in the post-exilic era, about a millennium after Moses (if he existed at all, which they doubt!).

The traditional view – Mosaic authorship

Moses is clearly the central human figure in the Pentateuch. He does not appear in Genesis, which forms an introduction to the books which follow, but he dominates Exodus to Deuteronomy. Exodus opens with the story of his birth, and Deuteronomy closes with the account of his death and burial. To modern readers this looks more like a biography than an autobiography, but as ancient writers could write about themselves in the third person, this does not rule out Moses as the chief author. Indeed, early Jewish writers held that he even wrote the account of his own death, surely not impossible if he was the greatest of the prophets.

Many passages in the Pentateuch seem to be intimately tied to the person of Moses. He is the one who ascends Mount Sinai to be given the Ten Commandments and to be told all the laws about sacrifice and everyday life with which the Pentateuch is filled. Time and again laws are introduced with a remark like 'The LORD called [said] to Moses' (e.g. Lev. 1:1). It is therefore natural to conclude that Moses probably put this material into writing. This is expressly stated to be the case in the book of Deuteronomy. Chapters 1 – 30 consist of three farewell speeches by Moses to the people of Israel and then 31:9 says, 'Moses wrote down this law and gave it to the priests'. It is therefore easy to infer that the bulk of Exodus to Deuteronomy was written by Moses himself, and since Genesis introduces the later books, it too presumably was at least edited, if not composed, by him.

The main critical view

From the late nineteenth century a quite different view of the origins of the Pentateuch came to dominate biblical scholarship, the so-called documentary theory. Its dominance is largely the achievement of J. *Wellhausen, whose brilliant synthesis of earlier scholars' ideas in his *Prolegomena to the History of Israel* (1878) captivated his contemporaries. Wellhausen argued that the Pentateuch is made up of four major sources, (J, E, P, and D). These four sources originated at different times and in different places, but one by one they were woven together until the present Pentateuch was produced.

J, the Yahwistic source, is characterized by its use of God's name Yahweh, usually rendered the LORD. It makes up about half the stories in Genesis and small parts of the narrative sections in Exodus and Numbers. According to Wellhausen it originated in the southern kingdom of Judah in the ninth century, but many later writers prefer to suppose it was composed about a century earlier in the days of David or Solomon.

E, the Elohistic source, is characterized by avoiding the use of God's name Yahweh, but simply speaking of God (Heb. *elohim*). It makes up about a third of the stories in Genesis and small parts of the narratives in Exodus and Numbers. Wellhausen argued it originated in the northern kingdom of Israel in the eighth century, but later scholars prefer to put its composition about 100 years earlier. Towards the end of the eighth century, soon after the fall of Samaria, somebody brought this E document to Jerusalem, which led to it being added to the J source. This created the Yehowistic (JE) document.

Next to be produced was the Deuteronomistic source (D). As the name suggests it is much the same as the book of Deuteronomy, or at least the legal parts of it. It was written to promote or justify the reforms of King Josiah, which took place in Jerusalem in 622 BC, as described in 2 Kgs 22 – 23. This D source was subsequently tacked on to the end of the JE document, perhaps in the sixth century.

Finally came the Priestly source (P) written as its name implies to deal with issues dear to priests, e.g. the Sabbath (Gen. 1), circumcision (Gen. 17), genealogies and laws about ritual, especially sacrifice. It comprises much of Exod. 25 – Num. 36 and is thought to have been drafted by priests in exile or soon after their return, i.e. about 500 BC. Some time afterward, the P source was amalgamated with the earlier JED material and so the present Pentateuch emerged, perhaps in Ezra's day i.e. in the mid-fifth century.

The argument in favour of this theory is complex and develops in two stages. First, Wellhausen split the material into sources using various criteria, such as different terms for God and other things, apparent contradictions and duplications (e.g. Gen. 12:10–20 versus Gen. 20), and variations in style and genre (e.g. genealogies versus narrative). Then, having determined that there were different sources, he attempted to correlate them with different stages in the development of Israel's

religion. He tied D to Josiah's reform and tried to show that JE corresponded to religious practice before Josiah, and P to practice in the post-exilic era.

The documentary hypothesis implies that the present Pentateuch gives a misleading account of the period it purports to describe and projects into the past conditions of much later times. This did not trouble sceptics like Wellhausen. More devout scholars tended to appeal to the doctrine of inspiration as a guarantee of the authority, if not the historicity, of the Pentateuch. But the mid-twentieth century saw an attempt by mainstream scholars such as Noth and von Rad in Germany and Albright and others in the USA to show that although the written sources of the Pentateuch may be late, they are in fact based on reliable oral tradition, so that the Pentateuch does not give such a distorted picture of the past as the original documentary hypothesis implied.

Recent developments

Until the 1970s the documentary hypothesis wedded to a conservative view of oral tradition remained one of the 'assured' results of *biblical criticism. But since then the scholarly consensus has collapsed, even if it is still widely taught, because there is no agreed alternative. The dating of the sources has been challenged. Critical Jewish scholars hold that the P source is quite early, certainly not exilic. Radical European scholars maintain that the J source is very late. Others challenge the very principle of source analysis: Whybray has argued that the principles underlying the analysis are illogical and self-contradictory. Few today support the existence of the E source. Uncertainty reigns, as the world of biblical scholarship waits to see whether an agreed alternative theory of pentateuchal authorship will emerge.

Because the modern arcane debate has led to no consensus about the composition of the Pentateuch, the issue of authorship is of less concern to apologetics today than many others raised by these books, such as their relationship to *science and their stance on ethical issues.

Bibliography

G. J. Wenham, 'Pondering the Pentateuch: The Search for a New Paradigm', in D. W. Baker and B. T. Arnold (eds.), *The Face of Old Testament Studies* (Leicester and Grand Rapids, 1999), pp. 116–144; R. N. Whybray,

Introduction to the Pentateuch (Grand Rapids, 1995).

G. J. WENHAM

PENTECOSTAL CHRISTIANITY, see CHRISTIANITY, PENTECOSTAL AND CHARISMATIC

PERCY, WALKER

Walker Percy (1916–90), American novelist, was born in Birmingham, Alabama. Percy was orphaned at the age of fifteen, and adopted by William A. Percy, a close relative and noted Southern essayist. In 1937 he graduated from the University of North Carolina and four years later from the medical school at Columbia University, where his primary interests were pathology and psychoanalysis. In 1942 he contracted tuberculosis as a result of performing autopsies, and this resulted in a two-year recuperation. During this period he read both novels and philosophy, which led to the abandonment of his medical career for writing.

Percy's novels are heavily influenced by Roman Catholicism (see *Christianity, Roman Catholic), to which he converted in 1946, and existential philosophers, especially Søren *Kierkegaard. Because he viewed himself as writing in 'the Century of Death' (Hobson, p. 172), his heroes are journeying and searching for meaning in a world that is often meaningless and devalued. Moreover, he wrote to catch the attention of Americans' acceptance of *boredom and isolation as the norm. Thus, Percy, the writer and physician, 'diagnoses the spiritual illnesses of Western man by examining and dramatizing the illness of his hero' (Hobson, p. 163). He suggests his readers can rise above the mundane and acquire a fresh view of the world, which results in 'celebrating the ordinary, and transforming it from the merely boring to the mysterious' (Hobson, p. 13). While both *science, as a pseudo-religion, and Christianity have seemingly failed modern people in their quest for this elusive goal, Percy unashamedly advocates individual will, human *community and divine grace as key factors needed for the quest.

In addition to his six novels, Percy produced two volumes of essays. The first, *The Message in the Bottle* (1975), consists of writings focusing on alienation, faith and *language. While these essays are of a technical nature, 'The Message in the Bottle', 'The Man on the Train', and 'Notes for a Novel about the End of the World' are intended for the general and educated reader. The second set of essays, *Lost in the Cosmos* (1983), is a collection of popular writings on linguistic, philosophical and psychological themes.

Bibliography

L. Hobson, *Understanding Walker Percy* (Columbia, 1988); W. Percy, *The Moviegoer* (New York, 1998); *Lancelot* (New York, 1999); *The Last Gentleman* (New York, 1999); *Love in the Ruins* (New York, 1999); *The Second Coming* (New York, 1999); *The Thanatos Syndrome* (New York, 1999).

J. E. MᶜDERMOND

PERSON AND PERSONALITY

Humans beings have traditionally been given a place of incontestable honour at the centre of the cosmos. This view has been challenged by scientific discovery, first by Copernicus (who demonstrated that our planet and, thus, we who inhabit the earth, are not the centre around which the universe pivots) and then by Darwin (whose evolutionary biology located *homo sapiens* within the world of animals, with a genetic make-up that strongly resembles the creatures around us; e.g. at the level of genetic sequences, humans and chimpanzees are nearly 99% identical). The most recent challenge has come from neuroscience, with its tightening of the mind–brain link. Human attitudes and behaviour are increasingly regarded as the outcome of the complex and generative interplay of genetic code and human, especially relational, experiences.

The resulting portrait of human personhood impinges on Christian *theology especially at two points. First, from a neuroscientific perspective, it is unnecessary to postulate a metaphysical entity, such as a soul or spirit, to account for human capacities and distinctives. Secondly, at the level of molecular biology, any meaningful distinction between human beings and other animals is impossible to maintain. These conclusions raise potentially unsettling questions. In the absence of a 'soul', what is it that makes us authentically 'human'? Without a soul or spirit, do we not leave our humanity to be explained exclusively and exhaustively –

indeed, reductively – with recourse to genetics or neuronal activity? If the line between humanity and other living things cannot be drawn decisively through the discrete existence of the human soul, how is it possible to speak of the sacred worth of human beings? If we embrace some form of physicalism (i.e. if the person is a unified whole, without a separate, nonphysical 'soul'), then what of free will? Given the self-apparent finality of death for the physical body, without recourse to a separate entity or personal 'essence' that survives death, how can we maintain a reasonable doctrine of the afterlife? If personhood, our 'being someone', is a biologically anchored process, what happens to our traditional doctrines not only of humanity, but also of the church, of salvation and of mission? What does it mean to affirm that we are bearers of 'the divine image'? Thomas Metzinger observes, 'Implicit in all these new data on the genetic, evolutionary, or neurocomputational roots of conscious human existence is a radically new understanding of what it *means* to be human.'

Contemporary Christians are not of one mind with regard to the question of the make-up of the human person. In the philosophical literature, among the current options are those for which it is unnecessary to postulate a soul or spirit, to account for human capacities and distinctives, including, e.g., *nonreductive physicalism* (that human capacities and distinctives are explainable, in part, as brain functions, but their full explanation requires attention to human social relations, to cultural factors, and, most importantly, to God's action in our lives); *emergent *monism* (that what emerges in the case of humans from the one, material substance is a psychosomatic unity capable of mental and physical activity); and *constitutional monism* (that human persons are constituted by their bodies without being identical with the bodies that constitute them).

Those for which a soul or spirit remains central include, e.g., *emergent dualism* (that the mind/soul is both generated and sustained, as a discrete substance, by the biological organism, and its activities are subserved and enabled by the functioning of the organism); and *substance dualism* (that a human person consists of a body somehow joined to a soul, which is the real self, is fundamentally different from the body, and bears no necessary relation to it).

Although lacking the semantic sophistication of the philosophers, neuroscientists, Christians among them, almost exclusively speak of human life in terms of embodiment as physical persons. Typically, they do this on account of the complex and subtle dependencies of our thought processes on the state and functioning of our brains without any need to appeal to an immaterial soul. In championing the notion of psychosomatic unity, however, they are careful to avoid the reduction of e.g. mental states or spiritual awareness to neuronal interaction. As the debate matures, it becomes increasingly clear that such traditional Christian beliefs as creation 'in the image of God', human agency and responsibility, and life after death are not necessarily compromised, and may even be enhanced, by some physicalist positions. Indeed it is increasingly transparent that our most pressing task is not to 'defend the soul' but to put forward a constructive view of the human person grounded in Scripture.

One looks in vain to the OT and NT for speculative portraits of human nature, though the question 'What is humanity?' does appear in Pss. 8 (cited in Heb. 2:6–9); 144; and Job 7:17–18. Moreover, we find important orientation in Gen. 1:27–31 and 2:4–25.

In the biblical texts humans are 'defined' not in essential but in relational terms, i.e. unlike the philosophical stream running from *Plato and *Aristotle to *Descartes and into the present, Scripture is not concerned with defining human life with reference to its absolutely necessary 'parts', and especially not with explaining in what we may regard as a philosophically satisfying way the nature of physical existence in life, death and afterlife. Nevertheless, Scripture is profound in its presentation of the human person fundamentally in relational terms, and its assessment of the human being as genuinely human and alive only within the family of humans brought into being by Yahweh and in relation to the God who gives life-giving breath.

With respect to the rest of creation, Scripture affirms of humanity both similarity and difference. Humans are clearly like other living things in being created by God and thus in their relation to him and in their having been formed from the stuff of the earth. It follows from this that the life and destiny of human beings are necessarily bound up with those of all of creation (cf. Rom. 8:19–23). Additionally, although vegetation is for both humans and animals (Gen. 1:30), and animals share with humans the command to reproduce, increase, and fill the seas and the earth (Gen. 1:22), we find nothing in Scripture that would provide for the human exploitation of nature. The additional vocation given humanity, 'to subdue' the earth and 'to have dominion' over it (Gen. 1:26, 28), must be understood in the context of the order set forth in the creation account, a narrative in which there is no hint of either chaos or combat. True, the creation account imbues humanity with royal identity and task, but this is a nobility granted without conquest; its essence is realized in coexistence with, and cultivation of, all of life in the land.

Humans, then, are *like* the nonhuman creation, but also *unlike* it in being made in God's image. Humanity is thus defined in relation to God in terms of both similarity and difference: humanity is in some sense 'like' God, but is itself not divine. Humanity thus stands in an ambivalent position – living in solidarity with the rest of the created order and yet distinct from it on account of its unique role as the bearer of the divine image, called to a particular and crucial relationship with Yahweh and yet not divine. This phrase, 'image of God', has been the focus of diverse interpretations among Jews and Christians, ranging widely from some physical characteristic of humans (such as standing upright) to a way of knowing (especially the human capacity to know God) and so on. Whatever else may be said, God's words transparently affirm the creation of the human family in its relation to himself, as his counterpart, so that the nature of humanity derives from the human family's relatedness to God. The concept of 'image of God' takes as its ground and focus the graciousness of God's own covenantal relations with humanity and the rest of creation. The distinguishing mark of *human* existence when compared with other creatures is thus the whole of human existence (and not some 'part' of the individual). Humanity is given the divine mandate to reflect God's own covenant love in relation with God, within the covenant *community of all humanity, and with all that God has created.

Interestingly, against the tide of modern thought concerning the nature of the human self (with its emphasis on self-sufficiency, self-determination, self-referentiality and self-legislation), the natural *sciences have begun to emphasize, along with the Scriptures, *both* the sameness of humanity in relation to other animals (evolutionary biology) *and* humanity's distinguishing characteristics, the latter focusing above all on the human capacity for and experience of rich, textured forms of personal relatedness.

The second emphasis of the biblical witness affirms the human being as a bio-psycho-spiritual unity. Scripture does not locate this singularity in the human possession of a 'soul'. Indeed, within the OT, 'soul' (*nephesh*) refers to life and vitality, not life in general but as instantiated in human persons and animals. It is not a thing to have but a way to be. To speak of loving God with all of one's 'soul' (Deut. 6:5), then, is to elevate the intensity of involvement of the entirety of one's being. The creation account employs the term 'soul' (*nephesh*) with reference to both the human being and to 'every beast of the earth', 'every bird of the air' and 'everything that creeps on the earth', i.e. to everything 'in which there is life (*nephesh*)' (Gen. 1:30; author's translation). This alone demonstrates that 'soul' is not for the Genesis story a unique characteristic of the human person, and Gen. 2:7 might best be translated, 'The LORD God formed the human being of the dust of the ground, breathed into his nostrils the breath of life, and the human being became fully alive [*nephesh*]'.

Consequently, it is inappropriate to think of the Christian mission as 'saving souls' when this is taken as anything other than 'human recovery'. Premium must be placed on the health and integrity of human community, Christian discipleship must be understood in terms of fully embodied life (as opposed to a narrow focus on one's interior life as though it were the locus of the 'true self'), and such Christian practices as pastoral care, *preaching, discipling and spiritual formation must be cast so as to account for persons as bio-psycho-spiritual unities.

Bibliography

W. S. Brown *et al.* (eds.), *Whatever Happened to the Soul? Scientific and Theological Portraits of Human Nature* (Minneapolis, 1998); R. A. Di Vito, 'Old Testament Anthropology and the Construction of Personal Identity', *Catholic Biblical Quarterly*, 61 (1999), pp. 217–238; J. B. Green (ed.), *What about the Soul? Neuroscience and Christian*

Anthropology (Nashville, 2004); J. B. Green and S. L. Palmer (eds.), *In Search of the Soul: Four Views of the Mind–Body Problem* (Downers Grove, 2004); N. H. Gregersen *et al.* (eds.), *The Human Person in Science and Theology* (Grand Rapids, 2000); P. Hefner, *The Human Factor* (Minneapolis, 1993); M. A. Jeeves (ed.), *From Cells to Souls: Changing Portraits of Human Nature* (Grand Rapids, 2004); T. Metzinger, 'Consciousness Research at the End of the Twentieth Century', in T. Metzinger (ed.), *Neural Correlates of Consciousness: Empirical and Conceptual Questions* (Cambridge, MA, 2000), pp. 1–12; R. J. Russell et al. (eds.), *Neuroscience and the Person* (Vatican City State/Berkeley, 1999); C. Schwöbel and C. E. Gunton (eds.), *Persons Divine and Human* (Edinburgh, 1991); F. L. Shults, *Reforming Theological Anthropology* (Grand Rapids, 2003); C. Taylor, *Sources of the Self: The Making of Modern Identity* (Cambridge, MA, 1989).

J. B. GREEN

PETER ABELARD, see ABELARD, PETER
PETER LOMBARD, see LOMBARD, PETER

PHENOMENALISM

Phenomenalism is the view that all that can be known for certain is the content of one's own experience, or possible experience. However, a phenomenalist need not be committed to the additional thesis that there are no physical objects, only that if there are, they are constituted by sense data. This distinction is important, and needs some unpacking. There is a difference between realist sense data theories and phenomenalist theories of sense data. Sense data theories of perception are typically realist, i.e. they claim that the sense data that a particular person (call him Gary) perceives corresponds to some real physical object that exists irrespective of whether Gary senses it or not. So, if Gary sees a red ball, the sense data of redness and roundness pertain to some physical object external to Gary, that causes Gary to have the sensations of redness or roundness that he does have. However, phenomenalist theories of sense data do not claim that Gary experiences an object that *causes* him to have certain sensations of redness or roundness. Instead, all it claims

is that physical objects just are collections of sense data. Gary's ball is just a collection of the properties of redness, roundness and so on. There is nothing more than this sum of sense data that generates these sensations in Gary's brain.

Bishop *Berkeley is usually credited with being a phenomenalist (Jonathan *Edwards was another, who came to conclusions remarkably similar to those of Berkeley). He held to a sense-datum version of phenomenalism as a constituent of his *idealism. His view was that objects are constructed out of the data of sensory experience, and such objects consist in the properties that make up data of a particular sensory experience. They are 'given'. To return to the red ball: it produces the sensory data of redness and roundness, and has a certain weight and smoothness on touching it. But is there more to the ball than my immediate sensory experience of it? Sense-datum phenomenalists seem to think not. Objects of perception are made up, like an onion, of layers of sense data that I receive. But there is nothing more to the onion than its various layers. Nor is there more to the object of perception than the different sorts of sense data I have of it. This view sits within Berkeley's idealism, which states that objects 'out there' are really only ideal, being held in being by the divine mind.

Recent philosophers who have defended a version of phenomenalism without this idealist component include C. I. Lewis and A. J. Ayer. The young Ayer of *Language, Truth and Logic* believed that Berkeley had rightly hit upon the fact that 'material things must be definable in terms of sense-contents', but he thought Berkeley was wrong to define this in terms of ideas alone. Instead, Ayer maintained that though there are material objects, such objects can only ever be verified in terms of certain sense data by which we are able to experience them. Ayer developed his phenomenalist theory against the metaphysically realist conception of physical objects. According to Ayer, the problem with the realist view of perception was that it postulated objects that are unobservable entities and, therefore, unverifiable entities. Take, for example, the fossilized remains of an unknown dinosaur that lies buried under the seas of some continental shelf, never to be found. Realists claim that there are many such objects, which exist irrespective of whether they are ever discovered or experienced by human beings. For phenomenalists like Ayer, such sentiments are literally meaningless, since they are unverifiable. And until and unless such an object can be verified through sense data, any sentence that claims to state facts about such an object has no meaning. (It is worth noting that Ayer later revised his views, rejecting the phenomenalism he had previously defended.)

The philosophical problems with phenomenalism are commonly thought to be fatal to both its theistic and atheological varieties. Here are several common objections. First, there are difficulties with trying to express things about unperceived objects purely in terms of sense experience. How can a person express abstract truths like 1 + 1 = 2 in a *purely* sensory way? What about expressions of time and place? How can one express the possible existence of a red ball in the next room at noon today in ways that will distinguish it from other, similar rooms and similar red balls at similar times?

Secondly, for phenomenalism to succeed, it must be able to show that the existence of a physical object like a red ball is a sufficient condition for the occurrence, in the right circumstances, of certain sense data such as 'redness' or 'roundness', or whatever. Moreover, where there are certain sense data ('redness', 'roundness' and so on), this must be a sufficient condition for the existence of a physical object. But phenomenalism does not appear to be equipped to satisfy either of these conditions. For although it might be that Gary is pretty sure there is a red ball before his eyes, there is no logical reason why Gary might not be being deceived. He could be hallucinating, for instance, or the ball could be an illusion of some kind. Or it might be that, when put in a certain situation, he is unable to see the ball though it is present, due to some psychological problem or malfunction. Finally, it might be that Gary's attention is drawn elsewhere, so that he fails to pick out the existence of the data of the ball in his immediate vicinity. So phenomenalists cannot rule out the logical possibility that their senses are deceiving them. Nor can they rule out the possibility that they have not picked up on the existence of something, though it is there before them. Thus, phenomenalism cannot meet the requirements of the two conditions outlined.

Thirdly, there is the Wittgensteinian objection about private *language. Language, according to *Wittgenstein, depends upon rules and conventions understood through use in a particular *community. If I say, 'Here is a red ball', this is meaningful where other people speak my language and share the same understanding of the words in the sentence and the object it refers to, the ball. However, this is not possible for phenomenalists. Their perception of a red ball and its expression in the sentence 'Here is a red ball' cannot be checked against other such expressions, since phenomenalists are insulated from any other person's experience. They cannot ever know whether what they perceive as a red ball is the same as another person's experience of a red ball, since there is no neutral vantage point from which phenomenalists can check their experience. It is rather like having to check the time of one's watch without having any means of recourse to another timekeeper to check it against. Phenomenalists are locked into a prison of their own perceptions and can never escape that prison to compare their experience with someone else's.

Christian theists like Berkeley and Edwards, who have taken up and defended phenomenalism as an aspect of their idealism, can perhaps overcome some, but arguably not all, of these problems. Phenomenalism remains, contrary to Berkeley's insistence, a deeply counterintuitive notion and one that has found few contemporary defenders. Christian thought has, in the main, steered well clear of this theory, in part at least because of its tendency toward *solipsism (the view that all that is real are the contents of my mind, and that everything else – including everyone else – is the creation of my own mind). Instead, Christian theism has in the main utilized metaphysical views whose emphasis is on the reality of some external world, and its creation and conservation by the triune God. These crucial theological doctrines are undermined in the atheological version of phenomenalism, since God is not reducible to a sense datum. Nor is he part of empirical experience in the conventional sense of that word. In fact, the atheological version of the theory seems to militate against the verification of any spiritual world apart from one's own inner life and experiences. The attraction of the idealist version of phenomenalism, which in both Berkeley and Edwards' estimation seeks to safeguard the sovereignty of God over his creation, cannot offset the fact that it is, in the final analysis, a philosophical, and perhaps theological, cul de sac.

Bibliography

A. J. Ayer, *Language, Truth and Logic* (Harmondsworth, 1936); *The Problem of Knowledge* (Harmondsworth, 1956); G. Berkeley, *Principles of Human Nature and Three Dialogues* (Harmondsworth, 1988); R. Chisholm, 'The Problem of Empiricism', *Journal of Philosophy*, 45 (1948); J. Edwards, *Scientific and Philosophical Writings* (New Haven, 1980); C. I. Lewis, *An Analysis of Knowledge and Evaluation* (La Salle, 1946).

O. D. CRISP

PHILO

Philo (c. 20 BC – AD 50) was an Alexandrian Jewish philosopher and writer, and a contemporary of Jesus of Nazareth. He was a prominent member of the large Jewish community in Alexandria, and in AD 39 was a member of a Jewish delegation sent to Rome to plead the case for Jewish religious rights in Alexandria before the emperor Caligula. His *Legatio ad Gaium* gives an account of this visit. Little else is known of his life, but his thought was widely influential in early Christian circles, and although he was known as Philo Judaeus ('Philo the Jew') it was Christians rather than Jews who preserved his works.

The thirty-eight extant works include extensive expositions of the five books of Moses, philosophical treatises, and a variety of historical and apologetic writings, including a life of Moses, which is the nearest approach to classical biography in early post-biblical *Judaism.

Philo was a natural Greek speaker and read the OT in Greek, though he could discuss the meaning of Hebrew names. His works explain and defend Judaism to the Greek philosophical world and also encourage his Hellenistic fellow-Jews to value and maintain their heritage by promoting Judaism as the true philosophy. He developed an elaborately allegorical interpretation of the OT laws and history, so that the down-to-earth regulations of the Mosaic law are seen to represent philosophical concepts and ideals, especially drawn from the *Platonic, Pythagorean and Stoic traditions. His allegorical interpretation did not exclude a literal understanding (as he accused some over-enthusiastic Jewish allegorists of doing), but enabled him to find a more important 'inner meaning' which could be commended to the non-Jewish philosopher.

Philo was a biblical expositor rather than a systematic theologian. His Judaism was essentially orthodox, but also creative. His *monotheism is clear, but in order to account for the involvement of a transcendent God in the created world he made use of the concept of God's Word (*Logos*), through which the world was created and sustained, and in one remarkable passage he spoke of the *Logos* as 'neither uncreated nor created, but midway between the two extremes, a surety to both sides'. He refers to the *Logos* as 'God's first-born' and even 'a second god'.

Within the NT, echoes of Philo's thought may be found especially in the prologue of John's Gospel and in the letter to the Hebrews (which probably comes from the same Alexandrian Jewish background, though earlier claims of direct influence from Philo are now less in favour). Early Christian Fathers, especially those of Alexandria such as Clement and *Origen, drew on Philo's works in their attempts to reconcile their faith with Greek philosophy.

Bibliography

Works, Greek text with English translation by F. H. Colson, G. H. Whittaker and R. Marcus, Loeb Classical Library, 12 vols. (London, 1929–62); P. Borgen, 'Philo of Alexandria', in *Anchor Bible Dictionary* (New York, 1992), vol. 5, pp. 333–342; E. R. Goodenough, *An Introduction to Philo Judaeus* (New Haven, 1962); S. Sandmel, *Philo of Alexandria: An Introduction* (New York, 1979); R. Williamson, *Philo and the Epistle to the Hebrews* (Leiden, 1970).

R. T. FRANCE

PHILOSOPHY OF MIND

The philosophy of mind is one of the most important and active areas in contemporary philosophy. Its principal aim is to gain an understanding of the nature of the mind, especially the phenomenon of consciousness, and the relation between the mind and the body. Schopenhauer described the mind–body problem as the 'world-knot', both because the problem is so mysterious and hard to solve, and because it appears that almost all the other problems of philosophy are connected to it.

The philosophy of mind can also be construed more broadly to include analysis of various dimensions of the mind, including such mental activities as perceptions, emotions and volitions.

Historically, probably most philosophers, as well as ordinary people, have held to some form of dualism on the mind–body problem. Dualistic views see the mind (or soul, often used synonymously with mind) as an entity or substance that is distinct from the body. *Plato infused this metaphysical dualism with a value dualism that saw the soul as the superior 'spiritual' part of a human being, with matter being the lower, degrading aspect. Plato held that the soul was naturally immortal and thus akin to divinity. *Descartes also argued that the mind or soul must be distinct from the body; the soul is a 'thinking thing' while the body is an 'extended thing'. Mind and body have essentially different properties. God has the capacity to cause the soul to exist without the body, and the soul cannot be part of the body if it can exist apart from it. However, Descartes did not argue that the soul was naturally immortal, but only that it could survive the death of the body if God willed it to do so.

Descartes's dualism was a form of interactionism, since the soul and body, though distinct substances, constantly affect each other. However, many philosophers have thought the idea of a non-material soul interacting with a material body to be problematic. Even today this problem is regarded as the most daunting issue facing a dualist, although, for a Christian philosopher, it is hard to see how one could in principle rule out such interaction, since Christians believe that God is a spirit and yet can act upon the world. Nevertheless, the problem of interaction has motivated a host of alternatives to interactionist dualism, including views such as occasionalism (which makes God the active causal agent in every event) and the theory of the pre-established harmony, both of which hold that no genuine causal interaction takes place between mind and body. More common views include *materialism (or physicalism, a term that some use indistinguishably with materialism but that others distinguish), epiphenomenalism, which holds that mental events are a kind of by-product of physical causes but are themselves causally impotent, *idealism, which denies the full reality of material things, and neutral *monism, which holds that what we call mind and body are two different aspects or appearances of one underlying reality.

The last one hundred years have seen a great flourishing of various forms of materialism. Understandably, philosophers who are committed to materialism as an overall metaphysical theory are confident that some form of materialism must be true in the philosophy of mind as well. This confidence does not, however, extend to particulars. That is, materialists have generally disagreed among themselves, and continue to do so, about which form of materialism is true and how to account for mind, especially the phenomena of consciousness and intentionality (the ability of the mind to conceive of meanings). Thus, in the early and middle twentieth century, behaviourism, which views mind simply as behaviour and dispositions to behave in various ways, was popular. The growth of neuroscience in the late twentieth century led to the popularity of the mind–brain identity theory, or central state materialism. The burgeoning of computers led to the popularity of functionalism, which views mental states simply as entities that are defined by the particular role or function these entities play in our lives. Finally, some materialists, sometimes dubbed the mysterians, hold that although materialism is true, the true nature of the mind is mysterious; we do not, and perhaps cannot, understand how physical things can have such attributes as consciousness. The diversity of explanations of mind given by materialists make it highly plausible that the tendency towards materialism is being driven by commitments to global metaphysical theories rather than by insight into how the mind can be physically explained.

Christian interest in the philosophy of mind has been driven by two main concerns. Some have argued that consciousness, or some aspect of the mind, cannot be physically explained, and have used this claim as part of an apologetic argument directed against materialism, perceived as the major rival of a theistic world-view. Of course, a defence of the soul as a non-physical entity does not by itself establish a religious world-view, but one might reasonably believe that it is difficult to account for a non-material mind if the universe consists solely of physical particles.

Perhaps even more important has been Christian concern with the possibility of the resurrection of the body and life after death.

Christian thinkers have usually attempted to avoid both Platonic dualism, which, with its low view of the body, makes the resurrection of the body seem pointless or even a bad thing, and materialism, which many have believed makes any kind of life after death impossible. Certainly, Christians who accept the traditional view that humans continue to exist in an intermediate state between death and the resurrection would appear to be committed to some form of moderate dualism.

Recently, however, a number of Christian philosophers have attempted to defend the claim that a materialistic view of the human person is consistent with belief in the resurrection. Some deny the intermediate state and hold to a gap theory, in which a person temporarily ceases to exist and then is reconstituted later in a resurrected body. Others have argued for an immediate-resurrection theory, in which there is no gap but the resurrection occurs immediately after death in a dimension of time and space different from our current universe. In both cases, however, it is arguable that the lack of continuity provided by a substantial soul creates problems for the identity of the resurrected person with the person who died.

Biblical scholars have rightly stressed in recent years the way in which the Bible sees human persons in a unified, holistic way. Some theologians and Christian philosophers have been led by this to support some form of neutral monism, or what is sometimes called non-reductive materialism. One interesting position in this context is the traditional view of *Thomas Aquinas, who held that a human person is a composite of body and soul. For Aquinas, the soul does survive death, but since full human personhood requires both a body and soul, the person does not exist, strictly speaking, after death until the resurrection. Whether this is a form of dualism or not is a much-debated question. It is clearly different from the views of both Plato and Descartes, but it may still be properly designated as a dualistic view.

It is in any case far from obvious that the unity of the person rules out some form of dualism. Human persons may be embodied souls, with minds that require bodies in order to function as God intended. Such a view may allow for the close connection and dependence that, contemporary neuroscience has discovered, holds for the relation between mind and body without denying that the mind is a distinct reality.

C. S. EVANS

PIERCING

The biblical references to piercing are in the context of the *slavery of Israelites, where the mark in the ear denotes ownership in perpetuity (Exod. 21:6). This slavery seems to have been permitted, but was in turn qualified, by Lev. 25:39ff., so that longer service, but not seven-year involuntary or lifelong voluntary 'slavery', was countenanced. There is no mention of the consensual ritual humiliation of the slave, perhaps on the grounds that it would contradict the dignity of the status of God's people as liberated from Egypt. Perhaps it is more pertinent to point out that any disfiguring of the body as made in the image of God was disapproved of. Cutting or marking the body is mentioned only in the context of mourning (Lev. 19:28) and was prohibited. It seems to symbolize death and looking to ghosts, and the Israelites, as God's children, should never think of the death of a near one as separating him or her from God's protection and so should not need to indulge in such desperate grief. Tattoos denoted slavery, and texts were not to be written on the body but put in phylacteries and placed on arms and foreheads (Deut. 6:8). Yet circumcision (Lev. 12:3), the sign of the covenant, is an interesting exception as the identity entrance marker for a people who belong by faith, not purely by descent.

Tattoos and piercings are not always driven by definable psychological distress but are often done to strengthen class or group solidarity. The thrill which comes from breaking a taboo can be read as the adventure of boundary-crossing; the ritual is ascetic, quasi-sacrificial and involves something akin to initiation into a group of those who look different, with a progression from simple (e.g. nose) to advanced (genitalia) piercing. The pleasure comes not so much from the enhancement of physical sensation as from control over one's body (the disenfranchised individual here at least can exercise power) and the re-creation of one's identity. Piercings and tattoos are often used to mark specific events in one's life and remind one of the body's ability to heal itself and to be changed. While often a mark of rebellion, they can become the type of conformist nonconformity and be reduced to just copycat behaviour.

If piercings and tattoos signal anything, then it is often pain, discomfort and death in a world that perhaps has enough of those. There seems to be an objectification of bodies and thus of the person by making them more the object of gaze and, in the case of certain piercings, by making them machines with levers the easier to 'turn on'. While piercing *could* operate to enhance a loving and covenantal relationship with oneself and others, it *might* often encourage the opposite.

Bibliography

M. Featherstone (ed.), *Body Modifications* (Sage, 2000), pp. 51–76; J. Milgrom, *Leviticus 17–22* (New York, 2000); G. Wenham, *Leviticus* (London, 1979).

M. W. ELLIOTT

PLATO

Plato (427–347 BC), the founder of Western idealist philosophy, grew up in a culture pervaded by a Greek *polytheism that was being deeply challenged by the materialistic philosophy of Democritus, his older contemporary. Plato, too, criticized Greek religion, but he was a deeply religious philosopher, respectful of the religious authority of the Greek poets. He argued that an adequate explanation of the natural world required both a realm of supernatural Forms, highest of which is the Good (*Republic* VI), and a divine 'craftsman' to order this world after the pattern of these Forms (*Timaeus*). Although Plato never quite combined this divine agency with the Good in one ultimate being resembling the biblical God, many scholars argue that he moved far enough in that direction to be counted as the father of philosophical *theism. That this was an easy next step is evident from *Aristotle, his student, whose god, although not a creator, was both a living, thinking being and the ultimate Form.

Plato was also the first to defend theism against *atheism, so that he is likewise the father of theistic apologetics. This modern term is derived from 'apology', which in Greek means 'defence'. It appears as the title of Plato's account of *Socrates' defence of philosophy at the trial in which he was convicted and sentenced to death. It reappears in the NT (1 Pet. 3:15) and again as the title of *Justin Martyr's early defence of Christianity against hostile attacks of pagan philosophers. Significantly, the Church Fathers often defended Christian theism with ideas that originated in Plato, ideas that have persisted in Christian apologetics to the present.

The centrepiece of Plato's apologetics is *natural theology. Although he did not use this specific term, Christian theologians use it to distinguish theology based on reason from revealed theology based on faith. Plato's arguments reflect its larger meaning: theology derived from the rational study of the *nature* of the world. Plato develops three such arguments (*Laws* X). First, he argues against atheism by linking it with materialistic philosophy, which tries to explain bodily motion in terms of mechanistic concepts alone. However, says Plato, since bodies are only moved by other bodies, mechanistic concepts fail to account for the origin of motion, let alone its orderliness. Such an account requires the principle of life and thought: the soul, which materialists reduce to matter or ignore altogether. The soul (or mind) is an intelligent mover unmoved by external bodies; hence it is the original source of their motion and its intelligibility. So impressive is the orderliness of motion in the world that there must be a 'best soul', its ultimate cause, which Plato calls 'god'. Here lie the rudiments of the *cosmological arguments for the existence of god, which found their classic form in the 'Five Ways' of *Thomas Aquinas and reverberate today in the thinking of those who advocate 'intelligent design'.

Secondly, Plato answers the attack on theism from the existence of *evil, especially in its most poignant form, the apparent neglect by a good and powerful god of human beings and their moral life. Why do the good suffer and the wicked prosper? All evil is disorder, says Plato, which cannot be attributed to god who, as the 'best soul', is wholly good. But there are other souls, less perfect, responsible for the disorder in the world. This account of evil anticipates the Christian 'free will defence' first elaborated by *Augustine, and influentially articulated today by Alvin Plantinga. In this argument, evil does not originate in God but in rational creatures to whom God has given free will. Plato adds the important corollary that god rules over all things, so that good eventually will triumph over evil, a belief that anticipates the Christian doctrine of providence.

Thirdly, from these conclusions Plato argues against the cynical view that religion is an attempt by humans to bribe god into winking at their evildoing. That view ignores god's wisdom, justice and providence and also that human beings actually belong to god and exist for the same purpose, to overcome evil with good. Thus god is their guardian, ally and helper, not a venal adversary to be appeased by gifts.

The role of natural theology in Christian apologetics is rather diminished in today's postmodern era. Subsequent to the patristic age, it reached its apogee in the medieval theology of Thomas Aquinas, which was followed by a thoroughly rationalist revival among modern Enlightenment theologians and philosophers. However, Martin Luther had already sown the seeds of a later Protestant reaction against natural theology, which resulted in the two highly significant but quite disparate reactions against reason in religion to be found in Immanuel *Kant and Søren *Kierkegaard. The Reformed tradition after John *Calvin, although more hospitable to natural theology than the Lutheran, has lately voiced its own critique of natural theology in a movement called 'Reformed epistemology'. Alvin Plantinga led the way with a seminal article, 'The Reformed Objection to Natural Theology' (1980). More recently, the 'openness of God theology' has challenged not only the natural theology tradition in apologetics but many of the orthodox conceptions of the divine nature itself, which it regards as due to the unfortunate influence of Greek philosophy upon the history of Christian theology. In one way or another, all these reactions echo the Pauline query, 'Has not God made foolish the wisdom of the world?' (1 Cor. 1:20).

Bibliography

R. M. Hare, *Plato* (Oxford, 1990); A. Plantinga, 'God, Evil, and the Metaphysics of Freedom', in *The Nature of Necessity* (Oxford, 1974); 'The Reformed Objection to Natural Theology', *Proceedings of the American Catholic Philosophical Association*, 54 (1980), pp. 49–63; Plato, *The Republic* (Book VI), *Timaeus, Laws* (Book X) in B. Jowett, *The Dialogues of Plato*, 2 vols. (New York, 1937); C. G. Rutenber, *The Doctrine of the Imitation of God in Plato* (New York, 1946); J. Sanders et al., *The Openness of God* (Downers Grove, 2000); Thomas Aquinas, 'The Existence of God' and 'Whether God can be Known in this Life by Natural Reason', in *Summa Theologica* (Part I; Q. 1. A. 3 and Q. 12. A. 12) in *Basic Writings*, vol. 1 (New York, 1945); N. P. Wolterstorff, 'The Migration of the Theistic Arguments: From Natural Theology to Evidentialist Apologetics', in R. Audi and W. J. Wainwright (eds.), *Rationality, Religious Belief, and Moral Commitment* (Ithaca and London, 1986).

D. J. HOITENGA

PLURALISM, see RELATIVISM AND PLURALISM

PLURALISM, RELIGIOUS

The influx into Western nations of immigrants from former colonies and advances in telecommunications during the twentieth century have heightened awareness of the religious diversity of humankind. The missiological and theological consequences of this heightened awareness have been significant. Mainline churches have largely lost a sense of calling to world evangelization, and contemporary theology has tended to marginalize the person and work of Christ.

In exploring the challenges raised by religious diversity, we shall find it useful to draw a number of distinctions. First, we may distinguish between *universalism and particularism. Universalism is the doctrine that every human being will partake of God's salvation; particularism is the view that only some will do so. A second distinction is that between accessibilism and restrictivism. Christian restrictivists maintain that salvation is available only through an appropriate response to God's special revelation, which today involves a faith response to the gospel of Christ. Christian accessibilists maintain that for those who have not had the benefit of special *revelation, salvation is available through their appropriate response to God's general revelation in nature and *conscience. Finally, we may distinguish between *exclusivism, inclusivism and pluralism. Christian exclusivism is the view that people in fact appropriate God's salvation only on the basis of Christ's work and through explicit faith in him. Christian inclusivism is the view that people appropriate God's salvation only on the basis of Christ's work but not always through explicit faith in him. Pluralism is the view that people appropriate God's salvation through a multiplicity of conditions and means in various religions.

These different schools of thought are obviously closely related, but it is important that we do not conflate them. For example, although we are apt to associate restrictivism with particularism, this would be a mistake; some restrictivists are universalists because they envision the possibility of a reception of the gospel after death. Or again, we are apt to think that pluralism implies universalism; but that need not be the case, since the pluralist may regard some religions as inefficacious channels of salvation.

The question, then, is what problem is posed by the reality of religious diversity and for whom? The recurring challenge seems to be laid at the doorstep of the Christian particularist. The phenomenon of religious diversity is taken to require the truth of universalism, and the main debate then proceeds to the question of which form of that doctrine is the most plausible. Many opt for a pluralistic universalism. But why think that Christian particularism is untenable in the face of religious diversity?

Some of the objections to Christian particularism seem to be textbook examples of logical fallacies. For example, it is frequently asserted that it is arrogant and immoral to hold to any doctrine of religious particularism because one must then regard all persons who disagree with one's own religious viewpoint as mistaken. This objection seems to be a case of argument *ad hominem*, i.e. trying to invalidate a position by attacking the character of those who hold to it. In any case, the objection is a double-edged sword, since the pluralist also believes that his own viewpoint is right and that all adherents to particularistic religious viewpoints are wrong, thereby convicting himself of arrogance and immorality.

Or again, it is frequently alleged that Christian particularism cannot be correct because religious beliefs are culturally relative, e.g. if a Christian believer had been born in Pakistan instead of Great Britain, it is likely that he would have been a Muslim. But the objection seems to be a case of the genetic fallacy, i.e. trying to refute a position by discrediting the way in which it came to be believed. If one had been born in ancient Greece, it is likely that one would have believed that the sun orbits the earth, but that does not imply that our belief

in heliocentrism is false or unjustified. And once again, the objection is a double-edged sword, for if the pluralist had been born in Pakistan, he would likely have been a religious particularist. Thus, on his own analysis his pluralism is a false belief which is merely the product of his being born in late twentieth-century Western society.

Thus, some of the arguments against Christian particularism are unimpressive. When these objections are answered by defenders of Christian particularism, however, then the real issue does tend to emerge. That issue is the fate of unbelievers outside one's own particular religious tradition. Christian particularism consigns such persons to *hell, which many people take to be unconscionable.

But what exactly is the problem here supposed to be? Is it supposed to be simply the allegation that a loving God would not send people to hell? It seems not. Scripture indicates that God wills the salvation of every human being (2 Pet. 3:9; 1 Tim. 2:4), and the only factor that could abort God's intention for humanity is human free will, for it is logically impossible to make someone freely do something. Therefore, even an all-powerful God cannot make people freely believe in him for salvation. If we make a free and well-informed decision to reject God's every effort to save us, then God cannot be held responsible for our intransigence. The lost, therefore, are self-condemned; they separate themselves from God despite God's will to the contrary.

Is the problem then supposed to be that a loving God would not send people to hell because they were uninformed or misinformed about Christ? Again, this does not seem to be the heart of the issue. For here the Christian particularist may endorse some form of accessibilism. He may argue that according to the Christian view, God does not judge people who have never heard of Christ on the basis of whether they have placed their faith in Christ. Rather God judges them on the basis of his general revelation in nature and conscience that they do have. This is not to say that people can be saved apart from Christ. Rather it is to say that the benefits of Christ's atoning death could be applied to people without their conscious knowledge of Christ. While the NT gives little ground for optimism about there being many, if any at all, who will actually be saved through their response to general revelation alone, the point remains that salvation is universally accessible, so that the problem posed by religious diversity cannot be simply that God would not condemn persons who are uninformed or misinformed about Christ.

It would seem therefore that the real problem is why an all-powerful and all-loving God has not arranged things so that every created person would hear the gospel and freely respond to it and be saved. This allegation is a version of the problem of *evil, a sort of soteriological problem of evil. The universalist seems to be alleging that it is impossible for God to be all-powerful and all-loving and yet for some people to never hear the gospel and be lost. In other words the statements that (1) 'God is all-powerful and all-loving' and (2) 'Some people never hear the gospel and are lost' are logically inconsistent.

The free-will defence ought to be as relevant to this problem as to the general problem of evil. For we can ask, why think that (1) and (2) are logically incompatible? After all, there is no explicit contradiction between them. But if (1) and (2) are said to be implicitly contradictory, one must be assuming some hidden premises that would serve to bring out this contradiction and make it explicit. The question is, what are those hidden premises?

The logic of the problem of evil would suggest that they must be something akin to (3) 'If God is all-powerful, he can create a world in which everybody hears the gospel and is freely saved' and (4) 'If God is all-loving, he prefers a world in which everybody hears the gospel and is freely saved.'

Since, according to (1), God is both all-powerful and all-loving, it follows that he both can create a world of universal salvation and prefers such a world. Therefore such a world exists, in contradiction to (2).

Both of the hidden premises must be necessarily true if the logical incompatibility of (1) and (2) is to be demonstrated. But are these premises necessarily true?

Consider (3). It seems uncontroversial that God could create a world in which everybody hears the gospel. But so long as people are free, there is no guarantee that everybody in such a world would be freely saved. In fact, there is no reason to think that the balance between saved and lost in such a world would be any better than the balance in the actual world. It is possible that in any world of free creatures

which God could actualize, some people would freely reject his saving grace and be lost. Hence, (3) is not necessarily true, and so the argument is fallacious.

Now what about (4)? Is it necessarily true? Let us suppose for the sake of argument that there are possible worlds actualizable by God in which everyone hears the gospel and freely accepts it. Does God's being all-loving compel him to prefer one of these worlds over a world in which some persons are lost? Not necessarily, for these worlds might have other, over-riding deficiencies that make them less preferable. For example, suppose that the only worlds actualizable by God in which everybody freely believes the gospel and is saved are worlds with only a handful of people in them. Must God prefer one of these sparsely populated worlds over a world in which multitudes believe in the gospel and are saved, even though that implies that other persons freely reject his grace and are lost? This is far from obvious. So long as God gives sufficient grace for salvation to all persons he creates, God seems no less loving for preferring a more populous world, even though that implies that some people would freely resist his every effort to save them and be damned. Thus, the second assumption is also not necessarily true, so that the argument is doubly fallacious.

But we can push the analysis a notch further. We may try to show positively that it is entirely possible that God is all-powerful and all-loving and that many persons never hear the gospel and are lost. All we have to do is find a possibly true statement which is compatible with God's being all-powerful and all-loving and which, together with (1), entails that some people never hear the gospel and are lost.

As a good and loving God, God wants as many people as possible to be saved and as few as possible to be lost. His goal, then, is to achieve an optimal balance between these, to create no more of the lost than is necessary to attain a certain number of the saved. But it is possible that the actual world (which includes the future as well as the present and past) has such a balance. It is possible that in order to create this many people who will be saved, God also had to create this many people who will be lost.

It might be objected that an all-loving God would not create people who he knew would be lost, but who would have been saved if only they had heard the gospel. But how do we know there *are* any such persons? It is reasonable to assume that many people who never hear the gospel would not have believed the gospel if they had heard it. Suppose, then, that God has so providentially ordered the world that *all* persons who never hear the gospel are precisely such people. In that case, anybody who never hears the gospel and is lost would have rejected the gospel and been lost even if he had heard it. No-one could stand before God on the judgment day and complain, 'All right, God, so I didn't respond to your general revelation in nature and conscience! But if only I had heard the gospel, then I would have believed!' For God will say, 'No, I knew that even if you had heard the gospel, you would not have believed it. Therefore, my judgment of you on the basis of nature and conscience is neither unfair nor unloving.'

Thus, it is possible that (5) God has created a world which has an optimal balance between saved and lost, and those who never hear the gospel and are lost would not have believed in it even if they had heard it. So long as this statement is even possibly true, it shows that there is no incompatibility between an all-powerful, all-loving God and some people's never hearing the gospel and being lost. Furthermore, these answers are attractive because they also seem to be in line with biblical revelation (Acts 17:24–27).

Now the universalist might concede the logical compatibility of God's being all-powerful and all-loving and some people's never hearing the gospel and being lost, but insist that these two facts are nonetheless improbable with respect to each other. People by and large seem to believe in the religion of the culture in which they were raised. But in that case, the universalist may argue, it is highly probable that if many of those who never hear the gospel had been raised in a Christian culture, they would have believed the gospel and been saved. Thus, the hypothesis we have offered is highly implausible.

Now it would, indeed, be fantastically improbable that by happenstance alone it just turned out that all those who never hear the gospel and are lost are persons who would not have believed the gospel even if they had heard it. But that is not the hypothesis. The hypothesis is that a provident God has so arranged the world. Given a God endowed with middle knowledge of how every free creature would respond to his grace in whatever circumstances God might place him, it is not at all implausible that God has ordered the world in the way described. Such a world would not look outwardly any different from a world in which the circumstances of a person's birth are a matter of happenstance. The particularist can agree that people generally adopt the religion of their culture and that if many of those born into non-Christian cultures had been born in a Christian society instead, they would have become nominally Christian. But that is not to say that they would have been saved. Since a world providentially ordered by God would appear outwardly identical to a world in which one's birth is a matter of historical and geographical accident, it is hard to see how the proposed hypothesis can be deemed to be improbable apart from a demonstration that the existence of a God endowed with middle knowledge is implausible. Since objections to middle knowledge are inconclusive at best, Christian particularism remains undefeated.

Bibliography

Faith and Philosophy, 14 (1997), pp. 277–320; P. Griffiths, *Exploring Religious Diversity* (Oxford, 2000); H. Netland, *Encountering Religious Pluralism* (Downer's Grove, 2001); P. L. Quinn and K. Meeker (eds.), *The Philosophical Challenge of Religious Diversity* (Oxford, 2000).

W. L. CRAIG

POINTS OF CONTACT

Christian apologetics – by its very nature as a means of convincing unbelievers of the truth, rationality, wisdom and pertinence of the Christian world-view – must find points of contact with the various kinds of unbelievers it addresses. 'Point of contact' refers to what is shared cognitively and existentially between Christians and non-Christians concerning matters of *logic, *morality, intuition, longing and *imagination (see also *Common ground). It is sought by the Christian apologist in order to build a bridge between what the unbeliever now believes and what he or she ought to believe and follow in order to embrace Christian *theism and confess *Jesus Christ as Lord. Establishing points of contact is a first step in both theistic arguments and appeals to Christian evidences (such as the reliability of the Gospels, and the resurrection of Christ). It is also essential in negative apologetics, which seeks to expose logical weaknesses in non-Christian world-views. The skilful apologist uses aspects of the unbeliever's knowledge (such as logic) against other aspects of the unbeliever's unbiblical world-view (such as naturalism).

Points of contact may be contrasted with another central plank of all Christian apologetics – antithesis. Just as apologists seek to find and capitalize on points of agreement with their unbelieving audiences, they must also explain clearly the points of disagreement and contradiction between Christianity and other world-views. Paul affirms antithesis when he contrasts the one true gospel with impostors (Gal. 1:6–9). Jesus does the same when he claims that ultimately one is either with him or against him (Matt. 12:30).

The rejection of points of contact

Some Christian thinkers have denied the possibility of points of contact for several reasons. Apologist Cornelius *Van Til and his followers claim that the *noetic effects of sin are so vast that there is no epistemological point of contact between the believer and the unbeliever. The former presupposes Christian theism as the explanation for *reality, and the latter appeals only to autonomous thought that rules out the biblical God in principle. Van Til does admit, however, that there is a metaphysical point of contact between believer and unbeliever, since both live in God's universe and are made in God's image. This metaphysical point of contact makes apologetic *reasoning possible with unbelievers. This concept is questionable, however, because a shared ontology does little to promote communication between world-views that are taken to have nothing in common epistemologically. A snail and a human live in the same world, but their access to that world radically differs. Moreover, Van Til and his school use reason in their apologetic attacks on the illogic non-Christian world-views (negative apologetics) and expect non-Christians to be able to discern the illogic of their own unbiblical world-views. This covertly presupposes epistemological points of contact.

Fideists of various stripes have also negated points of contact on the assumption that faith is a supernatural bestowal owing nothing to reason or evidence. Faith is, rather, a kind of epistemological island – self-supporting and solitary with respect to the world of intellectual life. This theme is salient in the earlier writings of theologian Karl *Barth, who denied general *revelation and thus that there was any intellectual point of contact between the faithful and unbelievers. One preaches to unbelief, instead of employing arguments (which would require intellectual points of contact to be successful). Faith is a mode of knowing that gains no support from the fallen reasoning of human philosophy. Therefore, to employ philosophical arguments (which may borrow concepts from pagans such as *Plato or *Aristotle, for example) to prove God's existence is an act of unfaithfulness. Barth claimed that all divine revelation was found in Christ alone. There is no general revelation in nature and, therefore, no legitimate *natural theology (which trades on the knowledge of God available to all and found in the natural world). Christianity is not even a 'religion', but the abolition of religion as a radical *revelation* from God.

Scriptural examples of points of contact

Barth's approach, while rightly concerned about using arguments not found explicitly in the Bible, overemphasizes the noetic (or intellectual) effects of sin on the intellect. The first two chapters of Romans make clear that God is somehow disclosed through creation and *conscience to his creatures (see also Acts 14:15; Ps. 19:1–6). While Paul stressed the transcendent source of the gospel and its offensiveness to unbelievers (1 Cor 1 – 2), he did not dispense with discovering points of contact with the unconverted, both Jew and Gentile. The book of Acts shows that, with the Jews, Paul reasoned from the Hebrew Scriptures that Jesus was the promised Messiah. With Gentiles, Paul appealed to what could be known of God from creation, conscience and *history, even apart from the Hebrew Scriptures.

When preaching at the Areopagus on Mars Hill (Acts 17:16–34), Paul began with establishing a theistic world-view before proclaiming the particular truths about Jesus. His use of points of contact – in this case, an undeveloped and insufficient theism – was central in this task. Through his efforts, Paul gained a hearing from several in attendance (17:34). There is no indication that Paul's efforts were a failure or that he was dishonouring God in this apologetic venture, as some fideists claim.

The Logos of God

The prologue of the Gospel of John further reveals an appeal to points of contact in

Scripture itself. The word John uses for the pre-incarnate Christ is 'the Word' (or *logos* in Greek). This term was widely known and used in Greek philosophical circles by Heraclitus and others. From *logos* we derive our word 'logic' and all words ending in -ology, such as 'sociology' and 'theology'. In Greek philosophy *logos* generally referred to an immanent and *impersonal* ordering principle in the cosmos, a principle that provided coherence. *Logos* makes the world a universe instead of a multiverse, a cosmos instead of a chaos. John harnesses a word rich in philosophical meaning for a unique purpose. The true Logos is personal and transcendent as well as cosmic. John says of the Logos: 'Through *him* all things were *made*; without *him* nothing was *made* that has been *made*' (John 1:3; emphasis added). Carl *Henry puts this into perspective: 'The Logos of the Bible is personal and self-revealed, transcendent to man and the world, eternal and essentially divine, intrinsically intelligible, and incarnate in Jesus Christ.' Moreover, the Logos is 'the foundation of all meaning, and the transcendent personal source and support of the national, moral, and purposive order of created reality'. The Logos became flesh and made his dwelling among us, John declares (1:18). In his prologue, John connects Christ to a well-known philosophical concept and takes that concept far beyond what any Greek philosopher ever imagined. He uses the *logos* concept as a strong bridge to the Greek mind, as well as a profound challenge to it.

Apologetic shock therapy

But even before staking out significant points of contact with unbelievers, apologists must sometimes jolt their audience out of the spiritual lethargy and stupefaction that blinds people to the significance of the gospel. Blaise *Pascal (1623–62) tried to accomplish this rude but redeeming awakening by various means, including parables, dialogues and epigrams. Knowing that mortals fear death at some level (despite our avoidance of the topic), he tells a parable: 'Imagine a number of men in chains, all under sentence of death, some of whom are each day butchered in the sight of the others; those remaining see their own condition in that of their fellows, and looking at each other with grief and despair await their turn. This is an image of the human condition.' Rather than allowing them to divert themselves from thinking of distressing matters beyond human

control, Pascal forces his reader to face them honestly and thereby to become open to a transcendent source of liberation. Instead of diverting themselves, his readers are incited to 'seek God'. Pascal puts the matter even more sharply when he says, 'Between heaven and hell is only this life, which is the most fragile thing in the world.' Death may be followed by eternity, and this life is precarious.

Similarly, Søren *Kierkegaard (1813–55), although a fideist in some ways, employed a variety of literary styles in order to jolt his readers out of religious complacency and bring them to the place of spiritual honesty before God. His point of contact was not an arsenal of objective evidence for the historicity of the Christian faith, but the subjective world of sinful creatures at odds with themselves, with their neighbours and with God. His account of the subjective dynamics of sin in *The Sickness Unto Death* is a powerful existential apologetic. While he was a critic of Kierkegaard, Francis *Schaeffer (1912–84) employed a related shock strategy in *The God Who Is There*, where he wrote of 'taking the roof off' the non-Christian's world-view by exposing its often shocking logical implications.

Truth

One point of contact that is necessary for apologetic endeavours, particularly in the post-modern situation, is the concept of *truth itself. Especially in religious matters, many contemporary Westerners claim that truth is relative to and dependent upon individuals and communities. Put another way, truth is constructed for various purposes. Therefore, religious truth is a matter, not of objective facts, but of human perspectives and interpretations. There are different religious truths that serve different purposes; therefore, no one religion can claim superiority. In fact, some postmoderns create a smorgasbord kind of spirituality, combining various traditions with little concern for logical consistency or historical pedigree.

Those of this mindset cannot accept the Christian world-view as true and authoritative. Instead, Christianity becomes one of many 'religious preferences' with no privileged status, and is allowed only on these relativistic terms. Nevertheless, the concept of objective truth is not alien to the most postmodern person. We apply it to matters of health ('Is the biopsy negative or positive?'), to transportation ('Did the mechanic fix my car?'), and to basic moral concerns ('Female genital mutilation is wrong'). These kinds of examples provide the conceptual point of contact necessary to present Christianity as offering objective truth-claims (even before those claims are defended as rationally compelling and true). Just as Caesar either crossed the Rubicon or did not, Jesus Christ either rose from the dead or did not.

Therefore, a true statement is one that matches the facts; a false statement fails to do this. If apologists can locate a point of contact on the concept of truth, they can move on to consider other areas of agreement between unbelievers and Christians. Of course, unbelievers come equipped with a plethora of non-Christian world-views, from the religious to the secular to the agnostic. In order to find a point of contact, the apologist must be an astute listener as well as a diligent student of the major world-views – theism, pantheism, *polytheism and *naturalism – and their various manifestations. The number and types of point of contact between the Christian and non-Christian differ from person to person. However, given God's general revelation in creation and conscience (Rom. 1 – 2) and the fact that all people are made in God's image and likeness (Gen. 1:26), we can find several. Apologists can also strive to find various cultural and personal affinities with those whom they wish to see converted to Christ.

Logic

First, one of the capacities that distinguishes humans from animals is their ability to reason. Humans do not merely react instinctively to situations, but are able to assess them rationally according to logical principles. These God-given abilities are fundamental to all points of contact, since one must be able to think logically about them. The question of the nature of rationality in a comprehensive sense is a complicated one, but need not concern us. Suffice it to say that when the human mind is working properly it uses the basic principles of logic for analysis.

These principles of logic are not deduced or inferred from other principles that are more basic or more certainly known. These principles must be presupposed or assumed in order to communicate or think intelligibly; they stand behind all rational thought and language. They are not arbitrary or whimsical. They are fundamental principles or laws of thought, not groundless speculations or *ad hoc* notions. They

are neither Eastern nor Western, neither male nor female, nor are they pigmented. They are eternal and essential principles by which our minds were created by God to function. They are rooted in the perfect reason and comprehensive knowledge of God himself (John 1:1). These are three indispensable logical principles: the laws of identity, non-*contradiction and excluded middle.

These logical principles are not the province of Western philosophers only. They function in all religions and philosophies and at a very commonsensical level. Apologists should abide by these principles and can count on the fact that people can recognize their validity. Further, the basic argument types, induction, deduction and abduction – all used in the apologetic enterprise – are readily understood by people who sufficiently attend to their structures. Of course, any number of subjective factors can inhibit one's appreciation of a good argument and solid evidence, as Jesus himself pointed out (John 5:44). Logic should be used, not as a club, but as a prod to open up new avenues to truth. For example, if someone wants to affirm both Jesus and Buddha as spiritual masters, one should point out that their world-views are contradictory. Therefore, they cannot both be correct in their most essential teachings.

Conscience

Conscience or a sense of morality provides a powerful point of contact, despite the widespread acceptance of moral *relativism in the West. Human beings know certain moral truths simply by being human, by having a God-given conscience. Paul reveals that 'the work of the law is written on the heart', whether or not one has received special revelation (Rom. 2:14–15). Moreover, the prophet Amos appeals to the morality of pagan nations – without the Mosaic Law – in his oracles against them (Amos 1 – 2). C. S. *Lewis begins *Mere Christianity* by arguing for the reality of moral law beyond mere social convention and personal preference: 'We know that men find themselves under a moral law, which they did not make, and cannot quite forget even when they try, and which they know they ought to obey.' Lewis argues that this moral law transcends instinct and custom, yet it is an escapable element of our consciousness. In *The Abolition of Man*, he refers to it as 'the Tao', by which he means *natural law. If there is an objective moral law knowable through conscience, this raises two salient apologetic questions: first, what is the source of that law?, and secondly, how can one find forgiveness and moral strength even as a violator of that law?

If one finds points of contact on basic moral principles and virtues, the next apologetic move involves discerning if the unbeliever's world-view can rationally support and explain these moral realities. In many cases (such as naturalism and pantheism) it cannot do so. Then the apologist may gently show unbelievers that they must either give up their moral belief or accept a sufficient basis for it. The Christian God provides moral meaning for the universe and persons through his character as an all-wise Law-giver. In this way, one can use points of contact to move to defending Christian theism.

Longing

Christians may also find points of contact with unbelievers by appealing to an inchoate sense of longing for *transcendence – an inner emptiness not satisfied by the things of this world. Ecclesiastes, which powerfully exposes the folly of worldly sources of ultimate satisfaction, speaks of people having a sense of 'eternity in their hearts', but without full knowledge of it (Eccl. 3:11). *Augustine famously said in *The Confessions*, 'Thou hast made us for thyself, and our hearts are restless until they rest in thee.' Likewise, in *Pensées*, Pascal wrote of the 'infinite abyss' within the human soul that can be filled only by 'an infinite and immutable object', namely, God himself. In *Surprised by Joy* and *The Weight of Glory*, C. S. Lewis eloquently wrote of the quest for a 'joy' that transcends this world, but is faintly tasted here as well. He takes this as indicating an objective need of the soul for God. The prophet Isaiah capitalizes on this inner poverty of those sojourners east of Eden when he cries: 'Come, all you who are thirsty, come to the waters; and you who have no money, come, buy and eat! Come, buy wine and milk without money and without cost. Why spend your money on what is not bread, and your labour on what does not satisfy?' (Isa. 55:1–2). In appealing to this point of contact, apologists will need to block the claim – made by Feuerbach, Marx, Freud and others – that these spiritual longings are nothing but a product of wishful thinking that has no basis in objective reality.

Imagination

Christian apologists typically use points of contact as starting points for explicit logical arguments for Christianity. However, the imagination can be a fruitful point of contact with unbelievers, especially for those with a literary or imaginative bent. This should not surprise us, given Jesus' ingenious and arresting use of parables. Those who have little interest in tackling covert defences of Christianity may be drawn nearer to a Christian sensibility through the fictional works of modern apologists such as C. S. Lewis, G. K. *Chesterton and Dorothy L. *Sayers, and through literary classics by Dante, Milton, George Herbert and others. These creative works commend the Christian world-view without explicitly defending it through philosophical argumentation. As John Stackhouse puts it, 'Stories and poems can be allusive, suggestive, implicative polyvalent, and surprising. They can arouse interest, offer an alternative viewpoint, even create a longing in more people than discursive argument can.'

Godly character

Lastly, godly character – marked by faith, hope, and love – is a necessary ingredient for finding points of contact with unbelievers. God has constituted his creatures to notice, appreciate and be attracted to people of compassion and wisdom (John 13:34–35; see also Matt. 5:4–16). Those who take up their crosses and follow Christ in the power of the Holy Spirit will find unbelievers asking them for the reason for the Christian hope that they have (1 Pet. 3:15).

Bibliography

W. Corduan, *No Doubt About It: Basic Christian Apologetics* (Nashville, 1997); C. S. Lewis, *The Abolition of Man* (London, 1944); *Mere Christianity* (London, 1943); *The Weight of Glory and Other Addresses* (London; 1949); G. R. Lewis, *Testing Christianity's Truth Claims* (Chicago, 1976); F. A. Schaeffer, *The God Who Is There* (Downers Grove and London, 1968); J. G. Stackhouse, *Humble Apologetics: Defending the Faith Today* (New York, 2002).

D. GROOTHUIS

POLANYI, MICHAEL

Michael Polanyi (1891–1976) was born in Hungary and became both a physical chemist and a social scientist, engaging in teaching and research in the universities of Oxford, Chicago and Manchester. He was made a Fellow of the Royal Society in 1944. In 1946 he wrote an original and controversial contribution to the *philosophy of *science, *Science, Faith and Society*. Polanyi demonstrates in that work that science must be understood as a social enterprise, which is carried forward by a *community of inquirers who are united by a common belief-system, rather than by the absolutely objective application of some abstract scientific method. Scientific faith, he argues, consists in a discipline which is imposed by scientists on themselves in the interests of discovering an objective, impersonal *truth. Yet scientists must presuppose, by faith, that such truth exists and can be found. He criticizes both authoritarianism and scepticism, proponents of which schools of thought, so he believed, were attacking science itself in their assault on those who argued that real science must involve subjectivity and valuing, rather than merely reading off observable data and organising them as facts. In other words, Polanyi understood science in many ways to be an art, which must follow rules of art. 'The rules of scientific enquiry leave their own application wide open, to be decided by the scientist's judgment ... In each such decision the scientist may rely on the support of a rule; but he is then selecting a rule that applies to the case, much as the golfer chooses a suitable club for his next stroke ... He must recognise as authoritative the art which he wishes to learn and those of whom he would learn it ... This is the way of acquiring knowledge, which the Christian Church Fathers described as *fides quaerens intellectum*, "to believe in order to know"' (*Science*, pp. 14–15). These ideas were later developed in his books *The Logic of Liberty* (1951), *Personal Knowledge* (1958), *The Study of Man* (1959), *The Tacit Dimension* (1964), *Knowing and Being* (1969) and *Meaning* (1975). In these works, Polanyi builds bridges between natural sciences and theological science, and shows in the process how all scientific methodology must be understood in the social context.

In establishing his case, Polanyi rejected the universalism of the eighteenth-century *Enlightenment rationalistic approach to science, thereby accepting three premises as essential to the ongoing debate about scientific methodology. First, he accepted the impossibility of verifying any of the universal statements commonly held by people, while agreeing on the potential falsifiability of all truth-claims. Secondly, he did not assert that eternal truths are automatically upheld, and in fact demonstrated that they can be effectively denied by modern man. Belief in such truths can only be sustained by an explicit profession of faith, in Polanyi's view, so that tradition is indispensable in every area of human inquiry. In this way, thirdly, he acknowledged that we all have to begin our intellectual development by accepting, uncritically, a large number of traditional presuppositions, which means that we should feel responsible for cultivating the particular strain of tradition into which we have been initiated.

This has a number of implications for *theological methodology and Christian apologetics. First of all, Thomas F. Torrance (*Theological Science* [Oxford, 1969]) has pointed out the essential difference between the kind of inquiry which is appropriate in theology and that which is apposite in the other sciences, when we consider the kind of verification or demonstration which is required. Theologians cannot investigate God by experimentation through human controls, he argues, and cites Polanyi's reference to the Christian doctrine of the resurrection of the dead. If this belief could be experimentally verified, this would disprove its miraculous nature, for, as Polanyi states, 'to the extent that any event can be established in terms of natural science, it belongs to the natural order of things ... It is illogical to attempt the proof of the supernatural by natural tests, for these can only establish the natural aspects of an event and can never represent it as supernatural' (*Personal Knowledge*, p. 284). Secondly, as a realist in philosophical terms, Polanyi accepts truth as existing independently of his knowledge of it and therefore accessible to all kinds of people. Yet he admits his inability to compel anyone to see the truth as he sees it. In describing how our love of truth is bound up with adherence to traditional practice within a particular community of inquiry, he also appreciated that his involvement in that community was an act of ultimate conviction, which stemmed from a 'conversion' experience. In this way, while the Christian apologist might recognize his or her inability to convince an unbeliever by rational argument, the possibility of conversion is open. 'Though powerless to argue with the nihilist, he may yet succeed in conveying to him the intimation of a mental satisfaction which he is lacking; and this intimation may start in him a process of conversion' (*Science*, p. 81). Thirdly, we should be unashamed to engage in the art of Christian apologetics from within our distinctive theological traditions, whether they be catholic, reformed, liberal or conservative, yet be prepared to learn from those whose tradition is different from our own, and to have common cause in areas where the essence of the historic Christian faith is under attack from proponents of other ideologies, religious or secular.

In addition, Polanyi's famous dictum on tacit knowledge, 'We know more than we can tell', is also an important insight for the contemporary practice of apologetics. Intuition is not only a key aspect of scientific inquiry, but it is also essential to the art of theological debate. There are some aspects of biblical truth which should never be presented as either logical or reasonable, in other words. When lovers express the wonder of their love for each other, they just know, by intuition, that they are in love. It cannot be established by any other so-called scientific criteria which would be at all convincing to them. A kiss, after all, is more than just the 'meeting of lips with an incidental exchange of fluids and micro-organisms', however scientifically accurate such a description might be. In the same way, how can we begin to formulate satisfactory arguments to establish, beyond a reasonable doubt, that 'God is Love'? All the evidence we may amass to support and defend such a statement, from the witness of creation as well as from the *revelation found in Scripture, will fall on deaf ears, apart from an intuitive awareness of the presence of God in human experience. In theological terms, such personal knowledge is the result of what John *Calvin termed 'the inner witness of the Holy Spirit'. He held that the words of Scripture were the result of a mysterious working (inspiration) of the Spirit, who guided the writers to communicate information and opinions (revelation) from God to people, so that the apostle Paul could claim that 'All Scripture is God-breathed' (2 Tim. 3:16), i.e. the origin of Scripture is in God's Spirit. But Calvin emphasized that the message of the Bible had to be impressed upon the mind and *conscience of the hearer or reader, so that the truth revealed through the biblical authors had an effect in the lives of believers. As scientific discovery is the realization of knowledge of that which is there, in the natural world, so spiritual illumination is the realization in experience of the God who is there, as mediated by the Spirit through the given revelation in Christ and the Scriptures which bear witness to him. Polanyian philosophical insights can, therefore, be very effective in informing apologetic arguments and expectations today.

Bibliography

M. Polanyi, *Science, Faith and Society*, 2nd edition (Chicago, 1964); V. S. Poythress, *Science and Hermeneutics* (Leicester, 1988).

G. R. HOUSTON

POLYTHEISM

The term 'polytheism' was coined to refer to the religious beliefs and practices of ancient Mesopotamia, Egypt, Greece, Rome and Scandinavia. Today any system of religious belief bearing significant similarity to these paradigmatic examples is classified as polytheistic. Usually the most easily identifiable similarity is that several gods are objects of cultic reverence. In many parts of the world polytheism remains common and presents challenges to Christian apologetics.

It is popularly assumed that *atheism, *monotheism and polytheism represent the full spectrum of religious belief. Terms built on the same etymological pattern are employed as subspecies of either monotheism (e.g. pantheism) or polytheism (e.g. henotheism). Classifying religious belief systems strictly by counting gods is attractive but proves inadequate given the great variety of religious belief. The problem is partly relieved by stipulating distinctions and employing supplemental terms like deism, dualism, monism, polydaemonism and totemism. Even so, some religions remain difficult to classify with a strict quantitative criterion without causing distortion and confusion.

This might seem counterintuitive, since everyone believes in either no gods, one god or many gods. However, despite their etymologies, polytheism and monotheism are not merely quantitative descriptors. They actually receive their primary meaning from reference to paradigmatic examples. As concepts they contain an important qualitative element. Furthermore, when speaking of how many gods are 'believed in' we must avoid taking this in the sense of 'belief in the existence of'. The more relevant sense of belief is 'devotion and cultic reverence for, worship'. For a religion or system of belief to be properly classified as polytheistic we should consider not only the number of gods said to exist, but also the nature of those gods and whether they are objects of worship. On these criteria a few religions turn out to be neither polytheistic nor monotheistic, but something else (e.g. traditional Mormonism).

Polytheistic religions generally consider their deities to be gendered and metaphysically finite. Each has *authority over specific areas of nature or society such as fertility, war, love, healing and the underworld. Gods can also have authority over specific trades. Each deity is accorded distinct cultic devotion appropriate to his or her position in the pantheon and importance to a society's needs. Polytheistic gods are not always exemplars of moral virtue and can have rivalries with one another. Often the gods that are worshipped are a second or third generation who have assumed their positions upon defeating a preceding generation in primordial combat. The ordering of the world and humanity's creation are sometimes explained as the results of such combat. These characteristics are common but some are not found in certain polytheistic religions. One idea that does seem to be universal is that the basic elements of the world have always existed in some form. As a result, no god is omnipotent. Many religions also count forces like fate and magic among the primal elements and see even the gods subject to them.

A polytheistic deity has historically been referred to as a 'god' but not a 'God'. Christians are sometimes accused of pejorative labelling for continuing this usage. However, linguistically 'god' and 'God' are different words. They are partially synonymous homonyms. Both refer to suprahuman beings that are objects of cultic devotion. Every 'God' is a 'god', but most 'gods' are not a 'God'. Unlike 'god', 'God' has no true plural. English has developed this usage to capture the fact that the gods of polytheistic and monotheistic religions are different sorts of beings.

Both ancient and contemporary polytheistic religions display a tendency to develop forms that posit some kind of unity between the gods. Sometimes the gods of the pantheon are considered parts of an organic whole, analogous to the human body, which is composed of individual parts with distinct functions. More often the gods who are worshipped are considered manifestations of a hidden high god, an impersonal divine reality or a philosophical principle. Because of this, some scholars mistakenly reclassify these religions as monotheistic. However, there remain significant differences between an omnipotent creator and a very powerful god who may be behind the gods. Even when high gods are praised as creators of the world, they are in reality mere craftsman; invariably they fashion the world from uncreated materials. Moreover, the unity attributed to the gods does not lead to unity of devotional practice. The various gods continue to be objects of distinct cultic reverence.

This search for underlying unity provides Christians with an entry point for discussion where design and *cosmological arguments may prove useful. In Romans Paul attributes polytheistic idolatry to the human tendency to suppress the truth about God (Rom. 1:18). This truth is suppressed by a futility in thinking associated with unrighteousness (1:18, 21). Paul does not have in mind all that can be known about God but specifically that people can know the truth about God's eternal power and nature (1:19–20). This refers primarily to God's oneness and uniqueness as creator and sustainer of the world (cf. Deut. 6:4; 1 Cor. 8:5–6; Col. 1:1–17). This truth is 'clearly seen' in what God has made (Rom. 1:19–20). When polytheistic religions attempt to unite the gods, this verifies that there is a deep intuitive sense of God's oneness and power. It is suppressed, but not without tension. Christians can appeal to these intuitions and show that their fulfilment is found in the Christian God.

Polytheists are not without arguments for the superiority of polytheism over monotheism and atheism. Most often cited is immunity against atheistic arguments from *evil. The polytheist agrees that there is no omnipotent, omniscient God responsible for creating the world, but denies atheism. Some evils can even be attributed to the gods and their competing interests. But evading the argument from evil exacts a high price. Evil is made a natural part of an uncreated universe. It is woven into the fabric of things and thus cannot be eradicated. Christianity, however, promises a future when God will rule over all and redeem the world from the corruption and suffering that characterize it (Rev. 21:1–4). This eschatological hope is a real possibility because the God of Christianity is an omnipotent creator who is not limited by the constraints of an uncreated reality. He has the power to bring about the eschatologically new and he promises one day to exercise that power (Rev. 11:17–18; cf. 4:11; 11:14).

The Japanese philosopher Takeshi Umehara and Western neo-pagans argue that polytheism fosters a responsible *environmentalism, whereas monotheism is an important cause of the environmental crisis. Monotheism empties nature of its divinity and allegedly places humanity in the centre of everything. Nature consequently becomes an object that humans are free to exploit. In contrast, polytheistic religions see humanity as one part of nature equal with all others. Nature is filled with the divine and gods have responsibility over specific aspects of nature. One must therefore be mindful of these gods in one's treatment of the environment.

Such claims contain a valid critique of the deism that has often functioned in the West as a surrogate for robust Christianity. But Christian monotheism is creational monotheism; the one God cares for the world and cares about what we do with it. Humanity is assigned a special role in the world and given dominion over the rest of creation (Gen. 1:28). This does not mean the world exists for humanity to do as it pleases. Rather, humanity is given the role and authority of a caretaker responsible for cultivating what belongs to another. Those who wantonly destroy the environment are guilty of the grave sins of disobeying God's foundational assignment to the race and defiling his handiwork. For this reason 'destroying those who destroy the earth' will be one of God's great eschatological acts of judgment (Rev. 11:18).

Lastly, polytheists contend that their religions promote peace, whereas monotheism destroys it. Monotheistic religions make universal truth-claims. They demand that all people worship one God. The monotheistic faiths send missionaries to convert people, sometimes forcibly. In the process, families are torn apart and rich cultures destroyed. Wars erupt because the monotheistic faiths disagree about which is the one true religion. Polytheism, however, supposedly rejects exclusive claims to universal religious truth. Each people group can have its own gods and customs. The beliefs and practices of different peoples can be tolerated and respected.

Christians should admit to making universal and exclusive truth-claims but point out that the polytheist's argument makes claims that are no less universal and exclusive. What matters is whose claims are true. The idealized portrait of polytheistic cultures assumed in these claims can readily be falsified. Conflict and wars are no less common in polytheistic than in monotheistic cultures. Though secular anthropologists decry doing so, Christians can also point to egregious cultural evils perpetuated within polytheistic societies that the advent of Christianity has eradicated in many places.

Bibliography

Y. Kaufmann, 'Pagan Religion', in The Religion of Israel: From Its Beginnings to the Babylonian Exile (ET, Chicago, 1960); B. N. Porter (ed.), One God or Many? Concepts of Divinity in the Ancient World (Chebeague Island, 2000); R. J. Z. Werblowsky, 'Polytheism', in M. Eliade (ed.), The Encyclopedia of Religion (New York, 1987).

C. MOSSER

POPMA, KLAAS JAN

Klass Jan Popma (1903–86), idiosyncratic and creative Reformed Christian scholar, lived in the Netherlands all his life. He received his PhD in classical studies from the University of Leiden and then completed his doctoral comprehensives in philosophy at the Free University in Amsterdam. Classicist, theologian, Bible scholar, philosopher and literary critic, Popma also wrote poetry and novels. All of his publications except one were in Dutch. He took his own position on many issues in the Reformed tradition to which he belonged. During a period spanning over half a century, he published at a furious pace, often seeing something in print – for the most part Bible studies and book reviews – twice or more times a month. He taught Reformational Philosophy at the University of Groningen from 1948 and at the University of Utrecht from 1955. Popma's most important mentor in Reformation thought was D. H. Th. *Vollenhoven, who together with his brother-in-law Herman *Dooyeweerd, initiated that philosophical tradition in the broader spiritual wake of Abraham *Kuyper. Popma's abiding scholarly interest was the place and task of academic theology. All his other work, in the many fields of expertise, is held together by a pervading sense of his vocation to test the spirits.

The significance of Popma for apologetics is his thematic preoccupation with *culture in all its dimensions and in any historical period from the perspective of the gospel. Niehbur's *Christ and Culture* could also have been the title of Popma's life. His desire was to help believers to learn to critically appreciate their cultural heritage as well as the contemporary cultural scene. He neither despised nor uncritically adopted any phase of human culture, whether it had Christian or pagan roots and regarded culture as God's gift to all, both tainted by sin and redeemed by grace. Hence the need to be both appreciative and critical of both Christian and secular culture.

Popma's most substantial publication is a seven-volume commentary on the Heidelberg Catechism called *Life View*. True to the author's idiosyncratic character, this work displays his erudition in all his fields of expertise, and does not easily fit into any category. It can perhaps best be characterized as a collection of observations about the Christian life of faith, occasioned by the Catechism. A goldmine of worthwhile aphorisms and unique insights, the work must be read on its own merits and could well serve as an apologetic notebook.

H. HART

POPPER, KARL

Karl Popper (1902–94) was born in Vienna and became a British subject in 1945. A scientist and philosopher, he was fully committed to the centrality of *science and its world-view. But he never joined the Vienna circle of the logical positivists, and he rejected their view that all non-scientific statements are meaningless. This was partly because he did not share their approach to issues of meaning as such, and also because he did not believe that scientific statements were verifiable in any of the ways the positivists required. Thus, he was willing to allow for the meaningfulness of ethical and metaphysical statements.

Popper argued that Einstein's theories necessitated a new understanding of how science operates. The old view, held since *Bacon and beloved of the positivists, was that science was able to give us certain knowledge through careful observation, the forming of hypotheses and experimental confirmation. Popper used the example of *Newton to show that this was not so. When Newton advanced his theories, they explained the behaviour of the planets perfectly except for some discrepancies in the behaviour of Uranus. These discrepancies could be explained, however, by postulating the existence of an unknown planet in a specific location. Sure enough, Neptune was then discovered in that location. This was universally seen as conclusively establishing the truth of Newton's system. However, said Popper, Einstein is now accepted as showing that Newton's system was not true after all. Even such impressive confirmation was unable to establish it in any definitive way. Thus, no scientific theory can, according to Popper, ever be established, and there are no grounds for having the confidence in scientific facts that people have felt for so long.

Further, induction as a method of finding truth has been discredited, and no amount of confirmatory observations can establish *truth. What is more, a large number of confirmations of a scientific hypothesis does not even increase the probability of it being correct. Scientists had assumed that repeated confirmation made the truth of a hypothesis more likely, even if it did not definitively prove it. Popper challenged this. Given that just one black swan exists, the truth of the hypothesis 'All swans are white' is no more established by observing a million white swans than by observing ten.

The observations of scientists are to be seen as tests with a view to falsification, rather than a means of confirmation. The scientist starts with a conjecture or intuition and then devises tests in an attempt to refute it. Until it fails a test, the conjecture is allowed to stand as a working hypothesis. If there are other different conjectures which explain the data equally well and have not been refuted, choice between the conjectures becomes a matter of personal preference. Popper extended the criterion of potential falsification to all areas of human knowledge and belief, and personally attacked both Freudians and Marxists for failing to take seriously data that potentially falsified their world-views.

Popper's concessions over the nature of scientific 'fact' opened the way for even more radical approaches, like that of Thomas Kuhn, and offered Christian apologists new ways of marrying the Christian and scientific world-views, in that the scientists are no longer to be seen as claiming definitive truth for their statements. Popper's position required apologists to take seriously their own 'openness'. However psychologically certain they may be of their own beliefs, they must be prepared to concede that at least something would falsify their position. For example, if Christ is not risen, their faith would be in vain.

Popper's concession, developed further by Kuhn, that scientists operate with conjectures rather than with hard facts, allows Christian apologists to place the Christian and strictly scientific world-views on an equal footing. Both are explanatory hypotheses for the data adopted 'by faith'; both may be allowed to stand provided they are not falsified after careful testing. Choice between them may be a matter of personal preference or, better, on the grounds of comprehensiveness in explaining all the data, including those of value, morals, human personhood and the like.

Bibliography

K. Popper, *The Logic of Scientific Discovery* (London, 1959).

P. HICKS

POSTMODERNITY

Postmodernism has been so freely applied by both its proponents and detractors that it has become virtually meaningless, but it tends to be associated with anything that overturns traditional standards and promotes *relativism (moral or otherwise). Before being applied to such thinkers as Jacques *Derrida, Michel *Foucault, Jean-François *Lyotard and Richard *Rorty, it was earlier used by literary critics and architects. 'Postmodernity' is more appropriate than the term 'postmodernism', since 'ism' implies a uniformity that postmodern thinkers clearly do not share. If anything unites postmodern thinkers, it is their reaction to modern (or *Enlightenment) thought, but that reaction takes different forms and degrees. Drawing a clear line between postmodern and modern thought seems impossible, for modern thinkers often have postmodern aspects to their thought, and postmodern thinkers both criticize and continue modernity. But, of course, modernity itself was never a unified phenomenon.

At the risk of oversimplifying the case,

modern thought could be characterized by three closely connected elements. First, modern thinkers usually place strong emphasis on the autonomy of the individual, assuming that human beings both are and ought to be free to define themselves. An important result of this is the denigration of tradition and *authority, so that each individual must decide right from wrong, *truth from falsity. Secondly, modern thought tends to have strong confidence in the powers of reason to make decisions. Thirdly, reason is defined as objective (i.e. universal). As long as one uses the right 'method', then individuals can, at least in theory, come to conclusions that all rational beings can endorse.

All of these aspects are strikingly evident in the thought of Immanuel *Kant, who gives us the 'motto' of enlightenment as 'think for yourself' in his essay 'What is Enlightenment?' Admittedly, Kant complicates this exhortation when he speaks of reason as having limits and even claims to limit reason so as to allow room for faith. But reason still remains the supreme test. Thus, in *Religion Within the Bounds of Reason Alone*, Kant reduces God to the moral lawgiver and Christianity to a moral system. Being convinced in the objectivity of reason, Kant thinks we can make rational decisions in a purely detached manner. Surprisingly, Kant describes his philosophical reorientation as a 'Copernican revolution', though it has exactly the opposite effect of making the human self become the centre of the universe. Instead of seeing the mind as mirroring the world, in the *Critique of Pure Reason* the mind becomes central to organizing ('interpreting') experience through concepts the mind creates. Kant considers his philosophy to be 'transcendental' in two senses, because the 'organization' brought about by thought is necessary for there to be any experience at all (making human interpretation central to knowledge) and this structure of knowing is universal for people in all times and places. Kant assumes that anyone, anywhere, at any time, who reasons aright will come to the same conclusion. But, if Kant is right that we always interpret the world in a particular way, then we never know it as it *really* is. Hence, Kant makes his famous distinction between the 'phenomenal' world (the world as it appears to us) and the noumenal world (the world as is). Thus, knowledge for Kant is objective in the sense of being universal but not objective in the sense of existing apart from the subject.

Even in Kant's lifetime, Johann Fichte had already undermined his insistence on the universality of truth. Emphasizing Kant's idea that the human self is radically free, Fichte argues that our minds organize the world on the basis of our personal needs, so that many different ways of viewing the world are possible, no one being truly 'correct'. Following both Fichte and Kant, G. W. F. *Hegel's *Phenomenology of Spirit* shows human *history to be a progression of world-views, none of which are absolutely true or false, even though each reveals a certain degree of truth (and some are more true than others). 'Truth' ends up being the sum total of all perspectives.

Given these 'modern' views, it is hardly surprising that the so-called first 'postmodern' thinker, Friedrich *Nietzsche, questions the very notion of truth as universal. But Nietzsche's attack is not simply against the moderns but against the entire philosophical tradition's claims that that truth is 'static' (as in *Plato's Forms) and can be fully known. Nietzsche dismisses these arguments as pretentious and unfounded. Although Nietzsche is often interpreted as simply denying the existence of truth, his attack is more accurately against a Platonic conception of truth. Of course, Nietzsche (wrongly) assumes that Christianity is simply a version of Platonism, so he takes his criticism of Platonism to be likewise against Christianity. However Nietzsche defines truth (a question open to scholarly debate), he clearly thinks that human beings only have a perspective on it. What we call truth is inevitably contextual and historical, not the final word. Nietzsche may be postmodern in questioning truth and rationality, but he is perhaps the apotheosis of the modern view of the self, partly in reaction to the decline of Christianity. In pronouncing the death of God in *The Gay Science*, he sees himself as simply making it clear that Christianity is no longer a vital cultural force. Admittedly, Nietzsche vehemently criticizes Christianity (particularly in *The Antichrist*), but how close those barbs come to hitting true Christian belief and experience is not easy to determine. Nietzsche's attacks were not so much against vibrant Christianity but against those who held to Christian morality without its metaphysical commitments. Since German Lutheranism of Nietzsche's day was rampant with such Christians, his criticism is understandable. But Nietzsche also wishes to replace Christianity with something that affirms life. As much as

Nietzsche sees Jesus as someone to emulate (and criticizes his followers for distorting his teachings), he cannot accept Jesus' call to love our enemies and give up our innate desire to take control. What Nietzsche means by the 'will to power' is disputed by scholars, but it is certainly difficult to reconcile with Jesus' willing renunciation of *power.

The idea that human knowing is historical and contextual is certainly continued in the thought of Martin Heidegger. But, more importantly, Heidegger seriously undermines such basic philosophical dualisms as subject/object and *realism/*idealism in *Being and Time*. For Heidegger, the human person (whom he calls *Dasein*) is related to the world in such an interconnected way that speaking of subject and object distorts that relationship. Neither realism (the view that the world exists independently of our relations to it) nor idealism (that we in effect 'create' the world) adequately describes that relationship. Thus, Heidegger sees the realism/idealism argument as simply misguided, since neither terms are adequate. In his later texts such as 'The Onto-theo-logical Constitution of Metaphysics', Heidegger makes the distinctly postmodern move of questioning the very project of metaphysics (theorizing concerning 'being'), arguing that it has been characterized by what he terms 'onto-theology'. Following Nietzsche, Heidegger claims that Western *metaphysics has reduced God to simply the 'greatest being'. But Heidegger sees this as an attempt to control God, so that God becomes an 'explanation' to fit the philosophers' purposes. In his 'Letter on Humanism', Heidegger expands this by saying that even reason has been a way of controlling the world and elevating human beings. Heidegger wishes to de-centre the self and make philosophy into a kind of poetry that attempts to think about being and truth without making pretentious claims to know it.

Reacting to the centrality of the self in modernity, Hans-Georg Gadamer rehabilitates the concepts of tradition and authority in *Truth and Method*. Gadamer sees Kant's ideal of thinking for oneself as impossible and undesirable. Instead, we are highly dependent upon the judgments and ideas passed on to us, so the self never stands, nor decides, alone. Further, Gadamer argues that authority may be legitimate, and recognizing legitimate authority is itself an act of reason. Although we should be

willing to examine the assumptions and prejudices of our culture, Gadamer sees thinking as
closely connected to our own historical and
cultural horizon, so reason and understanding
are never pure. But, even if understanding is
always contextual, Gadamer insists that true
understanding of other contexts is possible by
way of a 'a fusion of horizons'.

Jacques Derrida is most closely associated
with his idea of deconstruction, an idea that
has been used in the academy to justify irresponsible scholarship and relativism of various
sorts. But, strictly speaking, deconstruction is
the idea of unbuilding in order to examine a text
or a theory, which can be used for good or ill.
Derrida's early philosophy (see e.g. *Speech and
Phenomena* and *Of Grammatology*) particularly focuses on the possibility of complete
perception, knowledge and communication by
way of examining concepts and *language. For
Derrida, concepts and language present us not
with the thing in its fullness (either as phenomena or noumena) but with only a 'trace' of it.
While Derrida has widely been interpreted as
denying notions like truth and *morality, his
later philosophy focuses on them. To his critics,
he responds that such have been his concerns all
along. In 'Force of Law: The Mystical Foundation of Authority', Derrida claims not only
that *justice is beyond deconstruction but that
'deconstruction is justice', since deconstruction
illuminates the ways in which acts of justice fall
short of justice itself. Likewise, Derrida argues
that all attempts to speak adequately of God
fail, leaving us with but a 'trace' of who God is.
In *The Gift of Death*, Derrida argues that true
morality (which he finds exemplified by Christianity) demands a sacrifice of oneself for the
other, and true belief is ultimately faith (not
reason).

Derrida would readily admit that Emmanuel
Levinas was the primary impetus for his turn to
issues of morality and faith. In *Totality and
Infinity*, Levinas claims that Western thought
has always been about dominating the other.
Whereas metaphysics or epistemology have
traditionally been seen as 'first' philosophy,
Levinas replaces them with *ethics, in which
recognition of the true 'otherness' of the other
is central, and the relation to the other is
construed in purely non-economic or non-
reciprocal terms. In stark contrast to Kant's
conception of enlightenment, Levinas thinks
that reason only begins when the self no longer
attempts to think for itself but instead allows

its thinking to be put into question by the
other.

The extent to which one can follow the
modern imperative of thinking for oneself and
acting as a free agent proves a driving concern
for Michel Foucault. Both in his personal life
and scholarship, Foucault continually tests the
boundaries of thought and action by investigating the ways in which reason is shaped by
*culture and institutional practices (see e.g. *The
Origin of Things*), all the while seeking ways to
escape from that influence. Rather than seeing
concepts as simply benign, Foucault argues that
they are always used to exert power, and his
detailed research into, for example, medical and
penal institutions (see *Discipline and Punish*)
makes that clear. Towards the end of his life,
Foucault began studying the role *sexuality had
played throughout history. Through that study,
he became interested in the Stoics and their
ways of taking control of the self, particularly
practices of self-discipline. Had Foucault not
died relatively young, his thought might have
taken a very different direction.

Many of the preceding themes can be found
in the American philosopher Richard Rorty. In
Philosophy and the Mirror of Nature, he
attacks the idea that human knowledge can
mirror nature and dismisses *foundationalism
(the ideal of providing a foundation for human
knowledge) as a vain hope. Often quoted as
defining truth as 'what our peers will let us get
away with saying', Rorty speaks of himself as
an 'ironist', someone who holds to certain
beliefs all the while knowing that they are not
true in any sense other than the pragmatic
sense of 'useful for the moment'. Whereas in
his early philosophy Rorty still held to the idea
of philosophical argumentation, in his later
philosophy (e.g. *Contingency, Irony, and Solidarity*) he claims that there can be no real
'arguments' but simply 'redescriptions' of
things, poetic metaphors that make positions
seem appealing. Although Rorty is usually (and
rightly) labeled a relativist, he thinks such
terms as 'true rationality' or 'relativism' ultimately make no sense in a context where there
is no God and nothing is sacrosanct because
there is no meaningful alternative (which the
term 'relative' requires). Rorty's postmodern
view of the self takes over the Nietzschean idea
of poetization of the self but without the
romantic overtones.

Probably the most prominent Christian postmodern philosopher is Jean-Luc Marion, who

shows how postmodern insights can be applied to Christian thought. In *God without Being*, Marion argues that our claims to knowledge of God always run the risk of placing a conceptual schema on God that results in 'conceptual idolatry'. Arguing that God is above even 'being' (so that God is *not* defined as 'the greatest possible being'), Marion affirms not the God of the philosophers but the God of faith. For Marion, any concept of God that claims to present us with God in his fullness is idolatrous, for God always escapes our grasp. In contrast to idols, icons give us a 'trace' of God, whom no concepts can 'capture'. Marion attempts to steer a middle course between an unwise silence (when all talk about God is silenced) and unguarded chatter. A wise silence recognizes the limitations of one's speech and attempts to say only what one can legitimately say, the question being not so much 'what' one says of God but 'how'.

At this point, it should be clear just how complicated both modernity and postmodernity are. Probably the best advice is to beware of any simple acceptance or rejection of either. On the one hand, while modern thought does affirm the existence and possibility of knowing truth, its definition of truth tends to be limited to whatever is empirically provable. Thus modern thought has, on the whole, been inimical to Christian belief. While the Enlightenment emphasis on critical inspection of one's beliefs is admirable in a sense, the goal of 'thinking for oneself' has often been linked to an agenda. Gadamer bluntly points out that 'enlightenment critique is primarily directed against the religious tradition of Christianity – i.e. the Bible'. Further, not only does the modern conception of the self as autonomous seem incorrect descriptively, it also is incompatible with a Christian view of the person in which individuals find their identity as members of the body of Christ. Finally, although Scripture clearly affirms the value of human rationality as part of what it means to be made in God's image, the modern confidence in human reason is deeply at odds with the biblical emphasis on the limits of human ability.

On the other hand, the postmodern reaction is sometimes equally as questionable and incompatible with Christianity. Not only do some postmodern thinkers take the modern conception of the self to its absolute extreme (e.g. Nietzsche and Foucault), but the rejection of the abilities of human reason is sometimes so severe as to eliminate the possibility of knowing truth at all. Yet there are many aspects of postmodern thought that can benefit believers. The emphasis on a de-centred self is a helpful corrective to the presumptuous claims of modernity and resonates with Christian teachings concerning the danger of pride. Even a thinker like Nietzsche, however antagonistic he may be towards Christianity, is instructive, for his penetrating critique of the failings of Christians is sometimes all too true. Further, the postmodern denial of the pure objectivity of reason is not so far away from the Christian idea that knowing the truth is closely linked to being a virtuous person, since sin can easily cloud our minds. While the questioning of the power and purity of reason by postmodern thinkers is appropriate, one need not go to the extreme of concluding that there is only contingency. It is one thing to affirm the contingency (or historicality) of reason, and quite another to hold that reason is merely contingent and in no sense universally valid. Christians should heartily endorse the postmodern recognition of the limits of rationality (and the *humility of spirit that recognition should entail), but without concluding that there either is no truth or that we are incapable of knowing truth.

Bibliography

B. E. Benson, *Graven Ideologies: Nietzsche, Derrida, and Marion on Modern Idolatry* (Downers Grove, 2002); D. Lyon, *Postmodernity* (Minneapolis, 1999); J.-F. Lyotard, *The Postmodern Condition* (Minneapolis, 1985); R. C. Solomon, *Continental Philosophy Since 1750* (Oxford, 1988).

B. E. BENSON

POWER

Power is a fundamental reality of God, creation and human living. Its use and misuse, especially by and within Christian structures and relationships, is of critical apologetic importance, since it reflects the nature and power of the gospel. In the Christian tradition, power is exemplified in God, the 'maker of all things visible and invisible', who 'raises up' the downtrodden and helpless, and in Christ overcomes death. This living Lord's ultimate act of power is the transformation of this present age into a 'new creation' in Christ.

That God is 'omnipotent', 'all-powerful', is generally taken as axiomatic in the Western theological tradition. 'Power' here generally means 'force', and the exercise of power the unflinching imposition of might. The concept of deity involved comes close to caricaturing the God revealed in *Jesus Christ, though it has found ecclesiastical support. Where Christian institutions and the social order are closely interwoven, divine power can be commended as a resource for a 'quiet and peaceable' life, as the 1662 *Book of Common Prayer* of the Church of England envisaged. Christians who experienced that church as oppressive repudiated such an association and sought the separation of church and state. In centuries since, wider interrogations of divine power have arisen, partly from its use and abuse to sustain oppressive political structures, partly from rejection of religion itself in the face of disasters (e.g. the Lisbon earthquake, the Thirty Years War).

The biblical namings of God as 'almighty' appear to support this assumption. Further, to confess 'Jesus Christ is Lord' (1 Cor. 12:3; Phil. 2:11; cf. Acts 2:36) assumes his status as all-powerful 'head over everything' (Eph. 1:22). When set within Christ's ministry and the pattern of the acts of God as a whole, however, the scriptural testimony to divine power looks very different. The story of Abram and Sarai is paradigmatic: remarkable promises are made (Gen. 12:1–3, 7; 15:44–46; 17:1–8), unexpected births follow, and they are protected from life-threatening danger (Gen. 12:10–20; 14; 20), as is their only son Isaac (Gen. 22). Such demonstrations of divine power are not portrayed as examples of a general concept but personal encounters with the living God. Mary celebrates the overshadowing 'power of the most High', and the angel's 'nothing is impossible with God' (Luke 1:37) is no philosophical observation, but one with her song of praise of the Lord who scatters the proud and lifts up the poor, according to the promise made to our forebears, 'to Abraham and his descendants forever' (Luke 1:55).

The scriptural testimony has deeper levels, however. Israel's historical encounter with God embraced both exodus and exile. In the former, God's power delivers them from slavery, desert dangers and predatory marauders. In contrast, in the exile it is by *God*'s action that people, land, temple and royal family are devastated, issuing in a profound theological crisis (cf. Lam. 2:1–17). If the fact that 'the LORD is a warrior' is Israel's strength and might (Exod. 15:2), this same Lord could 'become their enemy' because of their evil (Isa. 63:10; and note Exod. 17; 32 – 33, Josh. 7 and 1 Sam. 4 – 6 for similar 'two-sided' divine action). This theological pattern, of the Lord able to act in ways that far exceed human understanding, but doing so according to the divine character of justice, compassion and mercy, is the fundamental witness of the Scriptures to power (cf. Isa. 40:12–31). It is seen existentially in the close intermingling of lament and praise within the Psalter. Praise alone may be full of power, but does not question the *status quo*; lament alone forgets the Lord with whom Israel is in covenant; their inter-mingling reflects the two-sided scriptural pattern of the exercise of God's power.

This two-fold pattern is most fully set out in the ministry of Jesus, who exercised God's power in relation to nature, disease, the demonic and even death. Yet this power is consistently deployed for the good – consideration is shown even to unclean spirits (Mark 5:11–13). Further, its chief manifestation is not seen in 'signs and wonders', but in the way he 'resolutely set out for Jerusalem', for passion and death (Luke 9:51), until his 'hour' had come to die on a cross (John 12:27–33). In Christ, and crucially in his death and resurrection, the divine 'exodus' (Luke 9:31) and 'exile' (Matt. 27:45–50) come together. Jesus refused the way of power, remaining silent in the face of the powers at his trial, to deploy God's power through death, to destroy this 'last enemy', and so bring God's reconciling liberation to all. Such 'power in weakness' was what Paul and his apostolic team sought to live out in their ministry: depending on God's powerful grace and rejecting any power of themselves as 'boasting', they proclaimed the gospel of Christ in ways that were commendable and costly, so that his power might save, build up and correct (Rom. 1:16–17; 3:27–31; 2 Cor. 3:1–6; 4:1–15; 10:1–18; 11:16–33). This outlook dominates Revelation, in which the victorious 'Lion of the tribe of Judah' is the 'Lamb, who was slain' (Rev. 5:5–10); those who conquer do so by the 'blood of the Lamb' and their faithful testimony even to death (Rev. 12:10–11). The power of God is thus definitively displayed in the 'weak' and 'foolish' cross of Christ, the definitive *revelation of God's powerful love (1 John 4:10–19).

For much of the church's history this pattern has not been to the fore, and a close connection between God and power has been viewed as a strongly positive element in apologetic. Where human beings are oppressed, or face disaster, danger or death, faith in an omnipotent deity offers hope, empowerment and meaning. When churches are persecuted, believe they are in danger of persecution, or even sense that they may be losing their place in society, faith in Christ as 'all-powerful' (*pantocrator*) forms an inescapable element (cf. the Eastern churches' millennium-long heritage of living under pressure). Yet such an association can become problematic, as has become the case since the First World War and Hiroshima, in which 'Christian' nations were implicated.

The particular context in which power is considered is thus of prime importance in shaping a particular apologetic response. Since the mid-twentieth century, 'liberationist' approaches to social order (notably post-colonialism and feminism in the West), democratic concern to disperse power (e.g. 'the principle of subsidiarity' in European political life) and the rise of numerous interest groups in consumer societies, form examples of changing contexts to which Christian reflection and use of power necessarily speak. Where there is radical scepticism about all institutions, power itself comes to be viewed as invalid and intrinsically abusive. This not uncommonly happens in faith communities where high ideals of relationship exist and structures of *authority are viewed as unnecessary. Here disillusionment and even abuse commonly emerge from the very real implicit power structures which subsist in all communities.

In Christian theology, the resurgence of explicitly trinitarian doctrine has in part been shaped by the need to respond to totalitarian regimes (of both 'right' in Karl *Barth and 'left' in Jürgen Moltmann) in which power is all. Such totalitarianisms are seen as expressions of the deistic 'omnipotence' assumptions about God which have undergirded much Western philosophy and society for centuries, but stand in tension with the self-revelation of the trinitarian God in Christ. Where Christian communities are too closely aligned to structures or patterns of power, distancing or questioning will be necessary, and the exile paradigm is relevant here. Where they share the dangers and sheer banality of much daily personal and community life, the proclamation in word and deed of the power of God forms a crucial part of apologetic, and an exodus orientation is significant here. Ideally, both paradigms are held together, as in the ministry of Christ.

In pastoral practice, apologetic responses need to be formed 'on the run' as particular situations are encountered, often with balancing responses needed at the same time: dealing with a colleague who has admitted having sex with church teenagers, supporting a persecuted non-Christian faith community, listening to a radical feminist recently bereaved, counselling someone whose 'power (non-)healing' has produced a crisis of faith. What really matters for apologetics in practice is that such ministries be experienced as 'power with' and 'power for' rather than 'power over'. Only then can Christian apologetics be received as gospel, good and powerful news which brings Christ's authentic peace, goodness and harmony in a troubled world.

Bibliography

K. Barth, *Church Dogmatics* 11/1 (Edinburgh, 1957); D. G. Bloesch, *God the Almighty* (Carlisle, 1995); A. Case-Winters, *God's Power: Traditional Understandings and Contemporary Challenges* (Louisville, 1990); J. Moltmann, *The Trinity and the Kingdom* (London, 1977); C. H. Sherlock, *The God who Fights: The War-Tradition in Holy Scripture* (New York, 1993); G. Studdert Kennedy, *The Hardest Part* (London, 1921); H.-R. Weber, *Power: Focus for a Biblical Theology* (Geneva, 1989).

C. SHERLOCK

PRAGMATISM

Pragmatism is a theory of meaning that seeks to establish meaning with reference to its actual effects on human experience and action. While having roots in philosophers as disparate as *Kant and *Nietzsche and British empiricists such as John *Locke and John Stuart *Mill, pragmatism as a developed philosophy is found primarily in the works of the American philosophers Charles S. Peirce (1839–1914), William *James (1842–1910) and John *Dewey (1859–1952).

Pragmatism may be described as an uneasy alliance between British *empiricism, with its emphasis on the basis of knowledge in sense experience, and German voluntarism, with its stress on the free choice and action of the individual. Like empiricism, pragmatism rejects any notion of *a priori* *truth in favour of an *epistemology founded upon sense experience. At the same time, however, it wishes to maintain the significance of human free will in the face of determinacy. This means that no truth can be regarded as self-evident, as the truth of a notion is dependent solely upon its practical consequences, and yet this emphasis on the practical and empirical is counter-balanced by the rejection by pragmatists (such as James and Peirce) of any understanding of human beings which renders us as nothing more than mechanisms in thrall to the laws of a mechanistic universe. Human existence and knowledge is not solely a matter of cause and effect, of practical consequences and experience. James in particular was horrified by the idea that we might be 'wholly conditioned', or that 'not a wiggle of our will happens save as a result of physical laws'.

In his 1879 work *The Sentiment of Rationality* James explores a theme already suggested by Kant, that humanity by nature has a tendency to move beyond evidence, to operate as agnostic. He says that, 'The absurd abstraction of an intellect verbally formulating all its evidence and carefully estimating the probability thereof by vulgar fraction, by the size of whose denominator and numerator alone it is swayed, is ideally as inept as it is actually impossible.' Here we see the importance of the exercise of the individual will – we are not simply responding to stimuli or working solely with what is given in experience.

James is also indebted to Kant (via the neo-Kantian F. A. Lange) for the view that the world we experience is a representation, a construct that is determined by our act of apprehension. What is significant here is again the balance between an emphasis on experience (the processes of external reality and their practical effects) and an emphasis on action (the exercise of human will and understanding). Lange, drawing on the burgeoning new discipline of *psychology, understood reality as a complex of that which is external to us and that which we bring to reality in the act of apprehension as we 'supplement reality'.

For many people pragmatism has connotations of meaning or truth being established by usefulness – 'I will believe this if it does me good.' Some basis for this view might be found

in Peirce, who, in many respects, marked out the principal tenets of pragmatism. For Peirce, following Alexander Bain, inquiry and meaning have to do with the habitual belief of a biological organism in the utility of things and ideas, this utility being specifically with respect to its survival. So, the quest for understanding and its conclusions are driven by biological instincts and needs. In other words, meaning is not inherent within a concept or object but rather issues out of its behaviour and effect when the survival driven organism engages with it. So, pragmatism is a philosophical method for clarifying meaning construed in this way. Peirce goes on to classify this pragmatic habit of mind as 'belief' in a way reminiscent of both *Hume and Kant and in a way which has a very contemporary ring to it in a postmodern context. Truth, even scientific truth, argues Peirce, is always provisional and thus ultimately fallible.

William James also argues for the significance of belief. In *The Will to Believe* (1879), he argues that even scientific hypotheses are initially founded upon belief, for prior to any evidence having been gathered in support, the scientist must exercise sufficient belief in a theory to pursue evidential support for it. James concludes that in the debate between *theism and *materialism there is no good reason for rejecting theism and thus, pragmatically, it makes perfect sense to maintain a theistic belief system. James was concerned to limit the application of *science and particularly to find a basis for the exercise of human freewill.

So, in many respects Pragmatism can be seen as a rejection of rational *idealism where truth is seen as eternal and one. It emphasizes the way we experience, see and understand the world as the source of meaning and belief. This raises the issue of *relativism and change and the possibility of progress. James makes this point, 'the world is characterised by change and truth, and meaning must be remade as we construct new concepts out of our new experiences of the world' (*A Pluralistic Universe*, 1909).

James believed in the potential for improvement in the world via an exercise of the human will which, as we have seen, is not seen by pragmatists as determined. The orientation towards an improved future found in Kantian-inspired thinkers like James and *Ritschl was taken up by John Dewey, who was also influenced by the Darwinian evolutionary outlook.

Dewey referred to his own brand of pragmatism as instrumentalism. For him ideas are instruments for adjusting life, in both its natural and social mode. It is here that we see the ethical implications of pragmatism most clearly. *Ethics is seen as the adjusting of human behaviour towards more satisfying ways of living, i.e. we change our behaviour and our evaluation of how we should behave in order to improve our lives. This modification takes place at the natural and social level rather than at any metaphysical one. Dewey was dismissive of any system of thought, such as idealism and classical *theology, which he saw as disengaging itself from a truly human environment. Ultimately, for Dewey, what is true is what works, and what works is established by a philosophical analysis of real problems resulting in a practical resolution or consummation. To this end, it could be said that philosophers are principally concerned with inquiry rather than truth. It is the process of investigation, analysis and inquiry that is at the heart of Dewey's conception of truth, and here we see the residue of his early interest in *Hegel. However, unlike Hegel, for whom the process of thought leads ultimately to absolute truth, for Dewey there is no such resolution.

So the primary focus for human inquiry is the immediate situation, not some abstract notion of eternal *absolutes. Dewey was very concerned that education should start from the foundations of actual human experience (here we see the links with empiricism again) so that what we learn improves our ability to function and survive in the world. Truth, for Dewey, becomes a matter of effect rather than one of fact; whatever hypothesis works is the truth.

Although we might not want to associate him too strongly with Dewey's instrumentalism, the German Protestant theologian Wolfhart *Pannenberg (who is also much indebted to Hegel) makes a similar point. Pannenberg argues that religions – and indeed the gods that they represent – ought properly to be tested and judged on the basis of their ability to improve our understanding of the world and our place in it. In other words, religions ought to be tested on pragmatic grounds, on whether they 'work' or not. However, Pannenberg clearly sees the process of inquiry as resolving itself in a future destiny, truth and ultimately God. His emphasis on actual experience and on beginning 'from below' is combined with concern for and confidence in 'absolute truth'.

This article has talked about the importance of experience to pragmatism, but this raises questions about how experience might be defined. What kind of experience? What counts as experience?

For Dewey it is important that actual human experience should not be confused with abstract philosophical reflection upon experience. Hearing a piece of music, for example, is not the same as an analysis of the component notes that make up that piece. Indeed, this observation forms the basis of Dewey's critique of empiricism, which he see as providing a sterile, spectator picture of the world which is in a very real sense inaccurate. It could be said that Dewey is seeking to establish the distinction between experience in the real world and experience generated under laboratory conditions. Thus, the frequently established division between theory and practice is, according to Dewey, a false one as true knowledge is successful practice. On this basis, Dewey offers a critique of the educational convention that divides vocational training from academic education. Education, he argues, is to do with training the intellect so that it might make the best sense of the world, thereby improving the human condition. We only learn about what is best for us and for the world by actual lived experience, and we can only effect change for the better if we know how to engage practically with the physical world. Armchair theorizing, argues Dewey, provides neither an accurate insight into the nature of the world nor the capacity to act in it effectively. Dewey is antagonistic to the passive 'spectator epistemologies' characterized by Greek idealism and, indeed, *Enlightenment *rationalism, on the ground that they encourage the notion of human powerlessness in the face of the absolute.

Dewey accepts Peirce's understanding of truth as fallible and thus always provisional (a view also found in Pannenberg and Moltmann). Dewey is somewhat wary of using the word 'true' at all, preferring the more guarded and less absolute phrase 'warranted assertability'. In this way, Dewey also prefigures the postmodern concern with the death of the 'grand-narrative'.

The apologetic utility of pragmatism is quite apparent when we consider its concern to establish the practical utility of a set of beliefs or courses of action. The Judeo-Christian tradition has always maintained that it provides the best possible insight into the human condition such that we might live the best possible lives in the world in which we find ourselves. All religions, as Pannenberg has argued, stand or fall on their ability to illuminate the world and make the best sense of our place in it. While issues of truth, right belief and devotion to God are undoubtedly of great concern to the Judeo-Christian tradition, there is clearly a pragmatic dimension to be found also as we are encouraged to 'taste and see' – clearly a pragmatic injunction. There are echoes here of the work of the seventeenth-century philosopher and Christian apologist Blaise *Pascal. Pascal argued in his famous 'wager' that belief in God is pragmatically reasonable in so far as God either exists or does not exist and that a choice one way or another is logically inevitable, just as a choice between heads or tails on a flipped coin is inevitable. Pascal goes on to argue that if you choose to accept belief in God, the possible outcomes are blessed eternal life if the wager pays off or oblivion if it does not, while if you choose not to accept God it is simply oblivion. The long and the short of it is that you might as well make the choice for God as you have nothing to lose and everything to gain, a very pragmatic argument indeed. Of course, Pascal goes on to argue that once the choice is made then God vindicates it through a real felt relationship with the believer.

There has been a suspicion since the nineteenth century that the influence of Greek thought, both metaphysical and epistemological, upon Christianity may have been less than helpful. Liberal protestant theologians such as *Schleiermacher, Ritschl and *Harnack have argued that the passive absolutism found in *Platonic idealism, for example, has tended to distance Christianity from the world focusing its attention on otherworldly ideals. As Dewey points out, this inclination encourages not only a sense of powerlessness to effect change in the world but also prompts an attitude towards the human perception of truth that is inappropriate to our context and condition. The charge that it is 'so heavenly minded it is no earthly use' is one to which the church has often laid itself open.

Pragmatism reminds us that the Christian tradition should not only be about what is true and what is right but also about what works

best. Christian theologians in the twentieth century have demonstrated significant concern to do justice to this aspect of Christianity, for example, Pannenberg's concern with actual experience and human *history, and the emphasis of Moltmann and liberation theologians on praxis reflect some of the insights of pragmatism in the way they see the truth and meaningfulness of Christianity as truth and meaningfulness which must be accessible for and related to actual human experience and need.

However, these theologians are not claiming that meaning and truth are established entirely or solely on the basis of their effects and value within human experience. Many Christians would be worried by a questioning of the 'status' of the truth of their beliefs and the relativistic nature of some pragmatic thought. Is Christianity true because it 'works' or does it 'work' because it is true? And is it true for those for whom it does not seem to work? There is a balance, if not a tension and a *paradox here which Pannenberg and Moltmann locate, in a sense, in Christ. The expectation that Christ has the potential to transform people's lives is based in the belief that Christ is the presence of God in human history and experience. And yet the belief that Christ is the presence of God is partly based on the way in which this belief offers potential to meet the human need for meaning and hope.

Bibliography

A. J. Ayer, *The Origins of Pragmatism* (London and Oxford, 1974); W. James, *Pragmatism* (New York, 1995).

M. ALSFORD and S. E. ALSFORD

PREACHING AND APOLOGETICS

In one sense all preaching is apologetic, in that its aim is to commend the gospel and to change people's attitudes and behaviour. However, much preaching has a largely pastoral dimension, in that it is mainly addressed to the converted and its purpose is to build them up in their faith. It is better not to draw rigid distinctions between different kinds of preaching; all preachers speak to mixed groups composed of people at all stages of faith and none. Nevertheless, there is a kind of preaching which, in the words of 1 Peter 3:15, is 'prepared to give an answer to everyone who asks you to give the reason for the hope that you have'. The word the NIV translates 'reason' is *apologia*, and an apologist is one who defends the gospel against misrepresentation and establishes its credibility and reliability. This article will look briefly at how apologetic preaching developed, and then address some of the contemporary issues which make apologetic preaching both particularly difficult and necessary.

Apologetic preaching is a major feature of the book of Acts, and Paul's sermon on the Areopagus, in Acts 17:22–31, is perhaps the most striking example of this. Here we have many of the features of good apologetic preaching: engaging with and challenging his hearers' world-view (vv. 22–23); the use of the biblical doctrines of creation and providence (vv. 24–26); the 'God-shaped blank' in human lives (vv. 25–28); the attempt to limit God (vv. 29–30); and the resurrection and judgment (v. 31). The OT canon is presented here, but, since Paul is speaking to non-Jews, it is implicit rather than explicit. Paul's preaching here is marked by boldness, confidence in the truth of the gospel and a conviction of its relevance to human history.

In the early church there were a number of significant 'apologists', such as *Justin Martyr, author of *Apology 1*, with its appendix, and *Apology 2*, which concentrates mainly on Christ as Logos. These works appeared in the second half of the second century. Justin also preached widely in many cities, including Rome. The most significant figure, as in much else, was *Augustine (354–430), the greatest Latin theologian and one of the most significant influences on all subsequent *theology. Himself a convert, he well understood the need to commend the faith to unbelievers. More than a third of his work consists of sermons, although what survives is only a fraction of the 8,000 sermons he is reputed to have preached. Augustine refuted Manichean errors, especially dualism and the lack of the objective reality of evil. His conflicts with donatism and Pelagianism, although in one sense 'in-house' matters, nevertheless had an apologetic thrust in that they developed a total theology and world-view.

Much apologetic work in the succeeding centuries was not specifically associated with preaching, and yet work such as that of Augustine, *Anselm (c. 1033–1109) and *Thomas Aquinas (1224–74) was vital in giving theological underpinning to apologetic efforts.

Preaching was one of the great marks of the Reformation, especially in the sermons of Luther (1483–1546) and *Calvin (1509–64), and their work provides indispensable foundations for later apologists. Their emphasis on the exposition and application of Scripture modelled the necessity of truly biblical theology in the apologetic task.

In the late seventeenth and early eighteenth centuries, the impact of the Enlightenment on the intellectual life of Europe and America produced a climate hostile to Christianity, and this had a profound effect on apologetics. David *Hume (1711–76) challenged the rationality of belief in miracles and the arguments from the world order for the existence and nature of God. Immanuel *Kant (1724–1804) argued that God is beyond our capacity to understand, and that theology therefore is properly concerned with human religion. Theology thus becomes anthropocentric, and Scripture is seen as descriptive of human religion but as having no objective *authority. This cuts the nerve of preaching, not least apologetic discourse, yet we must remember that the preaching of John Wesley (1703–91) and George Whitefield (1714–70) demonstrated that evangelistic and apologetic preaching could have a powerful impact at a time when the climate of opinion was unfavourable.

In the twentieth century, apologetics tended to flow in two different streams. Paul *Tillich (1896–1965), Rudolf *Bultmann (1884–1976) and John Robinson (1919–83) tried to distinguish what they perceived as the core gospel from its supernatural accretions and thus to make the gospel more credible to modern people. Much preaching to this day reflects that world-view; tends to major on *ethics and social issues and lacks a truly supernatural dimension.

The other stream is most powerfully represented by C. S. *Lewis (1898–1963), who championed a thoroughly supernatural Christianity in his apologetic works, such as *The Screwtape Letters* (1941), *Miracles* (1947), *Mere Christianity* (1952), and his 'Narnia' stories. Lewis was also a preacher, and his extant sermons show a lucid and imaginative command of English, a ruthless *logic and a deep understanding of human nature.

Today's preachers face a world often described as 'postmodern', of which term a bewildering array of definitions abounds. All agree, however, that there is a radical difference between the dogmatism of modernism and the ambivalence of postmodernism. Preaching has to take account of the vastly changed situation; in particular, there is a renewed need for apologetic preaching which will engage with the contemporary scene.

Here it is necessary for preachers to become theologians; all the great apologists who preached did so from a basis of a rich and developing theology. Apologetic preaching gives a theological world-view. In the contemporary world, the biblical world-view is increasingly unknown, and contemporary preachers need to set it out if the apologetic task is to be undertaken effectively.

Certain aspects of the contemporary age bear directly on the task of apologetic preaching. The Internet has produced an explosion of information which threatens to drown us in an avalanche of words and pictures. Further, this is an era of great scepticism, when faith of all kinds in institutions, leaders, systems and world-views is not popular. It is an age of *relativism, which is prepared to accept the gospel as a view of reality but not as the full *revelation of God. All these combine to create a situation in which effective and unashamed presentation of the gospel is very difficult.

It is easy to caricature preaching at this point: on the one hand, preaching to the faithful, with no relationship to the surrounding *culture, and, on the other, complete engagement with the culture with minimal biblical content. That such extremes exist cannot be denied; but among most preachers, certainly in the evangelical world, there is a genuine desire to preach in a way which is both biblically faithful and relevant to the contemporary world. Since this world is pluralist, multicultural and relativistic, there are a number of implications for the preacher who wants to engage in a prophetic and incisive way with the culture.

The first is an awareness of the vocabulary used. Words such as 'God', 'Spirit', 'sin', 'spirituality', 'peace', 'love' and many others will often be understood in a way far removed from their biblical use. The focus in much modern thinking is on self-awareness and self-fulfilment which will make us more at one with ourselves, with God, however understood and with the earth. In such a culture, a call to repentance and faith will be heard as a call to grow to our full potential rather than to turn away from our sins. Preachers have to teach

a biblical world-view and show people the coherent plot-line of the Bible as a necessary foundation for the apologetic task. A preacher who simply parrots the phraseology of earlier generations will not be understood.

A second and related area is the growing biblical illiteracy of our culture, where even formerly familiar Bible stories are completely unknown. Paul's method on the Areopagus, already mentioned, has significance here. The biblical world-view can be presented and then demonstrated from biblical narrative and other literary genres. An awareness of the diverse literary genres of the Bible is vital in preaching its message to the whole person.

A third area is *secularization. In the national media the concern is with politics, entertainment, celebrities, sports and, if significant enough, international affairs. If religion is mentioned at all, it is usually to mock at hypocrisy, failure and alleged obsession with sex. This means that preachers in Western societies are not so much attacked for fanaticism as dismissed as irrelevant.

A fourth area is *pluralism and its challenge to the uniqueness of Christ. There is a tension here between the preacher's basic conviction and the contemporary dislike for dogmatism. One way forward, common in apologetic preaching, is to ask questions about *Jesus and also to demonstrate his centrality in the Bible's plot-line. Jesus' question, 'Who do people say I am?', is at the heart of apologetic preaching, and it is the preacher's task to provide people with means to answer that question responsibly. The riches of the Gospel accounts, both in their distinctiveness and in their unity, need to form a regular part of preaching programmes, and all the huge issues of revelation, life, death, sin and the future will be raised frequently. Issues of poverty, compassion and integrity, which bulk large on the contemporary scene, will also be dealt with.

A fifth area which is inimical to effective apologetic preaching is the perceived weakness and unattractiveness of much of the church. It is true that 'spirituality' has become a buzz word, but that hardly extends to an affection for the church. Contemporary spirituality is often more at home with aromatherapy, holistic medicine, green issues and meditation than with churches and their practices. In bookshops, the section on spirituality will often contain books on reading tarot cards and other occult practices. Preachers will recognize this and see it as evidence of the deep spiritual hunger which can be satisfied only by God himself. Preachers must make sure that their apologetic becomes flesh as they expound 'the unknown God' to hearers.

These issues have certainly created a difficult situation for apologetic preaching, but they have also provided many opportunities for an incisive, rich and comprehensive presentation of the gospel. There are at least four areas which provide scope for such preaching.

The first is the growing interest in story and the increasing need for people to have a story which will make sense of their individual stories. Just as Augustine, in *The City of God* (413–26), provided a narrative based on the seven day-ages of the world, into which he fitted events such as the fall of Rome, so the contemporary preacher needs to present the big picture of God's purposes from creation to new creation and to make sense both of international and national events and of our community and personal lives. The large story will be seen to 'resolve' the smaller stories.

The second is the opportunity to provide hope in an age of doubt and despair. Two elements of the gospel are particularly relevant here. One is the plot-line of the story, which shows a God whose loving purposes stretch from creation to new creation. The other is the resurrection, which guarantees completion of the story. These are relevant not merely for individual faith but for building a framework of hope in the chaos of the world.

The third is the intellectual and spiritual challenge of proclaiming *truth in an age of relativism. This will not simply be propositional truth, although that will be a necessary foundation. It will involve passion as well as clarity, *imagination as well as meticulous exegesis, and a Christian lifestyle as well as Christian proclamation.

The fourth is the opportunity to support the church's primary task of evangelism and mission. In the cultural climate outlined above, apologetic preaching will have a function to prepare the way for the work of the evangelist. Perhaps a better way to put it would be to say that apologetic preaching is an inextricable part of evangelistic preaching. Apologetic preaching, with its broad group of the overall narrative of salvation, makes the case for the gospel and why people should believe it.

Plainly, preaching in the twenty-first century will need to engage vigorously with all the challenges and opportunities of an increasingly pluralistic age. It will draw heavily on all the resources available from contemporary apologetic writers, but will not deny itself the insights of the great figures of the Christian centuries, such as Augustine and C. S. Lewis.

Bibliography

D. A. Carson, *The Gagging of God* (Leicester, 1996); C. Chang, *Engaging Unbelief* (Leicester, 2000); G. Johnston, *Preaching to a Postmodern World* (Leicester, 2001); C. A. Loscalzo, *Apologetic Preaching: Proclaiming Christ to a Postmodern World* (Leicester, 2000); A. C. Thiselton, *Interpreting God and the Postmodern Self* (Grand Rapids, 1995); W. H. Willimon and R. Lischer (eds.), *Concise Encyclopaedia of Preaching* (Louisville, 1995).

R. S. FYALL

PREDESTINATION

'Predestination' is the process whereby God knows and plans in advance what he intends to do and then carries out his plans, especially with regard to the salvation of those whom he intends to save. If human beings have this capacity for forward planning, manifestly so must God. Problems arise because of the scope and nature of God's foreordination.

The 'classical' understanding

The doctrine arises from various biblical texts which appear to require it (Acts 2:23; 4:28; Rom. 8:29–30; Eph. 1:5, 11). The NT affirms the inability of sinful human beings to save themselves from their sin. Rather, God is said to choose certain of them to be saved ('election'), and send his Son to die for them, with the implication that he passes over the others and leaves them to their fate. There is accordingly some kind of *causality exercised by God over the former group so that they inevitably come to faith and continue in faith.

The 'classical' theory, associated particularly with *Augustine and *Calvin, goes beyond this in that it affirms the total, absolute control of God over all that happens. He plans in every detail all that he will do and carries it out exactly as planned. Human beings believe themselves to be free, within certain limits, to make their own choices and to carry them out. However, if predestination of this kind is a fact, then all our choices and actions are in fact foreordained by God, and although we act as though we are free, in reality we cannot choose and act otherwise than God has planned that we should. The classical doctrine solves the problem of free will by a philosophical theory called 'compatibilism', which affirms that, *paradoxically, God can foreordain human choices and yet human beings can act freely.

The things that happen include many actions that are wholly or partly *evil; God is opposed to them and he will judge the actors. How, then, is evil related to his will? Did he purpose it, or did he have to plan to deal with it as a limitation on what he could do, or is there an element of contingency at this point in his planning? The theory solves the problem of evil by denying that God is the cause of evil but affirming that in all cases he can work it into his plans and use it for his own ends.

Problems with the 'classical' understanding

This doctrine creates problems for the apologist in that it leads to an understanding of the nature and action of God which is out of character with other aspects of the biblical picture.

First, it solves the very real problem of how it is that some people hear the gospel and respond to it, while others do not, by arguing that it is God's will that they should respond or fail to do so. In so choosing, God acts justly, for the elect are saved by his mercy, which he is free to exercise as he pleases, whereas the others suffer the justly deserved consequences of their sins. However, this makes God's love appear arbitrarily selective, despite the scriptural assertions that he wishes to save all people (2 Pet. 3:9). If a human judge showed mercy by pardoning every fourth convicted criminal brought before him while condemning all the others, this would be considered intolerably unjust. So the fundamental problem raised by predestination to salvation is that it appears to make God behave unlovingly and unjustly to those whom he does not save, in that for no apparent reason he does not extend his love to them. The defence that he can choose those to whom he shows grace and is not under obligation to show it to all goes against Scripture.

Secondly, relationships between God and human beings are reduced to an impersonal level. They are treated by him as objects who behave as he predetermines. Their relationships with him are determined by his power and not by genuine love. By contrast, the biblical picture of what actually happens is that, through his agents, God makes a loving appeal to people to respond to his offer of reconciliation, and they may then respond with faith. If *determinism is at work, however, then it is not ultimately a case of love awakening a response but rather of people responding to God because God has foreordained their response and acts to bring it about.

It is arguable that human choices and actions can be foreseen by somebody else and yet still be free. However, there is a difference between an outside observer foreseeing what I will do, and God as the Creator foreseeing it, since in the latter case his foresight is linked to the fact that he has created me in such a way that I will behave in this manner.

Thirdly, and similarly, prayer is depicted in the Bible as a process in which human beings make petitions to God, and he responds to them; because of their prayers he does what he would otherwise not have done. According to 'classical' predestination, God himself causes the prayers to be uttered and thus gives the impression of responding to prayers that he had decided to cause. So the person praying is in effect a puppet whose strings are controlled by God. Prayer makes no difference to God's plans; it is simply part of what he plans.

Fourthly, God himself is controlled by his own predestination, since the divine programme necessarily includes not only what human beings do but also God's own responses to them and his causation of what they do. It is as if God writes a script for a play involving both himself and them as actors, and then lets it run; he himself is the prisoner of his own script! But in the Bible God appears to act freely and to take fresh directions as necessary.

Alternative understandings of predestination

The traditional alternative to 'classical' predestination is associated with Jacobus Arminius, who claimed that God foreordains what will happen on the basis of his foreknowledge of how human beings will freely behave. Karl *Barth has argued for the predestination of all people in God's election of his Son, but they may rebel against his choice. Other important contributions are the 'open theism' of Clark Pinnock and the 'middle knowledge' proposal of W. L. Craig. In fact, it is possible to understand predestination in a more biblical and less vulnerable manner.

First, some contemporary forms of the classical theory understand God's predestination as a causal *determinism* of *all* that happens. But predestination does not necessarily apply in detail to *all* events. God can leave a great deal of decision-making to human beings so that they are free within certain constraints. Human freedom may be like that of a flock of sheep within a pen; inside the pen they have freedom to move around as they wish, but they are constrained by the pen from moving outside its boundary. God does not need exhaustive knowledge of every detail of what will happen in the future. But this does not prevent his knowing what will ultimately happen. The chess-master may not know exactly what moves the novice will make, but he does know that, whatever the novice does, he himself will be able to make successful countermoves and win the game. Similarly, evil may have some 'free play', but in the end God will certainly overcome it.

Secondly, the classical doctrine is stated in terms of a philosophical theory of *determinism* that involves ideas about foreknowledge, the relation of God's existence to time, and freedom and causation. It is never wise to tie Christian doctrine to a specific philosophical system, especially when the issues are so intricate and there is so much difference of opinion, even among Christian philosophers, regarding them.

Thirdly, salvation is entirely the gift of God, initiated by him, but the human response that is made possible only by the divine initiative is a genuine response. God's relations within human beings are genuinely personal: he persuades by love rather than coerces by force; the human responses to his love are genuine responses and not pre-programmed responses like those of a computer, which cannot do anything else but respond according as it has been programmed. Yet various factors may affect that response. For example, the loving prayers of their family and friends may be a powerful element in the salvation of some people. So God works by calling people through the gospel accompanied by the power of the Holy Spirit rather than by some subpersonal kind of causation.

Fourthly, it is arguable that the biblical teaching on election, on which the 'classical' theory is alleged to rest, affirms God's purpose to create a people for whom he intends salvation without specifying all the individuals who will form part of that people. This does not rule out God's choosing of certain people to be called to salvation and service (Jeremiah, Paul), although they may have been free to reject his calling. Faced by the overwhelming amount of evidence in Scripture that God treats people on a personal level in genuine relationships, the better course is not to argue that the existence of the predestinarian language forces us to regard this 'dialogue' language as purely anthropomorphic and empty it of significance by affirming causal determinism, but rather to accept the 'dialogue' language as primary and to recognize that the statements of total divine sovereignty and foreknowledge are rhetorical and not to be misunderstood literally.

Finally, we face two inexplicable facts. One is that not all people are given the opportunity to respond to the gospel. The other is that many people fail to respond to the gospel. The classical understanding locates the explanation of these sad facts in the secret, inscrutable and apparently arbitrary will of God, who, in an act of 'double predestination', chooses some but bypasses others for no good reason. Granted that the latter face the just reward of their sins (since they are held to be responsible for these), it is difficult to avoid the impression that God distributes his mercy unjustly. But love and *justice cannot be separated; love itself must act justly. Therefore, it is preferable simply to recognize the unpredictability and irrationality of evil as a *mystery that we cannot fathom and also to recognize that, as finite human beings, we cannot fully understand the relationship between divine action and human action.

Neither the 'classical' nor the alternative type of solution is free from problems and difficulties. Neither view can fully explain why it is that God does not act otherwise than he does to bring evil to a speedier and complete end. Both views assert that God will finally overcome evil and destroy it. The latter view, in my opinion, commends itself as raising less intractable problems about the goodness of God than the former.

Bibliography

D. Basinger and R. Basinger (eds.), *Predestination and Free Will* (Downers Grove, 1986); J. K. Beilby and P. R. Eddy (eds.), *Divine Foreknowledge: Four Views* (Downers Grove and Carlisle, 2001); W. L. Craig, *The Only Wise God* (Grand Rapids, 1987); P. Helm, *The Providence of God* (Leicester and Downers Grove, 1994); I. H. Marshall, 'Predestination in the New Testament', in C. Pinnock (ed.) *Grace Unlimited* (Minneapolis, 1975), pp. 127–143.

I. H. MARSHALL

PRESUPPOSITIONAL APOLOGETICS

Presupposing God in apologetic argument

Presuppositional apologetics may be understood in the light of a distinction common in *epistemology, or the theory of knowledge. In any factual inquiry, it is important to distinguish between the ideas we have prior to the inquiry and those we gain in the course of the inquiry. No-one, of course, embarks on an investigation with an empty mind. If indeed we had done no previous thinking, nothing would motivate us to seek further information.

While a process of inquiry often corrects ideas we held previously, it is also true that our previous ideas often serve as assumptions governing the inquiry: defining the field of investigation, determining the methods of study, governing our understanding of what results are possible and thus limiting what conclusions may come from the study. So there is usually a dynamic interaction in any study between assumption and investigation: the investigation corrects and refines our assumptions, but the assumptions limit the investigation.

There are some kinds of assumptions we usually consider immune from revision. Among these are the basic laws of *logic and mathematics. What factual discovery could possibly persuade us that 2 + 2 is not equal to 4? The same is true of basic ethical principles, especially those governing the inquiry itself. For example, no factual discovery could legitimately persuade a researcher to be less than honest in recording data.

What about religious faith as an assumption governing human thought? Scripture teaches that believers in Christ know God in a supernatural way, with a certainty that transcends that obtainable by investigation. *Jesus himself reveals the Father to those he chooses (Matt. 11:25–27). Believers know God's mysteries by *revelation of his Spirit, in words inspired by the Spirit, giving them 'the mind of Christ' (1 Cor. 2:9–16; cf. 2 Tim. 3:16). So, by believing in Jesus, they *know* that they have eternal life (1 John 5:7).

In many respects, this supernatural knowledge contradicts the claims of people who do not know the true God. There is an opposition between the wisdom of God and the wisdom of the world (1 Cor. 1:18 – 2:16; 3:18–23). Wicked people (including all of us, apart from God's grace) 'suppress' the truth of God, exchanging it for a lie (Rom. 1:18, 25). The apostle Paul claims that his supernatural knowledge is powerful to 'demolish arguments and every pretension that sets itself up against the knowledge of God' so that he can 'take captive every thought to make it obedient to Christ' (2 Cor. 10:5). Spiritual warfare in Scripture, then, is intellectual as well as moral.

So when some claim that Christ will not return because 'everything goes on as it has since the beginning of creation', Peter opposes them, not by an empirical inquiry to ascertain the relative uniformity of physical law, but by citing the Word of God, his source of supernatural knowledge (2 Pet. 3:1–13).

The supernatural revelation of Scripture, therefore, is among the assumptions, what we may now call the presuppositions, that Christians bring to any intellectual inquiry. As Christians, may we revise those presuppositions in the course of an inquiry? We may certainly revise our *understanding* of those presuppositions by inquiring further into God's revelation in Scripture and nature, but we may not abandon the *authority of Scripture itself, as long as we believe that Scripture is God's Word. God must prove true, though every man be a liar (Rom. 3:4). Nor may we abandon the most fundamental truths of Scripture, such as the existence of God, the *deity of Christ and salvation by the shed blood of Jesus, without denying Christ himself.

Indeed, Christians believe that the very meaningfulness of rational discourse depends on God, as everything depends on God. Indeed, it is Christ in whom 'all things hold together' (Col. 1:17) and 'in whom are hidden all the treasures of wisdom and knowledge' (Col. 2:3). It is the 'fear of the LORD' that is 'the beginning of knowledge' (Prov. 1:7) and 'the beginning of wisdom' (Ps. 111:10; Prov. 9:10).

These facts pose a problem for apologetics. Non-Christians do not share the presuppositions we have discussed. Indeed, they presuppose the contrary, as they suppress the truth. The job of Christian apologists, trusting in God's grace, is to persuade non-Christians that the biblical presuppositions are true. What sort of argument can we use? If our argument presupposes the truths of Scripture, then our conclusions will be the same as our presuppositions. We will argue from Christian presuppositions to Christian conclusions. Since unbelievers will not grant the Christian presuppositions, however, they will not find the argument persuasive. But if we present an argument that does not presuppose the truths of Scripture, how can we be faithful to our Lord? And how can we produce an intelligible argument unless we presuppose those conditions that are necessary for intelligibility?

Many schools of apologetics (sometimes called 'classical' or 'traditional' or 'evidentialist') either ignore this question or take the second alternative and present arguments that avoid any use of distinctively Christian presuppositions. When they take the second alternative, they defend their faithfulness to biblical revelation by saying that the presuppositions they adopt are neither distinctively Christian, nor distinctively non-Christian, but 'neutral'.

Presuppositional apologists claim that there is no neutrality, invoking Jesus' saying that 'no-one can serve two masters' (Matt. 6:24). There can be no compromise between the wisdom of God and the wisdom of the world. Unbelief leads to distortion of the truth, exchanging the truth for a lie, and only by trusting God's Word can we come to a saving knowledge of Christ (John 5:24; 8:31; 15:3; Rom. 10:17). This trusting entails presupposing, accepting God's Word as what it is, the foundation of all human knowledge, the ultimate criterion of *truth and error (Deut. 18:18–19; 1 Cor. 14:37; Col. 2:2–4; 2 Tim. 3:16–17; 2 Pet. 1:19–21). So the apologetic argument, like all human inquiries into truth, must presuppose the truths of God's Word.

The problem of circularity

The presuppositionalist then faces the problem mentioned earlier. If he proceeds from Christian presuppositions to Christian conclusions, how can his argument be persuasive to a non-Christian? And how can he avoid the charge of circularity? Presuppositionalists have given different answers to this question.

Edward J. *Carnell, who is sometimes described as a presuppositionalist, affirms the *Trinity as the 'logical starting point' which 'gives being and meaning to the many of the time-space universe' (Introduction, p. 124). But his apologetic method treats the Trinity not as an ultimate criterion of truth, but as a hypothesis to be tested by 'both logic and experience' (Lewis, Truth-Claims, p. 179). He never indicates in any clear way how logic and experience themselves are related to Christian presuppositions.

Gordon H. Clark, who accepted the label 'presuppositionalist', holds that Scripture constitutes the 'axiom' of Christian thought, drawing an analogy between religion and geometry. The axiom, or first principle, cannot be proved. But axioms of different world-views can be tested to determine their logical consistency and to determine which of them is most fruitful in answering the questions of life. (See Clark, A Christian View, pp. 26–34.)

Clark admits that more than one system of thought could be logically consistent and that fruitfulness is a relative and debatable question. So Clark's method is more an exploration than a proof. By renouncing proof, he avoids the circularity of having to prove the axiom by means of the axiom. But if Christianity is not provable, how can Paul say in Rom. 1:20 that the clarity of God's self-revelation leaves unbelievers without excuse?

Cornelius *Van Til accepted the 'presuppositionalist' label somewhat reluctantly but admitted straightforwardly that the argument for Christianity is in one sense circular. Van Til believes, however, that the non-Christian's argument, too, is circular: 'all reasoning is, in the nature of the case, circular reasoning. The starting-point, the method, and the conclusion are always involved in one another' (Defense, p. 101). It is part of unbelievers' depravity to suppress the truth about God (Rom. 1:18–32; 2 Cor. 4:4), and that depravity governs their *reasoning so that unbelief is their presupposition, which in turn governs their conclusion.

How, then, can believer and unbeliever debate the truth of Christianity, given that the issue is already settled in the presuppositions of both parties? Van Til recommends a kind of 'indirect' argument whereby 'the Christian apologist must place himself upon the position of his opponent, assuming the correctness of his method merely for argument's sake, in order to show him that on such a position the "facts" are not facts and the "laws" are not laws. He must also ask the non-Christian to place himself upon the Christian position for argument's sake in order that he may be shown that only upon such a basis do "facts" and "laws" appear intelligible' (*Defense*, pp. 100–101).

But in this strategy, how do apologists argue that non-Christians' 'facts' are not facts and their 'laws' not laws? Should we argue on presuppositions acceptable to the unbeliever? If so, then on Van Til's account, we can reach only non-Christian conclusions. Should we argue on Christian presuppositions? Then the problem of circularity returns, but may be addressed in the following way.

As Van Til says, circular argument of a kind is unavoidable when we argue for an ultimate standard of truth. One who believes that human reason is the ultimate standard can argue that view only by appealing to reason. One who believes that the Bible is the ultimate standard can argue only by appealing to the Bible. Since all positions partake equally of circularity at this level, it cannot be a point of criticism against any of them.

Narrowly circular arguments, like 'the Bible is God's Word, because it is God's Word', can hardly be persuasive. But more *broadly* circular arguments can be. An example of a more broadly circular argument might be: The Bible is God's Word, because it makes the following claims, includes the following predictions that have been fulfilled, presents these credible accounts of *miracles, is supported by these archaeological discoveries, etc. Now this argument is as circular as the last if, in the final analysis, the criteria for evaluating the Bible's claims, its predictions, its accounts of miracles, and the data of *archaeology are criteria based on a biblical world-view and epistemology. But it is a broader argument in the sense that it presents more data to non-Christians and challenges them to consider it seriously.

God created our minds to think within the Christian circle of hearing God's Word obediently and interpreting our experience by means of that Word. That is the only legitimate way to think, and we cannot abandon it to please the unbeliever. Good psychologists will not abandon reality as they perceive it to communicate with delusional patients; so must it be with apologists.

In the final analysis, saving knowledge of God comes supernaturally. We can be brought from one circle of reasoning to another only by God's supernatural grace.

Transcendental argument

Van Til and those who closely follow him hold that apologetic argument must be *transcendental*. He also calls it 'reasoning by presupposition' (*Defense*, p. 99). A *transcendental argument tries to show the conditions that make anything what it is, particularly the conditions or presuppositions necessary for rational thought. This understanding of apologetics underscores Van Til's conviction that the Christian God is not merely another fact to be discovered alongside the ones we already know, but is the fact from whom all other facts derive their meaning and intelligibility.

Van Til is convinced that his transcendental argument is very different from traditional proofs for God's existence and the usual treatments of the historical evidences for Christianity. He speaks of his argument as 'indirect rather than direct' (*Defense*, p. 100), as a *reductio ad absurdum* of the non-Christian's position, rather than a direct proof of the Christian's. He intends to show that the alternatives to Christian *theism destroy all meaning and intelligibility and, of course, that Christian theism establishes these. These statements, however, raise some questions.

First, is it possible for an apologist to refute *all* the alternatives to Christian theism? Van Til thinks that it is possible, for in the final analysis there is only one alternative. Either the biblical God exists or he does not. And if he does not, Van Til claims, there can be no meaning or intelligibility.

Secondly, is a negative or *reductio* argument the only way to show that Christian theism alone grounds intelligibility? Van Til thinks it is. But if, say, *Thomas Aquinas was successful in showing that that the causal order begins in God, then God is the source of everything, including the intelligibility of the universe. Aquinas' argument, then, though it is positive rather than negative, proves Van Til's transcendental conclusion. And similarly if, say, physical law is unintelligible apart from the biblical God, why should we not say that physical law *implies* the existence of God? In that way, any transcendental argument can be formulated as a positive proof.

Finally, is the transcendental argument a simplification of apologetics? Presuppositionalists sometimes seem to suggest that with the transcendental argument in our arsenal we need not waste time on theistic proofs, historical evidences, detailed examinations of other views and the like. But presuppositionalists, like all apologists, have to answer objections. If the apologist claims that physical law is unintelligible without the biblical God, he will have to explain why he thinks that. What other possible explanations are there for the consistency of physical law? What does each of them lack? How does the Christian view supply what is lacking in the other explanations? Thus the presuppositional transcendental argument can become as complicated as more traditional arguments. And the presuppositionalist may often find himself arguing in much the same way traditional apologists have.

Conclusion

Despite these difficulties, the presuppositional approach has two advantages. It takes account of what Scripture says about our obligation to presuppose God's revelation in all our thinking and about the unbeliever's suppression of the truth, and it understands that according to Scripture the goal of apologetics must be to convince people that God's revelation is not only true, but the very criterion of truth, the most fundamental *certainty, the basis for all intelligible thought and meaningful living.

Bibliography

G. L. Bahnsen, *Van Til's Apologetic: Readings and Analysis* (Phillipsburg, 1998); E. J. Carnell, *An Introduction to Christian Apologetics* (Grand Rapids, 1948); G. H. Clark, *A Christian View of Men and Things* (Grand Rapids, 1952); J. M. Frame, *Apologetics to the Glory of God* (Phillipsburg, 1994); *Cornelius Van Til: An Analysis of His Thought* (Phillipsburg, 1995); G. R. Lewis, *Testing Christianity's Truth-Claims* (Chicago, 1976); C. Van Til, *The Defense of the Faith* (Philadelphia, 1967).

J. M. FRAME

PRINCETON THEOLOGY

'Princeton theology' is the name given to the teachings of Presbyterian theologians at Princeton Theological Seminary in the nineteenth and early twentieth centuries. It was characterized by a strong adherence to the Reformed faith, in particular as expressed by the Westminster Confession.

The seminary out of which this theology emerged was established following a resolution of the Presbyterian General Assembly in 1812. Located beside Princeton College (at this point, known as the College of New Jersey), Princeton Theological Seminary was to provide specialized training for ministers so that they would be equipped with a knowledge of Holy Scripture and able to make a learned defence of the faith and refute assaults from those promoting deism. The General Assembly appointed a board to oversee the new institution and supervise its faculty, who, in turn, were to 'truly believe' and teach in accordance with the Westminster Confession and Catechism.

By its centenary in 1912, it had enrolled over a thousand more students than any other seminary in the United States, and, even with the establishment of other seminaries, Princeton remained the most influential centre of training for the Presbyterian ministry. Through its *Biblical Repertory* and *Princeton Review* (later renamed the *Presbyterian Quarterly* and *Princeton Review*), the views of the Princeton theologians reached into the homes of many ministers and lay leaders. Although many of the seminary faculty were active on various church committees, and were in great demand as guest preachers, the greatest influence of Princeton came directly from its theology; it was the dominant (but not only) intellectual force on nineteenth-century American Presbyterianism. The close relationship which the seminary enjoyed with Princeton College, where its theology shaped much of the academic life, helped enable Princeton Seminary to exercise a considerable influence on the American intellectual community at large. However, the final third of the nineteenth century witnessed a rapid deterioration and decline in this relationship and a growing marginalization of the seminary and its theology.

A host of very able Bible scholars and theologians served on the faculty; among the most influential were Archibald Alexander, Charles *Hodge, A. A. Hodge and B. B. *Warfield. For some commentators, these four men constituted the Princeton theology. Even during the nineteenth century, people already spoke of the 'Princeton theology' as something distinctive but, on more than one occasion, Charles Hodge boasted that 'an original idea in theology is not to be found' in the pages of the *Princeton*

Review. For him, Princeton's distinctiveness came through its unchanging commitment to the *Calvinism of the Reformation. However, although the Princeton theologians saw themselves as guardians of this traditional Calvinism, they did not merely restate the teaching of the seventeenth century but rather expressed its truth in new terms which could relate meaningfully to 'Victorian' America.

The desire to remain totally faithful to classical Calvinism and yet to engage with contemporary society was clearly seen in Archibald Alexander (1772–1851), the first professor appointed to Princeton Seminary. He drew heavily upon the seventeenth-century Swiss theologian Francis Turretin, and made his *Institutes* a key text for all students at Princeton. Nevertheless, Alexander recognized the need to combat the new twin dangers of *rationalism and religious enthusiasm. Influenced by *Scottish common sense philosophy, he believed that 'God has so constituted our minds that we cannot avoid believing in certain truths as soon as they are presented to the mind'. Consequently, Alexander attempted to use these truths to make a rational defence of Christianity against sceptical critics such as David *Hume. In defending Christian truth, Alexander placed a strong emphasis on the absolute reliability of the Bible. Yet, as he surveyed new religious practices, he realized that religious enthusiasm was more likely than rationalism to 'spread extensive mischief' among the ordinary people, and so he insisted that all options and experiences 'must be judged by the standard of the Word of God'. Alexander did acknowledge the place of emotion and experience in the Christian life and the necessity of the direct work of the *Holy Spirit. Indeed, he was himself converted during the 1789 revival, and he retained a commitment to a personal piety which engaged the emotions but which was blended with rational truth. Among his most notable works was *Thoughts on Religious Experience* (1841).

Charles Hodge (1797–1878), who was in turn a student, friend and colleague of Alexander, was appointed to Princeton in 1820 and taught there for some fifty-eight years. In 1840 he became professor of exegetical and didactic theology, and in 1851, upon the death of Alexander, succeeded him as professor of didactic and polemical theology. As editor of the *Princeton Review* over many years,

Hodge engaged in various disputes with a wide range of adversaries, who included, among others, Charles Finney (1792–1875). Finney's emphasis on human ability to repent and on the perfectability of human nature clashed with the traditional Augustinian view of total depravity championed by Hodge. Since, in Finney's approach, everything appears to depend upon the exercise of the individual's will, Hodge argued that 'Christ and his cross are practically made of none effect'.

Apart from theology, Hodge wrote frequently on Presbyterian ecclesiastical affairs. A convinced 'Old School' Presbyterian, Hodge disagreed with the attempts by the 'New School' to promote a modified Calvinist theology and increase interdenominational cooperation on social issues. Nevertheless, he adopted a moderated stance at the time of schism in 1837, when the minority 'New School' were expelled from the Presbyterian Church. However, in his battles with New England theologians, such as Edwards Amasa Park (1808–1900) of Andover Seminary, Hodge was devastating. In his writings against Park, Hodge provided the fullest account of his understanding of the need for a proper balance between objectivity and subjectivity in the Christian faith. Concerned about allowing emotions to control theology, he stated that one cannot have truth in feelings and error in intellect at the same time.

His three-volume *Systematic Theology* (1871–73) represented the fruits of a lifetime's teaching at Princeton. Dealing with a vast array of theological issues, it was to prove extremely influential and, until very recently, served as a key text at conservative Presbyterian seminaries. It has been criticized by some for being too rationalistic and for playing down the work of the Holy Spirit. However, given that the volumes emerged partly as the work of theological disputes, they may simply reflect, at some points, the nature of such disagreements. Thus, if taken in isolation, there can be an overemphasis on certain aspects of the faith, and so it is important to take into account the other writings of Hodge before attempting to evaluate his overall contribution to the Princeton theology. For example, his Bible commentaries and devotional writings for the laity stress the need for a personal experience of the Holy Spirit, while his book *The Way of Life* (1841), commissioned by the American Sunday School Union, treated the Bible as self-authenticating rather than seeking to prove its truthfulness.

Hodge's son, Archibald Alexander Hodge (1823–86), taught didactic and polemic theology from 1877 until his death. A. A. Hodge's work was not as intellectually overwhelming as his father's approach to *theological method. He shared his father's view of theology as a science and likewise believed in the unity of scientific and biblical knowledge. He is perhaps best remembered for the essay he wrote in 1881 with Benjamin Breckinridge Warfield (1851–1921) on the inspiration of Scripture. The article restated many points previously expressed by various Princeton writers on the propositional character of biblical truth, and affirmed that 'the Scriptures not only contain, but are the Word of God', and hence were absolutely without error in their original autographs. Yet they were keen to guard against any mechanical dictation theory of inspiration, and Warfield stressed that the Bible came about through a process of concursus, whereby human actions and the working of the Holy Spirit coincided. The two authors also displayed an impressive ability for engaging with the latest higher-critical theories from Europe, which challenged their supernatural view of Scripture.

Interesting, because of changes in the intellectual climate and a growing hostility to the concept of divine *revelation, the 1881 article laid greater emphasis on demonstrating the truthfulness of Scripture than did Charles Hodge's essay of 1857 on the same subject. A. A. Hodge and B. B. Warfield gave less prominence to the internal testimony of the Holy Spirit as a means of validating the Scriptures, since the new critical scholars merely dismissed such an argument as fideism. This more evidentialist approach was indicative of Warfield's attitude to apologetics. Possessing one of the most penetrating theological minds of his generation, Warfield sought to gather evidence and to use rational argument in defence of supernatural Christianity. In contrast to the presuppositionalist approach of Dutch Reformed scholars such as Abraham *Kuyper, Warfield placed great importance on the need for apologetics to establish the reasonableness of belief before building up the theological system. As a result, Warfield, and indeed the Princeton theology in general, have been criticized for being unduly influenced by Scottish common sense philosophy and thus according

too high an importance to the role of the mind. Furthermore, in recent years, some evangelical scholars have even accused Warfield of lapsing into rationalism.

Without doubt, Warfield and the Princeton theology owed much to Scottish common sense philosophy; but then so, too, did virtually the entire intellectual elite in nineteenth-century America. However, it is simplistic to overplay its influence at Princeton. For example, unlike scholars of the New Haven theology, who made aspects of the philosophy crucial to their ethics, the theologians at Princeton did not allow it to control their theology. In an age when supernatural Christianity was increasingly being regarded by the academy as a superstitious relic, Warfield sought to present it as rationally credible. Yet even he, who placed less stress than his predecessors on *religious experience, taught that 'mere reasoning cannot make a Christian', for only the Holy Spirit can do that. Alongside rationality, he laid even greater emphasis on personal piety, and, while addressing theological students in the Princeton Chapel, he reminded them that they 'must keep the fires of religious life burning brightly in your hearts; in the most inmost core of your being, you must be men of God'.

In spite of all its efforts, the Princeton theology was unable to prevent *secular humanism sweeping the intellectual elite, or to halt the growing liberalism within Presbyterianism, or to defeat doctrinal revision of the Westminster Confession of Faith. It was observed by J. Gresham *Machen (1881–1937) that when Warfield died in 1921, the old Princeton and its theology died with him. Machen himself was a formidable theologian who, during his twenty-three years at Princeton, attempted to promote traditional Christianity. His *Christianity and Liberalism* (1923) was one of the best statements in the twentieth century against the innovations of liberal or modernist Christianity. In 1929, when the board at Princeton was reorganized to break the controlling influence of classical Calvinism, Machen left to found Westminster Theological Seminary in Philadelphia. With him went some colleagues, a number of students and the tradition of Princeton theology.

In addition to Westminster, the Princeton theology continues to find expression through newer institutions such as Covenant Seminary and Reformed Theological Seminary. Meanwhile, its teaching on inerrancy of Scripture has, until recently, exercised widespread influence throughout evangelical Christianity of whatever denomination.

Bibliography

A. W. Hoffecker, *Piety and Princeton Theologians* (Phillipsburg, 1981); A. McGrath, *A Passion for Truth* (Leicester, 1996); M. A. Noll (ed.), *The Princeton Theology* (Grand Rapids, 1983); J. B. Rodgers and D. K. McKim, *The Authority and Interpretation of the Bible* (San Francisco, 1979); D. F. Wells, *Reformed Theology in America* (Grand Rapids, 1985); J. D. Woodbridge and R. Balmer, 'The Princetonians and Biblical Authority', in J. D. Woodbridge and D. A. Carson (eds.), *Scripture and Truth* (Grand Rapids, 1983).

B. A. FOLLIS

PROGRESSIVE REVELATION, see REVELATION

PROJECTIONISM

With the rise of atheism in the nineteenth century in Europe, it became necessary to explain why people in all times and places could and did believe in a supernatural being. L. *Feuerbach (1804–72) was the first to explain it as 'projection', as faith giving reality to humanity's deepest wishes.

We strive after happiness and harmony. In ourselves, however, we find only weakness, so we project an all-powerful God. We look to ourselves and find mortality, so we project an immortal life in *heaven. We feel alone and small, so the desire for a godly father arises. We feel unloving and search in heaven for a perfect love. What we fail to be – perfect love, immortal, almighty, righteous and holy – we expect from our God.

For Feuerbach, theology was in effect anthropology, teaching nothing about God – for he is not there – but only about realities in the human mind. Believers can colour the object of their faith with their own dreams and hidden wishes or fears. God does fulfil our deepest longings, but as soon as this is turned around and the idea of projection is taken as the only explanatory principle we speak of projectionism.

Karl Marx based his view of society on Feuerbach's philosophy, saying that religious projection was the result of self-alienation, brought about via the alienation of society from the means of production and thus of people from the products of their own work. This made self-realization impossible, so we have dealt with this by projecting our inner selves on to the screen of eternity in heaven where the church had promised a golden future. Such a religion was 'the opium of the people'. No wonder that F. *Nietzsche went on to speak about the death of God.

Sigmund *Freud incorporated Feuerbach's ideas into his *psychology. He observed that in religious belief people project images, thoughts and fears that they themselves suppress deep in their subconscious. They cope with their helplessness against the forces of nature by projecting a God in human form, thus continuing their childhood situation of fear for their father combined with expecting all their help from him. For Freud, religion is a neurotic remainder from childhood. Carl *Jung also saw religion as projection but as having a positive influence on health and psychological balance. In the twentieth century the idea of projectionism was the main explanation of why people believe. Karen Armstrong, a contemporary writer on religious issues, has said that she 'expected to find that God had simply been a projection of human needs'. What she discovered was not that this is not true but that somehow this projection does relate to 'Something'. In Holland this led to the term 'something-ism' as the form of projectionism in a postmodern time.

Psychological criticisms

There is some truth in Freud's observation that we can pollute our relationship with God by what he calls projection, but the real question is: is faith in God itself a projection? His argument depends on the supposition that people have a hidden suppressed need to *affirm* the existence of God. The problem, however, is that there are also a lot of people with a need to *deny* God. Was Freud one of these? There is also a suppressed need to deny especially the fatherly characteristics of God, which could be illustrated in the philosophy of *Spinoza.

More recent psychological research no longer sees religion as a projection. Rumke, in his book *The Psychology of Unbelief, Character and Temperament in Relation to Unbelief* (London, 1952), comes to the opposite conclusion and claims that where people do not [want to] believe, or cannot believe, it can always be traced back to a neurotic or psychological disorder. He says that he discovered that the refusal to believe in God can go back to an inability to trust, rooted in hurts in the past. Projectionism loses its explanatory power somewhat if it can be used to account for two contradictory points of view.

Philosophical criticisms

There is a hidden philosophy behind the psychological criticism of religion. Supposing that there is no God, we naturally move into a world-view that constructs a *reality of two layers – an outer objective world in which the law of cause and effect applies, and the personal subjective world of the human consciousness, which must give meaning to the, in itself, meaningless outer world. Western society has lived with this dichotomy since *Descartes. It belongs to the presuppositions of 'modernity'. The human mind has to give meaning to the outer reality of a space-time world of cause and effect. Imagine that the world-view without a God was true: what sort of world would that be, and can you live with it?

In the first place it is not true, because meaning is intrinsic, just as the smell of a good meal is not something that rises up from the human subject in order that he or she might like the food that we need to survive, but is intrinsic to the meal itself. This can, however, be accepted only when we believe that there is a higher hand that made them for each other. The denial of that leads to the presupposition of modernity (which *Dooyeweerd characterized as a tension between 'nature' and 'freedom'), which cannot be proven scientifically because it precedes the intellectual reflection. Secondly, it is impossible to live with that world-view. It is just too much for the shoulders of humankind to bear, to be the ultimate giver of meaning.

It is also interesting to follow the purely rational thinking of a philosopher like Eduard von Hartmann, a non-Christian, who rightly observed that 'it is totally correct that things do not exist because men want them to'. While desire for something will not bring it into being, it does not follow that all I desire therefore does not exist (like a love relationship with a woman who loves me), and fortunately she exists.

The latest criticism of projectionism from a philosophical viewpoint comes from Charles Taylor. He argues that the philosophical presuppositions behind this theory are based on the nineteenth-century modernist presumption that it is 'always and everywhere wrong for anyone to believe anything upon insufficient evidence', but he asks the intriguing question whether it is more reasonable, in the presence of the religious hypothesis, 'to yield to our fear of its being an error, than to yield to our hope that it may be true'. He also suggests that there are some domains in which truths will be hidden from us, unless we go at least half way toward them, like 'Do you love me?' They reveal themselves to me only if I open myself up to them.

Biblical responses

The Christian faith is based not on emotional feelings or suppressed desires but upon historical facts in which God reveals himself to us as explained and proclaimed in the words of his prophets. Faith should be based not on what the Israelites felt to be true about God, but on the fact of God's self-*revelation. In the OT Israel believed in God because they 'saw' his works and all that he had done for them (Pss. 98:3; 111:2).

Doing what is presupposed in the theory of projection, humans creating their own god or taking anything out of creation and making it their god, was expressly forbidden by the second of the Ten Commandments (Exod 20:4; cf. Deut 4:16). This applies to mental images as well (see Ps. 50:21, where the Lord says, 'You thought I was altogether like you. But I will rebuke you'). The deepest reason why it is forbidden is that it is a rebellious reversal of the order of creation (Gen. 1:28). Also, the 'attractive' features of the Christian God that might incline someone to project his existence as a narcotic to help them face the threatening character of life are not only balanced and neutralized by the 'threatening' features of God but are overwhelmingly outweighed by the *traumatic* experience of encountering God (see Isa. 6:5).

In the NT we find the same to be the case. Faith comes from hearing the word of God (Rom. 10:17), and the good news on which it is founded comes from those who have seen and heard the events to which they bear *witness (1 John 1:1; cf. 1 Cor. 15). Seeing the risen Lord for themselves was the one thing that convinced the confused and disappointed disciples after the resurrection. In 2 Pet. 1:16, the apostle Peter says, 'We did not follow [projections of the human mind] when we told you about the power and coming of our Lord Jesus Christ, but we were eye-witnesses of his majesty.'

Faith may be accompanied by deep feelings, but it is not *built* on it. As we read the Bible we can examine its integrity and look for evidence of its being true to reality. The life and crucifixion of Christ are some of the most documented events in history. Faith is based on historical facts and therefore fulfils our deepest longings.

Bibliography

L. Feuerbach, *The Essence of Christianity* (ET, New York, 1957); H. Küng, *Does God Exist? An Answer for Today* (London, 1996); F. A. Schaeffer, *The God Who is There* (London, 1968); R. C. Sproul, *The Psychology of Atheism* (Minneapolis, 1974); C. Taylor, *Varieties of Religion Today* (Cambridge, MA, 2001).

W. G. RIETKERK

PROTESTANTISM, see CHRISTIANITY, PROTESTANT

PSEUDEPIGRAPHA

The term 'pseudepigrapha' is conventionally used to designate a wide range of Jewish writings from the post-biblical period, but not including the *Apocrypha, the Qumran literature or the rabbinic writings. The most widely used collection, edited by J. H. Charlesworth, contains fifty-two works and fragments of a dozen others, the majority dating from between the second century BC and the second century AD. They are preserved in various languages (Greek, Syriac, Latin, Ethiopic, Armenian), many having been translated from a Hebrew or Aramaic original. The term 'pseudepigrapha' ('of fictitious authorship') does not strictly apply to all these works as, while most purport to present the visions and writings of ancient figures such as Enoch, Moses, Solomon, Elijah and Ezra, others (e.g. *3* and *4 Maccabees*) carry no ascription of authorship.

None of these books was widely regarded as *canonical (though *1 Enoch* was preserved among the scriptures of the Ethiopian Church), but their influence can be traced in much early Christian writing, including a number of passages of the NT. For example, 1 Pet. 3:19–20 is best understood in the light of the Enoch literature, and the epistle of Jude both quotes directly from *1 Enoch* and draws on the *Testament of Moses*. Together these works illustrate the wide range of Jewish ideas and groups which existed alongside what we think of as 'mainstream' *Judaism around the NT period. Some of the writings as we have them show signs of significant Christian editing.

Four main categories of writing may be distinguished among the pseudepigrapha (though not all fit into one of these). One example in each category must suffice to give the flavour of the genre.

1. Apocalyptic works

Apocalyptic was a popular form of Jewish writing especially in the period 200 BC–AD 200; the NT book of Revelation is the nearest Christian equivalent. They generally purport to relate the experiences of an OT worthy such as Enoch, Ezra, Baruch or Elijah, who was granted privileged access to the secrets of heaven in a vision or trance-journey. They are typically full of strange imagery and cosmic phenomena, often constructing elaborate historical schemes to explain God's ultimate purpose. They tend to dismiss the present world-order as hopelessly corrupt, putting all the emphasis on God's imminent and decisive intervention to deliver and restore his people.

Probably the most widely influential of the apocalypses is *1 Enoch*, which consists of five originally independent Enochic writings, the earliest of which comes probably from about 200 BC, the latest from the first century AD. Originally in Hebrew or Aramaic, the combined volume (roughly the length of Genesis) was preserved in Ethiopic. Part 1 narrates Enoch's mission to the Watchers (the fallen angels of Gen. 6:1–4, now imprisoned) and other travels in the supernatural world; part 2 (the latest, and the only part not represented among the Qumran texts) gives an extended vision of the triumph of the Son of Man; part 3 is a cosmological treatise on the heavenly bodies; part 4 sets out the history of the world, past, present and future, in the form of animal symbolism; part 5 is a more varied collection of visions, including a detailed world history set out in weeks (cf. Daniel). *1 Enoch* formed the basis for two later Enoch books, *2 Enoch* (late first century AD, preserved in

Slavonic) and *3 Enoch* (in Hebrew, perhaps fifth century AD).

2. Testaments

These purport to give the last words of famous OT characters, in which they typically recall and draw lessons from their own life stories, predict the future course of events for their descendants, and exhort them to live as God's people. Testaments of Abraham, Isaac, Jacob, Moses, Solomon, Job and Adam are preserved.

The *Testaments of the Twelve Patriarchs* gives the last words of each of the twelve sons of Jacob, drawing on, but going far beyond, the tribal blessings of Gen. 49. It originated in the second century BC, and is preserved in Greek and Armenian. There are a number of clearly Christian interpolations, especially in the *Testament of Levi* with its vision of a messianic priest, but the work as a whole represents pre-Christian Jewish piety and expectation.

3. Expansions of the Old Testament

The OT stories were retold constantly within Judaism, and they grew in the retelling. The process can be seen in the Aramaic targums and in its most extended form in *Josephus' Antiquities*. The pseudepigrapha contain several examples of such expansions. Some cover considerable areas of the OT story, notably *Jubilees* (see below), and the *Biblical Antiquities* (better known as *Pseudo-Philo*), which covers Genesis to 1 Samuel; others give legendary expansions on a particular story or character, such as *Joseph and Asenath* or the *Lives of the Prophets*.

The book of *Jubilees* was probably compiled in the second century BC, and was well known at Qumran. It records the revelation received by Moses at Sinai in the form of an angelic account of the history of the world up to that point. The most distinctive feature is the author's preoccupation with the sacred calendar, which he urges his readers to uphold. God himself observed the sabbath at creation, and the whole history is organized into a scheme of sabbaths, 'weeks' of seven years, and jubilees, which are prominently superimposed on the narrative.

4. Psalms and prayers

These are modelled on those of the OT, some purporting to be further psalms of David,

others prayers of famous people such as Joseph and Jacob. The eighteen *Psalms of Solomon* were written in the first century BC, probably by a Pharisaic author in Jerusalem. They explore familiar themes from the OT psalms but focus especially on hope for the future and include, in Psalm 17, one of the most elaborate expressions in pre-Christian Judaism of the hope of a Davidic Messiah who will deliver and restore Israel as God's holy people.

Bibliography

R. H. Charles (ed.), *The Apocrypha and Pseudepigrapha of the OT*, vol. 2 (Oxford, 1913); J. H. Charlesworth (ed.), *The OT Pseudepigrapha*, 2 vols. (London, 1983–85); G. W. E. Nickelsburg, *Jewish Literature between the Bible and the Mishnah* (London, 1981); C. Rowland, *The Open Heaven: A Study of Apocalyptic in Judaism and Early Christianity* (London, 1982); E. Schürer, *A History of the Jewish People in the Age of Jesus Christ*, new edition ed. G. Vermes *et al.*, vol. 3 (Edinburgh, 1986–87), pp. 177–379, 470–808; H. F. D. Sparks, *The Apocryphal OT* (Oxford, 1984).

R. T. FRANCE

PSEUDEPIGRAPHY IN SCRIPTURE

'Pseudepigraphy' is the term used to describe writing presented as being written by someone other than the actual writer (i.e written under a *pseudonym* – an alternative name). It is a practice with a long history, and is clearly in evidence in various ancient writings, e.g. the *Testaments* of Adam, or Abraham, or Moses, which pass off historical review as the foresight of the named figure. No-one was deceived by this, it was a literary convention of the day (the early centuries AD, in these cases). The debate over the existence of pseudepigraphy in Scripture focuses on the question of how acceptable particular instances of this practice might have been in the context of *canonical writings.

Although it is relatively common to answer this question with either a sweeping affirmation or denial, there are various different cases to consider. Three examples will be noted, though in cases such as the Psalms or the four Gospels there are also relevant issues concerning the reliability of various ascriptions, and Jer. 36 gives one insight into the complex process of authorship!

1. The Pentateuch

The five books of the Torah are sometimes known as 'the five books of Moses', and this tradition evidently goes back to NT times, where Jesus is presented as attributing scriptural words to Moses (e.g. Mark 7:10). However, nothing in the five books themselves makes Mosaic authorship obvious, and although there are passages where Moses may well have been the author, there are clearly those where he was not, such as the accounts in Genesis (presumably handed down in tradition), or Deut. 34 recounting his death, or the attribution of unique humility to Moses in Num. 12:3 (which looks very odd indeed if written by the man himself). It is clear that in Jewish tradition words can be attributed to a rabbi when they were in fact uttered by his later student or disciple, if those words capture the rabbi's teaching on a particular matter. If this tradition was indeed in place by the time of the NT, then we can explain references to the Mosaic nature of the *Pentateuch without requiring Mosaic authorship. The older critical argument that writing was not sufficiently developed in the time of Moses to permit him to have written anyway seems now to be unfounded.

2. Daniel

The authorship of Daniel has long been an interpretative battleground, focusing on the question of whether the sixth-century setting of the stories in Dan. 1 – 6 is the same as the background to the later visions. In fact there is little to suggest that Daniel was the author of chapters 1 – 6, since anyone could have written the stories down, and the question of the link with the first-person narrated material in chapters 7 – 12 concerns primarily the nature and scope of apocalyptic literature and prophecy rather than issues of authorship *per se*. The non-deceptive presentation of historical review as backdated prophecy is well attested in ancient literature, and therefore no theory of scriptural inspiration need discount this possibility in Dan. 11, and thus Daniel could well be in part pseudepigraphic.

3. Paul's letters

Much of the energy of the pseudepigraphy debate has been expended on the question of Pauline authorship of certain of the thirteen NT letters which bear his name, particularly concerning the so-called 'deutero-pauline' letters (Eph., Col., 2 Thess.), and the three pastoral epistles. Here several factors invite consideration.

There are undeniable stylistic differences between the letters (more so, in fact, in the case of 1 and 2 Pet.), but these could easily be explained by the differing degrees of liberty afforded to the amanuensis, the one who actually wrote out the full text as dictated or sketched out by Paul.

Similarly, the letters exhibit several theological differences. Ephesians and Colossians focus on the church and the scope of salvation, and the pastorals on church order, whereas elsewhere Paul's distinctives are more clearly the gospel, salvation itself, reconciliation and so forth. This is inconclusive evidence regarding authorship. To challenge Pauline authorship on this basis is inevitably open to the charge of circular reasoning, and does not allow sufficient scope for Paul to have developed his thinking over time. Nevertheless, it is certainly striking how much 1 Timothy and Titus, for example, emphasize the propriety of upholding sound doctrine in a way which seems, at best, highly unusual for the Paul of Romans and Galatians.

One of the factors influencing the acceptance of a book into the NT canon was some kind of assurance of an apostolic link in the chain between the events of Jesus' life, death and resurrection and the witness to those events in the book concerned. It was not necessary to establish apostolic authorship (e.g. Mark, Jude), but if Paul himself did not write 1 Timothy, then this point requires that the actual writer was consciously attempting to represent Paul faithfully. This is the view usually held by those arguing for pseudepigraphy here. For example, Ephesians, as a kind of summary of Paul's teaching, is at least 'Pauline'. We may say that, historically speaking, writing in someone else's name was certainly a practice of the time, and that it could have been a transparent one which deceived nobody. Equally, however, authorship was not unimportant to the early church, and here the weight of evidence seems to support a very early date for believing that the authors were all named appropriately in all the letters.

To be more precise, the evidence from the early church regarding attitudes to pseudonymity indicates a strong line being taken on questions of apostolicity, and it is difficult to disentangle the literary issue of authorship from the theological one of authentic apostolic validation. Thus Tertullian (c. 160–220 AD) condemned the author of the *Acts of Paul* for attempting to pass off the work as Pauline, and the claim that it was done 'for the love of Paul' was deemed irrelevant. Yet Tertullian himself confidently attributed Mark's Gospel to Peter as regards its substance. Serapion, Bishop of Antioch (c. 200 AD?), is cited by *Eusebius as first accepting and then rejecting the *Gospel of Peter*, but this may be due to what was deemed its unorthodox theological content as well as to the re-evaluation of its authorship, and it is difficult to be sure of cause and effect in this reasoning. Overall, the evidence is inconclusive, as so often with historical inquiry, but it is perhaps fair to say (with Porter) that recent investigation has shown how tenuous is the historical basis for claiming that pseudepigraphy would have been an acceptable practice in the early church for writings deemed apostolic and/or canonical.

It is debatable how far one's view of Pauline or Petrine authorship of the canonical letters today makes much substantive exegetical difference, since to a considerable extent saying something in Paul's name makes exactly the same point as if Paul said it. A survey of commentaries written with differing convictions suggests that there is often no real difference, other than on this single point itself.

As a general conclusion, it must be said that a great deal of apologetic energy has been spent 'defending' traditional attributions of authorship, which have not themselves proved to be self-evident. Whether clarity over authorship is an important apologetic goal perhaps depends more on one's assumptions regarding the link between faithful witness and accurate reportage, than on the clear evidence of the biblical documents themselves, and ultimately it seems to be our concept of 'authorship' which needs to be more flexible to take into account ancient writing practices.

Bibliography

K. D. Clarke, 'The Problem of Pseudonymity in Biblical Literature and Its Implications for Canon Formation', in L. M. McDonald and J. A. Sanders (eds.), *The Canon Debate* (Peabody, 2002), pp. 440–468; D. G. Meade, *Pseudonymity and Canon* (Tübingen, 1986); S. E. Porter, 'Pauline Authorship and the Pastoral Epistles: Implications for Canon', *Bulletin for Biblical Research*, 5 (1995), pp. 105–123.

R. S. Briggs

PSYCHOLOGY

Psychology has been defined in many ways. For much of the twentieth century psychology was defined as the *science of behaviour. Earlier, and again more recently, psychology has also emphasized internal experiences, such as sensations, perceptions, feelings or emotions, motivations and thoughts. Today, most definitions of psychology include both elements. Thus, we will define psychology as the science of behaviour and mental processes.

Psychology as the science of behaviour is concerned with public and observable events. Behaviour is studied in organisms ranging from planaria to people. As the science of mental processes, psychology is concerned with such private experiences as the emotions of fear, guilt and *depression, and thoughts. Psychology as a science of mental processes is largely limited to the study of humans. Together, behaviour and mental processes comprise external-objective and internal-subjective frames of reference respectively. They form complementary aspects of functioning that fit together into a whole picture. While focus on mental processes rather than behaviour is more comfortable for Christians who emphasize human freedom, a balanced Christian approach needs to hold these two perspectives in tension.

Psychology is a broad discipline with many distinct sub-fields that have important benefits for contemporary society. Among the areas addressed by psychology are sensation, perception, behavioural neuroscience, learning, consciousness, *language and thought, memory, human development, intelligence, motivation, social relationships, personality, psychopathology, psychotherapy, stress and health. Most introductory psychology texts address each of these (e.g. see Myers, *Psychology*); a few also explore the psychology of religion.

The psychology of religion is an often neglected domain of psychology. Scientific study cannot shed light on whether God exists or on what is morally right or wrong. However, it can investigate what people believe and whether their behaviour is consistent with their beliefs. It can also investigate the relationship of religious faith and psychosocial functioning. For example, psychological research shows that religious persons are less likely to commit crimes, to abuse substances and probably less likely to commit suicide. Religious persons also cope more effectively with many kinds of adversity. Religious practices such as prayer are among the most common ways people deal with adversity.

Psychological research is valuable in many ways. For example, cybernetics, the science of human-machine interactions, aids in designing the instruments and controls of modern aircraft for optimal pilot effectiveness. Neuro-psychological assessment can sensitively test for the adverse effects of medications or environmental toxins on human functioning, can identify the effects of injury and illness on brain function more finely than even the best imaging techniques, and can aid in planning remedial interventions. Psychotherapy has been shown to help persons suffering from anxiety, depression, or more serious psycho-logical disorders.

Psychological advances, however, can be used both to benefit and to harm. For example, psychological testing helps in the selection and placement of military personnel and missionary candidates. But psychological testing can also be used in the service of discrimination against social and cultural minorities as when a test for police or safety personnel is inadvertently or intentionally biased against applicants from minority groups. Psychological techniques can be used for emotional healing or in coercive 'programming' and brainwashing.

Psychology is a controversial topic among Christians. Some Christians contend that psy-chology is of the devil while others view psychology as God's good gift. Five factors are central to these controversies: world-views, faith, *morality, boundaries and coherence.

World-views. Everyone has a world-view that answers questions about what exists, how we know it, how it works, what is morally right or wrong and who we are as persons. World-views are largely formed before we can speak articulately. They profoundly shape our views of ourselves and the world, often in subtle ways. All data are interpreted through world-view lenses and data errors tend to reflect world-view biases. Thus, most disagree-ments about psychology – or *theology – stem from world-view disagreements.

Much of the objection to psychology among Christians revolves around the world-views of prominent psychologists. Sigmund *Freud, B. F. *Skinner, Carl Rogers and Albert Ellis each rejected Christianity. Doubtless their world-views influenced their approach to psychology in ways that are troublesome to many Christians.

Faith. Surprisingly, psychology and theology converge in sharing faith in the sense that all scientists must have faith that the future will be like the past. All scientific data are *history in the sense that it was collected in the past, but scientists are really concerned about predicting or controlling the future. Further, all data is interpreted in the context of the interpreters' world-views. Thus science weds world-views with history and foretelling the future.

Christians also believe that the future will be like the past – but only while this earth remains. The faith of Christians is first in the God of the future. But for many psychologists, God cannot be brought into the laboratory. They trust in science. Science, or perhaps their own capacity to know, is their primary object of faith. From a Christian perspective psychology is over-reaching – thus becoming a false God.

Morality. Christians generally believe that morality is ordained by God and applies to everyone. In contrast, some psychologists assume that morality is situational, simply a social convention. Christian concerns about psychology have focused mostly on psycho-pathology and psychotherapy. Some Christians view anxiety and depression as sins and view psychology as offering a counterfeit to evangel-ism and discipleship. Others view anxiety and depression as non-moral ills; for them counsel-ling is viewed as a God-given tool that can be thoughtfully used by Christians to facilitate human functioning and well-being, but must be used with care.

Several recent studies suggest that counsel-ling or psychotherapy may enhance spiritual well-being and that gains in spiritual well-being occurred whether or not the therapists or clients were Christian. Such results may seem surprising, but if humans function holis-tically, it seems reasonable that any benefits to human functioning will affect the whole person in favourable ways.

Boundaries. Christian theology addresses questions about humans, particularly in rela-tionship to God and secondarily in relationship to fellow humans and the world; psychology is concerned about humans in relationship to themselves, each other and the world around them – including non-human organisms. Each field has distinctive domains, but they converge in their focus on humans. Theological anthro-pology (or the doctrine of humanity) and the psychology of human development, human differences, personality, psychopathology and psychotherapy seem to overlap. Just as the differences between biology and chemistry blur in biochemistry, the boundaries between theology and psychology are not clearly delineated. To further complicate matters, theologians and psychologists may at times be addressing the same issues, but from different perspectives.

Coherence or unity of truth. All human knowing is imperfect – even our Christian beliefs. Psychology provides data that both support and challenge Christian beliefs. In principle, findings in psychology should be coherent with findings in theology. Logically, both could be wrong – or right. But both theology and psychological science have limitations. As fallen persons in a fallen world, we 'see through a glass darkly'. Our seeing and knowing is improved when we use all the tools of knowing available to us to focus the light and sharpen our insights (see Prov. 27:17).

Christians believe that the Bible is true and that it should in principle be fully consistent with all true psychological discoveries. Because Christians are diverse, the notion that the Bible is true has a variety of meanings for them. First, the biblical text is believed to be historically accurate, and the discovery of primary documents dating to the first century and earlier provides evidence that the biblical record has survived the centuries with little change. Secondly, the Bible provides a history of the Jewish people. Thirdly, the Bible contains spiritual truth contained in allegory, metaphor and symbol, but should not be taken literally. Fourthly, the Bible is considered to be literally true, and many Christians believe the Bible is inerrant in its original documents. Finally, combining elements of the above notions, and perhaps the best view of the Bible as truth, is the view that the Bible conveys truth through a variety of literary mechanisms, including axioms, history, parables, poetry, principles, proverbs and stories. Interpretation of the Bible requires the use of good hermeneutical principles that take into account the text, its historical and social context, its literary style, its authorship and its intended readership. In many respects this approach to the Bible is much like the way we read our morning newspapers. Interpretations derived from the Bible (or theology), then, can be compared with interpreted truth derived from psychological

science and human experience. Comparing theology with theory and experience forms the basis for examining the coherence among these sources of knowing.

Psychology presents challenges to Christians, but Christian beliefs can also bring insights to psychology. For example, recent psychological findings show that those involved in stable marriages find greater sexual fulfilment as well as being generally more contented or happy. This challenges the conviction among some psychologists that the path to human contentment requires greater freedom of sexual expression. Christian beliefs, based on Scripture, can provide a starting place to guide our scientific investigation of human, and non-human, psychological functioning. In practice, of course, our fallen human condition means that our knowing may be flawed in both theological and psychological disciplines and consistencies between the two may not always be apparent. Because of these limitations, discrepancies between the two disciplines should prompt us to review our thinking in both theology and psychology.

Bibliography

D. G. Benner and P. C. Hill, *Baker Encyclopedia of Psychology and Counseling*, 2nd edn (Grand Rapids, 1999); R. K. Bufford, 'Consecrated Counseling: Reflections on the Distinctives of Christian Counseling', *Journal of Psychology and Theology*, 25 (1997), pp. 110–122; R. G. Hood, B. Spilka, G. Hunsberger and R. L. Gorsuch, *The Psychology of Religion: An Empirical Approach* (Englewood Cliffs, 1996); M. R. McMinn, *Psychology, Theology, and Spirituality in Christian Counseling* (Wheaton, 1996); D. G. Myers, *Psychology*, 6th ed. (New York, 2001); D. Powlison, 'A Biblical Counseling View', in E. L. Johnson and S. L. Jones (eds.), *Psychology and Christianity* (Downers Grove, 2000).

R. K. Bufford

QUEST FOR THE HISTORICAL JESUS, see JESUS, HISTORICAL
QUR'AN, see ISLAM

RACISM

At the beginning of the twentieth century the world-view of most societies in the West included the notion that humanity was improving. By the end of the century this myth of progress had been shattered, not merely by two world wars, but especially by a series of events indicative of a tendency in human beings towards racial hatred. From our vantage point at the beginning of the twenty-first century, it is virtually impossible to reflect on the nature of the human condition, or on the nature of God, without reference to two of our epoch's most extreme manifestations of racism: Auschwitz and apartheid.

Racism is fundamentally the attempt to advocate the intellectual or ethical superiority of one group of people over another, based on supposed racial or cultural differences. Thus, in Rwanda Hutus and Tutsis were distinguished primarily by height, build and facial features. In South Africa, the apartheid system was based on skin colour. In Nazi Germany religion, language, bodily characteristics and lineage were all determinative in the Nazi quest for separation and racial purity.

From time to time, racism or racially motivated nationalism has been combined with Christian ideas. When *slavery flourished in the southern United States, for example, many slave owners called themselves Christians, attended church and even used biblical texts to give credence to the institution of slavery. They were supported by theologians such as R. L. Dabney. The anti-Semitism of the Nazi period was not completely unrelated to some views of Martin Luther centuries before. The apartheid system was defended by arguments relying on biblical texts and ideas. It is not unusual, therefore, for a critic to raise the objection that the Bible and Christianity are either fundamentally racist or that they lend support to racist ideas.

The Christian's first response should be to admit that churches and individual Christians have often failed in this area. Our faith in Christ does not remove us from our cultural contexts. If the culture itself is infected with racist ideas, it would be strange if Christians who live and breathe that culture are not affected by it. We must also concede that certain scriptural texts are difficult to understand and have been twisted in the attempt to show that they support racism. At the same time, we must insist that the canon of Scripture taken as a whole is opposed to racist ideas and racial discrimination. The Bible witnesses to a God of love who 'hates nothing that he has made'.

'Problematic' texts

Certain biblical texts and ideas are problematic and must be addressed. These are the so-called 'curse' of Ham (Gen. 9:20–27), the issue of the conquest of Canaan, the apparent favouritism implied by God's choice of Israel, texts in the OT which imply that Israelites allowed slavery, and texts in the NT which discuss slavery without explicitly condemning it.

The 'curse of Ham' in Gen. 9 has been used in racist rhetoric to attempt to demonstrate that the peoples of Africa are under God's curse and may legitimately be enslaved (Gen. 9:27). This reading of Gen. 9 ignores key elements in the story. First, the curse for Ham's action (probably rape) is not applied to all of Ham's children but only to Canaan (9:25–27). The peoples of Africa who are said to be descended from Ham (Cush and Egypt, Gen. 10:6) are not mentioned in the curse of Gen. 9:25–27. The story cannot be used to justify the slavery of African peoples. More importantly, the story must be read as proleptic judgment on the Canaanites – not as innocent victims of their ancestor's sin, but as those who themselves are guilty of gross violations of God's will. This brings us to the second set of texts.

The command of God to punish the Canaanites is one of the most difficult problems of biblical theology. It must be noted that God does not command the conquest of Canaan simply because he wants to clear some land to give it to Israel. The Israelites are commanded to fight because the Canaanites have come under God's judgment in spite of God's many years of patience (Gen. 15:16). The punishment for sin is death (Gen. 2:17; Rom. 6:23) and *in this case* Israel functions as God's instrument for punishing sin. Later in the biblical story Israel herself will be judged for sin (Isa. 10:5–6). It may also be the case that what is envisioned in the conquest is not the extermination of all of the inhabitants of Canaan, but only their rulers (the Heb. word in question has the root meaning of 'those who sit' and this can sometimes mean 'rulers' rather than 'inhabitants').

Has God shown racial favouritism by choosing Israel? Two answers must be given to this question. First, God's choice of Israel does not imply that God considers Israel to be superior to other peoples. Israel's election is presented by Scripture simply as God's sovereign choice, not as something that was merited: 'The LORD did not set his affection on you and choose you because you were more numerous than other peoples . . . it was because the LORD loved you' (Deut. 7:7–8). Secondly, God's purpose in the election of Israel was the salvation of all nations. Far from being a sign of God's exclusiveness, Israel's election is integral to God's plan for creation. To Abram God says, 'All peoples on earth will be blessed through you' (Gen. 12:3). Isaiah declares Israel to be 'a light for the Gentiles' (Isa. 42:6). This trajectory allows Paul to proclaim repeatedly that 'God does not show favouritism' (Rom. 2:11).

Slavery was a pervasive reality in the ancient world. Of course its existence in ancient Israel and the lack of explicit condemnation of the institution in the NT is troublesome. It needs to be said, however, that the Bible's tolerance of slavery is not an uncritical acceptance. The Torah forbids the enslavement of Israelites (Lev. 25:42–55) and warns against the oppression of slaves, since Israel herself suffered oppression in Egypt (Deut. 15:15). Specific legislation protected slaves within Israel's borders and even included them in the covenant festivals (Exod. 12:44; 20:10; Deut. 16:11–14). In the NT 1 Tim. 1:10 lists slave-trading as a vice and, in Philemon, Paul argues that the runaway slave Onesimus is actually a brother in Christ – a view which would eventually lead Christians to the conclusion that the institution itself must be abolished.

A biblical theology of race

The trajectory of Scripture is racially inclusive. Most important is the clear biblical witness that God is 'one'. As opposed to the many gods of the nations which are bound to particular places, the God of Israel is the maker of the sea and the dry land (Jon. 2:9). For Paul the clear implication of this monotheistic belief is that God is not the God of the Jews only: 'Is he not the God of the Gentiles too? Yes, of Gentiles too, since there is only one God' (Rom. 3:29–30). This basic tenet implies that the God who made all, cares for all. God wills the salvation of all (1 Tim. 2:4) and, in Christ, dies for all (John 3:16). He makes no racial distinctions. The one God who created all people made them in his image. The doctrine of the *imago Dei*, the 'image of God' (Gen. 1:26–28), implies a radical equality between persons of all races. God has not chosen a particular race as the bearer of his image: 'From one man he

made every nation of men' (Acts 17:26) and has stamped all with his image. All races and nations are called to image his glory to the world.

The legal material in Scripture also emphasizes the equality of races. The Torah commands Israel to 'love your neighbour as yourself' (Lev. 19:18). The concept of 'neighbour' is not limited to those who are members of Israel, for the 'alien', the stranger, even the slave is worthy of love (Lev. 19:34; Deut. 10:18). As Jesus makes clear, even the enemy is included in the command to love (Matt. 5:44; Luke 10:25–37).

Perhaps the most eloquent testimony to God's racial inclusivity is presented in the book of Jonah, a reminder that Israel's election was never meant to be exclusive but a vehicle for God's mission. Paul is especially clear that God's purpose has always been for all nations to come to faith in the God of Israel and that in Christ this promise has come to fulfilment: 'there is neither Jew nor Greek, slave nor free, male nor female' (Gal. 3:28; cf. 1 Cor. 12:13; Eph. 2:11–22; Col. 3:11).

This new way of viewing the racial dimension of humanity in Christ is, however, an eschatological reality. A multicultural people has come into existence in Christ, but it has come into being in the midst of a world still filled with hatred. In the resurrection racial, cultural and linguistic distinctions will no longer be a basis for fear and hatred but the means of celebration as 'a great multitude that no-one could count, from every nation, tribe, people and language' give praise to God (Rev. 7:9; cf. 21:26).

These biblical themes have led Christians throughout the ages to condemn racism in its many forms: William Wilberforce and the Clapham Sect worked for the abolition of slavery in the British Empire; Desmond Tutu and a host of people around the world argued and worked against South African apartheid on biblical grounds; Martin Luther King led the Civil Rights movement in the United States; in their different ways Dietrich Bonhoeffer, Corrie ten Boom and Maximilian Kolbe witnessed to the love of God in Christ in the face of Nazism. The same biblical story can empower the church to resist the evil of racism today.

Bibliography

M. Brett (ed.), *Ethnicity and the Bible* (Leiden, 1996); C. Catherwood, *Whose Side* is God On? (New York, 2003); C. S. Cowles et al., *Show Them No Mercy: 4 Views on God and the Canaanite Genocide* (Grand Rapids, 2003); R. Gagnon, *The Bible and Homosexual Practice* (Nashville, 2001); N. Gottwald, *The Tribes of Yahweh* (Maryknoll, 1979); S. Haynes, *Noah's Curse: The Biblical Justification of American Slavery* (Oxford, 2002); C. Wright, *Living as the People of God: The Relevance of Old Testament Ethics* (Leicester, 1983).

G. LeMarquand

RAHNER, KARL

Karl Rahner (1904–84) is regarded by many as the foremost Roman Catholic theologian of the first half of the twentieth century. Born in Freiburg, Germany and entering the Jesuit order in 1922, he espoused the spirituality of *Ignatius Loyola as of 'more significance' to him 'than all learned philosophy and theology inside and outside the Order'. Even so, philosophically, his thinking was also shaped by *Thomas Aquinas and the Thomist tradition and, in the 1930s, by Martin Heidegger, in spite of the latter's Nazism. From 1937 Rahner held a range of posts as professor of theology over the next thirty-four years in Innsbruck, Munich and Münster, as well as working as a parish priest and pastor for much of his life. His 'philosophical theology' from the 1950s onwards both anticipated and enabled the more inclusive vision of the Second Vatican Council. In 1965 he founded the international journal *Concilium* in conjunction with Edward Schillebeeckx.

Theologically, Rahner is regarded as one of the foremost neo-Thomists in that he does not view the Christian faith as primarily a matter of intellect or will but, rather, as the experience of encounter with *Jesus Christ. For him that experience was made real through the senses and *imagination as he engaged with the Ignatian Spiritual Exercises. Thus, without denying the value of a 'descending' Christology, in which God reaches down to humanity through the incarnation, Rahner postulates an 'ascending' Christology which starts with human experience and aspiration and reaches up through the God/Man Jesus Christ towards unity with the Godhead. This 'transcendental' theology is not a grasping of a belief-system but a being grasped by the One whose

*mystery (or 'incomprehensibility') we strive towards. This perspective resonates with the 'unsearchability' of God's judgments (see e.g. Isa. 55:8 and Rom. 11:33).

For many Christian apologists Rahner's concept of 'anonymous' Christians is seen as especially controversial. And yet his notion, in which the *Holy Spirit is seen to be abroad in God's world, not least within non-Christian religions, leading people to a responsiveness to Christ even though Jesus as an historical reality is unknown to them, can be viewed as in accord with Pauline teaching in Rom. 2:12–16. As Rahner puts it, 'anyone who has let himself be taken hold of by this grace [of the Father in his Son] can be called with every right an "anonymous Christian"' (*Theological Reflections*, vol. 6, p. 395).

Bibliography
P. Burke, *Reinterpreting Rahner: A Critical Study of His Major Themes* (New York, 2002); W. V. Dych, *Karl Rahner* (London, 1992); G. A. McCool (ed.), *A Rahner Reader* (London, 1975); K. Rahner, *Foundations of Christian Faith: An Introduction to the Idea of Christianity* (ET, London, 1978); *Theological Investigations*, 20 vols (ET, 1961–81).

R. Hurding

RAMM, BERNARD

Bernard Ramm (1916–92) epitomized the evangelical goal of providing a cogent apologetic for classic Christianity in the face of the changes transpiring in modern culture.

Ramm's plans for a career in science were interrupted just prior to his entering university by a life-transforming conversion. As a result, he pursued studies in speech, philosophy and *theology, completing his PhD at the University of Southern California (1950) with a dissertation entitled 'An Investigation of Some Recent Efforts to Justify Metaphysical Statements from Science with Special Reference to Physics'. Ramm taught apologetics and theology at several evangelical institutions, most notably the American Baptist Seminary of the West (1959–74, 1978–86).

Three major areas – apologetics, Bible and *science, and theological *authority – captured Ramm's attention. In his early books, *Problems in Christian Apologetics* (Portland, 1949), *Types of Apologetic Systems* (Wheaton, 1953) and *Protestant Christian Evidences* (Chicago, 1953), he pursued an 'evidentialist' approach, seeking to provide evidences for the truth of the Christian faith by appeal to data that can be verified, at least in theory, by everyone. By 1958, however, Ramm was moving towards a course correction, spelled out in *The God Who Makes a Difference* (Waco, 1972). Convinced that no set of individual facts could prove the faith, he now put forth Christianity as a hypothesis. He also introduced a distinction between 'certitude' and '*certainty': although a believer can gain full spiritual certitude about the great truths of personal salvation, the historical dimension of the Christian faith can be relegated only a high degree of probability.

Ramm charted his proposal for an evangelical engagement with *science in *The Christian View of Science and Scripture* (Grand Rapids, 1954). He called for a return to the 'noble tradition' that viewed God as the author of both creation and redemption and, therefore, assumed the agreement between true science and the Bible. To demonstrate this agreement, Ramm not only harmonized science with Scripture, but he also declared that the Bible contained culturally conditioned statements and that the biblical writers were not teachers of science in the modern sense.

Ramm's third interest, which also served the apologetical goal of demonstrating the truth of the Christian faith, emerged in *The Pattern of Religious Authority* (Grand Rapids, 1958), *The Witness of the Spirit* (Grand Rapids, 1959) and *Special Revelation and the Word of God* (Grand Rapids, 1961). In his later years, Ramm turned his attention to constructive theology. But even this was consistent with his apologetic orientation. For him, constructive theology was apologetic by nature and necessitated a conversation with science.

Bibliography

S. J. Grenz and R. E. Olson, *Twentieth-Century Theology* (Downers Grove, 1992); B. Ramm, *The Evangelical Heritage* (Grand Rapids, 2000).

S. J. GRENZ

RATIONALISM

Rationalism is both something of which Christians are sometimes accused and something they may attribute to others. The word covers a cluster of ideas, and it matters which idea from the cluster is meant. Someone may be a 'rationalist' in one respect but not others. Moreover, the term often carries strong pejorative or approving overtones. Pejoratively, rationalism is associated with a somewhat arrogant use of human reason, while the approval often refers to a certain tough-minded desire to think things out independently. This provides a further reason for clarification, that one may know precisely what is being approved or condemned.

It is helpful first to distinguish rationalism from a commitment to being rational. Rationality focuses more on providing reasons for actions or beliefs and a commitment to some form of classical logical process, such as accepting the law of non-contradiction. Thus understood, Christian *theology has frequently been strongly rational (e.g. *Thomas Aquinas [c. 1224–74) and Francis Turretin [1623–87]) without necessarily being rationalist. Thus, Turretin stresses that human reason may and should be used as an auxiliary to the Bible, but not as an alternative or superior source of knowledge: reason is the minister of the Word, not its master. Rationality and rationalism are, nevertheless, related in their common use of reason. A key question, therefore, is whether and in what areas human reason is viable. Theologically this raises the issue of the effects of the fall. If one thinks sin has not affected the capacity for rational thought, one will tend to regard the ability of human reason far more optimistically, and this may mean regarding rationalism more favourably. However, given passages like Rom. 1:18–32 and Eph. 4:17–24, sin has often been regarded as fundamentally irrational (a kind of *dementia* in *Augustine's terms), and this curtails appeals to reason as a free-standing and independent instrument for human understanding. Secular counterparts to this question about the viability of human reason exist in the hermeneutics of suspicion generated by *Freud's psychoanalysis, Marx's class analysis and *Nietzsche's philosophy.

A second distinction lies between a more technical meaning and the everyday use of 'rationalism'. In everyday terms, rationalism readily suggests (sometimes approvingly, sometimes not) the supremacy and adequacy of human reason. The more technical sense refers to the philosophical movement including R. *Descartes (1596–1650), B. *Spinoza (1637–77) and G. *Leibniz (1646–1716). At its most modest, this movement had several characteristic themes: caution regarding the reliability of physical sense data (a theme found in the pre-Socratic philosopher *Parmenides and later *Plato), a prizing of intellectual reason as a way of comprehending the universe more deeply than mere sense data permits, a conception of the universe as an ordered and intelligible system, a high regard for mathematics, and an inclination to the view that there is a reason for any phenomenon. It is helpful here to note rationalism's relation to the revival of scepticism in the Renaissance period and thereafter. Rationalism in Descartes can be partly characterized as an attempt to meet scepticism's strongest formulations by reference to indubitable truths beyond unreliable sense data.

Given these themes, rationalism may be cast in terms of a series of important oppositions, of varying intensity. First, rationalism can be seen as in opposition to *empiricism because it stresses the primacy of data derived from the senses. In its stronger forms rationalism moves primarily or purely from the *a priori* principles not given by *sense perception. Just as strong empiricism is vulnerable to the charge that it downplays the 'processing' of sense data, so strong rationalism downplays the extent to which thought depends on sense data.

Secondly, rationalism is opposed to judgments formed for aesthetic or emotional reasons (a version of *Romanticism), because these are individual and subjective rather than universal. Hence, partly, rationalism's association with a certain sterility and inability to explain the richness of human experience. This in turn relates to the charge that rationalism implies certain dualisms, especially a mind-body dualism and an individual-external world dualism. The fear is that in both dualisms, the latter partner in each pair is devalued. Perceptions also arise that rationalism is characteristically 'black-or-white' and emotionally impoverished. The obvious question is whether a rationalist God can love.

Thirdly, rationalism is set against the supernatural, because rationalism suggests that 'natural' explanations are to be sought for the resurrection, for example, rather than accepting direct divine intervention. In this sense one might describe David *Hume (1711–76) as a 'rationalist', a title he would otherwise be reluctant to accept. Rationalism as anti-supernaturalism often involves a closed universe in which events are completely self-contained and self-referring and which, therefore, excludes direct divine interaction with the universe. This rationalism closely approaches atheism or implies a strongly deistic conception of God (but is a far cry from the rationalism of Descartes). The obvious apologetic challenge to such rationalism is how one would know if God indeed did act. Such action seems to have been ruled out *a priori*. This exclusion would only be sustainable if we had good reason for imagining that human *a priori* reasoning was demonstrably reliable in relation to God and his will. It is precisely that reliability that Rom. 1:18–32 envisages as unattainable because of sin.

Finally, rationalism is seen in opposition to *revelation, because rationalism allegedly requires one should not be under *authority but exercising independent judgment. Classic Christian belief has, of course, insisted on the need for revelation if we are to know the truth about God and his will. Several points arise. First, there is an issue of viability. *Kant (1724–1804), associated with this kind of rationalism, apparently assumes that human reason has such capabilities that we need no 'authority' (see his essay of 1784, 'What is Enlightenment?'). It is just this that the Bible questions in respect of God and his will. Further, it is hard to see how Kant's assumption can be adequately confirmed, unless, of course, God were to speak, saying we had correctly understood him (which would, naturally, be revelation). Secondly, Kant's 1784 essay hints strongly that such intellectual autonomy is ethically desirable – it should not be forgotten that rationalism can rely on ethical justification and involve ethical demands. The corollary of this is that reliance on revelation is unethical or at best a wilful immaturity. This suggests a view of the relation between Creator and creature that undercuts the dependence of created beings on their Creator. Thirdly, as *Thomas Aquinas long ago noted, it is entirely apt and intellectually hygienic to accept words on authority when those words are given by God (*Summa Theologiae* 1a.1.8.), that is, by an all-wise and truthful speaker.

This opposition to revelation, or to the need for revelation, is important. Rationalism in this sense readily implies a willingness to weigh the words of the Bible against human intellectual judgment. Thus, one might hear biblical teaching about the Trinity rejected because it is thought impossible, or moral instructions disregarded since modern understandings take a different view. The tendency is to seek external grounds for agreeing with the Bible rather than obeying it.

The current cultural climate of postmodernism is unfavourable to rationalism in many of the above senses. The idea of a universal reason sits uneasily with suspicion towards meta-narratives, in which *truth and reason can be readily seen as constructions with absolutist tendencies which serve particular purposes and agendas (note especially F. *Nietzsche's and M. *Foucault's reflections on truth and power). On this view 'reasons' readily become 'rationalizations'. For this reason the charge that Christian belief is 'rationalist' can be devastating in a postmodern context, and is associated characteristically with Christian claims that some truths (e.g. Jesus is God's son) are absolute. The obvious Christian counter-question is whether such charges do not assume absolutely that God is not a completely truthful speaker.

Certain apologetic techniques have been charged with rationalism. This charge relates to the idea that if proper evidence is produced in favour of Christian faith, a listener will, as a rational being, inevitably come to faith. The key word is 'inevitably'. Put this way there is indeed an assumption that sin has not corrupted the human reason, to which presuppositional apologists rightly object. There remains, though, the proper use of evidence as an intellectually ethical way of commending Christian faith (note the stress on this in 1 Thess. 2:3–8 and 2 Cor. 4:2) which God may graciously use to bring people to belief.

For Christian apologists the oppositions between rationalism and the supernatural and between rationalism and revelation are particularly important. In both these areas rationalism is associated with human independence and autonomy. It is at this level that there is a curious kinship between rationalism and its apparent opposite, irrationalism. Despite their difference over the viability of reason, both share, as C. Van Til argued, a paramount ethical value in human autonomy: they differ over the ways in which that value is defended.

Bibliography

H. I. Brown, *Rationality* (London, 1988); J. Cottingham, *The Rationalists* (Oxford, 1988); J. M. Frame, *Apologetics to the Glory of God* (Phillipsburg, 1994).

M. J. OVEY

REALISM

The debate about realism involves some of the most fundamental questions in philosophy and *theology. The term 'realism' has a number of different applications in the literature, depending upon which area of philosophy is under scrutiny. But there is a common idea that these different uses of 'realism' share. This is that there are things which are independent of the mind, and therefore 'real' as opposed to 'ideal', 'relative' or a matter of linguistic convention. What is confusing about realism is not just that it has a number of different guises, but that a person can be a realist in one area, and an anti-realist in another. For example, one could be an anti-realist with respect to *ethics, but a realist with respect to *science as, arguably, the logical positivists were.

Moreover, some theists retain the kernel of realism – the independence of *reality from personal experience of it – in other metaphysical theories. Bishop *Berkeley is an example of this. His *idealism means that all that is perceived of the external world by human agents are the ideas of sense data, matter being a fiction. However, the ideas of experience which Berkeley refers to are supplied by God, in whose mind they reside, and who ensures that things continue to exist, even when there is no-one there to perceive them, such as when I cease to perceive my chair on leaving my study. For Berkeley, there is always the divine perceiver, who continues to think of the ideas that make up this world, even when we do not. Thus, theists like Berkeley have sometimes been dubbed 'immaterial realists'. 'Immaterial' because all that can be known of an object is ideal, but 'realist' in the sense that a given object still has an existence beyond a particular perceptual experience of it, since all such objects continue to exist only as they continue to be thought of by the divine mind. However, since Berkeley's theory is dependent on the mind, it is not conventionally realist.

*Kant famously advocated another kind of overlapping position with respect to realism in *epistemology. He claimed that there is an empirical realm in space and time in which we can have a knowledge of material objects that is real. But this does not entail the additional transcendental realist thesis, that the existence and nature of a particular material thing is wholly independent of our knowledge of them. Instead, he advocated the view that, transcendentally speaking, humans are idealists. That is, there is an empirical realm of phenomena (things as they appear to us) which is realist, but there is an additional realm of noumena (things are they are in themselves) of which we can have no certain knowledge at all. This is because perception of empirical things leads only to knowledge of appearances, not of things in themselves.

Realism has also been used in philosophy of *language, where it is wedded to a correspondence theory of truth. This means that a particular sentence that expresses something about the world is meaningful if and only if it corresponds to something 'out there'. So, if Wayne says 'This is a large monkey-wrench' and he is holding a large piece of metal shaped like a monkey-wrench, then what he says corresponds to something that exists outside of himself, in this case, the wrench. This is opposed to anti-realism, which is the view that entails a coherence view of truth. This means that Wayne's utterance about the monkey-wrench has meaning just so long as it coheres with other, related notions in his language. So, Wayne may be participating in a language game in which 'monkey-wrench' has meaning, say, the language game of a mechanic. But this does not necessarily mean that his language game corresponds to what non-mechanics call a monkey-wrench. It might be that what he calls monkey-wrench would be understood by non-mechanics as an adjustable spanner, double-headed fork or some other such thing. The distinction here depends upon the weight given to the relation of a linguistic act to some object independent of that act. The realist emphasizes the independence of the object to which the linguistic utterance is related. The anti-realist emphasizes the relation of the utterance to other utterances, often, in *Wittgensteinian terms, in a particular language game.

In addition to metaphysical, epistemological and linguistic uses of realism, there is an ethical use in moral realism. This view claims that there are certain moral principles that are objective, mind-independent realities. These principles may be moral truths such as 'Love is a virtue', or *moral values, such as 'Adultery is worse than fornication.' They have often been thought to be ideas in the divine mind, although some versions hold that these principles are independent even of the mind of God. In Christian thought, such moral realism has been central to the tradition advocated, for example, by those committed to a divine command theory of ethics (that God commands certain moral truths like the Ten Commandments, which must be obeyed). But it is not wedded to one particular meta-ethical theory. One could, like Jonathan *Edwards, be a moral realist and virtue ethicist, although moral realists cannot be relativists unless they hold that there are objective moral principles that humans do not have access to, thereby combining moral realism with epistemological scepticism.

One important problem for theistic moral realists pertains to a version of the Euthyphro dilemma, a problem for the objectivity of moral truths. This takes the following form: Does God command what is good, or is what is good what God commands? If God commands what is good, then his commands appear arbitrary (what makes this good and that *evil? Could God have made murder good and pacifism evil?). But if what is good is what God commands, then it seems that God appeals to some standard of goodness independent of himself. This is also problematic, if Christians believe that God is the source of all goodness. One potential solution is to claim that God commands that which is the expression of his character, and his character is essentially good. This resolution grasps both horns of the dilemma, but it has not convinced everyone. For instance, it still leaves the problem of moral values like jealousy or pride unaccounted for. Some Christian thinkers, like *Augustine, have attempted to account for such negative moral values by claiming that they are privations of some positive moral principle, such as benevolence.

Realism also stands opposed to *relativism. This species of philosophical corrosive comes in different varieties. However, relativists are committed to the view that there is no one objective value or truth, no 'God's eye view' from which we can survey different experiences and truth claims to ascertain whether they match that which is real or not. Philosophers such as Richard *Rorty have advocated a pragmatic approach to this question, taking what works, rather than what corresponds to some objective reality, as their touchstone. There are other influential philosophers whose views seem to lead to relativistic consequences, such as W. V. O. Quine and Wittgenstein, although this is disputed. Nevertheless, Quine's holism, the view that all beliefs a person holds in an interrelated web are theoretically revisable, even truths of *logic, appears to lean towards relativism. The later Wittgenstein's theories on the therapeutic nature of philosophy in disentangling linguistic knots and the notion that language must be seen in the context of a particular language game rather than as corresponding to some absolute reality which it denotes, has been widely influential. Whether this entails some form of relativism is less clear.

In stark contrast to relativism, the Christian gospel speaks of a God who creates reality independent of any experience we may have of it. This points towards a realist understanding of the metaphysical nature of things, although, as we have indicated this can be understood in very different (even idealist) ways. Moreover, those who endorse a propositional view of revelation seem to be committed to some realist version of language, with a correspondence theory of truth. Thus, what can be known from the propositions of Scripture about say, the nature of God or salvation, corresponds in some way to the nature of God or salvation. It is not merely the convention of a particular community for whom certain words have certain meanings and uses. And it appears that the majority voice in the Christian tradition has consistently held to moral realism in some shape or form, even when the standard of moral value is not located in the divine nature.

Bibliography

G. Berkeley, *Principles of Human Nature and Three Dialogues* (Harmondsworth, 1988); J. Edwards, *Ethical Writings* (New Haven, 1989); A. C. Grayling, *An Introduction to Philosophical Logic* (Oxford, 1997); D. Groothuis, *Truth Decay* (Leicester, 2000); P. Helm (ed.), *Divine Commands and Morality* (Oxford, 1981); *Faith and Reason* (Oxford, 1999); J. Hick, *An Interpretation of Religion* (London, 1989); R. Kirk, *Relativism and Reality, A Contemporary Introduction* (London, 1999); T. Kuhn, *The Structure of Scientific Revolutions* (Chicago, 1996).

O. D. CRISP

REALITY

Philosophically, this term refers to the way things actually are, in contrast to their appearance. Reality is independent of appearance. Appearance does not determine reality in two ways. First, while there may be widespread agreement on the nature of reality, based on appearance, it is always possible that reality may be different from appearance. Secondly, reality does not require appearances. In the famous *Kantian illustration, if a tree falls and no-one is there to hear the noise, can we be sure there is a noise? Intuitively we answer in the affirmative. It is more likely that the right kind of observer is not present than that there is no noise. Perhaps reality is beyond all the investigations we are capable of making, which presuppose it as a basic premise.

Challenges to such a view of reality have come from various corners. Bertrand *Russell claimed that the distinction between appearance and reality is 'one of the distinctions that cause most trouble in philosophy' (*The Problems of Philosophy*). Why is this, especially when in ordinary experience the trouble is rarely there? *Phenomenalism is the position held by Russell (following John Stuart Mill), the view which holds that real, physical objects are logical constructions from our experiences. Russell set forth a programme whereby experience could be constructed to render physical objects. The project is thought to have failed, because it could not avoid circularity. Postmodernism in various guises suggests that there are no real meta-narratives that can be trusted, but only the more playful surface and style. But, it has been pointed out, such a postmodern understanding is itself a meta-narrative. Post-structuralism denies any fixed meaning, and in its more radical forms (such as deconstruction) denies any connection between *language and the outside world and rejects the idea of any fixed *truth or reality to be investigated. But, again, is not language required even to make such a claim?

Perspectivism, originating in *Nietzsche's philosophy, holds that truth is only a matter of one's perspective, tied to culture, language, human feeling or, more recently, gender and sexual orientation. *Foucault understood science and reason to be instruments of power, rather than ways to achieve reality. Instead of subject and object, we have subject and abject, owing to the human tendency to be cruel.

While there are valuable insights here, it is reductionist and tends to throw out the baby with the bath water. In *Hinduism and *Buddhism it is generally taught that we are in bondage to life, death and rebirth, giving us the illusion that suffering and evil are real. Once we gain release from this cycle and become detached, we will find that the illusion will vanish. The reality of suffering and evil, however, is not so easily dismissed from our experience.

Reality thus emerges as a stubborn fact, a state of affairs the denial of which is self-refuting. Yet the question emerges, how may we move from reality to a correct evaluation of its nature? Several answers from a Christian basis have been given. *Thomas Aquinas, borrowing from *Aristotle, held that God's existence could be demonstrated from the contingency of the world. According to the family of proofs known as the *cosmological argument, in all of the natural world we have dependency. It follows that this world of dependent beings must be grounded in a necessary being, an unmoved mover, or God. While there is a common-sense appeal to this approach, at the technical level it falls short of being a conclusive demonstration. It cannot show that this necessary existence is any different from the contingent existence of dependent things. Put as a question, why does contingency require an independent source? How would we know that God is not himself dependent?

Another type of answer is known as *foundationalism. In general this view holds that knowledge can be founded upon the secure warrant of experience and reason. *Descartes claimed that he had found an indubitable basis for existence in the fact of human thinking. In its Christian variant, because of God's *revelation we can be sure the world and our knowledge of it make sense. As bearers of the image of God, we have the capacity to see things as they are. This view has been opposed in a number of ways. Coherentism believes that truth is not the correspondence of our propositions to what is 'out there', but the consistency with which one proposition fits into other propositions. Some apologists, like Francis A. *Schaeffer, thought one could hold both to foundationalism and coherency. But generally, coherentism has not been able to recognize objective criteria whereby we may judge propositions to be consistently held. The strongest opponent of foundationalism in our times comes from the various types of postmodernism. The general idea is that we can no longer believe in the *grand récit*, the all-encompassing account of reality, because all such views have led to oppression. Again, postmodern thinkers have failed to prove their point without falling back into some sort of objective criteria.

There is a third way which avoids the Scylla of foundationalism and the Charybdis of postmodernism. It is the way of analogical knowledge. Not to be confused with either Thomas Aquinas' or Karl *Barth's use of the term, analogical knowledge means 'thinking God's thoughts after him'. This means one may unashamedly begin with the God of revelation, but recognize both our human finitude and our sinfulness. We can know truly, though not exhaustively. We can know what God reveals, without either the arrogance of univocal thought or the false humility of equivocal thought. This approach eschews postmodernism because it does hold to objectivity. But it is not a return to foundationalism because it puts knowledge within a covenant relationship, not claiming a rationalist or empirical rock of indubitability. Neither does analogical knowledge fit within the various forms of realism, including critical realism, because it recognizes that all facts are preinterpreted facts, originating in God. So, if one wants to say 'My view squares with reality', that is acceptable, depending on the nature of that reality. In order for knowledge to have any warrant, that reality must posit the distinction between Creator and creature.

Bibliography

T. E. Hill, *Contemporary Theories of Knowledge* (New York, 1961); C. Van Til, *A Christian Theory of Knowledge* (Phillipsburg, 1969).

W. EDGAR

REASON

Reason is perhaps the most important intellectual tool that human beings have for discovering the *truth or of getting in touch with *reality. While some might think that *revelation is a better tool for discovering the truth, consider that one must judge which revelation is the correct one (if any at all). Even if one were to settle on the Bible as the word of God, one must judge when and if God is speaking, how God is speaking and what is being said. Settling on revelation and then interpreting texts all require the judicious use of reason. Human beings must use reason if we are to have any chance of discovering the truth. In this essay 'reason' and 'rationality' are taken as synonymous.

Although rationality may assist our quest for truth, there is no rigid connection between rationality and truth. Nonetheless, reason aims at the truth. The goal of being rational is to acquire true beliefs. We are truth-seekers and reason is a means to the end of truth. Although reason aims at the truth, it is not an infallible guide to the truth. So, reason seeks but cannot guarantee the finding of the truth.

Preliminaries

Before we discuss the nature of reason or rationality, let us consider three issues.

1. Rationality is a matter of *how* one believes, not *what* one believes. One could irrationally believe something that is true. For example, one could believe that there are craters on the moon not because one attended carefully to the scientific evidence but because one's invisible friend told one so. And one could rationally believe something that is false. For example, it was rational 2,000 years ago to believe that the earth was flat and that the sun, planets and stars revolved around the earth; these beliefs were rational but false.

2. Rationality is person and situation specific. That is, what is rational for one person at a particular time and place might not be rational for another person at a different time and place. This is supported by the example of the earth's being flat. This was rational for most people to believe 2,000 years ago but is no longer rational for most people to believe now. It follows that concerning belief in God, we should not ask, 'Is belief in God rational?' as if the question of the rationality of that belief were timeless and eternal without reference to any actual believers. The question more properly should be, 'Is belief in God rational for this or that person (in this or that socio-historical situation)?' Recognizing that rationality is person and situation specific does not entail *relativism. Relativism holds that truth is culturally relative. But just because a belief may be rational for a person in a given situation does not make that belief true.

3. Rationality does not help us decide which of our or anyone else's beliefs is rational. God may know which of our and others' beliefs are rational or irrational, but human beings lack cognitive access to all of the experiential inputs, background assumptions, beliefs and conditions that rational belief involves. Lacking that sort of information precludes finite human beings, in most cases, from determining if others' beliefs are rational.

Rationality and the demand for evidence

Many people take rationality to be simply a matter of assembling available evidence and assessing its relevance for other beliefs. Rational beliefs are those which can be logically inferred from the evidence. According to this view of reason, the rationality of belief in God – that is, belief in an omnipotent, omniscient, perfectly good creator – is answered in terms of a positive or negative assessment of arguments for the existence God. This approach to reason and belief in God achieved ascendancy in the *Enlightenment era.

Enlightenment thinkers rejected the medieval reliance on *authority as a guide to religious, moral, political and scientific truth. They subjected each of these domains to the searching criticism of reason; if a belief could not survive the scrutiny of reason, it was rejected as irrational. This has resulted in four positions on Christian belief. First, some claim that reason supports traditional Christian beliefs; this view was held by, for example, John *Locke, William *Paley and many contemporary apologists. Secondly, some claim that reason supports more revisionary Christian beliefs; thinkers such as *Kant hold this view. Thirdly, some, such as W. K. Clifford, claim that belief in God is irrational because of the lack of evidence for God's existence. And fourthly, David *Hume, *Voltaire and J. L. Mackie claim that reason can be used to disprove God's existence because God's existence is incompatible with the existence of *evil.

Critique of the Enlightenment view of reason

These Enlightenment thinkers assume classical *foundationalism, a culturally dominant but defective understanding of reason. Classical foundationalism attempts to elucidate the structure of rational beliefs and their relationships to one another. Imagine a pyramid with a large but solid foundation and subsequent levels that are supported by the foundational level. In the same way, foundationalism assumes two kinds of beliefs. There are foundational level or basic beliefs, which are not based on evidence or argument, and non-basic or inferential beliefs, which rest on the foundations, i.e. can be inferred from other beliefs. Not all basic beliefs are rational, so classical foundationalism offers criteria for determining which of our beliefs are properly or justifiably basic. Properly basic beliefs are a special set of beliefs which are clearly true; these include beliefs that are self-evident or evident to the senses. Self-evident beliefs include, for example, logical and mathematical truths. Beliefs that are evident to the senses include 'grass is green', 'honey tastes sweet', and 'sandpaper feels rough'.

Classical foundationalism has been applied to belief in God. Since God's existence is neither self-evident nor evident to the senses, according to classical foundationalism it requires the support of evidence in order to be considered rational. If the evidence is lacking, belief in God is irrational. This claim that belief in God is irrational due to lack of evidence has been called 'the evidentialist objection to belief in God', and goes as follows: belief in God is rational only if it is supported by sufficient evidence; there is insufficient evidence to believe in God; therefore, belief in God is irrational.

Note that the conclusion is not 'God does not exist'. Even if God does exist, so the objection goes, it would still be irrational to believe in God because of the lack of evidence. So the evidentialist objection to belief in God, with its attendant assumption of classical foundationalism, has generated a powerful critique of belief in God.

Classical foundationalism, however, is irretrievably flawed according to its own standard as it is neither self-evident nor evident to the senses. In addition, it cannot be inferred from beliefs that are self-evident or evident to the senses. If classical foundationalism were true, it would be irrational to accept it! The second defect of classical foundationalism is that it entails scepticism about the world. We cannot infer anything about the existence of the external world, the past, the future, other persons and so on given the basis of the slim body of evidence that classical foundationalism permits. So, classical foundationalism must be rejected as the proper structure of rational belief.

Reidian rationality

Thomas *Reid, the eighteenth-century Scottish philosopher, offered an alternative account of reason that better suits our actual cognitive equipment. Reid recognized that most of our beliefs are basic and that they are produced immediately in us when one of our dispositions, or inclinations, to believe is triggered. These dispositions include both the perceptual faculties mentioned above and other cognitive 'triggers' that produce belief in other persons, such as the past, the future and memories. It should be noted at this point, that none of these beliefs could be established on the basis of an argument with premises that are self-evident or evident to the senses. The beliefs these dispositions produce are immediate and not based or dependent on an argument. Consider how much of what you believe is based on testimony, on what others tell you (your parents, teachers, books, newspapers and so on). We are disposed to believe what others tell us and, in addition, we have a reasoning disposition that causes us to accept one proposition that we didn't previously believe upon judging that some propositions we already believe provide good evidence for that proposition.

Reid takes reason to include all of our belief dispositions, most of which produce beliefs immediately and not by inference. Rational beliefs, then, are those which are produced by our cognitive faculties in the appropriate circumstances. Appropriate circumstances are necessary for rational belief. For example, the belief that there are craters on the moon is irrational in certain circumstances (if it is based on the testimony of your invisible friend) and rational in other circumstances (if it is based on the testimony of someone with a PhD in astrophysics).

In order to grasp reality, we must use and trust our cognitive faculties or capacities; they are the sum total of our rational powers. But we also know that we get things wrong, and our rational powers are not infallible. Reid suggests that we can trust the conclusions of reason until we have good justification to believe that they are false. If you have good cause to suspect one of your immediately produced beliefs, then you must bring the reasoning disposition to bear on the problem. Reasoning may help you sort through the competing beliefs and determine which one(s) should be rejected.

Reid's general approach to rational belief is to trust the beliefs produced by your cognitive faculties in the appropriate circumstances unless or until you have good arguments for rejecting them. According to classical foundationalism, most beliefs are guilty (irrational) until proven innocent. According to Reid, our beliefs are innocent (rational) until proven guilty.

Reid's approach does not resolve the problem that our cognitive faculties produce false beliefs in matters of fundamental human concern such as the nature of morality, the nature of persons, social and political philosophy and belief in God. This suggests that, if we are sincerely seeking the truth on these matters, we should be willing to do two things which may help us attain true beliefs and eliminate false beliefs. First, we ought to seek, as best we can, supporting evidence for immediately produced beliefs of fundamental human concern. Secondly, we ought to be open to contrary evidence to root out false beliefs. So, to summarize, if we are concerned to acquire true beliefs and root out false ones we should *trust* the conclusions of reason, *seek* supporting evidence and *be open* to contrary evidence. It is indeed frightening to realize that trusting our cognitive faculties may produce rational but false beliefs, and this approach offers some hope that we can, at least partially, avoid this danger.

Reason and belief in God

Can belief in God be rational for a person? The evidentialist objector contends that belief in God cannot be rational for any person in any situation because there is not adequate evidence in favour of God's existence. The two assumptions of this objection, that rational belief in God requires evidence and that there is not sufficient evidence, are both questionable, if not plainly false.

Consider first the claim that there is not sufficient evidence for the existence of God. Recently, many theistic arguments have found new life among philosophers. These include new versions of the *cosmological argument, the argument from the fine tuning of the cosmos to permit human life, the *moral argument, epistemological arguments and arguments based on *religious experience. And some thinkers offer theories that put all of these kinds of arguments together and claim that they mutually reinforce the likelihood of God's existence. The evidence

adduced or the metaphysical principles involved may not be readily apparent to all rational creatures, but they may be reasonably held by a person and if so, that person could reasonably hold what follows from those premises. It is surely defensible to claim that belief in God could be rational based on the evidence.

But what of the evidentialist assumption that belief in God must be supported by evidence in order to be rational? The deficiencies of the Enlightenment view of reason with its attendant assumption of classical foundationalism have been exposed. Can belief in God be properly basic? That is, can belief in God be rational for a person even if it is unsupported by evidence?

Reformed epistemologists such as Alvin Plantinga and Nicholas Wolterstorff have argued along Reidian lines that belief in God could be rational without the support of theistic arguments. They recognize that in the vast majority of cases of rational belief, humans must simply trust their intellectual equipment. In addition, they claim that humans have, as *Calvin puts it, a *sensus divinitatis* (sense of the divine) that produces belief in God immediately in people. Calvin claims that regardless of the culture, God seems to have implanted knowledge of himself within people's minds and hearts. Like our other beliefs, this immediately produced belief is 'innocent until proven guilty'. That is, belief in God could be rational for a person, even if unsupported by an argument, unless that person has good grounds for giving it up. How so? Suppose that belief in God was produced in a person in the appropriate circumstances (say, while on a mountaintop that person has an overwhelming sense of the majesty of creation), a belief not produced through a recitation of the argument from design but one that simply welled up within that person at that time. Suppose further that this person was not aware of reasons which would count against belief in God (e.g. the argument from evil) or was aware of the argument from evil but was also aware of its defects. In such a case, this person has an innocently produced belief in God without adequate reason to cease believing in God. If all of our assumptions were to be true, given the Reidian conception of rationality we have developed, this belief in God would be rational.

Conclusion

A Reidian concept of reason that is more suited to human beings' cognitive equipment has been developed and defended. This holds that belief in God may be properly basic, i.e. belief in God may be rational without the support of evidence or argument. Nonetheless, it would still be reasonable to search for supporting evidence for that belief and also to be open to contrary evidence. So evidence may not be required for belief in God to be rational, but it may nonetheless continue to play an important role in the life of the believer.

Bibliography

K. J. Clark, *Return to Reason* (Grand Rapids, 1990); A. Plantinga, *Warranted Christian Belief* (New York and Oxford, 2000); W. J. Wood, *Epistemology* (Downers Grove, 1998).

K. J. CLARK

RECONSTRUCTIONISM

Christian Reconstructionism is also sometimes known as 'Dominion Theology'. It is closely related to Theonomy, and denotes a theological, social, political and ethical movement calling for the transformation of civil society along biblical lines modelled upon the Mosaic (OT) civil polity. Popular among certain segments of conservative evangelical, fundamentalist, Pentecostal, Reformed and Presbyterian Christians in North America, the movement has gained adherents and influence among social conservatives since its development in the mid-1950s. Christian Reconstructionism is also closely associated with the elements of the Christian Right social and political movement, and many of its leaders credit Reconstructionism as their intellectual and spiritual inspiration. Reconstructionists blur distinction between modern civil polities and the Israelite theocracy. They typically hold that the United States was founded as a Christian nation, but their version of post-millennialism anticipates a massive societal collapse, out of which will arise a new republic modelled upon Reconstructionist principles.

History

The first and most significant proponent of Reconstructionism was Rousas John Rushdoony (1916–2001), the son of a Presbyterian minister. Rushdoony had become committed to cultural transformation by 1959. Most, but not all, of the most notable leaders of the movement, including theologian Greg L.

Bahnsen (1948–95), economist Gary North (Rushdoony's son-in-law), pastor and politician Joseph Morecraft, and authors James Jordan, Gary DeMar, Andrew Sandlin and Kenneth Gentry, have been closely associated with Rushdoony at some point. Of these proponents, only Bahnsen, a Presbyterian minister who taught *presuppositional apologetics briefly at Reformed Theological Seminary (Jackson, MS), rivals Rushdoony's influence on and authority for the movement. Nevertheless, this is not a centralized or hierarchical movement.

Philosophy

The philosophical influences on Reconstructionism are found chiefly in the writing of the former prime minister of the Netherlands and theologian Abraham *Kuyper (1837–1920), Westminster Seminary's Cornelius *Van Til (1895–1987) and the Dutch philosopher Herman *Dooyeweerd (1894–1977). It should be noted, however, that Van Til was a vigorous proponent of *common grace; he expressed grave reservations about Reconstructionist social theory and patently rejected post-millennial eschatology in favour of amillennialism. Reconstructionism may be analysed as a right-wing political and cultural version of Kuyper's cultural transformationalism. Kuyper proposed both a clear antithesis between belief and unbelief and a strong doctrine of common grace. Among Reconstructionists, however, common grace is generally rejected. Further, where traditional Reformed theology and piety distinguished between two kingdoms, that of the 'left hand' (culture) and that of the 'right hand' (cult), over which Christ is said to be Lord but where the duties of Christians are said to be distinct, in Reconstructionism cult tends to serve *culture. Rushdoony and North, particularly, have written pointedly against this and other traditional Reformed distinctions.

For Rushdoony, the problem of the 'one and the many' is the most basic philosophical issue. Following Van Til, he appealed to the equal ultimacy of the one and the many in the Christian doctrine of the *Trinity as the solution to the problem. In his social theory, his corollary was the principle that the citizen and the state are equally ultimate.

Theology

Reconstructionists argue that, though *Jesus fulfilled and abrogated the penalties of the Mosaic ceremonial laws, he did not do the same for the civil statutes and penalties. Therefore, according to Reconstructionism, they are still applicable today by civil authorities.

The Reconstructionist biblical hermeneutic shares strong similarities with fundamentalism. It also tends to read the Bible as a guide for science, society and education rather than as a history of redemption and a normative and saving revelation.

Most Reconstructionists are predestinarian. Some are traditional Protestants in soteriology; others, however, have rejected faith alone as insufficient for a Reconstructed society.

Problems

Doubtless the colonial Puritans hoped to establish a sort of theocracy. It is also a fact that the eighteenth-century American republic was formed under the influence of the Enlightenment and in the wake of the collapse of Christendom. Since the late eighteenth century, most American Christians have embraced religious pluralism as a matter of civil politics. Having committed itself to the myth of a Christian America, however, Reconstructionism rejects religious *pluralism in civil affairs.

Because Reconstructionists generally regard the classical Reformed theologians as having been tainted by the unholy influence of *Aristotle (384–322 BC), they also reject the traditional Reformed arguments from *natural law. Reconstructionists have been ambivalent about John *Calvin (1509–64). They have alternately claimed him as an inspiration and critized his theology and politics where they do not support the Reconstructionist agenda. They seem not to recognize his throughgoing commitment to natural law and the substantial continuity between his views and those of the Westminster Assembly (1647) expressed in the Westminster Confession (19.4).

Reconstructionism poses distinct problems for Christian apologists attempting to communicate the faith in a postmodern cultural context. Reconstructionism seems to confirm the worst fears of many post-structuralists, who see it as an attempt to impose Christianity upon an unwilling culture and to subvert or overtly destroy cultural and religious pluralism through the use of civil *authority gained legitimately or illegitimately. It confirms the worst suspicions of many that Christians are not actually interested in the well-being or salvation of persons, but in the acquisition and use of political power.

Christianity concerns not the human will, but the divine revelation of salvation in Christ. Considered historically, Reconstructionism is an aberration. The earliest patristic theologians argued for the truth of Christianity and for its toleration by civil authorities, but not for its *imposition* on Greco-Roman society. Even post-Constantinian theologians such as *Augustine (354–430) argued for an antithesis between the city of God and the city of man, maintaining that Christians live in the latter but belong to the former. Later, some medieval theologians supported the Crusades, but others argued that the faith is for 'persuading, not imposing'. Protestant theologians such as Martin Luther and John Calvin accepted the Pauline antithesis between 'this age' and 'the age to come', but argued that Christians belong to and have different responsibilities in the kingdom of God and the kingdom of man. Even at the height of Christendom, the imposition of Mosaic civil statues and penalties was rejected as inappropriate.

Reconstructionism is conditioned by the rise of American *power in the twentieth century. It is an unfortunate response to modernity and is foreign to Scripture and historic Christian teaching. We should confess that Christians have been tempted by power, but the faith really concerns Jesus the crucified (and raised) and his kingdom, not the acquisition of temporal power.

Bibliography

G. L. Bahnsen, *No Other Standard: Theonomy and Its Critics* (Tyler, 1991); *Theonomy in Christian Ethics* (Phillipsburg, 2nd edn, 1977); W. R. Godfrey and W. Barker (eds.), *Theonomy: A Reformed Critique* (Grand Rapids, 1990); R. J. Rushdoony, *Institutes of Biblical Law*, 2 vols. (Vallecito, 1973, 1982); D. S. Watson, 'Theonomy: A History of the Movement and an Evaluation of Its Primary Text' (master's thesis, Calvin Theological Seminary, Grand Rapids, 1985).

R. S. CLARK

REDACTION CRITICISM, see BIBLICAL CRITICISM

REDUCTIO AD ABSURDUM

Reductio ad absurdum is also known as *reductio ad impossibile* and, for short, *reductio* or

'RAA'. *Reductio* can occur in any of several forms: a rule of deduction, a theorem about deducibility, an axiom of a calculus, or a theorem of entailment. In its form as a rule of deduction *reductio* allows one to proceed from an assumption from which one may deduce a *contradiction (a pair of formulae, one of which is the negation of the other) to the negation of the assumption. Strictly speaking, *reductio* should be distinguished from the formally similar principle of indirect proof, which allows one to proceed from a negative assumption from which one may deduce a contradiction to the un-negated form of the assumption. Sometimes *reductio* is used as the name of the more general principle that one may proceed from an assumption from which one may deduce a contradiction to any proposition that contradicts the assumption, but in fact this usage obscures the fact that the principle of indirect proof is not valid in intuitionistic *logic, whereas *reductio* is. In classical logic the rule of double-negation elimination, the rule that allows one to proceed from the negation of a negation of a formula to the un-negated formula itself, allows one to dispense with the principle of indirect proof, but the rule of double-negation elimination is not valid in intuitionistic logic either. (One could equally dispense with *reductio* in favour of the principle of indirect proof and the rule of double-negation introduction.) Strictly speaking, one should also not confuse *reductio* with *modus tollens*, which is the rule that allows one to proceed from a conditional and the negation of its consequent to the negation of its antecedent. One can, however, deduce everything one could deduce by using *modus tollens* by using *reductio* and *modus ponens* instead, and the validity of *modus ponens* is not seriously questioned.

The apologetic use of *reductio* is clear. If you can show that a principle of your opponent leads to a contradiction, your opponent will have to relinquish his or her principle and accept its negation instead. There are examples of the use of *reductio* in the Bible. A concise example of a *reductio* is to be found in 1 Cor. 5:9–10. Paul has written to the Corinthians in an earlier letter that they should not associate with sexually immoral people. He now considers the interpretation that he meant that they should not associate with 'the people of this world who are immoral' (10a). Paul wishes to show that this was (obviously) not his

meaning. He does this by assuming, for the sake of a *reductio*, the proposition whose negation he wishes to prove. (This is a quite general strategy for a *reductio*.) So he assumes that he *did* mean that they should not associate with the people of *this* world who are immoral. Paul then shows that 'in that case' an absurdity follows: 'you would have to leave this world' (10b). Paul, naturally enough, does not bother to spell out the formal contradiction by pointing out that we already know that we should not leave this world, and he leaves it to his readers to draw the inference of the *reductio*: that his meaning was *not* that the Corinthians should not associate with those of this world that are immoral. Paul uses the principle of indirect proof a few chapters later (in 1 Cor. 15:12–20) when discussing the resurrection of the dead. Here he wishes to show that there *is* a resurrection of the dead against those of the Corinthians who have been saying that there is *no* resurrection of the dead (12b). Paul supposes, for the indirect proof, that the negative claim of the confused Corinthians is in fact correct – 'if there is no resurrection of the dead' (13a). (Again, it is the usual strategy for the use of the principle of indirect proof to assume the negative proposition whose un-negated form you wish to prove.) He then shows that it follows from this negative assumption, among other things, that 'Christ has not been raised' (13b). Paul, however, knows this to be false – 'But Christ has indeed been raised from the dead' (20a). So, Paul shows that the assumption that there is no resurrection leads to the contradiction that Christ has both been raised and not raised from the dead. It follows that the assumption was false and one may deduce the un-negated form('There is a resurrection of the dead') of the assumption ('There is no resurrection of the dead'), just as Paul wanted.

Bibliography

M. Machover, *Set Theory, Logic and Their Limitations* (Cambridge, 1996), 8.8.9–17.

D. J. HILL

REID, THOMAS

Thomas Reid (1710–96) was the major intellectual force behind the philosophical movement known as Scottish Common Sense Realism, an epistemological stance developed as a response to the radical scepticism of David *Hume.

Reid was born in Strachan, Kincardineshire, and studied at Marischal College, Aberdeen, where he was librarian from 1733 to 1736. He spent some time in the ministry of the Church of Scotland (New Machar, Aberdeenshire, 1737–51) before moving on to an academic career, being first regent at the University of Aberdeen (1751–1764), where he co-founded the Aberdeen Philosophical Club; and finally professor of moral philosophy at Glasgow (1764–96), a post he was awarded on the merits of his first major work, *An Inquiry into the Human Mind on the Principles of Common Sense* (1764).

Reid's early philosophy was shaped by the *empiricism of John *Locke and, more significantly, by the *idealism of George *Berkeley. He later came to reject the positions offered by their approaches after studying the work of Hume, and came to formulate his own position in opposition to that of his great contemporary.

Reid's philosophy is based upon the notion that human beings possessed certain intuitive beliefs which shaped the human view of *reality. Central to these was the idea of the immediacy and reliability of perception: when a person smells a flower and experiences an agreeable sensation, then human nature leads the person to conclude that the flower possesses some property which causes this sensation, and that the mind thus has an immediate acquaintance with the object causing the sensation. This is argued in opposition to those idealists and sceptics for whom the sensation, and not, for example, the flower itself, was the immediate object of perception.

In the sphere of morals, Reid's common sense approach leads him to argue that human beings have an intuitive sense of basic *morality, of right and wrong, and that moral judgments are thus more than simple expressions of feeling or emotional responses to certain circumstances.

Reid's importance lies in the influence he had on the development of Scottish Common Sense Realism, a philosophical trajectory which had a profound influence on generations of Scottish ministers and which came, through its impact upon professors such as Charles *Hodge at Princeton Theological Seminary, to shape profoundly the theology of nineteenth-century American Presbyterianism, particularly with regard to a strongly realist view of *language, though this was modified (as is often not noted) through the Princetonians' appropriation of classic Reformed theology.

Bibliography

M. Dalgarno and E. Matthews (eds.), *The Philosophy of Thomas Reid* (London, 1989); K. Lehrer, *Thomas Reid* (London, 1989); T. Reid, *Thomas Reid's Lectures on Natural Theology*, ed. E. H. Duncan (Washington, 1981); *The Philosophical Orations of Thomas Reid*, ed. D. D. Todd (Carbondale).

C. R. TRUEMAN

RELATIVISM AND PLURALISM

Relativism and pluralism have in common an opposition to absolutism, i.e. they both contain the denial that there are certain kinds of universal truths. Usually relativism is used in discussing ideas about objective *reality, and pluralism is used in the context of religion and *culture. However, the terms often overlap; there can be discussion of cultural relativism, or *truth pluralism, in which the first discusses culture and the second objective reality. This article will use pluralism to discuss religion or belief systems about the divine and relativism for all other areas.

Relativism

Relativism is the general thesis that the truth of some statement – whether it is about *morality, or God, or art or even *science – is true only relative to the individual or group holding it to be true. The idea that cannibalism is wrong might be true within one culture, but not another; the statement 'Dali's paintings are beautiful' might be true for one viewer, whereas the statement 'Dali's paintings are grotesque' might be true for another. Most people can accept this level of relativism. The question is whether relativism should be extended to far more basic propositions. Can we say there is no ultimate truth at all? Can one human validly say 'The earth is round for me', while another says 'The earth is flat for me'? Can one reader understand Shakespeare as brilliant Elizabethan writing, while another reader just as validly understands the same works as fascist manifestos of oppression?

There are aspects of relativism which within certain limits provide useful statements of common sense and promote a certain intellectual humility. Reflection on the doctrine of relativism has helped us have a more sophisticated view of how people come to their beliefs. In this sense, relativism need not be an attack on the validity of reason, but a helpful tool in reflecting on the context in which reason becomes possible. This is something which Christian missionaries have had to grapple with in practice for centuries – how to communicate a universal truth in a way that another culture with different cultural assumptions will understand it.

Relativism as a serious epistemological and moral thesis has arisen in the last few centuries. As Europeans gained greater understanding of the diversity of cultures within the world and academic disciplines such as anthropology and sociology arose in response, it became more clear that there were different ways of looking at the world. It was no coincidence, however, that as the Western intellectual world moved further away from God, relativism became more prevalent. Without the Christian world-view, it becomes much harder to defend the idea of objective standards of right and wrong, good and *evil, beauty and ugliness. Ultimately, without the Christian world-view, *epistemology almost inevitably moves to relativism (as we are seeing now in our universities).

Christian epistemology is based on a God who creates and who communicates. Christians believe in an objectively real creation. This is the basis for a realist ontology. Moreover, the Bible teaches that humans were created in the image of God and appointed as rulers of the world under him. This gives a basis for a realist epistemology, for part of ruling the world in the image of God is the ability to understand and order the world. The universe is not a random place in which humans are an accident; it was created to be habitable for humans, with a nature that can be understood by human minds.

The universe is also a moral place. There are ethical standards, decreed by God in accordance with his nature. Humans, as part of creation, resonate with those moral standards although they habitually ignore them. It is not surprising that despite the vast array of civilizations throughout human history, certain standards of relationship and respect for life keep reappearing. There are universal ethical rules, because there is an ethical God who has established them.

Moreover, Christians have a God who communicates and who has made communication possible through *language. Since Babel this communication has been more problematical, as a judgment on humans for their rebelliousness, but it has not become impossible. A Christian world-view, then, gives a basis for the reality of meaning and understanding and the ability to speak and be understood.

Without these doctrines, however, our theories about the world – how we come to understand it, how we should regard ourselves and each other and how we communicate – must be based simply on observation. This is much more difficult, for the world is fallen and confused. As the writer of Ecclesiastes reflects, it is difficult to make sense of the apparent regularities of the world. We seem to live in an objectively ordered world, but how can we be sure? Why should we be confident that our minds can tell us anything reliable about the world? How can we know if what we understand from another person is actually what they intended? Without the doctrine of creation as the basis for such confidence, we are thrown into *doubt about these things. We are thrown into relativism.

Relativism about the nature of objective reality holds that there are no universal truths about the world, just different ways of interpreting it. In some matters, this seems quite harmless. For example, regarding preference in flavours of ice cream, I can happily acknowledge that what is true for you – your view that licorice-flavoured ice cream is delicious – is not true for me. On reflection, however, there is no obvious reason why such a stance should be limited to ice cream. You might perceive the world as one in which magic works, whereas I see the world as science describes it. Can I say I am right and you are wrong? For most of the Western world, common sense seems to dictate that the scientific view is the right one, since refrigerators seem to work and magic spells do not. Philosophically speaking, however, we cannot guarantee that any one viewpoint is so privileged as to be right.

The most basic criticism of the extreme relativist position – that there is no absolute truth about anything – is that this is self-referentially incoherent. That is, to be a relativist about fact is to maintain that there is no such thing as objective knowledge of facts independent of the knower; but this statement itself asserts an objective fact. In logical terms, strict relativism about truth contravenes the law of *contradiction. The statements 'P is true' and 'Not P is true' can both be considered valid if there are two thinkers. It takes considerable mental gymnastics to hold such a system. To negate it, however, one must have some universal criteria that guarantees that the law of contradiction must be upheld.

Moral relativism holds, similarly, that there are no universally valid moral principles; all moral principles are valid only relative to culture or individual choice. Each society has its own value system, the meaning of which can be sought only within that system, and any comparison of systems is illegitimate. Again, the weakness of this position is that it is itself a universal standard. It seems that the only right view is to hold that there is no right view! Less radical versions of relativism about value might insist that we cannot judge a culture's standards of right and wrong until we fully understand that culture. Indeed, if we have no externally imposed standard of morality, we can do no more.

If this world is all we have, and there is no greater revelation to help us understand it, we are left in the uncomfortable position that relativism is the best we can do. It becomes self-referentially incoherent eventually, but without *absolutes there is no guarantee of an alternative epistemology. The world seems to be real, some ways of understanding it (such as the scientific way) seem to work best, and we seem to be able to understand each other. These things would tend to deny relativism. However, without any greater schema to justify such standards, we must be content to say we can never be confident of them. They are simply the standards that work for us.

Pluralism

Pluralism as a term has various usages (e.g. as an ontological theory opposed to both *monism and dualism) but is more generally a religious cousin of relativism. Pluralism is relativism applied to religion. Even more than a convenient matter of social arrangement, pluralism generally asserts that, despite surface or cultural differences, all religions ultimately have the same message (usually taken to be one of divinely inspired peace and love) and all believers will eventually reach the same spiritual end point. Pluralism has a pleasant aura of humility around it, and it is often held up as a positive alternative to the perceived arrogance of those who claim that their belief, and their belief only, is true.

There are a number of logically possible responses to the observable fact that there are many religions. Over the last century or so, secularism has presented a simple answer: they are all wrong. The plurality of religions is not taken as a sign of possible truth of the supernatural, but as a sign that they are all human inventions. Thinkers such as Marx, *Freud, Durkheim and, more recently, socio-biologist E. O. Wilson have variously asserted that religion is a way in which mankind solves certain psychological or social problems. It is a projection of human desires, a method of gaining a feeling of security against fear of the unknown, or an evolved trait useful for survival as a group. The differences between religions are simply different strategies humans have developed in order to feel better.

Members of different religions quite rightly feel rather offended by this blithe dismissal of their beliefs. Assuming that something about religion is true, however, requires a resolution of the various truth claims. Most religions have traditionally asserted that they alone are true; the back-to-fundamentals sections of traditional religions still do. Some traditions have come to an accommodation with other religions. Vatican II allowed for some measure of truth or salvation-power in other religions but affirmed Roman Catholicism as the most valid form of religion.

Another alternative is to adopt a form of pluralism and say that in some sense all religions are true. It has become popular to do this in a fairly careless manner, ignoring the logical problems of relativism and simply asserting the truth of conflicting claims. In a postmodern spirit of play, many people feel happy to select various parts of different religions in a syncretistic muddle, or hop between different views depending on the circumstances. This kind of arational pluralism often goes along with the view that faith is a matter of personal experience or preference, not a matter of trusting one's life to a philosophy that is demonstrably true.

Such casual pluralism is popular, probably because it makes few intellectual demands upon the believer, but also because it seems to have a morally superior air of tolerance and acceptance. This perceived humility is a deception, however, and is in fact far more arrogant than any fundamentalist statement. For to claim that all religions lead to God, one must be in the position of God, able to see that this is where all the paths converge. From the vantage point of being on the path on the ground, you are in no position to judge where any of the others are going.

However, pluralism has considerably greater problems than that. It founders on the content of the different religions themselves. The philosophies that come under the heading 'religion' are remarkably diverse. There are on view a vast range of conceptions of God, his/her nature and what God wants of us. There are mutually exclusive teachings on how to live in such a way that heaven or nirvana or enlightenment are to be achieved. Indeed, these states that are the final goal can be completely different from each other. To top it off, on some points it is logically impossible for all religions to be true, for they make specifically contradictory truth-statements.

For instance, if the Hindu way of fasting, meditation and yoga is followed, obeying the teachings of one's enlightened master and worshipping an array of deities and past masters as manifestations of the divine, one might be very healthy, but one will not reach Yahweh's heaven or Allah's paradise. Those who believe they are experiencing reincarnation endless times as they progress towards the losing of their selves in universal perfection will not be following the teachings of Christ. In reality, practising one religion generally excludes you from following another, just as believing in one will necessarily require rejecting another.

One of the most striking counter-examples of pluralism is the death of Christ itself, an event which divides the world's two biggest religions, Christianity and Islam. The Bible asserts that Jesus died, in fact, this is the central and essential fact on which Christianity depends. The Qur'an, however, asserts that Jesus did not die but was replaced on the cross. This is a clear disagreement on a specific issue; both views cannot be true. Even for a diehard relativist this direct opposition poses problems, for the two religions come from similar religious assumptions – monotheism, a personal God, a series of prophets – and, most importantly, the two religions share a belief in and respect for history and belief in the law of contradiction. These are not two incommensurable cultures making claims of fact which cannot be compared. Both cultures hold a view of history as linear, accessible and real. Their claims about history cannot both be true.

It has been relatively recently that another, more serious kind of pluralism has arisen. This newer view, propounded by writers such as John *Hick, holds that there is a true divine reality, and that the differences between individual religions can be explained as different cultural interpretations of that one reality. This does not assert blandly that all religions are true, but that all religions are equally right and equally wrong; equally right in seeking to worship the divine (and effective in reaching that goal), and equally wrong in the incomplete pictures or doctrines in which they try to understand the divine. In philosophical terms, the noumenal Real is experienced within different religious traditions as a range of gods or experiences. They are not illusions but empirically real manifestations of the noumenal.

This theory overcomes the problems of simple pluralism, in that differences of fact in different religions become unimportant. The details of religious belief or practice are always an inadequate phenomenal perception of the one reality to which no-one has direct access. The experience of an impersonal force, or a personal God, a God who died or a prophet who did not, are all equally valid and equally inaccurate experiences of the inaccessible divine.

The problem with this view, of course, is that it pronounces the believers of most of the world's religions totally wrong. Although Muslims believe that God is one and that his prophet is Mohammed, they are deluded. Buddhists who believe they have reached enlightenment and now understand true reality are equally deluded. Practitioners of each religion could rightly object that they understand their own religion better than some outside theorist. Also, like many views which try to reconcile conflicting truth-claims, this pluralism in the end fails to be truly pluralist. In effect, it sets up a new religion with absolute, exclusive claims, claims that all other religions do not understand the truth, only the religion of pluralism does.

Bibliography

J. Dickson, *If I Were God, I'd Make Myself Clearer* (Sydney, 2003); D. Papineau (ed.), *The Philosophy of Science* (Oxford, 1996); J. W. Sire, *The Universe Next Door: A Guide to Worldviews* (Leicester, 1977).

K. R. BIRKETT

RELIGIONS OF CHINESE AND JAPANESE ORIGIN

China and Japan are the point of origin for distinctive folk religions, Daoism, Confucianism and Shinto. These religions are of early origin and have many adherents, both in China and Japan and wherever Chinese and Japanese people have settled.

Chinese religions

The earliest religious beliefs in China are classified generically as traditional religion, which provides the basis for the other indigenous religions in China (namely, Daoism and Confucianism) and has never been supplanted by other religions as the dominant communal religion of the Chinese people. Thus, many religious ideas and practices are common among all Chinese people. They are often mixed with activities drawn from all religions.

Chinese traditional religion

This diverse complex of religious beliefs and practices has no centralized administration or enforced uniformity. To the extent that there are common traits, they are the result of China's cultural homogeneity going back to the Shang dynasty (c. 1766–1122 BC) and long periods of political unification under imperial rule. Chinese traditional religion has two major aspects: folk religion and ancestor religion. Both of these emerged from a distinctive early Chinese world-view predicated upon the activities of an agrarian society.

In Chinese thought, unlike in the West, there is no clear distinction between the temporal and the spiritual, but rather a continuum exists between the two. Gods and humans are in a mutual relationship and, by contrast with Christianity, gods can be obligated to act in certain ways if people make the proper appeals. Essentially, the Chinese world-view is a naturalistic universe without a divine creator or lawgiver pervaded by a vital energy (*qi*), resulting in a reverence and respect for nature. The universal natural order and *reality behind appearances (*dao*) manifests itself through cyclical patterns, processes of growth and decline, and a bipolarity where opposites are complementary rather than in opposition (known as *yin* and *yang*). In contrast, Western thought identifies good and *evil as opposed and events are viewed in a linear time perspective. Chinese tradition also recognizes a Supreme Ruler in *Heaven (*Tien*) who, rather than being a creator or lawgiver or causal force, is an impersonal controller of the world order. The goal is to achieve regularity and prosperity in change. Each person is an integral part of the wholeness of the universe and the focal point of nature's functioning.

Chinese folk religion derives from this basic world-view and involves nature worship as an essential part of everyday life and concerns. The religious practices centre on many local gods and invisible forces and beings who collectively maintain the cosmic order and who may be petitioned for protection, assistance and success in the endeavours of individuals, families and community affairs. While lacking a permanent clergy, there are many temples of various sizes and locations dedicated to these gods, who assist in such matters as protection from natural disasters, providing good health and childbirth, and bringing monetary or agricultural success. Everywhere in China, this emphasis on protection and prosperity has resulted in the predominance of the god of the hearth in each home, the god of soil, and the city god.

Common religious practices include the use of shamans and divination. Mediums, both men and women, are trained to intercede with the spirits in order to assist in people's lives or in governmental affairs. Various divination techniques are also employed, such as oracle bones in ancient times and the use of *feng shui* (geomancy) to determine the ideal natural location for buildings and tombs based upon the cosmic flow of *yin* and *yang*. Some gods are responsible for monitoring and recording both the good and the evil deeds of humans. However, unlike the Christian God, Chinese gods are not primarily intended to provide guidance in morals and *ethics, which are defined more by family and society.

Throughout Chinese history, one of the most important parts of traditional religion is the emphasis on ancestors. Family constitutes the focal point of Chinese rituals, and it is premised on the dual ideas that ancestral spirits, especially the family's oldest male members, continue to look out for family interests in death as in life, and that success comes not only by individual effort but by soliciting the support of ancestral spirits, which are considered part of the family and constantly present at the family altar. This ancestor religion is considered the universal religion of the Chinese people, resulting in the family being the defining trait of

Chinese civilization. As such, proper burial rites and sacrifices are essential to get spirits to act beneficently and to prevent them from turning malevolent.

In addition to recognizing one's own ancestors, Chinese people in the past were expected to recognize those of their ruler in order to ensure continual prosperity and success of individuals and society. The Chinese ruler, in a similar way to the OT concept of kingship under God's anointing but not as a deity, is considered to be expected by heaven to adjudicate its will in temporal affairs and to rule for the benefit of all people. This importance of the ruler and his ancestors for earthly success provides a strong historical and religious sanction for Chinese political unity.

Confucianism

Confucianism, indigenous to China and also known as the Literati tradition, is based on the writings of Confucius (551–479 BC) and his followers. Confucius did not view himself as a religious leader or prophet but rather as a moral and political philosopher. His central concern was to explain how a person who wants to be good should live when times are not conducive to the proper moral life. As the great teacher, Confucius looks to the Chinese past for his moral examples. While he is generally indifferent to Chinese folk religion, Confucius emphasizes ancestral spirits both within the family setting and on the national level regarding proper respect for the rulers and government. His practical ethics and emphasis on family and moral government constitute his major contribution to China and have led Western philosophers and theologians to view him favourably.

According to Confucians, the universe operates on rational, moral principles. Their *dao* consists of the moral and ethical order of society as the ideal human condition. There is no recognition of a concept of original sin, but rather, through education and practice of the ancient virtues, the good in each person will be accentuated and eventually peace and prosperity in society will emerge. This ideal consists of qualities like righteousness, loyalty, integrity, modesty, honour and courtesy, traits which are also admired by Western ethicists.

Confucianism had specific expectations for society's political leaders and by extension for all Chinese people. One principle was *ren* or *jen*, which entailed compassion for all people and was expressed in everyday life by obedience to the rightful ruler, respect for parents and elders, loyalty to friends and care for all people. *Li* (propriety) as taught by Confucius was promoted through training in the classical Confucian texts, which taught one how to behave properly. The greatest expectation was on the 'superior man' or gentleman, a member of a select group in society, who through education had cultivated his character and through his exemplary behaviour was qualified to govern and to lead society in its cultural development.

It was not until the Han dynasty (206 BC–AD 220) that Confucius' teaching was given official sanction and implementation by the imperial government. At this time the essentially secular Confucian teachings were given a more religious and metaphysical dimension in order that Confucian teaching might compete better with the pre-existing Chinese folk religion, the newly developing Daoism and the recently introduced *Buddhism. It took many centuries for Confucian ideals to be incorporated into Chinese government and to be generally accepted throughout society beyond the upper social classes. It was not until the Sung dynasty (960–1279) that Confucianism gained a metaphysical structure comparable to other Chinese religions of the time. The establishment of Confucian temples and rites as well as the relating of Confucian values and the ideal person with Daoist and Buddhist values and enlightened persons made Confucianism a more developed religious system.

Another gradual development from the Han dynasty onward was the increasing identification of Confucianism as the state religion alongside other religions practised by the government rulers. Essential Confucian support for imperial power included the emperor mediating between heaven and earth, and his ensuring that all necessary rituals, ceremonies and ancestral recognitions were performed.

Daoism

The basic statement of Daoist beliefs, *Daode jing*, is ascribed to Laozi, who lived in the sixth century BC and is revered by Daoists as their great Immortal. However, it is only in the early centuries AD, during times of political upheaval, that Daoism was transformed from a myriad folk beliefs into a more consolidated, aristocratic religion with encouragement from the state. From the sixth to the thirteenth centuries, Daoism gained support from the emperors of the Sui, Tang and Sung dynasties, resulting in increased prestige, growth of its clergy, the production of Daoist texts, and its expansion through the establishment of temples and monasteries throughout China and even into Korea and Japan. During this period, Daoism became firmly established as a distinct religious movement within Chinese culture, while at the same time its reciprocal borrowing and inter-relationship with Buddhism and Confucianism resulted in the complementary religious mixture that characterizes Chinese society.

Daoism's ideals of seeking *immortality and longevity contributes profoundly to Chinese poetry, drama and fiction. It also encouraged personal self-cultivation, healthcare sciences, preventative medicine and exercise. This results from classical Daoist beliefs about attaining immortality and is based on the understanding of the *dao* as the ultimate concept explaining the universe's functioning and human behaviour. When operating properly, the *dao* is a natural order where conforming to nature esteems personal quietude and inaction in regulating the self and the state, in sharp contrast to the Confucian emphasis on action.

While it is difficult to generalize about such a diverse collection of beliefs and practices, the underlying premise of Daoism is that life is good and to be enjoyed. One's objective should be to free one's self from physical limits to attain immortality, or at least longevity, and the enjoyment of the mundane pleasures of this world or by interaction with the immortals in space. This may be facilitated with the aid of spirits and gods drawn from folk religion or originating in Daoist writings and stories. This liberation can be fostered through such practices as religious rituals, meditation, exorcism, astrology, alchemy, occult rites and physical exercises like yoga or *qigong*. The intent through these practices was to control both beneficent and malevolent spirits in the body, and thus influence the body's relationship to the cosmos, since one's body is a microcosm of the universe.

Despite Daoism's variety of beliefs and customs, its many sects and local variations around temples and monasteries, and its lack of central *authority or administration, it has proved to be a vital religion in China to the present day. Recently, Daoist texts and practices have drawn attention and adherents

around the world, especially through Falun Gong and New Age movements.

Japanese religion

The Japanese religious scene has been greatly influenced by its adaptation, from the sixth century onwards, of foreign religions, especially Confucianism and Buddhism via China and Korea. Confucianism contributed its ethics, governmental structure and legal procedures, its family and social expectations, centralized imperial rule and its extensive social and political literature. Buddhism introduced a sophisticated religious, artistic and philosophical tradition, developed over many centuries with extensive written texts, established rituals and clergy and an emphasis on the afterlife.

These religions entered a Japan with loosely formulated religious institutions and a folk religion that would emerge as Shinto, an indigenous religion closely related to traditional beliefs in Japan before the introduction of Buddhism and Confucianism. Shinto influenced Confucianism and Buddhism, as they also helped shape Shinto.

Shinto, a religion unique to Japan, developed out of prehistoric practices going back at least two thousand years. Shinto especially identifies with the *kami* of Japanese folk religion. On this basis it serves to preserve much of Japan's ancient heritage and has traditionally been closely associated with the emperor and the nation. The concept of *kami* (sometimes translated 'deities') is a complex notion lacking a full theological explanation of their existence or essence, but is probably best thought of as a sacred quality or numinous energy (not a transcendent force) which any object, place or creature may possess, such as shrines, local spirits and natural forces, deified heroes, ancestors or rulers. *Kami* infuse nature with a spiritual presence and are considered the source of life and blessing.

Shinto has no founder, corpus of sacred texts or systematic theology. Its tradition is based on history and local practices such as seasonal activities, festivals, rites of passage and shrine activities. Besides its recognition of *kami* in various manifestations, Shinto is characterized by a few other concepts. One is a desire to seek purity and avoid pollution or impurity (as close as Shinto comes to an idea of sin) by taking part in religious ceremonies and going on pilgrimages. Another aspect of Shinto is its identification with the divine creation of Japan by the Sun Goddess and the centrality of this myth to the establishment of the imperial line from divine parents as the focal point of the Japanese nation. Each emperor is considered a *kami* and should be worshipped and respected as such. Likewise, he leads the nation in certain Shinto ceremonies and represents the sacred origin and continuity of Japan.

In modern Japan, Shinto and Japanese Buddhism have both stimulated the creation of new religions. Often these new religions contain influences from Shinto, Buddhism and popular religion and they often begin with an influential founder who propounds an innovative approach or interpretation and organizes followers around this new teaching. Many also actively proselytize outside Japan. The largest of the Shinto-related new religions is Tenri-kyo (Religion of Heavenly Origin), which was was founded in 1838 and teaches a pure and harmonious life where humanity will eventually live in union with their chief deity, the Lord of Heavenly Reason. Soka Gakkai, originating in 1930, draws heavily on the application of Buddhism to culture and education in order to achieve personal happiness and a peaceful world. It has had significant involvement in politics and education. Thus, Shinto and Japanese religions have manifestations both in their more traditional forms and in various new religious movements drawing on these historical practices.

Conclusion

Since religions of Chinese and Japanese origin have significantly different roots and development than Western religions, there are wide variations in their theological perspectives. In brief, Christianity's claims to exclusivity of religious allegiance, its uncompromising monotheism, its insistence on God's transcendence over his created natural world, and the reality of sin as an offence to God requiring the reconciling work of Christ, all conflict with the polytheistic and syncretistic practices of Asian religions in which individuals often practise a mixture of folk religion with Buddhism, Confucianism and Shinto. A personal relationship with a personal Creator and Redeemer as in Christianity is an alien concept because of general Asian beliefs in the inherent goodness of human nature, in the temporal intervention of ancestral spirits, and in the merging of the spiritual and temporal realms.

These are imposing theological gulfs to be bridged.

Bibliography

H. B. Earhart, *Japanese Religion: Unity and Diversity* (Belmont, 1982); *Religious Traditions of the World* (New York, 1997); L. G. Thompson, *Chinese Religion: An Introduction* (Belmont, 1996).

C. W. WEBER

RELIGIOUS EXPERIENCE AND MYSTICISM

Much current Western interest in these topics combines a general concern for them with ignorance of, or dismissal of, any Christian elements. The apologetic challenge is to confront this apparent paradox. An essential, if preliminary, part of the apologetic task is one of definition. 'Religious experience' and 'mysticism' (and for that matter, 'spirituality') have been understood in so many ways that it is necessary to try to distinguish the main meanings.

Religious experience can be defined both narrowly and broadly. For example, within Christianity it is sometimes maintained that we can only believe in God *in spite* of experience, as 'we walk by faith, not by sight' (2 Cor. 5:7, RSV). But this view, it may be argued, besides forgetting that we do at least see partially (cf. 1 Cor. 13:12), neglects the fact that walking by faith is itself a religious experience. The witness of Jeremiah, Job, or *Jesus in the garden of Gethsemane, suggests that even the experience of God's absence is a real experience, as real as estrangement from a loved one or a bereavement. Furthermore, the laments in the Psalms remind us that God's absence can be experienced corporately (cf. Pss. 44; 60; 74; 79; 80) as well as individually, whenever his people, perhaps under persecution or the pressures of secularism, find themselves forced to ask 'How shall we sing the LORD's song in a foreign land?' (Ps. 137:4, RSV).

The first, narrower, view defines religious experience quite strictly in terms of particular and often dramatic or unusual events which are recognizable from Scripture or mystical *theology, or from certain characteristics like the senses of 'encounter' with the 'Holy' identified by Martin *Buber (1878–1965) and

Rudolph Otto (1869–1937). The second, broader, view defines religious experience more generally in terms of the responses of people who are open to understanding any part of their experience of life and the world around them in a religious way, whether or not it occurs in a religious context.

Mysticism can also be defined in several ways. On one hand, religious experiences of either type can be described as 'mystical' on account of their intensity or apparent content. On the other, reports of 'nature mysticism' suggest there are experiences of bliss or ecstasy that have no connection with religion. This, together with the existence of accounts of destructive or even demonic experiences, suggests that it is unhelpful to attempt to cover everything by one concept. Even within Christian theology, there are several understandings of mysticism.

1. It can mean, as it did in the Middle Ages, simply personal experience of God. In this sense, every medieval theologian was a mystic because he wrote about what he himself experienced. Eastern Orthodoxy takes a similar view. Writers who understand mysticism in this way as a loving awareness or knowledge of God, see nothing unusual in describing Jesus and Paul as mystics and their teaching about prayer, union with God in Christ, or life in the *Holy Spirit as mysticism. For them, mysticism is concerned with the *mystery of God, understood and expounded in an irreducibly trinitarian way, that is not to be confused with talk of 'union with the One' in other religions.

2. A more restricted usage of the term confines it to experience and description of the higher stages of mystical prayer which, like other gifts of the Spirit, are given as God wills to some and not to others. In this context, mystical theology is distinguished from ascetical theology, which describes the stages of prayer from the beginnings to the 'prayer of loving attention' or 'simple regard' that goes beyond words. Many writers on prayer consider this latter type of contemplation is open to every Christian.

3. Protestant writers, though well aware of the relationship between theology and experience of God, have usually been reluctant to speak of mysticism. The term 'mystical' has suggested confusion with the Graeco-Roman mystery religions, identification with Neoplatonism and the errors of Gnosticism and quietism or the modern equivalents of syncretism, subservience to the current world-view, seeking secret knowledge restricted to the favoured few, or withdrawal from concern with the world. Some mystics may have laid themselves open to such charges, sometimes through their attempts to describe the indescribable, but it is impossible to categorize all mystical teaching in this way. Each example must be examined in context and assessed on its own merits.

This brings us to the second apologetic task: discernment. Since all human experience has both an objective and a subjective side, every religious experience invites assessment of its source, nature and interpretation.

The NT writers present Christianity as a way of life to be experienced and not just a theory to be believed, yet they are not naïve or uncritical about the compelling nature of religious experiences. Jesus and the apostles were not the only miracle-workers of their time. Even within the church it was necessary from the beginning to 'test the spirits', to see if they were from God, in terms of their effect on love, truth and unity in the fellowship (cf. 1 Cor. 12 – 14; 1 Thess. 5:21; 1 John 4).

Such doctrinal and ethical tests have been applied ever since to both individual and corporate religious experience. Roman Catholic mystical theology has assumed that all religious experience, whether apparently ordinary or extraordinary, would be discussed with one's spiritual director. Protestants have tended to stress the individual's direct access to God, but there is a tradition of personal direction or counselling of a more occasional and less authoritative kind in the letters of some of the Reformers and Puritans. Noteworthy too is the Quaker and early Methodist practice of group discernment which has been revived in some modern Christian communities.

Movements within the church which stress the importance of experience also invite assessment. Jonathan *Edwards (1703–58), for example, chronicled the eighteenth-century New England Awakening in his *Narrative of Surprising Conversions* (1737), and later in *A Treatise Concerning Religious Affections* (1746) gave his mature reflections on its significance. His careful discrimination between its positive and negative features was a forerunner of the approach followed by William *James (1842–1910) in *Varieties of Religious Experience* (1902), which set the tone for modern study. More recently, Pentecostal and charismatic experience such as the Toronto

Blessing have been carefully evaluated in studies which these days supplement theological concerns (including understandings of *revelation and *natural theology) with psychological and sociological criteria, philosophical analysis and comparison with drug-induced experiences.

To understand mysticism as personal experience of God (see 1 above) is to reject the modern view that Christianity has little to say about it or that it is a peripheral concern for Christians, but to affirm that it is not a technique for spiritual advancement. People now described as Christian mystics did not set out to be mystics, but to be more faithful believers, as the extensive tradition of Western mysticism and spirituality testifies.

A survey of Western mysticism down to the thirteenth century would include the Fathers from *Augustine (354–430) to Bernard of Clairvaux (1090–1153), Francis of Assisi (1182–1226) and his disciple and biographer *Bonaventura (c. 1217–74), not forgetting the mystical side of *Thomas Aquinas (1225–74). Bernard's devotion to the humanity of Christ, maintained in the writings of Aelred of Rievaulx (1110–67), had lasting influence in European mysticism. The other major influence was the apophatic theology of *Dionysius, translated from Greek into Latin by *Eriugena in the ninth century and into a modified English version in the late fourteenth century by the anonymous author of *The Cloud of Unknowing*. *The Cloud* (which also introduced English readers to the third contemporary influence in European mysticism, the school of St Victor) appeared c. 1370, between the works of Richard Rolle of Hampole (c. 1295–1349) and the other flowers of English mysticism – *The Scale of Perfection* (Walter Hilton, d. 1396), *Revelations of Divine Love* (Julian of Norwich, c. 1342–1416) and *The Book* of Margery Kempe (c. 1373–1433).

Mysticism also flourished during this period in movements of spiritual renewal in Germany and Flanders inspired by Meister Eckhart (c. 1260–1327), John Tauler (c. 1300–61) and Henry Suso (c. 1295–1366). These three were involved with the Rhineland Friends of God (which produced the *Theologica Germanica*, an anonymous plain man's guide to mysticism, which Luther later printed) and indirectly contributed to the Brethren of the Common Life in Flanders by their influence on Jan van Ruysbroeck (1293–1381). Ruysbroeck's disciple Gerard Groot (1340–84)

founded the Brethren, thus promoting a spirituality which achieved lasting expression during the following century in the writings of Thomas à *Kempis (1380–1471), especially his *Imitation of Christ*.

If some of the writings mentioned above suggest that a mystic is concerned only with the inner life of the soul, such an impression would be corrected by a study of the lives of Italian and Spanish mystics such as Catherine of Siena (1347–80), Catherine of Genoa (1447–1510), Ignatius of *Loyola (1491–1556) or Teresa of Avila (1515–82). The latter, a Carmelite reformer, produced, like her disciple the poet John of the Cross (1542–91), analyses of the stages of the mystical life which have never been surpassed. Twentieth-century wrestlings with the relation between mysticism, prayer and action stretch from Dietrich Bonhoeffer (1906–45) to liberation theology. It is a substantial theme in Thomas Merton (1915–68), and a concern of Karl *Rahner (1904–84) and Jürgen Moltmann (b. 1926).

This Western mystical tradition deserves not just to be better known, but to be expounded in *language appropriate to hearer and subject-matter. There is a need to recover what the medievals possessed but, it may be argued, was lost at the Enlightenment: a religious language that illuminates rather than circumscribes mystery and involves the people using it. In this view, the defining element of Christian mysticism, the doctrine of the *Trinity, is not to be approached as an intellectual puzzle, or even primarily as an intellectual defence, but more as a mystery that 'invites expansion of the mind and heart ... that leaves us happy, singing and giving thanks. It is not a wall placed in front of us, but a doorway through which we go to the infinity of God' (Leonardo Boff, *Trinity and Society* [London, 1988], p. 159).

The strong link between mysticism and prayer is one pointer to achieving this. The apologetic task includes inviting people to share the context in which the language used makes most sense. As the traditional saying goes, *Lex orandi, Lex credendi*, 'law of praying, law of believing', i.e. worship influences theology and vice versa. If an invitation to attend a prayer or worship group was not appropriate, it could be equally valuable to explain and demonstrate meditative or prayerful reading (a quite different activity from what our print and computer screen culture usually understands as reading). And if the inquirer is not ready for that, poetry, which is also an important element of the literature of Christian mysticism, could be a useful bridge.

All that has been argued so far about the need to found apologetics on a contextual, if not insider's, understanding of Christian religious experience and mysticism has parallels in the approach required in intra-religious dialogue. Debate on, e.g. the assertion that comparative study of religion shows that all religious or mystical experience is fundamentally the same, needs to be informed by, among other things, patient study of the descriptions and claims made within the religions concerned.

Bibliography

G. Griffith-Dickson, *Human and Divine: An Introduction to the Philosophy of Religious Experience* (London, 2000); D. Hay, *Religious Experience Today: Studying the Facts* (London, 1990); C. Jones, G. Wainwright and E. Yarnold (eds.), *The Study of Spirituality* (London, 1986); G. Mursell, *English Spirituality*, 2 vols. (London, 2001); P. Sheldrake, *Spaces for the Sacred* (London, 2001), pp. 119–146; (ed.), *The New SCM Dictionary of Christian Spirituality* (London, 2005); N. Smart, *The Religious Experience* (Englewood Cliffs, 1996). Earlier literature can be traced through the bibliographies in R. Woods (ed.), *Understanding Mysticism* (London, 1981), and S. B. Ferguson and D. F. Wright (eds.), *New Dictionary of Theology* (Leicester and Downers Grove, 1988), pp. 449 (Mystical Theology), 579 (Religious Experience).

P. N. HILLYER

RESURRECTION OF JESUS

The almost unanimous testimony of Christians from NT times onwards is that *Jesus' resurrection is the centre of Christianity. The best example is 1 Cor. 15, where the apostle Paul asserts that the resurrection is an indispensable part of the gospel message, and that salvation is achieved by responding in faith to Jesus Christ in light of this truth (vv. 1–4). Christian belief is vain unless Jesus was raised from the dead (vv. 12–20).

Two historical facts, probably the best established events in the NT, are affirmed by virtually all critical scholars. First, that Jesus died by crucifixion. Even John Dominic Crossan asserts

that the crucifixion is 'as sure as anything historical can ever be' (*Jesus: A Revolutionary Biography* [San Francisco, 1994], p. 145). Secondly, that the earliest Christians thought that they saw Jesus alive after his death. Reginald Fuller states that the fact that Jesus' disciples came to believe in the resurrection 'is one of the indisputable facts of history . . . a fact upon which both believer and unbeliever may agree' (*The Foundations of New Testament Christology* [New York, 1965], p. 142). What data support such critical convictions?

A crucial source

For decades, the centre of critical attention on the resurrection has been 1 Cor. 15, written approximately twenty-five years after Jesus' death. Almost never is the book's date or its Pauline authorship questioned, no matter how radical the researcher. Most scholars agree that in vv. 3–7 numerous factors indicate that Paul recorded an ancient oral tradition that is much earlier than the book itself. In fact, the vast majority of critical scholars date the origin of this tradition to within eight years of the crucifixion. Paul probably heard it during his stay in Jerusalem with Peter and James, the brother of Jesus, after his conversion (Gal. 1:18–19). Interestingly, these three apostles are the only named individuals in the list of Jesus' appearances (1 Cor. 15:5, 7, 8).

So the assertion of Christ's resurrection found in 1 Cor. 15:3–7 is an exceptionally early tradition from a very short time after the events, and could very well have been received by Paul from those who knew Jesus when he was alive. Historian Hans von Campenhausen writes, 'This account meets all the demands of historical reliability that could possibly be made of such a text' ('The Events of Easter and the Empty Tomb', *Tradition and Life in the Early Church* [Philadelphia, 1968], p. 44). C. H. Dodd emphasizes, 'The date, therefore, at which Paul received the fundamentals of the Gospel cannot well be later than some seven years after the death of Jesus Christ. It may be earlier' (*Apostolic Preaching*, p. 16).

Confirming Paul's testimony

We have said that many critical scholars acknowledge the historicity of Jesus' crucifixion and the disciples' conviction that they had seen him afterwards. It is generally thought that this early testimony cited by Paul provides the best evidence for the resurrection appearances. The apostles' belief that Jesus appeared to them after death is confirmed by four arguments from Paul.

1. Paul explains that he preached material that he had received from others, including a list of Jesus' appearances to numerous eyewitnesses (1 Cor. 15:3–7). If Paul received this information from Peter and James, as we have suggested, then this tradition is further corroborated by additional apostolic *authority.

Paul's testimony in Gal. 1:18–20 is very relevant. Describing his time spent with Peter in Jerusalem shortly after his conversion, Paul uses the term *historeo*, which most likely indicates an investigative inquiry. Paul also saw James, an unbeliever until he met the risen Jesus. The immediate context argues that the conversations these three men had concerned the nature of the gospel (vv. 11–16), which included Jesus' resurrection (1 Cor. 15:1–4). Dodd remarks that just a few years after Jesus died, Paul 'stayed with Peter for a fortnight, and we may presume they did not spend all the time talking about the weather' (*Apostolic Preaching*, p. 16).

Confirming Paul's claim to have received this testimony from others, we have literary indications that the material in 1 Cor. 15 did not originate with him. Stating what is the position of critical scholarship as a whole, Jewish scholar Pinchas *Lapide lists eight linguistic considerations for the non-Pauline nature of this material (*Resurrection*, pp. 97–99).

Still, it should be carefully noted that our conclusions do *not* depend on knowing the exact date and circumstances regarding this tradition. We do know that Paul learned it very early, as 1 Corinthians was written c. AD 55–57 and was preceded by Paul's initial trip to Corinth (c. AD 51), some 20 years after Jesus' death. At the very least, this report was derived from a source that Paul considered authoritative. So, this tradition is exceptionally early, an indicator that certain believers thought that Jesus had appeared to them after his death.

2. Paul reports that he himself was also an eyewitness to an appearance of the resurrected Lord (1 Cor. 15:8; cf. 9:1). Critical scholars acknowledge that here we have the actual testimony of one who claimed to have seen the risen Jesus. Additional corroboration of Jesus' appearance to Paul is contained in the three accounts recorded in Acts 9:1–9, 22:1–11 and 26:9–19.

3. Paul was not one to leave loose ends. Fourteen years after he first visited Peter, he again returned to Jerusalem in order to further corroborate the truth of the gospel. After meeting with the apostles Peter, James and John, Paul learned that his message was accurate (Gal. 2:1–10). So the 'pillars' of the church acknowledged the authenticity of Paul's central teaching.

Outside confirmation is provided by a similar discussion described in Acts 15. Again the topic was Paul's gospel proclamation. Peter and James the brother of Jesus were also involved. Again, the apostolic judgment indicated the accuracy of Paul's gospel preaching (vv. 7–21). Scholars debate whether this was the same meeting as described in Gal. 2, but this is a moot point. We either have confirmation of Paul's account, or a third trip to Jerusalem just so Paul could make absolutely sure that his preaching of Christ's death and resurrection was truthful! At any rate, the apostolic leaders substantiated Paul's gospel message.

4. After delivering to the Corinthians the early tradition that listed some of Jesus' resurrection appearances, Paul made a highly significant declaration. He reported that the other apostles were preaching the same message he was regarding Jesus' appearances (1 Cor. 15:11–15). Here we have Paul's testimony that these resurrection appearances were also being proclaimed by Jesus' original apostles.

We have more than one non-Pauline confirmation of this last claim. Other early traditions appear to be embedded in some of the preaching recorded in Acts. Although some scholars disagree, a number of others have noted the marks of early Christian preaching that predates the composition of the book. For example, Dodd argues for 'a large element of Semitism' and 'a high degree of probability' that there was an Aramaic original behind this material (*Apostolic Preaching*, pp. 19–20). More crucially, the messages are stated succinctly, with little embellishment, which is generally thought to be indicative of earlier layers of preaching. These texts record important details regarding Jesus' resurrection, like the fact that he appeared to groups of people (Acts 2:22–33; 3:14–15, 26; 4:10; 5:30; 10:39–43; 13:27–37). All but the last is attributed to the apostle Peter's teaching.

John Drane summarizes the importance of the Acts traditions, 'The earliest evidence we have for the resurrection almost certainly goes back to the time immediately after the resurrection event is alleged to have taken place. This is the evidence contained in the early sermons in the Acts of the Apostles ... But there can be no doubt that in the first few chapters of Acts its author has preserved material from very early sources' (*Introducing the New Testament* [San Francisco, 1986], p. 99).

Another witness to the resurrection comes from the Gospel accounts. They affirm at length that after his death Jesus' followers claimed to have seen him alive. This is far too broad a subject to be dealt with here, but suffice it to say that there are good reasons to trust these texts. From a critical viewpoint, Dodd argues that several of these narratives represent early tradition, and that they also merit careful consideration because of their lack of common mythical tendencies ('The Appearances of the Risen Christ: An Essay in Form-Criticism of the Gospels', *More New Testament Studies* [Grand Rapids, 1968]).

To summarize, we have presented nine lines of evidence for the apostles' teaching that Jesus appeared to them after his death. Four of these are drawn from two Pauline texts, while the other five are non-Pauline arguments. The texts we used are either apostolic and eyewitness, or drawn from other early testimony. Of the nine arguments, the four Pauline ones are the strongest in critical terms. Few, if any, scholars hold that Paul was totally mistaken at all four points. Dodd summarizes, 'Thus Paul's preaching represents a special stream of Christian tradition which was derived from the main stream at a point very near to its source ... anyone who should maintain that the primitive Christian Gospel was fundamentally different from that which we have found in Paul must bear the burden of proof' (*Apostolic Preaching*, p. 16).

The empty tomb

Although not quite as widely accepted as the Pauline data, a majority of critical scholars have noted the strong testimony in favour of Jesus' tomb being found empty a few days after his burial. Of the many reasons frequently cited for this conclusion, four will be briefly mentioned:

1. In the NT period, women could occasionally testify in law courts, but more regularly they were not allowed to serve as *witnesses in

crucial matters. So, the fact that women are depicted in all four Gospels as the earliest witnesses to the empty tomb is very significant, since their word would have been widely rejected. The discovery of the empty tomb by the women is, therefore, very likely to be true, as anyone making up the story would have put men in the main roles.

2. To proclaim the message of Jesus' resurrection in Jerusalem would have been ridiculous unless Jesus' tomb was actually empty. If the tomb was still closed, or if a body could have been produced, the message that Jesus had been raised *from the dead* would have been impossible to justify. The disciples chose the worst possible place for their proclamation, if their claims were false.

3. The early, pre-Pauline testimony in 1 Cor. 15 states that Jesus died, was buried, raised, and then appeared. It declares, in essence, that what was placed in the ground later reappeared. This sequence strongly implies an empty tomb, as does Paul's specific language in 1 Cor. 15:12 and Phil. 3:11, 21.

4. If Matthew is correct that the Jewish leaders spread the story that the disciples stole Jesus' body (Matt. 28:11–15), as confirmed by *Justin Martyr and *Tertullian, then we have 'enemy' attestation for the empty tomb. Such a claim was never widely accepted, largely since liars do not make good martyrs, and also because this thesis directly contradicts the critically recognized fact that the disciples really believed that Jesus had appeared to them. But the story nonetheless admits that Jesus' tomb was found empty.

The empty tomb is a tenth argument that supports the historicity of Jesus' resurrection. For those who would deny it, other explanations are necessary, but very difficult to viably construct. Historian Michael Grant admits, 'the historian ... cannot justifiably deny the empty tomb ... the evidence is firm and plausible enough to necessitate the conclusion that the tomb was indeed found empty' (*Jesus: An Historian's Review of the Gospels* [New York, 1977, 1992], p. 176).

Conclusion

The historical evidence for Jesus' resurrection is weighty. We have presented ten separate arguments for the historicity of this event, the vast majority being accepted by most scholars. The apostles' testimony that they saw the risen Jesus is early and hard to disprove. It is further confirmed by the fact that these same men were later willing to die specifically for this claim; that both Paul and James were unbelievers until they saw the risen Jesus; and the existence of the empty tomb. All of this must be explained adequately, if the fact of the resurrection is to be disputed.

Surprisingly, comparatively few recent critical scholars think that the resurrection can be explained naturally. (For a response to the most popular option, see the Habermas article cited below.) Rather, it is usually conceded that the known facts refute these alternative views. J. D. G. Dunn thinks that 'alternative explanations of the data fail to provide a more satisfactory explanation' (*The Evidence for Jesus* [Louisville, 1985], p. 76). Stephen Davis agrees, 'the alternative theories that have been proposed are not only weaker but far weaker at explaining the available historical evidence' ('Is Belief in the Resurrection Rational?: A Response to Michael Martin' *Philo*, 2.1 [1999], pp. 57–58). Of course, many still reject the resurrection. But many other critical scholars are at least open to it. In fact, perhaps more scholars accept the resurrection in some sense than at any time in the last 200 years.

Most succinctly, the evidence indicates that Jesus died, but was still seen afterwards. Since naturalistic theories fail to explain these two aspects, the best conclusion is that Jesus was raised from the dead.

For Christians, this matter is not dependent upon scholarly opinion. The truth that Jesus was raised from the dead is central to their faith. More than any other theological teaching, NT writers assert that Jesus' resurrection guarantees the believer's resurrection and eternal life (Phil. 3:20–21; 1 Pet. 1:3–4; 1 John 3:2). Further, it is God's ultimate answer to evil and suffering (1 Cor. 15:53–57). In short, because Jesus lives, believers will too (John 14:19).

Bibliography

W. L. Craig, *Assessing the New Testament Evidence for the Historicity of the Resurrection of Jesus* (Lewiston, 1989); C. H. Dodd, *The Apostolic Preaching and its Developments* (Grand Rapids, 1980); R. Fuller, *The Formation of the Resurrection Narratives* (New York, 1971); G. Habermas, 'Explaining Away Jesus' Resurrection: The Recent Revival of Hallucination Theories', *Christian Research Journal*, 23.4 (2001), pp. 26–31, 47–49; *The Historical Jesus: Ancient Evidence for the Life of Christ* (Joplin, 1996); G. Habermas and A. G. N. Flew in T. Miethe (ed.), *Did Jesus Rise from the Dead? The Resurrection Debate* (San Francisco, 1987); P. Lapide, *The Resurrection of Jesus: A Jewish Perspective* (Minneapolis, 1983); G. Osborne, *The Resurrection Narratives: A Redactional Study* (Grand Rapids, 1984); N. T. Wright, *The Resurrection of the Son of God* (Minneapolis, 2003).

G. R. HABERMAS

RESURRECTION OF JESUS, IMPLICATIONS OF

In discussions of *Jesus' resurrection, the historical evidence favouring this event frequently takes centre stage. Yet the NT has much to say about the doctrinal and practical implications of this event, as well. It grounds both *theology and the daily practice of the Christian life. The resurrection showed that Jesus' teachings were true, and the life-changing implications of this truth touched lives everywhere it was proclaimed.

The resurrection event validated Christian theology, indicating the truth of its doctrine. It also energized the routine of the Christian life, providing the motivation to live triumphantly. In this grand event, evidence, doctrine and practice move in harmony.

Jesus' resurrection and Christian theology

In the NT, Jesus' resurrection was the chief indication that his teachings were true. Even some cursory reflecting indicates why this was the case. If Jesus was raised from the dead, someone else acted upon him, since dead men do very little! But raising the dead is impossible in natural terms. So it makes the most sense to think that God was involved. Why would God perform such an event, if not to indicate that Jesus' teachings were true?

This approach is even more plausible in light of Jesus' own teachings. He taught that his *miracles indicated the truth of his message (Mark 2:10; Matt. 11:21). In particular, the resurrection would be his chief sign even for unbelievers (Matt. 12:38–40; 16:1–4). This event was at the heart of Jesus' central proclamation (Luke 24:44–48; cf. Acts 1:3). Especially in light of his teachings about his divine identity and that one's response to him determined where one spent eternity, when he was raised from the dead, the evidence pointed to an act of God, who raised Jesus from the dead in order to confirm this message.

From another angle, Jews thought that a true prophet could be distinguished from a false prophet (Deut. 13:1–5; 18:18–22). If Jesus was raised from the dead, this must indicate that God looked with favour upon his message. Otherwise, God would have raised a heretic from the dead, given Jesus' unique teachings. So early believers concluded that the resurrection was God's stamp of approval on his son. (For a more precise, scholarly treatment of this issue, see Habermas, *The Risen Jesus*.)

This same general approach is found in the NT. In Acts 2 we are told that Peter, in the first sermon after Jesus' resurrection, proclaimed that Jesus' miracles indicated that he was approved or accredited by God (2:22). In particular, God raised him from the dead (2:23–31), specifically to indicate that his teachings were true and that Jesus was precisely whom he claimed to be (2:32–36). Therefore, Peter encouraged his audience to respond to Jesus' message (2:37–41).

In another early message, we are told that Peter applied the key text in Deut. 18:18–19 directly to Jesus, who fulfilled its criteria (Acts 3:21–23). Peter concluded that Jesus was God's chosen spokesman, as indicated by his resurrection (3:24–26). Paul also preached the same message. The Creator God demanded repentance in light of Jesus, evidencing these truths by raising him from the dead (Acts 17:24–31).

In Romans, Paul reproduces some ancient credal teachings that proclaim the relationship between Jesus' resurrection and Christian theology. That Jesus was truly the Son of God, Christ and Lord was indicated by his resurrection (Rom. 1:3–4). Jesus died for our sins and his resurrection provided our justification (Rom. 4:25). Further, believers will be raised like Jesus (Rom. 8:11). It is a central component of the gospel (Rom. 10:9).

The resurrection actually furnishes a foundation for Christian theology as a whole. Paul taught that without it there is no distinctly Christian doctrine: preaching and teaching are useless, sins are unforgiven, and our deceased loved ones have perished (1 Cor. 15:12–18). In fact, our entire faith would be vain (15:14, 17), and Christians would be the most pitied persons (15:19). The resurrection even grounds our *ethics, rescuing it from hedonism (15:32).

Many other examples of the resurrection guaranteeing theological truth could be provided. In the middle of John's resurrection narrative, the reader is told that Jesus' miracles indicate that he is the Messiah, the Son of God, which should prompt faith (John 20:31). More frequently than any other doctrine, believers were told that they would be raised just like Jesus (e.g. Acts 4:2; 1 Cor. 6:14; 15:35–54; Phil. 3:20–21; 1 John 3:2). The resurrection secures *heaven for believers, promising that this hope will never fail (1 Pet. 1:3–4).

In short, the resurrection of Jesus provided the foundation for Christian theology. It grounded the central doctrines, helped define their parameters, and secured an eternal future for believers.

Jesus' resurrection and Christian practice

Not only does Jesus' resurrection ground theology, but the NT also repeatedly links this event to practising various aspects of the Christian life. This is clear from a number of passages, some of which we will highlight.

In his major treatise in 1 Cor. 15, Paul's argument moves from the historical truth of Jesus' resurrection (15:1–11), to this event being the foundation of the Christian faith (15:12–23), and the basis for the believer's own resurrection (15:35–53). Then the apostle turns to practical issues. Because Jesus has been raised, death has been conquered. Startlingly, Paul even taunts death, proclaiming that it no longer has the last word. It no longer has any sting! Death has been subjugated by Jesus Christ (15:54–57).

Then Paul concludes that, because of the resurrection, believers should stand firmly in their faith, without ever being moved. Moreover, they should be involved in ongoing work for the Lord (15:58). Without pausing, Paul provides details in the next few verses (16:1–4), where he commands that offerings be taken for poor believers (cf. Gal. 6:9–10). His argument for the resurrection, then, proceeds from historical evidence all the way to victory over death, steadfastness and the very practical labour of supplying others' necessities. As Paul teaches earlier, believers will be rewarded for their labour (1 Cor. 3:8–15).

The resurrection grounded other practical areas, too. It accounted for the transformations in the lives of Jesus' disciples (Acts 4:32). Even unbelievers like James the brother of Jesus (1 Cor. 15:7) and Paul (Gal. 1:13–16) came face to face with the risen Jesus and were changed for ever. The resurrection gave birth to the church, as believers celebrated the day on which Jesus was raised (Acts 20:7; 1 Cor. 16:1–2). Evangelism was based chiefly on the commands of the risen Jesus (Matt 28:19–20; Luke 24:47–49; Acts 1:8). This extends to daily needs, as well. Because Jesus was raised from the dead, believers can gain mastery over sin (Rom. 6:6–10; 8:9–11), and so can live for God (Gal. 2:19–20).

We have seen that for Jesus his resurrection was the chief sign even for unbelievers (Matt. 12:38–40; 16:1–4). When John the Baptist struggled with doubts, Jesus reminded him of the miracles that he had performed (Luke 7:18–28). We are told that, when Lazarus died, Jesus addressed Martha's grief with the truth of his resurrection (John 11:21–27). Later, he counselled his own disciples with his own resurrected presence (Luke 24:13–24, 36–42; John 20:19–21). Thomas's questions were also answered the same way (John 20:24–29).

For Paul, suffering and persecution were remedied by the truth of Jesus' resurrection (2 Cor. 4:7–18). Other writers agree (cf. Heb. 11:35), even saying that we should rejoice in our suffering since the resurrection has secured heaven for us (1 Pet. 1:3–9). What a hope, produced by this glorious event!

One reason for such advice is that Jesus came to free us from the fear of death, to which we were in bondage all our lives (Heb. 2:14–15). Paul knew that, because of the resurrection (2 Cor. 4:14), to die was to be at home with the living Jesus (5:8). This result is far better even than living longer (Phil. 1:21–23). After all, Jesus' death and resurrection make us citizens of heaven (Phil. 3:10–21). At present we have a foretaste of this hope (Eph. 2:6–7).

Conclusion

The NT connects Jesus' resurrection and its meaning to most major doctrines and even many areas of Christian practice. This event indicates that Jesus' teachings are true and ought to be applied.

The resurrection can be compared to a gorgeous, multi-faceted diamond. Turn it one way and find historical justification for the central fact of history. From another angle, we discover reasons to believe key doctrines. Move it again, just slightly, and we view the theology itself. Give it one more twist, and watch it invigorate personal existence. The resurrection confronts the entire Christian life, grasping our lives and bidding us to be transformed by its truth. In its wake, we are never the same.

Bibliography

G. R. Habermas, *The Resurrection: Heart of New Testament Theology* (Joplin, 2000); *The Resurrection: Heart of the Christian Life* (Joplin, 2000); *The Risen Jesus and Future Hope* (Lanham, 2003); R. N. Longenecker (ed.), *Life in the Face of Death: The Resurrection Message of the New Testament* (Grand Rapids, 1998); T. Lorenzen, *Resurrection and Discipleship: Interpretative Models, Biblical Reflections, Theological Consequences* (Maryknoll, 1995).

G. R. HABERMAS

REVELATION

In biblical and Christian usage 'revelation' means primarily God making himself known cognitively and relationally (active sense), and secondarily the communicated information and instruction whereby he does this (passive sense).

Triune God

God himself, the eternal, infinite, sovereign Lord, active in creation, providence and grace, is the source and subject of revelation. Through biblically recorded events and teachings he has disclosed not merely his purposes and plans, but also the transcendent glory of his own true identity. He has shown himself by his actions to be the triune Yahweh, within whose unitary being the personal threeness of the Father, the Son and the *Holy Spirit is as much a fact as their substantive oneness, and whose work in the world is done by these three persons acting together. Mysteriously but genuinely and authentically, the one God is plural. The three persons of the Godhead, relationally distinct though identical in powers and character, are he, and he, the Almighty One, self-sustained, self-programmed, self-named and self-announcing, is they. (See Gen. 1; Exod. 3:1–15; 34:5–8; Isa. 6; 40:12–31; 44:6 – 45:25; Matt. 3:16–17; 28:18–20;

John 14 – 17; Eph. 1:3–14; Rev. 1.) Divine revelation should be explicated in trinitarian terms.

Jesus Christ

In the Bible this triune God, who orders and permeates the entire creation (Ps. 139; Acts 17:24–28), is highlighted as saving lost sinners, indwelling Christians and the believing community, and guaranteeing to his people a hope of glory. (See Isa. 43:25; 44:21–23; Matt. 1:21; Luke 15; John 14:15–23; Rom. 8:9–17; Eph. 2; Titus 1:1–4; 2:10–14; 3:4–7; 2 Pet. 3:8–13; 1 John 3:2; Rev. 7:9–17; 21:1 – 22:5.) The central topic of revelation is redemption, and the focal figure in redemption, as indeed in creation, is *Jesus Christ of Nazareth, who was and is God the Son, now and for ever incarnate. He said that he and the Father were in solidarity together, so that seeing and knowing the one is seeing and knowing the other (John 10:30; 12:45; 14:7–11). He entered and left this world in miraculous ways (virginal conception and birth; bodily resurrection and ascension), died on the cross for our sins, and now lives and reigns for us beyond this world. He will one day reappear in triumph to raise the dead, renew the universe, declare final destinies, and bring believers into the fullness of the salvation that they have already experienced in part in fellowship with him through the Holy Spirit. (See Luke 1:26–38; 24; Acts 1:1–11; John 1:1–18; Rom. 8:18–30; Gal. 2:20; Eph. 5:25–27; Col. 1:13–23; Heb. 1:1–4; 2:9–18; 9:24 – 10:25; 1 John 1:1–3.) Divine revelation should be viewed theocentrically and Christologically.

Covenantal history

God gave this revelation by punctuating the ordered flow of almost two millennia of world *history with words and deeds that had decisive significance for creating, sustaining, disciplining, purging and revitalizing for himself a people, that is, an ongoing community of faithful worshippers. This people was and is God's Israel, once Abraham's progeny, now Christ's church, a global, multi-ethnic, multi-form fellowship of faith with Christ as its head, life and hope. (All this is laid out in Paul's teaching, especially Rom. 6:1–14; 11; 15:7–13; Gal. 3:1–14; 6:14–16; Eph. 2:12 – 3:13; 4:1–16; Col. 1:18, 24–29; 3:1–4; 1 Tim. 1:1.) The historical heart of God's revelation is the covenantal promise to Abraham 'to be your God and the God of your descendants' (Gen. 17:7). This promise was renewed to Abraham's descendants at Sinai (Exod. 19:4–6; cf. Jer. 11:4) and embodied in many later promises of renewal (Jer. 24:7; 30:22; 31:33; Ezek. 11:20; 36:28; 37:27; Zech. 8:8). It was reformulated through Christ as a new covenant (1 Cor. 11:25; 2 Cor. 3:6), with Christ as its permanent mediatorial priest and his death as its permanently valid sacrifice for the sins of penitent believers. This new covenant conveyed better promises than before (not an earthly inheritance, but a heavenly land to enjoy for ever) and richer resources of help in need through Christ's interventions from his throne (Rom. 8:34; cf. Heb. 2:17–18; 4:14–16; 7 – 10; 11:13–16). Divine revelation should be conceived in terms of this historical covenantal process.

Revealed truth

This process revealed truth: *truth of statement and testimony, as opposed to falsehood, misconception and lies, and truth of fact and *reality, as opposed to unreality, fantasy and illusion. Both these aspects of truth were regularly expressed by the Greek word-group used in the LXX and the NT (alētheia, truth; alēthēs, true; alēthinos, genuine; alethōs, truly), and both meet when Paul calls the vitalizing gospel of Christ 'the truth' (Gal. 2:5; 5:7; Eph. 6:14; 2 Thess. 2:10; 1 Tim. 2:4; 6:5; 2 Tim. 2:15; Titus 1:1) and when John describes Jesus as 'full of . . . truth' (John 1:14) and reports him saying that the Father is 'true' (John 7:28; 8:26; 17:3) and that he himself is 'the truth' in person (14:6). Because Jesus is 'the truth', he is both 'the way' leading to the Father and 'the life' of all his worshipping followers (cf. John 20:28). New Testament Christianity is built on this twofold truth-claim. Divine revelation should be classed as revealed truth in both senses.

Holy Scripture

Post-apostolic believers in every age learn of God's revelation through the canonical Scriptures of the Old and New Testaments. These constitute an interpretative record of the Creator's redemptive words and works in the world's past history and a declaration of the promises for now and hereafter that he bases on them. Ordinarily, it is through the interpreting of this material within the believing community, by its *preaching, teaching, witness and catechesis, both formal and informal, that knowledge of what is revealed is mediated. The church on earth is called to be the witness and a keeper of the Scriptures by labouring to draw out and apply their message, while submitting to their *authority and *power to judge, correct and augment all human attempts to grasp and share what they say. For Holy Scripture is in truth the living word of the living God, the source and substance of his continued communication; it is in essence God witnessing to himself in and through the witness to him of divinely guided human writers. This is clear from the way in which Jesus and the NT writers cite, interpret and apply OT passages and generalize about the OT as a whole and how through Christ the OT prophecies are fulfilled. (See Matt. 5:17–19; 19:4–5; 26:53–56; Mark 12:36; Luke 18:31–33; 22:37; 24:25–32, 44–47; John 10:35; Acts 4:25; 17:2, 11; 28:25; Rom. 1:2; 9:17; 15:4; 16:26; 1 Cor. 10:1–11; Gal. 3:8, 22; 2 Tim. 3:15–17; Heb. 3:7; 4:3–7; 10:15–17; 12:5–6; 13:5–6; 1 Pet. 1:10–12; 2 Pet. 1:19–21; 3:15–16.)

All Scripture is divine instruction in some form, teaching and illustrating truth about God and godliness, and is as such canonical, that is, a rule for faith and life. The books of both Testaments were written to call forth responses of faith, obedience and praise towards God, and must be interpreted in terms of their aim. Christ in effect gave the church its original *canon, namely the OT, which he claimed in broadest terms to be fulfilling and which the apostles evidently passed on to the infant churches in its LXX form.

Apostolic teaching was taken as the key to understanding the OT, so it is no wonder that as apostolic writings about Christ and the Christian life emerged they were circulated and set alongside it as the completion of God's self-disclosure in writing. Divinely revealed truth should be equated with, and identified as, biblical teaching.

Biblical interpretation

Canonical Scripture needs to be canonically interpreted, or its revelatory content will be muddled or missed. Such interpretation is a work of faith and prayer that elucidates the Bible according to its nature as God-given instruction for the whole church, embodied in many different literary and communicative forms (narrative, teaching, prophecy, poetry, proverbs, letters and visions). The aim of all interpreters should be: to draw from each passage, by contextualized grammatical-historical exegesis in light of genre recognition, what each biblical writer meant his readers to learn about God and godliness; to follow such topical and chronological links as Scripture itself provides between its documentary units; to synthesize the teaching of all the books of the Bible harmoniously, as the totality of God's revelation, always bearing in mind the historical context and sometimes fragmentary character of particular divine disclosures and human compositions; to correlate initial conclusions with the world church's heritage of biblical reflection and wisdom, which is a valuable resource for testing, correcting and augmenting preliminary understandings; to apply biblical teaching about God and godliness to modern people, taking account of cultural differences between Bible times and ours; to seek light and help from the Holy Spirit throughout the process, knowing that otherwise God's revealed truth will inevitably be misconstrued and misapplied.

Holy Spirit

While God's linguistic, mind-to-mind self-disclosure in and through biblical testimony is meant to be grasped intellectually, his revelatory action is not complete until he comes to be personally known in a responsive relationship, through the communicative agency of the Holy Spirit. The Spirit, who inspired, that is determined, the words of the whole canon as he did the words of the biblical prophets, now authenticates these writings to God's people as having the flavour of wisdom and truth from God (the image is *Calvin's) and guides them into the reality of truth (cf. John 14:17, 26; 15:26; 16:13–14). He does this by giving both a conceptual grasp of biblical teaching and an inward certainty that the God, the Christ, the salvation and the eternity in heaven or hell of which Scripture speaks are real indeed and demand the active acknowledgment of penitent trust in the living Christ and endless adoring gratitude to the Father for his redeeming love (Rom. 12:1; Eph. 5:20; Col. 1:12; 2:6; 3:15–17). This reality is realized through regeneration, the act of new creation within the believer (2 Cor. 5:17; Gal. 6:15) whereby spiritual blindness, deafness and hardness (unresponsiveness) of heart are ended, what God publicly presents in the gospel is personally received, and in the obedience of faith sinners know God as they move from death into life (see Jer. 31:34; Luke 1:76–79; 2:25–32; John 3:3–15; 17:3; Rom. 6:1–14; Gal. 4:8–9; Phil. 3:8–11; 1 John 2:3–6; 3:14; 4:7–10). This illuminating and regenerating work of God is specifically spoken of as revelation in Gal. 1:12, 16 (see also Matt. 11:25; 16:17; cf. 13:11–16; 2 Cor. 4:6). Accounts of divine revelation are incomplete when they fail to celebrate the work of the Holy Spirit leading the unregenerate through conceptual into relational knowledge of God.

General revelation

To explain the universality of the guilt for which the gospel revelation of the righteousness of God is the remedy (Rom. 1:16–17), Paul affirms a universal human awareness of God the Creator whom all should worship and who will justly punish all who have failed to seek him and to live by his moral standards (Rom. 1:18 – 2:11). This awareness is mediated by the majesty, beauty and apparent rational design of the created order (Rom. 1:19–20; cf. Pss. 19:1–6; 139:13–16), by the goodness apparent in timely rain and fruitful fields (Acts 14:17), and by the spontaneous self-judgments of *conscience (Rom. 2:14–15). It also persists (so Paul implies) at the back of the human mind despite the idolatry and immorality into which our fallen race actually plunges (Rom. 1:21–25, 32). The usual name for this awareness, which the Holy Spirit will not allow anyone totally to lose, is general or natural revelation, as distinct from the disclosure of saving grace in Christ (special revelation). Seeing general revelation as regularly distorted or ignored, Paul does not envisage a '*natural theology' being built on it as a stepping-stone to faith in Christ, as latter-day apologists sometimes do. Paul invokes general revelation only to establish the guilt of not worshipping God or living morally.

Deviations

'Revelation is the first fact, the first mystery, and the first category of theology' (Latourelle), and rejecting God's revelatory action, as described above, has far-reaching consequences. While the coherence of this classical Christian synthesis is clear and full, and the historical and rational case for it, both extrinsic and intrinsic, remains strong, two types of deviation are current. The first reduces revelation by philosophical and scientific scepticism; the second relativizes it by theological and religious *pluralism. The former, stemming from Renaissance and *Enlightenment *rationalism, effectively shrinks God, calling into question his triunity (so Socinianism and much recent liberalism), his sovereignty over human actions (so Arminianism and today's process theology, and 'open' theism), his *miracles and redemptive intrusions into his world (so Deism, ancient and modern), his use of *language to tell people things (so *Kant and Fichte and most twentieth-century theology), and the credibility of all Scripture as a witness to him (so most *biblical criticism). The end product of all this is a depersonalized, dethroned, silent and distant God whom we can get on without, and a Jesus who, whatever else he is, is not a divine Saviour. The other deviation, growing out of earlier *Romanticism and today's global multi-religious mix, posits a non-cognitive essence of religion underlying all particular religions, namely an alluring sense of the transcendent (sometimes faraway and abstractly conceived, sometimes immanent and mystically felt). On this view, all teachings of all faiths are just so many myths, pointing to this transcendent reality, however conceived. They are myths that evoke awareness of the divine, enforce moral and spiritual lessons and enrich the conscious identity of those whose myths they are, but they are not, nor do they need to be, factually based.

Both these trends exchange human experience for the Bible and the Christian *creeds as the arbiter of religious reality. Both rest religion on human ideas and inklings, and both dismiss a priori the claim that true knowledge of God depends on divine instruction given and action taken in world history, and quite specifically on the divine incarnation in Palestine two millennia ago. And both, claiming to fit Christianity into its appropriate frame, actually dismember it, by denying the key significance of Jesus Christ as the Saviour of those who by faith come to know him and, through him, the Father. The denial usually takes the form either of *universalism, which holds that Christ's atoning achievement saves everyone, whether they believe or not, or of naturalism, which sees no need for atonement, recasts Jesus as simply one of the world's great teachers and models of religion, and affirms that religious practice is what saves religious people. In both cases, the Christ of biblical revelation is lost, and Christianity effectively becomes a natural religion with a natural theology based on human intuitions emerging from human culture.

Bibliography

P. A. Avis (ed.), *Divine Revelation* (Grand Rapids and Cambridge, 1997); J. Baillie, *The Idea of Revelation in Recent Thought* (New York, 1956); R. T. Beckwith, 'Canon', and E. J. Schnabel, 'Scripture', in T. D. Alexander and B. S. Rosner (eds.), *New Dictionary of Biblical Theology* (Leicester and Downers Grove, 2000), pp. 27–43; M. Bockmuehl, *Revelation and Mystery in Ancient Judaism and Pauline Christianity* (Tübingen, 1990); B. Demarest, *General Revelation* (Grand Rapids, 1982); G. Fackre, *The Doctrine of Revelation* (Edinburgh and Grand Rapids, 1997); C. Gunton, *A Brief Theology of Revelation* (Edinburgh, 1995); P. Helm, *The Divine Revelation: The Basic Issues* (London, 1982); R. Latourelle, *Theology of Revelation* (New York, 1966); H. Netland, *Dissonant Voices* (Grand Rapids and Leicester, 1991); 'Revelation' in C. Brown (ed.), *New International Dictionary of New Testament Theology* (Carlisle, 1988); B. B. Warfield, *Revelation and Inspiration* (Grand Rapids, 1981).

J. I. PACKER

RITSCHL, ALBRECHT BENJAMIN

Albrecht Benjamin Ritschl was born in Berlin in 1822. He studied at Bonn, Halle, Berlin, Heidelberg and Tübingen, and became professor of *history in Bonn (1852–64) and subsequently professor of systematic theology in Göttingen from 1864 until his death in 1889.

Ritschl taught that Christianity must feed upon concrete facts and events. When it takes flight from historical realities, it becomes either mysticism or rationalism. He rejected metaphysical speculation, subjective experience and mysticism. *Metaphysics he considered an inadequate effort to put faith into philosophical conceptions, insisting that Christian faith should be based on the *revelation of God in *Jesus Christ. The subjective experience of believers was rejected as being insufficient to provide a ground of faith and knowledge. He considered mysticism to be unhistorical and lacking the significance of Jesus as mediator of the relationship between God and humans. It also downplays the Christian *community as the place where God reveals himself. For Ritschl, mysteries could be acknowledged, but, as by their nature they transcend knowledge, nothing more can be said of them.

Ritschl insisted that religion should be understood on a concrete historical foundation. Thus he gave importance to the Bible as a concrete historical fact, especially to the NT, which involves the work of Jesus Christ.

In his *epistemology, Ritschl denied to human reason the power to arrive at a scientific knowledge of God. Consequently, religion cannot have an intellectual foundation but solely a practical-moral one. Religious knowledge was seen as fundamentally distinct from scientific knowledge. Scientific knowledge is the product of religious faith and, as such, is bound up with the practical interests of the soul. For Ritschl, religion was practice, not theory.

Knowledge and faith are not only distinct domains; they are independent of and separated from each other. While knowledge rests on judgments of existence, faith proceeds on independent 'judgments of value'. Such judgments affirm nothing concerning the core nature of God or his actions; rather, they refer simply to the usefulness and fruitfulness of religious ideas.

Ritschl focused on the impact of God's work among human beings and on the kingdom of God as the supreme good. It was the Christians' vocation to take dominion over the world. He saw religion as being known only in community. Sin was seen as an egotistic tendency in all human beings, and thus was understood, not as inherited, but as universal.

Bibliography

K. Barth, *From Rousseau to Ritschl* (ET, London, 1959); H. R. Mackintosh, *Types of Modern Theology* (London, 1937).

C. CAMPBELL-JACK

ROMAN CATHOLICISM, see
CHRISTIANITY, ROMAN CATHOLIC

ROMANTICISM

The Romantic period is usually located between the years 1780 and 1830. Amongst the most cherished ideas of the Romantics were those that secured and enhanced individuality and particularity. The spirit within every human being must be set free from the intellectual formulas and dogmatism which imprison the mind and determine the boundaries of knowledge and experience. The shackles of restraint have imprisoned the human spirit for far too long. As *Rousseau stated so eloquently, 'Man is born free but is everywhere in chains.'

According to Romanticism, new and exciting horizons await the experience of the human consciousness and the inquiry of the human mind. Each individual life is unique and sacred and accumulates and verifies its most valuable knowledge through immediate sensation. There is an unshakable confidence in human intuition, cognition, ingenuity and judgment. The Romantics were in open rebellion against the formal and static strictures of the Augustan era, believing that the unrestrained experiential, intuitive and imaginative activities of humans provided a truer expression of life in all its spontaneity and unpredictability. The human will is free, the ultimate *reality is spiritual, and nature, which is usually personified, is a reflection of the human soul. People must be allowed to rediscover themselves in a sense of the infinite and in an exploration of the irrational elements in the human personality.

The importance of the impact of Romanticism on Christian thought throughout the nineteenth and into the twentieth century cannot be overestimated. Although non-Christian in its origin, Romanticism adopted some Christian vocabulary and values, so that at times the boundaries between them became blurred and created considerable confusion. This is illustrated in the work of the theologian F. D. E. *Schleiermacher (1768–1834), who is generally accepted as 'the father of modern Protestant theology'. He located the initiating font of religion in 'feeling', claiming that the distinctive element in religious experience is characterized by 'the consciousness of being absolutely dependent, or, which is the same thing, of being in relation to God' (Christian Faith, p. 12). Sin is the loss of this feeling of total dependence. Such a framework could not cope with the possibility of God giving himself to us as an objective person or with objective revealed *truth. As Schleiermacher states, 'any possibility of God being in any way given is entirely excluded' (ibid. p. 18). The uniqueness of Christ is the result of the 'constant potency of his God-consciousness, which was a veritable existence of God in him' (ibid. p. 385). Christian doctrine becomes no more than 'an account of religious affections set forth in speech' (ibid. p. 76).

The person responsible for introducing German philosophical Romanticism to the United Kingdom was the poet and theologian Samuel Taylor Coleridge (1772–1834). Like Schleiermacher, Coleridge redefined key theological terms. For him, *revelation proceeds from within the person. There is no such thing as propositional revelation. All revelation 'is *ab intra*'. The divine light is present in each individual so that religious truth becomes a matter of 'beholding' intuitively rather than knowing personally. True faith is 'a light, a beholding of truth', and reason is the faculty of beholding. *Theology is 'the objectification of the subjective spirit of Christianity' (J. D. Boulger, *Coleridge as a Religious Thinker*, p. 188). *Authority is subjective, and the Bible must be read like any other book. To discover the truth contained in the Bible one needs to adhere to the dictum that, 'Whatever finds me is true.' To have possession of the Bible is a great boon, but it is not essential. Indeed, Coleridge can state, 'Be only, my friend! As orthodox a believer as you would have abundant reason to be, though ... the Bible ... had been concealed from you' (*Confessions*, p. 10). We accept as truth that which we approve, 'Like a just Monarch [God] refers his own causes to the judgments of his High Courts [and] he has been graciously pleased to forbid our receiving aught that is not stamped with the great seal of Conscience and countersigned by the Reason' (*Aids to Faith*, p. 97). The Bible confirms intuition rather than informs our ignorance, corrects our error and introduces us to the God of truth.

Confusion concerning vocabulary and parallels in ideas and values brought more problems than benefits to Christian thought. No harm came from being reminded by Romanticism that lifeless orthodoxy and formalism are a disservice to true religion; indeed, they are the very antithesis of evangelical faith. True faith is personal and experiential. But, whilst the individual experience of revelation is essential for that revelation to impact me, the truth of revelation is objective and is true whether I perceive and receive it or not. Scripture is the record of this revelation. Furthermore, Christ is not only special because of his God consciousness, he is unique because he is the eternal Son of God who became incarnate and died to atone for our sin on Calvary. The *Holy Spirit is a divine person, not an influence who can be brought to the surface of our lives like water from a well.

The Romantic approach to the Bible should have alerted the discerning thinker to the vital difference between the authority of Scripture and its interpretation, and how homiletics may totally undermine a professed acceptance of its authority. Many have yet to learn this lesson. Equally devastating was the error which Coleridge and others foisted on the undiscerning in driving a wedge between light and truth. Truth is the element whose presence makes light the true light. Divorced from scriptural truth, light may become a synonym for darkness for, 'Satan himself masquerades as an angel of light' (2 Cor. 11:14). Christ is the embodiment of true light, and it is in contrast to the truth which he speaks that the pseudo light of the devil is exposed as darkness. Christ is the 'Truth' and the 'Light', both elements being inseparable in the unity of his person. To experience Christian salvation is to know God in the person of his Son Jesus Christ as he is revealed to us in Holy Scripture.

Bibliography

J. D. Boulger, *Coleridge as a Religious Thinker* (Yale, 1961); S. T. Coleridge, *Aids to Reflection* (London, 1825); *Confession of an Inquiring Spirit* (London, 1840); D. Jasper, *The Sacred and Secular Canon in Romanticism* (Basingstoke, 1999); S. Prickett, *Romanticism and Religion* (Cambridge, 1976); J. F. D. Schleiermacher, *The Christian Faith* (London, 1928).

J. H. ELIAS

ROOKMAAKER, HENDERICK (HANS) ROELOF

Hans Rookmaaker (1922–77) was a charismatic teacher and mentor, his grey suit and sharp cut trousers in memorable contrast to the colourful, bohemian dress of the art students he was popular with. In the UK he inspired the creation of The Arts Centre Group, for Christians professionally involved in the *arts and media. As a leading art historian he contributed significantly to his specialism and also educated a whole generation of evangelicals who had grossly neglected the arts and media. The main platform for his wide influence was his close association with Francis *Schaeffer and the L'Abri communities. The publication of his *Complete Works*, in six volumes (2002–3), has provided for the first time a full picture of the wide range and depth of his thinking on art, *music, creativity, contemporary *culture and

the Christian world-view. Someone once said of him, 'He spoke simply, because he thought deeply.' His integration of so many interests – philosophical, aesthetic, musical, cultural and biblical – is without parallel in his generation of evangelicals. He could be searingly critical, as when he was invited to speak at Bob Jones University. Looking around the auditorium, he said, 'I don't see any black people here.'

Rookmaaker had an aristocratic upbringing in the Dutch colonies of Indonesia and in The Hague before joining the Royal Dutch Navy, attending the Marine Officers' School in Den Helder. During the Second World War he was captured by the Nazis while distributing papers for the Dutch underground press. Later in an officers' prison camp in Poland, he became a Christian after reading the Bible in isolation and then being introduced to the Christian philosophy of Herman *Dooyeweerd (1894–1977), whose ideas he freely adapted and popularized in his lectures, discussions with students, and publications.

While he was in prison, his Jewish fiancée, Riki Spetter, was deported to Auschwitz and perished there. One of Riki's close friends was Anky Huitker, who sheltered several Jews, and whom Rookmaaker married after the war. They had three children. Rookmaaker's first intellectual passion was music, but he decided to explore art history, which had been neglected by Christian scholarship.

In 1948, while a student of art history at the Municipal University of Amsterdam, he met Francis Schaeffer, then in his thirties. Schaeffer became something of a mentor to the student, and they kept in touch after the Schaeffers settled in Switzerland. Later, Rookmaaker set up L'Abri discussion groups, which eventually led to the founding of the Dutch L'Abri branch at Eck en Wiel.

After graduating in 1952, Rookmaaker began doctoral research on the origins of modern art, eventually published as *Synthetist Art Theories* (1959). In his preface to a new edition in 1972, he wrote: 'The arts of the twentieth century cannot simply be equated with the modern movement characterized in its different streams by Cubism, Dada, Surrealism, Abstract Expressionism, Pop, Op, and Neo-Dada. This modern movement is not a style, but more an attitude, a spiritual insight, a feeling for the predicament of humankind. Modern art is defined by its content, not its style.'

He lectured in the history of art at Leyden University from 1958 to 1965, after which he took on the Chair of Art History at the Free University of Amsterdam, a Calvinistic institution. He remained there from 1965 until his sudden, untimely death in 1977.

Important for the formation of his thinking was the period from 1949 to 1956 when he served as art critic for the daily paper, *Trouw*. Once or twice a week he wrote columns reviewing artists and exhibitions, developing an informed Christian response to contemporary art based upon careful observation and receptivity. This paralleled his doctoral exploration of the origins of modern art in Gauguin and his circle of painters. Rookmaaker realized that the achievement of modern art lay in its shaping of a new pictorial language. He distinguished content and style, critiquing what he saw as the gnostic and dehumanizing features of post-Christian world-views, but appreciating the art. In 1959 he observed, 'Art is art, not philosophy or life and world view, however much art may have to do with these as well.' Art was neither to be justified nor dismissed solely on the basis of its message. Art was irreducible, yet connected to society, belief and our very humanity.

Rookmaaker's next book, written in Dutch, was *Jazz, Blues, Spirituals* (1960), reflecting his musicological interests. Between 1956 and 1966 he had edited a history series for Fontana Records of old Jazz, Blues and Spirituals – including recordings of Clarence Williams, King Oliver, Ma Rainey and Blind Willie Johnson. In 1961 he met the black Gospel singer Mahalia Jackson. The next year he published, also in Dutch, *Art and Entertainment*, which passionately argued for Christian involvement both in the 'high' and the 'low' arts – the entire world of the media which has so shaped the modern world.

His first publication which had a wider impact was *Modern Art and the Death of a Culture* (1970), which was read throughout the world. It revealed Rookmaaker's facility to move freely and with a sense of urgency between the worlds of high art, the media, music and biblical faith. The book was lauded by Malcolm *Muggeridge, yet was controversial (a) in popularizing art history and (b) in suggesting that *modernism was at its end. It took another fifteen years or so before Rookmaaker's views were shown to be accurate, as thinkers throughout the West

proclaimed the end, not only of modernism, but of history, of art and of Western tradition. Rookmaaker's hope in the kingdom of heaven was lacking in these postmodernist voices. His emphasis was on the West as post-Christian, rather than as postmodernist, and on the idea of divine judgment. His theme was God's presence in *history, blessing as well as judging humanity.

Bibliography

G. Birtwistle, 'H. R. Rookmaaker: The Shaping of his Thought, an Introduction', in H. R. Rookmaaker, *Art, Artists and Gauguin (Complete Works)*, vol. 1, xv–xxxiii; C. Duriez, interview with Hans Rookmaaker, *Crusade* magazine, April 1972; M. Hengelaar-Rookmaaker (ed.), *The Complete Works of Hans Rookmaaker*, 6 vols. (2002–3); L. Martin, *Hans Rookmaaker: A Biography* (1979).

C. DURIEZ

RORTY, RICHARD

Truth and language

Richard Rorty is a pragamatist about *truth. He claims that our statements have limited chances of *verification, including that statement itself, but also including any a more traditional opponent may make. Truth, unlike things, is always conditioned by how those things appear to us and interact with us: there is no truth where there are no sentences, and all truth comes 'through us'. A major influence here was the philosopher Donald Davidson, who 'has helped us realize that the very absoluteness of truth is a good reason for thinking "true" indefinable and for thinking that no theory of the nature of truth is possible'. Truth is the unknowable 'God'. So statements outlining the best courses of action given any situation are what qualify as truths. The only way ahead is one that echoes Jesus and his teaching about recognizing people's characters from their actions, that 'one interpretation may be better than another because it more effectively satisfies certain desires or fulfils such and such a purpose'. It is not such a shameful thing to subordinate truth to human interests! Refreshingly, Rorty dismisses the priority of philosophers and says philosophy should stop confronting and interrogating to look for the structures and allow conversation with our knowledge, life and culture (including literature), for these are the things which give vision through being close to life as lived now. After the horrors of the twentieth century, reason is no guide, as no such thing as 'reason' exists as a faculty any more than 'will' or 'emotion' does. Instead Rorty proposes that we do better to get away from such faculties to 'imaginative power' as the force which drives *morality and reconstitutes ways of seeing things. 'I am hungry' is not expressive of something internal but a means of helping others to predict our behaviour. *Language could not hope to mirror states of consciousness, much less things in the world, except perhaps for the banal (e.g. 'the cat sat on the mat'). One could object, however: but is not a lot of existence banal?

Ethics

Rorty's work strikes the Christian reader as warm, perhaps a re-heated Christian morality, if thoroughly without a vertical reference. He seems to espouse a sort of virtue *ethics, although it is given a slant 'moral progress as a progress of sentiments'. Rorty opposes the idea that what we desire is, on the face of it, wrong and always needing restraint. Moral development is seen as enlarging what feels natural to the self, or to do things which, not to do, would make us uncomfortable, which he suggests is a bit like the motivation for both Christian and Buddhist sainthood.

Picking up from *Dewey's faith in the family/*community, ethics is about extending our boundaries of sympathy more and more, taking people off the list of 'them' and adding people to our list of 'us'. Sentimental education is required, although just how one gives that to nationalist mass-murderers he does not detail. He claims that such people are not less rational but rather deprived of security and sympathy (although that may be to confuse the issue of their state of mind with its cause). It is about finding little commonalities which stitch communities together rather than one big human commonality such as 'all human beings have rationality or the image of God'. Against the idea that there is a human essence, Rorty prefers to see himself as a cluster of currents rather than a solid self, which is a form of freedom. Solidarity may not be the recognition of a core self, but we can still call the action inhuman if it betrays the principle by which

Rorty defines humans: those who *can* feel more for each other than any other species. Thus we 'disentangle Christ's suggestion that love matters more than knowledge from the neo-Platonic suggestion that knowledge of the truth will make us free'. It is not just a detail that Rorty here confuses the sayings of Jesus and Paul (as Platonist).

Reasons for behaving

The fundamental premise of Rorty's *Philosophy and Social Hope* is that 'a belief can still regulate action, can still be thought worth dying for, among people who are quite aware that this belief is caused by nothing more than contingent historical circumstance'. Yet, as he admits, 'Christianity has taught the West to look forward to a world in which there are no [strangers]'.

Rorty thinks that one can still loathe cruelty without thinking there is such a thing as 'cruelty' standing behind history. Indeed, it is better not to hate or love ideals too much. And yet is there not a need for an authority to be believed in to inspire, guide and help performance? Perhaps we will not be able to tell for a while whether making people who no longer think that they are swearing tell the truth before God will have led to less truthfulness and even conscious deceit in the courtroom. Rorty often asserts that we need to look to the future and not to the past (although there is a past which he is always talking about – he is a historian of ideas.)

Rorty admits that his younger consciousness was puzzled by how one can be devoted to social justice and also marvel at 'orchids' (wonder at the universe). Now he thinks one should give up trying to hold them together. Only religion can hold reality and justice in a single vision, but he is not religious. For him, religion is something to do with one's solitude and should not enter into the world of social/political argument. What it has to lose is any metaphysical baggage while keeping a vague sense of 'God'. Pragmatist theists 'do have to get along without personal immortality, providential intervention, the efficacy of sacraments, the virgin birth, the risen Christ, the covenant with Abraham', for these would control our environment and those things are better seen as mysteries. *Kierkegaard's belief in incarnation is compared to a mother's belief in the goodness of her sociopathic son. But believing in God is being in love without reason; it has and should have nothing to do with predicting and controlling anything. It is to be excluded from public discourse: the dualism between private and public is absolute. What this all tends to mean is that orchids get our passion and the social vision our pity and our talk: there is no one greater 'good'.

Bibliography

R. B. Brandom (ed.), *Rorty and His Critics* (Oxford, 2000); A. Malachowski, *Richard Rorty* (Chesham, 2002); R. Rorty, *Philosophy and the Mirror of Nature* (Oxford, 1980); *Contingency, Irony and Solidarity* (Cambridge, 1989); *Philosophy and Social Hope* (London and New York, 1999).

M. W. ELLIOTT

ROUSSEAU, JEAN-JACQUES

Jean-Jacques Rousseau (1712–78) was an influential but rather unrepresentative thinker of the Age of *Enlightenment. He challenged the optimistic view of human progress which often marked that age and harked back to an idyllic, primeval state of innocence in which humanity was free from the corruptions of civilization. The basic goodness and wonder of nature, physical or human, was fundamental to Rousseau's thought and sensibility. In extolling sensibility in its relation to reason, Rousseau distinguished his position from that of the French *philosophes* (philosophers); in extolling nature, and the place of humanity within it, he was a precursor of *Romanticism. Indeed, his impact on that movement was considerable: the cosmically homesick, but resolutely self-defining individual, is essentially there in Rousseau. Yet reason was certainly important to him, and freedom was fundamental to his aspirations, thus identifying him in important respects with the century to which he belonged.

A native of Geneva, Rousseau never knew his mother, who died just after he was born. This, allied with his inheritance of his father's romantic temperament, largely accounts for the sentimental and searching note which marked his life and literature. Public controversy over his work and personal quarrels somewhat characterized a life spent in several countries outside Switzerland, especially France. His religious views often featured in all this commotion. In religious conviction,

Rousseau can be regarded as standing broadly in the tradition of Deism, with a romantic colouring. Yet labels are slippery things here: on his account of things, Rousseau was an adherent of 'Theism in its truest form', which is 'limited to the *inner* worship of the Supreme God and to the eternal obligations of morality' which together constitute 'the pure and simple religion of the Gospels' (*The Social Contract*, IV.8). His views received famous expression in *Emile*, a treatment (in novel form) of the principles of education published in the same year as *The Social Contract* (1762), which advocated natural religion through the 'Profession of Faith of a Savoyard Vicar' contained in a section of it. But if he was strongly opposed to the traditional supernaturalism represented by the church, he was also the enemy of the materialistic scepticism represented by a wing of the *philosophes*. Rousseau was transparently passionate in religious conviction, and emphasized the role of innate *conscience in the apprehension of religious reality. Complex and self-absorbed, marked by pathos and paranoia, he was capable of powerful lyrical evocation of the deep unitary harmony of God, self and nature. Now, as then, it is difficult to remain indifferent to his literature, often loathed or loved. His self-revelation to readers included his autobiographical *Confessions* (1770).

Rousseau's political thought found particularly creative expression in *The Social Contract*, an attempt at developing a theory of popular sovereignty which embraced the ideals of liberty and equality and was celebrated as an ideological underpinning of the French Revolution. And the nature and course of the Revolution has led some people to see in it, and therefore in Rousseau, the prototype of modern totalitarianism. However, his political thought has given rise to a number of different and conflicting interpretations, being regarded either as championing or as threatening social and political freedoms. Here one must distinguish between the logic and the intentions of the work. Whatever certain formulations suggest and wherever the logic of his system leads, Rousseau's libertarian and egalitarian aims were not intended to support a totalitarian regime. He celebrated the republican glory of Rome, as he conceived it, and, as a Genevan patriot, gave highest praise to *Calvin's political wisdom and genius. 'Whatever changes time may bring to our religious observances, so long as the love of country and of liberty is a living reality with us, the memory of that great man will be held in veneration' (*The Social Contract*, II.7). Rousseau's interest in the self means that there is a strand in his work that encourages individualism, as opposed to totalitarianism, although a *heroic* individual, like Napoleon, might be taken as the synthesis of apparently opposing tendencies.

Rousseau's writings and interests ranged considerably, including articles on music and botanical observations apart from the better known works on social themes. He rejected intellectual endeavours whose ultimate aim was not self improvement or social improvement. In this, he influenced the thinking of no less a person than Immanuel *Kant on the fundamental purpose of philosophical work. It is easy to discount the larger portion of Rousseau's work today, but it would be a mistake to do so. Quite apart from its importance for intellectual history, it reveals, if in an extreme and idiosyncratic form, the profound longing for an integrated life which constitutes both the pathos and the hope of the sensitive human being.

Bibliography

K. Barth, *Protestant Theology in the Nineteenth Century* (London, 1972); R. Grimsley, *Jean-Jacques Rousseau* (Brighton, 1983); P. Riley (ed.), *The Cambridge Companion to Rousseau* (Cambridge, 2001); R. Wokler, *Rousseau* (Oxford, 1995).

S. N. WILLIAMS

ROYCE, JOSIAH

Josiah Royce (1855–1916) was born in impoverished circumstances in Grass Valley, a mining community in the Sierra Nevada mountains of California. He received his philosophic education in the university of his home state, at Johns Hopkins, and at Göttingen, where he studied under Lotze. He became professor of the history of philosophy at Harvard (1878) and one of the most influential American philosophers of the period of classical American philosophy from the late nineteenth to the early twentieth century. Along with F. H. Bradley he was one of the two most important of the English-speaking idealist philsophers.

Royce developed a religiously oriented brand of absolute *idealism. In his earliest writings Royce was inclined to follow *Kant in denying the possibility of ultimate metaphysical solutions except by ethical postulates, but in his first book, *The Religious Aspect of Philosophy* (1885), he comes out as a fully fledged metaphysical idealist.

This book made a profound impression, especially with Royce's arguments that the very possibility of error cannot be formulated except in terms of an absolute *truth or rational totality which requires an absolute knower. Like the individual parts of a sentence, all things find their condition and meaning in the final totality to which they belong. This means that the world must thus be either through and through of the same nature as our mind, or else utterly unknowable. But to affirm the unknowable is to involve oneself in contradictions.

It is possible to know truth beyond ourselves because we are a part of the logos, or world-mind. Science successfully depends on description, but appreciation must precede description, and consequently ideals must be deeper than mechanistic scientific accounts. The natural order of the world has to be also a moral order. Our ethical obligation is to the moral order, and in the view of Royce this takes the form of loyalty to the great *community of all individuals.

Despite the fact that his intellectual environment at Harvard was increasingly dominated by the *pragmatism of which his close friend William *James was a leading proponent, Royce remained committed to idealism. However, the later Royce tended to give the themes of his idealist thought a more naturalistic social foundation in contrast to the abstract metaphysical foundation evident in his earlier writings. This may well have been due to the influence of the pragmatist Charles S. Peirce.

Bibliography

J. Clendenning, *The Life and Thought of Josiah Royce* (Vanderbilt, 1998); G. Trotter, *On Royce* (California, 2001).

C. CAMPBELL-JACK

RUSSELL, BERTRAND

Bertrand Russell (1872–1970) was a British philosopher, mathematician and later prominent social and political activist, who developed an extraordinary range of social and political interests in his long life and who, despite being among the most prominent philosophers of his age, later came to repudiate many of the philosophical positions he had at one time or another held. Key philosophical work included the theory of descriptions, concerned with names and reference, the theory of types, and the (logical) foundations of mathematics (in his major work with A. N. *Whitehead, *Principia Mathematica*, 1910–13). He was especially influential in various forms of *logical positivism and in generating interest in the related work of the early *Wittgenstein. In later life he was a strong campaigner for nuclear disarmament and an ardent pacifist.

Of particular interest to Christian apologetics, however, is Russell's persistent and vehemently expressed *atheism, which is perhaps better understood as a concerted philosophical response to his Christian upbringing. His later attempts to live out various social forms of his anti-religious beliefs, such as extended family/school communities which deliberately eschewed any Christian moral basis, were generally unhappy, although one could not fault him for lacking the courage of his convictions.

The reader looking for an articulate account of his atheism on a level with his many other writings will perhaps be disappointed by the main presentation of his argument, a celebrated essay entitled 'Why I am Not a Christian', originally given as a lecture in 1927. In it he claims that religion is the cause of great misery; there are no satisfactory proofs for the existence of God; there is persistent and violent disagreement among the religious; Christian teaching provokes fear in its adherents and despises non-Christians. These are not entirely unfair points, but neither are they particularly original, and they certainly do not engage with the core elements of traditional Christian faith. Typically for its logical-positivist time, though with no little panache, this and related pieces reduce Christianity to a series of disconnected truth-claims which are then, of course, shown to be empirically unverifiable. With the benefit of hindsight this seems to tell us as much about Russell's evaluative framework as about Christianity.

Readers aware of such perspectives in his work will nevertheless find his *History of Western Philosophy* (1946) immensely enjoyable, while his *Problems of Philosophy* (1912) remains an admirable brief introduction to some key questions.

Bibliography
B. Russell, *Why I am Not a Christian and Other Essays on Religion and Related Subjects* (London, 1957); R. Monk, *Bertrand Russell*, 2 vols. (London, 1996–2001).

R. S. Briggs

SAGAN, CARL EDWARD

Carl Sagan (1934–96) was one of the leading scientists of the twentieth century, both in his capacity for fundamental research and in his outstanding ability as a popularizer of *science and public spokesperson for the scientific community. He was professor of astronomy and space sciences and director of the Laboratory for Planetary Studies at Cornell University. Trained in both astronomy and biology, he made key contributions to the study of planetary atmospheres, planetary surfaces, the history of the earth and exobiology. He also played a leading role in the *Mariner, Viking, Voyager* and *Galileo* spacecraft expeditions to the planets. An influential advocate of the search for extraterrestrial intelligence (SETI), he defended its importance both to the public and to funding bodies. He co-founded and served as president of the Planetary Society.

His television series *Cosmos* was seen by 500 million people in sixty countries, and the accompanying book was on the *New York Times* bestseller list for seventy weeks. He was the author of a number of other best-selling science books including the novel *Contact*, which became a major motion picture. At the time of Reagan's Star Wars project, Sagan became an outspoken critic, raising the scenario that a major nuclear exchange could lead to a smoke-shrouded, deeply frozen earth, the so-called 'nuclear winter'.

His importance for Christian apologetics is fourfold. First he challenges the church to take science seriously. He emphasized the importance of scientific literacy and education, demonstrating in his own work the fascination that people have with the big questions of science, whether our own origins or alien life. He reminds scientists of the importance of communication and of the opportunities for apologists to engage with people's interest with the universe. Secondly, he presented science in a way that engaged not just the intellect but also the *imagination, stressing its wonder and awe. For those who want to communicate the Creator of such a universe, the challenge is to use both intellect and imagination likewise. Thirdly, Sagan represented many in Western culture who want to find evidence. While backing SETI, he was at the same time publicly highly sceptical of alien visitation or the paranormal, stating that 'extraordinary claims require extraordinary evidence'. He wanted people to ask the difficult questions in science, politics, economics and religion. This sense of questioning and the importance of evidence even in a postmodern context is important to note for apologetics. Fourthly, Sagan was seen by some Christians to be a militant atheist. While it is true that he was highly critical of the claims of faith healing, creationism and the structures of the church, his position was more one of *agnosticism. His wife and collaborator Ann Druyan writes of his final illness, 'Contrary to the fantasies of the fundamentalists, there was no deathbed conversion, no last-minute refuge taken in a comforting vision of a heaven or an afterlife. For Carl, what mattered most was what was true, not merely what would make us feel better.' Sagan was committed to truth but did not see that truth in Christianity or *atheism. He wrote, 'To be certain of the existence of God and to be certain of the nonexistence of God seem to me to be the confident extremes in a subject so riddled with doubt and uncertainty as to inspire very little confidence indeed. A wide range of intermediate positions seems admissible, and considering the enormous emotional energies with which the subject is invested, a questioning, courageous and open mind seems to be the essential tool for narrowing the range of our collective ignorance on the subject of the existence of God' (*Broca's Brain*, 1979, p. 311). Christians will want to affirm the honesty of a questioning, courageous and open mind, but to say that science is not enough. Indeed, only the self-revelation of God can give us dependable truth about himself, and that is supremely shown not in the cosmos but in Jesus.

Bibliography

C. Sagan and I. S. Shklovskii, *Intelligent Life in the Universe* (New York, 1966); C. Sagan and R. Turco, *A Path Where No Man Thought: Nuclear Winter and the End of the Arms Race* (New York, 1990); C. Sagan, *Broca's Brain: Reflections on the Romance of Science* (New York, 1979); *Cosmos* (New York, 1980); *Contact: A Novel* (New York, 1985); *The Demon-Haunted World: Science as a Candle in the Dark* (New York, 1996); *Billions and Billions: Thoughts on Life and Death at the Brink of the Millennium* (New York, 1997).

D. WILKINSON

SARTRE, JEAN-PAUL

Jean-Paul Sartre (1905–80) was France's leading existentialist philosopher, a social and left-wing political activist, and an influential writer and playwright. Among his best-known works are *Being and Nothingness*, *Nausea* and *Critique of Dialectical Reason*.

Foundational to Satre's philosophy was the assumption that God does not exist, and this non-existence sets the agenda for both philosophy and life. If God existed, Sartre acknowledged, we would have a basis for meaning, *truth and morals, and for human existence and living. Since there is no God, we have none of these things. 'The existentialist finds it very troublesome that God does not exist, because with him disappears all possibility of finding values in an intelligible world; nor can there be any *a priori* good ... for we are precisely on a plane where nothing exists but men. I am very much vexed that this should be so' (*Existentialism is a Humanism*).

In a world without God 'man makes himself'. '*Existentialism is a humanism', that is, its philosophy rests solely on human beings. The individual alone must assert her or his freedom and humanness in the face of an absurd and hostile world. Everything else starts with a fixed essence or nature that makes it what it is. But for human beings, existence precedes essence; what we are is not given, we have to create it. We are nothing other than what we make of ourselves.

This freedom and responsibility to create our own essence is both glorious and terrifying. But the terror outweighs the glory as so much is at stake. We hang on the brink of nothingness; we are without essence and absurd. We have no-one to guide or help us. If there were a God, we would not be alone. But we are alone, 'alone in the midst of a monstrous silence, alone and free, without recourse or excuse, irrevocably condemned, condemned to be free'.

Sartre did much to highlight the absurdity

and hopelessness of a world without God. In response we might point out that in fact it is unrealistic to consign everything to absurdity and hopelessness, since in real life we find that the world and human beings operate within a given structure that is in fact coherent and meaningful. Nor do we have the wide freedom to create meaning and truth and values that Sartre suggests. Though we are able to exercise freedom, we cannot create all things; much of the creating has already been done.

Bibliography

S. Priest (ed.), *Sartre: Basic Writings* (London, 2000).

P. HICKS

SATAN, EXISTENCE OF

The existence of Satan has long been the object of the sceptics' doubts and of the scoffers' derision. 'Modernity', Edouard-Henri Wéber writes, 'usually refers the devil back to mythological superstition, and theologians prefer to remain silent on that topic.' The doctrine, however, must be clearly perceived before it can be judged as true or false.

Contours of Christian belief

The name 'Satan' is a mere transcription of *śāṭān*, the Heb. word used in the OT for an 'adversary', 'accuser', especially in a judicial situation (e.g. Ps. 109:6). In three passages, it is used for a seemingly superhuman agent: for Job's slanderer among the angelic beings in the divine court (Job 1:6–12; 2:1–7), for the one who incited David to sin (1 Chr. 21:1) and for the high priest's accuser, who was standing by his side before the Lord to accuse him (Zech. 3:1). The Septuagint translates *śāṭān* with *diabolos*, which has the same basic meaning. The inter-testamental period in *Judaism saw the development of demonology, and of Satan (also called Belial[r] and Beelzebul[b] amongst other names). He was recognized as the prince of all demons, the arch-foe of God and of the elect and the fountainhead of *evil both moral and physical. Persian influence may have helped in the process, especially through the Zoro-astrian model of the conflict between Spenta Mainyu and Angra Mainyu, the good and the hostile spirits, who both emanated from Ahura Mazda, but deep differences warn us not to overplay such an influence. An emphasis on

Satan, and on his emerging consort or avatar, Antichrist, is typical of apocalyptic literature.

The NT took over most of the current vocabulary and representations of Judaism, and it pictures Christ's work of redemption as victory – a paradoxical victory won through shed blood and shameful death – over the devil. (In Rev. 12, Michael is represented as the champion because the battle is waged in heaven, but however we construe his relationship to *Jesus Christ, v. 11 makes it clear that the decisive weapon of the Satan's defeat is the 'blood of the Lamb'.) The alliance of Satan, the evil one (the translation to be preferred in Matt. 6:13 and John 17:15), with the flesh and the world is noteworthy, and 'the whole world' is under his 'control' (1 John 5:19). Eph. 2:2 calls him 'the ruler of the kingdom of the air', who arouses unceasing rebellion throughout humankind. Paul also uses the phrase 'the god of this age' (2 Cor. 4:4), which should be understood in the subjective sense, as Satan effectively usurps God's role in human life (see 1 Cor. 8:5–6 for the distinction between what is true subjectively and what is true objectively). The symbolism in the book of Revelation elaborates the theme of the ape-like imitation of the trinitarian God by the devil. Not only is the first beast clearly a counterfeit Christ (13:3; 17:8), but this Antichrist receives his power and mission from the dragon as Christ does from the Father. The second beast is a prophetic agent who provides the inspiration for his universal worship, a parody of the Holy Spirit's role on behalf of the Lord Jesus. The 'dragon' probably recalls the Leviathan of OT passages (Isa. 27:1). This identification of the devil is joined with that of the 'ancient [or "original", *archaios*] serpent' of Gen. 3 in Rev. 12:9 and 20:2, something to which Paul also witnesses (Rom. 16:20; cf. Gen. 3:15; Luke 10:19; 2 Cor. 11:3).

Christian belief responds to the biblical data. It affirms the existence of a 'personal' and supreme agent of evil, the evil one, also called the devil or Satan, who is active among created 'spirits' in an invisible layer of the universe. From a Christian, monotheistic perspective, existence may be postulated only of the Creator and his creatures, and 'everything God created is good' (1 Tim. 4:4). So, orthodox doctrine has always been that Satan was created a good spirit (under another name) and *became* evil at some later point. This has been taught by church councils and countless teachers, starting with Tatian and including *Augustine, *Thomas Aquinas and *Calvin, down to Pope Paul VI, who spoke of the devil, on 15 November 1972, as 'alive, spiritual, perverted and perverting'. It was, apparently, *Tertullian who introduced the questionable exegesis that reads Satan's initial rebellion into Isa. 14:12–20 and Ezek. 28:12–19 to buttress this understanding (*Against Marcion*, 2.10; 5.11, 17). In the wake of this interpretation, the Latin translation *lucifer* for Isaiah's 'morning star' (lit. 'bright one', an allusion to the planet Venus as a metaphor for the past glory of the king of Babylon) came into use for the devil. This cannot be relied upon. There are, however, other scriptural indications which do confirm the doctrinal construction. In 1 Tim. 5:21 there is a reference to election among *angels; 2 Pet. 2:4 and Jude 6 speak of angels having forsaken their *archē* ('principle' or 'authority'). Christian doctrine, here, agrees with first-century Judaism, and also finds an echo even in the Qur'an, where Satan (also called Eblis, a name probably derived from *diabolos*) rebels as he refuses to bow down before Adam. He becomes the tempter and the arch-enemy, and is then cursed and stigmatized as the 'stoned' one (2.32ff.; 4.117f.; 7.10–17; 15.31–35).

René Girard, therefore, is inaccurate when he writes that traditional Christian theology refuses Satan the status of 'being' or 'real existence'. This is rather Girard's own choice, as he interprets the biblical character Satan as the 'mimetic' mechanism (scapegoating) personified. Since *Schleiermacher opened the way, Protestant liberalism (e.g. P. *Tillich) has argued against traditional teaching with regard to the person of Satan. Theologians of modernistic leanings usually agree with Christian Duquoc that Satan is 'a symbol that prevents trivialising evil … a regulative figure of our own self-understanding, not a person, a tempter'. Georges Tavard labours hard in the name of hermeneutics to undermine a literal reading of Bible and tradition.

Karl *Barth produced a daring piece of speculation when he rejected outright the idea that the devil and demons were first created and later fell from their original estate. Yet the demythologization he employs does not deny their existence but represents them as the dynamic form and expression of 'nothingness', and for that very reason, they are not nothing. 'Nothingness' itself is produced as a kind of counterpart of creation, as what is rejected by God's choice and by his approval of being which he creates.

Efforts to deny proper existence to Satan (and to the demons) as far as Scripture is concerned are hardly convincing. They appear to succeed, under the guise of hermeneutics, only when an alien world-view and unbiblical presuppositions are forced upon the texts. Barth's invention conflicts with the biblical references to a rebellion among angels, and also with several texts that assign the status of creatures to hostile spiritual powers (Rom. 8:38; Col. 1:16; cf. Gen. 3:1). Georges Tavard criticized Barth's solution as 'purely verbal' and spotted 'the influence of latent Manicheism' in it. The whole theory about 'nothingness' has received devastating blows at John *Hick's hands (*Evil and the God of Love*, pp. 132–150) and even Paul Ricœur has called it 'weak compromise'.

Against unsatisfactory attempts at revision, therefore, Christian belief should be defined by the twofold affirmation of Satan's creation as a celestial being (2 Pet. 2:10; Jude 8), and of his subsequent apostasy through which he became the supreme evildoer. The first element involves Satan's distinct existence and, more generally, the rejection of Manichean dualism. Despite recurring temptations in the Manichean direction, the Christian faith denounces the deceptive symmetry of God (or Christ) and the devil and a 'substantial' view of evil. Especially, the medieval and popular representation of the devil as the master and quasi god of *hell lacks biblical warrant: the 'lake of fire' is the punishment prepared *for* the devil (Matt. 25:41; Rev. 20:10). The second element rules out fatalism, since, in the evil one himself, actual evil issued from the exercise of created freedom, and it also rules out any optimistic reduction of evil to some wrong choices made by human individuals. Both elements, also, are opposed to the speculative interpretation of Satan as 'the dark YHWH', the black side of God, as it denies both creaturely status and ultimate malignity.

Accurately delineating the Christian belief in the existence of Satan and warding off misconstruals already contributes to its defence. Bringing to light its agreement with Scripture entails that the arguments in favour of scriptural trustworthiness indirectly establish that demonology. In this light, one may challenge the widespread unbelief about Satan and explanation in terms of *mythology. On what ground are they founded? Where does this modern assurance of knowing more about the invisible world than the Bible come from? Seldom is *any* basis for such an assurance apparent. From a formal standpoint, at least, biblical references are vastly different from mythological talk. Neither is the metaphysical and logical consistency of the Christian view demonstrably jeopardized, at least if one allows that the prior and more general doctrine of evil is worth some consideration.

Positive arguments point to aspects of experience that are best accounted for in the framework of the traditional doctrine of Satan. The first deals with direct, particular, evidence; the other two, with the import of general dimensions of the human plight.

Special evidence of demonic activity

Since Satan is called 'the prince of demons', the claim that has been made by many pastors, exorcists and 'possessed' people (mainly after deliverance) that they have encountered evil spirits, identified them and fought against them as real agents, is apologetically relevant. Johann Christoph Blumhardt's famous experience, with the cure of the demonized Gottliebin Dittus (after a two-year struggle), changed his theology and led him to a strong affirmation of the spirit world. Others have undergone similar changes; for example, Pfarrer Otto Rodenberg, whose pastoral encounter of powers of darkness overturned the demythologizing hermeneutics he had been taught. The quality of many witnesses, the details in their accounts, lend credibility to what they say (e.g. C. P. Wagner and F. D. Pennoyer [eds.], *Wrestling with Dark Angels: Toward a Deeper Understanding of the Supernatural Forces in Spiritual Warfare* [Venture, 1990]; D. R. Jacobs, *Demons* [Scottdale, 1972]).

Prejudice is so strong, however, against receiving such a testimony, that many dialogue partners will remain unmoved. There are also intrinsic weaknesses in the experiences invoked. In a number of cases, a purely psychiatric explanation is plausible. Despite the very stringent criteria set up for exorcists in long-established churches, the suspicion may be raised that the strangest phenomena might have natural causes. To a high degree, communal beliefs and expectations shape the expression of inner disturbances. The direct empirical proof of the existence of Satan is not as powerful as it might seem.

The more-than-human dimensions of evil

The experience of sinfulness appears to witness to a power, a depth and a sweep far beyond what can be traced back to the individual heart's decisions. The phenomenon of temptation strongly suggests that a tempter is at work. The phenomenon of sinful behaviour includes that of bondage and being driven by mad impulses to unimaginable extremes of evilness, almost against the sinner's will, witnessing to the force of another factor. Paul Ricœur unfolds the significance of the Genesis serpent and later Satan by pointing to the 'already there' of evil, to its prevenient tradition that moulds each awakening consciousness, and then to what he calls 'a cosmic structure of evil'. The *quantity* of human evil reaches supra-human proportions; it defies and crushes any attempt at imagination. The *quality* lies beyond words and people spontaneously cry out 'Devilish!' in response to the refinements of cruelty, the distortion of all values and the way the best intentions of moral agents are thwarted or, worse, channelled into the commission of heinous crimes. Is not a Satan uncovering himself in all of this?

Admittedly, one may criticize the argument. The evidence is almost co-extensive with human life, and so complex that no-one can dream of mastering its import. Psychology and social sciences do offer alternative explanations, referring, for example, to mechanisms of projection. Nevertheless, a persuasive case may be made that all their schemes fall short of a satisfactory account of the sinner's experience. There is a satanic residue of otherness and excess that is unexplained.

One may not evade the argument by reducing the status of Satan to that of an expression, in mythological symbol, of evil's supra-human dimensions as perceived in experience. This treatment fails to meet the theoretical challenge of how one accounts for these dimensions. Unless the tragic view is adopted (see below), there is no answer, and 'as if' talk cloaks the fact that thought is shirking its duty. Since there is moral evil before, above and beyond the exercise of human will, and evil happens only through created freedom, there must be a supra-human evil agent; there must be a devil.

The non-metaphysical character of evil

The 'tragic' view, which Ricœur regards as ultimately invincible, strictly assigns evil to a 'dark' side of deity, to a malevolent part of divine nature. But the reference may be broadened and extended to all systems that interpret evil as a constituent part of *reality as such, as a matter of essence and principle: all *metaphysical* explanations of evil. Apart from the tragic view in the strict sense (intra-divine dualism), these include dualism of the Manichean line and more moderate forms such as the Neo-*Platonic one (the uncreated principle of matter is the source of evils). Evil is said to be an element in being, or another being, or 'non-being' understood as real, as a metaphysical factor. In such perspectives, Satan remains at best as its symbol.

A systematic critique of metaphysical explanations has been offered by H. Blocher, *Evil and the Cross: Christian Thought and the Problem of Evil* (ET, Leicester, 1994). Some writers call metaphysical evil the limitations of finite existence; whether felicitous or infelicitous; this use is not at issue here. Objections are raised against theories which explain moral evil and its consequences, 'capital' evil in Christian eyes, as entailed by an essential ingredient of reality (whether a bad god, non-being, finiteness, etc.). Analysis reveals that they tend to deny, overtly or covertly, the evilness of evil, and hence the turn they often take to optimistic conclusions. The opposing non-metaphysical view traces back the actuality of evil to the use (misuse and abuse) of freedom. In view of supra-human evil in experience, it infers a devil.

Apart from the logical impossibility that two first principles, or *absolutes, could ever meet (for they have nothing in common, no common space even to collide, within or without God), several arguments carry considerable weight. Metaphysical interpretations of evil will account for (interdependent) features of experience. The bond between moral evil and freedom is one of the most persistent data of *conscience: guilt dissolves in natural necessity and 'tragic' views look suspiciously like attempts at self-excuse. Any symmetry between good and evil must be exposed as an illusion. Even Manicheans, probably the most consistent dualists of all, still refrained from calling the evil principle 'god'. The deep non-symmetry corresponds to the creaturely status of Satan, the liar, not the lie: the evil one is *not* 'evil in person'. Satan is not omnipresent or omniscient. Jonathan *Edwards could write, 'Although the devil be exceedingly crafty and subtle, yet he is one of the greatest fools

and blockheads in the world, as the subtlest of wicked men are.'

When one further explores the experience of moral evil, one endorses the perception of the Church Fathers and especially Augustine that evil is no substance with existence *per se*; it is relative and parasitic; it is the perversion, privation and corruption of the good. And so it is in Satan, according to Christian doctrine.

Several recent writers, while they speak of the devil in personal terms, add the qualification that his is an empty, depersonalized personality. While this emphasis may be used to elude the biblical and traditional affirmation, it highlights a legitimate theme for reflection, with some apologetic relevance.

The personality of the angels, and therefore of Satan, while it plainly implies created freedom and the ability to plan and to act, seems to lack an essential dimension of personality as it is realized in God and in God's image-creature: a bond of ontological community. The persons in the Trinity are one essence, numerically. Human persons are of one essence, specifically. But angels are pure individuals, each with his own essence; they are not members of one another. Is their personality less perfect? It might explain the biblical language of *forces* in their case (winds, powers) and a possible correspondence with animals.

Furthermore, though it is no ingredient of being, sin destructively affects being, as the metaphor of corruption implies. As Satan contributes to the depersonalization of his children-slaves and foolishly consenting victims, he must undergo the same process and become a vacuous, stultified personality, a personality deprived of the core of personal life: love.

Bibliography

Special issues of journals: *Churchman*, 94.3 (1980), pp. 197–253; 'Satan', *Lumière et Vie*, 15.78 (May–August 1966); 'Le Diable sur mesure', *Lumière et Vie*, 42.212 (April 1993).

K. Barth, *Church Dogmatics*, III/3 (Edinburgh: original 1950), §§50–51; G. Bazin and 32 others, *Satan*, Etudes Carmélitaines (Bruges and Paris, 1948); R. Girard, *Je vois Satan tomber du ciel comme l'éclair*, Biblio-Essais (Paris, 1999); J.-L. Marion, *Prolégomènes à la charité* (Paris, ²1991); P. Ricœur, *La Symbolique du mal* (Paris, 1960; ET, *The Symbolism of Evil* [Boston, 1967]); J. B. Russell, *The Devil: Perceptions of Evil from Antiquity to Primitive Christianity* (London,

1977); *Satan: The Early Christian Tradition* (London, 1981); *Lucifer: The Devil in the Middle Ages* (London, 1984); *Mephistopheles: The Devil in the Modern World* (London, 1986); G. Tavard, *Satan* (Paris and Ottawa, 1988); E.-H. Wéber, 'Démons', in J.-Y. Lacoste (ed.), *Dictionnaire critique de théologie*, (Paris, 1998), pp. 310a–311b.

H. A. G. BLOCHER

SAYERS, DOROTHY L.

Dorothy L. Sayers (1893–1957), English writer, was born in Oxford. She received a scholarship to Somerville College, Oxford, where she studied modern languages. In 1915 Sayers graduated from Oxford with first class honours. She left academia to work at Blackwell Publishing and later served as a copywriter for a London advertising firm. Although she wrote numerous theological essays, plays and poetry and translated Dante's *The Divine Comedy*, she is best known for her fourteen crime fiction volumes.

Her crime fiction period began in 1923, with the publication of *Whose Body?*, and ended in 1937 when *Busman's Honeymoon* appeared in print. Between 1938 and 1946 her attention focused on theological essays and plays of a religious nature. This shift of genres has caused some to conclude she experienced a conversion in the late 1930s; however, she 'appears to have been a committed, orthodox Christian from the beginning of her career' (Kenney, p. 184). Neither should one assume the change was motivated by a desire to write 'serious' literature. In fact, Sayers utilized crime fiction to explore the complexities of the human condition and its affairs in the rawest forms. She argues that to ignore humanity's sad state of affairs leads to chaos, crime and death. The alternative is to stress human responsibility and, in particular, the positive value of work. Clearly, her central character, Lord Peter Wimsey, is a model worker who finds his detective undertakings a source of great joy. Through his sleuthing activities on behalf of the needy, Wimsey depicts how good work in the chaotic world overcomes *evil.

Sayers' later writings addressed theological matters and the future of Western culture. In particular, she focused on church-goers' complacency and derided England as 'being only "nominally Christian"' (Kenney, p. 186).

For example, in 'The Dogma is the Drama' (*Creed or Chaos?*) Sayers explores religious ignorance in modern society and argues it is filled with people who are ignorant of Christ's teachings, but who do practise the 'Seven Deadly Virtues'.

Bibliography

D. Coomes, *Dorothy L. Sayers: A Careless Rage for Life* (Colorado Springs and Oxford, 1992); D. Gaillard, *Dorothy L. Sayers* (New York, 1981); C. Kenney, *The Remarkable Case of Dorothy L. Sayers* (Kent, 1990); A. Loades (ed.), *Spiritual Writings* (London, 1993); D. L. Sayers, *Creed or Chaos?* (Manchester, 1996); *The Man Born to be King* (San Francisco, 1990); *The Mind of the Maker* (Westport, 1971).

J. E. MᶜDERMOND

SCHAEFFER, FRANCIS

Francis August Schaeffer (1912–84) was born in Philadelphia, Pennsylvania, the only child of working-class parents. They were merely nominal Christians, and Schaeffer himself became an agnostic while at high school. However, at the age of eighteen, after reading the Bible over a period of six months, he was converted to Christianity. He was convinced that it was the Bible, and not the philosophy which he had also been reading, that provided the answers to life's deepest questions.

Despite opposition from his father, Schaeffer began studying at Hampden-Sydney College in Virginia with a view to ordination. He graduated *magna cum laude* in 1935, and in the same year married Edith Seville, the daughter of former missionaries in China. Schaeffer attended Westminster Theological Seminary for two years before transferring to Faith Theological Seminary, from which he graduated in 1938. He was the first minister to be ordained by the newly-established Bible Presbyterian Church, which emerged from the disputes between evangelicals and liberals within the mainstream denominations.

In 1948, after three pastorates spanning ten years, the Schaeffers moved to Switzerland as missionaries serving under the Independent Board for Presbyterian Foreign Missions. They resigned from the Mission Board in June 1955, convinced that the Lord was leading them to be a demonstration of his reality, and opened their home as L'Abri (Shelter). Over the years that followed, this became a place where thousands – many of them young and disillusioned – experienced and accepted the truth of Christianity. The publication of several books (from 1968 onwards) and the production of two film series brought Schaeffer to the notice of a much larger audience. By the 1970s he was widely regarded by evangelicals as one of the leading apologists for the faith. He was also an outspoken critic of *abortion. The work of L'Abri continued to develop with the establishment of other branches throughout Europe, Korea and the United States. Schaeffer died in 1984 after a six-year battle with cancer.

His apologetics

Schaeffer's apologetics developed from his conversations with individuals and not from any theoretical methodology. Indeed, he saw himself primarily as an evangelist who covered intellectual and cultural questions in order that he might reach people influenced in their thinking by anti-Christian concepts and values. He was convinced that a change in the concept of *truth, and of how people come to a knowledge of truth, was the most crucial problem facing Christianity and its evangelism. He believed that before one could effectively share the truth of the Christian gospel with a person, one needed to deal with the non-Christian presuppositions that affected how they reasoned. Thus he placed considerable emphasis in his apologetics on a critique of contemporary thought since the time of *Hegel and its shift from absolute to relative truth. Schaeffer also sought to show individuals how their personal presuppositions were inconsistent with the truth of the external world and the nature of mankind. Unlike Cornelius *Van Til, under whom he had studied at Westminster, Schaeffer maintained that one could discuss truth with a non-Christian without his or her first accepting the existence of God as an essential presupposition.

Schaeffer's emphasis on the primacy of ideas and his analysis of modern thought has been strongly criticized by a number of evangelical writers as simplistic or even inaccurate. However, he opened up the whole question of ideas, how we think and what influences our thinking, to the ordinary Christian. By freeing *epistemology from an academic elite, Schaeffer made it available to the rank-and-file Christian as an apologetic tool. Furthermore, he never claimed that his books contained the final word on any subject but that they put the issues on the table for discussion. The fact that many evangelical scholars were inspired to address intellectual and cultural questions is testimony to the effectiveness of Schaeffer's ministry.

His spirituality

Schaeffer has also been criticized for being too rationalistic in his apologetics, in that he gives the impression of trying to *argue* a person into the kingdom of God. This fails to recognize, however, that *how* he conducted his apologetics was as crucial as *what* he said. For Schaeffer, prayer and the *Holy Spirit were central to the everyday life of L'Abri, and this spirituality underpinned his apologetics. Indeed, L'Abri had been established to be a demonstration of the reality of God, and, as Edith Schaeffer later noted, those who visited it could not 'shake off' the truth of what they had experienced there.

His relevance

In an age that disputes the very notion of objective truth, is there a role for the apologetics of Francis Schaeffer? His insight that all people live according to some sort of value system; his willingness to engage with the individual and so build a personal apologetic bridge; his utter commitment to the absolute truth of the Bible as containing the only answer for all people; and his emphasis on *community and love in Christian relationships as the final apologetic; all this is extremely relevant to a society in search of the relational but in need of true meaning.

Bibliography

S. R. Burson and J. L. Walls, *C. S. Lewis & Francis Schaeffer* (Downers Grove, 1998); L. T. Dennis (ed.), *Letters of Francis Schaeffer* (Eastbourne, 1986); F. A. Schaeffer, *The God Who is There* (London, 1968); *Escape from Reason* (London, 1968); *True Spirituality* (Wheaton, 1971); *He is There and He is not Silent* (London, 1972).

B. A. FOLLIS

SCHLEIERMACHER, FRIEDRICH

Friedrich Daniel Ernst Schleiermacher (1768–1834), known as the father of liberal theology, was nevertheless one of Christianity's most ardent advocates. The Moravian piety of his childhood was later complemented with the study of rational dogmatics and an enthusiastic embracing of *romanticism. He read *Kant and translated *Plato, and is known especially for his systematic theology, *The Christian Faith* (1821–2, 1830–1), and his early work *On Religion* (1799, 1821), the first great apology for Christianity in modern times.

Coming of age in a period of political and social instability, Schleiermacher was motivated by his own youthful doubts and his search for a faith with integrity, yet in continuity with the confessions of the historic church. All of this combined with his artistic temperament to give him a sense of solidarity and friendship with the literary despisers of religion. Indeed he affirms his strong call to the task of apology. He has been driven to his work, he says, 'all petty notions' crushed with 'heavenly power'.

Schleiermacher's apologetic strategy is three-fold. He first attempts to draw a bridge between the artistic spirit and the religious one, and secondly, to ground religion not in knowing or doing, but in intuition. Thirdly, he gives a stunning indictment of institutional Christianity and its ties to the State. This last endeavour can at times sound like a dismissal of all ecclesial institutions, but Schleiermacher's own personal commitment to the church (he advocated the union of Reformed and Lutheran churches in the 'Old Prussian Church') and the centrality of ecclesiology within his later dogmatics mitigates any of his earlier more individualistic leanings. Today, as was true in the early nineteenth century, many an apology for faith must start with a distancing from much that goes on in the public square.

The bridge Schleiermacher builds between art and religion is through the common sense of the transcendent. The central thesis of *On Religion* is encapsulated in the famous words of the third edition, that 'true religion is sense and taste for the Infinite'. The basic premise of *On Religion*, that we contemplate all things 'in and through the Infinite' (Oman, p. 36), was to be articulated in *Christian Faith*, as the sense of 'absolute dependence'. The sense and taste of which Schleiermacher speaks are not feeling, so much as pre-cognitive intuition of the universe. Religion is thus not *primarily* the doing and the knowing one sees in its public face. Hence Schleiermacher draws links between the tacit passions and aspirations of artists, scientists and intellectuals, and those of religious faith. Both aspire to see the parts in terms of the whole, whatever is said or done around

the edges. Art and religion should be fellow travellers, he argues, not enemies – art without faith is barren.

Schleiermacher's theology differed from older Protestant pre-Enlightenment theology in starting with human intuitions and in de-emphasizing the fallenness of our reason and passion. While *Calvin begins by pointing out the providence of the Creator, even 'an awareness of divinity', by which nature instructs us, he nevertheless insists that we cannot know God this way, and turns to Scripture as our only point of *revelation. Where Calvin asserts the broken *imago Dei*, Schleiermacher begins with the fragile, corruptible but nevertheless present god consciousness in all. Importantly, though, god consciousness was never confused with faith. Rather, under the converting influence of the word proclaimed, this becomes the sense of sin and grace that characterizes the Christian state.

Why then, has Schleiermacher not been heralded as the apologist of the age? The answer lies partly in his irenic inclusiveness. Also it is easy to draw links between Schleiermacher's sense of absolute dependence and *Feuerbach's God as human projection. Moreover, Schleiermacher's optimism and post-millennialism were not sufficiently Christ-against-culture for the hard times and increasing apostasy that characterized the early twentieth century.

Jaroslav Pelikan explains that Schleiermacher has been overlooked because he so often appeared to be betraying his cause. Pelikan argues persuasively, however, that this betrayal is in the cause of the gospel. He identified with the world outside of faith in order that he might reorient that world to his own ends. His successors have misinterpreted or reinterpreted his ends and developed a theology of *culture. Karl Barth was the twentieth-century foil of Schleiermacher, insisting that humanity and creation are never naturally a revelation of the totally Other that is God. Schleiermacher's methods of identification and solidarity are now more commonplace in missions, but his passion for apologetics has been ignored by those who, like him, still desire to convert the world.

Bibliography

J. Calvin, *Calvin: Institutes of the Christian Religion* (Philadelphia, 1960); B. A. Gerrish, *The Prince of the Church: Schleiermacher and the Beginnings of Modern Theology* (Oregon, 2001); J. Pelikan, 'The Vocation of the Christian Apologist: A Study in Schleiermacher's

Reden', in E. H. Rian (ed.), *Christianity and World Revolution* (New York, 1963); F. Schleiermacher, *The Christian Faith* (ET, Philadelphia and Edinburgh, 1976); *On Religion: Speeches to Its Cultured Despisers* (ET, New York, 1958 [J. Oman, tr.]; Cambridge and New York, 1988 [R. Crouter, tr.]).

N. HOGGARD CREEGAN

SCHOLASTICISM

Derived from the Latin term *schola* ('school'), 'scholasticism' names a movement in medieval Christian European learning, especially in philosophy and *theology. More narrowly, it names the method of that movement. Scholasticism is noteworthy for being highly systematic and original in expression (making it dependent on refined technical vocabulary), while at the same time exhibiting careful deference to intellectual tradition (taking account of both Christian authorities and non-Christian philosophers, especially *Aristotle). Although there have been revivals and varieties of neo-scholasticism, and although medieval philosophy after *Augustine is sometimes loosely called scholastic, scholasticism is primarily identified with the high Middle Ages (mid-twelfth to mid-fourteenth centuries).

Historical context

Scholasticism developed out of a medieval learning already marked by attention to faith and tradition. The medieval church, in schools sponsored by cathedrals and monasteries, provided intellectual havens, free from purely practical and worldly concerns, where scholasticism could develop. Moreover, because of the universality of its claims, the church was also the primary motive of medieval learning. Christian faith was universally regarded as the highest wisdom, and although other 'secular' disciplines were recognized as having their proper spheres, they were understood as ordered under ultimate theological ends. The Augustinian concept of *fides quaerens intellectum* ('faith seeking understanding') captures the sense in which medieval philosophy itself can be called 'Christian', not because rational speculation was curtailed and forced to serve dogmatic religious claims, but because the mysteries of the Christian faith were the most fundamental and inspiring sources of intellectual wonder, providing a rich field of philosophical questions which the Christian thinker had a special interest in pursuing according to the gift of his natural reason.

A general consciousness of tradition also accounts for the continuity and ambition of medieval speculation. Learning was understood as the assimilation of an inherited fund of wisdom, and individual disciplines tended to be organized around authoritative texts. Reading, expositing and commenting on these texts were the primary means of mastering and joining the intellectual tradition. And, as a living tradition, it did not constitute merely a mechanism for the repetition of a closed set of ideas, but an initiation into the practices of continuing inquiry.

Scholastic method

Historians have variously identified Boethius (c. 480–524), *Eriugena (ninth century) and *Anselm (1033–1109) as the 'first' scholastics, insofar as each wrote Latin works which used Greek philosophical concepts in the explication of Christian faith. But more properly, scholasticism is noted for a distinctive literary style, reflecting a formal method, and in this sense Peter *Abelard (1079–1142) and Alexander of Hales (c. 1185–1245) are its more immediate ancestors. Abelard's *Sic et Non* ('Yes and No') presented a compendium of claims from authoritative sources – Scripture and the early Church Fathers – intentionally highlighting apparent inconsistencies as problems for theologians to solve. Perhaps taking cues from the methods of Islamic commentators, Alexander expounded a theological textbook by Peter *Lombard by composing a series of *quaestiones* ('questions') raised in the work. This format allowed Alexander to systematically handle particular issues, presenting opposing views and responding to anticipated objections.

The *quaestio* format became the characteristic method of scholastic discourse, since it gave the author a straightforward medium for defending a particular thesis while accounting for varieties of opinion and answering opposing views. In this sense, it can be considered a stylized descendant of philosophy's ancient literary form, the dialogue, fostering the back-and-forth of dialectic while directing it to the clear defence of discrete theses.

The literary form of the *quaestio* is reflected in another scholastic pedagogical practice, the oral *disputatio* or disputation. In addition to expositing texts, a master would conduct a public debate about particular theses, posed in the form of questions. Students would offer objections or responses (arguments for the negative and affirmative of the question), and the master would summarize the different arguments and offer his own solution.

These scholastic literary and oral forms transformed medieval learning. The medieval *lectio* or reading of a text was originally a running commentary on it, but as teachers strove to give more systematic exposition, they could not avoid controversial points and apparent contradictions. Rather than just commenting on the words of the texts, then, a scholastic reader could organize his exposition around particular questions raised by the text. This allowed for the acknowledgment, and proposed resolution, of difficult points, and gave the commentator more freedom to choose how to present material. Arranging sets of questions became a preferred method not just for organizing theological *summae* ('summaries', usually of the whole of theology), but also for composing more in-depth investigations of particular topics (*quaestiones disputatae*, 'disputed questions'). Thus, while medieval academic expositions had never been the slavish repetition of received doctrine, the scholastic *quaestio* format made them even better suited for dialectical progress, systematic organization and theoretical innovation.

The rise of scholasticism

The establishment of the first universities in the twelfth century is one of the most significant circumstances contributing to the development of scholasticism. In Paris and in Oxford, cathedral and monastery schools began coordinating their programmes and creating formal affiliations. Universities were given the privileges of official guild status, so that they not only had standardized curricula and authority to licence teaching, but also enjoyed a new degree of independence from both political and ecclesiastical oversight.

The second great influence on the emergence of scholasticism was a flood of newly discovered Aristotelian writings. A few of Aristotle's logical works had been available in the West for some time, and they had become fundamental to much of the medieval liberal arts curriculum, sufficient to establish Aristotle's authority. The rest of his *logic, along with his more substantive writings (*Nichomachean Ethics*, *Metaphysics*, *On the Soul*, among

others) were, however, unknown. Having been preserved in Arabic, these began to appear in translations into Latin, together with translations of formidable commentaries by Arabic philosophers (especially Avicenna and *Averroes), in the late twelfth and early thirteenth centuries. While Aristotle's philosophy was sometimes seen as a threat to traditional Christian learning, most medieval thinkers aspired to articulate an integrated picture of revealed and philosophic wisdom, and so they set themselves to the challenges of reconciling Aristotle's profound insights with Christian revelation, and of arbitrating rival, controversial interpretations of Aristotle found in his Muslim commentators.

Major figures and fundamental questions

*Thomas Aquinas is justly regarded as the most outstanding of scholastic thinkers, but other prominent figures in scholasticism include *Bonaventure, Albert the Great, Roger Bacon, *Duns Scotus and William Ockham. These, and others, represent a broad diversity of views, and this article is no place to sketch all their respective positions and review their differences, but it is possible to point to some common concerns and make general comments about some recurring themes in scholastic thought.

Although still informed by the Augustinian and neo-*Platonic tradition, it is fair to say that the style and content of scholastic philosophy was primarily shaped by the Aristotelian conceptual framework and the Aristotelian ambition of organized, systematic and comprehensive rational inquiry. Aristotelian logic, insofar as it was understood as the art of *reasoning, was the basis of the arts or philosophical education, and was considered the essential tool of theologians. Moreover, both philosophers and theologians were concerned with apparent conflicts between Aristotle and Christian faith. Particular points of controversy stand out, such as the *immortality of the soul, the creation of the world, and the providence of God, but in fact scholastic thinkers were concerned with the full range of philosophical and theological questions.

Because of the importance of logic, it has seemed to some that the underlying theoretical concern of scholastic philosophy, and of medieval philosophy more generally, was the so-called 'problem of *universals'. In fact the problem is really a set of problems about the meaning of general terms, what the mind conceives when it forms a general concept and how the significate and the concept are related to the individual particular things named by the general term. These are in turn naturally connected with such issues as the nature of the intellect, the nature of *reality and the nature of the connection between the two. Thus, while the problem of universals was raised explicitly in the context of logic (in connection with Porphyry's introduction to Aristotle's logical works), it was connected to the full spectrum of philosophical concerns, from philosophy of *language, *metaphysics and *epistemology, to philosophical *psychology, philosophy of *science, *ethics and aesthetics.

Another fundamental underlying concern of scholasticism was the relationship between philosophy and theology and between faith and reason. An Enlightenment prejudice has inspired the charge that scholasticism was dogmatic and fideist, and post-Reformation prejudice has sometimes led to the opposite charge that scholasticism was rationalistic, but in fact the scholastics were careful to avoid both extremes. The scholastics were sophisticated philosophers and as such generally regarded reason as having a genuine and proper domain, and in this sense their philosophical reflection was not constrained by external religious *authority. At the same time, scholastics were deeply faithful Christians who, far from being rationalists, regarded reason as in principle compatible with and crucially complemented by, revealed truths of faith. Thus, for instance, Thomas Aquinas could defend the authority and autonomy of reason, arguing against a double-truth theory according to which the truths of faith sometimes had to trump different truths apprehended by natural reason. In doing so he could insist, as in the *Summa Contra Gentiles*, that reason has a twofold apologetic task: to prove those aspects of the Christian faith that are available to it and to reveal as inconclusive any argument against the mysteries of the Christian faith.

Scholasticism's decline and legacy

An adequate account of the decline of scholasticism is beyond any brief summary, but reference must be made to a number of internal and external contributing pressures. In the first place, the very success of the scholastic method in facilitating discussion and focusing attention on *first principles of philosophy and theology

meant that it touched delicate issues and often provoked controversy. Disagreements about the interpretation of Aristotle and concern about the pedagogical dangers of certain interpretations even led the bishop of Paris (in 1270 and 1277) to formally condemn particular philosophical and theological theses.

The refined specialization of scholastic philosophy and theology was also both a strength and a weakness. Systematic theology served a particular purpose, but later theologians, especially reformers, emphasized other modes of reflection. Meanwhile, late-medieval universities began experiencing a kind of 'secularization', with more students aiming for careers in law and medicine and thus diminishing the need for the sophisticated philosophical distinctions employed by theologians. Furthermore, scholastic Latin, which as the technical language of a guild had become a standard and unifying tool of learning throughout Europe, was increasingly criticized for being less lovely than literary classical Latin. Eventually, new works in Europe's vernacular languages would find broader appeal outside the universities.

Other social factors displaced the authority of scholastic learning. The scientific revolution, for instance, called into question the entire traditional canon of the universities, even if in principle scholastic philosophical insights should have survived, and even helped to explain, new findings of empirical science. Broader political and economic changes in Europe also contributed to the decline of scholasticism. Indeed, much of the so-called decline of scholasticism was less a degeneration of scholastic practice than a shift in perspective, as larger cultural developments directed the attention of European intelligentsia to new forms of intellectual discourse outside the universities, where scholasticism continued in some form for centuries.

By the fifteenth and sixteenth centuries, scholasticism had many explicit opponents. These included Renaissance humanists, early modern philosophers and, of course, Protestant reformers. Thus, specialized and technical scholastic discourse was mocked as gibberish by thinkers who wrote in the vernacular to non-academic audiences, and the philosophy of Aristotle was disparaged by both Luther and *Calvin. These voices stand, however, more as reflections of the already declining authority of scholasticism than as substantive criticisms of the method or findings of scholastic philosophy and theology. Even if, by the time of the Renaissance and Reformation, scholastic discourse had proved incapable of maintaining its influence in a changing world, scholasticism at its best should be regarded as both intellectually successful and genuinely Christian. As an intellectual project, it consisted of an admirable, intergenerational community of thinkers, a tradition providing continuity and the context for creativity. As a Christian project, scholasticism boldly insisted on the unity of truth, and walked a difficult line between *fideism and *rationalism to allow reason a proper, if incomplete, domain of knowlege, confirmed and complemented by the knowledge of faith.

Bibliography

J. Marenbon, *Later Medieval Philosophy (1150–1350)* (London, 1987); J. Pieper, *Scholasticism: Personalities and Problems of Medieval Philosophy* (New York, 1960); J. Rickaby, *Scholasticism* (New York, 1908); W. Turner, 'Scholasticism', in *The Catholic Encyclopedia*, vol. 13 (New York, 1912).

J. P. HOCHSCHILD

SCHOPENHAUER, ARTHUR

The historical importance and forceful character of the philosophy of Arthur Schopenhauer (1788–1860) is often underestimated. Wagner, *Nietzsche, *Wittgenstein and, less directly, *Freud, were amongst those he influenced. He followed *Kant up to a point, in making a distinction between the thing-in-itself and the world of appearances foundational in his philosophy. But he proceeded to identify the thing-in-itself with 'will', and his major work was titled *The World as Will and Representation* (1818). By 'will' Schopenhauer did not mean anything personal, but something more akin to a blind, impersonal, purposeless force or energy which is expressed in the seething and transient world that we experience but whose inner character is unknowable. Yet Schopenhauer can describe the operation of 'will' with a vitality that gives it a mystical, if not a personal, hue.

Schopenhauer has been called the 'philosopher of pessimism'. Struck, early in life, by the misery of the human condition, he regarded suffering as the fundamental quality of life. Relief from the endless striving which makes up our existence is available through aesthetic contemplation. In principle, disinterested contemplation can free the intellect, awarding it a 'sabbath from the penal servitude of willing'. The *Platonic element in Schopenhauer's thought emerges here, for in this kind of contemplation we have access to the world of eternal Ideas. However, this is not a direct cognition of *reality; we are still trading in the world of 'representations'.

Schopenhauer promulgated one of the earliest systematically atheistic philosophies in Europe. He was certainly the first to incorporate Eastern thought into such a scheme on a major scale. *Buddhism helped to inspire his thinking about suffering, striving and existing; *Hindu thought enriched his account of a unitary reality behind the world of appearances. Schopenhauer maintained that, resigned to the commotion of existence, we should direct our actions by compassion, something he expounded with considerable power and applied to animals as well as to humans. He found connections both between Christian and Indian ideas of love and their respective ideas of salvation as an other-worldly negation of this world. These interpretations, however, are in some important respects either mistaken or questionable.

On the whole, Schopenhauer has received less attention than some other luminaries of his century, and this fact has tended to obscure the quality of his work. Quite apart from anything philosophically persuasive it contains, its bittersweet lyricism conjures up a resigned nostalgia that envelops the cosmos in a kind of bleak beauty. We have to appreciate it to understand the philosophy embodied in Wagner's developing music, Nietzsche's desperate affirmation of existence when he eventually reacted against Schopenhauer, antecedents to Freud's exploration of the unconscious and Wittgenstein's brooding mysticism. There is also profit in studying, on its own terms, the interweaving of atheistic and Eastern strands and their relation to Christianity in Schophenhauer's philosophy.

Bibliography

C. Janaway, *Schopenhauer* (Oxford, 1994); *The Cambridge Companion to Schopenhauer* (Cambridge, 1999); B. Magee, *The Philosophy of Schopenhauer* (Oxford, 1997).

S. N. WILLIAMS

SCHÜSSLER FIORENZA, ELISABETH

Elisabeth Schüssler Fiorenza, the foremost feminist biblical scholar of the twentieth century, was born in Germany in 1938. She came from a Catholic background, and went to the USA in 1970 to pursue a theological career when there proved to be no openings for a female theologian in Germany. Since 1988 she has been the Krister Stendahl Professor of Divinity at Harvard Divinity School.

The subtitle of her major book *In Memory of Her: A Feminist Theological Reconstruction of Christian Origins* gives a clear indication of the overall aims of her work. The driving insight is that, in contra-distinction to Jesus' own often radically liberating treatment of women, Christian tradition has tended to privilege the male perspective, gradually 'writing out' authentic women's spiritual experience in favour of male-centred (or 'androcentric') norms and canons. As a result, she claims, 'only those traditions and texts that critically break through patriarchal culture and "plausibility structures" have the theological authority of revelation'. The resultant 'reconstruction' of Christian origins seeks to focus on women's experience of a 'discipleship of equals'. It involves a renegotiation of the Christian *canon (as evidenced in the commentary *Searching the Scriptures* [1993–4], which she edited), and a recovery of, for example, a pre-Pauline vision of equality subsequently buried in Gal. 3:28.

Schüssler Fiorenza is perhaps the most articulate and compelling of all feminist biblical scholars. Her hermeneutic is clear in her influential Society of Biblical Literature presidential address (1988), which argues for the recognition that all biblical scholarship represents an advocacy position of some kind, with the attempt of the mainstream to label 'feminist' criticism as a fringe interest simply being a failure of white male scholarship to recognize its own biases. Her interests in *justice and equality have been in evidence in her work on the book of Revelation.

Feminist scholarship challenges any (largely male) Christian tradition which is self-perpetuating and uncritical, and Schüssler Fiorenza's work clearly represents such a challenge. Nevertheless, her work raises the issue of how to evaluate her own alternative vision once the guiding canonical vision of Scripture has been critiqued and effectively replaced. It is difficult to avoid the conclusion that what is ideologically acceptable to the feminist agenda has become the filter through which Scripture is screened, and the price one must pay for this particular reconstruction is considerable. Further, the best Christian thinking has always engaged in reflective self-critique (e.g. in the light of the cross) without thereby validating all advocacy positions. In short, one may (and should) be alert to the issues raised by feminist theological reconstruction, especially when tied to (valid) notions of justice and equality, and many forms of Christian discourse do need severe critique. The challenge, however, is to allow such critique to be guided overall by the cross and by notions of justice informed by the specific *revelation of God in Christ as recorded in the canon, and such a critique cannot be co-opted to any one ideological agenda.

Bibliography

E. Schüssler Fiorenza, *In Memory of Her: A Feminist Theological Reconstruction of Christian Origins* (London and New York, ²1994); 'The Ethics of Biblical Interpretation: Decentering Biblical Scholarship', *Journal of Biblical Literature*, 107 (1988), pp. 3–17; *Revelation: Vision of a Just World* (Minneapolis, 1991); *Rhetoric and Ethic: The Politics of Biblical Studies* (Minneapolis, 1999).

R. S. BRIGGS

SCHWEITZER, ALBERT

Albert Schweitzer (1875–1965) was an Alsatian theologian and biblical scholar who stunned the academic world in 1906 with his now classic work *Von Reimarus zu Wrede* (*The Quest of the Historical Jesus*). Schweitzer demonstrated that the portrait of *Jesus that had become dominant in nineteenth-century German Protestant thought was a construction of post-Enlightenment liberalism and bore little resemblance to historical fact. In place of this artificial construct, Schweitzer insisted that the historical Jesus had been a radical Jewish prophet who believed that the world was approaching an apocalyptic doom. This vision turned out to be false, but after his death, Jesus' disciples restructured his teaching to make it a more durable ethic, without, however, removing all trace of its origin.

Schweitzer's importance for apologetics is that he redirected the main thrust of Jesus research at a time when *Enlightenment values were being increasingly questioned. After the catastrophe of the First World War, there was a new public for his eschatological emphasis, which spoke to a world which felt that it was teetering on the edge of some cosmic disaster. Schweitzer's Jesus was a confrontational figure, who rejected the prevailing social norms in favour of a life of radical obedience to the word of God and the sacrifice which such obedience would inevitably entail.

Schweitzer's picture of Jesus relied heavily on the first two Gospels, which he regarded as completely authentic, when viewed against the background of contemporary Judaism. This went against the prevailing ideas of the time, alongside which Schweitzer emerges as very conservative in his views. Certainly his emphasis on Jesus' Jewish background is undeniable, and it has now become a fundamental ingredient of all Gospel research. According to Schweitzer, Jesus was called to a messianic destiny, but would not (and could not) be revealed as Messiah until the kingdom of God actually came. On the other hand, Schweitzer completely rejected the church's understanding of Jesus, including the picture given of him by the apostle Paul. He believed that church dogma, including such fundamental doctrines as the atoning death of Christ, were made up after the event, and therefore have no value for understanding Jesus himself. In theological terms, therefore, Schweitzer conformed to the liberalism of his time, and even expressed surprise that his views should have been popular with contemporary Anglo-Catholics like F. C. Burkitt, who was one of his earliest admirers and who did much to spread Schweitzer's views in the English-speaking world.

Bibliography

J. Brabazon, *Albert Schweitzer: A Biography* (New York, 1975); A. Schweitzer, *Out of My Life and Thought* (ET, Baltimore and London, 1990); *The Quest of the Historical Jesus* (ET, London, 1910).

G. L. BRAY

SCIENCE AND THE BIBLE

Introduction

In the institutions of science, some will insist that adherence to prior commitments is incompatible with scientific research. Implicitly, faith and reason define two different approaches to knowledge. The relationship between them is the central question for any apologetic regarding science and the Bible.

Thomist or Kuyperian?

After Galileo, intellectuals have been increasingly controlled by the humanist tradition (the tradition flowing from the *Enlightenment commitments to human autonomy, specifically to the autonomy of human reason). Even those who have sought to defend the Christian faith have often done so on the basis that it is 'reasonable', i.e. that it can be defended on the basis of natural phenomena (*naturalism) and human reason (*rationalism). A popular argument has been to say that God has two books: the Bible, interpreted by theologians, and the book of nature, interpreted by scientists. This argument flows from the foundational decision to adopt a Thomist rather than a Kuyperian approach to Bible-science issues.

A Thomist approach (after *Thomas Aquinas) separates the natural (or secular) from the supernatural (or religious) and restricts the scope of the fall and redemption to the supernatural realm. In the natural sphere, human reason is a true (if insufficient) guide to attaining *truth. By contrast, a Kuyperian approach (after the Dutch Christian leader, Abraham *Kuyper) takes everything, apart from God himself, as falling within the scope of the fall and redemption.

The 'two books' approach is essentially Thomist, assuming a (religiously) neutral world where timeless truths, valid for all peoples and cultures, are communicated in two different ways. Tacitly, faith doesn't come into it. If, however, every person lives by faith and faith is foundational to both the practice of science and that of scriptural exegesis, then our *first* calling as Christian apologists is to scrutinize both in the light of a biblical world-view.

The last half-century's work in the history and philosophy of science has abundantly supported this, showing very clearly that pre-scientific commitments enter decisively into the scientific enterprise at every stage. Hence, for a Kuyperian, science/religion debates are never between different categories of knowledge, but always between two fusions of faith and knowledge. Christian apologists must scrutinize both the empirical data and the world-views that select and interpret the data.

Faith and evidence

Many discussions proceed as if empirical evidence is neutral and can be used as an objective arbitrator between opposing positions. The apologist must probe deeper and should always give due credit to relevant evidence, while also scrutinizing the undergirding world-views. Indeed, if operating by faith (within a world-view) is part and parcel of being human, then *all* evidence has been selected and interpreted in faith contexts. The example of design is a case in point.

Design

Christian theists will affirm that the universe is designed – that God created it in accordance with predetermined purposes. (This issue is separate from that of evolution and special creation.) Darwinian evolutionists generally assume that design is merely apparent, that every biological organism and feature originated by chance in unsupervised processes. They claim that Darwinism can account for most, if not all, of the current evidence about life on earth. As far as they are concerned it is the defenders of design who must come up with new evidence.

Christian apologists should not accept this way of posing the challenge. Many of those who contributed the evidence used to support Darwinism were theists who believed in design. Much of the evidence can be rigorously interpreted in design as well as non-design ways and so is irrelevant to a choice between those perspectives. Indeed, it is highly unlikely that any of the sciences would have developed to their present sophistication if, during the past two centuries, students had constantly been told that there was no design in nature. Even logic demands a design approach. The proposition of no design can be established only by eliminating every possible hypothesis of design. Since it offers no incentive for such drudgery, it is not surprising, for example, that Darwinism delayed research into some so-called 'vestigial' organs by a century or more. The daily confirmation of the fruitfulness of the design assumption in science has considerable apologetic force.

Biblical language

Since the sixteenth century by far the most important approach to the relationship of biblical interpretation and the natural sciences has been that based on the idea of accommodation. This term can be used in two quite different ways. The first sees an accommodation of Scripture to the culture and world-view of the original author and recipients. The science identified in the Bible will be judged primitive and erroneous and as merely the vehicle for theological truth. The second limits accommodation to a popular and phenomenal use of *language, i.e. to the everyday language of the people that is either never meant woodenly (e.g. 'the four quarters of the earth'; Isa. 11:12) or, more often, simply describes things as they appear (e.g. 'the sun had risen over the land'; Gen. 19:23).

The apologist must not regard the phenomenal language as primitive or erroneous. Three important points should be made. First, the law-like uniformities (e.g. the sun rising and setting) on which we base our everyday reasoning have been observed by billions of people over thousands of years. That is a much larger support base than is enjoyed by any modern scientific theory. While the theories of modern science provide more precise information, the price paid for that precision is that they are less likely to be true.

Secondly, while our everyday observations may be open to more than one theoretical explanation, this does not impugn their truth. They remain the basic data that any theory must explain.

Thirdly, it must be recognized that the scientific evidence is often ambivalent. For example, at one time most scholars believed the sun orbited a stationary earth, at a later time most believed that the earth orbited a stationary sun, still later most believed that the sun also moved. But today, post-Einstein, we believe that it is not a question that can be answered through scientific investigation. There are no direct proofs of the earth's motion. Ultimately, the question is not even scientifically meaningful.

These necessary comments are not to disparage science, but to appeal for a chastened science that admits its grounding in faith commitments. That accepted, even the most literalist of biblical exegetes has to rely on the hard work of scientific research to resolve most of the issues. The Bible says almost nothing about astronomy or *cosmology. It does not describe continental drift, plate tectonics or volcanoes. It says nothing about fossils or whether Noah's flood produced all, some, or none of them. It does not tell us how much variation is possible in living organisms, or what the limits to that variation might be. It propounds no theories of God's action in the world, of the relationship of *natural law and miracle, or of *determinism and free will. In all of these areas Christian scholars have considerable freedom, but need much humility as they seek to come to tentative conclusions using the best tools of philosophical analysis and scientific research available. In contrast, secular scientists are usually the fundamentalists. Many are pre-committed to philosophical naturalism (the theory that the universe, the entire realm of nature, is a single closed system of material causes and effects, with nothing outside or beyond it, or, at least, nothing that can influence it) and evolutionism (the theory that the universe is a unity through being a continuity in time and space) that allows little or no room for manoeuvre. This is the fundamentalism that apologists must expose and critique.

Conclusion

In the modern era it has become virtually the orthodox position amongst Christian apologists to reject many traditional readings of biblical passages because of their presumed incompatibility with modern science. This ignores the foundational role of faith. If we are considering Scripture, then any interpretation (or reinterpretation) must be justified in terms of valid exegetical approaches consistent with a Christian philosophical framework based on biblical faith commitments. The same applies to science. By failing to discern and critique the naturalistic and rationalistic faiths that shape secular science we have often overrated what science is capable of showing. There are severe limitations on human *reasoning and scientific theorizing, especially when it comes to cosmology and origins.

These issues are not peripheral to modern apologetics. By failing to recognize the dominance of naturalism and rationalism, we have imbibed much of it into our lives. Through the media, and in school and college, young people are initiated into this same naturalism. Even in homes where the parents are committed Christians, it is hard, to the point of impossibility, for children to maintain belief in the reality of the biblical story. Outside of home and church they will live out the secular religion. If, against the odds, they maintain a Christian commitment, they will almost certainly have become secularized Christians. To an ever-increasing extent their homes and churches will be secularized too. Never before has this apologetic issue been so crucial.

Bibliography

J. Byl, *God and Cosmos* (Edinburgh, 2001); R. A. Clouser, *The Myth of Religious Neutrality* (Notre Dame, 2nd edn, 2005); N. R. Pearcey, *Total Truth* (Wheaton, 2nd edn, 2005); N. R. Pearcey and C. B. Thaxton, *The Soul of Science* (Wheaton, 1994); J. M. van der Meer (ed.), *Facets of Faith and Science*, 4 vols. (Lanham, 1996).

A. J. JONES

SCIENCE AND FAITH

Perception and paradox

Few questions have had a more fundamental influence on the current mind-set of doubt about Christian belief than science. In a survey by the Church of Scotland in 1995, the three main reasons why people did not believe were suffering, the church and science. It is not so much that science has rendered Christian belief untenable but that it seems to have made it unnecessary. The assumption is that *cosmology and evolutionary theory explain how we come to be here, making belief in God no more than an optional extra for those inclined that way. Science is perceived to have done away with the need to believe in God in order to explain origin, and *technology is able to meet our needs for material security. It is, therefore, no longer necessary to believe in God today in order to make sense of the world.

This being the case, to suggest that science and belief in God belong *intrinsically* together is often greeted with astonishment. Yet it is the truth, and shows a remarkable paradox. Some of the greatest scientists in history have been Christians or explicitly God-fearing, like Galileo, Copernicus, *Newton, Boyle, Dalton, Faraday, Maxwell and Kelvin, and, generations after Darwin and Einstein are popularly supposed to have explained everything, many of today's scientists still believe in God – for example, Sir John Houghton, scientific co-chair of the Intergovernmental Panel on Climate Change, and Francis Collins, director of the international Human Genome Project. Scientists often seem to have less of a problem with religious faith than those in the arts and social sciences. A poll of American scientists by the scientific journal *Nature* revealed that the percentage of those who believed in a God one could pray to was as high as in a similar survey of eighty years ago. In recent years there has been something of an intellectual rapprochement between science and the idea of belief in the supernatural. With a few vociferous but unrepresentative exceptions, the scientific community does not appear to have quite the fundamental problem with Christian belief that cultural stereotypes would lead one to expect. Reports of the death of God have been greatly exaggerated! The problem seems to be more with what the culture *thinks* science is about, an idealized view that demands critique.

Home truths about science

Science has been turned into an idol, making truth-claims beyond its capacity. In reality, it is just one particular, organized way of asking questions about the world and looking for answers and can speak only about certain things and in certain ways, typically things which can be measured by controlled experiment and repeated time and again. Science splits complex phenomena into small enough parts to be examined, deduces hypotheses and tests them. Within these bounds, it is extremely successful. Outside of them, it is silent. This is one of the reasons why we should not write off *miracles as 'unscientific'. Science can verify only what can be reproduced. By definition, miracles are unrepeatable events, so science can say little about them, one way or the other. God is perfectly capable of intervening in a universe which he created from nothing.

Scientific theories are always provisional and contingent. They are apt to change, open to being proved false as well as true. *Popper argued that in order to be considered scientific a theory must be capable of being falsified. Some theories, like the earth being flat, are eventually shown to be false. Even fundamental theories, like Newtonian mechanics, need reappraisal when new data emerge. Theories can only describe what we might expect to happen, based on the data currently available. They can never prescribe what *must* happen. Science is a detective, not a law enforcer. The grand framework theories, like evolution and cosmology, typically have to make more sweeping hypotheses than more narrowly focused ones like the laws of motion.

Some of their assumptions remain unproven and may even be untestable, and thus, on Popper's criterion, are not strictly scientific. In short, science has limits.

Explaining it all away

Despite this, many people make the mistake of assuming that once one has explained something in scientific terms, that is all there is to it. If one can explain something 'religious' using science, one has 'explained it away'. This approach has been applied to any number of miracles in both the Old and New Testaments. So, the fact that the parting of the Red Sea can be explained in terms of 'nothing but' natural phenomena is taken as proof that God did *not* do it (because 'there's a simple explanation'), rather than a description of how he did it. This is the fallacy memorably described by Donald MacKay as 'nothing buttery'. If we have a rational scientific explanation for something, like the eye or genetic inheritance, then it is assumed to be superior to any other way of describing it. It becomes 'nothing but' the scientific description.

This is profoundly mistaken. Ernest Lucas imagines two people walking along a cliff top when, out at sea, a bright red light suddenly shoots across the sky. One of the people is a physicist who happens to have some measuring equipment handy with which to calculate the trajectory, velocity and wavelength of the light and so is able to give a detailed description of what took place. The other is a Boy Scout who says to himself, 'That's a distress flare, I must run to the coastguard!' Both people gave an accurate and valid description of what they saw, but they each had different aims in mind. This illustrates the principle of 'complementarity', that there can be complementary ways of looking at the world, of telling different sorts of stories, none of which can claim it does not need the others.

Different ways of knowing

Mathematics, science, historical records and personal experience represent different ways of knowing. The Christian claims are grounded mainly in the last two. The way God revealed himself in Christ is accessible not by experimentation, but only from ancient documents, which have to to be assessed in the appropriate way. The way we know God is the way we know people, by experience. Science and Christian belief can be seen as complementary accounts, but, as in the Red Sea example, there is often an underlying subtext of people *wanting* to disprove the supernatural and using science as a tool to do so.

Science says a lot about mechanisms and processes, cause and effect, but its reductionism is a poor tool to describe the major realities of life – human relationships, love, beauty, meaning, purpose and so on. If a scientist says that the smile in a friend's eyes is nothing but a physiological effect which gives us a pleasant hormonal reaction and that anything more is just our construction upon *reality, would we not think he had missed the point? Our normal human 'construction' is the reality, and the scientist's 'reality' is a construction, useful only within the narrow confines of the scientific method.

This typifies the sleight of hand that can take place where science is taken out of its own realms and used to play philosophy. True science knows its limits. It can answer 'How?' questions, but it has no tools to address 'Why?' questions, like 'Why is the universe there at all?' or 'Why is the universe so orderly that we can do science?' Questions such as 'Why is there so much suffering?', 'What is the meaning of life?' or 'Who am I?' go beyond what science can talk about into realms where there are no measurable data or controlled experiments. *Logical positivism sought to shut down such questions as unscientific and therefore meaningless, but God invites us to look at the universe and ask them (Rom. 1:18–20). The final source of authority is where the infinite became the personal, where the Word became flesh, where the author of creation became human, died and rose again to restore humankind to God. In doing so, Christ has affirmed for all eternity the value of the created order in God's eyes.

Humankind is able to begin to comprehend the universe because the God who created it also took human form. This provides the explanation for Einstein's remark that the most incomprehensible thing about the universe is that it is comprehensible. The fact that we can conceive in our minds interpretations about the cosmos which correspond with reality is a presupposition of science which the scientist daily takes on faith. Science still unconsciously relies for its most basic assumption on a Christian understanding about the nature of reality and of being human, not on its own logic, or on other world religions. Here is one

of the strongest pointers from science to a Christian apologetic.

Science and faith: partners over values, reality and nature

Science and the Christian faith are partners. Early modern scientists talked about practising science as 'thinking God's thoughts after him', and of a God revealed in two books, the book of Scripture and the book of nature, each of which in different ways tells us truths about God and reality. *Enlightenment *rationalism displaced this by a human-centred view which elevated science to the status of an idol capable of making supreme truth-claims to rival God and pointing to the great hope for the future of humankind. This idol is now rightly seen to have feet of clay. The postmodern critique has undercut this optimism by pointing to where it has gone wrong and airing doubts about where our scientific knowledge is taking us. This presents a vital apologetic opportunity. Science is very good at solving problems, but it does not tell us what to do with the answers. It may discover something remarkable, like the energy in an atomic nucleus, but it will not tell us whether to make a bomb, a nuclear power station or a cancer treatment out of it, or whether to leave it alone. In themselves, the bewildering advances in the biosciences know no moral limits or how to set their discoveries in the wider human context. People have realized we need to have a source of values to drive science, and science itself cannot give them to us; it was not designed to do so, but rather to work within the values which faith in Christ can provide as its guide and gatekeeper.

Science is not neutral. The social sciences reveal that science is not as cold, dispassionate and logical as is supposed. Although objectivity is a genuine goal, it is practised by real, finite, fallible people who inevitably do not leave all their own presuppositions, preferences, drives, aversions and blind spots outside the laboratory door. Value questions do play an important part, e.g. in selecting areas for research, what the scientist is looking for, which data are reported to whom and what claims are made about them. Speculation and intuition both play a part. Some ideas, like the quantum theory, required great imaginative leaps. Elegance is valued as a characteristic of a good mathematical solution. Science also has a social dimension. The peer-review process is fundamental to science, but can also mean that peer pressure and even fashion play more of a role than the idealized view of objective science would suggest. Today's generally accepted ideas of plate tectonics and global warming both had long periods in the wilderness, doubted by the current orthodoxy, before they emerged as mainstream theories.

Yet science cannot be used by an elite group of experts to control knowledge in order to hold on to power. It has to correspond to reality. Whether a heterodox scientist remains a crank or the pioneer of the next generation's understanding ultimately rests on whether the data match up. Perhaps the scientific discipline of looking at the evidence and responding accordingly leads to Christ more easily than a sceptical mind-set of literary criticism and deconstruction. Thus in a postmodern world of scepticism, science and faith are natural partners, because both share the Christian belief in a communicable and intelligible external reality, and both find themselves under fire.

Complementarity or contradiction?

The picture of complementarity of science and the Christian faith should not gloss over the conflicts between Galileo and the medieval Catholic Church, Darwin and Victorian Christians, or current 'creationists' and the American educational system. Was the retreat of the liberal theological tradition from admitting the supernatural element in the Bible an accommodation to the spirit of the age of rationalism, or a genuine response to the light of science?

There are some myths to dispel. Colin Russell argues that much of the supposed conflict between science and Christian faith is little more than a myth, put about by Thomas Huxley and his friends in a Victorian secret society called the X-Club, whose minutes reveal that its aims were to promote the standing of science by systematically attacking religion. According to contemporary accounts, the famous debate between Huxley and Bishop *Wilberforce over evolution was a rather inconclusive affair. It was portrayed by opponents of Christianity, however, as a victory for science over outdated dogma, and the image has stuck to this day. In school we are taught that God has been associated with a simple explanation which we grow out of when we encounter what science 'tells us'. A lot of what has passed as a 'scientific' view is a statement of atheistic beliefs, presented as if they were the result of science.

The conflict has, however, been generated from the Christian side also. For example, the Catholic Church in Galileo's time made the mistake of having a prior theory to which it was committed and of reading science as a means of verifying it. It so wedded itself to the Aristotelian model of the universe as an expression of Genesis that it built dogma upon it. When Galileo's observations undermined *Aristotle, the church was left with an unsustainable position, which it took centuries to admit. Similarly, some contemporary American fundamentalists decided to take on evolution with the 'creationist' approach typified in the writings of Whitcomb and Morris. This has found little following amongst scientists in the UK who are Christians. It is fair to point out genuine inconsistencies in the basis for evolutionary theory, but the alternative evidence cited for a young earth and the effects of the flood has seemed to many scientists to be very weak. The young-earth creationist model locks its proponents into certain literalistic interpretations of Genesis which many conservative Christians do not consider warranted by the text. Humility is required. Parts of Gen. 1 – 3 pose quandaries which call for human interpretation. For instance, there is light on the first day, but no sun until the fourth; what does it mean that God rested on the seventh day, when elsewhere we are told that he sustains 'all things by his powerful word' (Heb. 1:3)? No interpretation of such texts can rightly claim infallibility. Similarly, we should be careful how quickly we reinterpret basic Christian truths because of the latest ideas in physics or genetics, or cite evidences which seem to support Christian belief, e.g. indications of intelligent design in the universe. These things are always contingent. We should hold lightly to the contemporary views of science. At the end of his famous book *A Brief History of Time*, Stephen Hawking speculates about finding a set of equations that would represent a scientific theory of everything. But he reflects that they are only equations, and asks, 'What is it that breathes fire into the equations and makes a universe for them to describe?' The most powerful apologetic of all is to ask why anything exists.

Science and the Christian faith are partners in truth but are perceived to be in conflict. This presents a hard task for the apologist because it is based not on an argument about facts but on impressions and plausibility. There is also a moral barrier. Science appeals to the inclination of fallen humanity to avoid God. Since belief in God implies moral challenges as well as providing explanations, if science can provide a plausible alternative for the latter, we think we can avoid the inconveniences posed by the former. To such thinking the apologist must and can respond.

Bibliography

M. A. Jeeves and R. J. Berry, *Science, Life and Christian Belief* (Leicester, 1998); E. Lucas, *Can We Believe Genesis Today?* (Leicester, 2001); A. E. McGrath, *Dawkins' God* (Oxford, 2004); M. Poole, *A Guide to Science and Belief* (Oxford, 1995).

D. BRUCE

SCIENTIFIC DATING

Scientific dating of the Earth and its geological strata provides a remarkably consistent picture of their great ages, using a wide variety of different techniques that allow cross-checking. A selection of some of the most significant dates is shown in the table (from Alexander and White, *Beyond Belief*, p. 97). Two striking features stand out: the Earth is only one-third the age of the universe; and although living organisms have existed on Earth since soon after its formation, humans have been present for only a tiny portion of its history.

Significant dates in the history of the universe

	Years ago/date
Origin of the universe	13,700 million
Origin of the solar system (= origin of Earth)	4,566 ± 2 million
Oldest known mineral on Earth	4,404 ± 8 million
Oldest known rock on Earth	4,000 million
Earliest evidence of life on Earth	3,850 million
Earliest microbial fossils on Earth	3,500 million
Oldest multicellular animal	575 million
Earliest known eutherian mammal	135 million
Earliest hominid (*Australopithecus*)	5 million
Early modern *Homo sapiens*	160,000–154,000
Birth of Christ (comet, historical records)	5 BC
Crucifixion of Christ (lunar eclipse, historical records)	AD 33

The simplest and most direct dating methods involve counting annual layers, such as growth rings in trees, which provide a chronology back to 8,500 BC, or annual layers in ice cores, which extend back more than 200,000 years. Although many people have heard of carbon-14 radiometric dating, fewer are aware that over forty other isotopic systems, each applicable to different ages and materials, may be used to date material from a few hundred years to as much as a few billion years old. Other dating methods use such factors as the influx of cosmic radiation, the speed of light or the background microwave radiation in deep space to deduce ages.

Although the precise dates in the table will be refined as measurements are improved and as new dating methods become available, they are unlikely to change radically. To many Christians, the perspective these place on our position in the time-frame of the universe remains humbling and strikingly illustrates both the assertion of the Bible that God made humans as the pinnacle of his creation and the profligacy and power of God's creative activities – the God who pronounced that all he created was good and pleasing to him.

A different approach to dating the Earth, based solely on information in the Bible, is to add up the genealogies, starting from Adam. Archbishop James *Ussher (1581–1656) famously calculated that Adam dates from 4004 BC. Some uncertainty comes from unknown life spans of individuals in the genealogies, and the possibility of missing or duplicated people in the biblical lists, but an estimate of about 10,000 years since Adam is widely accepted. This is consistent with scientific ages for the first settled agricultural peoples, to which the accounts of Adam and Eve and their descendants refer. The biblical chronology of more recent historic events also fits well with scientific dating through *archaeology and other methods. The problem with reconciling the scientific age of the Earth and the biblical account is not in the period since Adam, but in the assumption that the six days described in Genesis account for the entire history of the universe prior to Adam in six literal days.

There are some Christians for whom the great age of the Earth revealed by scientific dating has conflicted with their interpretation of the Bible, and who believe that the scientific dates must be incorrect. They hold that the acceptance of these dates undermines belief in the Creator God. The Creation Research Society, developed in the mid-twentieth century, embodies such views and has sought to find evidence that the Earth is only 10,000 years old. A major objective of this society has been to attempt to demonstrate the incorrectness of conventional scientific explanations for the geology and age of the Earth, and instead to postulate a young Earth and a flood geology (which seeks to explain the Earth's strata and the fossil sequences therein as a result of the Noachian flood) as better scientific explanations. These efforts over the past half-century have failed to meet with acceptance by the scientific community, largely because they do not address a vast range of interlocking observations which are explained by an old Earth. The difference between an age of the Earth of 10,000 years and one of more than 4,000 million years is not easily overlooked, and it is difficult, even for the non-scientist, to believe that the scientific dates could be that wrong.

Other Christians who have wished to uphold the integrity of the biblical accounts of God's creative activities have taken various approaches to reconcile the Genesis account and scientific results. One such is to postulate that the universe only *appears* to be old, but was actually created 10,000 years ago with all the fossils in place, and with light travelling from distant galaxies created instantaneously in flight. Philosophically, such a hypothesis cannot be disproved, since God is all-powerful and could indeed have created us yesterday with our memories intact. It runs counter, however, to everything else we know about God: his truthfulness, consistency and faithfulness towards us, and it is difficult to believe that he would so thoroughly deceive us.

Alternative methods that have attempted to achieve reconciliation mainly centre around interpretation of the genre of the Genesis passages dealing with the six days of creation. One suggestion is that they refer to six successive days when God revealed his creative work to the writer of Genesis. This, however, seems to be a contrived reading of the text and has not gained much support.

Another approach has been to treat the six days not as literal twenty-four-hour periods, but as long periods of time stretching to billions of years, so that they can then accommodate the great scientific age of the universe. The weakness of this explanation is that the order of creation described in the Bible does not match the order in which we know things happened from observation of the geological and astronomical record, e.g. in Genesis trees appear before marine creatures (Gen. 1:11, 20), which is contrary to the fossil record, and evening and morning appear before the sun and moon (Gen. 1:5, 14). In other words, this part of Genesis does not appear to be a scientific/historical account of the sequence of creation, but rather to be proclaiming fundamental truths about God's purposes in his creation and his own relationship to it.

The structure of the Genesis story itself points to the idea of a planned and ordered creation. As many commentators have pointed out, the first three days describe God giving his creation shape and form, with the next three days filling up that shape. This literary and theological interpretation is a more helpful way of reading the account than trying to press it into a twenty-first-century interpretive framework. Scientific literature is so familiar to us that we tend to accept it as the norm for descriptions of the world around us. But scientific narrative as a literary style, at least in the way we understand it now, did not begin until the seventeenth century with the first scientific journals. We should therefore avoid trying to fit the first few chapters of Genesis into a modernist Procrustean bed.

The great truths that the Genesis account proclaims include the assertion that God created the universe because he chose to do so, but that he exists outside his creation: he is transcendent. Further, he is active and present in his universe: he is immanent in it. God repeatedly proclaims that his creation is good, and when he created humankind, he said that it was 'very good'. People were brought into being at the summit of his creation in order to have relationship with him and to be stewards of his creation on his behalf. These are the bedrock truths on which stands our understanding of God's relationship with his people. The rest of the Bible then develops an account of God's dealings with humankind, of our rebellion and his great rescue made possible through the death of his Son, Jesus.

From the beginning God has made us capable of understanding the world around us and of manipulating and interacting with it through our scientific and technological abilities. Of course, we can use that ability for good or for evil. We should not be frightened of what science uncovers; all truth is God's truth. There are legitimate areas for differing interpretations of Gen. 1 – 2, but the great truths of Genesis are that God made us for relationship with himself, and that we are not accidental products of a meaningless universe. It is these truths that all Christians ought to unite to proclaim.

Bibliography

D. Alexander and R. S. White, *Beyond Belief: Science, Faith and Ethical Challenges* (Oxford, 2004); E. Lucas, *Can We Believe Genesis Today?* (Leicester, 2001); D. Wilkinson, *The Message of Creation* (Leicester and Downers Grove, 2002).

R. S. WHITE

SCIENTISM, see MATERIALISM (PHILOSOPHICAL/METAPHYSICAL)

SCOTTISH COMMON SENSE REALISM

Basic issues

Scottish common sense realism (SCSR) was a tradition of philosophy which represented a reaction to the philosophy of David *Hume, and an attempt to ground knowledge and *morality in a realist *epistemology which avoided the radical scepticism of Hume. Key figures in the development of the tradition were Thomas *Reid (1710–96), Dugald Stewart (1753–1828), Sir William Hamilton (1788–1856), and James *M'Cosh (1811–94), the last of whom wrote an influential history of the movement, *The Scottish Philosophy* (1874).

Basic to the SCSR position is the idea that certain beliefs, principles or laws are universal and intuitive and exist prior to any reflexive observation of them in action. This view enabled its advocates to argue that the objects of knowledge were not ideas or sensations caused in some manner by a *reality itself inaccessible to direct knowledge, but in fact the reality itself. Thus, the real, external world not only possessed an integrity of its own but was also directly accessible to the knower because of the way human nature was itself constructed. In arguing along these lines, SCSR pitched itself against the *idealism of *Locke, which itself lay in the background to the far more radical position of Hume. For Locke, when we see an object, its properties cause sensations which are themselves the immediate objects of our knowledge; for Hume, when we

see an object, we have no direct knowledge of the object but can only infer its existence from the image or sensation we have of the object; for Reid and other adherents of SCSR, in the same situation we do not have inferential but real, direct knowledge of the object itself.

In the field of morality, SCSR provided parallel arguments to those relevant to epistemology, with human nature possessing basic universal moral principles, with an innate sense of right and wrong. This does not mean that all human beings have equally developed moral senses, and those who are mature may well have clearer moral vision than the immature. In addition, human beings are able to defy their moral sense, to be confused about what their moral sense is saying in a given circumstance, and to be misled by bad examples and training. Nonetheless, when presented with good *moral values, even the most hardened and immoral individual can be brought to see the superiority of the way of the good. For this reason, innate principles of morality do not obviate the need for moral instruction.

Significance for theology

SCSR was ultimately of less significance for philosophy proper than for the influence it wielded over the theological world, where its significance was considerable. It was, after all, a system which was easily adaptable to the cause of orthodox Christianity, since God can be regarded as the source for the common sense principles which are part and parcel of human nature. Realist epistemology, as an antidote to scepticism, also offered obvious support to Christian beliefs which seemed to assume universal direct epistemological and moral access to a world which possessed its own order and not simply one imposed upon it by the structure of human perception. In addition, belief in God could itself be maintained as precisely one of those innate principles, in line with Paul's teaching on the universal knowledge of God in human nature which is suppressed by sinners not for intellectual but rather for moral reasons. Finally, the appeal to universal, innate moral principles was clearly akin to traditional Christian notions of a universal moral accountability to God in accordance with biblical standards.

Inevitably, given its Scottish locale, SCSR had a particularly significant impact upon Presbyterian theology in the nineteenth century.

Thomas Chalmers, for example, wrote the preface to Thomas Brown's *Lectures on Ethics*, and appears to have been positively influenced by other SCSR writings, though its importance has sometimes been exaggerated in a manner that excludes other obvious influences on his thought. More significant still was the influence of Scottish emigrant, John Witherspoon, an adherent of SCSR and the president of the College of New Jersey (later Princeton University) in 1768. This helped to ensure that SCSR was a decisive influence on both the shape and content of the curriculum at both the College (later University) and at the Theological Seminary. Indeed, the tradition was further reinforced by the later appointment of M'Cosh, a leading advocate of SCSR and former student of Chalmers, as chair of philosophy and president in 1868. At the Seminary, the basic principles of SCSR were picked up and integrated into a thorough system of Reformed theology by Charles *Hodge, a long-time admirer of Chalmers and the first generation of the intellectual leadership of the Free Church of Scotland.

It is probably through the work of Hodge that later generations of evangelicals imbibed much of SCSR. Hodge's statement that the Bible was a book of facts and that the theologian's relationship to this was analogous to that of the scientist and the natural world, indicated clearly both the *Baconian and the SCSR roots at least of the terminology of his theology. Yet the appropriation of philosophical paradigms and principles by theologians is rarely a straightforward exercise. Theology is such an eclectic discipline that, while much has been made of the impact of SCSR on the theology of Princeton prior to the reorganization in 1929, the use made of it by Hodge and company must be seen as part of their wider theological exercise. For example, the basic theological textbook at Princeton prior to Hodge's own *Systematic Theology* was Francis Turretin's *Institutio Elencticae Theologicae*. This work contains a number of distinctions, e.g. that between archetypal theology (God's infinite knowledge of himself) and ectypal theology (that theology which is true yet finite and designed for human capacity), which serve at least to attenuate some of the realism of SCSR and which are at least hinted at on occasion by Hodge. Nevertheless, having said this, Princeton became well known for the development of evidentialist apologetics built upon epistemological *realism and *inductive method, via the work of the Hodges and, more importantly, B. B. *Warfield. This has led some to argue that the Princeton view of Scripture, associated with notion of infallibility (or, to use the later term, inerrancy) is itself in part a product of SCSR. That the doctrine was articulated by Warfield in a manner which depended to some extent on the *empiricism of SCSR is beyond doubt; but it is arguable that the central thrust of what he was trying to say was a well-established position within the church and was not necessarily dependent upon SCSR for its truth value.

Current significance

SCSR has been attacked from both within and without the evangelical Christian world. Kantianism clearly leaves no room for the kind of realism for which it argues, and the same is true for the theological trajectories which take their cue from *Kant, such as the classic liberalism of *Schleiermacher. In addition, recent criticism of all attempts to create meta-narratives to explain reality, echoing in a strange way the scepticism of Hume, reject precisely the kind of principles upon which SCSR builds, such as (at the most basic level) any universal notion such as human nature.

The rejection of the principles of SCSR is not, however, confined to non-evangelical thought. For example, advocates of *presuppositional apologetics, such as Cornelius *Van Til, have pointed to the problems inherent with any system of belief which does not take seriously the status of the knower in terms of presuppositions and moral relation to God. In doing so, he argues that the *evidentialism of old Princeton, of which the principles of SCSR were themselves an important part, itself depends upon a view of human nature which does not take seriously human sinfulness. In doing so, he implicitly charges SCSR with holding to an incipiently Pelagian view of human nature.

Nevertheless, recent years have seen the development of Reformed epistemology by Alvin Plantinga, Nicholas Wolterstorff and their followers, who represent a movement with some potent similarities to SCSR. Plantinga's argument that *theism can be taken as a properly basic belief which requires no prior justification is similar to the kind of position being argued for by Reid, and recent work shows its proponents engaged in self-conscious dialogue with the thought of Reid and others in the tradition.

Bibliography

A. Broadie, *The Tradition of Scottish Philosophy* (Edinburgh, 1990); S. A. Grave, *The Scottish Philosophy of Common Sense* (Oxford, 1960); H. Laurie, *Scottish Philosophy in its National Development* (Glasgow, 1902); N. Wolterstorff, *Thomas Reid and the Story of Epistemology* (Cambridge, 2001).

C. R. TRUEMAN

SECULAR HUMANISM

The term 'humanism' refers to several different endeavours related to human dignity and development: the traditional areas of study called 'humanities', the Renaissance humanism of *Erasmus and Leonardo da Vinci, humanitarian efforts for the poor and needy, and humanist philosophies that stress personal fulfilment and well-being. In this latter sense, Christianity, Marxism and *existentialism have all been called humanisms. Secular humanism is a naturalistic philosophy that developed in reaction against theistic and other supernaturalist approaches, and was influenced by groups like Ethical Culture, the American Humanist Association and (in Britain) the Rationalist Press Association, as well as unitarian clergy.

In 1933 thirty-four American humanists published a Humanist Manifesto, among them the influential philosopher John *Dewey, whose own view of religion is reflected in the document. Religious humanists, it declared, regard the universe as self-existing, not created, and humankind as a product of natural evolutionary processes. Modern *science has made unacceptable any supernatural or cosmic guarantees of human values. But humanist religion seeks the complete fulfilment of human personality in a free and universal society, and makes that its social passion. By adopting the scientific spirit and method in formulating its hopes and plans, humankind will have the power to achieve its dreams. It must set intelligence and will to the task.

History soon showed this to be overly optimistic as subsequent events revealed the depths of human depravity, the seeming endlessness of poverty and suppression of human rights, and the dangers of nuclear and biochemical disaster. Scientific progress was seen to bring evil as well as good. So in 1973 an international group of 114 scientists and scholars published Humanist Manifesto II. They included well-known figures like philosophers A. J. Ayer and Anthony *Flew, ethicist Joseph Fletcher, biologists Francis Crick and Jacques Monod, psychologists Edward Ericson and B. F. *Skinner and author Isaac Asimov. Humanism was no longer presented as either a religion or a creed but as a shared social vision for the future.

Manifesto II is less optimistic, more detailed, and has a more international emphasis than Manifesto I. It has two main themes: the need to combine scientific methods with compassion, and the ultimate ideal of fulfilled potential for every human person. Traditional religion, it is claimed, lacks rational basis, and its insistence on unchanging moral norms impedes human progress. *Ethics must rather be situational, an application of creative intelligence to life's problems. In every situation, human freedom consonant with social responsibility should be maximized and differing lifestyles tolerated. Civil liberties, participatory democracy and economic well-being need to be extended, the world community must renounce force and work together on problems of ecology and economic development, and every person should become a member of this world community in practice as well as theory.

In 1980, yet another statement appeared, A Secular Humanist Declaration, in response to critical attacks by authoritarian clerics who denounced secular humanism as a dangerous and morally corrupting philosophy devoid of any moral framework. Drafted by philosopher Paul Kurtz and endorsed by other scholars and writers, it affirmed that humanism's first principle is a democratic commitment to free inquiry, free from both religious and political control. While it recognizes the central importance of *morality, it opposes absolutist ethics. The secular humanist ethic is relevant to a changing society in a scientific age; it is rationally based, not subjective as some critics assert, for objective standards emerge in the process of ethical deliberation. The critics who attack secular humanism are in effect attacking reason and science, and refusing to tolerate the diversity that democracy and free inquiry require.

The rhetoric by both sides in this debate tends to overstate the issues, as if they have nothing in common. Plainly, secular humanists share with Christians some weighty ethical concerns: for world peace, for the environment and scarce resources, for civil liberty and tolerance of diversity, for economic development and the elimination of hunger, for international co-operation and the development of a world community that transcends the limitations of national self-interest. They both lament irresponsible drug use and sexual behaviour. Secular humanists are strongly opposed to what they see as the anti-intellectual gullibility of narrow-minded believers, and this is something that thoughtful Christians also resist. Humanists reject supernaturalist religions, but they still recognize that religion expresses an ultimate concern that may give meaning and direction to life, and its altruistic feelings and common hopes may contribute to building *community. That was what the religious humanism of the 1933 manifesto had retained.

Contrasting beliefs

The underlying differences between Christianity and secular humanism, however, are crucial, and they reveal two overall features of secular humanist thought: the Christianity it criticizes is often a simplistic kind of anti-intellectual faith rather than a theologically informed historical orthodoxy, and the alternative it offers is rooted in eighteenth-century *Enlightenment ideas. On the justification of belief, for example, secular humanism requires the rule of reason alone, independently of all *revelation, *authority, and tradition. This is *rationalism: it was inspired by the rise of modern science, and in effect it often came to mean the rule of science alone. Revealed religion by definition cannot meet this requirement, and is accordingly rejected. But given the subtle influences which shape our beliefs, even a secular postmodern mentality finds that kind of rationalistic objectivity impossible, along with the Enlightenment demand that we proportion belief to the evidence. Christians are likely to agree, for they cannot separate reason from revelation, or from the long tradition of faith and thought that still informs their belief today. They would see revelation and reason as both God-given, and the capacity of one's beliefs to encompass related knowledge in a coherent and logically consistent fashion as highly important. On the other hand, the humanist who starts by denying even the possibility of divine revelation and then ignores the influence of a long and thoughtful tradition simply begs the question of religious belief. Revelation does not preclude reason but informs and enlightens it, using reason's God-given capacity to transcend the senses and reflect on the unseen.

Secular humanism contends that science must dictate our understanding of nature, and holds accordingly that, regardless of disagreements about the mechanisms involved, the universe is a product of natural evolutionary processes without any supernatural creator, divine purpose or providence. The human species emerged gradually from those processes, so that the entire personality is now a function of the biological organism in its social and cultural context. Christian responses to the evolutionist claim vary widely, from total rejection to an acceptance of evolutionary processes as the means God uses in his work of creation. The point is that natural evolutionary processes do not necessarily preclude a divine creator; it takes *naturalism to do that. *Theism and naturalism are mutually exclusive, but theism and natural science are not. Naturalism is not a conclusion necessitated by science, but a presupposition brought to it or added on. Reason and science alone are not the only bases for naturalistic belief any more than they are for religious beliefs. More personal and biographical factors are involved as well.

Naturalistic humanism takes a reductionist approach to the nature of persons: there is 'no separate soul', 'nothing but' natural processes, 'nothing but' biological causes, 'nothing but' a biological organism in a social environment. But the body-soul issue is much more complex than this implies. Christians too find the idea of 'separate' souls objectionable because of the brain-dependency of all our mental processes; it is more reminiscent of *Descartes than of the Bible. A 'separable' soul, perhaps, but not in this life a functionally 'separate' entity. More significantly, the biblical terms for 'soul' (OT *nephesh*; NT *psyche*) are also translated 'life' (and *nephesh* is used of animals as well as human beings), so it is not at all clear whether a soul-entity is intended or even necessary. The question is twofold: whether brain processes are both necessary and sufficient to explain all human functions and abilities, and how personal identity can survive until (and in) the final resurrection. A variety of responses have emerged among Christian theologians and philosophers, making the humanist's 'separate soul' appear to be little more than a straw man.

The naturalist's picture of human nature is very thin: fact without value, process without purpose, life without meaning. Why then are human beings to be respected and valued? The humanist says it is because of their powers, their capacity for reason and creative imagination and how they could develop. Humans are at the cutting edge of the evolutionary process, still developing, and they can devise ways of resolving problems and shaping the future. They are to be valued for their potential as rational beings in a changing world. So, it is not that persons have any intrinsic value, but they are valuable only because of some possible consequences of being human. By contrast, Christians value human beings because God does. He created us in his own image, as finite reflections of himself, and he loves us for ourselves, not just for any usefulness we may have. Human beings have intrinsic worth. Life has meaning, and its structures have purpose.

Ethics

The secular humanist ethic does not prescribe a particular morality, but rather applies scientific method and rational analysis to life's problems. It is, therefore, autonomous, situational and consequentialist. It is autonomous because any moral obligations are self-imposed. No God, no religious or secular authority, no natural order, no human tradition can impose its will, and so individuals are free to think for themselves and to act as they see fit. This approach is situational because in a changing world there are no fixed ends, moral rules become outdated, and *conscience is just a product of past social expectations. As situations change, so do the problems they pose, and their new complexities require scientifically informed solutions rather than invariable rules. This calls for a consequentialist approach because no human action is good or bad in itself, and so moral judgments depend on predictable outcomes. The contrast with a Christian ethic is obvious. Christian morality is not autonomous but theonomous, subject to divine *law. It is not situational, because the creation is structured in ways conducive to patterns of life that God intended. And it is not simply consequentialist because some things are good or bad in themselves.

This contrast comes out most clearly when we ask about the overall purpose, the highest end we are seeking, when we make particular decisions and shape a life for ourselves. While Christianity points to 'the kingdom of God and his righteousness', secular humanism points to the maximization of individual human freedom

in a globally democratic society. This elevation of individual freedom is typical of modern Western culture, and participatory democracy is its societal ideal. But will enlarging individual liberty ensure human compassion, social *justice, and moral improvement? Will it produce genuinely responsible people and actions? Democracy may well be the best political arrangement yet in human history, but it is no Utopia. It has proved to be notoriously inefficient, prey to individual and corporate self-interest, unable to secure economic justice for all, and it bears the marks alike of both human dignity and human depravity. Is this the highest end of humankind? How different is the promise of God's kingdom and his righteousness – a perfectly just and compassionate ruler and his perfected realm.

The ethical differences between humanism and Christianity all stem from naturalism's rejection of intrinsic meaning and purpose. For example, for the secularist, sex is in itself just a biological fact and a social context, and one is responsible for its biological and social consequences. *Marriage is no more than a human arrangement that has no larger moral significance. In Scripture, however, marriage is a divine ordinance with larger purposes, and sex celebrates the marriage bond by imaging Christ's love for his own. All of life has moral significance because it participates in the purposes of the Creator.

The contrast is not only about how we decide what is morally good, but also about motivation and moral obligation (why be good?). The secularist and the Christian may both be motivated in part by the satisfaction one finds in personal growth or helping other people, although, as a consequentialist, Paul Kurtz supposes that Christians must be motivated simply by fear of *hell and hope of *heaven. But are consequences the whole motivation story? Martin Luther realized that justification by faith frees us from concern about our own destiny, so that we can attend fully to life's earthly tasks. A Christian is then motivated more by deep devotion to a God who embodies every good rather than by consequences. The humanist rejects all but self-imposed obligations, while the Christian delights in what God wills, and finds it good.

The Enlightenment's rule of reason generated optimistic expectations of human progress, an optimism that was reinforced by modern *technology. While the 1980 Humanist Declaration recognizes that technology has had some unintended effects, its vision of a better world still depends on science and technology to save the environment, eliminate poverty, banish disease, improve our genes and further the evolution of humankind. There can be no guarantee that every human problem can be solved, but it calls every effort of intellect and will to the task of building this near-Utopia, and progress still seems inevitable. To the Christian, this is questionable. For all the promise in technology of every sort, humans still know only in part, make misguided decisions and too easily upset the natural and societal ecology. Human perversity too persists, seeking personal gain or *evil ends and making a mess out of our best-laid plans. Wars may or may not cease, biological and nuclear terrorism may be preventable, but crime and violence persist. The point is that one's view of *history can be no more realistic than one's view of human nature. Secular humanism has too optimistic a view of technology and its ability to recreate the future: because it is too optimistic about human nature, it is too optimistic also about the future. The Christian faces the uncertain future with realistic hope, because of faith in the providence of God over human affairs and assurance of human history's final outcome. Christianity and secular humanism represent two very different visions of the future, and offer two very different gospels. One says technology can save us, if we will trust human science and creative intelligence; the other says that only God can save us, and whatever science contributes in this life is a gift of his providence.

Bibliography

P. Kurtz (ed.), *Humanist Manifestos I and II* (Buffalo, 1973); *In Defence of Secular Humanism* (Buffalo, 1983); C. Lamont, *The Philosophy of Humanism*, 5th edn (New York, 1965); J. I. Packer and T. Howard, *Christianity: The True Humanism* (Waco, 1985).

A. F. HOLMES

SECULARISM

Secularism dispenses with religion and the supernatural, and the word can be seen as a descriptive term, a militant world-view or a social process.

As a descriptive term it portrays a society whose focus is this world rather than other-worldly. Values, meanings, concerns, morals and all aspects of community life are seen in terms of the material world as understood by contemporary *science. Nothing is based on belief in God or in any life other than this one. Most Western societies are said to be secular in this sense, even though the large majority of their populations would claim to have religious beliefs. In France, for example, where secularism is firmly entrenched, over 80% of the population claim to be religious believers, but the impact of their beliefs on French life as a whole is very small.

Seen as a militant world-view, secularism is a movement that consciously sets itself to destroy the influence of religion in all areas of public life. Though the movement tends to be dominated by atheists who clearly have a vision of a religion-free world, its adherents do not argue that religion should be forcibly abolished altogether. They allow that it can have a place as a private belief and way of life. What they cannot accept is that it should have any impact on society, politics, *morality, education or any other aspect of public life. All social and public organizations, they argue, should be based on their world-view rather than on any religious world-view. The ground on which secularists argue for the adoption of their world-view as the basis for all public institutions is that secularism is based on reason and science while the religious world-view is based on ignorance and superstition. Building society on reason and science, they say, will make it secure, happy, peaceful and strong, in contrast to societies built on religious beliefs, which are necessarily superstitious, intolerant and divisive.

Secularism as a process has its roots in Renaissance humanism and the *Enlightenment programme of seeking to understand the world without reference to God. Though it was a slow process, Western thought gradually moved over from a theocentric world-view, which understood the world and the human race in terms of God, to a humanistic world-view, which made human beings the basis of all understanding, value, morality and so on, without any need for God. Science set itself to find explanations that were contained wholly within the natural order. Moralists sought to find a basis for morality in society rather than in the commands or nature of God. The law of God was replaced by *natural law. Political theorists sought to develop concepts of the state as a purely human institution. Theologians even worked at developing a *natural theology. Leading thinkers such as Marx, *Freud, *Weber and Durkheim shaped ways of viewing the world that left no role for God. Social institutions such as schools, universities, hospitals, welfare organizations, all Christian in origin in the West, gradually drifted away from their religious roots and operated as this-worldly organizations. People at large, including many Christians, operated with a mind-set that was essentially secular. The observance of religious practices and church attendance declined. Until the middle of the last century, this process of secularism or *secularization was generally assumed to be inevitable and irreversible. In the last few decades, however, it has been recognized that this is not necessarily so. There is strong evidence that the loss of transcendent elements in our belief system leads to the impoverishment of life in general, and that those who find themselves in a strongly secular society will sooner or later seek for meaning and values in some form of religion, albeit not necessarily in traditional Christianity. The situation in China can be seen as an example, where despite (or perhaps because of) decades of fiercely imposed secularism there has been a phenomenal growth in deeply committed believers in Christianity.

Faced with secularism in any of its forms, Christians can respond in a number of ways. In the first place, they may choose to take on board the demands of the secularists and seek to adapt to secularism. This was a policy adopted by many nineteenth-century liberal theologians, and it reached its climax in the mid-twentieth century with books like John Robinson's Honest to God and the 'God is dead' movement. Spurred on by a conviction that 'man come of age' could no longer accept traditional concepts of God interfering in the world, those who took this line sought to remove the transcendent and supernatural elements from Christianity and thus make it acceptable to secular men and women. But to remove the supernatural from Christianity is to remove its heart. More than any religion it begins and ends with God; though deeply concerned with human life in this world, as the incarnation of Christ demonstrates, it can never be simply a this-world religion. What is more, there is good evidence that forms of Christianity that are emptied of the supernatural fail to answer the needs of those who

follow them. In the twentieth-century decline in churchgoing, sociologists noted, it was generally the churches that embraced liberalism that declined the most; churches that retained a strong sense of the supernatural declined the least, or, in the case of churches which particularly emphasized the supernatural, grew significantly. The English Church Census of 1989 revealed that churchgoing by those in the 'broad/liberal' tradition declined by 5% between 1985 and 1989, while in the same period churchgoing by 'evangelicals' grew by 3%, largely as a result of the strongly supernaturalistic charismatic movement.

A second possible response to secularism is to keep our Christian beliefs intact but at the same time to allow that the secularists' demand for the removal of all traces of religion from public institutions is a valid one. Christianity then becomes, as the secularists propose, a purely private affair, practised in isolation from all the rest of life. In particular, this would mean all severance of any ties between church and state. Those in favour of this response would argue that the power politics used by the state church in past generations and the forcible imposition of Christian values and concepts are contrary to the spirit and teaching of the NT. Others would argue that Christians cannot observe their faith simply privately. Christianity by its very nature affects the whole of life. While they readily accept that it is wrong to impose values and beliefs on others, Christians have as much right as anyone to seek to influence society and social institutions for good according to their own values and moral principles. In this they are doing precisely what the secularists have set themselves to do. Moreover, since for example, in the UK over 70% of the population claim to adhere to the Christian religion, they have a stronger mandate to do so than the secularists, who are very much in the minority.

A third way in which the Christian apologist will wish to respond to the secularists is to challenge their assumption that a society built on secularist values will be superior to one built on Christian values. In any such response we need to be prepared to admit that some so-called 'Christian' societies have in fact failed to put into practice the teaching of Jesus and the Bible, but at the same time, we can demonstrate that the true application of Christian principles does provide a basis for the kind of healthy and fulfilled society they desire.

A fourth area of response is to refute the accusation that all religion is unscientific, irrational and superstitious. Again, we will need to confess that some elements of Christendom may be open to such a criticism. But for the most part all the evidence is on the other side. No other world-view has been subjected to such thorough critique and careful scholarship as Christianity. Countless books have been written working through the implications of the scientific world-view. Christian thinkers are more concerned than anyone to eradicate any superstitious or irrational elements from their world-view.

It is arguable that the rise of secularism has given the Christian apologist a great opportunity to present the Christian world-view as a radical alternative. Most Western societies have emerged from a period in which they have seen themselves as essentially Christian, and, as a result, have felt little need to examine the claims of the NT. Now we are in a society where there is both widespread ignorance of the teachings of Christianity and an increasing disillusionment with the kind of belief system that secularism offers us. What is called for is not a watered-down version of Christianity that seeks to meet the demands of the secularists, but the offering of a full-blooded radical alternative that can be presented with grace and be shown to supply a viable and attractive alternative.

Bibliography

P. L. Berger, *The Sacred Canopy* (New York, 1967); S. Bruce, *Religion in the Modern World* (Oxford, 1996); H. Cox, *The Secular City* (London, 1965).

P. Hicks

SECULARIZATION

'Secularization' denotes the process in which religious beliefs, symbols and institutions have gradually lost their public status and influence within many modern industrial societies, notably those of Western and Central Europe. The process is exemplified in the widespread expectation today that political life should be kept entirely free of religious influences, though the same could also be said of economic affairs, media, education and other central sectors of modern society and *culture. While religious conviction undoubtedly survives in private life, and although religious beliefs occasionally surface in public rhetoric, religion has largely ceased to be a determining factor in a great many social practices. On the contrary, within secular societies such practices are for the most part geared toward safety, security, economic growth and other proximate ends. The methods and techniques employed in the pursuit of such ends, furthermore, are commonly pragmatic and practically atheistic.

Not surprisingly, the process of secularization tends – even among religious believers – to encourage a tacit shift of emphasis away from traditionally religious aspirations ('the world to come') towards secular, temporal and predominantly 'this-worldly' concerns. An example of this interesting shift is the condition Philip Rieff termed the 'triumph of the therapeutic', a state of affairs in which religious belief ceases to discipline and to direct life and is instead simply employed in pursuit of the more or less immediate experience of well-being. 'Religious man was born to be saved,' Rieff observed; 'psychological man is born to be pleased.'

Admittedly, the secularization of modern social life has liberated us from a great many repressive religious authorities, traditions and dogmas. The price we have paid for this new freedom has been high at the level of meaning, however. The process of secularization has effectively narrowed the range of human aspirations to the confines of the here and now, and the secular ideologies that have arisen to replace traditional religious beliefs provide little consolation in the face of suffering and death. As Peter Berger *et al.* observe: 'Modern society has threatened the plausibility of religious theodicies [i.e. attempts to make sense of death and evil], but it has not removed the experiences that call for them. Human beings continue to be stricken by sickness and death; they continue to experience social injustice and deprivation. The various secular creeds and ideologies that have arisen in the modern era have been singularly unsuccessful in providing satisfactory theodicies. It is important to understand the additional burden to modernity implicit in this. Modernity has accomplished many far-reaching transformations, but it has not fundamentally changed the finitude, fragility, and mortality of the human condition. What it has accomplished is to seriously weaken those definitions of reality that previously made that human condition easier to bear' (P. L. Berger, B. Berger and H. Kellner, *The Homeless Mind:*

Modernization and Consciousness [New York, 1973], p. 185).

Apologetic implications

The most obvious evangelical reaction to the process of secularization has been either to attempt to preserve what remains of the public influence of religion or to try to reinstate that which has been lost. In North America, for example, fundamentalist Christians have sought to preserve prayer within the public school system, to make 'creation science' mandatory within the secondary school curriculum, to erect explicitly Christian displays on federal, state and/or municipal properties, etc. Such attempts have not been without merit, for it is only to their peril that Western democracies forget the debt they owe to Christian ideas and institutions. Yet the apologetic emphasis might also be profitably placed upon the stubbornly pragmatic quality of contemporary social life as well as upon secularization's persistent constriction of human aspirations to the relatively short span between birth and death, for both are fundamentally depersonalizing. *Pragmatism, for example, often calls for the objectification of persons for the sake of convenience and social control. While perhaps conducive to effective management, rendering human beings as engineerable objects tends to empty the world of all but technocratic meanings and purposes. 'The unbelieving marrow of the capricious man', Martin *Buber observed in *I and Thou* (tr. W. Kaufmann [New York, 1970], p. 110) 'cannot perceive anything but unbelief and caprice, positing ends and devising means. His world is devoid of sacrifice and grace, encounter and presence, but shot through with ends and means.' The constriction of human aspirations to the 'here and now', furthermore, effectively obviates all human striving beyond that of simply seeking to secure creature comforts. It is fundamentally anti-heroic and uninspiring. In effect, limiting human aspirations to this world is to respond to the assertion that 'man does not live by bread alone' with the retort: 'On the contrary, people live quite well by bread alone so long as they can be distracted – by means of consumption, entertainment and therapy – from pondering the meaning of their lives.' The shortsightedness of such a view becomes apparent in the face of Jesus' rhetorical question, 'What good is it for a man to gain the whole world, yet forfeit his soul?' (Mark 8:36).

In the face of secularization Christians must be prepared to insist that truly human purposes cannot be limited to the *saeculum* – that is, to 'this age' – but must also extend into 'the age to come'. As Christians, we must be prepared, not simply to give an account of our hope, but also to give an account of the *possibility* of hope that extends beyond safety, security, material prosperity, *entertainment and other merely secular ends. This will not be possible if the churches have already succumbed to the 'triumph of the therapeutic', or if they have 'realized' Christian eschatology in any other way. Witness cannot be borne to Christian hope by mimicking secular products and services either. Rather, Christian witness must point beyond this world to the infinitely larger horizon of the kingdom of God. Christian ascetics down the ages have always recognized the importance of this relativization of the present, both in the interests of attaining to eternal life as well as for the sake of humanizing social conditions in this age. Indeed, it may well be that the apologetic response most appropriate within secularized societies is that of attempting to renew the habits and practices of the Christian ascetic tradition.

Bibliography

C. M. Gay, *The Way of the (Modern) World: Or, Why It's Tempting to Live as if God Doesn't Exist* (Grand Rapids, 1998); O. Guinness, *The Gravedigger File: Papers on the Subversion of the Modern Church* (Downers Grove, 1983); L. Newbigin, *Foolishness to the Greeks: The Gospel and Western Culture* (Grand Rapids, 1986).

C. M. GAY

SELF-REFUTING STATEMENTS

Several kinds of statements have been described as 'self-refuting':

1. Logical *contradictions, such as 'Socrates is mortal and Socrates is not mortal'. If the two occurrences of 'mortal' in this sentence are predicated of Socrates at the same time and in the same respect, then the sentence cannot be true. The first clause refutes the second, and vice versa.

2. Some self-referential statements, i.e. statements that refer to themselves, are self-refuting, such as 'All statements are false'. If that statement is true, then it is false.

3. Some statements refute themselves, not because of their explicit content, but because of the one who utters them, e.g. 'I am lying now'. Generally, there is no contradiction involved in saying that someone is lying. Replace the first person with the third, 'He is lying now', and the contradiction disappears. But in the first person the statement is self-refuting, because the very act of asserting something involves a claim to be telling the truth. So 'I am lying now' means, in effect, 'I am telling the truth, and I am also lying now', which is a contradiction.

4. There are other 'practical' forms of self-refutation that pertain more to the speaker than to the actual words he utters. If a person says that he hates beans, but he gorges himself with large helpings of them, observers may well claim that his behaviour refutes his statement. His statement itself is not self-refuting, but in an important sense the person has refuted himself. To argue against such practical self-contradictions is, of course, to argue *ad hominem*.

5. Some philosophical theories are said to be self-refuting because they set up conditions of meaning, rationality, and/or *truth that they themselves are unable to meet. For example, Ludwig *Wittgenstein in his *Tractatus Logico-Philosophicus* candidly admitted at the end that the propositions of his book did not measure up to his own criteria of meaning. He suggested that those propositions were a kind of ladder that one throws away after having used it to reach a higher vantage point. Later, the logical positivists insisted that a piece of *language cannot meaningfully state an empirical fact (either truly or falsely) unless it is empirically verifiable by methods akin to those of natural science. But many observed that this '*verification principle' itself could not be empirically verified in that way. That argument led to the demise of *logical positivism as an influential philosophical movement.

6. One philosophical view often accused of self-refutation is the general form of scepticism, which claims that there are no truths or that nothing can be known. This view is open to accusations of falling into the error noted above under (2), i.e. trying to state truly that there are no truths or claiming to know that nothing can be known. In response, sceptics may either abandon their scepticism, modify it to exclude their own claim (a move that can easily be criticized as arbitrary or self-serving),

or modify their view to allow for a few knowable truths. The last alternative might involve some sort of distinction between first-order truths and second-order truths (i.e. truths about truths), limiting scepticism to truth-claims of the first order. But it is hard to imagine any reason for first-order scepticism that would not apply equally to second-order scepticism. In any case, such a distinction naturally invites further arguments.

7. Immanuel *Kant argued that the truth of mathematics and *science cannot be proved by rational deduction (as *Leibniz) or by sense experience alone (*Hume), but rather by a 'transcendental' argument that shows the only conditions under which knowledge is possible. To deny this theory, Kant believed, is to deny the necessary conditions of knowledge while claiming to have knowledge, a self-refuting position. Similar claims, however, have been made for many epistemological theories, some very different from Kant's.

Christian apologists have often employed the concept of self-refutation against alternatives to Christian *theism. Gordon H. Clark, in *A Christian View of Men and Things* and other writings, is one of many apologists who emphasizes the logical contradictions of non-Christian thinkers, particularly those that entail scepticism. Stuart Hackett's *The Resurrection of Theism*, which develops a modification of Kant's *transcendental argument, is another example of an apologetic work in which this approach is prominent.

Francis *Schaeffer frequently employed the 'practical' sense of self-refutation (4). In *The God Who is There* (pp. 72–74) he refers to John Cage, who wrote 'random' music expressing his view that pure chance governs *reality. But Cage also collected mushrooms as a hobby, and he came to realize he would die if he applied his philosophy of chance to the gathering of mushrooms. In Schaeffer's view, Cage refuted himself in that his practice was inconsistent with his theory.

Cornelius Van Til often mentions in his writings (such as *Essays on Christian Education*, p. 89) a man he saw on a train whose little daughter was slapping his face. But she could not have reached him if he had not kept her on his lap. Van Til uses this incident to illustrate his view that the non-Christian cannot even argue against Christian theism without depending on it. To argue at all, even against Christianity, presupposes that the world is meaningful, knowable, and expressible in language. In Van Til's view, only Christian theism provides the conditions that make such rational discourse possible. Therefore, the unbeliever's very decision to argue against God refutes his position. This type of self-refutation is akin to (3) and (4) above, because the self-refutation is found not directly in the content of the assertion, but in the decision of a speaker to make that assertion.

Bibliography

G. H. Clark, *A Christian View of Men and Things* (Grand Rapids, 1952); S. Hackett, *The Resurrection of Theism* (Chicago, 1957); W. Hasker, 'Self-Referential Incoherence', in R. Audi (ed.), *The Cambridge Dictionary of Philosophy* (Cambridge, 1995), p. 721; F. Schaeffer, *The God Who Is There* (Chicago and London, 1968); C. Van Til, *Essays on Christian Education* (Phillipsburg, 1974); L. Wittgenstein, *Tractatus Logico-Philosophicus* (London, 1921, 1963).

J. M. FRAME

SENSE PERCEPTION, RELIABILITY OF

We can raise general questions about the reliability (i.e. the truth-conduciveness) of our cognitive, belief-producing sources such as perception, memory and introspection. Do these sources typically yield true rather than false beliefs? We may seek *evidence* that our cognitive sources are reliable in yielding true rather than false beliefs. In doing so, we aim to avoid circular *reasoning, where a source under question regarding its reliability is treated as if it were not under question. We thus ask what *non-circular*, or *non-question-begging*, *reason* we have to regard our cognitive sources as reliable, i.e. as trustworthy for acquiring truth and avoiding error. We then might seek to confirm the reliability of one cognitive source (say, auditory sensation) *without* relying on another cognitive source (say, visual sensation), because we have raised the same question concerning reliability about the latter source as about the former. Ideally, we aim to avoid circularity in answering our question about reliability.

Our question concerns the reliability of our cognitive sources such as perception, memory and introspection. In asking about *all* such sources, with regard to their reliability, we cannot rely on those sources to deliver non-question-begging, or non-circular, evidence of their reliability. Otherwise, an arbitrary circularity threatens. In addition, we cannot assume a position independent of our own cognitive sources to obtain a non-circular test of their reliability. We have no vantage point outside our cognitive sources from which we can assess their reliability. *Descartes suggested that the existence of a trustworthy God can underwrite the reliability of some cognitive sources. The suggestion is that if God is trustworthy, God would not allow for widespread unreliability in our cognitive sources. Such a suggestion calls for considerable argument, but an immediate problem arises. It seems that our reasonable acknowledgment of a trustworthy God, who ensures reliability in our cognitive sources, will rely on a cognitive source in question. In other words, such a cognitive source as perception, memory, or introspection will evidently play a role in our coming to know that a trustworthy God exists. In that case, a kind of circularity threatens Descartes's suggestion.

Our question about the reliability of our cognitive sources should be coherent. For instance, we should not demand non-question-begging evidence indicating the reliability of vision, for example, while we call into question, and thus refuse, any available evidence indicating the reliability of cognitive sources. That would be to demand that we stand somewhere to assess reliability while we are not allowed to stand anywhere. Such a demand would undermine itself owing to a kind of incoherence: call it demand incoherence. One can coherently question the reliability of all evidence available to us, and some sceptics do just this. In that case, however, one cannot coherently demand that we supply non-question-begging evidence indicating the reliability of our cognitive sources. If all available evidence (including that from our cognitive sources) is under question, then no evidence will be non-question-begging. So, a demand for non-question-begging evidence cannot coherently include unrestricted questioning of all available evidence. Any demand, then, that we establish the reliability of our cognitive sources must allow that some evidence should not be under question regarding reliability. Otherwise, a kind of incoherence threatens.

Fortunately, we have a firm place to stand in answering questions about evidence and reasonable belief: we may stand on our semantic, concept-forming intentions that give meaning to our terms. Consider the term 'epistemic reason'. *Philosophers of different outlooks share the general notion of an epistemic reason as a (possibly fallible) truth-indicator. An epistemic reason for a belief thus indicates, perhaps with only a degree of probability, that the belief is true. Our meaning-forming intentions (to use terms in a certain way) give semantic content to our talk of an 'epistemic reason for a belief'. Suppose we form the settled semantic intention to use 'truth-indicator' and 'epistemic reason' as follows: a visual experience, for example, of an *apparent* book in a situation with no accessible contrary evidence is a (fallible) truth-indicator and thus an epistemic reason for a visual belief that an actual book exists. This semantic intention, given its meaning-conferring role for us, could then serve as a directly accessible semantic truth-maker for our ascription of an epistemic reason for a visual belief that an actual book exists. It would then be part of what we mean by 'epistemic reason' that such an ascription captures an epistemic reason for a visual belief that an actual book exists. Our semantic intentions concerning 'epistemic reasons' may thus serve as ultimate, even if revisable, truth-makers for ascriptions of an epistemic reason.

What about sceptics who raise *doubts about the reliability and reasonableness of beliefs produced by our cognitive sources such as perception, memory and introspection? They might object that our semantic intentions can be 'mistaken', say in virtue of failing to capture language-independent justification. We can sidestep such an objection, however, because *reality (the objective world) does not settle how in particular we must seek *truth. For better or worse, it does not settle which specific variant (or specific concept) of justification, warrant, or knowledge is binding on a truth-seeker. Even so, one seeking to acquire truth and to avoid error should accommodate any necessary conditions for truth-acquisition (e.g. logical consistency in a belief) and for reliable and warranted belief.

Sceptics cannot convincingly hold non-sceptics to a specific concept or strategy of truth-acquisition that recommends scepticism. In particular, sceptics cannot cogently mandate an epistemic concept or strategy for us that undermines the aforementioned kind of epistemic reason (for visual beliefs) grounded in semantic intentions regarding 'epistemic reason'. One noteworthy problem for sceptics is that the aforementioned kind of epistemic reason is, so far as we can tell, at least as effective for judicious truth-acquisition as anything sceptics offer. In addition, sceptics have no stable foothold to propose that such a semantically grounded epistemic reason is defective as a fallible truth-indicator.

Sceptics cannot plausibly charge us with question-begging (or, circular reasoning) here. It is part of what we mean by 'epistemic reason' that the kind of ascription in question captures an epistemic reason for a visual belief that an actual book exists. So, we may now shift the burden of argument to the sceptic, and we may call this the sceptic's burden. We have, after all, produced a sceptic-resistant truth-indicator grounded in cognitively significant semantic intentions. We have also challenged inquirers to steer clear of demand incoherence. The sceptic's burden is now properly the sceptic's. Until this burden is met, we may endorse the reasonableness of some of the beliefs delivered by our cognitive sources. We may even endorse the reasonableness of belief in the reliability of some of our cognitive sources. It follows also that arguments for the reasonableness of theism have not been undermined by general sceptical worries about the reliability of sense perception.

Bibliography

W. P. Alston, *The Reliability of Sense Perception* (Ithaca, 1993); P. K. Moser, *Philosophy After Objectivity* (New York, 1993).

P. K. MOSER

SEXUALITY, see MARRIAGE, HOMOSEXUALITY
SHAMANISM, see PAGAN AND INDIGENOUS RELIGION

SHERLOCK, THOMAS

Thomas Sherlock, born in 1678, was the son of William Sherlock, the master of the Temple and dean of St Paul's. He succeeded his father as master of the Temple and later became the bishop of London in 1748.

Sherlock's writing had gained prominence in a debate with deists in 1725, where he was marked by some observers as the most powerful and rational opponent the deists faced. He published a volume of sermons entitled *The Use and Interest of Prophecy in the Several Ages of the World* in 1725 in response to Anthony Collins' deistic *Grounds of the Christian Religion*. Although he argued emphatically against the tenets of deism, Sherlock was praised for maintaining an even temper and a calm intellect despite opposition.

Sherlock opposed Benjamin Hoadly in the Bangorian controversy when Hoadly denied, in a sermon before the king in 1717, that the church had any doctrinal or disciplinary *authority. Sherlock eventually succeeded Hoadly as bishop of Bangor in 1728.

He published a strong apologetic in reply to Thomas Woolston's *Discourses on the Miracles*, titled *The Tryal of the Witnesses of the Resurrection of Jesus* (1729), which quickly ran through fourteen editions. In this, his most famous work, the 'claims of the witnesses of the resurrection are challenged by the prosecution in a courtroom setting. The defense argues its case and the jury renders its verdict as the author challenges [the reader] to do the same'. The ultimate question remains, 'What think ye of Christ?' Others, such as S. Greenleaf and J. W. Montgomery, have subsequently adopted the legal procedural method in apologetic argument.

Sherlock's most popular contemporary work was *A Letter to the Clergy and People of London and Westminster on occasion of the late Earthquake*, which appeared in 1750 and reads more like a novel than a sermon or letter. This work, which sold 100,000 copies in less than a month, denounced sin and appealed for changed hearts. Other popular sermon titles were 'Discourses on our Saviour's Miracles' (1729) and 'The Case of Insolvent Debtors, and the Charity Due to Them' (1728). Sherlock died in 1761.

Bibliography

Capstone Books, <http://www.capstonebooks. com/tryal.htm>; *The 1911 Edition Encyclopedia*, <http://33.1911encyclopedia.org/S/ SH/SHERLOCK_THOMAS.htm>; Sherlock, T., <http://www.bartleby.com/220/1508.html>; A. W. Ward *et al.*, *The Cambridge History of English and American Literature: An Encyclopedia* (New York, 1907–21).

J. C. ZELLMANN

SHINTO, see RELIGIONS OF CHINESE AND JAPANESE ORIGIN

SHROUD OF TURIN, see TURIN SHROUD

SIKHISM

Sikhism is a monotheistic religion, which holds that there is but one God, though he may be addressed by many names. The Mul Mantar, which is repeated at the beginning of every section of the Guru Granth Sahib, defines Sikh belief as 'There is but one God, the eternal truth, the creator, without fear, without enmity, timeless, immanent, beyond birth and death, self existent; by the grace of the Guru, made known.' Because God is formless he can never be incarnated in human form. A Sikh is defined as one who believes in the one immortal God, the Sikh Scriptures and the ten Gurus and their teaching.

Like Hindus, Sikhs believe in transmigration and the cycle of birth, death and rebirth. Our present status (good or bad) is determined by our past deeds. The Gurus taught that there is an almost endless round of 8,400,000 rebirths. Being born as a human gives the soul the opportunity to break that cycle through the grace of the Guru and meditation on the divine name. The soul must pass through five stages of development to reach the realm of bliss.

The Sikh concept of the world is similar to that found in *Hinduism. The world as we know it is not real but only a passing phase created by illusion (*maya*). According to Guru Nanak, 'This world is like a drama staged in a dream', emerging from God and merging with him again in endless cycles. Apart from God nothing is real and human beings are but puppets in his hands.

God records each person's destiny at birth on their forehead on the basis of their past deeds. The chances of attaining salvation in this life are remote, because destiny is unalterable. The scope for salvation is thus narrowed to a desperate hope that by God's grace his unalterable writ will be superseded. The longing for salvation is so intense in the prayers and songs of the Gurus, that it defies all the odds and finds hope in the mercy of God.

Critique of Sikhism

Sikhism arose out of Hinduism as a reform movement, protesting against the worship of many gods, idolatry, superstition, ritualism, priestcraft and casteism. Guru Nanak and the early Gurus devoted themselves to worship and meditation, singing the songs they composed in prayer to God, and incorporating in their scriptures the hymns of Hindu and Muslim devotees in tune with their theistic beliefs. Guru Nanak shared with *Islam the avowed belief in one God and its concomitant rejection of rival gods and idols. Sikhs believe that the formula *Ek Onkar* (One God) was given to Guru Nanak by God himself.

Sikhism is a religion of noble ideals and aspirations. However it has not been able to shake off its theological and philosophical dependence on Hinduism with regard to its views of God, creation, karma and transmigration. This is particularly serious in regard to its understanding of God. For though the Gurus had an intense longing to know God and desired a personal encounter with God, their formal conception of liberation (*mukti*) fell back on Hindu theories of fusion with a divine essence. They wrote of liberation as the soul merging into an impersonal Being. They took over the Hindu distinction between God as transcendent (*nirguna*) and God as immanent (*saguna*). Ultimately God is thought of as essentially transcendent, unapproachable and unknowable, to be described only in negative terms. Sikhs, like Hindus, believe that the universe emerges from and re-merges with the divine essence through immense cycles of time. Such a God is not the object of the songs of the Gurus, longing for the manifestation of the divine Name.

Similarly the Hindu doctrine of karma presented problems for the Gurus, who believed that sinners cannot attain liberation without the grace of God. 'If God's grace rests upon us, it is then that we obtain the Name. Of ourselves we cannot find it,' says Guru Nanak. Yet the karma doctrine decrees that only those who have earned the favour of God can receive it. Grace cannot be given, unless it is deserved by the good deeds of previous lives. According to the Gurus the bestowal of grace is a mystery, and there is no reason why some receive it and others do not. God's gift of grace helps human beings to recognize the Guru, but this is not salvation itself. The favour of God still needs to be earned through service, meditation and the repetition of the divine Name. From this it can be seen that grace in Sikhism is very different from the free gift of God available to all in the gospel of Christ.

Another aspect of Sikhism, which should not be ignored, is the ideal of the soldier-saint. The tenth Guru, Govind Singh, reshaped the heritage of the Gurus in this mode and gave Sikhism the form with which we are familiar today. This militant side of Sikhism has led in recent decades to the demand for a Sikh homeland in Indian Punjab, which in turn reinforces the identification of Sikhs as Punjabis. It is difficult to realize that at the time of the tenth Guru his followers were not all Punjabis but came from many parts of India. The militancy of many Jat Sikhs is not consistent with the devotional spirit of Guru Nanak or the aim to make Sikhism a world religion. It also makes some Sikhs more resistant to the appeal of Christianity.

Christian response

Pivotal to the Sikh hope of salvation is the role of the Guru. The Sikh Gurus knew that without someone to guide them they would never have attained the presence of God. Though human teachers and the company of the saintly were necessary, only God himself, as the divine Guru, could save them. 'May someone come and cause me to meet my perfect, true Guru,' says Guru Arjan Dev. 'My soul and body, I shall dedicate to him. Cutting my body into bits, I shall offer these as well to him.' Christ is the Sat Guru (the true Guru), not the knower of the way, but the way himself.

The major obstacle in the way of Sikhs recognizing Christ as the divine Guru is their belief that God is formless and cannot take human form. This conviction was formulated in the context of Hindu belief in *avatara*, connected with the worship of many gods. Christ is very different from Hindu avatars in a number of respects. Whereas Hindu incarnations are said to be gods like Ram or Krishna or lesser beings, in Christ the fullness of the Godhead was bodily displayed. Christians agree that God is formless, beyond all the limitations and confines of the created order, but being triune is able to remain formless and also, as the Word, to take flesh and dwell among us. The Sikh term for the Word is *Shabad*. It is said to be present in everything, but to be beyond human perception. In *Jesus the *Shabad* of God is revealed.

The Gurus' prayers focused on three desires: that God would grant them the divine Name (*Nam*), the vision of God (*darshan*) and liberation from the endless pain of transmigration (*mukti*). In Christ these three aspirations have been fulfilled and their realization offered to every living soul created in the image of God.

The Gurus' desire for the divine Name was not a simplistic quest for the right title for God or a human name by which they might approach God. For them the Name of God is not an abstract word but the key to the reality of God himself. Through the Name implanted in the mind the devotee is able to meditate on the immortal Lord. Jesus Christ is the eternal creator (*Akaal Purakh*), his is the divine Name, and 'there is no other name under heaven given to men by which they must be saved' (Acts 4:12).

Closely linked to the longing for the divine Name is the prayer for the vision of God. It is impossible to see the formless, unknowable creator. Nevertheless the Gurus' passionate longing could not be silenced by cold logic. 'Grant me a sight of thee,' cries Guru Nanak, 'and take me unto thine embrace'. How beautifully he would have responded, if he had encountered the risen Lord, through whom we see God in the face of Jesus Christ.

Liberation from the endless round of birth, death and rebirth is what the Gurus craved for. Listen to Guru Arjan Dev again: 'I have passed through many births and deaths. But without union with my beloved, no salvation is obtained. O Lord emancipate me.' Christ came precisely for the purpose of answering that longing of the heart. He achieved the costly liberation of mankind by bearing the sin of the world in his sacrifice on the cross. It is to the paradox of the crucified Guru that the gospel points the Sikh devotee in search of salvation.

Bibliography

R. Gidoomal and M. Wardell, *Lions, Princesses, Gurus* (Godalming, 1996); J. S. Grewal, *The Sikhs of the Punjab* (Cambridge, 1990); W. H. McLeod, *Sikhism* (London, 1997); H. S. Rahi, *Sri Guru Granth Sahib Discovered* (Delhi, 1999).

B. J. M. SCOTT

SIN, see EVIL, NOETIC EFFECTS OF SIN

SKINNER, B. F.

Born in 1904 in Susquehanna, Pennsylvania, and son of a lawyer, B. F. Skinner (1904–90) was raised in a middle-class Protestant family. He attended Hamilton College and planned a literary career, but soon enrolled in *psychology, completing his PhD at Harvard in 1931. Skinner taught at the University of Minnesota, Indiana University and also Harvard.

The father of modern behavioural psychology, Skinner is known for his emphasis on behaviour rather than mental processes. Considered the most prominent American psychologist of the twentieth century, Skinner sought to control, predict and interpret behaviour. He disliked formal theory and emphasized single-subject rather than group research. Skinner showed that most animal and human behaviour was operant rather than respondent, i.e. controlled by its consequence rather than elicited by the environment. He developed the Skinner Box, the cumulative recorder and the first teaching machines.

A prolific writer, Skinner published nineteen books. Perhaps most influential are *The Behavior of Organisms* (1935), an initial presentation of his theory and philosophy; *Science and Human Behavior* (1953), which applied his theory to everyday human activities; and *Verbal Behavior* (1957), his approach to cognition and experience. He also wrote extensively about his life and career. Skinner helped found the *Journal of the Experimental Analysis of Behavior* and the Division of the Experimental Analysis of Behavior in the American Psychological Association.

Skinner espoused materialistic humanism and was a signatory to the *Humanist Manifesto II. Beyond Freedom and Dignity* (1971) articulated Skinner's philosophy of social systems, *ethics and religion. Skinner viewed moral behaviour as simply the way a person had been taught to behave. At times Skinner's humanistic views seemed to shape his scientific conclusions, e.g. he concluded that punishment had harmful effects and did not work, a view others challenged.

Critics charged that Skinner reduced men to dehumanized robots without freedom or personal responsibility, undermined morals, fostered totalitarianism by his emphasis on control of human behaviour and confused his personal philosophy with psychology. He responded to his critics, most extensively in *Answers for My Critics* (in Wheeler, 1973).

Though a determinist, Skinner proposed that humans control their own destiny: 'Man himself may be controlled by his environment, but it is an environment which is almost wholly of his own making.' Thus he ended up advocating a view similar to that of *causality and responsible choice, a view held by many Christians. Though many view Skinner's religious perspectives as central to behaviour theory, behaviour theory need not embrace Skinner's world-view.

Skinner received many honours and over twenty honorary degrees. He was a fellow of the American Psychological Association and the Royal Society of Arts and member of the National Academy of Sciences, the American Philosophical Society, the American Academy of Arts and Sciences and the New York Academy of Sciences, among others.

Bibliography

R. K. Bufford, *The Human Reflex: Behavioral Psychology in Biblical Perspective* (New York, 1981); M. P. Cosgrove, *B. F. Skinner's Behaviorism* (Grand Rapids, 1982); J. G. Holland, 'B. F. Skinner (1904–1990)', *American Psychologist*, 47 (1992), pp. 665–667; J. A. Weigel, *B. F. Skinner* (Boston, 1977); H. Wheeler (ed.), *Beyond the Punitive Society* (San Francisco, 1973).

R. K. BUFFORD

SLAVERY

Slavery, or the ownership of a person or persons by another or others, appears to be as old as history itself. The earliest written records from Sumer indicate that those whom the Sumerians conquered, the Subarians, gave their name to the Sumerian cognate for 'slave'. Similarly, the first lawcodes, such as that of Hammurabi, contain sections dealing with slaves. The first biblical reference to slavery, Genesis 37:23–38, occurs when Joseph is sold to the Ishmaelites for twenty shekels. Slavery has been practised by virtually every society, some being slave-holding societies that simply tolerate the practice, and others being true slave societies, wherein the major portion of the economy is based on slave labour.

There are many variations on the concept of slavery. Servitude, or compulsory service, was an essential part of legal penalties for theft in ancient societies (e.g. Exod. 22:3), as well as for failure to pay debts. In theory, these forms of slavery were of limited duration, much like indentured servitude, although in practice the penalties could creep over into permanent status. That is why the great sixth-century Athenian lawgiver Solon abolished debt slavery in his *Shaking Off of the Burdens* in 509 BC. By this time, however, slave labour had become such an integral part of the Greek economy that the abolition of traditional debt servitude was simply replaced by a resort to buying chattel slaves from other cities or from foreign tribes. This engendered a shift from slavery as a circumstantial condition, theoretically possible for anyone down on his luck, to the view of slavery as an ethnic status. Thus *Aristotle (d. 322 BC) could view some people as 'slaves by nature' and designate a slave as a 'living tool'. The Roman writer Varro (first century AD) would later complete this trend by categorizing farming implements as 'mute' (such as ploughs), 'inarticulate' (such as oxen and other work animals), or 'articulate' (which were the slaves).

Slavery in Greco-Roman society was not confined to heavy labour. Certainly the Athenian silver mines at Laurium were stocked with slave labour; and the Romans actually considered slave labour in mining, the legal sentence of *damnatio ad metallum*, as a suitable variant on capital punishment. But equally common, and certainly more pervasive, was the use of slaves as a type of retirement account. Lacking workman's compensation and retirement provisions, the prudent worker would save up to buy a slave, so that, when no longer able to work, he might hire the slave out in his place. Since the slave might earn three times more than the cost of his upkeep, such a scheme proved financially rewarding for the elderly or disabled worker.

Slaves often rose to prominent positions in the Greco-Roman economy. Frequently, slaves were to be found as farm managers as well as bank executives. Most ships in the Roman Imperial fleet were commanded by slaves. In all these posts, the slave was thought to be more reliable than a free man because of his complete dependence on his master. While Demosthenes noted, in fourth-century BC Athens, that even the poorest of war taxpayers, who typically had plots of only six or seven acres, could still afford a slave, the talented ones fetched a hefty price. Nicias, a fifth-century BC mine-owner, found a slave capable of managing his business and was willing to pay one talent, or 6,000 times a daily wage, for him.

The advent of Christianity did not signal the end of slavery. Even though slave traders are mentioned in 1 Timothy 1:10 among the list of sinners suitably punished by God, the unmistakable thrust of the NT is to spiritualize slavery rather than eradicate it. Slaves and slave-holders are admonished to act Christianly toward one another, yet remain in their present status (1 Cor. 7:20–24). Passages such as Romans 6:16–18, suggested that, since all are slaves to something or someone, each Christian should now be a 'slave to righteousness'. Consequently, this spiritualization of slavery led to an incorporation of slave-holding into the church.

St *Augustine (354–430 AD) held that 'it is better to be a slave to man than a slave to sin', and slave ownership became no bar to holiness. St Martin of Tours (336–97 AD) was considered an extreme ascetic, in part because he had but one slave, while the fourth-century Christian matron Melania the Younger was considered quite holy when she kept only a few of her 8,000 slaves as she 'renounced the world'. Emphasizing this spiritualization, Pope Gregory the Great (540–604 AD) regularly signed himself 'Slave of the slaves of God' (servus servorum Dei). The practice of servitium, whereby those healed at a saint's shrine became the slaves of the church, grew to be so pervasive that the Sixteenth Council of Toledo, meeting in Visigothic Spain in 693, ruled that churches lacking a minimum of ten slaves could not have their own priest but must be attached to another parish.

As the Middle Ages progressed, and large-scale industries were replaced by manor-based farming, serfdom replaced slave labour in much of Europe. Along the frontiers, however, the Vikings carried on a brisk slave trade with the East, while Germanic warrior-settlers enslaved so many Slavs that their name (Sclavus) became the basis for the very word 'slave'.

With the great age of exploration in the fifteenth and sixteenth centuries, slavery underwent its own renaissance. The early conquistadors took their cue from Christopher Columbus (1451–1506), who remarked, as he watched the timid Taino Indians flee from a cannon salute he had arranged in their honour, 'How easy it would be to convert these people and make them work for us.' Soon the encomienda system encompassed the Spanish colonies in the New World. The native American slaves on these plantations largely gave way to hardier stock: African slaves purchased as the spoils of inter-tribal warfare and shipped across the Atlantic. Unlike the Greco-Roman system, this form of slavery on the encomienda, as well as the burgeoning plantations of the American South, was primarily racial and offered no opportunities for slaves to hold white-collar jobs as farm managers, bank executives or captains of seaworthy vessels. The old Roman practice of vernae, or keeping slaves born to slaves on the estate for life, which had been lightly used as a source of slave re-supply in ancient times, saw a tremendous, and profitable, rebirth on the US plantations.

The gulf between slave-owner and slave, now widened by racial and occupational barriers, led to a high degree of dehumanization of the mestizo and African workforce. The concomitant brutality of the systems led to an increasing sentiment for legal abolition. The *Enlightenment emphasis on 'the rights of man', such as the assertion by Jean-Jacques *Rousseau (1712–78) that we all inherit nobility from Noah, aided this growing movement. In the UK, a Christian call for abolition led by William Wilberforce (1759–1833) succeeded, and the Congress of Vienna (1814–15) abolished slavery by treaty in most of Europe. The independence struggles of the Latin American colonies in the early nineteenth century ended slavery there, but in the USA it took a bloody civil war (1861–65) to accomplish the task.

Slavery has, however, never been completely abolished worldwide, and continues in some countries, such as the Sudan, even today. Perhaps it is even more pernicious in its new, non-traditional forms. As Robin Winks (Slavery, p. 165) has pointed out, historians have assumed slavery to be a permanent condition and have not realized that it can be 'involuntary servitude for a term rather than for life'. The 'new slavery' of today often consists of children being enslaved for a period of months or years in labour-intensive manufacturing, or young women held in sexual slavery for a period of time and then discarded or 'freed'. The duration may be short in comparison to traditional, lifelong slavery, but the enslavement is just as real.

Slavery is rightly condemned across cultures and epochs as dehumanizing to both slave and master and conducive to many forms of abuse. Racial and sexual components in modern slavery create problems that can be deleterious to civilization as a whole. The Christian can, however, see in the complete submission of the slave a useful spiritual metaphor for the relationship of the believer to God, as a 'slave of Christ' (Eph. 6:5–8).

Bibliography

K. Bales, *New Slavery: A Reference Handbook* (Santa Barbara, 2000); R. Blackburn, *The Making of New World Slavery: From the Baroque to the Modern, 1492–1800* (London, 1997); D. B. Davis, *The Problem of Slavery in Western Culture* (Ithaca, 1966); M. I. Finley, *Ancient Slavery and Modern Ideology* (New York, 1980); P. Garnsey, *Ideas of Slavery from Aristotle to Augustine* (Cambridge, 1996); R. W. Winks (ed.), *Slavery: A Comparative Perspective* (New York, 1972).

B. W. REYNOLDS

SOCIALISM

Introduction: the principle of common ownership extended

Socialism's relationship to biblical faith is a complex one, sometimes standing in opposition to it and sometimes being claimed to be nothing less than Christianity put into practice. Although there is more than one way to define socialism, it usually revolves around a single form of common ownership of property to the exclusion of ownership by other communities and individuals. The assumption is that, because private property divides the earth's scarce resources unequally, many people are left with little or no means of subsistence and are thus faced with poverty and hunger. Socialism is viewed as a method of transcending such circumstances by ensuring that, within a given community, members will produce as much as they are able while the same members may withdraw from the common store of accumulated wealth as they have need. Or, as the Marxian dictum puts it, 'from each according to his ability; to each according to his needs' (Marx, *Critique of the Gotha Programme*, I.3).

The socialist challenge to Christianity

Although the book of Acts twice describes the early Jerusalem church as practising a rather extensive form of common ownership of property (2:44–45; 4:34–35), more recent socialists have often seen themselves standing in opposition to Christianity, as well as to all traditional religions. This opposition is most famously reflected in the writings of Karl Marx (1818–83), who, despite his Jewish background and his family's nominal conversion to Lutheranism, came to embrace *atheism as a logical concomitant of his adherence to Ludwig *Feuerbach's philosophical *materialism. Accordingly, Marx argues that human beings have created religion as a byproduct of their alienation from the concrete materiality of the world and from the products of their labour. As such, it is one more manifestation of the ideological distortions that plague human consciousness and prevent people taking their destinies in their own hands, particularly with respect to ending oppression. Marx's well-known observation that religion is the 'opium of the people' must be understood in this context. Putting an end to religion would, he assumes, serve to awaken the members of the oppressed working class to the reality of their plight and motivate them to do something about it. Concomitantly, ending oppression, which he sees accompanying the inevitable arrival of the classless society, would make religion unnecessary.

Friedrich Engels, though sharing the atheism of his long-time collaborator Karl Marx, nevertheless draws a parallel between the rise of Christianity during the Roman era and that of the labour union movement of his own day. Christianity, he argues, was originally a movement of oppressed slaves and poor people. Michael Harrington, continuing Engels' analogy, states that, with Constantine's conversion of Rome to Christianity, that religion became 'a religion of the rulers rather than of the ruled' (*Socialism*, p. 15). As such, it came to stand in opposition to efforts at changing society, particularly in revolutionary fashion.

Although not all socialists have by any means been atheists, the association between socialism and atheism stems in large measure from its modern origins in the French Revolution and its philosophical antecedents, which tended towards an anticlerical viewpoint hostile especially to the Church of Rome. Like other ideologies, such as liberalism, nationalism and radical democracy, socialism's rise and subsequent dissemination depended on the general climate of *secularism which had an increasing impact on Europe after 1789. In this respect, socialism was part of a much larger challenge to the Christian faith.

In the twentieth century the connection between socialism and atheism became especially acute in the various communist regimes that claimed to follow the Leninist variant of Marxism. Because adherence to traditional religions did not, as expected, become obsolescent after 1917, successive Soviet leaders subjected open believers to periodic persecutions of greater or lesser intensity. Indeed, such persecutions intensified the fear of *communism in the West, particular during the era of the Cold War (1945–89).

The Christian response to socialism

The response of Christians to the rise of socialism has taken at least three forms. First, there have been a number who have attempted to wed Christianity and socialism, retaining what its followers have seen as the ethical substance of the former while embracing the latter's political and economic programme. These include the Christian Socialism of nineteenth-century England, the social gospel of early twentieth-century North America, and the liberation theology of late twentieth-century Latin America.

Christian Socialism was largely a nineteenth-century British phenomenon which sought to implement a cooperative economic arrangement based on profit-sharing as a means of ameliorating the legitimate grievances of the industrial working class. It would come to have an impact on the formation of the Labour Party just before the end of the century. In North America the social gospel was especially influential within the historic Protestant churches, although in the United States it also had an impact on the (ultimately unsuccessful) Socialist Party itself and on the social reforms of Franklin D. Roosevelt's New Deal programme. The Canadian version of this movement influenced the denominations that became the United Church of Canada in 1925, as well as the Co-operative Commonwealth Federation (CCF), a social democratic party begun in the early years of the Great Depression. Liberation theology arose in the 1960s in Latin America, affecting both Protestant and Catholic churches. Liberation theologians apply Marxist class analysis to both the internal relationship between domestic rich and poor and the external relationship between the developed West and the poor countries of the South, especially Latin America.

A second Christian response to socialism has been characterized by determined opposition and a reaffirmation of its apparent adversary, *capitalism. This approach has often retained Marx's categories and even something of his

dialectic, but has obviously rejected his historical *determinism with its implicit soteriological framework. Among North American proponents of this view are the circle of Catholic neo-conservatives who claim to embrace what they call *democratic capitalism*, an expression used in particular by Michael Novak, a representative figure in this group.

A third response has come from Christians in especially the Roman Catholic and Reformed traditions, led by such thinkers as Pope Leo XIII (1810–1903, pope from 1878) and Abraham *Kuyper (1837–1920) respectively. Leo is best known for his social teachings as set forth in a series of ground-breaking encyclicals, culminating in *Rerum Novarum* (1891), subtitled 'On the Condition of the Workers'. Writing in the context of the dislocations engendered by the Industrial Revolution in Europe, Leo sought to set forth a distinctively Christian response to the challenge raised by the nascent socialist parties. To their call for the abolition of private property, Leo countered that ownership of property is rooted in the natural law and is the only source of economic security for members of the beleaguered working class. In place of the socialist tendency towards statism, Leo offered a principle which would later come to be known as *subsidiarity*, by which various human responsibilities are allocated to the lowest possible level within a social hierarchy, the state intervening only when the subordinate agents are unable to function adequately.

Kuyper, who founded the first Christian democratic party in the world and served as prime minister of the Netherlands between 1901 and 1905, drew on his own *Calvinist tradition and formulated the principle of *sphere sovereignty*, by which the pluriform agents in society, including individuals and communities, undertake their respective responsibilities in direct obedience to God's ordinances. Kuyper delivered an address to the first Christian Social Congress in 1891, in which he addressed *The Social Question and the Christian Religion* (translated and republished a century later as *The Problem of Poverty*). Here, in direct response to the socialist challenge in his own country, Kuyper advocated an important role for government in defending the rights of labour and ameliorating the plight of the poor.

It might finally be said that the rise of socialism, with its emphasis on social *justice and on securing the rights of the materially disadvantaged, has prompted Christians to look within their own traditions for resources serviceable to establishing and maintaining a more equitable economic arrangement.

Bibliography

G. Gutiérrez, *A Theology of Liberation* (New York, 1973); M. Harrington, *Socialism* (New York, 1970, 1972); D. T. Koyzis, *Political Visions and Illusions: A Survey and Christian Critique of Contemporary Ideologies* (Downers Grove, 2003); A. Kuyper, *The Problem of Poverty* (Washington, DC, and Grand Rapids, 1991); Leo XIII, *Rerum Novarum* (Rome, 1891); K. Marx and F. Engels, *Manifesto of the Communist Party* (1848); M. Novak, *The Spirit of Democratic Capitalism* (New York, 1982); W. Rauschenbusch, *A Theology for the Social Gospel* (New York, 1918).

D. T. KOYZIS

SOCIOLOGY

Sociology is an attempt to understand the way social relations are formed and maintained and change over time. Avoiding impressionistic or selective accounts, it seeks to explain social behaviour with a degree of objectivity and in a way that can be tested by others. Going beyond the merely descriptive, it investigates the causal basis of our social actions. Sociologists operate on several levels. On the micro level they may examine small and discrete examples of social interaction. Since, however, social relations often involve repeated patterns of behaviour or activities that cluster in certain areas, they also give attention to the way social institutions, such as the family, the education system, the criminal underworld or the media, function. On the macro level some consider how whole societies operate, including the values and arrangements that shape and hold them together. They may also engage in comparative or historical research. In every case it is a basic axiom of sociology that the whole is more than the sum of the individual parts.

Religion is one aspect of human social behaviour, and sociologists approach it in the same way as they might investigate the leisure industry or the workings of politics. A sociological explanation of human behaviour restricts itself to that which is empirically observable and consequently brackets out God or the supernatural as an explanation of religion. Good sociologists will take into account how religious people speak of their *religious experience and try to enter as fully as possible into the world of the believer – otherwise their explanations may be far removed from the reality experienced. By definition, however, their explanation is confined to the natural. This explains why sociologists often appear to write about religion in a reductionist way, i.e. in a way that reduces the supernatural experience of the believer to natural explanation. This reductionism is often referred to as 'nothing buttery' because the impression given is that religious behaviour is 'nothing but' the outworking of various social factors. It is, however, disingenuous, for even the most ardent sociologist must acknowledge that all *reality is complex and capable of explanation at a number of levels. The sociological level is one among many, albeit an insightful one and on occasions even the most significant one. Sociological explanation cannot be the only, or the total, explanation of the behaviour.

Sociological explanation of religion still owes much to the founding fathers of the discipline, who gave rise to a number of different schools of thought. Historically, the schools of conflict sociology, associated with Karl Marx (1818–83), functionalism, associated with Emile Durkheim (1858–1917), and social action, associated with Max *Weber (1864–1920), are significant. To Marx, society was based on material interests and advanced through the clash of opposites, of which the class system was a key expression. His views on religion are more complex than often assumed, but he certainly argued that it enslaved people in a state of false consciousness and was an instrument of oppression in the hands of the powerful. Durkheim stressed the cohesive factors that bound people into the collective and viewed society as a body or self-regulating system. To him religion was a major integrative, stabilizing force. Weber's approach continues to be the most fruitful. Striving for objectivity, he sought to understand social behaviour from the standpoint of the individual actor so that causal explanations would be well founded. He demonstrated the value of the approach in a wide range of studies in religion that include his work on the relationship between the Protestant (see *Christianity, Protestant) work ethic and modern rational *capitalism. His work remains even more useful because of his fascination with the rational principle on which the modern world was founded. Among the many contemporary debates that trace their roots back to Weber is that of *secularization, which is still too often used, in a way he would regret, as an ideological weapon to denigrate religion, rather than as an explanatory tool.

A key perspective relevant to the explanation of religion is that of social constructionism. Drawing on earlier roots, Peter Berger (b. 1929) (and Thomas Luckmann), argued that we are architects of our own identities, our interpretations of the world and the way we experience it. Although the social world appears to us, especially in early days, as a given, and although the way we see it is deeply inbred in us (so much so that we are not aware of it as other than 'factual'), in reality we construct our self and social worlds and the meaning we give to them. The way we do this has much to do with the significant social networks we inhabit. In these 'plausibility structures', as they are called, people we regard as significant feed us with particular interpretations, maintain their plausibility through conversation and the use of appropriate *language, underlined by rites and rituals, defend them with apt apologetics and impose sanctions on those who stray outside the fold. This perspective is frequently applied to religious practice and belief. So, is faith nothing more than a social construction? Is our experience of God nothing more than the way we have been led to see things, a social construction built with our own hands?

Social constructionism need not be intimidating to believers, or corrosive of religious practice. Strictly speaking, it describes a mechanism by which we gain knowledge of any kind. *Science, mathematics, *history, *psychology and sociology itself are all viewed as social constructions, alongside religion. All are equally secure, or equally vulnerable. This understanding helps us to relativize those who would relativize the Christian faith. Those who wish to argue that the believer's explanation of the world is 'merely' a social construction need to be cautious, since the same charge ricochets back on their own lack of faith. Unbelief is as socially constructed as belief.

The advocates of the approach say the question of the validity of a religious belief must be left to one side. The validity of a belief depends not on its social construction but on other factors, like the extent to which it makes sense of what humans actually experience and resonates with the 'reality' that they encounter. The process of assessing how much a belief corresponds to experienced reality also enables someone to choose between alternative ideas and means that it is possible to avoid the trap of *relativism. It is for these reasons that Berger advocates an inductive approach to *theology, i.e. one that starts with human experience, as preferable to either deductive or reductive approaches.

Not all are prepared to adopt a full-blown concept of social construction, believing that it is in danger of claiming too much. To accept that religious convictions and practices are socially conditioned is irrefutable. Consider the relationship between social background and denominational loyalty and the conditioning element soon becomes apparent. It is also much more easily compatible with the Christian belief in a living God who reveals himself to and communicates with his creatures, usually making himself known through intermediate channels, like prophets or the body of Christ, rather than directly.

The God of the Bible, though eternal spirit, is a God of creation and incarnation. He works in and through the world he has made and reveals himself in the arena of time and space. He operates not only in the physical world but through the social world as well. He is the Creator of rich and varied human *cultures – tainted though they all now are through the fall – and the various institutions of family, race, *law, economy and government in order that societies may be strong and healthy. Given this, it is not surprising that the practice and articulation of the faith should change over time according to the particular cultural contexts in which they operate. That is why sociologists are able to trace some congruence between, say, the charismatic movement and postmodern culture and say why phenomena like those demonstrated in the recent 'Toronto Blessing' might be said to resonate sociologically with contemporary culture. Such observations should not undermine faith but rather excite further wonder at the ever-contemporary and ever-creative God who relates to us in our day and culture.

To understand behaviour from a sociological viewpoint need not, therefore, be corrosive to faith although it may be challenging, even disturbing. Christians should not treat its findings with complacent indifference, since sociological research can help believers to see the social factors that predispose them to believe or behave in certain ways. It may alert them to the social channels through which the faith is mediated, and help, by raising sociological awareness, to distinguish between the principles that are divinely revealed and a particular way in which those principles have been applied, which can amount to no more than 'the tradition of the elders'. Sociology may highlight the social consequences that particular beliefs will have. It may also lead to a greater spiritual authenticity that enables believers to separate the wheat of divine action from the chaff of passing cultural fashions.

In recent days, sociology has relented in its quest for old-fashioned scientific objectivity and recognized that all who undertake research have a set of presuppositions on which they build. Hence there have emerged schools that self-consciously advocate Marxist sociology, feminist sociology, postmodern sociology and so on. That opens the door for the creation of a constructive Christian sociology in the future.

Bibliography

P. Berger, *A Rumour of Angels* (New York and Harmondsworth, 1970); D. A. Fraser and A. Campolo, *Sociology Through the Eyes of Faith* (San Francisco and Leicester, 1992); R. Perkins, *Looking Both Ways: Exploring the Interface between Christianity and Sociology* (Grand Rapids, 1987).

D. J. TIDBALL

SOCRATES

The Athenian philosopher Socrates (469–399 BC) saw himself as divinely called and divinely inspired. He wrote no book, but many of his ideas have been preserved in the writings of his younger contemporaries, *Plato and Xenophon.

In contrast to the Presocratics, the Greek philosophers who immediately preceded him, Socrates' interest was not in the nature of the world, but in moral and practical issues like virtue and right living. His method, for which he is famed, was that of dialogue. Typically he would ask someone for a definition of a specific virtue; he would then proceed to show by further questioning that the definition given was unsatisfactory. Though he doubtless had his own views, especially about the nature of virtue, Socrates did not normally teach them directly, preferring, we may assume, to enable his listeners to find the answers for themselves, once the poverty of their proposed definitions was exposed. Because of this, and because all our information about him is mediated through Plato and Xenophon, it is difficult to say with certainty just what Socrates himself believed. Although Socrates features in most of Plato's many dialogues, it is generally recognized that Plato used him as a front for his own ideas, and that these at times, particularly in the middle and later dialogues, diverged from those of the real Socrates.

After a time of political turmoil in Athens, the seventy-year-old Socrates was brought to trial, accused of rejecting the traditional Greek gods, introducing new gods, and corrupting the young men of Athens. He was found guilty and executed by poisoning. We have accounts by Plato and Xenophon of his robust defence ('apology') at his trial, where he sought to respond to specific allegations, and also to explain his sense of mission to the youth of Athens. After being sentenced to death, he made a further speech in which he showed no fear of dying and expressed calm faith in life after death.

Socrates has been recognized through the centuries as a type of the ideal philosopher: a humble seeker after *truth, willing to question everything, fearlessly exposing false ideas and poor arguments and committed to seek and follow goodness and truth wherever they may take him and at whatever personal cost. In the early Christian centuries parallels were drawn between Socrates and *Jesus. In the modern period the figure of Socrates was used in a variety of ways by philosophers, including *Hegel, *Kierkegaard and Nietzsche. Kierkegaard, for example, strongly contrasted Socrates and Christ. Socrates, he said, enabled his hearers to recall truths they already knew; Christ brought new truths. Socrates assumed that his hearers could receive truth and put it into practice; Christ knew that this was not so, and so came as saviour as well as teacher. Socrates deliberately directed his followers away from himself; Christ directed attention to himself and called for faith in himself as redeemer. *Nietzsche saw Socrates as the one who had stressed the priority of reason over against the higher values of earlier Greek culture, such as art, beauty and the sense of the tragic. In a wider sense he saw him as typifying any philosophy or religion which urged the subordination of our natural desires and feelings to reason or moral or social values or religious principles. As such he represented the wrong pathway that much of human history has followed.

Contemporary Christian apologetics can learn much from the Socratic method. Though the authoritative monologue of preaching undoubtedly still has a place where it is a faithful exposition of God's revealed truth to those who will accept it as such, most of the people we engage with today will be much more ready to engage in dialogue than to listen to a sermon. Socrates shows us that dialogue does not have to be indecisive. If we have a conviction, as Socrates had, that there is such a thing as truth, and that honest inquiry will lead us towards it, then we should be confident enough to enter into dialogue with those with whom we disagree. Socrates also shows us the value of exposing the weaknesses of alternative views before introducing our own answers, an approach used very effectively by Cornelius *Van Til and Francis *Schaeffer.

Bibliography

H. Tarrant (ed.), *The Last Days of Socrates* (London, 2003).

P. HICKS

SOLIPSISM

Foundational to the biblical world-view are God and relationships. If we are to understand anything, we must view it in the context of God, as only by starting with him as creator and upholder, standard-setter and judge, can we get the world or anything in it into true perspective. Without the God-perspective everything becomes meaningless. Indeed, without God, everything would collapse into nothingness.

So with relationships. The primary relationship is that between any object or person and God, but out of that relationship comes a whole network of relationships. It is relationships that give particulars or individuals meaning. As an isolated individual I barely exist, but as a person held in being and loved by God, known and loved by others, sharing life and experiences and knowledge and communication, relating, belonging, part of community – then my being becomes something rich and glorious.

By and large the medieval period maintained the biblical concepts of theocentricity and community. But the dawn of Renaissance humanism and its development in *Enlightenment *rationalism gradually replaced God with the 'I', and relationships and community with individualism. As a result, Western thought has hovered on the brink of an abyss for the past four hundred years. It is no exaggeration to say that unless God is the centre of my universe, ultimately, I am the centre, whether ontologically, morally, or epistemologically. If I have no relationship with him, I have no relationship.

The abyss that opens up when we reject God and relationship is solipsism. The word comes from the Latin for 'the self on its own'. At its crudest it states that I alone exist. In its more refined forms it refers to the belief that the only things I can ever have access to are the content of my own mind. I never see a table or greet a friend – all that happens is somewhere in my mind I have table-seeing or friend-greeting experiences. Though I may think that these experiences are evidence of the existence of objects other than myself, for all I know I may be dreaming or deceived by an evil demon or be a brain in a vat being fed programmed images of tables or friends that have no real existence.

No philosopher has ever adopted a consistently solipsistic approach; anyone who did would presumably never communicate the fact, since he or she would not believe in communication. Many, however, have assumed that the place we must start in our understanding of the world is our own mind, and have then discovered that if we start with our own mind it is virtually impossible to get beyond it. *Descartes notoriously started in this way and only escaped from solipsism by claiming to find in his mind a concept of God who then became the base for all other knowing. Few other philosophers have accepted his move from the individual self or mind to God and have struggled to find ways of moving from the self to anything. The centuries since Descartes have seen a steady trend away from *objectivism (*reality is outside of me and independent of me) to subjectivism (reality is in me, the subject, and dependent on me).

The pragmatic arguments against solipsism are strong. We all simply know that it is both impracticable and unbelievable. Apart from the moments when we indulge in philosophical scepticism, we are all quite sure the world around us, and other minds, exist. However, we still cannot locate the bridge between our inner experiences and things outside of us. We still cannot answer the question, 'How can I be sure that the content of my mind accurately expresses realities that are in the world?'

Christian apologetics' response to the threat of solipsism is the radical one of going back to building a world-view on God rather than on the contents of our own minds. Though this response seems open to the criticism, 'But the concept of God is only part of the content of your mind', we would seem to have as much right to posit a God who has made and illuminates our minds as to posit (as all philosophers have to do) just a world and other minds, and still be left with the puzzle of how their existence can become part of my inner experience.

Bibliography

C. Dore, *God, Suffering and Solipsism* (Basingstoke, 1989).

P. HICKS

SOLZHENITSYN, ALEKSANDR

Aleksandr Solzhenitsyn (b. 1918) was arrested in 1945 for criticizing Stalin and suffered eleven years of imprisonment and exile. After this he became a mathematics teacher and began to write. Encouraged by the destalinizing policies of the early 1960s, Solzhenitsyn wrote a short novel, *One Day in the Life of Ivan Denisovich* (1962). This was based on his own experiences and it describes a typical day in the life of an inmate of a forced-labour camp during the Stalin era. Solzhenitsyn's period of official favour proved to be short-lived, and ended with Khrushchev's fall from power in 1964. His criticism of repressive government policies met first with hostility and then with overt harassment from the authorities. A prayer of his remains from this period and shows how important his belief in divine providence was for him: 'How easy it is for me to believe in you, Lord! How easy for me to believe in you. When my spirit is lost, perplexed and cast down ... You give me a sure certainty that you exist, that you are watching over me.'

Solzhenitsyn began to circulate his work illegally in the form of *samizdat* (self-published) literature, as well as publishing ambitious novels abroad. These secured his international reputation and included *The First Circle* and *Cancer Ward* (both 1968). In 1970 Solzhenitsyn was awarded the Nobel Prize for Literature, but he could not receive it until after his exile in 1974. In 1971 he published *August 1914* (again outside the Soviet Union). This was an historical novel about Germany's crushing victory over Russia in their initial military engagement of the First World War. In 1973 the first parts of *The Gulag Archipelago* were published in Paris, after a copy of the manuscript had been seized in the Soviet Union by the KGB. ('Gulag' is an acronym formed from the official Soviet name for the system of prisons and labour camps which grew alarmingly during Stalin's regime, 1924–53.) After the publication of the first volume of *Gulag* in 1974, Solzhenitsyn was attacked in the Soviet press and arrested on treason charges. The second and third volumes of *Gulag* were published in 1974–5, and were followed in 1980 by *The Mortal Danger*, which set out to expose what Solzhenitsyn perceived as dangers of American misconceptions about Russia.

In presenting alternatives to the Soviet regime, Solzhenitsyn tended to reject Western emphases on democracy and individual freedom, and instead favoured the formation of a benevolent authoritarian regime that would draw upon the resources of Russia's Orthodox Christian tradition (see *Christianity, Orthodox). He took it for granted that morality, art, and life formed a seamless robe, and that our responsibilities in one are inseparable from our responsibilities in the other. This contrasted with fashionable modernist views in Western aesthetics, which asserted the detachment of art from moral considerations. In September 1974, following his enforced exile from Russia, Solzhenitsyn addressed the third council of the Russian Orthodox churches abroad, appealed for the unity of all branches of the Russian Church, and asked, 'How can we create a Church that would not be an instrument of the state, would not be spiritually subordinate to the power of the state, and would not be connected with political parties; a Church in which would flourish the best of our as yet unimplemented reforms, aimed at restoring the purity and freshness of primitive Christianity; a Church that would not merely exist for its own sake, but would assist all of Russia in finding its own, native, distinctive path away from the suffocation and darkness of today's world?' At the same time, he cautioned those active in the church outside Russia against the view that the state-recognized Orthodox Church in the USSR had fallen from grace and must be distinguished from the true or underground church: 'The contemporary Church in our homeland is captive, persecuted, oppressed, but far from fallen! It was resurrected by spiritual strength of which, as we can see, God did not deprive our people.'

Here we see affirmation of the fact that Solzhenitsyn is, first and foremost, a Christian writer, as Alexander Schmemann, of the St Vladimir's Theological School in the USA, has convincingly argued. The key is Solzhenitsyn's world-view, which is based on the unexpressed presupposition of creation, fall and redemption. His acceptance of the Christian doctrine of creation is seen in his perception and acceptance of the original goodness of the world and life, and his denial of the opposing position, which sees life and the world as absurd and meaningless. He also views the mystery of *evil as originating in the fall of humankind into sin, and holds to the realistic tradition in which Christianity is set apart from other religions and philosophies by the fact that it does not attempt to explain and neutralize evil. Far from advocating that believers should stoically resign themselves to evil powers, Solzhenitsyn's strategy for survival focuses on the fact that Christ was not crucified by impersonal forces, but by people, and that evil is real because it is the result of personal choices. His religious faith is not a humanistic optimism about progress or the ultimate victory of reason. On the contrary, it is because of the reality of God's being and purposes that nothing is inevitably closed, condemned or damned, and everything remains open. Hope triumphs over despair, for Solzhenitsyn. And this is demonstrated in his novels, which often depict the courage of Christian witness in the face of persecution. In *Gulag*, one heroine outwits the authorities and, in effect, preaches a sermon to her fellow employees, in an office where she is about to be interrogated.

Solzhenitsyn is also in no doubt that Christian commitment is an intrinsic part of his own life and thought as a Russian. Rather than accepting the Soviet propaganda that the masses have gladly accepted Marxism-Leninism as their religion, he asserts that the young people and intelligentsia of Russia, even

where they do not share the Christian faith, behave towards the church with a deserving respect, and treat communist ideology with cynicism and mockery. In contrast to the weakening Western churches, Russian Orthodox churches were overfilled in the 1970s, according to Solzhenitsyn, and in one region known to him, 70% of babies born were baptized. However, he recognized that the modern claim to have displaced religion is not confined to Marxism, but is also found in *secularization in the West, where life is no longer considered to be a *mystery to be lived but as a problem to be solved. In fact, Solzhenitsyn argues that secularization is itself full of *mythology, about the overcoming of evil, transformation of *culture and redirecting of selfishness. The greatest myth of *communism, concerning the need of continuous revolution, is also a myth, he asserts. Religions combat the evil which exists in all people, but revolutions can destroy only the bearers of evil and not the evil itself.

Solzhenitsyn's God, therefore, cannot be used to excuse human irresponsibility, nor to obscure truth and justify senselessness. His is not the God in whose name one can hate another, while at the same time loving and praising oneself. Solzhenitsyn's God is the living and true God: 'ineffable, incomprehensible, invisible and unfathomable', says Schmemann. He is the God who is. Because of that, the writer must confess his sins to this God, the living God, who is both righteous judge and merciful redeemer. Like *Augustine, Solzhenitsyn recognizes that human wickedness is not simply an expression of individualism. People live together in evil systems and structures, oppressed by idolatrous ideologies, which pervert cultures and can ruin entire periods of time. So we must confess not only our personal sin, but also those of our peoples and nations.

It may be argued with some justification, therefore, that Aleksandr Solzhenitsyn remains, at the time of writing, the greatest living literary apologist for the Christian faith. Unlike C. S. *Lewis, whose work emanated from a relatively secure academic life, the great Russian novelist and historian engaged in a very risky and costly defence of Christian orthodoxy under the constant threat of sanctions by a persecuting state. Solzhenitsyn's USSR citizenship was officially restored in 1990, enabling him to end his twenty-year exile and return to Russia in 1994.

Bibliography

N. C. Nielsen, *Solzhenitsyn's Religion* (Nashville, 1975); *Revolutions in Eastern Europe: Religious Roots* (Maryknoll, 1991).

G. R. HOUSTON

SOURCE CRITICISM, see BIBLICAL CRITICISM
SPECIAL REVELATION, see REVELATION

SPINOZA, BENEDICT DE

Benedict (or Baruch) de Spinoza (1632–77) was a Dutch philosopher, one of the chief figures of the 'rationalist' (as opposed to 'empiricist') tradition. Of Portuguese Jewish descent, he was expelled from his synagogue for unorthodoxy in 1656. His main work, the *Ethics*, published soon after his death, was an attempt to set out a complete system of *metaphysics and its ethical consequences in the deductive form used for Euclid's geometry.

According to Spinoza, there is only one ultimate substance, which can be called either 'God', as the source of all things, or 'Nature' as that of which all things are aspects. Since God is self-caused and necessary, *determinism follows. The goal of life, and true human happiness, are to be found in the 'intellectual love of God', i.e. rejoicing to understand the system of nature and accepting our place in it. God himself, however, is beyond love and hate, and it is not to be expected that he should love us. There is no reason to believe in any life after death, but in thinking adequately we share in God's understanding of himself, and so in his eternity.

Spinoza never founded a school and has had few followers (though many admirers, not least because of his personal attractiveness and integrity). Einstein called himself a believer in 'the God of Spinoza', but this was probably no more than belief in a God who did not intervene in the world.

Spinoza has been called 'a man drunk with God', yet he was regarded by many as an atheist. He did use religious-sounding language, and mean it, but in a most untraditional way, and certainly he had no belief in any revealed religion. He believed that religion's chief value is as a conveyor of moral truths to those unable to reason them out for themselves.

Consequently, his importance to apologetics lies less in his own thought than in the reaction to him. (For example, some of the thought of *Leibniz, who had met Spinoza and discussed his work with him, can be seen as the development of an alternative to Spinozism.)

Bibliography

S. Hampshire, *Spinoza* (Harmondsworth, 1951); B. de Spinoza, *Ethics* and *De Intellectus Emendatione* (ET, London, 1910).

R. L. STURCH

SPORT

No-one can seriously doubt the importance of sport in the modern world. The emphasis on physical fitness – jogging, going to the gym, aerobics etc. – is a modern phenomenon. While for some this can become an unhealthy obsession, the health benefits are undeniable.

With the benefit of satellite television, the football World Cup final is viewed by almost half the world's population. Sports stars are icons of the nation, instantly recognized, paid millions and used to sell anything from razors to racing cars, breakfast cereals to window frames. Top sportspeople can become millionaires with their first professional contract. Questions can rightly be asked about the fair distribution of wealth and the relative value that society attaches to playing professional football as opposed to, say, being a nurse. However, the same issues apply – arguably even more so – to the leaders of industry, whose salaries, benefits and severance packages raise as many questions.

Sport is more easily understood than defined. Sport is a hobby, a recreation, but can also be a job. It is certainly big business. It has psychological, physical and recreational value, and it can socialize and discipline us. The modern world has seen the emergence of both the sports spectator, whose sporting involvement is inactive and vicarious, and the growth and development of marathon running by literally tens of thousands of ordinary people.

The definition of sport used by the Council of Europe is 'all forms of physical activity, which, through casual or organised participation, aim at expressing or improving physical fitness and mental well-being, forming social relationships or obtaining results in competition at all levels'. According to the European

Sports Conference Charter, sport is 'an inalienable right of every person'.

A few years ago the Sports Council in the UK (now called Sport England) divided sport into four categories: competitive sport, physical recreation, aesthetic activities and conditioning activities. They further stated: 'Sport is its own justification. It is a vital element in our national *culture. It contributes to greater fitness, better health and a sense of personal well-being' (*The Case for Sport*).

There are a number of references to sport in the NT, mainly in Paul's letters (e.g. 1 Cor. 9:24–27; Gal. 2:2; 5:7; Phil. 2:16; 3:13–14; 1 Tim. 4:8; 2 Tim. 2:5; 4:7; Heb. 12:1–2). These reflect his readers' familiarity with the ancient Games but do not really help us much towards a biblical understanding of sport. They are no more a biblical justification for sport than Paul's references to slavery are a defence of that practice. While Paul saw clear parallels between Christianity and sport, and felt that Christians could take lessons for Christian living from the experience of the athletes of the day, nothing he says provides anything like a 'theology of sport'. The process of establishing such a theology must, therefore, be to take scriptural concepts and principles and apply them to sport.

The starting point is Gen. 1, which reveals God as the only Creator of all things. From the universe, sun, moon and stars, down to the smallest creature – all have their origin in Christ, including humans and their physical bodies. God is majestically in charge of the whole world. Everything that exists is created by God and is, in itself, good. That must include sport, our ability to play sport and our enjoyment of it. However, we live in a fallen and sinful world. All God's creation has been spoilt by human selfishness and sin, and this applies to sport no less – but also no more – than to any other aspect of God's creation. As Christians we believe in redemption through the death and resurrection of Jesus Christ, and this too must apply to sport as well as to the rest of human activity.

Grasping this truth about God as Creator and Redeemer must also affect our attitude to him. If he is the Creator of all things, we have an inescapable obligation to worship him in all things and at all times. This thought is well expressed in the words attributed to Eric Liddell, the 1924 Olympic gold medallist in the film *Chariots of Fire*, 'God made me for a purpose, but he also made me fast, and when I run, I feel his pleasure.' There seems no necessary reason why an example of sporting skill should not bring pleasure to God, pleasure in something that he has created. Sporting ability is as much a gift from God as other creative abilities like singing, painting and writing and can, by his Spirit, be redeemed in order to be used in worshipping him. Equally, all are capable of being used selfishly and for our own glory.

The last twenty years has seen the development of sports ministry, a strategy for Christian involvement with the world of sport and through sport to the wider world. There is now sensitive and appropriate Christian ministry at almost every major sports event. Local churches are seeing the world of sport as an important part of their mission field, as in many towns a sports club, rather than a church, is the focal part of the community.

Bibliography

P. Ballantine, *Sport, the Opiate of the People*, Grove Ethical Study, 70 (Cambridge, 1988); S. Connor, *Sports Outreach: Principles and Practice for Successful Sports Ministry* (Tain, 2003); G. Daniels and J. S. Weir, *Born to Play*, (Bicester, 2004); S. J. Hoffman (ed.), *Sport and Religion* (Champaign, 1992); A. Ladd and J. Mathisen, *Muscular Christianity* (Grand Rapids, 1999); G. Linville, *Contemporary Christian Ethic of Competition* (available from Overwhelming Victory Ministries, Canton, Ohio); L. McCown and V. J. Gin, *Focus on Sport in Ministry* (Marietta, 2003); S. Weir, *What the Book Says about Sport* (Oxford, 2000).

G. DANIELS and J. S. WEIR

STOKER, HENDRIK GERHARDUS

Hendrik Stoker (1899–1993) was a South African philosopher and psychologist. He matured intellectually as a Christian scholar under the influence of H. *Bavinck, J. D. du Toit, H. *Dooyeweerd, D. H. T. *Vollenhoven and C. *Van Til and made penetrating, progressive and original contributions to Christian apologetics, including theoretical analyses of apologetics. He also undertook a lifelong practical philosophical engagement with a variety of different intellectual, ideological and religious trends. His major works contain several significant applications of apologetics to various aspects of philosophy, such as his brilliant exposition of the unity of scholarship.

In his work on Calvinistic philosophy, Stoker analysed apologetics in detail, primarily as a methodical procedure. His main contribution is a well-grounded advocacy of the divergent possibilities, tasks and perspectives presented by basic theological apologetics, general philosophical apologetics and scholarly work on social life, communication, *law and politics, *ethics, etc.

Stoker sketched the methodological relevance of apologetics within an open philosophical system by distinguishing between synthetics, antithetics and irenics. Synthetics is the identifying and extracting of kernels of truth from various systems in a non-eclectic way. Antithetics is the investigation of the motifs, basis and legitimacy of methods whereby the intellectual struggle for scientific truth is conducted. The scope of antithetics includes the methodological consideration of *contradictions, polemics, elenctics and apologetics. The elenctic method involves an aggressive attack on contrary points of view (apologetics comprises a defence against such opinions). In both instances presuppositions play an important role. Irenics is the investigation of attempts to deal with common features of different systems and to transcend basic scientific differences for the sake of truth.

Stoker broadened his basic cosmological insights (known as the 'philosophy of the idea of creation') into a systematic and apologetic Christian viewpoint for the contemporary world. His contributions to the understanding of duty and *ethics, his novel application of the concept of the manifestation of *truth, and his method for probing the problem of truth are particularly important.

In several respects Stoker anticipated significant new approaches in both contemporary philosophy and apologetics, such as bridge-building and unmasking. Many of his insights are also still relevant in contemporary philosophical debates.

N. T. VAN DER MERWE

STRAUSS, DAVID FRIEDRICH

David Strauss (1808–74) was one of the most influential German theological writers of the nineteenth century, in spite of the fact that he spent most of his career outside the university system. He lectured briefly in Tübingen (1832–3), where his courses in philosophy and *ethics were very popular, but he grew tired of the constraints of academic life and resigned after less than eighteen months. At that time he was still very much under the influence of *Hegel and *Schleiermacher, but later on he adopted the more uncompromising *rationalism of the classical *Enlightenment. In 1839 he was called to a professorship at Zürich, but the opposition to him was such that he was pensioned off and spent the rest of his life as a freelance writer. The reason for the opposition lay in his book *The Life of Jesus* (1835), which basically argued that it is impossible to use the Gospels as historical sources. In sharp contrast to most of his contemporaries, who believed that the Gospels were generally reliable sources for the life of *Jesus and that it was possible to reconstruct a valid biography out of them, Strauss insisted that they contained little or nothing of historical value. Moreover, far from finding this a problem, Strauss regarded it as an important advance towards a new understanding of the spiritual principles which give the texts their true importance. What really matters, argued Strauss, is not the unrecoverable history of Jesus, but the *mythology which came to surround him, and which is the real stuff of the Gospels, despite Matthew's clumsy attempts to anchor Mark's account in some kind of history.

Strauss' commitment to this mythological interpretation made him completely blind to the eschatological dimension of Jesus' teaching, which was simply subsumed into the myth. Strauss had almost no critical sense, and completely ignored the problem of the origin of the church. It is this, more than anything else, which sets him apart from F. C. *Baur and the Tübingen school, with which he otherwise had certain significant affinities. Like Baur, under whom he studied, Strauss rejected the historicity of John's Gospel, though Baur was less comfortable with the overuse of the category of myth to which Strauss was committed. Nevertheless, Baur was sufficiently disturbed by the questions which Strauss raised about the nature of the Gospels to publish his own study of them, which in most respects must be seen as a rejoinder to Strauss.

Largely ignored and derided in his own day, Strauss came into his own in the early twentieth century, when many of his basic ideas were taken up and reworked by Rudolf *Bultmann and other 'demythologizers'. The survival of the category of 'myth', in spite of all the many problems of definition which the word contains, and regardless of the many subsequent defences of genuine historicity in the Gospels, demonstrates just what a powerful thinker Strauss was and how his influence lingers on, even in a fundamentally hostile intellectual climate.

Bibliography

D. F. Strauss, *The Life of Jesus Critically Examined* (ET, London, 1846), repr. with an introduction by P. C. Hodgson (New York, 1972).

G. L. BRAY

SUBSTITUTION, see ATONEMENT
SUFFERING, see EVIL
SUFFICIENT REASON, see REASON
SWOON THEORY, see RESURRECTION OF JESUS (APOLOGETIC FOR)

SYLLOGISM

A syllogism is a particular pattern of argumentation. The classic discussion of this form of argument is found in Aristotle's *Prior Analytics* and was integral to the study of *logic up until the first part of the nineteenth century. In the main form of syllogism the logical movement is from two premises to a conclusion. The first premise is typically the major one, e.g. 'All men are mortal'. The second premise is the minor one, e.g. 'Socrates is a man'. The conclusion inexorably follows that 'Socrates is mortal'. The main problem with such deductive forms of argument is securing the starting point, i.e. the truth of the major premise.

A syllogism as a pattern of argument raises three important questions. The first question asks, is the argument valid or invalid? Validity has to do with the logical form of the pattern and not the content, e.g. 'All humans are made of chocolate' – 'Socrates is human' – 'Socrates is made of chocolate'. This is a valid conclusion even though factually in error. However, as an example it raises a further important question: is it sound or unsound? All sound arguments are valid. They are put together correctly from a logical point of view. Not all valid arguments, however, are sound. Soundness has to

do with the truthful content of the major and minor premises as well as the correct logical form. An invalid argument may have truthful premises but gets the form wrong, e.g. 'All humans are mortal' – 'Blackie is mortal' – 'Blackie is human'. The conclusion is not logically necessitated by the premises. Blackie could be a dog. Formally speaking, this is the fallacy of the undistributed middle. George Mavrodes has suggested a third important question. Is the argument cogent or not cogent? With similarities to G. E. Moore, Mavrodes maintains that a cogent argument is one in which the premises are known to be true. Moore called such an argument a conclusive one. So a sound argument is also a cogent argument if the above pertains. This brings a person-relative dimension into the discussion of a syllogism. According to W. V. Quine, the great logician, of the sixty-four possible ways of combining the premises of a syllogism only fifteen are valid in form.

Knowing these distinctions (validity and invalidity, soundness and unsoundness, cogent and not cogent) and their relevance to various patterns of syllogistic *reasoning may help the apologist see that unbelief may have valid arguments against the existence of the theistic God and yet may responsibly judge such arguments as unsound and, therefore, not cogent.

There are two other major forms of syllogistic reasoning worth noting. The hypothetical syllogism has an 'if ... then' form, e.g. 'If I wash the car then the ground will be wet' – 'I washed the car' – 'Therefore, the ground is wet'. As with the categorical syllogism discussed at length above, there are valid and invalid forms of arguing this way. The disjunctive syllogism has an 'either ... or' form, e.g. 'Either it is raining or I will wash the car' – 'It is not raining' – 'Therefore, I will wash the car'. As with the other forms of the syllogism, this form has its valid and invalid patterns.

The study of the syllogism is a useful exercise. Aristotle was right to argue in his *De Interpretatione* that 'truth and falsity imply combination and separation'. Valid reasoning is the art of successful connection. Although quantification theory takes the modern logician further, Aristotle's fundamental insight remains.

However, some philosophers argue that the reasoning that is used in everyday life is unlike the idealized logic of Philosophy 101. Instead, everyday persuasion requires a working logic that is far less formal in structure. This also applies to the kinds of argumentation found in literary criticism, legal decision-making, history writing and theology. The apologist needs to be aware of the philosophical sophistication of the audience.

Bibliography

J. Baggini and P. S. Fosl, *The Philosopher's Tool Kit* (Oxford, 2003): A. Fisher, *The Logic of Real Arguments* (Cambridge, 2000); G. Mavrodes, *Belief in God* (New York, 1970); W. V. Quine, *Methods of Logic* (Cambridge, 1982).

G. A. COLE

TAOISM, see RELIGIONS OF CHINESE AND JAPANESE ORIGIN

TAUTOLOGY

In formal *logic a tautology states a logical truth but not a factual one, e.g. the claim that 'Socrates is Socrates'. That claim about Socrates is true by definition, and to deny it is to fall into self-*contradiction. Some philosophers argue that the truths of logic and mathematics are tautologies, i.e. they are true by definition and not because of the way the world is. The term 'tautology' also applies to speech or text where the same meaning is restated, using different words even in the same sentence, e.g. 'The comet was visible to sight'. The problem with tautology so defined is that of vacuity. Such utterances contain a redundancy. They appear to add something to what we are claiming about our experience of the world but in fact they do not. In the example above, the words 'to sight' add nothing to the word 'visible'. Sometimes, however, a tautology, though logically speaking uninformative, can be humanly speaking highly meaningful. For example, take this statement by the eminent British philosopher Gilbert Ryle: 'Men are not machines ... They are men – a tautology which is sometimes worth remembering.' In this case the tone of voice placing a particular emphasis on some words and not others makes the human difference. When the communication is written, then italics or bold type can help the reader see the point.

There was a period during last century when *logical positivism was rampant in Anglophone philosophy. During that period, the onus fell very much on the Christian to demonstrate that statements about God were meaningful rather than meaningless. A. J. Ayer, for example, maintained that only two sorts of statements were not nonsense, namely, tautologies as in mathematics and logic, and empirical statements. The former were true by definition, while the latter could be verified, so it was argued, by an appeal to sensory experience or where circumstances could be envisaged where such an appeal could be made. The Christian then had to show that talk of God was not empty tautology, and either need not be empirically verifiable or could be empirically grounded. But as the great American logician, W. V. Quine, and others, pointed out, the criterion of meaning used by logical positivists was itself neither true by definition nor capable of being verified empirically. The criterion suffered self-referential destruction. The logical positivist movement is now largely a curiosity in the history of ideas.

As far as Christian apology is concerned, the problem of tautology especially arises – so some claim – for those who argue for some divine command theory of Christian *ethics. On this view, in its classic form, God commands what is right and good, and what is right and good is that which is commanded by God. This view of God and ethics has been particularly appealing to Christians with a high view of scriptural authority. The God of biblical presentation is a speaking God from the very first chapter of the Bible (Gen. 1:3). Many of God's reported speech acts are commands. Most famously the Ten Commandments fall into that category (Exod. 20:1–17). On analysis – so the argument runs – this yields the following: 'God commands what God commands.' How can the right and good have any content if the Christian's claim is tautological?

One answer is to argue that God has a nature and that what God commands flows from and is consistent with God's nature, which is morally good. Moreover, if God is Trinity then God does not need a creation for relational values like love and righteousness to have reality. Love and righteousness have always been true of the nature of God. On this view one might argue that although the good (relationally defined) transcends each person of the Godhead, the good does not transcend the Godhead *per se*.

Bibliography

J. Baggini and P. S. Fosl, *The Philosopher's Tool Kit* (Oxford, 2003); N. L. Geisler and P. D. Feinberg, *Introduction To Philosophy: A Christian Perspective* (Grand Rapids, 1980); W. V. Quine, *Methods of Logic* (Cambridge, 1982).

G. A. COLE

TECHNOLOGY

Technology has a multifaceted relationship to apologetics. Technology, in itself, is not a world-view that is either hostile or compatible with Christian *theism. Therefore, there is no apologetic in relation to technology in the same sense in which there is an apologetic for Islam or for philosophical materialism. Technology is, rather, a set of humanly engineered practices that employ mechanical means to accomplish particular ends. (Technology also achieves ends neither intended nor desired by its creators.) Furthermore, there are various philosophies of technology that affect people's world-views – either tacitly or explicitly – in ways that bear on their estimation of Christianity. Technologies in contemporary Western cultures are enmeshed in *culture to such a high degree that they tend to shape our ways of being and thinking in ways that may marginalize Christian truth-claims.

Technology as displacing God

Some have taken technological developments, especially since the Industrial Revolution, to indicate the implausibility or irrationality of any supernatural world-view, Christianity or otherwise. Advances in medicine, transportation and communications, it is claimed, have effectively pushed God off the scene. An ancient agrarian culture, for example, may have sought God's hand for blessings for the harvest or for offspring, but modern technologies – pertaining to agriculture and reproduction, among many other things – have stepped in to take God's place. In *Jesus Christ and Mythology*, NT scholar Rudolph *Bultmann (1884–1976) boldly claimed in the middle of the twentieth century that anyone using electric lighting or a radio cannot accept the supernatural world-view of the NT. Therefore, these writings must be 'demythologized' – that is, their inner, existential meaning should be retained (somehow), but their literal portrayal of a world of *miracles, *angels, demons and *revelations must be rejected by any thinking modern person. Bultmann did not develop this argument very fully, and the claim that one who uses modern technology is thereby barred from rationally holding a biblical world-view seems almost to be a *non sequitur*. This is because the existence of natural technologies is compatible with the existence of a realm above the natural order that sometimes impinges on it. Nevertheless, this claim that technology refutes supernaturalism is still often made. Consider these comments made in reference to the God of *monotheism by philosopher Ray Billington in *Religion Without God* (2002): 'In our own time, study of our genetic structure, and, in particular, the discovery of the human genome, have thrown the question of God's place in the human life into even more intense relief. If we can now choose not only what sex we wish our children to be, but also whether they should be dark or fair, tall or short, brainy or just average, healthy or taking their chances as in the past, what role is left for God?' Billington is anticipating powers not yet possessed, but his point still stands.

Put more formally, the argument from modern technology to rejecting monotheism seems to be this:

1. Ancient cultures explained what they did not understand by positing the supernatural and sought supernatural support in these areas. Their ignorance of the laws of nature led to this supernatural interpretation.

2. Modern *science has explained almost all of these previously inexplicable phenomena on the basis of the laws of nature. Science is done without recourse to the supernatural and has, through this knowledge, conquered many previously uncontrollable areas of life through technological means.

3. Premise 2 shows that modern science trades on a non-supernatural conception of the cosmos.

4. Modern technology is dependent on modern science for its existence.

5. Therefore, (a) anyone who uses modern technologies is using something that owes its existence to a non-supernatural world-view.

6. Therefore, (b) one who uses and benefits from technology should hold a non-supernatural world-view in order to be rationally consistent.

Premise 1 is true but somewhat misleading. One need not have a modern scientific understanding of natural laws – say of gravity or hydraulics – to recognize events that transcend the unaided powers of nature. Ancient Israelite culture, for example, was not so superstitious as to be incapable of distinguishing an oddity of nature from a supernatural event. One need not understand hydraulics in order to recognize that Jesus' walking on water is an event that transcended the powers of water, air and flesh. As C. S. *Lewis pointed out in *Miracles*: 'Belief in miracles, far from depending on an ignorance of the laws of nature, is only possible in so far as those laws are known.' Joseph may have known little of gynaecology, but this did not hinder his recognition, after infidelity was ruled out, that Mary had conceived supernaturally. Premise 4 is unassailable. However, premises 2 and 3 (required for conclusions 5 and 6) are disputable. The notion that the history of science demonstrates that natural explanations inevitably trump supernatural explanations is false, or at least not yet proven. It is true that science has explained many previously inexplicable aspects of nature, such as the germ theory of disease, and that it has, in many cases, given us more control over nature.

However, some scientific discoveries seem to provide intellectual support for supernaturalism, instead of invalidating it. Consider two salient examples. First, Big Bang cosmology, which is well supported by several converging lines of evidence, reveals a universe that came into existence out of nothing about fourteen billion years ago. Unless something can come from nothing without a cause (a dubious principle at best, and one that even David *Hume rejected), the most plausible explanation for the cosmos is that a supernatural being originated the universe by an act of will. Second, as scientists uncover more of nature at the microscopic level, the more complex it appears. Life itself is an information system of vast complexity and specified function; a single cell has as much information as several sets of encyclopaedias. The notion of abiogenesis (life coming from non-life without a designer) is thus more difficult to sustain *given an increase in knowledge about the nature of life*. In this case God, as an intelligent designer, is invoked not to fill a gap in knowledge, but to explain a state of affairs less well explained otherwise.

But there is another reason why the kind of science that makes modern technology possible does not rule out a supernatural world-view. Our understanding of natural laws considers how objects act when left to their own unaided powers. Biblical supernaturalism leaves such laws as they are. (These natural laws were created by God, according to Christian theism.) For the normal and general workings of nature, these laws explain and predict how objects causally relate to one another under certain conditions. Supernatural intervention, whether at creation or through subsequent miracles, is, by definition, rare and distinguishable from the ordinary operations of nature. The fact that one uses a radio or the internet – technologies that depend on knowledge of natural laws – has no logical bearing on whether or not Christ rose from the dead, whether the Bible is divinely inspired, or whether God answers prayer.

Technology and secularization

Another argument, similar to, but not identical with, the first, may be employed against Christian theism (and religion in general) on the basis of the effects of technological improvements on the human condition. In the middle to later twentieth century a raft of sociologists predicted that, as societies became more technologically advanced (which is a vital element of the overall process of modernization), they would have less need for religion. Religion, they averred, was primarily a way of coping with an uncertain and dangerous world. As technology made the world less uncertain (especially through the increase in scientific knowledge) and less dangerous (through medical technologies and modern agriculture, for example), the need for religious orientations, compensations and expectations would diminish. This claim flows out of the generally secular orientation of the early sociologists, who tended to view religion as a second-order phenomenon. That is, religion owes its existence to other first-order social features that are more basic than religion itself. For example, Karl Marx claimed that religion was rooted in unjust social relationships. As those relationships were rectified (through revolution, in Marx's mind), the purported need for religious compensations (or 'opiates') would diminish and eventually cease. Marxism, as an explanatory model (and especially as a political ideology), has fallen into disfavour overall, but this general pattern of reasoning has not.

This argument looks something like this:

1. Modern technologies (as part of the process of modernization) radically undercut superstition and reduce the cultural power of

religion and replace it with a more scientific rationality.

2. As modern technologies develop and are implemented globally, religion will lose its cultural and intellectual power.

3. Religion is losing its cultural and intellectual power because of premise 2.

4. Therefore, religion is false and supported only by superstition, which is based on a pre-scientific world-view.

While much of sociological theory (officially) disowns any claim to philosophical judgments about the reality or unreality of religious beliefs and practices, sceptics and unbelievers often employ the *secularization thesis as a kind of empirical verification of the secular world-view. A recent textbook, *The Philosophy of Religion: A Critical Introduction*, by Beverly Clack and Brian Clack (1998), makes just this claim, and further argues for a non-realist view of religion, since any objective supernaturalism has been ruled out. The argument is that, as societies become progressively rational through scientific and technological means, the props of religion are kicked out. History, then, is on the side of irreligion and *secularism – assuming that the process of modernization continues apace throughout the world.

However, the secularization thesis has recently fallen on hard times (despite some retrenchment by ardent adherents such as Steve Bruce), thus challenging premise 3. Peter Berger, one of secularization theory's leading exponents (although a theist), has recently disowned it in the face of rather massive counter-evidence. He has, in fact, edited and contributed to a book entitled *The Desecularization of the World* (1999). While the thesis seems to hold true for Western Europe, which has become quite secular in the last two centuries, religion remains a potent force in the lives of many in the contemporary and developed world, particularly in modern South Korea and in the United States. (Sociologist Rodney Stark believes the 'American exception' is traceable to its political disestablishment of religion, which renders American religion flexible and creative in the face of potentially secularizing forces, such as technology.) Moreover, as many Third World countries modernize, they do not necessarily become more secular, as in much of Latin America, which has been massively affected by Pentecostalism. In fact, even so-called 'fundamentalist' movements worldwide employ communications technologies to further their ends and do not deem them a threat to their religious world-views.

Yet even if the world is becoming more secular – partially because of the omnipresence of all types of technologies – this fact in itself would not imply that any one religion, or that Christianity in particular, is false or irrational; that is, unless premise 1 is true: that religion is based on a superstitious world-view refuted by science. But to make that case, one would have to rely on the first argument addressed above, which was found to be fallacious.

Technology, culture and Christianity

Because of the prevalence of technology in the Western world and its immense effects on all of culture (including religious belief), Christian apologists should develop and apply a wise theology of culture able to make sense of technology in the contemporary world from a distinctively Christian world-view.

Although we have maintained that arguments from the facts of technology to the falseness or irrationality of Christianity (or religion in general) do not succeed, certain aspects of a technologically driven culture may make Christian belief more difficult to appropriate or less plausible for some. In our technologically saturated environment, technology can become an ersatz religion, which allows little access to genuine *transcendence. Cultural critique Neil Postman writes of those who trust in 'the god of technology'. Their faith in this god is shown in that they 'believe technology works, that they rely on it, that it makes promises, that they are bereft when denied access to it, that they are delighted when they are in its presence, that for most people it works in mysterious ways, that they condemn people who speak against it, that they stand in awe of it, and that, in the born-again mode, they will alter their lifestyles, their schedules, their habits and their relationships to accommodate it.' This false god often displaces and replaces the true God revealed in creation, Christ and Scripture with a humanly generated world of intense involvement, diversion and even obsession. Some technophiles become so absorbed in virtual worlds through various video games (especially fantasy role-playing games) that the realities of life and death, good and evil, heaven and hell, recede into the dim, off-screen background.

When technologies become diversions from matters of ultimate concern, apologists should alert those so deluded that the power will one day be turned off. The Psalmist affirmed that, while 'some trust in horses and some in chariots ... we will trust in the name of the LORD our God' (Ps. 20:7). The ancient point still stands: the products of all merely human *power and ingenuity, whether chariots or computers, are poor substitutes for a covenantal association with the Creator, whose power and goodness outstrip all finite aspirations. A strong apologetic for the truth and rationality of the Christian world-view provides a sharp critique of any humanistic alternatives.

Some thinkers entertain false hopes for final liberation through merely technological means. One group of extreme technological utopians known as Transhumanists or Extropians ('extropy' means the opposite of 'entropy') suppose that eventually all human limitations will be left behind through technological innovations. While atheistic, they shun despair and nihilism by placing their hopes in the unbridled powers of human achievements as they take evolution into their own hands and computers. Even death and entropy, they assert, will yield to their technological mastery of nature.

Apologists should name such misconceptions as idolatry. Mortality will not be mastered by merely mortal means – and eternity awaits us all. As *Pascal said in Pensées, 'Between heaven and hell is only this life, which is the most fragile thing in the world.' He further observed that, while our reasoning abilities place us above the rest of creation, we are still but 'thinking reeds', subject to decay and death. 'A vapour, a drop of water is enough to kill' us.

Technology has a dignified place in God's creation and should not be spurned by those endeavouring to live under Christ's comprehensive lordship. God created the universe as good, and humans as very good, made in God's own image (Gen. 1:26). Part of human uniqueness lies in the ability to reason and create cultural artefacts for the purposes of domination and stewardship (Gen. 1 – 2; Ps. 8). This activity includes technologies. Francis *Bacon's dictum from Novum Organum Scientiarum serves well: 'Man by the Fall fell at the same time from his state of innocence and from his dominion over creation. Both of these losses, however, can even in this life be in some parts repaired; the former by religion and faith, the latter by arts and sciences.' However, technological innovations will always be products of finite and fallen human beings, who are forever East of Eden apart from God's redemptive intervention in the life, death and resurrection of Jesus Christ. The fatal project of the tower of Babel (Gen. 11) serves as a ringing example of the human hubris that seeks to establish itself as the royalty of creation by its own power and ability.

Bibliography

A. Aldridge, Religion in the Contemporary World (Malden, MA, 2000); P. L. Berger (ed.), The Desecularization of the World: Resurgent Religion and World Politics (Grand Rapids, 1999); R. Billington, Religion without God (New York, 2002); S. Bruce, God is Dead: Secularization in the West (Malden, MA, 2002); P. Jenkins, The Next Christendom (New York, 2002); K.-M. Kwan, 'A Critical Appraisal of Non-Realist Philosophy of Religion: An Asian Perspective', Philosophia Christi, series 2, 3.1 (2001), pp. 225–235; N. Postman, Technopoly: The Surrender of Culture to Technology (New York, 1992).

D. GROOTHUIS

TEILHARD DE CHARDIN, PIERRE

Pierre Teilhard de Chardin (1881–1955) was a French Jesuit priest and paleontologist who sought to build bridges between Christian beliefs and those of *science, especially geology, biology and evolutionary theory. He studied philosophy, maths, geology, biology and paleontology, and spent some years in successful and influential field research in China and other parts of Asia. He was a sensitive man and was hurt by the refusal of the Catholic hierarchy to accept his ideas. He wrote prolifically; his more controversial writings were not published till after his death. His best-known work is The Phenomenon of Man (1955; ET, 1959).

Teilhard built on the ideas of Henri Bergson (1859–1941), who, while accepting evolutionary theory, had reacted against the mechanistic scientific world-view of his day and argued that the nature of the world is basically dynamic rather than inert. Behind evolution, he said, lies a creative or life force (élan vital), inaccessible to science, but the source and cause of everything. Teilhard sought to reconcile scientific evolutionary theory with Christianity by developing a concept of the dynamic evolution of the universe, from the 'Alpha point' of creation towards ever higher forms of consciousness, culminating in an 'Omega point' of union with God, which he identified as the full presence of Christ.

Teilhard viewed this process as possible because he saw no final distinction to be drawn between inorganic matter, such as rocks (the 'lithosphere'), organic matter (the 'biosphere'), and thinking conscious matter (the 'noosphere'). All are stages of the process. All that happens in the process is the action of God, the disclosure and increasing manifestation of Spirit. No piece of matter is to be seen as merely inert, because it is pregnant, at least potentially, with life through the presence of God, and thus is to be viewed as sacred. We share in the process of development, both by furthering knowledge and consciousness, and by expressing love and drawing together our fragmented world in the love of Christ.

The mid twentieth century was a time when most thinkers were urging the total separation of science and *theology; Teilhard's attempt to merge them aroused considerable interest but comparatively few followers. As the century progressed, however, attitudes changed. Science moved away from rigid mechanism; new spiritualities showed an openness to finding God in the material world. As a result, his broad ideas, if not the details, have subsequently won a considerable following.

P. HICKS

TELEOLOGICAL ARGUMENT

One of the five classical 'proofs' for the existence of God, the teleological argument emphasizes the belief that everything was created for a purpose. It is therefore closely linked to the aetiological argument, which says that everything created has a cause, since cause and effect are two sides of the same coin. In modern times, the teleological argument is generally known as the argument from design, and it is now probably the most popular of the classical 'proofs' used to defend the existence of God.

The roots of the teleological argument may be found in the creation narrative in Genesis, where the different parts of creation serve a purpose in the overall plan of God's universe. The philosophical difficulty is knowing whether (or to what extent) it can be said that this purpose is intrinsically necessary, or whether it is merely accidental, determined by an essentially random process and not by a preordained divine plan. In biblical times, this problem did not arise because everybody agreed that there was a divine mind behind the order of creation. Ps. 19 and Jer. 33:20–25 both emphasize what we would now call the laws of nature and tie them in very closely to God's preordained vision for his chosen people. As long as biblical *theism could be taken more or less for granted, the validity of the teleological argument was accepted as a matter of course, and little was said about it. Its development and probably also its popularity among modern theists seem to be very largely due to the widespread rejection of classical Christian theism since the Enlightenment of the eighteenth century and the corresponding need to find a credible justification for it.

The main opponent of traditional teleology was David *Hume (1711–76), who produced five arguments against it, some of which are still used today. Hume argued that even if it could be demonstrated that the world was created according to a prearranged design, it was not at all clear what caused the designer to come into existence. He also said that there is no reason why such a designer (if one exists) should correspond to the God of the Bible, because there was no intrinsic need for a designer to be perfect, omniscient or loving. There might even turn out to be more than one designer, a theory which might make it easier to explain conflicts caused by the existence of evil, for example. In Hume's mind, the existence of *evil was proof that if there were a single designer, he could not be morally perfect, and on those grounds the biblical God was excluded from consideration. Hume further rejected the use of analogies taken from the created order which are meant to show that the universe as a whole follows the same principles. It is one thing to say that the existence of a machine demands the supposition that an intelligent being created it, but this cannot be projected onto the universe because whilst there are many machines (which can be compared to one another) there is only one universe (which is therefore incomparable to anything else). Finally, Hume claimed that any coherent universe will appear to be designed as such by those who live in it, because they lack the perspective needed to imagine anything else.

Of all these arguments against design, the strongest (and the one most important in the eighteenth century) is the assertion that the supposed designer does not have to be the Christian God. There is no doubt that the God of the Bible has many characteristics which are not necessary in a designer, and it is equally certain that anyone who believes in God will be obliged to attribute the design of the universe to his all-knowing mind, whether this belief can be demonstrated by empirical evidence or not.

Hume's great opponent was William *Paley (1743–1805), whose book *Natural Theology* (1803) is often taken to be the classic expression of the teleological argument before the later nineteenth century. Paley was chiefly interested in the wonders of the interlocking mechanisms which he saw as the pillars of the universe, and to him is normally attributed the famous analogy of the watch and the watchmaker. Someone who finds a watch in a field knows that it must have been made by an intelligent being, so why does the same not apply to the even more complex mechanisms which we find in nature? Is it more plausible to believe that the wonders of this world were created by a supreme intelligence or that they emerged accidentally? To Paley the answer was obvious, and he argued that the regularity and sophistication of the natural order pointed towards a Creator who shared the same characteristics. As a Christian, Paley believed that this supreme intelligence had revealed himself in the Bible and shown that his character is great enough to embrace not only creation, but providence and redemption as well. He was untroubled by Hume's reductionism because he accepted that God must be so much more than just a cosmic designer, though of course he was that as well.

Paley's arguments held the field until 1859, when Charles Darwin published his theories of evolution which undercut them dramatically. Darwin believed in random genetic change and in natural selection, two processes which made it possible for higher forms of life to emerge out of lower ones. The mechanisms of the universe were not, therefore, an eternal given but rather an evolving process where chance was more important than design. The order and regularity of the universe as we see it could be attributed to the process of attrition which evolution involves, rather than to some foreordained divine plan. At the time, many people accepted the force of Darwin's arguments and support for Paley faded away. But if the older form of the teleological argument was no longer as strong as it had previously been, the essential premises of that argument remained valid and needed only to be restated to take evolution into account. For one thing, there was still the problem of the inorganic world, which was not subject to evolution, and yet which seemed to be perfectly designed to support life. Moreover, since evolution follows laws of its own which can be understood as part of an overall plan, the design argument can be recycled in a more sophisticated form.

This was actually done by F. R. *Tennant (1866–1957), and his general approach has been followed more recently by Richard Swinburne, who has moved away from the approach taken by Paley (which was based mainly on patterns of behaviour) to a time-based framework which stresses regularity of succession. According to this way of thinking, the fact that actions can be predicted with complete accuracy once the appropriate givens are known disproves the theory of purely random change and supports the idea that there is a mind governing the observed pattern. In the end he claims, the teleological argument comes out stronger for having faced the challenge of Darwinism and adapted itself accordingly. Swinburne also mentions the argument from beauty, which has seldom been put forward in recent years. To some extent, beauty is a subjective measurement, but there can be no doubt that people everywhere have found great beauty in the order of the universe, which makes it seem strange to deny the real existence of a coordinated harmony on which such notions of beauty are generally based.

Modern forms of the teleological argument are characterized by their appeal to the general order of nature rather than to the complexity of specific biological organisms. Because of this, they are seldom detailed arguments of the kind that would claim that the human ear was designed specifically for the purpose of hearing sounds produced in the natural order, and instead concentrate on the broader principle that the world is specially adapted to support forms of organic life. Analogies with things like watches tend to fall away, to be replaced by inferences which, taken together, point to intelligent design as the best explanation of *reality. Nowadays, defenders of the teleological argument have a tendency to draw their examples from chemistry or astronomy, rather than from sciences which are affected by Darwinian theories, because the theories which underlie the inorganic sciences appear to be less open to future revision.

The arguments concerning inorganic matter are much stronger and more numerous than might be imagined. This is because they tend to concentrate on pointing out that if the constants which we observe in physics and chemistry were variable to only a slightly greater degree than they are, life as we know it would not be possible. What is particularly impressive about this is that the natural laws in question are not all related to each other, but have apparently developed independently. How likely is it that such a remarkable conjunction would have occurred at random? Objectively speaking, the chances of this happening are so small that belief in an intelligent designer is by far the most rational conclusion, even if this does not 'prove' the belief in an absolute sense.

Objections to this form of the teleological argument exist, but they tend to lack serious force. For example, it has been argued that we should not be surprised to find intelligent life on earth because we are ourselves here to find it. If it did not exist, then neither would we, and so all our observations are contingent on our actual being. This is true as far as it goes, but that is not very far, since it does nothing to explain how we came into being in the first place. Instead, this objection reduces the whole issue to the level of the obvious and then sidesteps the real question altogether. Another common argument is that there may be many universes with different ground rules, each of which is capable of producing life forms according to its own criteria. Like different computer programmes, the incompatibility of these systems does not preclude each one from producing the desired result in its own way. Such an explanation may be theoretically possible, but it suffers from the total lack of any evidence which might support it. In the end, it is harder to accept this theory than it is to believe in an intelligent designer, and so the latter option wins out on grounds of probability.

In recent years, one of the more significant aspects of the teleological argument has been the way in which it is especially suited to the delicate task of harmonizing a religious view of life with the teaching of modern *science. It is a perspective which can be adopted by evolutionists and non-evolutionists alike, and avoids the difficulties commonly associated with so-called 'creation science' without abandoning the theistic perspective. It makes belief in the Christian God scientifically coherent without imposing belief in the details of the biblical *revelation, which both believers and unbelievers regard as a matter of faith, not of human *reasoning. It will always remain an argument open to objections of various kinds, but as its supporters maintain and hope, it is an argument which helps to make the theistic option scientifically respectable and which can therefore serve as a vehicle for introducing a Christian perspective into this important sphere of modern life.

Bibliography

S. T. Davis, *God, Reason and Theistic Proofs* (Grand Rapids, 1997); W. A. Dembski and J. M. Kushiner (eds.), *Signs of Intelligence: Understanding Intelligent Design* (Grand Rapids, 2001); R. Swinburne, *The Existence of God* (Oxford, 1991).

G. L. BRAY

TELEVISION

Television has created a media culture, which shapes the way people think, feel and behave, sometimes more than schools, families and churches. The information environment that characterizes the twenty-first century, for all of the new computer *technology is still defined by television, has grown from offering a handful of broadcast channels to making available hundreds of specialized networks and shows-on-demand, through fibre-optics, satellites, and the marriage of television and the Internet. Much of the population now gets their news, opinion and political discourse from television, rather than newspapers and books, and the way they approach issues and ideas is conditioned by the media through which they encounter them.

This means a different climate for Christian apologetics. Long, reasoned discourse tends to get tuned out by the television mind. Appeals to evidence, history or presuppositions seem to carry little weight with people used to channel-surfing through all of their options until they find something they like. Postmodernism owes less to university intellectuals and more to television in spreading its assumptions of *relativism, subjectivity and personal constructions of meaning.

Not that the television mind is immune from Christianity or is completely unsusceptible to religious persuasion. The classic obstacles to belief, such as *rationalism and *materialism, are also casualties of television. But Christian apologists will do well to consider how their audiences tend to think, as part of the process of changing their minds.

Media scholar Neil Postman contrasts the different mental processes involved in processing information through reading, which has been the major medium for apologetics, and television. Reading, he says, demands and brings into being sustained concentration, the development of long trains of thought and abstract *reasoning. Television, in contrast, cultivates in its audience a short attention span, immediate subjective response and concrete sensation. Whereas reading is rational and logical, television is best at creating purely emotional responses. Reading, says Postman, promotes continuity, the gradual accumulation of knowledge and sustained exploration of ideas. Television, on the other hand, fosters fragmentation, anti-intellectualism and immediate gratification.

It may take weeks to read through a book. A television programme, seldom more than an hour long, must grab its audience immediately or viewers will click on to something else. The programme is itself fragmented by its editing and by its commercial interruptions, which assault the viewer with an array of completely different and unrelated information packages lasting for only seconds. A reader's own mind and imagination are engaged when working through a book, imagining the characters and the action in a novel, thinking along with the author in a nonfictional treatise. Watching television simply involves tuning in the mind to a pre-packaged experience, in which the imagination and the ideas all belong to the producers and their corporate sponsors.

Television can indeed present intellectual content. Persuasion is its stock and trade, since much of the world's television is funded by corporate advertisements. News, the *arts, comedies and dramas, are on the air primarily for the sake of the commercials, and the whole economy of television rests on its ability to persuade customers to buy the sponsor's products. The rhetoric of television, though,

is different from that of language-centred media.

Complex political positions, though based on sophisticated policy analysis and involved chains of reasoning, must be conveyed in a 'thirty-second sound-bite'. What this means in practice is that political discourse gives way to the crafting of simplistic and emotionally charged imagery. Political commercials attempt to portray the opponent as a villain (as in the American presidential ad that took issue with one of the minor nuances of a candidate's environmental policy by saying, 'He wants to poison your water!'). The candidate paying for the commercial, on the other hand, with the help of 'image consultants' and spin doctors, is presented as the god from above, exemplifying all that is good, whose policies, seldom defined in thirty seconds, will be the salvation of the country. A little reflection, of course, shows such claims to be nonsense – and the public is famously cynical of campaign ads – and yet, reflection not being encouraged by the television mind, the public still responds to them, and image manipulation and negative advertising do win elections.

The classic epistemological dilemma of the conflict between appearance and *reality, explored with such urgency in Shakespeare and Spenser, is magnified by television. We believe what we see. And yet television, as a visual medium, *constructs* what viewers see. This construction presents a highly persuasive illusion of reality, but in fact is a product of the maker's biases, agendas and ulterior motives. For example, one American documentary programme did a consumer protection story on a particular truck, whose petrol tank would reportedly explode if another vehicle crashed into its side. Unfortunately, try as they might, no matter how many crashes they engineered into the test vehicle, the documentary makers could not get the truck to blow up. Finally, they installed ignitors to set off the petrol tank at the right moment. The documentary showed the truck exploding. Viewers, of course, assumed that the car company was guilty of manufacturing an unsafe product. They saw the explosion with their own eyes. And yet, what they saw was not true.

An exploding truck makes for better television than a flame-free car wreck or a 'talking-head' safety inspector, and television, as a visual medium, must create visual images and must express any ideas that it has to convey in visual terms. This alone means that television will have difficulty in conveying spiritual realities or matters of faith, 'the evidence of things not seen' (Heb. 11:1). Not just abstract ideas but also the labyrinthine ways of the inner life elude visual representation. The visual and the dramatic arts can indeed convey spiritual realities, through symbolism, indirection and evocation, but television, for the most part, does not have time for such subtleties.

Television works best as an entertainment medium, and even when it tries to be more ambitious, artistically or culturally, it must be, at least, entertaining, otherwise the programme will fail. Thus, as Postman has shown, *whatever* television presents – news, politics, education, or religion – must assume the characteristics of entertainment. The problem is not with the content of television, the sex and violence that bother many of its critics (though such things are intrinsically entertaining), rather, it is the form of television, as a visual entertainment medium, that is responsible for its effect on the human heart. Entertaining the public can, indeed, be a worthy goal, but when *everything* is reduced to entertainment – when 'I like that' or 'I don't like that' or 'That is boring' are sufficient reasons for belief or unbelief – the result is culturally and spiritually enervating.

Since not everything in the human condition is entertaining, television sometimes distorts its subject matter or, worse, conditions people to insist upon being entertained even when they are not watching television. Thus, school children often refuse or are unable to pay attention to their teachers unless they are as entertaining as the cartoon characters on educational television. Their parents, so used to being stimulated, are often in their real lives incapacitated by *boredom, which ruins marriages, inspires substance abuse, and is arguably the spiritual plague of our times.

The 'entertainment industry' has given rise to a pop culture, which is driving out both traditional folk cultures and the high culture. The former requires communities, with their own history and values, all of which are levelled out by the corporate consumerism, with its constantly changing fashions and customer pleasing *hedonism. The high culture requires reflection, thought and creativity, both to make and to appreciate its works, but these have little place in the mass produced, mass appeal economics that drives the pop culture.

Whereas radio, a purely linguistic medium, became a forum for the apologetics of C. S. *Lewis, Christian television has done little in the field of apologetics. In the early days of television, Archbishop Fulton Sheen, who began his work in radio, made the transition to television and became a hugely influential television personality, as well as an accomplished apologist. Though working mainly in the 'talking head' mode, a single person just speaking into the camera, an approach soon to be surpassed by the demands of a visual medium, Bishop Sheen was the master of a personal style that did communicate effectively to the 1950's television culture. Television tends to be personality, or even celebrity driven, and Christian television followed the pattern.

Soon it became evident that what worked best for religious television was not cerebral discourse, or even sermonizing, but dramatic spectacles. Mass evangelism rallies, such as those by Billy Graham, made for good television. The dramatic emotionalism of charismatic services worked well too, as in the sweaty intensity of the American Pentecostal firebrand Jimmy Swaggart or, even better, the miracle working healing services of an Oral Roberts. Viewers could see with their own eyes that young woman getting healed, a bit of concrete religious persuasion that was hard to deny. Just as the exploding truck was hard to deny.

Though the genre of the Christian talk show incorporates apologetic elements, and though Christian television does include overt apologists such as John Ankerberg, who stages debates and programmes on the truth-claims of Scripture, most Christian television is more concerned with evangelism than apologetics. The message is proclaimed, rather than proven, and the appeal, like all television, is to the heart rather than the mind. Not that this is theologically inappropriate, since most Christian traditions agree that conversion comes from the Holy Spirit working through the word, rather than through the fallen, limited human reason. But television Christianity is often noticeably lacking in doctrine, the biblical world-view, and spiritual depth and complexity, limits dictated by the medium, but which are often carried over into the real world, manifesting themselves in shallow piety and theologically vacuous churches.

Television, however, also has its casualties, and the yearning for authenticity and the contempt for fakery that characterizes today's younger generations may be a backlash against the artificiality that they have grown up with and that has made them cynical. Arguably, the rationalistic approach of much apologetics over the last century was a response to the rationalism that characterized modernity. Christianity, though, was never merely an abstract set of propositions, but rather a concrete *mystery centred on a God who is no abstraction but who became incarnate in the flesh of a tangible human being. He, in turn, bore in his body the sins of the world, died on a cross, and rose again, offering free salvation through the forgiveness of people's actual sins.

The postmodern television generation is open to things it does not understand and indeed in their spiritual seeking, they are actually attracted to religions of mystery. The vague *New Age mysticism of the talk shows plays well on television, and Christians would do well to counter it by recovering their own heritage of spirituality. Overrationalizing the faith may make it less appealing to the television culture, while highlighting its more mind-blowing doctrines (incarnation, atonement, the sacraments) may well strike an unexpected chord.

Though minds shaped by television tend to be relativist, they are often interested in hearing about 'other people's stories', 'what works for you'. This can be an invaluable opening for Christian apologists. To avoid making their audience defensive, triggering the complaint that 'You have no right to impose your religion on anyone else', they should present what they know to be true in a personal way, with reference to their own lives and their own spiritual pilgrimage. They should avoid the taboos of 'being judgmental', making everything negative fall back on themselves and their own sins and failures. They should be as concrete as possible, focusing on the tangibility of the faith, in the person of Christ and in his work on the cross, and in what he can tangibly mean in a person's life.

Defending the faith to postmodernist television fans may have to start with their particular mindset, though it should not stop there. Doctrine, ideas and abstractions can come later. They may have to be taught how to think in non-television terms. Those who have known only the little world of their television sets may wake up to a larger, richer universe than they ever imagined, realms of *truth and dimensions of life they never dreamed existed. This may well become part of the appeal of the Christian faith in an age of television.

Bibliography

J. Ellul, *The Humiliation of the Word* (Grand Rapids, 1985); M. McLuhan, *Understanding Media* (Boston, 1994); K. Myers, *All God's Children and Blue Suede Shoes: Christians and Popular Culture* (Westchester, 1989); N. Postman, *Amusing Ourselves to Death: Public Discourse in the Age of Show Business* (New York, 1985); *Teaching as a Conserving Activity* (New York, 1979); *Technopoly: The Surrender of Culture to Technology* (New York, 1993); G. Veith, *Postmodern Times: A Christian Guide to Contemporary Thought and Culture* (Wheaton, 1994); *Reading Between the Lines: A Christian Guide to Literature* (Wheaton, 1990); *The Spirituality of the Cross: The Way of the First Evangelicals* (St Louis, 1999).

G. E. VEITH

TEMPLE, WILLIAM

The life, thought and ministry of William Temple (1881–1944) bestride the first half of the twentieth century. Without doubt he was the most formative church leader in Britain in the middle of the century and a deeply respected leader in the wider European context.

His ministry embraced being headmaster of Repton School, rector of St James's, Piccadilly, and successively Bishop of Manchester, Archbishop of York and Archbishop of Canterbury (1942–44). Temple combined a massive intellect with a pastoral heart and a profound social conscience. Although his vocation took him into holy orders, he was deeply influenced by the political and social movements of his time and, although not active in party politics, was seen as a Christian Socialist by conviction.

Temple's book, *Christianity and Social Order*, published during the Second World War, sought to provide a set of Christian values to hold the community together for the task of building a new society once war was over. It is illustrative of his capacity to think on the large scale and to seek ways of understanding that brought divided things and peoples together. Temple chaired the famous Malvern

Conference of 1941, which gathered Christian leaders together to think towards a new and more socially cohesive future. He was genuinely catholic in his approach, wanting to give a foundation in Christian values to our common life. His thinking rang many bells with the vision and hopes of many in the 1940s and still inspires people today.

Temple worked hard in the field of ecumenical relations. His tireless work with Christian leaders in Europe helped to lay the foundations for the post-war establishment of the World Council of Churches and the British Council of Churches. The recent Porvoo Agreement between the Nordic Lutheran churches and the Church of England would have brought him much pleasure and built upon relationships established in his own time.

Temple had the capacity, not often evident in people of his intellectual ability, to communicate great truths in ways that gripped the common mind. His *Readings in St John's Gospel* proved an attractive road into serious Christian study for many ordinary lay people. St John's Gospel, with its sense of the given nature of the *mystery of divine love unfolded in the world in *Jesus Christ, takes us close to Temple's heart.

His death, so early in his time at Canterbury, was a great shock. The report *Towards the Conversion of England*, which came out in 1945 after his death, is the final testimony to his commitment to enable the people of England to receive and enjoy the Christian gospel in the emerging world of the post-war period.

J. GLADWIN

TENNANT, FREDERICK ROBERT

Frederick Tennant (1866–1957), Cambridge theologian and philosopher of religion, was educated at Caius College and was drawn to apologetics in response to attacks on Christianity by 'Darwin's bulldog', T. H. Huxley. He subsequently taught *science (1891–4), served as chaplain at Caius (1897–9), took a doctorate under James Ward, and became an Anglican rector (1903–13). Eventually he returned to Cambridge as a fellow of Trinity College and lecturer in the university (1913–38). His reputation was established by a trilogy of books on the relatively neglected doctrine of sin. In *The Origin and Propagation of Sin* (1902), *Sources of the Doctrines of the Fall and Original Sin* (1903) and *The Concept of Sin* (1912), Tennant accommodated Christian theology to the notion of human moral evolution, and attacked the orthodox doctrines of the fall, original sin and human depravity. The theology he espoused in these books has probably reduced historic evangelical appreciation for his separate works in apologetics.

These apologetic works include *Miracle and Its Philosophical Presuppositions* (1925), *Philosophy of the Sciences* (1932), *The Nature of Belief* (1943) and his two-volume *Philosophical Theology* (1928, 1930), which, Tennant admitted, 'takes reading'. He stood firmly in the British empirical tradition, unshaken by questions of the legitimacy of such an *epistemology in matters of religion. He was sceptical of the claims of *rationalism, *religious experience and biblical *revelation, and sought to establish *theism in the way scientific laws were established; 'science and theism,' he claimed, 'spring from a common root'. He expanded the design argument of William *Paley by underscoring the incredible complexity of life that science was progressively revealing. While no single piece of evidence was conclusive proof of God's existence, the cumulative weight of empirical evidence of an evolution-compatible 'cosmic teleology' was compelling. 'The multitude of interwoven adaptations by which the world is constituted a theatre of life, intelligence, and morality' strongly suggests 'purposive intelligence' (*Philosophical Theology*, vol. 2, p. 121).

In 1935 Tennant was appointed a fellow of the British Academy. John *Hick has described Tennant's design argument as 'probably the strongest presentation that has been written of this type of theistic reasoning'. His place in the history of apologetics is regularly acknowledged, but his works themselves are now seldom read. His basic approach has been perpetuated by Basil Mitchell, Richard Swinburne and, in some ways, by William Dembski and the contemporary 'intelligent design' movement.

Bibliography

P. Bertocci, *The Empirical Argument for God in Late British Theology* (Cambridge, 1938); J. Hick, 'F. R. Tennant', in P. Edwards (ed.), *Encyclopedia of Philosophy* (New York and London, 1967); B. Ramm, *Varieties of Christian Apologetics* (Grand Rapids, 1961);

D. L. Scudder, *Tennant's Philosophical Theology* (New Haven and London, 1940).

G. G. SCORGIE

TERRORISM

Terrorism involves destructive, frequently deadly, actions intended to modify people's behaviour by inducing terror. Terrorism cannot be defined in terms of a particular set of political goals or purposes, since it is a technique to which almost any group can resort, and it can come in any number of forms. It can involve murderous attacks on civilians, assassinations of political figures (who may or may not be seen as non-combatants) or destruction of property without intentionally killing anyone. It can be State sponsored, or it can be a technique adopted by organizations that oppose the State. It can be aimed at the general population, or at specific subsets of the population. Racial terror, for example, was a potent technique used by the Ku Klux Klan in the American South to control the behaviour of African Americans, and involved attacks on individuals as well as destruction of property. The Colombian M-19 guerillas use political assassinations to strike terror in government officials who oppose them.

Terrorism is generally mobilized for social or political means, and this distinguishes it from individual actions generated simply by a hatred of a particular person or group, or from random violence that is not intended to generate a response in others, or from other types of political assassinations. The central characteristic that distinguishes terrorism from other types of political violence is its indirect nature, so that the destruction or murders are not simply an end in themselves, but are intended to control the behaviour of others by generating fear. Terrorism is intended to send a message, and the destruction or killing is always a means to further that end.

Because terrorist acts are intended to create fear in certain individuals or in certain groups among a population, it can be an extremely potent political weapon, though not always a successful one. It is also immoral by its very nature, since it involves causing death or destruction, usually of non-combatants, in order to change the behaviour of some group. While there is legitimate debate about whether Christians can ever be justified in carrying out a political assassination, such as Dietrich Bonhoeffer's participation in a plot to assassinate Adolf Hitler, Christians are never justified in turning to terrorist tactics.

The label 'terrorism' is sometimes applied to actions that depart from the central characteristics of violence directed at controlling others' behaviour through fear, but the fewer of these characteristics are present, the more likely it is that the label 'terrorism' is being used to rhetorical effect rather than as an accurate description. Groups such as Al Qaeda, and the Red Brigades in Italy, are clearly terrorist organizations. Groups such as the Sierra Club and Right to Life are not. In between we find a variety of groups that are more or less accurately termed 'terrorist', depending on their willingness to use random violence to control others' behaviour. It is an important part of the duty not to bear false witness to refrain from calling organizations we disagree with 'terrorist'.

Although terrorism has been utilized for any number of political ends, it has become more popularly associated with religion in recent years. The destruction of the World Trade Center towers associated terrorist tactics with *Islamic belief. Likewise, the ethnic cleansing that occurred in the former Yugoslavia, the history of attack and counter-attack between Catholic and Protestant in Ireland, and the long and bitter history of Jews and Palestinians in Israel all provide support for the perception that religion is a, or perhaps the, cause of terrorism. But the claim that terrorism always has a religious basis is clearly false: State sponsored terror has been a weapon in any number of secular regimes. Likewise, the prevalence of terrorism adopted as a technique by both fascist and communist guerilla groups indicates that religious belief is not an essential precondition for terrorist activity.

Yet while it is important to note that religion is not a necessary component of terrorism, it is also important to note that religious fervour can be a potent inducement to terrorist activity, and sociological studies suggest that religiously inspired terrorism in recent years has been far more indiscriminate in killing civilians than secular terrorist groups. For many in the West the word 'terrorism' conjures up images of Islam, but terrorist groups that claim to be Christian, such as the various Christian Patriot paramilitary groups and the Christian Identity movement bear a striking resemblance to

Islamic terrorist groups in ideology and willingness to kill civilians. (Timothy McVeigh, executed for bombing the Oklahoma City Federal building, had numerous ties to the Christian Identity movement, a white supremacist organization that claims to be Christian and that interprets Scripture in ways that glorify violence and *racism.) Christians need to be clear in their condemnation of such activities. It brings no glory to God when the name of Christ is associated with violence directed at producing terror.

Clearly Christians should condemn terrorism, and just as clearly that condemnation should be accompanied by discerning judgment about the causes that generate the terrorist activity. The desperation that generates terrorism can be legitimate (though it need not be). In some cases, the sense of a particular group that they are politically powerless, and that the legal and social structures that oppress them can be addressed in no way other than terrorism, may be partly justified. The fight to end apartheid in South Africa included groups who resorted to terrorism. In such a situation, the desperation that led to violence can be understood without endorsing terrorism. In other cases, terrorism is used to protect financial and social interests, and this deserves unqualified condemnation. But in cases such as the fight against apartheid, Christian condemnation of terrorist tactics needs to be paired with serious and concerted efforts to change an unjust situation. Terrorism can thus call Christians to respond to injustice in an active and productive way.

Bibliography

C. Gearty, *Terrorism* (Aldershot and Brookfield, 1996); B. Hoffman, *Inside Terrorism* (New York, 1998); M. Juergensmeyer, *Terror in the Mind of God: The Global Rise of Religious Violence* (Berkeley, 2000); D. Rapaport and Y. Alexander (eds.), *The Morality of Terrorism: Religious and Secular Justifications* (Oxford and New York, 1982).

R. E. GROENHOUT

TERTULLIAN

Tertullian (c. 160/70 – c. 220) lived at a time when it was not just Christians who wrote 'apologetic' works, for such writings frequently appeared in defence of a variety of groups. Tertullian employed the genre, including the controversial style, very well. He illustrated the complexity of the would-be apologist's task, a complexity that is even greater today. His apologetics focused on four topics.

Verbal attack

The Apology, Tertullian's most famous work, skilfully responded to slander and political attacks on Christians. It debunked the idea that Rome's misfortunes sprang from the anger of the gods against Christians. So, in *To Scapula* governors hostile to Christianity had been compelled by local natural disasters to repent of their opposition to the faith. This tack opened up a startling possibility. Perhaps Christ was really the rejected friend of the emperor and of the Roman world. Perhaps, because of the Christians, God actually *protected* cities from destruction. The strength of this approach was that it avoided the trap of the unhealthy aloofness of the church from the world. God had actually placed Christians in a messy world to make a difference. The downside, through misuse, of this 'public theology' was the eventual alliance of church with empire, which today has finally made much of Europe disenchanted with Christianity.

Ethics

In *To the Nations*, Tertullian defended the integrity of the Christian community from caricature. Christians, he complained, often endured miscarriages of justice for alleged sacrilege or treason. They did *not* commit cannibalism and incest – but their pagan accusers did. This approach shows that Tertullian frequently depended heavily on the credibility of believers, not just on the technical winning of arguments. Even ancient paganism needed to observe challenging moral lives, if Christian claims were to be taken seriously. However, Tertullian was unduly concerned with sexual morality. The move badly skewed Hebrew and Christian spirituality and damaged the appeal of Western churches centuries later.

Religions

Tertullian could easily fall back upon established critiques of pagan *polytheism by the ancient world's philosophers. Did Roman gods not have the disadvantage of having been promoted by Roman society from the ranks of human beings themselves? Moreover, the classical gods were hardly an advert for civilized behaviour. They were merely demons and, when exorcized, they testified loudly to the truth of *Jesus. Equally, the burgeoning local and civil gods of the empire were parochial and narrow. These polemical hits owed more to Tertullian's fire than to his originality.

Philosophy

Despite his apparent disclaimers, Tertullian did plunder *philosophy for apologetic ends. He used its apparatus but rarely adopted its spirit. The philosophers read Moses, and were guided to share in his insights through God's universal 'seed' of true reason in human hearts. However, with the *truth now to hand *perfectly* in Christ, no synthesis could be further sought between philosophy and Christian *revelation. This is the likely meaning of Tertullian's famous rhetorical question, 'What has Jerusalem to do with Athens?' Was Christ not the completing and fullness of all philosophical striving after truth?

What, however, of Tertullian's equally famous description of the incarnation, as that which 'must be believed because absurd'? This saying, which has been debated for centuries, and even widely misquoted, is not a statement by the apologist of his general approach. It should not be turned into backing for apologetic paradox or irrational anti-intellectualism. It could mean, amongst several interpretations, that (a) we should *expect* the work of God to seem strange and inept to limited human minds, (b) anything worth saying can be given a paradoxical twist, (c) the incarnation points to God's doing things by stooping not by power, (d) something so unlikely, even inept, as the incarnation would not have been invented – so must be true.

In these ways Tertullian emboldened the faithful. He spoke to history and society and did not avoid difficult questions, though sometimes he answered them naively. However, through not entering the intellectual stratosphere tackled by the 'Greek' Christian apologists, he failed to provoke a deep questioning and lasting change in society.

Bibliography

M. Edwards, M. Goodman and S. Price (eds.), *Apologetics in the Roman Empire: Pagans, Jews and Christians* (Oxford, 1999); A. J. Guerra, 'Polemical Christianity. Tertullian's Search for Certitude', *Second Century*, 8 (1991), pp. 109–123; R. Kearsley, *Tertullian's Theology of Divine Power* (Carlisle, 1998); E. F. Osborn, 'The Subtlety of Tertullian', *Vigiliae Christianae*, 52.4 (1998), pp. 361–370; *Tertullian, First Theologian of the West* (Cambridge, 1997).

R. KEARSLEY

TEXTUAL CRTITICISM, see BIBLICAL CRITICISM

THEISM

The central core of theism is the belief in one eternal self-existent God, who brought the entire universe into existence and remains continually active in his creation, a being altogether wise and good, who alone is worthy of worship. Each of these attributes is important. Theism clearly differs from *atheism and *agnosticism, which deny or else doubt God's existence, and from *polytheism with its many deities rather than just one. It differs from ancient dualisms with their two eternal divinities, one rational and the source of order and good, the other irrational and the source of evil, and also from early Greek conceptions of a God who did not bring matter into existence, but only gave pre-existent elements the form and order that made the world good. It should, however, also be distinguished from eighteenth-century deism, which acknowledged God as the Creator who gave nature both order and existence but denied him any continued activity in nature through *miracles or special *revelation. Currently more important is theism's difference from pantheism, which sees no real distinction between God and nature and so calls into question God's personal attributes of wisdom and goodness and freedom to act. Without such attributes, faith has no focus, hope has no basis in reality and love finds no response. Only the theistic God is worthy of worship.

This central core of theistic belief is characteristic of the world's three major theistic religions, *Judaism, *Islam and Christianity. Their differences stem rather from what divine revelations they accept, i.e. from their sacred writings and the different 'prophets' they follow. A distinctively Christian theism therefore moves (like the Apostles' Creed) beyond the basic theism of 'God the Father almighty, maker of heaven and earth' to the person and work of Christ and the continuing activity of the *Holy Spirit. While Judaism and Islam reject this trinitarian theology, all three religions agree on theism's central affirmations and address similar questions about the God-creation distinction, life after death or the relation of religion to *ethics.

Theism, as a conceptual scheme, typically addresses these matters in philosophical terms. The apostle Paul drew on Greek ideas about God when he talked to philosophers at Athens (Acts 17), and both Jewish and Christian theologians in the ancient world used *Platonic ideas about God and the Logos in explaining the relation between God and creation. Such ideas were the currency of that day, and in many cases they proved invaluable both for apologetic purposes and for constructive theological thinking.

Theistic arguments

Throughout its subsequent history theism has been a major tradition in Western philosophy, and its arguments for the existence of God have varied in form with the philosophy of the times. *Augustine, for instance, argued in Platonic fashion from the existence of undeniable truths to the existence of God as the archetypal truth in which they all participate. *Anselm's *ontological argument claimed that 'that than which nothing greater can exist' (like Plato's idea of 'the Good') necessarily exists. *Thomas Aquinas leaned rather on Aristotelian premises about the natural order, posing five arguments to show that God is not only the efficient cause but also the formal and final cause of the whole creation. (*Aristotle himself thought of God only as final cause.) This kind of *natural theology has figured large in Roman Catholic apologetics ever since.

However, the breakdown of the medieval synthesis of Christian *theology with Greek philosophy undercut this kind of approach. Nominalists like William of Ockham rejected all theories of real *universals, allowing reference only to empirical particulars and whatever could be inferred from them. Martin Luther was schooled in that tradition and so had little use for Aristotle or for natural theology in Christian thought. *Calvin, on the other hand, maintained in his *Institutes of the Christian Religion* that the splendour of nature bears such clear witness to its Creator that even

human sinfulness cannot blot out the sense of a deity inscribed on human minds. 'Both heaven and earth contain innumerable proofs,' he wrote, but he was careful to emphasize that they lead only to the knowledge of God as Creator, not God as Redeemer.

Modern philosophy produced new versions of both ontological and causal arguments for the existence of God, the former in rationalists like *Descartes and *Leibniz, and the latter in more empirically oriented thinkers. But since mechanistic *science tried to explain things without Aristotle's formal and final causes, the new teleological arguments generally stressed only the orderliness of natural forces, or else they argued from analogies between natural phenomena and human artifacts. As William *Paley suggested, if on some primitive shore a stranger to civilization and technology stumbled for the first time on a watch, and over a period of time observed how amazingly it kept pace with day and night, and so how useful it could be, would he not then infer that someone had made it for a purpose? Causal arguments of this sort, however, address only nature's origin, not the continued activity of its Creator, and so they served the deism of that day more effectively than theism. Moreover, David *Hume was sceptical about our knowledge even of causation, for while we observe constant conjunctions of similar phenomena and so suppose them to be causally connected, we have neither empirical nor *a priori* knowledge of any causal force.

Immanuel *Kant, in his *Critique of Pure Reason*, argued that human knowledge is about phenomena only, so none of the arguments can prove whether in reality God exists, or not. But while speculative philosophy cannot demonstrate God's existence, it does provide a coherent idea of God, were he to exist. So, in his *Critique of Practical Reason* Kant developed a *moral argument instead. A sense of moral duty is by nature deeply engrained in human consciousness, yet this seems utterly inconsistent with our equally deep need for happiness. The two could only be reconciled in an afterlife where virtue is rewarded with happiness, but that requires a further postulate, namely that God in reality exists. In his *Critique of Judgment*, Kant later extended his case to include aesthetics, arguing that the teleology evident in nature's amenability to our moral and aesthetic feeling is best explained by a theistic world-view.

Moral arguments for the existence of God figured large in subsequent theistic apologetics, for Kant's idea of an ethical theism fitted well in the kind of metaphysical *idealism that developed in nineteenth-century Germany to explain the cultural creativity of the human spirit. It required developing an overall teleological world-view, rather than a line of argument focused simply on God's existence. Representative of this approach are William *Temple's *Nature, Man and God*, and his *Mens Creatrix*, where God is seen as the source and ideal of all good, truth and beauty. Meantime a growing interest in the *psychology of religion led to arguments from *religious experience for the existence of God. Like the medieval mystics, believers today take a realistic view of their meeting God, so the argument draws parallels between these experiences and realistic interpretations of *sense perception or our knowledge of other persons. Religious and moral and aesthetic experience are all seen as pointing to God, parts of a wider *teleological argument.

Twentieth-century philosophy was more oriented to logical analysis than system building, but by the middle of the century renewed attention was being given to informal *reasoning. Basil Mitchell observed that a rational case for theism need not take the form of deductive proofs or depend on strict probabilities. The case for theism is more like the reasons a historian gives for one interpretation of an event over another, or the literary critic's basis for accepting a particular interpretation of a text, or the reasons involved in a 'paradigm shift' in science. The point is to find the best coherent explanation, and in the case of conceptual schemes like theism this means the best overall world and life view. So, Mitchell advised a cumulative case approach in which all the various elements reinforce one another, those related to moral and religious experience as well as those adduced by the traditional arguments.

Are theistic arguments really necessary to justify theistic belief? *Enlightenment thinkers had supposed that rational beliefs must either be self-evident or else be derived from empirical or self-evident premises. *Scottish Common Sense Realism had objected that many of our beliefs arise naturally because of how our minds are made, and recent Reformed *epistemology extends this to belief in God. As Alvin Plantinga puts it, if our minds were functioning properly then belief in God would develop naturally; belief needs no further justification. Belief in God's existence, in fact, is properly basic to so much else. But our minds do not function properly.

Objections to theism

The most common objection to theism is the problem of *evil. If there is a God, and he is as powerful, wise, and good as theists say, then why is there so much evil and suffering? The atheist concludes that no such God exists, and some theists have opted for a finite God with limited power. However, the theistic tradition has offered two major responses. The 'free will defence', which goes back to Augustine, ascribes moral evil to free agents who have turned away from their Creator. This of course leads to further questions about the relation of human, and even demonic, freedom to God's foreknowledge and power. The 'greater good' argument envisions some larger divine purpose which both natural and moral evils eventually serve. Why did God make us so dependent and vulnerable, physically, emotionally, morally and in every way? What is our highest end?

Another common objection is that theism lacks coherence. The point may be that it is self-contradictory to claim, for example, that God is both one and three; or that it is meaningless to say that God is a free agent who created and sustains the universe. The first kind of objection is about logic; the second is about *language. Objections of the first kind were often addressed when the doctrine was first formulated: trinitarian doctrine distinguished the one 'essence' from the three 'hypostases', making plain that they are one and three in different regards, hence not self-contradictory at all. This requires the kind of clear thinking evident in recent philosophical theology, which uses philosophical methods and ideas to unpack and clarify difficult concepts or to resolve apparent contradictions. Objections of the second kind arise from the unusual nature of theological language, which lacks the kind of empirical grounding we now expect. Talk about God and creation uses language analogically rather than literally, in order to evoke understanding of what is literally 'supernatural'. A meaningful conceptual scheme therefore develops with the consistent use of such language, as it does with other than theistic *metaphysics.

A further objection comes from writers like *Freud and *Nietzsche, who see theism as the projection of some subconscious psychological need. This *ad hoc* argument is of course self-refuting, for the same could be said of atheism and almost any other position. Psychological needs do indeed influence our thinking, but this by no means implies that *reasoning serves only to mask them rather than contributing to the quest for truth. If theism is true and human reason is indeed a gift from God to people created in his image, then reason has a more positive function than that.

Traditional theism claims that God is omniscient and altogether wise, and this is the basis for a theistic understanding of truth. If the ultimate locus of truth is in the all-knowing mind of God, then truth is objective, independent of whether or not we know it. As Augustine put it, we do not judge it but it judges us. Moreover, God is the ultimate source of all we could possibly know, whether by natural means or by divine revelation. The *arts and sciences all depend ultimately on him, and find their purpose in his purposes for his creation. Humans are fallible, but in the providence of God everything true and good may still be said to come from God.

Like truth, the goodness of God is objectively real, and as the basis for theistic ethics it stands in contrast to the *relativism of much modern and postmodern thought. The motivation for a moral life is the love and goodness of God, the ideal of good character is 'godlikeness', the basis for moral obligation is the 'good and perfect' will of God, the ideal society is seen as a 'kingdom' of God. He alone is worthy of worship. But especially in Christian ethics the emphasis on sin and grace is crucial, and it distinguishes the Christian religion from mere theism.

Bibliography

E. L. Mascall, *He Who Is: A Study in Traditional Theism* (London and New York, 1943); B. Mitchell, *The Justification of Belief* (London and New York, 1973); T. V. Morris (ed.), *Divine and Human Action: Essays on the Metaphysics of Theism* (Ithaca, 1988); R. Swinburne, *The Coherence of Theism* (Oxford, 1977); K. E. Yandell, *Christianity and Philosophy* (Leicester and Downers Grove, 1984).

A. F. HOLMES

THEISTIC PROOFS

Theistic proofs are rational arguments for the existence of a monotheistic God which do not directly appeal to sacred scriptures for their cogency. These arguments claim that there are sufficient reasons to believe that *monotheism is objectively true. Monotheism affirms that there is only one God, who is a personal and perfect being of unlimited power and goodness and who created the universe out of nothing. This being is worthy of adoration and worship, distinct from the world but continuously involved in it, and capable of generating *miracles. The concept of God must be logically coherent for any argument or combination of arguments to establish the existence of such a being, since there are no possible arguments for incoherent concepts (such as square circles). Such theistic arguments have a long and complicated history, involving not only Christianity but other monotheistic religions as well. We will explain and evaluate the major types of theistic proofs and consider how they contribute to Christian apologetics.

Argument forms

The term 'proof' can mean an argument in which the premises deductively entail a conclusion such that the conclusion is secured beyond any doubt. That is, if the premises are true the conclusion must be true. So, a theistic proof in this sense would establish the existence of God in the same way that theorems are deductively derived from axioms in geometry. Some theistic arguments have such a deductive form. However, the phrase 'theistic proof' can mean any argument (even if inductive or abductive) for God's existence. Theistic proofs are also referred to as specimens of '*natural theology', which is distinguished from revealed theology (what can be derived by proper exegesis and theologizing from sacred texts). For example, the plan of salvation through *Jesus Christ is known through God's acts in *history and subsequently through the written biblical *revelation; it is not known through rational reflection on the creation alone. Theistic proofs thus form part of Christian apologetics, but not the whole of it. Their aim is to establish rationally the existence, and certain core attributes, of God. They do not fully fill out the Christian world-view, nor all of the attributes of the Christian God. Deism, not Christian *theism, claims that our knowledge of God is exhausted by what can be known about God through nature and unaided reason.

Types of theistic proofs

Theistic proofs are grouped into two main categories. Each category is a family of arguments, since there are various versions of each kind of argument. All of these arguments have been updated and made more analytically rigorous in recent decades. In fact, they are flourishing in the philosophical literature thanks to the works of philosophers such as Richard Swinburne, J. P. Moreland, and William Lane Craig. First, there are *a posteriori* or empirical arguments. These arguments, cosmological, design, and moral, depend on some evidence in the world as a basis from which to infer God's existence. A second kind of theistic argument is *a priori*. These *ontological arguments trade on the philosophical implications of the idea of God in itself, and not on states of affairs in the world. It argues that the very idea of God as a greatest possible being demands that God exists.

While the effectiveness of each kind of theistic proof must be evaluated individually, the apologist can combine several types of argument to form a cumulative case argument for theism that is stronger than the case of any argument taken by itself. One may use a *cosmological argument to establish the existence of God as creator, a *teleological argument for God as designer, a *moral argument for God as the source of the moral law, and so on. Each argument is like a witness in a trial; each testifies in its own way for the truth of theism. The larger case for Christian theism includes even more lines of converging evidence, such as the resurrection of Christ and *religious experience.

Cosmological arguments

Cosmological arguments come in three basic forms, but all argue from the fact of the universe to a cause of the universe. Thomistic cosmological arguments (deriving from *Thomas Aquinas) rely on notions received from *Aristotle. Any finite entity in the universe or any collection of entities (the universe itself) is a combination of actuality and potentiality. That which is finite might not have existed and is not the source of its own existence. Its essence (what it is) is not identical with its existence (that it is). Therefore, there must be a first cause that is non-contingent or necessary in order to support the series of finite states of being. This argument does not establish a temporal beginning of the universe, but rather a first cause that is first in metaphysical rank. According to Aquinas, the temporal beginning of the universe was a deliverance of biblical revelation and not established by theistic proof. Contemporary evangelical philosophers Norman Geisler and Bruce Reichenbach have advanced versions of the Thomistic argument.

Other cosmological arguments employ and adapt concepts formulated by *Leibniz, fundamentally the principle of sufficient reason. This principle has been given several forms, such as 'For any contingent entity, there is a sufficient explanation for why it exists' or 'Everything that exists has an explanation for its existence, either in the necessity of its own existence or in an outside cause'. From this, it is argued that the universe is not self-explanatory, but contingent. God explains the existence of the universe. But God himself requires no explanation outside of himself, since he is an eternal and perfect being (or necessary being). The strength of this argument relies on the status of the principle of sufficient reason. Richard Taylor has called it 'a principle of reason itself', while Bertrand *Russell has affirmed that the universe was 'just there' and in need of no explanation. However, the metaphysical implication of rejecting the principle of sufficient reason with respect to the cosmos is that the cosmos is meaningless. That entails *nihilism, which is an unacceptable and unlivable world-view for most. Furthermore, it seems arbitrary to search for explanations for anything in the universe, but not to seek an explanation for the universe as a whole.

The *kalam* cosmological argument was developed primarily by Muslim theologians in the Middle Ages, although the Christian Bonaventure endorsed it as well. Since the late 1970s, William Lane Craig as well as others have revived the argument. This argument depends neither on the metaphysical notions of contingency and necessity nor on the principle of sufficient reason. Unlike the Thomistic and Leibnizian forms, the *kalam* argument, if successful, secures the biblical doctrine of *creatio ex nihilo*. As stated by Craig, its form is simple and elegant: Whatever begins to exist has a cause – the universe began to exist – therefore, the universe has a cause.

This is a deductive argument. Craig takes the first premise to be a fairly non-controversial concept because *ex nihilo nihil fit* (out of nothing nothing comes). The alternative is that things pop into existence without a cause, which even the arch-sceptic David *Hume denied. The second premise is grounded on the impossibility of an actual infinite or the impossibility of crossing (or traversing) an actual infinite. This premise denies that the universe is composed of a beginningless series of linear events (which would require an actual infinite). An actual infinite must be distinguished from a potential infinite. The latter is a series that is always increasing, but which never reaches an upper limit. A verse from the hymn 'Amazing Grace' makes the philosophical point: 'When we've been there ten thousand years, bright shining as the sun, we've no less days to sing God's praise, than when we'd first begun.' The endless bisection of a line of finite extension is another example of a potential infinite.

An actual infinite, however, is complete and self-contained. According to J. P. Moreland, it 'is a set considered as a completed totality with an actual infinite number of members'. No new members can be added to it. This is what distinguishes it from a potential infinite. But this generates problems if one attempts to divide or subtract from actual infinities. For example, if a library with an actual infinite number of books is composed equally of red books and blue books, the subtraction of all the blue books will still leave an infinite number of books. But this is absurd. Similarly, if one subtracts all the odd numbers from the set of all natural numbers of an actual infinite set, the amount of numbers remaining is still infinite. This is logically unacceptable as well. Yet even if an actual infinite might exist, the *kalam* proponents argue that it could not be traversed through successive addition. One can neither count from one to infinity nor count down from infinity to one. There is always an infinite distance to travel, so one never arrives.

If the actual infinite does not exist and/or cannot be traversed, this means that the series of linear events in the universe must be finite. If the series is finite, it must have a beginning. If it has a beginning, the cause of the series must be outside of the universe. Craig argues that this cause is a personal being of immense power. The originator of the causal series is not subject to experiencing an actual infinity of moments if its existence does not involve a series of events.

Craig and others have sought epistemic support for creation *ex nihilo* through the scientific evidence for Big Bang *cosmology. Several converging lines of evidence have firmly established this cosmology, which is interpreted by most to require an absolute origination of the universe from nothing about fourteen billion years ago. Unless one posits that everything came from nothing without a cause, a supernatural Creator is the best explanation for what detonated the Big Bang.

Design or teleological arguments

Design or teleological arguments claim that features of the universe as a whole (both its laws and its constant features not constrained by laws) or various parts of it (such as living organisms or their parts) evidence an arrangement that is best understood as designed for goal-directed activity by a non-human mind. These facts cannot be accounted for on the basis of time, chance and impersonal natural laws. The data for design are diverse and numerous. They include design as order, purpose, simplicity, complexity and beauty at both the macroscropic and microscopic levels. Arguments from design have sometimes been construed as arguments from analogy. As William *Paley famously argued: we know that a watch is made by a mind – the universe resembles a watch (given its complexity and purposeful aspects) – therefore, the universe is designed. But arguments from analogy are subject to the suspicion that the items compared (a watch and the eye or the universe as a whole) may be significantly disanalogous, thus defeating the argument. However, Paley's design argument, as well as more recent versions, can be rendered as inferences to the best explanation, a stronger argument form. Given certain marks of design (whether in watches or the universe or the eye), design is a better explanation than merely chance and natural law.

Especially since Darwin's theory of natural selection, many have claimed that the apparent design of living things can be explained without recourse to intelligence, thus defeating the design argument. To this, some Christians (and others) have disputed the case for Darwinism itself (more below). Others have appealed to a 'larger teleological argument' that appeals to designed factors of the universe at large and not to the specifics of biology. Richard Swinburne has given an inductive or probability version of the larger design argument which accepts Darwinian evolution without endorsing *naturalism. Instead of arguing from analogy, Swinburne appeals to design as a better explanation for the overall design data than merely natural forces.

Two recent developments in science have bolstered the argument from design. First, on the macroscopic level, in the last several decades a host of cosmic constants have been discovered that are finely tuned to make life possible. Hugh Ross, an astronomer and apologist, has compiled over one hundred factors about the universe (the numbers have been steadily growing in the past two decades) that must all be in place (with very little margin of error) for it to be hospitable to life. Apologists argue that these factors, which are not constrained by natural laws to have the precise values they possess, indicate a designer who carefully crafted the cosmic details just so because it is amazing that this vast constellation of finely calibrated factors came about at all, when they might not have occurred. Given these cosmic constants, a theistic explanation is much more likely than an atheistic explanation. Naturalists attempt to escape theistic implications by way of the 'world ensemble hypothesis', which claims that vast numbers of universes (possibly an infinity of them) all exist independently of one another. By expanding universes, one expands possibilities. Our universe, then, was the lucky one, and there is no need for there to be a God in order to explain it. Swinburne takes this as 'the height of irrationality'. There is no evidence (and no possible evidence) for these other universes. They are posited simply to avoid theism, but theism is a simpler explanation and it receives evidential support from other theistic arguments as well.

Secondly, on the microscopic level, life is far more complex than Darwin ever knew. It contains oceans of information; a single human cell contains as much information as several encyclopedias. This is known as the 'information problem'. Consider DNA, which contains a literal message made up of letters (nucleotides), words (codons or triplets), sentences (genes), paragraphs (operons), chapters (chromosomes), and books (living organisms). Many theorists have abandoned chance as an explanation for abiogenesis (how life comes from non-life without intelligent agency) and are searching for exoteric natural laws that provide for the 'self-organization' of such highly complex systems. Francis Crick, realizing the impossibility of life

forming by itself from non-life, has posited the 'directed panspermia' theory, claiming that the earth was seeded with life by extra-terrestrials. This explanation leaves the origin of the extra-terrestrials unexplained and offers no independent evidence for their existence. The aroma of the *ad hoc* is in the air.

Biochemist Michael Behe argues that many microscopic molecular organisms, such as the bacterial flagellum, evince 'irreducible complexity'. This means that their function requires multiple interlocking parts, none of which is expendable to their function. Consider a mousetrap. Each part is necessary for its function. Behe argues that these 'molecular machines' – and they are literally machines – are not explicable on Darwinian terms, whereby each evolutionary change is incremental and unplanned. The metaphysical implications of irreducible complexity are significant: chance and natural law are not sufficient to explain many features of biology. A designing intelligence outside the natural processes must be introduced as a sufficient explanation.

William Dembski carefully develops the notion of 'specified complexity' as an indicator of intelligence behind the design of natural systems. If any natural system or entity cannot be explained by either chance or natural law (or some combination of the two), the only explanatory category remaining is intelligent design. Dembski is a key player in a new scientific research programme known as the Intelligent Design Movement (along with Behe, Phillip E. Johnson and others). Their metaphysical goals are modest – the reintroduction of design as a legitimate category for scientific explanation. However, their work contributes to the argument from design, since one may argue, along with intellectual support from the other theistic proofs, that this designing intelligence is the Creator.

Alvin Plantinga has developed a sophisticated epistemological version of the design argument aimed at defeating naturalism and establishing theism as the best explanation for human rationality. (C. S. *Lewis and Richard Taylor have given similar, but less rigorous, forms of this argument.) Plantinga argues that if our minds are merely the result of unplanned and brute natural forces, there is no reason to trust their deliverances. Our minds may have survival value, but this is not the same thing as possessing *truth through rationally reliable processes. Naturalists Richard *Rorty and Patricia Churchland agree that a Darwinian process can give no guarantee of truth to the mind. Therefore, Plantinga concludes, in order to justify the basic workings of our minds, we should believe in a rational and personal God who designed us to know both God and creation.

Moral arguments

Moral arguments claim that some aspects of *morality are best explained by the existence of God. They often appeal to *conscience to ground the reality of an objective moral law that transcends persons and cultures. They then claim that this moral law is better explained by the existence of God than by appeals to abstract impersonal principles of a Platonic nature. God is presented as the personal and moral source of the moral law, which is contained in his own being or character.

Although not as sophisticated as arguments given by Hastings Rashdall and R. W. Sorely, C. S. Lewis's moral argument in the immensely popular *Mere Christianity*, 'Right and Wrong as a Clue to the Meaning of the Universe', persuasively states the case that conscience indicates a law that stands in judgment of human attitudes and actions, which is not reducible to instinct or social convention. In *The Abolition of Man*, Lewis further argues that the moral law is evident in a wide variety of human societies through history and cannot be denied without abolishing the very idea of humans as morally significant beings capable of moral judgment.

Moral arguments face two significant challenges. First, if ethical *relativism is true, there is no objective moral law beyond individuals and communities. Conscience and ethical principles would be reduced to merely natural categories. But a careful analysis of moral sentiment and ethical judgments indicates the weakness of this view. Certain actions, such as rape and murder, are morally wrong, no matter what the social conditioning. Certain virtues, such as love and wisdom, are commendable as objective states of affairs.

Secondly, philosophers have argued that God fails to provide a metaphysical justification of the good. This is because if God's will is the creator of goodness, God could will anything, even murder, and it would thereby be good. But if God's will does not determine the good, then he loses his metaphysical supremacy before an abstract and impersonal moral law not of his own making. While some theists have opted for divine voluntarism (notably William of *Ockham as well as *Islamic thinkers), the more fruitful response is to articulate a *tertium quid*. The good is not variable according to God's arbitrary commands. Rather, God's commands are rooted in his eternally consistent character. Moreover, God's commands perfectly fit the nature of the world and the humans God created in his image. That God cannot command that we torture the innocent for pleasure is not a limitation on his character, but flows from the facts of own moral perfection and the qualities of his creatures.

Ontological arguments

Ontological arguments find their origin in a prayer of *Anselm in his *Proslogion*. Unlike *a posteriori* arguments, ontological arguments deduce the existence of God *a priori* from the concept of God as a perfect being or greatest possible being, apart from any experience in the world. If successful, the ontological argument is a 'winner-take-all' proof. In one move it ensures that God is perfect with respect to all the divine attributes. God possesses to the ultimate degree every attribute that it is better to have than to lack. Therefore, God is maximally powerful, maximally good, maximally knowing, and so on. The *a posteriori* arguments, on the other hand, deliver more piecemeal, but not insignificant, conclusions concerning God's attributes.

The argument takes two basic forms. The first version is a *reductio ad absurdum* argument. Anselm's definition of God is a 'being than which greater cannot be conceived'. But if God exists only in our minds, we can imagine a greater being: one that exists in objective *reality as well as in our minds. If so, then we can conceive of a being greater than one that merely exists in our minds. But this would be a being greater than the greatest possible being, which is absurd. Therefore, God exists in both the understanding and in reality. *Kant disputed whether or not existence is a genuine predicate that adds anything to a concept. If existence is not a predicate, the concept of God as the greatest possible being does not entail God's existence.

However, more recent versions of the argument developed by Charles Hartshorne, Norman Malcolm and Alvin Plantinga have capitalized on another of Anselm's ruminations, that a greatest possible being cannot be conceived not to exist, so exists necessarily. That is, God exists in all possible worlds. For this argument to work, the idea of a perfect being must be possible; it must be internally coherent and not contradict anything else more certainly known. Plantinga maintains that the premise that is it possible that a perfect being exists can be held rationally (that is, it is rationally permissible), but is not compelling (that is, rationally obligatory). Others, such as Stephen T. Davis, deem the argument to be stronger.

In the early years of the twenty-first century, the recent track record of theistic proofs is strong and their prospects are bright. Apologists should seize the day by providing the best arguments possible for the existence of God.

Bibliography

M. Behe, *Darwin's Black Box* (New York, 1996); J. Beilby (ed.), *Naturalism Defeated? Essays on Plantinga's Evolutionary Argument Against Naturalism* (New York, 2002); W. L. Craig, *The Cosmological Argument: From Plato to Leibniz* (Eugene, OR, 2001); *Reasonable Faith* (Wheaton, 1994); S. T. Davis, *God, Reason, and Theistic Proofs* (Grand Rapids, 1996); W. Dembski, *Intelligent Design: The Bridge Between Science and Theology* (Downers Grove, 1999); C. S. Lewis, *Mere Christianity* (London, 1943); J. P. Moreland, *Scaling the Secular City: A Defense of Christianity* (Grand Rapids, 1987); R. Swinburne, *The Existence of God*, 2nd edn (New York, 1991).

D. GROOTHUIS

THEOLOGICAL METHOD

Theology is not simply a list of dogmas to be believed but encompasses a framework for thinking about God and God's world and a vision for living in it. Theology must be lived in the life of the church and also lived in the midst of the world. As a result, it is a study of enormously complex and complicated dimensions. Compounding this reality is the bold intention to talk about God in an adequate and accurate manner. In this sense, theology ought to be the most ennobling and the most humbling of disciplines. The sad reality is that theology is also one of the most contested disciplines.

Theology finds a place as a discipline within the modern academy, which has meant that it has been required to reflect upon a 'proper method' of inquiry as a means to settle disputes. How does theology begin? What are the sources of theology? Why does it proceed as it does? Why should its conclusions be accepted? Who are the arbitrators of its disputes? But lest we also forget, the God who created us and created us to think about him, and thereby to think about how we think about him, imposes these questions upon us.

Theology and the speech of God

Theology which is distinctively Christian is not simply nor primarily human reflection on the meaning of life. It is centrally about listening to a divine word. Christians have long confessed that God is just the sort of being who not only creates and redeems but also communicates in intelligible ways. To the question, 'Where does theology begin?', Christians have confidently answered, 'It begins with the God who speaks and acts.'

The Great Tradition of *Christianity (Protestant, Roman Catholic and Eastern Orthodox) has long been convinced that God communicates in an intelligible manner, accommodating himself to the human intellect by using human language and human action. The primary location of this communication is the Bible. This is a central conviction of a theological method which begins 'from above'. By contrast, theologies that begin with human experience are referred to as theologies 'from below', characteristic most especially of liberal Christianity. The conflict between theologies 'from above' and 'from below' animated much of academic theology throughout the twentieth century.

In theologies from above, the divine speech comes in a variety of styles. God 'speaks' creation into being. God 'speaks' through the prophets. God 'speaks' with miracles. God 'speaks' through the providential ordering of redemptive *history. And God 'speaks' climactically in the living Word, *Jesus Christ. A theological method wrestles with how best to understand and interpret each of these divine speeches in the Scriptures.

Theology and history: tradition, culture and experience

Theology is a branch of history insofar as it depicts that relationship between God and ourselves across a time span from the beginning (creation) to the end (consummation), whose centre is the mystery that God has entered time in the person of Jesus Christ. A central part of the Scriptures is historical narrative, a recounting of selected events in the past. The story is filled with many sub-plots in order to shape the way we think about history and the meaning of history. Broadly speaking, God communicates that history moves with purpose, and that it moves towards a goal which may not always seem readily apparent. On the surface, life may seem meaningless, but underneath the very foundations of history, God is bringing all things to their proper consummation.

If theology is a discipline that begins with the divine speech, it also ought to pay attention to the human listener – a listener situated in a time and place. Theology has traditionally thought about the 'time and place' issue by speaking of the use of tradition, *culture (or experience) and reason in theology. Changing the earlier metaphor, the divine word/speech is like an arrow shot through the different layers of tradition, culture and experience, each of which resides, in some sense, within the human person. The speech of God comes through traditions, through cultures, and through individual experiences.

The theological use of the term 'tradition' simply signifies the means of passing on the message of the gospel from generation to generation. Every believer stands within a tradition. That tradition may be vast and varied (such as Roman Catholicism) or it may be fairly narrow and uniform (such as dispensational premillennialism). It may be well defined or it may be ambiguous; and, truth be told, most of us are influenced by a host of traditions.

The arrow of the divine speech also moves through a layer of enculturation. What is 'heard' and how we 'talk' are influenced by the web of habits and institutions that makes up culture. It is impossible to remove this influence, though it does not follow that theology is identical with one's culture, nor simply determined by one's culture. Theology ought to be humbly self-critical towards its own enculturation.

Theology is also lived out in the sub-culture of the church, often both distinctively different from and similar to the surrounding culture. The idolatries of the wider culture inevitably show up in the sub-cultures of the churches, because by nature people do not separate their sacred and secular experiences. The histories of Christians in the abolition movements of the eighteenth and nineteenth centuries and the civil rights movement of the twentieth century remind us that churches can and should take prophetic stances relative to the idolatries of their own time. Figuring out in the present how to do that is the hard part!

A sub-set of one's cultural habits is the individual experiences each of us goes through in the course of our lifetimes. These experiences shape us in profound and often unnoticed ways. We also ought to remember, however, that God has created us with a self-consciousness that enables us to transcend our own experiences while also being rooted in them. So, for example, growing up wealthy exerts a powerful influence upon how a person treats people and possessions. The many warnings in Scripture about wealth are powerful reminders of this.

It is worth paying careful attention to each of these layers, of tradition, of culture and of experience. The biblical *revelation stands in an authoritative position relative to these layers, but inevitably these layers influence the interpretation of that authority. These filters do not determine by themselves the nature of that authority, but they do exert a certain pull in the direction to which that authority moves in the life of the believer. The goal of theology is to bring the divine word into a position of judgment upon all of life, including the layers.

Whose truth, which theology?

In a world where everyone appears entitled to their own opinions, it may seem counterintuitive to claim that any theology is ultimately or finally true, though this is precisely the heart of Christian theology. People have become suspicious of any religious solution that appears as the 'only' one. Any attempt to locate one text (e.g. the Bible) as uniquely revelatory of God appears as intellectually and morally intolerant. In practical terms, there is no such thing as a 'consensus' of public opinion. In single congregations it seems difficult or impossible to develop a common mind on what is or is not essential about the Bible. In churches, public opinion is pluralized and polarizing. It is these contexts which put the modern problem of theology front and central – whose *truth and which theology can we believe?

As a means of defending theology, the temptation is strong to produce evidence of a philosophical or historical sort against the rationality of opposing claims and in favour of our own views. This is not entirely wrong-headed, but in a culture like ours, where notions of rationality are themselves contested, it may seem implausible to many to claim that any theological construct alone is rational. It might be wiser to pay attention to the impulse behind the initial objection: that taken-for-granted assumption that the gospel must be permitted to be interpreted in countlessly diverse ways. Let us call this the pluralist impulse.

Most often the pluralist impulse is defended by appeal to the fact of *pluralism: that there are multiple communities of faith, all with diverse sacred texts. But why should this be seen as a 'defeater' for an earlier way of understanding the gospel as simply true? Might not pluralism and its accompanying pluralist impulse be better understood from within the gospel? In other words, might there be a different (and more satisfying) way to understand difference?

The gospel is in fact one story among many competitors, but it is also a story which encompasses those other stories, precisely because God enters time (making it a story) and remains beyond time (making it a story about stories). The gospel is not only one set of interpretations, but also a way to understand the impulse to interpret in the first place. This is because the God who creates is also the God who interprets (once and for all).

The story of the gospel is centred on the person and work of Christ, and this unifying centre is the very centrifugal force which pushes the gospel outward, across the length and breadth and width of the globe. The gospel does not shy away from diversity but rather embraces it. However, the uniqueness of the God/Man, Jesus Christ, prohibits the interpreting of the gospel by means of many diverse and conflicting readings. The gospel is not merely one (contested) world-view but rather is a world to be inhabited, a story through which our (diverse) lives are told. By contrast, the pluralist impulse supposes that we create our own stories. The Christian story, however, is just that sort of story which uniquely subsumes all other stories in its shadow. To see this is to turn the pluralist impulse on its head and suppose that the Christian story alone accounts for there being so many diverse stories.

Conclusion

The Christian theological framework finds its shape, then, most definitively in the initiating communication of God. It ought not to underemphasize the expectations which the interpreter brings to that communication, but it likewise ought not to negotiate the fundamental starting point in the construction of theology. God is the Lord of history and the Lord of theology.

The biblical revelation is the court of last appeal for the theologian. A Christian theological framework is not merely our experience of the gospel but God's own interpretation of that redemptive experience. Theology in its form and substance as well as its function in the church ought to reflect the *authority of God as God.

Finally, theology ought to be framed within the context of doxology. Reflections upon God should be wrapped in praise and adoration of God. The entire theological endeavour must be understood in the context of knowing and worshipping God. Theology ought not only to serve our minds (though it must not do less than this) but must also be grounded in a heart prepared by God. A disinterested, dispassionate theological vision may capture the mind, but it will only impoverish the soul.

Bibliography

W. C. Gilpin, *A Preface to Theology* (Chicago, 1996); R. Lints, *The Fabric of Theology* (Grand Rapids, 1993); K. Vanhoozer, *First Theology: God, Scripture and Hermeneutics* (Downers Grove, 2002); F. Watson, *Text, Church, and World: Biblical Interpretation in Theological Perspective* (Edinburgh, 1994).

R. LINTS

THERAVADA BUDDHISM, see BUDDHISM

THOMAS À KEMPIS

Thomas à Kempis (1379–1471) was born in Kempen, a small diocese of Cologne. In his thirteenth year he left his home, never to see his parents again, and travelled to Deventer,

Holland, where he studied under the tutelage of the Brothers of the Common Life. In 1399 he travelled to Zwolle to visit his brother John, who at that time was prior of the Mount St Agnes monastery, a religious community founded by mystic Gerard Groot, committed to poverty, simplicity of life and good works. It was here that Thomas was ordained a priest in 1413 and where he would spend the better part of the rest of his life. His early training with the Brothers of Common Life shaped his entire life.

Overwhelmed by the passion of Christ, Thomas was devoted to the cross as the symbol of what Christ had done for him. He longed for a release from the flesh and denied himself many comforts and regularly scourged himself, lest the flesh overtake his thoughts, rendering him unworthy of the love of Christ. Thomas wrote, 'Christ's entire life was a cross and martyrdom, and will you look for rest and happiness? You are deluded if you look for anything other than affliction, for our entire mortal life is surrounded by crosses' (*Imitation of Christ*, p. 49). For Thomas, 'This is the highest wisdom: to see the world as it truly is, fallen and fleeting; to love the world not for its own sake but for God's; and to direct all your effort toward achieving the kingdom of heaven' (*Imitation of Christ*, p. 3).

Best known for his four books now under the general title of *The Imitation of Christ*, Thomas wrote to encourage personal devotion to Christ assisted by a life of meditation, measured conversation and self-denial. Although his self-denial may have been carried to an unwarranted extreme, Thomas's life and writings continue as a much needed reminder to Christians not to love the world nor the things of the world. If the authentic Christian life is the final Christian apologetic, then there is much to be learned from Thomas in ordering one's private and public life centred on God – to love the Lord with all one's heart, soul and mind.

Bibliography

D. Butler, *Thomas à Kempis: A Religious Study* (Edinburgh, 1908); J. E. G. De Montmorency, *Thomas à Kempis: His Age and Book* (Port Washington and London, 1906); V. Scully, *Life of the Venerable Thomas À Kempis* (London and New York, 1901); Thomas à Kempis, *The Imitation of Christ* (Macon, 1989).

B. A. LITTLE

THOMAS AQUINAS

Thomas Aquinas was born c. 1224 in Rocasecca, Italy. After early instruction with the Benedictine Order he studied at the university of Naples, where he entered the Order of Dominicans, and proceeded to further Dominican studies in philosophy and theology, first at the university of Paris and later at Cologne, where his appreciation of *Aristotle was stimulated by Albertus Magnus. On completion of his doctorate in 1256 he became a member of the theology faculty in Paris, where he remained until 1259. For some years Aquinas lectured in Dominican monasteries in the neighbourhood of Rome until he returned in 1268 to a further period of teaching in Paris. Summoned back to Italy to lecture and preach in Naples, he took ill and died in 1274 when travelling to a church council in France.

During the last twenty years of his life, Aquinas wrote voluminously, always in Latin. The task of understanding and expounding the philosophical foundations of Christian *theism provided the central motivation of his life. Although all of Aquinas' writings addressed philosophical and theological concerns, some were explicitly philosophical, others were works on philosophical theology and yet others were predominantly theological. Amongst the first category are *On Being and Essence* and *The Principles of Nature*; falling into the second category are *Summa Contra Gentiles* and *Summa Theologica*; whilst commentaries on *Job* and *Psalms* are prominent examples of the third category. One of the most important – and controversial – aspects of Aquinas' work was his assimilation of the philosophy of Aristotle and his re-working of the philosophical foundations of Christianity in the light of Aristotelian categories. Although *philosophy and *theology are closely inter-related in Aquinas' work, he viewed the two disciplines as being distinct and as having different methodologies. Philosophy proceeds from universally shared foundations, building on reason and on the knowledge provided by the senses. Theology, by contrast, builds on principles of truth revealed by the Bible and these are not universally shared. Philosophy itself, of course, has very diverse concerns. At times it takes a theoretical form, having truth as its object, and at other times it takes a practical form, serving to guide our choices and actions. However, Aquinas believed that at a deeper level all philosophy has a common argumentative structure, which gives to it a certain unity, and in his understanding of this he is again indebted to Aristotle. According to this view all philosophical inquiry moves from things which are clearly known, believed to be *universals, to things which are less well known, the particulars. Aquinas called this process 'the order of determination', and we may now sketch its outworking in some aspects of his theoretical and practical philosophy.

Metaphysics

A central aspect of the study of nature is an analysis of the nature of change. Aquinas followed Aristotle in analysing change in terms of the concepts of privation, matter and form, whether in substances, surfaces or places, and whether in relation to quantity or to quality. Such change, from privation to form, necessarily involves the existence of prime matter and a substantial form which underlies the process of change. An understanding of these leads us from physics to a study of *metaphysics. When fully developed, this analysis of change leads us to recognize the existence of a prime mover and to a belief in at least one thing which exists, not contingently but necessarily, and to a belief in God in whom existence and essence are identical.

Ethics

In his treatment of the practical aspects of philosophy Aquinas also followed Aristotle, both in method and in matters of substance. *Ethics takes as its starting point the pre-theoretical moral judgments which reasonable human beings share. However, ethics must do more than merely systematize the judgments, principles and ideals of rational agents because this would be to neglect the important, if obscure, fact that human *morality derives from, and so must ultimately be explained in terms of, participation of human reason in the underlying eternal law.

According to Aquinas, humans can find fulfilment only in the ultimate good, a concept which transcends all purely human conceptions of the good. Although distinct from what all humans actually seek, this alone provides for the fulfilment of the desires of rational human nature. Morality, therefore, is grounded in *natural law, the first precepts of which is that the good should be pursued and the evil should be avoided. The good, however,

has many constituents, and so natural law precepts enjoin on us, also, the things which are constituents of our own final good.

Philosophy of religion

Perhaps Aquinas' best known contribution to philosophy of religion is his 'five ways' or proofs of the existence of God. Each of these commences with premises which, although commending themselves to common sense, do not appear to presuppose theism. Each then moves, by plausible inferences to the conclusion that God exists. The first two ways rest on an analysis of change. There are changes in the world, or a series of changes, and since change requires a cause, we must recognize the existence of a first cause, which is God. The third way argues that although many things come into existence and pass away, not everything can be of this nature, and therefore there must exist a being who, not having come into existence, must always have existed. This being is God. The fourth way argues that since things possess properties to a greater or lesser extent, and since such gradations in many properties must be caused by something which perfectly exemplifies the property in question, there must exist a divine being who possesses all of these properties to perfection. Finally, things display purpose. However, purpose presupposes a mind that directs the purpose and this purposeful mind we call 'God'.

At least since the time of *Hume these arguments have been under a considerable cloud. Contemporary philosophers, including theists, are sceptical as to whether the conclusion of each of these arguments genuinely follows from the premises without the existence of God being somehow presupposed. In other words, it is questioned whether or not the arguments provide sufficient grounds for the rationality of theism. More recently it has been argued that the success of arguments such as the five ways is also not a necessary condition for believing in the rationality of theism.

Conclusion

Aquinas has had the misfortune of being in that small class of thinkers who have been badly treated by their friends and their enemies alike. Since becoming regulative of Roman Catholic teaching (see *Christianity, Roman Catholic), due to an encyclical issued by Leo XIII in 1879, his philosophy has been accorded a reverence which he himself would have found distasteful. By way of reaction, many philosophers neglect his genius and underestimate the greatness of his intellectual achievements. Aquinas belongs, without doubt, to the very first rank of philosophers.

Bibliography

F. C. Copleston, *Aquinas* (London, 1955); E. Gilson, *History of Christian Philosophy in the Middle Ages* (London, 1955); R. McInerny, *Thomas Aquinas: Selected Writings* (London, 1998); D. J. O'Connor, *Aquinas and Natural Law* (London, 1967).

H. BUNTING

THOMAS, GOSPEL OF, see GNOSTICISM

THOMISM

The many interpretations of the philosophy and theology of *Thomas Aquinas from his death to the present are known as 'Thomism'. The movement which inspired and followed upon Leo XIII's encyclical *Aeterni Patris* (1879) is often known as 'neo-scholasticism' or 'neo-Thomism'.

Thomas's thought originated in the context of thirteenth-century Augustinianism and Latin Averroism. Unlike the Augustinians of his time, who opposed using *Aristotle, Aquinas adapted and shaped fundamental concepts from Aristotle's philosophy for service in his theology. To do so, he had also to free these ideas from the additions deriving from *Averroes and others. Using the tools of philosophy, Aquinas gave an account of God's nature – the divine attributes and the *Trinity – that is still discussed today. His account of the human person as being a single substance composed of a body whose form is the rational soul was a significant advance over the Augustinian conception that had dominated Christian thought until his time. The moderate *realism of his account of human knowledge, rooted in a detailed *psychology, avoids the varieties of *rationalism, *empiricism and *idealism that have dominated modern thought. Thus, although seen as radical in his time, Aquinas has become for many in later centuries the most reliable teacher of Christian truth.

When Aquinas died, he had no disciples worthy of the name. Moreover, his innovations in theology were strongly opposed by the Franciscans and other Augustinians. In the context of the Averroist controversy, opposition to some of Thomas's views increased. Of the 219 propositions listed in the Condemnation of 1377, sixteen were from Thomas, mostly relating to his denial of universal hylomorphism, that every being is composed of both form and matter. Albert the Great and other Dominicans came to Thomas's defence, and by 1286 it was ordered that every friar should study and defend the teaching of Brother Thomas. By 1223 Thomas was canonized, and his followers turned to spreading his teaching in opposition to Scotism and nominalism. Aquinas' view of the harmonious relationship of nature and grace was only one theology among others in the late medieval world, and not the dominant one. It became known as 'the old way' as opposed to the 'modern way' of Ockham. In the fourteenth and fifteenth centuries, copies of Aquinas' writings multiplied, and Dominicans made his writings an essential part of the curriculum in their schools. Thomistic treatises on selected topics and compendia were written, but Thomists failed to meet the challenge of the new.

In the sixteenth century there was a new flowering of Thomism. Thomas de Vio, also known as Cardinal Cajetan, the opponent of Martin Luther at Augsburg, wrote an outstanding commentary on the *Summa Theologiae* (1507–20). In Spain professors began lecturing on the *Summa* and a major Thomist tradition developed. Francisco de Sylvestris (d. 1546), Domingo de Soto (d. 1560), and Domingo Bañez (d. 1604) are some of the outstanding commentators from Salamanca. More interest in Aquinas' writings was generated when the Jesuits (founded 1540) chose Aquinas as their primary source of scholastic doctrine. The Jesuits, however, were not so interested in recovering an authentic Thomas as in using his theology to address the issues of the day.

During the seventeenth century, Thomism shared in the decline of *scholasticism in general. The greatest Thomist of this time is John of St Thomas (d. 1644), who follows the order of the *Summa Theologiae* and uses material from Aquinas' works to discuss issues raised by Jansenism and spiritual writers of the time. Over all, Thomists of this period were either preoccupied with opposing nominalism or working out the details of particular doctrines.

During the *Enlightenment, Roman Catholicism (see *Christianity, Roman Catholic) was much weakened, and Thomism was almost unknown except in some seminaries. Apologetics, rather than theology, dominated the scene, and books were written against the new science, philosophy, politics and Protestantism. The suppression of the Jesuits and other religious institutions during the French Revolution added to the decline.

A rediscovery of the value of Thomas's writings began in the 1840s. Dissatisfaction with idealism and ontologism led in various centres across Europe to efforts to recover Aquinas' thought. After 1880, a neo-scholasticism, which was primarily Thomist, dominated Catholic theology and philosophy until Vatican II. This movement had a number of stages.

Leo III was convinced that returning to the philosophy and theology of Thomas Aquinas would revitalize Catholic teaching. Thomas's philosophy shows that natural reason can prove the existence of God and defends an understanding of the divine attributes that affirms the possibility of divine *revelation. This philosophy also provides apologetic arguments supporting the *church's claim to divine origin. It provides the organizational structure of a dogmatic theology and provides arguments to use against opponents of Christian teaching.

For Leo III, the scholastic doctors of the Middle Ages had gathered the wisdom of the fathers and put it in a form useful for future generations. Thomas is the greatest of these doctors, for in him human reason 'soared to the loftiest heights ... and can scarcely rise any higher, while faith can expect no further or more reliable assistance than it has already received from Thomas' (quoted by G. A. McCool, p. 8). The encyclical encouraged Catholic philosophers and theologians to study the old in order to meet the charges of modern philosophies and theologies.

Incorporated in the encyclical was a conception of *theology modelled on the Aristotelian understanding of *science, whose method consists in moving from *first principles to conclusions. This view has no place for history in theology, an awareness of which was growing in the German theology of the time. Also, Thomas's own work was not understood in its historical context, for developments in scholasticism and the differences between Thomas and his contemporaries were ignored. Even commentators such as Cajetan and Suarez were assumed to be completely faithful to Thomas in their writings.

With the publication of *Aeterni Patris*, scholars began to study the Middle Ages in depth. The result was not just a better understanding of Thomas and his world, but also a rejection of the ideal that had fostered the revival of Thomism. By 1900 a new generation of Thomists, building on the findings of their predecessors, distinguished the teachings of commentators like Suarez from those of Thomas, and in penetrating more deeply into the thought of Thomas found resources for dialoguing with contemporaries. Among others, Pierre Rousselot (1878–1915) and Joseph Marechal (1878–1944) focused on the dynamism of the intellect and dialogued with modern philosophers – *Kant and others – arguing that a truly critical philosophy can overcome scepticism and be the basis for a realist *metaphysics. So originated the movement known as transcendental Thomism. Bernard Lonergan and Karl *Rahner are the best-known exponents of this position in the last half of the twentieth century.

Equally influential, and especially effective in dialoguing with contemporaries, was Jacques Maritain (1882–1973) in his writings on knowledge, *ethics, politics and art. His philosophy of the human person and the common good remains a powerful statement against both individualism and collectivism. Maritain's Thomism was influenced by John of St Thomas and Cajetan, and, as the history of Thomism became better understood, it was recognized that some of the key positions that Maritain employed were not actually positions held by Thomas, but rather were developed by his commentators.

Another strand of Thomism that developed in the twentieth century was historical research into Thomas's thought and times. This development, too, led to surprising results. While many able historians participated in this research, the most influential of them was Etienne *Gilson (1884–1978). While studying the origins of *Descartes's thought, he discovered that the seventeenth-century philosophers owed their fundamental philosophical ideas to the theologians of the Middle Ages. Greek metaphysics had been reworked in the context of Christian theology, and Descartes and his followers had separated this philosophy from the context of Christian faith which had inspired it. Gilson's understanding of Thomas opposed the Aristotelico-Thomism of the seventeenth-century commentators. He also documented the variety of views in medieval scholasticism, thus destroying the illusion of a common scholastic doctrine. Studies on grace by Henry Bouillard and Henri de Lubac extended this historical depth into areas such as the understanding of nature and grace. They showed that Thomas's formulations of issues such as grace were intimately rooted in the problematic and language of his time, and not expressed in terms of a timeless philosophy.

Greater knowledge of the past led to the awareness that the genuine way to follow Thomas is to meet today's challenges in creative dialogue as Thomas did in relation to the Augustinians and Averroists in his own day. Thus, the third flowering of Thomism had a very different outcome from that envisioned by its founders. Nevertheless, the spirit and ideas of Thomas Aquinas continue to inspire philosophers and theologians today, not only among Catholics but among Protestants and others as well.

Bibliography

G. A. McCool, SJ, *From Unity to Pluralism* (New York, 1989); T. F. O'Meara, OP, 'Traditions, Schools, and Students', in *Thomas Aquinas: Theologian* (Notre Dame, 1997), pp. 152–200.

A. G. VOS

TIBETAN BUDDHISM, see BUDDHISM

TILLICH, PAUL

In America Paul Tillich's sparring partners were psychologists, and he saw himself in the succession of religious philosophers like Scheler. To overcome the gap between the spheres of *culture and church, he argues that life should be lived according to neither autonomy nor heteronomy ('rules coming from beyond ourselves') but 'theonomy' – a realm in which the structure and dynamics of our culture are transformed in the divine life. We are working towards a situation in which there is no sacred (cut off from life) nor secular (cut off from the source of life) but 'religious', understood as the foundation of ultimate concern.

'Correlation' was his term for the re-interpretation of Christian theological categories as religious symbols which latch on to ontological concepts; for instance, the Protestant principle of justification correlates to the full acceptance of self-criticism. For faith is no longer about finding a gracious, forgiving God (Luther) but is the quest for sense. Sin is not primarily about an immoral act but rather a state of alienation from self, an incurable existential anxiety. Our being in question demands a quest for being. This means a taking hold of oneself to find the ultimate meaning which gives meaning to all meanings, for without this we find that the present meaningful thing will quickly lose its meaningfulness. Rather than being a neurotic who avoids non-being by avoiding being, the alternative is to know oneself as accepted and to go out into the world ready to take existential anxiety upon oneself: this would be the dying which is followed by the rising in the Christian life.

Yet to see our limitedness as the cause of our guilt and hence anxiety is a partial view. Unfortunately, humans seem less bothered by perfectionism. Faith may well be about being grasped by the power of being, although in orthodox parlance that is better understood as 'grace'. Any anxiety about guilt, for Christians, may arise not simply from Puritanism but from the fact that we are indeed guilty.

Mysticism meant 'going down and within' rather than transcending this world and encountering an Other 'God'. Theology comes from religion as experienced, not from some allegedly other sphere by revelation. The revealed law is only a restatement of *natural law: being, *truth and goodness are the ways in which God as loving power (*erōs*) appears to the soul.

Tillich, in his desire to make sure that God is not understood as a being among others, tends to remove God from being a dialogue partner with human beings. As for Christology, occasional remarks such as 'The Christ is Jesus and the negation of Jesus' or 'The concrete Logos ... became flesh in Jesus' are elliptical.

Bibliography

D. Kelsey, 'Paul Tillich', in D. Ford (ed.), *The Modern Theologians* (Oxford, 1997); A. M. McLeod, *Paul Tillich: An Essay on the Role of Ontology in His Philosophical Theology* (London, 1973); A. Thatcher, *The Ontology of Paul Tillich* (Oxford, 1978).

M. W. ELLIOTT

TINDAL, MATTHEW

Matthew Tindal (1656/7–1733) was an English jurist, political writer and deist, who earned a reputation as a freethinker early in his life. His greatest influence, however, came in his latter years as author of *Christianity as Old as the Creation; or the Gospel, a Republication of the Religion of Nature* (1730), commonly referred to as the 'Deist's Bible'. Referring to himself as a 'Christian Deist', Tindal presented what was ostensibly a defence of the Christian faith in an argument that attacked the particularity of the Christian *revelation, and in so doing he drew more than 150 responses, the most notable of which were William Law's *The Case of Religion and Reason, or Natural Religion, Fairly and Fully Stated* (1731) and Bishop Joseph *Butler's *The Analogy of Religion* (1736).

Natural religion and revealed religion are the two sides of one true religion, Tindal maintained, the former an internal revelation of God to our reason, the latter an external revelation to us, a 'transcript of the religion of Nature'. As such, there is nothing new in the Christian revelation; rather Christianity is as old as God's original revelation, the creation.

The existence of 'a being of infinite wisdom and perfection' is self-evident, Tindal maintained. If God is absolutely perfect, then any revelation of God is perfect and intended entirely for human benefit, since nothing can be added to the happiness of a perfect being. God must, then, have revealed true religion in his original creation, and that solely for the sake of human happiness. Since that true religion, like God its author, is perfect, Christian revelation can only duplicate, but add nothing new, to natural religion.

Tindal's confidence in the power and reliability of human reason is enormous. Reason discovers the indubitable existence of a perfect being, accurately reads the revelation of that perfect being in nature, and may confidently and unerringly judge the pretensions of any 'instituted Religion' as it varies from the original 'Religion of Nature and Reason'.

Despite its popularity on the Continent, by and large both atheists and orthodox Christians find Tindal's arguments unpersuasive. Nature is hardly as perfect, or natural religion as transparent, as Tindal assumes, nor the existence of God so certainly delivered by reason alone. The perfection of human beings,

a doctrine entailed by his assumption that all that issues forth from a perfect being is originally and immutably perfect, is self-evidently false.

Bibliography

J. Herrick, *The Making of a New Spirituality: The Eclipse of the Western Religious Tradition* (Downers Grove, 2003); M. Tindal, *Christianity as Old as the Creation; or the Gospel, a Republication of the Religion of Nature* (London, 1730).

T. D. KENNEDY

TOLAND, JOHN

John Toland (1670–1722) was born in County Donegal, Ireland, and was educated at Glasgow and then Edinburgh University before he moved to England. Toland was one of the most influential deists of the early eighteenth century. His mark was made with the publication of *Christianity Not Mysterious* (1696), a work denounced as containing 'several Heretical Doctrines contrary to the Christian Religion and the establish'd Church of Ireland' and ordered burned by the Irish Parliament in 1697.

Reason, alone, must guide belief, according to Toland, and reason is satisfied only when we believe propositions that can be demonstrated. When a belief is proposed to us, we examine the arguments for that belief, and if we are unable to infer the belief from indubitable propositions, we must suspend belief. High probability is not good enough; we must be able to demonstrate the truth of our beliefs.

Reason's reign extends to religious belief and practice and enables us to pare superstition and the unnecessary accretions to true faith introduced by religious hierarchies from the core of religious truth. Thus, Christianity is not 'mysterious', that is to say, contrary to reason. 'Mystery' refers to that which is presented to us by *revelation alone, but the propositions of Christianity are neither incomprehensible nor unknowable, although for the moment they may not be known by reason. Hence the subtitle of *Christianity Not Mysterious*, 'That there is nothing in the Gospel contrary to Reason, nor above it: and that no Christian Doctrine can be properly call'd a Mystery'.

What is left of Christian belief after reason has stripped away all that is 'above or contrary to reason'? Toland is not expansive in answering this question. We do know, Toland argued in *Amyntor* (1699), that the earliest Christians accepted as canonical many writings of dubious authenticity. And, not unlike the Jesus Seminar of the late twentieth and early twenty-first centuries, Toland believed that a careful historical examination might lead us to 'the original plan of Christianity' in the NT. True Christianity is simple and rational, affirming the existence of a perfect Creator, who desires the happiness of his creation and directs creation towards happiness through the laws of nature and the rational moral teachings of the NT.

Toland is naïve in his confidence that we can and ought to believe only that which can be demonstrated. Clearer thinkers recognized that this assumption must end in scepticism. And these sceptics realized, as well, that a God who is every bit as mysterious as the leaf of a tree, but no more, can command little rational or emotional assent.

Bibliography

J. Champion, *Republican Learning: John Toland and the Crisis of Christian Culture, 1696–1722* (Manchester, 2003); J. Herrick, *The Making of a New Spirituality: The Eclipse of the Western Religious Tradition* (Downers Grove, 2003); J. Toland, *Amyntor: or, A Defence of Milton's Life* (London, 1699); *Christianity Not Mysterious* (London, 1696).

T. D. KENNEDY

TOLKIEN, JOHN RONALD REUEL

J. R. R. Tolkien (1892–1973), a close friend of C. S. *Lewis for nearly forty years, spent his early life in rural Warwickshire – the inspiration for his 'Shire' – just outside Birmingham. His father died while Tolkien was an infant. The family later moved into the city to be nearer to the Birmingham Oratory, founded by John Henry Newman. At twelve the boy lost his greatly talented mother. In the First World War Tolkien served in the trenches of the Somme until hospitalized to England.

While Tolkien was convalescing, his first work, *The Silmarillion*, developed rapidly. He sketched the early ages of his unfolding invented world of Middle-earth, populating it with people, languages, history and mythology. He was still writing his great opus when he died in 1973, but his son Christopher constructed an abridged and coherent version, *The Silmarillion* (1977) from the wealth of manuscripts (later published in *Unfinished Tales* and the twelve-volume *The History of Middle-earth*).

Tolkien's professional life followed the same course as his fiction, both inspired by a love of *language. He invented elven languages which in structure are proper human languages. After a spell working on the 'W' section of *The Oxford English Dictionary*, he began teaching philology. Initially he was reader then Professor of English Language at Leeds University. In 1925 he moved back to Oxford to take up the chair of Anglo-Saxon, meeting C. S. Lewis the following year. In 1945 Tolkien became Merton Professor of English Language and Literature, a post he retained until he retired in 1959.

Sometime around 1930 Tolkien began writing *The Hobbit* (published 1937), which was soon drawn into his history of Middle-earth. In turn, this demanded a sequel, and for over ten years he constructed *The Lord of the Rings*. Unlike *The Hobbit*, it was a book for an adult readership, a readership he almost single-handedly created (but with help from C. S. Lewis), as *fantasy had been relegated to children's reading. Tolkien played a large part in Lewis's move from atheism to Christian faith, and both men saw the rehabilitation of symbolic stories as a central apologetic strategy.

Tolkien conscientiously and meticulously crafted *The Lord of the Rings*, and its background *mythology and history of Middle-earth, to be consonant with Christian theology. Artfully, with a brilliant use of anachronism, he set forward his tales as taking place in the remote, pre-Christian northern Europe, full of prefigurings of the gospel, alive with Christian themes such as sacrifice, the ultimate defeat of *evil, providence, the renunciation of *power and prophecy. In the process he, like C. S. Lewis, became one of the most successful Christian communicators in the history of the church, remarkable in an age that had abandoned the Christian and Classical presuppositions of what he saw as the Old West.

Bibliography

H. Carpenter, *J. R. R. Tolkien: A Biography* (London, 1977); C. Duriez, *Tolkien and C. S. Lewis* (New York, 2003); T. A. Shippey,

J. R. R. Tolkien: Author of the Century (London, 2000).

C. DURIEZ

TRADITIONAL RELIGION, see PAGAN AND INDIGENOUS RELIGION

TRANSCENDENCE

The word 'transcend' comes from the Latin and means literally to 'climb across' or 'go beyond'. To transcend is thus to surpass or excel or move beyond the reach or grasp of something. Sometimes the term is 'transcendence' used epistemologically, as when something is beyond the reach of human knowledge, but in reference to the Christian doctrine of God, divine transcendence is used ontologically, and refers to God being beyond anything that is other than God. In Christian theology, what is other than God is, by definition, the creation.

It follows that divine transcendence needs to be understood in light of the Christian doctrine of creation. Historically, this has been a doctrine of *creatio ex nihilo*. *Creatio ex nihilo* means that in the primal act of creation (i.e. in God bringing contingent being to existence, and therefore in contradistinction to God subsequently ordering or designing the creation), God did not depend on any pre-existing entity separate from God – no pre-existing stuff, no autonomous principles, no other gods. Indeed, for God to have employed such an entity in the primal act of creation would have meant that something outside of God had a separate existence from God. Orthodox Christian theology, by contrast, affirms that there is but one God, that this God is the source of all being, and that nothing exists self-sufficiently apart from this God.

Creatio ex nihilo presupposes two things. First, that God is a personal being and not a principle, and secondly, that the world exists by a personal act, namely, an effected word spoken by God. The early theologians of the Christian church (like *Athanasius and the *Cappadocian Fathers) were all too aware of *Plato's *cosmology. The problem, in their view, with Plato's cosmology was just that, namely, Plato's world was a 'cosmos'. The cosmos of Plato, and of the ancient Greek philosophers more generally, was an ordered arrangement governed by principles that even the gods had to obey. The Christian God, by contrast, is absolutely free, and the world, as an absolutely free act by this absolutely free God, is not, at least in the first instance, a cosmos. Rather, it is a creation.

The logic here is inescapable and leads in either of two completely opposite directions. Either God is free, or God is bound. Unless God is absolutely free and the world is an absolutely free act of creation, there are principles that constrain God in creation. (The issue of God being bound by his nature is not a problem here so long as God's nature is not set over and against God – *Thomas Aquinas, for instance, identified God's essence or nature with God's existence.) Any such principles of cosmic constraint, however, are logically prior to God. But in that case the ultimate *reality is not God but those principles. One is, therefore, left with two mutually exclusive possibilities: either the ultimate reality is the one personal God or something else is the ultimate reality, like Plato's Forms or *Spinoza's Nature (writ large) or Alfred North *Whitehead's process (cf. process theology). Only the first possibility is consistent with orthodox Christian *theism. Transcendence provides the theological underpinnings for this first possibility. It is how Christian theology justifies the first of the Ten Commandments: 'You shall have no other gods before me' (Exod. 20:3).

Although transcendence is as important a Christian doctrine as one will find, there are two pitfalls connected with it that need to be avoided. The first is to forget that in the Christian doctrine of God, divine transcendence must always be balanced with divine *immanence. Immanence denotes the ongoing presence and activity of God in creation. God both transcends creation and is immanent in it. As immanent in creation, God sustains and preserves the creation, providentially guiding it not only in broad strokes but also down to the smallest details (e.g. God the Father cares even for the sparrow that falls to the ground, Matt. 10:29). Without immanence, transcendence leads to deism. Deism views God's relation to the world, after some initial act of creation, as that of an absentee landlord. Christian theism, by contrast, regards God as actively present and involved, moment by moment and from start to finish, in every aspect of creation.

The other pitfall connected with transcendence is to emphasize too much either God's control of the world or the world's autonomy from God. Because transcendence stresses the otherness of God from creation, the challenge facing a theology of transcendence is to understand the God–world relation in a way that gives proper due both to God and to the world. One faulty tendency is to exaggerate God's control of the world, making God directly responsible as causative agent for everything that happens in it (cf. the theological *determinism of hyper-Reformed theology, as in Huldreich Zwingli's *On Providence*). On this view, the creation is a prosthesis or puppet theatre of God. The other faulty tendency is to exaggerate the world's autonomy from God. On this view, the creation can thwart God's purposes, overrule God's commands and do things that God did not foresee (cf. open theism).

A proper understanding of transcendence therefore entails that God is one whose purposes cannot be frustrated, to whom the creation is subject in every detail, and for whom there are no surprises. At the same time, creation is free to explore new possibilities, even to the point of rebellion against its Creator. This combination of divine sovereignty and created freedom is a great *mystery. Unwillingness to live with this mystery leads to easy solutions that are no solution at all. In the worst case, God becomes either a tyrant or a milquetoast. The challenge for the Christian apologist is to show how divine transcendence is consonant with an all-powerful, loving Creator God, whose power is not arbitrary and whose love is not sentimental.

W. A. DEMBSKI

TRANSCENDENCE, SIGNS OF

By 'transcendence' we mean that which is beyond our *reality and which surpasses the *immanence of the here and now. *Transcendence and immanence belong together in a mutually reciprocal relationship. Our experience of the immanent is always in connection with our *imagination, our understanding and the conviction that there is something which transcends the present.

The boundary between immanence and transcendence is a dynamic one. Immanence, the accessible and attainable reality we experience, is on this side of the boundary. Transcendence is the reality that is inaccessible and unattainable. However, it is at the same time a reality that determines our existence and our whole world, beyond this boundary. Transcendence is 'beyond' this boundary, not merely as that which surpasses our immanence, but in the sense of an all-encompassing, 'above-all' dimension. Over this dimension is the only, paramount Personal Being, according to his own self-revelation.

Ultimately, because the immanent is not self-referential, that which is immanent always refers to that which is transcendent. It is the transcendent that reveals itself, and these self-revelations are the real, authentic signs (or signals) of transcendence. These signs of transcendence, which are references of the immanent pointing beyond itself, appear in a creation that has a cosmic perspective and in a *history that has a human perspective. Initially they appear in the human subject, who lives on the boundary of the immanent and transcendent.

Signs of transcendence as references of the immanent beyond itself

First, we may perceive signs of transcendence from *creation* with a cosmic perspective. Humans encounter the problem of the ultimate cause of being: why is there anything at all, and why is there not 'nothing at all'? Then there is the problem of the ultimate origin of the laws of the cosmos: on the one hand, the cosmos is founded in contingency; on the other hand, it is functioning in constancy. The reasonable order of the world refers beyond itself to a first and last Intelligence. There is also the problem of the teleological progress of the creation, which refers to an aim-giving will.

Secondly, we may see signs of transcendence in history. In humanity, that which is objectively spiritual became subjectively spiritual. In the creative audacity of humanity's risky freedom and the possibility of self-sacrifice (even unto death) of love, we discover the sole instance of genuine autonomy. History, in the midst of so many uncertainties and even regressions, demonstrates a clear progress throughout the existence of humanity.

Thirdly, we may deduce signs of transcendence from humanity and God. On an individual level we may point to finite humanity being in contact with infinity; the individual's search for an ultimate meaning; the will to surpass oneself constantly, in one's own life; arriving at the endless mystery of questioning oneself; and the readiness of self-sacrificing love.

On a collective level, we may note the demand for order – bringing forth a cosmos from the chaos; playing as a demonstratively ontological value (the birds sing much more, and the flowers are much more beautiful, than can be expected from the struggle for life); humour (in the sense of *Dostoevsky's 'to understand men, and to forgive fate'); the greatest gifts of grace: faith, hope and love in the Christian life; to be in partnership with God now, in the future and in eternity.

Signs of transcendence as the self-revelation of God

The main characteristic of twentieth- and twenty-first-century humanity's spiritual situation is the loss of transcendence. This confronts us with the boundary of existence. If we are perplexed, at this point of bewilderment we seek the 'beyond' of this situation, and the means of mastering it, or rather the Master himself, who overwhelms this jeopardy. This experience of the absence of the indispensable God is itself a major signal of transcendence. There is an infinite qualitative difference between non-experiencing the existence of God, and experiencing the non-existence of God (cf. Matt. 27:46; and see Job 16:9, where we find Job seeming to suggest that if God exists, he is Satan himself). Experiencing the non-existence of God means the unreality of transcendence for us in the bare, ultimate situation of our life, when 'only a God can save us' (Heidegger).

God's transcendence does not mean that he is beyond our existential possibilities or our cognitive faculties. According to his ultimate *revelation in *Jesus Christ, God is the centre of life. 'The church stands not at the boundaries, where human powers give out, but in the middle of the village' (Bonhoeffer). In Christ, we can see the main sign of transcendence at the centre: the real boundary between God and humanity is identical with the Christ, that point where God and humanity encounter one another. Christ is the divinely concentrated centre of transcendence (see Col. 2:9 and John 12:32). This is the universal signal of transcendence of the 'middle' for us.

The importance of Christ in the centre cannot be overemphasized. This is no self-isolated middle point, but a real, universal, eternal centre in immanent space and time. God meets us in Christ, as the transcendent personal reality.

Until the Enlightenment, *theology attempted to understand the transcendence of God as metaphysical. Since then, theology has posited the God of moral-ethical transcendence (*Kant), the God of absolute spiritual transcendence (*Hegel), the God of Christological, contemporary transcendence (*Kierkegaard), the God of inclusive transcendence (*Barth), the God of existential transcendence (*Bultmann), the God of universal, historical transcendence (*Pannenberg) and the God of eschatological future-transcendence (Moltmann). The transcendence of God is no longer an ideological upper storey high above, but is rather over-worldliness, world-penetration and world power once and for all. Without this transcendence, not only the divinity but also the reality of God is unreal. We must and can discover the real transcendence of God in every direction from the Christ-centre. We have seen that God is evident only in Christ, so the transcendence of God is first of all the *transcendence at the middle*, in the Christ-centre.

From Scripture, we know Jesus Christ as the immanent, incarnate transcendence of God. Divine justification, through which we become a new creation, is received by faith in the revealed Word of God. The history of revelation is found in the books of the OT and NT. We can then attain the transcendence of the Christ-centre by means of the *transcendence backward*, to be found in Scripture, in the biblical-theological sense of the two covenants.

The OT and NT affirm that it is the sole God above all who finally reveals himself in the Messiah. God, as the unconditional subject, comprises his omnipotence, omniscience, omnipresence, simplicity and eternity. Each divine attribute is freely and paradoxically concentrated in the incarnate, eternal love of God in Christ, therefore the transcendence at the centre refers to *transcendence upward*, in accordance with transcendence backward found in the Bible. The transcendence upward of the God of the biblical Christ-revelation transcends, and also penetrates, the whole visible and invisible world, as his sovereign will, Word and Spirit.

The wholly different essence and character of the divine presence in the world – over against the world – is guaranteed by the Creator's revelation. Creation by itself cannot reveal God, but God reveals himself in the depth of creation, if we have found him in Christ. Nevertheless, God's revelation in creation is echoed by creation itself, in an 'echo-revelation' (cf. Ps. 19). This means that there is a *transcendence downward*, concentrated in the transcendence in the centre of the Christ-revelation. We find it in the depth where only the Word can testify to the contingency of creation's being, the wonderful laws of its activity, the dangers that threaten its existence, and the necessities that cry out for redemption.

The testimony of the indispensable redemption – in the depth of the world – encounters the promise of the future eschatological new creation of the biblical revelation. This will be clear only from the *transcendence forward*, where the apocalyptic-eschatological dialectic of total redemption appears from the hiddenness of the Christ-centre (2 Pet. 3:13).

Bibliography:

L. Hegedűs, *A Study in the Concept of Transcendence* (Edinburgh, 1991); J.-P. Sartre, *Transcendence of the Ego* (ET, New York, 1962).

L. HEGEDŰS

TRANSCENDENTAL ARGUMENTS

Immanuel *Kant (1724–1804) is responsible for introducing the term 'transcendental' to philosophical discussion. Seeking to counter the scepticism of David *Hume, but unable to accept the methods of his rationalist teacher Christian Wolff, Kant came to advocate transcendental argument as a new means of grounding the *certainty of mathematics, *science and philosophy.

All of us, he argued, must concede that knowledge is possible. If not, there is no point to any discussion or inquiry. Now, given that knowledge is possible, said Kant, we should ask what the conditions are that make knowledge possible. What must the world be like, and what must the workings of our minds be like, if human knowledge is to be possible?

Kant argued that among the conditions of knowledge are the transcendental aesthetic, in which the mind orders sense experience into a spatio-temporal sequence, and the transcendental analytic, in which the mind imposes categories such as substance and cause upon experience. So we know by transcendental argument that the world (more precisely, the world of appearances, the phenomena, not the world 'in itself') is a collection of substances located in space and time, with causal relationships to one another. We do not get this knowledge from sense experience alone (Hume) or from rational deduction alone (*Leibniz, Wolff), but from an argument assuming the reality of knowledge and showing the necessary presuppositions of that assumption.

Transcendental argument became a staple of the writings of the idealist school that followed Kant, and from there it made its way into Christian apologetics. James *Orr (1844–1913) employed it. But the twentieth-century apologist who placed the most weight on the transcendental argument (which he sometimes called 'reasoning by presupposition') was Cornelius *Van Til (1895–1987).

Like Kant, Van Til was unhappy with *empiricism and *rationalism and with traditional ways of combining reason and sense experience such as that of *Thomas Aquinas. Kant found these approaches to knowledge logically invalid. But for Van Til they were also wrong in a distinctively theological way. Traditional methodologies applied to apologetics, said Van Til, assume that human sense experience and/or human reason can function adequately without God, that is, 'autonomously' or 'neutrally'. So, at the very outset of an apologetic argument, they concede the whole game. They adopt a presupposition contrary to the conclusion they wish to argue. They seek to gain knowledge of God by adopting a non-theistic *epistemology. The only alternative, Van Til argued, is to adopt a theistic epistemology when arguing for the existence of God. But that approach seems to be viciously circular: presupposing God in our epistemology and then using that epistemology to prove his existence.

Van Til answered the charge of circularity by claiming that every system of thought is circular when arguing its most fundamental presuppositions (e.g. a rationalist can defend the authority of reason only by using reason), and the Christian circle is the only one that renders *reality intelligible on its own terms.

From the second of these propositions, Van Til developed his own transcendental argument. He maintained that Christian *theism is the presupposition of all meaning, all rational significance, all intelligible discourse. Even when someone argues against Christian theism, Van Til said, he presupposes it, for he presupposes that rational argument is possible and that *truth can be conveyed through *language. The non-Christian, then, in Van Til's famous illustration, is like a child sitting on her father's lap, slapping his face. She could not slap him unless he supported her. Similarly, the non-Christian cannot carry out his rebellion against God unless God makes that rebellion possible. Contradicting God assumes an intelligible universe and therefore a theistic one.

How can we, then, defend the logical move from 'intelligible universe' to 'theistic universe'? Van Til rarely articulated his reason for that move; he seemed to think it was self-evident. In effect, however, he reverted at this point to apologetics of a more traditional type. Apologists have often noted that we could not know the world at all unless it had been designed for knowledge. If the world were nothing but matter, motion, time and chance, we would have no reason to think that the ideas in our heads told us anything about the real world. Only if a person had designed the world to be known, and the human mind to know it, could knowledge be possible. So Van Til at this point reverted to a traditional *teleological argument. He never admitted doing this, and he could not have admitted it, because he thought the traditional teleological (like the other traditional arguments) were autonomous and neutral.

If Van Til's transcendental approach is to succeed, however, it must abandon the assumption that traditional arguments are necessarily autonomous and welcome the assistance of such arguments to complete the transcendental argument. The traditional arguments are in fact necessary to establish the existence of God as a transcendental conclusion. And there is no reason to assume, as Van Til does, that anyone who uses an argument from design or *causality is presupposing a nontheistic epistemology. On the contrary, people who use these traditional arguments show precisely that without God the data of our experience suggesting order and causality are unintelligible.

What, then, does transcendental argument add to the apologist's arsenal, beyond the traditional arguments? First, it presents a goal for apologetics. The goal of the apologist is not only to show that God exists, but also who he is: that he is the source of all meaning and intelligibility in the universe. Further, it suggests apologetic strategies somewhat neglected in the tradition. Traditional apologists have often argued that causality, for example, *implies* God. A transcendental argument makes a stronger claim: that causality *presupposes* God. The difference between 'implies' and 'presupposes', according to Peter Strawson and Bas Van Fraasen, is that in the latter case God's existence is implied by either the assertion *or the denial* of causality. That is, not only does the existence of causality imply the existence of God, but even to deny (intelligibly, if it were possible) the existence of causality would be to invoke a framework of meaning that presupposes God's existence. Don Collett argues that the Strawson-Van Fraasen kind of presupposition is identical with Van Til's. So if creation presupposes God, even the denial of creation presupposes him, and the atheist is like the little girl slapping her father while sitting on his lap.

The Bible does make this kind of radical claim, that creation not only implies but presupposes God. For God is the Creator of all, and therefore the source of all meaning, order and intelligibility. It is in Christ that all things hold together (Col. 1:17). So without him everything falls apart; nothing makes sense. Thus, Scripture teaches that unbelief is foolish (Ps. 14:1; 1 Cor. 1:20). There are many arguments to be made on the way to that conclusion. Not every individual apologetic argument needs to go that far, but the apologist's work is not done until he reaches that conclusion, until he persuades the objector that God is everything the Bible says he is. That is to say that a complete argument for Christian theism, however many sub-arguments it contains, will be transcendental in character.

Bibliography

D. Collett, 'Van Til and Transcendental Argument', *Westminster Theological Journal*; J. M. Frame, *Cornelius Van Til* (Phillipsburg, 1995); I. Kant, *Critique of Pure Reason* (New York, 1958); P. Strawson, *An Introduction to Logical Theory* (London, 1952), pp. 174–179; B. C. Van Fraassen, 'Presupposition, Implication, and Self-Reference', *Journal of Philosophy* (1968), pp. 136–152; C. Van Til, *The Defense of the Faith* (Philadelphia, 1963).

J. M. FRAME

TRINITY

Though a foundational tenet of Christian belief, the doctrine of the Trinity has been historically a difficult and perplexing doctrine and one often considered unpractical. In more recent theological appraisal, however, it has become something of a treasure trove of Christian apologetic.

As a specific qualification of divine existence, the unique Christian understanding of God as the Trinity of Father, Son and *Holy Spirit has been accepted as a confession dependent upon *revelation. Here *Thomas Aquinas is classic, who, while conceding that human reason may establish something like a prime mover or first cause, regarded the more complex notion of the triune God to be a truth that transcended natural human discovery. A possible exception to this rule is Richard of St Victor's argument that God, as supreme charity, requires a plurality of divine persons, since love in its noblest expression is a predicate of persons in right relation. Indeed, Richard argued that God as love actually required *three* divine persons, since true charity entails a 'shared love' of two for a third. Richard's 'necessary reasons' for a trinity of persons, however, is best taken in the Anselmian sense of 'faith seeking understanding', similar to *Anselm's own ontological argument, presupposing and bolstering the truth of the Trinity, not a strict rational demonstration of it. Others have more modestly noted that 'God is love' (1 John 4:8) does seem to require a plurality of persons in God's eternal being (immanent Trinity), otherwise creation would be necessitated in order for God, as love, to fully actualize the divine life. That was the heresy of *Hegel. As a datum of special revelation, therefore, most challenges to the trinitarian confession have come largely from within the Christian community, broadly defined, or among near theistic neighbours.

A first and lingering challenge relates to the biblical basis of the doctrine. While the NT itself admits of no formal doctrine of the Trinity, the early church steadily discerned in Scripture the trinitarian conception. The key issue was the status of the person of Christ. By acknowledging his coequal deity with God the Father, the Council of Nicaea (325) ruled out the Arian position that the Son was a creature and thereby ecumenically endorsed a plurality of persons within the Godhead. The Holy Spirit was subsequently acknowledged as a third divine person by the second ecumenical Council of Constantinople (381), largely due to the efforts of the *Cappadocian Fathers (Gregory of Nyssa, Gregory Nazianzus and Basil of Caesarea). What has been known as the 'Cappadocian settlement' established

the trinitarian confession as three persons (or *hypostaseis*) in one divine essence (or substance, nature, deity, divinity, Godhead, God), though the precise connotation of 'person' and 'divine essence', as well as how three of the former constitute one of the latter, has long been debated in doctrinal history. The biblical basis of trinitarian doctrine was especially challenged in modern times by the rise of historical and *biblical criticism. The classical liberal *Harnack, for example, considered dogmas like the Trinity to be a weedy intrusion of Greek philosophy on the pure soil of the gospel. Though modern biblical scholarship is not always friendly to credal formulae, most scholars of confessional or evangelical persuasion are convinced that the trinitarian confession is a true reading of the biblical narrative, the necessary grammar of salvation, even if the distinct personhood and deity of the Son is much more explicit in Scripture than that of the Spirit, the so-called Cinderella of the Trinity. In fact, one of the challenges to trinity doctrine has been elaborating a robust trinitarianism that takes full account of the personhood and activity of the Spirit so as not to reduce it to a mere binitarianism of the Father and Son.

The Cappadocian settlement immediately ruled out the strict *monotheisms of both Arianism and Sabellianism, which finally only allow for one fully divine person in God. Arianism, in acknowledging the Father alone as fully divine, could worship Christ only as a lesser, creaturely grade of divinity; Sabellian modalism construed Father, Son and Spirit as historically progressive manifestations, or modes or roles of the one person who God is. The former, according to the Athanasian Creed, 'divides the essence', and the latter 'blends the persons', both of which positions indicate the heretical foul lines for 'right opinion' (orthodoxy) on the Trinity. While a trinitarian monotheism has always had to defend itself over against the strict *monotheisms of *Judaism and *Islam, which accuse it of polytheism, it has also had to contend with a persistent 'Christian unitarianism', as Arianism and modalism have reappeared in various guises throughout church history, if not in much popular Christianity. That simple defence would run as follows: biblical monotheism is the claim that the one true God is the Creator and therefore Lord of creation. Christians maintain that both creation and lordship are trinitarian affairs. Father, Son and Spirit (as the eternal immanent Trinity) are all on the side of the Creator and only together administer lordship over creation (as the economic Trinity).

Another major 'in-house' challenge for this doctrine concerns the quest for an appropriate and intelligible *analogy for the Trinity's threeness (persons) and oneness (one God). Popular analogies abound, and the Trinity has been likened to a shamrock, an egg or water in their triple parts or states. Augustine, the patriarch of Western trinitarianism, preferred a psychological analogy. Finding a key in *imago Dei* doctrine, *Augustine reasoned that if God is truly a trinity who creates humanity in the divine image and likeness, then some trinitarian imprint or vestige ought to be discerned in humanity. Since Augustine understood divine likeness to lie principally in the individual 'rational soul', with a little help from Platonic epistemology he identified a tripartite division of the human psyche into memory, understanding and will (or mind, knowledge and love, or some such variation) corresponding to Father, Son and Spirit respectively. While Augustine's psychological analogy has been dominant in Western trinitarianism, more recent Christian thinkers wonder whether the 'rational soul' is the best interpretation of the divine image in humanity, whether the soul really admits of three distinct parts, and, most importantly, whether a one-person analogy for the Trinity – the individual psyche – does not reinforce a 'blending of the persons'. The Cappadocian Fathers, on the other hand, experimented with social analogies, such as Gregory of Nyssa's 'three-man analogy' of Peter, James and John (three men but one shared humanity) or Gregory of Nazianzus' 'family analogy' of Adam, Eve and Seth. Whether the Cappadocians fully or coherently endorse a social analogy for the Trinity remains in dispute, but this tendency does underscore the general historical observation that the Eastern church tradition has allowed for a greater distinction among the trinitarian persons than has the Western tradition with its strong concentration on divine unity or oneness. Little wonder that the notion of *perichorēsis* – highlighting the sublime 'inness', 'fellowship', or 'communion' of the divine persons – of great currency and use in the present trinitarian discussion, had its origin and home in Eastern Orthodox thought. While the trinitarian confession was steadfastly preserved in Christian liturgy, more pronouncedly so in the Orthodox liturgy, certain medieval currents in both the East and the West did little to exploit the Trinity's theological, ethical and spiritual redolence.

In the West this was especially due to the ascendancy of the doctrine of the one God over the triune God. In something of an apologetic move to address the encroachment of both Aristotelian *rationalism and Islam, Aquinas placed in his two *Summae* consideration of the one God – *what* may be known about God *simpliciter* through human reason (*natural theology) – before the triune God, *who* is known only through special revelation (sacred theology). While his noble intention in initially clarifying a natural theistic point of contact was to show the limitations of human reason and the need for revelation to come to a full knowledge of God as triune, as disclosed in Scripture, the unintentioned effect was to make the Trinity secondary in importance to considerations of divine oneness (the one God). When the latter is defined by certain absolute properties derived *via negativa* – divine attributes such as strict *in*divisibility (simplicity), *im*mutability, *im*passibility, and *a*pathy – it puts in question divine characteristics one would be inclined to read off God's action in history (economic Trinity), by all scriptural appearances: that God is complex, not one simple, single thing; that God can change in certain respects; that God can be affected by the course of historical events; that God can suffer.

This methodological subordination of trinity doctrine to a philosophical *theism largely became the order of the day in both Catholic and Protestant doctrines of God, especially given the rationalistic challenges of the Enlightenment to both belief in God in general and Christian theology in particular. It was especially the assertion that God is both one, simple, indivisible spiritual entity and yet three distinct, discrete persons that aroused jeers of the 'incomprehensible jargon of the Trinitarian arithmetic, that three are one, and one is three' (Thomas Jefferson). And if incomprehensible, noted Immanuel *Kant, then hardly applicable, as he famously pronounced that the received doctrine of the Trinity has no practical relevance at all. This sentiment lingered well into the twentieth century, stigmatizing the Trinity as a doctrine that is at best *paradoxical or mysterious, at worst contradictory, but in any event hardly relevant.

Observing this moribund state of trinitarian affairs, Karl *Rahner lamented in the late 1960s that despite their orthodox confession of the Trinity, Christians are for all practical purposes 'mere monotheists'. But Rahner's lament that the Trinity had little part to play in the vast majority of Christian thought or spirituality became a rallying cry of the sentinel, as the last three decades have seen a resurgence of interest in the Trinity and its relevance for the life of the church and society at large. What occasions this ground swell of trinitarian thought, as signalled by a welter of publications, is a growing conviction that the Trinity is an eminently practical doctrine with crucial implications for Christian life. In this doctrine trinitarians are claiming to find the necessary resources to meet a wide range of practical concerns.

Key to this Western renaissance of trinitarian thought has been a more differentiated understanding of the divine persons, one that manifests a greater sympathy for Eastern trinitarianism, which in turn has opened up a much needed dialogue with Orthodoxy. By taking the redemptive history of Father, Son and Spirit as the appropriate point of departure for the Christian doctrine of God, in contrast to any supervening notion of divine oneness or unity that would impair their distinctions, trinity doctrine has been liberated from its subordination to a more philosophical theism (doctrine of the one God). Such is the force of Rahner's corrective axiom, 'The economic Trinity is the immanent Trinity and vice versa', i.e. bringing in close proximity our understanding of the historical actions of God with the being of God. This is a move that Karl *Barth had begun earlier in the twentieth century by locating the Trinity at the head (prolegomena) of his magisterial *Church Dogmatics* and making it the touchstone of his entire theology. In this way, Barth was a major stimulus in the twentieth-century renewal of trinity doctrine.

This move has resulted in a more dynamic or historically tempered doctrine of God. A trinitarian theism has led the way in rethinking certain classical divine attributes, particularly those derived *via negativa*: indivisibility, immutability, impassibility, apathy, eternality. Defined within a Greek metaphysical framework, such attributes conspired to paint a more static image of God that excited much of modern *atheism, especially of the protest variety. In response to a *Feuerbach, a Camus or an Ivan Karamazov, who can envision only a remote and distant deity, adored at the expense of creation and impervious to a world of absurdity and suffering (if not actually determinative of it), trinitarians insist that such a metaphysical construct is not the living God. Proposed instead is a trinity of divine persons who deeply participate in the ebb and flow of *history's weal and woe in sympathetic affirmation of creation. In this way the Trinity has come to play an important apologetic role in the dialogue with modernity, a timely resource in addressing the modern death of God (Nietzsche).

This trinitarian resurgence has also sponsored more relational accents in theology. Chief among these is a more relational or social view of the human person. Given that doctrines of God reinforce certain perceptions and patterns of human personhood, a more trinitarian conception of God with an emphasis on the *perichorēsis*, communion, fellowship, of the divine persons has been rallied to accentuate a more inter-personal view of humanity created in the divine image (as 'male and female'). Many view this as an important corrective to the socially corrosive 'autonomous individual' of modernity. The result has been a popular waning of Augustine's psychological analogy in favour of Richard of St Victor's full-orbed love analogy. In fact 'love' has become the preferred language for the 'divine essence' among trinitarians today. Few are the substantive statements on the Trinity that do not find in 'God is love' the most compelling description of, and entrance into, God's trinitarian being and action in history. In addition to anthropology, Christologies and ecclesiologies have become more pronouncedly trinitarian as the Trinity's implications are being explored for the broad range of theological topics. But even beyond concerns with more traditional doctrines, the Trinity has come to be considered salient to a diversity of issues, such as those concerning politics, social formation, economics, religious *pluralism, the practice of giving and the concept of *truth, to cite an important few. And this is how it ought to be, for the Christian vision of God should have redolence for all of life.

Given these developments, it is not surprising that more social doctrines of the Trinity have gained a considerable hearing. Harking back to the Cappadocians, social trinitarians have emerged from a broad range of theological traditions in the belief that the Trinity is best likened to a family, *community or society of persons. Though not without its controversy, the social analogy promises many advantages over other trinitarian constructs. For one, it claims to be the most consistent outcome of those more recent dynamic and relational gains in the doctrine of God in revision of more Greek-influenced categories. For another, it provides a more coherent account of the Trinity's threeness–oneness relation than the Western tradition has bequeathed us, one which falls in the fair territory of neither dividing the essence, nor blending the persons. As a more accessible understanding of the Trinity, the way becomes clear to see how the Trinity can function as an exemplary model for both the church and society at large, underscoring the relational nature and benevolent task of human personhood created in the divine image (cf. Gen. 1:26–28) and recreated in Christ (cf. John 17:20–23). The social conception of the Trinity offers a fundamental vision of God as a giving and open community of divine persons, one that invites us through Christ's sonship into its loving embrace as our true home. In this way, the Trinity grounds a personalist *metaphysics of communion and love that appeals to the deepest longing of the human heart, defining the meaning of life as the simply stated, but risky and arduous, project of learning to love.

Bibliography

L. Boff, *Trinity and Society* (tr. P. Burns, Maryknoll, NY, 1988); C. E. Gunton, *The Promise of Trinitarian Theology* (Edinburgh, 1991); J. N. D. Kelly, *Early Christian Doctrines*, rev. edn (San Francisco, 1978); A. E. McGrath, *Understanding the Trinity* (Grand Rapids, 1988); A. W. Wainwright, *The Trinity in the New Testament* (London, 1962).

T. R. THOMPSON

TROELTSCH, ERNST

Ernst Troeltsch, German liberal theologian, was born in Augsburg in 1865, and studied under the leading liberal Albrecht *Ritschl in Göttingen, where he developed as a systematic theologian. In this subject he was professor at Heidelberg from 1895 to 1915, and then taught philosophy in Berlin until his death in 1923. He worked across a range of disciplines and made influential studies of the social forms of Christianity through *history. His great methodological concern was to relate the classic Christian faith to the changed situation of modernity, and in this respect he demonstrated in particularly acute form the great strengths and weaknesses of liberal theology more generally: the desire to translate Christian convictions into terms comprehensible to modernity while thereby running the risk that the modern framework screens out essential elements of the Christian faith.

Troeltsch's historicizing approach to this problem dealt with the dilemma by effectively removing the essentials. In a work entitled *The Absoluteness of Christianity* he argued that the absoluteness in question was rooted in its unique fit with human nature, and did not consist in Christianity being 'absolutely' true, as in one truth for all time, because such a phenomenon was impossible.

Of most interest today are the three 'principles' by which he urged the study of Christianity as a religion to proceed. The principle of *criticism* requires a critical analysis and a probabilistic weighing up of all aspects of one's study. The principle of *analogy* posits fundamental continuity between the foundational events of Christianity and contemporary *religious experience. The principle of *correlation* effectively limits the framework of inquiry to a closed continuum of cause and effect, or condition and consequence. These principles have been much criticized, especially the second one for its apparent ruling out of the new, the unprecedented or even, perhaps, the supernatural. They do, however, in many ways accurately describe the methodology of historical criticism, leaving open to debate whether the study of Christianity as a religion can ever be capable of locating the coherent driving Christian convictions about God revealed uniquely in the life, teaching, death and resurrection of *Jesus Christ. Where Christian apologetics must also of necessity be engaged with this same slippery issue, it remains indebted to, though rarely in agreement with, Troeltsch's formulation of the matter.

Bibliography

V. A. Harvey, *The Historian and the Believer* (New York, 1966), pp. 3–37; E. Troeltsch, *The Absoluteness of Christianity* (ET, London, 1972).

R. S. BRIGGS

TRUTH, NATURE OF

An apologist claims to offer truth, but we live in an age when the nature, and even the existence, of truth are seriously questioned. Christian apologists need to clarify the nature of the truth-claims they are making for their message, and to convince their hearers of the validity of their concept of truth, before they can expect them to accept what they say.

Truth in Western thought

Historical Western thought has traditionally been dominated by one concept of truth, which predominated from *Plato until the twentieth century, and which has proved enormously fruitful. In this traditional concept truth was objective, something outside of us and independent of us; universal, the same the world over; eternal (if it is true today that the Berlin Wall fell in 1989, it will always be true; the 'fact' will never change); intelligible, something we as human beings are able to discover, comprehend and know.

Plato (c. 428 – c. 348 BC) was convinced of the objectivity of truth as something to be 'pursued' and 'discovered' and which exists independently of us. Much of our superficial knowing is tainted with error, largely because of the impermanence and comparative unreality of the things we see around us in the world. But behind the impermanent and unreal lies the real, which, for Plato, incorporated the true, the good and the beautiful. And human beings (especially philosophers, humanity at its best) have the innate ability to come to know what is real, since there exists in us something that corresponds to ultimate *reality. This ability is more than intellectual, though it certainly includes our reason, it is moral and aesthetic and involves our will and feelings. A philosopher is a *lover* of wisdom.

The holistic approach of Greek thought was paralleled in the Hebrew world-view, which was largely adopted by early Christianity. In Hebrew thought, truth is essentially a God-centred concept. Truth exists because God exists, and God is true. His nature is dependable, his ways are true and his words are trustworthy. Truth is more than correct propositions, though it includes such, it is also something we do. If we say 'Amen' (one of the Hebrew words for truth) to God's truth, we are committing ourselves to live by it. Truth that is not lived is not truth, it cannot

be divorced from goodness and *justice and right living. Because truth is rooted in God, it is personal and dynamic. *Jesus' claim to be the way and the truth and the life is significant, both for the paralleling of 'way' and 'life' with 'truth' and the linking of all three concepts with 'coming to the Father'. Truth is not an end in itself, but a means to finding God.

*Augustine (354–430) merged the Platonist and Christian traditions in his 'Christian philosophy', which dominated medieval thinking throughout the West. Truth, which is objective and to be located in God, is one. Some truths are given by God through *revelation in Christ and the Scriptures; other truths we can discover for ourselves, though even these probably need an element of divine 'illumination'. But both types of truth cohere into a consistent whole. In each sphere we have to take a certain amount on trust. Just as we believe many 'facts' about the world on the *authority of others, so we believe revealed truth on the authority of God. But our understanding, our God-given reason, always gets to work on such beliefs, checking them out and hopefully justifying them.

Building on Augustine, the Middle Ages retained a stable framework of God-given and rationally justifiable truth, but towards the end of the period a significant shift began to take place. It is seen to an extent in *Anselm (1033–1109), and more clearly exemplified in *Thomas Aquinas (1225–74). Where Augustine had stressed the significance of the role of God in all our knowing, the later Medieval thinkers began to stress the role of human reason and the fact that there is much truth we can discover without any intervention from God. So the role of God as the basis for truth began to be eroded. The increasing confidence in human reason expressed in the humanism of the Renaissance furthered this trend and set the stage for the *Enlightenment process of establishing truth solely on the foundation of human reason.

The Enlightenment was characterized by the supremacy of reason. The removal of God as the source and basis of truth was not a deliberate policy of most Enlightenment thinkers. Most of them gave God a significant place in their *epistemology. *Descartes (1586–1650), for example, made God foundational to his whole system, claiming that it was only because he could trust that God would not let him be deceived that he could depend upon his clear and distinct observations and rational processes at all. But the tide was flowing, and the amazing achievements of unaided human reason seemed to make God increasingly unnecessary. A significant point was reached with *Locke's (1632–1704) dictum that 'Reason must be our last judge and guide in everything.' 'Everything' included revelation, and so there were no longer two sources of truth, divine revelation and human reason, but only one. From now on reason was to stand in judgment over revelation.

The Enlightenment also witnessed the loss of objectivity. The recognition of human reason as supreme gave rise to another highly significant shift, which in effect brought about the downfall of the Enlightenment or modern concept of truth. While God was seen as the source and basis for truth, truth continued to be seen as essentially objective, something outside of us that we discover and submit to. The early Enlightenment continued to think of truth as objective, and used the language of discovery and submission. But by the nineteenth century this objectivity was being eroded. The increasing role of the *reasoning subject was emphasized. We have a hand in creating truth; rather than it shaping us, we shape it. Truth is not 'out there', it is in the thinking individual; it is not objective but subjective.

At the heart of this shift to subjectivity was the realization that if I as an individual make myself – my reason and my experiences – the key to reality and truth, I am for ever locked into the content of my own mind. I have no way of establishing the objectivity or universality of my beliefs. If my reason and my experience are ultimate for me, I have no criterion by which to judge their reliability and so the truth of my beliefs. I am shut up for ever in my own little world without any chance of knowing the truth of things-in-themselves.

Ironically, and not surprisingly, most Enlightenment thinkers failed to take on board the full implications of this shift to subjectivity. They still believed in the reality of the world around them, and in practice treated truth, especially scientific truth, as fully and reliably objective. *Hume (1711–76), who rejected God, escaped from the gloomy implications of his sceptical philosophy by ignoring them and enjoying a meal or a game. *Kant (1724–1804) took the issue more seriously, and attempted to mediate between Hume's empiricist critique and his own rationalist tradition. He was forced to concede

that on the basis of reason we can never know things around us as they are in themselves. Truth is no longer something that shapes us, and from now on, by a 'Copernican revolution', we will shape it. (He did go on to suggest that we can have some sort of knowledge of things in the real world and in themselves, but only through an utterly different sort of 'reason', which never intersects with the first.) The widespread acceptance of Kant's approach through the nineteenth century meant that, whatever happened in ordinary life, in philosophy truth had lost its objectivity and so its universality. Kant and many of his followers still clung to the hope that the shift to subjectivity would not remove truth completely. It was left to *Nietzsche, the forerunner of postmodernism, to make it clear that this was a forlorn hope.

Nietzsche (1844–1900) graphically described the results of losing God as the foundation for truth, and, indeed, for meaning, morals and life in general. It was as though the entire horizon has been wiped away and the earth has been unchained from its sun. We are plunging continually in all directions, with no up or down left, straying as through an infinite nothing, lost in empty space.

Nietzsche's response was that, having lost truth, we must create new truth for ourselves, a theme central to *existentialism. The conviction that the traditional concept of objective truth could somehow be salvaged, however, continued on into the twentieth century, especially among those whose philosophies were strongly influenced by the methodology of the scientists, who continued to assume the objectivity of their data. Thus the logical positivists sought to establish a dependable criterion for objective truth in a *verification principle, and Bertrand *Russell (1872–1970) tried to find a foundation in maths and logic. But the verification principle was rejected as inadequate, and Russell was forced to concede that the foundation he had sought for knowledge did not exist. In the last analysis everything has to be accepted on trust, and all our knowledge is built on assumptions we can never finally establish.

Though at the popular level *science is still looked on as dealing with objective truth, philosophers of science, from Popper and Kuhn onwards, have thus been forced to concede that its pronouncements are no longer to be seen as claims to objective truth; rather, they are an essentially pragmatic way of explaining our experiences, which we are free to accept or reject as we choose. Thus, philosophically speaking, the last bastion of objective truth has fallen, opening the way to the all-embracing *relativism of postmodernism.

Truth and Christian apologetics in a postmodern age

Confronted with a given culture, Christian apologists have always had a double task. They have had to present their message in terms understandable and acceptable to that culture, and at the same time they have had to preserve the distinctiveness of the message so as to be able to present it as a radical alternative.

Offering Christian truth

Enlightenment or modern culture, from which we are just emerging, made reason the test of truth for everything. Given that culture, Christian apologists justifiably set themselves to establish that Christianity was eminently reasonable, that the existence of God could be established by rational arguments, and so on. Christian truth was presented essentially as cerebral, facts to be believed and doctrines to be accepted. Since, despite the inroads of relativism and postmodernism, there are still many traces of Enlightenment *rationalism in our culture, such a rationalist approach may still have a place. Someone, for example, who is committed to a scientific world-view may well be prepared to think through a contemporary form of the cosmological argument.

The postmodern scene, however, presents us with the opportunity to do something different, something that seems more in keeping with the early Christian understanding of truth. For truth in the Bible is bigger than rational demonstration. It is personal, moral, dynamic and life-changing, as well as propositional and factual. Supremely, truth is God. So the apologetic task in a postmodern culture is to present truth in all its richness, not just as something narrowly rational. We are to live truth, and people need to experience the reality of Christ who is the truth in us and see the gospel as 'the power of God'. If 'community' and 'image' are buzz words in our culture, then truth needs be the characteristic of our Christian communities and our Christian image. The standard is set in Heb. 1:3 where it is said of the incarnate Christ that 'everything about him represents God exactly' (NLT).

This is by no means to deny the significance of truth presented as facts and doctrines. It would be impossible to be faithful to biblical Christianity without emphasizing the key importance of God being a God who speaks truth. In Scripture he has chosen to give us his truth in a form we can grasp with our minds. Here he speaks in words; here we find facts and on this basis we can build our doctrines. In all our apologetic the revelation of God in Scripture must remain normative. It is there we find how to live truth, or to be the true people of God, or to image Christ the truth.

A Christian approach to truth

It is highly unlikely that our culture will be able to survive without adopting some approach to truth to replace the lost Enlightenment concept. But at present, apart from a general pragmatism, no alternative concept seems to be winning much ground. This gives the Christian apologist an opportunity to offer a distinctively Christian alternative. In keeping with what we have seen above the key points of this might be:

Theocentricity. Just as we believe that God is the creator and upholder of the universe, we believe that truth, along with goodness, beauty, love, and much else has its origin and foundation in God. The individual ceases to be the centre of the universe, and the creator of what is true, and gives these roles back to God.

Objectivity. Truth is thus removed from the subjectivity of each individual, and we can return to the objective foundation for truth that was the key to Western thought for nearly two millennia. The consistency of the created universe is assured because God is faithful. The trustworthiness of truth is assured because God is true.

Richness. God is not monochrome, nor is his truth. It is rich and deep, transparent and mysterious, factual and moral, touching every part of life. We are not to separate God's truth from his other 'attributes'; it is holy truth, living truth, saving truth, and so on. No one truth may be detached from the whole; to do so is to distort it and destroy it.

Grace and revelation. In that he has made us in his image, God has enabled us to know truth, to think his thoughts after him. We have both the capacity to learn God's truth from the world around us, and to receive it by revelation, through Scripture and the *Holy Spirit.

Holism. Because God is much more than intellect, the receiving of his truth will be much more than intellectual. The paradigm here is meeting with Christ, which impacts every part of our personhood, not just our minds. Even 'scientific' truth is not to be taken as merely factual or cerebral. Sooner or later it must have, say, moral or personal implications.

How might we seek to demonstrate the 'truth' of this Christian concept of truth? Clearly, the old rationalistic approach will not do. Rather, we need to follow the way of holistic living of the truth described above, with the anticipation that this, validated by the work of the Holy Spirit, will lead others to the truth. But, as we have suggested above, where we find those who are willing to listen to reasoned arguments, we can follow the apologetic method that seeks to show that this approach to truth provides a more satisfactory and coherent explanation of what we actually find in the world than any other rival theory.

Bibliography

P. Hicks, *Evangelicals and Truth* (Leicester, 1998); W. J. Wood *Epistemology* (Leicester, 1998).

P. HICKS

TURIN SHROUD

The Turin Shroud, considered by many within the Roman Catholic community and beyond to be one of the most important of Christian relics, is preserved in the royal chapel of the Cathedral of San Giovanni Battista in Turin, northern Italy.

It consists of a linen strip, 14 ft 3 in. long and 3 ft 7 in. wide, bearing two images head to head of the body of a man of average height. It is as if a corpse had been laid on the lower half of the sheet and the other half of the strip was then folded back down over the head to cover the entire front of the body. What makes the shroud remarkable is that the sepia-tone marks on it, of the hands and feet, the back and the head of the corpse, indicate wounds consistent with crucifixion, scourging and even a crown of thorns. The face has a look of serenity upon it. Over the centuries, and still today, many (including some Protestants such as the NT scholar and former bishop of Woolwich, J. A. T. Robinson) have been of the conviction that this is the very shroud that covered the body of *Jesus when it was laid in the tomb.

The shroud first appeared in France in 1354, in the possession of the knight Geoffroi de Charnay. In the course of time it was moved to Chambery in south-east France, where, in 1532, it sustained damage by fire and water. It was moved to Turin in 1578. A recent, detailed history of the shroud is documented in Ian Wilson's, *The Blood and the Shroud* (1998), and the primary website summarizes Wilson's data.

Only very exceptionally has the shroud been open to public viewing, e.g. in 1931 to mark the marriage of Prince Umberto and in 1978 commemorating the four hundredth anniversary of its arrival in Turin. In 1998 over 2 million visitors viewed the shroud on the occasion of the centenary of Secundo Pia's first photograph, and there was a ten-week exhibition in 2000 to mark the Jubilee anniversary of the birth of Jesus.

Public fascination, both sceptical and endorsing, has been sustained by hundreds of books, articles in major journals such as *National Geographic* and *Time*, documentary films such as David Rolfe's *The Silent Witness*, national and international societies, conferences and symposia. Interest is not confined to the Christian world. An American Jew is editor of the principal Turin Shroud website, readily affirming his conviction that the shroud is the one that covered the body of Jesus. Another Jew, Rabbi Dan Cohn-Sherbok, argued in an article in *Expository Times* against its authenticity on the grounds that in the Jewish world of the first century bodies were wrapped in a way 'quite different' from that indicated by the shroud. An Internet search indicates over 20,000 results relating to the shroud. The leading website on the subject describes the shroud as 'the single most studied artefact in human history'.

Pia's first photographs of the shroud, taken in 1898, awakened a wider public curiosity in the shroud, both popular and scientific. Of particular interest to the scientific world was the dating of the cloth and its image, a subject of controversy from the beginning. Scientific investigation became more intense in the later decades of the twentieth century. A Shroud of Turin Research Project (STURP) was set up and in 1978 enlisted a team of scientists to subject the shroud to its most rigorous examination to date. The tests proved inconclusive. Then, a decade later, the shroud was carbon-tested by three separate laboratories in Zurich, Tucson (Arizona) and Oxford in an attempt to establish its date scientifically. With minor variations between the three laboratories, the tests indicated that the flax from which the shroud is made is of medieval origin, dating from between 1260 and 1390.

For many, the carbon-dating results are not conclusive, and these people continue to believe that the cloth is tangible evidence of the Jesus who was put to death by crucifixion in the first century. For others the tests settle the matter once for all: the shroud is merely a medieval curiosity. However, if the scientific evidence is taken as conclusive, the mystery of the shroud persists. If the image is not of Jesus, whose is it? Microscopic tests seem to indicate that the stains cannot have been added by paint or dye. The 'appalling possibility' has to be faced that another actual human being (of the thirteenth or fourteenth century) was deliberately subjected to a crucifixion-like execution with a view to simulating the wounds of Christ's Passion.

The shroud raises wider questions of faith and spirituality. For some Christians, tangible, visible evidences (even the most indirect) constitute important, even central, supports to faith. Another, recent example of such evidence is the limestone ossuary recently discovered in Jerusalem which bears the inscription, 'James, the son of Joseph, and brother of Jesus'. It has been hailed as 'the earliest archaeological evidence of Jesus'. As far as we can tell from the NT, the early church did not attempt to sacralize Jesus' tomb, nor any of his clothes or other possessions. The author of the fourth Gospel records Jesus as insisting instead that those are blessed who believe in him without 'seeing'.

Bibliography

B. Schwortz and I. Wilson, *The Turin Shroud: The Illustrated Evidence* (London, 2000); D. Sox, *The Shroud Unmasked* (Basingstoke, 1988); 'The Cult of the Shroud', *The Tablet* (Feb. 1998); I. Wilson, *The Blood and the Shroud* (New York, 1998); <http://www.shroud.com>.

G. MOLYNEUX

TYPOLOGY

Typology is a form of interpretation in which a text's description of a person, place, thing, event or institution provides a 'type', i.e. a foreshadowing of events either in one's own day or in the future. Biblical typology is grounded on the assumption that God is the ultimate agent behind events and thus there is a divine pattern to *history. Typology also assumes that God guides the actual description in Scripture so that the details of the description may hold significance beyond their meaning in the original context. Thus Paul finds in the collective singular 'seed', referring to Abraham's offspring (Gen. 13:15; 17:8; 24:7), a reference to Christ (Gal. 3:16).

Such correspondences occur within the OT itself, e.g. God says that he intends to be with Joshua as he was with Moses (Josh. 3:7). This relation is immediately emphasized by describing the parting of the Jordan River in terms drawn from the parting of the sea at the exodus (Exod. 15:8; Josh. 3:15). The repeated pattern signifies that the same God is at work accomplishing his purpose (Josh. 3:7, 10).

OT authors use correspondence to speak especially of God's great act of deliverance coming in the future. The exodus, for example, provides a pattern that will be repeated (Isa. 43:16–21; 48:20–21; 51:9–11; 52:11–12; Jer. 16:14–15; Hos. 2:15). Indeed, the coming salvation is so glorious that it will be a new creation (Isa. 11:6–9; 51:3; 65:17–25). Such imagery for the coming deliverance is used in the NT to reveal that God has now, in Christ, inaugurated the ultimate salvation.

The NT use of typology is grounded in Jesus' own claims that the OT speaks of him (John 5:39; Luke 24:44–47). He draws out numerous correspondences, for example, between his ministry and those of Elijah and Elisha (Luke 4:25–27). However, his own person and ministry do not simply repeat OT events, but rather they transcend that which God has done up to this point. Accordingly, Jesus claims to be greater than Jonah (Matt. 12:41), greater than Solomon (Matt. 12:42), greater than David (Mark 2:25–26), and greater than the temple (Matt. 12:6); and, indeed, his blood is the blood of the new covenant (Mark 14:24).

In addition to recounting Jesus' own use of typology the Gospel writers also appeal to it themselves. Consider, for example, Matt. 2:14–15, 'So he [Joseph] got up, took the child and his mother during the night and left for Egypt, where he stayed until the death of Herod. And so was fulfilled what the Lord had said through the prophet: "Out of Egypt I called my son." ' Matthew's quotation comes from Hos. 11:1, a passage that speaks of God's love for Israel (his 'son'), which was evident in the exodus from Egypt. In the original setting Hosea is not prophesying about the Messiah, but rather recalling Israel's history in order to speak to his own day. But in Hosea's description of God calling his son out of Egypt, Matthew sees a 'person' (Israel) and an event which form a pattern that is repeated in the life of Jesus, who is God's son in the ultimate sense. In the NT the fulfilment of the OT more often comes through such typology than through the fulfilment of explicit prophecies.

In NT typology the main focus is Christ, but types are also used for the church, matters of discipleship and future eschatology. Thus, while Paul uses typology to speak of the identity and significance of Christ, e.g. when he develops Adam as a type of Christ (Rom. 5:12–21), he also uses it to speak to such matters as the need for moral purity in the Christian community (1 Cor. 5:6–8) and the apostles' right to material support (1 Cor. 9:8–14), and as a way of teaching about baptism and holy communion (1 Cor. 10:1–22).

Such typological interpretations occur extensively throughout the NT. Indeed, in some books it is the main focus. For example, Luke and Acts together provide an extensive set of patterns drawn between the OT, Jesus and the church; the letter to the Hebrews develops Jesus' fulfilment of the OT priesthood and sacrificial system; and the book of Revelation uses a large collection of types to describe eschatological events and the future glory.

In modern scholarship typology is often distinguished from allegory. For many scholars 'typology' refers to patterns in history, while 'allegory' refers to arbitrary associations attached to words, images and even numbers. Thus, David fighting Goliath could be a type of Christ or the Christian, but an identification of David's five stones with weapons Jesus used against Satan, or which Christians may use in their spiritual warfare, would be an example of allegory. This distinction is useful, though the terms were not so neatly distinguished in ancient times. For example, Paul develops a complex set of patterns at one point (Gal. 4:21–31), which he calls an allegory (4:24), though his actual interpretation is more like typology as defined in some modern discussions.

In the NT and the early church, typology served to witness to the truth of Jesus through the continuity between God's acts and *revelation in the OT and now in Jesus and his church. This function made typology especially important in commending Christianity to Jews, but also helped counter the charge by non-Jews that Christianity lacked antiquity. Typology fell out of favour in some circles after the Enlightenment, but is presently stimulating much discussion in biblical studies and holds promise for apologetics as well.

One important contribution typology can make in the current setting is through its revelation of the beautiful coherent organic unity present in the midst of Scripture's diverse texts. Typology reveals the nature of the Scriptures, and the history to which they bear witness, to be analogous to the universe as the physical sciences are making it known to us. The complex networks of inter-dependence seen in the dance of the galaxies, in the ecosystems of the world, or in the life of a single cell, correspond to the network of typological references that unite the Bible in what Northrop Frye calls 'the great code'. Frye says, 'The typological organization of the Bible [is] unique: no other book in the world, to my knowledge, has a structure even remotely like that of the Christian Bible' (p. 80).

In an age when many scientists consider 'beauty' and 'elegance' as criteria of *truth, the beauty and elegance of the Bible as seen through typology are a mark of its truth. The signature marks of the Creator of the universe are seen also in the Scriptures, and, with the help of Scripture, may be seen within history as well. So typology's apologetic value endures, albeit varying in specific application from its use in earlier ages.

Bibliography

M. Fishbane, *Biblical Interpretation in Ancient Israel* (Oxford, 1985); N. Frye, *The Great Code: The Bible and Literature* (New York, 1982); L. Goppelt, *Typos: The Typological Interpretation of the Old Testament in the New* (ET, Grand Rapids, 1982); B. Lindars, *New Testament Apologetic* (London, 1961); F. M. Young, *Biblical Exegesis and the Formation of Christian Culture* (Cambridge, 1997; Peabody, 2002).

R. A. WHITACRE

UFOs, see NEW AGE

UNEVANGELIZED, SALVATION OF, see
WORLD RELIGIONS AND
CHRISTIANITY
UNIQUENESS OF CHRIST, see WORLD
RELIGIONS AND CHRISTIANITY

UNIVERSALISM

A universalist is one who maintains that every human being will finally be saved. The term 'universalism' can also be used in other ways, particularly to describe the view that salvation extends outside the bounds of Israel, encompassing the Gentiles; but here it is treated exclusively in the former sense. Traditionally, universalism has been opposed to the conviction that some will endure irreversible condemnation and endless punishment. However, there are alternative non-universalist positions, including the belief that some will be annihilated. A widely held position today is that dogmatic universalism cannot be affirmed, but that we may hope for the salvation of all, a position that can be described as 'hopeful universalism'. The scope of this article does not allow for discussion of the alternatives to the dogmatic-universalist position, although we shall touch on 'hopeful universalism'. This is a significant limitation, for our acceptance or rejection of universalism may be strongly affected by what we regard as the conceivable or likely alternatives.

Historically, there have been universalists in the Christian church from at least the second and early third centuries until today. Between *Origen at the beginning of this period, and major figures like *Schleiermacher and Erskine in the nineteenth century, these have included some, such as the German pietist Johann Bengel (1687–1752), who, while not being public and outright universalists, appear to have been definitely inclined that way. In the past, this has been very much a minority position, but adherence to it has increased over the last two centuries. Arguments advanced in favour of universalism are, generally speaking, of two kinds, which, of course, can be combined. The first are more narrowly exegetical, focusing on a number of NT texts that are held to support it, and reinterpreting those that appear not to do so. Pauline texts, particularly, are adduced in support of universalism. Supporting texts include Romans 5:18 (justification that brings life for all) and 11:32 (a divine purpose of mercy upon all); 1 Corinthians 15:22 ('in Christ all will be made alive'); Philippians 2:10–11 (universal confession of Christ); and Colossians 1:20 (everything reconciled through Christ). These are interpreted both in their immediate context and in conjunction with 1 Timothy 2:4 (God 'wants all men to be saved and to come to a knowledge of the truth') and 2 Peter 3:9 (God is 'not wanting anyone to perish'). What God desires he intends, and what he intends he brings about.

Texts which appear to say otherwise are explained in a variety of ways. Where they are not treated as early church additions (in the case of Gospel texts) or as evidence of canonical disunity on the question of universal salvation, two main strategies are possible. One is to treat them as statements of a logical or theoretical possibility, and not as declarations of what actually will be in the future. They are warnings about the destiny of the road being travelled, not predictions about the destiny of the traveller. Another is to treat them as declarations of what will be, but not of what permanently will be. Universal salvation follows, but does not replace, *hell.

The second kind of argument stems from broader theological considerations concerning the nature of God. Is it conceivable that divine love should not secure universal salvation? According to Scripture, God both desires it and has the *power to bring about what he desires. If all are not saved, God is defeated. It may be that a post-mortem process is required to bring those who have refused to receive God in this life to the point where salvation is attained. Judgment is an undeniable truth. But if the final outcome of all processes is not the salvation of all, either divine love or divine power (or both) is compromised. Since neither of these tenets should be given up or watered down, universalism follows.

Should Christians be universalists? Stephen Travis has written that 'he who has not felt deeply the attraction of universalism can scarcely have been moved by the greatness of God's love'. John Stott has also written of the everlasting suffering of hell: 'Emotionally, I find the concept intolerable and do not understand how people can live with it without either cauterising their feelings or cracking under the strain' (J. Stott and D. Edwards, *Essentials*, p. 314). Stott is resolutely non-universalist, pleading for the legitimacy of belief in the annihilation of some, following punishment, rather than unending punishment. But his words, coupled with those of Travis, indicate how wrong it would be to approach the question of universalism with emotional detachment. If God's love for sinners is immeasurably greater than ours, and his awareness of the state of condemnation immeasurably more acute than ours, does this not point towards universalism? At the least, should we not be hopeful universalists? We must appreciate the force of the case for giving a positive answer to these questions. Nevertheless, whatever the attendant perplexities, Scripture discourages us from doing so.

It is impossible, in short compass, to give a proper description, let alone examination, of the exegetical and theological issues involved. The exegetical difficulty with the universalist appeal to Paul is two-fold. First, the non-Pauline material in the NT appears to lend overwhelming support to a non-universalist reading of the texts. If that is indeed so, and Paul is indeed a universalist, the NT data are seriously discordant. Secondly, the Pauline texts sit alongside texts which are in harmony with the non-Pauline non-universalist material. Thus, Romans 2:7–9 contrasts two destinies; 1 Corinthians 6:10 describes those eschatologically excluded from the kingdom of God; Philippians 3:19 speaks of a destiny in destruction; and Colossians 3:6 speaks of God's eschatological wrath. These are just four examples from letters alleged to contain positive universalist teaching.

Universalists argue that these and many other texts do not actually contradict universalism, despite surface appearances. But it is also arguable that the texts adduced in its support do not affirm universalism either, despite surface appearances; and not everyone will see the surface in the same way. Hermeneutically, the question is sometimes framed in terms of whether we should be interpreting one set of texts in the light of others and, if so, which in the light of which. This description of procedure may be useful up to a point, but it runs the risk of viewing the material as two competing sets of passages, while an integrated and exegetically diligent reading of Scripture may not make it look that way. If Paul and other contributors to the NT did not believe that separation from God has the finality that it appears to have, according to several texts, it is strange that they expressed this conviction in a small number of texts not integrated into their teachings about judgment. This point is not conclusive; biblical authors are not all writing orderly treatises of systematic theology. But where a plausible explanation exists for the 'universalist' passages, the consistency and preponderance of biblical teaching on the finality of the condemnation of some people are weighty factors. (For a survey of principal 'universalist' passages, see H. Marshall in Parry and Partridge, *Universal Salvation?*) As for the treatments of the texts as warnings, rather than infallible predictions, would *Jesus or the biblical authors have issued warnings about a state which they thought that nobody would attain? It may well be that texts adduced in support of universalism indicate a comprehensive scope for Christ's work, a universally reconciled order and a wider reach for salvation than many have imagined. This applies to the extra-Pauline material too, notably Revelation 21:24–26. But the crucial issue is whether every single individual will be included within this grand design.

The force of the universalist case must surely be derived from broad theological considerations, rather than from particularly exegetical ones. Those of us who hold that biblical theology is normative for subsequent (including contemporary) theology, on the matter of universal salvation, must approach every issue with a due sense of our inability to penetrate beyond a certain point in our understanding. Consequences we say *must* follow from divine love, power, holiness or *justice should be strictly subordinated to what we believe God has done, is doing or promises to do. Although we are bound to think logically, we are also bound to regard as precarious the forging of some of the conceptual interconnections which go beyond the biblical data. Deuteronomy 29:29 gives us a sound theological rule: 'The secret things belong to the LORD our God, but the things revealed belong to us and to our children for ever, that we may follow all the words of this law.'

The strength of the theological case for universalism arises from the conjunction of three claims, roughly stated as follows: (1) that God loves all in a way that makes him desire to save all; (2) that God has the power to bring about what he desires, certainly including this desire; and (3) that, therefore, everyone will eventually be saved. This way of describing the issue demonstrates its connection with the problem of *evil and suffering. In the latter case, the conjunction in question is the one between (1) God's desire to prevent suffering; (2) God's ability to do so, and (3) the existence of suffering. It is widely held that point 3 is not compatible with points 1 and 2 together. If we deny point 3 in the universalist equation, we are told that points 1 and 2 cannot be maintained together. Yet many will hold that, in relation to suffering, we must maintain all three, however little we can explain their conjunction. We should view the question of universalism in the light of this question, for many will find it intellectually easier to affirm the co-existence of divine love and power with the non-salvation of the culpably impenitent than with the suffering of the relatively innocent.

The theological case for universalism is countered by convictions on the nature of human responsibility and human sin. Within the Protestant tradition, *Calvinists and Arminians have differed over the nature of freedom in connection with human responsibility. This is relevant to the question of universalism, for some will regard human freedom to reject God as crucial in a theological account of things. On any account of things, it is important to affirm human responsibility. God has so constituted humanity that his love and power operate in accordance with, not irrespective of, a measure of responsibility granted to those capable of exercising it. If that does not mean that we can posit certain *limits* to what God wants to or can do, neither does it mean that we can posit certain *constraints* upon what God must want to or must do, in the light of human responsibility. Speculation on the relation of divine action to human responsibility, however well grounded or near the mark, must be guided by the teaching of Scripture. The truth about human destiny cannot be derived from a consideration of divine love and power alone. It must be derived equally from a consideration of the nature of humanity, as divinely constituted.

It is also the case that hardly anything is more characteristic of our day than widespread failure to grasp the enormity of human sin. To sin is to ally oneself with that which is in extremest opposition to God. It is an assault, within the limits of human capacity to do so, on God, others and the world – on all that is good. We seldom actually see it in that light, even if our theological schemes declare it. This is one reason why it is far outside the boundaries of our comprehension to judge what God may or must do about sin, other than what we

can derive from Scripture or some manifest data. The reason why God will not save some may only become clear to us when the nature of sin is more fully revealed. Then, we may equally wonder why he has saved any, as the perfections of divine holiness and justice come into view, and we understand divine love and power anew in the light of the whole.

Should we be hopeful universalists? It seems harsh to deny it. Yet those exegetical factors which persuade some of us to reject universalism will persuade us also that Scripture does not encourage a hopeful universalism, if hope is built on expectation. If hope is built on desire, it may be different, and, where that desire is rooted in our understanding of divine love and desire, we may certainly be encouraged to keep searching the Scriptures to see if hope is warranted. The limits of our treatment kick in here, however, because the question of universalism is not adequately addressed without asking what alternative we propose, if we have one. While this cannot be done here, it is worth noting that we should certainly avoid confusing the universalist question with two others. The first is whether salvation is possible without hearing of Christ. A positive answer can (whether or not it should) be given to this question, without affirming the salvation of all. The second is whether those who are saved will be few. There is surely no reason to believe that we need more of an answer here than which Jesus gave his disciples in Luke 13:23–24.

What are the apologetic implications of rejecting universalism? Arguably, it causes problems, for it eternally and eschatologically compounds the problem of temporal suffering. Yet, the reverse is also arguable: if all will be saved, repentance may be robbed of its necessity and urgency, so that our apologia becomes an apologia for a hopelessly attenuated gospel. From the apologetic point of view, what surely needs to be emphasized is that the unity of God's perfections will be revealed in his future judgments and that we have grounds for believing this, so that we rightly walk now by faith and not by sight. The revelation of the exact nature of human responsibility also awaits its time. But if we are *now* told of our responsibility and *now* told that persistent and conscious sinning is the road to exclusion from God's presence, a non-universalist position should be no obstacle to Christian faith. 'Enter through the narrow gate. For wide is the gate and broad is the road that leads to destruction, and many enter through it. But small is the gate and narrow is the road that leads to life, and only a few find it' (Matt. 7:13–14). These words are patient of different exegeses up to a point, but their claim on our obedience is absolute and unmistakable.

Bibliography

K. Barth, *Church Dogmatics*; R. J. Bauckham, 'Universalism: A Historical Survey', *Themelios* 4.2 (1979); J. Hick, *Death and Eternal Life* (New York and London, 1976); I. H. Marshall, 'Does the New Testament Teach Universal Salvation?' in J. Colwell (ed.), *Called to One Hope: Perspectives on the Life to Come* (Carlisle, 2000); R. Parry and C. Partridge (eds.), *Universal Salvation? The Current Debate* (Carlisle, 2003); J. A. T. Robinson, *In the End God* (London and New York, 1969); T. Talbott, *The Inescapable Love of God* (Parkland, 1999); S. Travis, *Christian Hope and the Future of Man* (Leicester, 1980).

S. N. WILLIAMS

UNIVERSALS

The term 'universal' derives from the Lat. *universalis*, meaning 'pertaining or belonging to all or the whole', which is a translation of *Aristotle's Gk term *to katholon* of similar meaning. 'Universal' suggests a species, essence or feature predicated of like individuals, and contrasts with the terms 'individual', 'particular' and 'singular'.

Experience is always of individuals, while thought and speech use general terms and concepts. The 'problem of universals' is really a historically varied set of problems involving the ontological status of predicated commonalities and our ability to cognize individuals. Are species such as 'mankind' or features such as 'black' in some sense real? At stake is the basic accuracy of our concepts and the very possibility of general knowledge.

Positions on universals are historically three-fold: realism, conceptualism and nominalism, depending on whether universals are seen as primarily rooted in *language, thought or extra-mental reality. Realists see universals as in some sense mind-independent, existing in, or even prior to, individuals. Conceptualists identify universals with general concepts that have limited or no objective validity. Nominalists (from the Lat. *nomina*, 'names') see universality as characteristic of general terms and deny it of concepts or extra-mental items.

*Socrates (c. 470 – 399 BC) asked interlocutors for exact definitions of mathematical and axiological concepts. His student *Plato (427–347 BC) held that an important general term (common name, adjective, relation) corresponds to an immaterial, immutable exemplar or Form (*eidos*), existing apart from its exemplification by like individuals. His theory of Forms is found in *Phaedo*, *Republic* and *Parmenides*. *Aristotle (384–322 BC) moderated Plato's extreme realism of Forms by positing individualized forms of species and their accidental features as inhering in particulars. Abstract cognition grasps the basic form in separation from its individuating factors. Essences are the set of features defining individual membership in a species. However, Aristotle's *On Interpretation* cryptically defines 'universal' as 'that which is to be predicated of many subjects', which he at points identifies with species and genera while leaving their ontological status vague. Porphyry's (233–304) commentary on Aristotle's *Categories* asks whether species and genera exist in reality or only in thought, and, if they are real, whether they are corporeal or incorporeal, and in things or existing independently. Boethius (c. 480–524) represents Aristotle as holding species and genera to be 'understood as corporeal but subsisting in sensibles', i.e. inherent similarities are abstractly cognized. *Augustine (354–430) held that universals exist as exemplars of creation in God's mind. Hence, medieval thinkers would affirm universals as divine exemplars while denying that they are Platonic entities. Medieval debates over the precise ontology of universals achieved a range and technical sophistication many view as unmatched.

Peter *Abelard (c. 1079–1142) reports that Roscelin (1050–1120) thought that universals were no more than vocal words or 'emissions of the voice', and interprets William of Champeaux (1070–1120) as positing an extreme realism of the same essence inhering in like individuals that differ only in their accidents. Abelard mediates between these alleged extremes, saying that universals are general terms associated with concepts confusedly representing the same 'state of being' in like individuals. Though often labelled conceptualist, his position carries a semantic emphasis and denial of common essences, suggesting nominalism. *Thomas Aquinas (1225–74) in *On Being and Essence* holds that recognizably the same essence can inform both a mind as a concept and a thing as an Aristotelian individualized form, just as a book's information content is realized in separate minds, copies and editions. Aquinas' 'moderate realism' sees universality as accruing to concepts but having an objective basis in individualized forms. The mature *William of Ockham (c. 1290–1349) posits a reality of fundamentally singular and heterogeneous individuals. Universals are terms associated with singular acts of singular minds confusedly representing like individuals. Ockham's nominalisitic ontology and preference for empirical *verification prefigure classical British *empiricism.

Thomas Hobbes (1588–1679) declares universals to be names standing for groupings of individual images thought similar. John *Locke's (1632–1704) conceptualism holds that understanding attaches abstract ideas to general terms, while the real essences of things remain unknown. George *Berkeley's (1685–1753) emphasis on mental events as images inspired David *Hume (1711–76) to see universals as general terms connected to individual perceptions of similarities.

In the twentieth century, Bertrand *Russell (1872–1970) speculated that similarity itself might be an irreducible notion and hence a universal. Developments in mathematical logic brought questions about the ontology of logical and mathematical notions, e.g. numbers, classes and sets. Nelson Goodman (1906–98) cites a *paradox that every class and its members can form a larger one and so on to infinity, suggesting the denial of classes as entities. Others cite worse consequences in denying entitative status to logical and mathematical notions. American pragmatist Willard Quine (1908–2000) declares physical objects and universals to be culturally posited 'to simplify our account of the flux of experience'. *Wittgenstein and ordinary-language philosophers caution against seeking something that all individuals under a general term have in common. There might only be overlapping 'family resemblances' or perhaps variable meanings determined by individual usage and context. However, the current emphasis on language by analytic philosophers has not halted speculation on the ontological import of words and concepts. The problem of universals comprises perennial questions involving the

ontology and relatedness of thought, language and *reality.

Bibliography

R. Aaron, *The Theory of Universals* (Oxford, 1952); B. Blanshard, *Reason and Analysis* (La Salle, 1973); J. Cooper (ed.), *Plato: Complete Works* (Indianapolis and Cambridge, 1997); N. Goodman, *The Structure of Appearance* (Cambridge, 1951); G. Klima, 'The Medieval Problem of Universals', in E. N. Zalta (ed.), *The Stanford Encyclopedia of Philosophy*, <http://plato.stanford.edu/archives/win2004/entries/universals-medieval>; M. Loux (ed.), *Universals and Particulars: Readings in Ontology* (Notre Dame, 1976); R. McKeon (ed.), *The Basic Works of Aristotle* (New York, 2001); R. Miller and E. Synan, 'Universals', in *New Catholic Encyclopedia* (New York and London, 1967–89); W. V. Quine, 'On What There Is', in *From a Logical Point of View* (Cambridge, 1980); B. Russell, *Problems of Philosophy* (London, 1912); P. V. Spade (ed. and trans.), *Five Texts on the Mediaeval Problem of Universals: Porphyry, Boethius, Abelard, Duns Scotus, Ockham* (Indianapolis, 1994); H. Staniland, *Universals* (Garden City, 1972); Thomas Aquinas, *On Being and Essence* (trans. J. Bobik; Notre Dame, 1965); R. Van Iten (ed.), *The Problem of Universals* (New York, 1970); L. Wittgenstein, *Blue and Brown Books* (Oxford, 1958); N. Wolterstorff, *Universals* (Chicago, 1970).

P. WEIGEL

UNREGENERATE KNOWLEDGE OF GOD

Good teaching proceeds from the known to the unknown. So a good apologist will want to have some idea of what an inquirer already knows about God. Do non-Christians have any knowledge of the true God? If so, what do they know? In what ways does that knowledge manifest itself?

Scripture says that unbelievers know God (Rom. 1:21), but it also says they do not know him (1 Cor. 2:14; 15:34; 1 Thess. 4:5; 2 Thess. 1:8; cf. 2 Tim. 3:7; Titus 1:16; 1 John 4:8). Evidently, then, we must make some distinctions, for in some sense or senses, knowledge of God is universal, and otherwise it is not.

Rom. 1:18–32 is the classic text on this question. Here Paul stresses the clarity of

God's *revelation to the unrighteous. God reveals his wrath to them (18), and makes *truth about himself 'plain to them' (19), 'clearly seen' (20). That revealed truth includes his 'eternal power and divine nature' (20). It also contains moral content, the knowledge of 'God's righteous decree that those who do such [wicked] things deserve death' (32). Significantly, the text does not state that this revelation in nature communicates the way of salvation. Paul evidently believes that this additional content must come through the *preaching of the gospel (Rom. 10:13–17). Thus he warrants the traditional theological distinction between general revelation (God's revelation of himself through the created world) and special revelation (his revelation through prophecy, preaching, and Scripture).

The knowledge given by general revelation is not only a knowledge *about* God, a knowledge of propositions. It is a knowledge of God himself, a *personal* knowledge. For Paul says, not only that the wicked have information about God, but that 'they knew God' (21).

Nevertheless, according to Paul, the wicked do not make proper use of this revealed knowledge. Rather, they 'suppress the truth by their wickedness' (18). He continues, 'Although they knew God, they neither glorified him as God nor gave thanks to him, but their thinking became futile and their foolish hearts were darkened. Although they claimed to be wise, they became fools' (21–22). Paul describes their foolishness as idolatry (22–23). In his view, idolatry is not an innocent search for the divine or the result of honest ignorance; it is, rather, willfully and culpably turning away from clear revelation of the true God. So it is 'exchanging the glory of the immortal God for images' (23), exchanging 'the truth of God for a lie' (25). Because the unrighteous wilfully turned from God's clear revelation, God 'gave them over' (24, 26, 28) to serious sin, particularly of a sexual nature. Even then, however, the original clear revelation continues to function, for it serves as a standard of judgment. As Paul says, it leaves them 'without excuse' (20).

From this passage, we can understand the senses in which the unregenerate do and do not know God. They know God as they are confronted by his revelation. Other scriptures tell us that this revelation is found not only in the natural world, but in their own persons, for we are all made in God's image (Gen. 1:27). So God's revelation is inescapable. But apart from the special revelation and saving grace of God, people exchange this truth for lies and engage in such wickedness that they become enemies of God, not friends.

It is the grace of God that turns this enmity into friendship, so that people come to know God in a higher sense than the knowledge of Rom. 1:21. This is the knowledge of God that Jesus equates with eternal life in John 17:3. Many other passages too describe various kinds of knowledge that presuppose saving grace, such as Rom. 15:14; 1 Cor. 1:5; 2:12; 2 Cor. 2:14; 4:6; 6:6; 8:7; Eph. 1:17; Phil. 1:9; 3:8; 3:10; Col. 1:10; 1 Tim. 2:4; 2 Tim. 1:12; Heb. 8:11; 2 Pet. 3:18; 1 John 2:3–5, 13, 20–21; 3:14–24; 4:2–16; 5:2, 13, 19–20; 2 John 1:1. The unregenerate do not have this kind of knowledge. In this sense should we understand the passages that say they do not know God.

There have been two different accounts of unregenerate knowledge of God in the theological traditions. One, advocated by *Thomas Aquinas, says that this knowledge comes through our natural reason. In Aquinas' view, natural reason is sufficient to accomplish our earthly happiness, but a higher, supernatural knowledge is required for eternal life. Natural reason operates apart from divine revelation, but supernatural knowledge is based on revelation, which functions as a supplement to what we know naturally.

Reformed theologians have objected to this view, saying that God never intended our natural reason to function autonomously, or apart from his revelation. For one thing. all human knowledge comes through revelation, either general or special or both. Further, even before the fall, God supplemented Adam's natural knowledge with verbal revelation. And after the fall our natural knowledge requires both general and special revelation for its proper functioning. Left to our own devices, as Rom. 1 teaches, we suppress and distort the truth of general revelation. Only God's grace, operating through the gospel given in special revelation, can enable us to see general revelation rightly. So *Calvin spoke of special revelation as the 'spectacles' by which we understand general revelation.

Calvinists, therefore, have been more pessimistic than Aquinas about the unbeliever's knowledge of God. Aquinas regarded the pagan *Aristotle as a paradigm of natural reason, and he followed Aristotle closely in his proofs for

God and in other philosophical and theological matters. Followers of Calvin, however, have generally not thought that we can learn much about God from non-Christians. And, since the knowledge of God is integral to all human knowledge, some Calvinists, like Abraham *Kuyper and Cornelius *Van Til, have argued that non-Christian thought is radically distorted even in relatively non-theological subject matter. Yet the Reformed tradition (with significant exceptions) has generally also accepted the doctrine of '*common grace', in which God restrains non-Christians from the full implications of their rebellion against him and thus preserves in them some inclination toward civic virtue and true beliefs.

On the Reformed view, unregenerate knowledge of God needs more than supplementation. It needs a radical reorientation. The work of the apologist is not merely to add information to what the unbeliever already knows. It is, rather, to 'take captive every thought to make it obedient to Christ' (2 Cor. 10:5). This will involve questioning the unbeliever's basic world-view, the most basic presuppositions of his or her thinking. So Reformed presuppositional apologists have spoken of an 'antithesis' between believing and unbelieving thought, corresponding to the biblical distinction between God's wisdom and the world's foolishness. It has been difficult, however, for them to reconcile and balance their doctrine of antithesis with the doctrine of common grace. If there is such an antithesis, so that the non-Christian opposes the truth of God at every point, how can we ascribe to the non-Christian any knowledge at all?

This question is addressed in chapters 15 and 16 of J. M. Frame, *Cornelius Van Til* (Phillipsburg, 1995). To summarize, agreements between believers and unbelievers are never perfect agreements; they are always agreements with a difference. Believer and unbeliever can agree that the sky is blue, but the unbeliever tries to see this fact as a product of matter, energy, and chance. Christian and Pharisee may agree that God requires Sabbath observance; but the Pharisee will fail to see the mercy of God in the commandment and therefore the appropriateness of healing. Non-Christians, in other words, may agree with Christians on various matters, but, seen as a whole, their understanding of God is seriously distorted, and apologists must deal with that distortion.

The remainder of this article will consider how unregenerate knowledge of God is obtained, how it is suppressed and in what ways it continues to function, despite its suppression.

Rom. 1:20 tells us that this knowledge is gained from God's revelation 'from what has been made', that is, the entire created world, including human beings themselves. But how do people obtain this knowledge from creation? Some apologists have thought that this knowledge comes about through rational activity, particularly through *theistic proofs and evidences. But this understanding would limit the knowledge of Rom. 1 only to those competent to understand and be persuaded by those arguments and evidences. Paul, however, sees this knowledge as universal. Rom. 1 begins the argument that leads in Rom. 3:10–20, 23 to the conclusion that all have sinned and stand in need of God's grace. So the knowledge of Rom. 1 renders all human beings inexcusable (20). If that knowledge were less than universal, the conclusion of Rom. 3 would not follow from it.

So the knowledge of God by creation evidently reaches all, even those who are not competent to formulate or evaluate proofs and evidences. Evidently, we discern the general revelation of God by some form of intuition, an intuition that some are able to articulate and defend by proofs and evidences, but which does not depend on them. Alvin Plantinga says that we come to believe in God when our rational faculties are operating as God intended, and when they are placed in an environment naturally conducive to the formation of theistic belief. No better explanation of the process has been offered to date.

How do people suppress the truth of this revelation? It is tempting to think of 'suppression' in psychological terms, as when someone relegates an unwelcome truth to his subconscious or unconscious, but that is not the biblical picture. The enemies of God in the Bible often consciously acknowledge the existence of God (e.g. the Egyptians, Exod. 14:4), but according to Rom. 1, the suppression is seen in idolatrous worship and illicit sexual behaviour. The unregenerate deny their knowledge of God by their ethical rebellion. When Scripture describes the knowledge of God that comes by grace, that knowledge is always accompanied by obedience and holiness. John says, 'We know that we have come to know him, if we obey his commandments'

(1 John 2:3). Thus Scripture closely relates *epistemology to *ethics.

So the difference between unregenerate and regenerate knowledge of God may be described as ethical. The unregenerate represses his knowledge of God by disobeying God. This disobedience may lead in some cases to psychological repression, or explicit *atheism, but it does not always. The apologist should recognize, therefore, that the unbeliever's problem is primarily ethical, not intellectual. He rejects the truth because he disobeys God's ethical standards, not the other way around.

This ethical rebellion does, however, always inject an element of irrationality into the thinking of the unregenerate. To know God and his commandments, even his eternal power, and yet to rebel against him, is supremely futile. In this sense, unbelief is foolishness (Ps. 14:1). Consider *Satan, who knows God in some respects better than we do, yet who seeks to replace God on the throne. In some ways, Satan is highly intelligent and knowledgeable, but in the most important sense, he is supremely irrational. It is important for the apologist to understand that in the final analysis the position of the non-Christian is like this, often intellectually impressive, but at a deeper level ludicrous.

Non-Christians' suppression of the truth is never complete. They can never eradicate the truth completely from their consciousness. If they could, they could not live at all. For this is God's world, and all the world's structure, order and meaning is God's work. Further, as we have seen, God's common grace restrains the non-Christian's distortions of the truth. So even Satan uses the truth for his own purpose, and there are some unregenerate human beings who are relatively orthodox.

We can therefore expect unbelievers' knowledge of God to bubble up at times through their consciousness, despite their attempts to repress that knowledge. This happens in several ways. Unbelievers may sometimes explicitly display quite a lot of knowledge of the true God; they must assume that the world is not chaotic but is orderly and relatively predictable, even though this assumption in turn presupposes God; and in ethics, non-Christians often reveal a knowledge of God's law. Apologists like C. S. *Lewis and J. Budziszewski have pointed out that principles like 'Play fair', 'Don't murder', 'Be faithful to your spouse', and 'Take care of your family' are universally recognized. Although

many people violate these principles, they show they know them by making excuses or rationalizations, and by accusing others of violating the same principles.

In other words, they treat the moral law as law. Although some theorize that moral principles are mere feelings, conventions or instincts, no-one really believes that, especially when injustice is done to them. When someone treats us unfairly, we regard that unfairness as an objective wrong. But objective wrongs cannot be derived from mere instincts, feelings, conventions, evolutionary defence mechanisms, etc. Moral rights and wrongs are based on personal relationships, specifically relationships of allegiance and love, and that means that absolute moral standards must be derived from an absolute person. So develops the '*moral argument for the existence of God', but that argument is based on *conscience, a sense of objective right and wrong that is universal, that exists even in those who do not formulate it as an argument. Budziszewski also points out the terrible consequences that result from violating one's conscience. Apologists should draw on the data of the unbeliever's conscience to lead him or her to that greater knowledge of God, which is eternal life in Christ.

Bibliography

J. Budziszewski, *The Revenge of Conscience* (Dallas, 1999); *What We Can't Not Know* (Dallas, 2003); J. Frame, *Apologetics to the Glory of God* (Phillipsburg, 1994); *Cornelius Van Til* (Phillipsburg, 1995); *The Doctrine of the Knowledge of God* (Phillipsburg, 1987); C. S. Lewis, *Mere Christianity* (London, 1952); A. Plantinga, *Warranted Christian Belief* (New York and London, 2000); R. C. Sproul, *If There's a God, Why Are There Atheists?* (Wheaton, 1988).

J. M. FRAME

URBANIZATION

Urbanization as a socio-cultural process has raised numerous issues relative to Christian belief and practice. Believers need a framework for grappling with the issues raised by this process, making urbanization a matter of concern for Christian apologetics.

Urbanization can be understood from two perspectives. On the one hand, it is a process by which large numbers of people come to be concentrated in relatively small areas called cities. From this perspective urbanization finds its roots in the Industrial Revolution, which began in the eighteenth century and by now has become fairly worldwide. From a second perspective, urbanization can be understood as the social and cultural changes that have emerged from the demographic concentration in urban areas. It is this second perspective which has had an impact on Christian belief and practice, for within urbanization 'what is apparent is an accelerating change in the nature of change itself, speedily rendering not-yet-conventional wisdom inappropriate at best' (B. J. Berry, *Comparative Urbanization*, p. xv). These accelerating changes in society raise several challenges to Christianity.

Urbanization challenges to Christianity

One of the primary challenges urbanization brings to Christian faith is *pluralism. Pluralism is not merely the co-existence of varying cultures, races and nationalities, but rather the existence and integration of discrepant worldviews that take place in urban communities, organizations and institutions. Thus the individual now works and lives in an environment characterized by a multiplicity of fundamental and often conflicting outlooks on God, life and *morality. Pluralism tends to raise challenges to two fundamental commitments of the Christian faith: the uniqueness of Christ and moral *absolutes (or *universals). Pluralistic milieus tend to create a psychological outlook that challenges the idea that Christ is the only way to God (i.e. *universalism), and the notion that there are moral absolutes and constants rooted in God's character and action and mediated through divine revelation.

A second challenge to Christian faith is the loss of community within increasing urban anonymity. As people move from small towns and rural areas to cities, there occurs a loss of natural *community, with its built-in structures of accountability and personal identity. In the midst of the urban crowd, individuals are easily lost, experience fewer natural constraints on behaviour, and often find the setting to be lonely, despite the teeming masses. The loss of community within urban anonymity is further understood through Georg Simmel's classic essay on urban *sociology. He notes that urban life has a profound psychological impact upon the individual in that the urbanite is constantly bombarded by external stimuli. There is an 'intensification of neurotic agitation', with the constant stimulation from events, people, noise and activity. Thus, says Simmel, 'the metropolitan type of man ... develops an organ protecting him against the threatening currents and discrepancies of his external environment which would uproot him. He reacts with his head instead of his heart' (*Sociology*, p. 410).

This psychological response to stimuli and the loss of natural community tends to move people from affectional acceptance to intellectualized grappling with the Christian faith. While this has the potential to deepen one's commitment to historic Christianity, it also has the potential to engender questioning or cynicism towards the underpinnings or truthfulness of Christian claims. Moreover, hardened hearts (in this case resulting from the external environment), can make intellectual acceptance a significant challenge, for the mind and the affections interact together. Beliefs are never merely intellectual.

A third challenge to faith from urbanization is the emergence and proliferation of social problems. As cities grew, the demographic and cultural shifts were accompanied by major social problems such as crime, poverty, prostitution, health concerns, labour disputes, and social conflict between races and nationalities.

Within the urban context, social problems have been increasingly accounted for on the basis of sociological and psychological factors rather than by traditional theological explanations of human sin or fallenness. This shift allows one to understand human and societal behaviour entirely on a naturalistic basis, thus challenging historic faith. As theological understandings are challenged in their explanation of certain behaviours, theological perspectives are no longer deemed necessary in postulating solutions to the problems. Thus personal regeneration through Christ and the presence of the Holy Spirit are replaced by exclusive emphases on changing the environment and social structures that contributed to the social ills.

Responding to the urbanization challenges

Classical forms of apologetics have largely depended on rational arguments in responding to the challenges to biblical faith. With urbanization, however, it is not clear that the traditional forms of apologetics will always be well suited to the challenges.

Certainly, rational arguments will always have their place in any era, but urbanization reminds us that apologetics must also look to other forms of validating and upholding Christian truth and practice. In the face of pluralism, loss of community and social problems, the most viable defence of the gospel may well be an incarnational one. That is, for modern and now postmodern urbanites, the Christian faith is best understood and substantiated by a community of people who themselves embody the world-view, values and commitments of the gospel. Such an embodiment gives substance to and experiential evidence for the uniqueness of the Christian faith.

The church itself, through its narratives, rational reflections, rituals, experiences and moral behaviour, is an apologetic for the urban world (D. P. Hollinger, 'Church as Apologetic', pp. 182–193). Ideally, the unbelieving world can see within the church the Christian world-view incarnate. This is not a new form of apologetics, for the early church apologists frequently appealed to the distinctive Christian way of life as the most compelling evidence for Christian truth.

Robert Jenson has suggested that, in a socio-cultural context that finds belief in Christ difficult, we must find a fitting response. 'If the church does not find her hearers antecedently inhabiting a narratable world, then the church must herself be that world ... If the church is not herself a real, substantial, living world to which the gospel can be true, faith is quite simply impossible' ('How the World Lost Its Story', p. 22).

Bibliography

B. J. Berry, *Comparative Urbanization: Divergent Paths in the Twentieth Century* (New York, 1964); D. P. Hollinger, 'The Church as Apologetic', in T. R. Phillips and D. L. Okholm (eds.), *Christian Apologetics in the Postmodern World* (Downers Grove, 1995); R. W. Jenson, 'How the World Lost Its Story', *First Things*, 36 (Oct. 1993), pp. 19–24; G. Simmel, *The Sociology of Georg Simmel*, ed. by K. H. Wolff (London, 1950).

D. P. HOLLINGER

USSHER, JAMES

James Ussher (1581–1656), educated and later professor of divinity at the newly founded Trinity College, Dublin, became the Archbishop of Armagh, chief cleric of the Anglican Church of Ireland. A scholar above all, of exceeding ability and erudition (e.g. he identified the seven authentic letters of Ignatius from the spurious), Bishop Ussher's many and diverse works on theology, history and chronology constitute a lifetime *apologia* for Elizabethan Anglicanism during the turbulent Tudor-Stuart-Commonwealth years. Ussher's driving concern was to justify intellectually the providential role of the Protestant Church of England (see *Christianity, Protestant) as the true apostolic church in the apocalyptic struggle with the papal Antichrist (Roman Catholicism; see *Christianity, Roman Catholic). Among his many arguments, this included the need for an exact chronology of world *history to map the fulfilment of prophetic history, which he painstakingly delivered in his *Annales Veteris et Novi Testamenti* (*Annals of the Old and New Testament*). This chronology was used in the marginal notes of the Authorized Version of the Bible from the early eighteenth to much of the twentieth century. Ussher today is narrowly known for his dating of the dawn of creation at noon, 23 October 4004 BC, the precision of which has long since paled in the light of biblical scholarship and has been totally eclipsed by scientific perspectives. It is a date, however, still congenial to young-earth creationists, as well as to those who hold, as Ussher himself did, to the 'millennium-day' theory. The latter, based on the formula 'a day is as a thousand years' (2 Pet. 3:8), holds that God's creating in six days and resting on the seventh portends a human history of 6,000 years before Christ's return and millennial reign (Rev. 20). Such reckoning helped to stoke the hype surrounding the recent turn of the millennium, which came and went without cosmic incident.

T. R. THOMPSON

UTILITARIANISM

Social and political decisions are often made on a utilitarian basis. The greatest happiness of the greatest number is a practical way of deciding what should be done. It involves calculating pleasure and pain and deciding the consequences of choices. Such an approach is deeply seated in Western thinking, decision-making and social policies. Christians are generally uneasy about utilitarianism on the grounds of its basis, complexity in practice, reductionism and injustice, though some see it as an extension of the Golden Rule and recognize that happiness is part of God's good will for humanity. A Christian apologetic will offer a critical analysis and reflect on the role and nature of happiness and *justice.

A critique

To be a utilitarian requires careful calculation. The problem is that there is no clear unit of measurement for either pleasure or pain. Most people think that alleviating pain is more morally important than giving pleasure. Pain and pleasure are not equivalent and cannot be set off against each other. To do the calculation requires not just the unit of measurement but a high level of rationality. The sheer complexity of decisions, trying to think through all the possible results and likelihoods, requires extreme rational abilities. These calculations are also difficult in that utilitarianism is concerned about consequences. There is a tension within utilitarianism over whether the focus is the motive and aim of producing pleasure, or the aim of maximizing happiness as the end result. Some would argue that the end does not always justify the means. Torturing people even to save other's lives is morally wrong, as some means are wrong in themselves.

The problem with any and all consequentialist approaches is that we cannot predict or control the consequences of what will happen or what we and others will do. What happened to the World Trade Center on 11 September 2001, an event that even informed commentators on the response of radical Islam to American foreign policy had not anticipated, shows that it is extremely difficult to calculate consequences.

To try to overcome many of these criticisms, utilitarianism has spawned many variations, such as act, rule and preference utilitarianism. It is debatable how far these actually solve the problems or rather amount to having to judge each and every act in terms of happiness. It can be shown that different versions can lead to very different conclusions, depending on how you do the calculation. Different definitions of pleasure, happiness, utility and its basis are areas for discussion. Preferences are not necessarily good and seeking pleasure is not in and of itself morally positive.

The major critique of utilitarianism rests on the injustice to which it may lead. The execution of an innocent person could be justified if it would lead to the greatest happiness of the greatest number. Christians will acknowledge that the death of Jesus on unjust grounds has led to the good news of the gospel and happiness for those who accept Christ. But this does not alter the fact that simply trying to make the majority happy may lead to injustice. The cost of doing so, such as treating a few badly and immorally, would be justified, on the utilitarian view, as long as greater happiness than pain resulted.

There is a tension here between concern for the individual and concern for the *community and majority. The vulnerability of individuals is matched with a concern that the good life should not be just a matter of seeking pleasure and avoiding pain. Most *morality seems to be a matter of duty, responsibilities and often having to do what is difficult and painful. Utilitarianism can be reductionist in that people just become pleasure-seekers and mere units of pleasure measurement rather than autonomous, morally complex human beings.

Happiness and justice

Christians believe that happiness is not simply pleasure-seeking, but a fulfilment of the whole person in relationship with God and with others. The contrast between the sheer physicality and reductionistic view of human being at the heart of utilitarianism and the need for the satisfaction and fulfilment of every aspect of the complex amalgam of body, soul, mind and spirit which is humanity is very great. Likewise, true happiness is not a matter of satisfying the appetites, whether they are physical or mental, but a matter of wholeness or shalom in the context of right relationships.

Part of that relationship is that we are not required to try to work out morality on our own, but rather to recognize that God has revealed moral standards, embodied them in Christ and enabled humanity to fulfil them by the grace and power of the Holy Spirit. God is concerned for human well-being and that involves justice. At the heart of human morality is the need for justice in human relationships.

Christian realism about human nature, our shortcomings and frailties, contrasts with the optimism of utilitarianism, which seems to overlook the selfishness of each of us and our lack of loving concern for others. The need for help in motivating people to do and be good and to be concerned for the well-being of others seems obvious in human relationships. It is unclear how utilitarianism can provide that motivation. J. S. *Mill seems to argue that we are by nature concerned for the greatest happiness of others and that seeking our own pleasure will lead to the greatest happiness of the greatest number. This seems extremely optimistic on both counts. Even if it were in fact true, such a description does not justify any moral prescription of how we ought to behave. Mill himself recognized that another principle of justice or equity was necessary to save utilitarianism. This move destroyed its alleged simplicity and opened the door to different perspectives on humanity, happiness and morality.

Without denying that happiness and pleasure are important aspects of human being and moral decision-making, it is vital to emphasize the complexity of human nature and morality. Duty, responsibilities and justice in our dealings with each other are part not only of a divinely inspired morality, but of any adequate account of human *ethics.

Bibliography

J. S. Mill, *Utilitarianism* (Oxford, 1998); J. J. C. Smart and B. Williams, *Utilitarianism: For and Against* (Cambridge, 1973).

E. D. COOK

VAN TIL, CORNELIUS

Cornelius Van Til (1895–1987), Reformed theologian and apologist, was born in Grootegast, Holland. At the age of ten, he moved with his family to Highland, Indiana. The Van Tils affiliated with the Christian Reformed Church, and Cornelius attended denominational schools, the Calvin Preparatory School, Calvin College and (for one year) Calvin Theological Seminary, all in Grand Rapids, Michigan. He transferred to Princeton Theological Seminary and earned his ThM there in 1925, followed by his marriage to Rena Klooster. He completed his PhD at Princeton University in 1927. His dissertation, supervised by Archibald Allan Bowman, compared Reformed theology's view of God with the absolute of philosophical Idealism.

Van Til pastored a Christian Reformed church in Spring Lake, Michigan, taking a leave of absence to teach apologetics at Princeton Seminary during the academic year 1928–9.

The seminary offered him the chair of apologetics at the end of that period, but he returned to Spring Lake. He loved the pastorate and did not want to cooperate in the reorganization of the seminary mandated that spring by the General Assembly of the Presbyterian Church, USA. He believed that reorganization would purge the seminary's historic stand for orthodox *Calvinism and make it more representative of liberal theological viewpoints in the church. Those viewpoints included that of the Auburn Affirmation of 1924, in which 1,300 ministers declared that such doctrines as biblical infallibility, the virgin birth of Christ, his substitutionary atonement, his bodily resurrection and his literal second coming were human 'theories', not to be required of ministerial candidates.

Others opposing the reorganization included J. Gresham *Machen, author of *Christianity and Liberalism*, who left Princeton Seminary with others in 1929 to found Westminster Theological Seminary of Philadelphia, a school devoted to Presbyterian doctrine, but independent of denominational control. Van Til also joined the new school. He taught apologetics and systematic theology there until his retirement in 1972 and continued to teach occasionally until 1979.

In 1936, Machen was suspended from the ministry of the Presbyterian Church, USA, for founding and supporting a non-denominational, theologically orthodox mission agency. He then founded, with others, a new denomination, originally called the Presbyterian Church of America, later the Orthodox Presbyterian Church. In sympathy with Machen, Van Til transferred his ministerial membership from the Christian Reformed Church to the new denomination, where he remained the rest of his life.

Major influences on Van Til's thought were the Dutch Reformed theologians, particularly Abraham *Kuyper, who emphasized that Christ is Lord of all areas of human life. Kuyper disparaged apologetics because he thought it tended to put human reason above Scripture. Van Til's teachers at Princeton, however, emphasized that Christianity has nothing to fear from rational scrutiny and is fully capable of rational defence. Van Til sought to do justice to both these insights, by developing an approach to apologetics that was rational, but based on a distinctively biblical concept of rationality.

Van Til's studies of Idealism convinced him that all human thought is governed by presuppositions. (Hence, Van Til is sometimes called a 'presuppositionalist', though he was not enthusiastic about that label.) Ultimate presuppositions, he believed, cannot be proved by usual methods, since they serve as the basis of all proof. But they can be proved 'transcendentally', by showing that they are necessary for all rational thought and must be true if there is to be any meaning or order in the world. Van Til sought to reconstruct Christian apologetics so that it would establish the Christian God as the presupposition of thought, rather than one rational conclusion among many.

He disparaged the 'traditional method' of establishing Christianity by *theistic proofs and historical evidences, because he believed that that tradition began with data considered intelligible apart from God and thereby tried to prove God's existence. On the contrary, he argued, if we concede that anything is intelligible apart from the God of Scripture, we have lost the battle at the outset. So we should, rather, use a transcendental method, showing that the various forms of non-Christian thought ('would-be autonomous reasoning', as he put it) amount to meaninglessness, that they can account for precisely nothing, and that the Christian world-and-life-view can make sense of everything. For Van Til, then, the Creator–creature distinction is the key to *metaphysics, *epistemology and *ethics.

Some critics said that Van Til left no room for the use of evidence in apologetics. He replied that evidence is useful when used within a *transcendental argument based on biblical presuppositions. But is this not circular, to prove Christianity on the basis of Christian presuppositions? Yes, said Van Til, in a sense. But then every system of thought is circular when arguing its most fundamental presuppositions (e.g. a rationalist can defend the authority of reason only by using reason), and the Christian circle is the only one that renders *reality intelligible on its own terms.

Non-Christian thought, Van Til argues, collapses into meaninglessness, because of the *noetic effects of sin. The unbeliever knows God (Rom. 1:18–21) but suppresses the *truth (1:18, 21–32). Therefore, there is an 'antithesis' between Christian and unbelieving thought, between the wisdom of God and the wisdom of the world. Although the unbeliever knows and states truth on occasion, he does

that only by being inconsistent with his presuppositions and by relying inconsistently on the Christian world-view, or, as Van Til put it, by 'borrowed capital'.

Van Til's publications exceeded 300, including nearly forty books. Some of the most important are listed below.

Bibliography

Most of Van Til's writings, plus many audio lectures and sermons, can be found on the CD-ROM, *The Works of Cornelius Van Til* (published by Labels Army Co., available from P & R Publishers). On that CD, and also available separately, is the most complete bibliography of Van Til's works, *A Guide to the Writings of Cornelius Van Til, 1895–1987*, by Eric D. Bristley.

G. L. Bahnsen, *Van Til's Apologetic: Readings and Analysis* (Phillipsburg, 1998); J. M. Frame, *Cornelius Van Til: An Analysis of His Thought* (Phillipsburg, 1995); J. G. Machen, *Christianity and Liberalism* (Grand Rapids, 1923); C. Van Til, *Christian Apologetics* (Phillipsburg, 1975); *The Defense of Christianity and My Credo* (Phillipsburg, 1971); *The Defense of the Faith* (Phillipsburg, 1955; revised and abridged, 1963).

J. M. FRAME

VEGETARIANISM

Vegetarians believe that human beings should not eat the flesh of animals. The Christian tradition has generally viewed vegetarianism as unnecessary, though it has been a common ascetic practice for particular individuals and communities. In recent years theologians have argued that Christianity must rethink its attitudes to animals, including whether Christians should be vegetarian.

The legitimacy of killing animals for food has been defended with reference to the dominion given to Adam and Eve over the animals (Gen. 1:28), the explicit permission to eat animals addressed to Noah (Gen. 9:3), Jesus' rejection of the significance of diet (Matt. 15:11), and Peter's vision of the cleanliness of all animals (Acts 10:9–16). Some heretical sects, such as the Manicheans, considered the material world evil and abstained from eating meat on the grounds that it defiled the soul. *Augustine and others rejected such fastidiousness, citing Paul's teaching to the

Corinthians that avoiding meat offered to idols is mere superstition (1 Cor. 8:4–6). Perhaps the most important influence on current Christian views of animals, however, is *Thomas Aquinas' appropriation of the work of *Aristotle. In his *Politics*, Aristotle claims that animals are made for the sake of human beings, just as plants exist for the sake of animals. Citing this text and supporting scriptural verses, Aquinas reasons that it cannot be a sin to use a thing for the purpose it was intended, so it must be lawful for human beings to kill animals (*Summa Theologiae* IIa IIae, q. 64 a. 1).

As a result of this dominant emphasis, the *animal rights movement has often seen Christian theology as part of the cause of disrespectful and unethical treatment of animals, rather than part of the solution. Theologians have responded to this criticism in two ways. Some have affirmed the right of human beings to make use of animals, but recognized that Christians should be concerned about reducing the suffering this causes to animals and proposed incremental measures such as regulating the distance animals travel before slaughter, or the conditions of veal production. A second response has been to look at whether the traditional view that animals were made to be used by humans is sustainable. In this context, theologians note that Adam and Eve were originally given only plants and trees for food (Gen. 1:29), that the prophets look forward to a time when killing animals will be unnecessary (e.g. Isa. 11:6–9), and that the permission to eat meat given to Noah in Gen. 9 seems to be a reluctant concession to human sin. Human beings and animals are frequently seen in solidarity: they are common participants in the covenant made with Noah (Gen. 9:8–17) and will share together in the redemption of creation (Rom. 8:19–23). God tells Job in no uncertain terms that human beings know little of God's purposes for the rest of creation (Job 38 – 41). Those looking again at the Christian tradition have also found dissenting voices that affirm the value of animals, including St Francis, St Bonaventure and St Catherine of Siena. Particularly notable is St Basil the Great's petition in the fourth century asking God to help us realize that animals live not for us alone but for themselves and for God.

While we cannot know all God's dealings with other species, the Genesis narrative makes clear that human beings have a particular responsibility and vocation with respect to the created order in general and animals in particular (Adam's naming of the animals, Gen. 2:19–20, is significant here). The key issue in deciding how Christians should respond to vegetarianism is the character of this vocation. The traditional interpretation of the dominion given to Adam and Eve interprets this special role as hierarchical *authority and *power over the rest of the created order, but there are good reasons to reject this in favour of a model of stewardship where the emphasis is responsibility for creation rather than power over it. Beyond debates about the meaning of Hebrew terms here, the authority given to human beings must be understood in NT Christological terms, where lordship means service (see Phil. 2:5–9). The hierarchical model gives rise to no difficulties for killing animals for food, since human beings are free to do what they like with creation. Other Christians understand the special vocation of human beings as service to animals and the created order, and maintain it is much harder to justify eating animals except when absolutely necessary. Inuit hunters, at least in the past, could legitimately claim that killing seals or whales was necessary for their survival, but there are few others who could not obtain all their nutritional requirements without killing animals.

Christian thought on this issue must recognize the significance of the brokenness of God's relationship with his creatures, and of the relationships between creatures, as a result of the fall. Human beings cannot attain a perfect relationship with creation: even by eating vegetables they compete for scarce resources that other creatures could have thrived on. There is no moral purity to be found in this sphere, then, but instead a demand to find responsible ways of living in this fractured world that witness to God's graciousness to all creation.

Bibliography

A. Linzey, *Animal Theology* (London, 1994); C. Pinches and J. B. McDaniel (eds.), *Good News for Animals? Christian Approaches to Animal Well-Being* (New York, 1993); P. Singer, *Animal Liberation* (London, 1995); Thomas Aquinas, *Summa Theologica IIa IIae* (ET, New York, 1918), q. 64 a. 1, 3.

D. L. CLOUGH

VERIFICATION AND FALSIFICATION

The growth in human knowledge over the past few centuries has inevitably led to specialization. For most of human history it has been possible for one person to have a reasonable grasp of all areas of knowledge, of geography and maths and chemistry and *ethics and so on. But now the amount of knowledge is far in excess of any individual's grasp.

Francis *Bacon (1561–1626) was impressed with the progress of 'scientific' discoveries in his day, but argued that progress was being hindered by a confusion of methodologies; scientists' thinking was still dominated by old and irrelevant ideas and patterns of thought. These metaphysical cobwebs needed to be cleared away; *science required a distinct methodology, based on observation and experiment and a process of induction. Nothing should be accepted as true unless it has been established by a patient and careful process of verification. In particular, besides examining instances that appear to support their theories, scientists must make a study of anything that appears to contradict or falsify them.

Not all scientists after Bacon followed his advice. But the principle of careful verification and openness to falsification gradually became a key element of the scientific approach, and its success encouraged people to try to apply it in areas of knowledge outside science. Bacon himself sought to apply it to *law. By the nineteenth century it was being applied to just about all areas, and it was seen to be a mark of modernity and academic virtuosity to approach, say, *history, *psychology and even *theology 'scientifically'.

Philosophically speaking, it was well known that conclusive verification was unattainable. The process of observation and experiment, even a lengthy series of confirmatory experiences, could never finally establish a scientific hypothesis as true. No process of induction can prove the truth of its conclusion, but in practice, the scientific approach was accepted as infallible because it was seen as giving us facts, 'scientific facts' which, in contrast to the ideas and concepts of other ways of establishing knowledge, were dependable and sure.

So, increasingly, the scientific way of establishing *truth became the *paradigm for all areas of knowledge. The American pragmatist C. S. Peirce (1839–1914), for example, based a philosophical theory of knowledge on his experience as a professional scientist. His 'pragmatist principle' was designed to enable us to establish the meaning of an 'intellectual conception', and, derivatively, to test the truth of any given proposition and so to identify 'empty' metaphysical claims. Meaning is established, he said, by considering 'what practical consequences might conceivably result by necessity from the truth of that conception'; the sum of the consequences are 'the entire meaning of the conception'. The truth of a proposition is established by a thorough process of testing; it is established if it is 'ultimately agreed to by all who investigate'; what is established by universal agreement is 'the real'. If a hypothesis turns out to have no consequences following from it that we can test, then we are justified in dismissing it as 'empty'.

The move to apply the scientific methodology to all areas of human knowledge culminated in the short-lived but strident philosophical movement known as *logical positivism, which arose in Vienna in the 1920s and 1930s among a group of scientists and thinkers known as the Vienna Circle. Their approach was popularized in Britain by A. J. Ayer (1910–89) mainly through his book *Language, Truth and Logic* (1936). After the 1950s the movement declined rapidly.

Like Bacon, the logical positivists were implacably opposed to anything 'metaphysical', i.e. anything that could not be established on the principles of *logic and science. They saw their task as the elimination of *metaphysics and the establishing of a total world-view that was built on the methodology of science alone.

Starting from a basic assumption that the only source of knowledge is what we experience through our senses, they concluded that for any assertion to be meaningful it must be either analytic or such that it can be verified through some experience or observation. An analytic statement is one whose truth or falsehood depends entirely on the terms it contains, such as 'All bachelors are unmarried'. To have meaning, any non-analytic statement must be verifiable, and if it is not verifiable it is meaningless. It is non-sense, i.e. it makes no sense, it does not communicate. Though it appears to say something, it in fact says nothing at all.

To clarify their concept of verification, the logical positivists developed what they called the verification principle. At first this was stated in a 'strong' form, requiring conclusive verification, either actual or potential. So, for the statement 'This tree is 50 ft tall' to be meaningful it must be at least possible to measure it definitively and so prove conclusively that it is 50 ft tall. This, however, was too strict a definition, since it was clear that most scientific principles could never be conclusively verified.

A modified form of the principle replaced conclusive verifiability with conclusive falsifiability. Though we can never establish the proposition, 'All metals expand when heated', it is conceivable that we might discover a metal that contracts when heated, thus conclusively falsifying it. Given that, it can be accepted as meaningful. However, this form of the verification principle proved to be inadequate, since, as philosophers well know, it is always possible to bring in sceptical arguments about dreaming or hallucinating or a malignant demon to challenge the concept of conclusive falsifiability. How can we be conclusively certain we are not hallucinating when we observe the contraction of this special metal?

So the verification principle had to be pared down yet further, to a 'weak' form which simply said that for a statement to be meaningful it must be possible to think of some empirical evidence which could have a bearing on its truth or falsity. This seems a workable principle, but it turned out to be inadequate for the purposes of the logical positivists.

There was a further problem with the verification principle in that, for all its usefulness in eliminating metaphysical statements, it turned out itself to be nothing short of a metaphysical statement, in that it cannot be empirically verified. For all its dogmatism, logical positivism was not able to exist without metaphysics.

Despite its philosophical weaknesses, logical positivism was seen at the time as launching a formidable attack on all forms of metaphysics and especially on Christian theology. Applying the verification principle, Ayer specifically dismissed all the statements and concerns of metaphysics, theology, ethics, aesthetics and other issues of value as meaningless; thus all the problems associated with them are unreal and can be ignored. Ayer conceded that moral statements and value judgments and the like do appear to be meaningful, in that they do seem to communicate something. But, in keeping with his definition, he still insisted that they were meaningless and that the appearance of

meaning arises because these statements express our feelings or emotions. If I say 'Murder is wrong', I am expressing my negative feelings about murder, no doubt with the hope that whoever hears me will also feel negative about murder. But I am not actually saying anything meaningful.

Quite apart from the philosophical weaknesses in the logical positivists' approach, its popularity waned rapidly because of two additional features. The first was a growing dissatisfaction with such a reductionist worldview, coupled with a growing disillusionment with logic and science as the sole arbiters of all thought and knowledge. Many thinkers in the second half of the twentieth century realized that to dismiss issues of morals, values, aesthetics and metaphysics as meaningless was to take the heart from what it means to be human. The scientific world-view reduces us to machines. We are not machines, however, and there is far more to human life than the scientific.

The second feature was the development of science itself and of the philosophical understanding of what science is actually doing. Elements of subnuclear physics, for example, did not appear to follow the standard scientific paradigm assumed by logical positivism, and by the 1960s philosophers of science were realizing that the traditional stress on the rationality of the scientific world-view was open to serious challenge. The replacing of the *Newtonian world-view by the Einsteinian was a salutary lesson that a set of beliefs hailed by scientists as definitively established could, in the end, turn out to be false.

The debate over verification and falsification raises two major issues for Christian apologetics. The first is the extent to which we should expect or attempt to provide verification for our claims. The second is the issue of falsification. Should we concede that our claims could be shown to be false?

Christianity and verification

Though logical positivism itself has declined in popularity, there are still many who assume that the scientific criteria for meaningfulness or truth are ultimate and universal, and are quick to dismiss Christianity as a result. In presenting the case for the truth of Christianity it is open to the Christian apologist to begin by challenging such people's basic rationalist or empiricist presuppositions, or, alternatively, to choose to make a case for the truth of Christianity more or less from within those presuppositions, without, of course, having to concede that they are ultimately valid. One such approach might be to point out that it is in fact possible to provide at least some of the required verification for the meaningfulness and truth of Christian claims. 'Scientifically controlled' experiments have been conducted, for example, to test the effectiveness of prayer, giving rise, with some justification, to the conclusion that the claim that 'prayer works' is both meaningful and true. *Religious experience itself can be taken as a form of verification. I draw near to God; he draws near to me. Such verification is not to be expected to have the exact precision of a laboratory experiment; it is more like verifying the claim that 'September days in England are cooler than August days'. But some form of verification is seen as possible.

An alternative response is to insist that the validity of the verification approach as advocated by the positivists is limited to the area of science, or, at any rate, has no application in the area of Christian theology. This response could be a form of *fideism, claiming that religious convictions neither have nor require rational support. Or it could be a more *Wittgensteinian recognition that though the principles of verification that operate in the scientific sphere are inappropriate in the religious sphere, nevertheless Christian apologists can justifiably use appropriate religious verification. As *Pascal said, 'The heart has its reasons which reason does not know.' Thus within the religious sphere, or, more specifically, in the religious *community, there are criteria for verifiability which are specific to that sphere or community. So, for example, 'I heard God's voice' would be verified according to the community's understanding of what it means for God to communicate, rather than in terms of measuring decibels.

Thirdly, many Christians would claim that though some aspects of Christianity by their nature are beyond scientific verification, there is much that is not. God has intervened in history, he has acted in the world, and the events of salvation history are as open to 'scientific' testing as any events in history. The case for the resurrection of Christ, for example, can be established by the evidence concerning the empty tomb.

A fourth response would be to allow that the demand for verification is a valid one, but should not be applied piecemeal to the specific statements or beliefs of Christianity. Rather it is the whole package that should be subjected to verification. The total Christian world-view, with its manifold implications in every area of human life and understanding, should be assessed. Does it work? Is it consistent with our experience? Does it fit the facts? Is it comprehensive? Does it answer the questions that life raises? Does it do these things better than alternative world-views? We can hardly expect final and definitive answers to these kind of questions, but it may well be that they can offer a degree of verification of the Christian world-view as a whole.

Christianity and falsification

Should Christian apologists concede they they may be wrong, i.e. that their claims are falsifiable? There is a strong case that they should, though it needs to be emphasized that saying this in no way impugns their sincerity or their total conviction that their claims never will in fact be falsified. I am totally convinced of the reality of the external world around me and have every right to seek to persuade a doubter that it is really there. But, philosophically speaking, in the last analysis I have to concede that my belief in a real external world may be false. All my life may have been a dream; I may be a brain in a vat.

The problem with setting our Christian beliefs totally beyond falsification is that in so doing we implicitly allow any other set of beliefs the same incorrigible status. There is no way we can show that believers in the Great Pumpkin are mistaken. We are locked into the worst sort of subjective fideism. In order to be able to challenge other beliefs, we need to allow our beliefs to be open to challenge.

In what way might we concede that the Christian world-view is potentially falsifiable? Antony *Flew, in a historic discussion towards the end of the period of logical positivism, asked, 'What would have to occur or to have occurred to constitute for you a disproof of the love of, or of the existence of, God?' While conceding that many events, such as the Holocaust, might appear to cast doubts on these things, apologists would claim that they are not conclusive disproofs, since a loving God may transform their evil into greater good. But they could certainly concede some form of eschatological falsification; it is conceivable that in the next life we should discover that

God is, after all, totally evil, or, just possibly, that he does not exist. An alternative line of falsification is hinted at in Paul's words, 'if Christ has not been raised, your faith is futile' (1 Cor. 15:17). If it were established beyond all reasonable *doubt that Christ never lived or that the resurrection never happened, our faith would be falsified.

For Christian apologists to concede that some such falsification is philosophically conceivable in no way reduces their commitment to the truthfulness of the Christian world-view. There is no contradiction between saying, 'If it were to be shown that the resurrection never happened, the claims of the gospel would be shown to be empty', and saying, 'In fact Christ has been raised from the dead and the gospel is true.' Any concessions we may make to those who demand the possibility of potential falsification can be made in the complete confidence that the truth of the gospel never will in fact be falsified.

Bibliography

A. J. Ayer, *Language, Truth and Logic*, 2nd edn (London, 1946); A. Flew *et al.*, 'Theology and Falsification', in A. Flew and A. MacIntyre, *New Essays in Philosophical Theology* (London, 1955).

P. HICKS

VIRGIN BIRTH, see DIVINE BIRTH STORIES
VIRTUAL REALITY, see CYBERSPACE
VISIONS, see TRANSCENDENCE, SIGNS OF

VOLLENHOVEN, DIRK HENDRIK THEODOOR

D. H. T. Vollenhoven (1892–1978), a Dutch *Calvinist philosopher, theologian and mathematician, pioneered, together with his brother-in-law Herman *Dooyeweerd, the philosophical tradition once called 'cosmonomic philosophy', now referred to as Reformational thought. Both started to work on this project well before their appointment to the Free University in Amsterdam in 1926.

Vollenhoven started his career as a pastor. He articulated most of his systematic philosophical conceptualizations in a short summary known as *Isagogie* or *Introduction*, written primarily because he taught introductory philosophy to all incoming students. His appointment was focused in history of philosophy, and that work gave him the reputation of devoting his career to a systematization of the history of philosophy as a network of interrelated ontologies, cosmologies and anthropologies. Each philosopher was primarily understood in terms of a *type* of ontology and then distinguished from others who shared that ontology by the *spirit* of the time in which the ontology was worked out. This spirit of the time Vollenhoven characterized as the prevailing religious orientation of the philosopher to whatever essentially determined the fundamental nature of all *reality. By following types as constancies through time, and prevailing spirits as successive periods, he constructed a table of a rich historical variety of interrelated philosophical conceptions that differs markedly from the division of historical philosophies into materialist or idealist, rationalist or empiricist, and other overly simple divisions.

Vollenhoven was known for his irenic spirit and his exemplary piety. These traits induced him to stop working on certain developments in Reformational thought that potentially conflicted with the views of the then dominant Reformed theology. For most of his life he was chair of the Association for Calvinistic Philosophy. As a Reformational philosopher he differed from Dooyeweerd on important points, published after the death of both in the *Report on Divergencies*. Perhaps most important was their difference concerning God's law as it determined creation. Vollenhoven placed more stress on that law as law of love, and less on law as order of creation. Hence, contrary to Dooyeweerd, he had room for an evolving universe because the order of things was not already fixed before things came to be.

Three North American philosophers received their PhD degrees under Vollenhoven and also continued his work, viz. H. Evan Runner, Calvin G. Seerveld and Hendrik Hart. Seerveld in particular made creative use of the historical method developed by his teacher. Other philosophers who continued his work are James Olthuis, Robert Sweetman and John Kok.

Bibliography

D. H. T. Vollenhoven, *Calvinism and the Reformation of Philosophy* (Amsterdam, 1933); *History of Philosophy*, vol. 1

(Franeker, 1950); *Necessity of a Christian Logic*, (Amsterdam, 1932); *Introduction to Philosophy*, ed. J. H. Kok and A. Tol (Iowa, 2005).

H. HART

VOLTAIRE

François-Marie Arouet, usually known as Voltaire (1694–1778), is often taken to embody the French *Enlightenment of the eighteenth century. In a clever, readable, diversified authorship, he advanced a form of rational, enlightened humanism, designed to promote progress and benevolence. This he contrasted to the teaching and practice of the church, which mounted superstitious beliefs and tyrannous practices on the back of Scriptures peppered with fallacies, absurdities and immoralities. Nowhere was the Enlightenment attack on the church fiercer than in France, and nowhere was it pressed more pointedly than in the work of Voltaire. In terms of the guild of classical philosophers, he is not in the front rank, but he knew how to make his points and, along with other *philosophes* of the time, he favoured a candid and practical presentation over the lumbering treatises of theorists. 'Never will twenty-folio volumes produce a revolution; it is the portable little books of thirty sous which are to be feared.'

Voltaire was not irreligious. He was strongly influenced at an early stage by what he witnessed in England, whose political freedoms he envied and whose philosophical, scientific and religious thinkers (*Locke, *Newton, Samuel *Clarke) he profoundly admired. English deism encouraged his own brand of deism, essentially a rational and natural religion. He was thus neither a sceptic nor a materialistic atheist in the fashion of many of his intellectual compatriots, and he publicly opposed, for example, the *naturalism of Baron Paul d'Holbach (1723–89). Voltaire's understanding of divine providence was reflected or shaped in response to the Lisbon earthquake of 1755. Its major literary expression is probably his best-known work, *Candide* (1759), which satirizes the claim that this is the best of all possible worlds, associated especially with the great German philosopher, *Leibniz (1646–1716). Its conception was simple and its execution effective.

It is tempting to dismiss Voltaire today as the product of a superficial Enlightenment *rationalism that is increasingly a spent force in a postmodern era. One should not. His work clearly indicates why Christianity became socially and intellectually discredited in many European eyes. Further, perceptions of the Bible of the kind found in Voltaire accompany or underlie many contemporary critiques of Christianity. His work, therefore, commands apologetic attention in principle, even if we shall not meet it at the front line of engagement, and constitutes a constant reminder that intellectual claims against Christian teaching have been historically allied to moral complaints against ecclesiastical practice.

Bibliography

A. O. Aldridge, *Voltaire and the Century of Light* (Princeton, 1975); T. Besterman, *Voltaire* (Oxford, 1976); I. O. Wade, *The Intellectual Development of Voltaire* (Princeton, 1969).

S. N. WILLIAMS

WAR, see PACIFISM

WARFIELD, BENJAMIN BRECKINRIDGE

Benjamin Warfield (1851–1921) was born into a wealthy family on their estate near Lexington, Kentucky. After graduating from the College of New Jersey (later Princeton University) in 1871, Warfield toured Europe for a year before announcing his desire to train for the Presbyterian ministry. In 1876, following his studies at Princeton Seminary, he married Annie Pierce Kinkead and they travelled to Europe. During this visit, they were caught in a violent thunderstorm and Warfield's wife was so severely traumatized that she never fully recovered. For the next forty years, Warfield faithfully cared for his semi-invalid wife and was never away from their home for more than a few hours at a time. Warfield served briefly as assistant minister before teaching New Testament at Western Theological Seminary near Pittsburgh. After nine years, he moved to Princeton Seminary, where he taught didactic and polemic theology for the next thirty-five years.

A prolific author, Warfield became one of the most distinguished Reformed theologians in America and, years after his death, continues to exercise a considerable influence on evangelical theology. Warfield is perhaps best known for his polemic work on the divine inspiration of Holy Scripture, which he articulated most famously in an essay written in 1881 with A. A. Hodge. While restating many points previously expressed by various Princeton writers, this article displayed a new precision in expounding the doctrine of *biblical inspiration and an impressive ability to engage with the latest higher-critical theories. Warfield asserted that the Scriptures not only contain, but are, the Word of God and hence are absolutely errorless in their original autographs.

Although Warfield's writings on inerrancy remained influential among evangelicals throughout the twentieth century, he has come under attack in recent years from some evangelical writers. They claim to trace a strongly rationalist tone in his writings which, they believe, flowed from *Scottish common sense philosophy. This philosophy permeated nineteenth-century Princeton, and Warfield certainly absorbed much of it from studying under James *McCosh. However, it is questionable that he allowed it to control his thinking, much less shape his theology; for, alongside Warfield's strong emphasis on reason, was a piety which involved a stirring-up of the heart, will and emotions, and he remained a firm advocate of supernaturalism in Christianity.

For Warfield, attempting to harmonize scientific developments with Scripture (such as accepting a modified version of evolution) owed less to *rationalism and more to the outworkings of the Reformed faith. Indeed, defending traditional *Calvinism, with its stress on our need of grace, was his overriding concern. He criticized both liberals for their *naturalism and evangelical enthusiasts for their perfectionism, believing that both exalted human ability and thereby diminished God's glory.

Bibliography

B. B. Warfield, *Works of Benjamin B. Warfield*, 10 vols. (New York, 1927–31; Grand Rapids, 1981); M. Noll (ed.), *The Princeton Theology 1812–1921* (Grand Rapids, 1983); M. Noll and D. Livingstone (eds.), *B. B. Warfield on Evolution, Science and Scripture* (Grand Rapids, 2000); D. Wells (ed.), *The Princeton Theology* (Grand Rapids, 1989).

B. FOLLIS

WATTS, ALAN

Alan Watts (1915–73) was one of the most influential Western writers on Eastern spirituality and perhaps the most significant figure to contribute to the introduction of Eastern religious ideas to the West. Best known for his work on Zen *Buddhism, he also wrote about Vedanta and Daoism. Although it is apparent to anyone who takes the time to read his work that he had a deep understanding of the traditions about which he wrote, he has often been criticized for failing to study sacred texts in their original languages and, more importantly, for not treading the disciplined, often ascetic, path followed by many devotees.

Watts was born to Christian parents on 6 January 1915, in Kent, England, and from an early age his mother spoke to him about the Orient and particularly about missionaries in China. This led to an interest in both Christian theology and also Eastern religion and culture. While attending the King's School, close to Canterbury Cathedral, he decided that his future was in the church. However, also during this period, the teenage Watts began pursuing his interest in Eastern thought. He began attending the Buddhist Lodge, where he soon met the influential Japanese Zen Buddhist layman D. T. Suzuki (1870–1966). Greatly impressed by Suzuki, at the age of sixteen he produced his first essay for the journal of the Buddhist Lodge, *The Middle Way* (of which he would soon become the editor).

In 1938 Watts married Eleanor Everett and moved to New York. While fascinated with Eastern spirituality, his early interest in the priesthood had not left him. In 1941 he enrolled at the Seabury Western Theological Seminary in Evanston, Illinois, and in 1944 was finally ordained, becoming Episcopal Chaplain at Northwestern University. However, six years later, in 1950, he left both the church and his wife, and, after a short time in New York, moved to California with his second partner, Dorothy Dewitt, to take up a teaching position at the Academy of Asian Studies in San Francisco. From this time on, Watts wrote some of the most influential works on Zen Buddhism ever produced in the West, the most significant being *The Way of Zen* (1958) and the pamphlet *Beat Zen, Square Zen, and Zen* (1959). In 1960 he made a national television series in America, *Eastern Wisdom and Modern Life*, which marked the beginning of his rise to fame as the guru of the counterculture movement. Perhaps more than anyone else, it was Watts who turned young Western minds towards the East during the sixties.

Central to Watts's spirituality is the notion of faith as openness. One should not have faith in God, the Buddha, religious texts, or indeed anyone else. Rather faith is a state of being open to the truth, whatever that might be. It is not a matter of obedience, of 'keeping the faith', of clinging to God, but of letting go, of contemplation, of non-attachment, of waiting. And, as he describes in *The Joyous Cosmology* (1962), psychedelic *drugs can assist this form of 'faith', in that they facilitate consciousness expansion. (It should be noted that, unlike Timothy *Leary, Watts's use of hallucinogens was very limited, his interest being far more focused on the development of spirituality.)

True faith leads to an understanding of the true self. Deeper than an individual's superficial self, with its appetites and desires, there is the true self. An awareness of this self leads to the realization that one's self is continuous with the whole of existence. You are all that exists. There is no transcendent God standing over against the self – the self is divine and eternal. Therefore, in his writings Watts consistently presents an explicit challenge to the Judeo-Christian 'monarchical image of God, with its implicit distaste for religious insubordination'. Watts speaks passionately of oneness with God and the universe. Making much of *Jesus' claims to divinity in the Gospel of John, he argues that Jesus taught that all humans are divine: 'the Gospel of Jesus . . . was simply, "Wake up everybody and find out who you are!" . . . It is important for the human being to realize that . . . he is God or one with God, as is plainly taught by the Hindus and hinted at by the Buddhists.'

From the perspectives of Christian theology – especially the doctrines of creation, sin and salvation, which assume a clear distinction both between God and the created order and also between God and humanity – there are some fundamental issues that Watts's thought fails to address. Watts's philosophy, variations of which can be found in much contemporary alternative spirituality, collapses the divine into the human and thereby undermines Christian soteriology. Of course, it should be remembered that, although Watts began his theological reflection from within a Christian context, he was not seeking to construct a Christian theology. Hence, although he appreciated Jesus' contribution to spirituality (as many alternative religionists do), he radically reinterpreted the significance of Christ and the message of the Gospels from an Eastern perspective. Christ and other Christian doctrines are detraditionalized, i.e. they are detached from their original contexts and reinterpreted in terms of a Westernized form of Eastern self-spirituality. Hence, Jesus becomes a reflection of the sacralized self.

Bibliography

A. Watts, *The Culture of Counter-culture* (Boston, 1997); *The Joyous Cosmology* (New York, 1962); *This is It* (New York, 1962); *The Way of Zen* (Harmondsworth, 1962).

C. H. PARTRIDGE

WEBER, MAX

Max Weber (1865–1920), the German political economist and sociologist, exercised a formative influence on the social sciences for much of the twentieth century.

He was born in Erfurt, the son of a lawyer and politician who became a National-Liberal member of the Prussian House of Deputies. Both his parents came from religious families and Weber's mother (to whom he was closest) was a liberal Lutheran. Eventually obtaining a law degree from Berlin, Weber also studied at Heidelberg and Göttingen. He held faculty positions in political economy at Freiburg (1895) and then accepted a similar position at Heidelberg a year later. Weber battled depression, a condition that became so debilitating between 1897 and 1903 that it kept him from academic work.

Though influenced by the systems of *Hegel, Marx and the utilitarians, Weber reacted against grand theories and stressed that sociologists must focus primarily on the actions of individuals. Instead of uncovering universal laws, Weber sought to understand how human actors interpreted their actions within the larger social context. Unlike Marxian analysts, he was confident that social scientists could practise a 'value-free' method if they avoided mixing their mores and concerns with those of their subjects.

One of his most important works, *The Protestant Ethic and the Spirit of Capitalism* (appearing in German first in 1904/5) modelled Weber's distinctive approach to the *sociology of religion. Here, Weber sought to explain the relationship between economic development and otherworldly religious beliefs. Probing the Reformed emphasis on predestination, Weber concluded that the Calvinist laity responded to the uncertainty of their election with frenetic activity to confirm their calling. What Weber termed their 'inner-worldly asceticism' gave believers a measure of assurance and prompted them to transform their surroundings. Weber followed this study with works on non-Western religions in a parallel attempt to reveal the social and economic ramifications of certain religious beliefs. His last major study, *Wirtschaft und Gesellschaft* (published posthumously in 1922), dealt with (among other subjects) the different forms of domination that distinguished the exercise of authority. Weber identified three ideal types as charismatic, traditional and legal. Subsequent scholars sometimes employed these types in an ahistorical way foreign to Weber.

Weber's thinking has exercised an enormous influence among academics; his idea of a value-free social science was taken up and reshaped by positivist-minded social scientists who held sway in academia until the 1960s. His interpretation of the relationship between Protestantism (see *Christianity, Protestant) and *capitalism was controversial and continues to stimulate scholarly debate. Although Weber's debt to Christian thought has been largely ignored, a recent study concluded significantly that 'his work ... arose from a religious stimulus that consciously acknowledged the value of a Christian world view, and that he worked throughout his life on problems set for him by his faith tradition' (Swatos and Kivisto). Weber's work illuminated how what he termed a modern 'disenchantment of the world' could undercut traditional faith. Christians can garner many insights from Weber's analysis of the problematic nature of modernity and it implications for religious belief.

Bibliography

R. Bendix, *Max Weber: An Intellectual Portrait* (1960); P. Honigsheim, 'Max Weber: His Religious and Ethical Background and Development', *Church History*, 19, pp. 219–239; A. Mitzman, *The Iron Cage: An Historical Interpretation of Max Weber* (1985); W. H. Swatos and P. Kivisto, 'Max Weber as "Christian Sociologist"', *Journal for the Scientific Study of Religion*, 30 (1991); M. Weber, *The Protestant Ethic and the Spirit of Capitalism* (1930); *The Sociology of Religion* (1963).

G. HARP

WELLHAUSEN, JULIUS

Julius Wellhausen (1844–1918) is undoubtedly the single most influential figure in modern OT scholarship. He was professor at Greifswald, Halle and Marburg, before moving to Göttingen in 1892, where he remained until forced to retire because of poor health in 1913. His reputation rests on his *History of Israel*, which appeared in 1878 and went through several subsequent editions, beginning in 1883. All these later versions bear the longer title *Prolegomena to the History of Israel*, which is how the work is generally cited today.

Wellhausen's genius was his ability to take the theory that the *Pentateuch, the heart of OT religion, was a composite of different sources, and weave them into a credible 'documentary hypothesis'. This hypothesis has been challenged and modified many times over since Wellhausen's day, but in spite of this, his version of it remains the starting point for all modern Pentateuchal criticism. Wellhausen began with the existing theory that the Pentateuch had at least four distinct sources, E (the 'Elohist'), J (the 'Yahwist'), P (the 'priestly writers') and D (the 'Deuteronomist'). But instead of accepting the generally held view that the Elohist represented the basic strand or *Grundschrift*, Wellhausen claimed that this honour belonged to a priestly code which was largely co-extensive with, but not identical to, P. He also believed that someone had combined E and J before they were merged into the *Grundschrift* and that D was essentially the text that the high priest Hilkiah supposedly found in the temple in 621 BC.

Wellhausen believed that P could not have been composed before the exile, and therefore inclined to a late dating of the Pentateuch, though of course he recognized that many strands in it went back to a much earlier period. He also downplayed the role of oral tradition in the process of transmission, preferring to rely on the existence of a series of earlier documents. Given that writing was then regarded as a fairly late development, this inevitably distanced the texts in time from the events which they purported to describe. Wellhausen accepted that someone like Moses had existed, but he did not believe that that figure had had anything to do with the composition of the Pentateuch.

Criticism of Wellhausen's theory has centred mainly around his late dating of P, and the modern realization that writing was much older than previously thought has supported those who advocate an earlier, pre-exilic dating scheme. But even so, Wellhausen's hypothesis retains enormous influence, and may be said to have made all previous study of the question redundant.

Bibliography

D. A. Knight (ed.), 'Julius Wellhausen and his *Prolegomena to the History of Israel*', *Semeia*, 25 (1982); E. W. Nicholson, *The Pentateuch in the Twentieth Century: The Legacy of Julius Wellhausen* (Oxford, 1998).

G. L. Bray

WHITEHEAD, ALFRED NORTH

Alfred North Whitehead (1861–1947) was one of the most creative philosophers of the twentieth century. Born in Kent, Whitehead was educated at Trinity College, Cambridge, and taught mathematics there for twenty-five years. His early publications culminated in the three-volume *Principia Mathematica* (1910, 1912, 1913), written with his former student, Bertrand *Russell. After moving to University College, London, he went on to Harvard University from 1924 to 1937, where he turned his attention to *metaphysics. Among his many publications in philosophy, his *magnum opus* was *Process and Reality* (1929).

Metaphysics and God

Whitehead produced a unique system to reflect the new scientific reality of Einstein's theories about space and time. The foundational elements of the process of *reality are events. Each takes the form of the previous one and becomes itself by a novel coming together by its own subjective form. This totality of process is God in his finite 'consequent' nature of physical experiencing. This demands the reality of a mental, 'primordial', absolute pole, which contributes the initial aims of each

event. Thus Whitehead thinks of God as bi-polar and the resulting system is panentheistic: the universe is God, but God is more than it. Every event is God's action and yet also uniquely its own determination.

Theological influence

Whitehead has had little influence in philosophy itself. However, along with Charles Hartshorne, his views produced a process theology. This system seeks to provide solutions to several intractable problems in apologetics by seeming to offer a God more intimately related to human beings, persons who are freely co-creating, and an easier solution to the problem of *evil.

John Cobb, Schubert Ogden, Norman Pittenger, Lewis Ford and others have worked out a theological system that has been attractive to some evangelicals. There are, however, several difficulties which would prevent any application to evangelical theology. First, Whitehead's bipolar God, in addition to the general logical problem of a being both finite and infinite, cannot be squared with a sovereign Creator, distinct from the universe. Second, since God contributes only the initial causality of an event, process theology forfeits Scripture as uniquely inspired. Third, panentheists, for similar reasons, reject the incarnation. This event cannot be any more divinely instigated than any other. Finally, in rejecting Christ's deity, process theology lacks a *Trinity.

One can hardly imagine a list of doctrines more crucial to evangelical theology, and since all of panentheism's attractions are integral parts of a total metaphysics, one cannot simply pick out the bits and pieces one likes.

Bibliography

J. Bracken and M. Suchocki (eds.), *Trinity in Process* (New York, 1997); D. Brown, R. E. James and G. Reeves (eds.), *Process Philosophy and Christian Thought* (Indianapolis, 1971); J. Cobb and D. R. Griffin, *Process Theology: An Introductory Exposition* (Philadelphia, 1976; Belfast, 1977); L. Ford, *The Lure of God* (Philadelphia, 1978); L. Ford, *Transforming Process Theism* (New York, 2000); R. Gruenler, *The Inexhaustible God* (Grand Rapids, 1984); C. Hartshorne, *Man's Vision of God and the Logic of Theism* (Chicago, 1941); V. Lowe, *Understanding Whitehead* (Baltimore, 1966); S. Ogden, *The Reality of God* (London, 1966); N. Pittenger,

The Word Incarnate (New York, 1959); A. N. Whitehead, *Process and Reality* (London, 1929).

W. D. BECK

WILBERFORCE, SAMUEL

Samuel Wilberforce, born in 1805, was the son of William Wilberforce, abolitionist, member of Parliament, and philanthropist. He was educated at Oxford and ordained an Anglican priest in 1829. He published a variety of works during his time as rector on the Isle of Wight, including *Letters and Journals of Henry Martyn* (1837); with brother Robert, the *Life of William Wilberforce* (1838); the *Correspondence of William Wilberforce*; a children's work still in print today, *Rocky Island and Other Stories* (1840); and a *History of the Protestant Episcopal Church in America* (1844).

Wilberforce was brought up an evangelical, and although he was later a supporter of the High Church party, he did not align himself with the Oxford Movement or the Tractarians, but tried to find a middle ground between High and Low Church factions. Along with John Henry *Newman, Wilberforce's brother-in-law Henry Manning and his three brothers converted to the Roman Catholic Church, while Wilberforce remained an Anglican. Eventually, the differences between Wilberforce and the Oxford Movement became so marked that John Henry Newman refused to accept Wilberforce's contributions to the *British Critic*. In October 1845, he was made bishop of Oxford.

Wilberforce was critical of liberal biblical scholars and dissenters and gained notoriety for his frequently unpopular roles in debate, where he earned the nickname 'Soapy Sam' for his elusive style. His most famous encounter came with Thomas Huxley in 1860 at a meeting of the British Association during which Wilberforce and Huxley debated Darwin's theory of evolution. Although some accounts of this debate portray Wilberforce as an ill-informed cleric, he was in fact vice-president of the Association, conversant with current *science and Darwin's work, and the author of a skilful critique of *The Origin of Species*. The debate was of high quality, and neither side could justly claim victory.

Wilberforce established Cuddesdon Theological College, one of the first Anglican theological colleges, in 1854. He also supported building Anglican religious communities and churches, improved organization in his own diocese and began the movement to modernize the language of the King James Version of the Bible in 1870. This eventually led to the Revised Version, published from 1881 to 1895.

Wilberforce was killed by a fall from his horse in 1873.

Bibliography
J. H. Lienhard, 'Soapy Sam and Huxley', <http://www.uh.edu/engines/epi1371.htm>; S. Meachem, *Lord Bishop: The Life of Samuel Wilberforce, 1805–1873* (Harvard, 1970); 'Samuel Wilberforce', *Essays Contributed to the Quarterly Review*, 2 vols. (London, 1874), vol. 1, pp. 92–95; 'Samuel Wilberforce', <http://www.pitts.emory.edu/Archives/text/mss099.html>

J. C. ZELLMANN

WILLIAM OF OCKHAM, see OCKHAM, WILLIAM OF

WILLIAMS, CHARLES

Charles Williams (1886–1945) became a friend of C. S. *Lewis in the 1930s, and it was Lewis who introduced him to J. R. R. *Tolkien and their Oxford literary club, the Inklings. Williams was admitted into the circle after Lewis and his friends discovered his supernatural novel, *The Place of the Lion*, one of seven, the last of which was read to the Inklings in the months before his sudden death in 1945. He exerted a deep and lasting influence on Lewis.

Williams's sometime arcane writings become more accessible in the light of the books Lewis wrote under his influence. There are many elements consciously drawn from Williams in Lewis's *That Hideous Strength*, *The Great Divorce*, *Till We Have Faces* and *The Four Loves*. Lewis was particularly influenced by Williams's novel *The Place of the Lion*, his Arthurian cycle of poetry (including *Taliesin Through Logres*), and his theological understanding of *romanticism, especially the experience of falling in love. Williams's writings encompassed fiction, poetry, drama, theology, church history (his *The Descent of the Dove* impacted on the poet W. H. Auden's conversion and his 1940 poem, 'New Year Letter'), biography and literary criticism. His imaginative exploration of orthodox Christian theology is even timelier for the twenty-first century than it was in the 1930s and '40s. With today's wide exploration of spiritualities, including paganism, and insatiable appetite for books on mind-body-spirit themes, Williams uncannily fits. He once employed the Tarot Pack as a plot device, and one novel concerns a magical stone from the crown of King Solomon. The stone has the power to transmit a person anywhere in time and space. (Williams shared with Tolkien and Lewis an interest in time-and-space travel.)

Williams was evacuated in 1939 to Oxford with the rest of the staff of the London office of the Oxford University Press. Lewis arranged for him to teach in the University English School, a rare honour for someone who could not afford to complete his degree. Oxford University recognized Williams as a literary critic in 1943 with an honorary MA. In his *Preface to Paradise Lost*, Lewis acknowledged his debt to Williams's interpretation of Milton. T. S. *Eliot, who admired Williams's novels, also praised his work on Dante, as did Williams's friend Dorothy L. *Sayers (who made a lively translation of *The Divine Comedy*). After his death, Lewis published a commentary on Williams's unfinished cycle of Arthurian poetry. There has always been a small but enthusiastic readership for his books.

Bibliography

H. Carpenter, *The Inklings: C. S. Lewis, J. R. R. Tolkien, Charles Williams and their Friends* (London, 1978); G. Cavaliero, *Charles Williams: Poet of Theology* (Basingstoke, 1983); C. Duriez and D. Porter, *The Inklings Handbook* (London, 2001); A. Hadfield, *Charles Williams: An Exploration of His Life and Work* (Oxford and New York, 1983); T. Howard, *The Novels of Charles Williams* (San Francisco, 1983).

C. DURIEZ

WITCHCRAFT, see PAGAN AND INDIGENOUS RELIGION

WITNESSES, CRITERIA FOR

The NT places great reliance on eyewitness testimony to *Jesus' claims and to the truth of his message, e.g. 1 John 1:1; 2 Pet. 1:16, and the frequency of the words *martyreō* and *martyria* ('witness') in the Fourth Gospel.

In courts of law, firsthand testimony, as opposed to hearsay, is the chief means of introducing admissible evidence, and even so-called 'real evidence' (the smoking gun) or documentary evidence requires that a foundation be laid in sound testimonial evidence. Evidential standards in the law have been developed and refined over the centuries in response to unarguable human need, and there is remarkable consistency across legal systems in requiring sound testimonial evidence in order to reach just conclusions.

The ancient Persian *Digest of a Thousand Points of Law* begins with a detailed chapter on the law of evidence, insisting, as does the common law, on 'independent and convincing proof' to support allegations, and setting forth detailed criteria for distinguishing reliable from unreliable testimony (declarations against interest as opposed to self-serving declarations, etc.).

In Roman law, when the witnesses for the parties gave conflicting testimony on any point, it was the duty of the judge, not to count the number on each side, but to consider which of them were entitled to the greatest credit, according to the well-known rule, *Testimonia ponderanda sunt, non numeranda*. Roman law also provided that the benefit of the doubt should be given to the defendant rather than to the plaintiff.

Jewish evidential standards were, if anything, even more rigorous than those of Roman law at the time of Christ. For Jewish tribunals of the first century, 'all evidence must be direct, and not circumstantial or presumptive. Be the chain of evidence ever so strong, if not all links are forged by direct eye-testimony, and that of at least two competent witnesses, the accused cannot be adjudged guilty' (S. Mendelsohn, *The Criminal Jurisprudence of the Ancient Hebrews, Compiled from the Talmud and Other Rabbinical Writings, and Compared with Roman and English Penal Jurisprudence* [1891], para. 82).

What, then, are the evidential standards pertinent to the question of the reliability of the testimonies to Jesus Christ as found in the primary documents of the NT?

In courts of law, admissible testimony is considered truthful unless impeached or otherwise rendered doubtful. This is in accord with ordinary life, where only the paranoic goes about with the bias that everyone is lying. The burden, then, is on those who would show that the NT testimony to Jesus is not worthy of belief.

In their standard work on the subject, *Criminal Law Advocacy* (New York, 1984), McCloskey and Schoenberg offer a fourfold test for exposing perjury, involving the determination of *internal* and *external defects in the witness himself or herself on the one hand and in the testimony itself on the other*. Can the NT witness to Jesus be impeached by way of these four standard criteria?

1. Internal defects in the witness refer to any personal characteristics or past history tending to show that the witness is inherently untrustworthy, unreliable or undependable. There is no reason whatsoever to conclude that the *apostolic witnesses to Jesus were tainted with criminal records or suffered from pathological lying. If anything, their simple literalness and directness is almost painful. Nor do they have any of the characteristics of mythomanes (2 Pet. 1:16–18).

2. Did the apostolic witnesses suffer from external defects, i.e. motives to falsify? Surely no sensible person would argue that they would have lied about Jesus for monetary gain or as a result of societal pressure. After all, they lost the possibility both of worldly wealth and of social acceptability among their Jewish peers because of their commitment to Jesus. But might that very affection for and attachment to Jesus serve as a motive to falsify? Not when we remember that their master expressly taught them that lying was of the devil (John 8:44).

3. Turning to the testimony itself, we ask if the NT writings are internally consistent or self-contradictory. Certainly, the four Gospels do not give identical, verbatim accounts of the words or acts of Jesus. But if they did, that fact alone would make them highly suspect, for it would point to collusion. The several accounts are complementary, not contradictory. To use NT translator J. B. Phillips' expression, the internal content of the NT records has 'the ring of truth'.

4. Finally, what about external defects in the testimony itself, i.e. inconsistencies between the NT accounts and what we know from archaeology or extra-biblical historical records? Unlike typical sacred literature, myth and fairy-tale ('Once upon a time . . . '), the gospel story begins and ends in *history (Luke 3:1–3).

Modern archaeological research has confirmed again and again the reliability of NT geography, chronology and general history. Thus, no one of the four elements of the McCloskey-Schoenberg construct for attacking perjury allows us to impugn the veracity of the NT witnesses to Jesus.

Furthermore, a point well understood by trial lawyers but seldom by laymen needs to be stressed, namely, the extreme difficulty of successful lying in the presence of a cross-examiner. As F. F. Bruce declared (*The New Testament Documents: Are They Reliable?* [London, 1960], pp. 45–46): 'It was not only friendly eyewitnesses that the early preachers had to reckon with; there were others less well disposed who were also conversant with the main facts of the ministry and death of Jesus. The disciples could not afford to risk inaccuracies (not to speak of wilful manipulation of the facts), which would at once be exposed by those who would be only too glad to do so. On the contrary, one of the strong points in the original apostolic preaching is the confident appeal to the knowledge of the hearers . . . Acts 2:22. Had there been any tendency to depart from the facts in any material respect, the possible presence of hostile witnesses in the audience would have served as a further corrective.'

In short, even if the NT witnesses to Jesus were the kind of people to engage in deception (which they surely were not), *had* they attempted it, they could not have got away with it. Admittedly, they were never put on a literal witness stand, but they concentrated their preaching on synagogue audiences, thus putting their testimony at the mercy of the hostile Jewish religious leadership. That audience had the means, motive and opportunity to expose the apostolic witness as inaccurate and deceptive if it had been such, and the fact that they did not can only be effectively explained on the ground that they *could not*.

Legal standards of evidence, such as have here been applied to the NT witnesses to Jesus Christ, must not be ignored by believers or unbelievers. Since courts of law exist to decide the most intractable conflicts in society, to jettison legal methodology is to melt the very glue that holds society together.

Simon Greenleaf, the greatest of the nineteenth-century common-law experts in legal evidence, summarizes in the following terms: 'Let the [Gospel] witnesses be compared with themselves, with each other, and with surrounding facts and circumstances; and let their testimony be sifted, as if it were given in a court of justice, on the side of the adverse party ... The result, it is confidently believed, will be an undoubting conviction of their integrity, ability, and truth.'

Bibliography

C. A. J. Coady, *Testimony: A Philosophical Study* (Oxford, 1992); J. W. Montgomery, *Human Rights and Human Dignity* (Edmonton, 1995), especially ch. 6; *The Law Above the Law* (Minneapolis, 1975) (includes Simon Greenleaf's *Testimony of the Evangelists*); D. F. Ross, J. D. Read and M. P. Toglia (eds.), *Adult Eyewitness Testimony: Current Trends and Developments* (Cambridge, 1994).

J. W. MONTGOMERY

WITTGENSTEIN, LUDWIG

Ludwig Wittgenstein, Austrian philosopher, was born in Vienna, 1889, and died in 1951 in Cambridge, England, where he had lectured from 1930. Wittgenstein's unusual life involved training as a mechanical engineer, in which sphere he worked during the First World War, and then encompassed two different periods as an active philosopher. The first culminated in his only book published in his lifetime, the *Tractatus Logico-Philosophicus* (1921), a dense and difficult work set out in numbered propositions and sub-points, which argued for a 'picture theory' of *language where every word matched some corresponding *reality. He carefully defined how philosophical analysis allowed the building blocks of language to construct more complex sentences up to a certain point, and then suggested more briefly that the sphere of *ethics and human values lay beyond the reach of such language, concluding with: 'What we cannot speak about we must pass over in silence.' This was widely misconstrued as simply a form of *logical positivism: rigour regarding verifiable facts and the consigning of religious language to the scrap-heap of mystical nonsense. Such a reading, expressed in Bertrand *Russell's preface to the book, went unchecked in part because Wittgenstein 'retired' from philosophy at this point, and taught at a rural primary school in Austria. In retrospect, however, his argument was more likely that the rigours of logical language are simply not equipped to deal with what matters most in human experience.

On his return to philosophy in Cambridge, he took up a monastic-style residence in one bare room, and effectively devoted himself to thinking, in an effort to lay bare the ways in which language works in human interaction. Some see this second period as a direct rebuttal of his first, but there is a definite continuity of key themes, and it is the style of the work which changes. All of this later work was, unfortunately, published posthumously, most vividly in *Philosophical Investigations* (1953), but with many more personal reflections, including some religious reflections, in a collection entitled *Culture and Value* (2nd edn, 1998). The style is loose and conversational, appealing to how we say this or that, how we see things, and how we navigate our way through our shared experiences. Several emphases may be noted.

Wittgenstein struggles with talking appropriately about language while having only language itself as a medium in which to do so. He articulated one significant way in which philosophy could remedy its own confusions, which had arisen, he thought, because philosophy developed theories which were in fact undercut by the very way they were formulated. In particular, his so-called 'private language argument' suggested, for reasons to do with knowing whether you had followed a conventional rule correctly, that the existence of language itself presupposed a speaking community, and therefore most philosophical speculation about scepticism (and especially *solipsism) was mistaken.

In his last work, published as *On Certainty* (1969), he similarly explored *certainty as the bedrock of knowing how to proceed through life. Certainty is to do with conviction and practice (or, as he liked to say, a 'language game' embedded in a 'form of life'), and not an impossible epistemological ideal. Typically, Wittgenstein offers resources to those confused by the apparently all-conquering sweep of philosophical theories about *truth and knowledge which seem to overturn our shared stock of human experience. Perhaps, he says, our experiences deserve more serious philosophical sympathy: nothing turns out to be harder than to say what is the case.

Although not a Christian, Wittgenstein famously once remarked that he saw every problem 'from a religious point of view'. He made only brief inroads into applying his 'ordinary language' analysis to such topics as the language of prayer or faith-confession, but this has been picked up by various philosophers of religion with some limited results. An unfortunate development has been the misappropriation of the idea of a 'form of life' (which Wittgenstein saw as a specific activity such as praying or promising) to such a thing as 'religion', which has led to the suggestion that religion is its own 'language game', divorced from any shared criteria with other human activities. This is the route of 'Wittgensteinian fideism', which, in contrast to Wittgenstein's own work, offers little of promise to Christian apologists.

Bibliography

F. Kerr, *Theology After Wittgenstein*, 2nd edn (London, 1997); N. Malcolm, *Wittgenstein: A Religious Point of View?* (London, 1993).

R. S. BRIGGS

WORLD RELIGIONS AND CHRISTIANITY

In the course of the twentieth century the issues raised for Christian apologetics by the existence of other religions moved from being of marginal concern to become a major challenge. At the beginning of that century, Western civilization was widely regarded as superior to all other cultures and its global triumph was confidently expected. The spread of civilization was to go hand in hand with the success of missionary Christianity, with the result that the non-Christian religions would simply fade away. Lurking behind such assumptions (whether consciously or not) were ideas derived from social Darwinism, which, when applied to the history of religions, consigned vast numbers of the world's population to an earlier, primitive stage in the development of the human race. Missionaries who had spent years actually working in other cultures frequently challenged these assumptions, since their encounter with people of other faiths, especially in the East, convinced them of the antiquity and abiding strength of these religions. At the Edinburgh Missionary Conference in 1910 there were eloquent warnings of the danger of identifying Christianity too closely with modern culture, and participants drew attention to the enduring attractiveness of other faiths elsewhere in the world. There were also voices which suggested the inadequacy of the received theological responses to this challenge.

During the twentieth century, the situation just described changed completely. The violence which scarred Europe throughout this time, combined with a deepening sense of cultural malaise, led to widespread questioning of earlier claims concerning the superiority of Western civilization. In so far as it had been complicit in this culture, Christianity became vulnerable to the postmodern critique and, in an ironic twist, found itself increasingly viewed as an old, once powerful but now fatally weakened religion. In the meantime, the non-Christian faiths refused to follow the evolutionary script and, through various movements of renewal and revival, discovered new opportunities for growth and political influence. They continued to be significant in their ancient heartlands, but also became powerful forces in the West, where the combination of a perceived spiritual crisis and the phenomenon of *globalization provided them with an historically unprecedented missionary opportunity.

The nature of the apologetic challenge

In this situation, the non-Christian religions present a series of apologetic challenges to Christian *theology and mission. First, there is the obvious challenge of *their persistence and strength*. We might designate this as the *there-ness* of the religions, a situation in which the phenomenon of religious *pluralism has become an undeniable aspect of contemporary reality. This context demands Christian theological reflection in areas such as the doctrine of providence, eschatology and expectations of the outcome of the work of Christian missions. Certain models of mission, according to which large areas of the world are classified as already 'reached' while others constitute the final frontiers to be conquered, seem to be rendered redundant by this new reality. However, the challenge to serious theological and missiological reflection which this new context demands still remains to be faced.

Secondly, the religions pose questions for Christian apologetics in the realm of *ethics*. The apparently symbiotic relationship between Christianity and the project of modernity has led to difficulties in distinguishing Christian ethical values from those emanating from the secular Enlightenment. Generally speaking, Western churches have colluded in the severing of *moral values from the realm of facts, the latter being established (so it was believed) through scientific investigation and experiment. As a result, religion and *morality were relegated to the level of personal preferences and in the ensuing vacuum, issues of ultimate *truth and value came to be determined according to public opinion. In this situation, Western Christians have often found themselves defending social values which bear little relationship to the gospel of *Jesus Christ. Other religions, especially *Islam, vigorously reject the privatization of faith, insisting that human life should not be split into sacred and secular categories, nor should God be excluded from the public sphere. Here, as elsewhere, the Christian encounter with other religions may prove to be less a threat to faith and more a challenge to faithfulness.

Non-Christian religions have also presented an ethical challenge with respect to comparative studies of the social impact of conversion. Ethnographic studies of primal societies have suggested that the combined impact of Christianization and modernity has weakened traditional moral restraints and resulted in the appearance and spread of previously unknown antisocial practices. Recent moves toward the imposition of *sharia* law in Muslim contexts have been partly motivated by the fear of the spread of the ethical confusion observed in adjacent, Christianized areas. In such situations, Christians often appear to be theologically defenceless, frequently responding with an apologetic for precisely the secular values which are at the root of the problem.

Thirdly, the supreme challenge remains, of course, the issue of *truth*. Traditional Christian claims concerning the nature of *revelation and the uniqueness of Jesus Christ are threatened from two directions. On the one hand, postmodernism leads to the suspicion that all such claims to possess absolute truth involve the distortion of reality and the suppression of counter-evidence. All-embracing narratives, whether religious or secular, are said to be developed in the interests of those who possess privilege and power. On the other hand, the encounter between different religions has created an unprecedented awareness of rival claims to truth, all of which may be held by their adherents in absolute terms. Taken together, these developments have created a situation in which a representative voice can claim, 'Never again will a single story be told as though it is the only one' (John Berger).

Theology, mission and the religions

The problem for Western Christians in this new cultural context is that there is not much within their received theological traditions that is relevant to this challenge. While Christendom remained the dominant cultural force within Europe, there seemed to be little need to reflect theologically on the status of the non-Christian religions. There are notable exceptions, including *Thomas Aquinas, whose *Summa contra Gentiles* was written in response to an enquiry from a missionary working among Muslims concerning the factors in this religion which predisposed his receptors to reject the gospel. The work of Aquinas thus pointed in the direction of a missionary theology developed in dialogue with other religions. However, this could not seriously challenge the traditions of a monopolistic religious institution which exercised rigid controls on both the definition of truth and the path to salvation. For centuries, the only frontiers between Western Christianity and other religions were those created by the internal encounter with Jews and heretics and the external confrontation with Islam, both experiences resulting in bitter and tragic histories.

Consequently, when, in the fifteenth century, European explorers began to open up new worlds, mission was equated with ecclesiastical expansion and it was assumed that the Catholic faith would displace the newly discovered paganisms. In the event, these encounters proved to be the turning point in the history of theology and mission, since they revealed the inadequacy of Western theology when put to the test on these new frontiers of mission. This was as true for Roman Catholic missionaries such as Bartholemeo des Las Casas in South America and Matteo Ricci in China as it was to be, at a later stage, for Protestant missionaries such as William Carey and Henry Martyn in India and Persia. Mission thus came to be, in Andrew Walls's phrase, the 'learning experience' of the Western church, placing previously unknown questions on the theological agenda and exposing the extent to which inherited traditions had themselves been shaped, and sometimes distorted, by the Western cultural experience.

Learning from the Fathers

If contemporary mission studies provides one key resource in the search for a credible apologetic in relation to the non-Christian religions, another is to be found in the rich veins of theological reflection which can be mined in patristic studies. For the early Fathers, the issue of the relationship between Christ and the religions was unavoidable and thus constitutes a major strand in their theology. Indeed, the contrasting positions emerging in modern debates on this subject, often classified by the terms 'exclusivist' and 'inclusivist', are clearly anticipated in the works of the Greek Christian apologists and their successors. *Justin Martyr and *Tertullian stand as paradigmatic figures in this period. The former was able to adopt a positive view of aspects of pre-Christian religion by means of a Logos Christology which enabled him to recognize the work of the eternal Word of God throughout time and space, while the latter's fear of the demonic elements in paganism led him to adopt a radical 'Christ against the religions' position. Discussions like these, together with the work of later Fathers, especially the profound reflections of *Origen, offer rich materials to be quarried afresh, so that Christians confronting the challenge of religions at the *end* of Christendom can draw on the experience and wisdom of the Fathers who faced similar challenges *before* Christendom.

Contrasting approaches in the modern period

Following the so-called Age of Discovery, information concerning other religious faiths increased, resulting in the emergence of a radically new view of the world and its peoples. As a result, the theology of religions was placed firmly on the Western theological agenda, a fact reflected in the comment of the English theologian and hymnwriter, Philip Dodderidge, that the issue of the salvation of 'pious pagans' was 'much disputed' in the early eighteenth century. Later, as the Protestant missionary movement spread across the world, the flow of information resulting from the encounters with primal traditions, with the ancient religions of the East, and with Islam turned into a veritable flood, posing fresh challenges not only for theologians but also for the emerging historical and social sciences.

As in the earliest centuries of the Christian era, the theological response to this challenge has been divided. On the one hand, the figure of Karl *Barth, with his radical opposition to human religion, looms over this discussion. No matter how noble and good humankind's religions may appear to be, according to Barth they constitute the absolute antithesis of the divine revelation given in Jesus Christ. Barth defines religion as *unbelief*, treating it as a human construct erected in opposition to God and as the means of escape from him. The religions belong in the shadows of human ignorance and sin, so that there can be no point of contact between them and Christ, and no possibility that he fulfils the felt needs of Muslims or Hindus. Barth's insistence that God's revelation 'does not link up with a human religion', but rather contradicts and replaces it, seems to veto the possibility of a Christian apologetic in relation to other faiths. The only valid approach to devout adherents of the non-Christian religions is a proclamation requiring conversion in a form that involves complete discontinuity with the religious past.

At the opposite end of the theological spectrum we discover Barth's contemporary, Rudolf Otto. Unlike Barth, Otto had experienced deep and prolonged encounters with people of other faiths and possessed a profound knowledge of the mystical traditions of the East. Whereas the Barthian approach is founded on certain biblical and dogmatic assumptions concerning the religions, Otto insists that a Christian theology of religions cannot be constructed apart from a missionary dialogue with those religions. If it is to be credible, theology must describe the *phenomena* of the religions accurately and fairly, and it must account for the discoveries made through the study of the history of religions, their sacred texts, and the witness of devout adherents concerning their encounters with the 'holy'. For Otto, all genuine religion has at its core an experience of the *numinous* – an overpowering sense of our creatureliness in the light of the transcendent glory and otherness of God. Although the Bible remains normative in defining and evaluating such experiences, it is undeniable that they are to be found across history and in different cultures. Indeed, Otto insists that orthodox Christianity has itself frequently suppressed this vital core of religion, becoming 'one-sidedly intellectualistic and rationalistic'.

Towards a synthesis

Karl Barth and Rudolf Otto stand as paradigmatic figures in the modern development of the theology of religions. The positions they articulated, negative and positive, can be traced through to today, together with a range of mediating views located at different points on this spectrum. However, in a globalized world the question of the theological status of religions is becoming more urgent than ever before, as the movement of peoples around the world, whether the freely chosen travels of rich tourists or the tragic journeys of immigrants prompted by economic necessity, expose the majority of Christians to experiences of religious pluralism once limited to missionaries working in exotic locations. In other words, the theology of religions is no longer simply a missiological concern but a pastoral one as well.

The question to be addressed in this context is whether it is possible to achieve a synthesis of the positions we have described. The South African missiologist, David Bosch, observed that both of the emphases we have outlined are to be found in the Bible. The *negative* critique of human religion, so vividly articulated by Karl Barth and his followers, rests upon a scriptural foundation in the work of Israel's prophets and in the witness of Christ himself; but the *positive* evaluation of *religious experience described in Rudolf Otto's classic book *The Idea of the Holy* can also claim biblical warrant in the appearance of 'godly pagans' throughout the narratives of both the OT and NT. What is needed, according to Bosch, is a theology of religions that avoids absolutizing either of these positions and insists that *both* strands run through the Bible in constant tension with each other. Religion bears witness to the fact that human beings carry eternity in their hearts and are touched by the love and mercy of God. At the same time, religion may degenerate into mere idolatry and serve ideological interests completely at odds with the values of the kingdom of God. At its worst, religion becomes demonic, justifying what is evil and surrounding human wickedness and violence with a halo of sanctity. In this situation, apologetics demands great discernment and wisdom, since the reality of the manifestation of religion in particular contexts may require either a stance of prophetic opposition and resistance or the humble and gentle witness of those who recognize holiness when they encounter it, yet are still bound to point to the crucified one in whose presence all our righteousness 'is as filthy rags'.

By their fruits you will know them

We return, finally, to the ethical challenge mentioned earlier. The long history of the interaction between Christianity and other religions is marred by the failure of the church to allow its practice to be shaped by the teaching and example of Jesus. As a historical religion, Christianity has not been immune to the process of degeneration and demonization to which we have referred above. People belonging to other faiths have often noticed the contrast between profession and practice, which has then created a credibility gap which they have been unable to cross. For example, near the end of his life the Jewish philosopher Martin *Buber confessed that he had come to believe in Jesus of Nazareth as the Messiah, but when asked why he had not been baptized as a Christian he replied, 'I cannot see what the Christian Church as an Institution has to do with Jesus Christ.' In the encounter with other religions, apologetics can never be simply a search for the right words, but must involve a living demonstration of transforming power of redemptive love in the lives of the disciples of Christ and within the community that humbly and gratefully bears his name.

Bibliography

L. Newbigin, *The Gospel in a Pluralist Society* (London, 1989); R. Otto, *The Idea of the Holy* (Oxford and New York, 1950); D. A. Pittman *et al.* (eds.), *Ministry and Theology in Global Perspective: Contemporary Challenges for the Church* (Grand Rapids and Cambridge, 1996); R. J. Plantinga (ed.), *Christianity and Plurality: Classic and Contemporary Readings* (Oxford and Malden, MA, 1999).

D. W. SMITH

WORLD-VIEW

The English 'world-view' is a translation of the German *Weltanschauung*, a word first coined by Immanuel *Kant. It has been a key term in Western intellectual discourse since the early nineteenth century. Since the end of that century it has also become common to speak of a Christian world-view, denoting by that term an overall Christian view of things which is broader and less discipline-specific than 'theology', while highlighting those aspects of biblical religion which make it a competitor of culture-transformative ideologies like Marxism and liberalism. As such, it has become a key category in culturally engaged contemporary Christian apologetics. In what follows we shall briefly sketch the history of the concept, describe its strategic value for apologetics, highlight two key themes of a Christian world-view, identify world-view differences among Christians, and consider the dangers of linking the Christian message with a 'world-view'.

History

The German word *Weltanschauung*, initially an incidental coinage of no special significance, quickly became a pivotal notion in the thought of German *Idealism and *Romanticism. It was transmitted from Kant via Fichte to Schelling, *Schleiermacher, A. W. Schlegel, Novalis, Jean Paul, *Hegel and Goethe. By the 1840s it had become a standard item in the vocabulary of the educated German, denoting a global outlook on life and the world – akin to philosophy, but without its rational pretensions. Beginning in the 1830s, the notion of *Weltanschauung* began to penetrate other languages. By the end of the nineteenth century (when the word reached a crescendo of popularity in the German-speaking world), it had made its way into virtually every speech community in the Western world, either as a loan translation or as a direct loanword. In English the German word has been assimilated in both ways: the anglicized equivalent 'world-view' is documented since 1858, and the loanword *Weltanschauung* is not infrequently encountered as well. It seems that 'world-view' was an idea whose time had come.

As the word and its associated concepts spread, it began to play a crucial role in a number of different academic disciplines. Ever since *Kierkegaard (who used the freshly coined Danish equivalent *verdensanskuelse*), philosophers have reflected on the relationship of the new concept of world-view to the ancient one of philosophy. Are these two words for the same thing, or do they refer to different things? In discussions of this issue (for example by Dilthey, *Nietzsche, Husserl, *Jaspers and Heidegger), 'philosophy' usually retains its ancient association with rational and scientific thought, with its claim to universal validity, whereas 'world-view' has connotations of a more personal and historically relative point of

view. In the natural *sciences the idea of an underlying pre-theoretical framework which guides scientific concept-formation and theorizing, whether it was labelled 'world-view' or not, came to prominence in the work of Michael *Polanyi and Thomas Kuhn. In the social sciences, 'world-view' or its equivalent loomed large in *psychology (*Freud and *Jung), *sociology (Marx and Engels, Mannheim, Berger and Luckmann), and anthropology (Kearney and Redfield).

In Christian usage, 'world-view' was initially associated with the work of two thinkers: the Scottish Presbyterian theologian James *Orr and the Dutch Reformed polymath and statesman Abraham *Kuyper. The key works are Orr's *The Christian View of God and the World as Centring on the Incarnation* (1893), and Kuyper's *Calvinism: Six Stone Lectures* (1899), both of which have been frequently reprinted. Each in his own way presented Christianity as an all-embracing and intellectually robust view of *reality which had implications for human life far beyond theology and the church, and which collides at many points with the secular ideologies of the day. Although Orr has had isolated followers on this point in the English-speaking world (notably Gordon H. Clark and Carl F. H. *Henry), Kuyper has had a greater impact, largely through the movement of Dutch neo-Calvinism which he initiated (a movement associated with such names as Herman *Bavinck in theology, and Herman *Dooyeweerd in philosophy), and which has had considerable influence outside of the Netherlands in recent decades (e.g. in the work of Francis *Schaeffer and Chuck Colson, as well as that of many Christian philosophers).

Strategic value

The strategic value of the idea of a Christian world-view is that it implicitly repudiates the notion that Christianity can be relegated to an academic discipline (theology), or to a private realm of morality or spirituality, and that it is therefore out of place in the public arena of the university or the marketplace of social and political ideas. In a word, it asserts that the gospel makes a claim to 'public truth' (Lesslie *Newbigin) and has direct cultural relevance. Furthermore, especially in its Kuyperian form, it makes the claim that all *culture is shaped by world-views, and that all world-views are rooted in a kind of religious commitment. The picture that emerges is not the Enlightenment dualism of fact versus value, science versus religion, public versus private, but an across-the-board contest between different religiously motivated world-views struggling for cultural hegemony. This overall conception has the further corollary, of great relevance for apologetics, that every domain of culture represents a meeting place, a point of contact, between rival world-views, including the Christian one. The practical effect of the consistent employment of the notion of Christian world-view is therefore that any aspect of contemporary culture (movies, say, or *globalization, or childrearing practices), becomes an occasion for addressing the dominant world-view which they embody, and how that world-view compares with the Christian one. It is clear that such a conception tends to favour a presuppositional approach to apologetics over an evidentialist one, since it sees rationality itself, and the capacity to properly weigh evidence, as embedded in an underlying world-view which cannot itself be adjudicated by rules of reason and evidence.

Two key themes

In reflecting on the salient features of a Christian world-view in the context of the modern West (i.e. in asking ourselves which aspects of the fundamental biblical teaching concerning the nature of the universe and humanity's place within it which are especially relevant to the intellectual and cultural heirs of the Renaissance and *Enlightenment), it is useful to draw attention to two basic biblical themes which stand at right angles to the dominant tradition of modern secular thought in the West: creation and spiritual warfare, both broadly conceived.

The biblical idea of creation refers to something much broader than God's handiwork in the physical universe; it includes the entire range of the human world as well. It is not only the structure of the atom, or the process of photosynthesis, which displays God's creative artistry in the world, but also the structure of the family, or the process of concept-formation and emotional maturation. In fact, the idea of an all-encompassing world order, of divine origin and specifically including, and therefore setting limits to, human life, is found not only in the Bible but also in almost all cultures outside of the modern secular West. However, it is a characteristic feature of the central tradition of humanist thought since the Renaissance that it

has denied, with ever increasing radicality, the idea of a divinely instituted order which holds for all of reality. Increasingly, whatever order there is in the world has been attributed to humanity, not God. In contrast to this, the Christian world-view, rooted in the Scriptures, maintains the sovereignty of God over everything, both in the human and the non-human worlds. Everything, from ice crystals to art and politics, is called to fit God's creational design. Thus, biblical religion encourages humans to find their way in a fundamentally ordered and meaningful world; *secular humanism challenges humans to make their way in an essentially chaotic and meaningless world.

A significant feature of the biblical idea of creation is also that God's order continues to impose itself even on those who refuse to acknowledge it. An aggressively secular culture may seek to deny all God-given standards for family life or protection of the environment, but the very nature of created reality forces some conformity to, and recognition of, those standards. A common-law marriage or homosexual partnership may in many ways be a caricature of God's creational design for marriage, but it nonetheless bears unmistakable traces of that design, e.g. in the deeply ingrained longing for fidelity. Similarly, the most irreligious freethinker may nevertheless attach a very high value to cogent argument and honest facing of the evidence, thereby implicitly conceding that there are given standards of thought which need to be respected. It is this last feature which in an important sense provides justification for the evidentialist tradition in apologetics. An appeal to rationality and evidence, even across a religious divide, does not fall on altogether deaf ears. Because of a common creation, the embeddedness of all discourse in prior world-view commitments does not make meaningful communication impossible between adherents of different world-views.

The second salient theme of a Christian world-view is that of spiritual warfare, once again taken in a comprehensive sense. It refers to what Kuyper called the 'antithesis', the opposition between flesh and spirit, between the kingdom of darkness and the kingdom of God, as this works itself out in every dimension of human existence, privately and publicly, individually and collectively, devotionally and culturally. Here again the contrast with modern *secularism is particularly marked, because the latter has sought to restrict religious differences to a private and marginal zone and to deny their relevance to the arena of public discourse. Thus, religion has no place in politics or art, education or business. But the Christian world-view takes seriously the biblical teaching that God lays claim to all of life, and is opposed at every point by the counterclaims of his adversary. Ultimately, there is no spiritual neutrality in either scholarship or literature, sports or agriculture, art or journalism. Everywhere there are forces which seek either to honour the Creator's intent or to replace it with a substitute. To use *Augustine's terms, the contest between the *civitas terrena* and the *civitas Dei* cannot be restricted to just one domain of human life.

These twin themes of creation and spiritual warfare, both taken in a comprehensive sense, represent crucial aspects of biblical religion which are at odds with the dominant currents of Western secular thought and experience, whether 'modern' or 'postmodern'. Since they are comprehensive in scope, they also give rise to points of friction, i.e. opportunities for religious dialogue, wherever a world-view-sensitive Christian engages contemporary secular culture.

Different Christian world-views

In speaking of a Christian world-view, it is also important to recognize that 'world-view' can be used in a more restricted sense to refer to differences among Christians with respect to their attitude to 'the world'. If we restrict ourselves to the traditions of historic Christian orthodoxy (defined in terms of adherence to the ecumenical *creeds of the early church), it is possible to distinguish four such world-views, each defined by a different construal of the relation between church and world, or Christ and culture, or (more fundamentally) to grace and nature. Three of these can be called dualistic, in that they conceive of 'grace' (a shorthand formulation for everything involved in the redemption in Christ or the kingdom of God) as either opposing or supplementing or flanking 'nature' (a shorthand formulation for everything involved in God's good but fallen creation). In varying degrees, these Christian world-views allow for a dichotomy or separation between a sacred and a secular realm of life. The fourth, in the tradition of *Irenaeus, Augustine and *Calvin, construes grace as restoring nature, of entering into it like a medicine in order to recover its original health. This more integral view thus resists any suggestion that

'sacred' and 'secular' can be correlated with distinct realms of human life.

The dangers of 'world-view'

Finally, it is necessary to consider dangers in the Christian use of the concept of world-view. To begin with, the intellectual pedigree of *Weltanschauung* and its derivatives is suspect. It is a term that is associated with the rise of historicism in early nineteenth-century Germany. As a consequence, 'world-view' often had the connotation of the historically contingent, the private and personal, as opposed to the universal validity achievable in philosophy. To speak of a Christian world-view therefore has the danger of subtly suggesting that the claims of the gospel are historically relative, or merely private and personal – the very notion of religion which 'Christian world-view' seeks to counter. Furthermore, the concept of a Christian world-view could easily be taken as suggesting that Christianity is primarily a matter of ideas, and thus does not sufficiently emphasize that the Christian religion is primarily a relationship with the person of *Jesus Christ, or else that it calls for radical discipleship embodied in action. Finally, the idea of a Christian world-view perpetuates the old Greek preference for metaphors of seeing over those of hearing, whereas the Bible generally emphasizes hearing rather than seeing.

All of these objections signal genuine dangers in the notion of a Christian world-view. However, they need not compel the abandonment of the category. Like many other basic concepts of suspect pedigree (e.g. 'philosophy', 'essence', 'providence'), the term 'world-view' needs to be redefined in Christian usage, explicitly disavowing certain features (in this case historicist *relativism) of its pagan or humanist roots. To a large extent this has already happened through Christian usage since Orr and Kuyper. Furthermore, it needs to be emphasized throughout that the cognitive dimension of Christianity (including its 'world-view' aspect) is only relatively important. That is to say, it is important, but only relative to the centrality of the person of Christ, and to other dimensions of obedient action (thinking itself, of course, is also a kind of action). As for the privileging of 'seeing' metaphors, we should beware of false dilemmas, and remember that Scripture, too, occasionally privileges seeing over hearing (e.g. Job 42:5). The world-view aspect of the Christian religion does not define its essence, but focuses on one of its features – a feature which can be crucially important for certain purposes, not least apologetic purposes.

Bibliography

P. S. Heslam, *Creating a Christian World-view: Abraham Kuyper's Lectures on Calvinism* (Grand Rapids and Carlisle, 1998); D. K. Naugle, *Worldview: The History of a Concept* (Grand Rapids, 2002); A. M. Wolters, *Creation Regained: Biblical Basics for a Reformational Worldview* (Grand Rapids, 1985); 'Nature and Grace in the Interpretation of Proverbs 31:10–31', in *The Song of the Valiant Woman: Studies in the Interpretation of Proverbs 31:10–31* (Carlisle, 2001).

A. M. WOLTERS

ZEFFIRELLI, FRANCO

In 1973 Zeffirelli (b. 1923) directed *Brother Sun, Sister Moon*, a decidedly romanticized biopic of St Francis of Assisi. Critics bemoaned its saccharine, almost flower-child-like presentation of Sts Francis and Claire, not to mention the folk soundtrack provided by Donovan, but audiences adored the film. The central themes of peace, simplicity and compassion seem to resound as loudly today with audiences as they did when the film was released. These themes would resonate well with a group studying either St Francis or even what it means to live a Christ-like life. Perhaps the most memorable scene in the film finds humble Francis kneeling before the ostentatious papal dais. In a stunning move Pope Innocent III descends from his throne to kneel beside the young friar.

What many consider Zeffirelli's masterpiece is not one of his wide-screen epics, but rather the *television mini-series *Jesus of Nazareth* (1977). Full of verbatim biblical quotations and relatively little apocryphal material, *Jesus of Nazareth* pleased critics and audiences alike. Once again, the grand scope of Zeffirelli's production brought the characters and events to brilliant realization. The staging is impeccable, as is the cast of extras, who seem refreshingly Semitic when compared to those in other films of the life of Christ. The six-hour format allowed Zeffirelli and his co-writers enough latitude to produce this thorough-going and devout retelling of Christ's life.

The presentation of Jesus, in a memorable performance by Robert Powell, is both well balanced and well conceived, not overly emphasizing either his humanity or his divinity. The crucifixion scene alone sets the film apart from so many others and stands as one of the best-produced accounts of the events on Calvary. One need look no further than *Jesus of Nazareth* to find a beautifully wrought and gracefully accomplished film adaptation of the life of Christ. One might compare this presentation of Christ with some of the other, less faithful renderings.

D. S. RUSSELL

ZEN BUDDHISM, see BUDDHISM

ZOROASTRIANISM

'Zoroastrianism' is from the Gk translation of 'Zarthushti', a religion grounded in the ancient Indo-Iranian traditions of south central Asia. The founder, Zarathushtra (Zoroaster in Gk), was born around 1000 BC to a priestly family (probably Magi) in Persia (Iran), and his teachings are contained in a series of books collectively known as Avesta. The most ancient part of these is the Gathas, which contain hymns that are attributed directly to Zarathushtra himself. According to M. Boyce in *Textual Sources for the Study of Zoroastrianism* (Manchester, 1984), the Gathas are composed in an archaic form of language and contain many words of unknown or uncertain meaning, which makes them extraordinarily difficult to translate.

Put simply, the concepts contained in the Gathas consist of one creator God and Lord of Wisdom named Ahura Mazda. Related to this central concept is that of Amesha Spentas, variously translated as Holy Immortals or archangels but best thought of as attributes of Ahura Mazda. These consist of Spenta Mainyu (the holy spirit), Vohuman (good purpose or thought), Asha (truth, righteousness), Armaita (devotion, love, faith), Khshathra (sovereignty, divine power), Armetat (immortality) and Haurvatat (wholeness, salvation), collectively known as the Heptad. The most important of these is Asha (truth, righteousness), which is upheld by Spenta Maiynu as opposed to Angra Mainyu, who is the upholder of falsehood. Zarathushtra's adherents have to choose Asha and are helped by Vohuman to show it through their good thoughts, words and deeds. This is why the religion is still referred to as 'the good religion' (*Beh deen* in Parsi).

Angra Mainyu, or the *evil spirit, is twinned with Spenta Mainyu, or the holy spirit, in only one verse in the Gathas, which describes twin spirits appearing at the beginning of time. One chooses to follow either one or the other. The battle between these two spirits within the lives of people is all-important to Zarthushtis. The rewards and punishments of those choosing good or evil are mainly in the life hereafter, but the adherents are assured of the help of the Heptad. Most of the other concepts, such as judgment, *heaven and *hell, the end times and the kingdom of Ahura Mazda, are strikingly similar to those found in the Judeo-Christian traditions. The concept of a saviour or *saoshyant*, though weakly developed, is also found in the Gathas.

The adoption of Zarthushti by the Magi was probably crucial to its survival to this day. These priests, however, brought in a considerable number of their own beliefs, such as reverence of fire, purity rituals and exposure of the dead. For a thousand years (500 BC–AD 650) Zarthushti played a dominant role in the spiritual as well as the political lives of the peoples of the Middle East, and it is said to have influenced *Judaism as well as early Christianity.

Christian encounters with Zarthushti started with the spread of Christianity into Persia as early as the first century. Recent translations of Syriac manuscripts of the Assyrian (Nestorian) church indicate a rich early apologetic literature, such as Bardaisan's 'Dialogue on Fate', written in AD 196 as a direct response to Zarthushti criticism of Christianity. Tatian (110–180) was also born in the Parthian Empire, though his writings were mainly directed to the Greeks. Despite several periods of persecution, Christianity flourished in the form of the Assyrian church alongside the Zarthushti faith in Persia and even outlasted that religion. Both, however, were eventually buried in the sandstorm of *Islam. There were no substantial encounters between them from that period until the coming of the Protestant missionaries in the mid-nineteenth century.

Persian Zarthushti refugees fleeing from Muslim persecution came to western India in the eighth century, and in the course of time established themselves as a highly influential community known as the Parsis, who were particularly numerous in Bombay. They attracted John Wilson's attention in 1828. He was a Scottish missionary who chose an adversarial approach and engaged the community in a series of highly publicized discourses through the medium of newspapers, pamphlets and open debates. He also published a book on the Parsi religion in which he meticulously answered all the criticisms from Parsis. Directing his main attack on the Vendidad, one of the books of the Avesta, he denounced Zarathushtra as an impostor and his religion as Satan's. A second missionary to the Parsis, James Hope Moulton, came to Bombay in 1915. He also conducted a series of lectures and open debates amongst the Parsis and wrote a book about Zoroastrianism. In contrast to Wilson, he confirmed Zarathushtra as a prophet from God and said that his teachings contained truths that only needed 'fulfilment by Christ'. During the intervening period we know of two Parsi converts to Christianity, Sorabji Khersetji and Dahnjibahi Nauroji, who engaged actively with their compatriots and wrote to defend and promote Christianity to the Parsis. The significant message which these converts tried to convey to the Parsis, and which may have influenced Moulton, was that one did not have to reject Parsi culture and traditions altogether if one accepted Christ.

The Zarthushti religion has gone through many changes over its long history. The most recent started in the nineteenth century as a process of reform, which split the community into two: the reformers, who wished to go back to the fundamental tenets of Zarathushtra as contained in the Gathas, and the traditionalists who, though conceding to modernization, wished to retain most of their old rites and rituals. Modern Zarthushtis live mostly in Iran and India but substantial numbers can now be found in Europe, Canada and the USA (mainly the west coast). Despite very close contact with the 'Christian West' over the past century, there have been very few converts to Christianity.

Bibliography

J. H. Moulton, *The Treasures of the Magi* (Oxford, 1917); D. Nauroji, *From Zoroaster to Christ* (Edinburgh, 1909); C. Sorabji, *Therefore* (Oxford, 1924); J. Wilson, *The Parsi Religion as Contained in Zend-Avesta and Propounded and Defended by the Zoroastrians of India, Unfolded, Refuted, and Contrasted with Christianity* (Bombay, 1843).

F. NAMDARAN

Index of names

Index of subjects

Index of articles

W. C. Campbell-Jack (Ph.D., Edinburgh) is minister of Possilpark Parish Church (Church of Scotland) in Glasgow, Scotland.

Gavin McGrath (Ph.D., Durham) is associate minister at St. Luke's Anglican Church, Wimbledon Park, London. He is the author of *A Confident Life in an Age of Change*.

C. Stephen Evans (Ph.D., Yale) is Distinguished University Professor of Philosophy and the Humanities at Baylor University in Waco, Texas. In

addition to his many publications in philosophy, he is the author of *Why Believe?* and *The Historical Christ and the Jesus of Faith: The Incarnational Narrative as History*.